THE ANNUAL REGISTER
Vol. 241

THE ANNUAL REGISTER ADVISORY BOARD

CHAIRMAN
D.S. LEWIS

EDITOR
ALAN J. DAY

ASSISTANT EDITOR
VERENA HOFFMAN

JOHN BEETLESTONE
Emeritus Director of Techniquest, Emeritus Professor, University of Wales
NOMINATED BY
THE BRITISH ASSOCIATION FOR THE ADVANCEMENT OF SCIENCE

JAMES BISHOP
Editor-in-Chief, The Illustrated London News

M. R. D. FOOT
Formerly Professor of Modern History, University of Manchester
NOMINATED BY
THE ROYAL HISTORICAL SOCIETY

MICHAEL KASER
*Emeritus Fellow of St Antony's College, Oxford,
and Honorary Professor, University of Birmingham*
NOMINATED BY
THE ROYAL INSTITUTE OF INTERNATIONAL AFFAIRS

ALASTAIR NIVEN
Director of Literature, British Council
NOMINATED BY
THE BRITISH COUNCIL

RICHARD O'BRIEN
Principal, Global Business Network
NOMINATED BY
THE ROYAL ECONOMIC SOCIETY

Popperfoto/Reuters

Welcome to Kosovo (13 June): A young Kosovar Albanian girl greets a British soldier arriving in Priština with NATO-led K-For peace-keeping forces.

both Popperfoto/Reuters

[Top] *Relief for East Timor* (20 September): Australian troops arrive in Dili in the vanguard of an international peace-keeping force.
[Bottom] *Devastation in Turkey:* two major earthquakes in August and November killed thousands of people and did massive structural damage.

THE ANNUAL REGISTER

A Record of World Events
1999

Edited by
ALAN J. DAY

assisted by
VERENA HOFFMAN

FIRST EDITED IN 1758
BY EDMUND BURKE

Keesing's Worldwide
PRINT · CD-ROM · ONLINE

THE ANNUAL REGISTER 1999
Published by Keesing's Worldwide, LLC, 4905 DelRay Avenue, Suite 402,
Bethesda, MD 20814, United States of America

ISBN 1-886994-32-3

©Keesing's Worldwide, LLC 2000
All rights reserved; no part of this publication may be reproduced,
stored in a retrieval system, or transmitted in any form or by any
means, electronic, mechanical, photocopying, recording or otherwise
without either the prior written permission of the Publishers or a licence
permitting restricted copying issued by the Copyright Licensing Agency,
90 Tottenham Court Road, London, W1P 9HE, UK

British Library Cataloguing in Publication Data
The Annual Register—1999
1. History—Periodicals
909.82'8'05 D410

ISBN 1-886994-32-3

Library of Congress Catalog Card Number: 4-17979

Set in Times Roman by
ROCK CREEK PUBLISHING, BETHESDA, USA

Printed in Great Britain by
MPG BOOK DIVISION, BODMIN

CONTENTS

	CONTRIBUTORS	vii
	IGO ABBREVIATIONS	xiv
	PREFACE TO 241st VOLUME	xv
	EXTRACTS FROM EARLIER VOLUMES	xvi

I		OVERVIEWS OF THE YEAR	
	1	Global Issues and Regional Realities	1
	2	The International Economy	8

II		WESTERN AND SOUTHERN EUROPE	
	1	i United Kingdom 16 ii Scotland 43 iii Wales 46 iv Northern Ireland 48	16
	2	i Germany 55 ii France 59 iii Italy 63 iv Belgium 67 v The Netherlands 69 vi Luxembourg 70 vii Ireland 71	55
	3	i Denmark 74 ii Iceland 76 iii Norway 77 iv Sweden 79 v Finland 80 vi Austria 82 vii Switzerland 85 viii European Mini-States 88	74
	4	i Spain 91 ii Gibraltar 94 iii Portugal 95 iv Malta 98 v Greece 100 vi Cyprus 103 vii Turkey 107	91

III		CENTRAL AND EASTERN EUROPE	
	1	i Poland 110 ii Baltic Republics 113 iii Czech Republic 117 iv Slovakia 119 v Hungary 120 vi Romania 123 vii Bulgaria 126	110
	2	i Albania 128 ii Bosnia & Hercegovina 131 iii Croatia 134 iv Macedonia 136 v Slovenia 137 vi Yugoslavia 138	128
	3	i Russia 144 ii Belarus, Ukraine, Moldova 149 iii Armenia, Georgia, Azerbaijan 152	144

IV		AMERICAS AND THE CARIBBEAN	
	1	United States of America	154
	2	Canada	171
	3	Latin America: i Argentina 175 ii Bolivia 177 iii Brazil 178 iv Chile 179 v Colombia 181 vi Ecuador 182 vii Paraguay 184 viii Peru 185 ix Uruguay 186 x Venezuela 187 xi Cuba 188 xii Dominican Republic and Haiti 189 xiii Central America and Panama 190 xiv Mexico 194	175
	4	Caribbean: i Jamaica 195 ii Guyana 196 iii Trinidad & Tobago 197 iv Barbados 198 v Belize 198 vi Grenada 199 vii The Bahamas 199 viii Windward & Leeward Islands 200 ix UK Dependencies 202 x Suriname 204 xi Netherlands Antilles and Aruba 205 xii US Dependencies 206	195

V MIDDLE EAST AND NORTH AFRICA

1	Israel	207
2	i Arab World and Palestinians 211 ii Egypt 214 iii Jordan 216	
	iv Syria 219 v Lebanon 221 vi Iraq 222	211
3	i Saudi Arabia 225 ii Yemen 227 iii Arab States of the Gulf 229	225
4	i Sudan 234 ii Libya 237 iii Tunisia 238 iv Algeria 240	
	v Morocco 242 vi Western Sahara 244	234

VI EQUATORIAL AFRICA

1	i Horn of Africa 245 ii Kenya 249 iii Tanzania 250 iv Uganda 252	245
2	i Ghana 254 ii Nigeria 256 iii Sierra Leone 259 iv The Gambia 260	
	v Liberia 261	254
3	i West African Francophone States 262 ii Central African Franc Zone States 270	262

VII CENTRAL AND SOUTHERN AFRICA

1	i Democratic Republic of Congo 275 ii Burundi and Rwanda 278 iii Guinea-Bissau, Cape Verde and São Tomé & Príncipe 280 v Mozambique 282 vi Angola 283	275
2	i Zambia 285 ii Malawi 286 iii Zimbabwe 287 iv Botswana, Lesotho, Namibia and Swaziland 290	285
3	South Africa	297

VIII SOUTH ASIA AND INDIAN OCEAN

1	i Iran 302 ii Afghanistan 304 iii Central Asian Republics 308	302
2	i India 314 ii Pakistan 321 iii Bangladesh 324 iv Nepal 327 v Bhutan 330 vi Sri Lanka 331	314
3	i Mauritius 333 ii Seychelles, Comoros and Maldives 335 iii Madagascar 338	333

IX SOUTH-EAST AND EAST ASIA

1	i Myanmar (Burma) 339 ii Thailand 340 iii Malaysia 342 iv Brunei 344 v Singapore 344 vi Indonesia 346 vii Philippines 349 viii Vietnam 350 ix Cambodia 352 x Laos 353	339
2	i China 354 ii Hong Kong SAR 363 iii Taiwan 365 iv Japan 368 v South Korea 372 vi North Korea 374 vii Mongolia 376	354

X AUSTRALASIA AND THE PACIFIC

1	i Australia 379 ii Papua New Guinea 383	379
2	i New Zealand 385 ii Pacific Island States 387	385

XI INTERNATIONAL ORGANIZATIONS

1	United Nations	393
2	i Defence Organizations 403 ii Economic Organizations 410	403
3	i The Commonwealth 413 ii Francophonie and CPLP 416 iii Non-Aligned Movement and Developing Countries 419 iv Oranization of the Islamic Conference 422	413
4	European Union	424
5	i Council of Europe 433 ii Organization for Security and Cooperation in Europe 435 iii European Bank for Reconstruction and Development 438 iv Nordic, Baltic and Arctic Organizations 439 v Other European Organizations 441	433

6	i Arab Organizations 444 ii African Organizations and Conferences 447 iii Asia-Pacific Organizations 451 iv American and Caribbean Organizations 455	444
XII	**RELIGION**	459
XIII	**THE SCIENCES**	
1	Scientific, Medical and Industrial Research	465
2	Information Technology	471
3	The Environment	476
XIV	**THE LAW**	
1	i International Law 484 ii European Community Law 489	484
2	Law in the United Kingdom	492
3	United States Law	498
XV	**THE ARTS**	
1	i Opera 501 ii Music 503 iii Ballet & Dance 506 iv Theatre 509 v Cinema 514 vi Television & Radio 517	501
2	i Visual Arts 521 ii Architecture 525	521
3	Literature	528
XVI	**SPORT**	534
XVII	**DOCUMENTS AND REFERENCE**	
1	Kosovo Agreement and UN Resolution	544
2	NATO's New Strategic Concept	550
3	The Sharm el Shaikh Memorandum	560
4	UK Labour Government	564
5	US Democratic Administration	565
6	International Comparisons: Population, GDP and Growth	566
XVIII	**OBITUARY**	567
XIX	**CHRONICLE OF PRINCIPAL EVENTS IN 1999**	595
	INDEX	608

MAPS AND TABLES

K-For Deployment in Kosovo	142
The War in Chechnya	146
East Timor	348
United Nations Peace-keeping Missions	400

CONTRIBUTORS

EXTRACTS FROM PAST VOLUMES — **M.R.D. Foot,** Former Professor of Modern History, University of Manchester

PART I
GLOBAL ISSUES AND REGIONAL REALITIES — **John M. Roberts,** Former Vice-Chancellor of the University of Southampton and Warden of Merton College, Oxford

THE INTERNATIONAL ECONOMY — **Victor Keegan,** Assistant Editor, *The Guardian*

PART II
UNITED KINGDOM — **Alan J. Day,** MA, Editor, *The Annual Register*

UK ECONOMY — **Robert Fraser,** MA, Consulting Editor, *Keesing's Record of World Events*

SCOTLAND — **Charlotte Lythe,** MA, Senior Lecturer in Economic Studies, University of Dundee

WALES — **Gwyn Jenkins,** MA, Keeper of Manuscripts and Records, National Library of Wales, Aberystwyth

NORTHERN IRELAND — **Sydney Elliott,** BA, PhD, Senior Lecturer in Politics, The Queen's University, Belfast

GERMANY — **Charlie Jeffery,** PhD, Deputy Director, Institute for German Studies, University of Birmingham

FRANCE — **Martin Harrison,** Professor of Politics, University of Keele

ITALY — **Stephen Gundle,** Senior Lecturer in Italian, Royal Holloway, University of London

BELGIUM, NETHERLANDS, LUXEMBOURG — **Peter Dixon,** Historian at European Commission

REPUBLIC OF IRELAND — **Louis McRedmond,** MA, BL, Journalist, historian and broadcaster

DENMARK, ICELAND, NORWAY, LUXEMBOURG — **Alastair H. Thomas,** Professor of Nordic Politics, University of Central Lancashire

FINLAND — **David Smith,** PhD, Lecturer in Contemporary History and International Relations; member of Baltic Research Unit, Department of European Studies, University of Bradford

AUSTRIA — **Angela Gillon,** Researcher in West European affairs

SWITZERLAND — **Hans Hirter,** PhD, Editor, Année Politique Suisse, University of Bern

EUROPEAN MINI-STATES — **Stefania Zerbinati,** MA, Researcher in European affairs

SPAIN, GIBRALTAR — **Richard Gillespie,** PhD, Professor of Iberian and Latin American Studies, University of Portsmouth

PORTUGAL — **Antonio de Figueiredo,** Knight Commander of Portugal's Order of Freedom; Portuguese author, freelance journalist and broadcaster

MALTA — **D.G. Austin,** Emeritus Professor of Government, University of Manchester

GREECE — **Richard Clogg,** MA, St Antony's College, Oxford

CYPRUS	**Robert McDonald,** Writer and broadcaster on Cyprus, Greece and Turkey
TURKEY	**A.J.A. Mango,** BA, PhD, Orientalist and writer on current affairs in Turkey and the Near East

PART III

POLAND	**A. Kemp-Welch,** BSc(Econ), PhD, Senior Lecturer, School of Economic and Social Studies, University of East Anglia
BALTIC REPUBLICS	**John Hiden,** Professor of Modern European History and Director, Baltic Research Unit, University of Bradford
CZECH REPUBLIC, SLOVAKIA	**Sharon Fisher,** MA, Analyst specializing in East European political and economic affairs
HUNGARY	**George Schöpflin,** Jean Monnet Professor of Politics and Director, Centre for the Study of Nationalism, School of Slavonic and East European Studies, University of London
ROMANIA	**Gabriel Partos,** Eastern Europe Analyst, BBC World Service
BULGARIA	**Stephen Ashley,** MA, DPhil, BBC World Service News Programmes
ALBANIA	**Richard Crampton,** PhD, Professor of East European History and Fellow of St Edmund Hall, University of Oxford
FORMER YUGOSLAV REPUBLICS	**John B. Allcock,** MA, PhD, Head of Research Unit in South-East European Studies, University of Bradford
RUSSIA, BELARUS, UKRAINE, MOLDOVA AND CAUCASUS	**Stephen White,** PhD, DPhil, Professor of Politics, University of Glasgow

PART IV

UNITED STATES OF AMERICA	**Neil A. Wynn,** MA, PhD, Reader in History and American Studies, University of Glamorgan
CANADA	**David M.L. Farr,** Professor Emeritus of History, Carleton University, Ottawa
LATIN AMERICA, CARIBBEAN	**Peter Calvert,** MA, PhD, Professor of Comparative and International Politics, University of Southampton

PART V

ISRAEL	**Joel Peters,** BSc, DPhil, Senior Lecturer in Politics and Government, Ben Gurion University of the Negev, Israel
ARAB WORLD, EGYPT, JORDAN, SYRIA, LEBANON, IRAQ	**Christopher Gandy,** Formerly UK Diplomatic Service; writer on Middle Eastern affairs
SAUDI ARABIA, YEMEN, ARAB STATES OF THE GULF	**George Joffé,** Senior Research Fellow, School of Oriental and African Studies, University of London
SUDAN	**Ahmed al-Shahi,** DPhil, Social anthropologist and independent researcher
LIBYA, TUNISIA, ALGERIA, MOROCCO, WESTERN SAHARA	**Richard Lawless,** PhD, Emeritus Reader in Modern Middle Eastern Studies, University of Durham

CONTRIBUTORS

PART VI

HORN OF AFRICA	**Patrick Gilkes,** Writer and broadcaster on the Horn of Africa
KENYA, TANZANIA, UGANDA	**William Tordoff,** MA, PhD, Emeritus Professor of Government, University of Manchester
GHANA	**D.G. Austin** (see Pt. II, Malta)
NIGERIA	**Guy Arnold,** Writer specializing in Africa and North-South affairs
SIERRA LEONE, THE GAMBIA, LIBERIA	**Arnold Hughes,** Professor of African Politics, Centre of West African Studies, University of Birmingham
FRANCOPHONE AFRICA	**Kaye Whiteman,** Former Publisher, *West Africa*

PART VII

CENTRAL/SOUTHERN AFRICA ZIMBABWE	**Robin Hallett,** MA, Writer and lecturer on African affairs **R. W. Baldock,** BA, PhD, Editorial Director, Yale University Press; writer on African affairs
NAMIBIA, BOTSWANA, LESOTHO, SWAZILAND, SOUTH AFRICA	**Greg Mills,** MA, PhD, National Director, South African Institute of International Affairs

PART VIII

IRAN	**Keith McLachlan,** BA, PhD, Emeritus Professor, School of Oriental and African Studies, University of London
AFGHANISTAN	**D.S. Lewis,** PhD, Editor, *Keesing's Record of World Events*
CENTRAL ASIAN REPUBLICS	**Shirin Akiner,** PhD, Lecturer in Central Asian Studies, School of Oriental and African Studies, University of London
INDIA, BANGLADESH, NEPAL, BHUTAN	**Peter Lyon,** BSc(Econ), PhD, Reader Emeritus in International Relations and Senior Research Fellow, Institute of Commonwealth Studies, University of London; editor, *The Round Table,* the Commonwealth journal of international affairs
PAKISTAN	**David Taylor,** Senior Lecturer in Politics with reference to South Asia, School of Oriental and African Studies, University of London
SRI LANKA	**Charles Gunawardena,** Former Director of Information, Commonwealth Secretariat, London
SEYCHELLES, MAURITIUS, MALDIVES	**Harry Drost,** Writer and translator on European and Third World affairs; editor, *The World's News Media*
MADAGASCAR AND COMOROS	**Kaye Whiteman** (see Pt. VI, Ch. 3)

PART IX

MYANMAR (BURMA), THAILAND, VIETNAM, CAMBODIA, LAOS	**Jonathan Rigg,** PhD, Reader in South-East Asian Geography, University of Durham
MALAYSIA, BRUNEI, SINGAPORE	**Michael Leifer,** BA, PhD, Emeritus Professor of International Relations, London School of Economics and Political Science
INDONESIA, PHILIPPINES	**Norman MacQueen,** Head of Department of Politics, University of Dundee

CONTRIBUTORS

CHINA, TAIWAN, HONG KONG	**Robert F. Ash,** MSc(Econ), PhD, Director, EU-China Academic Network and Chiang Ching-kuo Professor of Taiwan Studies, School of Oriental and African Studies, University of London
JAPAN	**Ian Nish,** Emeritus Professor of International History, London School of Economics and Political Science
KOREA, MONGOLIA	**Alan Sanders,** FIL, Former Lecturer in Mongolian Studies, School of Oriental and African Studies, University of London

PART X

AUSTRALIA	**James Jupp,** MSc (Econ), PhD, FASSA, Director, Centre for Immigration and Multicultural Studies, Australian National University, Canberra
PAPUA NEW GUINEA	**Norman MacQueen** (see Pt.IX, Indonesia & Philippines)
NEW ZEALAND, PACIFIC ISLAND STATES	**Stephen Levine,** PhD, Associate Professor and Head of School, School of Political Science and International Relations, Victoria University of Wellington

PART XI

UNITED NATIONS	**David Travers,** BA(Wales), Lecturer in Politics and International Relations, Lancaster University; Specialist Adviser on UN to House of Commons' Foreign Affairs Committee
DEFENCE ORGANIZATIONS	**Paul Cornish,** Newton Sheehy Lecturer in International Relations, Centre of International Studies, University of Cambridge and Fellow, Wolfson College, Cambridge
ECONOMIC ORGANIZATIONS	**Robert Fraser** (see Pt. II, UK Economy)
COMMONWEALTH	**Derek Ingram,** Consultant Editor of *Gemini News Service*; author and writer on the Commonwealth
NON-ALIGNED MOVEMENT AND GROUP OF 77	**Peter Willetts,** PhD, Professor of Global Politics, Department of Sociology, The City University, London
ORGANIZATION OF THE ISLAMIC CONFERENCE	**Darren Sagar,** MA, Deputy Editor, *Keesing's Record of World Events*
EUROPEAN UNION	**Michael Berendt,** Expert on affairs of the European Union
COUNCIL OF EUROPE	**Christopher Shaw,** MA, Secretary to UK delegation to Parliamentary Assembly of the Council of Europe
ORGANIZATION FOR SECURITY AND COOPERATION IN EUROPE	**Adrian G.V. Hyde-Price,** BSc(Econ), PhD, Institute of German Studies, University of Birmingham
EUROPEAN BANK FOR RECONSTRUCTION AND DEVELOPMENT	**Michael Kaser,** MA, DLitt, DSocSc, Emeritus Fellow of St Antony's College, Oxford, and Honorary Professor, University of Birmingham
NORDIC/BALTIC/ARCTIC ORGANIZATIONS	**David Smith** (see Pt. II, Finland)
OTHER EUROPEAN ORGANIZATIONS	**Marc Cole-Bailey,** Writer on European affairs
ARAB ORGANIZATIONS	**George Joffé** (see Pt. V, Saudi Arabia, etc.)
AFRICAN ORGANIZATIONS AND CONFERENCES	**Kaye Whiteman** (see Pt. VI, Ch. 3)
ASIA-PACIFIC ORGANIZATIONS	**Darren Sagar,** MA,(see above)

CONTRIBUTORS

AMERICAN AND CARIBBEAN ORGANIZATIONS

Peter Calvert (see Pt. IV, Latin America etc.)

PART XII
RELIGION

Geoffrey Parrinder, MA, PhD, DD, Emeritus Professor of the Comparative Study of Religions, University of London

PART XIII
MEDICAL, SCIENTIFIC AND INDUSTRIAL RESEARCH
INFORMATION TECHNOLOGY

ENVIRONMENT

Martin Redfern, Chief Producer, BBC Science Radio Unit
David Powell, A Director of Electronic Publishing Services Ltd and Interactive Media Publications Ltd
Julian Coleman, Journalist, broadcaster and radio producer specializing in the environment, development and science

PART XIV
INTERNATIONAL LAW

EUROPEAN COMMUNITY LAW

LAW IN THE UK

LAW IN THE USA

Christine Gray, MA, PhD, Fellow in Law, St John's College, Cambridge
N. March Hunnings, LLM, PhD, Editor, *Encyclopedia of European Union Law: Constitutional Texts*
David Ibbetson, MA, PhD, Fellow and Tutor in Law, Magdalen College, Oxford
Robert J. Spjut, JD, LLM, Member of the State Bars of California and Florida

PART XV
OPERA

MUSIC

BALLET/DANCE

THEATRE
CINEMA
TV & RADIO
VISUAL ARTS
ARCHITECTURE
LITERATURE

Charles Osborne, Author; opera critic, *The Jewish Chronicle*
Francis Routh, Composer and author; founder director of the Redcliffe Concerts
Jane Pritchard, Archivist, Rambert Dance Company and English National Ballet
Jeremy Kingston, Theatre critic, *The Times*
Derek Malcolm, Film critic, *The Guardian*
Raymond Snoddy, Media Editor, *The Times*
David Cohen, MA, Art critic and lecturer
Paul Finch, Editor, *The Architects' Journal*
Alastair Niven, Director of Literature, British Council; formerly Literature Director of the Arts Council of England

CONTRIBUTORS   xiii

PART XVI
SPORT   Tony Pawson, OBE, Sports writer, *The Observer;* cricket, football and fly-fishing international

PART XVIII
OBITUARY   James Bishop, Editor-in-Chief, *The Illustrated London News*

PART XIX
CHRONICLE OF 1999   Verena Hoffman, Assistant Editor, *The Annual Register*

MAPS AND DIAGRAMS   Michael Lear, MJL Graphics, N. Yorks, YO14 9BE

ACKNOWLEDGMENTS

THE Editor gratefully acknowledges his debt to a number of institutions for their help with sources, references and documents, notably the NATO Secretariat in Brussels and the UN Secretariat in New York. Acknowledgment is also due to the principal sources for the national and IGO data sections (showing the situation as at end-1999 unless otherwise stated), namely *Keesing's Record of World Events* (Keesing's Worldwide), the *1999/2000 World Development Report* (Oxford University Press for the World Bank) and the *Financial Times* (London). The Board and the bodies which nominate its members disclaim responsibility for any opinions expressed or the accuracy of facts recorded in this volume.

ABBREVIATIONS OF NON-UN INTERNATIONAL ORGANIZATIONS

AC	Arctic Council
ACP	African, Caribbean and Pacific states associated with EU
ACS	Association of Caribbean States
AL	Arab League
ALADI	Latin American Integration Association
AMU	Arab Maghreb Union
ANZUS	Australia-New Zealand-US Security Treaty
AP	Amazon Pact
APEC	Asia-Pacific Economic Cooperation
ASEAN	Association of South-East Asian Nations
Benelux	Belgium-Netherlands-Luxembourg Economic Union
BSEC	Black Sea Economic Cooperation
CA	Andean Community of Nations
Caricom	Caribbean Community and Common Market
CBSS	Council of the Baltic Sea States
CE	Council of Europe
CEEAC	Economic Community of Central African States
CEFTA	Central European Free Trade Agreement
CEI	Central European Initiative
CIS	Commonwealth of Independent States
COMESA	Common Market of Eastern and Southern Africa
CP	Colombo Plan
CPLP	Community of Portuguese-Speaking Countries
CWTH	The Commonwealth
EBRD	European Bank for Reconstruction and Development
ECO	Economic Cooperation Organization
ECOWAS	Economic Community of West African States
EEA	European Economic Area
EFTA	European Free Trade Association
EU	European Union
G–8	Group of Eight
GCC	Gulf Cooperation Council
IOC	Indian Ocean Commission
Mercosur	Southern Cone Common Market
NAFTA	North American Free Trade Agreement
NAM	Non-Aligned Movement
NATO	North Atlantic Treaty Organization
NC	Nordic Council
OAPEC	Organization of Arab Petroleum Exporting Countries
OAS	Organization of American States
OAU	Oganization of African Unity
OECD	Organization for Economic Cooperation and Development
OECS	Organization of Eastern Caribbean States
OIC	Organization of the Islamic Conference
OPEC	Organization of the Petroleum Exporting Countries
OSCE	Organization for Security and Cooperation in Europe
PC	Pacific Community
PFP	Partnership for Peace
PIF	Pacific Islands Forum
SAARC	South Asian Association for Regional Cooperation
SADC	Southern African Development Community
SELA	Latin American Economic System
UEMOA	West African Economic and Monetary Union
WEU	Western European Union

PREFACE

As John Roberts points out in his political overview of the year, 1999 was not strictly speaking the last year of the twentieth century or of the second millennium. Nevertheless, the powerful symbolism of the imminent arrival of the year 2000 persuaded the world that a moment of transition was at hand and therefore stimulated an outpouring of surveys and analysis both of the twentieth century and of the past thousand years of human history. In that spirit, the present volume highlights the fact that *The Annual Register* has chronicled nearly a quarter of the second millennium (from 1758 onwards) by publishing, on the immediately following pages, extended extracts from past volumes. The first is from the 1775 AR's treatment of the American War of Independence; the last an extract from the 1963 volume's coverage of the assassination of President Kennedy. In between, other extracts illustrate how the AR has recorded the major political, military, social and scientific developments of the past 241 years.

In its main sections, this volume records how the last year of the nineteen-hundreds made a full contribution to the century's record as the most violent and turbulent in recorded history. Full coverage is given to the Europe's first conflict between states since World War II—the mobilization of NATO forces against Yugoslavia to stop perceived 'ethnic cleansing' in Kosovo—and also to Russia's rather more bloody action against Chechen separatist rebels on its southern flank. Further afield, the human miseries of East Timor's struggle for independence from Indonesia are chronicled, as are the latest round of open hostilities between India and Pakistan over Kashmir and the never-ending tribal wars of the African continent.

On a brighter note, relative economic progress is another theme of the 1999 AR, led by the remarkable continuing boom in the United States and extending both to Western Europe and, to a lesser extent, to the Asian economies recovering from near meltdown in 1997. Within the European Union, the historic launching on 1 January 1999 of a single currency, the euro, by 11 of the 15 member states appeared to assist the process of economic recovery by the participants, as this volume records. Yet the record of the year again confirmed that the maintenance of economically prosperous and stable societies is, so far, an achievement confined to relatively few countries, with the result that the successful ones increasingly felt themselves to be redoubts of civilization in a dangerous world.

Also catalogued in these pages is the year's exceptional record of devastating natural disasters in many parts of the globe, some caused or at least aggravated by human interference with the environment. And the darkest cloud of all—the fast-developing scourge of the deadly AIDS virus, particularly in Africa—meant that, as the second millennium ended, millions would not live long into the third.

Sadly, the Obituary section of this volume includes an entry for H.V. (Harry) Hodson, former Editor of the AR, who died on 27 March 1999 at the age of 92.

EXTRACTS FROM PAST VOLUMES

224 years ago

1775. *War in the American colonies.* [London, 20 January] Lord Chatham moved an address to his majesty, for recalling the troops from Boston. This motion was ushered in and supported by a long speech, in which he represented this measure as a matter of immediate necessity; an hour now lost in allaying the ferment in America, might produce years of calamity; the present situation of the troops rendered them and the Americans continually liable to events, which would cut off the possibility of a reconciliation.... The question was rejected by a vast majority.

200 years ago

1799. *Death of George Washington.* [Mount Vernon, 14 December] The illustrious general George Washington died, at his seat, at Mount Vernon, the 14th of December 1799, in the 68th year of his age, after a short illness of about twenty-four hours. His disorder was an inflammatory sore throat, which proceeded from a cold, of which he made but little complaint on the 13th. The next morning, about three o'clock, he became ill. Dr. Graick attended him in the morning, and Dr. Dick, of Alexandria, and Dr. Brown, of Port Tobacco, were soon after called in. Every medical assistance was offered, but without the desired effect. His last scene corresponded with the whole tenor of his life. Not a groan nor a complaint escaped him, in extreme distress. With perfect resignation, and a full possession of his reason, he closed his virtuous life.

194 years ago

1805. *Battle of Trafalgar.* [21 October] At twenty minutes past twelve the action became general; — It had been the intention of lord Nelson to have penetrated the adversary's line, between the tenth and eleventh of his ships in the van; but finding it so close, that there was not room to pass, he ordered the Victory, which bore his flag, to be run on board the ship opposed to him, and the Temeraire, his second, also ran on board of the next ship in the enemy's line, so that these four ships formed one mass, and were so close, that every gun fired from the Victory set the Redoubtable. to which she was opposed, on fire; whilst the British sailors were employed, at intervals, in the midst of the hottest action, in pouring buckets of water on the flames in the enemy's vessel, lest their spreading should involve both ships in destruction! An instance of cool and deliberate bravery not to be paralleled in ancient or modern history.

184 years ago

1815. *Battle of Waterloo.* [18 June] The Prussian pursuit was most active and vigorous. The Marshal [Blucher] had ordered that the last man and the last horse should join in it, and nothing could be more complete than the discomfiture of the French. ... Such was the battle of Waterloo, one of the most warmly contested, and most decisive, in modern military history. It shed the highest lustre on the British army, and raised their great commander [Wellington] to the summit of martial reputation. In his own modest narratives his name has rarely appeared, but all the private accounts of this engagement were filled with anecdotes of his extraordinary coolness in the most trying circumstances, and of the intrepidity with which he exposed himself where the danger was most urgent.

179 years ago

1820. *Death of George III.* [29 January] Seldom has so much private virtue adorned a throne, as in the person of George III. It may be said of him with truth (and no higher praise can a king of England receive), that he had not among his subjects a worthier man than himself. His habits of temperance, of early rising, and of regular exercise , enabled him to retain long, and to enjoy fully, the blessings of the vigorous constitution which he had received from nature. His pleasures were all simple and innocent; they consisted chiefly in the gratification which his domestic affections found in the bosom of his numerous family, varied by the sports of the field, amd by agricultural pursuits. He had no propensity to vain or ostentatious expense, though the splendour of his court was maintained with due decorum. As a husband, as a father, as a master, he was a model worthy of the imitation of his subjects.

150 years ago

1849. *The Bermondsey murder.* Thus, by the magic of modern science, which in this case is made the handmaid to retributive justice, intimation of a murder is conveyed from London to Edinburgh, with a description of the suspected person; and ere the superintendent of police in the former city can return to his office, a message has arrived from the northern capital, with a speed that equals the velocity of the thunderbolt, announcing that the presumed culprit [Mrs Manning] is in the hands of the law, with the damning evidence of her guilt upon her.

117 years ago

1882. *Death of Charles Darwin.* Darwin, it is said, like Murchison, was a keen fox-hunter in his youth, and that it was in the field that his great habits of observation were first wakened.... In 1859 was published what may be regarded as the most momentous of his works, "The Origin of Species by means of Natural Selection," which called forth the most alarmed anathemas from all who regarded themselves as especially orthodox in both science and religion. By slow degrees, however, the tempest thus roused calmed down, and before many years had passed Mr. Darwin's theory was very generally accepted by investigators of all schools.

100 years ago

1899. *The Dreyfus Affair.* [Paris] From the outset there was a practically universal opinion in this country that Captain Dreyfus was the victim, in the first instance, if not of an actual conspiracy among highly placed members of the French headquarters staff, at any rate of a series of stupendous blunders, the parties to which afterwards stuck at nothing in order to protect themselves and one another from exposure. This view received much confirmation from the course of the trial at Rennes. Little, if anything, which in any English court would be admitted as evidence was offered by any of the witnesses against the prisoner ... The indignation of the British public was natural, and indeed justifiable, but it was expressed in not a few quarters with a vehemence and want of discrimination which were certainly unfortunate.

84 years ago

1915. *The Dardanelles Landing.* Perhaps the most important event of the war which occurred during the summer months was the landing of an Army in the Dardanelles. High hopes had been entertained that the combined forces of the Army and Navy would succeed in forcing their way past the forts which guarded the Straits. These hopes were greatly encouraged by the success of the very difficult and costly operation of landing the troops: few persons in England then doubted that Constantinople would be at the mercy of the Navy before the summer was over. As time went on and the Army failed to make any material advance, the prevailing optimism gradually changed to despondency; and criticism of the Government with reference to the matter gradually became more frequent and ominous.

83 years ago

1916. *Battle of Jutland.* [31 May–1 June] Having regard to the size of the fleets engaged, the losses were small, and the battle was of an inconclusive character, neither side being able to claim anything in the nature of a final victory. In so far, however, as the German fleet was driven back to port with wounds not less severe than those which it inflicted upon the detached portion of the British fleet with which it first came into contact, the advantage rested with the British. The British navy still ruled the seas, and though it was true that Admiral Scheer never hoped to wrest the command of the seas from the British in one blow, he was so little satisfied with the result of his attempt to begin destroying the British fleet in detail, that up till the end of the year under consideration he never issued forth again on the same errand.

EXTRACTS FROM PAST VOLUMES

82 years ago

1917. *Revolution in Russia.* The Bolsheviks secured control of the Petrograd Soviet, and of the Soviets in Moscow and other large towns. On November 7 a coup d'etat was carried through in Petrograd. A naval detachment acting under M. Lenin's orders, seized the Official Petrograd Telegraph Agency, the State Bank, and the Marie Palace, where the so-called Interim Parliament had been sitting. On the following day all the other important buildings in the capital were seized. M. Kerensky fled, and M. Tereshtchenko was arrested. M. Lenin became chief of the new Government, or "Commissaries of the People," as they styled themselves. Proclamations were issued by the Petrograd Soviet declaring that the policy of the new Revolutionary Committee included (1) the offer of an immediate democratic peace; (2) the transference of private landed estates to the peasants; (3) the concentration of all power in the hands of the Soviets, pending (4) the convocation, at an early date, of the Constituent Assembly. A certain M. Trotsky, who had been President of the Petrograd Soviet since the Bolsheviks had secured a majority on that body, became Foreign Minister in the new Lenin Cabinet.

76 years ago

1923. *Abortive Munich putsch.* In company with General Ludendorff, who had long been likewise a leading figure in the *"volkisch"* circles of Munich, [Hitler] seized von Kahr and von Lossow at a meeting in a brewery on November 8, and proclaimed a new German Government, to be established by a *"volkisch"* rising. Herr von Kahr at first announced himself an adherent of the rebels, styling himself "Viceroy of the King of Bavaria." But on the very next day he joined the Bavarian militia against Hitler and Ludendorff. These, as it proved, had greatly overestimated their following, and they had to capitulate.

70 years ago

1929. *New speed records.* [11 March] Mr. H.O.D. Segrave, in his Irving special racing car, Goblin Arrow, set up a new world record at Daytona Beach, Florida, with an average speed of 231.36226 miles an hour. [10 September] A new air-speed record was reached by a British seaplane above Southampton Water of 355.8 miles an hour, as compared with the previous highest flying speed of 318.6 miles an hour.

67 years ago

1932. *Discovery of the neutron.* [Cambridge, England] First place in the records of a year of quite unusual scientific achievement must be given to the discovery of the neutron, a particle of mass 1.0067 and charge 0 consisting of a proton (i.e. the positively charged nucleus of a hydrogen atom) and an electron in close union - much closer than in the ordinary hydrogen atom which has, otherwise, the same constitution. The possibility of the existence of such particles was pointed out by Lord Rutherford in 1920

66 years ago

1933. *Book-burning by Nazis [Berlin]* In May the Nazi students organised a strong movement against what they termed "Non-German Culture," which reached its height on May 10 in Berlin with a bonfire of books whose opinions did not please the students, including the works of some of the foremost authors of the present day. This outbreak was characterised all over the world as an illustration of inexcusable barbarism.

59 years ago

1940. *Start of the London blitz.* In one of his speeches in August, Mr. Churchill had expressed his confidence that, if put to the test, the people of London would show no less power of resistance than the population of Barcelona had done during the Spanish Civil War. This prediction proved quite correct. Londoners in the mass showed a cheerful courage in face of suffering and an adaptability to new conditions which won universal admiration. The calamities inflicted by the raids produced no sign of panic, but only an intense desire for revenge. They also created a spirit of fellowship and of mutual help which went far to counteract their evil effects. The barriers between classes were loosened, social antipathies were softened, and community of suffering led among other things to a great mitigation of the anti-Jewish feeling in the East End, in spite of efforts by Fascists and pro-Nazis to keep it alive.

58 years ago

1941. *Barbarity of German rule.* The rights of man have been done away with in all countries under direct or indirect German rule. The sufferings of the occupied Slav countries are reminiscent of the darkest chapters in the record of mankind. The torture of Poland surpasses even the atrocities of the Conquista.

54 years ago

1945. *Discovery of Nazi prison camps.* In the course of their advance into the interior of Germany the British and American armies came across some of the Nazi prison camps which had been in evil repute for the barbarous treatment accorded to the unfortunate inmates. They found the actual conditions more terrible and gruesome than the worst that had been reported, especially at the two largest camps at Belsen and Buchenwald. The accounts of them sent home by Press correspondents shocked the British public beyond measure and raised to a white heat its indignation against the Nazi regime and party, and even against the German people in general.

The atomic bomb. While everyone was glad that the war had been shortened, the means which had been used to shorten it gave rise to profound misgivings. The potentialities of mischief inherent in the atomic bomb could not be overlooked, and the question was bound to arise whether human ingenuity had not created a demon which human wisdom would be unable to control.

50 years ago

1949. *Communist victory in China.* Though it had conquered all China, therefore, the new regime was still faced at the end of the year with immense problems. Internally these included the consolidation of the regime's political position, the maintenance of the remarkably high level of self-abnegation and incorruptibility which had been attained by the C.P.C. and its supporters during their long struggle, and the reconstruction and development of the economy of the country, all of which involved vast social changes. Externally the regime had still to secure recognition from much of the world...and to eliminate the last vestiges of the era of 'unequal treaties'.

47 years ago

1950. *United Nations and Korea.* The United Nations' fifth year of existence was the most dramatic since the founding of the organization. Opening in the uneasy but static atmosphere caused by the deadlock over Chinese representation, the year saw U.N. suddenly galvanized by the Korean conflict into an act without precedent in history—the launching of international military action against an aggressor State in the name of a world organization.

43 years ago

1956. *The Hungarian Uprising.* The country, naturally, saw only that the hated Soviet tyranny had returned. The fighting which followed the treacherous Russian coup was on a scale and of an intensity far exceeding that of the preceding week. The Soviets employed heavy artillery and bombers, and their troops, many of whom were Asians, used their arms ruthlessly and indiscriminately. The Hungarian freedom fighters, most of whom were of young or even of tender age, fought back with the reckless courage of fury and despair, while the workers and miners backed the combatants by a general strike of extraordinary completeness.

37 years ago

1962. *Nobel Prize for discovery of DNA*. The breakthrough had come on two fronts. First, in determining the structure of deoxyribonucleic acid—called DNA for short. It had been known for several years [since 1953] that the long thin strands of DNA in the nuclei of all living cells were the carriers of hereditary information from one generation to another, and that they controlled the structure of the rest of the cell in which they were embedded.... The prize for medicine was shared by Dr Francis Crick [Cambridge University]..., Dr Maurice Wilkins of King's College, London, and Dr J.P. Watson of Harvard.

36 years ago

1963. *Assassination of President Kennedy.* [Dallas, 22 November] No American will forget the year 1963. On 22 November, during the course of what had been an unimportant and little remarked political visit to a number of cities in Texas, President John Fitzgerald Kennedy was assassinated while driving in an open car through the streets of Dallas. It was an act as senseless as it was abhorrent, and if there was a reasoned motive in the mind of the assassin it will probably never be known, for the man accused of the crime was himself shot dead two days later....President Kennedy was youthful and vigorous in spirit, and in his short term of office he had succeeded in restoring the confidence of the people in themselves, and the confidence of other nations in the United States.

THE ANNUAL REGISTER
FOR THE YEAR 1999

I OVERVIEWS OF THE YEAR

1. GLOBAL ISSUES AND REGIONAL REALITIES

LIKE many of its predecessors, the penultimate year of the twentieth century was bloody and violent. It ended, too, with natural disaster on a terrifying scale. Sadly, none of that made it distinctive. In the course of time, too, a non-lethal—and, at least to that extent, peaceful—event in its closing weeks might well affect the lives of more people in the long run than fighting in Chechnya or floods in Venezuela. At the beginning of December the World Trade Organization (WTO) met in Seattle amid the shouts of demonstrators and drifting tear-gas in the streets outside. Some of those taking part in the uproar were questioning, among other things, whether this ostensibly benevolent and to most human beings unknown institution should exist at all. Having the WTO in town brought to the surface for many the intolerably persistent division of the world into rich and poor, North and South, developed and undeveloped, and other gratifyingly simple antitheses hawked about in recent years.

The WTO had been expected to help somewhat to overcome such divisions by advancing the cause of Free Trade, a creed which ten years or so earlier some had credulously believed to lie at the heart of the End of History then heralded. Others had believed it would steadily close the gap between rich and poor. To many, though, the visible outcome seemed to have been more Unfair Trade, arrangements (or the absence of them) which penalized poorer economies and meant in practice safeguarding and promoting the interests of global corporations and American economic hegemony. In 1999 itself, the United States had blocked international agreement on the control of genetic modification of foodstuffs, and had engaged in the 'banana war' with the European Union (EU) at the expense of poor former colonial nations. Some disliked, too, the efforts made by the United States to get China into the WTO, seeing in it only the greed of those attracted by a market of a billion potential consumers and the danger of imposing on them many allegedly damaging and much-blamed social and economic consequences of unbridled capitalism. That China's rulers seemed cautiously keen to join up was only additional reason for mistrust, they thought.

In the end, the main beneficiary of the fiasco in Seattle was probably President Clinton. Wary of the possible electoral fickleness of American trade unions, he succeeded in blurring the embarrassing fact that it was in their own vested economic interest, as well as that of their members' employers, that they had demanded minimum wages and better conditions for the overworked, underpaid and often under-age industrial labour of the Third World. Nothing could be done in the WTO meetings, for good or ill and that perhaps showed an essential continuity too. The losers were the world's poor, but they had not been there to demonstrate and their spokesmen had not been heard.

The excitement aroused by the WTO, even if brief and damaging to economic well-being, was symptomatic of the on-rolling continuity of so much of world history despite the efforts of well-meaning or self-interested alike. In Africa, certainly, such continuity was depressingly evident. The judgments made in *The Annual Register* a year ago (see AR 1998, p. 6), that its problems then looked as insoluble as ever and were perhaps also as much disregarded, can be renewed. Behind them lies the reality that 1999 had brought civil war, rebellion or forcible changes of government, often at terrible cost, to Algeria, Angola, Chad, the Congo, the Democratic Republic of the Congo, Guinea-Bissau, Niger, Nigeria, Sierra Leone, Somalia, and Uganda, while Ethiopia and Eritrea were almost continually fighting one another. It was only a small offset to this that the Republic of South Africa peacefully and without difficulty achieved its second general election and its first change of president in June; there too, though, friendly observers found ample cause for concern in the problems facing the young state.

On other continents, too, events had a similar and deplorable familiarity. There was fighting in Afghanistan, Sri Lanka and even Papua New Guinea. Confrontation came to conflict once more between Indian and Pakistani forces in May. Almost contemporaneously, the huge and sprawling republic of Indonesia both provided a tragic example of political failure in not maintaining peaceful procedures for the assumption by East Timor of an independence already conceded to it in principle, and witnessed a continuing series of smaller-scale massacres in its northernmost province. As the year closed, these appeared to be spreading through the Moluccas. When, finally, the UN assumed responsibility for East Timor, it was in ruins, without a government, terrorized by bandits resisting the coming of independence, without government, police or even crops to gather in.

All this should have made for pessimism, but in a few places there were grounds for moderate satisfaction. In Ireland there met the first institutions providing for the representation of the whole island in some governmental functions as well as a new assembly for Northern Ireland. This was part and parcel of the process of devolution which was also giving representative institutions to Scotland and to Wales. The closing of the history of the United Kingdom was at last beginning to come into sight without, remarkably, much fuss being made except in Ulster. Another historic British institution, the House of Lords, also underwent mutilation in the name of good government without public outcry. Perhaps the British did not mind silently withdrawing from their history; they had, after all, said goodbye to empire with relatively little stress.

At the year's end even the Middle East looked a little less explosive. An eagerly awaited and at once realised change in temperature followed the Israeli general election in June which initiated a search for coalition under Mr Barak, who also quickly engaged in vigorous personal diplomacy with leaders of Arab states, even exchanging compliments with Syria, the old enemy. The Palestinian leader, Mr Arafat, was assured that the agreements of the previous year would be carried out; he helped by cautiously delaying the threatened proclamation of an independent Palestinian state, while the Jewish lobby in New York conceded that it no longer felt it had to oppose one in principle. As December ended, new talks were about to open in Washington between the Israeli government and the Syrians. The world waited with fingers crossed, no-one's, one may presume, more firmly than Mr Clinton's.

There could even be found some signs of comfort in a wider Islamic context. For all the attacks on Christian communities in Indonesia, the Islamic contribution to Russia's difficulties in the North Caucasus and the barbarities of Taleban Afghanistan, less was heard of extreme pan-Islamicism. An Islamist party showed poorly in the April Turkish general election and this can hardly have failed to contribute to the willingness the EU at last expressed in December to consider Turkey for membership. In Iran, President Khatami appeared to hold his ground against more intransigent religious leaders and in March, unprecedentedly, he called on the Pope in the Vatican during the first visit paid by any Iranian leader to the Western world since the revolution of 1979. Possibly more menacing than ideological or even nationalist extremism, in fact, was the onset of a second year of drought in the Middle East. It might be that long-standing quarrels focused on Israel would before long be displaced by others much more divisive, over water.

If there was a general political theme which hung over the whole year, it was an old one. For all the many and noisy challenges to governments which exploded the world round, the state, and with it the most successful political idea of the last two centuries, national sovereignty, was obviously alive and well. Russians and Chinese found it easy to agree that the protection of human rights should not be allowed to infringe national sovereignty, and said so bluntly and often. Coincidentally and almost risibly (given the differing magnitudes of what might be at stake), the French government flatly declared that it would not withdraw its ban on the importation and sale in France of British beef. From the noisy exchanges of Tweedledum and Tweedledee diplomacy as reported in the popular press, this propelled the ball into the court of the embarrassed Brussels Commission, which had now to contemplate the necessity of legal proceedings against France. The latter's assertion of national sovereignty flouted international law in the familiar shape of EU treaty obligations. The Russians and Chinese did not need to go so far. They simply denounced what they saw as a questionable and dangerous doctrine touted by some other national governments whose own interests were not at stake.

Nonetheless, in their different ways, all three governments were asserting the same priority, just as was, in yet another mode, the United States, by its refusals to ratify international agreements about atmospheric pollution or the creation of an international court to deal with war crimes. Russia was able to assert its interests and rights against a more confident domestic background than for some time, even if when the year was over it was still hard to see where Russia was really going. Its internal state could then be judged to look more promising than when it began—it was no longer expected, for example, that Russia would default on its debts. True, continuing uncertainty and uneasiness over Boris Yeltsin's health, emotional state, possible involvement in corruption and highly personalized style of politics (in August he dismissed his fourth Prime Minister in 17 months) had all given rise to concern. Yet the floundering Russian economy was in no more obvious peril in December than it had been in January. Mr Yeltsin was by then fortunate, too, in being able to preside over what could be represented as a military victory and was certainly a winning of the upper hand in the new campaign launched against the Chechens in September. This evidently quickened the patriotism of many Russians who recalled historical struggle with the Chechens and resented the terrorist bombings they attributed to them. It also pleased the generals who found recompense for their humiliation four years before in steadily obliterating Grozny, the Chechen capital. It was another way of making clear, too, that the outside world (which to Mr Yeltsin meant, above all, NATO) had little power to affect the fate even of the refugees from Grozny, let alone the political destinies of their country, and could do nothing to change the will of the Russian government or the direction of its policy.

Russians liked Mr Yeltsin's trumpetings about non-interference in Russia's affairs or those of its friends. Whether the military and political outlook for the Russian Federation was or was not in fact brightened by events in the northern Caucasus, the December elections returned a Duma less likely to quarrel with the President than had been its predecessor. Mr Yeltsin could now look forward to easier relations with the politicians in the few months of office left to him. It was all the more surprising, therefore, that he resigned on New Year's Eve. Whether this would prove an advantage to Vladimir Putin, his Prime Minister and chosen successor in tackling the major problems of institutional reform, corruption and organized crime which Russia faced at almost every level was not clear: one of Mr Putin's first steps was to sign a decree granting Mr Yeltsin and his family immunity from prosecution; but it suggested that he would win the presidential election to be held in March 2000.

Early in the year, attempts to impeach their elected Presidents had aborted both in Russia and the United States. Even before the US Senate hearings began, it had been almost certain that Mr Clinton would escape conviction or severe censure, and perhaps any censure at all for his abuse of his office and devious behaviour. The Republicans were embarrassed by the Americans' evident lack of enthusiasm for impeachment, the Democrats by having to argue in the President's defence that the charges against him were not grave enough to warrant impeachment, even if he were guilty of them. Mr Clinton demeaned himself by the quibbling argument that, in the technical terms set by relevant legal proceedings, he had not had 'sexual relations' with Ms Lewinsky, but the Senate rejected the charge of perjury and went to a tied vote on the question of alleged obstruction of justice. America then resumed normal politics.

These often turned out to be frustrating both for Mr Clinton and for others, as Congress showed itself increasingly hostile to legislation put forward by the White House. Though excitement began to subside once the possibility of impeachment was out of the way, what had happened had sharpened party antagonism. The year unrolled in partisan stagnation and growing acrimony as potential presidential candidates began the struggle for nomination the following year. Meanwhile, 1999 could hardly have seemed a bad year to most Americans. Soon after it began, Mr Clinton once again presented a budget envisaging a handsome surplus. Thereafter, the economy continued to favour him. Although there continued to be talk of the danger of inflation, the year ended with the stock market still high and a diffused sense of well-being.

Mr Clinton's political weakness and preoccupation with electoral politics handicapped him in facing events abroad, too. As of Sarajevo in 1914, it might be asked why what happened in Kosovo in 1999 should so interest outsiders after fighting between Serbs and Albanians had begun there the year before. By February the sterile discussions of their representatives understandably preoccupied Europeans who feared the spread of disorder into neighbouring countries and possibly further. But only when the Serbians refused to admit a NATO 'peace-keeping' force to their territory and NATO forces finally began air operations against targets in Serbia without the authorization of the UN did the full implications of what was going forward emerge. It was, after all, a startling new departure in principle. No such international warlike operations had been seen in Europe since the days of the Holy Alliance. They were undertaken outside the territory of any NATO country (whose defence had been the original and always central purpose of the alliance) and were inevitably regarded as a threat in Moscow, already displeased by the very recent accession to NATO of Poland, Hungary and the Czech Republic.

The dangers were immediately apparent. The Russian Prime Minister denounced the bombing and voiced the sympathy of his fellow-Russians for the Serbs. Kosovar refugees began to pour into Albania and Macedonia in even greater numbers and soon in hundreds of thousands. Ordnance went astray and civilians, Albanian and Serb alike, began to be killed. Potential divisions and real weaknesses began to appear in the NATO ranks; the Italians and Greeks were particularly unhappy, while the US government remained unwilling to pay the price of its hegemonic power and hung back both from air operations which could endanger the lives of American personnel and from the ground campaign urged by the British. After the bombing of its embassy in Belgrade, the Chinese government announced it would oppose any peace proposals in the United Nations until the air strikes ceased. The possibilities of forcing surrender were not enhanced by the publication in May of an indictment of the Serb President and some of his colleagues on charges of war crimes by an international court.

Nonetheless, when bombing and Russian advice in Belgrade prevailed and the Serbians began to withdraw from Kosovo, tension relaxed somewhat. The United Nations became involved when its administration was set up in the province and NATO forces took up occupation duties there. Albanian Kosovars, soured by the experience they had undergone, eagerly turned on the minority of Serbs who remained there. New flows of refugees, this time Serb, began, with their concomitant miseries and sufferings, while returning Kosovars hurried back to towns and villages devastated by the bombing campaign and by Serbian demolitions and atrocities. 'K-For', the NATO-led international ground force operating at last under a UN resolution, could not ensure order, or enforce peaceful behaviour. Worse still, at Pristina airport it seemed as if there was a danger at one moment of Russian and British forces coming into conflict with one another.

All in all, the Kosovo operation could not be counted as an out-and-out success. Yet nor was it clearly, far less wholly, a failure. The attackers achieved their aim of forcing the government of Yugoslavia to change its behaviour towards its Albanian subjects in Kosovo, an aim which was a particular embodiment of the growing concern in some Western circles to advance what they saw as the protection of human rights. In the end Serbia had been excluded from the government of one of its own provinces in the name of that principle. Yet the cost was huge in the damage inflicted on the economic and governmental infrastructure of the Serbian republic, in the killing of innocent Albanians and Serbs, and in the misery of hundreds of thousands of refugees. A military victory, nonetheless, had been achieved at almost no cost in casualties to the NATO forces, even if at enormous expense. But few rejoiced over it and it had left great power relations tainted. Not unlike the Gulf War, it combined technical success with public relations failure.

The outlook was uncertain and ominous; by the end of the year, Europe's first major military operation of the century conducted wholly and ostensibly in defence of human rights had saddled the UN with an embarrassingly open-ended moral commitment to reconstruction and occupation in Kosovo. It had not provoked change in the Serbian government; its leader (and the original author of most of his countrymen's miseries, for they could be traced back to his speech ten years earlier which promised that Kosovo should be retained by Serbia willy-nilly), Slobodan Milošević, was still in office. His country, difficult to see at the outset as anything but the morally guilty party because of its treatment of the Kosovars, had won back some of the moral advantage by the end of the fighting thanks to the tenacity shown by its population under bombardment and the errors and excesses of the attackers, to say nothing of the Americans' unwillingness to risk casualties or engagement on the ground. Meanwhile, their evident fear of casualties had encouraged Russian and Chinese support for the government in Belgrade and had led to talk for the first time since the previous decade of the danger of a third world war.

The Kosovo episode had further and particularly wounded American relations with China, which, even before the crisis, were at best limping somewhat. The bombing of the Belgrade embassy was less important than the alarm the

Chinese government felt and showed from the start over the legal issue. Though its hectic recent rate of economic growth had fallen off, China was still changing fast, though not always in ways easy to recognize or judge. Much was easily overlooked by foreigners obsessed by the ten-year anniversary of the Tiananmen Square massacre (which, thanks to massive police precautions, passed off quietly, as did the celebrations of a half-century of the People's Republic). Matters such as the lifting of the ban on Walt Disney films and governmental admissions that there had been wrongful judgments in the judicial system were trivial but should perhaps have been given more careful appreciation. So should have been the turmoil of disagreement and debate evident within the ruling Communist Party over further relaxing on restraints on external trade. But cautious and crablike steps towards modernity, even if deliberate, were not enough for those who wanted to coerce China over its human rights record, and to denounce its government's aggressive and bullying government of Tibet, its harrying of religious sects, or even its intransigence over the old issue of Taiwan, still of major symbolic and commercial importance to some Americans. The Taiwanese government was, of course, left in still more stark isolation after the resumption in December of Chinese sovereignty in Macao, the last colonial possession left on the old territory of the Chinese empire. This was a milestone on a very long historical road; Macao, after all, had been the first colonial enclave within the imperial borders.

By and large, therefore, Chinese-American relations deteriorated or at least showed no improvement during the year. The American announcement of a programme of 'theatre missile defence' looked in Beijing like a revival of the 'Star Wars' threats which had so impressed the Soviet authorities 15 years before. Nagging about human rights produced no effect there except irritation. American efforts to get China into the WTO bore fruit eventually in an agreement between the two countries (which had, nonetheless, still to go before a probably hostile Congress as the year ended) but the first visit by the Chinese Prime Minister to the United States fell far short of creating the goodwill which had been hoped of it. By then, the Chinese had already denounced the bombing of Yugoslavia as an assault on a sovereign state. American confidence was soon damaged further by allegations of Chinese espionage in the United States. Then came the Belgrade embassy disaster. In spite of a prompt American apology, for a moment there flickered on the horizon the suggestion of more than diplomatic breakdown. But in an age of trans-oceanic bombing strikes, Beijing's thinking no doubt dwelt more on the possible implications of Kosovo for Tibet than on those for Europe, and it should never have been expected that China's rulers would embrace a doctrine so potentially dangerous to them as the assertion of rights of intervention such as were claimed by NATO. In the event, it became clear that although Chinese dignity was affronted, Beijing would content itself with apologies, compensation and an affirmation (together with Moscow) of the sanctity of national sovereignty. But it seemed clear that Mr Clinton's administration had breathed new life into the Moscow-Beijing axis so painstakingly undermined by American foreign policy a quarter-century earlier.

Perhaps the European Union drew some benefit from the lessons of this episode. No doubt the sense of a loss of control of events in the former Yugoslavia contributed to its policy-making later in the year. It had opened with the introduction on New Year's Day of a common currency among a majority of the Union's members. The increased prosperity this was expected to bring and the next steps to be taken towards the enlargement of the Union were the main preoccupations of European leaders at that time. A year later, the new euro currency stood at substantial and disappointing discount from its issue value. Worse, there had been positive failures and much that looked like failure in the EU's working. Even in January, criticism in the European Parliament had led the president of the Commission to threaten resignation; Britons regretted that the British leader of the Socialist Group of parliamentarians appeared to fail to press home action to secure that he did so. But it was a sign that there might, after all, be creative responses in the making, and soon they came, after the commissioners' collective, and in some cases individual, discharge of their responsibilities was denounced in March. The whole Commission then resigned, a change warmly and widely welcomed, and a new president and Commission were appointed. As the year ended, the beneficial effects of this had still fully to appear, but it was a hopeful sign, and perhaps an important one, that a meeting of heads of EU governments in December decided to invite six more countries to join the list of those seeking membership and to launch the preparation of a European military force independent of NATO.

2. THE INTERNATIONAL ECONOMY

THE economy of the 29-nation OECD group—comprising nearly all of the biggest economies except China—expanded by nearly 3 per cent in 1999, compared with 2.4 per cent the previous year. The outcome for 1999 was almost double the rate forecast by the OECD in the first part of the year and represented one of the sharpest upward revisions in recent memory. During the most recent four years (1996-99) the OECD achieved average growth of 3 per cent a year, significantly greater than the previous five years, though somewhat short of the 3.8 per cent average recorded in the six years to 1989.

Following the pattern of recent years, world economic growth was inequitably distributed, although output growth among non-OECD countries, at 3.3 per cent, was actually greater than world growth as a whole, thereby correcting part of the maldistribution of previous years. The USA grew almost twice as fast as the European Union (EU) and nearly three times as fast as Japan. The one-sided nature of this expansion left the USA at the end of the year with a worrying current-account deficit equivalent to almost 4 per cent of GDP while the EU bloc and Japan wallowed in surpluses (in Japan's case of nearly 3 per cent of GDP).

In the Third World there were few bright spots. The predicted benefits from the Uruguay Round of tariff reductions proved to have been exaggerated, and the long-predicted turning-point for Africa did not happen, despite some individual success stories. The 1999 report of the UN Conference on Trade and Development (UNCTAD) noted that poverty and unemployment were once again on the increase in developing countries and that income and welfare gaps between and within countries had widened. However, the UNCTAD report relied on statistics for an earlier period. According to the Economist Intelligence Unit (in a report published at the turn of the year), Africa was starting to reap the benefit of 'prudent' fiscal policies, business-friendly reforms and a favourable movement in commodity prices, particularly of oil, which more than doubled in price during the year. The EU predicted that sub-Saharan Africa (the poorest region in the world) would become the fastest-growing region in 2000, with average growth of 3.9 per cent (led by Mozambique and Botswana with growth of 8 to 10 per cent).

Whereas the OECD gave a broadly enthusiastic picture of the world in 1999, featuring unexpectedly high growth accompanied by surprisingly low inflation, UNCTAD thought otherwise. It observed that the twentieth century had come to an end with the world 'deeply divided and unstable'. It regarded the failure to achieve faster growth that could narrow the gap between the rich and the poor as 'a defeat for the entire international community'.

The main reason for the upward revision in world growth in 1999 was regarded by some economists as the international economy's greatest potential problem—the astonishing performance of the US economy. It expanded by around 4 per cent in 1999, thereby confounding critics who had been predicting its fall from grace for several years. Its importance to the world economy was underlined by the fact that at the end of 1999 it accounted for over 35 per cent of total OECD gross domestic product—almost equivalent to the cumulative GDP of the next five biggest economies (Japan, Germany, France, Italy and the United Kingdom). During the most recent four years the US economy had recorded average growth of 4 per cent a year, a rate that would normally be considered to be so far above its productive potential as to guarantee overheating and inflation. In fact, consumer price rises over the same period fell from 2.9 to 1.6 per cent, which hardly suggested that a new inflationary spiral was about to begin.

America's stunning performance gave rise to a global debate during the year about whether the world, led by the USA, had embarked on a new era of high growth and low inflation as a result of the twin effects of globalization and the Internet. Protagonists of the 'new economy' approach argued that globalization made it more difficult for companies to raise their prices because there were so many alternative sources of supply around the world that were easily accessible. At the same time, the expansion of the World Wide Web—which was approaching critical mass in major industrialized countries—was exerting strong downward pressure on prices.

There were two main reasons for this trend. First, the nature of the Internet cuts out the middle person in a transaction, thereby reducing prices—although ironically some of the biggest early success stories on the Web, such as Amazon.com, the world's biggest bookseller, were themselves intermediaries.

In some cases, such as the delivery of music in digital forms, the 'product' could be dispatched instantaneously from someone's house to millions of customers all over the world, thereby removing the need to employ people in factories manufacturing disks or in the wholesale or retail chains.

However, this concept of 'evaporating inflation' was challenged by traditional economists, who claimed that globalization and the Internet had not triggered any significant increase in the underlying rate of productivity growth and that, far from ushering in an golden era of economic growth with low inflation, the Internet could bring about a recession in the very country, America, that was leading the digital revolution. In brief, the argument of the traditional economists was that the surge of consumer spending behind US economic growth was the result of the paper wealth created by the boom in Internet-related stocks on Wall Street (see also XIII.2). The Nasdaq composite index, which tracks most of the high tech stocks, rose more than 80 per cent in 1999, while the Goldman Sachs Internet index more than doubled. This had made people feel wealthier and they had been quite prepared to launch themselves into a debt-driven spending spree because of the security of their share portfolios. But, it was argued, the whole process would be thrown into reverse once the unsustainable rise in Internet stocks inevitably burst. In these circumstances, the argument continued, US consumers would be forced to start saving more of their incomes, triggering a collapse in consumer demand that would reverberate around the world.

Among other positive influences on world growth in 1999 were an unexpectedly robust recovery in key parts of Asia, including South Korea and, to a lesser extent, Japan, where growth was expected to be almost 1.5 per cent in 1999 compared with the unprecedented contraction of 2.8 per cent in 1998. China, whose relatively closed economy enabled it to escape the worst of the Asian recession, managed very respectable growth of 7 per cent. This was well down on the 10 per cent average of the recent past but impressive in the circumstances. Russia, despite its endemic political problems and economic chaos, surprised Western critics by achieving positive economic growth of nearly 2 per cent following yet another sharp contraction of almost 5 per cent the previous year.

Monetary policy in the OECD area, led as usual by the US Federal Reserve, was dominated by the question whether the world had embarked on a new era of low inflation. If it had, then the traditional response of central banks—to raise interest rates at the first signs of an economy starting to expand too fast—could prove fatal. Monetary policy only affects the real economy after a time lag of up to 18 months. So if a central bank were to raise interest rates to quell a prospective increase in inflation that would never have happened, then the economy in question could be propelled into a totally unnecessary recession instead of a period of extended growth.

Alan Greenspan, chairman of the US Federal Reserve, had been elevated to a near god-like status in the financial markets for the way he had resisted pressures to raise interest rates because of his belief that new technologies could be raising the rate at which the US economy could expand without generating inflation. Time and again in previous years he had resisted the knee-jerk reaction to raise interest rates at the first sign of turbulence. But even he felt obliged to apply three quarter point increases during the year, to 5.5 per cent from 16 November, to prevent the economy running into capacity restraints that could stoke up inflation. At the end of the year it still looked like a very awkward balancing act, as Mr Greenspan had to engineer a slowdown in the economy without inducing a crash in shares that could propel the economy into a dangerous downswing.

One of the puzzling things to emerge during 1999 was the expansion of what was dubbed the 'black hole' in international statistics. This arose from the fact that world imports (as recorded in trade data) were rising much faster than exports. The result was that, instead of exports equalling imports on a global scale, as they are supposed to do, a gap in the global current account emerged. The gap was $9,000 million in 1997 but by the end of 1999 had risen to over $92,000 million—or roughly equivalent to the current-account deficit of the USA. Eventually this discrepancy will have to be allocated between nations, so it could be that the US trade deficit will turn out to be less than was recorded.

The EU group of countries suffered a setback to long-awaited hopes of recovery in 1999 but was growing in confidence towards the end of the year. Economic growth in both the EU as a whole and the narrower 11-nation currency union of 'Euroland' was a modest 2.1 per cent in 1999, well below the rate of 3 per cent at which most economists reckoned could be achieved without stirring up serious inflationary pressures. Among the major countries, France, Germany and Italy all recorded lower growth in 1999 with only France (2.4 per cent) exceeding 2 per cent. It was clear, therefore, that European countries were still feeling the after-effects of having been forced to contract their budget deficits severely in order to qualify for monetary union under the terms of the Maastricht Treaty. Nevertheless, employment rose in Euroland by 1.5 per cent (compared with an OECD average of 1.1 per cent), while aggregate EU unemployment dropped from 10.1 per cent in 1998 to 9.4 per cent in 1999.

Proponents of the single European currency launched at the beginning of 1999 (see XI.4) were surprised when the value the new euro declined sharply against other currencies (by about 14 per cent against the US dollar) instead of appreciating, as they had expected. But this had the effect of injecting some much-needed competitiveness into a currency which in the opinion of some critics had been launched at too high a value against the dollar. By the end of the year the economies of Euroland had recovered sufficiently to induce the new European Central Bank (ECB) to raise interest rates by 0.5 per cent on 4 November, to 3 per cent. This was the bank's first test in dealing with potentially inflationary pressures. With inflation running at only 1.3 per cent a year in the euro area (notwithstanding the decline in the exchange rate), the ECB's first move against inflation was described by the OECD as 'pre-emptive'.

In Germany, the economic slowdown towards the end of 1998 continued into 1999, before an acceleration in the second half of the year as exports started taking over from business investment as the engine of expansion. During the year the federal government announced spending cuts equivalent to 0.4 per cent of GDP in order to boost fiscal prudence and generate some money for tax cuts and labour reforms (such as using the proceeds of an energy tax to cut pension contributions). The government hoped that this would help consolidate the recovery, which resulted in growth of 1.4 per cent in 1999 compared with 2.2 per cent the previous year.

Recovery in France got underway in the spring and was sustained by a rise in house-building, exports and business investment. GDP increased by 2.4 per cent compared with 3.4 per cent in 1997. Unemployment fell from 11.8 per cent to a (still very high) 11.1 per cent, against the background of inflation remaining at the subdued level of around 1 per cent. In Italy, GDP growth slowed from 1.3 to 1.0 per cent due to rising imports and falling exports. Unemployment remained stubbornly high at 11.9 per cent in the first quarter but dropped to around 11 per cent by the end of the year, and employment expanded strongly as well.

Although the United States rightly gained most of the plaudits for economic management in 1999, the United Kingdom also did much better than expected. Most economic forecasters (except, interestingly, the Treasury itself) had expected the UK economy to slow down significantly and even to contract in 1999. In the event, GDP expanded by around 2.2 per cent in 1999 or roughly the same as the previous year (see also II.1.i). This meant that Labour's 'Iron Chancellor', Gordon Brown, had avoided an actual recession during the downswing of the economic cycle—in contrast to the previous Conservative administration, which had suffered two periods of negative growth during the downswings.

During the year the buoyancy of consumer spending in Britain—up almost 4 per cent—offset the effects of diminished exports aggravated by the strength of the pound. Employment continued to increase notwithstanding the slowdown in economic activity and unemployment continued on its long downward trajectory, reaching levels not attained for over 25 years. By the end of the year unemployment was down to almost 4 per cent and inflation down to only 1.5 per cent (or even lower if calculated the same way as in the rest of the EU). However, there were sufficient clouds on the horizon—mainly a surge in house prices, particularly in the south-east, and a potentially worrying rise in average earnings (to 4.9 per cent)—to prompt the independent monetary policy committee of the Bank of England to start a new cycle of higher interest rates.

But this did not disguise the fact that the UK economy, thanks partly to the relatively benign state it was left in by the Conservatives, was performing better than it had for decades. At the end of 1999 the UK was enjoying a rare combination of steady growth without inflation, against the background of rapidly-improving public finances as the accounts headed towards a substantial budget surplus. There were also signs that manufacturers were responding to fears that the strong exchange rate might prevail for much longer. Companies like Marks & Spencer, BMW and J.C. Bamford started to increase the raw materials and components they imported from abroad, in order to counter the effects of the strong pound on their competitiveness.

The Russian economy recorded positive growth of around 2 per cent in 1999—not very much but representing a huge improvement in terms of the previous decade. In only one of the previous ten years had the economy showed positive growth (the modest 0.8 per cent recorded in 1997). Between 1989 and 1998 Russia's economy contracted by over 45 per cent. If it were to maintain growth of 2 per cent it would take Russia 25 years to recapture its 1989 level of GDP. But the achievement of 1999 should not be underrated. If it proves to be the long-awaited turning-point, then Russia may be entering the era of sustained positive growth that some economists have predicted. Among the positive trends in 1999 was a strong 7 per cent recovery of industrial production (helped by the earlier weakening of the rouble), strong exports, better tax collection and the high price of oil.

However, on the darker side, there was an increase in the illicit export of capital—closely associated with money laundering—with the result that the International Monetary Fund postponed one tranche of its financial assistance. Russia's banking system was still in chronic need of restructuring, partly because the process of reform was hampered by powerful pressure from businessmen and politicians with vested interests in bankrupt banks. The political situation in Russia was in turmoil for most of the year, with much of the increased oil revenues going to finance a debilitating war in Chechnya (see III.3.i). Monthly inflation fell to 3 per cent and even 2 per cent. The country also had a large current-account surplus of approaching $18,000 million.

But behind these financial figures there lurked increasing human tragedy in Russia. Real incomes in the middle of the year were estimated to have fallen by 13 per cent compared with a year earlier. According to the OECD, the proportion of families below the official subsistence line increased from 28 per cent to 38 per cent of the population. Unemployment reached 14 per cent in February before falling back later in the year.

The Russian crisis had bad rippling consequences for surrounding countries formerly part of the Soviet Union, including Belarus, Kazakhstan, Moldova and Ukraine. Moldova's economy contracted by 5.3 per cent, marking a cumulative contraction of over 55 per cent since 1994. Ukraine's economy contracted by another 1.7 per cent, preserving its dismal record of not having experienced any positive growth since the break-up of the former Soviet empire.

There was better news for those former satellites that were not so geographically bound up with Russia and which had started their reform programmes with more enthusiasm. Hungary grew by 4 per cent and Poland, helped by more political stability, expanded by 3.8 per cent, while the Czech Republic's zero growth for 1999 disguised the fact that it appeared to be emerging from the devaluation-induced recession of 1997-98.

In the South American region, real aggregate GDP growth declined, by more than 1 per cent, for the first time in 15 years. A few countries escaped mildly, notably Brazil, where growth was only slightly negative; but most, including

Argentina, Chile, Venezuela, Ecuador and Colombia, suffered severe recessions without any obvious signs of early recovery. Beleaguered by debt refinancing problems, Argentina contracted by 4 per cent despite having conquered inflation. Brazil's inflation rate increased from 1.8 per cent in 1998 to almost 8 per cent in 1999, but this was a modest outcome in the wake of a devaluation of almost 40 per cent.

Recovery among the so-called 'dynamic Asia economies' was faster than expected in 1999, just as their fall from grace the previous year (when GDP had contracted) had been worse than expected (see AR 1998, pp. 10-12). Fiscal stimulus at home and export growth abroad—helped by an upturn in global demand for electronics products partly associated with fears about the 'millennium bug' (see XIII.3)—were the main engines of growth. One of the most spectacular recoveries was in Thailand, where the economy expanded by over 4 per cent in 1999 after a 10 per cent contraction in 1998. Hong Kong, which had contracted by 5 per cent in 1998, managed to record small positive growth by the end of the year, as did Indonesia, which had shrunk by no less than 13 per cent in 1988. Malaysia turned negative growth of 7.5 per cent in 1998 into positive growth of 4.5 per cent in 1999.

The economy of South Korea (the only Asian member of the OECD apart from Japan) surged forward by 9 per cent in 1999 after shrinking by almost 6 per cent the previous year. Recovery was led by a 9 per cent recovery in private spending, almost making up the fall of the previous year. Unemployment, however, at 6.5 per cent was more than double the pre-crisis level and prompted a sharp rise in public spending to cope with it.

Although there were still structural weaknesses in parts of the 'dynamic Asian economies' there was a feeling in 1999 that the crisis of the previous year had been overblown and had not been justified by the economic fundamentals of the region, which were still positive. The exception was Japan, whose economy had completely dominated Asia for several decades until the 1990s, in which, apart from the exceptional growth of over 5 per cent in 1996, it became becalmed in the economic equivalent of the Doldrums. Having suffered an unprecedented contraction of 2.8 per cent in 1998, the Japanese economy seemed to have rebounded upwards in the first half of 1999, thanks to a succession of government stimulation measures; but it slowed down in the second half to produce overall growth of barely 1 per cent.

According to the *Financial Times*, the cumulative total of Japanese stimulation packages since 1992 was a staggering Y18,000,000 million. This was the main reason why the country's gross debt as a proportion of GDP had shot up from 60 to 130 per cent since 1991. Fragile recovery at the end of 1999 was threatened by a rise in the value of the yen, denting the power of Japan's still formidable manufacturing and high-tech sectors. Yet Japan still had a lot going for it, including a savings ratio at 12 per cent (almost five times higher than that of the USA), low or negative inflation and a $130,000 million trade balance (compared with a US deficit of $354,000 million).

In China, a slowdown in the first half of the year was reversed by a fresh public spending package and a pick-up in exports thanks to a revival of world trade. Growth at 7 per cent was well down on the double figure increases that China had become accustomed to, but which were unsustainable over a long period. In 1999 the country was still enjoying a current-account surplus of $11,000 million (1.1 per cent of GDP) and very low inflation. In fact, prices actually fell by 2.8 per cent during the year in response to the effects of export price cutting during the Asian recession. All in all, China's relatively closed economy and active fiscal policies enabled it largely to shrug off the effects of the Asian meltdown—and the country's economic links with Taiwan helped that country to avoid the worst of the downturn as well.

The 1999 Nobel Prize for Economics went to the Canadian-born professor Robert A. Mundell for his work in the 1960s on 'monetary dynamics and optimum currency areas [which] has inspired generations of researchers'. Based on his analysis of exchange rates and the way they affect monetary and fiscal policy, his opposition to floating exchange rates and espousal of the merits of fixed-rate zones was one of the factors leading to the creation of the euro as the single currency for the 11-nation Euroland at the start of 1999.

II WESTERN AND SOUTHERN EUROPE

1. UNITED KINGDOM—SCOTLAND—WALES—NORTHERN IRELAND

i. UNITED KINGDOM

CAPITAL: London   AREA: 244,100 sq km   POPULATION: 59,000,000 ('98)
OFFICIAL LANGUAGES: English; Welsh in Wales   POLITICAL SYSTEM: parliamentary democracy
HEAD OF STATE: Queen Elizabeth II (since Feb '52)
RULING PARTY: Labour Party (since May '97)
HEAD OF GOVERNMENT: Tony Blair, Prime Minister (since May '97); for cabinet list see XVII.4
MAIN IGO MEMBERSHIPS (non-UN): NATO, CWTH, EU, WEU, OSCE, CE, OECD, G-8
CURRENCY: pound sterling (end-'99 £1=US$1.61)
GNP PER CAPITA: US$21,400 by exchange-rate calculation, US$20,640 at PPP ('98)

THE Labour government elected in May 1997 with a huge parliamentary majority remained politically dominant in 1999, thanks in part to the largely undiminished personal popularity of Prime Minister Tony Blair but also because of the failure of the main opposition Conservative Party to make much impact under the leadership of William Hague. The recovery of the UK economy from near-recession in the winter of 1998-99 also boosted the government's standing. Labour's constitutional revolution brought the election of legislatures in Scotland and Wales in May (see II.1.ii; II.1.iii) as well as the abolition of hereditary peers in the House of Lords in November. In addition, the Northern Ireland peace process at last yielded the inauguration of a new power-sharing executive for the province in December (see II.1.iv). On all these fronts, however, the government was exposed to criticism that there were flaws in its new constitutional prescriptions.

In the external sphere, the Blair government took a leading role with the United States in the use of NATO military power against Yugoslavia over Kosovo, while also seeking to promote the creation of an independent defence capability within the European Union (EU). However, the government's claim to be 'at the heart of Europe' continued to sit uneasily with Britain's non-participation in the EU's new single currency (the euro). Also embarrassing towards the end of the year was the refusal of France to accept an EU decision to lift the three-year-old ban on the export of British beef.

CONSTITUTIONAL REFORM. Labour's devolution project reached partial fruition with the election of a Scottish Parliament and a Welsh National Assembly in May and the inauguration of varying degrees of autonomy in the two parts of the UK on 1 July. Both devolved governments were effectively controlled by Labour, in Scotland in formal coalition with the much smaller Liberal Democrats and in Wales as a minority administration. The Labour heads of the two governments, Donald Dewar in Scotland and Alun Michael in Wales, were both the favoured candidates of the Blair leadership in London, to the chagrin of the Scottish and Welsh opposition parties (and many Labour supporters). As the year progressed, the criticism was increasingly heard that the Blair government had not thought through its devolution scheme and had 'control freak' instincts towards the devolved administrations. Eyebrows were also raised when successors to Mr Dewar and Mr Michael as UK Secretaries of State for Scotland and Wales were appointed, respectively John Reid and Paul Murphy. What exactly, many wondered, would these Westminster cabinet ministers and their large departments be doing now that most of their responsibilities had been transferred to Edinburgh and Cardiff? More fundamentally, the contentious 'West Lothian question' remained unresolved, namely why should Scottish MPs at Westminster continue to vote on matters affecting England when English MPs could no longer do so on Scottish domestic affairs?

The government was also accused of being less than transparent in its determination to abolish the hereditary component of the upper house of the Westminster parliament and to replace it with an interim chamber pending the enactment of definitive reform (see AR 1998, pp. 17-8). Published on 20 January, the House of Lords Reform Bill specified that, while losing their law-making role, the hereditaries would retain their titles and would be able to vote in general elections, as well as stand for election to the House of Commons. The five royal dukes—the Duke of Cornwall (Prince Charles), the Duke of Edinburgh (Prince Philip), the Duke of York (Prince Andrew), the Duke of Kent and the Duke of Gloucester—would cease to be members of the upper chamber, whereas the 24 bishops of the Church of England would retain their seats, as would the 12 law lords. Presenting the plans, Leader of the Commons Margaret Beckett said that the government would adhere to the 'Cranborne compromise' of December 1998, providing for the retention of up to 92 ex-hereditary peers in an interim chamber consisting mainly of life peers (see AR 1998, pp. 28-9), if reform proceeded by consent; but she warned the Tory majority in the Lords that the compromise, to be enacted by means of government amendments to the reform bill, would not be extracted by 'pitched battle'.

Also announced was the establishment of a Royal Commission which would make proposals on the final shape of the Lords, having regard to 'the need to maintain the position of the House of Commons as the pre-eminent chamber of Parliament'. An accompanying White Paper said that the broad options were a wholly nominated chamber, one directly or indirectly elected, or a combination of the two—it being made clear that the government's preference was for the third option. Other aspects on which the Commission would make recommendations included representation for non-Anglican religious traditions and whether the new second chamber should retain the Lords' status as the highest court in the land. The influential peer Lord Wakeham was appointed to chair the Royal Commission, the government's calculation being that his status as a former Conservative cabinet minister would confer a measure of cross-party consensus on reform proposals.

It proved difficult to obtain consensus on the actual reform bill, however, as Tory peers continued to deplore abolition of the hereditaries before anyone knew how a new second chamber would be constituted. In June and July the Tory majority in the Lords inflicted major defeats on the government by passing important amendments to the bill and voting to refer it to the Lords' Committee of Privileges for a ruling on its constitutionality. When parliament resumed after the summer recess, the noble Committee found no legal objection to the bill, with the result that the Tory peers abstained when it was given a third reading on 26 October by 221 votes to 81. But the version adopted by the Lords included amendments not acceptable to the government, so a nail-biting final fortnight of the 1998-99 session was guaranteed. The third reading debate was enlivened by a protest by the Earl of Burford, who leapt upon the Woolsack and denounced the bill as 'treason'. Eldest son of the 14th Duke of St Albans (whose title was first conferred upon the illegitimate issue of the 17th-century liaison between King Charles II and his mistress Nell Gwynn), the protesting earl had not yet inherited his father's title and so had been present in the chamber as an observer. More than one commentator opined that his conduct provided the clearest possible justification for abolishing the hereditary peerage.

There followed a period of brinkmanship in which final enactment of the Lords reform bill became enmeshed procedurally with the government's determination to overturn amendments passed by the Lords to other important legislation, notably its flagship Welfare Reform and Pensions Bill. This measure had already provoked the biggest Labour revolt so far in the Commons on 20 May, when 67 Labour backbenchers had voted against the third reading in protest in particular against a tightening of the rules for eligibility to disability benefits. Ministers therefore warned the Lords that, unless the other measures were enacted in the current session (and therefor did not lapse), the 'Cranborne compromise' clauses would not feature in the final version of the Lords bill passed by the Commons. After the Commons had rejected the Lords' amendments to the welfare reform bill on 3 November, Labour rebels in the Lords secured the reinstatement of the important ones on 8 November, whereupon the Commons again overturned them the following day. For a short time there was talk of the Lords insisting on their amendments. However, the rebel Labour peers opted to defer to the will of the Commons, thereby facilitating the further passage of the Lords bill in the Commons on 10 November, minus the Lords' amendments disliked by the government but including the 'Cranborne compromise' clauses. The bill received the royal assent in the Lords on 11 November. On that day, therefore, over seven centuries of parliamentary history came to an end with the exit of the hereditary aristocracy from Britain's legislature.

As provided for in the bill, elections were held in the Lords in late October and early November for 90 of the 92 ex-hereditary seats which would survive in the interim chamber, in which two additional seats would be held by the present hereditary incumbents of the offices of Lord Great Chamberlain and Earl Marshal. Candidates for the elective seats, each of whom was required to produce a 75-word 'manifesto', were elected by the whole house in the case of 15 office-holders (deputy speakers and committee chairs) and by outgoing hereditaries by party group in the case of the other 75. As intended, the balloting yielded 51 Conservative, 30 crossbench, five Liberal Democrat and four Labour victors. The outgoing house of 1,330 members (including 750 hereditary peers) was accordingly replaced by an interim chamber with 670 members, of whom 233 were Conservatives, 183 Labour peers, 159 crossbenchers, 54 Liberal Democrats and 41 'others' (including bishops and law lords).

The government's timetable for definitive reform of the second chamber envisaged that the recommendations of the Wakeham Commission would be considered by a joint committee of the Lords and Commons in 2000, following which the government would table legislation. Lord Wakeham was supposed to publish his proposals by 31 December, but that deadline was missed and the report promised for January 2000. The leaking to the press in September of the main thrust of his proposals, envisaging that most members of the second chamber would continue to be appointed rather than elected, was accompanied by press reports of divisions in the Commission on the desirable proportion of appointed to elected members.

LONDON MAYORAL CONTROVERSIES. Also given the royal assent on 11 November was the Greater London Authority Bill providing for the direct election of a mayor and 25-member assembly for London in May 2000, as approved by the capital's voters in May 1998 (see AR 1998, p. 18). By then, however, the Blair government could have been forgiven for regretting that it had ever embarked upon this enterprise, as the Labour Party got itself a remarkable tangle over the choice of its mayoral candidate. Nor was there much comfort for the Tories in Labour's London travails: little more than a week after the bill's enactment the official Conservative candidate, millionaire novelist Lord (Jeffrey) Archer of Weston-super-Mare, was forced out of the mayoral race, finally disgraced by new disclosures about his chequered past.

The descent of Labour's London selection procedure into near-pantomime began in mid-year, amidst increasingly desperate efforts by the Blair leadership to prevent left-wing MP Ken Livingstone becoming the party's mayoral candidate. Having been leader of the Greater London Council (GLC) until its abolition by the Thatcher government in 1986, Mr Livingstone was regarded by Downing Street as a godfather of the 'loony left' which had made Labour unelectable in the 1980s. The problem, however, was to find a candidate who could successfully challenge the popularity of 'Red Ken' in London Labour circles. After much reported arm-twisting by the leadership, then Health Secretary Frank Dobson announced his candidacy on 8 October, three days before leaving the cabinet in a reshuffle (see below). Notwithstanding Mr Dobson's protestations to the contrary, cynical press commentators suggested that he had been persuaded to run in London only on discovering that he would lose his cabinet portfolio in any case.

The Downing Street spin-doctors then applied their skills to promoting Mr Dobson as the candidate favoured by the Prime Minister and to trying to undermine Mr Livingstone. The more they spun, however, the more Mr Livingstone's popularity appeared to rise, not only in Labour circles but also among London voters at large. On 12 October Labour's national executive committee (NEC) responded by drawing up a procedure for selection of the party's candidate that was widely seen as making things more difficult for Mr Livingstone. Instead of the promised 'one member, one vote' election by the 68,000 London party members, the decision was to be taken by an electoral college of three equally-weighted sections consisting of (i) party members, (ii) affiliated trade unions and other organizations, and (iii) London MPs, MEPs and candidates for the new London assembly. In addition, aspiring candidates would require approval from a special NEC vetting panel before their names could go forward to the electoral college. Supporters of Mr Livingstone described the procedure as a 'fix' and a 'stitch-up', similar to the one by which the Labour leadership had secured the election of Mr Michael as Welsh Labour leader in February (see II.1.iii).

The Labour NEC vetting committee met on 17 November and quickly endorsed the candidacies of Mr Dobson and former actress Glenda Jackson, who had vacated her junior ministerial post in July in order to run. But Mr Livingstone was required to make a second appearance before the panel the following day because of doubts as to whether he supported official Labour policy in all respects. His particular difficulty was that he was on record as being opposed to the government's plans for the partial privatization of the London Underground, arguing instead for a bond issue to raise the capital needed for modernization of the system. When pressed by the vetting panel to give an undertaking to support party policy, Mr Livingstone responded that the London election manifesto had not yet been written and offered to play a constructive role in its drafting if he became Labour's candidate. A factor in his eventual endorsement by the panel was that Mr Dobson had urged that he be allowed to stand, in the realization that his own cause would be further damaged if there were not a genuine contest for the Labour candidacy.

Shortly after the conclusion of the Labour panel's deliberations on 18 November, it was announced from Downing Street that the Prime Minister's wife, Cherie Blair (45), was expecting their fourth child. Mr Blair's spokesman rejected media suggestions that the announcement had been timed to divert media attention from Labour's London fiasco, and did not have long to wait before the London spotlight was genuinely directed elsewhere. On 20 November Lord Archer withdrew as the Conservative candidate in light of imminent press disclosures that he had suborned a potential witness in his successful libel action against *The Star* in 1987, when he had been awarded damages of £500,000 over the newspaper's reports of a liaison between him and a London prostitute. The following day the *News of the World* published detailed evidence from a former Archer associate showing that in 1987 the novelist had persuaded the associate to provide a false alibi for the evening he was initially alleged to have spent with the prostitute. In fact, *The Star* had later changed the cited date of the liaison to the previous evening, for which Lord Archer had another alibi and so had not needed to use the false testimony in court. But this circumstance did not mitigate against the gravity of Lord Archer's offence, the disclosure of which ensured his political downfall less than two months after Conservative Party members in London had elected him as their mayoral candidate by a resounding 71.2 per cent vote.

Announcing his withdrawal from the London race, Lord Archer accepted that he should not have arranged the false alibi, but claimed that he had done so to protect a 'close female friend' with whom he had been dining on the evening in question. He again denied that he had had sex with the prostitute. Nevertheless, amid intensive media re-examination of the events of 1987, the police opened an investigation into a possible conspiracy to pervert the course of justice, while *The Star* demanded that Lord Archer pay back the £500,000 libel award plus £2.5 million in costs and interest. Things got worse for Lord Archer on 28 November when a former aide, whose delivery of a cash payment of £2,000 to the London prostitute had featured prominently in the 1987 trial, claimed that he had received £40,000 from his then boss to leave the country to avoid being subpoenaed. The former aide also accused Lord Archer of misleading the court about the state of his marriage to Mary Archer, whose performance in the witness box in 1987 had persuaded the judge, in a celebrated summing-up, to wax lyrical about her 'fragrance' and to suggest to the jury that her husband could not possibly have felt any urge to stray. Further press exposés in December focused on Lord Archer's alleged recent termination of a three-year-old affair with a London actress.

Mr Hague reacted angrily to the new disclosures, asserting that Lord Archer had 'let the party down' and ordering that he be deprived of the Tory whip in the Lords. The Conservative leader nevertheless came under strong criticism for not having heeded earlier warnings that Lord Archer should be investigated by the party's 'ethics and integrity committee' (set up by Mr Hague himself) before he was allowed to stand in London. On 23 November the party decided that it would re-run its selection procedure for a mayoral candidate. But Tory agony in London was not yet over for the year. On 12 December a party committee excluded former junior transport minister Steven Norris from the new list of approved nominees, despite his having been runner-up to Lord Archer in the first selection process. Two days later Mr Norris was reinstated by decision of the party leadership, notwithstanding misgivings about his complicated marital and extra-marital affairs. On 15 December a meeting of London Tories elected Mr Norris as one of two Conservative nominees from whom the new party candidate would be chosen in January 2000.

The year therefore closed with only one London mayoral candidate of the major parties being known, namely Susan Kramer of the Liberal Democrats. A businesswoman and transport specialist, Mrs Kramer used the discomfiture of the other two parties to advance her cause, although with little apparent prospect of victory in May 2000.

ELECTIONS, GOVERNMENT CHANGES AND PARTY AFFAIRS. Considering that it was in mid term, the Labour government could take some satisfaction from the party's electoral performance in 1999. Labour remained by far the strongest party in local government in countrywide polling on 6 May, although the Conservatives overtook the Liberal Democrats as the country's second party and the Liberal Democrats made some inroads in northern Labour heartlands, notably by capturing Liverpool. Labour also successfully defended three Commons seats in 1999 by-elections, albeit with the lowest turnout in any post-war election (19.6 per cent) in Leeds Central on 10 June and despite a 23 per cent swing from Labour to the Scottish National Party (SNP) in Hamilton South on 23 September (see II.1.ii). The victor in Leeds Central was Hilary Benn, son of veteran Labour left-winger Tony Benn, although himself an avowed 'Blairite'. On 27 June Mr Benn senior (74) announced that he would retire from the Commons at the next general election, so that he had 'more time to devote to politics and more freedom to do so'.

The only real blot on Labour's electoral landscape was its heavy defeat in the European Parliament elections on 10 June. In a record low turnout of 23.1 per cent (easily the lowest in the EU), Labour's share of the vote slumped from 44.2 per cent in 1994 to 28.0 per cent and its representation from 62 to 29 seats, while the Tories advanced from 27.8 to 35.8 per cent and doubled their seat tally to 36. Benefiting from the introduction of proportional representation (PR) in multi-member constituencies (see AR 1998, pp. 18, 29), the Liberal Democrats improved from two European seats to 10 despite dropping from 16.7 to 12.7 per cent of the vote, while the Green Party obtained national representation for the first time by electing two candidates on a vote share of 6.3 per cent. With the SNP retaining two seats in Scotland, Plaid Cymru winning two in Wales and three MEPs being elected from Northern Ireland (see II.1.iv), the other three seats went to the UK Independence Party (UKIP), which achieved a 7 per cent vote share for its platform of opposition to further European integration and the euro.

One consequence of Labour's dismal showing in the Euro-elections was to strengthen opposition within the party to the introduction of PR for general elections in Britain. As the 1998 Jenkins Commission recommendations for electoral reform (see AR 1998, pp. 24-5) gathered dust on the shelf, Home Secretary Jack Straw was not the only cabinet minister to declare a preference for the existing 'first-past-the-post' system. There was therefore little prospect of a referendum on PR, promised in Labour's 1997 election manifesto, being called before the next general election, and the Prime Minister maintained an inscrutable silence on the issue.

Labour's drubbing in the Euro-polling was quickly followed at the end of June by much negative press comment about the appointment of Labour supporter and financial backer Greg Dyke as the next director-general of the BBC (see XV.1.vi). Amid renewed claims that 'Tony's cronies' were getting all the top jobs, it was widely anticipated that Mr Blair would carry out a major mid-year cabinet reshuffle with the aim of regaining political impetus. When it was announced on 28-29 July, however, the reshuffle involved only one cabinet post (the Welsh Secretary) and was instead concentrated on the junior ministerial ranks, in which nearly half the jobs changed hands. The Prime Minister's spokesman doggedly insisted that a big cabinet reshuffle had never been intended at this juncture, but media commentators were agreed that Mr Blair had been thwarted, at least for the time being, by the resistance of certain senior ministers to being moved to new responsibilities.

Whatever his frustrations, Mr Blair remained untroubled by any threat to his popular standing from the leader of the opposition. The Tory gains in the local and European elections in May-June dampened talk of a leadership challenge to Mr Hague, and a shadow cabinet reshuffle on 15 June demonstrated his new authority, notably in that the formidable right-winger Anne Widdecombe was promoted to become home affairs spokesperson. But the image of 'sleaze' and corruption which had so damaged the 1992-97 Major government continued to haunt the party in opposition. The infamous 'arms to Iraq' affair and related scandals were reprised when former Conservative cabinet minister Jonathan Aitken received an 18-month prison sentence on 8 June, after he had pleaded guilty to perjury in his unsuccessful libel action against *The Guardian* newspaper in 1997 (see AR 1997, p. 482). More damagingly for the Tory leadership, the business affairs of party treasurer Michael Ashcroft, appointed by Mr Hague, came under intense media scrutiny from July, *The Times* in particular asking questions about the role in British politics of this US-based multi-millionaire with extensive business interests and political connections in Belize. On 21 July Mr Ashcroft issued a libel writ against *The Times*, accusing the newspaper of a conspiracy to smear him and denying categorically that he condoned drug-trafficking or money-laundering in the Caribbean. The litigation was later resolved 'to mutual satisfaction' and the writ withdrawn (as announced on 9 December), but only after *The Times* had disclosed on 23 November that Mr Ashcroft was making donations to the Conservative Party at a rate of £1 million a year from a trust fund in Belize.

Labour's annual conference in Bournemouth on 26 September–1 October, marking the start of the party's centenary year, featured a remarkable attempt by the Prime Minister to rally the country to his 'New Labour' or 'Third Way' project. After blaming 'the forces of conservatism' in general and the Conservative Party in particular for most of the evils of the 20th century, Mr Blair also laid into 'the cynics, the elites, the establishment, those who will live with decline, those who yearn for yesteryear, those who just can't be bothered, those who prefer to criticize rather than do'. There was much more in the same vein, culminating in a call for everyone to join 'the forces of modernity and justice' represented by New Labour, in which 'party and nation [are] joined in the same cause for the same purpose: to set our people free'. Described as 'pure Billy Graham' by one observer, the speech also attracted criticism from normally pro-Blair commentators for its messianic overtones, as the new conference procedures introduced in 1998 (see AR 1998, p. 23) again ensured that there was little rank-and-file dissent on policy issues. After delegates had voted on 27 September to 'refer back' sections of an economic policy document supporting the use of private finance to fund public-sector projects, the vote was re-taken the next day and went in favour of the leadership. On the other hand, pre-conference elections for the Labour NEC resulted in the return of veteran left-winger Dennis Skinner.

Liberal Democrats listened in vain for any reference in Mr Blair's speech to the calling of referendums on PR for general elections or on joining the euro. Both objectives had been reaffirmed at the Liberal Democrat conference held in Harrogate on 19-23 September, under the new leadership of Scottish MP Charles Kennedy (39), who had succeeded Paddy Ashdown in August. Mr Ashdown had unexpectedly announced his intended departure on 20 January, after 11 years in the post, claiming that he had achieved many of his objectives. In a leadership election among party members, Mr Kennedy had defeated four other candidates, the results announced on 9 August giving him victory in the fourth round of counting by 56.6 per cent against 43.4 per cent for London MP Simon Hughes. Having come to the Liberal Democrats via the now defunct Social Democratic Party, Mr Kennedy pledged to build a 'strong, independent [and] progressive' party but rejected grass-roots calls for the Liberal Democrats to position themselves to the left of Labour. He also favoured continued political cooperation with the Labour government on constitutional and social issues, despite Labour's foot-dragging on national PR and Mr Blair's silence on the date of a euro referendum.

The annual conference of the opposition Conservatives, held in Blackpool on 4-7 October, featured an attempt by Mr Hague to set out a credible policy framework for the future; but he was again upstaged by former Prime Minister Baroness Thatcher, while continuing deep internal divisions on Europe were also in evidence. Launching a 'common sense revolution' depicted as moving the party back to the 'Thatcherite' principles of the 1980s, Mr Hague set out five guarantees to voters: a 'taxpayers' guarantee' that taxation would fall as a proportion of GDP over the period of the next Conservative government; a 'sterling guarantee' that the party would oppose membership of the euro during the next parliamentary term; a 'can work, must work guarantee' that those unemployed for more than eight weeks would lose welfare benefits if they refused a job offer; a 'parents' guarantee' allowing parents to dismiss unsatisfactory head teachers and school governors; and a 'patients' guarantee' under which National Health Service (NHS) hospital appointments would be prioritized according to treatment need. Expanding on EU policy, foreign affairs spokesman John Maples told the conference that an incoming Conservative government would 'stop the slide to a super-state' by renegotiating the Treaty of Rome so that member states had the right to opt out of EU policies and directives unrelated to the EU's core role as a trading bloc.

Seen as the most overtly Eurosceptic line so far advanced by the party, the new EU policy was condemned by former Deputy Prime Minister Michael Heseltine as potentially leading to the 'incalculable folly' of withdrawal from the EU, while former Chancellor of the Exchequer Kenneth Clarke asserted that the 'extremism' of the Eurosceptics was 'quite contrary to the traditions of Tory internationalism'. Later in October Mr Heseltine and Mr Clarke joined with Mr Blair and Mr Kennedy in launching the cross-party 'Britain in Europe' movement, which aimed to promote the benefits of EU membership in general and of UK participation in the euro in particular. For his part, Mr Hague launched 'the battle for the pound', promising 'to give voice to the deepest instincts and feelings of the British people' in defence of the currency.

The undoubted centre of attention at the Conservative conference, for both the media and the delegates, was Lady Thatcher, whose denial of press reports that she was privately critical of Mr Hague's performance only served to highlight the original reports. Addressing a fringe meeting on 6 October, she delivered a forceful appeal for the immediate release of the former Chilean dictator, General Pinochet, contending that his arrest in London in October 1998 had been 'judicial kidnapping' (see below). The former Prime Minister had already been in the headlines for asserting at an earlier social gathering in Blackpool that 'in my lifetime all the problems have come from mainland Europe, and all the solutions have come from the English-speaking nations across the world'. Party officials insisted afterwards that Lady Thatcher had been referring to the two world wars and not to post-1945 European history.

The party battle was briefly suspended in the wake of a devastating collision between two trains near London's Paddington Station on 5 October, resulting in 31 deaths and 244 passengers being injured. Although the death toll was much lower than initially feared, it was Britain's worst rail disaster since 1988 and political leaders were unanimous that lessons must be learnt from the apparent inadequacy of safety procedures. More controversial was whether the rail companies privatized by the previous Conservative government under very generous terms were neglecting safety in the interests of maximizing profit. As Secretary of State for the Environment, Transport and the Regions, Deputy Prime Minister John Prescott took charge of the government's response, setting up two inquiries into the crash. But he came under increasing opposition and media criticism for his erratic performance and for allegedly not being the master of his extensive ministerial brief.

Mr Blair's delayed cabinet reshuffle was announced on 11 October, its most controversial aspect being the rehabilitation of Peter Mandelson only ten months after his resignation as Trade and Industry Secretary following disclosures about an undeclared personal loan (see AR 1998, pp. 29-30). Mr Mandelson replaced Marjorie (Mo) Mowlam as Northern Ireland Secretary, Mr Blair's reported desire being to have a more subtle political operator in the post at a critical time for the province's peace process (see II.1.iv). But it was also clear that the Prime Minister wanted Mr Mandelson back in the fold well in advance of the next general election, to ensure that his famed public relations skills would be available to the Labour cause. It was subsequently announced that Mr Mandelson would spearhead the party's re-election campaign, in tandem with Chancellor of the Exchequer Gordon Brown. That Mr Brown and Mr Mandelson were not the best of Labour Party friends was apparently not thought to be a problem by Mr Blair.

Dr Mowlam became Minister for the Cabinet Office and Chancellor of the Duchy of Lancaster in succession to Jack Cunningham, having apparently failed to persuade Mr Blair to give her a major departmental job. Mr Cunningham left the government, as did Health Secretary Frank Dobson (to run for the London mayorship—see above) and Defence Secretary Lord (George) Robertson of Port Ellen, the latter in consequence of his appointment as NATO secretary-general in August (see XI.2.i), when he had been made a life peer. The new Health Secretary was Alan Milburn, who was succeeded as Chief Secretary to the Treasury by Alan Smith, while Geoffrey Hoon became Defence Secretary. Mr Hoon had previously been Minister of State for Foreign and Commonwealth Affairs and Mr Smith Minister of State for Employment.

The government's legislative programme for the 1999-2000 parliamentary session, set out in the Queen's Speech on 17 November, contained over 30 proposed bills, the extensive agenda being widely seen as signalling that the session would the last full one before the calling of general elections for the spring of 2001. The list showed that Home Secretary Straw was going to be busiest at the Commons dispatch box, introducing the government's long-awaited freedom of information bill as well as bills to limit the right to opt for trial by jury, to extend mandatory drug testing of offenders, to extend anti-discrimination legislation to the police and other public services, and to introduce new rules on the funding of parties and their expenditure, as recommended by the Neill Committee in October 1998 (see AR 1998, p. 25). Also within Mr Straw's brief, the government promised that it would give parliamentary time to a further private member's bill to ban fox-hunting (the previous such measure having lapsed in 1998 despite being approved by an overwhelming majority in the Commons).

Other forthcoming legislation would include the government's first major transport bill (see below); yet another bill to equalize the age of consent for heterosexuals and homosexuals at 16 years (two previous such attempts having been defeated in the Lords—see AR 1998, p. 27); a bill to give people greater access to the countryside and to increase protection for wildlife; several bills to make improvements and reforms in the provision of education and social services; a bill to enable the Post Office to improve its performance and to compete more effectively in UK and overseas markets; and a bill to assist the rescue of viable businesses in short-term difficulties and improve the procedure for disqualifying unfit company directors.

Having given his most effective parliamentary performance to date in the debate on the Queen's Speech, Mr Hague a week later had the mixed pleasure of welcoming former Tory Defence Secretary Michael Portillo back to the Commons. The most spectacular Tory casualty in the 1997 general election (see AR 1997, p. 20), Mr Portillo won a by-election on 25 November for the central London seat of Kensington and Chelsea, achieving a swing from Labour to Conservative of 4.4 per cent. The vacancy had arisen because of the death in September of Alan Clark, former junior Tory minister and celebrated diarist (see Pt XVIII: Obituary). In declaring his candidacy on 9 September, Mr

Portillo had sought to lay to rest persistent rumours about his sexual orientation, admitting that he had had 'some homosexual experiences as a young person'. Now a married man, he had overcome some resultant misgivings among Kensington and Chelsea party members, receiving the Conservative nomination on 2 November by 530 votes out of 840 cast. In light of media speculations that he was a potential 'Thatcherite' contender for the Conservative leadership, Mr Portillo made a point of asserting that he would never challenge Mr Hague. But this pledge did little to dispel political talk that he was 'leader in waiting' of the Tory party.

By then Mr Hague was suffering the deep embarrassment of the disgrace of Lord Archer in London (see above); and things were to get worse for the Conservative leader before the year ended. In what was seen as a major coup for the Blair government, former Tory front-bench spokesman Shaun Woodward announced on 18 December that he was switching to the Labour Party, on the grounds that the Conservative Party had become too right-wing under Mr Hague's leadership. Hitherto regarded as a rising Conservative star, Mr Woodward had been greatly upset on being dismissed by Mr Hague as front-bench spokesman on London on 2 December, for refusing to toe the party line of opposition to Labour plans to repeal section 28 of the 1988 Local Government Act forbidding the 'promotion' of homosexuality by local education authorities. Secret negotiations between the aggrieved MP and Labour officials had produced Mr Woodward's defection announcement, in which he asserted that the Conservative Party 'has clearly now abandoned its commitment to one-nation politics'. Whereas the Prime Minister described Mr Woodward as a politician of principle and judgment, Mr Hague denounced him as an unprincipled 'careerist' and challenged him to fight a by-election, as did his angry constituency party in Witney. Mr Woodward responded that he did not intend to resign his Commons seat, the transfer of which increased Labour's ranks to 419 and its overall majority to 180.

The Prime Minister was therefore entitled to take some satisfaction from the political year as he sat with Queen Elizabeth in the newly-constructed Millennium Dome at Greenwich on New Year's Eve helping London and the country to celebrate the advent of the year 2000. His own position and that of his government remained impregnable, and opinion polls of voting intentions continued to show Labour far ahead of the Tories. At the same time, fears that the £758 million Dome might prove to be costly white elephant (see XV.2.ii), and an embarrassing series of hitches which marred the great event as the world watched, were perhaps indicative of more difficult times ahead for the government.

SECURITY AND ESPIONAGE CONTROVERSIES. A number of security and espionage controversies caused aggravation in government circles in the course of the year, beginning on 13 May with what Foreign and Commonwealth Secretary Robin Cook condemned as the 'deeply irresponsible and dangerous act' of the publication on the Internet of a list of over 100 officers of the MI6 external intelligence service. Mr Cook told the Commons that the presumed source was ex-MI6 employee Richard Tomlinson, whom he described as nursing a 'deep-seated and irrational grievance' against his former employers. Then resident in Switzerland and possessing dual UK and New Zealand citizenship, Mr Tomlinson had been dismissed from MI6 in 1995 and had received a one-year prison sentence in 1997 for seeking to publish a book on MI6 in breach of the Official Secrets Act. In addition to mounting a damage-limitation exercise to protect the named MI6 agents, British officials secured the withdrawal of the offending US website, while acknowledging that the list was circulating on the Internet beyond any government control. It emerged that the previous week Britain had obtained an injunction from a Swiss court barring Mr Tomlinson from disclosing any information obtained when he was an MI6 employee. Mr Tomlinson himself admitted that he had threatened to publish a list of MI6 agents but denied responsibility for the actual disclosure, suggesting on 16 May that MI6 itself might have been the perpetrator with the aim of discrediting him.

The affair took a new turn when the *Sunday Times* of 16 May reported that MI6 was investigating evidence that Mohamed al-Fayed, the controversial Egyptian owner of Harrods department store in London, had assembled data on MI6 officers in connection with his belief that the organization had been responsible, at the behest of Buckingham Palace, for the death of Princess Diana and his son Dodi Fayed in Paris in 1997 (see AR 1997, pp. 4-5). Ten days earlier Home Secretary Straw had rejected Mr al-Fayed's application for UK citizenship on the grounds of his 'serious want of probity'—a decision described by the Egyptian as stemming from the British establishment's vendetta against him. The *Sunday Times* quoted Mr al-Fayed as acknowledging that he had received information from Mr Tomlinson, but a spokesman subsequently denied that the Harrods owner had been responsible for the material published on the Internet.

Mr al-Fayed again voiced his conspiracy theories following the publication on 3 September of the official French judicial report on the Paris car crash in which Princess Diana and Dodi Fayed had been killed. The report concluded that the crash had been an accident attributable to the drunken state of the driver (who was also killed) and not to pursuing photographers. The findings were welcomed by lawyers of former bodyguard Trevor Rees-Jones, the only survivor of the crash, who was claiming damages against Mr al-Fayed. In contrast, the latter said that he would appeal against the report and on 17 September gave an interview to BBC Radio in which he repeated his claim that Diana and his son had been killed by MI6 agents to prevent the mother of the future king marrying a Muslim.

More embarrassment for the government arose in mid-September when *The Times* and a BBC television programme named a clutch of UK citizens who had allegedly acted as agents for the Soviet bloc during the Cold War but had never been prosecuted. The disclosures in *The Times* came from a forthcoming book by Cambridge University academic Christopher Andrew based on information provided to the UK intelligence service by Vasili Mitrokhin, a former chief archivist of the Soviet KGB who had defected to Britain in 1992 and had later cooperated with Mr Andrew. The BBC programme's allegations were derived from records found in the archives of the former East German security service, the Stasi.

The most important former agent named in the so-called 'Mitrokhin archive' was Melita Norwood (code-named 'Hola'), now an 87-year-old great-grandmother living in south London, who was said to have been recruited as a committed Communist in 1937 and to have passed information on the UK nuclear weapons programme to Moscow while working as a secretary at the Non-Ferrous Metals Research Association in the 1940s. In media interviews following the disclosures, Mrs Norwood was unrepentant about her past role, explaining that her motivation had been ideological and not pecuniary. Also named by the *The Times* were two deceased Labour MPs (Raymond Fletcher and Tom Driberg) as well as John Symonds, a former Metropolitan Police officer said to have worked in various countries in the 1970s as a KGB 'Romeo agent' charged with seducing women who had access to state secrets. Those identified in the BBC programme were mainly college lecturers alleged to have been recruited by the Stasi during exchange visits to Leipzig under the former regime.

Having called in the director-general of the MI5 internal intelligence service to brief him on the Mitrokhin case, Mr Straw on 13 September announced that at his request the parliamentary intelligence and security committee would investigate the security services' handling of information provided by the defector. In a lengthy statement, the Home Secretary disclosed that he had been 'made aware in general terms' of the Mitrokhin material when he took office in 1997 but had not been informed of the allegations against Mrs Norwood until December 1998, whereupon the Attorney-General had advised in April 1999 that 'the last opportunity' for a prosecution had been when the Mitrokhin evidence had been received in 1992. It emerged that Mr Blair, the titular head of the security services, had also been told about Mr Mitrokhin's defection on becoming Prime Minister but had not been briefed about his specific allegations until shortly before the exposé in *The Times*. As was to be expected, the Conservative opposition made a great clamour about the revelations, deploring the fact that none of the alleged agents had been prosecuted and urging the government to bring them to trial where sufficient evidence existed. Under some pressure, Mr Straw announced on 21 October that the Crown Prosecution Service had been asked to look at the cases of Mrs Norwood and four others. On 20 December, however, the Solictor-General confirmed that no action would be taken in the courts because it was 'clear that any prosecution would fail'.

Meanwhile, Mr al-Fayed had again found a public stage for his allegations about MI6, this time in a High Court trial of a suit by former Conservative junior minister Neil Hamilton claiming that the Egyptian businessman had libelled him in a 1997 television programme about the 'cash for questions' parliamentary scandal under the previous Tory government (see AR 1997, pp.

16-17). The sometimes chaotic High Court proceedings in November and December featured a deluge of accusations and counter-accusations, Mr al-Fayed's four days of testimony featuring a vigorous reassertion of his belief that MI6 had murdered Princess Diana and his son and that the plot had been instigated by the Duke of Edinburgh. On the substantive libel issue before the court, the jury on 21 December found against Mr Hamilton, who therefore faced financial ruin. *The Economist* of 23 December commented that Mr al-Fayed had won a 'Pyrrhic victory', having been 'further exposed as a deeply unsavoury fantasist'.

RACE RELATIONS, POLITICAL ASYLUM AND IMMIGRATION. A major theme of the year was the state of race relations in Britain and whether or not there was 'institutional' prejudice against non-white ethnic minorities in the police and other parts of British society. The catalyst was the publication on 24 February of the report of an independent judicial inquiry by retired High Court judge Sir William Macpherson into the police investigation of the unsolved murder of black teenager Stephen Lawrence, who had been stabbed to death on a south London street in April 1993. It found that there had been serious deficiencies in the conduct of the murder inquiry related to 'professional incompetence, institutional racism and failure of leadership' within the Metropolitan Police, and submitted a list of 70 recommendations for legislative and other remedial action.

The fact that no-one had been convicted of the Stephen Lawrence murder had become a *cause célèbre* for the black community, partly as the result of a determined campaign for 'justice' for their son by parents Doreen and Neville Lawrence. Although the police had eventually charged five white males with the murder, the Crown Prosecution Service (CPS) had not proceeded with the case, because identification evidence by Stephen Lawrence's companion at the time of the murder had been unreliable. Mr and Mrs Lawrence had then launched a private prosecution against three of the five suspects, but it had collapsed in 1996 when the evidence of the companion had been ruled inadmissible because of its inconsistencies and doubtful provenance. A subsequent coroner's inquest, at which the five youths had refused to answer questions on the grounds that they might incriminate themselves, had found on 13 February 1997 that Stephen Lawrence had been unlawfully killed 'in a completely unprovoked racist attack by five white youths'. Released during the inquest, a police surveillance video secretly filmed in a flat occupied by the youths had shown them brandishing weapons and making anti-black assertions. On the day after the inquest's conclusion, the *Daily Mail* had taken the highly controversial step of naming the five youths as the murderers, publishing their photographs and challenging them to sue the newspaper. In June 1998 the five suspects had been compelled to appear before the Macpherson inquiry, which had been established by Home Secretary Straw in July 1997 following Labour's election victory; but a High Court ruling had protected them from being asked questions pertaining to their guilt or innocence. On that occasion violent demonstrations against the five suspects had been led by British members of the US-based militant black separatist Nation of Islam movement.

The 335-page Macpherson report gave a detailed account of 'a series of errors, failures and lack of direction and control', as well as 'insensitive and racist stereotypical behaviour', in the early stages of the police investigation of the murder of Stephen Lawrence. Naming the five 'prime suspects', the report suggested that they should have been 'more obvious targets for early arrest', continuing that the catalogue of police errors could only be accounted for by 'pernicious and institutional racism' within the Metropolitan Police. Institutional racism was defined in the report as 'the collective failure of an organization to provide an appropriate and professional service to people because of their colour, culture or ethnic origin'.

The report's 70 recommendations began with several on 'openness, accountability and the restoration of confidence' in the police, including independent investigation of complaints and the application of 'the full force' of race relations legislation to all police officers. Other recommendations included the creation of 'a comprehensive system of reporting and recording racist incidents' (to be defined as 'any incident which is perceived to be racist by the victim or any other person') and full recording of all 'stop and search' actions by the police. The most controversial recommendations were that 'consideration' should be given to (i) granting the Court of Appeal the power to permit further prosecution of the same person after acquittal 'where fresh and viable evidence is presented', and (ii) an amendment to the law 'to allow prosecution of offences involving racist language or behaviour, and of offences involving the possession of offensive weapons, where such conduct can be proved to have taken place otherwise than in a public place'. Soon after publication of the report, the discovery that one of the its appendices inadvertently listed the names and addresses of some of the witnesses who had assisted the police obliged the Home Office to withdraw the appendix, but only after many copies of the original version had been distributed and published on the Internet.

Presenting the Macpherson report to the Commons on 24 February, Mr Straw committed the government to achieving 'permanent and irrevocable change' in the sphere of race relations, but made it clear that he did not support calls for the resignation of the Metropolitan Police Commissioner, Sir Paul Condon, who was due to retire at the end of the year in any case. A month later, on 23 March, Mr Straw announced that he was taking personal charge of a government 'action plan' to implement recommendations made in the report with the aim of 'building an anti-racist society'. At the same time, he indicated that he had doubts about the suggested abolition of the long-established 'no double jeopardy' rule and the criminalization of racist utterances in private, both of which issues had been referred to the Law Commission for its opinion. He also specifically rejected the Macpherson proposal that schools should compile and publish inventories of racist incidents involving schoolchildren.

In what appeared to be a far-right riposte to the Lawrence inquiry report, a series of three nail bombs exploded in London in the second half of April, the first targeted at Afro-Caribbeans in Brixton, the second at Bangladeshis in the East End and the third at homosexuals in a Soho public house. The first bomb injured 39 people and the second six, while the more deadly Soho bomb on 30 April killed two people outright and injured 66 others, one of whom one died later. The police received claims of responsibility from several shadowy far-right groups, but these were quickly discounted. On 5 July a 23-year-old white man was committed for trial at the Old Bailey on murder and other charges related to the bombings, the police reportedly believing that he had acted alone.

As well as sparking initiatives to improve ethnic minority recruitment in the critical area of policing, the Macpherson report set a fashion for the discovery of 'institutional racism' in many other sectors of British society. The armed forces, the prison and fire brigade services, the education and mental health authorities, the Crown Prosecution Service, the Ford motor-car plant at Dagenham, even the Anglican Church and the Ramblers' Association—all came under the spotlight for admitted or alleged discrimination against ethnic minorities, witting or unwitting. In the educational field, a survey published by the Office for Standards in Education (Ofsted) on 10 March concluded that many schools in England and Wales were institutionally racist, despite the best intentions of most teachers, and that this factor explained the under-achievement of Afro-Caribbean, Muslim Asian and Gypsy pupils, especially boys. Teachers' representatives responded that it was unhelpful to deploy the 'institutional racism' label in the case of schools, contending that teachers were in the vanguard of seeking to build a tolerant multicultural society. They also rejected claims that the high proportion of Afro-Caribbean boys being expelled from schools was a manifestation of unwitting racism among teachers.

Even more controversial in the second half of the year were crime figures indicating that one effect of the Macpherson report was police reluctance to combat black criminality for fear of being accused of racism. Official figures showed that in the period April to June violent crime in London had risen by 25 per cent compared with the second 1998 quarter, while the Met Commissioner acknowledged on 8 August that muggings and other street crime in London had increased by 35 per cent since publication of the report. Other figures showed a 50 per cent reduction in police 'stop and search' operations, which had come under criticism in the report for being disproportionately carried out on members of ethnic minorities. A Police Federation spokesman, representing rank and file officers, commented that the police were increasingly unwilling to tackle non-white suspects because of the climate created by the Lawrence case. Black community leaders, however, rejected any connection between rising crime rates and the Macpherson report and also claimed that non-whites were still being unfairly targeted in police 'stop and search' actions.

Underlying such controversies was the issue of whether there was disproportionately high criminality among non-whites, in particular young Afro-Caribbean males. The conviction evidence indicated that there was, in that British prisons contained ten times more blacks than whites proportionate to population numbers. But black spokesmen insisted that this disproportion stemmed from the racist bias of the criminal justice system in general and of the police in particular. Those seeking to make an objective judgment were not assisted by the authorities' policy of not specifying the racial identity of people arrested by the police on criminal charges.

The unresolved tensions in race relations were again apparent in early December when Mr Straw published the government's Race Relations (Amendment) Bill, intended to update the 1976 act for the first time. As recommended by the Macpherson inquiry, the new bill proposed that anti-discrimination legislation should be extended to cover all public services presently excluded, notably the police and immigration officers, so that members of the public would be able to sue if they believed that they had been victims of overt racist conduct. The Commission for Racial Equality and other race relations bodies voiced strong criticism of the draft bill on the grounds that it would do nothing to combat indirect or 'unwitting' racism. Mr Straw responded that he was reluctant to accept changes to the bill that might lead to a flood of 'mendacious' claims. In the post-Macpherson climate, however, it was thought unlikely that he would be able to resist pressure for a more inclusive definition of racial discrimination.

The parents of Stephen Lawrence remained convinced that police racism, witting or unwitting, had been the key factor in the failure to bring their son's killers to justice. On 21 December they issued writs against 42 named officers of the Met, including Commissioner Sir Paul Condon, claiming damages for deficiencies in the police investigation of the murder. A Scotland Yard spokesman stated that the legal costs of the officers and any damages awarded against them would be borne by the Met.

The Blair government was also discomforted in 1999 by controversies surrounding political asylum and immigration policy bearing similarities with those surrounding race relations. The monthly rate of asylum applications rose inexorably, reaching a record total of 71,160 for the year, an increase of over 50 per cent on the 1998 figure, while the number of outstanding applications and appeals stood at 102,000 at end-1999, also a record. According to Home Office estimates, inclusion of applicants' dependants increased these figures two or three times. The government was therefore exposed to opposition Conservative charges that it had allowed Britain to become a 'soft touch' for bogus asylum seekers. From the other direction, it was lambasted by refugee and race relations organizations for maintaining an illiberal approach on asylum and immigration questions.

Among new asylum seekers in 1999, refugees from Yugoslavia, most claiming to be ethnic Albanians from Kosovo, formed the largest group, followed by Somalis, Sri Lankan Tamils, Afghanis, Turkish Kurds and Pakistanis. The year also saw a sharp increase in the number of Czech and Slovakian Gypsies (Roma) arriving in Britain and claiming asylum on grounds of persecution at home. Among those awaiting a decision on their status or appealing against expulsion orders, some cases dated back to 1990 and delays of up to four years were common for the holding of first interviews. According to Home Office figures, only 17 per cent of asylum applicants processed in 1998 were found to be genuine refugees, although a further 12 per cent were allowed to stay on humanitarian or compassionate grounds. Other figures indicated that in the late 1990s less than 10 per cent of those refused asylum or permission to stay had actually been deported, the remainder having disappeared into the general population.

Most asylum seekers took up residence in London, but the county of Kent also entertained a large number because many arrived at Dover and other Channel ports. With a normal population of about 30,000, Dover housed an estimated 1,400 refugees by mid-1999, many having reached Britain hidden in cross-Channel lorries, while others were apparently given tickets to Dover by the French authorities in Calais. After the Kent County Council leader had warned of a 'tinder-box' situation in the Channel ports, clashes between refugees and Dover residents on 13-14 August resulted in 15 people being injured, about half of them requiring treatment for knife wounds. Local residents complained that the police did not enforce the law against carrying offensive weapons where asylum seekers were concerned.

The stock response of ministers was that the asylum and immigration policy inherited from the previous Conservative administration had been 'a shambles', which was 'taking time to sort out'. The government hoped that this 'sorting out' would be achieved by its new Immigration and Asylum Bill, which completed a contentious parliamentary passage in November. But the measure was not due to come into force until April 2000, so that ministers conceded that the situation was likely to get worse before it got better. Tabling the bill on 9 February, Mr Straw had promised that it would deliver 'an integrated approach to immigration and asylum which will be fairer for all, including the taxpayer, firmer when dealing with abuse, and faster in reaching decisions'. Its two most controversial provisions were that asylum seekers would be dispersed around the country and obliged to live in designated accommodation, and that they would receive welfare benefits mostly in the form of vouchers rather than cash. Under other clauses, a single appeals procedure and speedier deportation would be instituted, the aim being to reduce the time taken to accept or reject asylum applications to a maximum of six months by 2001; firms of legal 'advisers' on immigration would be regulated, with the aim of combating abuse of the system and racketeering; lorry drivers who brought in illegal immigrants would liable to fines of up to £2,000; and local authority registrars would be given new powers to stop bogus marriages between illegal immigrants and UK citizens.

Predictably, refugee organizations condemned the bill's dispersal plan as a recipe for 'ethnic cleansing', while some Labour MPs and peers came out against the payment of welfare benefits in the form of vouchers. Mr Straw conceded in July that the cash component of such payments would be increased from £7 to £10 a week per adult, but the House of Lords effectively rejected the relevant clause on 20 October, whereupon the government used its Commons majority to secure enactment of the bill in the desired form on 11 November. By then, however, an important part of the measure had been potentially undermined by a Court of Appeal ruling on 23 July that three applicants for political asylum from Algeria, Somalia and Sri Lanka could not be returned to France or Germany, from where they had travelled to Britain, because those countries were not 'safe' places to send refugees facing non-state persecution. Under the June 1990 Dublin Convention, EU members had agreed that asylum applications must be made in the first EU state reached by a refugee; but whereas Britain accepted non-state persecution as grounds for an application, France and Germany considered only those citing persecution by state authorities.

The dilemma of the well-intentioned in this area was perhaps best illustrated by the issue of forced marriage in the British Asian community. The establishment of a Home Office working party on forced marriage was announced on 4 August, prompted by evidence of an increasing number such unions, most involving British Asian girls being sent by their families to the Indian subcontinent to marry on the basis of a financial contract so that the men could gain entry to Britain. A factor in the increase was the Labour government's relaxation of the previous administration's 'primary purpose' immigration rule under which those marrying UK citizens abroad had not obtained automatic right of entry. Appointed to chair the working party, Bangladeshi-born Labour peeress Baroness Uddin stated that she was already convinced that forced marriage was 'not a major problem' and accused the UK media of sensationalizing the issue. The Southall Black Sisters, an Asian women's support group in west London, responded that the problem was 'very common' and was largely ignored by the police and social services for fear of being accused of interference with ethnic minority cultural practices.

THE ECONOMY IN 1999. During 1999 the UK experienced generally favourable economic conditions, with a recovery of growth, low inflation and falling unemployment, although in the latter part of the year fears of overheating led to a reversal of the steady decrease of interest rates, while the weakness of the new euro currency introduced among 11 EU member-states on 1 January (see XI.4) caused some pressure on UK exports. The Labour government maintained throughout this period the policy of 'prudent management' pursued since the administration was formed in May 1997.

Interest rates as agreed by the monetary policy committee of the Bank of England fell from the end-1998 level of 6.25 per cent to 6 per cent on 7 January, to 5.5 per cent on 4 February, to 5.25 per cent on 8 April and to a 22-year low of 5 per cent on 10 June. However, as the Bank identified indicators of overheating of the economy (notably above-inflation rises in average earnings, sharply increased consumer spending, a marked drop in unemployment and a boom in house prices), rates were subsequently increased again to 5.25 per cent on 8 September and to 5.5 per cent on 4 November.

The relationship between the euro and sterling affected UK trade not only with 'euroland' but also with other parts of the world where exports from the 11 euro countries became relatively more competitively priced. In the course of the year the value of the euro against the US dollar fell from around US$1.16 to around parity; after allowing for some net depreciation of sterling against the dollar during 1999 (from about $1.64 to $1.61, with a sharper drop in the middle of the year), the value of the euro against sterling dropped by about 12 per cent and the overall value of sterling appreciated accordingly.

The question of the UK's possible eventual participation in the euro continued to be a major political issue, still without resolution at the end of the year. In a clear signal of the government's attitude, Prime Minister Blair on 23 February unveiled a 'national changeover plan' to prepare the country for the possible replacement of the pound sterling, at the same time reiterating that a government decision to join the euro would require approval in a referendum. It was repeatedly stressed that, while the government was in principle in favour of joining a 'successful' euro, certain key economic tests as enunciated in 1997 had to be passed. However, no official assessments were divulged about how Britain was faring against these tests, as public opinion hardened into a two-to-one majority in favour of preserving the pound.

The UK had a continuing large deficit (on a balance of payments basis) in its trade in goods during 1999. Over the year as a whole the aggregate deficit amounted to £26,320 million, compared with £20,537 million in 1998. After taking into account a reduction in the positive balance of trade in services, the overall trade and services deficit was almost doubled from £8,352 million in 1998 to £15,442 million in 1999. Other official figures showed that the annualized increase in retail prices, on an all-items basis, dropped sharply during 1999, from 2.8 per cent in December 1998 to a 36-year low of 1.1 per cent in September, and in December 1999 stood at 1.8 per cent. The low figure for September led to the basic state pension being raised by only 75p a week as from April 2000.

For most of 1999 the headline rate for the increase in average earnings was between 4.5 and 5 per cent (slightly lower than in 1998). On 1 February the annual pay review awards for some 1.3 million public sector employees were announced, averaging 4.1 per cent but including also 12 per cent increases for junior nurses. Unemployment as registered by the claimant count criterion and on a seasonally adjusted basis fell broadly through 1999 from just over 1,300,000 to just over 1,150,000 (from 4.5 to 4.0 per cent), and in December numbered around 1,164,000 on this basis—a level not experienced for 20 years.

The London stock market showed in the course of 1999 an even greater net growth than in 1998, as registered by the increase in the FTSE 100 index. After finishing 1998 at 5882.6, the index showed an initial drop in 1999 but by late February had passed its mid-1998 high of 6179.0, rising to almost 6600 by late April. In October the index fell below 5900, but it then increased sharply to close with a final spurt to 6930.2 at the end of the year. This represented a net rise of nearly 18 per cent over the course of the year as against about 15 per cent in the previous year.

The Chancellor of the Exchequer, Gordon Brown, presented his third budget on 9 March, covering the 12-month period to 5 April 2000. This reiterated earlier forecasts that economic growth in 1999 would be in the 1-1.5 per cent range and that the annual inflation target remained at 2.5 per cent. Effective April 2000, the basic rate of income tax would be further reduced from 23 to 22 per cent, while from April 1999 the first £1,500 of an individual's taxable income would bear a rate of only 10 per cent. Moreover, the rate of corporation tax for a company with profits of up to £10,000 would be limited to 10 per cent from April 2000. A new energy tax was introduced, and heavy increases were made in duties on cigarettes and tobacco and on petrol and most other road fuels and in vehicle excise duties (the latter two elements giving rise to a series of large-scale protests by lorry drivers during the period from March to May). A new child tax credit would be introduced in 2001 (following the phasing out of the married couple's tax allowance). The income level at which national insurance contributions were payable would be increased, and measures were introduced to ease the way back into work for those aged over 50.

In his pre-budget report presented on 9 November, Mr Brown estimated that the UK economy would have grown by about 1.75 per cent in 1999 (i.e. by rather more than forecast in the March budget) and that growth in 2000 would be between 2.5 and 3 per cent. Macroeconomic indicators continued to be generally favourable, and in the current 1999-2000 financial year a budget surplus was projected of some £9,500 million, with a total surplus of £33,000 million expected in the three-year period to 2002.

On 7 May Mr Brown announced that the UK intended to sell over half of its stock of gold over the medium term, in order to achieve a better balance in the Treasury's portfolio by increasing the proportion of the reserves held in currencies. About a sixth of the UK's reserves of some US$37,000 million was then held in the form of gold, and it was planned to sell over 400 tonnes of Britain's 715-tonne holdings (the last major sale of gold by the UK having been in the late 1960s and early 1970s). In the weeks immediately after the Chancellor's announcement—unusual in that governments' gold sales were usually not foreshadowed in advance—the market price of gold sank by about 10 per cent to its lowest for 20 years (US$263 per troy ounce), although at the end of 1999 it stood again at the level at which it had opened the year of around US$290. The first two sales, each of 25 tonnes, took place in early July and late September.

The government's long-awaited draft Transport Bill was announced at the opening of the 1999-2000 parliamentary session on 17 November. While a major part of the bill dealt with road traffic in towns and cities, it also provided for the partial sale of the National Air Traffic Services (air traffic control) and the formal establishment of a Strategic Rail Authority. Sir Alastair Morton had been appointed chair of this embryo board on 25 February, effective 1 April. Subsequently Tom Winsor was on 23 March appointed rail regulator, effective early July. The government's programme for public and private expenditure over the next 10 years of some £80,000 million on transport was announced on 13 December. While detailed plans for the future financing of

London Underground were still under consideration, the Jubilee Line extension was formally opened on 20 November.

During 1999 there were many major mergers and takeovers involving UK companies. The mobile telephone company Vodafone in January bought the US AirTouch cellular company for £38,000 million, while in November Vodafone-AirTouch launched a record hostile bid for the German Mannesmann telecommunications and engineering company, at a figure then estimated at £79,000 million. Mannesmann had earlier, in October, acquired the UK Orange cellular company for nearly £20,000 million. Oil giant BP-Amoco, itself created in 1998, announced in April that it had agreed a $26,800 million takeover of the US company Atlantic Richfield (Arco), to form the world's second largest non-state oil company after Exxon-Mobil of the USA; however, because of regulatory problems in the United States the proposed merger had still not been implemented by the end of the year.

The most fiercely-fought takeover battle of the year began in September when the Bank of Scotland announced a £21,000 million hostile bid for the much larger National Westminster Bank (NatWest). As the battle raged, a speedy consequence was that NatWest aborted its recently-announced £11,000 million intended acquisition of the Legal and General life assurance company. The Bank of Scotland bid was itself overtaken in late November by a £26,500 million bid from the Royal Bank of Scotland, and no conclusion had been reached by the end of the year. In other important consolidations in June, Lloyds TSB bank had announced a £7,000 million takeover of the Scottish Widows life assurance company, while the world's third largest steel company (later named Corus) was formed through the agreed merger of British Steel and Hoogovens of the Netherlands.

EXTERNAL RELATIONS AND DEFENCE. Britain went to war in Europe on 24 March as a leading participant in NATO's 'Operation Allied Force', involving heavy air strikes against targets in Serbia intended to force the government of the Federal Republic of Yugoslavia to halt its alleged 'ethnic cleansing' of the majority ethnic Albanian population from the Yugoslav province of Kosovo (see III.2.vi). Prime Minister Blair took the lead in proclaiming the 'justness' of the war and received the support of all other major party leaders except Alex Salmond of the Scottish National Party, who described the NATO action as 'unpardonable folly'. Some prominent Labour and Conservative parliamentarians also had serious doubts, focusing on the absence of any UN mandate for the action. Other commentators questioned the wisdom of effectively promoting separatism among the predominantly Muslim Kosovar Albanians.

The doubts increased as the weeks passed and the Yugoslav government refused to yield to the aerial onslaught, which featured a number of embarrassing 'mistakes', notably the bombing by US planes of the Chinese embassy in Belgrade on 7 May. Also awkward for NATO was the predictable intensification of Yugoslav security measures in Kosovo, the resultant mass exodus of

Kosovar Albanians accelerating the 'ethnic cleansing' that NATO was supposed to be preventing. The Blair government therefore heaved a collective sigh of relief when Belgrade finally accepted NATO terms in early June and agreed to withdraw its forces from Kosovo. They were replaced, this time with UN endorsement, by an international security force (K-For), with Britain taking the leading role in terms of numbers and command. The first British fatalities in the action occurred on 21 June when two soldiers of a Gurkha field squadron were killed near Pristina when trying to defuse unexploded NATO bombs.

The Kosovo campaign served to highlight deficiencies in the ability of European NATO armies to engage in rapid deployment actions, amidst analyses showing that, whereas aggregate defence expenditure by NATO Europe approached the US level, operational capability lagged far behind. The Blair government was therefore bolstered in its advocacy of a 'European defence identity', finding particular support for the proposal in Paris and taking it further at a UK-French bilateral summit in London on 25 November. It was clear, however, that the French government did not share London's view that the proposed integrated force should remain under the NATO umbrella and therefore under a degree of US control. No clear resolution of these issues was apparent in the decision of the EU Helsinki summit in December that by 2003 member states collectively should be capable of the rapid deployment of up to 60,000 troops (see XI.4). Meanwhile, Britain had contributed 300 Gurkha soldiers to the Australian-led UN peace-keeping force deployed in East Timor from late September (see IX.1.vi; XI.1), being the only EU participant in this operation.

Queen Elizabeth undertook four state visits in 1999, the first to South Korea in April and the others to Ghana, South Africa and Mozambique before and after the Commonwealth Heads of Government Meeting held in South Africa in November (see XI.3.i). The South Korean authorities welcomed the royal visit—the first by a British monarch—as boosting the country's international credibility. However, UK-South Korean relations were later strained when a Korea Air (KAL) cargo jet crashed after takeoff from Stansted Airport in Essex on 22 December, killing the crew of four, and it was discovered that the plane had been carrying 425 kilos of depleted uranium as ballast. In light of KAL's poor safety record, the government ordered the Civil Aviation Authority to carry out random checks on the airline's flights into Britain.

Incoming state visits numbered only two in 1999, the first by President Göncz of Hungary in June and the second by President Jiang Zemin of China in October. The latter visitation, intended to cement UK-Chinese relations in the wake of the handover of Hong Hong to China in 1997, proved to be highly controversial, as demonstrations by Chinese human rights and pro-Tibet campaigners met with a heavy-handed police response. The demonstrators claimed that the British authorities were kowtowing to China in suppressing anti-Jiang protests, while a Chinese spokesman complained that the British authorities were not doing enough to that end. Both Prime Minister Blair and Foreign Secretary Cook were reported to have raised human rights questions with the Chinese visitors, though with no perceptible result. Prince Charles appeared to make his own protest by failing to attend a banquet at the Chinese embassy on 21 October.

Britain's external relations in 1999 were complicated by interminable legal wrangles over whether former Chilean dictator General (retd) Augusto Pinochet Ugarte, arrested in London in October 1998 (see AR 1998, pp. 37-8), should be extradited to Spain. On 24 March seven law lords decided by six to one to uphold the Lords' abortive ruling of November 1998 that General Pinochet could be extradited, but only on three charges related to alleged crimes committed since Britain became a party to the UN Convention Against Torture in 1988 (see also IV.3.iv). Invited by the law lords to reconsider his earlier decision that extradition proceedings could go ahead, Mr Straw in fact reaffirmed it on 15 April. After the High Court had rejected an appeal against Mr Straw's decision on 27 May, formal extradition proceedings at Bow Street Magistrates' Court resulted in a decision on 8 October that the General could be extradited to Spain. An appeal against this decision was due to be heard in March 2000. A further twist developed just before Christmas when the Home Office disclosed that General Pinochet was to undergo an independent medical examination to establish whether he was fit enough to stand trial. At year's end, therefore, the former dictator remained under police supervision at his rented house in Surrey, still uncertain about his future.

In other spheres, Britain's relations with Spain remained clouded by the Gibraltar issue (see II.4.ii), whereas an old dispute over fisheries reached a resolution of sorts in the House of Lords. On 28 October five law lords unanimously upheld a 1998 Court of Appeal ruling that Spanish trawler owners were entitled to compensation from the UK government in respect of the 1988 Merchant Shipping Act, which in July 1991 had become the first UK legislation to be struck down by the European Court of Justice (see also XIV.4). Enacted by the then Conservative government, the 1988 act had sought to preserve UK fishing quotas for British fishermen under the EU's common fisheries policy in the face of 'quota-hopping' by Spanish and other non-UK trawler owners. The compensation bill to British taxpayers resulting from the law lords' ruling was expected to total up to £100 million.

Even more irksome for Britain was the refusal of France to lift its ban on British beef exports despite an EU decision in July that such exports could be resumed. The EU ban had been imposed in March 1996 because of the probable link between bovine spongiform encephalopathy (BSE, or 'mad cow disease') in British herds and the fatal new variant Creutzfeldt-Jakob disease (nvCJD) in humans (see AR 1996, pp. 17, 392-3). The Labour government had made much of initial EU decisions to lift the ban, first for Northern Ireland in June 1998 and then for the rest of the UK in November (see AR 1998, pp. 35-6), but there had then been further delay while EU inspectors had confirmed that British safeguards were in place. Announced on 14 July, the resultant European Commission decision that exports (of deboned beef from animals aged six to 30 months) could resume from 1 August was further trumpeted by Mr Blair as a success for Labour's cooperative approach to Europe. The satisfaction was short-lived, however, as it became clear that the French government had no intention of abiding by the EU decision, while Germany also dragged its feet on lifting its ban on British beef.

The French government based its continuing refusal to lift the ban on a recommendation by its statutory food safety agency that it would be 'premature' to do so. In early October France presented a large dossier to the Brussels Commission and called for a new scientific study of the evidence, being backed by the German government. Having failed to make any progress on the issue with French counterpart Lionel Jospin at the EU summit in Tampere, Finland, Mr Blair declared on 15 October that 'the present situation is entirely unacceptable'. A week later Agriculture Minister Nick Brown called on shoppers to boycott French food because of the 'indefensible' French ban, having earlier announced his own personal decision not to consume French products until the ban was lifted. Amidst rising anger in the UK beef industry, farmers laid plans for blockading French goods at British ports, whilst some supermarkets refused to stock French apples. French farmers responded on 26 October by mounting a three-hour blockade of UK lorries at the Channel Tunnel terminal in Calais.

The further scientific study demanded by France resulted in a unanimous decision by a European Commission committee on 29 October that the 'new' French evidence did not support any change in the earlier decision that British beef was now safe. However, the French government insisted that it needed time to study the latest findings, while on 30 October seven of the 16 German *Land* governments announced their opposition to any speedy lifting of Germany's ban, on the grounds that new BSE cases continued to appear in British herds. Legislation to lift the German ban required approval not only by the *Land* parliaments but also by the federal upper house consisting of representatives of the *Länder*.

The French government's decision, announced on 9 December, was that its ban on British beef would remain in place, on the grounds that its food safety agency had again refused to recommend that it should be lifted. Attending another Finnish EU summit in Helsinki, Mr Blair described the French decision as 'totally wrong' and pledged the government's support for compensation claims against France by British beef producers. M. Jospin responded that he was accountable 'first and foremost' to the French people and was not worried by the prospect of legal action against France. In London, the Conservative opposition directed particular criticism at the 'deeply disappointed' Agriculture Minister, recalling that since July Mr Brown had repeatedly claimed that the French ban was about to be lifted thanks to British diplomacy and the government's pro-European credentials.

On 30 December the Brussels Commission confirmed that legal proceedings against France would begin in January 2000 with the lodging of relevant documents at the European Court of Justice in Luxembourg. The vigorous response in Paris was that France intended to launch a counter-suit against the Commission for allegedly breaching its duty to safeguard public health when it rejected the French submission that British beef was still unsafe. Earlier in the month the Commission had requested 'urgent clarification' from Germany on legislative delays in the lifting of the German ban on British beef.

Developments in the British armed forces in 1999 were dominated by the experience of participation in the Kosovo action, which raised question-marks over some of the provisions of the 1998 defence review and planned cuts in military expenditure (see AR 1998, p. 39). Particular concern was focused on the inferior quality of British rifles and other equipment reported by soldiers in the field, the Ministry of Defence responding that the apparent deficiencies would be studied. A more speedy outcome of the Kosovo operation was a government decision in October to increase the death-in-service benefit payable to families of Gurkha soldiers from Nepal to the level applicable to British soldiers. This was followed in December by a doubling of Gurkhas' retirement pensions to nearer the rates for British soldiers.

Two European court rulings in 1999 concerned military practices in Britain, the first a defeat for the government and the other a victory. On 27 September the European Court of Human Rights ruled unanimously that the discharge of four British military personnel in 1993-94 because of their homosexuality had been unlawful under the European Convention of Human Rights. Substantial compensation was expected to be awarded against the Ministry of Defence, which had defended its longstanding policy of excluding homosexuals on grounds of operational effectiveness and rank-and-file morale. Obliged to accept the ruling, the UK government announced that all pending cases for the discharge of homosexuals would be 'put on hold' while a new code of conduct was drawn up allowing for their participation in the armed forces.

The government victory was the rejection by the European Court of Justice on 26 October of a claim by a British female cook that she had been the victim of unlawful employment discrimination when the Royal Marines had refused to recruit her because she was a woman. The Court found that, while armed forces in EU countries were normally required to abide by equal treatment rules, exceptions were permissible in the case of front-line fighting units such as the Royal Marines, all of whose members, including cooks, were required to be ready for hand-to-hand combat.

ii. SCOTLAND

CAPITAL: Edinburgh   AREA: 78,313 sq km   POPULATION: 5,125,000 ('98)
OFFICIAL LANGUAGES: English/Gaelic   POLITICAL SYSTEM: devolved administration within UK
HEAD OF STATE: Queen Elizabeth II (since Feb '52)
RULING PARTIES: Labour Party & Liberal Democrats (since May '99)
HEAD OF GOVERNMENT: Donald Dewar (Labour), First Minister (since May '99)

THE major event in Scotland during the year was the coming into being of the Scottish Parliament. Elections were held on 6 May, and the newly-elected members (MSPs) were sworn in on 12 May. Dr Winnie Ewing (MSP for Moray), who presided over the meeting as the oldest member, opened proceedings by declaring 'the Scottish Parliament, which adjourned on 25 March 1707, is hereby reconvened'.

The elections were conducted on a combination of 'first-past-the-post' for constituencies and 'top-up' members by proportional representation in each of seven regions. Each elector received two ballot papers, one for the constituency member and the other for the regional top-up list; in the latter the elector selected the party but not the individual. Each party had determined its list of possible top-up candidates, in order of priority, for each region. A total of 73 members were elected to represent constituencies, and eight for each region from the top-up lists.

The outcome was that no party had an overall majority. The constituency members were predominantly from the Labour Party (53 members), the remainder being 12 Liberal Democrats, seven Scottish Nationalist Party (SNP) members and one independent (Denis Canavan, a Westminster Labour MP who stood as an independent in Falkirk West). The effect of regional top-up was predominantly to increase the number of SNP members (by 28) and to give the Conservatives 18 members; the Liberal Democrats gained another five members and Labour three. Also elected from the regional lists were one Scottish Socialist Party member (Tommy Sheridan) and one Scottish Green Party member (Robin Harper, who thereby became the first Green to be elected to any UK parliament). Overall, therefore, the Parliament consisted of 56 Labour members, 35 SNP, 18 Conservatives, 17 Liberal Democrats and three others.

After a week of negotiation, an alliance between Labour and the Liberal Democrats took office, with the SNP (led by Alex Salmond, member for Banff & Buchan) installed as the main opposition. The First Minister was Donald Dewar (Labour member for Glasgow Anniesland) and his deputy was Jim Wallace (Liberal Democrat member for Shetland). Mr Dewar presided over a cabinet of 11 members, including two Liberal Democrats, while Lord (David) Steel of Aikwood, the former Liberal Democrat leader, was elected Presiding Officer (Speaker). The main difficulty in striking the alliance was the conflict between the Labour and Liberal Democrat parties over student tuition fees, the problem being referred on 2 July to an independent committee of inquiry chaired by Andrew Cubie. The publication on 21 December of the Cubie Report threatened the stability of the alliance as the year ended, although both sides declared their desire to preserve it.

The new Parliament did not get off to a very good start in the eyes of much of the electorate. Expectations that it would quickly address serious matters were frustrated by the relatively technical business which occupied much of its first few months. The opening ceremonies were duly dignified but restricted in their impact to Edinburgh. The protracted negotiations on the government alliance did not help; and the first business of the Parliament was to determine matters about the salaries and expenses of the MSPs, who very shortly thereafter went into the summer recess. To make matters worse, when the Parliament reconvened the MSPs were awarded commemorative medals. However, the Parliament did establish the framework for its future, setting up 16 committees, all of which plunged into their work with enthusiasm. The desire for openness and informality were translated into well-received arrangements for public access, both physically and electronically, and the new Parliament dispensed with the more obscure aspects of Westminster parliamentary procedure.

Local council elections also took place on 6 May. Although held on a first-past-the-post basis, they resulted in no fewer than 17 of the 32 councils having no single political party in overall control. Labour lost seven councils and the SNP two, while a further eight were already governed by a coalition or by independent councillors. Although neither the Liberal Democrats nor the Conservatives controlled any councils, each party saw its number of councillors rise by over a quarter.

Most people delivered their verdict on the European Parliament elections on 10 June by staying at home. Scotland was for the first time a single constituency, its eight members being elected from party lists by proportional representation. The 25 per cent of the electorate who did vote elected three Labour, two SNP, two Conservative and one Liberal Democrat MEPs. The outcome gave further encouragement to the Conservatives that their political fortunes in Scotland might be recovering.

The weary electorate of Hamilton South was called into action again on 23 September, to vote in a Westminster parliamentary by-election occasioned by the appointment of UK Defence Secretary George Robertson as secretary-general of NATO and his elevation to the peerage as Lord Robertson of Port Ellen (in his native Islay). The voters elected another Labour member, in the person of Bill Tynan, although a 22.6 per cent swing almost gave the seat to the SNP. A second by-election had been averted in March by the clearing of Labour MP Mohammad Sarwar (Glasgow Govan) of the various electoral fraud charges against him (see AR 1998, p. 41).

Scotland produced its own version of the 1998 'cash for access' scandal at Westminster (see AR 1998, pp. 20-21) when *The Observer* of 26 September published the transcript of undercover interviews with two employees of a public relations firm who claimed that they could arrange direct access to Scottish ministers. The resultant controversy generated strains between Mr Dewar and his successor as UK Secretary of State for Scotland, John Reid, whose son Kevin Reid was one of the two lobbyists involved. Whereas Mr Reid declared that his son had acted 'honourably', Mr Dewar insisted on referring the case to the Scottish Parliament's standards committee for a formal investigation. Published on 18 November, the committee's report cleared ministers of any improper conduct but expressed concern about conflicting evidence given by witnesses, amidst press reports of growing intrigue and infighting within the Scottish Labour establishment.

Two decisions by Scottish courts in 1999 had potential major UK significance. On 21 October Sheriff Margaret Gimblett instructed a jury at Greenock to acquit three women charged with damaging the Trident nuclear submarine base at Faslane on the River Clyde, on the grounds that the UK nuclear weapons programme was, she believed, 'illegal under international law'. Pledged to remove nuclear weapons from Scotland, the SNP welcomed the acquittals, which were seen as certain to stimulate even greater anti-nuclear protest at Faslane. The second decision, throwing the Scottish legal system into some disarray, came on 11 November when the High Court in Edinburgh ruled that the tenure of 130 temporary sheriffs (judges) was in breach of the European Convention of Human Rights because they had been appointed for one-year terms by the executive and therefore were not wholly independent. The temporary sheriffs in question, responsible for about 25 per cent of the workload of Scottish courts, were immediately dismissed, as recruitment of new permanent sheriffs was hastily instituted. However, legal analysts were agreed that the ruling raised a question-mark not only over past judgments by temporary sheriffs but also over the status of their equivalents in England and Wales appointed by the Lord Chancellor, a member of the UK executive.

The Scottish economy continued to grow in 1999, but at a slower pace than that of southern England, prompting concerns that UK economic policy might be damaging manufacturing exporters. European Union (EU) regional policy was reformed over the summer, reducing the areas of Scotland likely to receive EU funding. The top level of assistance would no longer be available to the Highlands and Islands. Although the effects were to be tempered by a gradual reduction of assistance, the long-term implications for the fragile highland economy, and for some of the other areas likely to lose out, were the subject of anxious analysis.

On the other hand, Scottish morale was improved in 1999 by successes in sport. The Scottish rugby union team unexpectedly won the last Five Nations championship, while Paul Lawrie even more unexpectedly won the Open Golf championship at a windswept Carnoustie course in July (see Pt XVI).

iii. WALES

CAPITAL: Cardiff   AREA: 20,755 sq km   POPULATION: 3,000,000 ('98)
OFFICIAL LANGUAGES: Welsh & English   POLITICAL SYSTEM: devolved administration within UK
HEAD OF STATE: Queen Elizabeth II (since Feb '52)
RULING PARTY: Labour Party (since May '99)
HEAD OF GOVERNMENT: Alun Michael, First Secretary (since May '99)

THE year began and ended with doubts being expressed as to the suitability of Alun Michael to lead Wales into a new era of devolved government. Mr Michael had been appointed Secretary of State for Wales in October 1998 following the sudden resignation of Ron Davies (see AR 1998, pp. 25-6, 42-3), but he was challenged for the leadership of the Labour Party in Wales by Rhodri Morgan, the MP for Cardiff West, who had been controversially overlooked by the Prime Minister when forming his administration in 1997. An acrimonious election for the leadership ensued, with the winner expected to become the First Secretary of the new National Assembly for Wales, which was to come into existence in May. In the contentious electoral college system used by the Labour Party, Mr Morgan received substantial support from Labour's ordinary members, while Mr Michael was backed by most Welsh MPs. Those trades unions which balloted their members also tended to support Mr Morgan, but several union executives, including the powerful Transport and General Workers' Union, refused to conduct a membership ballot and backed Mr Michael. The Prime Minister openly supported the Secretary of State and pressure was exerted by the Labour Party centrally to ensure a victory for Mr Michael. This caused considerable bitternesss and accusations of what one senior Labour politician called 'an old Labour fix'.

On 20 February the result of the ballot was announced with Mr Michael winning narrowly, although Mr Morgan was by far the more popular choice among constituency parties. The apparent unfairness of the election, together with the lukewarm attitude to Mr Michael by many party activists who felt that he was being controlled from London, had a damaging effect on the Labour campaign during the elections for the National Assembly held on 6 May. Enthusiasm among Labour Party workers was minimal and many voters in traditional Labour constituencies failed to vote. Consequently, in one of the most surprising results in recent Welsh political history, Labour failed to win an outright majority in the Assembly.

The major beneficiary of Labour divisions and defections was Plaid Cymru, which captured several Labour strongholds previously considered impregnable, including the Llanelli, Rhondda and Islwyn constituencies. On a low turn-out (46 per cent), Labour won a total of 28 of the 60 Assembly seats, of which one, that of Mr Michael himself, was secured through the proportional representation (PR) system which accounted for 20 of the seats. Plaid Cymru was the second largest party with 17 seats (eight through PR), the Liberals won six seats (three through PR) and the Conservatives won only one constituency seat, Monmouth, and eight through PR. Although, inevitably, many of the new Assembly members were inexperienced, several Westminster MPs were also elected, including Ron Davies, Rhodri Morgan and John Marek (Labour) and Dafydd Wigley, Cynog Dafis and Ieuan Wyn Jones (Plaid Cymru). Also of significance was the high proportion of female Assembly members elected (24 out of 60), a consequence of selection procedures designed to ensure a fairer gender balance which had been applied by all the main parties apart from the Conservatives, who returned no female members.

The National Assembly held its first historic meeting on 12 May in Cardiff. Although it lacked legislative and tax-raising powers, it was to be the body which would now take most of the decisions affecting the lives of the people of Wales. Mr Michael, who was elected First Secretary, decided not to form a coalition with one of the opposition parties, but trusted that the new much-vaunted inclusive style of politics, together with Plaid Cymru's desire that the Assembly should be successful, would ensure the survival of his new minority government. The Assembly was officially opened by the Queen in a largely low-key ceremony at the end of May, while the transfer of power from the Secretary of State to the Assembly took place on 1 July.

Under the new constitutional arrangement, the role of the Secretary of State for Wales was now open to question and the following month Mr Michael resigned as Secretary of State to concentrate on his duties as First Secretary. He was replaced by Paul Murphy, MP for Torfaen, who had been an impressive junior minister in the Northern Ireland Office. Mr Murphy's belief, expressed in a speech soon after his appointment, that there had been a constitutional settlement and that no further powers would be transferred from Westminster to the National Assembly, was contrary to that advocated by many Welsh politicians who favoured Mr Davies's view that 'devolution was a process not an event'.

Mr Davies himself, despite being described as the architect of the Assembly, was not appointed to Mr Michael's first cabinet though, for a short time, he chaired the powerful economic development committee. He soon clashed with Mr Michael but in June, following further newspaper allegations about his private life, he resigned the chairmanship, while remaining an Assembly member. More controversial was Mr Michael's appointment of Christine Gwyther, a vegetarian, as Agriculture and Rural Development Secretary. There was much consternation among livestock farmers who found it difficult to see how a vegetarian might fight their cause, particularly at such a difficult time for the agriculture industry. Although defeated on a vote of censure in November, Ms Gwyther remained in office.

Mr Michael also remained in office although, by the end of the year, grave doubts persisted as to how long he might cling to power while the Assembly was, in many people's eyes, failing to make a credible impact on Wales. Much of the criticism was based on Mr Michael's inability to delegate, his lack of personality and, most significantly, his reluctance to forge distinctively Welsh policies, preferring instead to remain tied to those of the Labour government centrally. It was expected that he would be defeated on a vote of censure in the New Year were he to fail to secure from the Treasury additional matched-funding to take advantage of the European Union's 'Objective One' status granted to the most deprived parts of Wales.

Mr Michael was not the only party leader to be in difficulty. In August Rod Richards, over the years no stranger to controversy, was forced to resign the leadership of the Welsh Conservatives following an incident in London when he was alleged to have assaulted a young woman. He was replaced by Nick Bourne. The Plaid Cymru leader, Dafydd Wigley, was taken ill in December, and Ieuan Wyn Jones deputized for him while he recovered.

The elections for the European Parliament in June confirmed the advances made by Plaid Cymru the previous month. Taking advantage of the new electoral system designed to ensure proportional representation between the parties, Plaid Cymru captured two of the five Welsh seats, with Labour also winning two seats and the Conservatives one.

In the autumn Wales hosted the rugby World Cup, with the most important matches being played at the magnificent new Millennium Stadium in Cardiff (see also Pt XVI). Under its inspirational new coach, the New Zealander Graham Henry, the Welsh team had won eight consecutive international matches prior to the tournament; but it was knocked out at the quarter-final stage by the eventual champions, Australia.

iv. NORTHERN IRELAND

CAPITAL: Belfast   AREA: 18,843 sq km   POPULATION: 1,675,000 ('98)
OFFICIAL LANGUAGES: English, Irish & Ulster Scots
POLITICAL SYSTEM: power-sharing home rule within UK
HEAD OF STATE: Queen Elizabeth II (since Feb '52)
RULING PARTIES: Ulster Unionist Party (UUP), Social Democratic and Labour Party, Sinn Féin & Democratic Unionist Party (since Dec '99)
HEAD OF GOVERNMENT: David Trimble, First Minister (since July '98)

TURNING the Belfast 'Good Friday') Agreement of April 1998 (see AR 1998, pp. 45-6, 556-67) into a working set of institutions continued to prove difficult for most of 1999, until a breakthrough at last enabled the establishment of a power-sharing Executive in December and the inauguration of other bodies provided for in the agreement.

The necessary UK legislation, the Northern Ireland Act 1998, had taken until 19 November 1998 to enact, and outline agreement on a government structure of ten departments, with six North-South implementation bodies and six areas for cooperation, was not achieved until 18 December 1998. The final report from the inter-party negotiations on 15 February also made provision for a 60-member Civic Forum with a consultative role on social, economic and cultural matters and suggested that the North-South Ministerial Council (NSMC) should meet initially in Armagh and that the British-Irish Council should meet in London around the same time as the first meeting of the NSMC. The increase to ten departments meant some shuffling of functions from the previous six departments and the recruitment of four additional permanent secretaries.

After debate on 15-16 February, the Assembly voted by 77 to 29 to accept the report of the First Minister-elect and Deputy First Minister-elect, respectively David Trimble of the Ulster Unionist Party (UUP) and Seamus Mallon of the Social Democratic and Labour Party (SDLP). This cleared the way for the Northern Ireland Secretary of State, Dr Mo Mowlam, to accept the report on Standing Orders and to initiate the d'Hondt mechanism for the election of the Executive in advance of the proposed date for devolution on 10 March. The remaining work was the draft treaties between the United Kingdom and the Republic of Ireland to establish the British-Irish Council, its procedures and draft programme of work. When the Northern Ireland Office (NIO) introduced the Implementation Bodies (NI) Order 1999 on 9 March, the UK government had fulfilled its pledge to have the legislative basis of the new institutions completed ahead of the 10 March deadline for devolution. However, the problems of the previous autumn, namely implementing an Executive and the decommissioning of illegal weapons, remained. On 8 March, therefore, Dr Mowlam, postponed the deadline until Good Friday, 2 April.

In the interval attempts were made to produce an acceptable sequencing of the formation of an Executive and the decommissioning of paramilitary weapons. After two days of talks at Hillsborough Castle the British and Irish governments on 1 April issued a joint declaration on their view of the best way forward and gave the parties until 13 April to accept it. After it had been rejected by Sinn Féin (SF) and the Progressive Unionist Party (PUP) and criticized by other parties, Dr Mowlam pronounced that there was no basis for the formation of an Executive acceptable to both unionists and republicans. There were further inter-party talks on 28 April, but another suggestion from the British government was publicly rejected by the Irish government. After a further set of talks at Downing Street from 6 May, several parties thought they had got a deal on 14 May, but the UUP members of the Assembly elected in 1998 refused to buy into it.

The European Parliament elections on 10 June increased the pressure on UUP leader Mr Trimble, who was blamed by critics of the Belfast Agreement for the early release of paramilitary prisoners and the absence of decommissioning. The Rev. Ian Paisley of the Democratic Unionist Party (DUP) campaigned for unionist voters to treat the election as a re-run of the 1998 referendum to counter the claim that a majority of unionists had voted 'yes' on that occasion (see AR 1998, p. 47). The leader of the UK Unionist Party (UKUP), Robert McCartney, sought with some success to win disaffected UUP voters concerned at the perceived unbalanced implementation of the Belfast Agreement. In the event, the three sitting MEPs, Dr Paisley, John Hume of the SDLP and Jim Nicholson of the UUP, were re-elected, the DUP leader topping the poll for the fifth successive European election with 28 per cent of the vote. It was clear that a majority of unionists had supported Dr Paisley, the change since 1998 serving to undermine Mr Trimble's moral authority to speak for unionists.

UK Prime Minister Tony Blair launched another bid for agreement on 25

June by publishing a proposal and appealing directly to the public. He set 30 June as the new deadline, which he described as 'absolute' if devolution in Northern Ireland was to go ahead in phase with Scotland and Wales on 1 July (see II.1.ii; II.1.iii). However, resultant intensive talks were adjourned without agreement at 3.40am on 1 July. 'The Way Forward' document, published the next day, contained the 25 June proposals and proposed that the mechanism to elect an Executive should be triggered on 15 July to lay the Devolution Order on 16 July to come into effect on 18 July. It said that decommissioning could happen within days and that the international commission headed by General John de Chastelain (Canada) would report on progress in September. New legislation, the Northern Ireland Act 1999, proposed a 'fail-safe' device on decommissioning but government amendments did not meet UUP requirements and were withdrawn before the act was passed on 14 July.

Elected UUP members remained at their party headquarters on 15 July, staying away from the Assembly meeting convened by the Secretary of State for the election of the Executive. In their absence, six SDLP and four SF members were nominated when the unionist parties and the Alliance Party declined to make nominations. However, Dr Mowlam refused to confirm the nominations because they did not conform to a hastily-introduced standing order requiring that the Executive should consist of at least three unionists and three nationalists. Further, in a resignation speech from his position as Deputy First Minister-elect, Mr Mallon (SDLP) revealed the depth of the differences between his party and the UUP. In the aftermath of this disaster, the British and Irish governments stepped back from the process and asked former US senator George Mitchell to review the implementation of the Belfast Agreement. After a round of meetings with the parties on 21-22 July, the review was adjourned until 6 September.

There was no guarantee that all of the parties would take part in the review. Mr Trimble reserved his partys's position until the autumn, as the SF vented its anger on the UUP. SF negotiator Martin McGuinness said there was 'not a snowball's chance in hell' of meeting the May 2000 deadline for decommissioning. The SF's considered view of the peace process, expressed on 29 July, was that 'no-one should underestimate the depth of seriousness of the crisis we are facing'. The discovery on 27 July of a plot to import weapons for the Irish Republican Army (IRA) from Florida and the apparent execution of a Catholic taxi-driver by the IRA in early August (the organization's fifth suspected killing since the July 1997 ceasefire) called the sincerity of SF and the IRA into question. Disorder and destruction in Londonderry to the extent of some £4 million, after the Apprentice Boys march on 14 August, brought shades of the events 30 years previously which first brought the army on to the streets of Northern Ireland. The belief grew that the SF was insincere and that the IRA was working to a different agenda. Loyalists, who had walked away from confrontation at Drumcree in July, encountered confrontation from SF-inspired Catholic residents' groups in August. The lesson drawn by two loyalist paramilitary organisations, the Ulster Volunteer Force (UVF) and the Red Hand Commando, was that the conditions for decommissioning did not exist.

Having returned from holiday, Mr Trimble began to talk up the review process, urging Mr Mallon on 23 August to return as Deputy First Minister. However, Dr Mowlam's ruling three days later that there was not 'a sufficient basis to conclude that the IRA ceasefire has broken down' and that she would not use her powers under the Sentences Act to suspend prisoner releases, failed the test of public credibility. In addition, the leaks or constructive guesses about the content of the forthcoming Patten report on the Royal Ulster Constabulary (RUC), carried in the *Belfast Telegraph* from 25 August, produced such pressure on the Secretary of State that Mr Blair had to declare on 31 August that she had his 'full confidence'.

Despite the deteriorating political situation the UUP and SF executive committees both decided to take part in the Mitchell review which began on 6 September. The talks were adjourned on 9 September with the publication of the Patten report, which provided a strong campaigning issue within the unionist community by proposing that the RUC's name and symbols should be changed and that a new police force should be regionally accountable to elected representatives from both communities. Welcomed by republicans, the report was condemned by Mr Trimble as the shoddiest piece of work he had seen in his public life and as a 'gratuitous insult' to those who had served in the RUC. The first unionist protest against the report was held in the Ulster Hall on 18 September, unionists opposed to the Belfast Agreement being prominent at later rallies. The only harmony from Stormont in September was the music at a concert given by Luciano Pavarotti.

There was no breakthrough in time for the Labour Party conference at the end of September, but two decisions were taken soon after which were to prove important. First, on 11 October the Prime Minister moved Dr Mowlam to another cabinet post and replaced her in Northern Ireland by Peter Mandelson (see II.1.i). It was emphasized that there was no change of policy—no 'plan B'—but the change signalled the Prime Minister's close involvement in the situation, while his new Secretary of State was thought likely to have a better relationship with UUP than Dr Mowlam. Second, Mr Mitchell moved the review talks to London, to the residence of the US ambassador, Philip Lader. Despite initial reports of face-to-face meetings between Mr Trimble and SF leader Gerry Adams, there was no progress and the talks adjourned again on 15 October. When they resumed there were reports of a 'thaw' in relations and on 23 October it was decided to extend the talks beyond the original time allotted.

Political developments came to a head in the early weeks of November. On 2 November Mr Mitchell suspended the review and subsequently held meetings with Mr Blair, Irish Prime Minister Bertie Ahern and President Clinton of the USA. When talks resumed on 8 November, the SF revealed an offer by the IRA to appoint an official to liaise with General de Chastelain and his decommissioning body. After a further period for reflection, the review reconvened on 15 November to a series of choreographed statements. First, Mr Mitchell published an interim report saying that the pro-agreement parties shared the view that 'devolution should occur and the institutions should be established at the earliest possible date...and that decommissioning should occur as soon as possible'. Second, statements from Mr Trimble and Mr Adams on 16 November confirmed that significant progress had been made. The IRA then issued a statement on 17 November indicating that they would 'appoint a representative to enter discussions' with General de Chastelain following the establishment of the institutions provided for in the Good Friday Agreement. On 18 November Mr Mitchell concluded his review and asked the parties to embrace the opportunity for a lasting settlement and for the UUP and the SF to 'jump together'.

The focus then switched back to the UUP council meeting on 27 November to consider whether the party's demands on decommissioning had been sufficiently met to enter a power-sharing Executive with the SF. The council voted by 58 to 42 per cent in favour of the steps proposed in the Mitchell review. The majority was clearer than expected and was attributed to deputy leader John Taylor's last-minute support, a post-dated letter of resignation from Mr Trimble and the promise of a reconvened UUC meeting in February to review progress on decommissioning. The UUC decision was excoriated by DUP speakers at their annual conference on the same day for enabling the Executive to be formed with SF representatives before any decommissioning had been achieved.

Meeting on 29 November, the Assembly agreed to ignore the resignation of Mr Mallon in July and proceeded to elect ten departmental heads (ministers) using the d'Hondt procedure, with the party leader selecting the department as his turn came round. The outcome was an Executive comprising three UUP, three SDLP, two DUP and two SF members. The next day the Assembly appointed committee chairmen and deputies, again using d'Hondt, and allocated committee places proportionately. At the same time, the Northern Ireland (Appointed Day) Order to devolve power was approved at Westminster and came into effect at midnight on 1 December. Following a preliminary session of the NSMC at Stormont on 1 December, the next day, meeting in Dublin, Mr Mandelson and David Andrews, the Irish Foreign Minister, formally signed the treaties to create the NSMC, a relaunched UK-Irish Intergovernmental Council and a 'Council of the Isles' (representing the seven parliaments of the British Isles). At the same time, the Irish government promulgated amendments to the Republic's 1937 constitution approved in May 1998 removing the old territorial claim to the North in Articles 2 and 3 (see II.2.vii). The changing situation was symbolized by a meeting in Buckingham Palace on 2 December between Queen Elizabeth and the Irish President, Mary McAleese, who had been on a tour of Britain.

Progress was also evident on other aspects of the review. The IRA issued a statement on 2 December confirming that it had appointed a representative to enter discussions with General de Chastelain and a meeting took place at a secret location in the Republic two days later. On 8 December, moreover, the UVF also appointed a person to liaise with the decommissioning body.

The effect of the new institutions on administration were immediate. Two

Northern Ireland Office ministers, John McFall and Lord Dubs, whose responsibilities had been devolved, took their leave of the province. In addition, on 6 December Mr Mandelson declined to answer questions in the House of Commons on education and agriculture, two devolved areas. The new Assembly had another problem from 6 December, namely local criticism of a £9,000 pay rise for members as it moved from 'shadow' to full status. The committees began work on 8 December but sessions were initially private. The Executive also had the problems of agreeing a programme for government and of the fact that the two DUP members, Peter Robinson and Nigel Dodds, refused to meet in the same room as the SF ministers. On 14 December, moreover, there was a row between the smaller parties and the UUP and SDLP over their desire for two junior ministerial posts—which was eventually agreed by 49 votes to 38.

The two DUP ministers were missing from two historic events in mid-December. On 13 December a meeting of the NSMC in the Armagh city council offices brought members of the Northern Ireland Executive together with Irish ministers, who arrived in 11 Mercedes official cars. The meeting approved the interim heads for the six cross-border implementation bodies as well as an initial work programme. The second meeting, on 17 December, was the inaugural session of the new Council of the Isles at Lancaster House in London, at which parliamentary representatives from Britain, Northern Ireland, Scotland, Wales, the Irish Republic, the Isle of Man and the Channel Islands discussed drugs, social exclusion, transport, environment, e-commerce and the knowledge economy. On the same day the UK-Irish Intergovernmental Council met to discuss non-devolved matters, setting out a nine-point programme of work on human rights, policing and implementation of the Patten report, criminal justice, normalization of security arrangements, victims of violence, prison arrangements, drugs trafficking and broadcasting.

In his Christmas message Mr Mandelson said that life in Northern Ireland was returning to normal in an 'atmosphere of calm optimism', in what he described as 'the age of grown-up politics'. Christmas 1999 was certainly different from those of previous years, with only two paramilitary prisoners left in the Maze, 128 home on 12 days' leave and the rest fully released. A security paper published on 23 December suggested that a further 1,800 British troops could soon leave the province. The only reminder of the 'bad old days' was the abandonment of two races at Kempton Park in Britain on 28 December after a hoax bomb warning from the Continuity IRA.

The economy remained buoyant, with unemployment at the lowest level for 25 years, falling to 5.8 per cent seasonally adjusted by December, when a record number of 618,000 people were in employment. Business failures were at a six-year low and the Industrial Development Board (IDB) attracted 21 new projects by overseas investors, all of them in high-tech industries. There were generally optimistic economic forecasts. The First Trust Bank predicted a 'very positive' outlook, although it added that some sectors required attention. These included agriculture, where farm incomes were down by 79 per cent, beef and pig farmers being especially hit.

The manufacturing sector had shown recent expansion, although textiles had experienced job losses in a number of clothing and carpet manufacturers. The engineering sector was also expanding, though the Belfast shipyard was again in need of orders, while the TransTec engineering company in Londonderry was threatened with closure due to problems in the parent group. Overall, moreover, the Northern economy, despite the encouraging prospects, was not matching the rapid growth of the Republic of Ireland, so that one forecaster warned that the two economies were growing further apart in performance and structure.

2. GERMANY—FRANCE—ITALY—BELGIUM—
THE NETHERLANDS—LUXEMBOURG—IRELAND

i. GERMANY

CAPITAL: Berlin   AREA: 357,000 sq km   POPULATION: 82,200,000 ('98)
OFFICIAL LANGUAGE: German   POLITICAL SYSTEM: federal parliamentary democracy
HEAD OF STATE: President Roman Herzog (since July '94)
RULING PARTIES: Social Democratic Party (SPD) & Alliance 90/Greens
HEAD OF GOVERNMENT: Gerhard Schröder (SPD), Federal Chancellor (since Oct '98)
MAIN IGO MEMBERSHIPS (NON-UN: NATO, EU, WEU, OSCE, CE, CBSS, AC, OECD, G-8
CURRENCY: Deutsche Mark (end-'99 £1=DM3.14, US$1=DM1.95)
GNP PER CAPITA: US$25,850 by exchange-rate calculation, US$20,810 at PPP ('98)

IN a number of respects, 1999 signalled the opening of a new era in German politics. It saw the physical relocation of the centre of government from provisional and provincial Bonn to the 'real' capital city and metropolitan grandeur of Berlin. At the same time the new 'red-green' government elected in September 1998 (see AR 1998, pp. 51-2)—the first of the '1968 generation'— falteringly began to find its feet under the Social Democratic (SPD) Chancellor Gerhard Schröder and his Green Deputy Chancellor and Foreign Minister Joschka Fischer.

It was a government which broke new bounds in foreign policy, sending German forces to war for the first time since 1945 as the Kosovo crisis deepened in March (see III.2.vi) and winning plaudits for its skilful diplomacy in the resolution of the conflict. Domestically, though, it lacked clear policy direction, with both the SPD and the Greens suffering as a result a series of electoral setbacks. The shoots of recovery only emerged towards the end of the year as the leading opposition party, the Christian Democratic Union (CDU), became mired in a party funding scandal surrounding its former leader and elder statesman, Helmut Kohl, who had served as Chancellor from 1982-1998. This was arguably the real watershed in German politics. Herr Kohl's tragic disgrace closed the book on a political figure who had dominated German politics for nearly two decades.

The scandal also opened up the prospect of a brighter 2000 for a red-green coalition which had suffered an extraordinary year in public opinion trends. No other government in the post-war German state had suffered such a fall from favour so quickly after winning a *Bundestag* election. The rot started in early February—barely four months after the triumph of September 1998—when the sitting red-green regional government lost the election in Hesse (just) to a coalition of the CDU and the Free Democrats (FDP), a marginal SPD increase being cancelled out by a sharp Green setback. In June the SPD maintained its record of losing every election to the European Parliament to date to the CDU and its Bavarian sister party, the Christian Social Union (CSU), the Greens' share of the vote also falling. The SPD did much better in the Bremen state election in June, remaining dominant in the ruling SPD-CDU coalition. But the pattern of declining SPD and Green support was resumed in subsequent state elections. In September the SPD lost the Saarland to the CDU for the first time since 1985, surrendered its absolute majority in Brandenburg and came third behind the ex-communist Party of Democratic Socialism (PDS) in Thuringia and Saxony. In October it scored its worst ever vote in Berlin. The Greens had no partial consolations, losing votes in every election held in 1999.

The pattern of percentage votes obtained by the parties in elections during 1999 is shown in the table below (figures in parentheses showing the change from the previous result).

	SPD	CDU	Greens	FDP	PDS
Hesse (7/2)	39.4	43.4	7.2	5.1	-
	(+1.4)	(+4.2)	(-4.0)	(-2.4)	
Bremen (6/6)	42.6	37.1	8.9	2.5	2.9
	(+9.2)	(+4.5)	(-4.1)	(-0.9)	(+0.5)
Europe (13/6)	30.7	48.7*	6.4	3.0	5.8
	(-1.5)	(+9.9)	(-3.7)	(-1.1)	(+1.1)
Saarland (5/9)	44.4	45.5	3.2	2.6	0.8
	(-5.0)	(+6.9)	(-2.3)	(+0.5)	-
Brandenburg (5/9)	39.3	26.5	1.9	1.9	23.3
	(-14.8)	(+7.8)	(-1.0)	(+0.2)	(+6.8)
Thuringia (12/9)	18.5	51.0	1.9	1.1	21.3
	(-11.1)	(+8.4)	(-2.6)`	(-2.1)	(+4.7)
Saxony (19/9)	10.7	56.9	2.6	1.1	22.2
	(-5.9)	(-1.2)	(-1.5)	(-0.6)	(+5.7)
Berlin (10/10)	22.4	40.8	9.9	2.2	17.7
	(-1.2)	(+3.4)	(-3.3)	(-0.3)	(+3.1)

*including 9.4% for CSU

The extraordinarily poor run of election results for the federal coalition partners was largely self-inflicted. The SPD presented the image of a party unsure of its direction. This was crystallized in the first part of the year in the personal rivalry between Herr Schröder and his Finance Minister, Oskar Lafontaine. Herr Lafontaine's authority was bolstered by his simultaneously holding the post of SPD chairman and by his popularity among the party membership; Herr Schröder, by contrast, owed his position to his skill as an electoral tactician and was not highly popular in the party. This dual leadership structure was overlain by ideological difference. Though lacking a clearly recognizable political philosophy, Herr Schröder was associated with a project of 'Blairite' social democratic modernization. Herr Lafontaine, by contrast, was more deeply rooted in the ideological traditions of the SPD and sought to revive a broadly Keynesian approach to macroeconomic management. This ideologically divided, dual leadership structure was not a recipe for decisive and effective government, and was reflected in an atmosphere of drift and uncertainty over major policy issues such as tax and pensions reform.

Perhaps surprisingly, the problem was not resolved by Herr Lafontaine's abrupt and petulant resignation in March and his replacement as party leader by Herr Schröder and as Finance Minister by Hans Eichel, a technocrat more amenable to Herr Schröder's modernizing agenda. The debate between 'modernizers' and 'traditionalists' remained unresolved, and burst back to prominence with the publication of a joint policy paper by Herr Schröder and British Prime Minister Tony Blair on 9 June. Entitled 'The Way Ahead for Europe's Social Democrats', the Blair-Schröder paper was an unashamed and enthusiastic endorsement of the market economy and the promotion of competitiveness and entrepreneurship as the best framework for securing social democratic values in the era of globalization. For a British audience, the paper was an uncontroversial statement of post-Thatcher orthodoxy. In Germany, and in the SPD in particular, it was politically explosive, and sparked a highly public and divisive debate in the SPD about the values and goals of the party which continued for months.

This was arguably what Chancellor Schröder intended. He had sought with the paper to develop his vision of the SPD reaching into a 'new centre ground' (*neue Mitte*) and attracting new voter groups to compensate for its shrinking traditional electorate in the manual working class. What he had perhaps not expected was the breadth and volume of the debate he unleashed. It had the result both of disillusioning the SPD's traditional manual worker core electorate and, reflecting the unattractiveness of the party's obvious fractiousness, failing to reach into new voter groups. The net effect was deepening unpopularity and repeated electoral defeat.

The weaknesses of the Greens were less to do with a divided party leadership. Indeed, the three Green federal cabinet ministers were, despite occasional glitches, steadfast in their commitment to the responsible conduct of their government duties. This, though, was the cause of their party's electoral problems. The pragmatic realities of sharing power with the SPD all too often conflicted with, and typically ended up overriding, cherished Green political principles. Compromises on the liberalization of German citizenship law, on the timetable for phasing out nuclear power and on energy taxes had the effect of alienating traditional Green supporters. Most disillusioning for many Greens was the decision made by the red-green cabinet, carried out under the ministerial remit of Foreign Minister Fischer, to fight in Kosovo. This was revealed most dramatically at a special party congress called in May to debate the Kosovo issue, when Herr Fischer was paint-bombed into hospital and the party leadership could only speak to the congress from behind serried ranks of police bodyguards.

With the governing parties divided either in cabinet, or between party leadership and rank and file, there should have been easy pickings for the opposition parties. And generally there were—except that the FDP, whose neo-liberal 'turbo-capitalism' and lack of effective leaders since the retirement of Hans-Dietrich Genscher had left the party teetering on the edge of the 5 per cent electoral hurdle determining political survival or oblivion. The PDS by contrast, despite its tainted past as the ruling party of the former German Democratic Republic, continued to build on its pedigree as a party capable of articulating and representing a distinctive east German identity. Given its success also in clearing the nationwide 5 per cent hurdle in the June Euro-elections (as it did in the 1998 *Bundestag* election), it stood poised to take on a role of representing and legitimizing east German regional interests in national politics similar to that performed for Bavaria by the CSU.

It was a very good year for the CDU/CSU, until the end of November. The speed of their recovery in public and electoral opinion after, by German standards, a crushing defeat in the 1998 *Bundestag* election was quite remarkable. The recovery was not, though, based on especially robust foundations. It took off in the campaign for the February Hesse election in the form of a petition—which ultimately collected some five million signatures—directed against the plans of the SPD-Green federal government to liberalize Germany's antiquated law restricting the right of citizenship to those with German blood. The populist theme of the petition struck enough of a public nerve to overturn the eight-year-old red-green coalition in Hesse. However, the Christian Democrats' further electoral successes were hardly of their own making, reflecting instead the unpopularity of the federal government parties.

In these circumstances, the CDU arguably became lulled into complacency. In particular, it failed to review the reasons why it had lost the 1998 *Bundestag* election or to develop new strategies for a return to power. Its leader, Wolfgang Schäuble, was ill-equipped to launch a process of far-reaching party renewal, having been for over a decade an intimate insider of what became known as the 'Kohl system'. Despite its state electoral victories, therefore, the CDU remained vulnerable. This became clear when a party funding scandal enveloped Helmut Kohl in November. It came to light as an unanticipated by-product of a criminal investigation of a former CDU party treasurer indicating that Herr Kohl had run a network of secret accounts into which he had placed large-scale anonymous donations, and out of which he had dispensed patronage to regional branches of the CDU. Receiving anonymous donations and maintaining secret accounts contravened laws which the Kohl government had itself introduced and tightened in response to earlier funding scandals.

The effect on the CDU's public image was devastating. Herr Kohl's cavalier attitude to his own laws, a trickle of revelations about similar 'black' bank accounts (and anonymous donations to them) in regional branches of the party, and the former Chancellor's refusal to name his donors, even though this raised suspicions that his governments might have been 'bought' by private-sector interests, raised serious question-marks about the culture of probity in the party. These were reinforced by parallel parliamentary and criminal investigations launched into the 'Kohl system' in December. Inevitably, therefore, the tide of public opinion turned. It did so at the same time as Herr Schröder began to show signs of successfully meshing his modernizing agenda with the traditionalism of his party. The passing of a tough but business-friendly budget in November combined with the Chancellor's interventions in December to save jobs at Holzmann, an ailing building concern, to generate a new sense of potency and purpose. This reversal of fortunes was reflected in opinion polls showing the SPD as overhauling a rapidly-sinking CDU. The odds on an SPD victory at the federal level in 2002 were therefore considerably shorter at the end of the year than they had been at the start of it.

Perhaps unexpectedly, the Schröder government was rather more sure-footed in foreign policy than it was at home. After an initial period of unsteadiness caused in part by the 'export' of the Lafontaine-Schröder rivalry to the European level, and in part simply by inexperience, Germany's European Union (EU) presidency in the first half of 1999 was generally felt to have been well-managed. Joschka Fischer proved an inspired choice as Foreign Minister, deploying a diplomatic craft which belied his earlier, more turbulent persona in the Green movement. The results were manifold: the passing of the 'Agenda 2000' package of budgetary and policy reforms as an initial preparation for the eastern enlargement of the EU; the adept handling and resolution of the crisis surrounding the collective resignation of the European Commission in March; and the further institutionalization of the EU's common foreign and security policy (CFSP), in particular the appointment of the former NATO secretary-general Javier Solana as the EU's high representative for foreign policy (see XI.4).

However, the most remarkable foreign policy development in 1999 was the federal government's decision that German forces would participate in the NATO intervention against Serbia over Kosovo. This was an extraordinary decision, given the historically-grounded reluctance of post-war German policy-makers to contemplate the use of force in the international arena. It was all the more remarkable because large parts of the SPD and, in particular, the Greens were steeped in post-1968 pacifism. Amidst the inevitable domestic controversy raised by the Kosovo involvement, the steadfastness of the German contribution to the NATO mission was widely praised, and there was broad agreement on the justification: not to tolerate massive abuse of human rights (though the latter point was rather qualified by the end of the year by official German reticence to condemn Russian intervention in Chechnya). Arguably most remarkable, though, was the tireless effort invested by Herr Fischer in particular in pressing for a political resolution to the dispute, which was announced at the closing summit of the German presidency in June 1999.

ii. FRANCE

CAPITAL: Paris   AREA: 544,000 sq km   POPULATION: 59,000,000 ('98)
OFFICIAL LANGUAGE: French   POLITICAL SYSTEM: presidential parliamentary democracy
RULING PARTIES: Rally for the Republic (RPR) holds presidency; Socialist Party (PS), French Communist Party (PCF), Greens and other groups form government
HEAD OF STATE & GOVERNMENT: President Jacques Chirac (RPR), since May '95
PRIME MINISTER: Lionel Jospin (PS), since June '97
MAIN IGO MEMBERSHIPS (NON-UN): NATO, EU, WEU, OSCE, COE, OECD, G-8, Francophonie
CURRENCY: franc (end-'99 £1=F10.55, US$1=F6.54)
GNP PER CAPITA: US$24,940 by exchange-rate calculation, US$22,320 at PPP ('98)

A flourishing economy eased many problems—though sufficient remained to heighten tensions in an increasingly fragmented political scene. And the economy was indeed a success story. GDP grew by around 3.0 per cent over the year; industrial production boomed, partly reflecting the stimulus that depreciation of the euro gave to exports. (The euro slipped into operation at the turn of the year with minimal fuss, but its impact on daily life was as yet modest.) Retail prices rose by 1.3 per cent, earnings by comfortably more. Retail sales were buoyant. Even the stubbornly high level of unemployment inched down from 11.5 to 10.6 per cent. This was hailed as the first fruits of the 35-hour working week. Burgeoning tax receipts enabled the then Finance Minister, Dominique Strauss-Kahn, to claim in September that he was handing back 'the biggest tax cuts for a decade'. His budget increased spending on education, employment and 'solidarity' (though defence suffered a token reduction), cut VAT on house repairs and phased out the tax on rents.

Unusually, the year saw two major takeover battles—such matters being traditionally more likely to be fixed behind the scenes. One involved an eight-month three-way struggle between Banque Nationale de Paris, Société Générale and Paribas, and the other bid and counter-bid between oil giants Total Fina and Elf-Aquitaine, the former emerging the winner. Crédit Lyonnais was partially privatized in the autumn—a condition imposed by the European Union (EU) for allowing F120,000 million to be poured in to prevent complete collapse.

Introduction of the 35-hour week remained the government's major economic and social project. Further legislation was passed to bring in small employers, against their heated opposition. The Minister of Labour, Martine Aubry, claimed that 122,000 jobs had been created or saved; union reaction was more qualified, contending that full-time workers were being replaced with part-timers and that employers were introducing labour-saving technology and seizing their chance to impose onerous flexible working practices.

A government report on the equally delicate question of the retirement age and pensions suggested that increased life expectancies would make it impossible to pay the current working generation a full pension. It proposed to end retirement on a full pension at the age of 60 (earlier in some occupations), moving progressively to 66 years 7 months as soon as possible. Whether such a nettle would be grasped remained to be seen. Crime remained a major preoccupation. A government package of measures aimed to stem the rising tide of youth crime—nearly a quarter of crimes were committed by under-18s. Prime Minister Lionel Jospin promised 7,000 extra police, reorganization of a seriously outdated distribution of police, a fourfold increase in juvenile detention centre places, more youth centre educators and more judges to expedite the notoriously slow processes of the law. The government also introduced measures to strengthen the presumption of innocence, transfer the power to hold suspects on demand, limit preventive detention and improve defendants' access to lawyers. However, France refused to accept a European Court of Human Rights ruling that a man whose conviction had been marred by excessive delay and the absence of defence counsel should be retried.

Another hot potato was a bill to allow unmarried couples the same rights on material issues as married couples. These 'civil solidarity pacts', which were open to same-sex couples, were attacked as paving the way for homosexual marriages. Many politicians hesitated, whether from principle or calculation, but when a feared anti-gay backlash failed to materialize, and demonstrations against delay threatened electoral damage from another quarter, the bill was eventually approved.

President Jacques Chirac and M. Jospin supported a constitutional amendment to even the gender balance in parliament. (With only 59 women among the 577 deputies in the National Assembly, France ranked lowest in the EU apart from Greece.) The Senate, ever a bastion of conservatism, initially refused. However, heavy pressure from the President subsequently persuaded it to think again and the motion was adopted by 289 votes to 8. The parties did not wait for the constitutional formalities to be enacted: all the major formations except the National Front gave women parity or better in their Euro-election lists. A subsequent constitutional proposal to give greater recognition to regional languages failed when the President, with an eye to re-election, reversed his earlier support.

The approach of elections in France was frequently an occasion for parties to close ranks, however fleetingly. Not so this time. Most notably, the schism in the National Front (see AR 1998, p. 58) became a total split. At a rebel congress in January Bruno Mégret ousted Jean-Marie Le Pen as president. A bitter legal battle over the Front's finances, headquarters, title and logo ensued. At a by-election in March Front voters deserted in their thousands. The moderate right was also divided. Charles Pasqua, a Gaullist former minister, allied himself with the 'Eurosceptic' Movement for France, accusing President Chirac of 'betraying fundamental principles of Gaullism'. He later founded the Rassemblement pour la France (RPF), its initials evoking General de Gaulle's party in the early postwar years. The 'Europhile' Union for French Democracy refused to campaign with the neo-Gaullist Rassemblement pour la République (RPR), distrusting its leader, Philippe Séguin, a one-time opponent of the Maastricht Treaty. M. Séguin soon resigned, accusing friends of the President of plotting against him over his aspirations for the presidency. He was eventually succeeded by Michèle Alliot-Marie, first female leader of a major French party, whose success owed much to not being the candidate favoured by the President.

The centre-right entered the Euro-elections campaign tattered, fragmented and disorganized. In contrast, the governing coalition parties—Socialists, Communists and Greens—kept their tensions and rivalries in check and surmounted the tendency for Euro-elections to go against the government of the day. On a lowish 46.8 per cent turnout, the main parties of the left polled nearly 39 per cent—the Greens doing well, the Communists poorly. The mainstream right took 35 per cent of the vote, but M. Pasqua's breakaway movement overtook the official Gaullists. The rival National Fronts dismally shared under 10 per cent. However, the reduced turnout and the relative success of the anti-Paris, anti-EU 'Hunting, Fishing, Nature, Traditions' list carried a warning for the whole political class.

	votes	%	seats
Socialists	3,873,901	21.95	22
Rally for France and the Independence of Europe*	2,304,285	13.05	13
RPR-Defence of Liberties	2,263,476	12.82	12
Greens	1,715,450	9.72	9
Union for French Democracy	1,638,680	9.28	9
Communists	1,196,310	6.78	6
Hunting, Fishing, Nature, Traditions	1,195,760	6.77	6
National Front (Le Pen)	1,005,225	5.69	5
Workers' Struggle	914,680	5.18	5
Other lists (11)	1,545,317	8.44	0

*Consisting of the RPF and the Movement for France

The poisonous miasma of earlier scandals and controversy still lingered. The ex-mistress of Roland Dumas, president of the Constitutional Council and therefore the fifth-ranking personage in the land, admitted to having been paid large sums by the Elf-Aquitaine oil company to influence his decisions when he was Foreign Minister. Placed under formal investigation, M. Dumas refused to resign but was subsequently prevailed upon to take leave, though not before the Constitutional Council had ruled that a serving President of the Republic could not face trial in the ordinary courts for his actions before taking office. This effectively blocked the police from investigating M. Chirac's role in the scandal of fictitious posts at City Hall during his years as mayor of Paris. Several charges were dropped against former Prime Minister Alain Juppé, the city's head of finance during that period. M. Chirac's successor as mayor, Jacques Tiberi, resisted pressure to resign over the affair even after his wife appeared on charges of taking F200,000 francs from lobbyists for a useless report. In November Finance Minister Strauss-Kahn, arguably the government's most successful member (and probable Socialist candidate for mayor of Paris), resigned when placed under formal examination after allegations that, before becoming a minister, he had been improperly paid F603,000 by the Mutuelle Nationale des Étudiants de France and had forged documents to conceal the fact. He was succeeded by Christian Sauter, a former aide to the late President Mitterrand.

In March the president of the Assembly and former Prime Minister, Laurent Fabius, and two other former Socialist ministers were tried by the new Court of Justice of the Republic on charges of allowing haemophiliacs to receive contaminated blood in 1985. (A total of 1,348 out of 2,500 were infected, some 600 dying of AIDS.) He and another minister were acquitted and a former Health Minister, although found guilty on two counts, was freed without punishment. Even grimmer events were evoked when Maurice Papon unsuccessfully sued a historian who blamed him for the deaths of many Algerians at the hands of the police in 1961, when he was prefect of police. And on the eve of his appeal against conviction of complicity in crimes against humanity during World War II, M. Papon fled to Switzerland. He was speedily returned and his appeal rejected. More positively, the government's agreement to compensate Jewish children orphaned during the Holocaust and establish a memorial to the 76,000 French Jews deported to death camps, as well as a museum to record their experiences, was a further step in recognizing one of the darker episodes in France's recent history. Another, in a way, was the Assembly's belated recognition that events in Algeria between 1954 and 1962 amounted to a war rather than a mere police operation.

The most farcical scandal occurred in Corsica. The prefect, Bernard Bonnet, who had been appointed after the assassination of his predecessor, had made considerable headway in tackling separatist terrorism and the island's legendary levels of crime and corruption. In April a bungled arson attack on an illegally-built restaurant led to the arrest of an elite team of gendarmes, the head of the island's gendarmerie—and of M. Bonnet himself. M. Bonnet in turn alleged that two senior advisers to the Prime Minister were fully aware of his activities. Parallels with the 1985 *Rainbow Warrior* affair were inevitably made, but the matter had yet to come to trial. Further evidence of inefficiency and wrongdoing by the 'forces of order' emerged from two parliamentary inquiries in the autumn. There were further bomb attacks in Ajaccio in November.

It proved to be a bad year for disasters. In March 39 people died in a fire in the Mont Blanc road tunnel. In November 26 died in the south-west in the worst floods of the century. In December a tanker sank in the Bay of Biscay, severely polluting many miles of Breton tourist beaches and oyster beds. And, just before Christmas, the worst hurricane for decades caused over 80 deaths, devastated forests, damaged historic buildings and left several million people without power—many of whom therefore greeted the new millennium in chilly darkness.

The slow response to the tanker disaster was one of several issues causing strains within the disparate government coalition. When Michelin simultaneously announced a 17 per cent rise in profits and 7,500 job losses, M. Jospin responded angrily but insisted that the state could do little. However, pressure from his coalition partners soon spurred threats of punitive action against employers who abused their power. Green susceptibilities influenced a tougher line on genetically-modified (GM) crops and the refusal to accept the EU's lifting of the ban on British beef (see II.1.i). Other factors were public opinion, which was already sensitized by other food safety scares, and alarm among politicians over the implications for them of the contaminated blood trial. Direct action against McDonalds by farmers protesting at US sanctions over the EU's ban on hormone-treated meat also won widespread support.

Standing up to the United States invariably played well in France. Nevertheless, the President and Prime Minister supported allied action in Kosovo (see III.2.vi), against opposition from both left and right. France's combat role remained modest, not least because its forces were overstretched and the transition from conscription to professional forces was not yet complete. Diplomatically, the government opposed action that might alienate Russia. France's unease at the dominant role of the United States was certainly a major factor in its subsequent readiness to join with Britain in proposing an autonomous European defence force. In the controversy over sanctions on Iraq France continued to advocate a softer line than Britain and the United States.

But internal politics were now the main preoccupation, as politicians increasingly looked to the presidential campaign of 2002. Despite all vicissitudes, M. Jospin's stock stood high, whereas M. Chirac's position was increasingly uncomfortable. While personally popular, the President was blamed for electoral failure and his inability to check the Socialist government or unite the fragmented right—or even command his own party.

iii. ITALY

CAPITAL: Rome   AREA: 301,000 sq km   POPULATION: 57,500,000 ('98)
OFFICIAL LANGUAGE: Italian   POLITICAL SYSTEM: parliamentary democracy
HEAD OF STATE: President Carlo Azeglio Ciampi (since May '99)
RULING PARTIES: Left Democrats (DS) head centre-left coalition
HEAD OF GOVERNMENT: Massimo D'Alema (DS), Prime Minister (since Oct '98)
MAIN IGO MEMBERSHIPS (NON-UN): NATO, EU, WEU, OSCE, CE, CEI, OECD, G-8
CURRENCY: lira (end-'99 £1=Lit3,113.37, US$1=Lit1,931.73)
GNP PER CAPITA: US$20,250 by exchange-rate calculation, US$20,200 at PPP ('98)

ITALY was governed throughout the year by a centre-left coalition headed by the leader of the Left Democrats (DS), Massimo D'Alema. In general, Signor D'Alema enjoyed considerable success. His administration was competent and effective; it won credit for its conduct during the Kosovo crisis and for its continued pursuit of a rigorous financial policy. The Prime Minister also scored personal triumphs in securing the elections of Romano Prodi as president of the European Commission and of former Bank of Italy governor and Prime Minister Carlo Azeglio Ciampi as President of the Republic. However, in part because he had not won power through election himself, but had merely replaced Professor Prodi after the latter's resignation in December 1998 (see AR 1998, p.63), Signor D'Alema was continually beset with problems internal to the coalition. This situation affected public perceptions of his government and eventually led him to deliver an ultimatum to the parties in the form of his resignation in December.

The biggest issue of the year was the war in Kosovo (see III.2.vi). Because the government coalition included a variety of not very compatible forces, from the Communist splinter group led by Armando Cossutta to the rightist Democratic Union for the Republic (UDR) of former President Francesco Cossiga, as well as liberals, socialists, former Christian Democrats, Greens and others, international action against Serbia was potentially very divisive. Given, in addition, Italy's proximity to the arena of conflict and the Pope's insistence on the need for negotiation rather than bombing, direct participation in the air campaign was difficult. In order to fulfill his country's obligations as a member of NATO while also preserving government stability, Signor D'Alema pursued a twin strategy. On the one hand, he oversaw an extensive Italian commitment in terms of provision of air bases and of troops for peace-keeping and refugee protection duties, repeatedly stating that, as a large European country, Italy could not avoid playing a role. On the other, he was obliged to refer constantly to the need for peace and to call for a diplomatic solution to be pursued alongside the bombing campaign. On at least one occasion he urged a ceasefire, only to see his call rejected by NATO. He also favoured Russian attempts at mediation. Italian warplanes played a subsidiary role in the action, primarily intervening to defend Italian troops on the Kosovo-Albania border.

Within the government different strains of opinion emerged. While Defence Minister Carlo Scognamiglio took a pro-American line, Foreign Minister Lamberto Dini, who favoured a more independent position, was reproved for condemning the bombing of Serbian television in April. Signor Cossutta, whose ministers had very nearly quit the government over the campaign, went so far as to visit President Milošević in Belgrade. Because of these difficulties and the pressure of public opinion, Italy was regarded as the most reluctant of the alliance powers. NATO decisions were announced without the country being consulted, much to the annoyance of the government. Yet Italy made a significant contribution. Although it was not in the forefront of the action, it played a pivotal supporting role. Moreover, more than any other NATO country, it had to cope with refugees from the conflict zone. Some 10,000 were admitted in May alone.

Prior to the start of the campaign, there was friction between Italy and the USA over the acquittal by a US court martial of two pilots involved in an incident in Cemis in February 1998 in which 20 people had died when a low-flying US plane based in northern Italy had cut through the wires of a ski lift. Although the court martial decided it was an accident, Italians were outraged by what they saw as conduct endangering the public. When Signor D'Alema met President Clinton in Washington in March the incident was a major issue.

By contrast, the rapid election of Professor Prodi to the presidency of the European Commission the same month was viewed as a source of pride. Signor D'Alema proclaimed that Italy's pro-European outlook would no longer be seen as the result of an inferiority complex. The first Italian to hold the position, Professor Prodi was expected to introduce reform and restore confidence following the corruption scandals which forced his predecessor's resignation (see XI.4). However, in May Italy was warned by the European Union (EU) that its deficit was too high and officially invited to keep public spending under control. In view of the risk that the 1999 deficit would reach 2.4 per cent of gross domestic product, the objective of no more than 2 per cent (dropping to 1 per cent in 2001) was restated.

To lend credibility to the government's commitment to financial rigour, the experienced former Prime Minister Giuliano Amato was drafted in as Treasury and Finance Minister following the election in May of Signor Ciampi to succeed Oscar Luigi Scalfaro as Italian President for a seven-year term. The government's economic plan in July and budget in September did not raise taxes, but they heralded significant public spending cuts. The issue of pensions remained highly controversial, however. Signor D'Alema called for further reform even in the face of union opposition in this area shortly before the European elections in June. The trade union response was very critical and the poor result of the centre-left in the poll was attributed in part to the Prime Minister's intervention. Silvio Berlusconi's Forza Italia emerged as the largest party with 25.2 per cent and 22 of Italy's 87 seats, while the DS scored 17.4 per cent and won 15 seats. Two new groupings, the Bonino List (headed by the former European commissioner Emma Bonino) and the Democrats (formed in February by Professor Prodi together with the former magistrate turned politician Antonio Di Pietro and several city mayors) took 8.5 and 7.7 per cent respectively and seven seats each. The other 36 seats were distributed among 13 lists.

The extent of the government's commitment to privatizing publicly-owned enterprises was put in question by events surrounding Telecom Italia. Following what observers judged to have been a disastrous privatization, which resulted in large US and UK investment funds holding 40 per cent of shares, Olivetti launched a hostile takeover bid which the government was seen to favour, despite protestations of neutrality. The success of this bid gave Telecom a strong Italian ownership while also confirming the interventionist instincts of the coalition parties. Yet public enthusiasm for share issues continued unabated. In November shares to the value of 34.5 per cent of the capital of the electricity company ENEL were issued on the Milan stock market and some 3.8 million requests for shares were accepted.

Reform in other areas ran into obstacles. The issue of electoral reform suffered a setback in April when a referendum to abolish the 25 per cent proportional quota for the distribution of seats in parliament narrowly failed to reach the 50 per cent quorum. Although most parties, with varying degrees of enthusiasm, supported the aims of the referendum, it received relatively little publicity and was overshadowed by the Kosovo conflict. Reformers feared that this failure would halt moves towards the strengthening of bi-polar politics and would reinforce the hand of those, mostly smaller, parties which wanted to prevent the creation of more homogeneous majorities. The attempt by the government to introduce a bill to regulate electoral broadcasts and advertising by the parties (to replace the decree law of 1996) also ran into difficulties, as all possible schemes were rejected by opposition leader Signor Berlusconi as illiberal. One reform which was passed (by the necessary two-thirds majority in the Chamber of Deputies and the Senate) was a modification of the constitution to introduce direct election of the presidents of regional assemblies.

The right-wing opposition enjoyed a mixed year. While the government coalition won five by-elections held simultaneously in November in seats which the centre-left had won in 1996, the right scored an extraordinary coup in winning control of the municipality of Bologna. For decades the showcase of Communist local government, the city elected a right-wing independent, Giorgio Guazzaloca, as mayor in June local elections. The centre-left fared better in other cities, including Florence, but overall the right increased its vote in provincial assembly elections. Signor Berlusconi strengthened his position as a political figure by securing the admission of his party to the European People's Party. He also appeared to soften his opposition by supporting the election of Signor Ciampi to the presidency. But in other ways he remained a maverick figure. Although the conflict of interest issue concerning his massive business and media holdings was not considered pressing, his three first-degree convictions for corruption and continuing involvement in judicial investigations rendered him vulnerable. In November he was sent for trial with his associate and former Defence Minister Cesare Previti on charges of bribing Roman judges in the 1980s. He responded by repeatedly attacking investigating magistrates, especially those belonging to the Milan pool, who were denounced for carrying out a political persecution. As always, the judges were defended by Signor Di Pietro.

The acquittal in August of veteran politician Giulio Andreotti of the charge of ordering the murder in 1979 of the journalist Mino Pecorelli, and then his acquittal in October of charges of collaboration with the Mafia, added grist to the mill of those figures allied to the old system who regarded the whole anti-corruption drive of the early 1990s as illegitimate. Although some commentators were swift to point out that Signor Andreotti's acquittal did not absolve the country's elite for having failed to tackle the Mafia problem for several decades, others took it as proof that politically-motivated magistrates had conspired on the basis of scant evidence to bring down the country's elite. The air of restoration was confirmed by the increasing public expressions of sympathy for another former Prime Minister, Bettino Craxi, who remained beyond the reach of the law in Tunisia. Although convictions against him were confirmed in the course of the year, his ill-health led to calls for a pardon on humanitarian grounds.

At various points during the year there were appeals to relaunch the Olive Tree alliance which had been so successful in 1996. The reasons for this were threefold. First, following the departure of Professor Prodi to Brussels, the alliance had been overshadowed by a governing coalition that included forces external to the Olive Tree. Second, the creation of the Democrats had not widened the basis of support of the centre-left in the European elections, as had been hoped, but rather had further fragmented the left. Third, internal quibbling in the coalition was having a damaging effect on public opinion. When, in October, the Democrats signalled their willingness to join the government, a dispute broke out between those who wished to revive the Olive Tree and those, like Signor Cossiga, who opposed it. This led to a debate about the appropriate form and composition of the government which lasted until December. Various forces, including the Socialists, the Popular Party and Professor Prodi's allies, took the opportunity to call Signor D'Alema's leadership into question. In order to end the slow wearing-down of his administration, the Prime Minister demanded a clarification which resulted in his submitting a technical resignation and the swift formation on 22 December of a new coalition government under his continued leadership. While the Democrats took ministerial posts, the informal Trifoglio ('Three-Leaf') alliance of Signor Cossiga's supporters, the Republicans and the Socialists withdrew, although the last-mentioned agreed to abstain in parliament and not oppose the government.

This quick change left the government weakened numerically but strengthened politically, in that the coalition was more homogeneous. The intention was to pursue a coherent strategy in the period prior to the elections due to be held in 2001. It was agreed that the decision over who should lead the centre-left alliance into the poll would be decided at a future date.

iv. BELGIUM

CAPITAL: Brussels AREA: 30,500 sq km POPULATION: 10,200,000 ('98)
OFFICIAL LANGUAGES: French, Flemish & German
POLITICAL SYSTEM: federal parliamentary democracy based on language communities
HEAD OF STATE: King Albert II (since Aug '93)
RULING PARTIES: Flemish Liberals and Democrats (VLD/Flemish), Liberal Reform Party (PRL/Walloon), Socialist Party (SP/Flemish), Socialist Party (PS/Walloon), Flemish Greens (Agalev) & Walloon Greens (Ecolo)
HEAD OF GOVERNMENT: Guy Verhofstadt (VLD), Prime Minister (since July '99)
MAIN IGO MEMBERSHIPS (NON-UN): NATO, EU, WEU, Benelux, OSCE, CE, OECD, Francophonie
CURRENCY: Belgian franc (end-'99 £1=BF64.83, US$1=BF40.25
GNP PER CAPITA: US$25,380 by exchange-rate calculation, US$23,480 at PPP ('98)

SCANDALS had been the focus of attention in Belgium in 1998 and the year had ended with Willy Claes, formerly NATO secretary-general and before that a Socialist Deputy Prime Minister, receiving a three-year suspended jail sentence for corruption. In 1999 attention was directed more towards political change, the Social Christians being removed from office for the first time in 40 years as a result of a general election on 13 June.

The results for the 150-member federal Chamber showed that the opposition Flemish Liberals (VLD), with 23 seats, had overtaken the Flemish Social Christians (CVP), reduced to 22, as the largest party and that both Socialist parties, which were part of the outgoing coalition, had also lost ground. Both the French-speaking and the Flemish Greens (Ecolo and Agalev) made significant gains, as did the far-right Flemish Bloc and the Flemish nationalist Volksunie. The pattern was similar in simultaneous elections for Belgium's 25 seats in the

European Parliament.

The VLD leader, Guy Verhofstadt, accordingly replaced Jean-Luc Dehaene (CVP) as Prime Minister, with the Socialists remaining in a new coalition which also included the French-speaking Liberals (PRL) and both Green parties. The parties agreed on a 12-point programme including reduced taxation and maintaining the level of social security spending. It quickly became clear that a fundamental thrust of the new government's policy would be human rights, which were emphasized by the new PRL Foreign Minister, Louis Michel. The new approach showed itself at the World Trade Organization negotiations at Seattle in December (see XI.2.ii), when Belgium insisted on linking workers' rights with free trade.

Faced with a smaller deficit than previously forecast, the new government focused its economic plans on improving the employment situation, to which it committed BF6,100 million. Other promised measures included modernization of the public service and reform of the rules relating to political asylum. The latter reform was to involve simplification of procedures, regularization of those without papers living in Belgium, an effective expulsion policy and help for centres providing social support.

The year was marked in June by two public health scares which, partly as a reaction to the 'mad cow disease' (BSE) problem, were given a very high profile. The first concerned animal feedstuffs contaminated by dioxin and led to products from Belgian livestock being banned across Europe. In fact, the contamination was proved to have come from a single batch of feed. Immediately afterwards, drinks made by Coca-Cola were banned after some 100 people apparently fell ill after consuming them. However, this seemed to have been more a case of collective hysteria, perhaps triggered by an unpleasant odour resulting from the use of a fungicide.

One serious problem facing the new government related to the financing of the two linguistic communities in the discharge of the responsibilities for education. A highly-complex formula based on the number of pupils was found to settle the issue, partly because the Flemish liked the greater degree of fiscal autonomy it entailed.

Belgian support for European integration remained undiminished. All Belgian commentators welcomed the move at the European Union (EU) summit in Tampere (Finland) in October to develop common policies in the field of justice and home affairs through a more federal approach (see XI.4). At the December EU summit in Helsinki, Foreign Minister Michel called for a deepening of relations with the Maghreb (North African) countries as a way of balancing North-South relations and creating regional stability.

The Belgian monarchy and its role as a unifying force in the country were greatly enhanced by the marriage of Crown Prince Philippe to a Belgian aristocrat, Mathilde d'Udekem et d'Acoz. Their pre-nuptial entries into cities and towns throughout Belgium were the occasion for scenes of genuine popular rejoicing, only slightly marred by the revelation, probably inspired by opponents of the Belgian state, that over 30 years ago his father, King Albert II, had fathered an illegitimate daughter, now living in London.

v. THE NETHERLANDS

CAPITAL: Amsterdam   AREA: 37,000 sq km   POPULATION: 16,000,000 ('98)
OFFICIAL LANGUAGE: Dutch   POLITICAL SYSTEM: parliamentary democracy
HEAD OF STATE: Queen Beatrix (since April '80)
RULING PARTIES: Labour Party (PvdA), People's Party for Freedom and Democracy (VVD) & Democrats 66 (D66)
HEAD OF GOVERNMENT: Wim Kok (PvdA), Prime Minister (since Aug '94)
MAIN IGO MEMBERSHIPS (NON-UN): NATO, EU, WEU, Benelux, OSCE, CE, OECD
CURRENCY: guilder (end-'99 £1=f f3.54, US$1=f2.20)
GNP PER CAPITA: US$24,760 by exchange-rate calculation, US$21,620 at PPP ('98)

THE government coalition of the Labour Party (PvdA), the Liberals (VVD) and the centre-left Democrats 66 (D66) led by Wim Kok suffered a blow in provincial elections on 4 March. The opposition parties made strong gains, with the Green Left overtaking D66 as the fourth party and the ruling coalition being left with only a tiny majority in the Senate. The 46 per cent turnout was a record low for elections of this kind. The consequences were felt in May when the government failed to get the necessary two-thirds majority in the Senate for a proposal to introduce a binding referendum into the Dutch constitution. Crucially, former Liberal leader Hans Wiegel opposed the proposal and the government resigned. A mediator was appointed by Queen Beatrix and after a week of conversations with him the three coalition partners reached an agreement to reinstate the government under Wim Kok on the basis that the proposed law would merely introduce consultative referendums—which had the advantage of not requiring a two-thirds majority in the Senate.

The coalition parties also lost ground overall in elections for the 31 Dutch seats in the European Parliament on 10 June. Although the Liberals picked up some votes, the PvdA lost two of its eight seats and D66 two of their four, while the Green Left advanced strongly to four seats and the left-wing Socialist Party won a European seat for the first time.

The economy performed well, producing the first budget surplus for 25 years and 3 per cent economic growth. This success exposed differences in the coalition, with the Liberals wanting to reduce debt and taxes and their partners favouring priority for social welfare and education. The government brought forward tax changes giving most benefit to those near the minimum wage; while the top income tax rate was cut from 60 to 52 per cent, it was made more difficult to reduce total income liable to taxation. The VAT rate was increased from 17.5 to 19 per cent and there were significant rises in 'eco-taxes'.

In the traditional Queen's Speech in September considerable attention was given to European Union (EU) issues, stressing the importance of enlargement, the euro and the Netherlands' incorporation into integrated transport networks. Also covered were the more sensitive areas of political asylum and migration, on which the Netherlands was pressing for EU agreements alongside greater cooperation in the justice and police fields.

On the social side, an 87-year-old law was repealed when both houses of parliament voted to legalize brothels. More controversial were government plans to legalize mercy killing for people as young as 12. Following a serious riot in

Rotterdam when the local team Feyenoord won the football league championship, the Interior Minister called for a new law enabling the detention of high-risk hooligans.

There were several difficulties in agriculture, the responsible minister, Haijo Apotheker (D66), resigning on 7 June over problems in the pork sector. The introduction of an EU directive on nitrate levels was prevented by the strong resistance of the Liberals to the measure. This was notwithstanding the offer of a 750 million euro aid package to help farmers comply with the new rules, put forward by the new Agriculture Minister, Laurens Jan Brinkhorst (D66). There also remained the serious problem of cutting the manure waste produced by intensive livestock farming.

Also in the environmental sphere, a bitter dispute over a plan to produce natural gas in the Waddenzee natural area, famous for its birds and seals, was temporarily resolved by postponing a decision on the issue. A parliamentary report published in April on the 1992 crash of an Israeli El Al cargo jet on the Amsterdam suburb of Bijlmermeer (see AR 1992, p. 64) was critical of the government for misleading legislators and reacting sluggishly to health problems that could have been caused by released chemicals including sarin nerve gas.

The role of Dutch troops in not preventing the massacre of Muslims at Srebrenica in Bosnia in July 1995 (see AR 1995, pp. 125-6) remained a running sore in Dutch politics. An official report on the subject was still awaited at year's end.

vi. LUXEMBOURG

CAPITAL: Luxembourg   AREA: 3,000 sq km   POPULATION: 425,000 ('98)
OFFICIAL LANGUAGE: Letzeburgish   POLITICAL SYSTEM: parliamentary democracy
HEAD OF STATE: Grand Duke Jean (since Nov '64)
RULING PARTIES: Christian Social People's (PCS) & Democratic (DP) parties
HEAD OF GOVERNMENT: Jean-Claude Juncker (PCS), Prime Minister (since Jan '95)
MAIN IGO MEMBERSHIPS (NON-UN): NATO, EU, WEU, Benelux, OSCE, CE, OECD, Francophonie
CURRENCY: Luxembourg franc (end-'99 £1= LF64.86, US$1=LF40.25)
GNP PER CAPITA: US$43,570 by exchange-rate calculation, US$37,420 at PPP ('98)

THE main event of the year was the general election on 13 June, in which the right-wing liberal Democratic Party (DP) won 15 of the 60 Chamber seats, a gain of three, whereas the ruling Christian Socials (CSV) and Socialists (LSAP) slipped to 19 and 13 seats respectively. The DP benefited from opposition to a proposed reform of public sector pensions, as did the pensioners' Action Committee for Democracy and Justice (ADR), which advanced to seven seats. Jean-Claude Juncker of the CSV remained Prime Minister, heading a new coalition in which the DP replaced the LSAP.

The fact that former Luxembourg Prime Minister Jacques Santer was president of the European Commission when it felt obliged to resign in March following an investigation into maladministration (see XI.4) highlighted the issue within the country. But the affair did not stop Mr Santer from going on to head the CSV list in the June European Parliament elections and taking one of his party's two seats. The LSAP again won two seats and DP and the Greens again took one each

The economy remained in good condition, featuring a forecast public revenue surplus, the lowest unemployment rate (2.9 per cent) in the European Union (EU) and predicted GDP growth of 3.5 per cent for the year. Policy developments included the announcement in February of a national employment plan and proposals to reduce the residence qualification for citizenship from 10 to five years. Also envisaged was the establishment of an independent consultative commission on human rights and new procedures to allow for popular petitions to trigger referendums on draft legislation.

The tax issue remained to the fore, with Luxembourg opposing or trying to water down the proposal for an EU-wide 'withholding tax' on investments and savings respectively (see XI.4). There was also a row with Belgium, which Luxembourg accused of intimidating the Belgian employees of Luxembourg banks to break local rules on banking secrecy.

On 24 December Grand Duke Jean announced that he would abdicate in favour of his son Prince Henri, born in 1955. Having reigned since 1964, the Grand Duke was expected to the hand over the throne in September 2000.

vii. REPUBLIC OF IRELAND

CAPITAL: Dublin AREA: 70,280 sq km POPULATION: 3,750,000 ('98)
OFFICIAL LANGUAGES: Irish & English POLITICAL SYSTEM: parliamentary democracy
HEAD OF STATE: President Mary McAleese (since Nov '97)
RULING PARTIES: coalition of Fianna Fáil (FF) & Progressive Democrats (PD)
HEAD OF GOVERNMENT: Bertie Ahern (FF), Prime Minister/Taoiseach (since June '97)
MAIN IGO MEMBERSHIPS (NON-UN): EU, OSCE, CE, OECD
CURRENCY: punt (end-'99 £1=IR£1.27, US$1=IR£0.79)
GNP PER CAPITA: US$18,340 by exchange-rate and PPP calculation ('98)

ON 1 January the Republic adopted the euro as its currency unit at the rate of IR£1=Eur0.787564. The punt, destined to remain in circulation until mid-2002, was now effectively a local denomination of the euro at the agreed and irrevocable value. The decline in the value of the euro vis-à-vis other currencies, which soon set in, was accepted with equanimity since the corresponding strengthening of sterling and the US dollar aided a substantial increase in the Republic's exports, while the favourable exchange rate brought a boost in tourism to an all-time record level of six million visitors, generating earnings of some IR£1.8 billion.

An inherent fear, much reiterated by economic commentators and the Central Bank, was that serious inflation could develop to the detriment of the country's rapidly growing prosperity. The fear appeared to be realised as the annual inflation rate, following earlier fluctuations, reached 3.4 per cent in December, which was among the highest rates in the European Union. The commercial banks and building societies attracted criticism for contributing to inflationary pressures by the soft terms on which they were lending money, especially for house purchase at a time when house prices were soaring to unrealistic levels both in Dublin (where prices were said to parallel those in London) and in provincial centres. In practice, a considerable amount of house-purchase was being undertaken for investment and the relatively easy access to funds was inadequate to enable many even moderately well-off couples or families to find accommodation which they could afford. This was thought to be a major deterrent to the return to Ireland of skilled emigrants, badly needed in the labour-short health services, computer industry, business management and other activities benefiting from the booming economy, in which unemployment was no more than a fraction above 5 per cent.

The tension-fraught talks on implementing the 1998 Good Friday Agreement on Northern Ireland (see AR 1998, pp. 44-5, 70-1, 556-67), which repeatedly reached deadlock over the question of Unionist participation in an Executive including Sinn Féin without prior arms decommissioning by the IRA (see II.1.iv), caused frustration and anxiety in the Republic throughout the first half of the year. The Hillsborough declaration in April by the Taoiseach, Bertie Ahern, and the British Prime Minister, Tony Blair, failed to resolve the impasse, while the revelation in Florida of a conspiracy to smuggle guns for the IRA into the Republic in July threatened to undermine any lingering hope of a settlement. The despairing mood found reflection in a brief divergence of views between the two heads of government on the relative significance of decommissioning (stressed by Mr Blair) and the formation of the Executive (stressed by Mr Ahern). Their joint decision to recall former US senator George Mitchell to conduct a review of the means by which the Agreement might be implemented brought them on to common ground again and the eventual success of Mr Mitchell's efforts met with strong political and popular approval in the Republic.

The year closed with not only the establishment of the Northern Executive on 2 December but also of the North-South Ministerial Council on 13 December and a relaunched UK-Irish Intergovernmental Council on 17 December, both of them involving representation of the Republic's government in cooperative enterprises designed to benefit Ireland as a whole as well as the common interests of the Republic and the United Kingdom. A nagging doubt remained concerning the Unionists' own review of developments promised for the following February to decide whether they would continue their endorsement of the arrangements set in train, but this faded as the ministers of the Executive, including those from Sinn Féin, were seen to take up their portfolios with commitment. The Northern First Minister, David Trimble, travelled to Dublin to discuss matters of mutual concern with the Taoiseach and close contact was known to be continuing between Mr Ahern and Mr Blair.

Judicial tribunals investigating whether favours had been granted in return for payments to politicians provided headlines throughout the year. Most attention focused on the former Taoiseach, Charles Haughey, who transpired to have received some millions of pounds in gifts from wealthy entrepreneurs, mainly in the 1980s and early 1990s. No evidence of advantage gained by the donors of these funds emerged at the tribunal hearings, which were to resume in the new year. Meanwhile, another tribunal investigated allegations of corruption in local authority planning processes and an inquiry was ordered into offshore accounts held by businessmen in the Cayman Islands and suspected of being used for the evasion of Irish taxes.

The political system, tainted by the strong whiff of scandal, recovered in popular esteem in the autumn when hearings by the parliamentary public accounts committee were televised live. The committee members were seen to conduct sharp, well-informed questioning of Central Bank officials, directors and executives of commercial banks, revenue commissioners and senior civil servants to probe the extent of tax evasion through the use of bogus 'non-resident' accounts (see AR 1998, p. 73). The committee's report, published before Christmas, castigated the negligence, misjudgment and other deficiencies it identified in state and financial institutions, an outcome much to the satisfaction of citizens whose compliance in the past with a burdensome tax regime had helped to build the current successful economy in spite of the evasion of the same burden by those better equipped to carry it. Energetic steps to recover the lost taxation and the imposition of a levy on the banks, as recommended by the committee, were now awaited. These investigations represented the lancing of an abscess which had long been poisoning Irish society with suspicion and cynicism on the one hand and arrogant disdain for the law on the other. Exposure promised a vigilant watch against exploitation of privilege in the future and a consequently higher respect for democratically-elected authority. It was especially important that these consequences should have been brought about by investigatory mechanisms put in place by the state itself.

The sentiment that government should ensure equitable treatment for all reasserted itself in December when a wave of public outrage—not least among Fianna Fáil backbenchers—greeted the budget introduced by Finance Minister Charlie McCreevey. While extensive reductions in taxation and related measures offered benefits to virtually everybody, the 'one-income' family where one spouse chose to work in the home gained noticeably less advantage than the 'two-income' family where both spouses took paid employment. The unfairness of this provision, together with a perceived parsimony in assistance to the underprivileged, resulted in such strong protests that the minister had not only to revise the tax provisions but also to abandon important elements of his budgetary strategy.

The excess of Exchequer income over spending, which by year's end amounted to IR£1,200 million, gave wide scope for forward planning. The government's National Development Plan published in the summer projected ongoing infrastructural improvements in roads, transport, housing and health over the following six years. Privatization of state assets proceeded apace but a controversy over the sale of a major cable television distribution service to the Anglo-American group NTL and the sluggish Stock Exchange performance of Éircom (formerly Irish Telecom) shares following flotation raised some uncertainty about the sale of the national airline, Aer Lingus, envisaged by the

Transport Minister, Mary O'Rourke. Industrial relations in the public sector worsened somewhat, with work stoppages by police and nurses when pay increases fell short of expectations. The likelihood that a new national agreement on wages could be successfully negotiated between government, unions and employers became less certain in light of the budget controversy.

It was a relatively quiescent year in foreign affairs. The Republic remained neutral in the Kosovo conflict (see III.2.vi), although it concurred in the European Union's condemnation of Serbian actions in Kosovo. In October the Cabinet agreed to membership of the NATO-associated Partnership for Peace but with a firm undertaking not to join NATO itself. The Foreign Minister, David Andrews, energetically promoted human rights and aid for the Third World countries of Africa, especially Sierra Leone. He also took a close interest in East Timor, where the independence movement had strong support in Ireland as a result of several years of campaigning by a voluntary group, founded by a former Dublin bus driver, Tom Hyland.

The Attorney-General, David Byrne, became Ireland's member of the new European Commission in July; assigned responsibility for food policy, he soon found himself burdened with the scare over a range of Belgian produce and the continuing French ban on British beef (see II.1.i). The election to fill the Republic's 15 seats in the European Parliament resulted in Fianna Fáil 6, Fine Gael 4, Greens 2, Labour 1 and independents 2. This represented a loss of one seat by Fianna Fáil to an independent. In the new Parliament the independent Irish member, Pat Cox, was re-elected chairman of the Liberal group, as which he had played a leading role in voicing the criticism which led to the resignation of the Santer Commission in March (see XI.4).

3. DENMARK—ICELAND—NORWAY—SWEDEN—FINLAND—
AUSTRIA—SWITZERLAND—EUROPEAN MINI-STATES

i. DENMARK

CAPITAL: Copenhagen   AREA: 43,000 sq km   POPULATION: 5,250,000 ('98)
OFFICIAL LANGUAGE: Danish   POLITICAL SYSTEM: parliamentary democracy
HEAD OF STATE: Queen Margrethe II (since Jan '72)
RULING PARTIES: coalition of Social Democrats (SD) & Radical Liberals (RV)
HEAD OF GOVERNMENT: Poul Nyrup Rasmussen (SD), Prime Minister (since Jan '93)
MAIN IGO MEMBERSHIPS (NON-UN): NATO, EU, NC, CBSS, AC, OSCE, CE, OECD
CURRENCY: krone (end-'99 £1= DKr11.97, US$1=DKr7.42)
GNP PER CAPITA: US$33,260 by exchange-rate calculation, US$23,830 at PPP ('98)

ELECTIONS for Denmark's 16 seats in the European Parliament on 10 June again demonstrated the capacity of European Union (EU) membership to distort traditional party allegiances. Of the two ruling coalition parties, the Social Democrats (SD) were again the principal sufferers, retaining three seats but with less than half of their vote share in the 1998 national elections (see AR 1998, pp. 73-4), while the Radical Liberals (RV) retained one seat on an increased vote. Eurosceptic SD voters gave a further boost to the anti-EU June Movement, which gained a third seat, whereas the People's Movement against the EU lost one of two seats—indicating weaker outright opposition to the EU but stronger opposition to closer political union.

Continuing their recent decline, the Conservatives suffered the heaviest losses, down from three seats to one, despite trying five leaders in four years, the latest being Bendt Bendtsen. Their vote moved to the Liberals (Venstre), up from four seats to five, and to the Danish People's Party (DPP), which took 5.8 per cent of the poll and one seat for its anti-foreigner, anti-EU and anti-state message. In a turnout of 50.4 per cent (slightly above the European average of 49.4 per cent), the remaining Danish seat was retained by the Socialist People's Party.

The appointment of Development Minister Poul Nielsen as Denmark's EU commissioner in July caused a reshuffle among the Social Democrat members of Poul Nyrup Rasmussen's cabinet. Mr Nielsen was replaced by Research and Information Technology Minister Jan Trøjberg, who was himself succeeded by Birte Weiss.

Serious rioting erupted on 7 November in a district of Copenhagen housing many ethnic minority residents, in reaction to a court decision to expel a Turk following his conviction for theft. He had not applied for Danish citizenship, but this was the first expulsion order against someone born in Denmark. Following the court decision, inflammatory racial remarks were made by Mogens Glistrup, the founder and former leader of the far-right Progress Party (FP), who had been readmitted to the party by an FP congress the previous month. That decision had prompted the party's four MPs to resign from the party and to form the 'Liberty 2000' grouping, so that the FP faced probable extinction. Meanwhile, the DPP (formed by earlier FP dissidents in 1995—see AR 1995, p. 69) continued its advance, and by year-end had the support of 15 per cent of public opinion.

In mid-May the Faroe Islands maritime border was agreed, after 21 years of negotiation between the Faroes, Denmark and Britain, the Faroes gaining an additional 41 square kilometres of the North Sea believed to be rich in oil reserves. Elections in April 1998 having indicated a clear wish for greater Faroese autonomy (see AR 1998, p. 74), increased exploitable oil reserves strengthened the islands' economic independence.

ii. ICELAND

CAPITAL: Reykjavík   AREA: 103,000 sq km   POPULATION: 272,000 ('97)
OFFICIAL LANGUAGE: Icelandic   POLITICAL SYSTEM: parliamentary democracy
HEAD OF STATE: President Ólafur Ragnar Grímsson (since Aug '96)
RULING PARTIES: Independence (IP) & Progressive (PP) parties
HEAD OF GOVERNMENT: Davíd Oddsson (IP), Prime Minister (since April '91)
MAIN IGO MEMBERSHIPS (NON-UN): NATO, EFTA/EEA, NC, OSCE, CE, OECD
CURRENCY: króna (end-'99 £1=ISkr117.03, US1=Isk72.61)
GNP PER CAPITA: US$28,010 by exchange-rate calculation, US$22,830 at PPP ('98)

IN elections to the 63-member *Althing* held on 8 May, Davíd Oddsson's conservative Independence Party (IP) took 26 of the 63 seats (a gain of one) and remained the largest party with 40.8 per cent of the vote. Its coalition partner, the liberal Progressive Party (PP), lost three seats but retained 12 on a vote of 18.4 per cent. The majority IP-PP coalition therefore continued in office under Mr Oddson's premiership.

The main changes in the party system were on the left, where a United Left electoral alliance formed of socialists, social democrats and feminists took 26.8 per cent of the poll and 17 seats. As a result, the *Althing* became less fragmented than before. A new Left-Green Alliance took 9.1 per cent of the vote and six seats, while a new Liberal Party won 4.2 per cent and two seats. On a turnout of 84.1 per cent, the proportion of women in the *Althing* increased from 25 to 35 per cent.

The ruling coalition's victory was attributed to approval of its economic policies, which had delivered strong growth and low inflation. On returning to office, the government stated its aims to be to ensure economic stability, create conditions for continuing growth and increase national saving. Price stability and a better competitive position for Icelandic industry would be prerequisites for new jobs for the growing labour force, and would guide exchange-rate, monetary and fiscal policies. Responsibility for the Central Bank was transferred from the Ministry of Commerce to the Office of the Prime Minister, who had responsibility for coordinating economic policy. Treasury debts were repaid for yet another year. After four years of reduction, the Treasury debt-to-GDP ratio was expected approach 30 per cent at the end of 2000.

iii. NORWAY

CAPITAL: Oslo AREA: 324,000 sq km POPULATION: 4,500,000 ('98)
OFFICIAL LANGUAGE: Norwegian POLITICAL SYSTEM: parliamentary democracy
HEAD OF STATE: King Harald V (since Jan '91)
RULING PARTIES: Christian People's Party (KrF) heads minority coalition with Centre and Liberal parties
HEAD OF GOVERNMENT: Kjell Magne Bondevik (KrF), Prime Minister (since Sept '97)
MAIN IGO MEMBERSHIPS (NON-UN): NATO, EFTA/EEA, NC, CBSS, AC, OSCE, CE, OECD
CURRENCY: krone (end-'99 £1= NKr12.95, US$1=NKr8.04)
GNP PER CAPITA: US$34,330 by exchange-rate calculation, US$24,290 at PPP ('98)

PRIME Minister Kjell Magne Bondevik announced a cabinet reshuffle on 15 March, appointing Odd Roger Enoksen as Minister for Local Government and Regional Cooperation following his election to lead the Centre Party. Laila Dåvøy (Christian People's Party), previously head of the Nurses' Association and a determined strike leader, came in as Minister of Labour and Government Administration. She replaced Eldbjørg Løwer (Liberal), who became the first woman in any NATO country to head the Defence Ministry. The new Minister of Justice was Odd Einar Dørum, a veteran Liberal who was expected to speak strongly on crime prevention and immigration in the 2001 election campaign, in the context of an increasingly chauvinist Progress Party. The reshuffle was perceived to have strengthened the minority three-party coalition.

In June the state-owned oil company Statoil and Norsk Hydro (51 per cent state-owned) proposed purchasing Saga (20 per cent state-owned), but a counter-offer for Saga by Elf-Aquitaine of France succeeded. This development ended the agreed oil policy, in place since the early 1970s, that (i) Norwegian interests controlled about 80 per cent of oil and gas reserves on the Norwegian shelf, with the remaining 20 per cent being available to foreign owners, and (ii) the dominant Norwegian company was state-owned while the second-largest would be part state-owned. From 1984 the State Direct Financial Interest (SDFI) had received and invested the income from most of the state's oil interests. Statoil administered the SDFI, but had no disposal rights over the revenues, which were forecast to total $71,000 million in 2000. Saga had been privately owned in principle, although when the company had got into difficulties during 1998, Statoil had bought 20 per cent for the state.

Statoil proposed on 13 August to group all the state's oil interests, prior to a large public share offering. The proposed group would be the world's fourth-largest quoted oil company, with 17,000 million barrels of oil equivalents in reserves. At year end the Minister of Petroleum and Energy proposed to establish a new state oil company to manage at least half the SDFI, with assets of about NKr12,300 million. It would retain a strong state interest in the sector, although Statoil would be partly privatized.

In June Mr Bondevik announced plans to sell about $2,900 million of state-owned stocks, principally in banks and telecommunications. Other holdings included pharmaceuticals and wine and spirit distribution. The decision followed pressure from the conservative Right and the Progress Party, in return for their support for the 1999 budget.

In the September local elections the opposition Labour Party's vote of 28.7 per cent was 3.2 per cent lower than in 1995, 6.8 per cent lower than its 1997 parliamentary election result and its lowest since the 1920s. The three government parties—Christians, Centre and Liberals—also lost support compared to 1997. The main gainers were the conservative Right, who retained their place as second-largest party with 21.2 per cent, and the far-right Progress Party, which came third with 13.5 per cent. Turnout was low, at 56 per cent. Labour leader Thorbjørn Jagland faced sharp criticism within his party for its poor showing.

The budget proposed for 2000 was fiscally neutral. With slower growth forecast after the record expansion of 1993-98, there was a prospect for interest rate cuts and measures against unemployment. Real underlying growth in fiscal expenditure of 2.5 per cent was predicted, with government priority for development aid, health care, education, and new nursery places. The 1999 budget had been supported by the Right and the Progress Party, but for its 2000 budget the government obtained additional support from Labour. Some observers foresaw a centre-left coalition after the 2001 parliamentary election, but the three centre parties expressed no interest in the possibility.

In continuation of Norwegian mediation efforts in the Middle East, in September Terje Rød-Larsen was appointed a UN deputy secretary-general, to serve as the UN's coordinator for Middle East peace negotiations and as the Secretary-General's personal representative to the PLO and the Palestinian Authority. In October Prime Minister Bondevik held lengthy talks in Washington with US President Clinton, and on 1-2 November Mr Clinton visited Oslo for a summit meeting with Prime Minister Ehud Barak of Israel and Palestinian leader Yassir Arafat (see V.1; V.2.i).

Disaster struck on 26 November when the high-speed catamaran passenger ferry *Sleipner*, en route from Stavanger to Bergen, ran aground near Haugesund. Of the 89 passengers and crew, 16 were killed. The weather was rough, with waves over two metres high, and reportedly the ferry was not authorized to sail in waters higher than one metre. The ferry's life-saving arrangements were also criticized.

iv. SWEDEN

CAPITAL: Stockholm   AREA: 450,000 sq km   POPULATION: 9,000,000 ('98)
OFFICIAL LANGUAGE: Swedish   POLITICAL SYSTEM: parliamentary democracy
HEAD OF STATE: King Carl XVI Gustav (since Sept '73)
RULING PARTY: Social Democratic Labour Party
HEAD OF GOVERNMENT: Göran Persson, Prime Minister (since March '96)
MAIN IGO MEMBERSHIPS (NON-UN): EU, NC, CBSS, AC, PFP, OSCE, CE, OECD
CURRENCY: krona (end-'98 £1= SKr13.77, US$1=SKr8.54)
GNP PER CAPITA: US$25,620 by exchange-rate calculation, US$19,480 at PPP ('98)

IN February the government announced its intention, with effect from 2002, to cut annual defence spending by more than 10 per cent because of a perceived diminished military threat in the Nordic and Baltic region, following the collapse of the Soviet Union. The change would affect all three military services. In March General Owe Wiktorin, Supreme Commander of the Armed Forces, claimed that this would involve the loss of six army brigades, five submarines and eight squadrons of aircraft, a 50 per cent reduction of military units. On 20 October the government announced further details: 6,500 defence jobs would be cut, and SKr4,000 million per year would be saved. Some senior officers argued that reductions on this scale might require Sweden to abandon its long-held non-aligned status and join a military alliance such as NATO to ensure that its defence needs were met. On 15 November Defence Minister Björn von Sydow announced spending cuts, mainly on military hardware, of SKr12,000 million over the three years 2002-2004. This implied that over 10,000 military and civilian jobs would be shed.

In April Prime Minister Göran Persson (Social Democratic Labour Party) appointed Bosse Ringholm, previously chairman of the National Labour Market Board, as Finance Minister, following the resignation of Erik Åsbrink. Mr Persson had said on television that tax cuts of SKr15-20,000 million in 2000 were possible. Mr Åsbrink had complained that this undermined his position, as he had just negotiated with the Left Party and the Greens for a budget without tax cuts and with projected fiscal surpluses of 1.8 per cent of GDP in 1999 and 2.1 per cent in 2000.

In the European Parliament elections held in June, the Social Democratic Labour Party managed only 26.0 per cent of the vote (compared with 36.4 per cent in the 1998 national elections—see AR 1998, p. 78) and lost one of its seven seats. The Left Party moved ahead to 15.8 per cent and held its three seats, whereas the Green Party lost heavily, falling to 9.4 per cent and from four to two seats. The Centre Party lost one of its two seats, while the Conservatives, although slipping to 20.6 per cent, retained their five seats. Two parties made significant gains: the Liberals advanced to 13.8 per cent and from one to three seats, and the Christian Democrats, not previously represented in the European Parliament, obtained 7.7 per cent and two seats. The campaign was generally Eurosceptic, as evidenced by the low turnout of 38.8 per cent and by the Social Democrat and Conservative losses and the Left Party gains. The Social Democrats, as the government party, suffered from anti-government sentiment, as did its two support parties, the Left Party and the Greens.

On 16 June the Supreme Administrative Court upheld the government's demand that one of the two nuclear power reactors at Barsebäck must be shut. A 1980 referendum had decided to phase out nuclear power and the government had set 2010 as the deadline. The prospective closure of Barsebäck (located just across the Sound from Copenhagen) was welcomed in Denmark.

Two car bombs in three days sparked vigorous debate on how to deal with the far right. The first, in Stockholm on 28 June, seriously injured a journalist and his young son. Writing as Peter Karlsson, he had been investigating the far right, so the bomb was believed to have been planted by neo-Nazis and to be linked with the second, near Malmö, which seriously injured two policemen.

Carl Bildt resigned on 6 August as leader of the Conservatives (the Moderate Unity Party). He had been Prime Minister in 1991-94 and was a former international peace mediator in Bosnia. His successor was Bo Lundgren, an economist and parliamentary representative since 1975 with experience as junior minister of finance.

v. FINLAND

CAPITAL: Helsinki   AREA: 338,000 sq km   POPULATION: 5,200,000 ('98)
OFFICIAL LANGUAGES: Finnish & Swedish   POLITICAL SYSTEM: presidential democracy
HEAD OF STATE: President Martti Ahtisaari (since Feb '94)
RULING PARTIES: Social Democratic Party (SSDP), National Coalition (KOK), Left-Wing Alliance (VAS), Swedish People's Party (SFP) & Green Union (VL)
HEAD OF GOVERNMENT: Paavo Lipponen (SSDP), Prime Minister (since April '95)
MAIN IGO MEMBERSHIPS (NON-UN): EU, NC, CBSS, AC, PFP, OSCE, CE, OECD
CURRENCY: markka (end-'99 £1=Fmk9.56, US$1=Fmk5.93)
GNP PER CAPITA: US$24,110 by exchange-rate calculation, US$20,270 at PPP ('98)

FINLAND found itself in the international spotlight during the second half of 1999, when it held the presidency of the European Union (EU). This followed the country's emergence as a key mediator in the Kosovo conflict. The enhanced international profile contributed to the growing sense of self-confidence engendered by a buoyant economy and a stable political environment. In spite of a decline in exports to Russia and the former Soviet Union, economic growth continued at a level higher than the EU average, whilst inflation remained low. Unemployment, however, remained stubbornly high, and Paavo Lipponen's government was criticized for its failure to redress the economic disparities between the urbanized south and rural north. These issues were emphasized by the opposition Centre Party, which promised labour market reform and increased regional aid in its campaign for the parliamentary elections held on 21 March.

Despite registering a four-seat advance to 48 of the 200 *Eduskunta* seats, the Centre failed narrowly in its bid to become the largest parliamentary party and broker of a new coalition government. Mr Lipponen's Social Democratic Party (SDP) lost over 5 per cent of its vote and 12 seats compared to 1995, yet remained the largest grouping with 51 seats. The main victor was the conservative National Coalition (KOK), which advanced to 46 seats (a gain of seven), while the Greens and the Finnish Christian Union improved to 11 and 10 seats respectively.

KOK acquired added weight within the reconstituted 'rainbow coalition' government formed by Mr Lipponen in April. In the course of the electoral campaign, KOK had criticized SDP plans to increase corporation tax and introduce new taxes on capital and dividends. After lengthy negotiations, the two main coalition partners settled on a 1 per cent increase in corporation tax. In return, the SDP agreed that public spending would not be increased during the government's term. A decision on possible income tax cuts was delayed pending the outcome of autumn wage negotiations between trade unions and employers' organizations.

In broad terms, however, the new government maintained the previous course of economic policy, pledging to cut unemployment and further reduce the national debt. In keeping with the latter aim, the 2000 budget provided for a surplus of Fmk6,000 million. The government also announced plans to sell a further tranche of its shares in Sonera, the state-controlled telecommunications operator. An earlier, vastly over-subscribed offering of Sonera shares (see AR 1998 p. 81) became mired in scandal, leading to the sacking of the company's chief executive, Pekka Vennamo, and the resignation of Communications Minister Matti Aura in January. In effect, Mr Vennamo was found to have acquired 25,000 extra shares through his own private investment company, on top of the full allocation he obtained as a Sonera director.

For many, the lucrative share options enjoyed by Sonera directors were hard to stomach at a time when the government was calling for wage restraint to combat the risk of inflation. Despite the carrot of income tax cuts dangled by the government, the Central Organization of Trade Unions opted for sector-specific wage negotiations with employers rather than seeking the kind of centralized, national-level agreements concluded in 1995 and 1997. The latter were deemed to have been instrumental in keeping recent pay rises at a moderate level. Wage negotiations were still ongoing at the end of the year.

From July the government was required to focus much of its energies on the demanding task of exercising the EU presidency. Hopes that Finland would be able to advance its own distinctive agenda were overshadowed by a host of other pressing issues, most notably questions relating to the reconstruction and future status of Kosovo (see III.2.vi). Yet if the 'Northern Dimension' dear to Finland was sidetracked by events further south, the Yugoslav conflict further underlined Finland's credentials as an intermediary between Russia and the EU. The appointment of President Martti Ahtisaari as EU envoy for Kosovo was widely regarded as instrumental in securing Russian consent to the NATO-imposed peace plan. Through his role in the crisis, Mr Ahtisaari bolstered his flagging support amongst the Finnish electorate. By this time, however, he had already declared that he would not seek the SDP nomination for the January 2000 presidential elections.

The Kosovo conflict brought about a change in popular attitudes to NATO, with support for Finnish entry falling to 23 per cent by the end of the year. By contrast, plans for a separate EU 'crisis management force' enjoyed wide support, corresponding as they did to a longstanding Finnish-Swedish initiative. Changing attitudes to NATO partly explained the declining fortunes of early presidential front-runner Elizabeth Rehn (Swedish People's Party), the runner-up in 1994. But perhaps the main reason for the collapse in Mrs Rehn's support was that she began her campaign too early, only to be overtaken by an impressive field of late-comers. End-of-year polls gave the highest ratings to Centre Party leader Esko Aho (the only male amongst the four leading candidates), closely followed by popular Foreign Minister Tarja Halonen (SDP). The eventual winner was set to inherit a reduced brief, following parliamentary approval of a constitutional reform circumscribing the hitherto influential role of the President in domestic and foreign affairs.

vi. AUSTRIA

CAPITAL: Vienna   AREA: 84,000 sq km   POPULATION: 8,100,000 ('98)
OFFICIAL LANGUAGE: German   POLITICAL SYSTEM: federal parliamentary democracy
HEAD OF STATE: Federal President Thomas Klestil (since Aug '92)
RULING PARTIES: Social Democratic (SPÖ) & People's (ÖVP) parties
HEAD OF GOVERNMENT: Viktor Klima (SPÖ), Federal Chancellor (since Jan '97)
MAIN IGO MEMBERSHIPS (NON-UN): EU, OSCE, CE, PFP, CEI, OECD
CURRENCY: schilling (end-'99 £1= Sch22.13, US$1=Sch13.73)
GNP PER CAPITA: US$26,850 by exchange-rate calculation, US$22,740 at PPP ('98)

IN 1999 Austria continued to prosper but, with war in Kosovo and new waves of refugees flooding north, there was little sense of well-being. Gloom set in early, when on 23-24 February more than 30 people died in avalanches in the holiday villages of Galtur and Valzur and thousands of stranded tourists had to be airlifted out of Tyrolean ski resorts. On 29 May, moreover, 12 people died and many others were injured in a disastrous fire in the Tauern road tunnel. The general election on 3 October produced deadlock among the political parties, after a strong performance by Jörg Haider's right-wing Freedom Party (FPÖ), and by the end of the year there was still no agreement on a new coalition. On 29 December Galtur found itself again unwillingly in the international news after nine skiers died in yet another avalanche.

The FPÖ's electoral success in October was the culmination of a very good year for Herr Haider, in contrast to the problems encountered in 1998 (see AR 1998, pp. 82-3). His party performed well in three provincial elections held on 7 March in Carinthia, Tyrol and Salzburg, increasing its share of the vote in all three provinces and becoming the largest single party in Carinthia. Herr Haider was accordingly elected Carinthian state governor on 8 April. The FPÖ did less well in the European Parliament elections on 13 June, losing one of its six seats on a low turnout of just under 50 per cent, whereas the Social Democratic Party (SPÖ) improved from six to seven seats and the conservative People's Party (ÖVP) retained seven seats. The other two seats went to the Greens, a gain of one.

Having increased its vote by just over 9 per cent in the Vorarlberg election on 19 September, the FPÖ also polled strongly in the national elections two weeks later, relegating the ÖVP to third place in terms of votes, albeit by the narrow margin of some 400. The FPÖ had campaigned on an opportunist mix of financial promises, an appeal to those disillusioned with the political establishment, and blatant exploitation of widespread fears of being 'swamped' by foreigners. The SPÖ did badly, losing six seats, but remained the largest party in the federal lower chamber with 65 seats. The FPÖ and ÖVP won 52 seats each and the Greens 14.

The FPÖ's success prompted much hostile comment from abroad, the Israeli Foreign Minister indicating that Israel would 'reconsider' its relations with Austria if the FPÖ were given a role in government. Since the ÖVP leader, Wolfgang Schüssel, had already said that his party would go into opposition if it were beaten into third place, and the SPÖ had ruled out all cooperation with Herr Haider, the deadlock between the parties appeared complete. The FPÖ leader meanwhile showed some concern over his poor international image, rejecting accusations of Nazi sympathies and anti-semitism and apologizing on 12 November for 'past insensitive statements capable of misinterpretation'. On the same day a large anti-racism demonstration sponsored by the SPÖ and the Greens was held in Vienna to protest against the FPÖ and Herr Haider.

After two months of 'exploratory discussions' between the four parties elected to the new parliament, led by Federal Chancellor Viktor Klima as leader of the largest party, Herr Schüssel announced in early December that his party would after all participate in coalition negotiations with the SPÖ if six 'irreversible' conditions were met. The ÖVP was determined to drive a hard bargain, hinting that, if its demands were not satisfied, an ÖVP-FPÖ coalition could not be excluded. Public impatience at the endless manoeuvring for position, and at the prospect of yet another 'grand coalition' at the end of it all, were reflected in the findings in mid-December of an opinion poll on voting intentions if fresh elections were held. This put the FPÖ in the lead, with 31 per cent, as compared to the SPÖ with 30 per cent and the ÖVP with 26 per cent.

The key issues in contention between the prospective coalition partners were all of long standing, and all now further complicated by Austria's European Union (EU) membership. Among Herr Schüssel's 'irreversible conditions' was the vexed question of security policy, on which the ÖVP sought a move away from neutrality towards greater NATO participation and eventual membership in spite of increased public enthusiasm for neutrality in the wake of the Kosovo crisis. Other conditions were further budget and pension reforms to check the renewed upward trend in the budget deficit, also unlikely to appeal to SPÖ voters. This enthusiasm for budgetary discipline contrasted with the ÖVP's agreement, as a partner in the outgoing coalition government, to a generous but incompletely-funded tax reform bill passed on 17 June, introducing lower tax rates on wages and salaries and 'negative' tax with refunded social security charges for those outside the tax system. At the beginning of December caretaker Finance Minister Hans Edlinger (SPÖ) announced that every ministry's discretionary budget for 2000 would be cut by 20 per cent across the board, in order to pull the projected net deficit back towards the 2.7 per cent 'eurozone' permitted maximum.

Fortunately, the economy continued to perform strongly, with real GDP growth for the year estimated at 2.2 per cent, inflation almost non-existent at 0.8 per cent and the unemployment rate down to an estimated 4.3 per cent. EU membership remained generally unpopular, although the government was pleased in March with the outcome of the 'Agenda 2000' EU reform programme (see XI.4), which reduced Austria's net contribution to the EU budget from 0.4 to 0.3 per cent of GDP and provided Sch5,000 million in subsidies for Austria's border regions. But the use of anonymous savings accounts continued, in defiance of EU directives on money-laundering, and in October the European Court of Justice handed down two judgements against Austria in respect of its policies on public procurement. Although trade with the Central European candidates for EU membership continued to grow strongly, the Austrian public still largely saw enlargement as a threat to jobs and prosperity. Austrians were also suspicious of EU transport and energy policies, especially where nuclear power was concerned. Strongly-held views on the need completely to phase out nuclear energy caused disputes with the Czech and Slovak Republics during the year

The Kosovo conflict was the main foreign policy concern during the year, as Austria supported NATO's intervention (see III.2.vi), though not without misgivings. It offered help to large numbers of refugees, seconded 450 soldiers in June for service with the K-For international peace-keeping force and also provided a new UN high representative for Bosnia, Wolfgang Petritsch, to succeed Carlos Westendorp on 1 August. Another Austrian, Walter Schwimmer, became secretary-general of the Council of Europe in September, the third Austrian to hold this office (see XI.5.i). The state visits to Austria of the Chinese and Indian Presidents in March and November respectively were the first-ever such visits from either country, while President Klestil's visit to Iran in September was the first by an EU head of state since the Iranian revolution (see VII.1.i).

In November Bank Austria and its subsidiary, Creditanstalt, agreed a $40 million settlement to Holocaust survivors whose assets had been seized by their predecessor institutions under Nazi rule. In a separate agreement with Jewish organizations, Bank Austria established a $5 million humanitarian fund for victims of Nazi persecution from Austria.

vii. SWITZERLAND

CAPITAL: Berne   AREA: 41,300 sq km   POPULATION: 7,100,800 ('98)
OFFICIAL LANGUAGES: German, French, Italian & Rhaeto-Romanic
POLITICAL SYSTEM: federal canton-based democracy
RULING PARTIES: Christian Democratic People's (CVP), Radical Democratic (FDP), Social Democratic (SPS) & Swiss People's (SVP) parties
HEAD OF GOVERNMENT: Ruth Dreifuss (SPS), 1999 President of Federal Council and Interior Minister
MAIN IGO MEMBERSHIPS: OECD, OSCE, CE, EFTA, PFP
CURRENCY: Swiss franc (end-'99 £1= SwF2.58, US$1=SwF1.60)
GNP PER CAPITA: US$40,080 by exchange-rate calculation, US$26,620 at PPP ('98)

THE most important political event of the year was the general election for both chambers of the national parliament, held on 24 October. The most active party during the campaign, which was in general rather calm, was the Swiss People's Party (SVP). Under the leadership of Switzerland's most charismatic politician, Christoph Blocher, it continued its fight for deregulation and lower taxes, against any Swiss participation in international political institutions, such as the European Union (EU) or the United Nations, and a more restrictive policy against asylum seekers. The two other main conservative parties, the Radical Democrats (FDP) and the Christian Democrats (CVP), tried to present themselves as parties standing for realistic and practicable political solutions and therefore opposed to any extremist slogans. The Social Democrats (SPS) were unusually calm during the campaign. This was partly due to the fact, that their new leader, Ursula Koch, was averse to political confrontation in the mass media, and partly related to the rapid recovery of the Swiss economy, which annihilated their plan to focus on the problem of unemployment.

The election resulted as follows (1995 results in parentheses):

	% of vote	seats
Swiss People's Party (SVP)	22.6 (14.9)	44 (29)
Social Democrats (SPS)	22.5 (21.8)	51 (54)
Radical Democrats (FDP)	19.9 (20.2)	43 (45)
Christian Democrats (CVP)	15.9 (16.8)	35 (34)
Green Party	5.0 (5.0)	9 (8)
Swiss Liberal Party	2.3 (2.7)	6 (7)
Evangelical Party	1.8 (1.8)	3 (2)
Labour Party (PdA)	1.0 (1.2)	3 (3)
Swiss Democrats	1.8 (3.1)	1 (3)
Other parties	7.3 (11.5)	5 (13)

The SVP was the winner of the election. It gained 15 additional seats in the National Council and, measured by share of the votes, became the strongest party, beating the Social Democrats by 0.07%. Never since 1919, when the proportional distribution of seats for the National Council was introduced, had a party made a similar step forward in one single election. The SPS was able to mobilize some additional voters, but it nevertheless lost three seats. The big losers were not, as many had expected, the FDP and the CVP, which more or less maintained their positions, but the small parties of the far right. The Freedom Party lost all its seven seats and the Swiss Democrats lost two of their three. It would thus not be correct to summarize the outcome as a landslide to the right. What happened was mostly a concentration of the different right-wing formations into the successful SVP, whereas the left and the moderate conservatives suffered only small losses.

In the elections to the federal Council of States (*Ständerat*), consisting of two representatives elected from each canton by majority vote, the SVP was not able to challenge the dominance of the FDP and the CVP. With 18 and 15 respectively of the total of 46 seats, these two parties retained a comfortable majority. The SVP obtained seven seats (a gain of two) and the SPS six (up one).

The new parliament met in joint session of both chambers on 15 December to elect the government (Federal Council), its members being elected individually and (there being no function of Prime Minister in Switzerland) with equal rights in the decision-making process. All seven members ran for re-election for another term of four years, but the SVP, strengthened by its electoral victory in October, took up the fight for better representation than its existing single seat. Because the Federal Council had been composed since 1959 according to the electoral strength of the four major parties, the SVP first challenged one of the two seats of the CVP, which was now clearly the smallest of the four parties. When it became evident that there was no majority in parliament for this proposal, the SVP attacked one of the two SPS seats. However, the Social Democrats declared that, in the event of one of its representatives not being re-elected, the other one would resign.

The question now was whether the FDP and the CVP were willing to go along with the SVP and form an all-conservative government without the Social Democrats. This was clearly not the case, however, because only a small minority of the FPD supported Herr Blocher, the candidate for the SVP. In the event, therefore, all seven members of the Federal Council were re-elected. Federal Vice-President and Minister of Defence Adolf Ogi (SVP) was elected to the annually rotating post of President of the Federal Council for 2000.

The request of the SVP, as now the strongest conservative party, for one of the two CVP seats in the government was within the logic of the Swiss political system. But it did not generate any enthusiasm because both CVP federal councillors had been elected only half a year previously, and as a rule members of the government were sure to be re-elected unless guilty of important failures. Under these circumstances, the resignation announcement in January of the two previous CVP federal councillors, Flavio Cotti and Arnold Koller, had been a smart tactical move, because of the virtual certainty that the SVP would overtake the CVP in the coming elections. The ensuing election of two new CVP representatives on 11 March helped the party to defend those seats in December.

For the election in March, when the two seats for the CVP were still uncontested, the party presented several male and female candidates with the explicit wish that one of each sex should be elected. The parliament obliged and elected Joseph Deiss and Ruth Metzler. Herr Deiss, who became Foreign Minister, had represented the canton of Fribourg in the National Council since 1995. The political career of the 35-year-old Ruth Metzler, who became Minister of Justice, was a very steep one. Only three years previously she had been elected to the government of the tiny canton of Appenzell Innerrhoden; but she was not a member of the national parliament and was therefore, until the start of her campaign in February, practically unknown on national level.

Apart from the general election, the most important political issue in 1999 was parliamentary ratification of Switzerland's long-debated agreement with the European Union (EU). Among the seven different fields of mutual liberalization covered by the agreement, only two were really disputed: the opening of Swiss roads to 40-tonne trucks and unrestricted access to labour markets. To soften up the opposition, which came in the first case from the environmentalists and in the second case from the trade unions, the parliament voted in favour of so-called 'accompanying measures'. Thus, the railway companies would receive some additional subsidies to finance lower tariffs for freight trains through the Alps, to help them fight growing competition from road transport.

The second issue, free access to labour markets, seemed to be more crucial for acceptance of the agreement by Swiss citizens. With the number of the resident foreigners having reached 20 per cent the population and with 46,000 new asylum seekers arriving in 1999, it was evident that the small nationalist parties could easily mobilize opinion against the liberalization of immigration and had a good chance of victory in a popular vote if parliament did not adopt some measures of protection for domestic workers that were supported by the unions. As Switzerland had no state legislation on minimum wages, the trade unions were afraid that the unrestricted right of workers from the EU to look for employment in Switzerland would put the much higher Swiss salaries under pressure. They therefore demanded that their collective wage agreements with the employers should be applied generally, meaning that they would apply to all enterprises operating in Switzerland which had not signed such deals. The parliament did not go this far, but it decided that in cases where the usual salaries paid in an industry were extensively undercut the government would intervene.

At the end of the parliamentary deliberations, only some small groups from the far right and the far left were opposed to the ratification of the EU agreement. They collected the 50,000 signatures necessary for a popular referendum, which was scheduled to be held in May 2000. However, the SVP and Herr Blocher's organization 'Action for a Neutral and Independent Switzerland' (AUNS) did not support this initiative, even though they criticized the Federal Council for not being able to negotiate a better agreement with the EU.

The economy continued its recovery from the crisis of the late 1990s. The number of unemployed dropped from 124,309 at end-1998 to 91,041 in December 1999 (2.5 per cent of the workforce); this was the lowest number since 1992. After zero inflation in 1998, prices rose again in 1999 by 1.6 per cent.

viii. EUROPEAN MINI-STATES

Andorra

CAPITAL: Andorra la Vella   AREA: 460 sq km   POPULATION: 72,000 ('98)
OFFICIAL LANGUAGE: Catalan   POLITICAL SYSTEM: parliamentary democracy
HEADS OF STATE: President Jacques Chirac of France & Bishop Joan Martí Alanis of Urgel (co-princes)
HEAD OF GOVERNMENT: Marc Forné Molné, President of Executive Council (since Dec '94)
MAIN IGO MEMBERSHIPS (NON-UN): CE, OSCE
CURRENCY: French franc & Spanish peseta

Holy See (Vatican City State)

CAPITAL: Vatican City   AREA: 0.44 sq km   POPULATION: 875 ('98)
OFFICIAL LANGUAGES: Italian & Latin   POLITICAL SYSTEM: theocracy
HEAD OF STATE: Pope John Paul II (since '78)
HEAD OF GOVERNMENT: Cardinal Angelo Sodano, Secretary of State (since Dec '90)
MAIN IGO MEMBERSHIPS: OSCE
CURRENCY: Vatican lira (at par to Italian lira)

Liechtenstein

CAPITAL: Vaduz   AREA: 160 sq km   POPULATION: 32,000 ('98)
OFFICIAL LANGUAGE: German   POLITICAL SYSTEM: parliamentary democracy
HEAD OF STATE: Prince Hans Adam II (since Nov '89)
RULING PARTY: Patriotic Union (VU)
HEAD OF GOVERNMENT: Mario Frick, Prime Minister (since Dec '93)
MAIN IGO MEMBERSHIPS (NON-UN): EFTA/EEA, OSCE, CE
CURRENCY: Swiss franc
GNP PER CAPITA: US$45,000 ('98 est.)

Monaco

CAPITAL: Monaco-Ville   AREA: 1.95 sq km   POPULATION: 32,000 ('98)
OFFICIAL LANGUAGE: French   POLITICAL SYSTEM: constitutional monarchy
HEAD OF STATE: Prince Rainier III (since '49)
HEAD OF GOVERNMENT: Michel Lévêque, Minister of State (since Feb '97)
MAIN IGO MEMBERSHIPS (NON-UN): OSCE
CURRENCY: French franc

San Marino

CAPITAL: San Marino   AREA: 60.5 sq km   POPULATION: 25,500 ('98)
OFFICIAL LANGUAGE: Italian   POLITICAL SYSTEM: parliamentary democracy
HEADS OF STATE & GOVERNMENT: Captains-Regent Giuseppe Arzilli & Marino Bollini (Oct '99-March '00)
RULING PARTIES: Christian Democratic & Socialist parties
MAIN IGO MEMBERSHIPS (NON-UN): OSCE, CE
CURRENCY: Italian lira

IN ANDORRA, the centre-right Liberal Union (UL) government led by Marc Forné Molné remained securely in power. The construction of a new 4.5-kilometre road tunnel was started in 1999 to provide the main link between Andorra and France, as an alternative to the existing Puerto d'Envalira route. Worth 9,852 million pesetas, the contract was won by Acciona Unit Necso together with the concession holder, La Concessionaria Tunel d'Envalira.

In the HOLY SEE (Vatican), the year began with an historic meeting on 8 January between Pope John Paul II and Italian Prime Minister Massimo D'Alema of the Left Democrats, formerly the Italian Communist Party (PCI), who in October 1998 had become the first former Communist head of a West European government (see AR 1998, pp. 63-4). Signor D'Alema's audience was seen as symbolizing the end of the long struggle between the Church and communism, which in 1949 had impelled Pope Pius XII to excommunicate PCI members and supporters.

An official Vatican report on the mysterious double murder of the commander of the Swiss Guards and his wife in May 1998 (see AR 1998, pp. 88-9) was published on 8 February. It concluded that they had been killed by a Swiss Guards lance-corporal, Cedric Tornay, whose body had been found nearby and who had apparently committed suicide. Investigations had established that Lance-Corporal Tornay was a cannabis user and had a cyst on his brain, factors which were said to have brought on 'a fit of madness' in which he killed the couple.

The Vatican announced on 19 October that a panel of Catholic and Jewish scholars would review its World War II archives in order to clarify the wartime role of Pope Pius XII, said by critics to have failed to raise his voice against the Nazis. The decision followed the publication of *Hitler's Pope*, a book by British author John Cornwell, itself based on Vatican papers, portraying Pius XII as an antisemite. The Vatican responded by publishing *Pius XII and the Second World War*, claiming that the Pope's public silence had been a cover for secret activity to save Jews from the Nazi concentration camps.

The newly-restored Sistine Chapel dating from 1368, situated within the Vatican's Apostolic Palace, was inaugurated by Pope John Paul on 11 December, after 20 years of restoration work costing $3.1 million. Containing some of the world's most famous and precious frescoes by Sandro Botticelli, Luca Signorelli and Domenico Ghirlandaio, the chapel was the traditional location of the election of new popes.

The Vatican's condemnation of the availability of the abortion pill for victims of rape in the troubled Yugoslav province of Kosovo (see III.2.vi) provoked much controversy. Several international organizations called for the Vatican's expulsion from the United Nations for its unyielding opposition to such forms of abortion and to what many regarded as the right to reproductive health.

In LIECHTENSTEIN, the long-running controversy over royal prerogatives (see AR 1997, p. 79) intensified on 29 November when the European Court of Human Rights awarded costs and damages of 100,000 Swiss francs against Prince Hans Adam II, the reigning monarch since 1989, after finding that he had abused his subjects' right to freedom of speech. The case concerned Prince Hans Adam's refusal to reappoint a judge, Herbert Wille, who had been dismissed for proposing that the principality's Supreme Court should rule on constitutional matters rather than the monarch. However, an unrepentant Prince Hans Adam remained determined to secure constitutional changes that would strengthen his already extensive powers, notably in giving him full power to appoint judges. Intent on putting the issue to a popular referendum if necessary, the Prince therefore appeared as the year ended to be on a collision course with the Diet and the government of Mario Frick (Fatherland Union).

Liechtenstein overtook Britain in 1999 on the list of the richest royal houses in Europe. Prince Hans-Adam's family moved into second position, behind the Luxembourg royal family (with assets of the equivalent of £3,000 million) and ahead of the House of Windsor (with £2,700 million).

In MONACO, one of the world's richest men, Edmond Safra (68), died in a fire at his penthouse in Monte Carlo on 3 December. The Lebanese banker, who had created his Geneva-based financial empire in the 1960s, was about to receive $3,000 million from the sale of two financial institutions to the British bank, HSBC. After contradictory statements, Mr Safra's nurse Ted Maher, a former member of the US army special forces, admitted starting the fire, claiming that he had not intended to kill his employer but to settle differences with another nurse employed by the banker.

On 25 November Monaco, together with Italy and France, signed a treaty setting up the first whale sanctuary north of the Equator. Covering about 84,000 square kilometres, the sanctuary was to be created between the French and Monegasque coasts, the Ligurian coast of Italy and the islands of Corsica and Sardinia. Experts reported that 13 cetacean species lived in the area for some part of the year, including fin, sperm and pilot whales and four distinct dolphin species.

In a private civil ceremony in the Room of Mirrors at the Royal Palace in Monte Carlo on 23 January, Princess Caroline of Monaco (42) married Prince Ernst August of Hanover. The Princess's third marriage directly linked Monaco's reigning Grimaldi family to Queen Elizabeth II of England, a close relative of Prince Ernst August.

In SAN MARINO, a number of cases of young women marrying older men for their money caused the government to introduce a new regulation specifying that female domestic staff must be aged over 50. The government also called for a referendum to confirm a law abolishing the passing on of citizenship through marriage. The government argued that in a state with only 25,000 inhabitants and a high level of wealth, protection of citizens and their citizenship should be a priority.

The Republic of San Marino, together with Monaco and the Vatican, were included in the European Union's economic and monetary union under a recommendation by the European Commission that they should be allowed to use the new euro as their official currency. In return, the three states were expected to adopt EU legislation on euro banknotes and coins and to cooperate on measures against counterfeiting.

4. SPAIN—PORTUGAL—GIBRALTAR—MALTA—GREECE—CYPRUS—TURKEY

i. SPAIN

CAPITAL: Madrid   AREA: 505,000 sq km   POPULATION: 40,200,000 ('98)
OFFICIAL LANGUAGE: Spanish   POLITICAL SYSTEM: parliamentary democracy
HEAD OF STATE: King Juan Carlos (since Nov '75)
RULING PARTY: Popular Party (PP)
HEAD OF GOVERNMENT: José María Aznar López, Prime Minister (since May '96)
MAIN IGO MEMBERSHIPS (NON-UN): NATO, EU, WEU, OSCE, CE, OECD
CURRENCY: peseta (end-'99 £1= Ptas267.54, US$1=Ptas166.00)
GNP PER CAPITA: US$14,080 by exchange-rate calculation, US$16,060 at PPP ('98)

THE approach of a general election, scheduled for March 2000, was a decisive influence upon Spanish political developments during 1999. In late January the 13th congress of the governing People's Party (PP) saw electorally-driven moves by José María Aznar to distance the party from its right-wing origins and reposition it in the 'reformist centre'. The former Labour Secretary, Javier Arenas, noted for developing good working relations with the unions, replaced Deputy Prime Minister Francisco Alvarez Cascos as PP general secretary, while Industry Ministry Josep Pique, formerly a Catalan independent appointed to further the PP's ambitions in Catalonia, joined the party executive.

Sr Aznar's plan was to conquer the moderate centre of Spanish politics and in this way make the PP capable of winning an absolute majority of the seats in the *Cortes* at the general election. In this way he hoped to overcome his government's post-1996 reliance on parliamentary support from various nationalist parties, chiefly the Catalan Convergence and Union (CiU) alliance. However, the results of regional, local and European elections on 13 June, and of Catalan regional elections on 17 October, brought the PP disappointments, as the opposition Spanish Socialist Workers' Party (PSOE) regained ground that it had lost in the mid-1990s.

The Socialists suffered a blow on 14 May when their general election candidate, Josep Borrell, resigned in response to news of fraud investigations relating to former collaborators. This led to renewed party uncertainty until 24 July, when PSOE general secretary Joaquín Almunia was chosen to head the Socialist list of candidates for the next general election. Despite this temporary uncertainty, in June the Socialists managed to reduce the PP's lead from almost 10 per cent in the European Parliament election of 1994 to 4.4 per cent. Simultaneously, in the municipal elections, a number of provincial capitals changed hands from the PP to the PSOE, while in the regional contest the Socialists retook Asturias, and went on to gain Aragón and the Balearic Islands through coalition agreements with regional parties. The PSOE benefited from a realignment of support on the left: both from the electoral decline of the Communist-led United Left (IU) and, in the Catalan election, from collaboration with ex-communists, greens and independents. The progressive alliance headed by Pasqual Maragall in Catalonia attracted more votes than the CiU, but the latter ended up with more seats, which enabled Jordi Pujol to remain regional president, with support from the PP.

General election considerations led the PP to adopt a cautious response to the new Basque political situation created by the ceasefire declared by the separatist organization ETA in September 1998. In May government negotiators held a meeting with ETA representatives in Zurich, to no immediate effect. During the 14-month ceasefire, approximately 100 ETA prisoners were released early and 135 others were transferred to prisons closer to home. However, the central government took no political initiative to bring about multi-party talks within the Basque region of Euskadi.

Indeed, the PP's relations with the Basque Nationalist Party (PNV) deteriorated as the latter party, heading a nationalist coalition government at regional level, made concessions to the Basque Citizens party (Euskal Herritarrok), composed of ETA supporters, in an effort to draw them into a peace process. The most notable PNV overture to the radicals involved the establishment of an assembly (*Udalbiltza*) of nationalist councillors and mayors from the Basque areas of Spain and France, which met in Pamplona on 6 February. In the long run, however, these nationalist gestures were deemed insufficient by ETA, which on 28 November signalled its intention to return to a violent strategy from 3 December.

Although some 49 ETA activists were arrested during the 14-month ceasefire (19 in Spain, 30 in France), the organization used the break to reorganize and to establish an alliance with the so-called 'Breton Revolutionary Army'. In September a joint raid in Plevin, France, brought the allied organizations some 3,000 kilos of explosives. Shortly before Christmas, however, ETA suffered a setback: its plan to recommence hostilities with major bomb attacks in Madrid was frustrated when Spain's Civil Guard intercepted two vans carrying 1,700 kilos of explosives.

Towards the end of the year opinion polls pointed to public perceptions of a declining political situation, while inflation returned as a concern on the economic front. On 22 December the government secured parliamentary approval for its budget for the following year, despite the PNV voting with the opposition, but on the same day the PP suffered a serious setback when amendments it had introduced in the Senate to a new Aliens bill were rejected by the Congress of Deputies. The new law strengthened the rights of immigrants living in Spain, both those with and without legal status. PP isolation over this legislation left the party with a more conservative public image than it wished for in the run-up to a general election.

The government was keen for Spain to remain in step with its European Union (EU) partners on immigration issues and was lobbied hard by its own Ministry of the Interior to resist the pro-immigrant demands made by NGOs. Of particular concern to the right wing of the PP was the effect that the law might have on the future of Ceuta and Melilla (Spanish cities in North Africa claimed by Morocco). In July, following the triple election, Mustafa Aberchan had become Melilla's first Muslim president, with support from the populist Independent Liberal Group (GIL), which itself won in Ceuta. In December the Ceuta authorities threatened to rebel against the new law, while the PP announced that it would repeal the new legislation if re-elected. The government's parliamentary defeat strengthened the possibility of a return to Socialist-Nationalist parliamentary collaboration, as had existed under the previous administration.

Externally, Spain was preoccupied principally with European issues. Sr Aznar's government led a campaign to hold on to Spain's substantial allocations from the structural and cohesion funds of the EU, against German efforts to trim the community budget and redirect these funds primarily to central and eastern Europe, in view of the expected future eastern enlargement of the Union (see XI.4). In April, at the EU's Berlin summit, Spain had to settle for a smaller volume of aid from these funds than it had sought, but nevertheless retained substantial allocations for the period 2000-2006.

The Spanish government continued to place great emphasis on the cultivation of relations with France, the highlight of the diplomatic year being a two-day state visit by President Jacques Chirac in early October. Increased bilateral cooperation to combat terrorism and political collaboration over a series of issues within the EU underpinned the burgeoning relationship. During his visit the French President referred to Spain as a 'major ally' of France, and supported Spanish proposals for EU policy harmonization in the fields of justice and security, while Sr Aznar endorsed French defence proposals.

In June, at the Cologne summit of the EU, NATO secretary-general and former Spanish Foreign Minister Javier Solana became the EU's high representative for foreign and security policy (dubbed 'Mr CFSP'). Not pushed by Spain, his candidature was supported by France, Germany and the UK. In October, to pave the way for a merger of the EU and the Western European Union, Sr Solana was also named general secretary of the WEU, again with French support. Spain's own readiness to play a greater role in international defence and security undertakings had already been demonstrated in late April by Spanish participation in the NATO attacks on Serbia (see III.2.vi).

A second line of collaboration within the EU linked Madrid and London. Spain and the UK worked on joint proposals for EU economic reform, and an inaugural Anglo-Spanish summit was held on 10-11 April, notwithstanding bilateral tension over Gibraltar (see II.4.ii). In October a further Anglo-Spanish initiative led to joint proposals on extradition, submitted to the extraordinary EU summit meeting at Tampere, Finland. However, in mid-December the preparation of joint economic reform proposals for a special EU employment summit the following spring suffered a setback when Spain called off a bilateral meeting in Madrid, upset over British plans to meet a PSOE representative during the same visit.

In relation to Latin America, Spanish foreign policy makers remained preoccupied with relations with Chile and Cuba. On 14 September Spain rejected Chilean calls for international arbitration in the Pinochet affair (see II.1.i; IV.3.iv), despite the Aznar government's evident lack of enthusiasm for the former Chilean President's extradition to Spain to go ahead. In mid-November the ninth Ibero-American summit meeting, held in Cuba, decided to establish a permanent secretariat in Madrid, to coordinate cooperation programmes (see XI.6.iv). On this occasion King Juan Carlos became the first Spanish monarch ever to visit Cuba, but it was not an official visit, as had been envisaged at one stage. The Spanish government continued to receive opponents of President Castro's government, and during the summit itself Sr Aznar and other Spanish representatives met a group of Cuban oppositionists to discuss human rights issues (see also IV.3.xi).

ii. GIBRALTAR

CAPITAL: Gibraltar   AREA: 6.5 sq km   POPULATION: 33,000 ('98)
OFFICIAL LANGUAGE: English   POLITICAL STATUS: Crown Colony, parliamentary democracy
HEAD OF STATE: Queen Elizabeth II
GOVERNOR: Sir Richard Luce
RULING PARTY: Gibraltar Social Democrats (GSD)
HEAD OF GOVERNMENT: Peter Caruana, Chief Minister (since May '96)
CURRENCY: Gibraltar pound (at par with UK pound)

THE dispute over Spanish fishing access to waters off Gibraltar, which had flared up the previous August (see AR 1998, p. 95), remained a political focal point early in 1999. On 27 January the *Piraña*, a fishing boat from Algeciras, was detained off Rossia Bay for contravening local fishing restrictions. Spain immediately protested to the British ambassador and gave the UK 72 hours to ratify the Spanish interpretation of what had been agreed verbally by Foreign Ministers Robin Cook and Abel Matutes the previous October. At the end of January Spain instituted strict controls on the circulation of people, vehicles and merchandise at the frontier with Gibraltar, thereby causing long delays, affecting inhabitants of the Rock and also the Spaniards working there. Britain and Spain both complained to the European Commission about the actions of the other.

On 1 February, an agreement was reached between the Gibraltar authorities and fishermen's representatives from La Línea and Algeciras, under which limited Spanish fishing access was restored. The Spanish newspaper *El País* on 4 February claimed that Gibraltar's Chief Minister, Peter Caruana, was trying to use the dispute to force Spain to negotiate directly with him. The Madrid authorities refused to recognize the local agreement, but faced criticism at home for obstructing movement across the frontier. The PSOE came out against the government's 'confrontation' tactics, which also involved Sr Matutes stating on 4 February that he would not hold further talks with the UK on the future of Gibraltar, unless it was to discuss the Rock's reintegration with Spain.

As the tension between Spain and the UK gradually diminished, Gibraltar's authorities stepped up efforts to develop cooperation agreements with local authorities in neighbouring parts of Spain, concerning practical issues of mutual interest such as tourism, education, culture and sporting links. Although a planned meeting on 24 June between Mr Caruana and Jesús Gil, the mayor of Marbella, was called off owing to bail conditions affecting the latter politician, the Gibraltar Chief Minister did meet the new mayor of La Línea, Juan Carlos Juárez, who had been elected on the list of Sr Gil's GIL party. Four months later, on 26 October, Mr Caruana signed a declaration with the Socialist president of Cádiz province, Rafael Román, calling for the lifting of the border controls and announcing a collaborative venture with the University of New York to establish a Centre of Studies of the Straits of Gibraltar, with headquarters on both sides of the frontier.

On several occasions the Gibraltar dispute came up within the European Union (EU) context. Of particular concern to the UK was a European Court of Human Rights ruling on 18 February that Britain had violated the rights of citizens in Gibraltar by not allowing them to vote in elections to the European Parliament (EP). The ruling left the UK vulnerable to legal action for compensation by citizens living in Gibraltar, yet unable to grant them the vote without first obtaining an amendment to the treaty on elections to the EP. This would require the approval of all 15 EU member states, including Spain.

iii. PORTUGAL

CAPITAL: Lisbon   AREA: 92,000 sq km   POPULATION: 10,000,000 ('98)
OFFICIAL LANGUAGE: Portuguese   POLITICAL SYSTEM: presidential/parliamentary democracy
HEAD OF STATE: President Jorge Sampaio (since March '96)
RULING PARTY: Socialist Party (PS)
HEAD OF GOVERNMENT: António Guterres, Prime Minister (since Oct '95)
MAIN IGO MEMBERSHIPS (NON-UN): NATO, OECD, EU, WEU, OSCE, CE, CPLP
CURRENCY: escudo (end-'99 £1= Esc322.36, US$1=Esc200.01)
GNP PER CAPITA: US$10,690 by exchange-rate calculation, US$14,380 at PPP ('98)

THE first full year of what was regarded as a surprisingly smooth transition into the economic and monetary union of the European Union (EU) continued Portugal's striking record of stability and development since accession to the EU in 1986. Such success was perhaps comparable to the cases of Ireland, Spain and Greece, but for the Portuguese, coming as it did after the dislocation of the end of overseas empire, it was hailed by some as 'a miracle made in Brussels'.

Whereas the Portuguese had traditionally emigrated to find work, widespread infrastructural development in the 1990s, much of it EU-funded, was providing progressively higher rates of employment at home. Although Portuguese wage levels in 1999 were still, with those of Greece, at the bottom of the EU scale, GNP per capita income reached 74 per cent of the EU average, compared with 54 per cent in 1986. Moreover, the rate of economic growth in 1999, though falling from 4 to 3 per cent compared with 1998, was still one of the highest in the EMU participating countries.

Against this background, a widespread recognition that financial and socio-economic governance in one of the small EU member states was principally dependent on EU regulations resulted in reduced public attachment to party politics in Portugal, as evidenced by low participation in recent national and local elections. The main political division seemed to be not so much between right and left but between optimists who believed that the country's future was so bound up with the EU that national politics were irrelevant, and those who harboured fears that economic success was overly dependent on EU 'cohesion funds'. It was noted that Portugal, with 3 per cent of total EU population and about 1.5 per cent of its economic output, would continue to receive more than 10 per cent of EU regional and structural funds until 2006, when the present arrangement would come up for revision. Another worrying factor was that apparent economic success was dangerously based on an artificial credit boom rather than on increased industrial and agricultural production.

Such uncertainties, at least about the longer-term future, contributed to some party political realignments in advance of the parliamentary elections in October. In early March a new Left Bloc (BE) was formed, being described as a social movement rather than a conventional party. Consisting of fringe groups of radical leftists, feminists and ecologists, it sought to gather support from a new generation for which traditional socialism had reached an impasse. This was followed by the dissolution of the centre-right opposition Democratic Alternative (AD) alliance between the Social Democratic Party (PSD) and the Popular Party (PP), when the latter, led by newspaper editor Paulo Portas, decided to go it alone. Two months later the 22nd PSD congress elected former Foreign Minister José Manuel Durão Barroso as party president in succession to Rebelo de Sousa. On the traditional left, the almost unnoticed passing of the 25th anniversary of the April 1974 revolution reflected the trend towards consumerism rather than ideology or party politics. The Communist Party (PCP), although partially reinvigorated under the modernizing leadership of Carlos Carvalhas and by its electoral union with the Greens, had not recovered from the collapse of the Soviet bloc and of communist internationalism.

In the European Parliament elections held on 13 June the list of the ruling Socialist Party (PS), headed by former President Mário Soares, advanced from 10 to 12 of Portugal's 25 seats, while the PSD only just managed to retain its nine seats. The United Democratic Coalition (CDU) of the PCP and the Greens fell back from three to two seats, as did the PP. The most surprising aspect of the contest was the return to active politics of Sr Soares, who had announced that he intended to run for the presidency of the European Parliament once elected. His eventual defeat in this aim was a personal setback for the PS elder statesman, who had been hoping, despite his age, to start another political career on the European stage.

Campaigning for the parliamentary elections on 10 October was overshadowed by national agitation over the situation in East Timor (see below) and by the death on 6 October of renowned *fado* singer Amália Rodrigues, for whom three days of national mourning were declared (see Pt XVIII: Obituary). In the event, the PS government led by António Guterres was returned to power with 115 of the 230 Assembly seats (and 44.1 per cent of the vote), equal to the combined strength of the opposition parties. Of the latter, the PSD slipped to 81 seats (32.3 per cent), while the CDU advanced slightly to 17 seats (9.0 per cent) and the PP retained 15 seats (8.3 per cent). The new Left Bloc produced the only real surprise by winning two seats on a vote share of 2.4 per cent.

Announced on 21 October, the new Guterres government included a number of changes, the most significant being the replacement of Finance Minister António de Sousa Franco by Joaquim Augusto de Piña Moura, a former assistant secretary to the Prime Minister. A political independent, Sr de Sousa had played a key role in securing Portuguese participation in the euro single currency launched in January (see XI.4) but had been damaged by a dispute between the EU and Portugal over the government's abortive attempt to veto the takeover of the Portuguese Champalimaud financial group by Spain's Banco Santander Central Hispanoamericano (BSCH).

Amid stability at home, the dominant external event of the year was the unfolding of drama and tragedy 10,000 miles away in the former Portuguese colony of East Timor, annexed by Indonesia in 1975 but still regarded by the UN as legally a 'territory under Portuguese administration' (see IX.1.vi; XI.1). Portugal's initial diplomatic efforts were concentrated on rallying support within the EU and UN to pressurize Indonesia into agreeing to a referendum in the territory to enable its people to decide their future. Eventually held on 30 August under UN supervision, the referendum produced a massive 78.5 per cent majority in favour of independence from Indonesia, despite a last-minute offer of 'special autonomy' made by the new post-Suharto government in Jakarta. The violent reaction of the pro-Indonesian Timorese minority, aided by the Indonesian military, recalled the atrocities of the 1975 Indonesian invasion and gave rise to an unprecedented outburst of emotion in Portugal in support of the Timorese people. The government responded by giving its full support to the speedy deployment of a UN-sponsored peace-keeping force in East Timor from late September and the establishment of a UN transitional administration charged with taking the territory to independence.

The other major external event in 1999 was the formal return of Macao to Chinese sovereignty on 20 December, after 450 years of Portuguese colonial rule. The transfer had originally been scheduled for 31 December, but the Chinese government had eventually agreed to bring it forward so that the formal ceremonies would not clash with Christmas and New Year festivities in Portugal. As the Chinese side pointed out, the handover, accomplished without acrimony, marked the end of the last outpost of European imperialism in Asia. Both sides agreed that it heralded the start of a new relationship between China and Portugal.

Although Portugal's external interests were increasingly bound up with the EU, links with the countries of its former empire remained a major factor in Portuguese politics. The year ended with preparations being made not only for Portugal's occupancy of the EU presidency in the first half of 2000 but also for joint Portuguese-Brazilian commemoration on 3 May of the 500th anniversary of the landing of Pedro Alvares Cabral in what became Brazil. The Lisbon government hoped that one of the highlights of its EU presidency would be a Euro-African summit conference to highlight the problems of a post-colonial marginalized continent containing five of the far-flung nations of the Community of Portuguese-Speaking Countries (see XI.3.ii). At the end of the year, however, no agreement had been reached with the Organization of African Unity as the relevant African interlocutor for the planned summit.

iv. MALTA

CAPITAL: Valletta   AREA: 316 sq km   POPULATION: 378,000 ('98)
OFFICIAL LANGUAGES: Maltese & English   POLITICAL SYSTEM: parliamentary democracy
HEAD OF STATE: President Guido de Marco (since April '99)
RULING PARTY: Nationalist Party (NP)
HEAD OF GOVERNMENT: Edward Fenech Adami, Prime Minister (since Sep '99)
MAIN IGO MEMBERSHIPS (NON-UN): NAM, CWTH, OSCE, CE
CURRENCY: lira (end-'99 £1= Lm0.67, $US1=Lm0.41)
GNP PER CAPITA: US$9,440 by exchange-rate calculation, US$13,610 at PPP ('98)

THE underlying issue during the year was the island's relationship with the European Union (EU). The Nationalist Party government elected in 1998 (see AR 1998, pp. 99-100) had renewed its application for full membership and in February the European Commission published its 'update report' on Malta. It called for the immediate screening of Malta's legislation so that negotiations might start by the end of the year. There were no particular difficulties likely to be found. The government repeated its promise to hold a referendum on the terms and conditions of entry once they were known. The Labour Party under Dr Alfred Sant hardened its opposition, saying that even 'a narrow majority of 52 per cent' would not alter its determination to withdraw the application if it were returned to power. Since voting in Malta was usually balanced between the two parties at 49 to 51 per cent of the vote, the party's stance was critical.

The Church, often an important player, refused to take a stand on the EU issue. The three leading figures—Archbishop Joseph Mercieca, Gozo Bishop Nikol Cauchi and Auxiliary Bishop Annetto Depasquale—agreed that the decision to join was 'fundamentally a political one' and not, therefore, within the competence of the Church, although the Pope had stated that 'Europe needs Malta as a faithful witness'.

A delegation led by Dr Eddie Fenech Adami attended the Helsinki summit of the EU heads of government on 10-11 December. The Prime Minister noted that negotiations should have started after the Florence summit in 1996 but that the government was 'back in the position we were then'. Malta was now one of six new applicant states, together with Latvia, Lithuania, Slovakia, Bulgaria and Romania (see XI.4).

Party rivalry remained intense throughout the year. The Labour Party believed that it had been unfairly ousted from office by Dom Mintoff's defection in September 1998 and by the vagaries of the electoral system. The party therefore adopted a confrontational posture, including opposition to the government's nomination of the former Nationalist Foreign Minister, Professor Guido de Marco, to the presidency. There was also strident criticism of the government's privatization programme. The first major transfer from the public sector was on 10 June when the assets and liabilities of Malta's largest bank, the MidMed, were taken over by Midland Bank, subsidiary of HSBC. The net asset value was put at £114 million including some 60 offices and 1,800 staff. The sale was completed in November. The wheel had almost turned full circle, since many remembered the MidMed's origins in 1975 when the Labour government under Mr Mintoff took into state control the Maltese operations of Barclays Bank.

The government published its full privatization programme in a White Paper on the same day (23 November) as the budget. The businesses to be released to the private sector were listed as Malta International Airport, Malta Freeport, Public Lotto, the LibyanArabMaltese Holding Company and the Bank of Valletta. No decision was taken on the preferred method, only a promise to examine a number of options—including flotation on the stock market, a strategic sale to a single (private) company and a management buyout. Malta was proceeding cautiously down a familiar path.

The budget for 2000 was designed to generate revenue to reduce the island's deficit. As part of the preparation for EU membership, value-added tax (VAT) had been introduced in January and a partial privatization had brought in additional revenue. The budget now raised duties by 15 per cent on cigarettes, tobacco, petrol and diesel fuels and locally-produced alcohol, and by 5 per cent on telephone charges. There were increased contributions to national insurance. The removal of subsidies on bread and flour also hit the general consumer. Income tax was unchanged for incomes below Lm1,500, but increased by new 5 per cent bands from 15 to 35 per cent. Although the imbalance between revenue and expenditure had been reduced from the Lm54 million of 1998 to Lm21 million in 1999, Finance Minister John Dalli declared that it was 'vital that we move from deficit to surplus'.

The opposition condemned the budget, arguing that 'these measures will dent families' income more than Labour's budget for 1998'. They were, said Dr Sant, 'a deceit and a betrayal'. The government had been 'reduced to a puppet on strings pulled by Brussels'.

As relations between the parties grew worse, so the attitude of trade unions towards the Nationalist government turned sour. In August there was a long-drawn-out dispute over the question of termination benefits for workers employed in the state construction company, Kalaxkokk Enterprises. After the completion of the Malta Freeport Terminal, the majority of Kalaxkokk employees became redundant. The government offered compensation. The General Workers' Union (GWU) rejected the terms and called a number of sympathy strikes among the pilots, tug operators and stevedores working in the island's ports. Agreement was finally reached, but not before the conflict had spread to the international airport where the GWU mounted a series of damaging strikes, at the height of the tourist season, in support of its demand for recognition as the airport's chief negotiating body. There were angry scenes, the police were called in and the issue was settled only by recourse to the courts, which issued a prohibitory injunction against the union.

Malta was brought into a dispute over arms sales between Britain and Libya when spare parts for Scud missiles were discovered and seized by customs officials at Gatwick on 24 November. They were in 32 crates and disguised as car parts, and were said to be en route from Taiwan to Libya via London and Malta.

The Central Office of Statistics published a report on 5 December which showed that the rate of illiteracy was 11.2 per cent among adults aged 15 and over, broken down to 12.6 per cent for men and 10 per cent for women. The ratio was high despite the high spending (5.4 per cent of GDP) on education.

Among deaths in Malta during the year was that of the British actor Oliver Reed on 2 May.

v. GREECE

CAPITAL: Athens   AREA: 132,000 sq km   POPULATION: 11,000,000 ('98)
OFFICIAL LANGUAGE: Greek   POLITICAL SYSTEM: parliamentary democracy
HEAD OF STATE: President Kostas Stephanopoulos (since March '95)
RULING PARTY: Pan-Hellenic Socialist Movement (PASOK)
HEAD OF GOVERNMENT: Kostas Simitis, Prime Minister (since Jan '96)
MAIN IGO MEMBERSHIPS (NON-UN): NATO, EU, WEU, OSCE, CE, BSEC, OECD
CURRENCY: drachma (end-'99 £1= Dr531.07, US$1=Dr329.51)
GNP PER CAPITA: US$11,650 by exchange-rate calculation, US$13,010 at PPP ('98)

THE troubled relationship of Greece with its NATO ally Turkey dominated the political scene in 1999 (see also II.4.vii). At the time of the Öcalan affair in February, prospects for a rapprochement between the two countries appeared remote but 'earthquake diplomacy' during the summer months gave rise to a much-improved climate in relations.

The government, not wishing to add the Kurdish issue to a long list of bilateral differences with Turkey, had made it clear that it was not prepared to offer asylum to Abdullah Öcalan, the leader of the Kurdistan Workers' Party (PKK), after he had been dislodged from his Syrian refuge in late 1998 as a result of Turkish pressure (see AR 1998, pp. 64, 110, 229). Nonetheless, the Kurdish leader was illegally spirited into Greece by a retired army officer, questions therefore being raised as to who was really running the country. He then ended up being temporarily sheltered in the Greek embassy in Nairobi while apparently on his way to a more permanent refuge in the Seychelles. When the Kenyan authorities got wind of his presence, he was persuaded to leave the embassy to take a flight to Amsterdam. On 15 February, however, on the way to the airport, Mr Öcalan was abducted by Turkish agents and flown to Istanbul. His capture led to large-scale protests by Kurds, who directed their wrath against Greek diplomatic missions, over 20 of which were occupied, including the Greek embassy in London. The Turkish government accused the Greek government not only of harbouring the PKK leader but also of giving active support to PKK militants.

The Öcalan fiasco led to the downfall of the outspoken Foreign Minister, Theodoros Pangalos, as well as Interior Minister Alexandros Papadopoulos and Public Order Minister Phillipos Petsalnikos. In the ensuing reshuffle, George Papandreou, the son of former Prime Minister Andreas Papandreou, became Foreign Minister, while Vasso Papandreou (no relation) was appointed Interior Minister and Mikhalis Khrysokhoidis Public Order Minister. Evangelos Venizelos became Minister of Development, being replaced as Minister of Culture by Elisavet Papazoi.

Relations between Greece and Turkey in the aftermath of the Öcalan affair were extremely tense. But it soon became clear that the new Greek Foreign Minister was not going to continue his predecessor's confrontational style. Before long some conciliatory gestures were made. Mr Papandreou stated, for instance, that he had no objection if members of the country's Muslim minority chose to call themselves Turks, and not, as they were officially designated, Muslims. This declaration was heavily criticized, not least within the ruling Pan-Hellenic Socialist Movement (PASOK). There was also good cooperation between the two countries in handling refugees from the Kosovo crisis (see III.2.vi).

The catalyst for a radically improved climate in relations between the two countries, at least at the level of rhetoric, was the devastating earthquake of 17 August that caused large numbers of casualties and widespread damage in north-western Turkey. In Greece there was a massive upsurge of popular sympathy for the country's stricken neighbours. This rapidly translated into a number of initiatives launched to bring relief to the devastated areas. Such was the speed of the response that Greek rescue teams were in operation on the evening of the disaster. Turkish politicians were quick to express their gratitude.

On 7 September Greece itself was afflicted by an earthquake, measuring 5.9 on the Richter scale. Although not of the magnitude of the Turkish earthquake, it was nonetheless serious. The death toll was 143 and 100,000 were left homeless. The epicentre of the earthquake was located slightly to the north of Athens, where some 22 buildings, including factories built without planning permission, were totally destroyed. A preliminary survey found that, of 100,000 damaged buildings, 60 per cent were habitable and 32 per cent in need of repair, while 8 per cent could only be demolished. The authorities promised to prosecute those who had built sub-standard buildings in breach of building regulations.

Turkish rescue teams were equally prompt in their response to the Greek earthquake disaster. Thus was set in train the phenomenon that came to be known as 'earthquake diplomacy'. In early September Mr Papandreou stated in an interview that he wanted Greece to be 'the locomotive that will pull Turkey into Europe', while his Turkish counterpart, Ismail Cem, referred to what he termed an explosion of affection and expectation on both sides of the Aegean. But despite the warm rhetoric expressed by politicians and at the popular level, the launching of a number of initiatives to improve cooperation over non-contentious issues, and the decision at the Helsinki European Union (EU) summit in December to accord Turkey candidate status with respect to entry (see XI.4), there was little sign of substantive progress towards a resolution of the perpetual Cyprus problem (see II.4.vii) or of the numerous strictly bilateral differences between the two countries.

An important role in bringing about the improved climate in relations between the two countries had been played by Yiannos Kranidiotis, the Cypriot-born Alternate Minister for Foreign Affairs. Together with his son Nikos and four others, Dr Kranidiotis died on 14 September when the government plane in which he was travelling to a meeting of Balkan Foreign Ministers experienced a sudden loss of height on approaching Bucharest airport. He was replaced by Christos Rokophyllos.

A planned visit by US President Bill Clinton in November was severely curtailed in the light of fears for his security. Anti-American feeling had been rekindled during the Kosovo conflict, on which opinion polls consistently registered by far the highest levels of opposition to the bombing campaign of any NATO member state. During the conflict, albeit demonstrating a degree of unease over the development, the Greek government had demonstrated solidarity with its NATO partners, while avoiding a high-profile role in the conflict. It had originally been intended that President Clinton would spend three days in Greece, but in the event his visit, on 19-20 November, was postponed for a week and shortened to less than 20 hours, to avoid coinciding with the annual commemoration on 17 November of the student uprising of 1973 that helped precipitate the downfall of the military junta in 1974.

As it was, violent demonstrations preceded Mr Clinton's visit, which was characterized by extraordinary security measures. Opinion polls suggested that over 60 per cent of Greeks were opposed to the visit, which prompted further violent protests but otherwise went off without incident. Indeed, President Clinton managed, against the odds, to turn the visit into something of a success. He accomplished this feat by publicly apologizing for US support of the junta that misruled Greece between 1967 and 1974, and by expressing, in the course of a visit to the Acropolis, sympathy with Greek aspirations for the return to Greece of the Elgin Marbles in the British Museum and by undertaking to raise the issue with UK Prime Minister Tony Blair.

The austerity measures imposed by the government in its determination to prepare the ground for Greek membership of the EU's economic and monetary union, together with dissatisfaction over the perceived inefficiency of the state in dealing with matters such as rising crime and the annual rash of forest fires, took their toll on the government's popularity as registered in the elections for the European Parliament held on 13 June. There were few points of dispute between the two main parties over specifically European issues. The opposition New Democracy party's 36 per cent share of the vote (2 per cent lower than in the 1996 national election) secured nine of the 25 Greek seats. The ruling PASOK party, whose 32.9 per cent share was 8.6 per cent lower than in 1996, also won nine seats. The Communist Party of Greece, with 8.7 per cent (5.6 per cent in 1996), took three seats. The Democratic Social Movement (DIKKI), a left-wing offshoot of PASOK, with 6.8 per cent (4.4 per cent in 1996), secured two seats, as did the Alliance of Left and Progress (Synaspismos), with 5.2 per cent (5.1 per cent in 1996). Neither the right-wing Political Spring, which had previously held two seats in the European Parliament, nor the Liberals, established in May by the dissident New Democracy deputy Stephanos Manos, obtained representation. The 75 per cent turnout, partly explained by the fact that voting was in theory compulsory, contrasted with the low participation elsewhere in Europe.

The issue of the return of the Elgin Marbles to Greece was vigorously pursued by the Greek government, anxious to secure their return for the 2004 Olympic Games to be staged in Athens. In November a conference held at the British Museum in London to assess the effects of the 'cleaning' of the marbles shortly before World War II gave rise to acrimony. There was, however, no movement on the issue of return, Prime Minister Blair making it clear that the marbles would remain in the British Museum.

Two prominent figures associated with the military junta in power between 1967 and 1974 died in 1999. Colonel George Papadopoulos, the prime mover in the coup of 21 April 1967, died on 27 June (see XVIII: Obituary), while General Phaidon Gizikis, President of Greece when the junta collapsed in July 1973, died on 26 July.

vi. CYPRUS

CAPITAL: Nicosia   AREA: 9,250 sq km   POPULATION: 867,000 ('98): 663,000 Greek Cypriots in the south & 204,000 Turkish Cypriots and Turks in the north (acc. to respective Planning Bureaus)
POLITICAL SYSTEM: separate presidential/parliamentary democracies in Greek Cypriot area and in Turkish Republic of Northern Cyprus (recognized only by Turkey)
HEAD OF STATE & GOVERNMENT: President Glafkos Clerides (since Feb '93); Rauf Denktash has been President of Turkish area since Feb '75
RULING PARTIES: Democratic Rally (DISY) heads coalition with United Democrats (EDI) and independents in Greek Cyprus; National Unity Party (UBP) & Communal Liberation Party (TKP) form coalition in TRNC
MAIN IGO MEMBERSHIPS (NON-UN): (Greek Cyprus) NAM, OSCE, CE, CWTH
CURRENCY: Cyprus pound (end-'99 C£1= C£0.93, US$1=C£0.58); in TRNC Turkish lira
GNP PER CAPITA: Greek Cyprus US$20,000 at PPP ('98 est.); TRNC US$4,000 ('98 est.)

UN-sponsored negotiations for a constitutional settlement resumed, in the form of 'proximity talks', on 3 December, a week before European Union (EU) heads of government agreed to accept Turkey as a 13th candidate for membership (see II.4.vii; XI.4). The negotiations had been suspended since August 1997 when the Turkish Cypriot leader, Rauf Denktash, walked out of face-to-face talks with the Greek Cypriot President of the Republic, Glafkos Clerides, following a recommendation by the European Commission that

Cyprus be accepted as a candidate for accession while Turkey be put on hold. Dr Denktash claimed that the Commission position compromised the putative sovereignty of the Turkish Republic of Northern Cyprus (TRNC) because it had not been party to the application by the Greek Cypriot government of the Republic.

Until the change in EU policy, there had been stalemate in all efforts to revive settlement negotiations. Nevertheless, the Republic of Cyprus, which was included in the first group of six enlargement candidates, pressed ahead with its negotiations, hoping to accede by the beginning of 2003. The leadership of the TRNC abjured all efforts to engage the Turkish Cypriots in the negotiating process and instead developed a policy, in conjunction with Turkey, of matching every move of the Cyprus government towards EU accession with comparable moves towards integration of the TRNC with the mainland. This rejectionist stance was reinforced following the formation in May 1999 of a Turkish coalition government consisting of three chauvinist parties and headed by Bülent Ecevit, who as Prime Minister in 1974 had ordered the Turkish military intervention in Cyprus in the first place.

In February four EU member states—Germany, France, Italy and the Netherlands—entered reservations regarding the accession of the Republic of Cyprus on the grounds that its government would not be able to apply the *acquis communautaire* throughout the whole island unless there were a settlement. The government of Greece responded by saying that it would veto the accession of the other five candidate states if such impediments were put in the way of the application of Cyprus.

Throughout the first half of 1999 the UN head of mission in Cyprus, Dame Ann Hercus, continued to shuttle between President Clerides and Dr Denktash. Her technique was to tell neither side the views of the other but to relay their positions to UN Secretary-General Kofi Annan, who assessed them for points of convergence in the hope of finding a basis for the resumption of talks. Endorsing the Secretary General's efforts, the Cologne summit of the Group of 8 nations on 20 June called for comprehensive negotiations under UN auspices to begin in the autumn. This call was reiterated in Security Council resolution 1250 of 29 June (see also XI.1).

The Greek Cypriot leadership said that it would attend such talks provided that they were based on UN resolutions calling for a bi-zonal, bi-communal, federal state with a single citizenship and international personality. The Turkish Cypriot leadership, backed by Turkey, responded that it was only prepared to negotiate a confederation between two sovereign states. Such an arrangement would allow the Turkish Cypriots to conclude bilateral treaties with Turkey that would permit the continued stationing of Turkish troops on the island. When the Greek Cypriots rejected the confederation proposition, Dr Denktash and Mr Ecevit issued a joint declaration on 20 July (the anniversary of the Turkish invasion) saying that the TRNC and Turkey would develop relations 'with the target of integration set at the highest level'.

In February relations between Greece and Turkey had reached nadir when

Abdullah Öcalan, the Kurdish separatist leader, was captured by Turkish agents in Kenya, after having being afforded sanctuary at the Greek embassy (and being found to be in possession of a Cypriot passport). However, the incoming Greek Foreign Minister, George Papandreou, worked assiduously with Turkish counterpart Ismail Cem to repair relations (see II.4.v). The initiative was given impetus following earthquakes in Turkey in August and in Greece in September when both nations offered reciprocal aid. These gestures led to an outpouring of amity among opinion-makers and the previously hostile press of both countries. In the new climate, the Greek government was able to say that it could foresee lifting its veto on Turkey's EU candidacy provided that Turkey would undertake certain commitments regarding bilateral issues in the Aegean and provided that the EU did not make a settlement on Cyprus a precondition of the Republic's accession.

During an official visit to Washington in September, Mr Ecevit was urged by the Clinton administration to promote settlement talks in order to facilitate Turkey's EU candidacy. President Clinton reiterated this message in November during visits to Turkey and Greece that preceded and followed the Istanbul summit of the Organization for Security and Cooperation in Europe (see XI.5.ii). While Mr Clinton was in the region, the UN Secretary-General on 14 November issued invitations for the Cyprus 'proximity talks' in New York in December.

The Greek Cypriots accepted the invitation on the understanding that the talks would be 'substantive'. Dr Denktash, insisting that he would discuss only matters related to his equality at the bargaining table, first accepted, then demurred (claiming that he had not been invited in the same capacity as Mr Clerides), then re-accepted, apparently under pressure from Ankara. The formula for getting him to the talks was to refer to 'the parties' to the negotiations, thus circumventing his historical complaint that Mr Clerides was referred to as the President of Cyprus while he was referred to as a community leader. The proximity talks on 3-14 December were conducted under a news blackout. A second round was scheduled to begin on 31 January 2000 in Geneva, after which it was hoped that sufficient common ground could be achieved for a resumption of face-to-face negotiations.

Meanwhile, the EU summit in Helsinki on 10-11 December had set new ground rules for enlargement. It decided that negotiations would continue with the first six candidates (Cyprus, the Czech Republic, Hungary, Poland, Estonia and Slovenia) and open in 2000, earlier than previously planned, with the second six (Bulgaria, Latvia, Lithuania, Romania, Slovakia and Malta). Turkey was accepted as a 13th candidate, but negotiations with it would commence only when the Ankara government had satisfied the so-called 'Copenhagen criteria' on political and civil liberties, a process expected to take several years. The EU member states also accepted that a settlement on Cyprus should not be a precondition for accession and that Turkey should settle outstanding bilateral disputes with Greece in the Aegean by 2004 or submit to adjudication by the International Court of

Justice. This was sufficient for Greece not to employ its veto.

Turkey reluctantly accepted these conditions. Publicly both Mr Ecevit and Dr Denktash continued to insist that confederation (or a 'sovereignty association') was the only acceptable solution for Cyprus. There was therefore little present prospect for a positive outcome to continued talks. However, given the shifts in Greek-Turkish relations during the second half of 1999, it was possible to hope that there could also be an amelioration of relations between the communities on the island.

Greek Cypriot public opinion opposed the NATO military action launched against the Serbs in Yugoslavia in March (see II.2.vi). On 8 April Spyros Kyprianou, leader of the Democratic Party (DIKO) and speaker of the House of Representatives, took it upon himself to travel to Belgrade to take advantage of the good relations between the two Orthodox countries to secure the release of three US servicemen held prisoner. He was unsuccessful. The House subsequently threatened to overturn legislation introduced by the government to support an EU oil embargo and other sanctions against Yugoslavia, but backed down after President Clerides had insisted that the legislation was necessary for Cyprus to demonstrate its willingness to coordinate its foreign policy with its future EU partners.

Following the withdrawal of the EDEK Socialist Party in December 1998 (see AR 1998, pp. 107-8), the Clerides coalition government—now consisting of the Democratic Rally (DISY), the United Democrats (EDI) and DIKO dissidents—suffered further political reverses in 1999. Beleaguered by corruption allegations, Dinos Michaelides (a DIKO defector) resigned as Interior Minister in March, the resultant reshuffle featuring the appointment of Takis Clerides (a distant relative of the President) to the vital post of Minister of Finance. Three further resignations in August, prompted by internal wrangling in DISY and by allegations of ministerial impropriety in the acquisition of shares in a company recently listed on the booming stock exchange, necessitated another round of new appointments, including that of Socrates Hasikos as Defence Minister. The air of scandal and instability in the cabinet led to opposition demands for President Clerides to step down and to call early elections. He insisted that he would see out his term until February 2003.

In the TRNC, the unlikely coalition between the right-wing, pro-Turkish-integrationist National Unity Party (UBP) and the centre-left, pro-federal Communal Liberation Party (TKP) survived the year. Neither party supported the Turkish-backed confederation concept, but in February both were publicly forced to endorse it under pressure from Ankara and threats by Dr Denktash that he would resign as negotiator if they did not. Aged 75, Dr Denktash announced that he would seek re-election as TRNC president in polling due in April 2000 elections. The UBP leader, Dervis Eroglu, and the centre-left Republican Turkish Party (CTP) leader, Mehmet Ali Talat, said that they would oppose him (although after the resumption of the negotiations there was speculation that Mr Ergolu might stand aside to leave Dr Denktash unopposed in the rightist camp).

vii. TURKEY

CAPITAL: Ankara   AREA: 779,000 sq km   POPULATION: 64,000,000 ('98)
OFFICIAL LANGUAGE: Turkish   POLITICAL SYSTEM: parliamentary democracy
HEAD OF STATE: President Süleyman Demirel (since May '93)
RULING PARTIES: Democratic Left (DSP), Nationalist Action (MHP) & Motherland (ANAP) parties
HEAD OF GOVERNMENT: Bülent Ecevit (DSP), Prime Minister (since Jan '99)
MAIN IGO MEMBERSHIPS (NON-UN): NATO, OSCE, OECD, CE, OIC, ECO, BSEC
CURRENCY: lira (end-'99 £1= LT874,186.2 US$1=LT542,400.0)
GNP PER CAPITA: US$3,160 by exchange-rate calculation ('98)

TURKEY went through a year marked by natural disaster, economic hardship and, paradoxically, rising optimism fed by the belief that the will had been found to end political instability and put in hand a programme of reform.

On 11 January the veteran centre-left politician Bülent Ecevit, leader of the Democratic Left Party (DSP), formed a caretaker minority administration for the purpose of holding parliamentary and local government elections simultaneously on 18 April. His popularity soared when on 16 February a Turkish commando captured the Kurdish rebel leader, Abdullah Öcalan, and flew him to Turkey from Nairobi, where he had been hiding on Greek diplomatic premises after a sojourn in Italy. As Mr Öcalan was put on trial on the prison island of Imralı in the Sea of Marmara, his organization, the Kurdistan Workers' Party (PKK), staged violent protests throughout Europe, causing a drop of one fifth in the number of foreign tourists visiting Turkey during the year.

However, political gains outweighed economic losses, and on 18 April Mr Ecevit's DSP increased its share of the total vote from 15 to 22 per cent and came first with 136 seats in the 550-member parliament. The second beneficiary of the wave of nationalist euphoria set off by Mr Öcalan's capture was the far-right Nationalist Action Party (MHP), which doubled its share of the poll to 18 per cent and gained 129 seats. Other parties lost ground. The Islamist Virtue Party (FP) dropped from 158 to 111 seats, as its share of the total poll fell from 21 to 15 per cent; the centre-right Motherland Party (ANAP) saw its support drop from 20 to 13 per cent and its parliamentary strength from 132 to 86; its rival on the centre-right, the True Path Party (DYP), led by Tansu Çiller, suffered similar losses (dropping from 135 to 85 seats, as its share of the vote fell from 19 to 12 per cent), while the centre-left Republican People's Party (CHP), founded by the father of the republic Kemal Atatürk was, for the first time ever, excluded from parliament as it polled less than 10 per cent of the total vote, the minimum needed for parliamentary representation. The CHP leader, Deniz Baykal, resigned as a result and was replaced by the journalist Altan Öymen. The Kurdish nationalist People's Democracy Party (HADEP) increased its share of the vote fractionally from 4.2 to 4.75 per cent. This did not entitle it to any seats in parliament, but in local government elections it won control of 37 towns in the south-eastern provinces.

On 29 May Mr Ecevit formed a new coalition with the MHP and ANAP. The MHP leader, Devlet Bahçeli, became Deputy Prime Minister, while the ANAP leader, Mesut Yılmaz, stayed out of the government as he was under investigation on charges of administrative impropriety. Relying on its solid majority, the government secured parliamentary approval for a record number of reforms. In response to criticism of Turkey's record on human rights, military judges were removed from state security courts, the grounds for banning political parties were reduced, penalties were increased for officials guilty of torture, a partial amnesty was decreed and many prisoners of conscience were released. On the economic front, the government raised the minimum age of retirement, allowed international arbitration in disputes between the state and foreign companies, improved banking supervision, harmonized customs regulations with those of the European Union (EU) and passed a number of fiscal reforms.

The security situation improved. Mr Öcalan, who was sentenced to death on 29 June, called on his followers to end their insurrection, which had cost some 30,000 lives over 15 years, and to leave the country by 1 September. The sentence on the PKK leader was confirmed by the Turkish Court of Appeal on 21 October, but the government heeded the stay of execution decreed by the European Court of Human Rights of the Council of Europe in Strasbourg pending its ruling on the legality of the trial. However, the question of Mr Öcalan's fate caused tension within the coalition as the year ended. President Süleyman Demirel and Prime Minister Ecevit were in favour of waiting for the completion of the lengthy legal process in Strasbourg, while the MHP argued that the Turkish parliament should not be deprived of its right to confirm the death sentence—a right it had not exercised for 15 years.

On 17 August an earthquake registering 7.4 on the Richter scale devastated Turkey's industrial heartland. The provincial centres of Izmit, Adapazari and Yalova suffered heavy damage, as did the naval base of Gölcük, on the Sea of Marmara, and a suburb of Istanbul. More than 17,000 people were killed, 40,000 injured and an estimated 600,000 rendered homeless, as some 250,000 residences and workplaces were destroyed. On 12 November another 700 people were killed as an earthquake measuring 7.2 on the Richter scale struck the town of Düzce, which had already been damaged in the first earthquake. The disaster brought out inadequacies in administration: government services were slow to respond, and widespread disregard for planning and building regulations contributed to the heavy death toll. On the other hand, local voluntary organizations acted quickly and foreign aid was available promptly on a large scale. The immediate arrival of rescue teams from the USA, Europe and Israel made a deep impression. The international aid effort affected Turkish perceptions of the outside world. Unstinting help from Greece, which Turkey reciprocated when Athens was struck by an earthquake in September, helped to improve relations which had been soured by the Öcalan affair (see II.4.v).

The US administration played a major part in placing Turkey at the centre of international attention. When Prime Minister Ecevit visited Washington at the end of September he was assured of American support for Turkish efforts to join the EU, but was left in no doubt that the USA wanted a settlement of Turkey's disagreements with Greece over Cyprus and the Aegean, and also wished to see improvements in the observance of human rights and the conduct of the economy in Turkey. The message was reinforced in October when the EU Commission in Brussels recommended that Turkey should be officially named a candidate for full membership, but that no date should be set for the beginning of negotiations until basic criteria for membership were met. The following month President Clinton made a highly successful official visit to Turkey, where he attended the summit meeting of the Organization for Security and Cooperation in Europe (see XI.5.ii). In the margins of the conference, political agreements were signed for the construction of oil and natural gas pipelines from the Caspian basin to Turkey. However, finance for these projects had still to be arranged. On 10 December an EU summit meeting in Helsinki endorsed the report of its Commission and named Turkey an official candidate for membership on an equal footing with other candidates. The political dialogue with the EU, which Turkey had suspended two years earlier when candidate status was denied it at Luxembourg, was to be resumed, with particular stress on the settlement of problems with Greece and Cyprus (see II.4.vi), and on human rights. The Turkish government accepted the formula and Mr Ecevit flew to Helsinki to take part in a line-up of candidates.

At the end of December the International Monetary Fund (IMF) accepted Turkey's letter of intent on measures to fight inflation and opened a $4,000 million stand-by credit. Simultaneously the Turkish parliament passed an austerity budget, increasing taxes and aiming at a substantial primary surplus as a means of reducing inflation from around 60 to 25 per cent by the end of the year 2000. While the economy contracted in 1999 by an estimated 5 per cent and the public debt increased (partly as a result of increased expenditure and the fall in revenues occasioned by the earthquakes), the promise of better economic management led to a rapid rise in market confidence. Interest on treasury bills fell from over 100 to under 50 per cent, and the index of the Istanbul stock exchange, which stood at 2,598 points at the end of 1998, closed the year at a record level of 15,209 points.

Thus a year in which natural disaster struck, and living standards fell, closed on a note of remarkable optimism. Turkey's inclusion in Group of 20, the consultative group of aspirants to the club of rich nations, symbolized the widespread hope that the main obstacles to Turkey's political and economic development were finally being overcome.

III CENTRAL AND EASTERN EUROPE

1. POLAND—BALTIC REPUBLICS—CZECH REPUBLIC—
SLOVAKIA—HUNGARY—ROMANIA—BULGARIA

i. POLAND

CAPITAL: Warsaw   AREA: 313,000 sq km   POPULATION: 38,600,000 ('98)
OFFICIAL LANGUAGE: Polish   POLITICAL SYSTEM: presidential democracy
HEAD OF STATE: President Aleksander Kwasniewski (since Dec '95)
RULING PARTIES: Solidarity Electoral Alliance Movement (AWS) & Freedom Union (UW)
HEAD OF GOVERNMENT: Jerzy Buzek (AWS), Prime Minister (since Oct '97)
MAIN IGO MEMBERSHIPS (NON-UN): : NATO, OSCE, CE, PFP, CEI, CEFTA, CBSS
CURRENCY: new zloty (end-'99 £1= Zl.6.67, US$1=Zl.4.14)
GNP PER CAPITA: US$3,900 by exchange-rate calculation, US$6,740 at PPP ('98)

POLAND's centre-right coalition, in power since September 1997 (see AR 1997, p. 105), sustained its policies of market-led reform and a more-balanced state budget against a no-confidence vote in the lower house (Sejm) and increasingly vocal extra-parliamentary opposition, especially from the peasantry. The government thus kept the country on track for European Union (EU) accession, though West European leaders warned that its hopes of achieving full membership by the year 2003 were 'optimistic'.

The annual budget, passed on 9 January, forecast increased growth of 5.1 per cent, following the previous year's 4.8 per cent, reduced after the Russian financial crisis of August 1998. Annual inflation was set to fall from 9.5 per cent (1998) to 8.1 per cent. The country thus kept to the phased reductions aiming at a target of 4 per cent inflation in 2003. But the announced cut of the annual budget deficit from 2.8 per cent to 2.18 per cent of GDP aroused immediate controversy.

Farmers' protest groups renewed earlier actions in mid-January, blockading roads and border crossings for a third month. Their overall objective was to retain state subsidies for labour-intensive agriculture, currently employing 20 per cent of the workforce but contributing a shrinking proportion of GDP. Specific demands included higher tariffs on food imports and cheap credits to compensate for lower domestic food prices. On 28 January the government agreed to a 50 per cent increase in the state subsidy for pork. But rural protests continued, coordinated by a Farmers' Self-Defence Union led by Andrzej Lepper. On 8 February the authorities acceded to most of their demands, including an amnesty for all those who had taken part in illegal protests. A joint agricultural reform committee, drawn from both sides, was to consider the unresolved issues: rural debt, subsidies for other meats, dairy products and grain. But Mr Lepper rejected this agreement and announced further actions, to include a general blockade of movement in the countryside.

A second set of protests followed health service reforms introduced on 1

January. These aimed to bring market forces into a system virtually unchanged since the communist period. But the attempt to introduce consumer choice confused many patients, unclear where to attend for treatment. They also led to demands from health workers for substantial pay increases, to be offset by an increase in national insurance contribution from 7.5 per cent to 11 per cent of basic earnings.

The health service reforms led to ructions within the ruling coalition. The senior partner, the Solidarity Electoral Action Movement (AWS)—of which the Prime Minister Jerzy Buzek became chairman on 17 January—was challenged by its junior, the Freedom Union (UW), which demanded the removal of Deputy Health Minister Jacek Wutzow for mishandling the reforms. He was dismissed on 20 January, but health service strikes continued until an interim agreement was reached with protestors on 20 February.

The ruling coalition was also beset by issues of privatization. Far-reaching legislative proposals by the AWS to distribute state assets to private citizens were withdrawn, but conflict continued. The government was pruned in March, eight deputy prime ministers and all ministers without portfolio being removed. The cabinet was reduced to 17 members and ministerial advisers cut by two-thirds. Further casualties in face of popular protests included the Minister for Agriculture, who resigned on 15 March, and the Minister of Health, replaced by Franciszka Cegielska. Three days later Leszek Balcerowicz, Deputy Prime Minister and main architect (since 1989) of Poland's economic reform, faced a motion of no confidence in the Sejm, tabled by the Polish Peasant Party. This opposed the programme for reducing the state budget deficit, but the ruling coalition retained its programme by a vote of 228 to 180.

By contrast, there was parliamentary unity on foreign affairs. On 17 February the lower house ratified NATO accession by 409-7 (with four abstentions) and the Senate did likewise by 92-2. On 26 February the President Aleksander Kwasniewski and his Czech counterpart, Václav Havel, signed documents confirming this decision. A formal accession ceremony, including Hungary, took place on 12 March (see XI.2.i). Under a 15-year programme of modernization of the Polish armed forces, adopted in September 1997, there was to be an eventual reduction in strength to 180,000 and greater reliance on professionals. In 1998 Poland had some 141,600 conscripts in its total military complement of 240,650. From January 1999 the length of their compulsory military service was reduced from 18 to 12 months.

EU entry moved forward more slowly. On 6 September German Chancellor Gerhard Schröder, apologizing for the Nazi attack 60 years earlier, supported Poland's bid for full membership of the EU. But he stated that entry by 2003 was 'ambitious', and no timetable was forthcoming from Brussels.

Rural demonstrations resumed in mid-August and were dispersed by riot police, of whom over 80 were injured. On 25 August the Farmers' Self-Defence Union called for the resignation of both government and parliament, promising further 'social protest' if they did not comply. The organization declared a Peasant-National Self-Defence Bloc, which was intended to a 'third force' (with the Polish Peasant Party) in future elections. On 20 September health workers protested against the government's failure to honour wage increases agreed after earlier stoppages in July. This was followed by a mass protest in Warsaw on 24 September. This time farmers, miners and other industrial workers marched together to demand the resignation of the Prime Minister and Finance Minister.

Growing opposition in parliament put pressure on the Prime Minister to reshuffle his cabinet or resign. He rejected these alternatives, declaring that he would improve reforms of the health system and education and revise plans for privately-funded pensions. Reminding parliament that his government had two years left, he announced that it would complete its term of office. Even so, the ruling coalition was reshuffled on 11 October. Marek Biernacki was appointed Interior Minister and a two-year policy statement was issued.

Coal miners protested in Warsaw the next day at the lack of funding for the restructuring of their industry. This measure, announced in 1998, aimed to reduce the country's dependence on coal, which still provided most of Poland's energy. Part of the replacement was to be imported natural gas, set to reach 15 per cent of energy requirements by 2010. A government agreement with the miners was reached on 23 October.

Settling of accounts with the communist past came somewhat closer. Unlike the former East Germany, where Stasi files were put in the public domain, Poland proceeded cautiously with declassification of secret documents. On 5 May the Public Interest Ombudsman rejected claims of collaboration made against the Prime Minister, brought by the right-wing Confederation of Independent Poland–Fatherland (KPN-O), whose witnesses included secret service agents alleging they had employed him. Nonetheless, parliament agreed that the Ombudsman should be given access to former Ministry of Interior secret files for vetting purposes. Politicians who were shown to have lied about their previous collaboration with the communist authorities would be disbarred from public office for ten years. At the end of the year it was decided to transfer all secret service police records for the communist period to a National Remembrance Institute (IPN). This new body, under a council to be elected by the Sejm, would decide which documents to make public.

Two controversial episodes were revisited. The Supreme Court in Warsaw ordered the reopening of the 1995 trial of former communist leader (and former President), General Wojciech Jaruzelski. He was charged with ordering the use of force against peaceful demonstrations on the coast while Minister of Defence in 1970, with the result that 44 were shot dead and hundreds wounded. Similarly, the trial of 22 riot policemen accused of killing nine miners during the imposition of martial law in December 1981, proceedings against whom had ended inconclusively after almost five years, resumed in Katowice.

An emotive 'battle of the crosses' ended on 28 May when police and army units removed some 300 crosses erected by radical Catholics outside the former concentration camp at Auschwitz. The organizer of the planting of the crosses, veteran activist Kazimierz Switon, was to face public order charges.

However, the cross erected to commemorate the visit to the site by Pope John Paul II in 1979 remained. The Pope made his longest pilgrimage to his native land on 5-17 June, beginning in the Gdansk region, where he held a Mass before a congregation of 700,000. In an unprecedented address to parliament on 11 June, he endorsed Poland's bid for membership of the European Union, but observed that economic development must be based on ethical principles and spirituality.

ii. ESTONIA—LATVIA—LITHUANIA

Estonia
CAPITAL: Tallinn   AREA: 45,000 sq km   POPULATION: 1,500,000 ('98)
OFFICIAL LANGUAGE: Estonian   POLITICAL SYSTEM: democratic republic
HEAD OF STATE: President Lennart Meri (since Oct '92)
RULING PARTIES: Pro Patria Union, Moderate & Reform parties
HEAD OF GOVERNMENT: Mart Laar (Pro Patria), Prime Minister (since March '99)
MAIN IGO MEMBERSHIPS (NON-UN): OSCE, CE, PFP, CBSS
CURRENCY: kroon (end-'99 £1= K25.16, US$1=K15.61)
GNP PER CAPITA: US$3,390 by exchange-rate calculation ('98)

Latvia
CAPITAL: Riga   AREA: 64,000 sq km   POPULATION: 2,600,000 ('98)
OFFICIAL LANGUAGE: Latvian   POLITICAL SYSTEM: democratic republic
HEAD OF STATE: President Vaira Vike-Freiberga (since July '99)
RULING PARTIES: People's Party (TP) heads coalition
HEAD OF GOVERNMENT: Andris Skele (TP), Prime Minister (since July '99)
MAIN IGO MEMBERSHIPS (NON-UN): OSCE, CE, PFP, CBSS
CURRENCY: lats (end-'99 £1= L0.95, US$1=L0.59)
GNP PER CAPITA: US$2,430 by exchange-rate calculation ('98)

Lithuania
CAPITAL: Vilnius   AREA: 65,000 sq km   POPULATION: 4,000,000 ('98)
OFFICIAL LANGUAGE: Lithuanian   POLITICAL SYSTEM: democratic republic
HEAD OF STATE: President Valdas Adamkus (since Feb '98)
RULING PARTIES: Homeland Union (TS) heads coalition
HEAD OF GOVERNMENT: Andrius Kubilius (TS), Prime Minister (since Nov '99)
MAIN IGO MEMBERSHIPS (NON-UN): OSCE, CE, PFP, CBSS
CURRENCY: litas (end-'99 £1=L6.45, US$1=L4.00)
GNP PER CAPITA: US$2,440 by exchange-rate calculation, US$4,310 at PPP ('98)

THE turnout for the parliamentary elections in ESTONIA on 7 March proved to be the lowest since independence, with almost 50 per cent of the electorate staying away from the polls. Edgar Savisaar's tightly-organized Centre Party, drawing on the support of the less well-off and hinting at greater state intervention in the economy, headed the voting with 28 seats. However, the charismatic Mr Savisaar was thwarted from returning to government by the formation of a coalition commanding 53 of the 101 seats in the Riigikogu, between the Pro Patria Union, the Reform Party and the Moderates. The Moderates benefited from the support of the People's Party under Toomas Hendrik Ilves, who was appointed Foreign Minister in the new administration. Reform Party leader and former Bank of Estonia President Siim Kallas became Finance Minister, notwithstanding investigations into his role in the disappearance of moneys advanced by the central bank in 1993 to the now defunct North Estonian Bank. Mart Laar, head of the Pro Patria Union (successor to the Pro Patria party which had governed Estonia from 1992 to 1994 under Mr Laar's premiership), returned to the Prime Minister's office.

Mr Laar's cabinet was sworn in on 25 March, but none of the politicians matched the public approval ratings of President Lennart Meri, who celebrated his 70th birthday in April. His great success and outspokenness on major issues continued to mislead many into thinking that his position was more important than that of the Prime Minister. Interestingly, the ruling coalition voted in November against a bill sponsored by the Centre Party calling for direct presidential elections, although opinion polls suggested overwhelming public support for such a step.

Additional backing for the ruling coalition came when it also gained control of Tallinn in local elections on 17 October. In general, the administration firmly committed itself to sustaining Estonia's remarkable economic progress, although the Human Development Report released on 10 December by the UN Development Programme advised that greater attention should be given to issues thrown up by the reform process, such as economic and income stratification, unemployment, poverty, regional imbalances, gender inequality and rising drug abuse and crime.

Social problems were duly exploited by the opposition Social Democrats in LATVIA. During the spring Latvia's three social democratic political groups merged to form one Social Democratic Workers' Party under the chairmanship of Juris Bojars, who frankly admitted that 'you have to work with what you can get'. The price of Social Democratic support for Vilis Kristopans's minority coalition on a number of key issues, including increased defence spending in the budget, was the post of Minister of Agriculture. The Social Democratic group helped to scuttle opposition-sponsored votes of no confidence in Mr Kristopans on 20 May and on 2 June. However, there were cumulative blows to the shaky administration, including the defeat of its various presidential candidates in June by the Canadian-Latvian academic Vaira Vike-Freiberga in seven rounds of voting in the Saeima. In addition, a rift developed between Mr Kristopans and his coalition partners in the Union for Fatherland and Freedom/LNNK on how to reduce the yawning budget deficit. The beleaguered Prime Minister resigned on 5 July, whereupon parliament on 16 July voted to install Andris Skele of the People's Party (TP) as his successor. Mr Skele committed himself to tackling the financial and economic crisis on the basis of a programme already agreed between the TP and the Union for Fatherland and Freedom/LNNK.

In LITHUANIA, the opposition Lithuanian Democratic Labour Party (LDDP) launched a series of calls for Prime Minister Gediminas Vagnorius to resign, accusing him among other things of inept and corrupt handling of the energy sector. The large centre-right majority in parliament kept him in office until

May, when he was replaced by the immensely popular Conservative mayor of Vilnius, Rolandas Paksas. An active pilot, Mr Paksas was eventually brought to earth by a deal between the Mazeikiu Nafta refinery and the American-based Williams International oil company. Mr Paksas alone in his cabinet refused to approve the arrangement, which entailed Lithuania making a large loan to the Williams group, and he resigned on 27 October. Andrius Kubilius of the Conservative Party became Prime Minister on 3 November, Mr Paksas being consoled by a job created specially for him, as President Adamkus's envoy for special assignments.

The governments of all three Baltic states once more underlined in discussions in Riga in June their joint commitment to entry to both the European Union (EU) and NATO. Contrary to earlier indications, the closure of the Ignalina nuclear power plant did not become a formal precondition for Lithuania's further progress towards EU membership. Germany's Foreign Minister, Joschka Fischer, indicated an important shift in EU thinking when he called in Tallinn in early September for upgrading the so-called second group of EU aspirants, which included Lithuania and Latvia, so that they would be put on a par with Estonia, already in the first group. Such a procedure was adopted at the EU summit in Helsinki in December (see XI.4), this decision marking the effective abandonment of the unpopular notion that some countries, including Estonia, had been on a special fast track. Full preparedness for EU membership was made the sole condition for entry, achievement of which henceforth depended on the rate at which the Baltic and other aspirants could complete the harmonization of national legislation with that of the EU. Latvian Foreign Minister Indulis Berzins observed: 'The tier system was wrong and it was recognized as being wrong. Our idea is simple: the best should be first.'

As to NATO expansion, all three Baltic governments agreed to try to reach the unofficial average of NATO members' current expenditure on defence, namely 2 per cent of GDP. A report by US Congressional Research Services in February put Lithuania among the top three applicants for NATO entry, alongside Slovenia and Slovakia. Other encouragement for Baltic membership came from US Secretary of State Madeleine Albright, who in July hinted that invitations might be forthcoming by 2002. European voices were far more cautious, however. In contrast to his unqualified commitment to early EU entry for the Baltic states, German Foreign Minister Fischer said that NATO's main goal for the moment remained the tightening of ties between its members. Russia's attitude to further NATO enlargement was graphically expressed in August by the Deputy Chairman of the Russian Duma, Sergei Baburin, who asserted during a visit to the Russian enclave of Kaliningrad on the Baltic coast that Moscow should never allow the Baltic states to become fully-fledged members of NATO.

Russia contrasted its resistance to further NATO expansion with its acceptance of EU enlargement towards the Baltics. That did not prevent it from muddying the waters by further attacks on the alleged maltreatment of ethnic Russians in Estonia and Latvia. In this respect it was able to exploit EU concerns about language laws in these two states. In Estonia amendments coming into force in June established requirements for a minimum level of Estonian for public servants, local government workers and individual entrepreneurs—24 teachers in the heavily Russian-populated north-east of Estonia being immediately targeted as having an inadequate command of Estonian. In Latvia a requirement that ethnic Russian teachers should have Latvian language certificates came into force in January, and in July the Saeima passed legislation requiring all state and municipal public meetings to be conducted in Latvian. Criticism of such policies from the Organization for Security and Cooperation in Europe (OSCE) had some impact in Latvia, where incoming President Vike-Freiberga persuaded parliament to tone down the July law to reduce its impact on the private sector. An earlier proposal to ban multi-lingual public signs was also abandoned. The commitment of the Presidents of both countries to their respective national languages remained absolute, however: Soviet colonization in the past had after all come perilously close to making Estonians and Latvians minorities in their own lands.

The long shadows of history were also cast in January during the prosecution of a former Soviet security officer in Estonia for deporting families to Siberia, resulting in the first-ever conviction for crimes against humanity in Estonia. In Latvia too, there were charges of genocide mounted against former Soviet security officers. Placed alongside the Estonian and Lithuanian parliaments' denunciation of Moscow's action against the Chechen people (see III.3.i), the trials of former Soviet officials inevitably soured Baltic-Russian relations. However, such cases also highlighted the need for the Baltic peoples themselves to re-examine their own past more fully, in particular their role in war crimes conducted under Nazi occupation.

The worldwide public concern at the sudden though brief appearance in Britain at the end of the year of an alleged Latvian participant in World War II crimes, Konrad Kalejs, immediately threw up questions about Latvia's commitment to prosecuting Nazi as opposed to Soviet 'war criminals'. The Latvian Commission of Historians had already been criticized in November, for example, for the 'intermingling and confusion' of the Jewish Holocaust and Soviet atrocities. That the Latvian government was alive to the potential political damage of such issues was clear from its decision to reverse the policy it had adopted in 1998 and to distance itself officially from the commemoration in March for veterans of the wartime Latvian Legion.

iii. CZECH REPUBLIC

CAPITAL: Prague AREA: 30,450 sq km POPULATION: 10,500,000 ('98)
OFFICIAL LANGUAGE: Czech POLITICAL SYSTEM: parliamentary democracy
HEAD OF STATE: President Václav Havel (since Jan '93)
RULING PARTY: Czech Social Democratic Party (CSSD)
HEAD OF GOVERNMENT: Milos Zeman (CSSD), Prime Minister (since July '98)
MAIN IGO MEMBERSHIPS (NON-UN): NATO, OSCE, CE, PFP, CEI, CEFTA, OECD
CURRENCY: koruna (end-'99 £1= K57.88, US$1=K35.91)
GNP PER CAPITA: US$5,040 by exchange-rate calculation ('98)

IN the Czech Republic, the year was characterized by political controversy and economic problems. The ruling Social Democrats (CSSD) continued to have a difficult time passing legislation through the parliament because Prime Minister Milos Zeman's one-party government lacked a parliamentary majority. Although the country's economic problems and poor marks in meeting European Union (EU) accession requirements led to calls for the creation of a majority cabinet, no appropriate combination of parties could be found, mainly because of personality clashes among party chairmen.

The CSSD and the Civic Democratic Party (ODS) continued their 'opposition agreement', according to which the ODS tolerated the CSSD cabinet and promised not to back a vote of no-confidence in the government. However, the ODS refused to take responsibility for CSSD policies and refrained from supporting a number of legislative measures proposed by the government. The two parties planned controversial election law changes that would put their smaller competitors at a disadvantage as well as measures to reduce the powers of the President. A loose coalition of four small and medium-sized centre-right parties—including the parliamentary Christian Democrats (KDU-CSL) and the Freedom Union—continued their efforts to block their two bigger rivals. Independent businessman Vaclav Fischer's victory in a by-election on 28 August stripped the CSSD and ODS of their constitutional majority in the Senate.

Of three ministerial changes in 1999, the most important was the dismissal of Finance Minister Ivo Svoboda in July over a bankruptcy controversy and his replacement by Deputy Premier Pavel Mertlik. The other two were the exit of Deputy Premier Egon Lansky in November and of Health Minister Ivan David in December, the former being succeeded by Foreign Minister Jan Kavan and the latter temporarily by Deputy Premier Vladimir Spidla. The dismissal in January of the head of the Czech secret service (BIS), Karel Vulterin, for 'serious professional mistakes', was followed by the naming on television of the Prague head of station of the British MI6 intelligence service, who was said to have instigated the dismissal. In November the parliament approved the introduction of an ombudsman. It also adopted legislation permitting Czechs to hold dual citizenship and allowing Czechs living in exile to reclaim their citizenship.

By April public opinion polls showed that support for the ODS had surpassed that for the CSSD, and by July even the Communists had pulled ahead of the CSSD. In a sign of disillusionment with the 'opposition agreement', from October many polls put the Communists in first place. Calling for more discussion of public issues, a group of Czech intellectuals published an appeal entitled 'Impulse 99' in July. In commemorating the tenth anniversary of the November 1989 velvet revolution, former student leaders called on top political leaders to step down. These efforts were backed by more than 100,000 demonstrators in early December, but only Freedom Union chairman Jan Ruml resigned. At a party congress in May, Jan Kasal was elected KDU-CSL chairman.

Annual inflation increased slightly to just 2.5 per cent in 1999, while the unemployment rate rose steadily throughout the year and reached 9.4 per cent by December. One of the government's key priorities was to encourage economic growth, and gross domestic product grew by 0.8 per cent in the third quarter despite expectations of further decline. The cabinet attempted to put the blame for the country's economic problems on its predecessors. After considerable delay, the 1999 budget was approved in January, thanks to support from the opposition Communists and KDU-CSL.

In June the state's 66 per cent share of the Československa Obchodni Banka was sold to the Belgian bank KBC, marking the biggest sale in the history of Czech privatization. The government also made plans to privatize the two other banks that remained in state hands. In an attempt to save the Czech Republic's largest ailing firms, the cabinet approved a revitalization programme in April. After considerable deliberation, the government decided in May to complete the Temelin nuclear power plant, despite a European Parliament resolution that criticized the project. In a negative signal for foreign investors, the Bermuda-based CME began proceedings in August against the Czech Republic under the Bilateral Investment Treaty because of a controversy over private television station TV Nova.

Tensions continued to exist between Czechs and Roma (Gypsies). The construction of a wall separating a Romani community from a residential area in Usti nad Labem created considerable controversy before being pulled down in November. Church-state relations were also problematic, since the government questioned the Catholic Church's right to restitution of property confiscated in the communist era.

Although the Czech Republic's formal accession to NATO on 12 March symbolized its entry into the West (see XI.2.i), the country's commitment to that organization was questioned because of Czech politicians' lack of support for NATO air-strikes against Serbia over Kosovo (see III.2.vi). The Czechs were also criticized for damaging NATO unity when the Czech and Greek Foreign Ministers signed a joint initiative in May on the resolution of the Kosovo crisis. Moreover, the Czechs were repeatedly scolded for moving too slowly in adopting EU legislation, and the country received repeated warnings from EU representatives that the country was falling behind other first-round applicants. With social democratic governments in both countries, Czech-German relations warmed, marked by a series of high-level bilateral visits. Ties with Slovakia also strengthened considerably, and the longrunning dispute over the division of state property of former Czechoslovakia was finally resolved in November.

iv. SLOVAKIA

CAPITAL: Bratislava   AREA: 18,930 sq km   POPULATION: 5,600,000 ('98)
OFFICIAL LANGUAGE: Slovak   POLITICAL SYSTEM: parliamentary democracy
HEAD OF STATE: President Rudolf Schuster (since June '99)
RULING PARTIES: coalition of Slovak Democratic Coalition (SDK), Party of the Democratic Left (SDL), Party of the Hungarian Coalition (SMK) & Party of Civic Understanding (SOP)
HEAD OF GOVERNMENT: Mikulas Dzurinda (SDK)), Prime Minister (since Oct '98)
MAIN IGO MEMBERSHIPS (NON-UN): OSCE, CE, PFP, CEI, CEFTA
CURRENCY: koruna (end-'99 £1=K68.22, US$1=K42.33)
GNP PER CAPITA: US$3,700 by exchange-rate calculation ('98)

ALTHOUGH not an easy year for Slovakia, 1999 brought progress in politics, economic reform and foreign relations. Prime Minister Mikulas Dzurinda's government, which took office in October 1998 (see AR 1998, p. 120), faced economic problems, conflicts within the four-party ruling coalition, as well as the challenge of bringing Slovakia into the first group of countries in line for membership the European Union (EU). The government's greatest success was the decision of the EU's December summit in Helsinki to invite Slovakia to begin formal accession talks in 2000 (see XI.4).

By July the cabinet had met all the political criteria that the EU had recommended to the previous government as a condition for entry, including the approval of a law on the use of minority languages. Another important political achievement was the holding of direct presidential elections in May after a vacancy in that position for more than one year. The ruling coalition's candidate, Rudolf Schuster, defeated former Prime Minister Vladimir Meciar by a wide margin despite the fact that Slovakia was experiencing economic difficulties at the time of the elections. Mr Schuster claimed that he wanted to be the President of all citizens of Slovakia, and he criticized both the ruling coalition and the opposition. In August the new President refused to call an opposition-backed referendum on the minority language law and privatization of strategic firms that was widely considered to be unconstitutional.

In 1999 police reopened the investigation into several controversial cases involving representatives of the previous ruling parties, including the 1995 kidnapping of former President Michal Kovác's son (see AR 1995, pp. 108; 1996, pp. 103-4). However, these efforts were complicated by amnesties issued by Mr Meciar in 1998 while serving as acting President. The Dzurinda government resisted the temptation to place a political appointee at the head of the National Bank of Slovakia, and former deputy governor Marian Jusko took over the position of governor in July. In November President Schuster proposed nine new Constitutional Court judges and named Justice Ministry state secretary Jan Mazak as the court's new chairman, although they were not scheduled to take office until January 2000.

Several new political parties were formed in 1999, including Ivan Mjartan's Party of the Democratic Centre and Robert Fico's Smer (Direction) party. Mr Dzurinda's Slovak Democratic Coalition showed signs of strain since many deputies returned to their original parties. A series of public scandals brought a significant drop in the government's popularity, and there were calls for a cabinet reshuffle by mid-year. Transport and Telecommunications Minister Gabriel Palacka left office in August, being replaced by Jozef Macejko, and was followed in October by Economy Minister Ludovit Cernak, the latter's replacement being Lubomir Harach. The chairmanship of several parliamentary parties changed hands in 1999, with Pavol Hamzik being elected as Party of Civic Understanding chairman in July and Anna Malikova becoming Slovak National Party chairwoman in October. Throughout the year Mr Meciar's opposition Movement for a Democratic Slovakia topped public opinion polls.

After some hesitation, the Dzurinda government managed to take a number of unpopular but necessary steps to turn the economy around. The announcement in May of a 'revitalization program', which included an increase in the lower rate of VAT, an import surcharge, price deregulation and cuts in state administrative personnel, won praise from domestic and international analysts and put a halt to speculation against the Slovak currency. Because of increased demand for Slovak exports, the economy narrowly managed to avoid recession, although GDP growth fell to just 0.6 per cent in the third quarter. Unemployment grew to a high of 19.2 per cent in December, while annual inflation reached 14.2 per cent. The difficult economic situation was accompanied by increasing demands by the Confederation of Trade Unions, which in June sent Mr Dzurinda a long list of demands. In September approximately 40,000 trade unionists demonstrated in Bratislava.

Slovakia's warming relations with the EU were matched by improved ties with neighbouring countries. The Slovaks and Czechs resolved their dispute over the division of the state property of former Czechoslovakia in November, while Slovakia and Hungary agreed to rebuild a highly symbolic bridge over the Danube that had been destroyed during World War II. Nonetheless, Slovakia had difficulties with some Western countries because of an outflow of Slovak Roma (Gypsies) seeking asylum and with Austria because of delay in decommissioning the controversial Jaslovske Bohunice nuclear power plant.

v. HUNGARY

CAPITAL: Budapest   AREA: 93,000 sq km   POPULATION: 10,250,000 ('98)
OFFICIAL LANGUAGE: Hungarian   POLITICAL SYSTEM: parliamentary democracy
HEAD OF STATE: President Arpád Göncz (since Aug '90)
RULING PARTIES: Young Democrats (Fidesz) head coalition with Independent Smallholders' Party (FKGP) & Hungarian Democratic Forum (MDF)
HEAD OF GOVERNMENT: Viktor Orban (Fidesz-MPP), Prime Minister (since July '98)
MAIN IGO MEMBERSHIPS (NON-UN): NATO, OSCE, CE, PFP, CEI, CEFTA
CURRENCY: forint (end-'99 £1= Ft409.40, US$1=Ft254.02)
GNP PER CAPITA: US$4,510 by exchange-rate calculation ('98)

THE dominant event in 1999 for Hungary was the war in south-east Europe. Hungary had entered NATO as a full member only 12 days before the outbreak of hostilities on 24 March and neither the elite nor wider opinion was prepared for participation in war. Indeed, as some commentators were ready to point out, the situation was fraught with contradictions. For much of the 1990s the West had urged Hungary to make peace with its neighbours in order to qualify for membership of Western institutions. Having done so, Hungary immediately found itself at war with one of them, Serbia. Furthermore, Hungary had no real quarrel with Serbia and, if anything, had an interest in avoiding exacerbating the position of the Hungary minority there. Above all, there was real fear that, if it came to a land campaign, Hungary would be used as the invasion channel given its geo-strategic position abutting on northern Serbia.

In the event, Hungary adopted a cautiously supportive stance towards the hostilities. NATO air forces were, of course, given full overflying rights and US planes used bases in Hungary without any conditions. However, Hungarian opinion was deeply divided about the advisability and moral justification of the bombing, not least whether it was proper to launch a campaign of violence in support of human rights.

At the same time, the centre-right and the nationalists, with different degrees of emphasis, used the war as an occasion to raise the question of the ethnic Hungarian minority in the Serbian province of Vojvodina. The moderates, clearly including the government, sought to establish a linkage between Kosovo and Vojvodina, roughly to the effect that, if Serbs were thought unreliable in making provisions for the ethnic and human rights of their Albanian minority, would they be any better with respect to their Hungarians? However, the government made it very clear that Hungary was not in any way pursuing frontier revision, though the extreme right was less reticent in this regard. In fact, the Hungarian government admitted that its linkage initiative had failed. The West in general and the US in particular could only focus on one issue at a time, and that happened to be Kosovo.

The Prime Minister, Viktor Orban, did make a major speech in August in which he outlined his government's perspective on the question of Hungarians living beyond the frontiers of Hungary. He argued that all Hungarians belonged to the Hungarian nation and that the Hungarian state had an interest in their having 'full opportunity to education and cultural fulfilment' in the mother tongue. This formulation was evidently within the current conception of ethnic rights in Europe. Linked to this was the proposal to give voting rights to citizens of Hungary if they lived abroad, although the project would not enfranchise non-citizen ethnic Hungarians. It was envisaged that the status of ethnic Hungarians abroad, who faced serious curtailment of their right of entry under the Schengen rules of the European Union (EU) once Hungary had been admitted to full membership, would be settled over the next few years.

As far as relations with other neighbouring states were concerned, there was a cautious improvement with Slovakia. The Slovak government moved towards the restoration of some of the rights that the Hungarian minority had lost under the Meciar government (1994-1998), but was regarded as less generous and slower than it might have been. However, the joint decision to rebuild the bridge across the Danube at Esztergom-Sturovo, which had been blown up in 1944 and had never been reconstructed, was seen as a positive signal (see also III.1.iv). In the case of Romania, the Hungarian government had probably come to conclusion that it could expect little or nothing from the rather weak government in power in Bucharest as far as Hungarian-language university education, a central concern, was concerned. This had been a major issue in 1998 (see AR 1998, p. 123). Hence the decision to support a private ecumenical initiative to set up a Christian university with Hungarian as the language of instruction.

In its quest for EU membership, Hungary appeared to have faced up to the reality that because of obstacles within the EU the chances of membership by 2002 were nil. Mr Orban was critical of the slow progress, using strong language in an interview with *Tagesspiegel* in September, but there was no alternative. It was most unlikely, according to EU sources, that Hungary's negotiations for entry could be completed by 2001, and ratification would require another two years at least.

On the domestic political front, polarization was evident in attitudes between the centre-left opposition and the centre-right government. From the perspective of the former, the latter could do nothing right, its critiques being articulated in ever more vehement terms. Hungarian commentators used the terms 'cultural struggle' or 'cultural war' to describe the situation. In essence, the divide was over different visions of the nation and its place in Europe. The opposition sought to marginalize the national-cultural element in the Hungarian approach, seeing all manifestations of the nation as nationalistic or fascistic, while the moderate centre-right insisted that Hungarians had a national identity as well as other peoples and that it could not be neglected.

The entire issue debouched into the complex and sensitive area of anti-semitism. For the c.100,000-strong Jewish community, all references to Hungarian nationhood were suspect, tantamount to a first step towards Nazism, so that there were instances of overreaction and exaggeration of the threat to the Jewish community. All the same, the extreme right, which was indeed anti-semitic, encouraged these anxieties by its xenophobic language.

It was striking that the political atmosphere deteriorated despite relatively favourable economic figures. GDP expanded by an impressive 4-5 per cent in 1999, direct foreign investment continued (some $17,000 million having flowed into the country in 1990-98), and inflation was slowly coming under control (down from 14 per cent in 1998 to c.10 per cent in 1999). Hence the 'cultural war' was only indirectly linked to economic factors—to the fear on the left that the government would benefit from the upturn at the next elections due in 2002.

vi. ROMANIA

CAPITAL: Bucharest   AREA: 237,500 sq km   POPULATION: 23,000,000 ('98)
OFFICIAL LANGUAGE: Romanian   POLITICAL SYSTEM: presidential democracy
HEAD OF STATE: President Emil Constantinescu (since Nov '96)
RULING PARTIES: Christian Democratic National Peasants' Party (PNTCD) heads coalition including Hungarian Democratic Union of Romania (UDMR), Democratic Party (PD) & National Liberal Party (PNL)
HEAD OF GOVERNMENT: Mugur Isarescu (non-party), Prime Minister (since Dec '99)
MAIN IGO MEMBERSHIPS (NON-UN): OSCE, CE, CEI, PFP, BSEC
CURRENCY: leu (end-'99 £1=L29,413.5, US$1=18,250.0)
GNP PER CAPITA: US$1,390 by exchange-rate calculation, US$3,970 at PPP ('98)

POLITICAL turmoil, social unrest and economic recession were the dominant themes of Romania's year—a fittingly depressing end to the 1990s, which had disappointed the post-communist expectations of so many Romanians. From a violent miners' march on Bucharest in January to the appointment of a new Prime Minister, Mugur Isarescu, in December, Romania seemed to be lurching from one crisis to another with, at times, little sense of direction or unity at the top. The political and economic uncertainty further undermined public support for the parties in the broad-based governing coalition; and prompted a higher-than-ever proportion of people (61 per cent) to state in opinion polls that things had been better in the communist era.

The year began ominously with a bitter miners' strike in the traditionally militant Jiu valley. The dispute over pit closures and wage increases turned serious when the charismatic miners' leader, Miron Cozma, launched a march on Bucharest, and about 20,000 of his supporters broke through police lines. For a while it seemed possible that the march might lead to a repetition of the events of September 1991 when the miners went on the rampage in Bucharest, an action that had resulted in the dismissal of the reformist Prime Minister, Petre Roman (see AR 1991, p. 162). This time firm action by the security forces eventually halted the marchers at Cozia, 100 miles north of Bucharest; and lengthy negotiations led to a compromise deal.

The government was badly shaken by the events. Gavril Dejeu, the Minister of the Interior, was among officials dismissed for the initial failure of the police to halt the miners. He was replaced by Constantin Dudu Ionescu, a former deputy defence minister. Within weeks of the agreement, Mr Cozma, for long the scourge of reform-minded governments, was sentenced to 18 years' imprisonment by the Supreme Court for his role in the 1991 disturbances. The ruling replaced an earlier three-year sentence passed by the Appeal Court; both judgments were widely regarded as politically-motivated sentences handed down by judges with different loyalties.

The miners' action was followed by several waves of industrial unrest. During the worst of these, in May and June, strikes were held by workers in the steel industry, on the Bucharest Metro and in the tractor and helicopter plants in Brasov. They were followed by stoppages by staff in the health service and by teachers and lecturers. There was also a one-day general work stoppage on 24 May, although the response to the strike call was patchy. The unrest signalled deepening public dissatisfaction with the administration's economic policies. But in parliament Prime Minister Radu Vasile easily survived (by 248 votes to 147) a no-confidence motion proposed by the Party of Social Democracy of Romania just a few days before the general strike.

Even more impressive was the overwhelming parliamentary support (with just 12 votes against) for belated legislation on opening the files of the communist-era secret police, the Securitate. Under the new law, all citizens were to be allowed access to their own files. In addition, files on a large number of officials, civil servants and professionals—including judges, teachers and journalists—were to be made public.

In another step to deal with the legacy of the communist period, parliament began legislative moves in August to return to their original owners real estate that had been confiscated after World War II. Where restitution was no longer possible, compensation in the form of shares, government bonds or cash was to be made available. The law, adopted in December, granted the title 'Fighter in the Anti-Communist Resistance' to all those gaoled or punished during the years 1945-89, making them priority claimants for restitution. Legal moves also got underway to expand earlier half-hearted land restitution measures, this time returning to their former owners confiscated land with an upper limit of 50 hectares in each case. The government estimated that compensation claims would amount to the equivalent of about US$2,000 million; the opposition argued that the total might be 25 times more. In either case, the parlous state of the government's finances provided little scope to disburse such sums of money in a bid to render justice to the victims of communist rule and cement the governing coalition's support among the would-be beneficiaries.

The political impact of continuing economic difficulties was highlighted again when President Emil Constantinescu was booed during the traditional national day celebrations in Alba Iulia on 1 December. The President's discomfiture was closely linked to the government's growing unpopularity and a widespread perception that Prime Minister Vasile was failing to provide not just leadership but even effective coordination among the governing parties. Rivalries between the coalition partners, duplication of tasks between various ministries and an increasing disenchantment with Mr Vasile's personal style seriously undermined his position.

When Mr Vasile refused to yield to growing demands that he should relinquish his post, ministers belonging to his Christian Democratic National Peasants' Party (PNTCD) submitted their resignations on 13 December, allowing President Constantinescu to conclude that the government was no longer functioning. The President then nominated Mugur Isarescu, the governor of the Romanian National Bank (the central bank), as Mr Vasile's replacement. For a while Mr Vasile contested the President's decision on the grounds of its dubious legality, but in the end he gave in. Mr Isarescu won a resounding vote of confidence (305 votes to 35) on 21 December in a confidence motion that was supported by several opposition parties. The new Prime Minister, who had no party affiliation, was the only high-ranking Romanian official to have kept his post throughout the post-1989 period of transition. Indeed, his governorship of the central bank was merely suspended for the duration of his appointment as Prime Minister.

Mr Isarescu was widely respected for having been the architect of the macroeconomic stabilization programme of 1993-94 and for having established and safeguarded the central bank's independence. He took over a very difficult legacy. Although most economic indicators improved compared to the previous two years, 1999 still marked the third consecutive year of recession, this time with a drop of over 4 per cent in GDP. Inflation, though slightly reduced, still remained close to 50 per cent. Meanwhile, as some of the much-needed restructuring got underway, unemployment increased to 12 per cent of the labour force.

Despite Romania's continuing economic woes, there were some achievements in the sphere of privatization. Renault acquired a majority stake in Dacia, the car manufacturer, and the Romanian Development Bank was privatized early in the year. However, the deal with Renault was clinched with the help of some substantial tax breaks—a policy subsequently withdrawn from other investors on the IMF's insistence. As a result, the planned sale of the Petromidia refinery to a Turkish company fell through when the tax advantages were removed. The IMF was viewed, at times, as a hard taskmaster. In March it had suspended talks on a stand-by credit on the grounds that Bucharest was failing to meet a number of conditions. Eventually, it gave its approval in August for a $547 million stand-by credit to be disbursed in four tranches during 1999-2000.

The Romanian government gave its full support to NATO's bombing raids against Yugoslavia (see III.2.vi). In April parliament authorized the alliance to use Romania's air space, a policy which had little public support. Meanwhile, the previously overwhelming public backing for Romania's hoped-for membership of NATO declined considerably. In addition to the disruption of trade during the conflict over Kosovo, Romania also suffered longer-term losses. One of the most serious was caused by the destruction of bridges on the Yugoslav stretch of the Danube which cut the river in two. Romania therefore had to find more expensive forms of transport for shipments to key markets in Central and Western Europe.

In foreign affairs the year ended on a high note in December when Romania was included in the group of six additional applicant countries with which the European Union (EU) was to open accession talks early in 2000. The EU summit decision in Helsinki was a vindication of the government's strongly pro-European policy and a clear recognition of its loyalty to the West during the Kosovo conflict. A few weeks earlier Brussels had unveiled a huge three-year aid package, worth $2,400 million, which could go a long way towards helping to reform Romania's economy and society.

vi. BULGARIA

CAPITAL: Sofia   AREA: 110,000 sq km   POPULATION: 8,500,000 ('98)
OFFICIAL LANGUAGE: Bulgarian   POLITICAL SYSTEM: parliamentary democracy
HEAD OF STATE: President Petar Stoyanov (since Jan '97)
RULING PARTIES: Union of Democratic Forces (UDF) & People's Union (PU), allied as United Democratic Parties
HEAD OF GOVERNMENT: Ivan Kostov (UDF), Prime Minister (since May '97)
MAIN IGO MEMBERSHIPS (NON-UN): OSCE, CE, PFP, CEI, CEFTA, BSEC, Francophonie
CURRENCY: lev (end-'99 £1=L3.13, US$1=L1.94)
GNP PER CAPITA: US$1,230 by exchange-rate calculation ('98)

IN Bulgaria the invitation to begin accession talks with the European Union (EU) was seen as an overdue reward for the country's efforts for Balkan stability and its economic recovery under the Union of Democratic Forces' Prime Minister, Ivan Kostov. The offer was made to Bulgaria and four other former communist countries at the EU summit in Finland in December 1999 (see XI.4). Analysts said that there was little prospect of Bulgaria being ready for full EU membership before 2010; but the invitation was seen as sending a powerful message that Bulgaria's future was as a part of democratic Europe. The visit by President Bill Clinton in November was similarly perceived as another tribute to Bulgaria's successful transition from communism, as well as its contribution to NATO during the conflict over Kosovo (see III.2.vi). Mr Clinton was the first serving US President to visit Bulgaria.

The Clinton visit came at the end of a year that had seen an amazing rapprochement between Bulgaria and its western neighbour, Macedonia (see also III.2.iv). This began on 22 February when the two governments signed a declaration affirming that neither had territorial claims against the other. More significant was the Bulgarian authorities' first-ever recognition of Macedonian as a separate language, which allowed more than a dozen long-delayed cooperation agreements to be signed. The background to this reversal in Bulgarian policy was the change of government in Skopje in late 1998 (see AR 1998, p. 140). This had brought to power a centre-right coalition, headed by the main Macedonian nationalist party, the VMRO-DPMNE, which had repeatedly turned to Mr Kostov's UDF for tactical and policy advice. On 12 March the two governments concluded a defence agreement under which Bulgaria undertook to supply military equipment, including tanks, to Macedonia and to hold joint training exercises.

With the eruption of the Kosovo conflict, the new axis proved an important factor for stability in the southern Balkans. The Bulgarian government supported NATO in the conflict but sought guarantees that it would not become directly involved. One limiting factor on Mr Kostov was the enormous public disquiet in Bulgaria over NATO air-raids against Serbia—a country for which many people felt a strong cultural and ethnic affinity. Public alarm increased after 29 April when a NATO plane strayed off course and accidentally bombed a house in Sofia with an anti-radar missile. Denunciation of the NATO intervention was led by the Bulgarian Socialist Party (BSP); but it could not secure the passage in parliament on 7 April of a no-confidence motion against the government over assistance for NATO. The BSP similarly failed to defeat a government resolution on 4 May giving the alliance use of Bulgarian air space for its campaign. As a gesture to the public, NATO was asked to confine its warplanes to a west-east corridor and to avoid flying over Sofia and the Kozloduy nuclear power plant. In return, the alliance offered to upgrade the Bulgarian air defence system. On 22 March Bulgaria announced an ambitious army reform, cutting the military by almost a half to 45,000 personnel and upgrading the role of professional soldiers. The government said that the package was part of its effort to win full NATO membership.

The Kosovo war had a damaging impact on the Bulgarian economy, with the government saying in late April that its estimate of the cost—mainly in lost trade with Western Europe—was in excess of $13 million. The ban on oil exports to Yugoslavia, which Bulgaria imposed in April following an EU lead, also hit revenues and contributed to a widening of the annual deficit: by the year's end it stood at 8.3 per cent of GDP. On 22 April the World Bank undertook to supply additional aid worth some $275 million to support the balance of payments. Bulgaria profited from favourable credit treatment as a result of the success of its currency board in limiting annual inflation to a single digit figure. The deeper causes of economic problems, though, remained low investment and low productivity. There was a zero rate of growth in GDP—a disappointment after growth of 3 per cent in 1998. However, the burgeoning of the black economy—a process encouraged by the re-imposition of international sanctions against Serbia—meant that official statistics told only part of the story about annual trends.

With the new millennium opening with some 30 per cent of the industrial sector still in state ownership, international creditors urged the government to complete its programme of privatization as fast as it could. In particular, they demanded the sell-off of the country's largest bank, Bulbank, saying that its remaining as a state enterprise was an impediment to modernization of the entire financial sector. The government had managed to sell several of its more problematic installations. It sold the Neftokhim oil refinery at Burgas to a Russian firm and the Kremikovtsi steelworks near Sofia to a consortium of Bulgarians.

However, public criticism of the lack of transparency in the sale of state enterprises fuelled allegations of kickbacks, favouritism and tax-fraud; and spurred Mr Kostov into a major cabinet reshuffle on 21 December. Ten out of 16 ministers were dismissed as the Prime Minister sought to give a fresher, more energetic image to his team and to step up efforts to control corruption. The chief beneficiary was Petur Zhotev, who left his profession as a banker to become Economy Minister and the sole Deputy Prime Minister. Mr Kostov also appointed a new Internal Affairs Minister, Emanuil Yordanov, and a new Justice Minister, Teodosii Simeonov, with a view to intensifying the war against the country's criminal gangs.

The reshuffle was meant to improve UDF prospects in the next general election, due by April 2001. The UDF had been shocked out of its complacency by its setback in local government elections on 16 and 23 October. Hampered by a low turnout—which President Petar Stoyanov blamed on public disillusionment with self-serving and confrontational politicians—the UDF won the poll but captured just one-third of mayoral posts, half the target it had set itself. The UDF vote was 31.3 per cent, a loss of 1.25 million votes in comparison with its result in the 1997 parliamentary election. The BSP, which many had written off when its last, disastrous government fell in 1997, scored a respectable 29.4 per cent.

One consequence of the elections was the souring of relations between the UDF and the country's third party, the Movement for Rights and Freedoms (MRF), led by ethnic Turks. The MRF lost control of two important southern towns, Smolyan and Kurdzhali, despite its 11.1 per cent share of the poll. In Kurdzhali the mayoral election was fought on bitter ethnic lines, with the BSP backing the UDF simply to remove the ethnic Turkish MRF incumbent. Such conflicts dampened speculation that the UDF and MRF could negotiate a coalition deal, in the event of a hung parliament after the next general election.

The year finally saw the removal of another symbolic relic of communism. To much fanfare, the hideous, brutalist mausoleum in Sofia that had once housed the embalmed body of Bulgaria's 'little Stalin', Georgi Dimitrov, was demolished. The BSP was outraged, as were many intellectuals, who said that the building should have been reused as a museum to the excesses of the Soviet era.

2. ALBANIA—BOSNIA & HERCEGOVINA—CROATIA—MACEDONIA—SLOVENIA—YUGOSLAVIA

i. ALBANIA

CAPITAL: Tirana   AREA: 29,000 sq km   POPULATION: 3,500,000 ('98)
OFFICIAL LANGUAGE: Albanian   POLITICAL SYSTEM: parliamentary democracy
HEAD OF STATE: President Rexhep Mejdani (since July '97)
RULING PARTY: Socialist Party of Albania (PPS) holds presidency and heads government coalition
HEAD OF GOVERNMENT: Ilir Meta (PS), Prime Minister (since Oct '99)
MAIN IGO MEMBERSHIPS (NON-UN): OSCE, PFP, CE, CEI, BSEC, OIC
CURRENCY: lek (end-'99 £1=AL216.05, US$1=AL134.05)
GNP PER CAPITA: US$810 by exchange-rate calculation ('98)

ALBANIAN public life in 1999 was dominated by the Kosovo crisis and by the repercussions of widespread crime, corruption and collusion at home.

During the Kosovo emergency (see III.2.vi), Albanian policy generally conformed with the requirements of NATO. In January both major parties, the Socialist Party of Albania (PSS) and the Democratic Party of Albania (PDS), gave support to a parliamentary resolution calling for NATO intervention, and on 11 February Foreign minister Paskal Milo stated that Albania had no programme for a 'greater Albania'. Three days later Prime Minister Pandeli Majko told *Zeri i Popullit* that the United States, Albania's 'greatest ally', would protect Albania if its sovereignty were threatened. After NATO action had begun, the Albanian parliament on 9 April gave the alliance full authority over the country's air space, ports and military infrastructure. Albania earned the respect of most nations by its selfless accommodation of up to 350,000 refugees. To demonstrate national solidarity in the face of the threat to Albanian life in Kosovo, the leaders of the PDS announced in July that they would end the boycott of parliament they had imposed in September 1998 after murder of PDS deputy Azem Hajdari (see AR 1998, p. 131). In a moderation of previous policy statements on Kosovo, President Rexhep Mejdani told *Koha Jone* on 25 July that autonomy for the area within Yugoslavia might be feasible; this was more acceptable to the Western powers than the former insistence that independence for Kosovo was the only solution. The determination to please the Western powers continued after the end of the Kosovo war. On 28 September Albania ratified the Council of Europe's Convention on Minorities and on 9 December the Constitutional Court ruled in favour of the abolition of the death penalty.

Albania expected some reward for its good behaviour. There were indications that such expectations might be fulfilled. European Union (EU) officials in Luxembourg at the end of April promised that Albania would sign an association agreement with the EU 'very soon', whilst German Chancellor Gerhard Schröder encouraged Mr Majko to work towards membership of both NATO and the EU. On 25 May the EU commissioner in charge of foreign affairs told Mr Majko that the EU was willing to grant Albania preferential trade treatment and that the EU would discuss the timetable for the possible admission of Albania to the EU. On 22 September, when visiting Tirana, Herr Schröder thanked Albania for its stance during the Kosovo emergency and promised help in securing an association agreement; at the end of that month the United States announced that it would support Albania's bid to join the World Trade Organization (WTO). On 3 November the US Senate did grant permanent 'normal trade relations' to Albania. Albania also received direct financial assistance. International donors meeting in Brussels on 26 May promised $200 million to help Albania cope with the refugee influx, and both the World Bank and the International Monetary Fund (IMF) continued to extend new loans and to augment agreed ones. An IMF delegation to Tirana announced on 2 November that the foreign assistance and hard currency flowing into the country after the Kosovo emergency was a major cause of the encouraging economic position in Albania, which could boast a growth rate of 8 per cent and virtually no inflation. But there were major disappointments too. In October France vetoed any moves to admit Albania to the WTO. More seriously, on 25 October Fabrizio Barbaso, the head of the EU department for the western Balkans, said in Helsinki that Albania remained unstable and that, before an association agreement could be signed, the country had to undergo more institutional and political reform.

A major reason for Signor Barbaso's reservation was the crime and corruption which still bedevilled Albania. In January *Zeri i Popullit* reported that there were 17,000 stolen cars in the country and that of the 300,000 vehicles registered in impoverished Albania 80,000 were Mercedes. Smuggling continued to be a major activity, the items involved including tobacco, stolen automobiles, arms, drugs and, most tragically, humans—most of them young women from Russia, Moldova, Ukraine and Belarus who were destined for the brothels of Western Europe. Crime was carried out by powerful, well-organized gangs. The gangs, like most of the population, had easy access to weapons: the government instituted a programme in 1999 to buy arms still illegally held after the anarchy of 1997, but by early December only 70,000 of an estimated 600,000 items had been recovered.

In some areas of the country lawlessness continued to reign. In January 400 armed civilians blocked the main road from Gjirokaster to Greece in protest at the government's inability to control local bandits. In the same month criminals in Vlora kidnapped the local chief of police and held him until the police had returned six speedboats impounded from smugglers. On 24 February judges suspended work in protest at the increasing violence against the judiciary in general and in particular at the serious wounding by unknown gunmen of the president of the Bar Association. In July there were ugly scenes as Albanians looted abandoned Kosovar refugee camps.

The authorities made some attempts to contain the problem. In January restrictions were placed on the use of small boats and in February the government decided to burn impounded boats rather than put them up for auction, which had meant that they were repurchased by mafia groups. The US government gave two patrol vessels to Albania and in the summer agreements were concluded with Italy and Greece on measures to intensify the campaign against the smugglers. In August the police claimed to have smashed a network smuggling prostitutes from Russia, Moldova, Ukraine and Romania to Italy via Albania, and in September the government announced that 12 organized gangs had been broken up in the last four weeks. The leader of one gang was Myrteza Caushi, also known as 'Zani', from Vlora, who had been released from gaol in March and then injured in a gangland shootout in July, after which he had escaped when police tried to arrest him in hospital.

As serious as crime itself were suspicions of official collusion with the gangs. An investigation into a former MP accused of drug smuggling was closed in February; the ring-leader of the gang involved was said to be the brother of a prominent politician. In October the former Premier, Fatos Nano, was absolved of charges of corruption and abuse of power carried against him in 1994 and for which he had served three years in prison. In the same month the newly-appointed Minister for Public Order, Spartak Poci, acknowledged that unidentified politicians had put pressure on the police and justice officials as a result of which several of the gang leaders arrested in the late summer had been released. It was also alleged that political influence was the main reason why the investigation into the murder of PDS deputy Azem Hajdari had been bogged down for over a year.

Public officials were suspected of corruption as well as collusion. On 20 August the Prime Minister ordered the Finance Ministry to check the personal business activities and wealth of high-ranking government, customs and tax officials. In September these officials were obliged to declare their personal wealth and that of their families together with the sources of that wealth. On 24 September the government agreed with the Organization for Cooperation and Security in Europe (OSCE) to wage a joint campaign against corruption, which was said to pose 'a great danger for the future development of Albania'. On 7 October the government set up a commission under then Deputy Premier Ilir Meta to fight corruption at all levels of government.

Accusations of corruption played an important role in conflict between and within both major Albanian political parties. In January former Premier Nano had resigned as leader of the ruling PSS, to be replaced by the incumbent Premier, Mr Majko. The latter became nationally and internationally respected during the Kosovo crisis, which he used in part to urge conciliation between the feuding political parties. Enjoying greater support in the party apparat, Mr Nano resented the idea of conciliating those who had imprisoned him in 1994 and reacted sharply in September when Mr Majko attacked politicians of all parties, including the PSS, for their links with crime. At its congress in October Mr Nano challenged Mr Majko for the leadership of the PSS and won. Mr Majko accordingly resigned as Prime Minister on 26 October, claiming that tensions within his own party made it impossible for him to do his job. He was succeeded by Ilir Meta, whose cabinet was little changed from that of his immediate predecessor.

Within the PDS, Sali Berisha also faced a challenge to his leadership from a younger deputy. Genc Pollo pushed for closer cooperation with other parties of the centre-right but found Mr Berisha's hold on the party machine too firm for a credible challenge to be mounted at the party congress at the beginning of October. Nevertheless, Mr Pollo continued to criticize his party boss, and in December the two exchanged allegations of corruption and self-enrichment at the public expense.

ii. BOSNIA & HERCEGOVINA

CONSTITUENT ENTITIES: Federation of Bosnia & Hercegovina and Republika Srpska (Serb Republic)
CAPITAL: Sarajevo   AREA: 51,129 sq km   POPULATION: 4,500,000 ('98)
OFFICIAL LANGUAGE: Serbo-Croat   POLITICAL SYSTEM: federal republic
MAIN RULING PARTIES: Coalition for a Single and Democratic Bosnia & Hercegovina (KCD),
  Accord Sloga) Coalition & Croatian Democratic Union (HDZ)
HEADS OF STATE & GOVERNMENT: Ante Jelavić (President of Republic of Bosnia & Hercegovina);
  Ejup Ganić (President of Muslim-Croat Federation); vacant (President of Republika Srpska)
PRIME MINISTERS: Haris Silajdzic & Svetozar Mihajlović (Republic of Bosnia & Hercegovina);
  Edhem Bicakćić (Muslim-Croat Federation); Milorad Dodik (Republika Srpska)
MAIN IGO MEMBERSHIPS (NON-UN): OSCE, CEI
CURRENCY: marka (end-'99 £1=M2.94, US$1=M1.86)
GNP PER CAPITA: n.a.

IN the Republika Srpska (RS) the struggle continued to secure the appointment of a Prime Minister. Successive nominees of President Nikola Poplašen faced opposition both from moderate and other ethnic opinion in the RS and from the office of the UN High Representative (HR), who continued to support the candidacy of Milorad Dodik. The question of this appointment became a test of the determination of the Bosnian Serbs to go their own way. On 3 March HR Carlos Westendorp finally dismissed Mr Poplašen, accusing him of having 'consistently acted to trigger instability'. Mr Dodik eventually resumed the office of Prime Minister on 15 March, having to deal with the refusal of Mr Poplašen to vacate the presidency. Every measure requiring the collaboration of both 'entities' of the Bosnian union resulted in a challenge to the Dayton framework—it was even necessary in February for the union House of Representatives to adopt a national anthem without words.

The determination of the international community to sustain the 1995 Dayton agreement was underlined on 5 March when an arbitration panel chaired by US diplomat Robert Owen announced its decision on the future of the disputed Sava river port of Brcko. After two previous deferrals of its decision in the interval since the Dayton agreement of 1995, the commission determined that Brcko should become an open city under multi-ethnic administration, rather than be awarded to the control of either 'entity'. A new civic administration took office in Brcko on 15 April, under a Serb mayor. A Serb boycott of union institutions in the RS, begun in response to the ruling, was abandoned on 3 June. The arbitration process was wound up in August, the city being successfully demilitarized without incident by the end of the year.

Sr Westendorp on 15 April endorsed the decision of the Independent Media Commission to close the RS television station Kanal S, because of its 'inflammatory' broadcasts. Having completed his term of office, Sr Westendorp was replaced as HR in September by former Austrian diplomat Wolfgang Petritsch. The office of the HR intervened to dismiss officials or impose decisions at several points during the year where the inter-ethnic constitutional process had been obstructed, or had failed to reach agreement. Senior officials of the international community, at the celebration of the fourth anniversary of the Dayton settlement on 20 November, described a united Bosnian state as a 'distant goal'.

A sign that there might be progress towards inter-ethnic reconciliation in the region came in June, when the long-standing dispute between Muslim and Croat members of the municipal authority in Mostar was settled, making provision for joint cantonal bodies and headquarters. On 14 September 30 Muslim families returned to their homes in the former Bosnia Serb capital of Pale in a widely publicized and highly symbolic occasion. Nevertheless, in September the UNHCR reported upwards of 800,000 displaced persons within Bosnia, and 350,000 abroad.

The merger announced on 6 December between Mr Dodik's Party of Independent Social Democrats (SNSD) and the Social Liberal Party (SLS) led by Rade Dujaković, was construed as a sign of the consolidation of moderate political forces in the RS. Nevethleless, the year ended with Mr Poplašen still refusing to vacate the RS presidency, having on 24 December called on the RS Assembly to dismiss Mr Dodik and his government.

Although political problems were no closer to resolution, the sense of military threat subsided. The mandate of the S-For peace-keeping force was extended for another year at the UN Security Council meeting on 18 June, it being subsequently announced that the force was to be reduced from 31,000 to 16,500. An International Crisis Group study estimated that the international involvement in Bosnia was costing around US$9,000 million annually.

The International War Crimes Tribunal at The Hague continued to prosecute those indicted of serious war crimes during the war of 1992-95, on 12 April opening the trial of Dario Kordic and five other Bosnia Croats accused of the murder of at least 100 Bosnian Muslims in the Lašva valley. The Bosnian Ministry of the Interior issued a warrant on 10 January for the arrest of Fikret Abdić, charged with war crimes, and requested his extradition from Croatia. Abdić had also been indicted by the International Criminal Tribunal for the Former Yugoslavia (ICT). Several arrests of indicted suspects were made during the year (both within Bosnia and abroad). Most notable of those arrested were Radislav Brdjanin (a Bosnian Serb who had served as a close associate of former Bosnian Serb leader Radovan Karadžić) and Colonel-General Momir Talić (a senior officer in the Bosnian Serb army). Several of those brought to trial received sentences during the year: most notably Goran Jelišić, the Bosnian Serb former commander of the Luka detention camp, who was sentenced to 40 years' imprisonment. The relative effectiveness of the measures against indicted war criminals was called into question dramatically, however, when in mid-September Mr Karadžić delivered a speech in the main square of Srebrenica, in a calculated snub to the war crimes process.

A report was issued by the UN on 15 November into the events surrounding the over-running of Srebrenica by Serb forces in 1995, despite its status as a 'safe haven', leading to the killing of more than 7,000 Muslim men and boys. The report concluded that force, including air strikes, should have been used earlier to prevent the city's capture, and was critical of the Security Council for 'error, misjudgment and an inability to recognize the scope of the evil confronting us'.

The fifth international conference of aid donors to Bosnia, held on 20-21 May, occasioned controversy because of its outspoken criticism of corruption and waste in the handling of financial assistance. The conference nevertheless agreed to aid amounting to US$1,050 million for 1999. The Customs and Fiscal Assistance Office revealed in February that smuggling, corruption and organized crime had emerged as a serious economic problem in Bosnia. Subsequently, a report of investigation carried out by the office of the HR revealed that up to $1,000 million of public money and international aid funds was unaccounted for since 1995.

The Bosnian economy showed signs of significant recovery during the year, in spite of disruption caused by the war in Kosovo (see III.2.vi), notably the closure of Sarajevo airport for three weeks in March and April to meet the needs of military traffic. The long-delayed privatization process was finally launched in May, beginning with 35 companies in the Muslim-Croat Federation, although problems were encountered because of the faulty distribution of privatization vouchers.

iii. CROATIA

CAPITAL: Zagreb   AREA: 56,538 sq km   POPULATION: 5,000,000 ('98)
OFFICIAL LANGUAGE: Croatian   POLITICAL SYSTEM: presidential republic
RULING PARTY: Croatian Democratic Union (HDZ)
HEAD OF STATE & GOVERNMENT: President (acting) Vlatko Pavletić (since Dec '99)
PRIME MINISTER: Zlatko Matesa (since Nov '95)
MAIN IGO MEMBERSHIPS (NON-UN): OSCE, CE, CEI
CURRENCY: kuna (end-'99 £1=K12.35, US$1=K7.66)
GNP PER CAPITA: US$4,520 by exchange-rate calculation ('98)

THE year marked the end of the Tudjman era, the only President of independent Croatia dying in office in December. The year therefore ended with a new political era beckoning, as the country prepared for parliamentary and presidential elections early in 2000.

At the beginning of the year President Tudjman delivered a 'state of the nation' address which was remarkable for its explanation of Croatia's troubles in terms of foreign intervention, particularly foreign espionage. Officials had to issue explanations indicating that the President (appearances to the contrary) accepted the 1995 Dayton settlement in Bosnia & Hercegovina (see AR 1995, pp. 126-8, 559-62). After closure of more than seven years as a consequence of war, border crossings between Croatia and the Yugoslav republic of Montenegro were reopened on 20 January, although the issue of the contested Prevlaka peninsula remained unresolved.

The position of the communications media in Croatia remained controversial. On 15 January a case was brought by journalists against the Ministry of the Interior, for the illegal tapping of their telephones, and in February the director of the state news agency HINA and a member of the directorate of Croatian Radio and Television (HTV) both resigned, alleging continuing government interference. A US State Department report to the Organization for Security and Cooperation in Europe (OSCE) in March also contained outspoken criticism of media repression in Croatia. An independent television company, Nova TV, received a licence to operate on 12 July, breaking the former monopoly of the state-run HTV. Many of the problems of the press related to the indebtedness of the state-owned distributing company Tisak. Since the principal victims of its situation were the opposition press, its financial difficulties were perceived to have a political dimension.

Agreement was announced with the US construction company Bechtel on 20 May for the reconstruction of part of the Zagreb-Split highway, in a deal worth US$990 million. Its political significance was notable, in that the route chosen would partially free Croatian overland transport from dependence upon Bosnia. The project was to be funded by a consortium of ten international banks.

Doubts about the probity of the government were also voiced in connection with the failure in May of the Komercijalna Banka, in which President Tudjman's wife Ankica was said to be implicated. The reappointment of Miroslav Tudjman (the President's son) to the position of head of the Croatian Intelligence Service on 2 July also excited debate about the inappropriate concentration of political influence in the presidential family.

The failure of the government to make progress in facilitating the return to Croatia of the estimated 300,000 ethnic Serb refugees displaced during the recent conflicts was criticized by Helle Degn, president of the OSCE parliamentary assembly, who concluded from a visit in January that the government had 'no real commitment to reconciliation'. Hopes for improvement in this direction were raised by the first post-war visit of the Serbian Orthodox Patriarch Pavle on 15 March, which included a meeting with President Tudjman.

President Tudjman died on 10 December, following a long struggle against stomach cancer (see Pt XVIII: Obituary). International disapproval of his regime was apparent from the general absence of other heads of state at his funeral. A former general in the Yugoslav army, Franjo Tudjman had risen to prominence as a revisionist historian associated with the 'Croatian Spring' of 1971-72. He had subsequently formed the Croatian Democratic Union (HDZ), leading the party to victory in the first contested elections in 1990 and Croatia to independence from Yugoslavia in 1992. His advocacy of the unification of ethnic Croats into one state had greatly complicated resolution of the status of an independent Bosnia & Hercegovina. His obdurate insistence on distancing Croatia from its Yugoslav past had resulted in its international economic and diplomatic isolation.

Among the expectations raised by this death was the hope that Croatia's record of reluctance to cooperate with the International Criminal Tribunal for the Former Yugoslavia (ICT) might improve. The USA had threatened Croatia with economic sanctions if cooperation with the tribunal did not improve. Several cases were concluded during the year, however, in which both Croats and ethnic Serbs were arraigned on war crimes charges in Croatian courts, and on 9 August Vinko Martinović was extradited to The Hague to face charges before the ICT.

Elections to the *Sabor* (Assembly), which had already been planned for January 2000, were not rescheduled because of the President's death, and the selection of his successor was left to be determined following their outcome. Pending the elections, the function of President was undertaken by Vlatko Pavletić, Speaker of the Assembly.

The Kosovo war (see III.2.vi) hit the Croatian economy hard, especially its crucial tourism sector. On 27 September an IMF delegation began an extended visit to Croatia in order to negotiate an 18-month stand-by arrangement for US$200 million, which would partially compensate for the government revenue losses resulting from the war. On 4 October the sale of a 35 per cent stake in the Croatian telecommunications company HT to Deutsche Telekom eased the government's liquidity difficulties.

iv. MACEDONIA

CAPITAL: Skopje AREA: 25,713 sq km POPULATION: 2,000,000 ('98)
OFFICIAL LANGUAGE: Macedonian POLITICAL SYSTEM: presidential republic
HEAD OF STATE & GOVERNMENT: President Boris Trajkovski (since Dec '99)
RULING PARTIES: coalition of Internal Macedonian Revolutionary Organization–Democratic Party for Macedonian National Unity (VMRO-DPMNE), Democratic Alternative (DA) & National Democratic Party (NDP)
PRIME MINISTER: Ljubco Georgievski (VMRO-DPMNE), since Nov '98
MAIN IGO MEMBERSHIPS (NON-UN): OSCE, PFP, CE, CEI
CURRENCY: denar (end-'99 £1=D96.46, US$1=D59.85)
GNP PER CAPITA: US$1,290 by exchange-rate calculation, US$3,660 at PPP ('98)

MACEDONIA's delicate inter-ethnic relations made a shaky start to the year when President Kiro Gligorov declined to sign an amnesty releasing political prisoners, including the ethnic Albanian mayors of Gostivar and Tetovo. On 4 February his decision was over-ridden by the Sobranje (Assembly) and the two were released.

Macedonia made pointed demonstration of its distance from Yugoslavia when on 28 January it was announced that diplomatic relations had been established with Taiwan. In reply, China used its UN Security Council veto to block further extension of the mandate of UN Preventive Deployment Force (UNPREDEP), which ended on 1 March (see XI.1). The military base at Kumanovo used by UNPREDEP, however, had in November 1998 become the logistic centre for the observer mission to Kosovo of the Organization for Security and Cooperation in Europe (OSCE). The deteriorating situation in Kosovo actually resulted in a heightened international presence in Macedonia, particularly when in February Kumanovo became the local headquarters for the creation of an 'extraction force' for use in the event of the outbreak of full-scale war.

When NATO's campaign of air bombardment against Yugoslavia began on 24 March (see III.2.vi), a flood of ethnic Albanian refugees began to leave Kosovo, many of them crossing into Macedonia, which by the end of May was estimated to be sheltering nearly 250,000 (although some in transit to Albania). This influx caused great anxiety because of its possible destabilizing effect upon relations between the Macedonian Slav majority and the ethnic Albanian minority, estimated at nearly a quarter of the population of the republic.

The Kosovo war was also of significance for Macedonia in terms of the enhancement of its international recognition. However, the accidental death on 28 August of Minister without Portfolio Radovan Stojkovski in a collision involving a K-For vehicle driven by Norwegian soldiers became the occasion for fierce controversy regarding the legal jurisdiction under which the case could be investigated.

The economic reconfiguration of the Balkans continued to take shape with the signing on 7 July of an economic cooperation agreement between Macedonia and Albania, covering energy supplies, mining and transport. The republic's international stability was enhanced by improvement in its relations with Greece, and the conclusion on 8 July of a military training and cooperation agreement with Bulgaria.

Macedonia ended an era with the retirement of President Gligorov, who had been a significant figure in Macedonian politics since 1945 and the first head of the independent state. Following a campaign spoiled by allegations of malpractice, which compelled the partial re-run of the second round of voting, Boris Trajkovski of the ruling Internal Macedonian Revolutionary Organization–Democratic Party for Macedonian National Unity (VMRO-DPMNE) was inaugurated as President on 15 December. His success was aided by significant support among Macedonia's Albanian minority. A new government took office on 27 December under the continued premiership of Ljubco Georgievski, including representatives of VMRO-DPMNE, the Democratic Party of Albanians and the Democratic Alternative.

v. SLOVENIA

CAPITAL: Ljubljana   AREA: 20,251 sq km   POPULATION: 2,000,000 ('98)
OFFICIAL LANGUAGE: Slovene   POLITICAL SYSTEM: presidential republic
HEAD OF STATE & GOVERNMENT: President Milan Kucan (since April '90)
RULING PARTIES: Liberal Democracy of Slovenia (LDS), Slovene People's Party (SLS) &
   Democratic Party of Pensioners (DeSUS)
PRIME MINISTER: Janez Drnovsek (LDS), since April '92
MAIN IGO MEMBERSHIPS (NON-UN): OSCE, CE, PFP, CEI
CURRENCY: tolar (end-'99 £1=T319.89, US$1=T198.48)
GNP PER CAPITA: US$9,760 by exchange-rate calculation ('98)

ON 1 February a new association agreement came into force between Slovenia and the European Union (EU), taking Slovenia a step closer to its major foreign policy objective of membership of the EU. New legislation removed previous obstacles to EU membership in the areas of foreign investment and insurance. However, concerns remained regarding Slovenia's ability to meet the Maastricht criteria for membership of the euro single currency, particularly in relation to inflation.

The National Assembly passed a vote of no confidence in Interior Minister Mirko Bandelj on 16 February. He was accused of attempting to limit the powers of committees of the Assembly. The controversy revealed serious divisions within the ruling coalition, which were confirmed by other ministerial resignations. Similar political turmoil was also apparent among the conservative opposition parties, however, with inconclusive discussions continuing about a possible merger between the Slovene Christian Democrats and the Slovene People's Party. With parliamentary elections due in 2000, the political outlook for the opposition depended upon the outcome of these negotiations.

US President Clinton undertook an official visit to Ljubljana on 21-22 June. US investment in Slovenia continued to be low in relation to other states of the region, but American officials promised support for Slovene efforts at closer integration with European institutions.

Slovenia's relations with neighbouring Croatia remained uneasy, both in relation to the future of the shared Krško nuclear installation and the issues relating to their common borders. Expectations of an improvement were encouraged by the death of Croatian President Franjo Tudjman in December (see III.2.iii). Despite Slovenia's energetic efforts to distance itself in general from the Balkans, economic ties with the region continued to expand. Overall economic recovery was damaged by the regional impact of the fighting in Kosovo, which resulted in a significant decline in tourism.

vi. FEDERAL REPUBLIC OF YUGOSLAVIA

CONSTITUENT REPUBLICS: Montenegro (13,812 sq km), Serbia (88,316 sq km)
CAPITAL: Belgrade   AREA: 102,128 sq km   POPULATION: 10,640,000 ('98)
OFFICIAL LANGUAGE: Serbo-Croat   POLITICAL SYSTEM: federal republic
RULING PARTIES: Socialist Party of Serbia heads coalition in Serbia; For a Better Life alliance heads coalition in Montenegro
HEAD OF STATE & GOVERNMENT: President Slobodan Milošević (since July '97)
PRESIDENTS OF REPUBLICS: Milan Milutinović (Serbia), Milo Djukanović (Montenegro)
PRIME MINISTERS: Momir Bulatović (Yugoslavia); Mirko Marjanović (Serbia); Filip Vujanović (Montenegro)
MAIN IGO MEMBERSHIPS (NON-UN): OSCE
CURRENCY: new dinar (end-'99 £1=ND18.71, US$1=11.61)
GNP PER CAPITA: n.a.

FIGHTING in Kosovo worsened from 2 January following the breakdown of the ceasefire between Serbian government and ethnic Albanian forces (see AR 1998, pp. 145-6). A week later eight Serb soldiers were captured by the Kosovo Liberation Army (KLA), although later released in a prisoner exchange negotiated by the chairman of the Organization for Security and Cooperation in Europe (OSCE), Knut Vollebaek. On 15 January a Serbian offensive near Stimlje killed 15 KLA fighters. The fragile position of the OSCE observer mission was underlined by the death of one of its members. Following the discovery of the mass killing of 45 ethnic Albanian civilians at the village of Racak, near Priština, General Wesley Clark (Supreme Allied Commander of NATO) warned that the situation could deteriorate into all-out war.

On 18 January the head of the OSCE monitoring mission, William Walker, was ordered to leave by the Yugoslav government because of his handling of the Racak incident. On 20 January a meeting of the Foreign Ministers of the Contact Group for Yugoslavia (the USA, the UK, France, Germany, Italy and Russia) urged President Milošević to reconsider the expulsion order, advanced the level of alert for potential NATO air-strikes against Yugoslavia and moved NATO naval forces into position.

On 30 January the Contact Group urged the Yugoslav government and the Kosovars to attend talks at Rambouillet (France). The Albanian side hoped to secure a formal ceasefire as a precondition for negotiation (which the Yugoslavs had previously refused), while the Yugoslavs demanded a prior commitment to the integrity of state borders. Under constant diplomatic and military pressure, talks were opened on 6 February chaired by the US ambassador to Macedonia, Christopher Hill. After two extensions of the deadline for agreement (reflecting the depth of difference within the Albanian delegation as well as between the two sides), the talks were suspended on 23 February, to be reconvened on 15 March. Fighting continued, and there was a build-up of Yugoslav armed forces along the border of Kosovo.

Following the resignation of Adem Demaqi from the Albanian negotiating team on 2 March, the high command of the KLA decided to accept the Rambouillet proposals, and the Kosovars indicated that they were prepared to sign the draft agreement. When talks reconvened the Yugoslav delegation demanded changes relating to the political arrangements for power-sharing, which were unacceptable to both the Albanian side and the Contact Group. Negotiation was abandoned on 19 March and the 1,300-strong international peace-monitoring mission was withdrawn from Kosovo. A major offensive by Yugoslav troops commenced, aimed at securing control of key areas and driving out the Albanian population. The senior US negotiator, Richard Holbrooke, visited Belgrade in a last-minute attempt to persuade President Milošević to accept the Rambouillet proposals, but without success. As a consequence, on the evening of 24 March NATO forces began 'Operation Allied Force'—a massive aerial bombardment of Yugoslav military installations.

NATO was widely criticized for bypassing the UN, but a Russian-sponsored resolution in the Security Council calling for the cessation of bombing failed (by 12-3) on 24 March (see also XI.1). The Milošević government remained defiant, and throughout March the range and number of targets in Yugoslavia were steadily escalated beyond strictly military facilities, to include communications, infrastructure and manufacturing capacity deemed likely to aid the Yugoslav war effort. The loss of a US F-111A 'Stealth' warplane on 27 March raised questions about the political and financial costs of the action, and launched a debate regarding the campaign's reliance upon air power alone. The response of the Milošević government to NATO pressure was to launch an intensive campaign to drive the ethnic Albanian population from Kosovo. On 30 March the UN High Commissioner for Refugees (UNHCR) reported that since the bombing started 94,000 people had left.

The bombing campaign was also questioned because it was likely to blunt internal opposition to the Milošević regime and diminish the possibility of exploiting political divisions between Serbia and Montenegro. Whereas Vuk Drašković, leader of the Serbian Party of Renewal, agreed to enter a government of national unity, Montenegrin President Milo Djukanović consistently refused to break off relations with NATO governments. As the military campaign extended into April, the impact of NATO's policy of targeting bridges across the River Danube began to have an impact upon the trade of the other riparian states.

Bad weather limited the effectiveness of a many NATO air sorties, while the strict rules of engagement adopted also slowed the progress of the air war. On 14 April controversy erupted over the bombing in error of a convoy of refugee vehicles near Djakovica, and over other stories reporting substantial 'collateral damage' involving civilians. The numbers of refugees displaced by 'ethnic cleansing', and challenges to NATO claims that air-launched 'smart' munitions could be used to minimize civilian casualties, combined to fuel public debate about the need to deploy ground forces. These issues continued to test the solidarity of NATO governments.

At the Washington summit meeting of NATO leaders on 23-25 April to mark the alliance's 50th anniversary (see XI.2.i), divisions over the implementation of further economic sanctions, and the possibility of using ground troops against Yugoslavia, became public. Two days later the Foreign Ministers of the European Union (EU) states agreed to the reimposition of an oil embargo on Yugoslavia, despite the reluctance of Italy and Greece.

In late April it was estimated that some 750,000 displaced persons were seeking refuge within Kosovo itself, that more than 300,000 had fled to Albania, and that over 160,000 had taken refuge in Macedonia. At the end of the month the UNHCR abandoned its policy of seeking to accommodate the refugees within Europe.

Despite NATO bombardment of targets in Montenegro, the high profile of the Yugoslav army in the republic and rumours of an impending military coup, the Montenegrin government continued to distance itself from the Serbs. On 28 April, Mr Drašković was dismissed from the federal government because of his outspoken criticism of President Milošević. Earlier pro-government demonstrations dwindled. Attempts were made to silence opposition media: Slavko Curuvija, editor/proprietor of *Dnevni Telegraf* and *European*, was assassinated on 11 April (one of several cases of political violence).

Two visits to Belgrade by Russian envoy Viktor Chernomyrdin failed to produce any new proposals which could be internationally acceptable. On 7 May the Foreign Ministers of the Group of 7 countries met in Bonn, together with Russian representation (making the Group of 8), and agreed a set of proposals for ending the war. That night, however, the Chinese embassy in Belgrade was seriously damaged during NATO raids on Belgrade, four of the staff being killed and 20 injured. The event, admitted as an error by NATO, raised concern about the likely response of China, as a member of the UN Security Council, in subsequent decision-making in relation to the Kosovo crisis.

During early May the KLA began to make military gains against the Yugoslav forces, supplied from northern Albania and taking advantage of NATO aerial activity. Meetings between President Milošević and the leader of the moderate Democratic League of Kosovo (DLK), Ibrahim Rugova, fed expectations that the Yugoslavs were exploring means of bringing the conflict to a close.

Although the North Atlantic council meeting of 25 May began planning for the deployment of ground forces, differences of interpretation of the G-8 proposals prevented agreement on a draft Security Council resolution. Pressure on the Yugoslavs was eased, and the 'ethnic cleansing' of Kosovar Albanians continued. Russia's Mr Chernomyrdin and the Finnish representative of the EU, Martti Ahtisaari, began a round of 'shuttle diplomacy' in the search for a mediated solution based upon the G-8 proposals.

The indictment of Mr Milošević and other Serb leaders by the International Criminal Tribunal (ICT) for the Former Yugoslavia at The Hague on 27 May, for crimes against humanity, was variously interpreted as adding to the international pressure on the Yugoslav government or as likely to stiffen their reluctance to cooperate. On 2 June, however, the Yugoslavs announced their acceptance of the Chernomyrdin-Ahtisaari package, which provided for the withdrawal of Serb forces from Kosovo, the deployment of a NATO peace-keeping force under UN auspices and the safe return of refugees. The following day the agreement was ratified by the Serbian legislature. NATO action against Serb forces in Kosovo continued, however, until a 'Military Technical Agreement' had been concluded on 9 June (see XVII.1). The UN Security Council adopted Resolution 1244 the following day, accepting the peace plan, whereupon NATO suspended its 78-day bombing campaign. NATO 'K-For' units began to enter Kosovo on 11 June. The IMF estimated that the cost to Yugoslavia of the war could be as high as US$150,000 million; the cost in economic disruption to neighbouring states $2,250 million; and the cost to NATO countries of conducting the war $7,000 million.

The 50,000-strong K-For contingent (including 12,000 from the UK) was responsible for peace-keeping; the EU accepted responsibility for reconstruction; the OSCE for the establishment of democratic institutions; and UNHCR for the return of refugees. A UN 'Interim Administration Mission for Kosovo' (UNMIK), headed by the French former minister Bernard Kouchner, undertook the running of the justice system and public utilities. The province was divided into five military zones, each under control of a main national contingent and under the overall command of Lieut.-General Sir Michael Jackson (UK). Both sides to the conflict represented the agreement in terms of victory: President Milošević insisted that 'we never gave up Kosovo' and that the borders of Yugoslavia remained intact; the Albanians interpreted the provisional status of the agreement as marking the first step towards independence for Kosovo.

The deployment of K-For was generally uneventful, with one exception. On 12 June a convoy of 200 Russian troops reached Priština and surrounded the airport. NATO had resisted proposals for direct Russian participation in the force on the grounds that a Russian sector might prepare the ground for a partition of the province. Negotiation between US Defence Secretary William Cohen and his Russian counterpart delivered a statement on 18 June, accepting a Russian contingent distributed between the US, German and French zones. The withdrawal of Yugoslav forces from Kosovo was completed ahead of schedule on 20 June.

The return of refugees proceeded rapidly, the UNHCR reporting the return of roughly half of those who had left by 29 June. There were still around 350,000 in the Balkan states, however, including 209,000 in Albania alone, together with numbers in countries out of the region. Fear of reprisals set in motion a counter-flow of Serbs and others out of Kosovo: although the KLA was brought under K-For control, there were frequent attacks (often by organized armed gangs) and threats issued against the local Serb population. The fears of the Serb population of the province were heightened by the initial refusal of the

K-FOR DEPLOYMENT IN KOSOVO

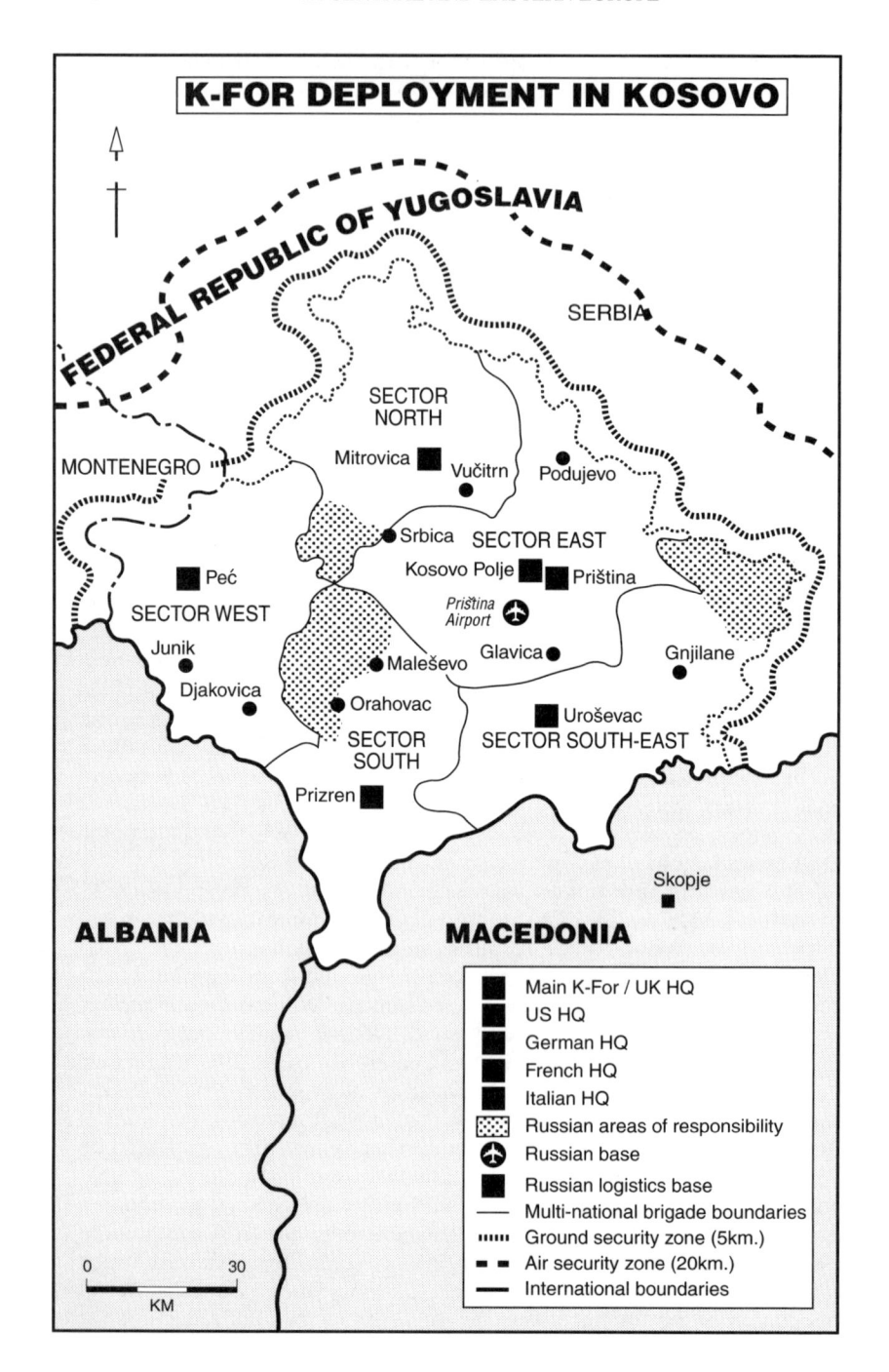

■	Main K-For / UK HQ
■	US HQ
■	German HQ
■	French HQ
■	Italian HQ
▨	Russian areas of responsibility
✈	Russian base
■	Russian logistics base
—	Multi-national brigade boundaries
⋯⋯	Ground security zone (5km.)
– –	Air security zone (20km.)
—	International boundaries

moderate DLK to participate in the Transitional Council, handing leadership of the new administration to the political head of the KLA, Hacim Thaci. The DLK only agreed to join the Council on 13 August.

The end of the war permitted the ICT to extend its investigation of war crimes into Kosovo. By the end of June more than 30 reports of major atrocities were under investigation, including the discovery of more than 500 dead at Orahovic and more than 700 at the Trepća mines near Mitrovica. Inter-communal violence continued throughout the year, stimulating Serb emigration and inflicting regular casualties on K-For personnel. Mitrovica was the scene of repeated ethnic clashes, culminating in riots during October. Attempts to foster the reintegration of educational and other facilities failed. In September it was reported that paramilitary units from Serbia had returned to the province. Relations between the two communities deteriorated further when former KLA units were adopted by UNMIK as the backbone of a new civilian Kosovo Protection Corps. An OECD report on peace-keeping efforts in the province, published in December, admitted that attempts to maintain law and order had been largely ineffective.

The ending of the war saw signs of growing dissent in Serbia, including the first open criticism of the Milošević regime by the hierarchy of the Orthodox Church. The New Democracy party announced its withdrawal from the ruling coalition. Opposition forces were never sufficiently strong or integrated, however, to pose a serious threat to the Socialist Party of Serbia, which was compelled to lean increasingly upon its coalition partner, Vojislav Šešelj's ultra-nationalist Serbian Radical Party, in a reshuffle of the cabinet on 12 August. The EU attempted to exploit political differences within Yugoslavia through its 'fuel for democracy' plan, whereby the oil embargo would be lifted to permit deliveries to cities where local government was controlled by the opposition. The first of such deliveries reached Niš on 7 December. Western economic pressure was mitigated to some extent by Chinese loans estimated at $300 million and by Russian support for fuel imports.

The war in Kosovo drove deeper the wedge between the Serbian and Montenegrin governments. On 5 August the Montenegrin government published proposals for a restructuring of the federation, including control over its own currency and defence forces. Montenegrin hopes for economic development were boosted in September by involvement of the Swiss-based Glencore in the ailing AKP aluminium plant. Dissatisfaction with the federation was sharpened by the steady depreciation of the Yugoslav dinar and the return of inflation. The continuation in force of the 'outer wall' of (largely financial) sanctions against Yugoslavia was particularly resented by Montenegrins. Discussion of these proposals between politicians from both republics, on 25 October in the resort of Sveti Stefan, were inconclusive. In November the Djukanovic government defied Serbian objections and introduced a dual monetary system based upon the German Deutsche Mark. The level of tension between the two republics was indicated by the unexplained short-term seizure by the federal army of Podgorica airport on 8 December.

3. RUSSIA, EASTERN EUROPE AND THE CAUCASUS

i. RUSSIA

CAPITAL: Moscow   AREA: 17,075,000 sq km   POPULATION: 146,000,000 ('98)
OFFICIAL LANGUAGE: Russian   POLITICAL SYSTEM: federal republic
HEAD OF STATE & GOVERNMENT: President Boris Yeltsin (in office since June '91, resigned on 31 Dec '99); Vladimir Putin became acting President
RULING PARTIES: fluid coalition
PRIME MINISTER: Vladimir Putin (since Aug '99)
MAIN IGO MEMBERSHIPS (NON-UN): CIS, OSCE, G-8, CE, PFP, CBSS, BSEC, AC
CURRENCY: rouble (end-'99 £1= R44.40, US$1=R27.55)
GNP PER CAPITA: US$2,300 by exchange-rate calculation, US$3,950 at PPP ('98)

AN eventful year for Russia saw a general election and the dramatic resignation at the end of December of President Boris Yeltsin. But although the Kremlin could feel satisfied with the unexpected success of reformist parties in the Duma election, there was little sign of a wider improvement in an economy that had contracted almost continuously since the end of communist rule. Russia's economic difficulties were associated in part with a deepening crisis of crime and corruption, and during the year a spectacular series of reports on money-laundering through a New York bank reached close to the Kremlin itself, which made a series of attempts to dismiss the procurator-general who was conducting the investigation.

The year also saw a resumption of hostilities with the breakaway Chechen republic, following a series of explosions elsewhere in the country: a war that, by the end of the year, was proving increasingly difficult and expensive to win. The tactics of the Kremlin government, and of the troops on the ground, led in turn to a widening dispute with the Western powers, concerned by the apparent violation of human rights in what was acknowledged to be a constituent part of the Russian Federation. Mr Yeltsin, in his farewell address to the Russian people at the end of the year, asked for their forgiveness; it was certainly clear that he had left a difficult legacy for his successor, who was due to be elected at early presidential elections at the end of March 2000.

There had been deepening tensions during the year between an increasingly infirm President and his political opponents. In May Mr Yeltsin ordered the resignation of the Primakov government, formed as recently as September 1998 (see AR 1998, pp. 150-1). At the same time, he nominated Sergei Stepashin, formerly First Deputy Premier, as acting Prime Minister. Yevgenii Primakov had helped to stabilize the Russian economy after the financial collapse of August 1998, and had also established better relations between government and Duma. He had also instigated an anti-corruption campaign against the financial magnates or 'oligarchs', some of them closely connected with the Yeltsin court, and had been widely seen as a future President. It was his protection of the prosecutor-general, who was conducting an investigation into high-level corruption, that was thought to have precipitated his dismissal. The Duma, in the event, approved Mr Stepashin on the first vote by 301 to 55, with 11 abstentions, and it failed to support any of the five counts of impeachment that had been raised against the President in May. The charge that was thought most likely to succeed was that Mr Yeltsin had illegally launched the war against Chechnya in 1994, but in the event all the votes fell short of the two-thirds majority of the entire legislature needed to approve them.

President Yeltsin dismissed his fourth government in 17 months in early August when Mr Stepashin made way for Vladimir Putin, the head of the Federal Security Bureau and Secretary of the Security Council, who was named not just as Prime Minister-designate but also as Mr Yeltsin's preferred successor to the presidency. In a televised statement the Russian President explained that he had chosen Mr Putin because he would be 'able to consolidate society and, drawing support from the broadest political forces, ensure the continuation of reform in Russia', and because he would also be able to unite around himself those who were 'to renew Great Russia in the new, 21st century'. No reason was given for the dismissal of his predecessor, who had held the post for only three months and who was generally considered to be competent. Mr Stepashin himself told newspaper interviewers that he had been dismissed because he had refused to 'service the interests of a certain group that decided I was not reliable enough'.

Mr Putin's background in the security services made him an important ally of the President's entourage in these circumstances. Born in 1952, Mr Putin had studied law at Leningrad University and had then joined the KGB, working for Soviet intelligence in East Germany and rising to the rank of colonel. He returned to Leningrad in 1990 to work for Mayor Anatolii Sobchak and then moved to Moscow to work in the presidential administration, becoming head of the Federal Security Bureau in July 1998. His nomination, in the event, was approved by the Duma on 16 August by 232 votes to 84, with 17 abstentions. In a speech before the vote, Mr Putin explained that the new government's priorities would include the payment of public sector workers and pensioners, strengthening of the defence sector, further assistance to farming and fighting economic crime. He also warned against 'spinelessness' in relation to the Russian regions and the North Caucasus in particular, and promised to defend the interests of Russians in the other former Soviet republics.

The Duma election on 19 December took place against a background that would ordinarily have been expected to place the President and his government at a serious disadvantage. National income had declined steadily since 1990, improving slightly in 1997 but then plunging again in August 1998 when Russia defaulted on its international obligations and the rouble dropped sharply against the dollar (see AR 1998, pp. 13, 149-50). Nor was there much confidence that the government would be able to resolve these difficulties. For a start, it had been extraordinarily unstable, with five different Prime Ministers between March 1998 (when the long-serving Viktor Chernomyrdin had been dropped) and August 1999 (when Mr Putin had taken over). But by December the Putin government had established a surprisingly strong position, assisted by the Prime Minister's apparently decisive action in the North Caucasus, which was itself covered uncritically by the Russian media (though not by the foreign press). Indeed, it was the developing crisis in the region itself and its implications for the rest of the country that came to dominate the entire campaign.

The crisis was precipitated when Islamic fundamentalists from Chechnya entered Dagestan in early August, capturing three mountain villages just over the border on 7 August and four more shortly afterwards. Russian forces began to retaliate on 13 August and the Chechens were forced to retreat, but their leader, Shamil Basayev, promised that they would switch to 'military-political' methods, widely understood as a threat of terrorism. A bomb exploded in the Manezh shopping centre in central Moscow on the night of 31 August, injuring 30 (one died later), following which an army hostel in Dagestan was bombed on 4 September, 36 servicemen being killed. Further explosions on 7 and 13 September ripped apart two residential blocks in Moscow, killing some 200 people (many of them children) and injuring hundreds more. Another residential explosion in the southern town of Volgodonsk killed 17 people on 16 September.

Under these circumstances there was considerable popular support for the resumption of hostilities against the breakaway Chechen republic in what the Russian government insisted on describing as an 'anti-terrorist operation'. Air strikes were launched against supposed rebel strongholds in late September, and ground forces began to advance across the border. Meanwhile, a range of security measures were taken against resident aliens in other parts of the country, and many thousands were forced to leave Moscow after a re-registration exercise that targeted Caucasians in particular.

As voting took place on 19 December, federal troops were on the outskirts of Grozny, the capital of Chechnya. Abroad, Russian spokesmen were rebuffing Western objections to the military action, insisting that Russia had every right to restore federal authority on its own territory. Western criticism, indeed, served if anything to strengthen the more assertive, 'Russia first' approach in foreign policy that had been apparent since Mr Primakov took over the Foreign Ministry in early 1996, and that had been apparent in the Russian government's vigorous attacks on the NATO bombing campaign in Yugoslavia. Attending a summit of the Organization for Security and Cooperation in Europe (OSCE) in Istanbul (see XI.5.ii) in mid-November, President Yeltsin insisted that the West had 'no right to criticize us for Chechnya'. And during a visit to Beijing on the eve of the election, he saw fit to 'remind' President Clinton that Russia was still a great power with a 'full arsenal of nuclear arms'. In their joint statement, the Russian and Chinese Presidents insisted on a multi-polar world in which the United States could not impose its wishes unilaterally (see also IX.2.i). 'Not since the time of the fall of the Berlin Wall', *Izvestiya* commented on 19 November, had 'Moscow and the West been so far apart'. By contrast, the pre-election period saw a strengthening of Russia's relations with the other members of the Commonwealth of Independent States, particularly the signing and all-but-unanimous ratification of a new union treaty with Belarus (see III.3.ii).

There were several entirely new parties or alliances in the Duma election. One was the Union of Right-Wing Forces, headed by former Prime Minister Sergei Kirienko, former Deputy Prime Minister Boris Nemtsov and Duma deputy Irina Khakamada. More enigmatic was a centrist grouping called Unity (Yedinstvo), which had come into existence in late September as a movement of regional governors with the support of the Kremlin, and with the evident purpose of securing a more 'loyal' Duma than in the recent past. The Unity list was headed by Emergencies Minister Sergei Shoigu, who enjoyed numerous opportunities to appear on television in connection with his official duties. For Mr Shoigu, Unity was 'not a political party' but an 'association of sensible people, fed up with seeing others decide their fate'; its ideology, he told interviewers, was actually 'the absence of ideology'. What mattered most was that it was a movement very closely associated with the Putin government: the Prime Minister himself declared that 'as a citizen' he would be voting for it (whereupon its ratings immediately improved), and Unity itself accepted that it could be called 'the party of Putin'.

The parties of the left and centre-left were represented by another new grouping, Fatherland–All Russia (Otechestvo–Vsya Rossiya, OVR). OVR was another association that had no other purpose than to fight the coming elections, but it drew upon two components that had a little more reality: the Fatherland party, founded in late 1998 by Moscow mayor Yuri Luzhkov, and a movement of governors and regional elites known as All

Russia. Its list was headed by former Prime Minister Primakov, followed by Mr Luzhkov and St Petersburg governor Vladimir Yakovlev, with fourth place going to Yekaterina Lakhova, leader of Women of Russia. 'We don't want to go back to the command system that went bankrupt', Mr Primakov told the new party's founding congress at the end of August, 'nor do we want to nationalize everything, but we do want to use the levers of the state to regulate the economy in the interests of growth, honest business and the welfare of taxpayers'. The more orthodox left was represented, as in previous elections, by the Communist Party, and nationalist opinion by the erratic Liberal Democratic Party headed by Vladimir Zhirinovsky.

In all, 26 blocs were listed on the ballot paper in the party list competition, with a total of 3,736 candidates; a further 2,300 sought election as independent or party-sponsored candidates in single-member constituencies. The final results took some time to emerge, but from an early stage on election night it was apparent that pro-Kremlin parties, particularly Unity, had performed much better than expected. The winner, as in 1995, was the Communist Party, and with a larger share of the vote (24.3 per cent of the party list vote and 114 of the 450 seats altogether). But Unity followed closely with 23.3 per cent and 73 seats in all; then came Fatherland–All Russia, but with a smaller share of the vote than the polls had predicted (13.3 per cent and a total of 66 seats). The Union of Right-wing Forces did rather better than expected with 8.5 per cent of the vote and 29 seats altogether, and the Zhirinovsky Bloc came in fifth with scarcely more than half of its 1995 vote but still above the threshold (6 per cent and 17 seats). Yabloko, however, failed to achieve the breakthrough it had hoped for: its party-list vote was down to 5.9 per cent and it won just 20 seats. No other parties or blocs exceeded the threshold.

The outcome was a new Duma that was expected to be much more supportive of the new Prime Minister. However, much depended on the independents, who had once again won most of the individual constituencies, to become the second-largest 'party' with 105 seats. As the year ended they were being energetically courted by both sides.

ii. BELARUS—UKRAINE—MOLDOVA

Belarus
CAPITAL: Minsk   AREA: 208,000 sq km   POPULATION: 10,500,000 ('98)
OFFICIAL LANGUAGES: Belarusan & Russian   POLITICAL SYSTEM: presidential
HEAD OF STATE & GOVERNMENT: President Alyaksandr Lukashenka (since July '94)
RULING PARTY: Belarusan Patriotic Movement (BPR)
PRIME MINISTER: Syargey Ling, Prime Minister since July '94
MAIN IGO MEMBERSHIPS (NON-UN): CIS, OSCE, PFP, CEI
CURRENCY: Belarusan rouble (end-'99 £1=BR1,450,529.7, US$1=BR900,000.0)
GNP PER CAPITA: US$2,200 by exchange-rate calculation ('98)

Ukraine
CAPITAL: Kyiv   AREA: 604,000 sq km   POPULATION: 50,090,000 ('98)
OFFICIAL LANGUAGE: Ukrainian   POLITICAL SYSTEM: democratic republic
HEAD OF STATE & GOVERNMENT: President Leonid Kuchma (since July '94)
RULING PARTY: Inter-Regional Reform Bloc (MBR) links ruling circle
PRIME MINISTER: Viktor Yushchenko (since Dec '99)
MAIN IGO MEMBERSHIPS (NON-UN): CIS, OSCE, CE, PFP, BSEC, CEI
CURRENCY: hryvna (end-'99 £1=K8.41, US$1=K5.22)
GNP PER CAPITA: US$850 by exchange-rate calculation ('98)

Moldova
CAPITAL: Chisinau (Kishinev)   AREA: 34,000 sq km   POPULATION: 4,500,000 ('98)
OFFICIAL LANGUAGE: Moldovan   POLITICAL SYSTEM: democratic republic
HEAD OF STATE & GOVERNMENT: President Petru Lucinschi (since Jan '97)
PRIME MINISTER: Dumitru Braghis (since Dec '99)
MAIN IGO MEMBERSHIPS (NON-UN): CIS, OSCE, CE, CEI, PFP, BSEC
CURRENCY: Moldovan leu (end-'99 £1=ML18.80, US$1=ML11.67)
GNP PER CAPITA: US$410 by exchange-rate calculation ('98)

IN BELARUS, there was little sign of a reconciliation between an increasingly authoritarian President Lukashenka and his political opponents. The latter continued to challenge the legitimacy of the November 1996 referendum that had extended the President's term of office (see AR 1996, p. 133), and in January they convened a session of the Supreme Soviet (which Mr Lukashenka had dismissed) and called for presidential elections to be held on 16 May, when the President's original term would have expired. The initiative was supported by all of Belarus's opposition parties but denounced by the Justice Ministry, which insisted that it had no legal force, and its organizers began to suffer from a series of repressive measures. Viktar Hanchar, the chairman of the opposition Central Electoral Commission, was arrested on 1 March; his wife reported that he had been tortured while in prison. Former Prime Minister Mikhas Chygir, a candidate in the unofficial presidential elections, was arrested at the end of March and charged with larceny and abuse of office. The other candidate in the elections, exiled leader of the Belarusian Popular Front Zyanon Poznyak, was not eligible to stand because he had lived abroad for three years. Opposition parties boycotted the elections to local councils that took place in April.

The elections to the presidency that took place in May were claimed to have secured a 53 per cent turnout, but Mr Poznyak objected to the procedure for balloting and withdrew his candidacy, and the whole exercise was pronounced invalid because of 'irregularities'. In July, nonetheless, the speaker of the opposition

Supreme Soviet was declared the country's 'acting President', and up to 5,000 people took part in a public demonstration in Minsk to mark what would have been the end of President Lukashenka's legitimate terms of office (more than 50 being arrested). Mr Hanchar himself disappeared on 16 September; he had been among the organizers of the alternative presidential elections and had been a prominent critic of the President Lukashenka. His disappearance followed those of the former head of the National Bank, who had been under house arrest, in April, and of a former Interior Minister in May. Mr Chygir was indicted in late September on charges of exceeding his authority, abuse of authority and negligence.

A more broadly-based 'freedom march' was organized on 17 October by opponents of the President; it ended in skirmishes between demonstrators and police and in the arrest of 93 demonstrators. The march, which had attracted an estimated 15,000 participants, was the largest oppositional demonstration since April 1996. The protesters demanded the resignation of Mr Lukashenka and opposed the proposed union treaty with Russia (see below); in addition, they demanded the release of political prisoners, and to know the whereabouts of two opposition leaders. Nine newspapers were closed down during the month because of technical breaches of the regulations.

More positively, the year saw a resumption of normal relations with European Union member countries, five of which resumed their representation in Minsk in January following a seven-month absence caused by a dispute over diplomatic residences (see AR 1998, p. 154). The US ambassador returned a little later (in May) for a preliminary visit. And in June the IMF re-established its permanent representation.

At a ceremony in Moscow on 8 December Presidents Lukashenka and Yeltsin formally signed the long-delayed union treaty under which Belarus and Russia were to become a confederal state (see AR 1998, pp. 153-4), although the timing and mechanism remained vague.

Politics in UKRAINE were dominated, as in Russia, by an election, in this case a presidential one, as President Kuchma's four-year term of office expired at the end of October. In order to secure nomination, candidates had to secure at least one million signatures in their support. Any candidate who won more than half the vote in the first round would be elected; if none did so there would be a second round, in which a simple majority would be sufficient. In the first round on 31 October President Kuchma was up against opponents, including several hardline Communist candidates who attacked the West, denounced privatization policies and argued that Ukraine should join the union between Russia and Belarus (see above). Mr Kuchma, who denounced the proposed merger as a 'dead end', won 36.5 per cent of the first-round poll, which was the largest individual vote but short of a victory without a run-off. The first-round runner-up, with 22.2 per cent, was Petro Symonenko, the Communist Party leader, who promised a referendum on the new union if he was successful. International observers declared the election largely free and fair, although it was clear that Mr Kuchma had exploited his control over the state apparatus and control over the media to disadvantage his opponents.

In the second round on 14 November Mr Kuchma scored an unexpectedly decisive victory with 56.3 per cent of the vote, 37.8 per cent opting for Mr Symonenko. Voter turnout was higher in the second round than in the first, at 75 per cent; this was thought to be a consequence of a two-week anti-communist propaganda campaign that had been unleashed by Mr Kuchma's campaign staff with the help of almost all the non-leftist parties and movements. In addition, the inter-round appointment of former Prime Minister Yevhen Marchuk as Secretary of the National Security and Defence Council swung the 8 per cent of the vote he had received in the first round behind Mr Kuchma in the second. It was a manoeuvre, some noted, that appeared to have been copied from Boris Yeltsin's similar stratagem in the 1996 Russian presidential election.

The Supreme Council rejected President Kuchma's first nomination for the premiership in mid-December, but on 22 December Viktor Yushchenko, the head of the National Bank, was approved by a large majority, with Communist deputies abstaining. Mr Yushchenko (45), a career banker with an American wife, was thought to have a good relationship with the IMF and Western financial circles. 'The cabinet', he told deputies, 'must become the political leader of reforms'.

MOLDOVA also experienced political instability during the year. On 1 February Ion Ciubuc resigned as Prime Minister, a post he had held since early 1997. He said that he was unable to consolidate his cabinet due to its diverse composition and blamed ministers for splitting along party lines. After a number of false starts, President Lucinschi nominated the outgoing Deputy Prime Minister and Minister for Economy and Reform, Ion Sturza, of the Movement for a Democratic and Prosperous Moldova (MDPM). The new government was approved in mid-March, based on the MDPM, the Party of Revival and Accord of Moldova and the Party of Democratic Forces.

There was a non-binding referendum on 23 May on the introduction of a fully presidential system of government under which the President rather than parliament would appoint the Prime Minister. Although 60 per cent of participants were reported to have supported the change, the turnout was only 56 per cent, below the 60 per cent threshold required for it to be valid. President Lucinschi insisted that, despite the failure of the referendum, he would work to change the constitution by setting up a commission to draft amendments.

Having lost its parliamentary majority, the Sturza government fell on 9 November on being defeated in a vote of confidence. Several weeks of political confusion ensued during which two new administrations proposed by President Lucinschi failed to obtain sufficient support. On 21 December, however, the parliament approved a new cabinet headed by Dumitru Braghis, hitherto Deputy Prime Minister for Economy and Reform, whose key ministers were unchanged. The new Prime Minister promised to continue the previous government's reform programme, while President Lucinschi said that increased efforts would be made to reduce tax evasion and fight organized crime.

iii. ARMENIA—GEORGIA—AZERBAIJAN

Armenia
CAPITAL: Yerevan   AREA: 30,000 sq km   POPULATION: 4,000,000 ('98)
OFFICIAL LANGUAGE: Armenian   POLITICAL SYSTEM: democratic republic
HEAD OF STATE & GOVERNMENT: President Robert Kocharyan (since Feb '98)
RULING PARTIES: Pan-Armenian National Movement heads ruling coalition
PRIME MINISTER: Aram Sarkisian (since Nov '99)
MAIN IGO MEMBERSHIPS (NON-UN): CIS, OSCE, PFP, BSEC
CURRENCY: dram (end-'99 £1=D836.39, US$1=D518.95)
GNP PER CAPITA: US$480 by exchange-rate calculation ('98)

Georgia
CAPITAL: Tbilisi   AREA: 70,000 sq km   POPULATION: 5,500,000 ('98)
OFFICIAL LANGUAGE: Georgian   POLITICAL SYSTEM: democratic republic
HEAD OF STATE & GOVERNMENT: President Eduard Shevardnadze (since Oct '92)
RULING PARTIES: Citizens' Union coordinates fluid coalition
MAIN IGO MEMBERSHIPS (NON-UN): CIS, CE, OSCE, PFP, BSEC
CURRENCY: lari (end-'99 £1=L3.16, US$1=L1.96)
GNP PER CAPITA: US$930 by exchange-rate calculation ('98)

Azerbaijan
CAPITAL: Baku   AREA: 87,000 sq km   POPULATION: 7,600,000 ('98)
OFFICIAL LANGUAGE: Azeri   POLITICAL SYSTEM: democratic republic
HEAD OF STATE & GOVERNMENT: President Geidar Aliyev (since June '93)
RULING PARTY: New Azerbaijan Party (YAP)
PRIME MINISTER: Artur Rasizade (since July '96)
MAIN IGO MEMBERSHIPS (NON-UN): CIS, OSCE, PFP, BSEC, OIC, ECO
CURRENCY: manat (end-'99 £1= M7,051.19, US$1=M4,375.00)
GNP PER CAPITA: US$490 by exchange-rate calculation, US$1,820 at PPP ('98)

ARMENIA held parliamentary elections on 30 May, on the basis of a new and controversial law under which 80 members of the legislature would be elected through single-member constituencies, while the remaining 51 were chosen through a national party-list contest with seats allocated on a proportional basis. In the elections the Unity Bloc, comprising the Republican Party and the People's Party, received 41 per cent of the vote, gaining 55 seats in the 131-seat Assembly. The Communist Party took 12 per cent and the Right and Accord Bloc 8 per cent. In early June Armen Darbinian, Prime Minister since April 1998 (see AR 1998, p. 156), announced his resignation, President Kocharyan appointing Defence Minister Vazgen Sarkisian, leader of the Republican Party, to take his place.

There was still greater political drama when Mr Sarkisian, parliamentary speaker Karen Demirchian and six other officials were shot dead by gunmen during a televised parliamentary debate on 27 October. The gunmen, it was thought, had either been reacting to the government's strong line on corruption, or to the apparent progress of negotiations with Azerbaijan over the disputed enclave of Nagorno-Karabakh. On 1 November five men were charged with murder and acts terrorism in connection with the killings. President Kocharian appointed Mr Sarkisian's younger brother Aram to the premiership on 3 November. The new Prime Minister pledged to continue the policies which his late brother had promoted.

GEORGIA continued to be affected by political instability during the year, although the position of President Shevardnadze was strengthened by a parliamentary election at the end of October. There were 17 arrests in May following the discovery of a new plot against the President; all those detained were reported to have links with the former head of state security, who had been forced to flee the country in 1995 following charges that he had been involved in an assassination attempt. Another 13 were charged in May with state treason as a result of another attempt to assassinate the President in February 1998. The parliamentary election on 31 October, however, gave the pro-Shevardnadze Citizens' Union of Georgia 41.9 per cent of the total vote, while the other two parties to achieve the 7 per cent threshold for representation, the Revival bloc and the Industry Will Save Georgia bloc, secured 25.7 and 7.8 per cent respectively. President Shevardnadze declared that the majority had voted for 'the country's independence, stability and its further development'. The results also strengthened Georgia's drift towards a greater distancing from Russia (Georgia having left the CIS collective security treaty when it expired in May) and towards a closer relationship with the Western powers. 'If I'm re-elected next year', remarked the Georgian President, 'we'll be knocking on NATO's door by the end of my second term in 2005'.

The third Caucasian republic, AZERBAIJAN, had no general election in 1999, but it also experienced political instability in the form of a series of trials of political opponents of the government. A case against former President Abulfaz Ali Elchibey was closed in February, but former Prime Minister Surat Guseinov was sentenced to life imprisonment in the same month on charges that included high treason. A further 22 opposition leaders were sentenced in February to prison terms for their part in an illegal demonstration in Baku the previous November. Like Georgia, Azerbaijan pursued an increasingly independent line in foreign affairs during the year. It also withdrew from the CIS collective security treaty because of Armenia's continuing occupation of Nagorno-Karabakh, and as a protest against recent armaments contracts between Russia and Armenia.

President Aliyev was able to sign contracts to develop potential oilfields in the Caspian Sea totalling an estimated US$10,000 million when he visited the United States in April. Also with potential long-term implications for oil development, a framework document providing for a feasibility study on the construction of an oil pipeline from Baku to the Turkish port of Ceyhan was signed on 19 November. This agreement satisfied the West, as well as those who signed it; but it threatened to isolate Russia still further from the future destinies of the region.

IV THE AMERICAS AND THE CARIBBEAN

1. UNITED STATES OF AMERICA

CAPITAL: Washington, DC   AREA: 9,372,614 sq km   POPULATION: 271,645,000 ('99)
OFFICIAL LANGUAGE: English   POLITICAL SYSTEM: democratic federal republic
HEAD OF STATE & GOVERNMENT: President Bill Clinton, Democrat, since Jan '93 (*for full cabinet list see* XVII.5)
RULING PARTIES: President is a Democrat; Congress is controlled by Republicans
MAIN IGO MEMBERSHIPS (NON-UN): NATO, OSCE, OECD, G-8, OAS, NAFTA, APEC, AC, CP, PC, ANZUS
CURRENCY: dollar (end-'99 P1=US$1.61)
GNP PER CAPITA: US$29,340 ('98)

As the year opened only one event seemed to matter to the media, if not always to the American people, namely the impeachment trial of President Bill Clinton. Following his impeachment by the House of Representatives (see AR 1998, pp. 170-1), Mr Clinton became the first President to be tried by the Senate since Andrew Johnson in 1868. However, given the balance of political parties and the requirement for a two-thirds majority to secure a conviction, an acquittal seemed a foregone conclusion and public impatience with the procrastination of the politicians was widespread. Once the President had been acquitted, the affair which had dominated national and international news for months was soon displaced from the headlines by the conflict in the Balkans, a series of shooting outrages and a chain of natural and man-made disasters.

An estimated 90 people died between 2 and 6 January when severe snow storms crossed the Midwest. At the end of the month California and other west coast states had their first snow in 20 years. A tornado which hit northern Louisiana on 3 April laid waste the town of Benton, killing 10 people. On 4 May the worst tornadoes to hit America in a decade devastated parts of Oklahoma and Kansas, killing at least 47 people and injuring hundreds more. A suburb of Oklahoma city was almost totally destroyed in the storms President Clinton promised immediate federal aid for the affected areas. A heatwave during July was thought to be responsible for more than 190 deaths as different states, mainly in the east, experienced record high temperatures. On 2 August President Clinton announced emergency measures to provide aid to farmers for their livestock, as well as air-conditioning for the elderly and the poor.

An estimated 3 million people were evacuated from their homes in Florida, Georgia and South Carolina as Hurricane Floyd hit the east coast between 13 and 17 September. Fortunately, it did not reach the force predicted, although considerable damage was done. Some 60 deaths were attributed to the storm, most of them in the widespread flooding. Some of the same areas were hit again on 17-18 October when Hurricane Irene came ashore. At least seven people died in South Florida.

Some commentators suggested that the extremes of weather were due to the 'greenhouse effect' and changing climate (see XII.3). The same causes were suggested for the spread of the mosquito-borne West Nile disease, first thought to be St Louis encephalitis, and malaria to New York in September. Parts of New York city were sprayed with disinfectant to counteract the disease, after four people and thousands of birds had died.

A series of air disasters captured the headlines during the year. On 2 June nine people died when an American Airlines plane crashed while landing during a thunderstorm at Little Rock, Arkansas. On 16 July the entire country virtually came to halt following the death of John F. Kennedy Jr, his wife Carolyn, and her sister Lauren Bessette, when the light aircraft piloted by Mr Kennedy en route to a wedding crashed into the sea near Martha's Vineyard, Massachusetts. The precise cause of the accident remained unknown, but pilot error appeared to have been a key factor. The ashes of the three deceased were scattered at sea on 22 July. Mr Kennedy, the son of the assassinated President, born just weeks after his father's election, became embedded in the nation's consciousness when as a three-year old he saluted his father's coffin (see XVIII: Obituary). At the memorial service in New York attended by the Clinton family and many other leading politicians on 23 July, Senator Edward Kennedy said that, like his father, 'this John Kennedy…had every gift but length of years'. Senator Kennedy further observed: 'From the first day of his life, John seemed to belong not only to our family but to the American family. The whole world knew his name before he did.'

Almost similar expressions of grief followed the death of the popular golfer Payne Stewart, twice winner of the US Open, when his Learjet crashed on 25 October in South Dakota. The aircraft, on a flight from Orlando, Florida, to Dallas, Texas, had apparently flown out of control for 1,500 miles. Four other people were killed with the golfer. It was believed that a sudden loss of air pressure might have been responsible.

On 31 October an Egyptair Boeing 767 crashed south-east of Nantucket island off Massachusetts following takeoff from John F. Kennedy Airport, New York. All 217 people on the plane died. Because the airliner had apparently plunged 33,000 feet without any distress call or warning, the disaster was at first feared to be the result of a terrorist attack. Warnings of a possible bomb attack had apparently been given to several US agencies some months earlier. However, other suggestions focused on a possible fault in the plane's thrust reversers. Information from the recovered flight recorders revealed that the aircraft's engines had been switched off during the descent, and this led to speculation that a pilot might have committed suicide. This scenario seemed to be supported by the sound on the voice recorder of one of pilots repeating a Muslim prayer minutes before the disaster occurred.

Other accidents also briefly caught the headlines: 11 people died in the worst train crash since 1996 when an Amtrack train collided with a truck near Bourbonais, Illinois, on 15 March; 20 people died and at least 23 were injured when a bus crashed off an elevated highway outside of New Orleans on 9 May;

11 students were killed at the Texas Agricultural and Mining University on 18 November in the collapse of a huge pyramid of logs which they were building for a bonfire to mark the start of the football season.

On 14 December it was announced that an American institution, the famous 'Peanuts' cartoon featuring the characters Charlie Brown, his dog Snoopy, and friends Linus and Lucy, which began in 1950, would cease at the end of year because their creator Charles Schultz was suffering from cancer. The end of the year also brought the sad news that former President Ronald Reagan was no longer able to make sense of a conversation and could not receive visitors as a consequence of Alzheimer's disease. Mr Reagan's illness had first been diagnosed in 1994.

IMPEACHMENT AND POLITICS. Congress reconvened on 6 January and the trial of President Clinton opened the following day before the full Senate chaired by Supreme Court Chief Justice William Rehnquist. An agreement on how to proceed was reached on 8 January by members of both parties led by Republican majority leader Trent Lott and Democratic leader Tom Daschle. Under the terms of the agreement the prosecution and defence would each be allowed 24 hours to present their arguments. The senators would then have up to 16 hours to question both sides. The contentious issue of whether to call witnesses, or whether to dismiss the case, would be decided at that point.

The 13 trial 'managers' from the House of Representatives, led by Henry Hyde, chair of the judiciary committee, presented their opening arguments against the President on 14-16 January. Their argument was that the President had been guilty of 'egregious and criminal' conduct which could be classed as 'high crimes and misdemeanours'. They claimed that he had committed perjury and had attempted to pervert and obstruct the course of justice during the Whitewater investigations and hearings, particularly with regard to his relations with the White House aide Monica Lewinsky (see AR 1998, pp. 159-60, 161-62, 164-65, 577-81).

Lawyers acting on behalf of President Clinton offered their arguments on 19-21 January. They suggested that even if the prosecution case was true it did not meet the 'rigorous' constitutional standard for impeachment, in that the actions described were of a private rather than public nature. They also argued that some of the issues presented by the House managers had already been dismissed by the lower chamber and that Ms Lewinsky's own previous testimony demonstrated that there had been no attempted cover up. They maintained that the Senate should apply the standard of 'beyond reasonable doubt' rather than that of 'clear and convincing' evidence of guilt used in the initial impeachment proceedings. Finally, they claimed the President had not committed perjury when he had denied 'sexual relations' with Ms Lewinsky because he had adhered to the definition agreed in the Paula Jones case (see AR 1998, p. 164).

On 19 January the impeachment proceedings were suspended while President Clinton delivered his sixth annual State of the Union address before Congress. In a remarkably upbeat performance Mr Clinton made no reference to the impeachment but pointed to his administration's positive achievements, beginning with 'the longest peacetime economic expansion in our history'. The President highlighted high home ownership, low unemployment and the balanced budget. He also pointed to falling rates of violent crime and to success in cleaning the environment. Addressing the need 'to meet our historic responsibility to the 21st century', Mr Clinton drew attention to the 'ageing of America' and the likely future inability of federal Social Security to provide full benefits to the elderly. He proposed that 60 per cent of the budget surplus for the next 15 years should be committed to Social Security to overcome this problem. The President further suggested that 'one out of every six dollars in the surplus for the next 15 years' should be invested in Medicare. Additionally, the President called for the use of budget surpluses to establish universal savings accounts to strengthen investment and provide further pension provision, and for tax credits for those families needing long-term care.

Mr Clinton also called for improvements in educational standards and said that no child should graduate from high school in future if he or she could not read. He demanded more performance testing of teachers and greater empowerment of parents. Among the many other measures requested by the President were increasing the minimum wage by a dollar an hour over two years, tax credits and subsidies for working families, a patients' bill of rights, the extension of health insurance to smaller businesses, and increased efforts to improve mental health. The President also urged Congress 'to resist the tobacco lobby' and to hold tobacco companies accountable for smoking-related health costs. He asked Congress to strengthen gun controls and to take more action to limit the access of children to guns, and to approve the Non-Discrimination Act and the Hate Crimes Prevention Act to end discrimination or violence because of race, religion, ethnic background, gender or sexual orientation.

In foreign affairs Mr Clinton said trade barriers ought to be torn down and markets opened and called for a 'new round of global trade negotiation to expand exports of services, manufactures and farm products'. He reaffirmed America's commitment to bringing peace in Northern Ireland, Bosnia, Kosovo and the Middle East, to containing Iraq and to reducing nuclear arsenals. He called upon the Senate to approve the Comprehensive Nuclear Test Ban Treaty, but said it was 'time to reverse the decline in defence spending'.

Finally, Mr Clinton urged communities to launch projects 'to save our history, promote our arts and humanities [and] prepare our children for the 21st century' as part of the millennium celebrations, and called upon the country to look forward to the next century as 'a new dawn for America'.

President Clinton's address was regarded as a great public relations success that focused on more important issues than the impeachment, with which the public seemed thoroughly bored. Interest was revived, however, when a US district court judge ordered Monica Lewinsky to begin informal discussions with the House prosecutors about her possible testimony in the trial. Ms Lewinsky was interviewed for two hours in a hotel in Washington DC on 24 January. The following day a Senate motion to dismiss the case against the President was rejected by 56 votes to 44 with only one Democrat voting against. A motion to begin the deposition of witnesses was passed by the same margin following an agreement that only three witnesses would be called and that none would be questioned for more than nine hours. It was also agreed that no questions of a sexually explicit nature would be asked.

On 1 February Ms Lewinsky was interviewed under oath by a team of prosecutors followed by lawyers for the White House. Vernon Jordan, the President's friend and confidante, gave a deposition on 2 February, followed by White House aide Sidney Blumenthal on 3 February. Following a vote on 4 February in which the Senate decided against hearing live evidence from Ms Lewinsky, the Senate heard her videotaped deposition. In the course of her questioning, shown on television on 6 February, a demur Ms Lewinsky objected to the description of an encounter with the President as 'a salacious occasion', saying that she did not feel comfortable characterizing what the President had said as either truthful or untruthful. None of the evidence heard seemed likely to affect the outcome of the trial. The Senate's final deliberations behind closed doors began on 9 February.

On 12 February the Senate acquitted President Clinton of the charges of perjury and obstruction of justice brought in the two articles of impeachment. Voting on both fell far short of the necessary two-thirds majority needed to convict the President. In the first vote, on the article alleging perjury, ten Republican senators joined with 45 Democrats in declaring the President not guilty; the remaining 45 Republicans voted guilty. The vote on the second article, alleging obstruction of justice, ended on a 50-50 tie with five Republicans voting with the Democrats. A move to bring a motion of censure against the President failed for procedural reasons.

Shortly after the vote had taken place, a clearly emotional President Clinton appeared in the White House rose garden before the television cameras. He said that he was 'profoundly sorry' for what he had said and done 'to trigger these events and the great burden they have imposed on the Congress and the American people'. Declaring himself 'humbled and very grateful for the support and prayers' he had received, the President declared that now 'must be a time of reconciliation and renewal for America'. Asked if he would forgive his opponents, Mr Clinton replied: 'I believe any person who asks for forgiveness must be prepared to give it.' Aides had earlier made it clear that in the event of a successful outcome to the trial the White House would be a 'gloat-free zone'.

Just a week after his acquittal by the Senate President Clinton faced further allegations about his past sexual conduct when Juanita Broaddrick, a former campaign worker, told the *Wall Street Journal* that he had raped her in a Little Rock hotel in 1978. The story had been subject to rumours as early as 1992 and had first resurfaced in a tabloid magazine in January. Ms Broaddrick had denied it in an affidavit to Paula Jones's lawyers but repeated her original claim in an interview on NBC television on 24 February.

On 3 March an audience of 70 million watched a two-hour interview with Monica Lewinsky broadcast on ABC television. During the interview Ms

Lewinsky apologized to the country and to Mr Clinton's family for her part 'in last year's ordeal'. Although she was not particularly critical of Mr Clinton, she said that she would 'never have an affair with a married man again'. The interview coincided with the publication of *Monica's Story*, a biography written by British author Andrew Morton in which Ms Lewinsky accused the independent counsel, Kenneth Starr, of descending to the 'realms of malevolence'.

The President suffered further embarrassment on 12 April when a US district court judge in Little Rock, Arkansas, ruled that he had given 'intentionally false testimony' when he told Paula Jones's lawyers in January 1998 that he had not had a sexual relationship with Ms Lewinsky. Mr Clinton was declared to be in civil contempt of court, even though his testimony had not affected the outcome of the case, which had been the dismissal of a harassment suit. White House lawyers accepted that the President, although technically correct, had been misleading. The President was subsequently fined $90,000.

Also on 12 April a jury in the US District Court acquitted Susan McDougal of obstruction of justice in the Whitewater investigations (see AR 1996, p.144; 1998 p. 163). Apparently a central figure in the Whitewater affair, Ms McDougal had been imprisoned for refusing to testify before a grand jury in 1996, but had repeated the action in 1998. She argued that Mr Starr, the independent counsel, had been motivated by political consideration. In a related case, on June 30 the former Associate Attorney-General, Webster Hubbell, pleaded guilty to charges of lying to Whitewater investigators and was sentenced to a year's probation. Mr Hubbell had previously served an 18-month prison sentence for fraud (see AR 1998, pp. 163, 168).

On 12 June Governor George W. Bush of Texas, son of former President Bush, officially announced his intention to seek the Republican nomination for the presidential election in 2000. His platform included traditional Republican policies of tax cuts, privatization of welfare and increased military spending. While the governor committed himself to free trade (which some fellow Republicans opposed), he did not comment on contentious abortion or gun control issues.

Speaking in his home town of Carthage, Tennessee, Vice-President Al Gore announced his intention to seek the Democratic nomination for the presidency on 16 June. Seeking to distance himself from Bill Clinton, he said: 'Any two individuals are very different, and certainly the President and I are. I felt what the President did, especially as a parent, was inexcusable.' He suggested that his campaign would focus on 'the crisis in the American family', but committed himself to tighter gun control and support for women's choice in abortion. Opinion polls showed the Vice-President lagging behind Governor Bush by a considerable margin but ahead of challengers for the Democratic nomination.

The first test for Republican candidates came with the Iowa straw poll on 14 August. Although this had no official standing, a number of potential candidates competed for votes in the hope that a good showing would boost their public standing. They included Governor Bush; former Vice-President Dan Quayle; conservative Pat Buchanan; former governor of Tennessee Lamar Alexander; former head of the US Red Cross Elizabeth Dole, wife of Bob Dole, the unsuccessful Republican candidate in 1996; Senator Phil Gramm; multi-millionaire media boss Steve Forbes; and the black conservative talk-show host Alan Keyes. Mr Bush was clearly victorious, securing almost twice as many votes as his nearest rival, Mr Forbes, who had spent $2 million in the campaign. Mrs Dole came third, revitalizing a campaign that had appeared to be flagging.

Mr Gore's campaign seemed to be struggling during the summer, and he faced a strong challenge from Senator Bill Bradley, who announced his own candidacy on 8 September. Mr Bradley, a famous former basketball player, offered a liberal platform of increased healthcare for those without health insurance, a reduction in child poverty, tighter gun controls and the reform of campaign financing. Having earlier declared himself the 'underdog', on 6 October Mr Gore moved his campaign office from Washington DC to Nashville, Tennessee, in an attempt to refocus his image and distance himself from the Clinton administration. Mr Gore, notoriously rather stiff and wooden in delivery, also tried to present a more relaxed image and promised a 'rip tootin' campaign that's gonna win in the year 2000'. He received a boost later in October when the AFL-CIO union organization indicated that it would support him.

On 27 September Senator John McCain, whose account of his five-and-a-half years as a prisoner-of-war during the Vietnam War, *Faith of My Fathers*, was a best-seller, joined the race for the Republican nomination. Former Vice-President Quayle had meanwhile announced his withdrawal from the competition following his poor showing in Iowa, and on 20 October Mrs Dole announced that she could no longer afford to continue in the race. Having at one time appeared to be the strongest challenger to Mr Bush, Mrs Dole argued that the campaign finance laws favoured candidates with huge personal fortunes such as Mr Forbes and the Texas governor. Nevertheless, suggestions that Mr Bush had used cocaine during his youth, and his apparent inability to be precise in answering questions about such matters, contributed to a decline in his lead over Democratic rivals in the opinion polls. Mr Bush was not helped by reports that political connections had enabled him to serve in the Texas Air National Guard rather than serve in Vietnam.

One of Mr Bush's rivals, Pat Buchanan, muddied the political waters when he announced on 25 October that he would seek the nomination of Ross Perot's Reform Party in the presidential contest. Criticizing the 'identical twin' two-party system which had produced 'hollow men', he called upon a 'peasant army' of 'forgotten Americans' to save the United States from disappearing into 'a godless world order.' Millionaire Donald Trump also left the Republicans and joined the Reform Party, indicating that he might challenge Mr Buchanan, claiming that the latter had the support of 'the really staunch wacko vote'. In the course of a radio conversation with Howard Stern on 10 November, Mr Trump suggested that a one-off 14.25 per cent tax on individuals or trusts worth more than $10 million would raise $5.7 trillion and erase the US national debt.

On 18 October Kenneth Starr resigned as Whitewater independent counsel. He was to be succeeded by his deputy, Robert Ray, who would be responsible for the final report and any further indictments arising from the investigations. Figures released by the General Accounting Office revealed that the total cost of the investigation since August 1994 stood at $47.2 million.

There was much speculation through the year concerning the state of the Clintons' marriage and their future after they left the White House. In March Hilary Rodham Clinton abruptly cut short a skiing trip to Utah amid rumours of stormy arguments between the couple, whereas in May they made a public point of holidaying together in Florida. In an article published in *Talk* magazine at the start of August, Mrs Clinton spoke for the first time since the impeachment trial about her marriage. She suggested that the President's behaviour was due to his childhood experience, pointing out also that the Lewinsky affair followed the deaths of his mother and mother-in-law, and the suicide of a close friend. She said her husband, who was guilty of 'sins of weakness' rather than malice, was 'working on himself very hard' and had 'become more aware of his past and what was causing this behaviour'.

There were indications through the year that Mrs Clinton might run for election to the Senate and challenge the Republican mayor of New York, Rudolph Giuliani, in a contest for the seat to be vacated by Democrat Daniel Patrick Moynihan on his retirement in 2000. Mrs Clinton seemed to have acquired considerable public support as a result of her steadfast loyalty to the President, and in September she and Mr Clinton arranged to purchase a home in New York. Criticism of the initial mortgage arrangements, in which an associate was reportedly providing $1.35 million as collateral, led to the declaration that the purchase would take place without such a loan.

Mrs Clinton's still officially-undeclared candidacy ran into further problems in late November as her lead in the polls slumped badly after she had alienated various key groups of potential constituents. She antagonized Puerto Ricans after withdrawing her support for an amnesty for gaoled terrorists; she angered Catholics by failing to speak out against the picture of the Virgin Mary decorated with elephant dung in the British 'Sensation' art exhibition (see XV.2.i); and she upset the Jewish community by failing to criticize an accusation by Suha Arafat (wife of the Palestinian leader) that the Israelis were poisoning Palestinian women and children, made during President Clinton's visit to the Middle East (see V.2.i). After polls published on 21 November showed that Mayor Giuliani, who had also yet to declare his candidacy, had a significant lead over Mrs Clinton, some senior Democrats suggested that she should withdraw from the race. However, on 23 November Mrs Clinton indicated that she intended to run, announcing on 7 December that she was preparing to move to New York once the festive celebrations in the White House were over.

The biggest demonstrations in America since Vietnam occurred in Seattle, Washington state, on 30 November-1 December when protesters disrupted the World Trade Organization's opening meetings (see also XI.2.ii). Over 100,000 anti-free trade activists, pro-labour supporters, environmentalists and anarchists blocked central Seattle, where they became involved in violent confrontations with riot police. A considerable amount of damage was done as protesters became involved in violent confrontations with police, while other demonstrators attacked and looted city-centre shops. Heavily-armed riot police using tear gas and mustard spray struggled to disperse the crowds. President Clinton, who arrived on 2 December as the city centre was completely sealed off, said he had some sympathy with the demonstrators but could not condone lawlessness. The Seattle police were criticized by some observers for their heavy-handed response. The police chief, Norm Stamper, who was also criticized for failing to anticipate the violence, resigned on 7 December.

The Lewinsky affair resurfaced on 13 December when Linda Tripp went on trial in Maryland following her indictment in July for illegal wiretapping. It was Ms Tripp who first made public the affair between Monica Lewinsky and the President when she reported details of Ms Lewinsky's telephone conversations with her to *Newsweek* in 1997. Ms Lewinsky appeared in court on 16 December and claimed that she had felt 'violated' when she discovered that her conversations had been recorded.

During a televised debate with Bill Bradley on 19 December, Vice-President Al Gore challenged his opponent to halt all television and radio campaigning until the nomination was decided. He also offered to hold twice-weekly debates. Mr Bradley declined, but suggested that such offers were an acknowledgement that Mr Gore was facing a real challenge. Mr Gore appeared to have a substantial lead in national opinion polls, and was reported to have already secured the votes of almost a quarter of the delegates to the Democratic national convention. However, the two men were neck-and-neck in some northern states, including New Hampshire, where the first primary was scheduled for 1 February 2000.

That Governor Bush would achieve a victory in New Hampshire also seemed less certain following an interview on 3 November in which he had been unable to name the leaders of several major nations. A lacklustre performance on two later televised debates cast further doubts concerning his intellectual ability. A poll in New Hampshire early in December showed Senator McCain leading among Republican voters by 38 to 36 per cent. National opinion polls still showed the senator lagging far behind Mr Bush, but his supporters hoped that a good result in New Hampshire could narrow the gap.

US airports were put on a state of high alert following the arrest on 17 December of an Algerian, Ahmed Ressam, who was carrying bomb-making equipment across the Canadian border. The US State Department had warned that followers of the Afghanistan-based Saudi Islamic militant Osama bin Laden might launch attacks over the holiday period. On 19 December KLM flight 644 from New York to Amsterdam was diverted to Boston and searched following a bomb threat. Additional customs inspectors and police were deployed at ports of entry after a series of further arrests at Canadian border crossings. Many cities increased security for the New Year celebrations, while Seattle city centre was closed and scheduled events cancelled.

In his millennium message, released on 30 December, President Clinton once more celebrated the nation's economic achievements and success as 'a leader in promoting peace and human rights across the globe'. He called for national unity and urged Americans to 'honour the past, imagine the future' as he offered his best wishes for the celebration.

SOCIAL AND LEGAL AFFAIRS. Racial tensions in New York city came to the fore following the shooting of an unarmed black West African immigrant, Amadou Diallo, by white police officers early in February. Mr Diallo was hit by 19 bullets. The police offered no immediate explanation for the shooting, which became the focus of organized public protest. Four members of the New York Police Department's special crimes unit were subsequently charged with second-degree murder. The case brought into question police commissioner Howard Safir's hard-line policy on street crime, which was thought to have reduced reported crime rates by 70 per cent in five years, although there had been a 40 per cent rise in complaints against the police. Mayor Giuliani also faced criticism for failing to criticize the shooting of Mr Diallo and for describing protesters as 'silly'.

On 25 May a former New York city policeman, Justin Volpe, pleaded guilty to a vicious attack on a Haitian immigrant, Abner Louima, in 1997 (see AR 1997 p. 159). Mr Louima had been badly beaten and sodomized by Volpe and other police officers, who had at first covered up the attack behind the 'blue wall of silence'. Volpe changed his plea after fellow officers gave evidence against him and was sentenced to 30 years in prison on 13 December. Another officer, Charles Schwartz, was awaiting sentence. The police were again accused of using excessive force after Gary Busch, a mentally-ill Jewish man, was shot and killed on 30 August when four police officers responded to his attack with a hammer by firing at least 12 bullets at him. Hundreds of Hassidic Jews took to the streets to protest.

The Los Angeles Police Department (LAPD) also suffered embarrassment during the year following revelations of widespread corruption emerging from an official inquiry. Rafael Perez, a police officer who admitted stealing cocaine intended as evidence, accused other officers of covering up crimes and of shooting suspected criminals. By November two officers had been dismissed and 13 had been suspended pending inquiries. It was believed that up to 3,200 criminal cases might have to be reviewed in the light of the apparently widespread corruption in the LAPD.

On 25 February John William King, a self-confessed white supremacist, was sentenced to death for the brutal murder of James Byrd, a black man dragged behind a truck outside Jasper, Texas, in June 1998 (see AR 1998, p. 174). Lawrence Brewer was also convicted and sentenced to death on 23 September, while a third man, Shawn Allen Berry, who claimed that he had been too afraid of his companions to prevent the murder, was convicted on 18 November.

There was controversy concerning the use of the death penalty in March when Walter LaGrand, a 37-year-old German citizen, was executed by gas in Arizona for the 1982 murder of a bank manager during a robbery. His brother and co-defendant Karl, who had been executed by lethal injection in February, had become the first German to be executed in the United States since World War II. The governor of Arizona, Jane Hull, had refused to grant stays of execution pending an appeal by the German government to the International Court of Justice. The German government argued that the two men, who had been resident in America since childhood but had never assumed US citizenship, had been denied the right to assistance from their embassy, contrary to the Vienna convention. In a similar case in June, Canadian citizen Joseph Faulder was executed in Texas. He too had not been given access to consular services at the time of his arrest. The US authorities claimed that they did not know of his Canadian citizenship until after the event.

Dr Jack Kervorkian, widely known as 'Doctor Death', was convicted of murder by a court in Pontiac, Michigan, on 26 March after a television programme had shown him administering a lethal injection to a terminally-ill patient in 1998. He was sentenced to between ten and 25 years' imprisonment on 13 April.

The campaign against tobacco companies continued. On 10 February a jury in the San Francisco superior court awarded $50 million in punitive damages against the Philip Morris company to a smoker of Marlboro cigarettes who had developed lung cancer (see also XIV.3). This amount was subsequently halved on 6 April, but on 30 March a court in Portland, Oregon, awarded a record $80 million in damages against the same company in favour of the family of Jesse Williams, who had died of cancer in 1997 after smoking Marlboro cigarettes for over 40 years.

In October the Philip Morris company did admit that 'smoking is addictive' and that there was 'overwhelming medical and scientific consensus' linking cigarettes to lung cancer and other diseases. The admission, contained in the company website, was part of a public relations campaign to prevent the government from imposing further stringent controls on cigarette sales and advertising.

In June Manjit Basuta, a 44-year-old British nanny, was convicted by a court in San Diego, California, of causing the death of a 13-month-old child in her care by shaking. Under a new law, Ms Basuta faced a possible mandatory sentence of 25 years, but on 5 August Judge William Kennedy suggested that such a penalty could be considered 'cruel and unusual punishment'. However, after hearing further arguments Judge Kennedy decided that a prison sentence rather than probation was appropriate, and on 1 October imposed the maximum sentence on Ms Basuta, commenting that she had 'a dark side'. Supporters of Ms Basuta in Britain complained that her trial had generated none of the public concern surrounding the similar case of Louise Woodward (see AR 1997, pp. 154-5; 1998, p.174), attributing the disinterest to the fact that Ms Basuta was of Asian origin.

Demands for gun controls were fuelled once more by different shooting incidents during the year. The whole nation was shocked on 20 April when 17-year-old Dylan Klebold and 18-year-old Eric Harris shot and killed 13 of their schoolmates at Columbine high school in Littleton, Colorado, before killing themselves. The two teenagers had also planted bombs in and around the school. Diaries and video tapes found after the shooting showed that the two youths had planned the attack for some time out of a sense of social exclusion. Suspicions that they had been aided by friends forming part of a so-called 'Trenchcoat Mafia' were apparently unfounded.

On 27 April President Clinton suggested new legislation to raise the legal age for handgun possession from 18 to 21 and to make parents legally liable when children committed crimes with family guns. He also suggested tightening the background checks required before gun sales were concluded. Despite much criticism, the annual convention of the pro-gun ownership National Rifle Association (NRA) took place as scheduled in Denver on 2 May, but for one day rather than the planned three. The NRA president, actor Charlton Heston, denied that they or the 80 million 'honest gun owners' were responsible for what happened in Littleton. Later that month Thomas J. Soloman, aged 15, shot and wounded six of his class-mates at Heritage high school in Conyers, Georgia.

During the 4 July weekend holiday Benjamin Smith, a white supremacist, killed two people and wounded nine others in a series of apparently racially-motivated attacks in Chicago, Springfield, Champaign-Urbana and Bloomington, Indiana, before shooting himself. On 29 July Mark Benton shot and killed nine people in two securities and investments buildings in Atlanta, Georgia, after he had lost more than $150,000 trading on the financial markets. Benton, who had earlier killed his wife and two children, shot himself when cornered by police. On 5 August Alan Eugene Miller killed three of his fellow office workers in Pelham, near Birmingham, Alabama, before being arrested. Another attack on children occurred on 10 August when a gunman opened fire on a Jewish summer camp in a community centre on the outskirts of Los Angeles. Three young children and two women were wounded. On 11 August Buford Oneal Furrow surrendered to police in Las Vegas, claiming that the shooting was a 'wake-up call' for Jews. Furrow had links with the Aryan Nations and other right-wing racist groups.

On 16 September Larry Gener Ashbook, aged 27, opened fire on the congregation of a Baptist church killing seven young people. He then shot himself. There appeared to be no obvious motive for the shootings. On 2 November Bryan Uyesugi shot and killed seven workers in the Xerox plant in Honolulu, Hawaii. Uyesugi, a former employee of the company, was later captured by police. The following day an unknown man shot and killed two men in a Seattle boatyard before escaping.

The wave of shootings occasioned much public and political debate. President Clinton repeatedly urged the passage of tighter gun controls and on 1 June announced a federal study to investigate the links between the marketing of violent films and video games and child violence. The administration was very critical of Congress after the House of Representatives failed on 18 June to approve a much-amended juvenile crime bill which included several gun-control measures. The Senate had reversed itself and passed the measure the previous month in response to public reaction to the Columbine shootings. Vice-President Gore suggested that the Republican Party had 'handed the Speaker's gavel over to the gun lobby', while the President appealed to Congress to send him 'common-sense legislation' which would keep guns 'out of the hands of criminals and children'. In a speech on 9 September Mr Clinton said that too many American neighbourhoods were 'awash with guns', and called for the passage of legislation that would provide $15 million to fund local police 'buy-back' schemes offering $50 to anyone who handed in a useable weapon. A similar programme in Washington DC brought in over 2,300 guns in two days in August.

On 11 October the famous gun manufacturer Colt announced that it would cease to produce handguns. Seen as a response to various lawsuits brought by different cities against Colt as well as Smith & Wesson because of the high incidence of handguns used in domestic murders, the decision ended a history which began in 1835 when Sam Colt produced the first revolver.

Aaron McKinney, one of the two men accused of murdering Matthew Shephard, the gay student found tied to a fence in Wyoming in October 1998 (see AR 1998, p.174), was cleared of first degree murder, but found guilty of felony murder, kidnapping and aggravated robbery on 3 November. McKinney's friend Russell Henderson had pleaded guilty to murder and kidnapping in April in an attempt to avoid the death penalty and had given evidence against McKinney.

A court in Boulder, Colorado, decided on 14 October that there was not enough evidence to charge anyone with the murder of JonBenet Ramsay, the six-year-old child beauty queen murdered in December 1996 (see AR 1997, p. 155). The chief suspects were her parents, and many observers had anticipated a trial that would challenge that of O.J. Simpson (see AR 1995, p. 158) for the title of 'trial of the century'.

Further shooting incidents occurred at the end of the year. On 26 December 19-year-old Jonathan Erik Carter shot and killed Rev. Keith Blakely and wounded two elderly relatives in Miami. Rev. Blakely's daughter Angela had refused to go out with Carter, who later shot Jonathon Lott, a friend who had been assisting the police, and wounded two police officers before committing suicide. On 30 December a 36-year-old Cuban immigrant, Silvio Layva, was charged with murder after he shot and killed four fellow hotel workers and a woman whose car he attempted to steal in Tampa.

On 27 December the record producer and 'rap' singer Sean 'Puff Daddy' Combs and his actor/singer girlfriend Jennifer Lopez were charged with firearms offences following a shooting incident which left three people wounded in a Manhattan nightclub

ECONOMIC DEVELOPMENTS. As President Clinton continually pointed out, the American economy continued to expand, for the ninth consecutive year, with a growth rate of 3.5 per cent, unemployment at 4.5 per cent and a federal budget surplus of approximately $70 billion in January (see also I.2). Figures released in April showed that the number of people in receipt of welfare benefits had dropped by 14.1 million since 1993 to 7.6 million, the lowest figure since 1969.

In a $1,766,000 million draft budget for fiscal year 2000 (beginning on 1

October 1999) submitted to Congress on 1 February, Mr Clinton predicted a budget surplus of at least $76,000 million for fiscal year 1999, rising to S117,000 million in fiscal year 2000. The President proposed an increase in overall government spending of $39,000 million for 2000. Echoing his State of the Union address (see above), he called for a $1,000 annual tax credit to help families pay for child care and the cost of medical care for the chronically ill. The President also asked for a 55 cent increase on the price of 20 cigarettes, which would yield $34,500 million over five years. Almost 62 per cent of the budget surplus was to be used to bolster Social Security programmes, while 15 per cent would be used to strengthen Medicare. Another 11 per cent was to be set aside for pressing national needs, including education, law and order, and defence. Defence spending was to be increased by $12,600 million in 2000. Despite the optimism of politicians concerning the strength of the US economy, on 6 May Alan Greenspan, chairman of the Federal Reserve (the central bank), expressed some concern about 'imbalances in our expansion that, unless redressed, will bring this long run of strong growth and low inflation to a close'. He referred specifically to the US trade deficit and high share prices in a speech seen as a warning that interest rates might have to rise.

Wall Street reacted nervously on 12 May when Robert Rubin announced his retirement as Treasury Secretary, to take effect in July. Mr Rubin was widely credited, along with Mr Greenspan, with orchestrating the country's economic boom and overcoming the global financial crisis in 1998. It was believed that Mr Rubin might have left earlier but had been persuaded not to resign during the Lewinsky affair for fear of embarrassing the administration further. It was announced that he was to be succeeded by his deputy, Lawrence Summers.

As predicted, the Federal Reserve raised interest rates from June onwards in order to slow the economy and head off the risk of rising inflation. The short-term base rate was increased from 4.75 to 5.0 per cent on 30 June, the first rise since March 1997, and to 5.25 per cent on 24 August. A third rise on 16 November took the rate to 5.5 per cent, as unemployment reached its lowest level since 1970 at 4.1 per cent. Inflation in the 12 months from June 1998 was 2.1 per cent.

The President and Congress were locked in conflict over the budget for much of the year and faced the possibility of another government shutdown like that of 1995 (see AR 1995, pp. 154-5). On 30 July the Senate voted along party lines 57-43 to approve a $792,000 million plan to provide tax relief to many Americans. The bill expanded relief for middle income-earners, eliminated the 'marriage penalty', reduced estate taxes and provided additional relief for healthcare and education costs. A similar measure had been passed earlier by the House. President Clinton condemned the vote as 'the wrong choice for America's future', describing the cuts as 'too big and too bloated' and arguing that they would damage Medicare and other welfare programmes. On 23 September Mr Clinton vetoed the tax cuts enacted by Congress on the grounds that they would make it difficult for the administration to finance its own expenditure priorities, proposing instead cuts of $300,000 million over ten years.

The White House and Congress finally agreed on the fiscal 2000 budget on 18 November, with both Democrats and Republicans claiming victory. The budget as enacted included provision for payment of almost $1,000 million of unpaid US dues to the UN (see XI.1), more spending on teachers and community policing, and a reduction in the national debt of $147,000 million. However, Republicans could point to the cut of 0.38 per cent agreed on all federal programmes. Mr Clinton called the agreement a 'hard-won victory for the American people', signing the final agreement on 29 November.

There was considerable interest in the business world and beyond in the Justice Department's anti-trust suit against the huge computer software company Microsoft Corporation headed by Bill Gates (see AR 1998, pp. 172, 483). The Justice Department claimed that the company had used its domination of the computer software market to stifle competition, particularly by tying the Windows operating system to the Internet Explorer browser. On 5 November a US district court judge in Washington DC issued a 'finding of fact' accepting the majority of the allegations made against Microsoft (see also XIII.2). Unless an out-of-court settlement could be reached, further rulings were expected which could require the break-up of the company or require it to share information with its competitors.

On 12 November President Clinton signed legislation, passed overwhelmingly by Congress earlier that month, repealing the Glass-Steagall Act of 1933. This depression era legislation had prohibited banks from operating in insurance and securities. Its repeal was expected to lead to a wave of mergers and acquisitions in the financial services industry.

FOREIGN AFFAIRS. The most significant issue in foreign affairs was US involvement the crisis in Kosovo (see III.2.vi). Announcing American participation in the NATO air strikes against Serbia on 24 March, President Clinton described it as an act to prevent a wider war. Referring to the situation in Kosovo, he declared: 'Ending this tragedy is a moral imperative.' In an appeal for relief for Kosovar refugees on 5 April, he said that 'the ethnic cleansing of Kosovo cannot stand as a permanent event', and confirmed that the long-term goal was to ensure the return of the refugees to their homes.

Prior to the Washington summit to celebrate NATO's 50th anniversary (see XI.2.i), Mr Clinton met UK Prime Minister Tony Blair on 21 April to agree their policy and to ensure NATO unity following the bombing of Belgrade. Commenting on the conflict during the summit meeting, President Clinton declared: 'When we fight, we fight to prevail.' However, on 28 April the House of Representatives voted by 249-180 to require the President to seek congressional approval before committing ground troops in Kosovo. Republican opponents had also voted against supporting the bombing campaigns in a vote that tied 213-213 the same day.

The capture of three US servicemen by Serb forces on the Macedonian border on 31 March brought considerable pressure on the administration. The three men were released on 2 May following the intervention of Rev. Jesse Jackson, the African-American civil rights leader, who travelled to Belgrade to intercede personally with President Slobodan Milošević. He returned, amid much criticism, carrying a letter from Mr Milošević to President Clinton calling for a face-to-face meeting.

In a morale-boosting tour at the start of May, President Clinton visited NATO headquarters in Brussels and then went on to meet the three released servicemen. At a US Airforce base in Germany on 5 May he told servicemen and their families that America 'must stand in Kosovo for the common humanity of every living, breathing person on this continent. Our quarrel is with ethnic cleansing.' He described President Milošević as 'an evil despot'.

President Clinton expressed his 'regrets and profound condolences' following the bombing of the Chinese embassy in Belgrade on 7 May, which he described as a 'tragic mistake'. However, Secretary of Defence William Cohen and CIA Director George Tenet, who acknowledged that the attack was due to faulty intelligence, said that 'NATO intends to continue and intensify the air campaign'. Addressing the nation on June 10 on the cessation of the air strikes, Mr Clinton reiterated the view that in Kosovo 'we did the right thing'.

The President and his family travelled to Europe again for a week-long visit from 15-22 June. On 21 June Mr Clinton met with European leaders at the G-8 summit in Cologne (see XI.2.ii). Later that day, in Ljubljana (the Slovenian capital), the President announced agreement on a Stability Pact for south-eastern Europe providing economic assistance to Balkan countries. Mr Clinton made it clear, however, that Serbia would not participate while under the leadership of President Milošević. The Clintons travelled on to Macedonia, where they were received ecstatically during a visit to Kosovar Albanian refugee camps.

On 16 August the US consulate-general in Ho Chi Minh City, Vietnam, was formally reopened nearly a quarter of a century after its previous occupants had left by helicopter from the rooftop at the end of the Vietnam War. With a trade agreement having been signed the previous month, the reopening marked the final step in the normalization of relations between the two countries.

Relations with China were strained throughout the year. The Clinton administration was embarrassed in March by allegations that it had been slow to react to suspected spying at Los Alamos National Laboratory in New Mexico on behalf of China. Following a story in the *New York Times* on 6 March, the FBI began an investigation of Taiwanese-born Wen Ho Lee, who was dismissed from his post two days later for breaking security rules, although no charges were brought against him. A congressional report issued in May claimed that there had been systematic spying since the 1970s resulting in China gaining access to information about the neutron bomb and US nuclear warheads. On 24 August the deputy chief of intelligence at the US Energy Department, Notra Trulock, resigned because of criticism of his aggressive investigation of the spy allegations. His critics argued that there was no solid evidence against Wen Ho Lee and that he had been singled out because of his ethnic background.

US State Department officials warned Beijing against taking any military action during the build-up of tension between China and the Taiwan in July and August (see IX.2.iii). However, President Clinton personally telephoned President Jiang Zemin of China to reaffirm the US commitment to a 'one China' policy. It was announced on 31 August that China had accepted a payment of $4.5 million in compensation for the Belgrade embassy bombing. When President Clinton travelled to Auckland, New Zealand, for the Asia-Pacific Economic Cooperation summit on 12-13 September (see XI.6.iii), he had a meeting with President Jiang Zemin to discuss China's entry into the World Trade Organization (WTO) and other matters. The meeting, on 11 September, was apparently cordial and marked a relaxation in the tension that had existed since May. A bilateral agreement between China and USA with regard to Chinese entry into the WTO was finally reached on 15 November.

The President suffered a major defeat in foreign affairs on 13 October when, by a margin of 51 votes to 48, the Senate rejected the Comprehensive Nuclear Test Ban Treaty which he had signed in 1996 (see AR 1996, pp. 542-3). Seen as in part a rejection of any legal constraint on the installation by the USA of an anti-ballistic missile defence system, the vote was described by the President the following day as motivated by 'politics, pure and simple'. Although he declared that 'the fight is far from over', most observers believed it unlikely that the treaty could be brought back to the Senate before Mr Clinton departed from office in 2001.

The rift between President Clinton and Congress widened on 18 October when he vetoed a bill that would have reduced US foreign aid by $12,600 million. Mr Clinton justified his veto, the 28th of his presidency, on the grounds that the bill seemed to be 'the next big chapter in the new American isolationism', following the rejection of the test ban treaty.

In an agreement reached with the White House on 14 November, Congress agreed to release $926 million to pay back dues to the UN in return for a promise that federally-funded bodies would not lobby for liberalized abortion laws abroad. Seen as a major capitulation to the anti-abortion Republicans by the Clinton administration, the agreement was criticized by liberal Democrats and pro-abortion groups.

On 2 November President Clinton travelled to Oslo, where he met Israeli Prime Minister Ehud Barak and Palestinian leader Yassir Arafat at a memorial service for Yitzhak Rabin, the Israeli Prime Minister assassinated in 1995. Mr Clinton viewed the meeting as a positive step that 'revitalized the peace process', urging the two leaders to take advantage of the situation to 'finish the job' of achieving a lasting peace settlement (see V.1; V.2.i).

During a state visit to Turkey, President Clinton on 15 November pledged $1,000 million in loans to aid recovery following the country's devastating recent earthquakes (see II.4.vii). Mr Clinton praised the Turkish government for its progress on human rights and called for further steps to allow free expression.

Attending a summit of the Organization for Security and Cooperation in Europe (OSCE) in Istanbul, Mr Clinton on 18 November responded to a warning by Russian President Boris Yeltsin that the West should keep out of Chechnya (see III.3.i) by reminding Mr Yeltsin of the support given by the West for his resistance to the attempted Moscow coup in 1991 and by expressing 'respectful disagreement' with Russian actions in Chechnya. On 22 December US Deputy Secretary of State Strobe Talbott said in Moscow that the Russians were breaking 'the norms of international law' in their prosecution of the Chechnya conflict and that there were substantial disagreements between the two countries.

Mr Clinton flew from Turkey to Greece on 20 November for a visit which had been postponed because of security concerns and which was reduced from three days to one. The President apparently won over many of his critics when he apologized for US support for the military junta which ruled Greece in 1967-74 and made it known that he wanted to help to solve the Cyprus problem before his term of office expired (see II.4.vi) In his main speech in Athens he said: 'We are all Greeks, not because of monuments and memories, but because what began here two-and-a-half thousand years ago [i.e. democracy] has at last been embraced all around the world.'

On 15 December Mr Clinton hosted a meeting between Israeli Prime Minister Ehud Barak and Syrian Foreign Minister Faruq al-Shara at the White House in the hope of expediting a peace agreement between the two countries (see V.2.iv). The President described the meeting as 'a big step along the path' towards peace.

2. CANADA

CAPITAL: Ottawa   AREA: 9,9970,610 sq km   POPULATION: 31,000,000 ('98)
OFFICIAL LANGUAGES: English & French   POLITICAL SYSTEM: federal parliamentary democracy
HEAD OF STATE: Queen Elizabeth II (since Feb '52)
GOVERNOR-GENERAL: Adrienne Clarkson (since Oct '99)
RULING PARTY: Liberal Party (since Oct '93)
HEAD OF GOVERNMENT: Jean Chrétien, Prime Minister (since Oct '93)
MAIN IGO MEMBERSHIPS (NON-UN): NATO, OECD, OSCE, G-7, OAS, NAFTA, APEC, CP, CWTH, Francophonie
CURRENCY: Canadian dollar (end-'99 £1= Can$2.38, US$1=Can$1.45)
GNP PER CAPITA: US$19,290 by exchange-rate calculation, US$21,860 by PPP calculation ('98)

THE final year of the 20th century was one of stability for Canada. The threat of Quebec secession appeared to have eased, there were no major political issues dividing the country, economic conditions were the most buoyant in the decade and, for the first time in over a quarter of a century, the national government registered a surplus in its financial accounts, with more expected in future years. The governing Liberal Party under Prime Minister Jean Chrétien, in office since 1993, enjoyed broad popular support, with most Canadians applauding M. Chrétien's pragmatic style and prudent management of the economy. Holding 157 seats in the 301-seat House of Commons, the Liberal government had a slim majority, but its legislative position was strengthened by the divided state of the opposition.

The Reform Party, stressing a limited role for government and conservative social values, formed the official opposition with 58 seats. Its support was confined to the three prairie provinces and British Columbia in western Canada. The party formed to promote separatist views in national politics ten years before, the Bloc Québécois, held 44 seats, all from the province of Quebec. The Progressive Conservative Party (PCP), dominant under Brian Mulroney in the 1980s, but reduced to a 'corporal's guard' by the Chrétien Liberals in the election of 1993, still struggled to re-establish itself as a national party. Under the resumed leadership of former Prime Minister Joe Clark (61), who had not yet returned to parliament, the PCP held 19 seats, mostly from the Maritime provinces. It resisted overtures from the Reform leader Preston Manning to join a 'United Alternative' to the governing Liberals. Mr Manning pointed out that a good number of Liberal seats in Ontario, the party's base, had been won because the conservative vote was divided. But differences on social issues and a coolness between the two leaders kept the parties apart. Canada's socialist party, the New Democratic Party (NDP), found little support for its views among Canadians in 1999. It held 20 seats, mostly from the Maritimes, where it had mounted a strong stand against the Liberal government's cuts in unemployment assistance and social benefits. There were also three independent members in the Commons.

With an opposition often voicing the particular concerns of the regions from which it drew support, the Liberal government was able to capture the middle ground on most national issues. A loyal cabinet dominated by a core group of powerful ministers maintained M. Chrétien's steady course. The most important was Paul Martin, Minister of Finance, who was widely regarded as the Prime Minister's probable successor. M. Chrétien, however, showed no signs of retiring. He announced that he hoped to follow the example of his political hero, Sir Wilfrid Laurier, who had led a Liberal government in 1900, by bringing his own administration into the new millennium. Warming to the theme, he later declared that he hoped to lead his government through a third general election, likely to take place in 2001. In October Canada gained a personage of a different stamp in the appointment of Adrienne Clarkson (60) as the country's 26th Governor-General. Ms Clarkson, a broadcaster and commentator known for her graceful literary style and fervent nationalist convictions, followed a succession of ex-political figures in the vice-regal office. Of Chinese origin, she had come to Canada with her parents as a little girl after the fall of Hong Kong in 1942. She was expected to bring vigour and style to the largely ceremonial office.

Six of Canada's ten provinces held elections in 1999. With three sitting governments defeated and three returned to office, it was difficult to discern a trend in the results. In New Brunswick and Nova Scotia, Liberal administrations were defeated, in each case by the PCP. In Manitoba, the NDP opposition displaced a PCP government of 11 years' standing. Its neighbours,

Ontario and Saskatchewan, returned incumbent PCP and NDP governments respectively. Newfoundland continued a Liberal administration in office. Generally, the Liberal Party did poorly in the provincial elections, reflecting an historical Canadian tendency to support different parties at the provincial and federal levels.

Separatism was not a burning issue in 1999. Polls indicated that it attracted the support of about 40 per cent of decided voters within Quebec, the same percentage gained when the Parti Québécois (PQ) was returned to office in 1998. Led by Premier Lucien Bouchard, the PQ continued to emphasize economic growth and financial retrenchment in an effort to prepare the ground for a later referendum on independence. The provincial budget, brought down on 9 March, revealed the government's success in the second of these objectives. A year ahead of schedule, the government announced a balanced budget for the fiscal year 1998-99, ending 31 March. This result was partly due to an unexpected windfall in equalization payments from Ottawa, designed to maintain a uniform level of social services across Canada. It was Quebec's first balanced budget in 40 years. For several years budget trimming had been accomplished by severe cuts in medical services, and the strain began to show in 1999. The province's 47,500 nurses embarked on a 26-day strike in June, claiming that budget cuts had left them with salaries that were among the lowest in Canada. The Quebec government, which bargained centrally with all public-sector employees, offered the nurses a 5 per cent increase over the next three years, consistent with its budget-retrenchment guidelines. Although the nurses enjoyed wide public support, they eventually accepted the government's offer. Hard bargaining with other groups among the province's 400,000 public employees continued throughout the rest of the year. M. Bouchard's belt-tightening was expected to hurt the separatist cause, since sovereignty for Quebec had always been popular in the province's labour unions. Premier Bouchard continued to insist that he wanted another referendum on independence (the third since 1980) before the end of his present term. This pledge would mean another vote before 2003.

Prime Minister Chrétien, leading the national government, made it clear that his government's actions would be based on the Supreme Court of Canada's decision on the legality of secession, delivered in August 1998 (see AR 1998, pp. 180-1). Unilateral secession by a province was clearly illegal, but if the voters of Quebec, answering a clear question with a decided majority, supported separatism, then the federal government and the provinces would be obligated to negotiate the issue. M. Chrétien announced in November that his government would bring forward a parliamentary enactment (legislation or a resolution) spelling out the conditions that would govern future negotiations. The Quebec legislature would be free to define the wording of a referendum question, but the question would have to be acceptable to Ottawa. M. Chrétien declined to specify the level of support a successful referendum would have to secure, but hinted that a 60 per cent majority would be necessary to validate the momentous decision to divide the country.

Canada enjoyed a prosperous year in 1999, with an estimated expansion in gross domestic product (GDP) of between 3 and 3.5 per cent. There were several reasons for this. The prices of commodities, still an important sector of Canada's trade, recovered as the Asian economies began to regain strength. The booming US economy offered a ready market for an unprecedented 80 per cent of Canada's exports. Confidence, both in business circles and among consumers, returned to bolster economic growth. The Canadian dollar, battered against its American counterpart in 1998, held up steadily in 1999. The level of unemployment fell to 6.9 per cent in November, its lowest rate in 18 years. Inflation remained at a moderate level, the gain in the consumer price index hovering at around 2 per cent during the year.

Finance Minister Martin reported encouraging trends in his sixth budget, brought down on 16 February. For the second year in a row he was able to balance the budget, the first time this has happened since 1951-52. Mr Martin offered increased grants to the provinces for health, education and social service, totalling Can$2,500 million over the next three years. This would bring the level of funding to Can$15,000 million by 2000-01, the point which had been reached when the Liberal government began its budget-cutting programme in 1996. The Finance Minister offered only modest tax cuts, while promising more action on this front in the first year of the millennium.

Canada's defence forces, numbering 60,000 men and women, emphasized peace-keeping and humanitarian assistance in 1999. Some 4,000 served abroad on peace-keeping assignments in locations ranging from Haiti and the Middle East to central Africa. The bulk of Canadian peace-keepers were stationed in Bosnia & Hercegovina and in Kosovo, aiding international efforts to bring stability to these troubled regions. About 1,400 Canadians were serving in each theatre at year's end. In September 600 Canadian personnel were sent to East Timor to participate in the Australian-led force restoring civilian rule to the former Indonesian territory (see IX.1.vi). Canada provided military transport aircraft, infantry and a supply vessel to the East Timor operation. Canadian CF-18 aircraft also took part in the NATO action over Kosovo in the spring (see III.2.vi). From Aviano air base in Italy, they flew 618 bombing missions against Serb forces in Kosovo and against installations in Serbia itself.

It was evident that peace support duties were imposing a strain on Canada's defence forces, which had suffered under-funding for years. Criticism of Canada's performance in fulfilling NATO obligations occurred at meetings of the alliance in Toronto in September. Critics compared Canada's defence spending under the alliance to that of Luxembourg, the smallest partner in the organization. The Chrétien government pointed to the acquisition of new weapons systems and sophisticated frigates as a compensation for reduced manpower and defence spending. Lloyd Axworthy, the Minister of Foreign Affairs, took a dovish stance within the NATO alliance. He called on the major nuclear powers to reduce their armaments, stating that this would encourage efforts at global nuclear disarmament. It was unrealistic to expect lesser powers, such as India and Pakistan, to renounce nuclear weapons unless the great powers took the lead. Mr Axworthy also opposed the 'first-use possibility' of nuclear weapons in NATO's strategic thinking. His position was strongly opposed by the United States but received support from Germany.

During the summer months four shipments of illegal immigrants from Fujian province in southern China came ashore on Canada's Pacific coast. Transported on rusty trawlers carrying no flags, 600 young people survived a gruelling 40-day voyage to the shores of Vancouver Island and the Queen Charlotte Islands. Three of the vessels were apprehended at sea and escorted to Canadian ports but the fourth dumped its cargo on a remote beach. Under Canadian law the immigrants were entitled to a judicial hearing to determine their eligibility as refugee claimants. In the past many unauthorized Chinese immigrants had gone underground rather than show up for the hearings. It was believed that criminal gangs, who would eventually smuggle the migrants into the United States, had managed the operation.

3. LATIN AMERICA

ARGENTINA—BOLIVIA—BRAZIL—CHILE—COLOMBIA—ECUADOR—
PARAGUAY—PERU—URUGUAY—VENEZUELA—CUBA—DOMINICAN REPUBLIC
AND HAITI—CENTRAL AMERICA AND PANAMA—MEXICO

i. ARGENTINA

CAPITAL: Buenos Aires   AREA: 2,766,890 sq km   POPULATION: 36,000,000 ('98)
OFFICIAL LANGUAGE: Spanish   POLITICAL SYSTEM: federal presidential democracy
HEAD OF STATE & GOVERNMENT: President Fernando de la Rúa Bruno (since Dec '99)
RULING PARTY: Radical Civic Union–National Solidarity Front (since Dec '99)
MAIN IGO MEMBERSHIPS (NON-UN): OAS, SELA, ALADI, Mercosur
CURRENCY: peso (end-'99 £1=AP1.61, US$1=AP1.00)
GNP PER CAPITA: US$8,970 by exchange-rate calculation, US$10,200 at PPP ('98)

THE arrest of former military President General Reynaldo Bignone (see AR 1982, p. 82) was ordered by a judge on 21 January. The charge—involvement in the theft of babies born to detainees during the 'dirty war'—was not covered by the 1989 amnesty. Vice-Admiral (retd) Rubén Oscar Franco was arrested a few days later, after former naval captain Jorge Acosta had surrendered voluntarily. General (retd) Guillermo Suárez Mason was arrested on the same charge on 3 December. On 30 December the Spanish judge Baltasar Garzón issued international arrest warrants for 49 people alleged to be complicit in genocide, terrorism and torture, including former military Presidents Jorge Rafael Videla and Leopoldo Galtieri, effectively confining them to Argentinian territory.

The IMF had earlier agreed to relax conditions on its three-year loan under the extended fund facility to permit the fiscal deficit created by Argentina's 'dollarization' policy to rise in 1999 to US$5,000 million; in September the World Bank approved a further small basic guarantee facility to support operations on the world financial markets. However, the news that Labour and Social Security Minister Antonio Ermán González was receiving a personal pension from the President in addition to his salary forced his resignation on 21 May. He was replaced by José Alberto Uriburu and the Minister of Education and Culture, Susana Decibe, by Manuel García Sola.

On 22 March the Peronist Party (PJ) governor of Catamarca, Ramón Saadi, was defeated for re-election by Oscar Castillo of the Radical Civic Union (UCR), running as candidate of the opposition Alliance of the UCR and the National Solidarity Front (Frepaso). With Sr Saadi therefore out of the race for the PJ presidential nomination, the surprise withdrawal on 7 June of Adolfo Rodríguez Saá, current governor of San Luis, left the governor of Buenos Aires province, Eduardo Duhalde Maldonado, unopposed as the PJ's candidate.

However, in the presidential elections held on 24 October the conservative 62-year-old mayor of Buenos Aires, Fernando de la Rúa Bruno (Alliance) won a decisive victory, taking 9,039,892 votes (48.5 per cent) to 7,100,678 (38.1 per cent) for Sr Duhalde (PJ) and 1,881,417 (10.1 per cent) for Domingo Felipe Cavallo (Acción por la República, ApR). Simultaneous elections to renew 130 of the 257 seats in the 257-member the Chamber of Deputies resulted in the composition of the lower chamber becoming as follows: Alliance 127, PJ 101, ApR 12, others 17. The PJ nevertheless retained its majority in the Senate, with 40 seats to 21 for the UCR and three for Frepaso. In a surprise result, moreover, incumbent Vice-President Carlos Ruckauf (PJ) won the race to succeed Sr Duhalde as governor of Buenos Aires province, the nation's second most powerful political position. Sr de la Rua was sworn in as President on 10 December, appointing Rodolfo Terragno as his Head of Cabinet and José Luis Machinea as Economy Minister. In late December the new Congress approved an austerity budget cutting public expenditure by $1,400 million, a major tax reform programme and a federal revenue-sharing scheme.

One of the President-elect's first statements after his election confirmed his intention to maintain existing policy on the Falkland Islands/Islas Malvinas. In mid-January Foreign Minister Guido di Tella had offered to freeze his country's claims to sovereignty in return for a number of symbolic concessions, which once again the islanders were not prepared to concede. During an official visit to Argentina on 9-11 March Prince Charles, having earlier laid a wreath on the monument to the Argentinians who had fallen in the 1982 war, referred to the islanders' right to self-determination. Though this provoked criticism, it did not appear to surprise his hosts unduly. During a visit to London in May the Foreign Minister held talks for the first time with members of the Falkland Islands legislature, at their initiative. On 14 July, moreover, the UK and Argentine governments concluded an agreement ending restrictions on travel to the islands by Argentine citizens and re-establishing direct air links between the islands and the mainland from 16 October. On 1 November the British and Argentine navies began their first joint exercises since 1982.

The Senate had meanwhile, on 3 June, ratified the 1998 Continental Glaciers Treaty, ending the last remaining boundary dispute with Chile.

ii. BOLIVIA

CAPITAL: La Paz and Sucre   AREA: 1,099,000 sq km   POPULATION: 8,000,000 ('98)
OFFICIAL LANGUAGES: Spanish, Quechua, Aymará   POLITICAL SYSTEM: presidential democracy
HEAD OF STATE & GOVERNMENT: President Hugo Banzer Suárez (since Aug '97)
RULING PARTIES: Democratic Nationalist Action (AND) heads coalition with Civic Solidarity Union (UCS), New Republican Force (NFR) & Movement of the Revolutionary Left (MIR)
MAIN IGO MEMBERSHIPS (NON-UN): NAM, OAS, ALADI, SELA, AG, CA
CURRENCY: boliviano (end-'99 £1=Bs9.54, US$1=Bs5.92)
GNP PER CAPITA: US$1,000 by exchange-rate calculation, US$2,820 at PPP ('98)

DESPITE opposition from some 60 environmental groups in 25 countries, Hugo Banzer Suárez, jointly with President Cardoso of Brazil, on 9 February inaugurated the $2,000 million pipeline designed to carry some 8 million cubic metres of natural gas a year from Santa Cruz de la Sierra to São Paulo via Cuiabá, Brazil. In July the President was able to announce that a vast new gas field, estimated to contain 300,000 million cubic metres (equivalent of all Bolivia's existing proved reserves), had been located in the south by Petrobrás. However, the government's economic policies continued to provoke demonstrations by the Bolivian Workers' Central (COB).

On 31 March the Labour Minister, Leopoldo López, was forced to resign after allegations surfaced that he was linked with smuggling, while the commander of the national police, Ivar Narváez, resigned in May amid accusations that he had blocked investigations of corruption. A major reshuffle of the Cabinet followed on 21 June. In November the Argentine government agreed to pay US$224,000 compensation to the widow of former President Juan José Torres, who had been murdered in Buenos Aires in 1976 as part of 'Operation Condor'. Meanwhile, Congress had approved a new penal code, incorporating for the first time customary Quechua and Aymará law.

iii. BRAZIL

CAPITAL: Brasília   AREA: 8,512,000 sq km   POPULATION: 165,000,000 ('98)
OFFICIAL LANGUAGE: Portuguese   POLITICAL SYSTEM: federal presidential democracy
HEAD OF STATE & GOVERNMENT: President Fernando Henrique Cardoso (since Jan '95)
RULING PARTIES: Brazilian Social Democratic Party (PSDB) heads coalition with Liberal Front Party (PFL), Brazilian Progressive Party (PPB), Popular Socialist Party (PPS) & Brazilian Democratic Movement Party (PMDB)
MAIN IGO MEMBERSHIPS (NON-UN): OAS, ALADI, SELA, Mercosur, AP, CPLP
CURRENCY: real (end-'99 £1=R2.89, US$1=R1.79)
GNP PER CAPITA: US$4,570 by exchange-rate calculation, US$6,160 at PPP ('98)

BRAZIL recorded its second successive quarter of negative growth in the last quarter of 1998 and began the year in recession. The announcement by Itamar Franco, a former President and current governor of Minas Gerais state, of a 90-day moratorium on payment of his state's debt precipitated a major financial crisis. Emergency action by the federal government of Fernando Henrique Cardoso failed to halt capital flight; on 13 January the real was devalued and two days later allowed to float, thus ending the exchange-rate peg of the 'real plan' (see AR 1993, p. 175). The Chamber responded by passing a long-delayed civil service pensions bill and on 27 January approved the budget.

Early in February the government was therefore able to reach agreement with the IMF on adapting the stand-by programme agreed in December (see AR 1998, p. 187) to the floating rate regime. On 8 March the IMF managing director, Michel Camdessus, recommended approval for the government's 1999-2001 counter-inflationary strategy, so permitting a second credit disbursement of US$4,900 million. However, Francisco Lopes, who as newly-appointed governor of the Banco Central do Brasil had carried through the devaluation, was dismissed on 2 February and replaced by Arminio Fraga Neto, a Soros Foundation executive. At the same time Paulo Paiva was dismissed as Minister of Budget and Management, this resulting in the withdrawal of his Brazilian Labour Party (PTB) from the ruling coalition in March. Sr Lopes was arrested on 26 April after evidence of a $1.7 million foreign bank account was found in his apartment, but was freed by the Supreme Court the following day.

With his popularity on the wane, President Cardoso announced on 31 August a massive new spending programme designed to counter rising social unrest. Yet on 7 October the government was forced to announce a new package of measures to cover the anticipated budget shortfall caused by a Supreme Court ruling on 30 September that retired civil servants were not liable to make social security payments. Other measures followed, aimed at boosting consumer demand, and in November the Senate finally approved long-delayed tax increases.

Agripino Soares da Silva, the leader of the Rural Workers' Union who had led a mass protest in May against government land policy in the state of Pará, was found murdered some ten days later. On 18 June, after only three days in office, the new head of the federal police was forced to resign by allegations of complicity in torture in the 1970s and was replaced by the force's first black commander, Agildo Monteiro Filho. Meanwhile, however, the President had been able on 10 June to sign into law a bill creating a unified Defence Ministry under civilian control, with Elcio Alvares as minister. A cabinet reshuffle was announced on 19 July. Following the killing of Maria Dorcelina Folador, mayor of Mundo Novo in the state of Mato Grosso do Sul, who had resolutely opposed the drugs trade, a federal task force was established to combat organized crime.

Three days of national mourning were decreed for the death on 27 August of Dom Hélder Câmara, Archbishop of Olinda and Recife from 1964 to 1985.

iv. CHILE

CAPITAL: Santiago   AREA: 756,000 sq km   POPULATION: 15,000,000 ('98)
OFFICIAL LANGUAGE: Spanish   POLITICAL SYSTEM: presidential democracy
HEAD OF STATE & GOVERNMENT: President Eduardo Frei Rúis-Tagle (since March '94)
RULING PARTIES: Christian Democratic Party (PDC) heads Coalition for Democracy (CPD)
MAIN IGO MEMBERSHIPS (NON-UN): OAS, ALADI, SELA, NAM, APEC
CURRENCY: peso (end-'99 £1=Ch$853.88, US$1=Ch$529.80)
GNP PER CAPITA: US$4,810 by exchange-rate calculation, US$12,890 at PPP ('98)

THE decision of the UK law lords announced on 24 March, that Spain's application to extradite General (retd) Augusto Pinochet Ugarte was valid (see II.1.i), aroused predictable fury amongst the General's supporters. It had been revealed on 19 February that, at the urging of Chile's government, the Vatican had added its voice to those calling for the General to be released on humanitarian grounds. Their expressed concern, that the General's continued detention might harm Chile's national process of reconciliation, was later echoed by Baroness Thatcher in a public gesture of support for the former dictator (ibid.). Other prominent figures calling for the General to be allowed to return to Chile included former US Secretary of State Henry Kissinger and former US President George Bush.

The government announced on 19 March that it was suspending its weekly flights from Punta Arenas to the Falkland Islands in protest at General Pinochet's continued detention in Britain. However, on 19 May Foreign Minister José Miguel Insulza conceded that his department had acted improperly in issuing the former President with a diplomatic passport for a private visit. In a cabinet reshuffle on 21 June, therefore, he was replaced by Juan Gabriel Valdés, while Edmundo Pérez Yoma was recalled to the Defence Ministry to improve relations with the armed forces. After Spain had refused to intervene in the judicial process, Sr Valdés announced on 15 September that the government would ask the International Court of Justice to establish whether Spain really had jurisdiction.

Meanwhile, in an important development on 9 June, a judge of the Court of Appeal had ordered the arrest of five high-ranking retired army officers who had commanded the special unit known under the Pinochet dictatorship as 'the caravan of death'. The charge—of kidnapping 72 political prisoners in the weeks immediately following the 1973 coup—lay outside the scope of the 1978 amnesty law and could not be evaded, since in law the victims were considered to be still alive. Two more retired generals, Humberto Gordon Rubio, former head of the National Intelligence Centre (CNI), and Roberto Schmied, were arrested on 14 September for the abduction and murder of a trade union official in 1982. In October, moreover, General (retd) Hugo Salas Wenzel, another former head of CNI, was indicted for the killing of 12 alleged members of a guerrilla organization in 1987.

A further blow to the credibility of General Pinochet came with the declassification on 30 June by the US government of some 5,800 hitherto secret files conclusively demonstrating that his regime had fabricated the allegation that it was President Allende who had been planning a coup in 1973 (the so-called 'Plan Z') and confirming that the Nixon administration had been made fully aware of the human rights abuses committed under the General's authority. On 21 October, moreover, the president of the Supreme Court, Roberto Dávila, ruled that General (retd) Manuel Contreras Sepúlveda, former head of the Department of National Intelligence (DINA, the Pinochet regime's secret police), could be extradited to Italy on the conclusion of his current seven-year sentence for the 1976 murder of Orlando Letelier in Washington (see AR 1995, p. 172).

Power rationing was introduced from 1 April as drought reduced generating capacity; its spread to Santiago caused daily street demonstrations and two died in clashes on 11 September, the first anniversary of the 1973 coup not to have been observed as a public holiday. Unemployment, which had risen to 11 per cent in 1998, was widely believed to be higher, and on 3 September longstanding restrictions on currency movements were removed and the peso allowed to float against the US dollar.

Significantly, Senate president Andrés Zaldívar, of President Frei's Christian Democratic Party (PDC), was on 30 May heavily defeated in the presidential primary for the nomination of the ruling Concertación coalition by Ricardo Lagos Escobar. Sr Lagos was a former Socialist Minister of Public Works who had been briefly detained in 1986 following an unsuccessful assassination attempt on General Pinochet, the following year founding the Party for Democracy (PPD). In the first round of the presidential elections on 12 December, however, Gladys Marín Millie, the Communist Party candidate, gained sufficient votes (3.2 per cent) to deny Sr Lagos (with 48.0 per cent) outright victory against his right-wing opponent, Joaquín Lavín Infante (47.5 per cent) of the Independent Democratic Union (UDI). The run-off was scheduled for 16 January 2000.

On 9 April Cardinal Raúl Silva Henríquez, who as Archbishop of Santiago from 1961 to 1983 had sought to defend human rights during the Pinochet dictatorship, died on 9 April at the age of 91 (see Pt XVIII: Obituary). The last survivor of the Ona people of Tierra del Fuego, Virginia Choinquitel, died in early June.

v. COLOMBIA

CAPITAL: Santa Fe de Bogotá   AREA: 1,141,750 sq km   POPULATION: 41,000,000 ('98)
OFFICIAL LANGUAGE: Spanish   POLITICAL SYSTEM: presidential democracy
HEAD OF STATE & GOVERNMENT: President Andrés Pastrana Arango (since Aug '98)
RULING PARTIES: Social Conservative Party (PSC) heads Great Alliance for Change
MAIN IGO MEMBERSHIPS (NON-UN): OAS, ALADI, SELA, AG, CA, ACS, NAM
CURRENCY: peso (end-'99 £1=Col$3,021.94, US$1=Col$1,875.00)
GNP PER CAPITA: US$2,600 by exchange-rate calculation, US$7,500 at PPP ('98)

TALKS had been due to open on 7 January between President Andrés Pastrana Arango and the Revolutionary Armed Forces of Colombia (FARC), but the FARC leader, Manuel Marulanda Vélez ('Tirofijo'), failed to turn up. Right-wing death squads linked to the United Self-Defence of Colombia (AUC) then rampaged through villages across the country, killing some 150 civilians. The National Liberation Army (ELN), which broke off talks on 16 February, hijacked an Avianca Fokker airliner on 12 April during an internal flight from Bucaramanga to Bogotá; 15 of the 46 passengers were still held hostage at the end of the year. The ELN kidnapping of members of a church congregation in Cali on 30 June, however, rebounded when it was vigorously condemned by the Church; the hostages were eventually released, the last three not until 10 December.

Meanwhile, the President had made further concessions to the FARC concerning the withdrawal of troops in the south, on 18 February even proposing the disbandment of Convivir civilian self-defence units set up to protect rural areas. On 10 March the FARC admitted that its forces had murdered three US civilians who had been working with the U'wa community in the north-east. Despite this, two senior generals accused of links with the paramilitaries were retired and an unannounced meeting took place between the President and Sr Marulanda on 30 April, following which talks with FARC began on 6 May with a representative of the armed forces taking part for the first time. However, when the President declared permanent the military withdrawal from Meta and Caquetá (see AR 1998, p. 190), the Defence Minister, Rodrigo Lloreda Caicedo, resigned on 26 May with the backing of some 20 generals.

Soon afterwards, on 7 June, a political reform bill giving the President broad powers to further the peace process was defeated in Congress. Its members were not alone in believing that too many concessions had already been made, and on 12 July the President called off a visit to Boyacá after warning that his assassination was planned. By then an FARC attack on the AUC headquarters in the Nudo de Paramillo highlands, which drew army units into a series of ambushes, had been succeeded by a nationwide FARC offensive in which some 200 died. The previous day the AUC had murdered 16 businessmen in Boyacá. When on 27 July the two alleged AUC leaders were arraigned in Bogotá, it was only on the formal offence of the theft and destruction of identity documents.

By September the conflict had spread into Venezuela, Ecuador, Peru, Brazil and Panama, all of which mobilized forces to contain the conflict. The AUC, accusing Panama's National Guard of being in collusion with the guerrillas, threatened reprisals. As massive demonstrations took place for peace on 24 October, the government reopened negotiations with the FARC. A third round of negotiations began on 18 November and the FARC called a Christmas truce on 20 December, having on 12 December carried out an attack on a naval base at Jurado in which some 50 marines died and many were injured.

The economy continued in deep recession, not assisted by a major earthquake on 25 January which killed more than 900 people in the department of Quindío and left more than 250,000 homeless. Following heavy speculation, the peso was devalued by some 9 per cent on 28 June. However, on 24

September international financial institutions led by the IMF and Inter-American Development Bank agreed a loan of US$6,900 million to avert social crisis, the peso being allowed to float freely two days later. On 20 December the IMF approved a further three-year credit. US reports indicated that coca cultivation had increased by 28 per cent in 1998, but Washington commended President Pastrana for his efforts to combat the problem. For the first time in three years, the US government on 26 February certified Colombia (together with Mexico, Bolivia and Peru) as cooperating fully in the anti-drugs programme.

vi. ECUADOR

CAPITAL: Quito   AREA: 270,500 sq km   POPULATION: 12,000,000 ('98)
OFFICIAL LANGUAGE: Spanish   POLITICAL SYSTEM: presidential democracy
HEAD OF STATE & GOVERNMENT: President Jamil Mahuad Witt (since July '98)
RULING PARTIES: Popular Democracy (DP) heads coalition
MAIN IGO MEMBERSHIPS (NON-UN): OAS, ALADI, SELA, AG, CA, NAM
CURRENCY: sucre (end-'99 £1=S31,734.40, US$1=S19,690.00)
GNP PER CAPITA: US$1,530 by exchange-rate calculation, US$4,630 at PPP ('98)

ECUADOR began the year in economic crisis exacerbated by losses sustained in 1998 floods resulting from the effects of El Niño weather distortion. President Jamil Mahuad Witt decreed national mourning for Jaime Hurtado González, former presidential candidate of the Popular Democratic Movement (PMD), who was shot and killed, together with his nephew and a bodyguard, while leaving the National Assembly on 17 February. Arrests followed, linking the assassination to right-wing Colombian paramilitaries. The United Workers' Front (FUT) mounted massive demonstrations, widening into protests against government economic policy.

In early March anxiety about low world prices for the country's main export, oil, precipitated a 38 per cent fall in the exchange rate of the sucre and a run on the banks, which were closed on 8 March. Faced in addition with a general strike by trade unions, Indian organizations and grassroots activists of the Patriotic Front, the President proclaimed a state of emergency on 11 March, a partial freeze on bank withdrawals and a tough austerity programme. Following the withdrawal of support by the Social Christian Party (PSC) on 15 March, the programme passed Congress only with a bare majority and in revised form. The state of emergency lifted (except in Guayas, where it was extended for 60 days), the Banco del Progreso, Guayaquil, collapsed seven days later.

The launch on 14 April of the President's 'Ecuador 2000' plan, a substantial package of economic and social development measures, was inevitably marred by doubts about the cost of the proposals, given that servicing the country's US$16,000 million debt required 41 per cent of the annual budget. Announcing the conditions, the President triggered a strike by taxi and truck drivers and public transport workers and unrest which continued to spread after his proclamation of a state of emergency on 5 July. By 16 July he had been forced to cancel proposed fuel price increases, further concessions following before the state of emergency was lifted on 19 July. Ana Lucia Armijos resigned as Finance Minister and was replaced on 8 September by Alfredo Arizaga.

On 28 September Ecuador defaulted on $44 million in interest payments due on its 'Brady bonds', the first country to do so, triggering a demand by its creditors for accelerated repayment of capital. The government responded with a letter of intent to the IMF requesting a stand-by loan of $400 million to enable restructuring of the whole outstanding debt of $16,000 million, representing 110 per cent of GDP. In the 2000 budget approved by Congress on 25 November, 54 per cent of expenditure was earmarked for debt service. A number of cabinet changes were announced in mid-December, but the country remained in deep economic crisis at year's end.

Abroad, the Presidents of Ecuador and Peru jointly attended a ceremony in February for the placing in the Lagartococha area of the first of the 27 markers which were to delimit the common frontier finally agreed in 1998 (see AR 1998, p. 184). The Foreign Minister, José Ayala Lasso, resigned on 21 May and was replaced by Benjamín Ortiz, a well-known political writer. Sr Ayala, who was to represent Ecuador at the Holy See, was reported to have resisted the government's decision to vote against Cuba in the UN Human Rights Commission.

vii. PARAGUAY

CAPITAL: Asunción   AREA: 406,752 sq km   POPULATION: 5,000,000 ('98)
OFFICIAL LANGUAGE: Spanish   POLITICAL SYSTEM: presidential democracy
HEAD OF STATE & GOVERNMENT: President Luís González Macchi (since March '99)
RULING PARTIES: Colorado Party (ANR-PC) heads coalition with Authentic Radical Liberal Party (PLRA) and National Encounter (EN)
MAIN IGO MEMBERSHIPS (NON-UN): OAS, ALADI, SELA, Mercosur
CURRENCY: guarani (end-'99 £1=G5,346.82, US$1=G3,317.50)
GNP PER CAPITA: US$1,760 by exchange-rate calculation, US$3,650 at PPP ('98)

VICE-PRESIDENT Luís María Argaña Ferraro was assassinated on the streets of Asunción on 23 March when three men in military uniform opened fire on the car in which he was travelling. Tensions had been running high and the 66-year-old Sr Argaña and his supporters had just succeeded in regaining control of the headquarters of the ruling Colorado Party (ANR-PC), from which they had been expelled on 14 March by supporters of General (retd) Lino César Oviedo Silva and his protégé, President Raúl Cubas Grau. The latter were immediately accused by 'Argañistas' of being at least the 'moral instigators' of the crime, following which large crowds filled the streets demanding the President's resignation.

The President responded by replacing Interior Minister Rubén Arias Mendoza with his own brother, Navy Captain Carlos Cubas Grau, and by detaining General Oviedo, having earlier refused to obey an order of the Supreme Court to do so. On 26 March four died and 60 were injured when snipers fired on crowds holding a vigil outside Congress. By then, however, Congress had by initiated impeachment proceedings against the President. On

28 March, hours before the vote on the critical resolution, President Cubas resigned and fled to Brazil, where he was granted political asylum, while General Oviedo simultaneously sought and was granted asylum in Argentina. The president of the Senate, Luís González Macchi, immediately took the oath of office as interim President for the remainder of Sr Cubas's five-year term (i.e. until 2003).

President González Macchi appointed a cabinet of national unity including members of the Authentic Radical Liberal Party (PLRA) and National Encounter (EN), although the key posts went to ANR-PC members Miguel Abdón Tito Saguier (foreign relations), Walter Bower Montalto (interior) and Federico Zayas Chirife (finance and economy). On 6 April the President ordered the dishonourable discharge of General Oviedo, and in a major reshuffle of the armed forces command on 21 April General Expedito Garrigoza replaced General Guillermo Rolando Escobar Fariña as army commander. A week later the Senate voted to lift the parliamentary immunity of ex-President Cubas, orders being given to seek his arrest. General José Segovia Voltes, his Defence Minister, who had been charged with corruption, was granted political asylum in Uruguay early in May.

In July a judge ordered General Oviedo's arrest as an alleged 'moral co-author' of Sr Argaña's assassination. On 2 September, however, Argentina rejected for a second time a request for General Oviedo's extradition, though he was later ordered to be confined to Tierra del Fuego for breaching the terms of his asylum by giving a newspaper interview. The following day Foreign Minister Saguier resigned under pressure from Sr Argaña's widow and her son, Nelson Argaña, the new Defence Minister. He was replaced by José Félix Fernández Estigarribia. Meanwhile, on 3 July one of Sr Argaña's alleged assassins, José Villar Benítez, had been killed in a shoot-out with police; another, Pablo Vera Esteche, was arrested on 23 October.

Tensions between the Defence Minister and the armed forces commander, General Eligio Torres Heyn, led to the resignation of the latter on 11 October and his replacement by Rear-Admiral José Ocampo Alfaro. However, although 14 officers were arrested, the government denied rumours that an attempted military coup on 21 November had brought the President back a day early from the Ibero-American summit in Cuba (see XI.6.iv).

viii. PERU

CAPITAL: Lima   AREA: 1,285,000 sq km   POPULATION: 25,000,000 ('98)
OFFICIAL LANGUAGES: Spanish, Quechua, Aymará   POLITICAL SYSTEM: presidential democracy
HEAD OF STATE & GOVERNMENT: President Alberto Keinya Fujimori (since July '90)
RULING PARTIES: New Majority-Change 90 heads government coalition
PRIME MINISTER: Alberto Bustamante Belaúnde (since Aug '99)
MAIN IGO MEMBERSHIPS (NON-UN): NAM, OAS, ALADI, SELA, CA, AP
CURRENCY: new sol (end-'99 £1=NS5.66, US$1=NS3.51)
GNP PER CAPITA: US$2,460 by exchange-rate calculation ('98)

THE year began with the news of the capture on 31 December 1998 of Juan Carlos Rios, senior military commander of Sendero Luminoso (SL). On 14 July Oscar Ramírez Durand ('Feliciano'), leader of Red Path, its last known active faction, was also captured. Nevertheless, SL guerrillas attacked an army patrol near Satipo on 2 October. Meanwhile, up to 600 imprisoned members of the Túpac Amaru Revolutionary Movement (MRTA) staged a hunger strike in protest at their harsh conditions.

On 1 February the opposition nominated former President Alan García Pérez to head the party's list for the next congressional elections. If elected, Sr García, who was currently in exile following his conviction in 1995 on corruption charges (see AR 1995, pp. 176-7), would be exempt from further prosecution. Protests by cabinet members and leading members of the ruling New Majority–Change 90 alliance forced out Labour Minister Jorge Jamil Mufarech on 15 April for bringing corruption charges against customs officials. On 28 April a one-day strike against government economic policy and President Alberto Keinya Fujimori's intention to stand for a third term brought a strong response from trade unions and opposition political parties. On 24 June the IMF approved a three-year credit under the extended fund facility in support of the government's economic programme for 1999-2001.

Eight opposition parties, including the American Popular Revolutionary Alliance (APRA), had previously agreed to form a united front to oppose the President should he choose to run again; by September the two leading opposition candidates, Luis Castañeda Lossio of National Solidarity and Alberto Andrade of Somos Perú, were both complaining that government security personnel, ostensibly assigned to protect them, were in fact harassing their supporters. In August the President of the Council of Ministers, Víctor Joy Way Rojas, resigned to contest the legislative elections; a new cabinet was appointed on 13 August, headed by Dr Alberto Bustamante Belaúnde, with Efraín Goldenberg Schreiber as Minister of Economy and Finance. Dr Bustamante immediately showed himself sensitive to long-standing criticism of the government by human rights advocates, and on 4 November the President announced that in future Congress would have oversight of the National Intelligence Services (SIN), currently controlled by Vladimiro Montesinos.

Interior Minister José Villanueva Ruesta was appointed commander of the armed forces on 24 July in place of General César Saucedo Sánchez. On 4 February, in a speech to the Inter-American Defence College in Washington, President Fujimori called on the entire region to unite against the threat from Colombian guerrillas, who had crossed the Putumayo river into Peru on a number of occasions in recent months (see IV.3.v). In concert with the President of Ecuador, he also pledged that his government would abstain from arms purchases over the next four years.

ix. URUGUAY

CAPITAL: Montevideo   AREA: 176,200 sq km   POPULATION: 3,300,000 ('98)
OFFICIAL LANGUAGE: Spanish   POLITICAL SYSTEM: presidential democracy
HEAD OF STATE & GOVERNMENT: President Julio María Sanguinetti Cairolo (since March '95)
PRESIDENT-ELECT: Jorge Batlle Ibáñez
RULING PARTIES: Colorado Party holds presidency and heads government including Blanco Party, People's Government Party & Civic Union
MAIN IGO MEMBERSHIPS (NON-UN): OAS, ALADI, SELA, Mercosur, NAM
CURRENCY: new peso (end-'99 £1=NUr$18.74, US$1=NUr11.63)
GNP PER CAPITA: US$6,180 by exchange-rate calculation, US$9,480 at PPP ('98)

THE IMF on 29 March approved a stand-by credit facility to support the government's 1999 economic programme. Agriculture remained depressed, and in August Luis Brezzo replaced Ignacio Zorrilla as Minister of Agriculture, Fisheries and Stock-raising. The year, however, was dominated by presidential elections.

In the first round held on 31 October, Tabaré Vázquez, former mayor of Montevideo and candidate of the left-wing Progressive Encounter–Broad Front (EP-FA) coalition, obtained 38.5 per cent of the votes against 31.3 per cent for Jorge Batlle Ibáñez, who had secured the nomination of the ruling Colorado Party over Luis Hierro López, candidate of outgoing President Julio María Sanguinetti. Former President Luis Alberto Lacalle Ibáñez (1990-95) of the centre-right National (Blanco) Party (PN) obtained only 21.3 per cent (the worst showing in the party's history) and Rafael Michelini of the moderate left New Space (Nueva Espacio) only 4.4 per cent.

Despite offering reassurances to the financial sector that he would maintain Uruguay as the 'American Switzerland', Sr Vázquez was decisively defeated by Sr Batlle in the run-off contest on 28 November, the latter's formal coalition with the PN giving him 54.1 per cent of the vote to 45.9 per cent for Sr Vázquez. In legislative elections on 31 October the Senate results were: EP-FA 12, Colorados 10, PN 7, New Space 1; the new Chamber composition was: EP-FA 40, Colorados 32, PN 23, New Space 4.

x. VENEZUELA

CAPITAL: Caracas   AREA: 912,000 sq km   POPULATION: 23,000,000 ('98)
OFFICIAL LANGUAGE: Spanish   POLITICAL SYSTEM:presidential democracy
HEAD OF STATE & GOVERNMENT: President Hugo Chávez Frias (since Feb '99)
RULING PARTIES: Patriotic Front coalition
MAIN IGO MEMBERSHIPS (NON-UN): OAS, ALADI, SELA, CA, ACS, OPEC, NAM
CURRENCY: bolívar (end-'99 £1=Bs1,045.59, US$1=Bs648.75)
GNP PER CAPITA: US$3,500 by exchange-rate calculation, US$8,190 at PPP ('98)

PRESIDENT-ELECT Hugo Chávez Frías was received by US President Bill Clinton in January in the course of a regional tour to reassure allies of his democratic intentions. Sr Chávez was sworn in on 2 February, appointing

José Vicente Rangel, a former presidential candidate of the Movement Towards Socialism (MAS), as Foreign Minister and Luis Miquelena, founder of the Fifth Republic Movement (MVR), as Interior Minister. The new President's first act, a decree calling a referendum on his proposal for a Constituent Assembly, was approved by voters on 25 April by a large majority but on a turnout of less than 40 per cent. Elections for an Assembly were nevertheless held on 25 July and gave the ruling Patriotic Front coalition 121 of the 128 contested seats (out of 131), with no seats going to either of the two traditionally dominant formations, Democratic Action (AD) and the Social Christian Party (COPEI), both now in opposition.

Finance Minister Martiza Izaguirre Porras had been retained in office for the time being as a sign of stability in economic policy, but on 17 February a draft 'enabling law' was sent to Congress authorizing the President to enact a series of emergency economic measures. In March the Inter-American Development Bank suspended the disbursement of a US$350 million package while the future of the social security system was reviewed. The bill was approved with amendments by Congress on 27 March but was subsequently returned by the President, who threatened to declare a state of emergency and dissolve Congress if the amendments were not withdrawn. On 22 April Congress granted him all the powers requested except that of raising a new bond issue without its consent. In early May value-added tax was introduced by decree at a flat rate of 15.5 per cent. The Finance Minister resigned on 1 July and was replaced by her deputy, José Rojas. Soon afterwards the President announced a new public works programme intended to create 250,000 new jobs.

At the end of August conflict between the Constituent Assembly and Congress came to a head when the former tried to close the latter by emergency decree. On 6 September, however, agreement was reached guaranteeing the freedom of Congress to continue to legislate until a new constitution had been ratified. A further referendum held on 16 December gave a 71 per cent majority to the new constitution, although on another low turnout of 46 per cent. Changing the country's name to the 'Bolivaran Republic of Venezuela', the new text was described by President Chávez as strengthening democracy by enshrining basic civil and human rights, but was criticized by his opponents as concentrating power in the presidency.

The low turnout on 16 December was partly attributable to torrential rains which over the next three days resulted in the country's worst natural disaster of the century. Huge tracts of Vargas state were devastated by flooding and mudslides which buried shanty towns along the coast, including those of Caracas itself. President Chávez correctly laid the blame for the devastation on previous administrations, which had allowed unchecked development. Up to 50,000 people lost their lives and hundreds of thousands were left homeless before substantial international relief was mobilized.

On 2 October President Chávez reopened Venezuela's longstanding claim to some two-thirds of Guyana's national territory (see IV.4.ii).

xi. CUBA

CAPITAL: Havana   AREA: 115,000 sq km   POPULATION: 11,103,000 ('98)
OFFICIAL LANGUAGE: Spanish   POLITICAL SYSTEM: one-party republic
HEAD OF STATE & GOVERNMENT: President Fidel Castro Ruz (since Jan '59)
RULING PARTY: Cuban Communist Party (PCC)
MAIN IGO MEMBERSHIPS (NON-UN): ACS, SELA, NAM
CURRENCY: peso (end-'99 £1=Cub$33.85, US$1=Cub$21.00)
GNP PER CAPITA: n.a.

MARKING the 40th anniversary of the 1959 revolution, President Fidel Castro Ruz, in a speech in Santiago on 1 January, launched a scathing attack on free-market capitalism. Three days later some minor relaxations in the US embargo on Cuba indicated that President Clinton had bowed to congressional pressure not to create a national bi-partisan commission on policy towards Cuba. President Castro's call to fight crime, meanwhile, led the National Assembly of People's Power (ANPP) to approve substantially increased sentences for theft, corruption, drug-trafficking and prostitution. The Law for the Protection of National Independence, also approved on 16 February, increased maximum penalties for 'counter-revolutionaries' and 'collaboration' from 20 to 30 years' imprisonment and was justified as a necessary measure to combat increased subversion by US agencies.

On 25 February the Cuban Telecomunications Enterprise (ETECSA) suspended most of the country's telephone links with the USA after a US judge, in an unrelated case, had ordered the US companies involved to withhold payments due to ETECSA. The judge subsequently compounded the issue by ordering the money withheld to be paid to the families of the three Cuban-Americans shot down in 1996 when their aircraft deliberately approached Cuban airspace (see AR 1996, pp. 173-4). In March two Salvadoreans allegedly sponsored by the Cuban-American National Foundation (CANF) to carry out bombings of leading Havana hotels (in which an Italian tourist had died in 1997—see AR 1997, p. 179) were sentenced to death. In September two Cubans formerly resident in the USA were sentenced to long prison terms for an unsuccessful attempt to smuggle people out of the country.

Foreign Minister Roberto Robiana González was dismissed on 28 May and was replaced by Felipe Pérez Roque, previously the President's private secretary. No official explanation was given for the dismissal, which was attributed by exiled Cuban sources to President Castro's desire to be more closely involved in foreign policy formulation.

In a response to US use of domestic courts to inflict damage on Cuba, a group of organizations on 1 June started proceedings against the US government for some US$181,100 million in a court in Havana, obtaining judgment in their favour on 2 November. In September an agreement between Britain and the Cuban Central Bank opened the way for the resumption of export credit cover for UK exports to Cuba, as members of the Paris Club paid a secret visit to the island for talks on debt rescheduling.

In October Governor George Ryan of Illinois paid a five-day fact-finding visit to the island. In the last weeks of the year, however, Cuban-US relations were unexpectedly dominated by a bitter argument whether a six-year-old boy, Elian González, who had been picked up by US Coastguards after his mother and stepmother had been lost at sea trying to escape to the USA, should be returned to the custody of his father in Cuba.

xii. DOMINICAN REPUBLIC AND HAITI

Dominican Republic
CAPITAL: Santo Domingo   AREA: 48,400 sq km   POPULATION: 8,000,000 ('98)
OFFICIAL LANGUAGE: Spanish   POLITICAL SYSTEM: presidential democracy
HEAD OF STATE & GOVERNMENT: President Leonel Fernández (since Aug '96)
RULING PARTY: Dominican Liberation Party (PLD)
MAIN IGO MEMBERSHIPS (NON-UN): OAS, SELA, ACS, ACP
CURRENCY: peso (end-'99 £1=RD$25.38, US$1=RD$15.75)
GNP PER CAPITA: US$1,770 by exchange-rate calculation, US$4,700 at PPP ('98)

Haiti
CAPITAL: Port-au-Prince   AREA: 27,750 sq km   POPULATION: 7,500,000 ('98)
OFFICIAL LANGUAGE: French   POLITICAL SYSTEM: presidential democracy
HEAD OF STATE & GOVERNMENT: President René Préval (since Feb '96)
RULING PARTY: Lavalas Political Organization
PRIME MINISTER: Jacques Édouard Alexis (since Jan '99)
MAIN IGO MEMBERSHIPS (NON-UN): OAS, SELA, ACS, ACP, Francophonie
CURRENCY: gourde (end-'99 £1=G28.14, US$1=G17.46)
GNP PER CAPITA: US$410 by exchange-rate calculation, US$1,250 at PPP ('98)

PRESIDENT René Préval of HAITI told the nation on 11 January that he did not have the power to prolong the mandates of senators and deputies to September 1999, as they had requested, and that the new Prime Minister, Jacques Édouard Alexis, could legally appoint a cabinet. Anti-government demonstrations followed, but on 26 March, seeking to end nearly two years of uncertainty and following consultations with opposition parties (see AR 1998, p. 197), the President appointed M. Alexis' government by decree. The new Minister of Justice and Public Security was Camille Leblanc, while Emmanuel Fritz Longchamp retained the foreign affairs portfolio and Fred Joseph that of economy and finance. Agreement had also been reached on the formation of a provisional electoral council, but following the assassination on 1 March by unknown gunmen of Senator Yvon Toussaint, the main opposition Organization of the Struggling People (OPL) withdrew. The council decided on 11 June to void the results of the April 1997 Senate elections, but a presidential decree calling fresh elections in November was subsequently subject to postponement to 2000 by the electoral council.

In mid-September more than 30 opposition parties formed an alliance to contest the elections as the Haitian Civic and Political Front (Frontciph). On 7 October the Secretary of State for Public Security, Robert Manuel, resigned following disagreements with President Préval. His expected replacement, Jean Lamy, was assassinated the following day. Jean Coles Rameau, chief of police of Port-au-Prince, had been successfully extradited from the Dominican Republic in June, accused of killing five detainees.

In the DOMINICAN REPUBLIC, the Christian Social Reform Party (PRSC) decided in July to nominate former President Joaquín Balaguer Ricardo as its candidate for the 2000 presidential elections, despite his being 91 years of age and virtually blind.

xiii. CENTRAL AMERICA AND PANAMA

Guatemala

CAPITAL: Guatemala City   AREA: 109,000 sq km   POPULATION: 11,000,000 ('98)
OFFICIAL LANGUAGE: Spanish   POLITICAL SYSTEM: presidential democracy
HEAD OF STATE & GOVERNMENT: President Alvaro Arzú Irigoyen (since Jan '96)
PRESIDENT-ELECT: Alfonso Antonio Portillo Cabrera
RULING PARTY: Guatemalan Republican Front
MAIN IGO MEMBERSHIPS (NON-UN): OAS, SELA, CACM, ACS, NAM
CURRENCY: quetzal (end-'99 £1=Q12.35, US$1=Q7.66)
GNP PER CAPITA: US$1,640 by exchange-rate calculation, US$4,070 at PPP ('98)

El Salvador

CAPITAL: San Salvador   AREA: 21,400 sq km   POPULATION: 6,000,000 ('98)
OFFICIAL LANGUAGE: Spanish   POLITICAL SYSTEM: presidential democracy
HEAD OF STATE & GOVERNMENT: President Francisco Flores Pérez (since June '99)
RULING PARTY: National Republican Alliance (Arena)
MAIN IGO MEMBERSHIPS (NON-UN): OAS, SELA, CACM, ACS
CURRENCY: colón (end-'99 £1=C14.09, US$1=C8.75)
GNP PER CAPITA: US$1,850 by exchange-rate calculation, US$2,850 at PPP ('98)

Honduras

CAPITAL: Tegucigalpa   AREA: 112,000 sq km   POPULATION: 6,000,000 ('98)
OFFICIAL LANGUAGE: Spanish   POLITICAL SYSTEM: presidential democracy
HEAD OF STATE & GOVERNMENT: President Carlos Roberto Flores Facussé (since Jan '98)
RULING PARTY: Liberal Party of Honduras (PLH)
MAIN IGO MEMBERSHIPS (NON-UN): OAS, SELA, CACM, ACS, NAM
CURRENCY: lempira (end-'99 £1=L22.92, US$1=L13.77)
GNP PER CAPITA: US$730 by exchange-rate calculation, US$2,140 at PPP ('98)

Nicaragua

CAPITAL: Managua   AREA: 120,000 sq km   POPULATION: 5,000,000 ('98)
OFFICIAL LANGUAGE: Spanish   POLITICAL SYSTEM: presidential democracy
HEAD OF STATE & GOVERNMENT: President Arnaldo Alemán Lacayo (since April '97)
RULING PARTY: Liberal Alliance (AL)
MAIN IGO MEMBERSHIPS (NON-UN): OAS, SELA, CACM, ACS, NAM
CURRENCY: córdoba (end-'99 £1=C$19.82, US$1=C$12.30)
GNP PER CAPITA: n.a.

Costa Rica

CAPITAL: San José   AREA: 51,000 sq km   POPULATION: 3,600,000 ('98)
OFFICIAL LANGUAGE: Spanish   POLITICAL SYSTEM: presidential democracy
HEAD OF STATE & GOVERNMENT: President Miguel Angel Rodríguez Echeverría (since May '98)
RULING PARTY: Social Christian Unity Party (PUSC)
MAIN IGO MEMBERSHIPS (NON-UN): OAS, SELA, CACM, ACS

CURRENCY: colón (end-'99 £1=C479.54, US$1=C297.54)
GNP PER CAPITA: US$2,780 by exchange-rate calculation, US$6,620 at PPP ('98)

Panama
CAPITAL: Panama City   AREA: 77,000 sq km   POPULATION: 2,800,000 ('98)
OFFICIAL LANGUAGE: Spanish   POLITICAL SYSTEM: presidential democracy
HEAD OF STATE & GOVERNMENT: President Mireya Elisa Moscoso de Gruber (since Sept '99)
RULING PARTIES: Anulfist Party (PA) heads Union for Panama coalition
MAIN IGO MEMBERSHIPS (NON-UN): OAS, SELA, NAM
CURRENCY: balboa (end-'99 £1=B1.61, USP1=B1.00)
GNP PER CAPITA: US$3,080 by exchange-rate calculation, US$6,940 at PPP ('98)

IN GUATEMALA, the independent Historical Clarification (or Truth) Commission set up under the 1996 peace agreement (see AR 1996, p. 177) published its long-awaited report on 25 February. It concluded that the US Central Intelligence Agency (CIA) and US army advisers had financed and trained Guatemalan forces which had carried out 'acts of genocide' against the indigenous Mayan population. During a four-day visit to Nicaragua, Honduras, El Salvador and Guatemala on 8-11 March, US President Bill Clinton publicly expressed regret for the US role. Yet the government decided not to set up a commission to investigate the conduct of the army and security forces during the 36-year civil war, during which they had been responsible for 90 per cent of the recorded deaths.

Three prominent activists were murdered in the run-up to a referendum held on 16 May on constitutional amendments embodying provisions of the 1996 accords that the rights of the indigenous majority should be recognized and the power of the armed forces curbed. In a turnout of less than 20 per cent, the amendments were rejected by a margin of two to one, despite having been approved by Congress in October 1998 and then upheld in lawsuits in the Constitutional Court. In July Air Force General Marco Tulio Espinosa became Defence Minister, just two days after being named by a former judge as the 'intellectual author' of the assassination of Mgr Juan José Gerardi Conedera, auxilliary Bishop of Guatemala, in April 1998 (see AR 1998, p. 200). On 7 October Celvin Galindo, the state attorney investigating the case, resigned and fled to the United States.

In the first round of presidential elections held on 7 November, Alvaro Colom Caballeros of the New Country Alliance (ANN), incorporating the former guerrilla organization Guatemalan National Revolutionary Unity (URNG), came a poor third with 12.3 per cent of the vote. In the run-off on 26 December, on the other hand, Alfonso Antonio Portillo Cabrera of the ruling Guatemalan Republican Front (FRG), a populist who admitted having killed two men allegedly in self-defence in 1982, won decisively with 68.3 per cent of the vote to 31.7 per cent for the former mayor of Guatemala City, Oscar Berger Perdomo, of the National Advancement Party (PAN). In elections to the unicameral Congress on 7 November, the FRG won 63 of the 113 seats, the PAN 37, the ANN nine and others four.

In a landmark decision on 3 December, the Inter-American Court of Human Rights ruled that there was sufficient evidence that two Guatemalan police officers had tortured and murdered three youths and two adults in 1990, overruling a contrary decision of the country's Supreme Court. The ruling obliged the Guatemalan government to prosecute those responsible for the crimes and the miscarriage of justice, including any judges found to have acted negligently.

Along with Honduras and Nicaragua, Guatemala suffered a week of severe flooding in late September, the effects representing a serious setback to recovery from the 1998 hurricane disaster (see AR 1998, pp. 198-9).

The National Assembly of EL SALVADOR in early February ratified a constitutional amendment purporting to guarantee the right to life from the moment of conception. In presidential elections held on 7 March, the candidate of the ruling Nationalist Republican Alliance (Arena), Francisco Flores Pérez, won outright and was sworn in on 1 June, appointing María Eugenia Brizuela de Avila as Minister of Foreign Affairs and José Luis Trigueros as Minister of Finance. The opposition Farabundo Martí National Liberation Front (FMLN), the former guerrilla organization, had failed to capitalize on its success in the 1997 legislative elections (see AR 1997, p. 182), and its candidate, Facundo Guardado, who received only 28.88 per cent of the votes cast on a low turnout, resigned as a member of the FMLN national coordinating body. FMLN objections to the appointment of Mauricio Sandoval, former Secretary of Information, as chief of the national police, were ignored. Meanwhile, a lawsuit was initiated in the United States against two former Defence Ministers resident in Miami, Florida, for their role in the murder in December 1980 of three US nuns and a lay worker.

In NICARAGUA, a student demonstration in mid-April at the failure of the government of President Arnaldo Alemán Lacayo to observe the constitutional requirement to spend 6 per cent of the budget on university education turned into a riot when police shot and killed one student. On 4 May the government ordered a reduction in the price of diesel fuel to put an end to a paralysing transport strike. In September the World Bank approved Nicaragua's application for inclusion in the official list of heavily indebted poor countries (HIPC). Comptroller-General Agustín Jarquín was arrested on 10 November accused of fraud against the state, but claimed he that was being persecuted for exposing government corruption.

Ratification by the Honduran National Congress on 30 November of a 1986 maritime boundary treaty with Colombia to which Nicaragua objected precipitated a crisis which led to troop movements on both sides of the Honduran-Nicaraguan border and a request to Colombia to withdraw its military attachés from Managua.

President Carlos Roberto Flores Facussé of HONDURAS reshuffled his cabinet on 24 January, appointing Roberto Flores Bermúdez as Minister of Foreign Relations. On 27 February General Mario Raúl Hung Pacheco handed over the post of commander-in-chief of the armed forces to the President; the following day Edgardo Dumas Rodríguez was appointed as the country's first civilian Defence Minister. With the task of reconstruction after Hurricane Mitch in 1998 still hardly started, on 26 March the IMF approved a grant under the enhanced structural adjustment facility to support the government's economic programme. In April the Paris Club agreed to write off 67 per cent of the country's debt of $1,170 million to member countries and to postpone all debt service for three years.

In COSTA RICA, Alvaro Jiménez, a judge in San José, was detained on 15 March, charged with membership of an international drugs syndicate.

In elections held in PANAMA on 2 May, Martín Torrijos Espinoso of the ruling Democratic Revolutionary Party (PRD), son of the late General Omar Torrijos Herrera and running as candidate of the New Nation coalition, was defeated by Mireya Elisa Moscoso de Gruber, widow of former President Arnulfo Arias, of the Arnulfist Party (PA) running as candidate of the Union for Panama coalition. She gained 44.9 per cent of the vote to 37.6 per cent for Sr Torrijos, who was subsequently elected secretary-general of the PRD. Alberto Vallarino of Opposition Action obtained 17.5 per cent. The New Nation coalition gained 46 of the 71 seats in the new legislature. Sworn in on 1 September for a five-year term, Sra Moscoso promised to summon a constitutional convention.

In March a judge in Miami had reduced by ten years the 40-year sentence passed by a US court on former Panamanian leader General Manuel Antonio Noriega Moreno in 1992, opening up the possibility of his parole in 2000. On the other hand, President Moscoso on 3 September revoked the pardon granted by her predecessor to 33 of his former associates.

The year was above all the one in which Panama became a fully sovereign nation. On 5 May, in accordance with the Panama Canal Treaties of 1977, the US government closed the Howard airforce base and transferred the main operations of the anti-drugs programme to Florida. Amidst alarmist rumours in Washington about alleged Chinese designs on the canal, President Clinton and Secretary of State Madeleine Albright chose not to court political unpopularity at home by attending the final handover ceremony. Hence on 14 December it was former US President Jimmy Carter, on behalf of the US government, who signed over the canal to President Moscoso with the words 'It's yours'.

xiv. MEXICO

CAPITAL: Mexico City   AREA: 1,958,000 sq km   POPULATION: 97,000,000 ('98)
OFFICIAL LANGUAGE: Spanish   POLITICAL SYSTEM: federal presidential democracy
HEAD OF STATE & GOVERNMENT: President Ernesto Zedillo Ponce de León (since Dec '94)
RULING PARTY: Institutional Revolutionary Party (PRI), since 1929
MAIN IGO MEMBERSHIPS (NON-UN): OAS, SELA, ALADI, ACS, APEC, NAFTA, OECD
CURRENCY: peso (end-'99 £1=Mex$15.285, US$1=Mex$9.48)
GNP PER CAPITA: US$3,970 by exchange-rate calculation, US$8,190 at PPP ('98)

FROM 1 January the government ended the subsidy on tortillas, the price of which immediately rose by a third. In July the country's third-largest bank, Grupo Financiera Serfin, went into receivership and was put up for sale in December. Meanwhile, a divided Chamber of Deputies spent weeks arguing over the federal budget.

Raúl Salinas de Gortari, brother of former President Carlos Salinas de Gortari, was sentenced to 50 years' imprisonment on 21 January, having been convicted of ordering the killing in 1994 of José Francisco Ruiz Massieu, former secretary-general of the ruling Institutional Revolutionary Party (PRI). The latter's brother, former Attorney-General Mario Ruiz Massieu, committed suicide on 15 September while still under house arrest in New Jersey, USA, awaiting trial.

During his fourth pastoral visit to Mexico, Pope John Paul II met privately with President Zedillo. In public, his apostolic message defended the rights of excluded and indigenous peoples and denounced 'neo-liberalism' and globalization. The Zapatista National Liberation Army (EZLN) subsequently held a second unofficial national referendum on Indian rights on 21 March; later EZLN adherents peacefully and successfully resisted attempts by police to eject them from state buildings. A new insurgent group in Guerrero, the Indigenous and Peasant Revolutionary Army of National Liberation (ERIC-LN), was announced on 4 March. In October police arrested Jacobo Silva Nogales ('Comandante Antonio'), founder and leader of the Revolutionary Army of the Insurgent People (ERPI).

President Clinton paid a brief visit to Mexico on 4-5 February to sign agreements on control of drug-smuggling and violence on the US-Mexican border, subsequently recommending re-certification of Mexico's efforts to combat the drugs trade. Orders were given on 6 April for the arrest of the outgoing governor of Quintana Roo, Mario Villanueva Madrid, on charges of complicity with the Juárez drugs cartel. In hiding, Sr Villanueva declared the allegations false and part of a political vendetta. However, the shooting of television presenter Francisco 'Paco' Stanley on 7 June, in an apparent contract killing, again raised questions about the role of drugs interests. US-Mexican naval cooperation was suspended in November, shortly before the arrest on 29 November of Juan José Quintero Payán, regarded as number two in the Juárez cartel, and the excavation of mass graves of the cartel's victims near Ciudad Juárez.

In state elections in February the centre-left Party of the Democratic Revolution (PRD) obtained a third state governorship, that of Baja California Sur, although amid accusations of vote-rigging the ruling PRI held on to the governorships of Guerrero, Hidalgo and Quintana Roo. Charges of manipulation, moreover, marred the election of José Antonio González Fernández as the new PRI president on 30 March, following the withdrawal of the only other candidate, Rodolfo Echeverría. Similar charges delayed the choice of Senator Amalia Garcia Medina as the new president of the PRD. In November President Zedillo forced the resignation of Sr González as PRI president by appointing him Health Minister. He was succeeded by Sra Dulce María Sauri Riancho.

In elections on 4 July the PRI held on to the governorship of the crucial state of Mexico, though it lost the Pacific state of Nayarit to an opposition coalition, while on 26 September victory in Coahuila also went to the PRI. Talks aimed at forming a coalition of the PRD and the National Action Party (PAN) to contest the presidency foundered on 28 September amid recriminations, the PRD going on to nominate Cuauhtémoc Cárdenas Solórzano as its candidate in the 2000 presidential elections. In the PRI open primary on 7 November Francisco Labastida Ochoa won the party's presidential nomination with 61 per cent of the votes cast to 29 per cent for his main rival, Roberto Madrazo Pintado, who subsequently returned to the governorship of Tabasco.

On 15 June a powerful earthquake measuring 6.7 on the Richter scale shook central and southern Mexico but fortunately killed only some 19 people in the state of Puebla. No casualties were reported from a second large earthquake on 21 June which shook the capital itself. However, on 1 September an earthquake in Oaxaca registering 7.5 on the Richter scale killed at least 33 people, while severe flooding in the states of Hidalgo, Puebla, Veracruz and Tabasco at the beginning of October left at least 341 people dead and an estimated 271,000 homeless.

4. THE CARIBBEAN

JAMAICA—GUYANA—TRINIDAD & TOBAGO—BARBADOS—BELIZE—GRENADA—
THE BAHAMAS—WINDWARD & LEEWARD ISLANDS—UK DEPENDENCIES—
SURINAME—NETHERLANDS ANTILLES AND ARUBA—US DEPENDENCIES

i. JAMAICA

CAPITAL: Kingston   AREA: 11,000 sq km   POPULATION: 3,000,000 ('98)
OFFICIAL LANGUAGE: English   POLITICAL SYSTEM: parliamentary democracy
HEAD OF STATE: Queen Elizabeth II   GOVERNOR-GENERAL: Sir Howard Cooke
RULING PARTY: People's National Party (PNP)
HEAD OF GOVERNMENT: Percival J. Patterson, Prime Minister (since March '92)
MAIN IGO MEMBERSHIPS (NON-UN): OAS, SELA, ACS, Caricom, ACP, CWTH, NAM
CURRENCY: Jamaican dollar (end-'99 £1=J$66.40, US$1=J$41.20)
GNP PER CAPITA: US$1,680 by exchange-rate calculation, US$3,210 at PPP ('98)

THE presentation of the annual budget on 16 April by the Finance and Planning Minister, Omar Davies, brought three days of violent protests across the country. In Kingston, the capital, the army was called out in support of the police, but as the arson, looting and the blocking of roads spread, at least seven people were reported to have died, mostly at the hands of the police. A new tax on petroleum products, which had threatened to raise fuel prices by some 30 per cent, was the main target of the unrest, and the government agreed on 27 April to halve it. Though new taxes were also imposed on motor vehicle permits, cigarettes and alcohol, this meant that other ways would have to be found to finance the J$24,300 million deficit (US$661 million) expected in 1999. Although Prime Minister Percival Patterson's government planned to raise US$400 million on the international market in the 1999/2000 financial year, it had to withdraw an initial bond issue for US$250 million because of nervousness among financial institutions.

Faced with a further wave of violent crime which had claimed 505 lives since the beginning of the year, the government on 13 July deployed more security forces in the streets of Kingston than at any time since 1976. Much of the violence, the government claimed, was the result of the deportation of Jamaican-born criminals from the United States, Canada and Britain. On 16 August 80-

year-old Rose Leon, former Minister of Health and Housing and chair of the Jamaican Labour Party (JLP) from 1948 to 1960, was murdered in her home, apparently by burglars.

ii. GUYANA

CAPITAL: Georgetown   AREA: 215,000 sq km   POPULATION: 850,000 ('98)
OFFICIAL LANGUAGE: English   POLITICAL SYSTEM: cooperative presidential democracy
RULING PARTY: People's Progressive Party-Civic (PPP-C)
HEAD OF STATE & GOVERNMENT: President Bharrat Jagdeo (since Aug '99)
PRIME MINISTER: Sam Hinds (since Dec '97)
MAIN IGO MEMBERSHIPS (NON-UN): OAS, SELA, AP, ACS, Caricom, ACP, CWTH, NAM
CURRENCY: Guyana dollar (end-'99 £1=G$289.46, US$1=G$179.60)
GNP PER CAPITA: US$770 by exchange-rate calculation, US$2,680 at PPP ('98)

THE 20-member constitutional reform commission, created as part of the 1998 agreement between the ruling People's Progressive Party-Civic (PPP-Civic) and the opposition People's National Congress (PNC) (see AR 1998, p. 205), was sworn in on 22 January, with a mandate to report by July to the National Assembly on a wide range of constitutional issues. Ralph Ram Karran of the PPP-Civic was appointed chairman. However, tension between the rival parties remained strong, giving rise both to continued street protests and to a 56-day strike by civil servants.

A mild heart attack led to the hospitalization of President Janet Jagan on 30 June. With the need evident for further investigation and treatment in Trinidad & Tobago and the USA, she decided to resign on 11 August, when her chosen successor, Finance Minister Bharrat Jagdeo (35), was sworn in as the youngest President in the Americas. President Jagdeo retained responsibility for finance until 19 November, when Sasenarine Kowlessar was given day-to-day responsibility for financial affairs as Minister within the Office of the President.

The decision to grant offshore oil concessions to three foreign companies triggered a sequence of events which led in October to the reopening of Guyana's longstanding boundary dispute with Venezuela. On 13 July the Venezuelan Foreign Minister, José Vicente Rangel, sent a note reminding Foreign Minister Clement Rohee that, under the terms of an agreement between the two governments in 1966, no action which might imply or deny a claim to sovereignty should be initiated by either party without the agreement of the other. In September a further note indicated that Venezuela considered that one company, Century, had already started work, not only in the disputed area but in waters indisputably Venezuelan. Hence on 2 October President Chávez of Venezuela indicated that he wished to reopen negotiations which had been deadlocked since 1990.

iii. TRINIDAD & TOBAGO

CAPITAL: Port of Spain AREA: 5,128 sq km POPULATION: 1,320,000 ('98)
OFFICIAL LANGUAGE: English POLITICAL SYSTEM: parliamentary republic
RULING PARTIES: United National Congress (UNC) & National Alliance for Reconstruction (NAR)
HEAD OF STATE: President Arthur N.R. Robinson (NAR), since March '97
HEAD OF GOVERNMENT: Basdeo Panday (UNC), Prime Minister (since Nov '95)
MAIN IGO MEMBERSHIPS (NON-UN): OAS, SELA, ACS, Caricom, ACP, CWTH, NAM
CURRENCY: Trinidad & Tobago dollar (end-'99 £1=TT$10.06, US$1=TT$6.24)
GNP PER CAPITA: US$4,430 by exchange-rate calculation, US$6,720 at PPP ('98)

THE nine members of a drugs gang who had been sentenced to death in 1996 for the murder of four members of a family two years previously were hanged in batches of three on 4, 5 and 7 June, following a ruling by the judicial committee of the UK Privy Council on 26 May that hanging was not in itself inhumane. Given the strong support for capital punishment in the islands, sentiment in favour of a regional supreme court persisted—a sentiment likely to be strengthened by the murder on 31 December in his own home of Hansraj Sumairsingh, a leading businessman with close government connections. Suspicion remained in judicial circles, however, that proposals to reform the administration of justice, as advanced by Attorney-General Ramesh Lawrence Maharaj, were the prelude to more extensive political interference.

In a major cabinet reshuffle announced by Prime Minister Basdeo Panday on 20 October, Brian Kuei Tung became Minister of Finance, Planning and Development.

iv. BARBADOS

CAPITAL: Bridgetown AREA: 430 sq km POPULATION: 266,000 ('98)
OFFICIAL LANGUAGE: English POLITICAL SYSTEM: parliamentary democracy
HEAD OF STATE: Queen Elizabeth II GOVERNOR-GENERAL: Sir Clifford Husbands
RULING PARTY: Barbados Labour Party (BLP)
HEAD OF GOVERNMENT: Owen Arthur, Prime Minister (since Sept '94)
MAIN IGO MEMBERSHIPS (NON-UN): OAS, SELA, ACS, Caricom, ACP, CWTH, NAM
CURRENCY: Barbados dollar (end-'99 £1=B$3.19, US$1=B$1.98)
GNP PER CAPITA: US$7,890 by exchange-rate calculation, US$12,260 at PPP ('98)

IN a general election held on 20 January the ruling Barbados Labour Party (BLP) won 65.4 per cent of the votes cast and 26 of the 28 seats in the House of Assembly. The opposition Democratic Labour Party (DLP), with 34.6 per cent, won the other two. Prime Minister Owen Arthur, who was also responsible for defence and security, finance and economic affairs, on 24 January announced an expanded cabinet in which the Deputy Prime Minister, Billie Miller, held the portfolio of foreign affairs and foreign trade. The government's success was attributed to five years of uninterrupted economic growth. On 9 August, however, Elizabeth Thompson, the Health and Environment Minister, was dismissed and replaced by Philip Goddard, while Romell Marshall became Minister of International Trade and Business.

In mid-September thousands of dead fish, large and small, were washed up on the beaches. The cause of the phenomenon, previously observed on St Vincent, Grenada and Tobago, remained unknown.

v. BELIZE

CAPITAL: Belmopan   AREA: 23,000 sq km   POPULATION: 236,000 ('98)
OFFICIAL LANGUAGE: English   POLITICAL SYSTEM: parliamentary democracy
HEAD OF STATE: Queen Elizabeth II   GOVERNOR-GENERAL: Sir Colville Young
RULING PARTY: People's United Party (PUP)
HEAD OF GOVERNMENT: Said Musa, Prime Minister (since Aug '98)
MAIN IGO MEMBERSHIPS (NON-UN): OAS, SELA, ACS, Caricom, ACP, CWTH, NAM
CURRENCY: Belize dollar (end-'99 £1=BZ$3.21, US$1=BZ$1.99)
GNP PER CAPITA: US$2,610 by exchange-rate calculation, US$3,940 at PPP ('98)

IN his state of the nation address on 16 September, Prime Minister Said Musa was able to report some significant economic progress, notably new investment in various infrastructure projects, including some US$80 million earmarked for hurricane preparedness and upgrading storm shelters. With the banana dispute still unresolved, efforts continued to expand citrus production and shrimp farming was developing rapidly. The world market for sugar, however, remained depressed, though exports to Guatemala were rising.

On 7 April a World Trade Organization (WTO) arbitration panel, ruling on a complaint from the US government in support of its large transnational banana companies, had held that the European Union's banana import policy, which had come into effect on 1 January, still failed to comply with earlier WTO judgements, and authorized the imposition on EU countries of unilateral US sanctions (see XI.4).

vi. GRENADA

CAPITAL: St George's   AREA: 344 sq km   POPULATION: 100,000 ('98)
OFFICIAL LANGUAGE: English   POLITICAL SYSTEM: parliamentary democracy
HEAD OF STATE: Queen Elizabeth II   GOVERNOR-GENERAL: Sir Daniel Williams
RULING PARTY: New National Party (NNP)
HEAD OF GOVERNMENT: Keith Mitchell, Prime Minister (since June '95)
MAIN IGO MEMBERSHIPS (NON-UN): OAS, SELA, ACS, Caricom, OECS, ACP, CWTH, NAM
CURRENCY: East Caribbean dollar (end-'99 £1=EC$4.35, US$1=EC$2.70)
GNP PER CAPITA: US$3,170 by exchange-rate calculation, US$4,720 at PPP ('98)

IN a general election on 18 January which had been forced on the ruling New National Party (NNP) by the resignation of Dr Raphael Fletcher (see AR 1998, p. 208), the NNP led by the Prime Minister, Dr Keith Mitchell, unexpectedly took all 15 seats in the House of Representatives with 62.2 per cent of the votes cast. The opposition National Democratic Congress (NDC) and Grenada United Labour Party (GULP) gained 24.9 per cent and 12.0 per cent respectively but won no seats. In the new cabinet announced on 23

January, Dr Mitchell held the portfolios of finance and foreign affairs concurrently with the premiership, but there was a general redistribution of duties.

The 25th anniversary of independence in 1974 was an occasion for general celebration. In the budget presented in March plans were announced for a considerable increase in spending on infrastructural projects, including a new cruise ship port and the upgrading of 24 kilometres of road. In the course of the year both American Eagle and Air Jamaica opened flights to Pointe Salines. However, the results of a 1998 poverty survey showed that 30.8 of all Grenadians were officially poor.

In a further cabinet reshuffle on 1 November, the Prime Minister took over responsibility for national security, while Mark Isaac became Minister of Foreign Affairs and Anthony Boatswain Minister of Finance, Trade and Planning. On 1 December full diplomatic relations were established with Cuba.

vii. THE BAHAMAS

CAPITAL: Nassau   AREA: 14,000 sq km   POPULATION: 294,000 ('98)
OFFICIAL LANGUAGE: English   POLITICAL SYSTEM: parliamentary democracy
HEAD OF STATE: Queen Elizabeth II   GOVERNOR-GENERAL: Sir Orville Turnquest
RULING PARTY: Free National Movement (FNM)
HEAD OF GOVERNMENT: Hubert Ingraham, Prime Minister (since Aug '92)
MAIN IGO MEMBERSHIPS (NON-UN): OAS, ACS, Caricom, ACP, CWTH, NAM
CURRENCY: Bahamas dollar (end-'99 £1=B$1.61, US$1=B$1.00)
GNP PER CAPITA: US$10,460 at PPP ('98)

MILLIONS of dollars worth of damage was caused when one of the largest hurricanes ever reported in the Caribbean, Hurricane Floyd, tracked over the islands on 14 September. Although only one person died as a direct result, a further death occurred in Nassau when a woman was electrocuted as power was restored.

viii. WINDWARD AND LEEWARD ISLANDS

Antigua & Barbuda

CAPITAL: St John's   AREA: 440 sq km   POPULATION: 67,000 ('98)
OFFICIAL LANGUAGE: English   POLITICAL SYSTEM: parliamentary democracy
HEAD OF STATE: Queen Elizabeth II   GOVERNOR-GENERAL: Sir James B. Carlisle
RULING PARTY: Antigua Labour Party (ALP)
HEAD OF GOVERNMENT: Lester Bird, Prime Minister (since March '94)
MAIN IGO MEMBERSHIPS (NON-UN): OAS, ACS, OECS, Caricom, ACP, CWTH
CURRENCY: East Caribbean dollar (end-'99 £1=EC$4.35, US$1=EC$2.70)
GNP PER CAPITA: US$8,300 by exchange-rate calculation, US$9,440 at PPP ('98)

Dominica

CAPITAL: Roseau   AREA: 750 sq km   POPULATION: 74,000 ('98)
OFFICIAL LANGUAGE: English   POLITICAL SYSTEM: parliamentary republic

HEAD OF STATE: President Vernon Shaw (since Oct '98)
RULING PARTY: United Workers' Party (UWP)
HEAD OF GOVERNMENT: Edison James, Prime Minister (since June '95)
MAIN IGO MEMBERSHIPS (NON-UN): OAS, ACS, OECS, Caricom, ACP, CWTH, Francophonie
CURRENCY: East Caribbean dollar (see above)
GNP PER CAPITA: US$3,010 by exchange-rate calculation, US$3,940 at PPP ('98)

St Christopher (Kitts) & Nevis

CAPITAL: Basseterre   AREA: 260 sq km   POPULATION: 41,500 ('98)
OFFICIAL LANGUAGE: English   POLITICAL SYSTEM: parliamentary democracy
HEAD OF STATE: Queen Elizabeth II   GOVERNOR-GENERAL: Sir Cuthbert Sebastian
RULING PARTY: St Kitts-Nevis Labour Party (SKNLP)
HEAD OF GOVERNMENT: Denzil Douglas, Prime Minister (since July '95)
MAIN IGO MEMBERSHIPS (NON-UN): OAS, ACS, Caricom, OECS, ACP, CWTH
CURRENCY: East Caribbean dollar (see above)
GNP PER CAPITA: US$6,130 by exchange-rate calculation, US$7,940 at PPP ('98)

St Lucia

CAPITAL: Castries   AREA: 616 sq km   POPULATION: 160,000 ('98)
OFFICIAL LANGUAGE: English   POLITICAL SYSTEM: parliamentary democracy
HEAD OF STATE: Queen Elizabeth II   GOVERNOR-GENERAL: Perlette Louisy
RULING PARTY: St Lucia Labour Party (SLP)
HEAD OF GOVERNMENT: Kenny D. Anthony, Prime Minister (since May '97)
MAIN IGO MEMBERSHIPS (NON-UN): OAS, ACS, OECS, Caricom, ACP, CWTH, NAM
CURRENCY: East Caribbean dollar (see above)
GNP PER CAPITA: US$3,410 by exchange-rate calculation, US$4,610 at PPP ('98)

St Vincent & the Grenadines

CAPITAL: Kingstown   AREA: 390 sq km   POPULATION: 113,000 ('98)
OFFICIAL LANGUAGE: English   POLITICAL SYSTEM: parliamentary democracy
HEAD OF STATE: Queen Elizabeth II   GOVERNOR-GENERAL: Charles James Antrobus
RULING PARTY: New Democratic Party (NDP)
HEAD OF GOVERNMENT: Sir James F. Mitchell, Prime Minister (since July '84)
MAIN IGO MEMBERSHIPS (NON-UN): OAS, ACS, OECS, Caricom, ACP, CWTH
CURRENCY: East Caribbean dollar (see above)
GNP PER CAPITA: US$2,420 by exchange-rate calculation, US$4,090 at PPP ('98)

IN a general election held in ANTIGUA & BARBUDA on 9 March, the ruling Antigua Labour Party (ALP) won 52.9 per cent of the votes cast and 12 of the 18 seats in the new House of Representatives, a net gain of one seat from the opposition United Progressive Party (UPP), which won 44.9 per cent and four seats. The Barbuda People's Movement retained the single seat for Barbuda with 1.3 per cent.

In the new cabinet announced by Prime Minister Lester Bird, one new appointment attracted particular comment, that of his brother, Vere Bird Jr, who had been barred from public office in 1990 following allegations of involvement in illegal arms trading (see AR 1990, p. 101). He became Minister of Agriculture, Lands and Fisheries. Other new appointments included that of Errol Cort as Attorney-General and Minister of Justice and Legal Affairs, who in September followed other Caribbean states in announcing the government's intention to resume the use of the death penalty.

In March Ronald Sanders, high commissioner in London, was raised to the rank of ambassador-at-large with ministerial rank and later strongly criticized an OECD report claiming that competitive tax policies in Antigua & Barbuda were harmful.

The Prime Minister's father, Sir Vere Bird, who had served as Prime Minister from independence in 1981 until he retired in 1994, died on 28 June at the age of 89. He had made his political reputation in the 1950s as a trade unionist fighting for more pay for sugar cane workers and had been honoured on 1 January with the first knighthood of the country's new honours system.

Prime Minister Edison James of DOMINICA, who expressed his continuing support for the Windward Islands Banana Development and Exporting Company (WIBDECO), visited Spain, Portugal, Finland and Belgium in May to lobby for the maintenance of the European Union's banana quota. The economy had grown by 3.5 per cent in 1998, but criticism in July by opposition leader Rosie Douglas, that cabinet members were too much occupied in various private businesses, was supported by the Chamber of Commerce. Important developments included the launch in July of a nine-month programme to encourage young people to remain on the land and the purchase in August by the government of the Londonderry estate for EC$16 million to build an international airport.

The US Deputy Assistant Secretary of State for Western Hemisphere Affairs visited ST CHRISTOPHER (KITTS) & NEVIS, St Lucia and Barbados in May on a fact-finding tour about the banana industry.

In April the Organization of American States (OAS) launched an electoral and boundary reform project in ST LUCIA. In June the Prime Minister, Dr Kenny Anthony, announced his government's intention to execute the seven prisoners held on death row. There were angry demonstrations in Castries when, on the eve of a scheduled execution in September, Judge Suzie d'Auvergne commuted to life imprisonment the death sentence imposed on Morrel Cox nearly five years previously for a murder committed in 1991. In fact, although murders had risen to 17 (from 12 in 1997), statistics for 1998 showed that crime in general had fallen, while at the end of 1999 Police Commissioner Francis Nelson was able to report a further sharp fall in criminal activity.

A number of teething problems were encountered with the newly-privatized banana regime. The St Lucia Banana Corporation chairman, Patrick Joseph, complained in September that WIBDECO had been 'ripping off' farmers. Although he denied the charges, WIBDECO chairman Garnet Didier admitted that his organization was in arrears to the St Lucia Corporation. Mr Joseph had meanwhile refused to sign the memorandum of understanding needed to release some US$16.8 million of European Union funds to the struggling industry, so that a new organization, the Banana Industry Trust, had to be created for the purpose. Prime Minister Anthony had earlier complained that there had been some 'serious malpractice' under his predecessors from the ruling United Workers' Party, though he was careful to exempt them personally from blame.

In ST VINCENT & THE GRENADINES, Prime Minister Sir James Mitchell signed an agreement in April for the receipt of European Union 'Stabex' funds totalling US$44.4 million, to be used for sustainable growth of the economy and to reduce poverty. Earlier the islands' Cenotaph was removed from the position it had occupied for the previous 75 years to make way for further construction on the new Kingstown vegetable market.

Dr Ralph Gonsalves succeeded Vincent Beache as leader of the main opposition Unity Labour Party (ULP) in June. ULP deputy leader Ken Boyea called for the party to reassess its strategy of non-cooperation with the government following its narrow defeat in the June 1998 general elections (see AR 1998, p. 211), but was reproved. In September businessman Higman Peters announced the formation of the National Democratic Labour Party (NDLP).

ix. UK DEPENDENCIES

Anguilla
CAPITAL: The Valley   AREA: 96 sq km   POPULATION: 8,400 ('98)
OFFICIAL LANGUAGE: English   POLITICAL SYSTEM: representative democracy
GOVERNOR: Alan Poole
RULING PARTIES: Anguilla United (AUP) & Anguilla Democratic (ADP) parties
HEAD OF GOVERNMENT: Hubert Hughes (AUP), Chief Minister (since March '94)
MAIN IGO MEMBERSHIPS: OECS, Caricom (obs.)
CURRENCY: East Caribbean dollar (end-'99 £1=EC$4.35, US$1=EC$2.70)

Bermuda
CAPITAL: Hamilton   AREA: 53 sq km   POPULATION: 64,000 ('98)
OFFICIAL LANGUAGE: English   POLITICAL SYSTEM: representative democracy
GOVERNOR: Thorold Masefield
RULING PARTY: Progressive Labour Party (PLP)
HEAD OF GOVERNMENT: Jennifer Smith, Prime Minister (since Nov '98)
MAIN IGO MEMBERSHIPS: Caricom (obs.)
CURRENCY: East Caribbean dollar (see above)

British Virgin Islands
CAPITAL: Road Town   AREA: 153 sq km   POPULATION: 18,000 ('98)
OFFICIAL LANGUAGE: English   POLITICAL SYSTEM: representative democracy
GOVERNOR: David MacKilligin
RULING PARTY: Virgin Islands Party (VIP)
HEAD OF GOVERNMENT: Ralph O'Neal, Chief Minister (since May '95)
MAIN IGO MEMBERSHIPS: OECS (assoc.), Caricom (assoc.)
CURRENCY: East Caribbean dollar (see above)

Cayman Islands
CAPITAL: George Town, Grand Cayman   AREA: 259 sq km   POPULATION: 35,000 ('98)
OFFICIAL LANGUAGE: English   POLITICAL SYSTEM: representative democracy
GOVERNOR: Peter John Smith
MAIN IGO MEMBERSHIPS: Caricom (obs.)
CURRENCY: East Caribbean dollar (see above)

Montserrat
CAPITAL: Plymouth   AREA: 102 sq km   POPULATION: 3,000 ('98)
OFFICIAL LANGUAGE: English   POLITICAL SYSTEM: representative democracy
GOVERNOR: Frank J.Savage
HEAD OF GOVERNMENT: David Brandt, Chief Minister (since Aug '97)
MAIN IGO MEMBERSHIPS: OECS, Caricom, ACS
CURRENCY: East Caribbean dollar (see above)

Turks & Caicos Islands
CAPITAL: Cockburn Town   AREA: 430 sq km   POPULATION: 14,500 ('98)
OFFICIAL LANGUAGE: English   POLITICAL SYSTEM: representative democracy
GOVERNOR: John Kelly
RULING PARTY: People's Democratic Movement (PDM)
HEAD OF GOVERNMENT: Derek H. Taylor, Chief Minister (since Jan '95)
MAIN IGO MEMBERSHIPS: Caricom (assoc.)
CURRENCY: East Caribbean dollar (see above)

IN elections to the House of Representative of ANGUILLA on 4 March, the opposition Anguilla National Alliance (ANA) won 42 per cent of the vote and three seats, one more than in 1994. However, each of the two parties in the ruling coalition, the Anguilla Democratic Party (ADP) and the Anguilla United Party (AUP), retained two seats. Two seats were held *ex officio* by the Deputy Governor and the Attorney-General and two were nominated by the Governor. On 5 March Hubert Hughes was reappointed Chief Minister, the new Executive Council being sworn in four days later.

Prime Minister Jennifer Smith of BERMUDA, who in May had expressed concern at pressure from Europe for tighter financial regulation, in August ruled out independence in the current parliament and promised to end hanging. A massive advertising campaign was launched in the United States in April after it was announced that the Marriott Castle Harbour Resort was to close at the end of 1999. Cruise arrivals were up in the first months of the year, but government minister David Allen warned in August that rising crime levels could threaten the tourist trade. Islanders sustained some local damage from Hurricane Gert when it brushed the islands on 21 September, temporarily cutting electricity supplies.

In elections to the Legislative Council of the BRITISH VIRGIN ISLANDS on 17 May, the Virgin Islands Party (VIP) maintained its 13-year-long hold on power, taking 38 per cent of the votes and seven of the 13 seats, one more than in 1995. The National Democratic Party (NDP) gained 36.9 per cent and five seats and the Concerned Citizens' Movement (CCM) 4 per cent and one seat.

In May Peter John Smith was sworn in as the seventh Governor of the CAYMAN ISLANDS since they opted for dependent status in 1962. In July the Tourism Minister, Thomas Jefferson, had to be dispatched to London to lobby for the maintenance of tax haven status. In the same month, the government withdrew its controversial proposal to oust expatriate children from public schools (expatriates accounting currently for approximately half of the islands' 42,000 residents). The annual meeting of Commonwealth Finance Ministers was held in the islands on 21 September, three days after the annual 'clean-up day'.

A further violent eruption of the Soufrière Hills volcano on MONTSERRAT occurred at 6.30am on 13 January. A vertical ash cloud rose to some 20,000 feet and ash fell to the west over the area from Cork Hill to Plymouth. Then and on 20 January pyroclastic flows moved down the Tar river valley to the sea. By Sunday 21 March activity had declined sufficiently for regular daily bulletins to be discontinued, and on 23 April the travel advisory warning tourists against visiting the island was rescinded. A new ash cloud on 5 June was accompanied by a series of earth tremors, an alert being issued to inhabitants. A further explosion on 21 July sent ash drifting westwards and caused a fresh lava flow down the Tar river valley. However, although small rockfalls continued to occur, the worst appeared to be over.

In January the UK International Development Secretary, Clare Short, announced a £75 million aid programme, and from 1 May the British government paid the fares of returnees from other Caribbean territories. Plans were also announced for a two-year programme to reopen the W.H. Bramble airport rendered unusable in 1997 and to restore air links. During a visit by the UK Foreign and Commonwealth Office minister responsible for overseas territories, Baroness Scotland of Asthal), Chief Minister David Brandt admitted: 'We are fortunate in the sense that we are a dependent territory, because if we were independent I do not know who we could have depended upon.' Stray donkeys had become a serious pest, and in August Agriculture Minister Percival Austin Bramble tried to negotiate their sale abroad.

In elections held on 4 March for the 20-member Legislative Council of the TURKS & CAICOS ISLANDS, the ruling People's Democratic Movement (PDM) won 52.8 per cent of the vote and 10 of the 13 contested seats. The opposition Progressive National Party (PNP) gained 40.3 per cent of the vote, and only three seats. Apart from the Speaker's seat, which was not contested, the remaining members consisted of three *ex-officio* members and three nominated by the Governor.

x. SURINAME

CAPITAL: Paramaribo   AREA: 163,000 sq km   POPULATION: 420,000 ('98)
OFFICIAL LANGUAGE: Dutch   POLITICAL SYSTEM: republic
HEAD OF STATE President Jules Wijdenbosch (since Sept '96)
RULING PARTIES: National Democratic Party (NDP) heads coalition
HEAD OF GOVERNMENT: Vice-President Pretaapnarain Radhakishum (since Sept '96)
MAIN IGO MEMBERSHIPS (NON-UN): OAS, SELA, AP, ACS, Caricom, ACP, NAM
CURRENCY: Suriname guilder (end-'99 £1=Sf1,304.67, US$1=Sf809.50)
GNP PER CAPITA: US$1,660 by exchange-rate calculation ('98)

ANGER at the virtual collapse of the country's economy culminated in May in a week of protest against the government of President Jules Wijdenbosch. On 28 May the President accepted the resignation of his cabinet following a series of scandals. His action in reappointing them, however, provoked an even larger demonstration than before in the capital, Paramaribo. On 1 June the National Assembly voted to remove the President from office, a decision which he refused to accept. He did, however, agree to hold new elections no later than May 2000, and on 8 December accepted the resignation of the entire cabinet for a second time.

xi. NETHERLANDS ANTILLES AND ARUBA

Netherlands Antilles
CAPITAL: Willemstad (Curaçao)   AREA: 800 sq km   POPULATION: 205,000 ('98)
OFFICIAL LANGUAGES: Dutch, Papiamento, English
POLITICAL SYSTEM: parliamentary, under Dutch Crown
GOVERNOR: Jaime M. Saleh
RULING PARTIES: National People's Party (PNP) heads coalition
HEAD OF GOVERNMENT: Susanne Camelia-Römer (PNP), Prime Minister (since May '98)
CURRENCY: Neth. Antilles guilder (end-'99 £1=Naf2.71, US$1=NAf1.68)
GNP PER CAPITA: n/a

Aruba
CAPITAL: Oranjestad   AREA: 193 sq km   POPULATION: 94,000 ('98)
OFFICIAL LANGUAGE: Dutch   POLITICAL SYSTEM: parliamentary, under Dutch Crown
GOVERNOR: Olindo Koolman
RULING PARTIES: Aruban People's Party (AVP) & Aruban Liberal Organization (OLA)
HEAD OF GOVERNMENT: Jan Hendrick (Henny) Eman (AVP), Prime Minister (since July '94)
CURRENCY: Aruba guilder (end-'99 £1=Af2.84, US$1=Af1.76)
GNP PER CAPITA: US$16,640 by exchange-rate calculation ('98)

IN the NETHERLANDS ANTILLES, elections were held for the island councils of Bonaire in March, Curaçao, Saba and St Eustatius on 7 May and Sint Maarten on 21 May. The ruling government coalition led by Prime Minister Susanne Camelia-Römer increased its overall representation in Curaçao's island council to 13. Her National People's Party (PNP) won 22.1 per cent of the vote and took five seats, a gain of one; the Workers' Liberation Front led by Anthony Codett and the Labour Party People's Crusade of Errol Cova won four seats each. For the opposition, the Antillean Restructuring Party (PAR) of former Prime Minister Miguel Pourier won 22.7 per cent of the vote and five seats, one less than in 1995, while the New Antilles Movement (MAN) of former Prime Minister Don Martina managed only two seats, a loss of four. One seat went to a new evangelical Christian party, ORDU, led by Josephine Bakhius-Trinidad. Meanwhile, the Curaçao administration had requested central government help to meet a budget deficit of 73.2 million guilders (US$41.39 million) carried forward from 1998.

In the Saba council election the Windward Islands Popular Movement (WIPM) won four of the five seats and the Saba Labour Party one. On St Eustatius the Democratic Party (DP), with two seats, was defeated by the St Eustatius Alliance, with three. The Democratic Party–Sint Maarten (DPSM) won seven of the 11 seats on Sint Maarten, therefore forming the new government unaided. The outgoing Sint Maarten Patriotic Alliance/Serious Alternative People's Party (SPA/SAPP), senior party in the outgoing coalition, took only three seats and the National Progressive Party one.

The Customs Department of ARUBA recorded a new record for drug seizures in 1998.

xii. US DEPENDENCIES

Puerto Rico
CAPITAL: San Juan   AREA: 9,103 sq km   POPULATION: 3,870,000 ('98)
OFFICIAL LANGUAGES: Spanish & English   POLITICAL SYSTEM: democratic commonwealth
GOVERNOR: Pedro J. Rosselló
RULING PARTY: New Progressive Party (PNP)
CURRENCY: US dollar (end-'99 £1=US$1.61)

US Virgin Islands
CAPITAL: Charlotte Amalie   AREA: 342 sq km   POPULATION: 118,000 ('98)
OFFICIAL LANGUAGE: English   POLITICAL SYSTEM: democratic dependency
GOVERNOR: Charles Turnbull (independent)
CURRENCY: US dollar (see above)

TRANSFER of US Army units from Panama (see IV.3.xiii) to their new headquarters at Fort Buchanan and Roosevelt Roads naval air base on PUERTO RICO began in May and was completed by August. In April, however, two US Navy jets on a Kosovo training mission accidentally fired 500-pound bombs on Vieques Island, killing a security guard and injuring four other persons. The incident exacerbated the tense relationship between the US Navy and Vieques residents. The mayor of Vieques, Manuela Santiago, a pro-statehood supporter said that she wanted the military to leave the island, and a formal complaint was lodged by Governor Pedro Rosselló with President Clinton. The crisis worsened in May when a declassified US Navy document revealed that naval training exercises on Vieques had included use of ammunition tipped with depleted uranium. Although the Navy later agreed to cede back some of the land which it currently occupied, in July Governor Rosselló asked the UN to reinstate Puerto Rico on the official list of 'non-self-governing territories'. Meanwhile, improved air and cargo services to the island had been announced.

Former government workers in the US VIRGIN ISLANDS complained that they had been either dismissed or not rehired by the new administration of Charles Turnbull elected in 1998. State employees seeking a pay increase picketed the Senate in September to protest at government cost-cutting plans.

V MIDDLE EAST AND NORTH AFRICA

1. ISRAEL

CAPITAL: Jerusalem   AREA: 22,000 sq km   POPULATION: 6,000,000 ('98)
OFFICIAL LANGUAGE: Hebrew   POLITICAL SYSTEM: parliamentary democracy
HEAD OF STATE: President Ezer Weizman (since March '93)
RULING PARTIES: One Nation alliance of Israel Labour Party, Gesher and Meimad heads coalition with Shas, National Religious Party, Yisrael b'Aliya, Centre Party & Meretz
HEAD OF GOVERNMENT: Ehud Barak (Labour), Prime Minister (since July '99)
CURRENCY: new shekel (end-'99 £1=NSh6.70, US$1=NSh4.16)
GNP PER CAPITA: US$15,940 by exchange-rate calculation, US$17,310 at PPP ('98)

IT was a year of change and revival for Israel. On 17 May Ehud Barak secured a stunning victory in a general election, defeating incumbent Prime Minister Binyamin Netanyahu with a 400,000-vote majority, gaining slightly over 56 per cent of all votes cast. The change of government heralded a swift resumption of the peace process with the Palestinians and with the Syrians towards the end of the year (see V.2.i; V.2.iv).

Mr Barak's victory was as dramatic as it was surprising. At the start of the year it had been widely expected that Mr Netanyahu would win the election. This analysis was based on two assumptions: first, it was generally believed that, despite the criticism levelled at his style of leadership by his coalition partners and by disenchanted members of his own Likud party, Mr Netanyahu retained the confidence and loyalty of the voters who had swept him to power three years previously. Second, as opposition leader Mr Barak had failed to capture the imagination of the Israeli public and trailed Mr Netanyahu in the polls.

This was the second time the Israeli public had voted under the new electoral system whereby votes were cast both for a prime ministerial candidate and for a political party. As in 1996, Israelis continued to desert the two main parties and to vote for smaller, specific-interest parties. Whilst Mr Barak secured a resounding personal victory, his One Israel list—an alignment of the Labour Party, the Gesher movement headed by David Levy and Meimad, a moderate religious movement—did significantly less well, securing only 26 Knesset seats and 663,000 votes, barely a quarter of all votes cast. Mr Netanyahu's overwhelming defeat, which led to his immediate departure from public life, his resignation as Likud leader and from the Knesset, was mirrored by the dramatic collapse in the vote for Likud, which only just managed to retain its ranking as the second-largest faction with 19 seats.

At the outset of the electoral campaign there were five prime ministerial candidates: Mr Netanyahu, Mr Barak, former Defence Minister Yitzak Mordechai (who had recently left Likud to head the new Centre Party), Benny Begin (head of a right-wing National Unity list) and Azmi Bishara, a Palestinian Israeli. By election day the last three had withdrawn, leaving the Israeli public with just two candidates. In 1996 Mr Netanyahu had won the election by playing on the public's fears and insecurities about the peace process, famously promising 'peace with security', and by exploiting the people's lack of trust in then Labour leader Shimon Peres. The same strategy failed, however, in 1999. Mr Barak was not a soft target. As a former Chief of Staff and Israel's most decorated soldier, Mr Barak had unparalleled military credentials and was more than a match for Mr Netanyahu on security issues. At the same time, Israelis had become conditioned to the peace process with the Palestinians and to negotiating with Yassir Arafat. Allusions to the terrorist attacks of 1996 and to the existential threat posed by the Palestinians were no longer effective campaign tools.

Mr Netanyahu also miscalculated public sentiment on the domestic front by trying to exploit the rifts in Israeli society to his advantage. He accused the media of being captive to the left and tried to disadvantage his opponent by claiming that Mr Arafat hoped for a Barak victory. The 1996 Labour Party campaign had lost it the election. Mr Barak determined not to repeat the same mistake, running a faultless and highly professional campaign from start to finish. His first move was to enter the elections with as wide a coalition as possible, setting up the One Israel list with Mr Levy's Gesher movement and Meimad. In addition, he brought in a team of American electoral strategists who had worked for Bill Clinton and Tony Blair. They played down security issues and focused instead on the shortcomings of the Likud government in the areas of the economy, employment and health.

The 1999 elections were contested by a broad spectrum of political parties reflective of the divisions within Israeli society. Many new or relaunched parties emerged, such as Shinui, led by former journalist Yosef (Tommy) Lapid, which gained six seats; the Centre Party, which also won six seats; Israel Beitenu (Israel Our Home) led by Avigdor (Yvette) Lieberman, previously director of the Prime Minister's Office, which secured four seats; Am Ahad (the Workers' Party) led by Amir Peretz (head of the trade union movement), which won two seats; and Balad, an Arab party headed by Mr Bishara, which also won two seats.

The outstanding result of the election was the dramatic rise of Shas, the ultra-orthodox Sephardi party, from ten to 17 seats, making it the third largest party in the Knesset. Combined with the five seats of United Torah Judaism and the five of the National Religious Party (NRP), the total representation of the religious parties became 27 seats, nearly a quarter of Knesset total. Through the development of its own educational and welfare agencies, Shas had established wide-ranging social services in the predominantly lower-class, ethnically-Sephardi development towns and had become the main provider of affordable social services for the elderly and the poor. As a result, these towns, once Likud strongholds, became the main power-base of Shas.

An equally significant outcome was the emergence of a clearly-articulated bloc of secular parties in favour of a written constitution for Israel. This bloc included the new Shinui and Centre parties as well as Meretz, the long-established promoter of civil and secular issues. Shinui ran on a radically secular, anti-religious ticket, focusing on the issue of the separation of religion and state, and on contentious questions such as the exemption of yeshiva students from military service and the encroachment of Jewish orthodoxy on Israeli civil society. The Centre Party, established six months prior to the election and led by Mr Mordechai, Amnon Lipkin Shahak and former leading Likud members Dan Meridor and Roni Milo, focused on similar issues.

Two parties (compared with one in the last Knesset) now represented the Russian immigrant population of Israel. Yisrael B'Aliyah, which first entered the political arena in the 1996 election, retained its standing, dropping one seat to six. A new party, Israel Beiteinu, led by Avigdor Lieberman, ran on a right-wing ticket, appealing to Likud supporters within the Russian population disillusioned with former Soviet dissident Natan Sharansky, a member of the Netanyahu government.

Israeli Palestinians gave their support to three Arab parties, as opposed to two in the last election: Hadash, a Jewish-Arab party built on the former Israeli Communist Party; Ra'am, consisting of the Unified Arab List and the moderate faction of the Islamic movement; and Mr Bishara's Balad. Support for the Arab parties, which won ten seats in all (nine in the previous Knesset), rose only marginally.

The principal losers in the election were the right-wing parties. The National Unity Party, representing the settler movement, received only four mandates. This failure led Benny Begin, head of the list, to resign from the Knesset and to withdraw from political life. The representation of the NRP, which also ran on an essentially right-wing platform, was reduced by almost half, to only five seats.

A central theme of Mr Barak's election campaign was that he would be a 'Prime Minister for all'. The fragmented nature of the Knesset, however, presented him with difficult choices when it came to forming his coalition. Any choice would necessarily result in a trade-off in the issues he would be able to address and limit his freedom of manoeuvre. For the first time in the political history of Israel, a secular-based coalition was a possibility. Bringing in Likud and not the religious parties would have given Mr Barak a working majority and enabled him to deal with civic issues, the writing of a constitution and the separation of religion and politics. Such a course, however, would have been at the expense of his hopes for the peace process. The alternative, which he in fact chose, involved bringing in the religious parties, which allowed him to deal with the peace process but obliged him to wait on the religion/state issue.

Mr Barak's government commanded the support of 73 of the 120 Knesset members, in seven parties: One Israel, Meretz, the three religious parties (Shas, the NRP and United Torah Judaism), Yisrael B'Aliyah and the Centre Party. Taking the full 45 days allotted to him to form a coalition, Mr Barak proceeded with skill and patience, smoothing things over in order to enable the widely divergent factions to sit together. Of particular significance was the removal of convicted Shas leader Aryeh Deri from any leadership role, which enabled Meretz to back down from its initial refusal to join a coalition which included a convicted criminal. In order to persuade the religious parties to join the coalition, Mr Barak was forced to compromise on the issue of whether yeshiva students should be exempt from military service.

Mr Barak offered major portfolios to win over the coalition partners of his choice. Meretz obtained education and industry and trade, as well as the position of Deputy Finance Minister. Yisrael B'Aliyah wrested the Interior Ministry from Shas, which in return received four social welfare ministries (labour and social affairs, national infrastructure, health and religion).The Centre Party was given transport and the NRP housing.

With the Cabinet limited by law to 18 seats, few pickings were left for Mr Barak's own party. One of Mr Barak's first acts in government was thus to amend the law and expand his Cabinet to 24 members, thereby enabling additional posts to be given to One Nation representatives. Having promised Mr Levy the Foreign Affairs Ministry and having decided to keep the Defence Ministry for himself, the Prime Minister had only seven cabinet posts for the Labour Party. The Finance Ministry, sought by Shlomo Ben Ami and Yossi Beilin, was in fact given to his loyal supporter Avraham (Beiga) Shochat, while Mr Ben Ami and Mr Beilin were allotted internal security and justice respectively.

By choosing a coalition favourable to the peace process and retaining the Defence Ministry for himself, Mr Barak clearly indicated that the revival of the peace process would be at the top of his government's agenda. His immediate inheritance on the Palestinian front was the implementation of the Wye River accords signed in November 1998 (see AR 1998, pp. 219-21), but unilaterally suspended by Mr Netanyahu at the end of that year after the first of the three designated territorial withdrawals.

At the beginning of September, after weeks of negotiation, Mr Barak and Mr Arafat signed a modified version of the Wye accords, agreeing upon a formula for their renewed implementation. The signature at the Egyptian resort town of Sharm el Sheikh was witnessed by US Secretary of State Madeleine Albright, Egyptian President Husni Mubarak and King Abdullah of Jordan (see XVII.3). Under the new agreement, Israel and Palestine agreed to begin final status talks immediately, with the intention of drawing up a set of principles to guide the final status negotiations by 13 February 2000, with the target date for a final peace treaty set for 13 September 2000, seven years after the signing of the Oslo accords. The Sharm el Shaikh accords also included a timetable for three further redeployments of Israeli troops from the West Bank and the transfer of those areas to Palestinian control; for the release of 350 Palestinian prisoners held in Israeli gaols; and for the opening of two safe-passage routes betweeen the West Bank and Gaza—agreement on the first of which, the southern route, was reached on 5 October and which became operational on 25 October.

Mr Barak's election also raised hopes for an immediate revival of negotiations between Israel and Syria, suspended since March 1996. Indeed, in the immediate aftermath of Mr Barak's victory there were signals from Damascus that it was viewed in a positive light. Mr Barak in turn praised Syrian President Hafiz al-Asad. By autumn hopes for speedy reconciliation and progress had begun to fade. Nevertheless, behind the scenes intense diplomatic efforts were being made by the Americans to bridge the gap between the two sides. These bore fruit when President Clinton convened a high-level meeting in Washington on 15 December between Mr Barak and Syrian Foreign Minister Faruq al-Shara. The very fact that such a meeting could take place marked a significant breakthrough in Israeli-Syrian relations and led to intense speculation that the two sides were close to signing a peace treaty. However, the two-day White House meeting was essentially a confidence-building exercise and no substantive negotiations took place. The two sides agreed to meet at the beginnning of January 2000 in Shepherdstown, Virginia, for negotiations based on the Camp David model and aimed at drawing up a peace treaty.

The year was one of the most momentous in Israel's economic history, as inflation fell to its lowest level since 1968. By the end of the year the rate was below 2 per cent, a figure which surprised even the most optimistic analysts. High interest rates, however, drew much criticism from the industrial and commercial sectors, whose representatives attributed Israel's economic recession between 1997 and 1999 to the anti-inflationary measures of Professor Jacob Frenkel, the governor of the Bank of Israel. Professor Frenkel responded that only growth based on a low-inflation economy could be stable and consistent. His aim achieved, he surprised the markets by announcing his resignation after almost nine years as head of Israel's central bank.

2. ARAB WORLD AND PALESTINIANS—
EGYPT—JORDAN—SYRIA—LEBANON—IRAQ

i. THE ARAB WORLD AND THE PALESTINIANS

THE Arabs felt relief at Binyamin Netanyahu's replacement as Israeli Prime Minister by Ehud Barak in May (see V.1). But Mr Barak lacked complete control and faced crucial problems—Jerusalem, the status of Palestinians in the occupied territories (OT) and their hawkish Israeli settlers. Palestinian leader Yassir Arafat retained his wayward temperament and style (see AR 1998, p. 221) and faced Palestinian critics who had never accepted the Oslo agreements. The rulers of Egypt, Syria and Iraq were ageing and often inflexible. In Jordan, the untried Abdullah replaced King Husain, the Arabs' most experienced ruler (see V.2.iii).

As Mr Netanyahu expanded Jewish settlement in Jerusalem and the OT, Palestinian spokesmen again demanded a unilateral declaration of independence. Mr Netanyahu responded by threatening to annex the West Bank. Mr Arafat (but not all his colleagues) now opposed such a declaration, which Egypt, Russia and the USA urged him to avoid. On this, the Palestinian leadership's new line provoked hostility in the OT, while Amman received coolly Mr Arafat's suggestion of a Palestinian-Jordanian confederacy. At the UN, the USA and Israel were isolated in opposing a special UN conference and a ban on Jewish settlement in the OT—which Mr Netanyahu continued expanding and so enlarging Jerusalem as to separate it effectively from the West Bank.

Mr Barak promised to revive talks with the Palestinians and made them friendly gestures. But he lacked the political authority for a fundamental modification of Israel's stand, and his talks with the Palestine Liberation Organization (PLO) looked unlikely to produce a final settlement. The political balance in Israel meant that frontiers could not return to those of 1967 nor Jerusalem be once more divided, which some Palestinians were still demanding.

Mr Arafat first met Mr Barak on 11 July and again on 27 July. Mr Barak confirmed Israel's intention of implementing the Wye accords (see AR 1998, p. 222) but wanted, by a brief delay, to combine it with final talks on the trickiest issues—refugees, Jerusalem, Jewish settlements. Mr Arafat insisted that the Wye accords must be implemented in their entirety. Palestinian-Israeli talks culminated when, on 4 September, the two sides, witnessed by King Abdullah of Jordan, President Mubarak of Egypt and US Secretary of State Madeleine Albright, signed the important Sharm el Shaikh agreement (see XVII.3). It envisaged redeploying Israeli forces, releasing some Palestinians from Israeli gaols, safe passage for Palestinians (under Israeli control) around the OT, a new port at Gaza and new regulations in the emotionally-charged town of Hebron. The Israelis, as before, expected the Palestinians to arrest suspected terrorists and confiscate arms.

Anti-Palestinian activities by Jewish settlers persisted, and on 9 October the Palestinians boycotted further negotiations. They resented Israel's continued detention of Hamas men, whom they viewed as freedom fighters. Jewish settlements expanded. Mr Barak later cast doubt on the relevance of UN resolution 242 of 1967 (which had been accepted at Sharm el Shaikh) to the present situation. He said that the government would not allow new settlements in the OT, but existing ones could expand. A clear Arab-Jewish frontier—involving separation of the Israeli and Palestinian economies and thus damaging for the Palestinians, now dependent on the employment in Israel of 100,000 Arabs—was under study by the Barak government but opposed by Israeli business.

Jewish settlement continued. In December Israel issued tenders for another 500 Jewish homes in the OT, the figures showing that in a few months of 1999 Mr Barak had authorized more building there than his predecessor in the whole of 1998. Mr Barak later froze these expansions, but the Palestinians would not, initially, resume negotiations, despite a last-minute appeal to Mr Arafat by Mrs Albright. As 1999 ended, hopes of a settlement were weaker than after Mr Barak's election victory.

On Jerusalem, Mr Netanyahu's leading hawk, Ariel Sharon, declared in March that the original UN resolution for internationalization of the city was null and void: his new settlement at Har Homa seemed intended to enlarge it. His efforts to close the PLO's Jerusalem office were frustrated by the Israeli Supreme Court. Acting as current president of the European Union (EU), Germany protested in March at Israel's banning (ineffectually) of visits to that office by foreign delegations. Palestinian spokesmen were still talking of Jerusalem as the capital of an independent Palestine; in October the city's most influential Arab personality, Faisal Husaini, said that compromise there would damage Mr Arafat's credibility. At year's end Mr Barak described the city as the eternal and undivided capital of the Jewish state, but one which must be treated as the centre of three faiths.

In the OT, continual attacks on Israeli forces by anti-Arafat Arabs produced severe retaliations, Palestinian casualties being the heavier. Opinion polls showed falling Arab support for the peace process. Arabs were further antagonized by Israeli demolitions of Palestinian houses and by indulgence shown to Israeli soldiers who had killed Palestinians. Even after Mr Barak took office, the Israeli authorities still wanted to monitor sermons in mosques and vet the selection of imams, among other interference. Liberal Palestinians opposed the fundamentalists but criticized collective punishments imposed on them to combat individual cases. Two subjects—Israel's tendency to release common criminals rather than political prisoners and to restrict the movement of Palestinians around the OT—aroused particular resentment. The suggested bridge between Gaza and the West Bank was replaced, after the Sharm el Shaikh agreement, by permitted movement by road under supervision. In November the Israeli army dismantled an illegal Jewish settlement in the OT and the Israeli courts and public opinion removed other provocations.

Arbitrary or oppressive behaviour by the Palestinian police against Hamas and its adherents damaged the Palestinian cause. The Palestinian legislators wanted their own authorities to stop detaining political prisoners, some of whom went on hunger strike. Anxious not to irritate the Israelis, some Palestinian authorities seemed ready to erode press freedom. There was popular dissatisfaction with their less intransigent line towards Israeli occupation and their suspected corruption. The latter was also outspokenly attacked by the EU, which disliked seeing its generous help—the largest single source of Palestinian funds—wasted or embezzled.

Other Palestinian deficiencies were primarily administrative. In June Palestinian lawyers appealed to Mr Arafat to save the justice system from collapse: the only laws in force were out of date, courts were under-staffed and subjected to interference by the security authorities, lawyers under-trained. The new Palestinian administration was surveyed, sometimes critically, by an international task force including former heads of state. It commended the authority for establishing a legislative and administrative structure but criticized the lack of accountability, transparency and press freedom and censured the resultant corruption. Mr Arafat's vulnerability to such criticism was not lessened by his Christian-born, Sorbonne-educated wife, who attacked the Israelis and was rebuked by the State Department.

Christian influence in the traditionally multi-confessional Palestinian movement had been reduced by emigration. Confessional differences caused intra-Palestinian tensions—Christian-Muslim over a new mosque in Nazareth and inter-Christian over the Church of the Holy Sepulchre in Jerusalem. Palestinians believed that Mr Netanyahu's government had knowingly encouraged such tensions: the Vatican, too, accused Israel of fomenting them.

In February international donors to the Palestinian administration pledged $700 million to assist the Palestinian authority. The US government also hinted that it might increase its help to the Palestinians (and reduce what it was paying to Israel), while making clear that it expected the EU to support their economic development. In July the head of the World Bank met Mr Arafat in Gaza and approved the commitment of $54 million to new projects in the OT.

ii. EGYPT

CAPITAL: Cairo   AREA: 1,000,000 sq km   POPULATION: 61,500,000 ('98)
OFFICIAL LANGUAGE: Arabic   POLITICAL SYSTEM: presidential democracy
HEAD OF STATE & GOVERNMENT: President Mohammed Husni Mubarak (since '81)
RULING PARTY: National Democratic Party (NDP)
PRIME MINISTER: Atif al Ubayd (since Oct '99)
MAIN IGO MEMBERSHIPS (NON-UN): AL, OAPEC, OAU, OIC, NAM
CURRENCY: Egyptian pound (end-'99 £1=EP5.51, US$1=EP3.42)
GNP PER CAPITA: US$1,290 by exchange-rate calculation, US$3,130 at PPP ('98)

PRESIDENT Husni Mubarak, in power since 1981, was again preoccupied with the Palestine peace process (see V.1; V.2.i). At home, Islamic fundamentalism, though still powerful, seemed more manageable than before. Mr Mubarak changed Prime Ministers in October: the change was believed to herald a devolution of power to individual ministers and a reduction in state control of the economy. The large-scale export of natural gas came nearer.

The President seemed resolved to remain in power indefinitely. In May the (unelected) upper house of parliament pledged him *baya* ('homage', normally associated with monarchies), this action being copied by the chief trade unionist and, under threat of dismissal, by the schoolteachers. The elected lower house nominated Mr Mubarak on 3 June as the sole candidate for presidential elections, the left-wing and Islamist members abstaining. Their enforced acquiescence contrasted with latitude allowed in previous presidential elections. On 27 September Mr Mubarak was re-elected by 94 per cent of the votes cast and began his fourth term of six years, amid some calls for looser political controls.

Mr Mubarak remained, in the Arab-Israeli peace process, an important actor who could not be ignored. After Egypt's chilly relations with Binyamin Netanyahu, the new Israeli Prime Minister, Ehud Barak, was a welcome change. The President accepted that there would be a few weeks' delay in implementing the Wye agreement (see AR 1998, p. 222). His optimism diminished as the autumn went on. In London in November he said that the process was doing less well than expected and even that Mr Barak's government was bullying the Palestinians.

Egypt was dissatisfied with the response from Britain and Germany to an appeal for help in clearing Egypt of mines laid in World War II, and uncomfortable at having to join US forces in October's military exercises, to which the USA gave an anti-Iranian slant. Egypt was ordered to compensate the widow of a Libyan political exile kidnapped and killed in Cairo. A member of the Saudi royal family was prosecuted for assaulting the police.

Internal security was still overshadowed by fundamentalism. In February three Egyptians from Jama'at al Islamiyya connected with the 1997 Luxor massacre (see AR 1997, p. 209) and linked to its reputed Saudi financier, Osama bin Laden, were arrested in Uruguay. In Egypt itself many of the Jama'at were on trial (nearly half *in absentia*), some being Albanians handed over to Egypt by the Americans. Later in the spring, Jama'at leaders in and outside Egypt called jointly for a ceasefire in their conflict with the security forces (estimated to have already cost 1,300 lives) and for political pressure on the government which, they maintained, had not responded to their ceasefire call. In September the Interior Ministry claimed that 5,000 Islamists had been released in 1999 (though human rights groups said 15,000 were still in gaol) and announced that Egypt would allow the ageing Shaikh Omar Abdulrahman, imprisoned in the USA since 1996, to finish his sentence in Egypt. Other fundamentalists refused any accommodation: in September the police shot the leader and three others of the Jama'at's military wing, which was promptly reconstituted abroad. During the President's September visit to Port Said, the police shot dead an unarmed eccentric with a persecution complex trying to present a petition.

In October President Mubarak replaced the Prime Minister, Kamal Ganzuri, with Atif al Ubayd, a former minister, who planned to give more power to individual ministers and to accelerate economic reform, to which he reportedly saw the government's grip on banking and insurance as obstacles. Observers viewed his appointment as strengthening the reformers: Mr al Ubayd was said to speak 'the language of international business'.

Despite Mr Mubarak's autocratic instincts—a chaotic democracy, he said, was worse than dictatorship—his adviser Usama al Baz encouraged some businessmen to start a new party called Al Mustaqbil (The Future), perhaps connected with a developing conflict between technocrats and government party bosses. Some MPs were accused of dishonesty and two were arrested for running a gang of armed thugs.

By March there had already been 15 strikes, the biggest labour unrest for many years, which the opposition Wafdist paper was accused of encouraging. Civil servants, displeased by a reduction in benefits, also struck. There was opposition from civil liberties groups and academics to new laws which, they maintained, would turn non-governmental organizations into a branch of government—criticism supported by the new UN Commissioner for Human Rights. Twenty Islamists belonging to professional associations were arrested while attending a meeting and accused of infiltrating syndicates, parliament and local councils. This was followed on 20 October by the appointment of judges to supervise the elections to the lawyers' syndicate. There was also opposition to a new labour law ending Nasser's principle of jobs for life.

When a Boeing of Egyptair crashed off New York on 31 October, foreign newspapers suggested that the pilot had deliberately committed suicide (see IV.1). However, there was nothing in his background to support this suggestion, which caused indignation in Egypt.

The Egyptian pound was overvalued: US dollars were short and current account deficits were being met from the reduced dollar holdings of state banks. Earnings from tourism remained lower than before the 1997 Luxor disaster. But the government immediately rejected devaluation: inflation and the current account deficit were low and future income from gas fields looked promising. A joint Egyptian-British-Italian venture aimed to exploit large estimated gas reserves and there was also an agreement with a French company to establish two gas-powered generating stations.

There were growing doubts about the grandiose water project west of the Nile at Toshka in the far south (see AR 1998, p. 226). the press now claiming that it would not be ready for more than a decade: by then population would be up by another 20 million.

Egypt had its usual quota of unusual stories. In March a hospital was found to have sold organs from dead children to wealthy patients and rumours of an impending earthquake led thousands of people in Cairo to flee their homes and sleep in the open. The new year was celebrated at the Giza pyramids with a vast musical spectacle, but a scheme to accompany it by putting a golden cap on the Great Pyramid was abandoned after complaints that this would have Masonic and Zionist overtones.

Kamal ud Din Husain, one of the Free Officers behind the revolution of 1952, was buried on 20 June, having died at the age of 78. He had been Vice-President until 1964, when he had opposed Egypt's intervention in Yemen.

iii. JORDAN

CAPITAL: Amman   AREA: 97,000 sq km   POPULATION: 5,200,000 ('98)
OFFICIAL LANGUAGE: Arabic   POLITICAL SYSTEM: monarchy
HEAD OF STATE & GOVERNMENT: King Abdullah ibn al-Husain (since Feb '99)
PRIME MINISTER: Abdul Rauf Rawabidah (since March '99)
MAIN IGO MEMBERSHIPS (NON-UN): AL, OIC, NAM
CURRENCY: dinar (end-'99 £1=JD1.14, US$1=JD0.71)
GNP PER CAPITA: US$1,520 by exchange-rate calculation, US$3,230 at PPP ('98)

THERE was a change of monarch and style in Jordan and, in neighbouring Israel, a new government with a less hard-line Prime Minister (see V.1). King Abdullah could not inherit his father's unique prestige and was therefore more dependent on the USA.

King Husain returned from America on 25 January and abruptly appointed his son Abdullah as Crown Prince to replace his brother Hasan, whom he publicly accused of interfering with the army. The King's health then obliged him to return to the USA: when treatment there proved unavailing, he returned to Amman and died on 7 February (see XVIII: Obituary). Heads of state at his funeral included President Clinton and, surprisingly, President Asad of Syria. Queen Elizabeth was represented by Prince Charles, who later spoke at a memorial service in London attended by his father and several European sovereigns.

The new King, son of an English mother and educated largely in Britain and America, but married to a Palestinian, had been a professional soldier and spoke Bedouin Arabic. He forthwith dismissed four senior generals, the Prime Minister and several ministers close to Prince Hasan, the new government being headed by Abdul Rauf Rawabidah, former Deputy Premier and regarded as an arch-reformer. The King's first few months included visits to most Arab countries, Europe and the USA.

Israel's then Prime Minister, Binyamin Netanyahu, marked the new reign by recalling Jordan's links with, and sympathy for, Iraq. In March Israel announced that poor rainfall made it impracticable to supply Jordan with as much water as previously promised; this disagreement was later resolved. The King met the new Israeli Prime Minister, Ehud Barak, when the latter took office in July. In August a new Jordan bridge and a frontier crossing were opened. Later, after Jordanian deputies visiting a Muslim shrine in Hebron had been searched by Israeli police and attacked by Israeli settlers, the press association, committed to opposing peace with Israel, expelled Jordanian journalists who had visited it at Israeli invitation.

Only days after Husain's death, a Jordanian official rejected Yassir Arafat's proposed Jordanian-Palestinian confederation, saying that Israel must first evacuate the occupied territories (OT). Once King Abdullah took control, the government was readier to side with the Palestinian leader and less inclined to sympathize with his opponents in such groups as Hamas (see V.2.i). The Hamas offices in Amman, tolerated by King Husain, were in August closed as belonging to an illegal organization and many of its members arrested: they were later charged with, among other things, preparing armed operations in the OT. Later, after the King had asked his Premier to end the crisis with Hamas, six of its men, having abandoned a hunger strike, were told that if they wished to stay in Jordan they must leave Hamas. In November Jordan released them: some, including the prominent Khalid Mish'al (see AR 1997, p. 212), were flown to Qatar, at its ruler's suggestion; others were freed in Jordan. In December 11 Jordanians and two other Arabs were arrested on suspicion of planning terrorism after training in Afghanistan.

The new monarch improved relations with the Gulf states. Ambassadors were exchanged with Kuwait, which released Jordanians accused of collaboration with Iraq. Jordanian ministers discussed economic ties with Saudi Arabia, including the recruitment of Jordanian workers. The planned pan-Arab games in Amman were discussed with Saudis and Kuwaitis, the latter being disposed to boycott them because the Iraqis had been invited. The Gulf states would not, however, help to finance the games, with the result that Jordan's Finance Minister resigned.

Relations with other neighbouring states improved. In July the King visited Damascus and next month the Syrian Prime Minister came to Amman on the first such visit for years. Syria began to admit Jordanian newspapers and helped by supplying much-needed water. The King became the first Jordanian ruler to visit Beirut for 30 years. In November Jordan began to allow Iraqi exports through the port at Aqaba. Of Jordan's perennial influx of foreign workers, the then Prime Minister said in January that only 21,000 work permits had been issued since the previous October, but there were now up to a million of them in the country. By July work permits to foreigners had been cut by a third.

Jordan remained one of the more democratic Arab states. Twelve deputies voted in April against the new government. At July's municipal elections other opposition parties were upstaged by the powerful Islamic Action Front (IAF), the political wing of the Muslim Brotherhood. The IAF won 72 council seats and had seven mayors elected (being stronger in the towns than in the Bedouin-dominated countryside) and viewed the elections as fairly conducted. Turnout was 60 per cent overall but lower in the towns. Some journalists favouring the opposition were assaulted: one was arrested but released after four days. The King had reportedly ordered the police not to arrest journalists. On this and other occasions he disguised himself, à la Haroun al Rashid, to observe bureaucracy at work. In December the persistent East Bank/Palestinian divide produced a fight between football supporters from the two communities.

On leaving for Europe, the new King said that Jordan's financial difficulties were his hardest job. Debt repayment was taking a third of the budget: one-and-a-half million Jordanians were in poverty and a quarter of the workforce unemployed. Foreign debt was now $6,800 million. The King was believed to be seeking special treatment for Jordan; the Americans had already written off most of the $700 million owed to them, and King Abdullah now sought to halve Jordan's debts to the industrialized world. In May the Paris Club refused a simple write-off but agreed to rescheduling. Later there were other pledges of US assistance, and the World Bank approved further loans for the current year.

In June, citing a recent increase in government salaries and a fall in customs receipts, the government increased sales tax from 10 to 13 per cent; parliament approved only under protest. Privatization continued and it was now to extend to the railways. In November civil servants met businessmen to encourage cooperation between them, agreeing that privatization and private development should continue.

iv. SYRIA

CAPITAL: Damascus　　AREA: 185,000 sq km　　POPULATION: 15,000,000 ('98)
OFFICIAL LANGUAGE: Arabic　　POLITICAL SYSTEM: presidential
HEAD OF STATE & GOVERNMENT: President Hafiz al-Asad (since March '71)
RULING PARTY: Baath Arab Socialist Party
PRIME MINISTER: Mahmud Zuabi, Prime Minister (since Nov '87)
MAIN IGO MEMBERSHIPS (NON-UN) AL, OAPEC, OIC, NAM
CURRENCY: Syrian pound (end-'99 £1=SP72.53, US$1=SP45.00)
GNP PER CAPITA: US$1,020 by exchange-rate calculation, US$3,000 at PPP ('98)

THE ageing President, though still in full control, began to instal his son as successor. His initial welcome to a new Israeli government turned to caution. Syria still dominated Lebanon, though less rigidly. The President warmed towards the new King in Jordan (see V.2.iii) and again showed particular respect for Moscow. There was some tentative economic relaxation.

In January the Assembly dutifully nominated General Hafiz al-Asad as President for his fifth term of seven years: this was promptly ratified by 99.9 per cent of voters in a referendum. He retained all his constitutional powers, though his son Bashar al-Asad, by profession not a soldier but an eye-doctor, was now the chosen successor. He was received by the President of France, visited Saudi Arabia for talks on Palestine and acted as a kind of mediator between the Syrian government and its people.

From a television station in France, the President's unruly brother Rifa'at al-Asad in September denounced the arrest of his supporters in Syria. In October an illegal port of theirs in Lattakia was violently closed. Rifa'at was also suspected of having been behind an attack in Paris in November on the President's son-in-law.

President Asad's first reaction to Israel's election of Ehud Barak as Prime Minister (see V.1) was favourable: in June he described Mr Barak as an honest man who could deliver peace. He offered to accept some international presence on the Golan Heights after the area's return to Syria; warned dissident Palestinian groups in Damascus against military ventures; and suspended arms supplies to Hizbullah in southern Lebanon (see V.2.v). But he remained cautious and missed King Hassan's funeral in Morocco (see V.4.v) from reluctance to be drawn by President Clinton into premature talks with Mr Barak.

By August the Syrian attitude to Israel had perceptibly cooled. Bashar al-Asad said that Israel had not backed words with action and, when Israel deferred discussion of previous promises to leave the Golan, the government, through the Syrian press, called Israeli peace offers hollow and pressed the USA to break the deadlock. In late September both Syria and Israel were asking more than the other would concede, the Israelis in particular pressing for agreement on issues other than the Golan, whereas Syria insisted on the evacuation of the Golan as a precondition for further negotiations.

By December Mr Barak had replaced previous plans for unilateral evacuation of southern Lebanon with one to negotiate withdrawal later. US Secretary of State Madeleine Albright saw President Asad in Damascus on 7 December and arranged a meeting in America on 15 December between Syrian Foreign

Minister Faruq al-Shara and Mr Barak. This was chilly and inconclusive: Mr al-Shara denounced the Israeli occupation of the Golan whence, he said, half a million Syrians had been uprooted in 1967, as well as the anti-Syrian bias of the world's press. Discussion was to resume early in 2000.

As regards Syria's relations with the major powers, early in 1999 the US government partially restored services to Syria, which had been suspended the previous year after mass protests in Damascus against allied air attacks on Baghdad. But soon Washington was imposing sanctions on Russian firms for exporting arms to Syria, which it still classified as a supporter of terrorism. In February the Finance Minister was in Moscow discussing arms and President Asad himself went there on 5 July for the same purpose; the Russians still had large outstanding financial claims on Syria. The two governments joined to demand the return of the Golan Heights to Syria.

The Syrian government retained in principle its dominant position in Lebanon, though the new leadership there seemed less inclined than its predecessor to accept Syrian policy without question. There were moves towards a rapprochement with Jordan, the new monarch there being readier for it than his father. In April King Abdullah visited Damascus and agreed with President Asad to ignore past disagreements over Israel and reactivate their joint committee, which had not met for five years. They had negotiations over water supplies (see V.2.iii). Turkey was planning a dam which the Syrians and Iraqis feared would reduce the flow of the Euphrates river (see V.2.vi). Other Turkish-Syrian disagreements covered Turkey's close relations with Israel and their opposing attitudes on Kurdish nationalism.

The economy continued to be unsatisfactory. In March a reliable survey showed the GDP was contracting, population growing by 3.5 per cent a year, oil prices falling and rainfall inadequate. In the autumn a Syrian businessman pointed out that Syria was still too much a command economy in which foreigners were reluctant to invest. All this, especially the fall in oil income, was forcing Syria towards a more market-friendly system, a trend stubbornly resisted by a small group of ill-paid bureaucrats who had benefited, through bribery, from state control. Signs of improvement included a projected new law to encourage exporters, the removal of taxes on raw cotton and textiles and Iran's agreement to reductions in Syria's repayment obligations on debts of over $500 million. But there were unpaid debts of over $900 million incurred with the former East German regime. The Syrian Economics Ministry demonstrated Syrian ignorance of commerce by complaining that business was importing three times more than it exported.

v. LEBANON

CAPITAL: Beirut   AREA: 10,000 sq km   POPULATION: 4,000,000 ('98)
OFFICIAL LANGUAGE: Arabic   POLITICAL SYSTEM: presidential, power-sharing
HEAD OF STATE & GOVERNMENT: President Émile Lahoud (since Nov '98)
RULING PARTIES: government of national unity
PRIME MINISTER: Salim al-Hoss, Prime Minister (since Dec '98)
MAIN IGO MEMBERSHIPS (NON-UN): AL, OIC, NAM, Francophonie
CURRENCY: Lebanese pound (end-'99 £1=LP2,429.64, US$1=LP1,507.50)
GNP PER CAPITA: US$3,560 by exchange-rate calculation, US$6,150 at PPP ('98)

LEBANESE politics differed little in essentials from the year before. The government remained under Syrian supervision and partial occupation. Israeli forces still occupied an important area in South Lebanon where Iran had significant influence. In Beirut the presidency of General Émile Lahoud was now firmly established and later confronted a new and seemingly less intransigent government in Israel. The hopes thus inspired had not, by year's end, been fulfilled and the outgoing Israeli government's air-raids had seriously damaged Lebanon's economy.

Damascus, in agreement with Beirut, would still not contemplate Lebanon's making its own peace with Israel, thus recovering the security zone (SZ) in South Lebanon. This was advocated by some Lebanese who argued that the Syrian occupation had resulted from the 1967 war for which Lebanon was not responsible: but Syria, seeing the SZ as a bargaining counter, was expected to require Hizbullah, the Shia militia, to continue its operations until Syria had recovered the Golan. In September Maronite clergy and politicians urged the withdrawal of all foreign troops, Syrian as well as Israeli, from Lebanese soil: this line was also followed by a newly-launched multi-confessional party, the Lebanese National Front.

As the year opened, the then Israeli government said that Israel would withdraw from the SZ only if Lebanese forces would police the frontier and take over Israel's proxy militia, the South Lebanese Army (SLA), which had been trained by, and was cooperating with, the Israeli authorities. An Israeli human rights group revealed that 14 Lebanese had been found dead in an SLA prison after maltreatment. When Israeli military opinion began to contemplate leaving the SZ, SLA men naturally thought of seeking asylum in Israel. An American human rights organization accused Israel also of expelling hundreds of Lebanese from their homes in the SZ. Although the Israeli Labour Party had spoken while in opposition of bringing the troops home from Lebanon and Mr Barak had promised to withdraw from the SZ during his first year in office, he did not do so.

In South Lebanon Israeli occupying forces and the SLA were throughout the year attacked by, and suffered casualties from, Hizbullah guerrillas. In late February Israeli troops who had forcibly emptied a Shia village lost several officers, including a general, in Hizbullah attacks. The US government urged restraint on both sides. In June Hizbullah reacted to Israeli shelling by attacking the Israeli border town of Kiryat Shimona: the Israelis responded with massive air attacks on many Lebanese public utilities. Two power stations were hit, plunging Beirut into darkness. Damage was estimated at much more than in the 1996 raids (see AR 1996, p. 211). The Israeli high command had failed in its declared objective of deterring Hizbullah, whose attacks rose sharply thereafter.

There were still 350,000 Palestinians in Lebanon. About 40 per cent of them were under 15 years of age and 170,000 were still in camps, over half of them unemployed, while thousands of non-Arab nationals and nearly 300,000 Syrians and Egyptians had found work. The new government began to ease travel restrictions on Palestinians, but, unlike those in Jordan or Egypt, they were still not given citizenship or permanent residence. They included factions hostile to Al Fatah (the mainstream Palestinian leadership in the Israeli-occupied territories), which had earlier intruded into Lebanese politics and now tried to do so again. There were several violent intra-Palestinian hostilities which caused casualties, some fatal, in Lebanon, especially in the Ain al-Hilwa camp. In this connection, the personal representative in Lebanon of Palestinian leader Yassir Arafat was condemned to death *in absentia* and two of his lieutenants were arrested. One Palestinian faction opposed to the Oslo agreement attacked Israeli positions in the SZ.

The northern city of Tripoli had its own particular troubles, especially hostilities, sometimes fatal, between different groups of Sunni extremists and Muslim attacks on Greek Orthodox Christians.

The government of President Lahoud and Prime Minister Salim al-Hoss busied itself in removing traces of the previous regime dominated by Rafiq Hariri. Amid revelations of extensive corruption, many important people, including adherents of Mr Hariri, were dismissed. Former ministers and senior officials were arrested for peculation. There were even accusations that money voted to help those displaced by the Israelis in the SZ had been stolen. The President declared his intention to strengthen the structure of the state, to whose weakness he ascribed the long civil war. The huge property company Solidère now owed $220 million and its profits fell sharply: the company blamed this on government reductions in public investment.

Shafiq al-Wazzan, a former Prime Minister, died on 8 July. Although hostile to Israel, he had signed the still-born peace agreement of 1983.

vi. IRAQ

CAPITAL: Baghdad   AREA: 438,000 sq km   POPULATION: 22,000,000 ('98)
OFFICIAL LANGUAGE: Arabic   POLITICAL SYSTEM: presidential
HEAD OF STATE & GOVERNMENT: President Saddam Husain (since July '79), also Prime Minister
   & Chairman of Revolutionary Command Council
RULING PARTY: Baath Arab Socialist Party
MAIN IGO MEMBERSHIPS (NON-UN): AL, OPEC, OAPEC, OIC, NAM
CURRENCY: dinar (end-'99 £1=ID0.50, US$1=ID0.31)
GNP PER CAPITA: n/a

THE campaign of the Anglo-Americans ('the alliance') against President Saddam Husain left him firmly in power and was little supported at the UN. Sanctions harmed the Iraqi people rather more than Saddam and his regime, which was still firmly in place despite American backing for opposition groups.

The alliance's campaign to impose no-fly zones continued. In February there were almost daily raids and an attack on the Iraq-Turkey pipeline: the Iraqis soon claimed to have reopened it. Air defences, communications and pipelines were regularly attacked from bases in Turkey, Saudi Arabia and Kuwait: when the USA warned Iraq against attacking them, Saddam wrote to the Arab League offering reconciliation and sent his Foreign Minister round member states. Iraqi civilians were regularly killed and Iraq was accused of siting its missiles deliberately near civilian centres.

The US government tried, through the UN Special Committee on Iraq (UNSCOM), to infiltrate personnel and equipment in order to intercept Iraqi military communications. Leaked documents showed Washington privately urging its Arab friends to oppose lifting sanctions or reforming UNSCOM. There were American meetings with Iraqi political exiles, the State Department being under congressional pressure to resurrect an opposition which remained only half alive. In November the exiles were introduced to US officials and to Secretary of State Madeleine Albright herself.

The economic sanctions hit hardest at ordinary Iraqis, who tended to blame foreign governments rather than their own. Child mortality had doubled since 1989. Professional people were leaving the country. The sanctions aroused opposition abroad, especially from Russia and China and often from France. In October Christian leaders in Iraq asked the Archbishop of Canterbury to use his influence in ending them.

In response, the alliance began dangling the possibility of lifting sanctions to induce Iraq to abandon its non-conventional weapons: this would have required checking by UN inspectors, and Iraq refused to readmit them. It also steadily refused offers to replace UNSCOM, with its supposedly anti-Iraq chairman, Richard Butler, by another body and to finance the oil-for-food programme by raising the ceiling on oil exports, demanding instead a simple end to sanctions (see also XI.1).

In November the UN Security Council offered to extend the oil-for-food programme for 14 days while revised terms were considered. This Iraq rejected, in the justified hope of highlighting differences within the Council. On 22 November Iraq halted all oil-for-food exports and brought the oil price to its highest for several years. In the event, the allies could not secure unanimous Security Council support for the proposed bargain. A resolution acceptable to the allies, on which Russia, China and France abstained, offered an amplified oil-for-food programme but would not lift the blockade until Iraq readmitted UN inspectors. Iraq would not promise cooperation with a monitoring commission to be set up under the UN resolution.

As for other Middle East states, those which had suffered Iraqi aggression— notably Kuwait—wanted sanctions to remain. Attitudes elsewhere took account of public opinion, generally anti-Western. This applied to Egypt, despite Iraq's maltreatment of its nationals. Syria had fought with the allies in the Gulf war but was now to supply military equipment to replace Iraq's losses. The pro-allied Turks were disregarding sanctions by importing Iraqi oil directly by pipeline. Jordan's public opinion was unambiguously pro-Iraqi, but Deputy Prime Minister Tariq Aziz was rebuffed when he sought to use Amman (now under new management—see V.2.iii) as an intermediary with Washington. Gulf states (other than Kuwait) whose trade was prejudiced by the continued blockade of Iraq consulted primarily their own economic interests. In September Palestinian leader Yassir Arafat urged other Arab leaders towards a rapprochement with Iraq.

Iraq for its part, though sending its Foreign Minister round the Gulf states to offer reconciliation, asserted that its entry into Kuwait in 1990 had been a response to a conspiracy there: the Kuwaiti and Saudi peoples should overthrow their 'agent' regimes; the Turks should halt allied flights from Turkish bases; and OPEC should cut the Saudi oil export quota. When the Arab League's assembled Foreign Ministers would not condemn allied air attacks on Iraq, the Iraqi chairman walked out. The remainder promised to work for an end to sanctions but said that Iraq must obey the UN Security Council.

The Pope's proposal to visit Ur, Abraham's birthplace, vexed the alliance and was in December finally but reluctantly dropped. Another controversy surrounded Turkey's plan for a Europe-financed dam on the Euphrates river (see AR 1996, p. 214), which Iraq and Syria had long seen as detrimental to their interests. Advocates for Turkey—and the construction firms involved—replied that the dam, being designed to generate electricity, not to provide irrigation, would not deprive other states of water.

Some periodic violence was connected with the Shia minority, never popular with the Sunni-dominated regime. The murder, in the Shia holy city of Kerbela, of a prominent Shia divine with links to Iran, and of his two sons, caused demonstrations in Basra and elsewhere: four men were executed for the murders. The regime admitted disturbances but denied that many Shia had been killed. Six Iranian exiles died in an explosion near their headquarters. In September Deputy Prime Minister Taha Yazid Ramadan survived an assassination attempt.

Saddam's family were again involved in violence, real or reported. Saddam himself really did dismiss his cousin, Ali Husain al-Majid, commander of the southern region; other less reliable stories were of rivalries between Saddam's sons Husain Uday and Husain Qusay and of executions at an airbase near Baghdad.

Kurdistan was less in the news than before, the two rival factions reaffirming in September their adherence to the peace between them agreed in 1998 (AR 1998 p. 235), which had proved more effective than expected.

The oil industry remained, despite the blockade, the most important economic factor. In May the Oil Minister expected production to rise to three million barrels per day (bpd). Any further increase would depend on essential spares: without them, pipelines and terminals could break down and any raising of the limits would remain theoretical. However, this was not fully accepted by the UN Security Council, which in October refused an Iraqi request to be allowed to export more in order to pay for spare parts. Nevertheless, production in July was the highest since 1990.

The government emphasized the hardships imposed on ordinary people by the blockade. This argument was weakened when a ship intercepted by the Kuwaitis was found to be exporting baby food from Iraq. In May the Health Minister said that no medical supplies had arrived since December 1998: according to a UN source, they were simply not being distributed. But hardship was increasing, aggravated by drought, which lowered food production.

3. SAUDI ARABIA—YEMEN—ARAB STATES OF THE GULF

i. SAUDI ARABIA

CAPITAL: Riyadh   AREA: 2,000,000 sq km   POPULATION: 20,000,000 ('98)
OFFICIAL LANGUAGE: Arabic   POLITICAL SYSTEM: monarchy
HEAD OF STATE & GOVERNMENT: King Fahd ibn Abdul Aziz (since June '82), also Prime Minister
HEIR APPARENT: Crown Prince Abdullah ibn Abdul Aziz (since June '82), also First Deputy Prime Minister
MAIN IGO MEMBERSHIPS (NON-UN): AL, OPEC, OAPEC, GCC, OIC, NAM
CURRENCY: riyal (end-'99 £1=SRls6.04, US$1=SRls3.75)
GNP PER CAPITA: US$6,790 by exchange-rate calculation ('97)

THE year in Saudi Arabia was dominated by its role in the Organization of the Petroleum Exporting Countries (OPEC) and its own attempts to deal with the consequences of the collapse in oil prices in 1998 and early 1999. Crown Prince Abdullah's hints in 1998—that foreign companies might be allowed to enter Saudi Arabia's upstream sector (see AR 1998, p. 238)—were clarified during a visit by US Energy Secretary Bill Richardson in March. Ali al-Naimi, Saudi Arabia's Oil Minister, made it clear that no such access was envisaged at present: Saudi Arabia had sufficient capacity and Saudi Aramco was strongly opposed to foreign partners upstream, while seeking their help in adding value elsewhere in the production process. He added, however, that companies that now collaborated in downstream activities, particularly in gas-integrated projects, would enjoy priority attention were such developments to be considered. Towards the end of the year the ministerial petroleum committee under the Crown Prince evaluated projects put forward by a number of major companies, some of them trying to exploit the apparent 'back-door' into the upstream sector through associated gas production.

In March Saudi Arabia was able to persuade Iran to collaborate in reversing OPEC's calamitous policy that had resulted in a slide in oil prices to below $11 per barrel in the second half of 1998 and early 1999. The breakthrough came during a visit to the kingdom by Iranian Foreign Minister Kamal Kharrazi in early March, just before a state visit by the Iranian President, Mohammed Khatami. Mr Kharrazi agreed that Iran would accept quota cuts based on a production level of 3.6 million barrels per day (b/d), rather than its preferred level of 3.9 million b/d. One week later, on 10 March, OPEC member Venezuela and non-OPEC members Mexico and Norway agreed to support the proposed cuts, thus ensuring that sufficient oil was removed from the world market to force prices up. Saudi Arabia was looking for a $5 per barrel rise to cover its budget deficit of SRls44,000 million. The quota system was reaffirmed during OPEC's October summit in October (see also XI.2.ii) and was set to last until March 2000 at the least.

Saudi Arabia was also active in ensuring control over production and distribution. The imminent end of the Arabian Oil Company concession in the offshore Neutral Zone resulted in Saudi pressure on its Japanese partner in the concession to increase Japanese investment in the kingdom. Japan eventually offered $4,000 million, half directed towards basic industry, water and power projects and the balance for the Germany-to-Saudi Arabia railway project. The Kuwaiti part of the concession would not end until 2003. It was possible that Saudi Aramco might take over the concession itself. Saudi Aramco also purchased an additional 28.4 per cent of Ssangyong Oil, a South Korean refining and distribution company in which it already held a 35 per cent stake, in order to guarantee access to the South-East Asian market.

The crisis created by low oil prices had its repercussions both domestically and abroad. At the start of the year it was announced that oil payments for the Al-Yamamah project were to be cut from 800,000 b/d to 400,000 b/d, in an effective rescheduling of the outstanding payments to British Aerospace. Domestic petrol prices were raised in June by 50 per cent, although this had little effect on inflation, which continued at 1 per cent throughout the year. In September it became clear that the budget deficit for the year would be of the order of SRls15-25,000 million, rather than the anticipated SRls44,000 million ($800 million), although the kingdom would have little difficulty in financing this through its own resources (including $80,000 million in foreign reserves), as it had done over the past 12 years, during which the cumulative deficit had risen to $180,000 million. Even though sovereign debt rose by $2,300 million, as Saudia raised funding to complete its purchase of 61 new aircraft, Saudi Arabia had no significant foreign debt problem: since 1991 it had raised only a $4,500 million loan, now paid off, and a $2,600 million loan for Saudi Aramco.

Attention was paid to economic development during the year. Crown Prince Abdullah, increasingly in charge of government, set up a new Supreme Economic Council in September. This body was to advise government on strategic economic planning, particularly over increasing the role of the private sector and economic liberalization under the new 2001-2005 Plan adopted by the government in July. Preparations began for entry into the World Trade Organization, legislation being introduced in December to allow foreign investment and provide security for foreign investors. Saudi Arabia also accepted the guidelines of the Gulf Cooperation Council (GCC) on mutual investment and ownership rights, as well as the common rules of origin and common tariff—5.5 per cent on basic imports and 7.5 per cent on luxuries— which were agreed in November as the first step towards building a regional common market (see XI.6.1). In addition, legislation was introduced to require foreigners in the kingdom to pay for health insurance, which had previously been provided free of charge. Consolidation in the power and banking sectors was encouraged in June.

Although Saudi Arabia continued to support US policy towards Iraq during the year and refused to allow Iraqi aircraft to fly in pilgrims for the annual *haj*, the Saudi government became increasingly concerned about Gulf security issues as its relations with Iran improved. In part this mirrored the changes attendant upon Crown Prince Abdullah's increasingly prominent role in government, although King Fahd returned to the kingdom from convalescence in Spain in September. The King was not present for the burial of his son Prince Faisal, who died unexpectedly of a heart attack on 21 August. Despite four minor government reshuffles during the year, caused mainly by illness, government policy appeared to continue unchanged. In October Saudi Arabia secured the extradition from the United States of Hani Abderrahman Hussein al-Sayegh, who was suspected of involvement in the 1996 bombing of American military installations at Al-Khobar (see AR 1996, pp. 216-7) but who had refused to collaborate with US investigators.

The veteran blind Grand Mufti of Saudi Arabia, Shaikh Abdulaziz bin Baz, died in May aged 87 and was replaced by Shaikh Abdelaziz bin Abdullah al-Sheikh.

ii. YEMEN

CAPITAL: Sana'a AREA: 540,000 sq km POPULATION: 16,000,000 ('98)
OFFICIAL LANGUAGE: Arabic POLITICAL SYSTEM: presidential
HEAD OF STATE & GOVERNMENT: President (Field Marshal) Ali Abdullah Saleh (since May '90)
RULING PARTIES: General People's Congress (GPC) & Yemeni Alliance for Reform (Islah)
PRIME MINISTER: Abdulkarim al-Iryani (since April '98)
MAIN IGO MEMBERSHIPS (NON-UN): AL, OIC, NAM
CURRENCY: Yemeni rial (end-'99 £1=YRls257.43, US$1=YRls159.73)
GNP PER CAPITA: US$300 by exchange-rate calculation, US$740 at PPP ('98)

YEMEN started 1999 facing a major crisis in its relations with Britain after the Aden-Abayan Islamic Army had been responsible for the deaths of four tourists in a confrontation with the Yemeni army in December 1998 (see AR 1998, p. 239). The group's leader, Zine el-Abidine al-Mihdar, admitted responsibility for the incident in court in Zinjibar but warned of serious consequences were he to be executed for it. The court ignored his warnings and he was sentenced to death, the sentence being carried out by firing squad in October in Sana'a. The situation was complicated, however, by the arrest of eight young Britons of Arab and Pakistani origin and two Algerians in the Aden area as the new year opened. They were accused of links with the Aden-Abayan Islamic Army and of planning terrorism against targets in Yemen connected with Britain. The Yemeni government claimed that the arrested group was connected with a radical Muslim cleric in London, Abu Hamza al-Masari, and demanded his arrest. Although Mr al-Masari was investigated by the British authorities, no substantive evidence of criminal activity was found. The British nationals accused in Yemen were found guilty in August but three were subsequently released and expelled from the country.

Despite the introduction of a new law carrying the death penalty for kidnapping, local tribes continued their time-honoured practice of this form of negotiation with government, which was generally too weak to apply the law. Kidnaps of oil company personnel, tourists and aid workers occurred for short periods in January, February and October. More serious, however, was a spate of bombings during the year, both in the south of the country and in the capital. The central market in Aden was bombed in early June with two deaths, whilst ten people died in a water dispute between local tribes and the armed forces in the Sabir district of Taiz. August saw another upsurge in violence, with a bomb in a Sana'a market which killed six persons and another in a supermarket which killed two, including the owner, who was later suspected of having bombed his own store in an insurance scam. Other bombs exploded in Aden and Zinjibar in what were undoubtedly political initiatives against the Sana'a government. A helicopter accident in Hadrawmaut resulted in 17 deaths.

On 23 September Yemen held the first direct presidential elections ever held in the Arab world. As expected, incumbent Ali Abdullah Saleh won easily, with 96.3 per cent of the 3,577,960 votes cast. Two persons were killed and nine injured in election violence. The transparency of the elections had been somewhat undermined by the preliminary manœuvres, however. There were only two contenders for the post and the loser, Najib Qahtan al-Shabi, was also a member of the President's own political party, the General People's Congress, although he stood as an independent. Furthermore, the House of Representatives had on 21 August barred all other candidates because they had failed to surmount the barrier of 10 per cent support within the 301-member House, in which the GPC controlled 226 seats. The Islah party, coalition partners with the GPC, failed to field candidates and the Yemeni Socialist Party was in disarray since its leadership had split in March after a noisy congress in 1998. The President had prepared for the election by launching an anti-qat campaign in June and by announcing that he had given up use of the mildly stimulant drug, to which the vast majority of Yemenis were addicted, despite the immense damage done to the agricultural sector of the economy.

Despite the oil price crisis, and Yemen's dependence on the revenues from its oil output, the Yemeni economy continued to strengthen throughout the year, although the rial depreciated from 140 to 160 to the US dollar. The IMF, which had two structural adjustment agreements with Yemen, voiced its approval of Yemeni economic management in July, as the budget deficit declined to below 3 per cent of GDP and the annual inflation rate fell below 10 per cent. The current account was held in balance, compared with a $228 million deficit in 1998, and reserves rose to $1,200 million. The 2000 budget, which was approved on 1 November, anticipated a 32 per cent increase in revenues, from YRls294,400 million in 1999 to YRls388,950 million, as a result of increased oil production (419,000 b/d in 1999) and a 51 per cent revenue increase to YRls246,500 million. Expenditure was also set to rise by 26 per cent to YRls422,250 million (from YRls335,500 million the previous year), but the deficit would be significantly reduced by 19 per cent from its 10 per cent of GDP level in 1999.

In September Yemen signed up for its first independent power producer project and announced the award of private sector licences for its GSM mobile telephone network. In June past problems with Russia had been resolved by a debt repayment deal providing for the repayment of $426 million over 33 years at an interest rate of 1.19 per cent. This followed an agreement in 1998 covering the $7,000 million debt owed by the former state of South Yemen.

iii. ARAB STATES OF THE GULF

United Arab Emirates (UAE)
CONSTITUENTS: Abu Dhabi, Dubai, Sharjah, Ras al-Khaimah, Fujairah, Umm al-Qaiwin, Ajman
FEDERAL CAPITAL: Abu Dhabi   AREA: 77,000 sq km   POPULATION: 3,000,000 ('98)
OFFICIAL LANGUAGE: Arabic   POLITICAL SYSTEM: federation of monarchies
HEAD OF STATE: Shaikh Zayad bin Sultan al-Nahayyan (Ruler of Abu Dhabi), President of UAE (since Dec '71)
HEAD OF GOVERNMENT: Shaikh Maktoum bin Rashid al-Maktoum (Ruler of Dubai), Vice-President and Prime Minister of UAE (since Nov '90)
MAIN IGO MEMBERSHIPS (NON-UN): AL, OPEC, OAPEC, GCC, OIC, NAM
CURRENCY: dirham (end-'99 £1=Dh5.92, US$1=Dh3.67)
GNP PER CAPITA: US$18,220 by exchange-rate calculation, US$19,720 at PPP ('98)

Kuwait
CAPITAL: Kuwait   AREA: 18,000 sq km   POPULATION: 2,000,000 ('98)
OFFICIAL LANGUAGE: Arabic   POLITICAL SYSTEM: monarchy
HEAD OF STATE: Shaikh Jabir al-Ahmad al-Jabir al-Sabah (since Dec '77)
HEAD OF GOVERNMENT: Crown Prince Shaikh Saad al-Abdullah as-Salim as-Sabah, Prime Minister (since Feb '78)
MAIN IGO MEMBERSHIPS (NON-UN): AL, OPEC, OAPEC, GCC, OIC, NAM
CURRENCY: dinar (end-'99 £1=KD0.49, US$1=KD0.30)
GNP PER CAPITA: US$22,110 by exchange-rate calculation, US$24,270 at PPP calculation ('97)

Oman
CAPITAL: Muscat   AREA: 300,000 sq km   POPULATION: 2,300,000 ('98)
OFFICIAL LANGUAGE: Arabic   POLITICAL SYSTEM: monarchy
HEAD OF STATE & GOVERNMENT: Shaikh Qaboos bin Said (since July '70)
MAIN IGO MEMBERSHIPS (NON-UN): AL, GCC, OIC, NAM
CURRENCY: rial (end-'99 £1=OR0.62, US$1=OR0.39)
GNP PER CAPITA: US$4,950 by exchange-rate calculation, US$8,690 at PPP ('97)

Qatar
CAPITAL: Doha   AREA: 11,400 sq km   POPULATION: 742,000 ('98)
OFFICIAL LANGUAGE: Arabic   POLITICAL SYSTEM: monarchy
HEAD OF STATE & GOVERNMENT: Shaikh Hamad bin Khalifa al-Thani (since June '95)
MAIN IGO MEMBERSHIPS (NON-UN): AL, OPEC, OAPEC, GCC, OIC, NAM
CURRENCY: riyal (end-'99 £1=QR5.87, US$1=QR3.64)
GNP PER CAPITA: US$11,570 by exchange-rate calculation ('97)

Bahrain

CAPITAL: Manama   AREA: 685 sq km   POPULATION: 640,000 ('98)
OFFICIAL LANGUAGE: Arabic   POLITICAL SYSTEM: monarchy
HEAD OF STATE: Shaikh Hamad bin Isa al-Khalifa (since March '99)
HEAD OF GOVERNMENT: Shaikh Khalifa bin Sulman al-Khalifa, Prime Minister (since Jan '70)
MAIN IGO MEMBERSHIPS (NON-UN): AL, OAPEC, GCC, OIC, NAM
CURRENCY: dinar (end-'99 £1=BD0.61, US$1=BD0.38)
GNP PER CAPITA: US$7,660 by exchange-rate calculation, US$13,700 at PPP ('98)

THROUGHOUT 1999 all the Arab states of the Gulf had to come to terms with the implications of reduced oil incomes as a result of the collapse in oil prices in the second half of 1998. Even though prices recovered after March, when Saudi Arabia, Iran and Venezuela agreed on reduced production quotas for the Organization of the Petroleum Exporting Countries (OPEC) and were supported by Mexico and Norway (see V.3.i; XI.2.ii), Gulf budgets continued to reflect the consequences of reduced revenue flows throughout the year.

The 1999 budget in Oman, drawn up in January, was based on an oil price assumption of only $9 per barrel, spending cuts of 7 per cent and increased non-oil revenues up 7 per cent. But it still allowed for a deficit of OR631 million ($1,000 million)—twice that anticipated in the 1998 budget, which was forecast at OR295 million ($466 million) and actually reached OR311 million ($491 million)—after oil revenues dropped by 32 per cent and GDP by 10 per cent.

The Qatari 1998 fiscal year budget came in with a deficit of QR3,631 million ($1,000 million), around 10 per cent of GDP. The 1999 budget, however, envisaged a deficit of a mere $13 million, because of the inclusion of one-off receipts from the sale of 45 per cent of Qatar Telecommunications (Q-Tel) for $650 million, while promises were made of a budget surplus of $500 million in the subsequent financial year. No budget balance was expected for the next fiscal year either and cuts in labour levels and capital expenditures were promised.

The 1999 Kuwaiti budget, approved by the government in April and, reluctantly, by the newly-elected Assembly in July, included a 2 per cent reduction in expenditure to KD4,250 million ($13,700 million) and a deficit of KD2,026 million ($6,600 million), equivalent to 26 per cent of GDP and 8 per cent more than in 1998.

The UAE budget deficit for the 1998 fiscal year had been set at 17 per cent of GDP, envisaging a 24 per cent fall in revenues to Dh42,700 million ($11,600 million)—31 per cent in oil revenues, which declined to Dh37,000 million ($10,000 million)—and an 11.2 per cent rise in expenditure to Dh71,600 million ($19,100 million), which was spent on education, housing and social welfare. The same pattern was repeated in the 1999 federal budget.

Bahrain's budget followed a similar pattern to its neighbours, with revenues down 8.6 per cent and expenditure up by 4.5 per cent in the 2000 budget, published in March.

The spending constraints implied by reduced oil revenues had a marked effect on attitudes towards economic development throughout the year. Greater emphasis was placed on charging for service provision and on opportunities for privatization, and for co-opting the private sector into service provision, particularly in the power sector. The Kuwaiti economic reform plan, published in January, proposed cuts in subsidies and revenue growth through charges for state-supplied services. Although the IMF, in its annual Article IV review, praised Kuwaiti economic management, it argued for further reforms to restrain the budget deficit, despite the current-account surplus of 10 per cent of GDP and 2.2 per cent GDP growth in 1998. Its proposals included the privatization of telecommunications and transport—ideas adopted by the Kuwaiti government, which also proposed to privatize Kuwait Airways, the Kuwait Petroleum Corporation and the water and electricity utilities, now that public hostility to such changes had died down.

Qatar turned to independent power producer (IPP) projects to overcome its chronic power shortages, simply because the state could not afford major financial capital commitments in the electricity sector. The UAE followed a similar path, with the contract award for its first IPP project at the Taweelah A-2 site in March and a second planned at Suweilah.

In Oman the telecommunications sector was corporatized by royal decree in September as the Omani Telecoms Company in a preliminary step towards privatization, while Seeb International Airport and the National Transport Company were privatized. A second IPP, to follow the first awarded in 1996, was also commissioned. By the second half of the year these measures had begun to bear fruit. Confidence rose in the Muscat securities market, as did capital markets in Qatar, after the first-ever treasury bond issue was made in July, although in the UAE stocks had lost 15 per cent of their value by the end of the year, despite a rally in September which countered the previous year's losses. The ambitious Saadiyat Island project for a free-trade zone and a financial centre was initiated in September, with expectations of funding from the estimated $1 trillion investment pool and the $400,000 million worth of commodities trading available in the region.

Development plans in Qatar were rationalized as Rasgas and Qatargas came on stream to South Korea in September, even though the Enron deal for gas sales to India collapsed. Positive revenue streams were expected from North Field projects within three to four years, whilst foreign debt remained manageable at 117 per cent of GDP. Oman proposed a clutch of 14 private sector projects for which funding of $280 million was sought, and Kuwait enjoyed yet another current-account surplus.

Oil and gas developments were, however, the major symptoms of the impending recovery. Kuwait devoted much attention to its 'Project Kuwait' proposal for foreign participation in the upstream sector, with particular reference to new fields along its western and northern borders. The government was unapologetic about the clear strategic advantages of the proposal—that it would guarantee foreign support if Kuwait were threatened militarily in future. It also pointed out the technical advantages of technology transfer, an expansion of reserves, an increase in production capacity of 1 million b/d and the training of Kuwaiti nationals—60 per cent of the staff of any multinational or multinational consortium granted a 20-25-year concession were required to be Kuwaiti.

Public hostility continued, however, not least because Kuwait's constitution required oil and gas reserves to be nationally-owned assets. A major refinery overhaul scheme was also proposed in Kuwait, with emphasis being placed on expanding refinery capacity abroad.

Qatari gas in the North Field became the subject of an initiative—Project Dolphin—by the UAE Offsets Group, a company originally conceived to mobilize offset deals for the UAE's arms purchases but now a vehicle for investment opportunities. The project involved gas purchase through a swap arrangement with Mobil and eventual concessions in the North Field, with the gas being sold on to Dubai, Oman and Pakistan for use. It implied, incidentally, that the UAE had abandoned earlier proposals for gas purchases from Iran to compensate for domestic energy and gas shortages, although gas discoveries by Sharjah's Crescent Petroleum in October implied potential competition for Project Dolphin. Bahrain published elaborate plans to upgrade its 60-year-old refinery and to allow a private refinery to be constructed, whilst Texaco joined Chevron in seeking new sources of crude.

Political developments were also important for the Gulf states in 1999. The Kuwaiti Assembly was dissolved on 4 May, after it attempted to force the resignation of the Justice, Waqf and Religious Affairs Minister for printing errors in a Koran published by his ministry, on the grounds that the Assembly had abused its constitutional rights. New elections were called for 3 July, in the hope that a more amenable Assembly could be elected. In the interim, the government approved 60 Amiri decrees, including one giving women the right to vote and to stand for elective office after 2003. The elections were, however, a disaster for the government, as both its Islamist and its liberal opponents did well, leaving the government with only 16 of the 50 elective seats. The government resigned in the wake of the elections, but the new government showed only one substantive change—in the finance portfolio—and appeared to be dedicated to greater privatization of the economy.

The Amiri decrees were examined by the Kuwaiti Assembly at the end of November, but the political liberalization of women was prevented by a 41-22 hostile vote in which liberals—who were actually in support of the measure but disliked its introduction by decree—supported the Islamists. A subsequent liberal motion for the measure was defeated by 30 votes to 32, with two abstentions. Kuwait was also reminded of the danger of relying on immigrant labour at the end of October when Egyptian workers in Kheitan rioted after police intervened in a dispute between an Egyptian customer and a Bangladeshi shopkeeper. The police took nine hours to control the 60,000 rioters, and further trouble from the 200,000-strong Egyptian community in Kuwait was headed off by careful action by the authorities with support from Egypt.

In Qatar, elections for a new municipal council received a disappointing degree of support, with only half the eligible 40,000 voters bothering to register, although women were able to participate and there were six women amongst the 220 candidates. Although the council would only have advisory powers, it was expected to evolve into a national assembly with executive authority. A 32-member constitutional consultative committee was formed by the Amir in July to draft a new constitution within six months. In the same month, however, a reminder of the past emerged when Hassan bin Jassem bin Hamad al-Thani, a former minister, was arrested for involvement in the 1996 coup attempt which sought to remove the Amir from power after his own coup against his father one year before (see AR 1996, p. 223; 1995, p. 224). His trial, at the end of the year, was expected to result in a light sentence, as a gesture indicating the stability of the Amir's government. Opposition to the Amir continued, however, and a new opposition front was created in Paris in March. Qatar's support for freedom of the press was underlined in June when Kuwait shut down the offices of Al-Djezira Television, ostensibly for violating professional ethics but, in reality, because it had carried a comment by an Iraqi contributor that was critical of Kuwait.

The sudden death of the Bahraini Amir on 6 March from a heart attack, just after he had received US Defence Secretary William Cohen, resulted in the succession of Crown Prince Shaikh Hamad bin Isa al-Khalifa (49), the former head of the Bahraini defence force. Although no major change of policy was expected, and a new government in June showed little change, the Shia opposition leader, Shaikh Abdulamir al-Jamri, was freed in July, the day after he was sentenced to ten years in prison for supporting violent anti-government demonstrations. Shaikh Abdulamir, who had been imprisoned without trial for three years, helped his case by making an abject apology the day before. It soon became clear that the new Amir was determined to approach the liberalization of the Bahraini political system with great caution, although 300 Shia detainees were released and 12 political prisoners pardoned. Bahrain also made it clear that it was anxious to distance itself from too close a linkage with American policy over Iraq and that it now sought reconciliation with Iran.

The UAE continued to seek support for its opposition to Iran's occupation of the Tunbs Islands and Abu Musa. It protested in March against Iran's construction of a new town hall on Abu Musa and persuaded the GCC to condemn Iranian military manœuvres around the islands. The Arab League supported the protest but there was increasing evidence that individual Gulf states would not allow the issue to interfere with their national policies towards Iran. The matter came to a head in June when the UAE protested at apparent Saudi support for a negotiated solution, in the wake of a visit to the kingdom by the Iranian President, Mohammed Khatami. Saudi Arabia rejected UAE protests and, eventually, Qatar had to mediate a settlement to the disagreement, which had interfered with GCC business.

The outcome was that the UAE accepted the principle of negotiations or reference of the matter to the International Court of Justice at The Hague. Iran, however, insisted on bilateral negotiations with the UAE, something which the government rejected, seeking GCC support instead. By December the UAE was so disillusioned that it threatened to pull out of the GCC. It nevertheless agreed to moves designed to create a customs union and a regional

GCC free market within the next five years. The UAE was also prepared to accept Iranian feedstock into the Jebel Ali refinery. The gesture perhaps symbolized the relatively upbeat mood in the Gulf by the end of the year, compared with the gloom with which it began.

4. SUDAN—LIBYA—TUNISIA—ALGERIA—MOROCCO—WESTERN SAHARA

i. SUDAN

CAPITAL: Khartoum   AREA: 2,500,000 sq km   POPULATION: 28,400,000 ('98)
OFFICIAL LANGUAGE: Arabic   POLITICAL SYSTEM: Islamist/military regime
HEAD OF STATE & GOVERNMENT: President (Gen.) Omar Hasan Ahmed al-Bashir (since Oct '93), previously Chairman of Revolutionary Command Council (since June '89)
RULING PARTY: National Islamic Front (NIF)
MAIN IGO MEMBERSHIPS (NON-UN): AL, OAU, COMESA, OIC, ACP, NAM
CURRENCY: dinar (end '99 £1=D412.60, US$1=D256.00)
GNP PER CAPITA: US$290 by exchange-rate calculation, US$1,360 at PPP ('98)

ATTEMPTS, particularly by Egypt and Libya, to reconcile the present regime with Colonel John Garang, leader of Sudan People's Liberation Army (SPLA), and with exiled northern opposition leaders were unsuccessful. Continuing international isolation of Sudan, the unresolved and costly civil war in the south, a strong internal opposition and a power struggle between General Omar Hasan Ahmed al-Bashir, President of the Republic, and Dr Hasan al-Turabi, leader of the National Islamic Front (NIF), impelled the President to declare a three-month state of emergency on 11 December, to suspend the National Assembly and to offer the traditional political parties a role in Sudan politics. Rejecting suggestions that his action amounted to a coup, President Bashir said that new Assembly elections would be held at a date to be decided. At the end of December the President and Dr al-Turabi agreed to submit their dispute to the Constitutional Court with a view to resolving the crisis.

During the year the National Democratic Alliance (NAD) continued its military operations against the regime in eastern Sudan. Reports of meetings between the exiled leaders of the NDA and Dr al-Turabi were denied by the former. However, it emerged that Sayyid Sadiq al-Mahdi, leader of the Umma Party, was willing to reach a compromise with the government which the NDA regarded as a personal initiative.

Efforts to end the civil war were made by Egypt and Libya in January, by a personal initiative in May by former Vice-President Abel Alier, and by the regional Inter-Governmental Authority for Development (IGAD) in July. Moreover, Pope John Paul II and Dr George Carey, the Archbishop of Canterbury, agreed in February to work together to bring peace to the south. Leaders of southern Sudan continued their disagreement about the future of the south and its link with the central government. In January Kerubino Kuanyin

Bol defected from the SPLA, for the second time, and joined government forces. Gatwich Gatkouth, an ally of Riak Machar in the South Sudan Defence Force (SSDF), a group fighting the SPLA in collaboration with government forces, accused Mr Machar of disrespect for the law and pulled out of the alliance to establish his own 'SSDF-2'. The infighting within the SSDF reached a climax in November when 25 officers of the SSDF were killed in Bentiu by a rival pro-government faction, the United Army, during peace talks between the two groups.

In February Mr Machar resigned from the National Congress of the central government and established the United Democratic Salvation Party (UDSF), although he kept his government posts. The SPLA and the government declared ceasefires in April and August to allow relief convoys to get to the famine-devastated region of Bahr al-Ghazal. A positive move by the government and the SPLA to ban the use of mines was achieved in March in view of large casualties from these weapons. Despite these steps, fighting between government forces and the SPLA continued: a number of villages and small towns changed hands during the year. While attending the UN Human Rights Commission in Geneva in March, Colonel Garang stated the objective of his organization: to end the civil war and to achieve peace by the creation of two separate but confederal states.

While the Sudan government accused Egypt of supporting opposition groups and of continuing to occupy the border area of Halaib, the Cairo government was criticized for its rapprochement with the regime in Sudan. As a sign of improved relations, Sudan agreed in June to return to Egypt 20 irrigation works, the Khartoum branch of Cairo University and other properties which were taken over by the regime some years ago. The close relations between Sudan and Iran were enhanced by an agreement in March to further political and economic cooperation.

Ethiopia and Sudan agreed to normalize relations, and in February the Presidents of Ethiopia, Sudan, Egypt, Uganda, Tanzania and the Democratic Republic of the Congo agreed on an equitable use of Nile water resources. While Sudan lent support to opposition groups aiming to overthrow President Afewerki of Eritrea, Qatar hosted a reconciliation meeting in May between leaders of Sudan and Eritrea. However, leaders of the NDA stated that there would be no peace without a political solution.

Contacts took place in January seeking a settlement of the disputes between the United States and Sudan. US sanctions on the export of food and medicines to Sudan were lifted and the US assets ($24 million) of Salih Idris, owner of the pharmaceuticals factory bombed by US warplanes in 1998 (see AR 1998, p. 245), were unfrozen. On the other hand, Sudan rejected the US envoy appointed to mediate in the civil war and to examine the regime's human rights record. Britain was accused of obstructing Sudan's relations with the European Union but attempts were made to restore full diplomatic relations. Due to pressure from Sudan, the UN Committee on Non-Governmental Organizations voted for the withdrawal of the UN consultative status of Christian Solidarity

International (CSI), which was reported to have paid cash to free 1,000 young Christians alleged be held in slavery in Sudan. The Khartoum government accused CSI of encouraging the payments and rejected the description of those released as slaves.

In January Sudan's new Islamic constitution, a major source of contention between the central government and the southern Sudanese, was made law. Subsequent military setbacks for government forces in the south led to the dismissal of the Minister of Defence, the army commander and all his senior staff. General Abd al-Rahman Sirr al-Khatim was appointed as the new Defence Minister. Tribal clashes in January and February over grazing rights in Darfur, a frequent occurrence, left about 150 people dead and caused the flight of 7,000 refugees to Chad, as well as the internal displacement of over 100,000 people. To the disappointment of many Sudanese, in May the government allowed the return from Egypt of ex-President Jafar Nimairy, who was granted permission to establish his Alliance Party, calling for complete integration with Egypt. He was granted amnesty from prosecution for the crimes he committed while in power in 1969-85.

The completion in March of preparations for oil exports from the Heglig field in the Muglad Basin and the first shipment of crude from the new port of Basha'ir to Singapore were seen as a major achievement that would help the ailing economy. It was estimated that oil output would reach between 40,000 and 60,000 barrels per day. However, the 1,600-kilometre pipeline feeding oil exports was vulnerable to sabotage by opposition groups. In May the SPLA attacked oil installations at Leer in Unity state and an explosion on the pipeline near Atbara occurred in September. Moreover, the US government protested about the Canadian Talisman company's involvement in oil exploration and extraction, and Canada promised to investigate the company's role in Sudan's civil war.

Adherence to rescheduled debt payments and an improvement in economic performance led the International Monetary Fund (IMF) in August to lift its non-cooperation policy with Sudan, in operation since 1990, although Sudan's IMF voting rights remained suspended. Western financial investment in Sudan remained practically non-existent, but the Islamic Development Bank allocated $8 million to repair the power generator station at Roseires. Businessmen from the Gulf Emirates concluded trade agreements worth $50 million for Sudan to export meat, sugar and other agricultural products in exchange for industrial and chemical products. Further, in April the Emirates Telecommunications Corporation (Etisalat) acquired a majority share in Sudan Telecommunications (Sudatel) for $12.5 million.

ii. LIBYA

CAPITAL: Tripoli   AREA: 1,760,000 sq km   POPULATION: 5,330,000 ('98)
OFFICIAL LANGUAGE: Arabic   POLITICAL SYSTEM: socialist 'state of the masses'
HEAD OF STATE: Col. Muammar Qadafi, 'Leader of the Revolution' (since '69)
HEAD OF GOVERNMENT: Mohammed Ahmed al-Manqoush, Secretary-General of General People's Committee (since Dec '97)
MAIN IGO MEMBERSHIPS (NON-UN): AL, OPEC, OAPEC, AMU, OAU, OIC, NAM
CURRENCY: dinar (end-'99 £1=LD0.74, US$1=LD0.46)
GNP PER CAPITA: n/a

IN early April Libya finally handed over the two Libyan suspects in the 1988 Lockerbie bombing for trial in the Netherlands by a panel of Scottish judges under Scottish law. The decision followed months of intensive diplomatic efforts by South Africa and Saudi Arabia to persuade the Libyan leader, Colonel Qadafi, to accept the offer by the USA and UK for a trial in a neutral third country and their assurances about arrangements for the trial. While there was much speculation about the Libyan leader's motives in finally agreeing to surrender the two men, many analysts argued that economic factors played a key role. The two suspects, Al-Amin Khalifa Fahima and Abd al-Basset al-Megrahi, were handed over to Scottish authorities at Camp Zeist near Utrecht, a former US airbase, which became Scottish territory for the purposes of the trial, due to begin in February 2000.

A month earlier at a trial in Paris six Libyans (including Colonel Qadafi's brother-in-law) were found guilty *in absentia* of bombing a French airliner over Niger in 1989 and sentenced to life imprisonment. In July, after Libya paid $31 million in compensation to families of French victims, French officials issued a statement that the payment represented 'an acknowledgement by the Libyan authorities of the responsibility of their citizens'. Libyan cooperation in this case had been one of the requirements for the lifting of UN sanctions.

With the surrender of the two suspects in the Lockerbie bombing, the UN Security Council immediately suspended sanctions against Libya in place since 1992 (see also XI.1), but under pressure from the USA avoided a vote on whether to approve the permanent lifting of sanctions. The USA insisted that a formal lifting of UN sanctions would be premature before the trial of the Lockerbie suspects was completed. There was, however, no question of UN sanctions being reimposed. US sanctions against Libya—some of them dating from 1981—remained in place despite opposition from American business groups. In contrast, in September the European Union (EU) removed most of its remaining sanctions against Libya and agreed to Libyan participation in the Euro-Mediterranean partnership programme initiated at Barcelona in 1995. However, the EU's embargo on arms sales remained in place. In December Romano Prodi, the president of the European Commission, invited Colonel Qadafi to visit Brussels.

Several European countries moved quickly to strengthen political and economic links with Libya in the hope of gaining lucrative investment opportunities there. The day after the two Libyan suspects were handed over, Italy called for Libya's full integration into the international community, and in December the Italian Premier, Massimo D'Alema, became the first Western leader to visit Tripoli for seven years. In early July Britain announced that it was restoring full diplomatic relations with Libya broken in 1984 after a British policewoman was shot dead outside the Libyan People's Bureau in London. The decision followed a statement by Colonel Qadafi in which he accepted Libya's responsibility for the shooting and offered to pay compensation to the policewoman's family. In November Britain confirmed that compensation had been paid, and a British ambassador arrived in Tripoli the following month. UK trade delegations visited Libya in July and October.

Libya continued its diplomatic offensive in Africa, with Colonel Qadafi playing the role of regional peacemaker. He was particularly active in an attempt to end the war in Democratic Republic of the Congo between forces loyal to President Kabila and rebels backed by Rwanda and Uganda (see VII.1.i). For the first time in many years, the Libyan leader attended the Organization of African Unity (OAU) summit held in Algiers in July (see XI.6.ii) and persuaded the organization to hold a special summit in Libya in early September devoted to ways of resolving the region's conflicts. The special summit coincided with extensive celebrations to mark the 30th anniversary of the Qadafi regime.

At home the regime claimed to have contained Islamist militancy. Unconfirmed reports suggested that Libyan officials had held talks with members of two Islamist groups and had made overtures to the opposition in exile. According to the Libyan authorities, the cumulative effect of UN sanctions on the country's economy amounted to over $23,600 million. The Economy and Trade Minister stated that Libya would have to invest $35,000 million over the next five years to reach a target annual growth rate of 5 per cent. Substantial foreign investment would be sought not only in the hydrocarbons sectors but also in power, water, telecommunications and transport. At the same time, *Al-Zahf al-Akhbar*, a newspaper voicing the views of the revolutionary committees, issued a stern warning to foreign companies that profited 'at the expense of the Libyan people'.

iii. TUNISIA

CAPITAL: Tunis   AREA: 164,000 sq km   POPULATION: 9,250,000 ('98)
OFFICIAL LANGUAGE: Arabic   POLITICAL SYSTEM: presidential
HEAD OF STATE & GOVERNMENT: President (Gen.) Zayn al-Abdin Ben Ali (since Nov '87)
RULING PARTY: Constitutional Democratic Rally (RCD)
PRIME MINISTER: Mohammed Ghannouchi (since Nov '99)
MAIN IGO MEMBERSHIPS (NON-UN): AL, AMU, ICO, OAU, OIC, NAM, Francophonie
CURRENCY: dinar (end-'99 £1=D2.03, US$1=D1.26)
GNP PER CAPITA: US$2,050 by exchange-rate calculation, US$5,160 at PPP ('98)

EARLY in the year parliament approved a temporary amendment to the constitution which enabled leaders of opposition parties to stand as candidates in the presidential election so long as they had led their party for five consecutive years and their party had at least one seat in the Chamber of Deputies.

Previously, candidates for the presidency had to obtain the support of 30 members of parliament or mayors, which effectively ruled out anyone but the nominee of the ruling Rassemblement Constitutionnel Démocratique (RCD).

In Tunisia's first contested presidential election since independence, held on 24 October, two candidates opposed incumbent Zayn al-Abdin Ben Ali: Abderrahmane Tlili, secretary-general of the Union Démocratique Unioniste, and Mohammed Belhaj Amor, secretary-general of the Parti de l'Unité Populaire; but they obtained less than 1 per cent of the total vote between them. M. Ben Ali's victory was never in doubt, the presence of the other two candidates being a risk-free strategy to give the illusion of greater political pluralism. Moreover, the amendment was valid only for the 1999 presidential election, suggesting that new changes to the constitution might be introduced at a later date to allow President Ben Ali to stand for a fourth consecutive term in 2004. In parliamentary elections held at the same time, the ruling RCD secured a massive majority, with the weak and divided opposition parties attracting little support.

During demonstrations by high-school students in several towns in February, police arrested many of the demonstrators, several students were injured and unconfirmed reports indicated that a number had been killed. The replacement of Ridha Ferchiou as Education Minister by Abderrahim Zouari was believed to have been prompted by the unrest in high schools and universities. Further cabinet changes were made in April, notably the replacement of Mohammed Jeri as Finance Minister by Tawfik Baccar, formerly Economic Development Minister.

In mid-November President Ben Ali appointed Mohammed Ghannouchi as Prime Minister in place of Hamid Qarwi, who had held the premiership for a decade. The decision followed months of speculation that the President would appoint a new Prime Minister committed to a faster pace of economic reform. Hitherto International Cooperation and Foreign Investment Minister, M. Ghannouchi had also held the finance portfolio. Other cabinet changes included the transfer of Habib Ben Yahya from defence to foreign affairs, while Muhammad Jegham, who had headed the Presidential Office, became the new Defence Minister. Ali Chaouch was replaced as Interior Minister by Abdallah Kallel, who had been Justice Minister, and Fethi Merdassi succeeded M. Ghannouchi as International Cooperation and Foreign Investment Minister. Daly Jazi moved from the higher education portfolio to head a new Ministry of Communications, Human Rights and Relations with Parliament.

The Ben Ali regime maintained a tight grip on power and continued to display a relentless intolerance of any public criticism. In April a number of activists in the Union Générale des Travailleurs Tunsiens (UGTT) were arrested after criticizing the policies of the union's president, Ismail Sahbani, a supporter of President Ben Ali's economic policies. Later in the year gaol sentences were imposed on several members of the banned Parti Ouvrier Communiste Tunisien, which despite years of repression retained a core of support, mainly in the universities. Many of the defendants claimed to have been tortured while held in detention. Human rights activists continued to suffer harassment, the local press remained strictly controlled and foreign publications were subject to regular censorship.

In March President Ben Ali made a state visit to Morocco during which a free trade agreement was signed between the two countries. The president continued his efforts to revive the moribund Arab Maghreb Union (see XI.6.i), which he described as 'the irreversible fateful choice' for Tunisia. He subsequently held talks with Algeria's new President, Abdelaziz Bouteflika, and with Libyan leader Colonel Qadafi at the Organization of African Unity (OAU) summit in Algiers in July (see XI.6.ii). Colonel Qadafi visited Tunis on his return from the Algiers summit and the Tunisian President attended the special OAU summit in Libya in early September which coincided with celebrations to mark the 30th anniversary of the Qadafi regime. Tunisia repeatedly called for the lifting of sanctions against Iraq 'to end the suffering of the Iraqi people', and a number of senior Iraqi officials visited Tunis. A trade agreement with Iraq was signed in May.

The economy was reported to be President Ben Ali's priority for his third term of office. Economic growth remained strong, and in September the IMF observed that significant strides had been made towards an open market economy. Concern was expressed, however, that the government's drive for greater economic efficiency was incompatible with its pledge to create more jobs and that unemployment, already at a high rate, was set to rise.

iv. ALGERIA

CAPITAL: Algiers   AREA: 2,382,000 sq km   POPULATION: 30,000,000 ('98)
OFFICIAL LANGUAGE: Arabic   POLITICAL SYSTEM: quasi-military regime
HEAD OF STATE & GOVERNMENT: President Abdulaziz Bouteflika (since April '99)
RULING PARTIES: National Democratic Rally (RND), National Liberation Front (FLN), Movement for a Peaceful Society (MPS) & En-Nahda Movement (MN) form coalition
PRIME MINISTER: Ahmed Benbitour (since Dec '99)
MAIN IGO MEMBERSHIPS (NON-UN): AL, OPEC, OAPEC, AMU, OAU, OIC, NAM
CURRENCY: dinar (end-'99 £1=DA109.85, US$1=DA68.16)
GNP PER CAPITA: US$1,550 by exchange-rate calculation, US$4,380 at PPP ('98)

THE presidential election in April took place amidst high drama. The day before Algerians went to the polls six out of the seven candidates announced that they were jointly withdrawing from the election. They accused the authorities of initiating a massive fraud in favour of former Foreign Minister Abdulaziz Bouteflika, widely seen as the candidate favoured by the army chiefs. Fraudulent practices were alleged to have begun in the itinerant polling stations provided for the nomadic populations of the Sahara and more importantly in the special polling stations provided for the armed forces, where voting had already begun. The authorities rejected these allegations, and President Zéroual refused to cancel the election.

Officially, M. Bouteflika gained 73.8 per cent of the votes cast, with 60.25 per cent of eligible voters participating. Other sources, however, claimed that turnout had been a mere 23 per cent with M. Bouteflika obtaining only 28 per cent of the votes cast. A spokesman for the Front des Forces Socialistes declared that the election results had no credibility and were the work of military security; instead of an election, it declared, there had been 'a coup d'état by the ballot boxes'. Despite the protests of the opposition, M. Bouteflika accepted the presidency and, after 20 years in the political wilderness, was sworn in on 27 April. In May the six opposition candidates issued a 'Manifesto for Liberties and Democracy' but were prevented from organizing demonstrations, and their solidarity proved short-lived.

The new President quickly initiated contacts with senior members of the banned Front Islamique de Salut (FIS), and in June the movement's miltiary wing, the Armée Islamique du Salut (AIS), agreed to make their ceasefire (in place since October 1997) permanent and offered to cooperate with the security forces against their rivals, the Groupes Islamiques Armés (GIA). Abassi Madani, the FIS leader, who remained under house arrest, and the FIS constitutional council endorsed the agreement, but some FIS supporters complained that it did not provide a political solution to the conflict. Others demanded that *jihad* (holy war) should continue until their goal of an Islamic state had been achieved. Some 5,000 imprisoned Islamist supporters were released in July and both houses of parliament overwhelming adopted a law on civil concord offering an amnesty for Islamist militants not implicated in mass killings, rapes or bombings and reduced sentences for those who had taken part in such crimes so long as they surrendered to the authorities by January 2000.

In a referendum held in mid-September, 98.6 per cent of voters supported the President's peace initiative, according to the Interior Ministry, with turnout officially reported at 85 per cent. Families of victims of Islamist attacks denounced the new law, and the French-language press called it a 'shameful capitulation to Islamist violence'. Given the controversial circumstances of his election, some politicians accused M. Bouteflika of using the referendum to bolster his own legitimacy. Despite the President's peace initiative, the killing of civilians continued, although at a lower level of intensity. The GIA remained divided, and there were reports that some members of GIA breakaway groups had surrendered to the authorities or joined the AIS ceasefire. The assassination in November of Abdelkader Hachani, number three in the FIS hierarchy, was seen as a major blow to attempts at national reconciliation, and there was an upsurge of violence before the start of the Ramadan holy month on 9 December.

Despite a great deal of rhetoric, there were few signs that President Bouteflika exercised real power, as he sought to achieve greater freedom of action without risking direct confrontation with the military. Not until late December was a new government formed, headed by former Finance Minister Ahmed Benbitour (an independent) and including representatives of four parties which had backed M. Bouteflika's presidential candidacy and two others which had supported his peace initiative in the referendum. The formation in early December of a new Parti National pour l'Unité et l'Action was seen as an attempt by the President to create a political power base.

In July Algeria hosted a successful meeting of the Organization of African Unity and assumed the presidency for the following year (see XI.6.ii). At the end of the month President Bouteflika met briefly with new Israeli Premier Ehud Barak at the funeral of King Hassan of Morocco in Rabat (see V.4.v), placing Algeria for the first time within the Middle East peace process. But an improvement in relations with Morocco proved short-lived and renewed tensions prevented the long-awaited reopening of the land border between the two countries scheduled for late August. Moreover, Algeria's generals and not the President dictated policy on the disputed Western Sahara (see V.4.vi). Tensions with France following the presidential election soon subsided, and M. Bouteflika met French Premier Lionel Jospin at the UN General Assembly in September, the highest-level talks between the two countries since the military takeover in 1992.

The oil price recovery meant that debt repayment obligations could be met without further rescheduling, as well as encouraging international oil companies to proceed with a number of major oil and gas field development projects in Algeria.

v. MOROCCO

CAPITAL: Rabat   AREA: 460,000 sq km   POPULATION: 28,000,000 ('98)
OFFICIAL LANGUAGE: Arabic   POLITICAL SYSTEM: monarchy
HEAD OF STATE & GOVERNMENT: King Mohammed VI (since July '99)
RULING PARTIES: Socialist Union of Popular Forces (USFP) heads broad coaliton
PRIME MINISTER: Abderrahmane Youssoufi (USFP), Prime Minister (since Feb '98)
MAIN IGO MEMBERSHIPS (NON-UN): AL, AMU, OIC, NAM
CURRENCY: dirham (end-'99 £1=DH16.24, US$1=DH10.08)
GNP PER CAPITA: US$1,250 by exchange-rate calculation, US$3,130 at PPP ('98)

KING Hassan died of a heart attack on 23 July, shortly after being admitted to hospital in Rabat. The King had been in poor health for some years and had appeared exhausted after an official visit to France earlier in the month. He had recently celebrated his 70th birthday and had ruled Morocco for almost four decades (see Pt XVIII: Obituary). His eldest son, Crown Prince Sidi Mohammed, who succeeded him as Mohammed VI, announced his father's death to the nation on state television shortly after members of the royal family, government ministers and senior members of the armed forces had made the traditional oath of allegiance to the new monarch.

Hassan's funeral on 25 July was attended by many world leaders, including President Clinton of the USA and President Chirac of France. The funeral provided an opportunity for the new Israeli Premier, Ehud Barak, and Palestinian leader Yassir Arafat to hold their first meeting, amidst hopes for a revival of the Middle East peace process in which the late King had played an important mediating role.

In his last speech from the throne in March, King Hassan had praised Morocco's first opposition-led government appointed in February 1998 (see

AR 1998, pp. 253-4), declaring that the country's experience of *'alternance'* was an example to others but adding pointedly that it provided a new elite the opportunity to experience 'the hard reality of government'. In April the King replaced Abd al-Latif Filali as Foreign Affairs and Cooperation Minister by Mohammed Benaissa, Morocco's ambassador to the USA since 1993. M. Filali, a longstanding member of the King's inner circle, had occupied the post for 14 years and no reason was given for his removal. Only weeks before his death King Hassan had visited Premier Abderrahmane Youssoufi in hospital, where he had undergone surgery for a blood clot. Officially his condition was reported to be not life-threatening; nevertheless, concern was expressed whether the 75-year-old Premier would be able to maintain his heavy workload. His government was faced with persistent protests by the unemployed, especially graduates, and was criticized for the harsh methods adopted by the police to disperse demonstrators.

Little was known about Hassan's successor, the 36-year-old Mohammed VI, who as Crown Prince had always remained in his father's shadow. Although he had been groomed for the succession, his father had been reluctant to let him share power or to play a role in the armed forces, despite his rank as a four-star general. Addressing the nation for the first time, the new King pledged to support the multi-party system, economic liberalization, regional decentralization, the rule of law and respect for human rights and individual liberties. He reaffirmed his confidence in the Youssoufi government and in the principle of *'alternance'*.

The new monarch immediately demonstrated his wish for reconciliation and change. He adopted a populist style, very different from that of his late father, and quickly showed that he was not afraid of speaking out on social and economic issues, even the most sensitive, such as the importance of equal rights for women. Shortly after his succession the King granted an amnesty to thousands of prisoners and set up an arbitration body to determine compensation for the families of political opponents who had 'disappeared' or had suffered arbitrary detention. At the end of September the King granted permission for Abraham Serfaty, the country's most famous dissident, to return from exile in France.

In early November the King abruptly dismissed Interior Minister Driss Basri, who had held the post for two decades and whose influence extended well beyond the interior portfolio. He was replaced by Ahmed Midaoui, a former chief of national security. As the late King Hassan's right-hand man and loyal servant, M. Basri was closely identified with the repressive policies of the old regime. The King's decision was widely applauded and was seen as a clear break with the past and a sign of his desire for a faster pace of political change. But some expressed concern that greater political freedom might be exploited, notably by elements within the Islamist movement.

An improvement in relations with Algeria proved short-lived. In mid-August Algeria again accused Morocco of providing a haven for its Islamist opponents, after a brutal massacre of civilians by one of the Groupes Islamiques Armés near the Moroccan border. The long-awaited reopening of the land border between the two countries was cancelled, and the press embarked on a new round of mutual accusations.

Almost half of projected expenditure under the 1999-2000 budget, approved by parliament in July, was allocated to social provisions—health, housing, urban development, education, youth and sports. Debt-service payments remained a serious burden.

vi. WESTERN SAHARA

CAPITAL: Al Aaiún   AREA: 252,000 sq km   POPULATION: 164,000 ('82)
STATUS: regarded by Morocco as under its sovereignty, whereas independent Sahrawi Arab Democratic Republic (SADR) was declared by Polisario Front in 1976

AT the end of January Morocco and Polisario reached an agreement which allowed the recording of tribal groups not already included in the voter identification process to resume, but the UN Security Council warned Morocco that if it did not cooperate fully the mandate of the UN Mission for the Referendum in Western Sahara (MINURSO) would not be renewed and the UN would withdraw from the region. Polisario declared that if the referendum did not go ahead the alternative was war. In his speech from the throne in March King Hassan declared that Morocco remained committed to the UN peace plan for the territory and that the planned referendum would confirm 'the Moroccan nature of our Sahara'. Later in the year it was announced that the referendum, which had been scheduled for December, would be subject to a further delay and would not take place until July 2000. William Eagleton, a former US ambassador to Syria, replaced Charles Dunbar as MINURSO's head, and Eduardo Vetere became the new head of voter identification.

On the death of King Hassan in late July (see V.4.v), Polisario leader Mohammed Abdelaziz sent his condolences. Departing from the organization's usual rhetoric, he praised the late monarch for laying the foundations for 'a democratic and modern Morocco living in peace and harmony with its neighbours' and reiterated his commitment to the referendum process. In early November the abrupt dismissal of Moroccan Interior Minister Driss Basri by the new King, Mohammed VI, was seen as opening the way for a negotiated settlement to the conflict over the Western Sahara. King Mohammed was reported to be in favour of a compromise which would allow the Western Sahara a considerable degree of autonomy, including an elected local administration. Riots in Al Aaiún, the capital of the disputed territory, came as a shock to the Moroccan authorities, and it was suggested that the new autonomy proposals were aimed at avoiding the UN referendum and an uncertain result. The success of Rabat's latest strategy, however, depended on an agreement with Polisario and reconciliation with Algeria.

VI EQUATORIAL AFRICA

1. HORN OF AFRICA—KENYA—TANZANIA—UGANDA

i. ETHIOPIA—ERITREA—SOMALIA—DJIBOUTI

Ethiopia
CAPITAL: Addis Ababa   AREA: 1,128,000 sq km   POPULATION: 61,000,000 ('98)
OFFICIAL LANGUAGE: Amharic   POLITICAL SYSTEM: presidential
HEAD OF STATE: President Negaso Gidada (since Aug '95)
RULING PARTIES: Ethiopian Peoples' Revolutionary Democratic Front (EPRDF) coalition
HEAD OF GOVERNMENT: Meles Zenawi, Prime Minister (since Aug '95)
MAIN IGO MEMBERSHIPS (NON-UN): OAU, COMESA, ACP, NAM
CURRENCY: birr (end-'99 £1=Br12.89, US$1=Br7.99)
GNP PER CAPITA: US$100 by exchange-rate calculation, US$500 at PPP ('98)

Eritrea
CAPITAL: Asmara   AREA: 94,000 sq km   POPULATION: 4,000,000 ('98)
OFFICIAL LANGUAGES: Arabic & Tigrinyam   POLITICAL SYSTEM: presidential
HEAD OF STATE & GOVERNMENT: President Issaias Afewerki (since May '93)
SINGLE RULING PARTY: People's Front for Democracy and Justice (PFDJ)
MAIN IGO MEMBERSHIPS (NON-UN): OAU, COMESA, ACP, NAM
CURRENCY: nakfa, at par with Ethiopian birr (see above)
GNP PER CAPITA: US$200 by exchange-rate calculation, US$950 at PPP ('98)

Somalia
CAPITAL: Mogadishu   AREA: 638,000 sq km   POPULATION: 9,100,000 ('98)
OFFICIAL LANGUAGES: Somali & Arabic   POLITICAL SYSTEM: transitional
HEAD OF STATE & GOVERNMENT: disputed
MAIN IGO MEMBERSHIPS (NON-UN): AL, OAU, ACP, OIC, NAM
CURRENCY: shilling (end-'99 £1=SSh4,118.15, US$1=SSh2,555.16)
GNP PER CAPITA: n/a

Djibouti
CAPITAL: Djibouti   AREA: 23,000 sq km   POPULATION: 653,000 ('98)
OFFICIAL LANGUAGES: Arabic & French   POLITICAL SYSTEM: presidential
HEAD OF STATE & GOVERNMENT: President Ismail Omar Guellah (since April '99)
RULING PARTY: Popular Rally for Progress (RPP)
PRIME MINISTER: Barkat Gourad Hamadou (since Sept '78)
MAIN IGO MEMBERSHIPS (NON-UN): AL, OAU, ACP, OIC, NAM, Francophonie
CURRENCY: Djibouti franc (end-'99 £1=DF277.61, US$1=DF172.25)
GNP PER CAPITA: n/a

ETHIOPIA. Eight months of quiet along the disputed Ethiopian-Eritrean border was broken in February. Ethiopian forces launched a successful effort to retake Badme (seized by Eritrea in May 1998—see AR 1998, pp. 257-8), pushing 30 kilometres into Eritrean territory. An attempt to repeat this success two weeks later at Zalembessa was a disaster, as was an Eritrean attempt to retake Badme at the end of March; two further Eritrean efforts on the Badme front in May and June were repulsed with substantial losses. Casualties were heavy, estimates putting them at 30,000 or more on each side. The rest of the year saw only minor military activity. Ethiopian planes ineffectually bombed Assab and Massawa and the Sawa national service centre. There were artillery exchanges and small-scale operations all along the border.

International efforts at mediation made some progress, but did not produce a ceasefire. One day after the loss of Badme, Eritrea accepted the peace framework proposed by the Organization of African Unity (OAU) calling for deployment of military observers and demarcation of the border with the help of the UN, and for both sides to redeploy forces outside occupied areas, returning to the *status quo ante* of 6 May 1998. Ethiopia had accepted the OAU proposals when first drawn up.

In July both sides accepted the second stage—'modalities for implementation'. Further 'technical agreements' were presented in August. Eritrea accepted immediately, though it raised the issue of compensation for Eritreans deported from Ethiopia. Ethiopia requested clarification, wanting guarantees that Eritrea would withdraw from all areas seized in May 1998 and that the previous administration would be restored pending final agreement. Ethiopia's suspicions of Eritrean intentions were paralleled by Eritrea's belief that this was an attempt to get the disputed territories declared Ethiopian without demarcation. The OAU responded to Ethiopia's queries in December, but the issue remained unresolved at the end of the year.

The conflict widened during the year. Eritrea supported Djibouti's armed opposition, the Front for the Restoration of Unity and Democracy (FRUD), encouraging attacks on the railway line to Ethiopia in August and November. Eritrea also provided arms and training to the Oromo Liberation Front (OLF), funnelling 1,500 fighters into southern Ethiopia courtesy of Somali warlord Hussein Aydid, who visited Asmara in February. OLF activity led to joint Kenyan-Ethiopian security operations in June. By August Ethiopia claimed that it had killed or captured over 1,100 OLF fighters, and its response included military support for Hussein Aydid's opponents. By October Hussein Aydid was ready to change sides. He visited Ethiopia, and a few weeks later OLF leaders were deported to Eritrea, while the OLF's Mogadishu office was closed.

Ethiopia and Sudan supported external Eritrean opposition groups. In March ten Eritrean opposition movements launched the Alliance of Eritrean National Forces (AENF) in Khartoum, drawing support from Eritrean Muslims, although it had yet to organize its own military command. Following the improvement of relations between Sudan and Eritrea, the AENF was based in Ethiopia.

Deportations of Eritreans from Ethiopia, halted in February by renewed fighting, resumed in July, though at a reduced level. By December, according to Eritrea, a total of some 65,000 Eritreans had been expelled. An Amnesty International report in January strongly criticized the scale and the methods used. The organization accepted at the same time that 22,000 Ethiopians had left Eritrea, but said that there was no evidence to support claims that 40,000 had been seriously ill-treated and deported.

The economy of Ethiopia continued to deteriorate. Dismayed at rising military expenditure, donors began to reallocate aid funding. In September the World Bank announced a moratorium on further projects for both Ethiopia and Eritrea. Ethiopia's trade deficit in 1998-99 rose by over 60 per cent, with coffee earnings falling by nearly a third and imports, mainly military material and fuel, rising sharply. The conflict was funded by increased taxes (January) and a surtax and fuel price rises (December), by diverting funds and by voluntary contributions, amounting to an estimated $100 million. The diversion of resources, human and material, affected production. Ethiopia's food security deteriorated during the year. A failure of the short rains in March and April was followed by widespread drought, localized floods and pest infestations. Some 6.5 million people needed food relief by November. By year's end a further 300,000 people on each side had been displaced by the fighting.

In September Ethiopia announced a timetable for federal and state elections in May 2000; by December 38 parties had been registered. Professor Asrat Woldeyes, chairman of the opposition All Amhara Peoples Organization, released from prison on medical grounds in December 1998, died in the USA in May. In March prison sentences of up to 20 years had been passed on 23 of his co-defendants. In June Dr Taye Wolde Semayat, chairman of the Ethiopian Teachers' Association, was given a 15-year sentence. In both trials detailed allegations of torture were made. Eight journalists were in prison in December, with 31 more on bail. The Ethiopian Human Rights Council was finally allowed to register in May, and public hearings started in December on a draft proclamation to establish a government human rights commission and the office of ombudsman.

ERITREA. At the beginning of the year Eritrea's application to join the Arab League was rejected. Following mediation by Libya and Qatar, however, Eritrea and Sudan agreed in May to normalize relations, broken in December 1994. In August a joint security committee held its first meeting, and the two Presidents, in Tripoli in December, agreed to exchange ambassadors. The rapprochement effectively limited the activities of the Eritrean opposition AENF (see above). In December Eritrea accepted the maritime boundary between Eritrea and Yemen, announced by the arbitration tribunal which had awarded the Hanish Islands to Yemen in October 1998 (see AR 1998, pp. 240, 260, 494).

Eritrea's economy continued to decline in 1999, with over 250,000 soldiers mobilized, heavy spending on military hardware and a lack of activity at the ports, particularly Assab. Officials admitted in May that the growth rate had fallen by 50 per cent and that defence spending in 1999 was expected to double. The government increased taxes and issued zero interest bonds, launching an aggressive campaign to increase donations from Eritreans abroad, raising an estimated $350 million. Several areas were affected by drought; high-school students had to help to bring in the harvest. In November there was a national campaign to round up draft dodgers, all those aged 18 to 40 being required to do national service, while older age groups, up to 55, were also recruited for military training.

SOMALIA. Attempts to create regional administrations continued in 1999.

The 'Benadir' administration, set up in 1998 (see AR 1998, p. 260), collapsed in March, after Hussein Aydid switched his allegiance to Eritrea, leading Ethiopia to support his enemies. Ethiopia made several incursions into the Gedo region, and in June sent troops to help the Rahenweyne Resistance Army (RRA) to capture Baidoa. Hussein Aydid was seriously weakened, though his allies captured the strategic port of Kismayo a few days later. A Hawiye conference ending in July produced the Somali Consultative Conference (SCC), but failed to reconcile the Hawiye or to set up an administration.

In August the Somali Peace Alliance was launched by pro-Ethiopian groups, including 'Puntland' (see AR 1998, p. 260), the RRA and the SCC, with the aim of creating a unified military command. In December the RRA declared an administration in the Bay and Bakool regions. Hussein Aydid, failing to get more Eritrean support, had visited Ethiopia in October, agreeing to expel the Eritrean-backed Oromo Liberation Front (OLF) in return for an end to direct Ethiopian support for the RRA. In December he and other Mogadishu warlords, faced by increasingly powerful Islamic courts, again tried to set up a Benadir administration. In September President Ismail Omar Guellah of Djibouti proposed a new Somali conference, to include elements of civil society, with politicians and warlords attending only with a popular mandate. The regional Inter-Governmental Authority for Development (IGAD) summit in November endorsed the plan, but organization and funding remained uncertain.

A poor harvest in mid-year led to deteriorating conditions in southern and central Somalia. In October the UN estimated that 1.2 million people were at risk from food shortages, with 600,000 requiring urgent food aid.

The Republic of Somaliland, still unrecognized, benefited from the use of the port of Berbera to import relief food for eastern Ethiopia, and, in March, from the lifting of the livestock ban imposed by Saudi Arabia in 1998. No progress was made in settling Somaliland's dispute with the Darod administration of 'Puntland' over control of the Sol and Sanaag regions.

DJIBOUTI. President Hassan Gouled Aptidon (83) stepped down in April after 22 years in power. With several prominent figures banned, his Ethiopian-born nephew and designated heir, Ismail Omar Guellah, easily won the election on 9 April and reappointed long-serving Prime Minister Barkat Gourad Hamadou. The opposition alleged fraud, its candidate, Moussa Ahmad Idris, being arrested in September accused of supporting the armed opposition (the Front for the Restoration of Unity and Democracy, FRUD).

Relations with Eritrea deteriorated because of its support for the FRUD. President Ismail said in October that Djibouti was 'almost' in a state of war with Eritrea, the visiting French Chief of Staff reiterating France's full support. Ethiopia continued to provide internal security assistance.

Djibouti port showed much increased activity, rail freight to Ethiopia increasing by up 40 per cent in the first half of 1999. The government launched a three-year economic reform programme in July. In September a UN mission estimated that 80,000 people were in need of food aid due to drought. The IMF approved a $26 million loan in October.

ii. KENYA

CAPITAL: Nairobi   AREA: 580,000 sq km   POPULATION: 30,000,000 ('98)
OFFICIAL LANGUAGES: Kiswahili & English   POLITICAL SYSTEM: presidential
HEAD OF STATE & GOVERNMENT: President Daniel arap Moi (since Aug '78)
RULING PARTY: Kenya African National Union (KANU)
MAIN IGO MEMBERSHIPS (NON-UN): OAU, COMESA, ACP, CWTH, NAM
CURRENCY: shilling (end-'99 £1=Ksh117.33, US$1=Ksh72.80)
GNP PER CAPITA: US$330 by exchange-rate calculation, US$1,130 at PPP ('98)

PRESIDENT Daniel arap Moi's decision to take the constitutional reform process out of the hands of a 25-member commission to be nominated by political parties and civil societies and to hand it over to a parliament dominated by the ruling Kenya African National Union (KANU) raised a storm of protest. Church leaders, opposition MPs and their supporters staged a demonstration in Nairobi on 10 June and were dispersed by riot police. However, strong domestic and donor pressure led MPs on 11 November to pass, by a vote of 185 to 0, constitutional amendments which cut presidential powers and made the Parliamentary Clerk responsible to Parliament rather than, as hitherto, the President.

Once President Moi had stated that he would vacate office when his final term expired in 2002 (though he intended remaining chairman of KANU), politicians started jockeying for position. A powerful triumvirate formed around George Saitoti upon his reappointment in April as Vice-President, a post which he had held for nine years up to the December 1997 general election, after which it was left vacant. The other members of this pro-Moi (KANU-B) triumvirate were Joseph Kamotho, the Trade Minister and KANU secretary-general, and Nicholas Biwott, the wealthy Kalenjin Minister for East African and Regional Cooperation, who was subsequently given the tourism, trade and industry portfolio. However, Mr Saitoti's involvement in the Goldenberg scandal of 1991-93 (see AR 1993, p. 250) diminished his own chances of securing the presidency. His appointment as Vice-President discomfited the Luhyas, Kambas, Kisiis and other ethnic groups who had hoped that their own favoured 'son' would be appointed.

Another disgruntled person was Simeon Nyachae, the Finance Minister, who was demoted in a February reshuffle. The President shocked donors and the business community by announcing that Mr Nyachae was to change places with Francis Masakhalia, the Minister for Industrial Development, a respected economist but lacking his predecessor's political clout to push through unpopular reforms. Mr Nyachae resigned from the government and, as head of the KANU-A faction, became one of its most outspoken critics. A number of middle-level members of KANU also attacked the party leadership. Over 30 parties were registered, a late addition being the People's Alliance for Change in Kenya (PACK) in November.

In July the President, under pressure from the IMF and World Bank, undertook a sweeping reshuffle of senior civil servants. His most dramatic and unexpected appointment was that of Richard Leakey, the celebrated palaeontologist and conservationist, as head of Kenya's public service and secretary to the cabinet. Mr Leakey was charged with stamping out corruption, increasing civil service efficiency and cutting public spending, and thus of unlocking the credits which the IMF had held back for two years. A fearless critic of government and founder of the opposition Safina party, he was credited with transforming the Kenya Wildlife Service following his reappointment as director in 1998.

In presenting his budget on 10 June, Mr Masakhalia said that to achieve his objectives of economic recovery, poverty alleviation and employment creation, civil service and local government reform would be undertaken, privatization accelerated, and a Poverty Eradication Unit and an Anti-Poverty Trust Fund established. Value-added tax was reduced from 16 to 15 per cent and the top rate of tax from 32.5 to 30 per cent, bringing the rate into line with that in Tanzania and Uganda, Kenya's partners in the East African trade bloc. Some critics questioned whether the implementation process to reduce poverty would be effective, while others were disappointed that the minister had not said more about public sector reform, corruption and security—issues that were important to foreign investors. Crime was rampant, especially in Nairobi, and was discouraging tourism and investment.

In February Nairobi University and other students staged an environmental and anti-corruption protest over government plans to allow the Karuna forest on the outskirts of the capital to be developed as an up-market housing estate. The following month cattle rustling led to fighting in the drought-stricken north-west, leaving 100 dead, while the derailment of a train on the Nairobi-Mombasa line caused 32 deaths and hundreds of injuries. Over 300 people died in a malaria epidemic in the west and the lives of consumers were put at risk by fishermen in Lake Victoria who were alleged to be using chemicals to increase the size of their catch.

iii. TANZANIA

CAPITAL: Dar es Salaam/Dodoma   AREA: 945,000 sq km   POPULATION: 32,000,000 ('98)
OFFICIAL LANGUAGES: Kiswahili & English   POLITICAL SYSTEM: presidential
HEAD OF STATE & GOVERNMENT: President Benjamin Mkapa (since Nov '95)
PRESIDENT OF ZANZIBAR: Salmin Amour (since Oct '90)
RULING PARTY: Chama cha Mapinduzi (CCM)
PRIME MINISTER: Frederick Sumaye (since Nov '95)
MAIN IGO MEMBERSHIPS (NON-UN): OAU, SADC, ACP, CWTH, NAM
CURRENCY: shilling (end-'99 £1=Tsh1,284.53, US$1=Tsh797.00)
GNP PER CAPITA: US$210 by exchange-rate calculation, US$490 at PPP ('98)

PRESIDENT Benjamin Mkapa declared a 30-day period of national mourning following the death in London on 14 October of Julius K. Nyerere, Tanzania's first President and a statesman of world stature, widely respected for his moral integrity and his commitment to social justice (see Pt XVIII: Obituary). Drawing on experience since Mr Nyerere left public office in 1985, President Mkapa opted for a market-driven reform strategy rather than the state-controlled economy preferred by the 'the father of the nation'. With the support of the IMF and World Bank, significant achievements were registered in the tourist and mining sectors—commercial gold mining began in the Mwanza area—and in some privatized businesses. The budget returned to surplus, but the public sector needed restructuring and corruption to be eliminated if economic growth was to be achieved. In introducing the 1999/2000 budget, which was based on a performance-related system, Finance Minister Daniel Yona said that his priorities were health, education, water, the rehabilitation of roads and agricultural projects. Financial and fiscal management would be improved, inflation (down to single figures in January) further reduced, the privatization programme stepped up, civil servants' pay increased and unemployment cut.

In August President Mkapa announced Tanzania's withdrawal from the Common Market for Eastern and Southern Africa (COMESA) trading bloc because of his country's commitment to other regional organizations, notably the Southern African Development Community (SADC).The socio-political context gave cause for concern: a divided opposition on the mainland meant that Chama cha Mapinduzi (CCM), the ruling party, retained its former monopoly; social tensions, for example between Christian and Islamic communities, were increasing; and in Zanzibar there was mounting pressure to restructure the Union.

Zanzibar still suffered from the divisive effects of the 1995 election (see AR 1995, p. 245). In June the rival parties—the ruling CCM and the opposition Civic United Front (CUF)—signed a Commonwealth-brokered reconciliation agreement, under which the CUF ended its boycott of the House of Representatives and recognized Dr Salmin Amour as President. This climb-down was resented by some elements within the CUF. Tension between the parties resurfaced in September when, as in March, the CUF was accused of plotting a coup.

In mainland Tanzania internal division afflicted the opposition as a whole and individual opposition parties. Thus the National Convention for Construction and Reform (Mageuzi) lost its leader (Augustine Mzema) and other members to the Tanzania Labour Party. Towards the end of the year opposition leaders pressed for a nationwide debate on the future of the Union. Like the CUF and others in Zanzibar (though for different reasons), many of them wanted to scrap the present two-tier system and proposed instead the adoption of a federal system, with separate governments for Tanganyika, Zanzibar and the Union. Feelings on this issue ran high in Zanzibar, whose economy had not recovered from the collapse of the cloves market in the 1980s and was adversely affected by the Union government's recent decision to harmonize customs duties throughout the Union. Many islanders urged that Zanzibar should be made a free port. In the meantime, the outlook was bleak. In her June budget, Amina Salum Ali said that government spending would have to be cut and the size of the civil service reduced.

iv. UGANDA

CAPITAL: Kampala   AREA: 240,000 sq km   POPULATION: 21,500,000 ('98)
OFFICIAL LANGUAGE: English   POLITICAL SYSTEM: presidential
HEAD OF STATE & GOVERNMENT: President Yoweri Museveni (since Jan '86)
RULING PARTY: National Resistance Movement (NRM) heads broad-based coalition
PRIME MINISTER: Apolo Nsibambi (since April '99)
MAIN IGO MEMBERSHIPS (NON-UN): OAU, COMESA, ACP, CWTH, OIC, NAM
CURRENCY: new shilling (end-'99 £1=Ush2,425.61, US$1=Ush1,505.00)
GNP PER CAPITA: US$320 by exchange-rate calculation, US$1,170 at PPP ('98)

PRESIDENT Yoweri Museveni carried out a major reshuffle of the government in April. Kintu Musoke, Prime Minister since November 1994, stood down voluntarily and was replaced by former Education Minister Apolo Nsibambi, while seven other ministers were dropped. The President was accused by the opposition Uganda People's Congress and Democratic Party—which could exist but not campaign—of acting unfairly over the forthcoming referendum by putting forward prematurely his own preference for a 'democratic no-party' state as against a multi-party system. They challenged the legality of the Referendum Act on the ground that parliament was inquorate when the vote on it was taken in June and argued that it was in any case unconstitutional since it violated the concept of free and fair elections enshrined in the constitution.

Gerald Ssendawula, the Minister for Finance, presented his budget on 10 June and announced that government expenditure would increase by 25 per cent, with the main focus on poverty eradication; other areas of priority spending would include universal primary education, road construction and maintenance, health, water and sanitation. He anticipated that GDP growth would exceed 7 per cent in the next financial year, to match the 7.8 per cent in the current year. Coffee remained the country's main export earner. Mr Ssendawula promised that there would be no tax increases and said that defence expenditure would be cut by 22 per cent in the next financial year—a statement welcomed by the IMF. On the grounds of unwarranted expense, the President ordered the closure of all except six of Uganda's 24 diplomatic missions abroad by the end of the year. As a poor country with a good economic record and a government making a serious, though not yet successful, effort to stem corruption, Uganda continued to benefit from the 'heavily-indebted poor countries' (HIPC) initiative. It pledged to use the debt relief that it received to halve the pupil-teacher ratio in primary schools within 12 months and to provide permanent classrooms for all primary school children.

Though defence expenditure was cut, the security situation remained serious. In March eight foreign tourists, including four Britons, were killed by Rwandan Hutu *interahamwe* fighters in the Bwindi Impenetrable Forest National Park. Situated near the borders with Rwanda and the Democratic Republic of the Congo (DRC), the park was the home of the mountain gorillas that the tourists had come to see. President Museveni claimed that this tragic incident vindicated his decision in August 1998 to send troops into the DRC to protect Uganda's western border. In fact, most of the troops were deployed inside the Congo where, together with mainly Tutsi rebels, they sought to oust President Laurent Kabila (see VII.1.i).

The government also had to contend with three rebel groups. The Lord's Resistance Army (LRA) was a fanatical, professedly 'Christian' group led by Joseph Kony; it was based in Sudan and supported by the Sudanese government. The LRA's frequent raids into Gulu and other northern districts ruined the local economy and increased the disaffection of the Acholi people, who were erstwhile supporters of ex-President Milton Obote. Whereas Mr Museveni had hitherto been adamant that the LRA must be destroyed by military means, in May he offered Mr Kony an amnesty; however, it was unlikely that this would be taken up so long as the Sudanese government continued to support the LRA. The West Nile Bank Front (WNBF) was a second group, formerly armed from and based in Zaïre, but now also backed by Sudan. It was active in the West Nile area.

The Allied Democratic Forces (ADF), a third rebel group operating mainly in western Uganda, was made up of a fundamentalist Islamic sect known as *Tabliqs* and remnants of the rebel National Army for the Liberation of Uganda backed up by soldiers loyal to the former rulers of Rwanda and Zaïre. From early in the year the ADF launched a series of attacks in Bundibugyo district, which was cut off from the rest of the country by the Ruwenzori mountains. Local religious leaders tried to mediate between the government and the rebels, whose activities resulted in over 90 deaths and left some 70,000 people homeless. In November over 6,000 soldiers of the People's Defence Force, specially trained in mountain warfare, mounted a fresh offensive against the ADF. The latter and a new rebel group—the Uganda Salvage Rescue Front—were blamed for exploding bombs in the capital in February and again in April, causing many deaths and injuries. In most cases there was insufficient evidence to secure the conviction of terrorists brought before the courts.

2. GHANA—NIGERIA—SIERRA LEONE—THE GAMBIA—LIBERIA

i. GHANA

CAPITAL: Accra   AREA: 240,000 sq km   POPULATION: 18,000,000 ('98)
OFFICIAL LANGUAGE: English   POLITICAL SYSTEM: presidential
HEAD OF STATE & GOVERNMENT: President Jerry Rawlings (since Nov '92), previously Chairman of Provisional National Defence Council (since '81)
RULING PARTIES: National Democratic Congress (NDC) heads coalition
MAIN IGO MEMBERSHIPS (NON-UN): OAU, ECOWAS, ACP, CWTH, NAM
CURRENCY: cedi (end-'99 £1= C5,750, US$1=C3,400)
GNP PER CAPITA: US$390 by exchange-rate calculation, US$1,610 at PPP ('98)

FOR many Ghanaians the highlight of the year was very likely the arrival on 8 November of Queen Elizabeth, not only because of the intrinsic appeal of the visit but because it offered a welcome diversion from a gloomy year of economic troubles and political quarrels. The Queen addressed the national parliament and praised Ghana's democratic renaissance, noting that the forthcoming election in 2000 'will itself demonstrate the political change and freedoms which Ghana now enjoys'. Very large crowds struggled to catch a glimpse of the Queen and the Duke of Edinburgh who later held a *durbar* of chiefs, queen mothers and elders in Accra.

The newly-chosen *Asantehene* (traditional Ashanti ruler) was not present, being still in mourning after the death in Kumasi on 25 February of Nana Opuku Ware II (79) after almost 30 years on the Golden Stool. Otumfuor Osei Tutu II (a famous historical name) was installed as his successor on 1 April. He was not (it was said) the preferred choice of President Rawlings, but Ashanti had rarely been in step with the government in Accra.

Ashanti was a trouble to the government on a second front. The Ashanti Gold Fields Corporation was almost brought into default in October by the miscalculation of its chief executive, Sam Jonah, who had believed the world price of gold would fall. The company had taken out high-risk derivatives or 'exotics' as an insurance hedge against a fall. Instead the price had risen following decisions on gold sales in London and Europe. On 28 September the board of Ashanti declared that it could not meet its liabilities of US$450 million and was technically insolvent. As the third major mining company in Africa, Ashanti was of the highest importance, providing some 65 per cent of the Accra stock market capitalization.

The government was directly involved. Foreign Minister Richard Kwame Peprah and Mines Minister Fred OheneKena were both members of the Ashanti board. Battle was joined when Lonmin (formerly Lonrho), with 32 per cent of Ashanti shares against the government's 20 per cent (plus a 'golden' controlling share), bid $820 million for the company. On 9 October Mr OheneKena publicly supported a Lonmin takeover, only to be sacked from the government four days later. Intervention from Saudi Arabia by Prince Al-Waleed bin Talal bin Abdulaziz al-Saud came to nothing; and the company, its share price having fallen from $10 to $4, limped into the new millennium after a conditional three-year respite when its bankers were promised 15 per cent of the company's capital collateral. Other ministers affected included Kojo Yankah, Minister for the Ashanti Region, who resigned from the government after being removed from his post.

The overall economic picture was dark, as oil prices rose and cocoa prices fell. The country suffered both floods and drought and falling revenues. When the government tried to raise extra revenue by increasing student fees and hospital charges there were widespread protests. The combined opposition parties drew some 510,000 supporters to the Accra sports stadium on 25 November, when speakers berated the government's economic mismanagement. All five opposition parties were represented, including John Kuffour's National Patriotic Party and Augustus 'Goosie' Tanoh's Reform Party. President Rawlings cancelled the increases, but the problems remained. On 23-24 November the World Bank held a donors' conference in Accra at which there was talk of corruption and of the need to speed up economic reforms. Japan also sought to persuade Ghana not to apply for debt cancellation (under the 'heavily-indebted poor countries initiative') and threatened to withhold all its bilateral aid. The IMF put the funding gap for Ghana at some $183 million. Meanwhile, the cedi fell from 2,200 to $1 at the beginning of the year to 3,400 at the year's close.

The government was also weakened politically by divisions. A Reform movement began within the ruling National Democratic Congress and drew support from dissident members led by 'Goosie' Tanoh and Sam Garbah, who complained of corruption, patronage and the misuse of party organization. The underlying issue was still that of the presidential election for the year 2000 (see AR 1998, p. 267). Strongly entrenched in government, President Rawlings' supporters had elected him 'Life Chairman', but it was not clear what that meant. The President's preferred candidate as his successor was the Vice-President, John AttaMills, but would he be a President obedient to the 'Chairman'? By the end of the year, therefore, there was still everything to play for in Ghana's new democracy.

Towards the end of October a bizarre case began to unravel. The *Weekend Statesman*, owned by an opposition MP, published the transcript of a tape-recording—purportedly between 'Albert' and an unknown woman—which implicated members of the government in several unsolved crimes including bomb explosions and murder. The tape was subsequently broadcast on Joy FM radio in Accra, whereupon the government declared it to be a fake. The journalists and editor were threatened with prosecution but denied wrongdoing, saying that they had earlier handed copies of the tape to the police and the Attorney-General.

As if to underline the country's difficulties, it was forecast that the census in 2000 would show that the population had risen to 20 million, of whom half would be under 15 and one in five under five. How would these new Ghanaians be educated, fed and cared for?

ii. NIGERIA

CAPITAL: Abuja   AREA: 924,000 sq km   POPULATION: 121,000,000 ('98)
OFFICIAL LANGUAGE: English   POLITICAL SYSTEM: presidential
HEAD OF STATE & GOVERNMENT: President (Gen. retd) Olusegun Obasanjo (since May '99)
MAIN IGO MEMBERSHIPS (NON-UN): OAU, ECOWAS, OPEC, ACP, OIC, NAM
CURRENCY: naira (end-'99 £1=N161.25, US$1=N100.05)
GNP PER CAPITA: US$300 by exchange-rate calculation, US$820 at PPP ('98)

THE return to civilian rule and the election of General (retd) Olusegun Obasanjo as President at the end of February opened a new chapter for the country which, hopefully, could put behind it the long and miserable period of military rule. The new government faced huge tasks both in terms of building confidence among its own people and the international community, and in restoring an economy that had been reduced to a pale shadow of what it ought to be. A former military ruler and the only one to have restored civilian rule voluntarily (in 1979), General Obasanjo had announced in November 1998 that he would seek the nomination of the People's Democratic Party (PDP) as its presidential candidate (see AR 1998, p. 271), asserting that he was determined to overcome ethnic divisions and to keep Nigeria united.

Elections for 35 of the 36 state legislatures and governorships were held on 9 January, the PDP leading the poll to gain control of 20 states with just over 50 per cent of the votes cast. Prior to the elections, on 5 January, the All People's Party (APP) and the Alliance for Democracy (AD) had formed an electoral pact to fight the legislative and presidential elections. The APP won nine states with 36 per cent of the vote and the AD six with 14 per cent. Various presidential hopefuls announced their candidatures during January, but in the event the only two contenders were General Obasanjo for the PDP and Olu Falae for the APP–AD alliance.

Elections to the 360-member House of Representatives and the 109-member Senate were held on 20 February with the following results:

Party	House	Senate
People's Democratic Party (PDP)	206	59
All People's Party (APP)	74	24
Alliance for Democracy (AD)	68	20
Undeclared	12	6

The presidential elections, held a week later on 27 February, resulted in a convincing victory for General Obasanjo, who won 18,738,164 votes (62.8 per cent) against Mr Falae's 11,110,287 (37.2 per cent). The loser denounced the results as fraudulent. The Yoruba, despite the fact that General Obasanjo was a Yoruba himself, voted overwhelmingly for Mr Falae because they believed that General Obasanjo represented northern and military interests.

General Obasanjo was inaugurated as Nigeria's elected President on 29 May. In his acceptance speech he said that military rule had been a disaster, causing economic ruin and political discord, and that his government's main tasks would be to tackle corruption and restore the economic infrastructure. He suspended all contracts entered into under the outgoing Abubakar regime since 1 January, adding that they would be examined to determine their propriety and relevance. It was believed that many of them had been made fraudulently to benefit senior military figures. Charges had been made of widespread looting by the military in the period January to May.

On 3 June the new National Assembly was inaugurated. The Senate elected Evan Ewerem as its president and Harune Abubakar as his deputy, while Alhaji Buhari was elected speaker of the House of Representatives. At the end of June President Obasanjo announced his new cabinet, all of whose members were new except Adamu Ciroma (finance) and Chief Iyorchia Ayu (industry), who had both served under the late General Sani Abacha.

In a significant move to clear out people from the past, President Obasanjo on 10 June removed all senior military officers who had held political posts between 1985 and 1999, discharging 150 altogether. They were removed to ensure the permanent subordination of the military to the elected civilian government. The President also established an eight-member human rights panel to investigate abuses of human rights committed by the military since 1983, when it had overthrown the previous civilian government. On 21 July 200 officers were promoted or commissioned to fill the gaps left by the 150 who had been discharged. There was a significant promotion of officers from the south to senior posts in order to offset the preponderance of northern officers. In November 1998 the Abacha family had returned approximately US$750 million of an estimated $1.3 billion looted from government reserves by the late military ruler. Efforts to recover the balance of these funds were pursued through 1999.

Tensions between the western Yoruba and northern Hausa peoples mounted during the year. On 18-19 July inter-communal clashes occurred in Shagama near Lagos in which 66 people died, leading thousands of Hausa to flee to the north. In retaliation, on 24-25 July Hausas targeted Yorubas in the northern city of Kano, where 40 people were killed. Further violence erupted in late November with clashes in Lagos which led to over 70 deaths. President Obasanjo then ordered the police to shoot rioters on sight. Although a majority of Yorubas had voted for Mr Falae in the presidential elections, the northerners were now complaining that the President was favouring Yorubas in his government appointments.

The government announced major cuts in the military establishment in August. Defence Minister General Theophilus Danjuma said that the armed forces would be reduced by 30,000 to a total of 50,000 personnel—30,000 in the army and 10,000 each for the navy and air force.

In October the state of Zamfara became the first in Nigeria to announce the introduction of *sharia* law, which was intended to become operational in January 2000. The move caused apprehension in other parts of the country. The law was proclaimed in a packed square in the state capital, Gusau, by Governor Ahmad Sani Yerima, who said that 'without *sharia*, Islamic faith is valueless'. The state authorities promised that in any dispute between a Muslim and a Christian the Christian would be allowed to decide where the case should be judged.

In the economic sphere, the government in January abolished the dual exchange rate, which had allowed officials to buy US dollars at only 25 per cent of their commercial value. The price of petrol was reduced by 20 per cent to 20 naira a litre, reversing a huge rise imposed the previous December. On 24 March the Central Bank of Nigeria devalued the naira from N86.5 to N90 per US dollar. Between December 1998 and March 1999 the country's external reserves fell by more than a third, from $6,700 million to $4,000 million. At the beginning of May a privatization decree was passed to pave the way for the sale of major utilities, including electricity, telecommunications and oil refining. In June the Central Bank introduced exchange controls to defend the currency. As the new President quickly discovered, his main problem was the dire and deteriorating state of the economy, which required major investment in its manufacturing and construction sectors and a massive overhaul of its infrastructure.

An agreement was concluded with the International Monetary Fund (IMF) on 24 January for an economic reform programme, bringing to an end a ten-year stand-off between Nigeria and the IMF. It was agreed that economic restructuring would mean diverting funds from prestige projects into anti-poverty programmes and pursuing tighter monetary policy. In its first budget, presented on 22 July, the Obasanjo government emphasized that its priority aim was to reduce an inherited N265,000 million deficit by 90 per cent by the end of 1999.

The rise in world oil prices from mid-1999 proved a boon to the new government, with oil revenues effectively doubling to $35 million a day. At the same time, Nigeria began to produce liquefied natural gas (LNG) for the European market after a $3,800 million gas plant came on stream. By October agreements had been signed to supply gas to Italy, Spain, France, Portugal and Turkey. However, such production was threatened by unrest in the Delta region, where a tinder-box of discontent existed among local people who had argued for years that they had not received their share of the region's oil wealth and that oil operations had created huge pollution.

At the beginning of 1999 elections in Bayelsa state in the Delta region had been postponed because of unrest, while in February an oil pipeline was sabotaged and another bout of kidnappings of foreign oil workers occurred (although they were later released unharmed). In June the centre of Warri was seized by Ijaw youths and an estimated 200 people died in subsequent fighting before rival factions agreed to peace talks. Further violent clashes took place during September with 19 deaths in Bayelsa state and 16 in Ondo. These ongoing troubles threatened the oil production upon which the economy depended. At the heart of the problem was the complaint that despite Nigeria's huge oil output from the Delta region the people who lived there remained among the poorest, most neglected in the country. Violence appeared to have become endemic: at least 200 people were killed between January and September and some 50 Shell employees were kidnapped.

Nigeria's return to democracy provided a modest boost to the economy, but as General Obasanjo had said on taking office: 'I cannot right wrongs of 30 years in 30 days.' He faced two mammoth tasks: to restore the economy and to halt the ethnic violence which threatened the entire fabric of the state. By the end of the year an estimated 1,200 people had died in ethnic clashes since he came to power.

iii. SIERRA LEONE

CAPITAL: Freetown   AREA: 72,000 sq km   POPULATION: 5,000,000 ('98)
OFFICIAL LANGUAGE: English   POLITICAL SYSTEM: presidential
HEAD OF STATE & GOVERNMENT: President Alhaji Ahmed Tejan Kabbah (since March '96)
MAIN IGO MEMBERSHIPS (NON-UN): OAU, ECOWAS, OIC, ACP, CWTH, NAM
CURRENCY: leone (end-'99 £1=Le3,079.96, US$1=Le1,911.00)
GNP PER CAPITA: US$140 by exchange-rate calculation, US$390 at PPP ('98)

EXPECTATIONS of a rapid conclusion to the protracted civil war in Sierra Leone (see AR 1998, pp. 272-3) were once again dashed when rebel forces belonging to the Revolutionary United Front (RUF) and former Armed Forces Revolutionary Council (AFRC) launched a massive and unexpected attack on the capital, Freetown, on 6 January. Forces of the Economic Community of West African States Monitoring Group (ECOMOG) were able to drive them out within two weeks, but only after 3,000 civilians had been killed by the rebels and serious damage inflicted on the city. As the rebel forces remained within 20 miles of Freetown and appeared to control as much as 60 per cent of the country, despite repeated counter-attacks by ECOMOG troops and local militias, President Ahmed Tejan Kabbah came under mounting diplomatic pressure to restart peace negotiations with the rebel leaders.

Nigeria, which had borne the largest share of the cost of the ECOMOG intervention (some 900 lives lost and a daily bill of $1 million), repeatedly announced its intention to withdraw its forces; and the British government, Sierra Leone's other main financial backer, combined with Nigeria to persuade a reluctant President Kabbah to reopen abandoned talks with the rebel leaders in late January. A national consultative conference on the peace process was held in Freetown in April, attended by Liberian representatives. President Kabbah insisted on abiding by the terms of the 1996 Abidjan peace accord and the conference rejected rebel demands for a total amnesty for their widespread atrocities, a share of power in the government and the release of RUF leader Foday Sankoh. Nevertheless, these objections were subsequently overruled and a ceasefire agreement was negotiated on 18 May in Lomé, Togo, as result of mediation by other West African governments.

The principal decisions agreed to at Lomé were (i) a ceasefire to come into force on 24 May; (ii) fresh talks to start on 25 May; (iii) both sides to retain their existing territorial positions; (iv) humanitarian relief agencies to be allowed access into rebel-held areas; (v) prisoners to be released; and (vi) the UN to be asked to deploy monitors to supervise the disarmament and rehabilitation of combatants. A final peace agreement was signed in Lomé on 7 July. This provided for the release of Foday Sankoh, an amnesty for war crimes and rebel participation in the government (four ministries and four deputy ministries, together with the directorships of several parastatal organizations). Mr Sankoh was given vice-presidential authority with respect to overseeing the reconstruction of the key minerals industry. In what was meant to be a final gesture of reconciliation, both the RUF leader and Johnny Koroma of the AFRC publicly apologized for their followers' atrocities in a meeting with President Kabbah in Freetown in October; but the situation remained far from settled.

There was international condemnation of the blanket amnesty. Violent clashes continued to be reported in the north of the country and relations between the former rebel forces and the 6,000-strong UN force were jeopardized by the ex-combatants' fears of being arrested for war crimes and the refusal of the UN forces to pay for weapons surrendered. Divisions also appeared within the ranks of the ruling Sierra Leone People's Party, where President Kabbah was accused of weak leadership, particularly with respect to his ability to handle the ex-rebels in the enlarged cabinet.

Of equal concern was the poor response of the international community to providing funding for the UN presence and the wider programme of economic and social rehabilitation, though the IMF announced a $421 million aid package in December.

iv. THE GAMBIA

CAPITAL: Banjul   AREA: 11,300 sq km   POPULATION: 1,216,000 ('98)
OFFICIAL LANGUAGE: English   POLITICAL SYSTEM: presidential
HEAD OF STATE & GOVERNMENT: President (Col.) Yahya Jammeh (since Sept '96), previously Chairman of Armed Forces Provisional Revolutionary Council (from July '94)
RULING PARTY: Alliance for Patriotic Reorientation and Construction (APRC)
MAIN IGO MEMBERSHIPS (NON-UN): OAU, ECOWAS, ACP, CWTH, OIC, NAM
CURRENCY: dalasi (end-'99 £1=D18.66,US$1=D11.58)
GNP PER CAPITA: US$340 by exchange-rate calculation, US$1,430 at PPP ('98)

DESPITE his party's secure majority in the National Assembly, and his own diplomatic success in helping to broker a peace agreement in neighbouring Guinea-Bissau (see VII.1.iii), President Yahya Jammeh faced a number of difficulties during the year. His frequent claims to having restored democratic and honest government to The Gambia continued to be challenged by opposition parties and the independent press. His political intolerance was seen in continued official attacks on the press and members of the main opposition party, the United Democratic Party. Difficulties within the ruling Alliance for Patriotic Reorientation and Construction (APRC) also surfaced. There was a major cabinet reshuffle in June and the APRC secretary-general decamped in October with party funds. In the same month the President was forced to dissolve the controversial July 22 Movement, a pro-military organization set up after the coup of 1994. Its reputation for violence and intimidation against the opposition and growing indiscipline had made it an embarrassment and a threat to the government.

Financial scandals also resurfaced during the year, particularly concerning money obtained from the sale of free oil allocations provided by the late Nigerian head of state, General Sani Abacha, in return for diplomatic support, which had ended up in Swiss bank accounts. Controversy also surrounded President Jammeh's decision to spend substantial amounts of unaccounted money on his home village of Kanilai in the Foni district.

v. LIBERIA

CAPITAL: Monrovia   AREA: 97,750 sq km   POPULATION: 2,969,000 ('98)
OFFICIAL LANGUAGE: English   POLITICAL SYSTEM: republic
HEAD OF STATE & GOVERNMENT: President Charles Taylor (since July '97)
RULING PARTY: National Patriotic Party of Liberia (NPPL)
MAIN IGO MEMBERSHIPS (NON-UN): OAU, ECOWAS, ACP, NAM
CURRENCY: Liberian dollar (end-'99 £1=L$1.61, US$1=L$1.00)
GNP PER CAPITA: n/a

PRESIDENT Charles Taylor's continued involvement in the protracted fighting in neighbouring Sierra Leone (see VI.2.iii) earned him international condemnation. Liberia was accused by neighbouring states of supporting the main insurgent forces, the Revolutionary United Front (RUF), and generally acting as a destabilizing presence in the sub-region. Liberia's involvement, repeatedly denied by President Taylor, was partly retaliatory—Sierra Leone and Guinea had contributed soldiers to the ECOMOG West African regional intervention force in Liberia—and partly motivated by a desire to gain access to rebel-controlled diamond mining areas across the Sierra Leonian border.

All was not calm within Liberia itself, though, as dissident elements based in Guinea launched armed attacks on Lofa county in August-September. The insurgents called themselves the Joint Forces for the Liberation of Liberia and were believed to consist of elements of disbanded former rebel factions. A peace accord mediated by regional heads of state was signed by President Taylor and President Lansana Conté of Guinea at Abuja in Nigeria on 17 September. By then the domestic political situation was sufficiently stable to allow the remaining ECOMOG forces to withdraw in October, after ten years of peace-keeping and weapons monitoring.

Government reshuffles took place in February, May and September, and the heads of both the army and the police were killed in separate road and air accidents in September and November.

3. WEST AFRICAN FRANCOPHONE STATES—CENTRAL AFRICAN FRANC ZONE

i. SENEGAL—MAURITANIA—MALI—GUINEA—CÔTE D'IVOIRE— BURKINA FASO—TOGO—BENIN—NIGER

Senegal

CAPITAL: Dakar   AREA: 196,000 sq km   POPULATION: 9,000,000 ('98)
OFFICIAL LANGUAGE: French   POLITICAL SYSTEM: presidential democracy
HEAD OF STATE & GOVERNMENT: President Abdou Diouf (since Jan '81)
RULING PARTIES: Socialist Party (PS) heads government
PRIME MINISTER: Mamadou Lamine Loum (PS), since July '98
MAIN IGO MEMBERSHIPS (NON-UN): OAU, ECOWAS, UEMOA, ACP, OIC, NAM, Francophonie
CURRENCY: CFA franc (end-'99 £1=CFAF1,054.73, US$1=CFAF654.42)
GNP PER CAPITA: US$530 by exchange-rate calculation, US$1,710 at PPP ('98)

Mauritania

CAPITAL: Nouakchott   AREA: 1,000,000 sq km   POPULATION: 3,000,000 ('98)
OFFICIAL LANGUAGES: French & Arabic   POLITICAL SYSTEM: presidential
HEAD OF STATE & GOVERNMENT: President (Col.) Moaouia Ould Sidi Mohammed Taya
   (since Jan '92); previously Chairman of Military Council of National Salvation (from Dec '84)
RULING PARTY: Democratic and Social Republican Party (PRDS)
PRIME MINISTER: Cheikh El-Avia Ould Mohammed Khouna (since Nov '98)
MAIN IGO MEMBERSHIPS (NON-UN): OAU, UEMOA, AMU, AL, OIC, ACP, NAM, Francophonie
CURRENCY: ouguiya (end-'99 £1=OM359.93, US$1=OM223.33)
GNP PER CAPITA: US$410 by exchange-rate calculation, US$1,660 at PPP ('98)

Mali

CAPITAL: Bamako   AREA: 1,240,000 sq km   POPULATION: 11,000,000 ('98)
OFFICIAL LANGUAGE: French   POLITICAL SYSTEM: presidential
HEAD OF STATE & GOVERNMENT: President Alpha Oumar Konaré (since April '92)
RULING PARTY: Alliance for Democracy in Mali (ADEMA)
PRIME MINISTER: Ibrahim Boubakar Keita (since April '92)
MAIN IGO MEMBERSHIPS (NON-UN): OAU, ECOWAS, UEMOA, AL, OIC, ACP, NAM, Francophonie
CURRENCY: CFA franc (see above)
GNP PER CAPITA: US$250 by exchange-rate calculation, US$720 at PPP ('98)

Guinea

CAPITAL: Conakry   AREA: 246,000 sq km   POPULATION: 7,000,000 ('98)
OFFICIAL LANGUAGE: French   POLITICAL SYSTEM: presidential
HEAD OF STATE & GOVERNMENT: President (Gen.) Lansana Conté (since Dec '93); previously
   Chairman of Military Committee for National Recovery (from April '84)
RULING PARTY: Party of Unity and Progress (PUP)
PRIME MINISTER: Sidya Touré (since July '96)
MAIN IGO MEMBERSHIPS (NON-UN): OAU, ECOWAS, OIC, ACP, ACP, NAM, Francophonie
CURRENCY: Guinean franc (end-'99 £1=GF2,203.60, US$1=GF1,367.25)
GNP PER CAPITA: US$540 by exchange-rate calculation, US$1,760 at PPP ('98)

Côte d'Ivoire

CAPITAL: Abidjan   AREA: 322,000 sq km   POPULATION: 15,000,000 ('98)
OFFICIAL LANGUAGE: French   POLITICAL SYSTEM: presidential
HEAD OF STATE & GOVERNMENT: Gen. Robert Gueï, Chairman of National Committee of Public
   Safety (since Dec '99)
MAIN IGO MEMBERSHIPS (NON-UN): OAU, ECOWAS, UEMOA, ACP, NAM, Francophonie
CURRENCY: CFA franc (see above)
GNP PER CAPITA: US$700 by exchange-rate calculation, US$1,730 at PPP ('98)

Burkina Faso

CAPITAL: Ouagadougou   AREA: 275,000 sq km   POPULATION: 11,000,000 ('98)
OFFICIAL LANGUAGE: French   POLITICAL SYSTEM: presidential
HEAD OF STATE & GOVERNMENT: President (Capt.) Blaise Compaoré (since Dec '91); previously Chairman of Popular Front (from Oct '87)
RULING PARTY: Congress for Democracy and Progress (CDP))
PRIME MINISTER: Kadre Desiré Ouedraogo (since Feb '96)
MAIN IGO MEMBERSHIPS (NON-UN): OAU, ECOWAS, UEMOA, OIC, ACP, NAM, Francophonie
CURRENCY: CFA franc (see above)
GNP PER CAPITA: US$240 by exchange-rate calculation, US$1,020 at PPP ('98)

Togo

CAPITAL: Lomé   AREA: 57,000 sq km   POPULATION: 4,000,000 ('98)
OFFICIAL LANGUAGES: French, Kabiye & Ewem   POLITICAL SYSTEM: presidential
HEAD OF STATE: President (Gen.) Gnassingbé Eyadéma (since '67)
RULING PARTY: Rally of the Togolese People (RPT)
PRIME MINISTER: Eugène Koffi Adoboli (since May '99)
MAIN IGO MEMBERSHIPS (NON-UN): OAU, ECOWAS, UEMOA, ACP, NAM, Francophonie
CURRENCY: CFA franc (see above)
GNP PER CAPITA: US$330 by exchange-rate calculation, US$1,390 at PPP ('98)

Benin

CAPITAL: Porto Novo   AREA: 113,000 sq km   POPULATION: 6,000,000 ('98)
OFFICIAL LANGUAGE: French   POLITICAL SYSTEM: presidential
HEAD OF STATE & GOVERNMENT: President Mathieu Kérékou (since March '96)
MAIN IGO MEMBERSHIPS (NON-UN): OAU, ECOWAS, UEMOA, ACP, NAM, Francophonie
CURRENCY: CFA franc (see above)
GNP PER CAPITA: US$380 by exchange-rate calculation, US$1,250 at PPP ('98)

Niger

CAPITAL: Niamey   AREA: 1,267,000 sq km   POPULATION: 10,000,000 ('98)
OFFICIAL LANGUAGE: French   POLITICAL SYSTEM: republic
HEAD OF STATE & GOVERNMENT: President Mamadou Tandja (since Dec '99)
RULING PARTY: National Movement for a Development Society (MNSD)
PRIME MINISTER: Hama Amadou (since Dec '99)
MAIN IGO MEMBERSHIPS (NON-UN): OAU, ECOWAS, UEMOA, ACP, OIC, NAM, Francophonie
CURRENCY: CFA franc (see above)
GNP PER CAPITA: US$190 by exchange-rate calculation, US$830 at PPP ('98)

SENEGAL. Senegalese political life for much of the year was focused on the presidential elections due in February 2000. A foretaste of the action came in January, when for the first time there were elections for the Senate, the 64-seat second chamber introduced in the constitutional reform of 1993, but only now formally set up. The main opposition parties—the Senegalese Democratic Party of Abdoulaye Wade and the Democratic Renewal (RD) of Djibo Kâ—decided to boycott the elections, saying both that the Senate would be 'ruinous and useless' and that the results were 'false in advance'. The ruling Socialist Party accordingly took all 45 elected seats, while two small marxist parties won 6.5 per cent of the vote. In February Abdoulaye Diack was elected president of the new chamber.

New hopes that the presidential election would be a more interesting contest were raised in July when one of Senegal's best-known politicians, Moustapha Niasse, twice Foreign Minister and with a substantial following both in the ruling party and in the country, announced that he would be running against

President Diouf, the PS candidate, having created a new party, the Alliance of the Forces of Progress (AFP). By the end of the year the line-up of presidential candidates included not only incumbent Abdou Diouf but also MM. Niasse, Wade and Kâ, as well as trade unionist Mademba Sock. At the end of December there was an additional quickening of the already mounting tension because of the military coup in neighbouring Côte d'Ivoire (see below). The speculation was whether, in the event of a disputed election in Senegal the army might also be impelled to intervene.

Meanwhile, the vexed question of the peace process in the rebellious southern province of Casamance continued to drag on. Early in the year, following discussions between President Diouf and the leader of the Movement of Democratic Forces of Casamance (MFDC), Abbé Diamacoune Senghor, a new ceasefire and disarmament process was initiated. This was allied to the impending peace in neighbouring Guinea-Bissau, whose recent crisis had in part been triggered by connections between elements in the army and Casamance rebels. In March there was a return of MFDC militants who had been fighting in Guinea-Bissau with rebel General Ansumane Mane, but it was clear that only some were ready to be disarmed. At the end of April new fighting broke out, despite the holding of ultimately abortive peace talks between rival factions in the Gambian capital, Banjul.

Senegal also took great exception to a parallel call by Guinea-Bissau Prime Minister Francisco Fadul for a referendum in Casamance, especially since, as these events were unfolding, the withdrawal of Senegalese troops from the ECOWAS operation in Guinea-Bissau was completed (see VII.1.ii). This was to the great relief of the Senegalese government, which had been increasingly under fire over the intervention. Later in the year, following a new outbreak of violence in the area, fresh peace talks between the Diamacoune faction and that of 'southern front commander' Leopold Sadio were once again held in Banjul. Although these had the guarded blessing of the Dakar authorities, they similarly made slow progress, although a further round in December was claimed by the Gambians to have made significant advances.

MAURITANIA. The year began with political turbulence surrounding municipal elections and the charging of opposition leader Ahmed Ould Daddah with incitement and disrupting public order. He had been arrested in December 1998 after demanding an inquiry into the alleged dumping of Israeli nuclear waste in the country, but was released in mid-January. All opposition parties boycotted the elections, which they said were 'mocking the aspirations of the people'. In the circumstances, the ruling Democratic and Social Republican Party (PRDS) won the vast majority of seats and control of all the councils. The only other contestants were independent candidates and in many rural areas no-one stood against the PRDS at all. In some districts the elections were suspended because of alleged 'massive fraud'. In a trial held in April, M. Ould Daddah and other opposition figures were acquitted.

Relations with neighbouring Mali deteriorated in mid-year, following clashes between Peulh cattle herders and Soninke villagers. There was a reported build-up of Mauritanian troops on the border following attacks from Mali on army patrols. But tension was defused after talks, it being recognized that the problem was principally internal to Mali (see below).

Shortly after the summit of the Economic Community of West African States in Lomé, Togo, in December (see XI.6.ii), it was announced in Nouakchott that Mauritania would be withdrawing from the 16-nation grouping. Observers saw this as a sign that the country was moving more definitively in the direction of the sphere of influence of the Arab states of North Africa (Mauritania having left the franc zone nearly 30 years previously).

MALI. The continued poor relations between government and opposition, which had troubled Mali's democracy since the difficulties surrounding the presidential election of 1997, took a new turn at the beginning of the year. The convening of the long-promised 'national forum' on political and institutional problems in January was seen as a limited success in that only four of the 19 political parties belonging to the 'radical opposition' took part, alongside the ruling ADEMA party and parties of the 'presidential tendency'. International jurists and observers from a range of countries and international institutions were also present.

The event led to the easing of a split in one of the main parties, the former ruling Sudanese Union (US-RDA), with Bamou Touré's faction deciding to join that of Seydou Badian Kouyaté in participating in the forum, although the two tendencies continued to exist. Police, however, broke up the meeting of a grouping that continued to be opposed to the Forum, the Patriotic Renewal Movement, and the various opposition alliances continued to be at odds over whether to participate in the initiative.

Local elections in May saw ADEMA take 59 per cent of the seats in the four northern regions. There was no boycott this time, and a 45 per cent turn-out, which was considered unusually high for Mali. In mid-year clashes were reported in the north both between Peulh nomads and Soninke villagers near the Mauritanian border, and between Arabs and Kounta in the Gao and Kidal regions, in which many were killed. Some attributed the clashes to problems arising from the local elections, but the president of the National Assembly, Ali Diallo, blamed the proliferation of arms in the region.

GUINEA. The year was dominated by the detention, in the wake of the December 1998 presidential elections (see AR 1998, p. 279), of the main opposition leader, Alpha Condé, who remained in custody despite considerable international pressure. In January he was transferred to the central prison in Conakry and charged with plotting a coup d'état, but it was August before a decree setting up a special 21-member security court (including several army officers) to try him was promulgated. Although it had been asserted that the trial would begin in September, by the end of the year he had still not come to court.

M. Condé's colleagues in the opposition alleged that he had been arrested prior to the announcement of the election results, which gave incumbent President Lansana Conté a narrow victory—fraudulently obtained, according to the opposition. This accounted for the nervousness of the government over the trial, aggravated in the wake of the end-of-year coup in neighbouring Côte d'Ivoire (see VII.1.iii). It was recalled that President Conté was nearly overthrown by his own army in 1996 (see AR 1996, p. 256), and there was open speculation that he was once more at risk. Continuing to weigh heavily on the Guinean polity were the unresolved problems of Sierra Leone (see VI.2.iii), especially the 100,000 refugees still remaining there, and there were also reports of links between warlords in both Sierra Leone and Liberia and supporters of Alpha Condé in Upper Guinea.

CÔTE D'IVOIRE. The year ended with a dramatic twist that shook the whole region, and indeed all of Africa—the shock military coup of 24 December, in which the government of President Henri Konan Bédié was overthrown by a junta led by General Robert Gueï. The exact circumstances of the coup remained unclear in the aftermath, but it seemed clear that it began as a barracks mutiny by members of an elite para-commando unit protesting at not receiving pay due to them for service with the UN in the Central African Republic. However, it escalated so rapidly into a fully-fledged take-over—first of the TV-radio station, then of the President's office and then the of airport—that some suspected that the initial unrest triggered an existing plan for a coup.

The President had been in his home village of Daoukro and returned to Abidjan on 23 December on receiving news of the unrest. After some probably fatal delays, he received a delegation of mutineers early on 24 December, but only agreed to consider their demands. Not long after, at 11am, a broadcast was made on a commercial radio station by General Gueï, a former chief of army staff, who had been brought out of retirement from his village near Man in the far west of the country (possibly under a certain amount of duress). Describing himself simply as 'spokesman' of the dissident soldiers, he announced the removal of the head of state, the dissolution of the government, the National Assembly, the Constitutional Council and the Supreme Court, and the establishment of a nine-member National Committee of Public Safety (CNSP). Only later in the day was it announced that General Gueï was in fact the new head of state. He was by no means just a figurehead: although retired, he had much prestige in the army and the country, not least for his dignity after being dismissed in 1995 by President Bedié because of his unwillingness to see the army used for political purposes during the presidential elections of that year (see AR 1995, p. 259).

The announcement that General Gueï was the country's new ruler was the point at which M. Bédié and his family, and several members of the government, decided to go by underground passage from the presidential palace to the French ambassador's residence. Following hostile demonstrations by soldiers outside that building, it was decided to transfer the deposed President to the French military base at Port Bouët. Although M. Bedié made a broadcast (relayed by Radio France Internationale) calling for resistance to the coup, it seemed that none was forthcoming. In particular, the supposedly pro-Bédié gendarmerie was, like the other branches of the security forces, in favour of the coup.

A key factor was the lack of any serious French response. The French President and Prime Minister, it was true, were already abroad on holiday, and France was preoccupied both by the hurricane of 23 December and the wreck of an oil tanker on the Brittany coast (see II.2.ii). But the unwillingness of the Socialist-led government to intervene was clear: the only voice in favour of responding to M. Bédié's appeal for assistance in restoring constitutionality was that of President Chirac's African affairs adviser, Michel Dupuch. In these circumstances, France confined itself to sending reinforcements to the Port Bouët base, saying that this action was in case of risk to the French community. General Gueï responded by warning against any French intervention, and by exerting pressure for M. Bédié to leave. Thus on 26 December the ex-President and his entourage left for Lomé, Togo, from where, after an unsuccessful visit to Nigeria asking for assistance, he flew to Paris.

The new government rapidly restored order, following rioting and looting on 23-24 December. It soon became clear that, apart from General Gueï himself, three senior officers were playing a key role: General Abdoulaye Coulibaly, General Lansana Palenfo, and Lieut.-Colonel Mathieu Doué (the last seen as principal representative of the core mutineers). All political prisoners were released, including the parliamentary leader of the Democratic Republican Rally (RDR), Henriette Diabaté, who had been gaoled in November 1999 following a demonstration. More significantly, the party's presidential candidate for the October 2000 elections, Alassane Ouattara, returned from exile in France. A few weeks earlier a warrant had been issued for his arrest following a mounting political crisis, triggered by further legal attempts to deny him Ivorian citizenship, as had already been instituted prior to the elections of 1995 (see AR 1995, p. 259).

If there were political tensions behind the coup, the Côte d'Ivoire economy—the most important in francophone West Africa—was also in trouble. Revenues had slumped because of falling commodity prices, and the IMF had suspended assistance earlier in the year because of unhappiness at aspects of governance. In particular, the Bédié regime had appeared beset by a series of corruption scandals.

The coup was generally well-received in the country, apart from the political circles close to M. Bedié and in the ruling Côte d'Ivoire Democratic Party (PDCI), which was one of the main losers of the change of regime. Nonetheless, there was immediate international condemnation from France, the USA, the European Union and the Organization of African Unity, among others, even if this was increasingly tempered by calls for as short a period of military rule as possible.

Thus at the end of 1999 the unthinkable had happened: the country thought to be immune from a coup was under military rule. The haven of stability built up in the 33-year rule of the late President Félix Houphouët-Boigny, which was seen as a model economy and emerging market *par excellence*—where the stock exchange of the West African Economic and Monetary Union (UEMOA) had recently opened—was now on the brink of a year of deep uncertainty of a kind to frighten off investors in droves. As was remarked, it was 'the second death of Houphouët-Boigny'.

BURKINA FASO. In spite of efforts of President Blaise Compaoré to focus his country on development, the year was haunted by a political affair which was still unresolved at the end of the year. This concerned the murder in December 1998 of the journalist Norbert Zongo and three others (see AR 1998, p. 281). Dissatisfaction on the part of the public, the trade unions and a broad political spectrum led to a whole year of demonstrations. The root cause was the increasing certainty that the murders had been political, because M. Zongo had written too much about the way the President's brother, François Compaoré, had allegedly killed his chauffeur. A commission of inquiry reported in May that the evidence suggested murder, but the perpetrators were never pursued.

The effect of the crisis was nonetheless to awaken the fragmented opposition from its torpor and to generate pressures for a national government. President Compaoré responded partially by seeking proposals from a College of Elders, which included suggestions for a national government, the dissolution of parliament and the establishment of a 'truth commission'. However, by the first anniversary of M. Zongo's death in December (when 25,000 people visited his grave), all President Compaoré had been able to achieve was an inadequate government reshuffle and the establishment of commissions to consider constitutional reforms and 'possible scenarios for national reconciliation'.

TOGO. The dinosaur-like regime of President Gnassingbé Eyadéma, in power for 32 years, was able to maintain its political grip, in spite of continued deep international reserves about him and no evidence of real support in the country other than in his own northern area, which still dominated the army. Parliamentary elections in March were boycotted by the opposition, and a report by Amnesty International in May detailing many summary executions at the time of the 1998 presidential elections (see AR 1998, p. 281) did further damage, even if the Togo government did its best to contest its veracity. International donors, led by the European Commission, continued to hold back on the provision of aid.

A widely-criticized visit by President Chirac of France in July was said to have helped to achieve a breakthrough in bringing together government and all sections of the opposition. This was posited on President Eyadéma's agreement to organize another more transparent parliamentary election, and his apparent willingness not to stand again in the presidential elections of 2003. He also reportedly agreed to a genuinely independent electoral commission, a statute for political parties and an amnesty for former heads of state (the last being to protect his own position), as well as the establishment of a 'reconciliation forum'.

Up to the end of the year, however, progress was slow, with opposition parties still suspicious that the process might not be genuine. They observed that the veteran President was still trying to build an external position and to win back lost international credit, through the chairmanship of the Economic Community of West African States (ECOWAS)—for example promoting the Lomé peace talks on Sierra Leone (see VI.2.iii)—and securing the OAU summit for Lomé in 2000. His diplomacy fought a rearguard action, however, on the next treaty arrangement between the European Union and the African, Caribbean and Pacific (ACP) states, which looked finally lost to Lomé after 25 years during which the name of the Togolese capital had adorned four successive conventions.

BENIN. Benin's reputation as the pioneer of democracy in French-speaking Africa in the 1990s was maintained by the parliamentary elections of 30 March. These were marked by important gains by the Benin Resistance (RB) of former President Nicéphore Soglo, the principal opposition party, which won 27 of the 42 opposition-held seats. Since the presidential group won only 41 seats, the coalition of opposition parties had a slight majority in the new National Assembly, which meant that President Mathieu Kérékou was obliged to 'cohabit' with an opposition-led legislature. M. Soglo did not stand in the elections, so his wife, Rosine Soglo, became principal RB (and coalition) spokesperson in the Assembly. Adrien Houngbedji, whose Party for Democratic Renewal (PRD) won 11 seats, was elected president (speaker) of the Assembly.

NIGER. It was another dramatic year for one of Africa's poorest countries, featuring the assassination on 9 April of President Ibrahim Baré Mainassara at the military base in Niamey. Although Prime Minister Ibrahim Assane Maiyaki called the death an 'unfortunate accident', and it took two days for a successor regime to emerge, there were suspicions that the killing was linked to dissent within the army. The assassination was linked with the presidential guard, whose commander, Major Daouda Mallam Wanké, emerged on 11 April as head of a National Reconciliation Council (CRN), which gave itself a nine-month time-limit for returning to democracy.

No inquiry was held into the killing, and international condemnation was widespread, although there was broad support for the change, if not the manner in which it had happened. Widely known as 'the boss', General Baré Mainassara had come to power in a coup against what he called 'democratic disorder' three years before and had been pressurized into holding elections, which he had won amid wide allegations of rigging (see AR 1996, pp. 258-9). Even as an ostensible democracy, his regime had been autocratic and had faced increasing opposition from political parties and trade unions.

Similar pressures, including temporary suspensions of aid, compelled Major Wanké to stay within his deadline, ruling with the help of a constitutional council of elders and experts. a referendum on 18 July approved a new constitution by 89 per cent of a 31 per cent turnout, considered low for Niger. This provided for a presidential/prime ministerial structure, with more power for the prime minister than under the previous constitution overthrown in 1996 following a deadlock between the holders of the two posts. The referendum also approved an amnesty for all those involved in the death of General Baré Mainassara (though they were not named). This had been accepted by political parties, which accepted the military commitment to hand over power within the nine-month deadline.

In presidential elections held on 24 November there were seven candidates. The contest was won fairly convincingly by Mamadou Tandja, a retired colonel heading the National Movement for a Development Society (MNSD), a party which had been set up by a former military regime in the early 1990s but had never done very well at the polls until this time round. Colonel Tandja won just under 60 per cent of votes cast, with all his opponents, who included former President Mahamane Ousmane and another retired colonel, Moumouni Djermakoye, trailing far behind. The MNSD also obtained 55 of the 83 seats in the National Assembly, which on 31 December approved the President's nomination of Hama Amadou, the MNSD secretary-general, as the new Prime Minister.

The MNSD Assembly majority meant that the new President was not required to engage in the coalition politics which had bedevilled the previous civilian regime. He also benefited from the widespread view of observers that the elections had been fair and that voters had opted for him not simply as someone who could keep Niger's turbulent military under control but also to give him the clear popular mandate that had so far been lacking in the era of multi-party politics. There were certainly challenges before him, notably in restoring chaotic government finances and confronting a desperately serious economic situation.

ii. CHAD—CAMEROON—GABON—CONGO-BRAZZAVILLE— CENTRAL AFRICAN REPUBLIC—EQUATORIAL GUINEA

Chad

CAPITAL: Ndjaména   AREA: 1,284,000 sq km   POPULATION: 7,000,000 ('98)
OFFICIAL LANGUAGES: French & Arabic   POLITICAL SYSTEM: presidential
HEAD OF STATE & GOVERNMENT: President (Col.) Idriss Déby (since Dec '90)
RULING PARTIES: Patriotic Salvation Movement (MPS), Union for Renewal and Democracy (URD) & National Union for Development and Renewal (UNDR)
PRIME MINISTER: Nagoum Yamassoum (since Dec '99)
MAIN IGO MEMBERSHIPS (NON-UN): OAU, CEEAC, OIC, ACP, Francophonie, NAM
CURRENCY: CFA franc (end-'99 £1=CFAF1,054.73, US$1=CFAF654.42)
GNP PER CAPITA: US$230 by exchange-rate calculation ('98)

Cameroon

CAPITAL: Yaoundé   AREA: 475,000 sq km   POPULATION: 14,000,000 ('98)
OFFICIAL LANGUAGES: French & English   POLITICAL SYSTEM: presidential
HEAD OF STATE & GOVERNMENT: President Paul Biya (since Nov '82)
RULING PARTY: Democratic Rally of the Cameroon People (RDPC)
PRIME MINISTER: Peter Mafany Musonge (since Sept '96)
MAIN IGO MEMBERSHIPS (NON-UN): OAU, CEEAC, OIC, ACP, Francophonie, NAM
CURRENCY: CFA franc (see above)
GNP PER CAPITA: US$610 by exchange-rate calculation, US$1,810 at PPP ('98)

Gabon

CAPITAL: Libreville   AREA: 268,000 sq km   POPULATION: 1,181,000 ('98)
OFFICIAL LANGUAGE: French   POLITICAL SYSTEM: presidential
HEAD OF STATE & GOVERNMENT: President Omar Bongo (since March '67)
RULING PARTY: Gabonese Democratic Party (PDG)
PRIME MINISTER: Jean-François Ntoutoume-Emane (since Feb '99)
MAIN IGO MEMBERSHIPS (NON-UN): OAU, CEEAC, OPEC, OIC, ACP, Francophonie, NAM
CURRENCY: CFA franc (see above)
GNP PER CAPITA: US$3,950 by exchange-rate calculation, US$6,660 at PPP ('98)

Congo-Brazzaville

CAPITAL: Brazzaville   AREA: 342,000 sq km   POPULATION: 3,000,000 ('98)
OFFICIAL LANGUAGE: French   POLITICAL SYSTEM: presidential
HEAD OF STATE & GOVERNMENT: President Denis Sassou-Nguesso (since Oct '97)
RULING PARTIES: Congolese Movement for Democracy and Integral Development (MCDDI) is included in ruling coalition
MAIN IGO MEMBERSHIPS (NON-UN): OAU, CEEAC, ACP, Francophonie, NAM
CURRENCY: CFA franc (see above)
GNP PER CAPITA: US$690 by exchange-rate calculation, US$1,430 at PPP ('98)

Central African Republic

CAPITAL: Bangui   AREA: 623,000 sq km   POPULATION: 3,500,000 ('98)
OFFICIAL LANGUAGE: French   POLITICAL SYSTEM: presidential
HEAD OF STATE & GOVERNMENT: President Ange-Félix Patassé (since Sept '92)
RULING PARTIES: Central African People's Liberation Party (MPLC) heads broad coalition
PRIME MINISTER: Anicet Georges Doleguele (since Jan '99)
MAIN IGO MEMBERSHIPS (NON-UN): OAU, CEEAC, OPEC, OIC, ACP, Francophonie, NAM
CURRENCY: CFA franc (see above)
GNP PER CAPITA: US$300 by exchange-rate calculation, US$1,290 at PPP ('98)

Equatorial Guinea

CAPITAL: Malabo   AREA: 28,000 sq km   POPULATION: 432,000 ('98)
OFFICIAL LANGUAGES: Spanish & French   POLITICAL SYSTEM: presidential
HEAD OF STATE & GOVERNMENT: President (Brig.-Gen.) Teodoro Obiang Nguema Mbasogo (since Aug '79)
RULING PARTY: Democratic Party of Equatorial Guinea (PDGE)
PRIME MINISTER: Angel Serafin Seriche Dugan (since March '96)
MAIN IGO MEMBERSHIPS (NON-UN): OAU, CEEAC, ACP, Francophonie, NAM
CURRENCY: CFA FRANC (SEE ABOVE)
GNP PER CAPITA: US$1,500 by exchange-rate calculation, US$4,400 at PPP ('98)

CHAD. It was an uneasy year for Chad's President Idriss Déby as the prospect of a real improvement in his country's economic fortunes seemed as far away as ever. The root of the problem was the continued delay on the part of the World Bank governors in getting to grips with the crucial contribution of $110 million to the funding of the proposed pipeline from the Doba oilfields in southern Chad to the Cameroonian port of Kribi. This was in part due to pressure from the environmentalist lobby, which was mainly concerned about the Cameroonian rainforest; but there were also human rights campaigners worried about Chad's difficult political situation, in spite of an easing of tensions in the past three years.

A renewal of fighting in the Tibesti area following activities by a rebel group led by a former Defence Minister Youssouf Togoimi added to the uncertainties, highlighting the failure to give the go-ahead to the $3,000 million oil project. Though decided for perfectly correct business motives, the withdrawal from the oil consortium of both the French firm Elf and the Anglo-Dutch Shell in November (leaving the US Exxon to seek new partners) further undermined confidence and gave the World Bank an opportunity for further delay of the pipeline decision.

In December Ouaido Guelendouksia was replaced as Prime Minister by Nagoum Yamassoum, who formed a broad-based government which included two members of the military.

CAMEROON. Although it was not an election year, there were still many political undercurrents, and a remaining political sullenness dating back to the 1997 presidential election (see AR 1997, p. 264). The chairman of the Social Democratic Front, John Fru Ndi, held out against President Biya's attempt to include all groupings in a national government, to which most others had succumbed. The ending of a trial of 'treasonable' anglophone secessionists in Bamenda without any of the feared death sentences, while still exacerbating feelings in the short term, was seen as opening the way for an eventual political 'appeasement'.

An improvement in the economic situation, notably a stable growth rate of around 5 per cent, was seen as helping to calm the political situation, especially as this was achieved mainly on the basis of agriculture, since oil revenues were continuing to decline.

GABON. Following the excitements of the December 1998 elections (see AR 1998, p. 285), which the opposition rejected because of allegations of fraud, President Omar Bongo began his sixth term—which he said would be his last—in an atmosphere of economic crisis. The run-up to the election had been beset with social unrest, which continued well into 1999, despite the appointment of a new government headed by Jean-François Ntoutoume-Emane pledged to political reconciliation. For a country with large mineral revenues (especially from oil) to be suffering from huge deficits and an intolerable debt burden could only be due to mismanagement. Since 1998 this had led the IMF not to renew assistance, and the financial situation was worsened by the low oil price in the first part of 1999, although this aspect improved substantially later in the year. President Bongo continued to be impervious to the regular charges coming from Paris of his involvement in corrupt activities involving the former parastatal Elf company, a major partner in Gabon's oil industry.

CONGO-BRAZZAVILLE. The whole year was characterized by a situation of near-anarchy arising from the refusal of much of the southern part of the country to accept the forcible return to power in 1997 of President Denis Sassou-Nguesso (see AR 1997, pp. 265-6), who had ruled through a one-party state of military origin from 1978 to 1993. Through the year there were heart-breaking reports of the social breakdown and anarchy in Brazzaville, once one of francophone Africa's liveliest capitals, and the creation of a serious internal refugee problem, because of the warring militias of the President (the 'Cobras') and of principal opponent Bernard Kolélas (the 'Ninjas'). M. Kolélas continued to command wide support from the different Bakongo-related populations of the south. The other political player, the former elected President Pascal Lissouba, now in exile, had largely faded from the scene because of apparent lack of firm support on the ground.

The presence of Angolan troops, who had originally put him in power, helped President Sassou-Nguesso to maintain his regime in what would otherwise have been an intolerable situation for his northern supporters in the capital (located in the Bakongo heartland). After months of skirmishing, there was an evident military stalemate. Towards the end of the year a series of peace feelers were put out involving President Bongo of Gabon (married to M. Sassou-Nguesso's daughter), which led to a provisional settlement being arranged between the two rivals

CENTRAL AFRICAN REPUBLIC. The political focus of the year was the presidential election held on 19 September, after having been twice delayed mainly for reasons of administrative confusion. Against some expectations, incumbent President Ange-Félix Patassé won 51.6 per cent of the vote in the first round, so that a second round was not needed. As in the 1993 presidential elections, former President André Kolingba scored about 20 per cent and former President David Dacko 11 per cent, the other six candidates making little real impact. Following the election Anicet Georges Doleguele, originally appointed in January, was reappointed as Prime Minister of a broad-based government. All nine opposition candidates rejected the result of the poll, complaining of widespread rigging and of an 'electoral coup d'état' and calling for popular resistance, although there was little sign of this before the end of the year.

The mandate of the MINURCA UN force which had been present in the CAR since it replaced a purely francophone African force in 1998 (see AR 1998, p. 286) was extended in November for a further six months, because of continued uncertainties in the wake of the political turbulence surrounding the election. There were also persisting doubts about the capacity of the newly-retrained army to hold together, in view of its near disintegration under pressure in 1996-97. MINURCA's presence had been important in ensuring that the election took place peacefully.

EQUATORIAL GUINEA. The country's second multi-party parliamentary elections, held on 7 March, followed a similar pattern to the first in 1993. This was in part because the controls exercised by the ruling the Democratic Party of Equatorial Guinea (PDGE) were more firmly in place, while the opposition parties, after years of being under attack, were less able to operate effectively—and protested strongly at irregularities and at the arrest of their candidates. The result was, to the surprise of no-one, a landslide for the PDGE, which won 75 of the 80 seats in the new Assembly. The main opposition party, the Popular Union (UP), won four seats and Social Democracy one. The electoral commission claimed that the poll had an incredible 95 per cent participation.

Under legislation of 1998 requiring the dissolution of parties not represented in parliament, 11 unsuccessful parties would cease to exist. Court action by opposition parties seeking the cancellation of the election results was rejected in mid-April and seven opposition leaders were shortly afterwards prevented from leaving for Madrid. The country thus reverted to a traditional pattern of harassment.

Angel Serafin Dugan was reappointed as Prime Minister for a third time in July, the formation of his 'government of national unity' having been delayed by the holding in Malabo in June of a double summit of the Economic and Monetary Community of Central Africa (CEMAC) and the Economic Community of Central African States (CEEAC) (see also XI.6.ii). This prestigious event indicated just how much the increasingly important oil-producing state of Equatorial Guinea was being wooed by its neighbours.

VII CENTRAL AND SOUTHERN AFRICA

1. CONGO-KINSHASA—BURUNDI AND RWANDA—GUINEA-BISSAU, CAPE VERDE
AND SÃO TOMÉ & PRÍNCIPE—MOZAMBIQUE—ANGOLA

i. DEMOCRATIC REPUBLIC OF THE CONGO

CAPITAL: Kinshasa   AREA: 2,345,000 sq km   POPULATION: 48,000,000 ('98)
OFFICIAL LANGUAGE: French   POLITICAL SYSTEM: presidential
HEAD OF STATE & GOVERNMENT: President Laurent Kabila (since May '97)
RULING PARTIES: fluid
MAIN IGO MEMBERSHIPS (NON-UN): OAU, CEEAC, ACP, Francophonie, NAM
CURRENCY: Congo franc (end-'99 £1=CF7.25, US$1=CF4.50)
GNP PER CAPITA: US$110 by exchange-rate calculation, US$750 at PPP ('98)

AT the start of the year the civil war between President Kabila's government and rebels from eastern Congo which started in August 1998 (see AR 1998, pp. 289-90) was still producing bouts of intense fighting. Outside observers were prevented from reaching the battle-fronts, so it was impossible to get a clear picture of what was happening. But from the fragmentary evidence available, it was evident that rebels of the Congolese Democratic Rally (RCD) were still pursuing their advance into Katanga and eastern Kasai. At the same time, an independent rebel group, the Movement for the Liberation of the Congo (MLC) led by Jean-Pierre Bemba, was securing substantial successes in the north east. But the rebels found themselves faced with enemies in their rear. Between 9 and 16 January Bembe resistance fighters known as Mai-Mai, supported by Hutu guerrillas from Burundi, launched a vigorous attack on Bukavu, provoking the RCD to retaliate by killing 500 civilians in a village near Uviva in southern Kivu.

After five months of fighting the five African countries which had intervened in the Congo in August 1998—Uganda and Rwanda backing the rebels, Angola, Namibia and Zimbabwe the government—were coming to realize the cost both in money and casualties of being caught up in what was certainly not a popular war for their own peoples. Attempts to negotiate a ceasefire had begun the previous September (see AR 1998, p. 290). On 18 January the five states involved in the war met at Windhoek (Namibia) and agreed on the first stage towards a ceasefire. In March the Organization of African Unity (OAU) appointed the Zambian President, Frederick Chiluba, to coordinate regional efforts to find a peaceful solution. April brought a widening of the peace process, with Libyan leader Colonel Qadafi convening a meeting of African leaders at the Libyan town of Sirte, where President Kabila had the opportunity of meeting President Museveni of Uganda, who had consistently backed the rebels; the two leaders signed a peace agreement. Later it was reported that Uganda was training 1,500 Congolese troops as a step towards replacing its own contingent in the eastern Congo. On 7 April the UN Security Council passed a resolution calling for an immediate end to hostilities, the withdrawal of foreign forces and the engagement of all Congolese in a national dialogue that could lead to early elections.

President Kabila represented a major stumbling-block on the road to peace. He had an excessively exalted view of his own position, ordering that he should be known as 'the creator, the thinker, the initiator, the main craftsman and chief architect'—a choice of epithets clearly revealing the influence of his models, Mao Zedong and Kim Il Sung, the late dictator of North Korea. He accepted the need for a 'national dialogue or debate', but defined its agenda so as to exclude his political opponents. He was exasperatingly unpredictable except on one point—his paranoid hatred of the Tutsi, about whom he put out propaganda reminiscent in its vocabulary of Hitler's abuse of the Jews. Like his predecessor Mobutu Sese Seko, he was determined to cling on to power, yet he could not prevent international peace moves gathering momentum.

Rwanda's announcement on 29 May of a unilateral ceasefire in the Congo drew a cool response from the Kinshasa government, which insisted on the withdrawal of all 'uninvited forces'. Nevertheless, diplomatic activity resulted in 'summit talks' being convened by South Africa, Tanzania and Zambia in Lusaka in June, attended by members of the Kabila government and rebel supporters, along with representatives of other African states, the role of South Africa proving particularly important. On 11 July agreement was reached on an accord that provided for an immediate ceasefire, the incorporation of rebel troops in a national army and future discussions through a 'national dialogue' on the country's political system. The accord was signed by the Kinshasa government and by representatives of the five countries that had intervened in the civil war. But there was no signature from the RCD, whose members were facing an acute internal crisis, with the membership bitterly divided between ex-Mobutuists and 'renovators'. Wamba dia Wamba, leader of the RCD from its foundation, spoke for the 'renovators', only to be accused by the RCD executive committee of 'high treason' and removed from office after it became known that he had held talks with Presidents Mugabe and Kabila in Harare in June. But he could still count on the backing of Uganda and maintained a power base in the Kisangani area.

So the fighting went on. In early July both the RCD and its ally, the MLC, claimed substantial successes, the MLC taking Gbadolite, the town in Equateur province closely associated with former President Mobutu, who had built an airport there with a runway long enough for a Concorde. At the same time, the RCD claimed to have surrounded Mbuji-Mayi, the diamond-producing centre in eastern Kasai from which the Kinshasa government drew most of its revenue. A few weeks later, on the advice of its backer Rwanda, which was under pressure from the US government, the RCD (now led by Emile Ilunga) and its MLC ally signed the Lusaka accord and accepted the ceasefire. In September the ceasefire was reported to be 'practically intact', although both sides accused each other of violations.

On 11 October the joint military commission (JMC) formed by the OAU to monitor the peace process and chaired by General Lallali Rachid of Algeria held its first sessions in Kampala. The meeting was attended by all the warring parties and by representatives of the UN, the European Union, the OAU and Zambia. The JMC had a daunting task ahead of it. One of its first actions would have to be the sending back to Rwanda of ex-soldiers from the former Rwandan army and *interahamwe* militiamen: this was an essential precondition for participation by the present Rwandan government in the peace process. The Lusaka accord also laid down a timetable that required the withdrawal of all foreign troops by February 2000. It was expected that the UN would be actively involved, initially by sending in 500 peace monitors. The UN sent a 'technical mission' to Kinshasa in October; some of its members were allowed to tour rebel-held territory but were denied access to areas under government control. In December the OAU announced that one of Africa's most respected elder statesmen, former Botswana President Sir Quett Ketumile Masire, had been chosen to act as 'facilitator' for the peace process.

In October Wamba dia Wamba, one of the RCD's rival leaders, who had had inconclusive talks with his rival Emile Ilunga in Johannesburg in September, announced that he was setting up a new government based on the north-eastern town of Bunia. He himself would be 'President and Minister of Defence'. There would also be a new party, retaining the name RCD but adding the suffix 'Liberation Movement' (LM). In December the three rebel groups—RCD-Ilunga, RCD-LM and MLC—came together in Uganda and agreed to form a coalition.

By this time it was clear that the ceasefire had at least partially broken down. From the north-east came reports of Zimbabwean, Namibian and Congolese troops being surrounded near Ikeka and of a substantial government force attempting to reverse the situation. To re-equip his army, President Kabila had recently concluded an arms deal with China. The prospects of an enduring peace looked, as many Congolese had gloomily predicted, slight in the extreme.

ii. BURUNDI AND RWANDA

Burundi
CAPITAL: Bujumbura   AREA: 28,000 sq km   POPULATION: 7,000,000 ('98)
OFFICIAL LANGUAGE: French & Kirundi   POLITICAL SYSTEM: presidential
HEAD OF STATE & GOVERNMENT: President (Maj.) Pierre Buyoya (since July '96)
MAIN IGO MEMBERSHIPS (NON-UN) OAU, CEEAC, ACP, Francophonie, NAM
CURRENCY: Burundi franc (end-'99 £1=Fbu1,017.23, US$1=Fbu631.15)
GNP PER CAPITA: US$140 by exchange-rate calculation, US$620 at PPP ('98)

Rwanda
CAPITAL: Kigali   AREA: 26,300 sq km   POPULATION: 8,000,000 ('98)
OFFICIAL LANGUAGES: French, Kinyarwanda & English   POLITICAL SYSTEM: transitional
HEAD OF STATE & GOVERNMENT: President Pasteur Bizimungu (since July '94)
RULING PARTIES: Rwandan Patriotic Front (FPR) & Republican Democratic Movement (MDR) head coalition
PRIME MINISTER: Pierre-Célestin Rwigyema (MDR), since Aug '95
MAIN IGO MEMBERSHIPS (NON-UN): OAU, CEEAC, ACP, Francophonie, NAM
CURRENCY: Rwanda franc (end-'99 £1=RF541.63, US$1=RF336.06)
GNP PER CAPITA: US$230 by exchange-rate calculation, US$690 at PPP ('98)

BURUNDI. The war between the largely Tutsi army and various Hutu rebel groups, reckoned to have cost 250,000 lives since 1993, dragged on in 1999. 'The fighting nowadays is low-intensity', reported *The Economist* on 23 October, 'but it remains vicious, marked by massacres and arbitrary killings'. The fourth round in the negotiations between the government and moderate members of rebel groups—a process begun in June 1998 (see AR 1998, p. 292)—took place in Arusha, Tanzania, in the second half of January. Participants discussed reports compiled by three commissions on the roots of the conflict, security matters, and economic reconstruction and development. Towards the end of the talks, President Museveni of Uganda announced that enough progress had been made in the peace negotiations to justify the suspension of the sanctions imposed on Burundi by neighbouring states in July 1996. Further talks took place in Arusha in the first half of July, with four commissions discussing a wide range of issues. On some aspects, defined as 'areas of genocide, crimes against humanity, the return of refugees and political reconstruction', the talks were described as successful; less progress was achieved in the commissions discussing 'democracy and good governance', the judicial system and the security forces. Western donors financing the talks were concerned about their length and by the fact that there was still no agreement on a ceasefire, in part because of the many rifts in rebel ranks, with hardliners refusing to take part in the talks.

On 14 May five soldiers found guilty of the murder of the country's first elected President, Melchior Ndadaye, and six ministers in 1993 were sentenced to death by the Supreme Court; another 28 people (most of them soldiers), who had been involved in the murders, received prison sentences. Rebel attacks in the early part of the year appeared to come mainly from bases in Tanzania, mention being made of the large refugee camp at Kigoma. In September rebel activity intensified in what had hitherto been a relatively safe area, in the vicinity of the capital, Bujumbura. Some reports ascribed these attacks to Rwandan Hutu *interahamwe* (militiamen) who had been allowed by President Kabila's government to settle in the eastern Congo.

The Burundian government responded with the drastic decision to move 300,000 peasants to 'regroupment camps'. Conditions in the camps soon became so atrocious that aid agencies found it increasingly difficult to work in them and withdrew completely after two UN aid workers—one Chilean, the other Dutch—and seven Burundians had been ambushed and killed while on their way to visit a camp in a remote area in south-east Burundi. The state of the camps was brought to the notice of the UN Security Council in November. The Council urged the government of Burundi to abandon the regroupment policy, to which a military spokesman in Bujumbura replied that nothing could be done until the rebels abandoned their 'genocidal agenda'. Such developments augured ill for the peace process, which suffered another major blow with the death of Julius Nyerere in October (see VI.1.iii; Pt XVIII: Obituary). The former Tanzanian President had been the originator of the complicated scheme for peace talks and had played the major role in the progress of the negotiations.

RWANDA. Most developments in Rwanda could be seen as being in different ways consequences of the genocide of 1994. The primary motive for the army's involvement in the civil war in the Democratic Republic of the Congo (see VII.1.i) was the imperative need to put an end to the threat presented by Hutu ex-soldiers and militiamen still determined to 'liberate' their country from Tutsi domination. There was also the inevitably heavy cost of the war, on which the government released no information.

North-west Rwanda had suffered much from rebel attacks. Vigorous military action had bought a measure of security, though occasional clashes were still reported. To consolidate its position, the government embarked on a policy of 'villagization', a policy all too likely to cause deep resentment among peasant farmers.

Many tens of thousands of genocide suspects were still in detention centres awaiting trial. By November there had been 22 executions and there were 200 on death row. In terms of numbers, this figure was better than that of the International Criminal Tribunal for Rwanda, sitting at Arusha (Tanzania), which had only made five convictions. The low opinion of the UN and its agencies held by the Rwandan government found confirmation in a damning report on the role of the international community in the 1994 crisis, produced by an independent panel and presented to the UN Secretary-General.

A hopeful development was the first election of any kind to be held since 1994: Rwandans turned out in large numbers in March to take part in the most local of elections. The country was divided up into communities of 50 to 100 families. Each community elected a ten-member committee which would vote for officials to run larger units. Officials in Kigali described this initiative as 'an apprenticeship in democracy', leading towards the government's aim of creating a society in which 'there are no Hutus or Tutsis, only Rwandans'. On 9 June it was announced that the transitional government established in 1994 would be extended for another four years.

iii. GUINEA-BISSAU—CAPE VERDE—SÃO TOMÉ & PRÍNCIPE

Guinea-Bissau

CAPITAL: Bissau   AREA: 36,000 sq km   POPULATION: 1,161,000 ('98)
OFFICIAL LANGUAGE: Portuguese   POLITICAL SYSTEM: presidential
HEAD OF STATE & GOVERNMENT: President (acting) Malam Bacai Sanha (since May '99)
RULING PARTY: African Party for the Independence of Guinea and Cape Verde (PAIGC)
PRIME MINISTER: Francisco Fadul (since Jan '99)
MAIN IGO MEMBERSHIPS (NON-UN): OAU, ECOWAS, ACP, OIC, NAM, CPLP
CURRENCY: CFA franc (end-'99 £1=PG1,054.73, US$1=PG654.42)
GNP PER CAPITA: US$160 by exchange-rate calculation, US$750 at PPP ('98)

Cape Verde

CAPITAL: Praia   AREA: 4,000 sq km   POPULATION: 412,000 ('98)
OFFICIAL LANGUAGE: Portuguese   POLITICAL SYSTEM: presidential
HEAD OF STATE: President Antonio Mascarenhas Monteiro (since March '91)
RULING PARTY: Movement for Democracy (MPD)
HEAD OF GOVERNMEMT: Carlos Veiga, Prime Minister (since Jan '91)
MAIN IGO MEMBERSHIPS (NON-UN): OAU, ECOWAS, ACP, NAM, CPLP
CURRENCY: Cape Verde escudo (end-'99 £1=CVEsc176.85, US$1=CVEsc109.73)
GNP PER CAPITA: US$1,060 by exchange-rate calculation, US$2,950 at PPP ('98)

São Tomé & Príncipe

CAPITAL: São Tomé   AREA: 965 sq km   POPULATION: 142,000 ('98)
OFFICIAL LANGUAGE: Portuguese   POLITICAL SYSTEM: presidential
HEAD OF STATE & GOVERNMENT: President Miguel Trovoada (since March '91)
RULING PARTY: Movement for the Liberation of São Tomé and Príncipe–Social Democratic Party (MLSTP-PSD)
PRIME MINISTER: Guilherme Posser da Costa (since Dec '98)
MAIN IGO MEMBERSHIPS (NON-UN): OAU, CEEAC, ACP, NAM, CPLP
CURRENCY: dobra (end-'99 £1=Db3,736.94, US$1=Db2,318.63)
GNP PER CAPITA: US$280 by exchange-rate calculation, US$1,350 at PPP ('98)

GUINEA-BISSAU. In December 1998 President João Bernardo Vieira and General Ansumane Mane, the leaders of the two sides in the civil war that had torn Guinea-Bissau apart in the previous six months, had signed a peace agreement brokered by francophone members of the Economic Community of West African States (ECOWAS) (see AR 1998, p. 294). On 11 January President Vieira appointed a government of national unity with Francisco Fadul, an adviser to General Mane, as Premier. Sr Fadul was reluctant to assume office until the troops from Senegal and Guinea which had supported the President had been withdrawn. The arrival of 600 troops from Togo—the first, and as it turned out the only, substantial contingent in the planned ECOWAS Monitoring Group (ECOMOG)—was followed by the withdrawal of the Senegalese and Guinean detachments. At the end of January Premier Fadul announced that legislative and presidential elections, which under the agreement should have taken place in March, would be postponed until the end of the year.

In February the peace agreement seemed on the verge of breakdown with a violent outbreak of fighting in the capital, Bissau, but a ceasefire was hastily negotiated; the two leaders, President Vieira and General Mane, meeting in Lomé (Togo), pledged never to resort to arms again. This agreement held for little more than two months. On 6 May members of General Mane's personal guard unit broke into sealed containers at Bissau airport to recover weapons surrendered under the peace agreement. Thus rearmed, they stormed the presidential palace. President Vieira sought refuge in the Portuguese embassy and on 10 May signed an unconditional surrender.

On 14 May the speaker of the Legislative Assembly, Malam Bacai Sanha, was appointed acting President pending elections scheduled for November. He announced that the ousted President would be allowed to leave the country for Portugal, where he had been offered asylum. The coup caused panic in Bissau, where hundreds of people were reported to have been killed in the fighting, while thousands fled the city, On 7 June the last of the 718 ECOMOG troops left the country. In July a new constitution was introduced, limiting the tenure of the presidency to two terms and completely abolishing the death penalty.

In the first round of presidential elections on 28 November, the leader of the Social Renewal Party (PRS), Kumba Ialá, won 38.8 per cent of the vote, well ahead of Sr Sanha (23.4 per cent), who stood for the ruling African Party for the Independence of Guinea and Cape Verde (PAIGC), and ten other candidates. A decisive second round of voting was scheduled for 16 January 2000. In simultaneous Assembly elections, the PRS won 38 of the 102 seats, the Guinea-Bissau Resistance–Bafata Movement 28, the PAIGC 24 and five other parties 12.

CAPE VERDE. Cape Verde retained its reputation as one of the most stable of African states. Aid donors, particularly the IMF and the World Bank, regarded its governnment as 'a model pupil'. Since 1992 the country's economic growth rate had averaged 5.5 per cent, with average annual income per head in 1998 put at nearly US$3,000 by the World Bank's 'purchasing power parity' calculation, both figures among the best in Africa. Critics of the government complained that too much development money was spent in the area of the capital, Praia, where only 15 per cent of the population of over 400,000 lived. Holding 50 of the 72 seas in the National Assembly, the centre-right Movement for Democracy (MPD) was described by *Africa Confidential* as 'ruling quietly'.

Prime Minister Carlos Veiga, the country's most powerful politician, announced in April that in 2000 he would be giving up the party leadership, which he had held since 1991. At the same time, he talked about constitutional changes designed to give the office of the President, hitherto 'honorific not functional', a measure of real power. Critics saw this as a continuation of Sr Veiga's policy of centralizing power, a policy vigorously and freely criticized by politicians possessing firm regional bases.

SÃO TOMÉ & PRÍNCIPE. On 5 January President Miguel Trovoada swore in a government formed by the Movement for the Liberation of São Tomé and Príncipe–Social Democratic Party (MLSTP-PSD), which had won the general election of November 1998 with the largest number of seats (see AR 1998, p. 295). The long-running tension between the President and the ruling party had led Sr Trovoada first to veto the cabinet proposed by Prime Minister Guilherme Posser da Costa, then to demand the removal of two ministers on the new list. The party accused the President of exceeding his powers but eventually agreed to accept his demand.

In a cabinet change in March, Adelino Castelo David became Minister of Planning, Finance and Cooperation in place of Afonso da Graça Varela da Silva, whose departure was officially for personal reasons but was reportedly connected with corruption investigations. In a further reshuffle in July, Paolo Jorge Rodrígues do Espirito Santo was appointed Minister of Foreign Affairs and Overseas São Tomeans in succession to Alberto Paulino.

iv. MOZAMBIQUE

CAPITAL: Maputo   AREA: 800,000 sq km   POPULATION: 19,000,000 ('98)
OFFICIAL LANGUAGE: Portuguese   POLITICAL SYSTEM: presidential
HEAD OF STATE & GOVERNMENT: President Joaquim Alberto Chissano (since Nov '86)
RULING PARTY: Front for the Liberation of Mozambique (Frelimo)
PRIME MINISTER: Pascoal Mocumbi (since Dec '94)
MAIN IGO MEMBERSHIPS (NON-UN): OAU, COMESA, SADC, ACP, CWTH, OIC, NAM, CPLP
CURRENCY: metical (end-'99 £1=Mt21,287.40, US$1=Mt13,208.00)
GNP PER CAPITA: US$210 by exchange-rate calculation, US$850 at PPP ('98)

THE IMF and the World Bank's International Development Association announced on 30 June that Mozambique had met the requirements for receiving close on US$3,700 million in debt relief from its external creditors under the 'heavily-indebted poor countries' (HIPC) initiative. At the same time, the IMF approved a three-year-loan under the enhanced structural adjustment facility (ESAF) equivalent to $78 million. In July the Paris Club of creditor countries cancelled $2,200 million of the country's external debt, thereby reducing its annual debt service payments by $100 million. These decisions by donor nations and institutions were an indication of the high standing that Mozambique, with an average annual growth rate of 10 per cent, a stable currency and low inflation, had now achieved among developing countries.

With the successful conclusion of its second general election in December, Mozambique also impressed observers that it was achieving a remarkable degree of political maturity. The election was held on 3-4 December, but the electorate had to wait until 22 December for the ceremony at which the results were announced. There were only two candidates in the presidential election. Incumbent Joaquim Chissano (in office since 1986) won 52.3 per cent of the vote, against 46.6 per cent for Afonso Dhlakama, leader of the National Resistance Movement (Renamo). President Chissano's party, the

Front for the Liberation of Mozambique (Frelimo), took 133 of the 250 seats in the National Assembly and Renamo 117, while a clutch of minor formations failed to surmount the 5 per cent barrier to representation.

The result was narrower than had been expected. The newly-re-elected President accordingly promised to form 'a government of experienced people willing to undertake a constant dialogue with the nation'. This did not satisfy Sr Dhlakama, who claimed that Renamo had won the elections. So the results were referred to the Constitutional Court, with the loser threatening that if Sr Chissano put pressure on the Court to validate the result Mozambique would become 'ungovernable'. The President condemned this statement as intimidation, and received support from the conclusion of international observers that the elections had been free and fair.

v. ANGOLA

CAPITAL: Luanda AREA: 1,247,000 sq km POPULATION: 12,000,000 ('98)
OFFICIAL LANGUAGE: Portuguese POLITICAL SYSTEM: presidential
HEAD OF STATE & GOVERNMENT: President José Eduardo dos Santos (since Sept '79)
RULING PARTY: Popular Movement for the Liberation of Angola–Workers' Party (MPLA-PT) heads nominal coalition
MAIN IGO MEMBERSHIPS (NON-UN): OAU, COMESA, SADC, ACP, NAM, CPLP
CURRENCY: new kwanza (end-'99 £1=NKw8.98, US$1=Kw5.57)
GNP PER CAPITA: US$340 by exchange-rate calculation, US$840 at PPP ('98)

ANGOLA, the UN Secretary-General told the Security Council on 17 January, was on the verge of catastrophic breakdown; the statistics for malnutrition and disease were rising and the number of new internal refugees was put at 800,000 since the violent resumption of the civil war at the end of 1998 (see AR 1998, p. 299). The second crash of a UN plane—the first had occurred on 26 December (ibid.)—took place in the Huambo area on 2 January; forces of the National Union for Total Independence of Angola (Unita) were accused of involvement in both crashes. Given the worsening situation, the Security Council voted unanimously on 20 February to withdraw the 1,000-strong UN Observer Mission in Angola (UNOMA), which had been set up in 1997.

Early in the year a highly critical report on UN policy, 'Angola Unravels: The Rise and Fall of the Lusaka Peace Accord', was published by the New York-based Human Rights Watch. The UN was taken to task for failing to publicize breaches of the 1994 Lusaka peace accord and the arms build-up by both sides; Unita had found little difficulty in evading the arms embargo and so had been able to re-equip its armed forces. The UN had also 'failed to draw attention to the government's crude lack of interest' in a true peace. *The Economist* of 2 January reported that 'in territory abandoned by Unita, where people were desperate for food and medicine, the government sent in thuggish policemen who, without supplies of their own, stole the last local food stocks'.

Unita beat off two government offensives aimed at a taking Bailundo (home of the kings of the Ovimbundu, Angola's largest ethnic group, providing Unita with its firmest supporters) and Andulo (the home town of Unita leader Jonas Savimbi and Unita's most symbolic strongholds in the central highlands). Unita then went on the offensive, making substantial advances both in the central highlands and in the north-western province of Zaïre, where Mbanza Congo was occupied on 26 January. In May fighting intensified, with the government again on the offensive. Unita then devised new tactics that proved devastating for local civilians. In the past, both sides had left farmers to continue working their land; now they and their families were rounded up by Unita soldiers and marched off at gun-point to government-controlled towns. Unita then used the threat of ambush to cut off all road access to these centres, putting towns such as Huambo and Cuito, with their swollen populations, in a state of siege. The government had no means of providing food, so it was left to the international aid agencies, especially the UN's World Food Programme (WFP), to fly in supplies—an expensive and dangerous operation which severely strained already diminished budgets. Taken together, the UN agencies had asked for $67 million in 1999; by mid-year they had only been able to raise $25 million. Another brutal threat to the civilian population came when both sides resumed the laying of land-mines, forcing foreign charities to abandon most of their work of mine clearance.

Another round of intensified fighting began in September with government forces again aiming at Bailundo and Andulo. This time, to the surprise of many observers, they were completely victorious; Bailundo fell in mid-October, Andulo a few weeks later. On 15 November MPLA army commander General Matos claimed that 80 per cent of Unita's conventional capacity had been disrupted, with 15,000 tons of weapons now in government hands. In December successes were also achieved in the extreme south, where towns that had been in Unita's hands for 20 years fell to the government and Unita forces were reported to be retreating into Zambia and Namibia. In a broadcast on 31 December President dos Santos told his people: 'The sombre circumstances and despair resulting from successive wars and persistent economic decline are changing. The Angolan people are on the brink of a new era of hope.'

The war was not yet over, however. Unita had acquired a new generation of senior officers, tough young men who had spent all their lives in the bush and who felt a deep repugnance for the MPLA's urban elite, many members of which were of mixed-race or European origin. Unita had proved itself to be one of the most enduring guerrilla organizations in twentieth-century history. Moreover, the Luanda government had a shocking reputation for gross corruption. 'To notch up foreign bank accounts at the cost of the hunger, suffering, blood and death of others is a repugnant infamy', declared the country's Roman Catholic bishops, normally supportive of the government. On 28 August, reported *The Economist* of 4 September, 'President José Eduardo dos Santos marked his 57th birthday by raising his champagne glass and making a toast to "the fight against poverty and misery". In fact, alleviating human pain hardly features on the agenda of either of the bodies [MPLA and Unita] that wield power in Angola.'

On 15 October the UN Security Council passed a resolution to re-establish a UN presence in Angola through the opening of a UN Office in Angola (UNOA); its task was very broadly defined as being to 'liaise with the political, military, police and other civilian authorities with a view to exploring effective measurers for restoring peace, assisting the Angolan people in the area of capacity-building, humanitarian assistance, the promotion of human rights, and coordinating other activities'. The Angolan government took the view that UNOA, which had not yet been established at year's end, should confine itself to 'humanitarian activities and strengthening the government's human rights capacity'.

In December, at a conference of G-8 Foreign Ministers in Berlin, the British Foreign Secretary launched a scheme for curtailing the sale of stolen diamonds from regions such as Angola and the Democratic Republic of the Congo, where sales of illegal diamonds contributed to sustaining violent conflicts. The world's largest diamond company, De Beers, also announced that it was introducing measures to prevent the sale of illegal diamonds.

2. ZAMBIA—MALAWI—ZIMBABWE—BLNS STATES

i. ZAMBIA

CAPITAL: Lusaka   AREA: 750,000 sq km   POPULATION: 10,000,000 ('98)
OFFICIAL LANGUAGE: English   POLITICAL SYSTEM: presidential
HEAD OF STATE & GOVERNMENT: President Frederick Chiluba (since Nov '91)
RULING PARTY: Movement for Multi-Party Democracy (MMD)
MAIN IGO MEMBERSHIPS (NON-UN): OAU, COMESA, SADC, ACP, CWTH, NAM
CURRENCY: kwacha (end-'99 £1=K4,520.83, US$1=K2,805.00)
GNP PER CAPITA: US$330 by exchange-rate calculation, US$860 at PPP ('98)

'ALL is not well in Zambia', wrote *The Courier* (European Commission, Brussels) in a special country report in its issue for July/August. 'Structural adjustment is biting hard without bringing the benefits hoped for. Poverty and its associated ills—chronic malnutrition, poor amenities and bad health—affect 70 per cent of Zambians. The average family (eight members) food basket costs K228,000 [about £85] per month but most families earn less than K76,000 [about £30]. In the absence of jobs, the informal sector is mushrooming and so is the number of street children. AIDS affects 20 per cent of the population. As a result of AIDS and tuberculosis, many grandmothers on limited income have been forced to take responsibility for orphaned grandchildren. With 60 per cent of government revenues required to service the external debt burden, many of these problems are not being dealt with effectively.'

It was a quiet year for domestic politics, but the situation in two of Zambia's neighbours gave much cause for concern. The government had wisely not followed Zimbabwe's example of intervening in the civil war in the Democratic Republic of the Congo (see VII.1.i). Instead, President Chiluba played a leading role as a mediator in bringing the warring parties together and Lusaka provided the venue for the peace accord signed on 11 July. With Angola, relations were more difficult. In February the Angolan government accused Zambia of giving support to Unita with arms being smuggled across the border from a farm near the Zambezi river owned by a Zambian minister, Benjamin Mwila. Opposition parties used the incident to call for the resignation not only of Mr Mwila but also of the President and Vice-President.

A further twist to the alleged smuggling incident occurred at the end of February, when the Angolan government was widely blamed for a series of 16 bomb explosions in Lusaka which caused serious disruptions to the capital's water and electricity supplies. Another explanation, put forward by some opposition politicians and journalists, was that the bombs had been planted by the government as a means of uniting the country and providing an excuse to suppress dissent. A few days later two Zambians were arrested in connection with the bombings. On 9 March an article appeared in the *Lusaka Post* citing an unnamed military source as saying that the Zambian armed forces were incapable of withstanding an attack from Angola. Ten of the newspaper's staff, including the editor-in-chief, were arrested on a charge of espionage and the government obtained an injunction restraining the paper from publishing further articles on security issues.

On 14 April the President announced that an agreement had been signed with Angola to reduce tension and promote cooperation. The improvement in relations was carried further by another agreement signed on 17 June which reactivated the Joint Permanent Commission on Defence and Security. In December the Angolan government's offensive in south-eastern Angola (see VII.1.vi) brought a flood of refugees across the border into Zambia, and it was likely that there were armed Unita supporters among them.

The High Court in Lusaka on 17 September sentenced to death 59 soldiers charged with involvement in the 1997 coup attempt (see AR 1997, pp. 278-9).

ii. MALAWI

CAPITAL: Lilongwe   AREA: 118,500 sq km   POPULATION: 10,500,000 ('98)
OFFICIAL LANGUAGE: English   POLITICAL SYSTEM: presidential
HEAD OF STATE & GOVERNMENT: President Bakili Muluzi (since May '94)
RULING PARTIES: United Democratic Front (UDF) heads coalition with Malawi National Democratic Party (MNDP) & United Front for Multi-Party Democracy (UFMD)
MAIN IGO MEMBERSHIPS (NON-UN): OAU, COMESA, SADC, ACP, CWTH, NAM
CURRENCY: kwacha (end-'99 £1=MK74.83, US$1=MK46.43)
GNP PER CAPITA: US$200 by exchange-rate calculation, US$730 at PPP ('98)

AFTER decisively rejecting Dr Hastings Banda and his dictatorial policies in the general election of 1994 (see AR 1994, p. 302), 'Malawians', wrote *The Economist* , 'now take democracy and human rights for granted. But they are still horribly poor.' AIDS had cut average life expectancy to 43, and the country's first television station did not open until April 1999. The government could claim some reforms. It was encouraging small farmers to diversify and not be dependent on tobacco, the country's major export. Practical encouragement to improve productivity was given in the form of 'starter packs' containing fertilizers and hybrid seeds. The abolition of school fees and uniforms had almost doubled school enrolment. But by cutting subsidies it was impossible to continue Dr Banda's policy of cheap maize; and in the towns there was a serious increase in violent crime, so on balance many Malawians felt worse off.

Election preparations were hamstrung by confusion over registration, so that a postponement of several weeks was necessary. Eventually the presidential and legislative elections were held on 15 June. There were three candidates for the presidency: the incumbent President Bakili Muluzi of the southern-based United Democratic Front ((UDF), Gwanda Chakwanda for the coalition formed by the central-based Malawi Congress Party (MCP) and the northern-based Alliance for Democracy (AFORD) and Kamulepo Kalua of the Malawi Democratic Party (MDP). Between the parties there were no ideological differences: the issue was to decide who could govern the country most effectively.

The electorate decided to play safe. Mr Muluzi retained the presidency by winning 52.3 per cent of the vote, while Mr Chakwanda gained 45.3 per cent and Mr Kalua only 1.5 per cent. In the election for the 192 National Assembly seats (15 more than in 1994) the UDF won 93, MCP 66, AFORD 29 and independents 4. International observers declared the election to have been 'substantially free and fair', but political tension was reported to have remained high after the polls with outbreaks of political violence in the north.

iii. ZIMBABWE

CAPITAL: Harare   AREA: 390,000 sq km   POPULATION: 12,000,000 ('98)
OFFICIAL LANGUAGE: English   POLITICAL SYSTEM: presidential
HEAD OF STATE & GOVERNMENT: President Robert Mugabe (since Dec '87); previously Prime Minister (from April '80)
RULING PARTY: Zimbabwe African National Union–Patriotic Front (ZANU-PF)
MAIN IGO MEMBERSHIPS (NON-UN): OAU, COMESA, SADC, ACP, CWTH, NAM
CURRENCY: Zimbabwe dollar (end-'99 £1=Z$61.16, US$1=Z$37.95)
GNP PER CAPITA: US$610 by exchange-rate calculation, US$2,150 at PPP ('98)

ENDING its 19th year of continuous rule, Zimbabwe's ZANU-PF government appeared to be clinging to power rather than wielding it. An increasingly fragile economy, an inflation rate which topped 70.4 per cent in October, record unemployment and severe fuel and commodity shortages resulting from an acute foreign exchange crisis provoked widespread criticism within the country and outside it. Meanwhile the President, Robert Mugabe, blamed the economic crisis on a conspiracy of foreign interests seeking to destabilize Zimbabwe. This included a continued stand-off by the International Monetary Fund (IMF), which had halted payment of up to Z$6,500 million in loans pending improved government control over spending, inflation and the budget deficit.

The first crisis of the year involved the arrest on 12 January of Mark Chavunduka, editor of the independent newspaper the *Sunday Standard* . Having exposed an alleged attempted coup the previous month (see AR 1998, p. 303), Mr Chavunduka and a colleague were detained and subsequently tortured by military police. The illegality of the action provoked an appeal to the President by four Supreme Court judges seeking confirmation of the government's commitment to the rule of law. Mr Mugabe retaliated with a ferocious attack on the judiciary and called for the judges to resign. In the capital, Harare, a peaceful demonstration of lawyers and activists demanding 'zero tolerance for any erosion of human rights' was tear-gassed by riot police.

In March three US citizens were apprehended at Harare airport and charged with carrying arms and plotting to assassinate the President. When the visitors were eventually convicted on the single charge of attempting to board an aircraft while in possession of weapons, and sentenced to six months' imprisonment, the judge cited state torture of the detainees as a mitigating factor in the sentence.

The incidents signalled the government's frustration with the existing constitution, and presaged a full-scale review of the constitutional principles established at Lancaster House in December 1979 (see AR 1979, p. 257). Side-stepping the National Constitutional Assembly, an independent group of church and civil organizations established in 1997 to consider constitutional change, the government in May appointed its own Constitutional Commission, headed by Judge Godfrey Chidyausiku. At an estimated cost of Z$300 million, the 400 commissioners, either sitting MPs or individuals handpicked by ZANU-PF, sought to test the public view through a series of open consultations. But when draft proposals were tabled in November several commissioners claimed that dissenting views had been suppressed, particularly in relation to moves to curtail the powers of the President's Office. Mr Mugabe nevertheless chose to amend the proposals further, 'to reflect what the people want', and announced plans to submit the constitutional changes to a referendum early in 2000.

Despite the government's readiness to invoke the antiquated Law and Order (Maintenance) Act to threaten its critics and restrain fractious ZANU-PF MPs from what Mr Mugabe described as 'apostasy and treachery', open criticism of the government persisted. The most significant initiative was the formation in May of the Movement for Democratic Change (MDC), an attempt to construct a united front of workers, trade unions and peasant farmer organizations. The movement emanated from the Zimbabwe Congress of Trade Unions (ZCTU) which, though once closely allied to the ZANU-PF government, had in recent years successfully coordinated mass protest and industrial action (see AR 1997, p. 282; 1998, pp. 301-2). Three months later the MDC, led by ZCTU chairman Gibson Sibanda and secretary-general Morgan Tsvangirai, had already transformed itself into a plausible political party, the first such organization since independence to forge a viable national structure and constituency base. Mr

Tsvangirai, a leader of intelligence and charisma, claimed that the ZANU-PF government had lost the capacity and energy to govern, declaring: 'The entire lot must just be swept away.'

Joshua Nkomo, joint Vice-President and one of the pioneering figures of African nationalism, died on 1 July (see Pt XVIII: Obituary). As the focus of nationalist opposition among the Ndebele, Zimbabwe's second tribe, from the 1950s to the 1970s, he became leader of the Zimbabwe African People's Union (ZAPU), based in Matabeleland, eventually commanding a liberation army and universal support across a third of the country. Following the electoral victory of Mr Mugabe's Shona-based ZANU–PF in 1980, and five years of brutal suppression of ZAPU supporters, Mr Nkomo relinquished personal ambition and entered a government of national unity in 1987. The death of the man popularly known as 'Father Zimbabwe' risked reopening tribal animosities. Declaring that 'the giant has fallen', President Mugabe granted Mr Nkomo a hero's funeral and, in October, announced plans to compensate civilian victims of the notorious Gukurahundi military campaign of the 1980s. Meanwhile, in April, Simon Muzenda, the second Vice-President, was sued by the Zimbabwe Banking Corporation for bad debts of Z$3 million.

The single most costly, and unpopular, government policy was Zimbabwe's continuing intervention in the war in the Democratic Republic of the Congo (see VII.1.i). Despite rumours in June of moves towards peace, 10,000 Zimbabwean troops remained deployed in support of President Laurent Kabila, at an estimated cost of more than Z$2.3 million per day. In his budget statement of 21 October the Minister of Finance, Dr Herbert Murerwa, allocated Z$8,200 million to defence spending, an increase of 58 per cent on the previous year. The budget also provided for a 60 per cent increase in expenditure on health and for an AIDS levy of 3 per cent of taxation revenue. Zimbabwe's AIDS pandemic had reduced the country's population growth-rate from 3.3 per cent in 1980 to close on 1 per cent 20 years later and was now killing some 1,700 Zimbabweans each week. The budget deficit for the coming year was optimistically forecast at 3.8 per cent of GDP.

At the end of the year renewed threats of mass industrial action by ZCTU prompted an unbudgeted 80 per cent salary hike for all civil service workers, an increase of 192 per cent in the salaries of government ministers and MPs, and a proposal to pay substantial allowances to traditional chiefs and village headmen. The move was ridiculed by the MDC as a desperate attempt by the 75-year-old President to buy popularity in advance of the forthcoming constitutional referendum and the general election due in April 2000.

iv. BOTSWANA—LESOTHO—NAMIBIA—SWAZILAND

Botswana
CAPITAL: Gaborone   AREA: 580,000 sq km   POPULATION: 1,750,000 ('98)
OFFICIAL LANGUAGE: English   POLITICAL SYSTEM: presidential democracy
HEAD OF STATE & GOVERNMENT: President Festus Mogae (since March '98)
RULING PARTY: Botswana Democratic Party (BDP)
MAIN IGO MEMBERSHIPS (NON-UN): OAU, SADC, SACU, ACP, CWTH, NAM
CURRENCY: pula (end-'99 £1=P7.47, US$1=P4.63)
GNP PER CAPITA: US$3,600 by exchange-rate calculation, US$8,310 at PPP ('98)

Lesotho
CAPITAL: Maseru   AREA: 30,000 sq km   POPULATION: 2,400,000 ('98)
OFFICIAL LANGUAGES: English & Sesotho   POLITICAL SYSTEM: monarchy
HEAD OF STATE: King Letsie III (since Jan '96)
RULING PARTY: Lesotho Congress for Democracy (LCD)
HEAD OF GOVERNMENT: Bethuel Pakalitha Mosisili, Prime Minister (since June '98)
MAIN IGO MEMBERSHIPS (NON-UN): OAU, COMESA, SADC, SACU, ACP, CWTH, NAM
CURRENCY: maloti (end-'99 £1=M9.92, US$1=M6.16)
GNP PER CAPITA: US$570 by exchange-rate calculation, US$2,320 at PPP ('98)

Namibia
CAPITAL: Windhoek   AREA: 824,000 sq km   POPULATION: 1,600,000 ('98)
OFFICIAL LANGUAGES: Afrikaans & English   POLITICAL SYSTEM: presidential democracy
HEAD OF STATE: President Sam Nujoma (since March '90)
RULING PARTY: South West Africa People's Organization (SWAPO)
HEAD OF GOVERNMENT: Hage Geingob, Prime Minister (since March '90)
MAIN IGO MEMBERSHIPS (NON-UN): OAU, SADC, SACU, ACP, CWTH, NAM
CURRENCY: Namibian dollar/SA rand (end-'99 £1=N$9.92, US$1=N$6.16)
GNP PER CAPITA: US$1,940 by exchange-rate calculation, US$4,950 at PPP ('98)

Swaziland
CAPITAL: Mbabane   AREA: 17,350 sq km   POPULATION: 988,000 ('98)
OFFICIAL LANGUAGES: English & Siswati   POLITICAL SYSTEM: monarchy
HEAD OF STATE: King Mswati III (since '86)
HEAD OF GOVERNMENT: Sibusiso Barnabas Dlamini, Prime Minister (since July '96)
MAIN IGO MEMBERSHIPS (NON-UN): OAU, COMESA, SADC, SACU, ACP, CWTH, NAM
CURRENCY: lilangeni/emalangeni (end-'99 £1=E9.92, US$1=E6.16)
GNP PER CAPITA: US$1,400 by exchange-rate calculation, US$3,580 at PPP ('98)

THE year brought good and bad news for the southern African region. Although the conflicts in Angola and the Democratic Republic of the Congo (DRC) had, by year's end, drawn in Rwanda and Uganda from outside of the 14-member Southern African Development Community (SADC), along with the SADC member-states Zimbabwe, Zambia and Namibia (see VII.1.i), the region recorded positive economic growth during 1999. The statistics showed that SADC states had higher growth rates from the mid-1990s than the rest of sub-Saharan Africa.

Positive moves were also made to promote regional integration through the SADC. In September the South African parliament ratified a ground-breaking regional free trade deal due to come into effect on 1 January 2000. Covering the nearly R18,000 million of trade within the SADC, the agreement provided that goods with 10 per cent or less in tariffs would be duty free within six months. This applied to 60 per cent of goods traded. A second list of goods would ultimately become duty free within, officially, eight years, though officials expected this to be more like ten.

There had been some delay in the ratification of the SADC trade deal signed originally in 1997 (see AR 1997, p. 283), as a result of South Africa's focus on the negotiation of its free trade, development and cooperation agreement with the European Union (EU) ultimately completed in October 1999. This agreement covered 10,000 products and provided for the phased removal of tariffs on 95 per cent of South Africa's exports to the EU over ten years and on 86 per cent of EU exports to South Africa over 12 years. Conclusion of the accord was held up in its final stages of negotiation by wrangling over the use of the names port and sherry by South African producers (see AR 1998, p. 312).

There had also been related delays to the negotiation of a new revenue-sharing formula between the five Southern African Customs Union (SACU) members—South Africa, Botswana, Namibia, Swaziland and Lesotho. Negotiations had commenced in 1993 but had not been concluded by the end of 1999. As a result of the EU-South Africa agreement, the SACU revenue pool was expected to shrink by between R1,900 million and 3,500 million annually. Swaziland's share of SACU revenue was estimated to provide more than 50 per cent of total government income, Lesotho's more than 40 per cent, Namibia's some 30 per cent and Botswana's over 10 per cent.

The problems of security rivalry within SADC and its Organ on Politics, Defence and Security (see AR 1997, pp. 282-3) were also reportedly resolved as the result of a deal struck in Mbabane in October. The Organ was to be more closely integrated with overall SADC structures rather than acting as a separate summit and bureaucracy. Moreover, democracy appeared to have taken root during the region. Four countries staged successful multi-party elections in 1999—South Africa (see VII.3), Mozambique (see VII.1.v), Namibia and Botswana (see below).

Less positively, it was reported that over two-thirds of the SADC potential labour force remained unemployed. This was due to a lack of education, a low skills base, insufficient economic growth and ongoing regional conflicts. Estimates put the figure of the economically active population in SADC states at 50.7 million, but of these only 11.1 million were formally employed. The region had a population of about 180 million people, of whom an estimated 30 per cent lived in 'abject poverty'. These conditions were exacerbated by the developmental challenges posed by burgeoning rates of HIV/AIDS. The virus was expected to reduce life expectancy in southern Africa from an average of 59 in the early 1990s to just 45 between 2005-10.

BOTSWANA. An estimated 390,000 voters of the 800,000 eligible went to the polls on 16 October to elect a 40-member National Assembly, as well as local councillors, in the eighth general election since the country gained independence from Britain in 1966. Nine political parties registered for the elections, in which the party that polled the most votes in the 40 constituencies formed the government and appointed a President from among its members.

The ruling Botswana Democratic Party (BDP), which had governed the country since independence under the leadership of President Festus Mogae, was returned to power, winning 33 of the 40 seats, up from 26 in the 1994 election. The Botswana National Front (BNF) led by Dr Kenneth Koma, which had won 13 seats in 1994 but contested the latest event with only two seats after 11 of its MPs had broken away in 1998 to form the Botswana Congress Party (BCP), won six sets. The BCP, led by former BNF deputy leader Michael Dingake, managed to win only one seat. Mr Dingake had been a prominent members of the African National Congress in South Africa during the 1960s, spending 15 years in gaol.

Following the election, history was made in southern Africa in October by the appointment of a woman, Lena Mohohlo, to head the country's central bank. She replaced Baledzi Gaolathe, who had been appointed as Minister of Finance and Development Planning in the new cabinet. A number of women occupied senior positions in Botswana's government structures. One of Ms Mohohlo's deputies at the bank was a woman, and there were eight women among the BDP MPs, five of whom were in President Mogae's cabinet.

Worsening regional relations in southern Africa, in which Botswana was seen to have sided with South Africa against Zimbabwe, were reflected in the imposition in September by National Railways of Zimbabwe (NRZ) of tariff charges of up to 300 per cent per metric tonne on cargo to and from Botswana. The move was expected to cost Botswana Railways up to US$3.5 million in lost revenue during the 1999/2000 financial year.

In December the International Court of Justice at The Hague ruled in favour of Botswana in a territorial dispute with Namibia over an island along the Chobe river separating the two countries (see also XIV.1.i). The Court found by 11 votes to four that Kasikili/Sedudu island formed part of the territory of Botswana. The two countries had taken the case to the Court in 1996. Botswana had occupied the island in 1991 following Namibian independence in March 1990, though the origins of the dispute dated back to the colonial period. Namibia said that it would abide by the Court's ruling.

Botswana remained one of the countries worst hit by the HIV/AIDS epidemic. In September the UN Development Programme called for a more aggressive campaign in the fight against the disease. According to UN AIDS figures, more than 20 per cent of people between the ages of 15 and 49 were living with HIV or AIDS in Botswana. The number of children estimated to be infected had doubled between 1994 to 1997, to 7,300 among a population of just 1.7 million.

In October a pilot with the Air Botswana national airline, Chris Phatswe, who was reportedly suffering from AIDS, killed himself and destroyed the airline's fleet by flying an empty passenger aircraft into two others at Gaborone's Sir Seretse Khama airport. He had earlier been suspended from the airline on health grounds.

Following its election victory, the BNP promised to continue to adhere to its economic policies, including the maintenance of large foreign cash reserves to protect against droughts and food shortages. The country's reserves totalled US$5,600 million by the end of 1999, made possible by its diamond mines, which generated 80 per cent of export revenue and 30 per cent of GDP. However, the mining industry employed only 8,600 people, or 3.6 per cent of the workforce, compared with around 100,000 in the civil service. Severe drought hit the economy hard during 1999, most districts reporting a deficit of cereals by July.

Fears, too, remained over the financial health of Hyundai Motor Distributors (HMD), employing 900 workers at its assembly plant in Gaborone. HMD was indebted to the Botswana Development Corporation to the tune of US$23 million. The anticipated collapse of HMD was expected to have a dramatic impact on an economy already suffering from 20 per cent unemployment.

LESOTHO. South African and Botswanan peace-keeping troops withdrew from Lesotho in May amid concerns about the risk of leaving a security vacuum in a politically-charged environment. South Africa and Botswana had intervened militarily in September 1998 under the aegis of the Southern African Development Community (SADC), following violent opposition protest over alleged government rigging of the May 1998 election and an army mutiny which threatened to develop into a coup (see AR 1998, p. 306). The deployment had been resisted by elements of the Lesotho army, and areas of the capital, Maseru, were destroyed in looting before peace could be restored by the 3,000-strong intervention force.

Following the withdrawal, a small contingent of SADC troops remained in Lesotho to retrain the Lesotho army. A rapid reaction force of South African and Botswanan troops was also put on standby should instability re-emerge in the run-up to general elections in 2000. However, despite high-level representation from the ruling Lesotho Congress for Democracy (LCD), the multi-party Lesotho Interim Political Authority (IPA), established following the September 1998 violence, moved very slowly in preparing the country for elections. In September President Thabo Mbeki of South Africa said that it would be impossible to hold elections in Lesotho by March 2000 because the electoral system, security arrangements and other issues had not been finalized. He noted that the government and political parties in Lesotho had accepted the postponement. Lesotho's politicians had originally agreed that elections would be held within 18 months from October 1998. The Commonwealth secretary-general was charged with appointing a group of experts to look into the matter and finalize a date (see XI.3.i).

It was hoped that early elections would stem a loss of the foreign investor confidence necessary for economic reconstruction and growth. The construction phase of the Highlands Water Project, being built to transport water to South Africa, was scheduled for completion in 2003. Located 60 kilometres east of Maseru in the upper Senqunyane river catchment area, the project had become one of the largest employers in a country which faced high unemployment. Some 25 per cent of the male labour force worked in South Africa. The looting in September 1998 had cost 2,600 jobs, around 15 per cent of all employment in the commercial and industrial sectors.

The Ministry of Health noted that by the end of 1998 there were 7,317 reported AIDS cases in Lesotho, with 3,242 reported in 1998, a 30 per cent increase over the year. This was seen as a substantial under-estimation, however. It was anticipated that AIDS would lower life expectancy from 54 in 1998 to 45 by 2010.

NAMIBIA. Around 62 per cent of the Namibia's 878,000 registered voters went to the polls on 30 November to elect a President and a 72-member National Assembly. Although the newly-formed Congress of Democrats (CoD) hoped to put up a serious challenge to the ruling South West African Peoples Organization (SWAPO) of President Sam Nujoma, SWAPO swept to its biggest victory yet, winning 77 per cent and 76 per cent of the votes in the presidential and parliamentary polls respectively. Nine parties contested the election, the third since independence in 1990.

The result was surprising in view of much rhetorical opposition to Mr Nujoma's rule stemming from the high costs of Namibia's military intervention in the Democratic Republic of the Congo (DRC) on the side of President Laurent Kabila, allegations of corruption, low economic growth, high unemployment and few job prospects, the tense security situation in the Caprivi Strip to the north-east, and the controversy surrounding the President's change in the constitution enabling him to stand for a third term. Amid opposition allegations of vote-rigging, Mr Nujoma's main presidential opponent, the CoD's Ben Ulenga, a SWAPO dissident and former high commissioner to Britain, polled just 11 per cent, 1 per cent more than Katuutire Kaura of the Democratic Turnhalle Alliance (DTA). Mr Ulenga, once a member of SWAPO's central committee and deputy environment minister, had resigned his diplomatic post in London in 1998 and had formed the CoD in March.

In July a call by the Namibian National Society for Human Rights (NSHR) for the establishment of a truth commission to examine human rights abuses during the independence struggle was sharply criticized by SWAPO. It was alleged that over 4,000 Namibians who were in exile with SWAPO remained unaccounted for.

At least 18 Namibian soldiers died in the war in the DRC in 1999. Namibia had sent a force estimated at 2,000 personnel in 1998 costing the country US$150,000 a day. According to the International Committee of the Red Cross (ICRC), 11 soldiers were also being held as prisoners-of-war in the Rwandan capital, Kigali.

The cost of fighting in the DRC was expected to push up the budget deficit for 1998/99, while real economic growth was anticipated to remain low at 2.5 per cent during the year. A draft report from the Presidential Commission on Education, Culture and Training stated that by the year 2010 Namibia would have produced more than 200,000 secondary school leavers who would not find gainful employment. Unemployment grew to about 35 per cent in 1999, or 550,000 economically active people, 70 per cent of whom were rural women. The country's labour force was currently increasing by around 4 per cent a year, while formal employment growth was less than 2.3 per cent annually.

In September it was reported that Namibia's fisheries industry, the country's third highest export earner after diamonds and agriculture and employing up to 7,000 people, was under threat due to high levels of bacteria in its exports. In 1998 the industry had recorded growth of 18.6 per cent.

There were concerns that the HIV/AIDS epidemic would set back human resource development efforts, given expectations that many of those trained would fall victim to the disease. The infection rate in major population areas was estimated to be 35 per cent, though the government did not possess a visible programme for dealing with the crisis. Namibia's HIV infections were poised to break the 200,000 mark by the start of 2000, in a population of 1.6 million. The disease had cut an estimated five years off the average life expectancy in Namibia. In 1989 most Namibians were expected to live to the age of 57; by 1997 this had dropped to 52.

A flare-up of secessionist violence in Caprivi in August left the political situation tense in an area bordering on Angola, Botswana, Zambia and Zimbabwe. Historically, the region had been under the sway of the Lozi Barotseland kingdom in Zambia. Secessionists led by the Caprivi Liberation Army (CLA), aiming at incorporation within a revived Barotseland, claimed that the region had been marginalized by the Ovambo-dominated SWAPO, which also stood accused of dabbling in the region's ethnic politics with the aim of weakening the minority Mafwe influence in eastern Caprivi.

The Caprivi violence had regional security implications. There were reports of activity in the area by Angolan Unita forces, while Botswana was the destination of many Caprivi exiles, including CLA leader Mishake Moyongo, and Zambia had links with Barotseland. In August the leader of the Barotse Patriotic Front, Imasiku Mutangelwa, fled to the Lusaka residence of the South African high commissioner after being summoned to police headquarters in connection with his alleged remarks supporting secessionist violence in Caprivi. He was later handed over to the Zambian authorities.

Unita's stepping-up of its military activities in Caprivi during the year was interpreted as both a warning to the Windhoek government not to contemplate direct military intervention on the side of its old allies in Luanda, and also to recruit support for its own rebel campaign. In November Namibia granted the Angolan government access to its territory for launching attacks against Unita. In December, moreover, President Nujoma committed his forces to operations against Unita in Angola to assist in Luanda's big push against Jonas Savimbi's movement (see VII.1.vi). This resulted in scores of refugees in the northern areas of the country, and was likely to have a serious and negative impact on the region's tourist industry, which provided US$210 million in receipts in 1997.

A Namibian government project to extend the country's railway network to northern parts of the country and link it with neighbouring Angola commenced in 1999 and was scheduled for completion by 2005. Costing US$66 million and co-funded by the Kuwaiti government, the line would commence at Tsumeb and head for Ondangwa before proceeding to Oshakati, while a final section would link Ondangwa to Oshikango on the Angolan border.

SWAZILAND. Swaziland continued to stumble between political repression and reform. In September Bheki Makhuba, the editor of Swaziland's independent *Times on Sunday*, appeared in court on charges of defamation after writing an article about King Mswati's new fiancée. His arrest followed a story in his newspaper in September which said that the latest bride of King Mswati, chosen at a Reed Dance ceremony, was a 'high school dropout'. This was interpreted as meaning that she posed a risk of HIV/AIDS to the King in a country where around 30 per cent of Swazis were estimated to be living with the illness. Soon after the publication of the story, Mr Makhuba was forced to resign from his post.

During the year the government drafted legislation for a tough Media Bill on defamation of character. This led to the media rights watchdog *Reporters sans Frontières* (RSF) asking the French government to broach the subject of press freedom in Swaziland during an official visit by King Mswati to France in September. In addition, at least two journalists were allegedly threatened and forced to leave their posts on 28 October following an apparent illegal strike by workers at the Swaziland Television Broadcasting Corporation (STBC).

In May Swaziland's Constitutional Review Commission (CRC), appointed by King Mswati, started six months of canvassing people's views on constitutional issues. The 25-member CRC aimed at visiting 350 chiefdoms to receive submissions from individual citizens on the desirability of multi-party system versus traditional or conventional law. The CRC and the King were to interpret the results and the wishes of the people in preparing a draft constitution, which was to be presented to the people at a national meeting in 2000 prior to its adoption. Swaziland did not have a written constitution, the kingdom being governed under a decree made and passed in 1973 by King Mswati's predecessor, King Sobhuza II. The decree banned all political activity and organizations.

The Swazi central bank reported that the economy grew by just 2.3 per cent in 1998, compared to 3.7 per cent in 1997, with a population growth rate of 2.7 per cent. Direct foreign investment had declined, amounting to an estimated US$33.75 million in 1998. The report noted that government expenditure and expansion was not being matched by increased revenue, resulting in a budget deficit.

3. SOUTH AFRICA

CAPITAL: Pretoria   AREA: 1,220,000 sq km   POPULATION: 41,000,000 ('98)
OFFICIAL LANGUAGES: Afrikaans, English & nine African languages
POLITICAL SYSTEM: presidential democracy
HEAD OF STATE & GOVERNMENT: President Thabo Mbeki (since June '99)
RULING PARTIES: African National Congress (ANC) & Inkatha Freedom Party (IFP)
MAIN IGO MEMBERSHIPS (NON-UN): OAU, SADC, SACU, CWTH, NAM
CURRENCY: rand (end-'99 £1=R9.92, US$1=R6.16)
GNP PER CAPITA: US$2,880 by exchange-rate calculation, US$6,990 at PPP ('98)

THE inauguration of Thabo Mbeki as South Africa's second democratically-elected President on 16 June brought down the curtain on the rule of Nelson Mandela, who had governed since the first democratic elections in April 1994. For many South Africans this provided a moment to take stock on the accomplishments of the past five years and the challenges that lay ahead.

Elections to the 400-member National Assembly on 2 June enhanced the dominance of the African National Congress (ANC), which won 266 seats with a vote share of 66.4 per cent (compared with 62.6 per cent in 1994) and thus fell just one seat short of the two-thirds majority required to amend the constitution. A distant second place was taken by the mainly white Democratic Party (DP), whose 38 seats and 9.8 per cent vote share were achieved at the expense of the New National Party (NNP), successor to the ruling party of the apartheid era, which slumped to 28 seats and 6.9 per cent. The main surprise of the contest was the political survival of the mainly Zulu Inkatha Freedom Party (IFP), which retained third place in the Assembly with 34 seats and 8.6 per cent. The multiracial United Democratic Movement (UDM) won 14 seats and the remaining 20 seats were distributed among eight minor parties.

The ANC achieved an equally crushing victory in simultaneous elections for the nine provincial assemblies, retaining power in seven (with increased majorities in five) and also gaining ground in Kwazulu-Natal and Western Cape. The IFP remained the largest party in Kwazulu-Natal, while in Western Cape the ANC overtook the NNP to become narrowly the largest single party, but remained in opposition to a controversial coalition of the NNP and the DP.

The new Assembly formally elected Mr Mbeki as the country's President on 14 June, his nomination by the ANC being unopposed. Following his inauguration, an enlarged cabinet announced on 17 June continued the previous ANC-IFP coalition, although IFP leader Chief Mangosuthu Buthelezi turned down the post of Deputy President (which went to Jacob Zuma of the ANC) and instead continued as Home Affairs Minister. Also retained in their posts, to the satisfaction of the business community, were the white Ministers of Finance and of Trade and Industry, respectively Tevor Manuel and Alec Erwin, both members of the ANC. Shortly after the elections the ANC had entered into a formal alliance with the small Indian-led Minority Front (MF), whose single seat in the new Assembly gave the ANC the two-thirds majority needed to enact constitutional change without the support of any other party.

Mr Mbeki came to office promising an African renaissance for the continent. In spite of such rhetoric and high expectations of the role to be played by Africa's new leadership generation which he epitomized, South Africa's domestic success would remain the prime determinant of its foreign relations. Here two major and related challenges were evident during 1999: first, the need for South Africa to consolidate its liberal democracy and at the same time reform its economy to become globally competitive; second, the imperative to strengthen the state's ability to provide essential services. Many questioned whether President Mbeki could maintain domestic stability through the management of the social and political costs of necessary economic reform. To these issues could be added a central foreign policy task with immediate domestic implications, namely the need to stabilize a weak and rough regional neighbourhood.

The five years of the Mandela government had apparently left South Africa comparatively well-equipped, however, to handle these challenges. It possessed a strong and non-belligerent democracy, a highly-developed financial and physical infrastructure, and sensible, sound and conservative economic policies. However, not only was there an enormous apartheid-related backlog of development, but also the economy continued to fail to perform to the high expectations. After just 0.2 per cent real economic growth in 1998, estimates for 1999 were revised downwards from the initial expectations three years earlier of 6 per cent. In October Finance Minister Manuel predicted that the growth rate would reach 0.9 per cent during 1999.

In September the UN Conference on Trade and Development (UNCTAD) reported that the level of foreign direct investment in South Africa had plunged to about US$371 million in 1998—four times lower than 1997, dragged down by a slowdown in privatization-related transactions. This fall placed South Africa behind countries such as Nigeria, Egypt, Tunisia, Algeria, Zimbabwe and Angola (the top African direct investment recipients) and contributed to an overall decline of $1,100 million in foreign direct investment in the African continent to $8,300 million in 1998.

By 1999 black economic empowerment groups had effective control or a substantial interest in 53 companies listed on the Johannesburg Stock Exchange (JSE) with a market capitalization of more than R111,000 million. These groups had taken three years, from 1995 to 1998, to increase their stake on the JSE from zero to 10.3 per cent—compared with the 20 years that it took Afrikaners to achieve 10 per cent control. Yet South African income patterns remained skewed. The R38,000 million collected in income tax in 1998 came from only 1.6 million taxpayers. During 1999 the South African population was expected to reach 44.7 million, of which 77.4 per cent were black, 11.7 per cent white, 8.4 per cent coloured and 2.5 per cent Asian.

The Bank of England's decision in May to auction about half of its gold bullion holdings on the open market (see II.1.i), together with the International Monetary Fund's intention to sell 10 per cent of its gold stocks, combined to produce a major fall in the price of gold. This had a devastating impact on the South African gold industry. Already in July the gold price had dropped to a 20-year low of $260 an ounce. This resulted in massive retrenchments and mine closures in South Africa, although the decision in October by the G-7 nations to suspend the sale of gold in order to finance debt relief for the poorest countries provided some reprieve.

South Africa's economic challenges were compounded by the developing AIDS crisis. Life expectancy was expected to fall to 48 years in 2010, from 68 years under pre-AIDS projections, and the percentage of the workforce infected to rise from 11 per cent in 1999 to 18 per cent in 2005. By 1999 there were an estimated 50,000 new AIDS cases each month. Among the 20-29 male age group, the infection rate was estimated to be 40 per cent.

South Africa's potential pitfalls also included the state's low capacity to deliver, particularly in the criminal justice sector. So-called 'top 20' crimes, which included murder, robbery with aggravating circumstances, rape and burglary, increased by over 5 per cent between January and October compared with the same period in 1998. From the time of his first speech to parliament as President in June, Mr Mbeki made fighting crime a major priority. This served to boost morale amongst the 120,000-strong South African police service. A shift in emphasis from the policing side to the Directorate of Special Prosecutions reinforced the legal rather than the sharp end of the criminal justice system. The formation of an FBI-type Special Operations Directorate (known as the 'Scorpions') was also viewed as a positive long-term development.

The country's relatively low level of constitutional consolidation was seen as a further impediment to growth and delivery. This difficulty was exacerbated by the apparent ideological confusion among members of the ruling ANC/South African Communist Party (SACP) and the allied Congress of South African Trade Unions (COSATU). The conservative Growth, Employment and Redistribution (GEAR) economic policy (see AR 1998, pp. 309-10), to which Mr Mbeki's government remained wedded, was seen as incompatible with certain SACP/COSATU positions. In the course of the year the President scolded unionists and Communists at a number of their meetings.

In April the government statistics office provided figures showing that around 180,000 jobs had been lost nationally in 1998 through retrenchments and closures. By the start of 1999 there were almost 500,000 fewer jobs than was the case in 1994. The rate of unemployment was estimated to be 33 per cent, and was climbing at 3 per cent annually. In 1999 an estimated 38,700 jobs were lost in the third quarter alone. In December the government promulgated the Employment Equity Bill, which was designed to legislate affirmative action and greater racial and gender equality in the workplace, but which was widely seen as a deterrent to greater employment.

The establishment by President Mbeki of a Presidential Office with 330-plus personnel and his control over key appointments came under increasing focus during the year, being interpreted as showing a desire to centralize control. His unwillingness to entertain criticism also came under scrutiny. Yet the President's Office was not averse to equating condemnation of the government's record as often being racially-motivated attacks on the democratic order or the liberation struggle. These issues came to the fore in a public spat between the press and the President's chief of communications, Parks Mankahlana, in December.

In the foreign policy domain, the record of South Africa during the early days of the Mbeki presidency was characterized both by some external successes and by difficulties in trying to resolve bitter conflicts in the Democratic Republic of the Congo (DRC) and in Angola. Under President Mandela there had been little coherence to South Africa's foreign policy, which meandered between a need to repay old debts of assistance to the ANC and adherence to the *realpolitik* of encouraging deeper and wider trade and investment relations with traditional, largely Western allies. The establishment of a concerted policy process was complicated by Mr Mandela's virtually canonized international personality and exacerbated by the reorganization of the South African bureaucracy to allow integration with non-statutory elements.

In Africa, South Africa had been, under President Mandela, sensitive about providing leadership, preferring to kowtow to regional sensitivities inherent in South Africa's relative economic and political giantism. The South African economy was nearly four times the size of the rest of the other 13 member states of the Southern African Development Community (SADC) combined. By contrast, South African businesses had taken full advantage of the end of apartheid, dramatically expanding business links with Africa, at times much to the chagrin of local producers. In 1994-98 South Africa's annual trade with the rest of Africa rose 130 per cent, from R11,000 million to R25,000 million. With regard to trade with SADC countries, the balance was heavily biased in favour of South Africa. South African imports from SADC jumped sharply to R2,200 million in 1998 from just R611 million in 1990. while exports from South Africa to the other SADC members surged to R15,600 million (11 per cent of total exports).

Little had been achieved in the Mandela years towards remedying Africa's 'arc of instability', running from Sierra Leone in the west through Angola and the Great Lakes region to Sudan in the east. As a result, President Mbeki (a former head of the ANC's department of international relations) made foreign policy a priority issue early in his presidency. The appointment of former Health Minister Nkosazana Dlamini-Zuma, a Mbeki loyalist, as the Minister of Foreign Affairs was perceived as placing the portfolio squarely within the control of the presidency and out of the hands of the Foreign Ministry.

Dr Dlamini-Zuma led a strong South African diplomatic attempt to end the war in the DRC (see VII.1.i). However, although some progress was made initially, by the end of the year it appeared that these efforts had fallen prey to entrenched regional and ethnic interests. The pattern of South African arms sales in the region showed the extent to which Pretoria was losing its status as a regional honest broker. In September it was announced in parliament by the chairman of the National Conventional Arms Control Committee (NCACC), Professor Kader Asmal, that South Africa had supplied more than R60 million worth of arms to countries involved in the Congo conflict, although exports of weapons had been banned since the war started afresh in August 1998. Rwanda had been the largest customer, spending more than R30 million on armoured personnel carriers, guns and ammunition. The DRC had spent R1.8 million on magazines for weapons.

In the other direction, major arms purchases by South Africa were announced on 15 September at a cost of R21,300 million over eight years. The purchases included nine dual-seater Gripen and 12 Hawk aircraft from British Aerospace/Saab, to replace South Africa's existing Cheetah and Impala aircraft (options being taken on a further 12 Hawks and 19 single-seater Gripens); 30 light utility helicopters from the Italian manufacturer Augusta, to replace the French-built Alouette helicopters in service for over 40 years; four patrol corvettes from the German Frigate Consortium, to replace the navy's nine strike craft; and three submarines from the same consortium, to replace the navy's three 30-year-old Daphne-class submarines. If options to procure additional equipment were exercised, the total equipment cost would rise by R8,500 million to R29,800 million over 12 years. Industrial participation projects linked to the purchases would reportedly yield significant economic benefits for South Africa.

In October South Africa signed a trade, development and cooperation agreement with the 15-member European Union (EU) following four years of tough negotiations. Represented by Trade and Industry Minister Alec Erwin, South Africa hoped that the agreement would result in economic growth, while the EU's development commissioner, Poul Nielson, described it as a symbol of the commitment of the world's biggest trading bloc to post-apartheid South Africa. The deal provided for the establishment of a free trade area between the parties over 12 years, during which the EU would grant duty-free status to 95 per cent of imports from South Africa, while South Africa would cut its tariffs on 86 per cent of its imports from the EU. South Africa's neighbours in the region were, however, concerned that the arrangement would have a negative impact on their trade relations.

South Africa continued to play an important and high-profile role outside Africa, especially in the World Trade Organization (WTO) and the United Nations (see XI.1; XI.2.ii). It was announced in September that South Africa was joining a new group established to pursue discussions on key policy issues between the Group of Seven (G-7) countries and the largest emerging market economies. To be known as the Group of 20 (G-20), the new initiative was intended to provide a forum for discussion on financial regulatory issues as well as issues connected to reform of the international financial architecture (see XI.3.iii). In November South Africa hosted the 32nd Commonwealth summit in Durban (see XI.3.i).

VIII SOUTH ASIA AND INDIAN OCEAN

1. IRAN—AFGHANISTAN—CENTRAL ASIAN REPUBLICS

i. IRAN

CAPITAL: Tehran   AREA: 1,650,000 sq km   POPULATION: 63,500,000 ('98)
NATIONAL LANGUAGE: Farsi (Persian)   POLITICAL SYSTEM: Islamic republic
SPIRITUAL GUIDE: Ayatollah Seyed Ali Khamenei (since June '89)
HEAD OF STATE & GOVERNMENT: President Mohammed Khatami (since Aug '97)
MAIN IGO MEMBERSHIPS (NON-UN):: OPEC, ECO, CP, OIC, NAM
CURRENCY: rial (end-'99 official rate £1=Rls2,824.50, US$1=Rls1,752.50)
GNP PER CAPITA: US$1,770 by exchange-rate calculation

MOHAMMED Khatami's presidency remained secure and his popularity with the young people in Iran increased during the year. Yet the hardliners opposing him also had their successes in 1999, so that the reformists made only partial gains overall in their struggle to command the levers of political power. The local government elections on 26 February represented a heavy defeat for the hardliners, who took only 15 per cent of the vote against 85 per cent for independents and reformists, while more than 300 women won seats on the new regional councils. However, how much real authority would ultimately reside with the provincial assemblies was unclear.

Qorbanali Dorri Najafabadi resigned as Information Minister in February, following an admission by his department the previous month that its intelligence agents had been involved in recent deaths of dissidents. The episode suggested that the President might have an opportunity to begin to rid the political system of its many non-democratic institutions and of officially-sponsored political violence. An attempt by the conservative group in the *Majlis* on 1 May to impeach the Minister of Culture, Ataollah Mohajerani, failed by 14 votes, but a long-running campaign to rein in press freedom brought prosecution of many reformist writers and editors.

In reaction in particular to the closure of the reformist *Salaam* newspaper, students of Tehran University held a protest meeting on 9 July, which led to several days of bloody clashes between conservative groups, including security forces, and the reform-minded students. The troubles were ended only by the intervention of President Khatami—to the political discomfort of the hardliners—when in July the chief of the Tehran police was dismissed. The student riots shocked Iran, but fortunately did not lead to any domestic political instability. In May the government's grip on power was also tested when foreign tourists were abducted by bandits in south-eastern Iran, the incident indicating a lack of security in peripheral regions of the country.

The conservative forces were strongly entrenched within the political system and continued to fight back against the liberals in the regime. In November the reformist former Minister of the Interior and newspaper publisher, Abdollah Nouri, was sent to prison. Other newspapers that supported President Khatami also suffered closures and arrests of staff.

Political opposition from outside the regime was limited, though the Mujaheddine Khalq (MK) organization claimed in January that it had hit Ministry of Information offices with mortar bombs and in April assassinated an Iranian army general. In retaliation, there were hard-hitting Iranian attacks on MK bases in Iraq during the first half of June.

In foreign affairs, the Iranian government concentrated on improving links with regional states, notably the Arab countries of the Persian Gulf and Arabian peninsula. Prince Sultan bin Abdul Aziz, the Saudi Arabian Minister of Defence, made a formal visit to Iran on 13 May to meet Iranian counterpart Ali Shamkhani and senior political figures, including Spiritual Guide Ali Khamenei and President Khatami. Discussions took place on Arab-Iranian cooperation in regional affairs and laid the basis for President Khatami's state visit to Saudi Arabia on 15 May (see also V.3.i). Iranian military manœuvres in the Gulf in February and September and retaliatory Gulf Cooperation Council exercises did little to capitalize on this diplomatic activity or calm tensions. No progress was made in the year on the vital issue of settlement of Iran's dispute with the United Arab Emirates over sovereignty of Abu Musa and the Tunbs islands. Problems with Syria over the latter's debts, with Iraq over the return of prisoners-of-war and Iranian air raids on Iraqi territory, and with the Palestinian Authority over treatment of Islamic organizations provided other areas of Irano-Arab friction.

Relations with Turkey were unstable. A visit to Tehran in January by the then speaker of the Turkish Grand National Assembly, Himet Çetin, was followed by severe tension over Turkish claims in May that Iran was supporting Islamic groups in Turkey and that Tehran was harbouring Kurdish separatists leaders. Iran for its part was unsettled by the Turkish alliance with Israel and by Turkish military incursions into north-west Iran.

The Iranian government achieved two major advances with the European Union (EU) states. President Khatami made formal missions to Italy on 9 March and France on 28 October, signifying a normalization of contacts with the wider EU grouping. On 18 July Iran and the UK formally raised their diplomatic representation to ambassadorial status, officially ending the Salman Rushdie affair—albeit that some Iranian fundamentalist groups persisted in threatening assassination of the author of *The Satanic Verses*. Iran lent support in September to the Russian attempt to bring Chechnya under control (see III.3.i) and continued to develop its axis with Moscow on arms supplies and cooperation in nuclear power projects at Bushehr.

The only important area in foreign policy where progress was absent was in relations with the USA. There remained long-standing issues such as alleged Iranian involvement in the bombing of the Al-Khobar US military establishment in Saudi Arabia in 1996 (see AR 1996, pp. 216-7), Iranian activities against a settlement of the Palestine problem and Iran's pursuit of nuclear arms.

New difficulties included the persecution of Iranian Jews (13 of whom were arrested in June), which plagued any possible restoration of diplomatic links and the rescinding of US sanctions in the short term. In Iran official attitudes towards the USA slightly hardened during 1999, following accusations that Washington was involved in fomenting the student riots at mid-year.

Iran benefited considerably from the rising prices of its oil and natural gas exports, which earned an estimated $12,500-14,500 million in 1999 against an original forecast of some $10,000 million. Improving oil income gave opportunity for the repayment of some of the country's foreign debt of $14,000 million, especially since non-oil exports remained buoyant at approximately $4,000 million and imports decreased by value to $11,000 million. Economic growth at 3 per cent in real terms was patchy, with the state sectors (other than oil, gas and petrochemicals) in stasis. The situation was saved by strong development of the private manufacturing and retail trades, which universally across the country prospered greatly. Economic difficulties persisted with low personal incomes at $2,000 per head and high levels of unemployment. The currency continued to depreciate against the US dollar, though at a much slower rate than in the preceding year. The multiple exchange rate system survived, despite government disapproval, with a range of 1,750 to 8,680 rials per US dollar being available in December. Inflation fell to 25 per cent in the year but urban areas fared badly through rising property prices and house rental costs.

Privatization made slow progress in the face of opposition from entrenched political vested interests and the commercial obstruction emanating from the bazaar merchant groups. The President's attempt to push forward economic reform, including liberalization of trade and finance, brought only limited gains. The petroleum industry had a good year, with important contracts signed with Elf-ENI on 1 March for redevelopment of the Dorood oil field and with Shell on 14 November for the offshore development of the Soroush-Nowruz fields. In September it was announced that a 26,000-million-barrel oilfield had been discovered at Azadegan in Khorasan, south-west Iran. Cooperation with Azerbaijan in oil affairs led to a revival of schemes for Iran to play a significant future role as a transit country for Caspian oil (see VIII.1.iii).

ii. AFGHANISTAN

CAPITAL: Kabul   AREA: 650,000 sq km   POPULATION: 19,000,000 ('98)
OFFICIAL LANGUAGES: Pushtu, Dari (Persian)   POLITICAL SYSTEM: Islamic state
LEADERSHIP: Mola Mohammad Omar, Leader of the Taleban (in power since Sept '96),
   Mohammed Rabbani, Chairman of Interim Council (since Sept '96)
MAIN IGO MEMBERSHIPS (NON-UN): ECO, CP, OIC, NAM
CURRENCY: afghani (end-'99 £1=Af7,541.32, US$1=Af4,679.11)
GNP PER CAPITA: n/a

THE armed struggle between the government Taleban militia and the anti-Taleban coalition forces—the United Islamic Front for Salvation of Afghanistan (UIFSA), commanded by former Defence Minister Ahmed Shah Masud—continued throughout the year. Although the Taleban maintained the upper hand, controlling Kabul (the capital) and up to 90 per cent of the rest of the country, they could not achieve a decisive victory. The fighting was punctuated by several sessions of peace talks, but these failed to produce any lasting or significant agreement.

Although hampered by poor weather, the Masud forces began the year with local military successes prior to the opening of peace talks in Ashkhabad (the capital of Turkmenistan) on 10 March. Four days later the two sides agreed in principle to establish a broad-based government with a shared executive, legislature and judiciary, and to hold further talks in Afghanistan later in the year. Although the negotiations did not result in a ceasefire, the agreement was welcomed by the UN as 'a major step forward'. Nevertheless, as the weather improved in late March, there was a resumption of heavy fighting in several provinces. Hopes for peace also faded when, in a statement on 10 April, Taleban supreme leader Mola Mohammad Omar said that power could not be shared with those who 'have destroyed the country or have looted the state's treasury'. The statement was widely interpreted as a reference to General Masud, and was immediately followed by a UIFSA rocket attack against Kabul. On 12 April UN officials admitted that the peace process had collapsed.

Throughout April UIFSA forces claimed to have made territorial gains in several northern provinces, particularly Fariab; on 23 April they were reported to be in control of Bamian, a provincial capital some 100 kilometres west of Kabul. The Taleban counter-attacked in a number of provinces in early May, however, and by the middle of the month had recaptured Bamian. In mid-June UIFSA forces repelled a fierce Taleban attack in the northern province of Samangan and there was then a brief lull in hostilities as both sides reinforced their positions before resuming heavy fighting in the latter part of July.

The lull coincided with UN-sponsored peace talks held in Tashkent (the capital of Uzbekistan) on 19-20 July between Taleban officials and UIFSA representatives. The talks followed a meeting of the informal group—dubbed the 'two plus six', namely the USA, Russia, China, Iran, Pakistan, Tajikistan, Turkmenistan and Uzbekistan—which had agreed not to provide military support to any Afghan party. However, the talks failed to produce any agreement other than a reaffirmation of earlier commitments not to obstruct the delivery of humanitarian aid from foreign donors. A peace initiative sponsored by Pakistan led to a further series of meetings between UIFSA officials and Taleban representatives on 18 and 23 August in Dushanbe (the capital of Tajikistan), but no agreement was reached.

On 28 July Taleban forces attacked heavily-fortified UIFSA positions some 50 kilometres north of Kabul. Despite heavy casualties, they made significant gains, but by early August all of this territory had been recaptured by the UIFSA. A further brief lull occurred as both sides regrouped and resupplied their forces. Then, from 24 September, the Taleban launched fresh attacks in the north-eastern provinces of Takhar and Konduz. The attacks yielded no significant gains, however, and the intensity of the fighting diminished as the weather deteriorated towards the end of the year.

Domestically, there was little change within Afghanistan during the year, with the Taleban maintaining its tight control over the population and continuing to impose its extreme form of Islamic law. Public executions remained commonplace, and on 16 November new ground was broken with the first public execution of a woman. The condemned, a mother of seven, was shot in a crowded sports stadium in Kabul after being convicted of murdering her husband.

Mola Mohammad Omar's position as Taleban leader remained unchallenged, although on 24 August at least ten people were killed in a failed assassination attempt when a bomb hidden in a truck exploded close to his home. In general, however, it was anti-Taleban figures who were at greater risk, and a number were assassinated in exile in Pakistan during the course of the year. Nevertheless, serious doubts remained over the capabilities of the Taleban regime, as inefficiencies were exacerbated by the continued fighting, the Taleban's distrust of Western aid agencies, and by an earthquake on 11 February in Wardak province, south-west of Kabul, which killed over 50 people and destroyed more than 7,000 houses. In September UN officials warned of a serious food crisis developing within the country. In November Omar made a number of cabinet changes and replaced senior figures in both the military and regional government in a bid to improve efficiency and discipline.

Notwithstanding these problems, the Taleban was able to continue funding its military struggle through the profits derived from the production and exportation of heroin. The UN Drugs Control Programme (UNDCP) reported on 10 September that production of opium in Afghanistan—most of which was refined to produce heroin–had more than doubled in 1999, to 4,600 tonnes, thereby making Afghanistan the world's largest producer of the drug.

There was a slight relaxation in the Taleban's opposition to the education of girls with the opening of 13 girls' schools in Kabul. Although the new schools focused on religious instruction and the girls would be forced to leave when they reached the age of 12, the move was seen as a small step forward in a country where, hitherto, females had been effectively excluded from the education system by the Taleban.

The Taleban regime remained diplomatically isolated throughout 1999, with the UN continuing to withhold recognition. The regime also came under considerable international pressure over the presence in the country of Osama bin Laden, the Saudi-born Islamic militant who was wanted in the USA on terrorism charges which included the August 1998 bombing of US embassies in east Africa (see AR 1998, pp. 174, 176, 245, 318). In an interview in the US magazine *Time*, published on 3 January, bin Laden renewed his call for a *jihad* (holy war) against US and British targets in retaliation for their military action against Iraq. Bin Laden also made a series of cryptic remarks which were interpreted by many as an admission of his involvement in the embassy bombings.

In early February talks focusing on the bin Laden issue were held between Taleban and US representatives in Islamabad, Pakistan. On 9 February Taleban spokesmen stated that bin Laden would not be expelled from Afghanistan, but on the following day it was announced that the Taleban had restricted his ability to make public statements. Although Taleban leader Omar said on 14 February that bin Laden's whereabouts were unknown, unconfirmed reports suggested that he had been moved to a secure hiding place in southern Afghanistan.

Frustrated by the Taleban stance over bin Laden, US President Bill Clinton on 5 July signed an executive order which imposed financial sanctions against the regime. The move followed reports in June that groups linked with bin Laden planned further attacks on US diplomatic missions in Africa. Additional sanctions followed when, on 10 August, US officials seized assets belonging to Afghanistan's national airline Ariana. The pressure on the Taleban regime to surrender bin Laden was intensified on 15 October, when the UN Security Council voted to adopt resolution 1267 imposing limited sanctions against Afghanistan. Drafted by US officials, the resolution gave the Taleban until 14 November to hand over the wanted man. On 23 October the Taleban announced a willingness to hold direct talks with the USA over the issue, but stressed that any solution needed to be compatible with Islamic law and Afghan culture. When the UN deadline expired with bin Laden still at large, the UN imposed limited sanctions. The overseas assets of Ariana were frozen and a flight ban was introduced on all of Ariana's international routes. In Kabul angry crowds responded to the news of the sanctions with demonstrations against the UN.

The year ended with Afghanistan being thrust into the international spotlight by the hijacking on 24 December of an Indian Airlines aircraft by Islamic fundamentalists. The aircraft, on a scheduled flight from Kathmandu (the capital of Nepal) to New Delhi (the capital of India), was hijacked in Indian airspace by five armed men. Denied permission to land in Lahore (Pakistan), the aircraft touched down briefly at Amritsar (India), where one Indian passenger was stabbed to death. It then flew on to Lahore, where the Pakistani authorities allowed the plane to be refuelled. After an abortive attempt by the hijackers to reach Kabul, the aircraft landed at Dubai in the United Arab Emirates in the early hours of 25 December, when 27 passengers were released in exchange for fuel and food. Later that day the airliner flew on to Kandahar, in southern Afghanistan, where the hijack eventually ended on 31 December with the release of the remaining 158 passengers and crew. In exchange, the Indian government freed three Islamic militants imprisoned for their involvement in the separatist conflict in Kashmir. Once the hostages were safe, the hijackers and the freed militants were spirited away by Taleban officials.

iii. KAZAKHSTAN—TURKMENISTAN—UZBEKISTAN—KYRGYZSTAN—TAJIKISTAN

Kazakhstan

CAPITAL: Astana   AREA: 2,717,300 sq km   POPULATION: 17,000,000 ('98)
OFFICIAL LANGUAGES: Kazakh & Russian   POLITICAL SYSTEM: presidential
HEAD OF STATE & GOVERNMENT: President Nursultan Nazarbayev (since Feb '90)
RULING PARTIES: Fatherland Party (Otan) leads ruling alliance
PRIME MINISTER: Kasymzhomart Tokayev (since Oct '99)
MAIN IGO MEMBERSHIPS (NON-UN): CIS, PFP, OSCE, OIC, ECO
CURRENCY: tenge (end-'99 £1=T223.30, US$1=T138.55)
GNP PER CAPITA: US$1,310 by exchange-rate calculation, US$3,400 at PPP ('98)

Kyrgyzstan

CAPITAL: Bishkek   AREA: 198,500 sq km   POPULATION: 5,000,000 ('98)
OFFICIAL LANGUAGES: Kyrgyz & Russian   POLITICAL SYSTEM: presidential
HEAD OF STATE & GOVERNMENT: President Askar Akayev (since Oct '90)
RULING PARTIES: Democratic Movement of Kyrgyzstan heads loose ruling coalition
PRIME MINISTER: Amangeldy Muraliyev (since April '99)
MAIN IGO MEMBERSHIPS (NON-UN): CIS, PFP, OSCE, ECO, OIC
CURRENCY: som (end-'99 £1=S73.22, US$1=S45.43)
GNP PER CAPITA: US$350 by exchange-rate calculation, US$2,200 at PPP ('98)

Tajikistan

CAPITAL: Dushanbe   AREA: 143,100 sq km   POPULATION: 6,000,000 ('98)
OFFICIAL LANGUAGE: Tajik   POLITICAL SYSTEM: presidential
HEAD OF STATE & GOVERNMENT: President Imamali Rakhmanov (since Nov '92)
RULING PARTIES: People's Democratic Party of Tajikistan & United Tajik Opposition head precarious coalition
PRIME MINISTER: Akil Akilov (since Dec '99)
MAIN IGO MEMBERSHIPS (NON-UN): CIS, OSCE, ECO, OIC
CURRENCY: Tajik rouble
GNP PER CAPITA: US$350 by exchange-rate calculation ('98)

Turkmenistan

CAPITAL: Ashgabat   AREA: 448,100 sq km   POPULATION: 5,000,000 ('98)
OFFICIAL LANGUAGE: Turkmen   POLITICAL SYSTEM: presidential
HEAD OF STATE & GOVERNMENT: President (Gen.) Saparmurad Niyazov (since Jan '90)
RULING PARTY: Democratic Party of Turkmenistan (DPT)
MAIN IGO MEMBERSHIPS (NON-UN): CIS, PFP, OSCE, ECO, OIC, NAM
CURRENCY: manat
GNP PER CAPITA: US$630 by exchange-rate calculation, US$1,410 at PPP ('97)

Uzbekistan

CAPITAL: Tashkent   AREA: 447,400 sq km   POPULATION: 24,000,000 ('98)
OFFICIAL LANGUAGE: Uzbek   POLITICAL SYSTEM: presidential
HEAD OF STATE & GOVERNMENT: President Islam Karimov (since March '90)
RULING PARTY: People's Democratic Party (PDP)
PRIME MINISTER: Otkir Sultonov (since Dec '95)
MAIN IGO MEMBERSHIPS (NON-UN): CIS, PFP, OSCE, ECO, OIC, NAM
CURRENCY: sum (end-'99 £1=S1,047.60, US$1=S650.00)
GNP PER CAPITA: US$870 by exchange-rate calculation, US$2,900 at PPP ('98)

SEVERAL rounds of elections were held in the Central Asian states in 1999. The first was the presidential election held in Kazakhstan on 10 January. In a turnout of 87 per cent incumbent President Nursultan Nazarbayev was returned to office with a large majority, winning just under 80 per cent of the vote. His closest rival was Serikbolsyn Abdildin, leader of the Communist Party of Kazakhstan, who received 11.7 per cent. President Nazarbayev called the result 'historic' and 'a step towards democracy', but international observers were less impressed. The Organization for Security and Cooperation in Europe (OSCE) was so concerned about the numerous shortcomings in the election campaign that it declined to take part in the official monitoring process; it did, however, send a team of unofficial assessors.

Criticisms of the proceedings focused on such issues as the snap announcement of the date of the election and the subsequent brief period of time allowed for campaigning, which effectively prevented most prospective candidates from making proper preparations; on restricted access to the media for the incumbent President's rivals; on unduly onerous legal and administrative obstacles to free association and assembly, which impeded the registration of some candidates; and on lack of impartiality on the part of the state authorities, who provided support for the incumbent's campaign. Also, there was serious disquiet about the disqualification, on a minor technicality, of the candidacy of former Prime Minister Akezhan Kazhegeldin, whom many regarded as the only serious challenger to Mr Nazarbayev. A declaration issued by the German presidency on behalf of the European Union (EU) characterized the elections as a setback to the 'process of democratization and the development of the rule of law' in Kazakhstan.

In May the Kazakh parliament formally approved changes to the constitution, originally proposed before the election, regarding the President and parliament. They included the extension of the term of the office of the President from five to seven years. The *Majlis* (lower house of parliament) was enlarged by 10 seats, to be allotted on a party basis. In accordance with the recommendation of international organizations, measures were introduced to give the electoral commission greater independence from the executive.

Partial elections to the 39-member Kazakh Senate (upper house of parliament) took place on 17 September. There were 29 candidates for the 16 available seats. Once again, the proceedings attracted criticism from the OSCE. The main cause of complaint was lack of openness regarding the electoral procedures. Observers and media representatives were obstructed in their attempts to monitor the sorting of the ballot papers. Elections to the 77-member *Majlis*, held on 10 and 24 October, attracted even greater criticism. There were numerous allegations of irregularities, and in some cases outright falsitation. The Kazakh prosecutor-general acknowledged that there had been violations of the election rules, not only by individual candidates but also by the constituency-level electoral commissions and by the central electoral commission. Some of the election officials also filed complaints, clearly concerned about abuses that they were powerless to prevent. According to the official results, the pro-presidential Otan (Fatherland) party won 23 seats (with 31 per cent of the vote), the Civic Party 13 and the Communist and Agrarian parties three each, the remaining seats going mainly to independents. During the election process Kasymzhomart Tokayev was confirmed as the country's new Prime Minister in succession to Nurlan Balgimbayev, who had resigned on 1 October to return to the chairmanship of Kazakh Oil.

A presidential election in Tajikistan on 6 November resulted in a landslide victory for the incumbent, Imamali Rakhmanov. According to the central election and referendum commission, there was an almost 100 per cent turnout, with Mr Rakhmonov receiving 97 per cent of the vote. His only rival, Davlat Usmon (the Minister of Economics and Foreign Economic Relations), was the candidate for the Islamic Rebirth Party, the dominant element of the United Tajik Opposition (UTO); he received 2 per cent of the vote. However, the fact that the election was contested at all was somewhat unexpected, since the three would-be candidates were unable to collect the required 145,000 signatures of nominees. Mr Usmon himself failed to gather the necessary number of nominations, but was registered anyway. He complained to the Supreme Court, but was overruled. The other prospective candidates claimed that the results were rigged. Nevertheless, an influential UTO member, the prominent Muslim cleric Haji Akbar Turajonzade, voiced his support for the outcome. A new cabinet announced on 20 December was headed by Akil Akilov, former deputy governor of Leninabad, and again included some UTO members.

The final contests of the year were the parliamentary elections held in Uzbekistan on 5 December and in Turkmenistan on 12 December. Five parties, as well as representatives of selected groups (state organs and citizens' initiative groups), contested the elections for the 250-member Uzbek *Oli Majlis*. The People's Democratic Party (successor to the Soviet-era Communist Party) won 48 seats, followed by the Self-Sacrifice Party (Fidokorlar) with 34, Progress of the Fatherland (Vatan Tarkietti) with 20, Justice (Adolat) with 11 and National Renaissance (Milli Tiklanish) with 10; the remaining seats went to citizens' groups and unaffiliated candidates. In Turkmenistan, all the candidates belonged to the ruling Democratic Party of Turkmenistan. Most foreign human rights organizations declined to send monitors to either elections, a clear indication that they considered the proceedings to fall short of the required democratic standards.

While not holding elections in 1999, Kyrgyzstan got a new Prime Minister in April, when Amangeldy Muraliyev) was appointed to the post following the sudden death of Jumabek Ibrahimov only three months after his appointment (see AR 1998, p. 321).

Security concerns figured large in 1999. One manifestation of this was related to the role of Russia in Central Asia. On 3 February it was announced that Uzbekistan would not renew its membership of the collective security treaty of the Commonwealth of Independent States (CIS), due to expire on 15 April. It was explained that the treaty did not meet current requirements; also that the Uzbek government was opposed to Russia's military activity in some CIS countries—an apparent allusion to Russian involvement in Tajikistan. Russian border guards were withdrawn from Kyrgyzstan, by mutual agreement, at the beginning of the year. In July a timetable was agreed between Russia and Turkmenistan on a similar withdrawal of Russian border troops. Meanwhile,

Russia reinforced its border with Kazakhstan in order to keep out illegal immigrants from third countries (e.g. Afghanistan) and to try to stem the flow of narcotics. Check-points were doubled on roads, railways and airports.

Another aspect of regional security was the growing concern about terrorist activities. On 16 February the threat of terrorism became a reality when six car bombs exploded in the centre of Tashkent, the Uzbek capital, killing 13 people and wounding many more. The most serious explosion was in the entrance to the government building minutes before a cabinet meeting was due to begin, the President narrowly escaping injury. 'Terrorist and extremist religious groups' were accused, including Hizbullah, Wahhabis and the 'Party of Liberation' (a radical Islamic organization of Middle Eastern origin that had only recently surfaced in Central Asia). Large-scale arrests soon followed. International and local human rights organizations, however, voiced concerns that many of the detainees were in fact innocent of any involvement in the crime. Rather, it was suggested, they had attracted official displeasure either because they were devout Muslims (which was not against the law) or because they had in some way been critical of the government's policies.

In late August another dangerous terrorist incident erupted when a group of Islamic militants from Uzbekistan established themselves in the Kyrgyz part of the Ferghana Valley. They took several hostages, including four Japanese mining engineers who had been prospecting for gold in the region. For over a month the insurgents resisted the attempts of the Kyrgyz and Uzbek armed forces to dislodge them. They eventually fled to Tajikistan in early October, having first freed their prisoners. The crisis prompted a general tightening of security policy throughout the region. The Kyrgyz President and the secretary-general of the CIS Collective Security Council signed an agreement on the provision of CIS military aid to Kyrgyzstan.

The peace process in Tajikistan continued throughout 1999, though frequently hindered by delays and setbacks. In February President Rakhmonov ordered the drawing up of an inventory of all national (government) and UTO forces, as a first step towards amalgamating the two armies. However, the rate of integration was far slower than had been anticipated and was barely completed by the end of the year. During the year members of the UTO were gradually appointed to senior government posts, in accordance with the provisions of the peace agreement signed in June 1997 (see AR 1997, pp. 298-9). Some progress was made with the registering (or in some cases re-registering) of political parties; among those legalized was the (opposition) Democratic Party, banned since 1993. A referendum on amendments to the constitution was held on 26 September, a preliminary to the parliamentary elections scheduled for early in 2000. Two of the most sensitive questions concerned the legalization of religion-based parties and the restructuring of parliament (by transforming the current unicameral body into a bicameral body). The amendments were accepted, but only after heated negotiations between the main parties.

Relations between China and the Central Asian states were strengthened. The leaders of the 'Shanghai Five' (China, Kazakhstan, Kyrgyzstan, Russia and

Tajikistan) held their fourth summit meeting in Bishkek on 25 August, signing a joint declaration on regional security and cooperation. In particular, the signatories agreed to develop practical cooperation to combat international terrorism, narcotics and arms trafficking, illegal immigration and other forms of trans-frontier criminal activity.

On a bilateral level, progress was made on a number of issues between China and Kazakhstan. On 3 February the Kazakh parliament ratified agreements concerning, amongst other points, the settlement of disputed border areas in eastern Kazakhstan; out of 994 square kilometres of disputed territory, Kazakhstan received 56.9 per cent. The Kazakh Foreign Minister described the agreement as 'very advantageous' to his country, providing extra security guarantees. Kazakh opposition groups, however, were not satisfied; they denounced the agreement as 'shameful' and suggested that bribery was involved. During these discussions, progress was also made on the utilization of trans-boundary water resources. The Chinese announced plans to draw off some 10 per cent of the flow of the Cherny Irtysh river by the year 2010 (some 1 billion cubic metres of water a year). A joint commission was established to monitor the situation.

Agriculture performed slightly better than expected in most areas, though there were some problems. Kazakhstan was hit by a plague of locusts in the summer. The effects were particularly devastating in eastern Kazakhstan, where over a million hectares of land were affected. Pasture land and crops were severely damaged. However, the 1999 Kazakh grain yield, harvested in the late autumn, was almost double that of 1998, totalling some 16 million tonnes. In Turkmenistan the harvest was also good, fulfilling state procurement goals for the second year running. The Kyrgyz grain harvest totalled 1.7 million tonnes, ensuring a sufficient supply for human consumption and animal feed. However, although maize and barley yields were up, wheat was down. It was decided that the acreage under cultivation for winter wheat should be increased. In Uzbekistan the cotton crop was an improvement on the previous year's harvest, touching the 4 million tonne mark. In Tajikistan, though, cotton yields were far below target. Adverse weather conditions were blamed for the poor showing, though lack of finance to pay for fertilizers and pesticides was acknowledged to have been a contributory factor.

There was some improvement in the mining sector. The upturn in world gold prices, which began on 27 September, raised hopes of a boost for the Central Asian gold industry. The earlier slump in prices had resulted in most foreign companies cutting back their exploration and mining budgets by 50 per cent or more. Notable exceptions were Cameco and Hemco, which continued their activities in Kyrgyzstan according to schedule. However, the Central Asian gold producers were still vulnerable and, as a representative of the Kyrgyz Mining Association pointed out, in order to benefit from the price rally the tax and investment climate needed to be improved. A new joint venture, the Jer-Uy Gold Company, was established in October to mine the Jer-Uy field, the second largest gold deposit in Kyrgyzstan; the partners were the Norox Mining Company (owned by Oxus Resources of the UK and Normandy Mining of Australia) and the Kyrgyz State Gold Company.

In Kazakhstan the government was eager to sell the majority of its 37.6 per cent stake in Kaztsink, the country's largest lead-zinc mining concern; however, Switzerland's Glencore International, holder of the other 62.4 per cent of the shares, did not appear to be interested in increasing its holding. In north-eastern Kazakhstan the massive Ulba metallurgical plant announced that it would resume production of tantalum and superconductors by the end of the year. The plant had suffered from chronic under-financing. The Kazakh nuclear agency (Kazatprom), which owned 90 per cent of the enterprise, promised investments worth US$19 million in the production of tantalum, beryllium and uranium.

The Central Asian states continued to strengthen their foreign relations, underpinning diplomatic and economic negotiations with personal visits to and from the region by heads of state and senior government personnel. In January President Rakhmanov of Tajikistan visited Hanoi and signed a package of cooperation accords with Vietnamese President Tran Duc Luong. In February then Kyrgyz Prime Minister Ibrahimov undertook a 'working trip' to Germany, while in March President Akayev of Kyrgyzstan visited Italy. Also in March Uzbekistan hosted separate visits from Greek President Stephanopoulos, Georgian President Shevardnadze and Turkish President Demirel; at the end of March Uzbek Prime Minister Otkir Sultonov headed an official delegation to Japan, where the programme included meetings with a number of government ministers. In April senior representatives of Afghanistan's ruling Taleban visited Uzbekistan—the first such initiative—for talks on cooperation, trade and the resumption of Uzbek electricity supplies to Afghanistan. Tajik President Rahmonov went to Washington in mid-April and had meetings with a number of government agencies; later in the month he visited Russia for discussions with the mayor of St Petersburg.

Chinese Vice-Premier Qian Qichen toured the Central Asian states in early June and signed numerous cooperation agreements and aid packages. In July Kazakh President Nazarbayev and Kyrgyz President Akayev made separate visits to Turkey, each holding discussions with President Demirel on cooperation in various fields. In August the Tajik President, accompanied by a large ministerial delegation, paid a four-day 'goodwill' visit to China at the invitation of President Jiang Zemin; four major documents were signed, including agreements on trade, transport, the prevention of drug-trafficking and Chinese-Tajik border issues.

In November state visits were made by Uzbek President Karimov to China, by Kyrgyz President Akayev to Denmark and by Kazakh President Nazarbayev to Mongolia and China. Uzbek Foreign Minister Abdulaziz Kamilov visited Japan and had talks with Prime Minister Obuchi and other senior ministers; Japan agreed to make loans worth the equivalent of $50 million for the implementation of various infrastructual projects in Uzbekistan. In December President Nazarbayev also visited Japan, where he was received by the Emperor; further Japanese aid was pledged to Kazakhstan. President Nazarbayev also visited the USA, where he had meetings with, amongst others, UN Secretary-General Kofi Annan and Vice-President Al Gore.

At a multilateral level, the Central Asian states participated in a Foreign Ministers' meeting of the 16-member Conference on Cooperation and Confidence-Building Measures in Asia (CCCBMA) in Almaty, Kazakhstan, on 14 September, when a declaration was signed enshrining the principles of mutual respect for sovereignty and peaceful settlement of disputes. Originally proposed by President Nazarbayev, the CCCBMA was an attempt to create an Asian equivalent of the OSCE. Less productive was a summit meeting of the Central Asian Economic Union (CAEU)—of Kazakhstan, Kyrgyzstan, Tajikistan and Uzbekistan—held in Bishkek, Kyrgyzstan, in mid-June. Although the four Presidents approved joint investment projects worth $50 million and decided to coordinate their power grids, plans to establish a CAEU free trade zone were again postponed.

2. INDIA—PAKISTAN—BANGLADESH—NEPAL—BHUTAN—SRI LANKA

i. INDIA

CAPITAL: New Delhi   AREA: 3,287,000 sq km   POPULATION: 980,000,000 ('98)
OFFICIAL LANGUAGES: Hindi & English   POLITICAL SYSTEM: parliamentary democracy
HEAD OF STATE: President Kocheril Raman Narayanan (since July '98)
RULING PARTIES: Bharatiya Janata Party (BJP) heads multi-party coalition
HEAD OF GOVERNMENT: Atal Bihari Vajpayee (BJP), Prime Minister (since March '98)
MAIN IGO MEMBERSHIPS (NON-UN): SAARC, CP, CWTH, NAM
CURRENCY: rupee (end-'99 £1=Rs70.14, US$1=Rs43.52)
GNP PER CAPITA: US$430 by exchange-rate calculation, US$1,700 at PPP ('98)

INDIA held its third general election in as many years in September-October, as political competition ensured that politicians occupied centre stage in the nation's affairs. The year began with the government led by the Bharatiya Janata Party (BJP) apparently rudderless and unpopular. It ended with BJP leader Atal Bihari Vajpayee as a re-elected Prime Minister with an enhanced mandate to govern. It was also a year of marked ups and downs in Indo-Pakistan relations, the favourable prospects of the Lahore meetings in February soon giving way to armed clashes in Kashmir in May which ensured that the two countries were again opposed and reciprocally vituperative for the rest of the year. Otherwise, India's relations with immediate neighbours and generally in international arenas showed some mild improvements when compared with 1998.

In retrospect, it could be seen that the last quarter of 1998 had produced a shift in the internal dynamics of the BJP. Three events marked some of this shift. In December, ignoring howls of protest by protectionists within the BJP, the government had introduced a new law in parliament promising to open India's inefficient insurance sector to foreign investors and to greater competition. However, it was unable to get the bill passed. And a bill that promised to reserve one-third of the seats in parliament for women was blocked again (see AR 1998, p 330) by MPs demanding that the quota for women should include sub-quotas for women from disadvantaged castes and religious minorities. In another demonstration of its willingness to take decisions, the government had sacked India's naval chief, Admiral Vishnu Bhagwat, allegedly for refusing to carry out orders from Defence Minister George Fernandes. The dismissal raised a furore in parliament and in the media, but the government refused to back down.

Also significant was the induction of Jaswant Singh and Pramod Mahajan into the union cabinet in late December 1998, despite reported opposition by the hardline Hindu-nationalist Rashtriya Swayamsevak Sangh (RSS). Mr Singh, a confidante of Mr Vajpayee's who, as deputy chairman of India's Planning Commission, had been handling sensitive post-nuclear talks with United States in the wake of India's nuclear tests (see AR 1998, pp. 327-8), was appointed Foreign Minister. Mr Mahajan was put in charge of the important information and broadcasting portfolio. In sum, these moves consolidated the Prime Minister's political ascendancy and control of the BJP, whilst perhaps diminishing the influence of the RSS, a traditional source of BJP ideology and top leaders.

Sporadic attacks on Christians in Gujarat in January, and the burning alive of an Australian missionary and his two sons in Orissa the following month, brought into sharp relief the BJP's now rather uneasy and problematic relationship with militant Hindu nationalist groups. India's image as a tolerant, multi-religious republic was severely tarnished.

By February it seemed clear that Mr Vajpayee had tamed economic nationalists in the RSS and was firmly in charge. Finance Minister Yashwant Sinha presented an investor-friendly budget competently, in marked contrast to his fumbling performance a year earlier. Meanwhile, facing US pressure to improve relations with Pakistan, Mr Vajpayee decided to take a bus trip across the border and to confer with his Pakistani counterpart, Nawaz Sharif, on 20-21 February (see also VIII.2.ii). In Lahore the Indian and Pakistani governments signed three documents ostensibly charting the way for improving their relations. But Pakistan's army chief, General Pervez Musharraf, refused to receive Mr Vajpayee at the border, claiming a prior engagement with the visiting Chinese Defence Minister.

Just as it seemed that the BJP-led administration was learning how to govern decisively, it collapsed in April after Jayalalitha Jayaram, leader of the All-India Anna Dravida Munnetra Kazhagam (AIADMK) of Tamil Nadu, withdrew the support of her 18 MPs. A temperamental former film star, Jayalalitha had long been demanding that the union government should dismiss the state government, led by her rival, and intervene on her behalf in a number of pending corruption cases. The Union government refused, at least partly because such a step would almost certainly have been successfully challenged in court. On 27 March Jayalalitha demanded that Mr Fernandes be stripped of the defence portfolio for his role in the Bhagwat dismissal. Two days later she attended a party in New Delhi at which the president of the opposition Congress (I) party, Sonia Gandhi, was also present. When Mr Vajpayee refused to accede to her demands,

Jayalalitha on April handed a letter to President Narayanan indicating her withdrawal of support for the government, whereupon the President asked the BJP to prove its majority in parliament. Three days later, amid allegations of backroom deals and last-minute betrayals, the BJP-led government was defeated on a confidence motion by a single vote.

The President then called upon Congress (I) to form a government. But the opposition had found it easier to unite against the BJP-led coalition than it did to cobble together an alternative. Mrs Gandhi's attempt fell short by about 40 votes, as Mulayam Singh Yadav, a powerful regional leader from Uttar Pradesh (India's most populous state and until recently the political heartland of Congress) refused to support Mrs Gandhi, while most of the BJP's other coalition partners refused to be weaned away. Left with no alternative, the President dissolved India's 12th parliament only 13 months into its five-year term and called fresh elections. In the interim, the Vajpayee government was asked to continue in a caretaker capacity.

Despite losing the vote of confidence, the BJP emerged stronger from the April events. The inability of Congress (I) to form an alternative left it open to the charge of irresponsibly foisting an expensive election on India, the third in as many years. Sensing public sympathy for Mr Vajpayee over his one-vote defeat in parliament, the BJP in fact pressed for early elections. However, India's three-person electoral commission decided that heavy monsoons and flooding and necessary revisions of India's 605 million-strong voters' rolls meant that elections had to be held in September and October. Citing the need to move police and paramilitary forces from one part of the country to another, the commission said that the elections would be staggered over five weeks.

In the long run-up to the actual voting, several factors came together to help the BJP. Defeat by only one vote had given Mr Vajpayee the appearance of being a victim of opportunism and spite, while Mrs Gandhi was portrayed by much of the media as an immature politician in a hurry to grab office at almost any cost. The troubles of Congress (I) were to deepen. On 20 May the party split over the issue of the Italian-born Mrs Gandhi's origins. A few days earlier a small group of party members led by Sharad Pawar, an influential leader from the western state of Maharashtra, had demanded that Mrs Gandhi should declare publicly that she would not be a candidate for the premiership. Mr Pawar said that no-one other than 'an Indian born of Indian soil' should head India's government. This direct challenge to the authority of the Nehru-Gandhi dynasty brought swift retribution, as Mr Pawar and two other Congress (I) leaders were expelled from the party. With their expulsion, however, went Congress's hopes of capturing a majority of the 48 parliamentary seats in Maharashtra, India's third most populous state.

Another factor, erupting in May, was to impact on the elections. On 6 May India's military discovered that Pakistan-backed insurgents and, allegedly, Pakistani troops had occupied mountain ridges and gun emplacements several kilometres inside the Indian-administered part of the disputed state of Jammu and Kashmir, threatening to cut off the important Srinagar-Leh highway. On 27 May the battle to evict the intruders intensified as Pakistan shot down two Indian MiG-27 aircraft. This so-called 'Kargil conflict', named after the district where the incursion had taken place, became India's first televised war. Every day pictures of slain soldiers appeared on millions of television sets across India. Entire towns or villages turned out for funerals, as the people rallied round the flag. Official figures put the Indian death toll at more than 400, though unofficial estimates were significantly higher. By the middle of July it was clear that India had prevailed in Kargil. Faced with mounting military losses and intense pressure from the US government, Pakistan's then Prime Minister, Nawaz Sharif, agreed to back down. The Vajpayee government's handling of the war won it both international and domestic praise, enabling the caretaker Prime Minister to consolidate his position as India's most popular politician.

The BJP-led National Democratic Alliance (NDA) went into the polls under Mr Vajpayee's leadership. The BJP did not issue an election manifesto of its own, thereby not giving prominence to some of its earlier, more controversial goals. These included building a temple to the Hindu god Ram on the site of a mosque razed by Hindu militants in 1992, abolishing special constitutional protection for the Muslim-majority state of Jammu and Kashmir and discontinuing separate laws for religious minorities on such issues as marriage, divorce and inheritance. On 28 July Bal Thackeray, leader of the right-wing Hindu nationalist Shiv Sena party, was disenfranchised for six years by India's election commissioner. The decision came immediately after the Supreme Court had upheld his conviction by the Bombay high court for inciting hatred amongst communities whilst electioneering in 1997.

The outcome of the polling from 5 September to 3 October was a decisive victory for the NDA, giving Mr Vajpayee and his allies an overall majority in the new *Lok Sabha* (lower house of parliament). Overall turnout in the five phases of the polling was around 60 per cent, the distribtion of the 543 seats decided being shown in the table below.

Party	*Seats*
National Democratic Alliance	
Bharatiya Janata Party (BJP)	182
Telugu Desam Party (TDP)	29
Janata Dal United (JDU)	20
Shiv Sena (SS)	15
Dravida Munnetra Kazhagam (DMK)	12
Biju Janata Dal (BJD)	10
Trinamul Congress (TC)	8
India National Lok Dal (INLD)	5
Pattali Makkal Katchi (PMK)	5
Marumalarchi Dravida Munnetra Kazhagam (MDMK)	4
Shiromani Akali Dal (SAD)	2
Himachat Vikas Congress (HVC)	1

LC 1
MGDK 1
Manipur State Congress Party (MSCP) 1

Congress and allies
Congress (I) 115
All-India Anna Dravida Munnetra Kazhagam (AIADMK) 10
Rashtriya Janata Dal (RJD) 7
Muslim League (MUL) 2
RLD 2
Kerala Congress (Mani) (KECM) 1

Left alliance
Communist Party of India-Marxist (CPI-M) 33
Communist Party of India (CPI) 4
Revolutionary Socialist Party (RSP) 3
All-India Forward Bloc (AIFB) 2
Kerala Congress (KEC) 1

Other parties
Samajwadi Party (SP) 26
Bahujan Samaj Party (BSP) 14
Nationalist Congress Party (NCP) 7
Jammu and Kashmir National Conference (JKNC) 4
Akhil Bharatiya Lok Tantrik Congress (ABLTC) 2
All-India Majlis-e-Ihehadul Mushimoon (AIMIM) 1
Bahipa Bahujan Mahasangha (BBM) 1
Communist Party of India (Marxist-Leninist) (CPIML) 1
Janata Dal (Secular) (JDS) 1
MADMK 1
Peasants' and Workers' Party of India (PWPI) 1
Shiromani Akali Dal (M) (SADM) 1
Sikkim Democratic Front (SDF) 1
Samajwadi Janata Party (Rashtriya) (SJPR) 1
Independents 5

Total   543*

*Polling in four *Lok Sabha* seats in Bihar was postponed until 28 October because of flooding in the constituencies. Three of these were won by Congress (I) and one by CPI-M.

The combination of deliberate moderation and Mr Vajpayee's popularity enabled the BJP to stitch together an extensive coalition with the help, again, of regional parties. The BJP itself was not able to better its 1998 tally of 182 seats; with its allies, however, it commanded 303 seats, a comfortable majority. Congress (I) crashed to an all-time low of 115 seats, although an incipient revival in the Hindi heartland state of Uttar Pradesh gave the party some semblance of hope for the future. Mrs Gandhi won re-election for both seats that she contested. Her daughter, 28-year-old Priyanka Vadhra Gandhi, unlike her mother a fluent Hindi speaker, emerged as a rising political star of Congress (I). Pundits spoke of her as the natural heir to the political mantle of her grandmother, Indira Gandhi, but it remained unclear whether Vadhra would accept a formal position in the party.

The other big election winner was Andhra Pradesh's reformist chief minister Chandrababu Naidu. His Telegu Desam Party won 29 *Lok Sabha* seats and swept to a nearly two-thirds majority in the state assembly. Pundits interpreted his re-election in Andhra Pradesh as a vote of confidence for good governance. With the second largest number of seats in the NDA coalition, Mr Naidu was so placed as to be able to play a critical role in ensuring the survival of the government. He refused to join the government formally, however, preferring to support it from outside while concentrating on broadening his reform agenda in Andhra Pradesh. In other states, incumbents generally did not fare well. In Maharashtra the BJP-Shiv Sena alliance was replaced by one between Congress (I) and Sharad Pawar's Nationalist Congress Party. And in Karnataka Congress (I) swept aside the ruling Janata Dal, which had formed an alliance with the BJP.

The new government faced challenges as soon as it took office. The 12 October coup in neighbouring Pakistan (see VIII.2.ii) cast a pall over the ministerial swearing-in ceremony, Pakistan's new ruler, General Musharraf, being regarded by the Indian government as a hardliner and anti-India in his basic disposition. For the rest of the year Indo-Pakistan relations remained tense. Disagreement over Kashmir showed no sign of abating—rather the reverse. Anti-India militants launched an attack on the army's headquarters in Srinagar in November. At the end of the year an Indian Airlines airliner with 187 passengers and crew on board was hijacked by Kashmiri separatists during a flight from Kathmandu (Nepal) to New Delhi. The airliner then made several landings, one of the passengers being murdered by the hijackers at Amritsar and 27 others, mostly women and children, being released in Dubai. It ended up at Kandahar airport in southern Afghanistan (see also VIII.1.ii), where several days of negotiations resulted in a deal being struck for the release of three militant Muslim clerics in gaol in India for involvement with Kashmiri separatists. The remaining passengers were released after an ordeal that had lasted six days.

During 1999 relations with both the United States and China improved, though those with Pakistan soured after the meetings in Lahore in February had seemed to have begun charting a genuine detente. Confidential talks between Foreign Minister Singh and US Deputy Secretary of State Strobe Talbott continued in the first quarter of the year and seemed to hold out the prospect of bringing the two countries closer on a range of issues, including India's accession to the Comprehensive Nuclear-Test-Ban Treaty and closer bilateral economic and technological cooperation. The talks were suspended after the parliamentary defeat of the Vajpayee government in April, but were resumed later in the year with the return of the BJP-led coalition to office. The rejection of the test-ban treaty by the US Senate in October (see IV.1) raised questions as to whether India would sign the treaty, which earlier had appeared likely.

Nevertheless, US-India ties continued to improve. President Clinton waived some of the sanctions imposed on India after its nuclear tests in May 1998, while a flurry of visits between New Delhi and Washington laid the ground for a US presidential visit in 2000, which would be the first such visit since one by Jimmy Carter in 1977. At the same time, the resumption of large-scale funding from the World Bank and India's demand for access to US technology in space exploration and rocket science remained unresolved issues. The US government, for its part, appeared willing to accept that India would not roll back its nuclear programme, but wanted substantive assurances that it would limit its scope. This would mean not following India's 'draft interim' (*sic*) nuclear doctrine, released as a public document in August, which said that it would pursue a 'minimal nuclear deterrent' which would include the capacity to deliver nuclear weapons by air, sea and land. Earlier, in April, India had tested its medium-range Agni II missile, which was said to have a range of 2,500 kilometres and therefore to be capable of reaching much of China.

Despite the Agni II test firing, India's relations with China improved generally over the year. In 1998 Indian Defence Minister Fernandes had described China as India's top long-term potential threat. In 1999 the government tried to downplay anti-Chinese sentiment and Foreign Minister Singh visited Beijing in June. China's studiously neutral stance during the Kargil conflict in Kashmir was seen by India as a diplomatic coup.

Despite sustaining heavy losses in and around Kargil, India had refrained from crossing the line of control dividing the Indian- and Pakistani-held portions of Kashmir. This show of restraint earned it the goodwill of the US government, which was eager to prevent clash escalating into a larger war between two nuclear-armed adversaries. India's relations with Pakistan were generally strained and tense from May onwards. The clashes in Kargil effectively derailed what had come to be known as the Lahore process. India saw Pakistan's intrusion as a betrayal of trust and, with public opinion hardening against Pakistan, demanded that it stop arming and funding insurgency in India, a charge Pakistan denied. The coup in Pakistan in October set back relations even more. Rather than give Pakistan's new ruler recognition and international legitimacy, India refused to participate in a summit of the South Asian Association for Regional Cooperation scheduled to meet in Kathmandu in November, thus causing its indefinite postponement (see XI.6.iii).

Other disappointments for India's diplomats included continued chilly relations with Japan, which had reacted adversely to India's nuclear tests. At the same time, India's relations with its smaller regional neighbours remained on an even keel. It signed an agreement with Bangladesh allowing goods to be transported through that country to India's north-east. A free-trade pact was signed with Sri Lanka, though bureaucratic obstacles reduced its potential benefits.

The West Bengal state legislature voted unanimously on 20 July to change the official name of Calcutta, India's most populous city, to Kolkata. The rationale was that the name should reflect its ethnic Bengali pronunciation. In 1690 a young merchant of the East India Company, Job Charnock, had set up Britain's first permanent colony on the site of three villages, one of which was called Kali-Kata, from which Calcutta took its name. The state legislature also passed a motion to change the state's name to Bangla; however, this change required a constitutional amendment to become formally effective.

India's overall population was thought to have reached 1,000 million by mid-August, the 52nd anniversary of independence in 1947, when it was 345 million. With current annual growth of about 15 million, it was predicted that India's population would overtake China's within the next 20 to 30 years. A report from the Worldwatch Institute in Washington commented that the figure of 1,000 million was not a cause for celebration. Half of India's adults were illiterate, half of its children undernourished and a third of its population existed below the poverty line. Grain production had tripled since 1947, but food production was threatened by falling water tables, some estimates showing that underground water reserves were being used twice as fast as they were being replaced. Average per capita income was US$430 in 1998 (compared with $21,400 in Britain); but life expectancy had risen from 39 to 63 since independence.

Two severe cyclones battered the hitherto rather prosperous eastern state of Orissa during October, wreaking tremendous damage. Hundreds of thousands of people were made homeless, and it was estimated that thousands had died.

The distinguished Indian writer and polemicist Nirad Chaudhuri died on 1 August aged 101 (see Pt XVIII: Obituary).

ii. PAKISTAN

CAPITAL: Islamabad   AREA: 804,000 sq km   POPULATION: 130,600,000 ('98)
OFFICIAL LANGUAGE: Urdu   POLITICAL SYSTEM: military regime
HEAD OF STATE: President Mohammed Rafiq Tarar (since Dec '97)
HEAD OF GOVERNMENT: Gen. Pervez Musharraf, Chief Executive Officer of National Security Council (since Oct '99)
MAIN IGO MEMBERSHIPS (NON-UN): OIC, SAARC, ECO, CP, NAM
CURRENCY: Pakistan rupee (end-'99 £1=PRs83.61, US$1=PRs51.88)
GNP PER CAPITA: US$480 by exchange-rate calculation, US$1,560 at PPP ('98)

PAKISTAN in 1999 underwent interlinked crises in the political, economic and international spheres. A military coup in October ended the decade of always-fragile democratic rule that had begun with the death of General Zia in 1988; the economy hovered on the edge of financial disaster; and from May to July India and Pakistan engaged in fierce border skirmishing in Kashmir.

The Prime Minister, Nawaz Sharif, had started the year in apparent control of the situation. He had forced the resignation of the previous Chief of the Army Staff in October 1998, installing General Pervez Musharraf as his own choice (see AR 1998, p. 332). His own majority in the National Assembly was secure and he had managed to place chief rival Benazir Bhutto on the defensive through a series of legal cases involving corruption charges. It was clear, however, that there was resentment in many quarters over his perceived dictatorial style of government and exploitation of his position for personal and family gain. In the earlier part of the year there were clampdowns on journalists who had been critical of the government.

Following the setbacks in Kashmir (see below), army resentment of what was seen as Mr Sharif's failure grew, as did rumours of a coming coup. The Prime Minister decided to counter-attack by dismissing the chief of the army while he was abroad, in order to install his ally Lieut.-General Ziauddin on 12 October. The army immediately responded by arresting Mr Sharif. On 15 October a state of emergency was declared and General Musharraf appointed himself Chief Executive Officer of the country. Martial law was not formally declared, however, and the civilian courts continued to function under the authority of President Tarar. There was no popular resistance to the coup, and evident relief in many quarters at the end of what was seen as authoritarianism masquerading as democratic rule.

General Musharraf's initial statements insisted that the army would only hold power for a short while, so as to cope with the immediate economic crisis. A National Security Council was appointed on 26 October, along with a civilian cabinet, mostly consisting of technocrats. However, by the end of the year he had given no specific indication of any timetable. Attempts were made to tackle the economic crisis by a crackdown on high-profile loan defaulters, although inevitably with only limited success.

Mr Sharif himself was kept under arrest, along with some of his relatives and members of his cabinet. Serious charges were brought against him relating both to his conduct of government and to what was seen as a deliberate attempt to kill General Musharraf by refusing to let his plane land at Karachi on 12 October. At the end of the year he remained in prison.

While there was some criticism of the coup internationally, notably from the leaders of the Commonwealth, who suspended Pakistan from membership at their Durban meeting in November (see XI.3.i), it soon became clear that the USA and other countries would continue to maintain normal diplomatic relations.

In April Benazir Bhutto, still leader of the opposition Pakistan People's Party (PPP), had been convicted *in absentia* on corruption charges and sentenced to five years in prison, and the following month the Supreme Court refused to entertain an appeal unless she returned to Pakistan from abroad. Her husband, also convicted in April, remained in gaol throughout the year. His supporters claimed that he had been tortured. Although the opposition parties collectively had succeeded in coming together for anti-government demonstrations in September, they were unable to derive much benefit from the military coup, as many people saw all political parties and politicians as equally incompetent and corrupt.

Economic performance continued to be sluggish, partly because of the effect of the previous year's economic sanctions following the May nuclear tests (see AR 1998, pp. 333-4). The 1998/99 financial year figures showed growth at only 3.1 per cent against a target of 6 per cent. This reflected poor agricultural and manufacturing performance, as also low rates of inward investment. A poor cotton crop in 1998/99 affected the economy as a whole. The trade gap widened during the year. The budget included the imposition of a general sales tax as an attempt to raise additional tax revenue. This led, however, to a nationwide business strike on 4 September and to a subsequent climbdown by the government. The IMF had resumed its aid programme at the beginning of the year following its suspension after the 1998 nuclear tests, but withheld further payments later in the year. Factors at work included concerns about the possible political motivation behind charges of corruption in respect of private power projects initiated during Ms Bhutto's 1993-96 PPP government.

At the beginning of the year Indo-Pakistan relations had appeared to improve dramatically with the visit to Lahore by the Indian Prime Minister, who travelled across the land border by bus (see also VIII.2.i). Mr Vajpayee's visit led to the signing of the Lahore Declaration on 21 February, creating the prospect of a renewed dialogue not excluding the Kashmir question. The declaration pledged the two countries to work towards peace and stability, listing a number of confidence-building measures to be implemented. The mood of optimism was totally dashed in May, however, when the Indian army discovered that during the winter intruders had occupied positions on the Indian side of the line of control dividing Indian from Pakistani controlled Kashmir. The intrusion had taken place in the Kargil region and threatened communications with the Ladakh region further north.

India responded in late May with air strikes on militant positions, although it was careful throughout not to cross the line of control and risk both an escalation of the conflict and foreign intervention. Substantial fighting ensued as Indian troops struggled to push the intruders back from their superior positions. Casualties were heavy on both sides, some hundreds being killed. The diplomatic battle was equally fierce, with India seeking to convince the international community that the intruders included significant numbers of Pakistani troops and that the whole episode had been planned by the Pakistan army. Pakistan maintained its traditional position that it provided only political and diplomatic support to Kashmiri militants.

The Kargil fighting eventually came to an end after Prime Minister Sharif visited Washington on 4 July and, at President Clinton's instance, issued a statement calling on the fighters to withdraw. The withdrawal eventually took place over the following couple of weeks. Mr Sharif's decision provoked some political opposition, in particular from the Islamist Jamaat-i-Islami, which organized a major demonstration on 25 July.

Following the end of the Kargil fighting, on 10 August India shot down an unarmed Pakistani reconnaissance plane which was allegedly flying over Indian territory along the Sindh-Gujarat border. While Pakistan claimed that the plane had lost its way, India argued that it was a deliberate provocation. India responded to the October coup by cancelling a planned meeting of the South Asian Association for Regional Cooperation (see XI.6.iii), although General Musharraf had taken steps to reduce tension along the border. At the end of the year an Indian airliner was hijacked by militants demanding the release of a

Pakistani religious leader who had been captured in Kashmir. Following a brief stop at Lahore, the plane eventually reached Kandahar in Afghanistan (see also VIII.1.ii). The hijack was eventually resolved on New Year's Eve with the release of the religious leader and two other individuals. India immediately made it clear that it believed that the Pakistani intelligence service, the ISI, was behind the action.

iii. BANGLADESH

CAPITAL: Dhaka   AREA: 144,000 sq km   POPULATION: 126,000,000 ('98)
OFFICIAL LANGUAGE: Bengali   POLITICAL SYSTEM: parliamentary democracy
HEAD OF STATE: President Shahabuddin Ahmed (since July '96)
RULING PARTIES: Awami League heads coalition
HEAD OF GOVERNMENT: Sheikh Hasina Wajed, Prime Minister (since June '96)
MAIN IGO MEMBERSHIPS (NON-UN): SAARC, CP, OIC, CWTH, NAM
CURRENCY: taka (end-'99 £1=Tk82.20, US$1=Tk51.00)
GNP PER CAPITA: US$350 by exchange-rate calculation, US$1,100 at PPP ('98)

THIS was another year of unrelentingly feverish national politics. Neither Sheikh Hasina Wajed, the Prime Minister and leader of the Awami League (the core of the ruling coalition), nor former Prime Minister Begum Khaleda Zia, heading the principal opposition Bangladesh National Party (BNP), showed any serious disposition to end their politics of confrontation and mutual recrimination. Rather, it seemed as if their fierce rivalry intensified. National strikes, 'hartals', became more organized in 1999 and the government became tougher on the strikers. BNP spokesmen claimed that general strikes were the only way the opposition could carry on its campaign against the government because of tough police action against processions and public meetings.

The opposition's recurrent call throughout the year was for the government to resign and hold free and fair general elections. The government pointed out that elections did not have to be called until June 2001 and that they would be held at an appropriate time. Victories for government supporters in several by-elections generated predictable opposition accusations of vote-rigging. After a by-election in Tangail on 15 November even pro-government newspapers reported that there had been widespread coercion of voters by armed thugs and government officials. Such charges were echoed in reports by diplomatic and other independent observers.

Criticism of the Prime Minister and the government elicited strong reactions. Officials seemed to be immersed in trying to unearth conspiracies. On 5 October the Home Affairs Minister, Mohammed Nasim, said that there had been a plot to kill Sheikh Hasina on her return from a visit to Paris. He did not elaborate, but he accused the opposition of using propaganda to try to destabilize the country. A number of people were arrested by intelligence agencies without it being revealed how they were involved in any alleged plot. In a statement on 1 November Begum Khaleda accused the government of torturing people to extract false confessions implicating opposition leaders. She said that the actions of some officials had shown that the government was politically and morally bankrupt.

Having withdrawn from the ruling coalition in March 1998, the Jatiya Party (JP) led by former President Hussein Mohammed Ershad decided in April to end the JP's remaining links with Sheikh Hasina's government and henceforth to back the opposition BNP. The JP's decision, which was emulated by the right-wing Jamaat-e-Islami and the Islami Oikaya Jote (IOJ) alliance of four smaller Islamic parties, inspired the BNP-led opposition to declare itself even more determined to topple the government. There was a strong sense of *déja vu:* similar statements had been made by Sheikh Hasina when her Awami League was leading the opposition against Begum Khaleda's BNP government in the early 1990s. Mr Ershad's move caused a split in the JP, with former minister Anwar Hossain leading a breakaway group of 11 MPs (out of 35) that continued to support the government. On 3 November the Prime Minister ordered the confiscation of Mr Ershad's passport as he was about to fly to Beijing at the official invitation of the Chinese government.

As well as supporting—well nigh sponsoring—regular general strikes, which were estimated to cost the economy $50-$100 million per day, opposition MPs boycotted full National Assembly sessions. They complained that the speaker denied them reasonable opportunity to speak, an accusation which he repudiated. Continuing to attend the various parliamentary committees, opposition MPs also continued to draw all the benefits of their Assembly membership. Leaders of the four main opposition groupings met at the end of November, announcing an action plan built around their demand that the government should transfer power to a caretaker administration pending early general elections. Their focus on 'Bangladesh nationalism' and 'Islamic beliefs' threatened further polarization of the urban middle classes. The onset of the holy month of Ramadan in early December, and the associated suspension of political activism, gave the two sides some chance to negotiate. Sheikh Hasina said several times towards the end of the year that she was willing to hold talks. By the end of the year, however, no formal invitation had been extended to the opposition, so that political stalemate prevailed.

In the sphere of external relations, Bangladesh was elected unopposed in September to a non-permanent seat on the UN Security Council in 2000-01, having previously been a member in 1978-79. Regionally, Bangladesh continued to be involved in a new Asian grouping formed together with India, Myanmar (Burma), Sri Lanka and Thailand in 1997 and constituting the only regional grouping with members from both the Association of South-East Asian Nations (ASEAN) and the South Asian Association for Regional Cooperation (SAARC). The second ministerial meeting of the group had been held in Dhaka in December 1998 and a third was due to take place in New Delhi in 2000. The group's proposals regarding lower tariffs and their eventual complete removal was resisted by India, which said that Thailand would get the most benefit.

Bangladesh was due to host the 2001 summit of Non-Aligned Movement (NAM) in Dhaka, and then to take over the chairmanship of the NAM for three years. Meanwhile, following recent NAM practice, Sheikh Hasina enjoyed the prestige and influence of being one of the troika of NAM leaders, consisting of the current chairperson together with the immediate past and the prospective chairpersons. However, the looming problem of how to accommodate over 100 heads of state and government and their aides, not to mention representatives of international agencies and media people, had yet to be solved. Construction of three new five-star hotels in Dhaka suffered from serious delays, some local sources maintaining that such hotels could not be completed in less than three years.

The 1999 ministerial meeting of the Developing Eight (D-8) group of countries was held in Dhaka on 1-2 March. Consisting of Bangladesh, Egypt, Indonesia, Iran, Malaysia, Nigeria, Pakistan and Turkey, and therefore representing 65 per cent of the world's Muslim population, the D-8 aimed to develop closer economic cooperation among its members. President Shahabuddin Ahmed subsequently paid his first official visit to Turkey, which had launched the D-8 initiative in 1997 (see AR 1997, p. 401).

Having been devastated by unprecedented floods in 1998 (see AR 1998, pp. 335-6), the Bangladeshi economy was further damaged in 1999 by politically-inspired strikes which shut down industry and virtually halted manufacturing growth. In December alone, according to a senior executive at a leading private bank in Dhaka, the economy was paralysed for 10 days as strikes called by the opposition BNP and its allies forced businesses to close. Such turmoil meant that, despite some recovery in agriculture, the official GDP growth target of 6.5 per cent in the financial year ending 30 June 2000 was unlikely to be achieved. Most analysts believed that the growth rate was likely to be closer to 5 per cent, a marginal rise over the previous year's rise of 4.2 per cent.

Much of the improvement came from agriculture. According to the World Bank, the rice crop harvested in the August-September period produced a welcome 9.5 million tonnes, up from just 7.6 million tonnes in the flood-ravaged financial year 1998-99. With food prices making up the bulk of Bangladesh's consumer price index, a likely benefit of the bumper crop was that inflation would remain in check. Both exports and imports continued to lag in 1999. After achieving an impressive annual average growth of 17 per cent between 1990 and 1998, exports in 1998-99 stood at $5,300 million, barely 3 per cent up from a year earlier. The frequent shut-downs caused by political strikes, as well as patchy power supplies and poor infrastructure, together conspired to choke exports, of which garments were by far the most important (with a value of $3,000 million). Some Bangladeshi economists believed that an over-valued currency was also to blame for the slow-down in export growth, though two devaluations brought the Bangladeshi taka to 51 to the US dollar by the end of the year. More encouragingly, foreign exchange reserves remained stable at $1,700 million in October, enough to cover more than two months of imports.

The Finance Minister and some of his colleagues spoke repeatedly of the need to speed up the privatization process and to encourage new investment. But there were no decisive signs that such wishes were being translated into reality. State-owned enterprises, including power, railway, water transport and road transport corporations, continued to incur losses at an annualized rate of almost $500 million. Even so, according to a World Bank study released at the end of the year, Bangladesh was poised to receive sharply higher inflows of foreign direct investment, thanks to measures taken to liberalize its economy. Having been just a trickle a decade earlier, foreign investment was expected to rise to an annual average of about $780 million over the next five years, from around $400 million in the fiscal year 1997-98. The trend was expected to accelerate thereafter to an annual average of $900 million within a decade. Bangladesh had been hoping to attract investments from companies wanting to develop its large gas reserves. However, the World Bank study showed that investment in telecommunications, manufacturing and services could overtake energy investment by the year 2006. Liberalization of trade, foreign exchange and foreign investment regulations, as well as the current-account convertibility of the local currency, had helped to improve the climate for investment, the Bank said.

iv. NEPAL

CAPITAL: Kathmandu   AREA: 147,000 sq km   POPULATION: 23,000,000 ('98)
OFFICIAL LANGUAGE: Nepali   POLITICAL SYSTEM: parliamentary democracy
HEAD OF STATE: King Birendra Bir Bikram Shah Deva (since '72)
RULING PARTY: Nepali Congress Party (NCP)
HEAD OF GOVERNMENT: Krishna Prasad Bhattarai (NCP), Prime Minister (since May '99)
MAIN IGO MEMBERSHIPS (NON-UN): SAARC, CP, NAM
CURRENCY: Nepal rupee (end-'99 £1=NRs110.76, US$1=NRs68.72)
GNP PER CAPITA: US$210 by exchange-rate calculation, US$1,090 at PPP ('98)

SEEKING to bring an end to five years of unstable coalition government (see AR 1998, pp. 328-9), Prime Minister Girija Prasad Koirala of the Nepali Congress Party (NCP) on 15 January called a general election in May, six months ahead of schedule. The tactic worked, although Mr Koirala turned out not to be the beneficiary. The main voting on 3 and 17 May and delayed contests in some constituencies in June gave the NCP 111 of the 205 seats in the House of Representatives, enabling it to form a majority government. However, the new Prime Minister was Mr Koirala's long-time NCP rival Krishna Prasad Bhattarai (75), who had last held the top post in 1990-91.

The election gave a bruising to the mainstream leftish United Communist Party of Nepal–Marxist-Leninist (UCPN-ML), which declined to 71 seats, half what it had hoped for, while the breakaway Communist Party of Nepal–Marxist-Leninist (CPN-ML) failed to gain even a single seat. A split in the rightist National Democratic Party (NDP) also cost it dearly in the elections. The main NDP faction led by former Prime Minister Surya Bahadur Thapa managed to win just 11 seats; a splinter group led by former Prime Minister Lokendra Bahadur Chand failed to win a seat. Other smaller parties and many of the independent candidates were also marginalized in the polls.

A 16-member NCP cabinet was sworn in under Mr Bhattarai on 31 May. It was soon reduced to 15 members when Law and Justice Minister Tara Nath Ranabhatt resigned to contest elections for the speakership of the new House. In major changes announced on 30 June the Bhattarai administration more than doubled in size to 32 members (including eight ministers of state and five assistant ministers), as the government spread its workload in its focus on economic development and the elimination of corruption and lawlessness. In the reshuffle Mr Bhattarai relinquished four of his six portfolios, including home and foreign affairs, but remained Minister of Defence and Royal Palace Affairs. Dr Ram Sharan Mahat, a former Finance Minister, took over foreign affairs, the new Home Affairs Minister being Puma Bahadur Khadka, who was also made responsible for press and communications. A woman MP, Kamala Pant, took the social welfare and women's affairs portfolios. In a budget tabled in July, the new Finance Minister, Mahesh Acharya, announced a mix of fiscal reforms and populist measures which hinted at dilution of the pro-market economic policies introduced by the ruling NCP eight years earlier.

Commentators were generally agreed that the new administration contained a balance of new and experienced ministers representing a cross-section of Nepalese communities. But few people genuinely expected the government swiftly to meet its avowed aims of controlling terrorism, promoting economic development and eliminating corruption. Whatever the Prime Minister's problems within parliament, where some NCP elements were unhappy with his leadership, he faced larger and more intractable ones from outside.

The insurgency launched in February 1996 by the extreme-left Nepal Communist Party–Maoist (see AR 1996, p. 307) was spreading and still defied peaceful solution. Tentative attempts at negotiation proved fruitless. Stamping out the insurgency wholly by armed force was not practicable. By the end of 1999 it had claimed over 1,000 lives, and human rights groups and opposition politicians berated successive governments for the security forces' treatment of captured insurgents. The lack of an adequate legal framework hamstrung government efforts to deal with insurgency, and attempts to pass anti-terrorism legislation also met with criticism from both the opposition and human rights groups.

Adding to the government's travails was a resurgence of reactionary forces maintaining that the multi-party parliamentary system, adopted in 1990, was failing the country. Since 1990 the poor record of successive governments in dealing with the country's problems had provided much fuel for such reactionary arguments. The government responded by repeatedly claiming that these reactionary forces were thwarting its efforts and in effect supporting the Maoist insurgency. Another sore point was the position of the royal nominee to the National Council, parliament's upper house. Initially the choice was between Ramesh Nath Pandey, supported by the more right-leaning politicians, and the ruling party's Basudev Risal. Mr Pandey looked set to win the two-tier election, but ultimately Mohammed Moshin, the candidate of the NDP–Thapa, was elected.

Nepal continued to practise its 40-year-old policy of non-alignment, despite the tendency of both the ruling NCP and the opposition UCPN-ML to display deference towards India. On 17 June Prime Minister Bhattarai reaffirmed his country's non-alignment and declared that, while Nepal wanted to maintain close cordial relations with India and China, it aimed at staying friendly with all countries.

In fact, Nepal's relations with India were unsteady in 1999, despite the government's efforts to maintain an even keel. Although Nepal expressed concern over the India-Pakistan nuclear arms race (see VIII.2.i; VIII.2.ii), both NCP and UCPN-ML leaders openly supported controversial bilateral deals with India, including multi-billion dollar hydro-electric power (HEP) schemes. Meanwhile, India's hostility towards Nepal's third-country trade, involving the movement of goods over the Phulbari-Banglabandh region of India, remained a thorn in bilateral relations.

Indian Foreign Minister Jaswant Singh paid an official visit to Nepal in early September, the issues discussed including the HEP projects and counter-insurgency. However, an unresolved border dispute (along the extreme north-west frontier of Kalapani) was left virtually unmentioned. For the first time since his accession to the throne in 1972, King Birendra was officially invited by India's President to pay a state visit. In 1997 he and Queen Aishworya had been principal guests at celebrations to mark India's 50th anniversary of independence.

China sent a number of goodwill missions to Nepal in 1999, including a high-level military delegation, and several Nepalese political leaders visited China. Sri Lanka's President, Chandrika Kumaratunga, paid an official visit to Nepal in July, in her capacity as chairman of the South Asian Association for Regional Cooperation (SAARC). In September Nepal and Sri Lanka signed an air services agreement facilitating weekly two-way flights, in an effort to boost tourism and bilateral trade.

Nepal's longstanding cordial relationship with Britain continued in 1999, assisted by moves to improve the benefits and pensions of former Nepalese Gurkha soldiers who had served in the UK armed forces. After Mr Bhattarai, returning from the UN General Assembly in New York, had met UK Prime Minister Tony Blair in London in early October, Mr Blair announced on 27 October that the death-in-service benefit payable to families of Gurkhas was being increased immediately to the levels applicable to British soldiers. The decision followed the death of a Gurkha sergeant on active service in Kosovo in June and meant that his widow received £54,000 rather than £19,000. In December, moreover, the UK Ministry of Defence announced that the retirement pensions of the 3,500 Gurkhas currently serving in the British army would be doubled with immediate effect.

The SAARC grouping suffered a setback as a result of the military takeover in Pakistan on 12 October (see VIII.2.ii). India's refusal to attend the SAARC summit scheduled to be held in Kathmandu in November led to its indefinite postponement.

The political year ended with a resurgence of familiar party factionalism in parliament, where NCP members initiated moves to remove Mr Bhattarai from the NCP parliamentary leadership and thus from the premiership. The Prime Minister responded on 24 December by promising the NCP chairman that there would be a change of leadership 'soon'.

v. BHUTAN

CAPITAL: Thimphu   AREA: 46,500 sq km   POPULATION: 759,000 ('98)
OFFICIAL LANGUAGES: Dzongkha, Lhotsan, English   POLITICAL SYSTEM: monarchy
HEAD OF STATE & GOVERNMENT: Dragon King Jigme Singye Wangchuk (since '72)
MAIN IGO MEMBERSHIPS (NON-UN): SAARC, CP, NAM
CURRENCY: ngultrum (end-'99 £1=N70.14, US$1=N43.52)
GNP PER CAPITA: US$400 by exchange-rate calculation ('97)

THE most novel, and probably most exciting, event of the year for Bhutanese living in or near to the capital city, Thimphu, was the start up of television and an Internet service in June, as part of the silver jubilee celebrations commemorating King Jigme Singye Wangchuk's coronation 25 years earlier. At a brief Buddhist ceremony, Queen Ashi Dorji Wangmo Wangchuk, the eldest of four sisters married to the King, said that the time had come for Bhutan to be better connected to the outside world, but without compromising traditional values.

Thimphu was the only area immediately benefiting from the initial television programming, although the Bhutan Broadcasting Service said that it planned to expand transmissions to cover the whole country. The Internet service, DrukNet, would also eventually reach all 20 districts, many of which did not have paved roads. The King said that Bhutan could drop its old ban on television because significant progress had been made both in technological terms and as a society. But Bhutan's entry into the cyber age also reflected some of the problems still facing the country. The government-controlled broadcasts were in the national Dzongkha language (related to Tibetan and using Tibetan script) and in English, but not in Nepalese, which was spoken by a large minority living mainly in the south of Bhutan.

Indeed, since the late 1980s the government had initiated and maintained campaigns to strengthen national identity through a policy known as 'Driglam Namzha'. As well as promoting Dzongkha as the national language, this policy also prescribed the wearing of traditional Bhutanese dress for men and women of all ethnic groups—a policy much resented and questioned by Bhutan's Nepalese minorities.

There were many indications in 1999 that Bhutan's elites were determined to maintain their own distinctive way of life and governance. Following the King's dismissal of his entire cabinet and issuance of decrees regarding governance (see AR 1998, pp 339-340), much controversy, debate and bargaining had ensued. In July 1999, however, the National Assembly in effect broadly endorsed the King's proposals.

In mid-September Bhutan and Nepal resumed ministerial-level talks, after a gap of more than three years. In a joint statement issued from Kathmandu, the

Foreign Ministers of the two countries claimed to have agreed on a way to identify Bhutanese citizens from among the approximately 100,000 refugees languishing in camps run by the UN in south-east Nepal.

Bhutan's rather ill-equipped security forces were becoming increasingly preoccupied with internal civil strife, as years of political and ethnic violence in the Nepalese-dominated south showed no sign of abating. India was the first country of asylum for refugees originally from Nepal, with which Bhutan has no common border; but New Delhi was markedly wary of becoming involved in this issue. The return of thousands of disgruntled ethnic Nepalese had the potential to heighten political unrest in Bhutan, something which successive Indian governments had sought to avoid. India continued its policy of quietly providing defence assistance to Bhutan.

Bhutan encountered problems with the United States in 1999. Authorities in New York delayed a request by Bhutan to open a new consulate in Manhattan because of the country's alleged human rights abuses and the treatment of refugees now in camps in Nepal.

vi. SRI LANKA

CAPITAL: Colombo   AREA: 64,500 sq km   POPULATION: 19,000,000 ('98)
OFFICIAL LANGUAGES: Sinhala, Tamil, English   POLITICAL SYSTEM: presidential democracy
HEAD OF STATE & GOVERNMENT: President Chandrika Bandaranaike Kumaratunga (since Nov '94)
RULING PARTIES: Sri Lanka Freedom Party (SLFP) heads People's Alliance coalition
PRIME MINISTER: Sirimavo Bandaranaike (since Nov '94)
MAIN IGO MEMBERSHIPS (NON-UN): SAARC, CP, CWTH, NAM
CURRENCY: rupee (end-'99 £1=SLRs114.75, US$1=SLRs71.20)
GNP PER CAPITA: US$810 by exchange-rate calculation ('98)

PRESIDENT Chandrika Bandaranaike Kumaratunga won a second six-year term in elections held on 21 December, a year ahead of schedule. Three days earlier she had survived a terrorist bomb attack, which left her blinded in her right eye and killed 27 other people, including the woman suicide bomber. The attack bore the thumbprint of the Liberation Tigers of Tamil Eelam (LTTE), which had been fighting since 1983 to create a separate state out of Sri Lanka's northern and eastern provinces; it was similar in several respects to the attack in which an LTTE suicide bomber—also a woman—assassinated Indian Prime Minister Rajiv Gandhi in 1991.

President Kumaratunga's close shave with death could have moved some voters to support her out of sympathy; she could also have benefited, as alleged by her opponents and by some poll observers, from electoral malpractices. But these two factors alone could not account for her lead of over 8 per cent of the votes polled over her main challenger, Ranil Wickremasinghe, leader of the United National Party (UNP), whose vigorous campaign was reportedly helped by election 'specialists' from Britain's Conservative Party. The official results gave Mrs Kumaratunga, who was backed by the ruling People's Alliance (PA) headed by the Sri Lanka Freedom

Party (SLFP), 51.4 per cent of the vote against 42.7 per cent for the UNP candidate and an aggregate of 5.9 per cent for 10 other contenders.

Mrs Kumaratunga's victory was all the more impressive for two reasons. One was that, just before the election, government forces battling the LTTE in the north had suffered a major reverse that was expected to cost her votes. The other was that many Tamil voters had switched support to Mr Wickremasinghe, believing that, if elected, he would be more amenable to Tamil demands and allow the LTTE to run an interim administration in the island's north and east for two years. The election confirmed the dominance of the PA and the UNP, which together polled well over 90 per cent of the votes; it was a blow to smaller parties, notably the Janatha Vimukthi Peramuna (JVP), or People's Liberation Front, which received a mere 4 per cent. After two failed armed insurrections, in 1971 and 1988, this marxist group had opted for parliamentary politics and had gained up to 7 per cent of the vote in recent provincial elections; it had therefore been expected to do better in the nationwide presidential poll, perhaps even to emerge as a third force. A candidate from the extreme right of the majority Sinhalese community who was firmly opposed to concessions to the Tamil minority achieved only a derisory vote. The poll results suggested that most people would favour a political solution satisfying Tamil aspirations—but short of dividing the country into two states as demanded by the LTTE.

There was speculation that President Kumaratunga had sought early re-election because she feared that the UNP would defeat her government in a crucial vote by securing defections from the PA. However, once she called the election, parliamentary traffic was in the other direction, with five UNP MPs crossing to her side. After the election, there was speculation that the President would seek to attract more defectors to give the PA the two-thirds majority required to push through constitutional changes, including her proposals for devolving power designed to meet Tamil demands for autonomy, so far blocked by lack of UNP support (see AR 1998, p. 341). Alternatively, she had the option of calling an early parliamentary election—one was due by August 2000 in any case—and trying to increase the PA's strength on the back of her presidential triumph.

Immediately after her victory, President Kumaratunga coupled a warning that she would stamp out terrorism with an appeal to Mr Wickremasinghe to join her in efforts to settle the ethnic problem. He responded positively but asked her to spell out what she had in mind. The year therefore ended without a clear indication as to whether Sri Lanka's two major political parties would in fact set aside their traditional bitter rivalry to work out a bipartisan approach towards ending the island's ethnic conflict through a negotiated settlement with the LTTE.

The LTTE leader, Velupillai Prabhakaran, had earlier said that he was ready to negotiate, but once again there were qualifications. He wanted external mediation and, more importantly, a prior withdrawal of government forces from the area—nearly a third of the island—which he claimed for the Tamils. This condition was unlikely to appeal to any government in Colombo. In the run-up to the December poll the LTTE forced the army to abandon several camps and to vacate a large part of the northern Wanni region (which had been wrested from rebel control only recently), thus proving that the LTTE was still a formidable force. The débâcle was so serious that President Kumaratunga, who was also Defence Minister and commander in chief, set up an inquiry to find out why the government forces had suffered one of their worst reverses in the war.

The LTTE also continued to eliminate Tamil leaders who did not accept its claim to be the sole authentic representative of the Tamil people. On 29 July a suicide bomber killed Neelan Tiruchelvam, an MP of the moderate Tamil United Liberation Front (TULF) and an internationally-respected lawyer closely associated in the preparation of President Kumaratunga's proposals for devolution of power. The cause of ethnic reconciliation also suffered by the death, on 4 September, of A.C.S. Hameed, former long-time UNP Foreign Minister and a leader of the Muslim community, who had been active in efforts to achieve a negotiated end to the conflict with the LTTE.

The full effects of the 1998 South-East Asian economic crisis finally hit Sri Lanka in 1999, stunting economic growth, which fell to 4 per cent from 4.7 per cent in 1998 and a healthy 6.3 per cent in 1997. Garments, which had topped tea as the biggest export, faced stiffer competition from East Asian countries benefiting from currency depreciation, and tea itself suffered from low prices. Tourism was one of the few bright spots, with a significant rise in visitors, aided partly by a recovery in traffic from East Asia. However, the year ended with further terrorist bombs which threatened to reverse this trend. The war also continued to distort public expenditure, with military requirements taking up 5 per cent of GDP.

3. INDIAN OCEAN STATES

i. MAURITIUS

CAPITAL: Port Louis   AREA: 2,040 sq km   POPULATION: 1,160,000 ('98)
OFFICIAL LANGUAGE: English   POLITICAL SYSTEM: parliamentary democracy
HEAD OF STATE: President Cassam Uteem (since June '92)
RULING PARTY: Mauritius Labour Party (MLP) heads coalition
HEAD OF GOVERNMENT: Navin Ramgoolam (MLP), Prime Minister (since Dec '95)
MAIN IGO MEMBERSHIPS (NON-UN): OAU, COMESA, SADC, OIC, ACP, CWTH, Francophonie, NAM
CURRENCY: rupee (end-'99 £1=MRs40.96, US$1=MRs25.42)
GNP PER CAPITA: US$3,700 by exchange-rate calculation, US$9,400 at PPP ('98)

THE Mauritian economy, the most successful in Africa since the mid-1980s, suffered a major slowdown in 1999, following a boom of which the sugar, tourism and textile industries, together with offshore banking, had been the main pillars. The causes were adverse weather, which damaged the sugar crop, a lower than expected increase in tourist arrivals, disappointing textile exports and ethnic unrest which dented business and investor confidence. GDP growth for the year fell to 2.5 per cent from 5.3 per cent in 1998—although growth picked up again in the second half year, while inflation eased to 6.9 per cent by year end after peaking at 8.1 per cent in August.

The sugar crop was damaged by a prolonged drought in late 1998 and early

1999, and then by a cyclone. The harvest was the second worst in 40 years, down by over 40 per cent on the previous year in both volume and revenue terms. Tourist arrivals increased by 3.6 per cent in 1999 and earnings from the sector increased by 8.1 per cent in real terms. These lower than expected figures were attributed to political unrest (see below), a rise in muggings of tourists and relatively few bookings for the millennium holiday. The textile industry was undermined by fiercer competition from the recovering South-East Asian economies.

The 1999/2000 budget, presented by Finance Minister Vasant Bunwaree on 15 June, included measures to alleviate poverty, attract additional foreign investment (notably the creation of an investment board to promote Mauritius as a business location) and stimulate economic activity (including a harmonization of corporation tax at 15 per cent). Another main theme was the need to cut the budget deficit, which had hit 3.9 per cent of GDP in the 1998/99 fiscal year. This would be done primarily by reducing waste and improving efficiency in the public sector.

The event which cast a long shadow over the year in Mauritius was the ethnic unrest which followed the death in police custody of a popular Creole singer, Joseph Topize, known as 'Kaya'. He had been arrested on 18 February for smoking marijuana at a rally calling for the decriminalization of the drug. His death in policy custody three days later under suspicious circumstances—a head injury and bleeding, according to the post mortem—sparked four days of clashes in Port Louis and elsewhere between Creoles and the police and between Creoles and Hindus. Three people, including another well-known singer, Berger Agathe, were killed by police during the riots. The government subsequently launched inquiries into Kaya's death and into the causes of the unrest.

The riots were the worst in 31 years of independence and were said to expose the widening gap between rich and poor and the related underlying tensions between the island's two largest ethnic communities, the Creoles (mixed-blood descendants of African slaves) and Hindus, who accounted for just under a third and around half the population respectively. Many Creoles considered themselves disadvantaged and discriminated against by the Hindus and the smaller European and Chinese communities, which had benefited most from the economic boom.

In the political sphere, the two main opposition parties, the Mauritian Socialist Movement (MSM) and the Mauritian Militant Movement (MMM), formed an alliance on 26 January. They committed themselves to reducing public expenditure if they won the next election. On 25 September Prime Minister Navin Ramgoolam announced a minor cabinet reshuffle. The main change was the inclusion of Xavier Duval, leader of the Xavier Duval Mauritian Party (XDMP), which had formed an alliance with the ruling Mauritius Labour Party (MLP). M. Duval was appointed Minister of Industry, Commerce, Corporate Affairs and Financial Services.

ii. SEYCHELLES, COMOROS AND MALDIVES

Seychelles
CAPITAL: Victoria   AREA: 454 sq km   POPULATION: 79,000 ('98)
OFFICIAL LANGUAGES: Seychellois, English & French   POLITICAL SYSTEM: presidential
HEAD OF STATE & GOVERNMENT: President France-Albert René (since June '77)
RULING PARTY: Seychelles People's Progressive Front (SPPF)
MAIN IGO MEMBERSHIPS (NON-UN): OAU, COMESA, IOC, ACP, CWTH, Francophonie, NAM
CURRENCY: rupee (end-'99 £1=SR8.35, US$1=SR5.37)
GNP PER CAPITA: US$6,450 by exchange-rate calculation, US$10,530 at PPP ('98)

Comoros
CAPITAL: Moroni   AREA: 1,860 sq km   POPULATION: 531,000 ('98)
OFFICIAL LANGUAGES: Arabic & French   POLITICAL SYSTEM: military regime
HEAD OF STATE & GOVERNMENT: Col. Azili Assoumani (since April '99)
PRIME MINISTER: Bianfrifi Tarmidi (since Dec '99)
MAIN IGO MEMBERSHIPS (NON-UN): OAU, COMESA, OIC, ACP, CWTH, Francophonie, AL, OIC, NAM
CURRENCY: Comoros franc (end-'99 £1=FC781.67, US$=FC485.00)
GNP PER CAPITA: US$370 by exchange-rate calculation, US$1,480 at PPP ('98)

Maldives
CAPITAL: Malé   AREA: 300 sq km   POPULATION: 262,000 ('98)
OFFICIAL LANGUAGE: Divehi   POLITICAL SYSTEM: presidential
HEAD OF STATE & GOVERNMENT: President Maumoun Abdul Gayoom (since Nov '78)
MAIN IGO MEMBERSHIPS (NON-UN): SAARC, CP, CWTH, OIC, NAM, SADC
CURRENCY: ruffiya (end-'99 £1=R17.83, US$1=R11.06)
GNP PER CAPITA: US$1,230 by exchange-rate calculation ('98)

IN the SEYCHELLES, the economy continued to be troubled in 1999 by a high budget deficit (around 14 per cent of GDP) and a shortage of foreign exchange. The government continued its policies of diversifying the economy and generating revenues, while retaining the extensive welfare provisions which had brought the Seychellois the highest standard of living by far in Africa.

To boost the tourism industry, the government sponsored the launch of the Tourism Marketing Authority in April. The intention was to involve the private sector, in particular tour operators and hoteliers, more closely in the formulation and implementation of policy. The government also abolished a US$100 tax levied on all tourists and foreign nationals arriving at Mahé airport (see AR 1998, pp. 345-6). Tourism revenues and arrivals, which had hovered around $130 million and 130,000 respectively since 1994, dropped by 8 per cent in the first quarter of 1999, but picked up again subsequently and eventually broadly matched 1998 figures.

The main planks of economic diversification—fish processing and offshore financial services—continued to thrive. The Indian Ocean Tuna canning factory began operating at full capacity in late 1999. In the three years since its opening it had already become the country's largest single foreign exchange earner and its biggest employer; its turnover of around $100 million was already close to the earnings from the whole tourism sector. By the end of 1999, moreover, around 4,800 offshore companies had been registered in the Seychelles.

In January the poor state of the archipelago's coral reefs, which were a major tourist attraction and a major source of fish, was exposed in a report by an independent environmental organization, the Global Coral Reef Alliance. Rising sea temperatures due to global warming were the root cause of reef destruction, according to the report.

An investigation of the reefs in December 1998 had found that warming water had killed 80 per cent of the coral and badly damaged the rest. The damage was especially severe around the tourist islands of Mahé, Praslin and La Digue, where 95 per cent of the coral had died.

Dying coral reefs were first observed in the 1980s, but the rate of destruction accelerated in the late 1990s. Sea temperatures around the Seychelles, normally around 29°C, had risen to 33°C in recent years. The report also showed that low-lying islands in the archipelago faced severe beach erosion if the barrier reefs were to break apart.

On the sporting front, Africa's smallest country enjoyed a rare success in January when the football club Saint Michel United won a qualifying tie for the African Cup Winners' Cup by beating a Mauritian side. Saint Michel lost in the first round proper to the Zambian club Power Dynamos, losing 6-1 away but recording a 2-1 victory in the home leg.

The troubled history of the COMOROS took another twist on 30 April when the army seized power in the capital, Moroni, after three days of rioting. The army chief of staff, Colonel Azili Assoumani said that he had removed President Tajiddine Ben Said Massounde 'to preserve national unity and the traditional links uniting all the citizens of the country'. Elected institutions were dissolved and an executive body 'primarily of civilians and especially young technocrats' was set up. The coup was the culmination of nearly two years of tension following the efforts of two of the smaller islands, Anjouan and Mohéli, to secede. Fighting in December 1998 (see AR 1998, p. 347) had prompted a new round of mediation by the OAU, which led to a provisional accord being reached in Antananarivo, Madagascar, on 23 April granting considerable autonomy to the two secessionist islands. The Anjouanese did not sign, however, saying that they needed to consult their people. This led to the anti-Anjouan riots in Moroni which triggered the coup, although the strong Anjouanese component in the army might have increased pressure for a takeover. There had been earlier riots in Moroni in March against the alleged takeover of Grand Comore island by Anjouan, at the same time as it was trying to secede. Anjouan itself had been without any central government authority since September 1997 (see AR 1997, p. 323).

International reaction to the coup was negative, especially since the OAU called on the international community to reject any form of cooperation with the new junta. This was firmed up at the OAU summit in July, when the coup was condemned and heads of state agreed to exclude coup-makers from their counsels in the future (see XI.6.ii). There was also an end to any OAU mediation. An Arab League fact-finding mission took a markedly more neutral position than the OAU, its members saying that they were encouraged by the stability of the islands.

Sworn in as President in early May, Colonel Assoumani said that he would remain in power for at least a year to implement the Antananarivo accord. A 'national mediator' for Anjouan was appointed in the person of Lieut.-Colonel

Said Abeid, who was reported to be emerging as the new 'strong man' of Anjouan, having elbowed out the original secessionist leader, Foundi Abdallah Ibrahim. At a secret meeting later in the year between Colonel Assoumani and Lieut.-Colonel Abeid in Fomboni on Mohéli island, it was agreed to set up a commission to examine reservations about the Antananarivo accord. In the meantime, Lieut.-Colonel Abeid had organized elections on Anjouan in mid-August, resulting in the return of mainly hardline secessionists. There were complaints that polling took place under the eye of armed militia and was thus scarcely free and fair.

Following further talks between the central authorities and the secessionists, President Assoumani on 2 December appointed a new government under the premiership of Bianfrifi Tarmidi, hitherto Interior Minister. However, assertions that a 'national unity' administration had been formed were belied by a continuing impasse on the secession question, amid fears that a break-up was inevitable. Political parties in Moroni charged France with favouring separatism, but there was no evidence that the government in Paris was giving any encouragement to the idea of Anjouan following the path of Mayotte and connecting itself again with France—a position favoured by some of the Anjouanese secessionists.

The economy of the MALDIVES, sustained by increased tourist arrivals and higher international fish prices, continued to perform well in 1999. Provisional figures showed growth of 6.4 per cent, comparable to the 6.8 per cent and 6.2 per cent recorded in the previous two years. Some 429,000 tourists visited the Maldives in 1999, an increase of 8.4 per cent on 1998.

The tourism industry was shaken by two helicopter accidents in 1999. Five people were killed in a crash off the Rangali resort in January, and another crash in the same area in December cost the lives of 10 people. In both cases the helicopters were taking tourists to Malé airport.

A parliamentary election for the 40 elected seats of the *Majlis* was held on 19 November (the remaining eight members being appointed by the President). In the absence of political parties in the Maldives, the 130 candidates ran as independents. The turnout was 80 per cent, up from 74 per cent in the last election in December 1994 (see AR 1994, p. 349). Two candidates were elected unopposed.

As in previous years, there was growing evidence that the effects of global warming were damaging the fragile ecosystem of the low-lying Maldives archipelago. A study by an independent environmental organization, the Global Reef Alliance, published in January, showed that the average temperature of the ocean had risen sharply in recent years, with the result that long stretches of coral reefs suffered from severe 'bleaching', an early indication of their destruction. The report also showed that rising sea levels were threatening the beaches of one-third of the archipelago's 200 inhabited islands. Responding to the report, President Abdul Gayoom declared: 'Sea-level rise is not a fashionable scientific hypothesis. It is a fact'.

iii. MADAGASCAR

CAPITAL: Antananarivo   AREA: 587,000 sq km   POPULATION: 15,000,000 ('98)
OFFICIAL LANGUAGES: Malagasy & French   POLITICAL SYSTEM: presidential
HEAD OF STATE & GOVERNMENT: President (Adm.) Didier Ratsiraka (since Jan '97)
RULING PARTIES: Vanguard for Economic and Social Recovery (ARES) heads coalition
PRIME MINISTER: Tantely Andrianarivo (since July '98)
MAIN IGO MEMBERSHIPS (NON-UN): OAU, COMESA, IOC, ACP, Francophonie, NAM
CURRENCY: Malagasy franc (end-'99 P1=FMG10,371.30, US$1=FMG6,435.00)
GNP PER CAPITA: US$260 by exchange-rate calculation, US$900 at PPP ('98)

IN a largely quiescent political year, the continuing difficulties of the economy moved centre stage, part of the problem being the heavy burden of servicing a $3,500 million debt. The IMF foresaw in April that if no agreement were reached in coming months with the international donor community a serious financial crisis was unavoidable, involving cessation of payments by the state. Accordingly, a new monetary and financial strategy for 1999-2000 was embarked on at the end of August in agreement with the Fund, following a 10 per cent devaluation of the currency in June, which helped put relations with the Washington institutions back on course. The strategy involved strengthening financial markets and facilitating participation by small shareholders in the privatization programmes, which had been a source of discord between the Malagasy government and the IMF/World bank. A stock exchange was due to be set up in the year 2000.

IX SOUTH-EAST AND EAST ASIA

1. MYANMAR (BURMA)—THAILAND—MALAYSIA—BRUNEI—SINGAPORE—INDONESIA—PHILIPPINES—VIETNAM—CAMBODIA—LAOS

i. MYANMAR (BURMA)

CAPITAL: Yangon (Rangoon)   AREA: 676,500 sq km   POPULATION: 50,000,000 ('98)
OFFICIAL LANGUAGE: Burmese   POLITICAL SYSTEM: military regime
HEAD OF STATE & GOVERNMENT: Gen. Than Shwe, Chairman of State Peace and Development Council and Prime Minister (since April '92)
MAIN IGO MEMBERSHIPS (NON-UN): ASEAN, CP, NAM
CURRENCY: kyat (end-'99 £1=K10.07, US$1=K6.25)
GNP PER CAPITA: n/a

IN a significant development, Japanese Prime Minister Keizo Obuchi held talks with Burmese Prime Minister General Than Shwe at the ASEAN summit in Manila on 28 November and offered to help rebuild the country if political and economic reforms were put in place. This was the first such meeting with a major world leader since the massacres of 1988.

Myanmar's membership of ASEAN impeded relations between the Association and the European Union (EU). High-level meetings in January and February were cancelled because of objections about Myanmar's participation. Nonetheless, on 6-7 July a delegation from the EU held talks with the government and opposition groups. Relations between Myanmar and Thailand also deteriorated. On 1 October five armed activists belonging to the previously-unknown Vigorous Burmese Student Warriors group occupied the Burmese embassy in Bangkok, taking 89 hostages. They demanded that the State Peace and Development Council (SPDC) open negotiations with the opposition, release all political prisoners, and convene the constituent assembly elected in 1990. The Thai government negotiated a peaceful resolution to the crisis (see IX.1.ii) but not one to the SPDC's liking. The opposition National League for Democracy (NLD) condemned the hostage-taking but expressed sympathy for the group's aims.

In January radio broadcasts from Myanmar reported that thousands of NLD members had resigned from the party-apparently in response to a campaign of intimidation orchestrated by first secretary General Khin Nyunt.

On 27 March Michael Aris, British husband of pro-democracy leader Aung San Suu Kyi, died in the UK. Following the diagnosis in January that he had cancer, Mr Aris was denied a visa to see his wife. Ms Suu Kyi turned down an offer to visit him in the UK fearing that she would not be permitted to return; she decided not to attend his funeral for the same reason. Ms Suu Kyi made a rare public appearance on 19 July at the official ceremony commemorating the 52nd anniversary of the assassination of Aung San, Ms Suu Kyi's father. In July it was also reported that 19 people had been arrested for planning a march to commemorate Aung San's death, among whom were eight members of NLD member Kyaw Wunna's family, including his three-year-old daughter.

In April it was reported that Ms Suu Kyi had smuggled a video to the UN High Commissioner for Human Rights alleging that the situation in Myanmar had deteriorated and that 150 NLD MPs were held in custody without trial, along with 400 other party members. In May the SPDC gave its permission to the International Committee of the Red Cross (ICRC) to make private visits to 48 prisons in the country. The NLD criticized the agreement; it was reported that 350-500 political prisoners were transferred from Yangon's notorious Insein prison ahead of the ICRC's first visit there.

In separate and unrelated events, two British activists were arrested in Myanmar in August and September. James Mawdsley was sentenced to 17 years' imprisonment and Rachel Goldwyn to seven years; the latter was released within a month following intervention by her parents.

August saw the 11th anniversary of the 1988 uprising against the junta; there were reports of limited protests across the country to mark the event. There were also expectations that opposition groups would mount significant protests on 9 August, to mark the anniversary of the August 1988 massacre. These did not materialize to any significant extent.

In mid-year there were reports of large-scale movements of Shan and Karen people into Thai territory in response to government actions. An Amnesty International report in June highlighted the plight of the Shan and Karen at the hands of the government and maintained that human rights abuses had worsened since Myanmar joined ASEAN.

ii. THAILAND

CAPITAL: Bangkok   AREA: 513,000 sq km   POPULATION: 61,000,000 ('98)
OFFICIAL LANGUAGE: Thai   POLITICAL SYSTEM: constitutional monarchy
HEAD OF STATE: King Bhumibol Adulyadej (Rama IX) (since June '46)
RULING PARTIES: Democrat Party (DP) heads six-party coalition
HEAD OF GOVERNMENT: Chuan Leekpai, Prime Minister (since Nov '97)
MAIN IGO MEMBERSHIPS (NON-UN): ASEAN, CP, APEC, NAM
CURRENCY: baht (end-'99 £1=B60.56, US$1=B37.58)
GNP PER CAPITA: US$2,200 by exchange-rate calculation, US$5,840 at PPP ('98)

IN 1999 Thailand saw the first substantive glimmers of recovery after two years of economic recession. GDP expanded by 0.9 per cent in the first quarter of 1999, the first period of growth since the recession hit in mid-1997. Growth for the year was 4.2 per cent. While foreign direct investment remained weak, exports were up, inflation low, foreign reserves stood at US$32,000 million, and the current account was expected to show a surplus of $11,600 million at year-end. In November the government announced that it would not be drawing on the final $3,700 million of the IMF's $17,200 million rescue package agreed in August 1997.

For most Thais, however, the most significant event was King Bhumibol Adulyadej's 72nd birthday on 5 December, auspiciously marking the end of his sixth cycle of 12 years. There were widespread celebrations. In late December a censorship committee banned *Anna and the King,* a film recounting Anna Leonowens's time as governess in the court of King Mongkut, on the grounds that it broke Thailand's strict laws of *lèse majesté.*

Prime Minister Chuan Leekpai survived several challenges to his leadership. In January a series of bombing incidents in Bangkok was said to have been orchestrated by his political opponents in the military hoping to bolster a no-confidence motion against three government ministers in late January. The motion failed. In August more serious allegations emerged about financial irregularities at the state-owned Krung Thai Bank. Former bank president Sirin Nimmanahaeminda, brother of Finance Minister Tarrin Nimmanahaeminda, was implicated in the scandal.

The most serious challenge to Chuan's premiership came in a five-day censure debate in mid-December. The opposition New Aspirations Party (NAP) questioned Tarrin's association with the Krung Thai scandal, alleging that he tried to cover up the extent of the bank's bad loans to protect his brother. Again, the government won the day. The failure of NAP leader (and former Premier) Chaovalit Yongchaiyudh to mount an effective challenge contributed to the feeling that his days in politics were numbered. By contrast, telecoms tycoon Thaksin Shinawatra, leader of the opposition Thai Rak Thai Party, was felt to have improved his chances in the general election due no later than November 2000, by remaining on the sidelines.

The government's attempts to reform the legal and administrative structures underpinning the economy continued through 1999. In February the Senate passed a contentious new bankruptcy law making it easier for creditors to pursue their claims by creating a specialized bankruptcy court. In March the House of Representatives gave final approval to a privatization bill, while the Senate approved legislation permitting, for the first time, foreigners to own and lease land, albeit on a limited basis. The government also authorized the subsidized sale of five state-owned banks despite some opposition to the government's modest privatization programme.

Attempts to resolve the mountain of private-sector debt progressed slowly, with only a fraction of indebted companies entering the (central) Bank of Thailand's debt restructuring programme. The failure to reform the banking sector remained, analysts agreed, Thailand's main barrier to a sustainable recovery. In mid-year non-performing loans constituted 45 per cent of total lending, or $65,000 million, and fell only marginally during the course of the second half of the year.

After over 18 months of IMF-orchestrated fiscal austerity, on 30 March the government unveiled a B130,000 million ($3,500 million) stimulus package of tax cuts and spending plans. The IMF signalled its approval of the change in strategy. On 10 August a further stimulus package of B102,000 million ($3,000 million) was announced, aimed at encouraging new investment. These contributed to a budget deficit for the fiscal year to October of 7 per cent of GDP.

Relations with Myanmar deteriorated after five armed opposition activists occupied the Burmese embassy in Bangkok on 1 October (see IX.1.i). The government brokered a deal and, after releasing their 89 hostages, the dissidents were flown to a refugee camp on the border with Myanmar and released. The Burmese authorities closed the border with Thailand and in November the Thai government responded by expelling around 100,000 illegal Burmese immigrants living in border areas of the country.

Army commander-in-chief General Surayud Chulanont received plaudits for beginning the task of transforming the military. This included reducing the role of the army in business and introducing reforms designed to shrink the army from 230,000 to 190,000 by 2007 as well as cutting the number of generals, admirals and air force marshals from 1,600 to 1,000.

At the beginning of July internal squabbling led to the withdrawal of the Social Action Party from the ruling coalition, reducing Chuan's support in the House of Representatives by 20 and necessitating a cabinet reshuffle which was seen as strengthening the positions of Chuan's Democrat Party and the Chart Patthana Party.

In early March drought and weak rice prices brought thousands of farmers to Bangkok to demonstrate for a fairer deal. An explosion caused by leaking chemicals at a fruit-processing plant outside the northern town of Chiang Mai killed 23 people on 19 September. On 5 December Bangkok's first mass transit system opened in the notoriously congested capital, the $1,500 million Skytrain.

Puey Ungpakorn, arguably the architect of Thailand's modern economy, died in London on 28 July aged 83. He had been exiled to the UK after being branded a communist.

iii. MALAYSIA

CAPITAL: Kuala Lumpur   AREA: 132,000 sq km   POPULATION: 22,000,000 ('98)
OFFICIAL LANGUAGE: Bahasa Malaysia POLITICAL SYSTEM: federal democracy
HEAD OF STATE: Salahuddin Abdul Aziz Shah, Sultan of Selangor (since April '99)
RULING PARTY: National Front coalition
HEAD OF GOVERNMENT: Dr Mahathir Mohamad, Prime Minister (since July '81)
MAIN IGO MEMBERSHIPS (NON-UN): ASEAN, APEC, CP, OIC, CWTH, NAM
CURRENCY: ringitt (end-'99 £1=M$6.12, US$1=M$3.80)
GNP PER CAPITA: US$3,600 by exchange-rate calculation, US$6,990 at PPP ('98)

PRIME Minister Dr Mahathir Mohamad led his ruling Barisan Nasional (National Front) coalition to a fifth consecutive federal election victory on 29 November. His 13-party coalition secured 148 seats in a parliament expanded by one seat to 193 from the previous legislature. Although the Barisan Nasional achieved its declared goal of a two-thirds majority, its parliamentary numbers were reduced from 162 in 1995, while its overall share of the vote was reduced from 65 to 56 per cent. Moreover, major losses were experienced by its political core, the United Malays National Organization

(UMNO), which secured 74 seats compared with 88 in 1995. Of its main non-Malay partners, the Malaysian Chinese Association (MCA) secured 27 seats, compared with 30 in 1995, while the Malaysian Indian Congress (MIC) retained seven seats.

The main beneficiary of the Barisan Nasional's loss of support was the Barisan Alternatif (Alternative Front), an electoral pact established in June between the Parti Islam (PAS), the Democratic Action Party (DAP), the Parti Keadilan Nasional (National Justice Party) and the Parti Ra'ayat Malaysia (Malaysian People's Party). The PAS increased its federal parliamentary strength exceptionally from seven to 27 seats, while the non-Malay DAP secured 10 seats, one more than in 1995, although DAP leader Lim Kit Siang together with another party luminary, Karpal Singh, failed to secure re-election. Keadilan, established in April and led by Azizah Ismail, the wife of deposed and imprisoned former Deputy Prime Minister Anwar Ibrahim (see below), secured five seats. The left-wing Malay-based Malaysian People's Party failed to win any seats.

When the federal parliament reassembled in early December, the Alternative Front named Fadzil Noor, the PAS president, as the leader of the official opposition. The PAS also enjoyed electoral success in the concurrent elections for state legislatures, with the exception of those in Sarawak and Sabah, which had been held in September 1996 and in March 1999 respectively. It held on to office in Kelantan and secured victory additionally in the neighbouring state of Terengganu. In the earlier state elections in Sabah, the Barisan Nasional secured a victory with 31 out of 48 seats.

Dr Mahathir announced his new cabinet in mid-December, having a number of places to fill because four ministers and five deputy ministers had lost their parliamentary seats. In the event, its composition registered continuity with Daim Zainuddin retained as Finance Minister, Abdullah Ahmad Badawi as Deputy Prime Minister and Home Minister and Hamid Albar as Foreign Minister. Najib Razak, who secured re-election with a majority of only 241 votes, was transferred from the education portfolio to defence, while Tengku Razaleigh, a former Finance Minister and political rival of Dr Mahathir, who had failed in his allotted task of capturing the state of Kelantan, was not offered cabinet office. Towards the end of the month, Dr Mahathir, who had already indicated that he had embarked on his last term, announced that Abdullah Ahmad Badawi was his chosen successor. Mr Badawi had first been appointed Deputy Prime Minister in January.

In March the royal commission of inquiry into the injuries sustained by Anwar Ibrahim in September 1998 while in police custody (see AR 1998, pp. 352-3), concluded that the inspector-general of police, Abdul Rahman Noor, was wholly responsible. In April Anwar Ibrahim was found guilty of four charges of corruption (abuse of power) and sentenced to six years' imprisonment, provoking public disorder in Kuala Lumpur for several days. Later that month he was charged with a further count of sodomy, the trial being scheduled to begin in June. However, the trial was suspended initially because of unproven allegations by the former Deputy Prime Minister that he had been subject to arsenic poisoning and again indefinitely from mid-November.

In September a Canadian journalist, Murray Hiebert of the *Far Eastern Economic Review*, was sentenced to six weeks' imprisonment for 'scandalizing the court' in respect of an article published in January 1997 dealing with a legal case brought against a school by the wife of a judge.

iv. BRUNEI

CAPITAL: Bandar Seri Bagawan   AREA: 5,765 sq km   POPULATION: 314,000 ('98)
OFFICIAL LANGUAGES: Malay & English POLITICAL SYSTEM: monarchy
HEAD OF STATE & GOVERNMENT: Sultan Sir Hassanal Bolkiah (since '67)
MAIN IGO MEMBERSHIPS (NON-UN): ASEAN, APEC, OIC, CWTH, NAM
CURRENCY: Brunei dollar (end-'99 £1=B$2.69, US$1=B$1.66)
GNP PER CAPITA: US$25,090 by exchange-rate calculation ('97)

AUDITORS Arthur Andersen confirmed in July that Amedeo, the company formerly headed by the Sultan's brother, Prince Jefri, was unable to pay its debts and that its book-value assets were US$79 million, while its liabilities were US$3,700 million. The company was wound up by a Brunei court at the end of the month, leaving creditors without legal redress. A mitigating factor in Brunei's economic adversity was the significant rise in the world price of oil in the latter part of 1999.

v. SINGAPORE

CAPITAL: Singapore   AREA: 620 sq km   POPULATION: 3,000,000 ('98)
OFFICIAL LANGUAGES: Malay, Chinese, Tamil, English POLITICAL SYSTEM: parliamentary
HEAD OF STATE: President S.R. Nathan (since Sept '99)
RULING PARTY: People's Action Party (PAP)
HEAD OF GOVERNMENT: Goh Chok Tong, Prime Minister (since Nov '90)
MAIN IGO MEMBERSHIPS (NON-UN): ASEAN, APEC, CP, CWTH, NAM
CURRENCY: Singapore dollar (end-'99 £1=S$2.69, US$1=S$1.67)
GNP PER CAPITA: US$30,060 by exchange-rate calculation, US$28,620 at PPP ('98)

IN his National Day Rally speech in August, Prime Minister Goh Chok Tong indicated that the Deputy Prime Minister, Lee Hsien Loong, would be his likely political successor. On 1 September S.R. Nathan, formerly permanent secretary of the Ministry of Foreign Affairs and director of the security and intelligence division of the Ministry of Defence, succeeded Ong Teng Cheong as President. The official committee charged with screening presidential candidates took the view that since he was the only one of three applicants to meet the prescribed criteria, an election was not required. Ong Teng Cheong, who had been the first elected President, had earlier called a press conference to register his dissatisfaction with government cooperation in his constitutional role. That role was subject to a half-day parliamentary debate in late August.

In February Chee Soon Juan, leader of the Singapore Democratic Party, was sentenced to 12 days in prison and barred from standing for election for five years after being found guilty under the Public Entertainment Act of making an unlicensed speech in Singapore's business district. He had refused to apply for a licence under the act on the ground that free speech was guaranteed under the constitution. He had been imprisoned for seven days earlier in the month for a similar offence.

In May Lee Hsien Loong, Deputy Prime Minister and head of the Monetary Authority of Singapore, announced banking reforms intended to make Singapore a leading Asian financial centre. The reforms included reductions on limits to foreign ownership of local banks and a commitment to grant six full banking licences to foreign banks. By the end of the year, economic growth forecasts had been revised upwards to indicate the end of recession.

Relations with Indonesia deteriorated in February after President B.J. Habibie told Taiwanese journalists that Singapore was a country of 'real racists' because Malays were not allowed to assume officer rank in its armed forces. A marked improvement occurred, however, after he was succeeded by Abdurrahman Wahid in October (see IX.1.vi). President Wahid received a warm welcome when he visited Singapore in November on his first stop on a tour of ASEAN countries.

Singapore's relations with China soured, despite a visit by Premier Zhu Rongji at the end of the year. At issue was the failure of a joint venture to build a 27-square-mile industrial park in the eastern Chinese city of Suzhou with anticipated losses of S$90 million. The venture had been undermined by local officials who had set up a nearby rival park, despite the formal commitment of the central government. Senior Minister Lee Kuan Yew acknowledged the failure in September and indicated a new-found caution about investing in China.

Relations between Singapore and Malaysia continued at a low ebb after general elections in the latter at the end of November (see IX.1.iii). A contentious bilateral issue, unresolved by the end of the year, was that of the status of Malaysian shares traded in Singapore under an arrangement known as 'central limit order book' (CLOB). CLOB holding accounts had been frozen on the Kuala Lumpur stock exchange when Malaysia imposed capital controls in September 1998 (see AR 1998, p. 353). A number of offers from Malaysian companies to buy the shares at a heavily discounted price had been rejected out of hand by Singapore's Securities Investors' Association.

vi. INDONESIA

CAPITAL: Jakarta   AREA: 1,905,000 sq km   POPULATION: 204,000,000 ('98)
OFFICIAL LANGUAGE: Bahasa Indonesia   POLITICAL SYSTEM: presidential
HEAD OF STATE & GOVERNMENT: President Abdurrahman Wahid (since Oct '99)
RULING PARTIES: National Awakening Party (PKB) heads coalition
MAIN IGO MEMBERSHIPS (NON-UN): ASEAN, APEC, CP, OIC, OPEC, NAM
CURRENCY: rupiah (end-'99 £1=Rp11,362.50, US$1=Rp7,050.00)
GNP PER CAPITA: US$680 by exchange-rate calculation, US$2,790 at PPP ('98)

THROUGHOUT 1999 Indonesia battled to manage the aftermath of the sudden collapse of the Suharto regime the previous year (see AR 1998, pp. 355-6). The huge task of putting in place fundamental changes to the political system had to be undertaken against a background of political and inter-ethnic violence in various parts of the national archipelago. Meanwhile, the calamitous economic situation which had precipitated Suharto's departure persisted.

In January the country's electoral law was reformed to prepare the way for legislative elections. The poll, scheduled for 7 June, would determine the 462 elected members of the 500-strong House of Representatives (a further 38 seats being reserved for the military). By 19 May, when the campaign formally began, 48 parties had announced an intention to run. The Indonesian Democratic Party (PDI-P) headed by Megawati Sukarnoputri consistently led early predictions ahead of the 'official' party of the Suharto era, Golkar (Joint Secretariat of Functional Groups). Also in serious contention were the National Awakening Party (PKB) of moderate Muslim leader Abdurrahman Wahid (usually known as Gus Dur) and the National Mandate Party (PAN) of Amien Rais.

As the campaign opened, the three non-Golkar parties agreed an electoral pact which ensured that, despite the formidable machine which it still deployed, the party of the old regime was destined for the novel experience of opposition. The official result, announced at the end of July after a number of delays and confusions, gave the PDI-P 154 seats to Golkar's 120, with the PKB and PAN taking 51 and 35 respectively. The victory of Megawati's party led to the assumption, not least on her own part, that her nomination as President by the upper house, the People's Consultative Assembly (MPR), would follow automatically. In the event, however, a combination of factors denied her the post, which on 20 October went instead to Mr Wahid by a decisive margin. Golkar's nominee, the incumbent President B.J. Habibie, withdrew from the contest at the last moment, leaving a straight fight between the PDI-P and PKB leaders. Suspicions about her political attributes (basically, whether they extended beyond the Sukarno family name) as well as traditional Muslim resistance to a woman leader combined to deny Megawati the presidency. A spasm of rioting by her disappointed and incredulous supporters was ended when the MPR elected her to the vice-presidency the following day.

By the end of the year the new government team had yet to be tested, though doubts were soon expressed about President Wahid's capacities. Beyond his chronic poor health, his lack of governmental experience and a certain impetuosity of judgment gave cause for concern both at home and abroad. However, his initial policy pronouncements, undertaking to introduce greater regional autonomy and rein in the power of the military, showed at least an awareness of the main issues confronting the new, first truly post-Suharto regime. Similarly, his cabinet reflected a clear break with the past. A civilian was appointed as Defence Minister while the armed forces commander, the enigmatic though ambitious General Wiranto, was moved to a less powerful government post and replaced by a navy man in what was interpreted as a calculated weakening of the power of the army. There were also early indications that investigations into the financial affairs of the Suharto family, fudged and frustrated during Mr Habibie's presidency, would be reinvigorated.

Accompanying these political developments at the centre was a series of crises in the periphery. The most serious and destructive of these was in East Timor. In January Foreign Minister Ali Alatas had caused widespread surprise by suggesting that if the people of East Timor rejected greater autonomy within Indonesia the option of independence might be considered. At the same time, he announced that the Timorese independence leader, Xanana Gusmão, would be released from prison into house arrest in Jakarta to facilitate the negotiation process. Talks at the United Nations in New York took place in February and March between UN Secretary-General Kofi Annan, Mr Alatas and the Portuguese Foreign Minister, Jaime Gama. (Portugal was formally recognized by the UN as the 'administering power' in East Timor). These produced a plan for a referendum in the territory to be held in August which would decide between autonomy within Indonesia or independence.

From the beginning of the process there was widespread scepticism about Indonesia's motives and intentions—or more precisely the motives and intentions of different factions within the state. While the diplomatic process appeared to be forging ahead, the Indonesian administration in East Timor, with the cooperation of the armed forces, was arming and training anti-independence 'militias' which soon began a systematic campaign of terror against the pro-independence majority. The extent of government complicity in this remained opaque, but it clearly went high in the military hierarchy. For many officers East Timor was not just an issue of institutional pride but had developed into one of personal economic interest too, because they had developed their own 'business' activities in the territory.

Despite the deteriorating security situation, the vote on 30 August passed off relatively peacefully. However, when the extent of the majority for independence became clear (78.5 per cent on a 98.6 per cent turnout), the pro-Jakarta militias initiated an orgy of killing and destruction-with the obvious complicity of the Indonesian 'security' forces. Massacres and mayhem followed in what was evidently an intentional scorched earth policy. The UN mission was eventually forced to withdraw, leaving the majority of pro-independence Timorese to their fate. In New York the Security Council appeared paralysed, unwilling to intervene without Jakarta's agreement. In the meantime, the militias' spasm of violence continued unresisted in the territory.

Finally, following heavy pressure from Washington—including a suspension of military cooperation and a threat to future arms sales—President Habibie agreed to the presence of an international force. This 'International Force for East Timor' (INTERFET)—not a UN force as such but a UN-authorized 'coalition of the willing'—began to deploy under Australian leadership with some Asian participation on 20 September. Its arrival was, of course, far too late to prevent the almost total destruction of the territory's urban areas and a massive outflow of refugees. At the end of the year the UN was preparing to formalize its interim protectorate of the territory.

The extent of the conflict in East Timor overshadowed major outbreaks of violence in other parts of the archipelago. Separatist agitation and military repression continued in Aceh in northern Sumatra throughout the year, despite a much-vaunted 'apology' for past military misbehaviour by General Wiranto in March. To many associated with the old regime, particularly in the military, such outbreaks validated a 'domino theory' of national disintegration following the perceived 'weakness' of Mr Alatas and President Habibie over East Timor.

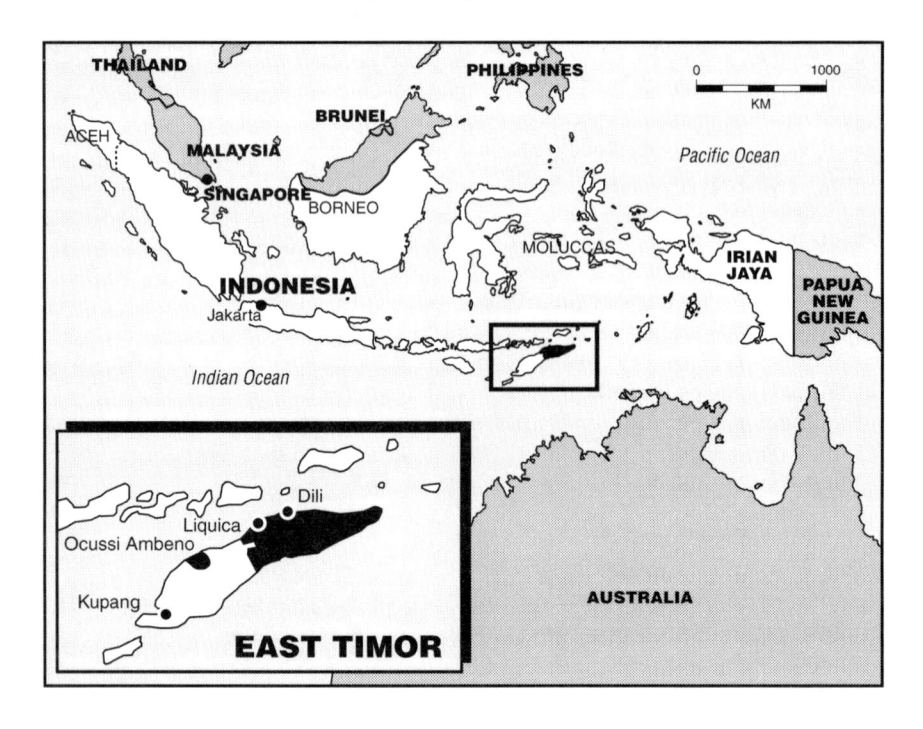

Meanwhile, on the spice island of Ambon the year had begun, and was to end, with major inter-communal violence between Christian and Muslim communities which Jakarta seemed unable to contain. Similarly, in March and April a gruesome blood-letting by indigenous Dayaks and Malays in the province of West Kalimantan on Borneo against migrants from Madura broke out and was brought under control only after another massive movement of refugees. The low-level insurgency of the indigenous Papuan people of Irian Jaya (west New Guinea) also continued sporadically during 1999.

It was therefore far from clear at the end of the year that the multiple crises of the previous two momentous years had yet peaked, let alone run their course.

vii. PHILIPPINES

CAPITAL: Manila   AREA: 300,000 sq km   POPULATION: 75,000,000 ('98)
OFFICIAL LANGUAGE: Filipino   POLITICAL SYSTEM: presidential democracy
HEAD OF STATE & GOVERNMENT: President Joseph Ejercito Estrada (since June '98)
RULING PARTY: Struggle of the Nationalist Philippines Masses (LMMP)
MAIN IGO MEMBERSHIPS (NON-UN): ASEAN, APEC, CP, NAM
CURRENCY: peso (end-'99 £1=P64.95, US$1=P40.30)
GNP PER CAPITA: US$1,050 by exchange-rate calculation, US$3,540 at PPP ('98)

DURING 1999 the general contours of the presidency of Joseph Estrada began to emerge. A largely unknown political quantity at the time of his election in 1998 (see AR 1998, p. 358), Mr Estrada's apparent populism raised initial hopes and misgivings in the country in equal proportions. In the event, a dangerous uncertainty of political instinct, along with an evident inclination towards old-fashioned Filipino 'cronyism', marked his first full year's performance in office.

Hostility to the President's style and performance momentarily reinvigorated the old spirit of people's power which had forced Ferdinand Marcos from office in 1986 (see AR 1986, pp. 297-8). In June former President Corazon Aquino and the Catholic leader Cardinal Jaime Sin denounced President Estrada for opening the presidential palace once again to the dubious business figures of the Marcos years and undermining and intimidating the press—in short, of attempting to reverse the achievements of 1986. On 20 August they managed to bring 150,000 on to the streets of Manila to drive their point home. President Estrada's lack of political instinct had already been demonstrated in the apparent unravelling of the delicate internal peace processes he inherited from his predecessor Fidel Ramos (see AR 1997, p. 336).

At the beginning of the year clashes began with the Moro Islamic Liberation Front in Mindanao, despite the existence of a ceasefire, as the government refused to accept the *de facto* reality of guerrilla-controlled zones. Then in February, following the probably unplanned and unauthorized abduction of a senior army general, President Estrada appeared set on a military 'solution' to the longstanding insurgency of the leftist New People's Army (NPA). Talks with the NPA's political organization, the National Democratic Front (NDF), were broken off by the government. The result was a threat of MILF military support for the NPA and a refusal by the NDF to resume negotiations with the government, even though the general and other hostages were released. By the end of the year both the MILF and the NPA were extending their guerrilla operations-a remarkable circumstance for the latter, which had been widely regarded as a spent force after the fall of Ferdinand Marcos and the end of the Cold War.

President Estrada had by then, apparently, abandoned the negotiation route.

A further divisive policy was adopted by the government at the end of May when the Senate agreed to the Visiting Forces Agreement (VFA). This opened the way for a resumption of the US military presence in the country which had been ended in 1991 (see AR 1991, p. 321). The government, concerned at the declining capacity of the national armed forces, looked to the military benefits of joint training exercises with the United States. A broad alliance opposed to the VFA soon emerged, however. Leftists and nationalists objected on political grounds, while the church was concerned about the damage to local communities which the re-establishment of foreign military garrisons would entail.

The government's anxiety to upgrade the capacity of the armed forces through the VFA was driven in part by the unresolved security problems over the contested Spratly Islands (see AR 1995, p. 328). During 1999 incidents of varying seriousness in the area of the islands occurred between the Philippines and China, Vietnam and Malaysia. Two Chinese fishing vessels were sunk with loss of life after 'accidental' collisions with Philippine patrol boats in May and July. The difficulties with Malaysia were aggravated by President Estrada's 'personal' support for its former Deputy Prime Minister, Anwar Ibrahim, after his dismissal and prosecution by Prime Minister Mahathir Mohamad (see IX.1.iii).

By the end of the year President Estrada's position, while not under direct threat, was not wholly secure. Ominously for him, political attention was focused increasingly on his widely-respected and independently-appointed (therefore untainted) Vice-President, the glamorous and formidable Gloria Macapagal-Arroyo (see AR 1998, p. 358).

viii. VIETNAM

CAPITAL: Hanoi   AREA: 330,000 sq km   POPULATION: 78,000,000 ('98)
OFFICIAL LANGUAGE: Vietnamese   POLITICAL SYSTEM: socialist republic
RULING PARTY: Communist Party of Vietnam (CPV)
HEAD OF STATE: President Tran Duc Luong (since Sept '97)
PARTY LEADER: Gen. Le Kha Phieu, CPV general secretary (since Dec '97)
HEAD OF GOVERNMENT: Phan Van Khai, Prime Minister (since Sept '97)
MAIN IGO MEMBERSHIPS (NON-UN): ASEAN, NAM, Francophonie
CURRENCY: dong (end-'99 £1=D22,609.70, US$1=D14,028.50)
GNP PER CAPITA: US$330 by exchange-rate calculation, US$1,690 at PPP ('98)

IN February the Communist Party of Vietnam (CPV) launched a concerted anti-corruption drive. In April the two ring-leaders among 74 government officials, some of them high level, accused of smuggling US$70 million of consumer goods into Ho Chi Minh City between 1994 and 1997, were sentenced to death. Six others faced life imprisonment. On 10 May the trial of 77 businessmen and civil servants accused of fraudulently obtaining state loans valued at $280 million opened in Hanoi. It was the country's largest-ever corruption trial. Almost three months later the trial concluded with six of the defendants sentenced to death, six to life imprisonment, and all of the remainder convicted. On 18 May general secretary La Kha Phieu attacked the 'degradation' in the party during a speech marking the birthday of Ho Chi Minh. In November Deputy Prime Minister Ngo Xuan Loc, along with a former central bank governor and customs chief, were dismissed for 'mismanagement'. The dismissed minister was ousted from the National Assembly in December. Some analysts saw him as a victim of a battle between 'reformers' (with whom he was closely allied) and 'conservatives' in the government.

There were significant developments in relations with the USA. On 25 July Trade Minister Truong Dinh Tuyen and US deputy trade representative Rich Fisher met in Hanoi and agreed to normalize trade relations. This marked the culmination of three years' discussions and was regarded as the most important development in trade relations between the two countries since the lifting of the US trade embargo in 1994. On 6-7 September US Secretary of State Madeleine Albright visited Hanoi and held discussions with Le Kha Phieu and Prime Minister Phan Van Khai. However, by year's end the trade agreement was still not signed-to consternation on the US side-apparently because of concerns among Vietnamese conservatives about the side-effects of such reform.

At the beginning of the year the central bank announced that it would allow the controlled depreciation of the non-convertible dong to bring it in line with market rates. In June foreign donors expressed concern at a meeting in Haiphong that economic reforms were not progressing fast enough. In 1999 foreign aid was expected to total $1,000 million, but foreign direct investment all but dried up, falling to below its 1992 figure. Also in June it was announced that two foreign insurance companies would be allowed to operate in Vietnam, while in December the Prime Minister indicated that state monopolies would be dismantled to stimulate the economy. In an attempt to bring greater transparency to public finances, on 10 June the government published details of its annual budget for the first time-and forecast a budget deficit for 1999-2000 of the equivalent of $935 million. Official figures indicated that the economy had grown by 4.8 per cent in 1999.

It was reported in March that the poor harvests of 1998 had induced near famine conditions in some areas of the northern and central regions. In mid-year expectations for the 1999-2000 crop year were high, but serious flooding in the central region in December left over 700 people dead and one million in need of emergency assistance.

In February the Chinese announced that they would begin clearing the estimated 800,000 landmines laid along the border with Vietnam following the border war of 1979. The ever-present conflict over sovereignty of the Spratly Islands brought Vietnam and the Philippines into conflict, just weeks before an ASEAN summit in Manila in November (see XI.6.iii).

ix. CAMBODIA

CAPITAL: Phnom Penh   AREA: 181,000 sq km   POPULATION: 11,000,000 ('98)
OFFICIAL LANGUAGE: Khmer   POLITICAL SYSTEM: monarchy
HEAD OF STATE: King Norodom Sihanouk (elected Sept '93)
RULING PARTIES: Cambodian People's Party (CPP) & United National Front for an Independent, Neutral, Peaceful and Cooperative Cambodia (FUNCINPEC)
HEAD OF GOVERNMENT: Hun Sen, Prime Minister (since July '97)
MAIN IGO MEMBERSHIPS (NON-UN): ASEAN, CP, Francophonie, NAM
CURRENCY: riel (end-'99 £1=R6,039.04, US$1=R3,747.00)
GNP PER CAPITA: US$280 by exchange-rate calculation, US$1,240 at PPP ('98)

ON 9 February the 'last' 4,332 Khmer Rouge (KR) soldiers surrendered to the government. Of these 1,700 were to be integrated in to the Royal Cambodian Armed Forces (RCAF) and the remaining 2,632 given a payment to aid their return to their families. A month later KR leader Ta Mok, along with a remnant group of supporters, was captured. Ta Mok was formally charged with genocide on 7 September, although no date was set for his trial. It was also reported that former KR leader 'Duch', who was arrested in May, had been charged with genocide.

The year saw the continuation of the long-running debate over whether-and how-former KR leaders should be tried. After Hun Sen had apparently offered an amnesty to KR leaders Khieu Samphan and Nuon Chea following their surrender in December 1998 (see AR 1998, p. 361), he backtracked in the face of criticism. In March UN Secretary-General Kofi Annan lent his support to a UN report recommending the creation of an international tribunal. Hun Sen remained opposed to such an idea. But in April Hun Sen appeared to relax his position and said that foreign judges might participate. On 21 June it was reported that Hun Sen had approached the UN special representative on human rights in Cambodia, Thomas Hammarberg, to request assistance with the trials. However, two months later Hun Sen rejected UN proposals that either five judges (two of them Cambodian) or seven judges (three of them Cambodian) would try the cases, saying that this would compromise the country's sovereignty. On 20 October Hun Sen seemed to agree to a US formula under which the tribunal would consist of three Cambodian judges and two foreign judges, but any verdict would have to be agreed by at least four of the five judges. A similar system was proposed for the appeal court: four Cambodian judges, three foreign and decisions requiring the agreement of five judges. However, given Hun Sen's tendency to change his mind, it was far from clear whether this formula would be implemented.

As a foretaste of what might follow, 7 June saw the trial of former KR commander Nuon Paet for his part in the abduction and murder of three foreign tourists in 1994. The trial lasted less than a day and Nuon was sentenced to life imprisonment. The trial was condemned as a sham by relatives of the tourists and by independent observers.

On 24 January Hun Sen resigned as commander-in-chief of the RCAF, handing over to General Ke Kimyan. He stated that plans to reduce the size of the military and police from 208,000 to 79,000 personnel were dependent on foreign assistance. In February Cambodia secured an aid package worth US$470 million from donor countries. At a meeting in June donors stated that they were satisfied with progress in introducing environmental and economic reforms, and restructuring the civil service and armed forces. In October the IMF approved a three-year SDR58.5 million loan under its enhanced structural adjustment facility (ESAF).

In January Hun Sen signalled his intention to take a firmer line against illegal logging and at the beginning of February eleven illegal sawmills in Kompong Speu were raided, their equipment confiscated, and sawmill buildings razed. In April 3,000 tonnes of toxic waste dumped by a Taiwanese firm were shipped back to Taiwan. The year also saw a number of reports highlighting the continuing pillage of the ancient temples of Angkor Wat. In August King Norodom Sihanouk appealed for international help to prevent further destruction. King Sihanouk's health continued to be a source of concern. The 76-year-old monarch spent two months in China undergoing medical treatment.

On 2 March the National Assembly agreed to the formation of a new, unelected 61-member Senate, which was promptly sworn in on 25 March. Nine days earlier the Indonesian government had confirmed that Cambodia would be admitted to the Association of South-East Asian Nations (ASEAN), having met the membership requirement of having an upper parliamentary chamber. At a meeting of ASEAN Foreign Ministers in Hanoi on 30 April Cambodia was formally admitted to the organization (see XI.6.iii).

x. LAOS

CAPITAL: Vientiane   AREA: 237,000 sq km   POPULATION: 5,000,000 ('98)
OFFICIAL LANGUAGE: Laotian   POLITICAL SYSTEM: people's republic
RULING PARTY: Lao People's Revolutionary Party (LPRP)
HEAD OF STATE: President (Gen.) Khamtay Siphandon (since Feb '98)
HEAD OF GOVERNMENT: Gen. Sisavath Keobounphanh, Prime Minister (since Feb '98)
MAIN IGO MEMBERSHIPS (NON-UN): ASEAN, CP, Francophonie, NAM
CURRENCY: new kip (end-'99 £1=KN10,556.60, US$1=KN6,550.00)
GNP PER CAPITA: US$330 by exchange-rate calculation, US$1,300 at PPP ('98)

DEPUTY Prime Minister and Minister of Finance Khamphoui Keoboualapha and the governor of the central bank, Cheuang Sombounekhanh, were both dismissed from their posts by President Khamtay Siphandon on 6 August, accused of economic mismanagement. Laos was unable to avoid being severely affected by the regional economic crisis and it was felt in some quarters that the reformist policies of Khamphoui and Cheuang had accentuated the country's vulnerability to external forces. Boungnang Volachit took on the finance portfolio and Soukhan Maharaj became central bank governor.

During 1999 the economy suffered from high inflation (unofficially as high as 150 per cent), a weak currency, a widening trade deficit (expected to exceed the 1998 figure of US$347 million) and low levels of foreign investment. The government tried to encourage Thai traders to take kip (the domestic currency) rather than Thai baht as a means of stabilizing the sliding currency. This effort failed to gain many converts. Even 'Visit Laos Year' 1999-2000 got off to a slow start. The rice crop for the year was 2.1 million tons, enough to meet the country's needs.

On 15 December 291 Laotian refugees living in Nakhon Phanom in northeast Thailand were compulsorily repatriated by the Thai government and the UN High Commission for Refugees, leaving just 118 awaiting final placement to a third country. The repatriation followed a meeting in Vientiane in July at which Laos reluctantly agreed to the exercise. Border disagreements continued to cloud relations with Thailand.

During the year there were several reports of Christians being imprisoned. Pro-democracy sources estimated that 40 'senior' church figures had been incarcerated. The government rejected such estimates as entirely unfounded.

2. CHINA—HONG KONG—TAIWAN—JAPAN—SOUTH KOREA—
NORTH KOREA—MONGOLIA

i. PEOPLE'S REPUBLIC OF CHINA

CAPITAL: Beijing   AREA: 9,600,000 sq km   POPULATION: 1,248,100,000 ('98)
OFFICIAL LANGUAGE: Chinese POLITICAL SYSTEM: people's republic
HEAD OF STATE: President Jiang Zemin (since March '93)
RULING PARTY: Chinese Communist Party (CCP)
PARTY LEADER: Jiang Zemin, CCP general secretary (since June '89)
CCP POLITBURO STANDING COMMITTEE: Jiang Zemin, Li Peng, Zhu Rongji, Li Ruihuan, Hu Jintao, Wei Jianxing, Li Lanqing
CCP CENTRAL COMMITTEE SECRETARIAT: Hu Jintao, Ding Guangen, Wei Jianxing, Wen Jiabao, Zhang Wannian, Luo Gan, Zeng Qinghong
CENTRAL MILITARY COMMISSION: Jiang Zemin, chairman (since Nov '89)
PRIME MINISTER: Zhu Rongji (since March '98)
MAIN IGO MEMBERSHIPS (NON-UN): APEC
CURRENCY: renminbi (RMB) denominated in yuan (end-'99 $1=Y13.34, US$1=Y8.28)
GNP PER CAPITA: US$750 by exchange-rate calculation, US$3,220 at PPP ('98)

IN the year of the 50th anniversary of the founding of the People's Republic, faltering growth against the background of serious deflationary pressures underlined the scale of the challenge facing the Chinese government in its attempt to maintain the momentum of economic reform and preserve social stability. Political concerns were also to the fore: not least, the uncompromising response to the activities of the quasi-religious Falun Gong sect highlighted the government's sensitivity to any form of behaviour that might be interpreted as a threat to its political authority. Meanwhile, China's efforts to extend its international influence met with considerable, but not universal, success. Thus relations with Japan remained at a low ebb, while President Lee Teng-hui's insistence that relations between the mainland and Taiwan should be pursued on a 'special state-to-state' basis halted progress towards closer cross-Strait ties (see IX.2.iii). The most serious incident affecting Chinese interests overseas occurred in May, when NATO forces operating in Kosovo accidentally bombed the Chinese embassy in Belgrade (see III.2.vi). This action cast a cloud over Sino-US relations for the rest of the year, although it did not prevent a major breakthrough from taking place in November, when Chinese and American trade negotiators announced that they had finally reached agreement on conditions for China's entry into the World Trade Organization (WTO).

Throughout 1999 the 'three stresses' campaign sought to inculcate better attitudes and an improved work style among Chinese Communist Party (CCP) officials by emphasizing the importance of theoretical study, politics and healthy conduct in combating inner-party corruption, ensuring compliance to the centre and infusing cadres with a proper ideological outlook. The urgency of the task was suggested by the revelation that over 130,000 cadres had been disciplined during 1999. Central to efforts to enhance political study was the integration of the theoretical canon of Marxism-Leninism-Mao Zedong Thought and Deng Xiaoping Theory ('building socialism with Chinese characteristics') with the reality of Chinese conditions. Jiang Zemin argued that it was political belief alone—defined in China's case as the commitment to socialism and communism, based on 'Marxist dialectical materialism and historical materialism'—that ultimately gave meaning to economic development. Premier Zhu Rongji meanwhile urged an intensification of the 'strike hard' campaign against crime and corruption, insisting that efficient administration by a 'clean, diligent, pragmatic...government' was essential to stable social and economic development.

At the end of April a silent demonstration by some 10,000 Falun Gong members outside Zhongnanhai, the walled compound of Chinese leaders in central Beijing, was the catalyst for a government-inspired campaign against the Buddhist-cum-Taoist, quasi-religious sect and its leaders. The seriousness with which this incident was viewed was highlighted in a statement, issued on behalf of the CCP central committee (CCPCC), that the demonstration had constituted the most serious threat to public order since the political upheavals of spring 1989. Officially, the growing organizational strength of Falun Gong was seen as evidence of an unfolding 'political struggle...[involving] hostile forces at home and abroad...against the party and government'. The response of the government was to detain large numbers-according to some reports, over 35,000 of its supporters-and to issue a series of decrees aimed at outlawing the sect and banning its activities. Such measures were, however, only partly successful and demonstrations continued. In two separate trials in November and December, prison sentences of between two and 18 years were passed on eight supposed Falun Gong ringleaders, variously found guilty of having helped organize the original April demonstration and used 'an evil cult to obstruct the law'.

Tight security arrangements, including the detention of prominent dissidents and the closure of Tiananmen Square, ensured that the 10th anniversary (4 June) of the 'Tiananmen massacre' (see AR 1989, pp. 339-40) passed without serious incident. At the end of the previous month, however, survivors and relatives of the victims of the upheavals of 1989 urged the government to undertake a criminal investigation of the officials responsible for those events, including former premier Li Peng. An unconfirmed Hong Kong source reported that Bao Tong (former aide to the disgraced former Chinese Premier and CCP general secretary, Zhao Ziyang) had also appealed to the Chinese leadership to reassess the events of spring 1989, urging them to resolve 'contradictions' that had subsequently emerged out of the simultaneous pursuit of a flexible, pragmatic economic strategy alongside conservative and repressive political policies.

Against the background of further downsizing of China's armed forces and in the light of the lessons of the Gulf War and Kosovo crisis, Defence Minister Chi Haotian reaffirmed the government's determination to use high technology in order to facilitate military modernization and strengthen its defensive and offensive military capabilities. Enhancement of China's strategic missile basis was an urgent priority and in August Japanese officials expressed concern about the potential impact on efforts to promote the non-proliferation and reduction of weapons of mass destruction of China's recent test launch of a new long-range inter-continental missile. The inclusion of many new weapons in a parade in Beijing to mark the 50th anniversary of the founding of the People's Republic underlined the recent rapid growth in China's military strength, including the ability to launch a destructive missile strike against Taiwan, even in the face of the latter's acquisition Patriot PAC-2 missiles.

Ideological, political and military preoccupations notwithstanding, it was a key economic issue-reform of China's state-owned enterprises (SOEs)-that was the focus of the fourth plenum of the 15th CCPCC (19-22 September). A subsequent CCPCC 'decision' acknowledged that the persistence of serious problems merely underlined the urgency of SOE reform. But it ruled out wholesale privatization (as Jiang Zemin remarked, 'a market economy is not a pretext for private ownership'). In particular, the CCPCC document insisted that the state sector would still play the dominant role in key industries and sectors of the economy-those affecting state security, natural monopolies, suppliers of public goods and services, and 'backbone enterprises in pillar industries'. Elsewhere, capital restructuring and other structural adjustments were permissible in the interests of developing a joint stock system and other mixed forms of ownership. Meanwhile, technological renovation and upgrading were the means whereby the first decade of the 21st century would see the emergence of 'powerful and competitive large enterprises and enterprise groups', capable of meeting global competition in terms of technology, product quality, productivity and profitability.

ECONOMY AND SOCIETY. At a macroeconomic level, the issues that featured most prominently during 1998 and 1999 were those of slowing growth and deflation. In recent years, GDP growth had experienced consistent annual decline—official Chinese estimates, which almost certainly overstated reality, showed the annual rate of growth to have fallen from 14.1 per cent (1992) to 7.1 per cent (1999). Until 1997 the declining trend was consistent with government efforts to cool an overheated economy. But in 1998, the retail price index fell by 2.6 per cent (but by almost 3.5 per cent in large cities)—a trend that continued, albeit at a slowing rate, in 1999. All three major sectors shared in GDP expansion in 1999, although industrial growth (8.1 per cent) again outstripped that of both agriculture (2.8 per cent) and services (7.5 per cent). The implied annual growth of average per capita GDP in 1998 was 6.8 per cent.

There was a consensus that deflationary pressures had become sufficiently serious to pose a threat to sustained, rapid development. Because of slow growth of farm incomes and rising urban unemployment associated with continuing large-scale layoffs from SOEs, domestic consumer demand in both rural and urban sectors remained sluggish. Survey findings also pointed to a change in urban residents' consumption patterns, as spending shifted from the purchase of durable consumer goods towards house purchases, education for their children (including study overseas), share buying, etc. Meanwhile, overseas markets in many parts of East and South-East Asia stayed relatively depressed during 1998 and 1999. The outcome of such trends was the emergence of excess supply in many industries, with stocks of manufactured goods rising by 5.5 per cent in 1998. Only thanks to stimulatory government efforts through increased infrastructural investment and pursuit of proactive financial policies, including the issue of over 200,000 million yuan (US$24,000 million) of treasury bonds, was a steeper decline in GDP growth avoided.

The most outstanding feature of agricultural growth in 1998 was the achievement, despite severe flooding (see AR 1998, p. 367), of a record grain harvest of 512.3 million tons—a 3.7 per cent increase above the previous year's level. Although total production in 1999 fell back to around 490 million tons, the recent run of fine harvests for the time being allayed fears that China might be compelled substantially to increase food imports, thereby threatening supplies to chronically food-deficient regions elsewhere in the world. From this perspective, it was notable that in 1998, China was again a substantial net exporter of cereals (both in volume and value terms).

In the industrial sector, foreign-funded enterprises contributed most to growth during 1998. By contrast, a 3 per cent fall in the growth of collectively-owned enterprises highlighted the declining role of what had once been the most dynamic sector of the Chinese economy There was a deterioration in industrial economic efficiency and, despite a rise in sales income, enterprise profits fell by 17 per cent, while losses increased by 22.1 per cent. More encouraging were sharp output rises of high-technology and high-value added goods (microcomputers, programme-controlled switchboards and communications equipment).

In 1998 there were major increases in investment in agriculture (by 47.8 per cent) and transport and telecommunications (up by 53.4 per cent). A 31.2 per cent rise in investment allocation to western China, compared with 14.9 and 16.8 per cent in coastal and central regions, underlined the commitment to reduce inter-regional economic and welfare differentials.

The most direct consequence of policies designed to rationalize China's

SOEs, and a major impediment to the swifter implementation of enterprise reform in recent years, was the sharp rise in urban unemployment. At the end of 1998 the number of registered urban unemployed was officially estimated to be 5.71 million—a gross underestimate of reality because of the exclusion of large numbers of unemployed urban migrants. In 1999 a further 11 million SOE workers lost their jobs. Although 4.92 million of these subsequently found new employment, the threat to social stability associated with such a high rate of layoffs, especially in some north-eastern and coastal regions, where SOEs had traditionally been concentrated, was again a source of pressing official concern. These same factors, as well as demographic pressures that were expected to raise China's elderly population from some 130 million to around 400 million between 2000 and 2050, highlighted the urgent need to provide more effective social security arrangements—an area in which significant, but limited, improvements continued to be made in 1999.

Official figures showing that the rate of natural increase of total population had fallen below 1 per cent in 1998 and 1999 highlighted the success of the government's recent demographic policies. In a single decade (1988-98), China's share of world population had fallen from a quarter to a fifth-a trend, which, if maintained, would generate zero population growth by the middle of the 21st century. During 1971-88 official birth control measures had been responsible for 338 million fewer births than would otherwise have occurred, thereby saving an estimated 7.4 trillion yuan (roughly equivalent to China's GDP in 1997).

A reversal, in 1998, of the previous year's acceleration of merchandise trade growth mainly highlighted the impact of the Asian financial crisis on the Chinese economy, as exports to Hong Kong, Japan and South Korea fell by 11.5, 6.7 and 31.3 per cent respectively. In the aggregate, the combined value of exports and imports fell by 0.4 per cent, compared with a rise of 12.1 per cent in 1997 (export growth alone fell from 20.5 per cent to a mere 0.5 per cent). Thanks, however, to a more pronounced decline in imports (by 1.5 per cent), China's overall trade surplus increased from US$40,400 million to US$43,600 million. The negative effect of the regional financial crisis was mitigated by a reorientation of exports from Asia (down by 9.9 per cent) to other parts of the world (shipments to Europe and North America rising by almost 12 per cent). But even allowing for the impact of the regional financial crisis, China's global ranking as a trading nation improved in 1998, taking it from tenth to ninth place as an exporter, and from twelfth to eleventh place as an importer. Its national foreign exchange reserves meanwhile also rose, by US$5,069 million, to reach US$144,959 million.

In 1999 an increase in the value of China's merchandise trade to a record level (US$360,700 million) and some recovery in exports concealed the sharp gap that had opened up between export and import growth. Preliminary results indicated that side by side with export expansion of 6.1 per cent, imports had risen by 18.2 per cent, thereby causing China's trade surplus to shrink by more than 33 per cent to US$29,100 million. An acceleration of export growth to 15.8 per cent in the second half of the year did, however, offer encouragement for the future.

China's disappointing trade performance was matched by declines in inflows of foreign capital. In 1998 utilized foreign investment of all kinds fell by 7.9 per cent, although foreign direct investment (FDI), constituting almost 80 per cent of all capital inflows, continued to show a marginal increase of 0.7 per cent (to US$45,400 million). The regional financial crisis was a major contributory factor, with FDI from within Asia falling by more than 8.6 per cent. Whether a 3 per cent decline in FDI from Europe, including European Union (EU) member states such as Germany and the UK, signalled a longer-term loss of confidence in China by some Western investors in China, it was too early to say, although FDI from the United States for the time being continued to rise steeply. In 1999, however, the USA, EU and Asia were all reported to have shared in a further decline, by 11.4 per cent, in total FDI.

Without underestimating the significance of such development indicators, the single most important economic event in 1999 was probably the Sino-US agreement, reached after years of tortuous negotiations, on the terms and conditions for China's entry into the WTO. On 15 November Chinese and US representatives signed a market access agreement, a copy of which was to be sent to the WTO secretariat. Although few details were forthcoming, it was revealed that the agreement provided specific undertakings on access to markets for agricultural and industrial products, and services. The chief US negotiator, Charlene Barshevsky, spoke of a 'profound historic moment' having been reached in Sino-US relations, while Shi Guangsheng (Minister of Foreign Trade and Economic Cooperation) predicted that China would join WTO within a year. He added that China would immediately accelerate its negotiations with EU member states in the interests of early accession.

The official Chinese response to the agreement was predictably upbeat. One analysis suggested that by 2005 WTO membership would boost GDP by 5 per cent, facilitating rises in foreign trade and FDI to US$600,000 million and US$100,000 million respectively. The Ministry of Agriculture welcomed the agreement, arguing that WTO membership would benefit the farm sector by facilitating agricultural restructuring and modernization, and enhancing China's farm export capabilities. But it conceded that accession would pose challenges for inefficient farmers, and elsewhere there were suggestions that demands for agricultural protectionism would intensify. In the industrial sector membership of the world trading body was expected to force Chinese SOEs to accelerate structural readjustment and make further improvements in management that would help create a modern enterprise system. Greater equity diversification was also thought likely to result, as more overseas funds were attracted various certain industries.

FOREIGN RELATIONS. In his annual work report on behalf of the government, presented on 5 March, Zhu Rongji once more stressed his government's determination to pursue an independent and peaceful foreign policy—a sentiment echoed in the remarks of Foreign Minister Tang Jiaxuan in his address to the 54th UN General Assembly in September. At the same time he warned that 'hegemonism and power politics' remained a continuing source of regional crises throughout the world. The situation in Kosovo was one such crisis, in which China unwittingly became directly involved, following the bombing by US-led NATO forces on 7 May of its embassy in Belgrade.

The bombing caused severe damage and three Chinese journalists were killed in the attack. Chinese sources described the incident as a 'barbarian act...a gross violation of China's sovereignty and a wilful trampling of...the norms of international relations', while defence experts rejected claims that the bombing of the embassy had been unintentional, insisting that the attack had been 'absolutely premeditated'. In Beijing the Chinese Foreign Ministry delivered a formal protest to the American ambassador, while Vice-President Hu Jintao called on the UN Security Council to convene an emergency meeting to consider the situation. Government sources announced the postponement of bilateral talks on arms control, international security and human rights issues. At a rally in the Chinese capital, Jiang Zemin referred to the 'three martyrs...[who had]...sacrificed their lives for peace, justice and their motherland', and placed full responsibility for the 'brutal act' on 'US-led NATO'.

The public response to the bombing was the organization of tens of thousands of protesters (mainly university students) in demonstrations in many provinces and cities, including Beijing, Tianjin, Shanghai, Chongqing and Chengdu. In the Chinese capital large numbers of students pelted the US embassy, with stones and rotten eggs. There were, however, no reports of foreign diplomatic personnel having been harmed.

On 14 May the Chinese and American Presidents held a telephone conversation, in which Bill Clinton apologized for the bombing and sent his personal condolences to the families of the dead and injured. He promised to carry out an investigation of the causes of the incident and reaffirmed his determination to restore Sino-US relations to the path of normal development. In response, Jiang Zemin again described the attack on China's Belgrade embassy as a serious infringement of China's national sovereignty, and a violation of the UN Charter and the norms of international relations.

Following negotiations in Beijing, a first agreement was reached at the end of July, whereby the US government undertook to pay US$4.5 million in compensation for casualties caused by the bombing. In December, following further talks, Chinese and US government representatives agreed on the further payment of US$28 million in respect to property losses and damage.

Throughout 1999 China's vigorous foreign relations offensive was very evident, with reciprocal high-level diplomatic visits between China and countries in Africa, Asia, Europe, Latin America, North America and the Pacific taking place throughout the year. Jiang Zemin undertook three diplomatic tours, including two involving visits to European countries. His visit to the UK in October was the first ever undertaken by a Chinese head of state and confirmed the steady development of bilateral relations since the return of Hong Kong to

Chinese rule. In London his talks with Prime Minister Tony Blair focused on ways to strengthen bilateral economic relations, as well as international issues (see II.1). Mr Blair apologized for the bombing of the Chinese embassy in Belgrade, but noted that Sino-British ties had since returned to normal. Subsequently, in France, Jiang held talks with President Chirac, in which it was revealed that China would purchase 28 Airbus airliners—a deal worth F15,000 million.

Chinese Defence and Foreign Ministry sources condemned NATO air strikes in Kosovo, blaming NATO for the deepening 'humanitarian disaster' and arguing that military intervention had merely deepened the regional crisis. An article in *People's Daily* even suggested that Kosovo had become a 'testing and demonstration site for high-tech weapons and...a big advertising film [for] the US arms industry'. The same source argued that the United States was taking advantage of NATO's eastward expansion in the wake of the collapse of the former Soviet Union in order to extend its sphere of influence in Europe, while transforming NATO's former defensive programme into an 'expansionist offensive strategy'.

Reciprocal high-level visits by senior officials, including Presidents Jiang Zemin and Boris Yeltsin and Premier Zhu Rongji, underlined further progress towards the development of a 'strategic partnership' between China and Russia. The signing of two more border agreements highlighted the continuing political rapprochement between the two sides, although with bilateral trade having fallen by 10.5 per cent in 1998, the more immediate concern was to find new areas of economic and trade cooperation.

In April Zhu Rongji undertook the first visit to the United States by a Chinese Prime Minister for 15 years. Earlier, the Chinese ambassador in Washington, Li Zhaoxing, noted that the value of bilateral trade had reached US$54,900 million in 1998, making the US China's second-largest trading partner, and China America's fourth-largest. According to the ambassador, two-way trade had provided 300,000 jobs for Americans, and about one million jobs for Chinese. In addition, over 26,000 US-invested projects had been established in China, with a contractual value of US$45,800 million.

Following his arrival in Los Angeles on 6 April, Zhu hoped that his visit would strengthen the common understanding reached in two earlier presidential summits and help overcome current 'obstructions' to closer bilateral ties. In Washington he held 'constructive and fruitful' talks with President Bill Clinton on a range of bilateral, regional and international issues, including human rights, China's accession to the WTO and the situation in Kosovo. Zhu stressed the sensitivity of the Taiwan question and urged the US government not to provide Taiwan with theatre missile defence (TMD) technology or other advanced weaponry. President Clinton reaffirmed Washington's one-China policy and its commitment to the three Sino-US joint communiques and other undertakings.

In September Presidents Clinton and Jiang Zemin held a summit meeting in Auckland, New Zealand, where they were attending the 11th Asia-Pacific Economic Cooperation (APEC) ministerial meeting (see XI.6.iii). Their discussions embraced a range of pressing issues, including questions relating to the bombing of the Chinese embassy, the situation in the Korean peninsula, Taiwan and China's membership of WTO.

In the wake of the new Japan-US Defence Cooperation Guidelines, a Chinese Foreign Ministry source warned Japan that the inclusion of Taiwan in the orbit of such cooperation was a violation of Chinese sovereignty and constituted interference in its internal affairs. Several rounds of talks between the two sides, including discussions between Jiang Zemin and Premier Keizo Obuchi, failed to resolve differences on this issue. Meanwhile, amidst expressions of Chinese outrage at claims by the newly-elected governor of Tokyo to the effect that reports of Japanese brutality during the 1937 'Rape of Nanking' were a gross distortion of the truth, Jiang Zemin impressed on Prime Minister Obuchi the need to learn from history and adhere to the 'path of peace and development'. The governor of Tokyo later attracted further condemnation when he referred to Taiwan as a 'state'.

Elsewhere in Asia, a stream of reciprocal high-level visits by senior government officials between China and countries in South, South-East and North-East Asia attested to the vigour of China's regional diplomatic offensive. However, the warming of cross-Strait relations, encouraged by the historic visits to Shanghai and Beijing made in 1998 by Koo Chen-fu (chairman of the Straits Exchange Foundation) and the expected return visit to Taiwan by his mainland counterpart, Wang Daohan (see AR 1998, pp. 374-5), ended abruptly when President Lee Teng-hui unexpectedly announced that relations between Taiwan and the mainland would henceforth be governed by a 'special state-to-state' relationship. Beijing's response was to launch a vituperative attack on Lee, to cancel Wang's visit and to suspend all cross-Strait non-governmental contacts (see also IX.2.iii).

Preparations for the recovery of Chinese sovereignty over Macao from Portuguese rule included the appointment of senior officials, among them Edmund Ho Hao Wah as Chief Executive, to the first government of the future Macao Special Administrative Region. In December, Portuguese President Jorge Sampaio and Jiang Zemin were present in Macao for the celebrations and ceremonies surrounding the return to China of the erstwhile Portuguese colony (see also II.4.iii). Following the formal transfer of government on 20 December—incidentally marking the end of the long history of Western colonial rule in Asia—Jiang reaffirmed his government's determination to uphold the principle of 'one country, two systems' and promised that the people of Macao would enjoy a high degree of autonomy.

ii. HONG KONG SPECIAL ADMINISTRATIVE REGION

CAPITAL: Victoria AREA: 1,073 sq km POPULATION: 6,687,200 ('98)
STATUS: Special Administrative Region of People's Republic of China (since 1 July 1997)
CHIEF EXECUTIVE: Tung Chee-hwa (since July '97)
ADMINISTRATIVE SECRETARY: Anson Chan (since July '97), previously Chief Secretary (since Sept '93)
MAIN IGO MEMBERSHIPS: APEC
CURRENCY: Hong Kong dollar (end-'99 £1=HK$12.53, US$1=HK$7.77)
GDP PER CAPITA: US$24,892 ('98)

A dispute about residency rights raised constitutional issues bearing on the relative powers of government and legal institutions in Hong Kong and the mainland. In the end, the ultimate authority of the National People's Congress (NPC) in Beijing to reinterpret the Basic Law of Hong Kong Special Administrative Region (HKSAR) was upheld—a decision that led some local legislators to infer the abrogation of the high degree of legal autonomy promised for Hong Kong under the terms of its return to Chinese rule in 1997.

The origin of the dispute, the ramifications of which lasted throughout 1999, lay in a controversial decision, taken by the Hong Kong Court of Final Appeal (CFA) in January, to overturn the provisions of immigration legislation officially endorsed shortly after the return of Hong Kong to Chinese sovereignty. Mainland sources were highly critical of the CFA's ruling, the alleged effect of which would be to grant an automatic right of abode in Hong Kong to at least 1.67 million people living in the mainland. PRC sources denied the authority of the CFA to make such a ruling ('the CFA's power to interpret the Basic Law is not inherent'), arguing that its power derived from the NPC. The more practical point was also made that the expected influx of immigrants into Hong Kong would place undue strain on SAR services, with 'evil' consequences for local society.

Against a background of continuing heated debate, HKSAR Chief Executive Tung Chee-hwa announced in May that the government intended to refer the matter to the NPC—a decision that caused some pro-democracy members of the Hong Kong Legislative Council to walk out of the debate in protest against what they regarded as a threat to the CFA's authority to interpret the Basic Law. The following month the NPC standing committee effectively overturned the CFA's original ruling, offering a reinterpretation of two sections of the HKSAR Basic Law. First, it argued that *à propos* discussion of entitlement to live in Hong Kong, reference (section 4, article 2) to 'people from other parts of China' meant 'sons and daughters of Chinese nationality born...[to]...citizens with Hong Kong permanent residency'—who would be required to obtain official approval before being allowed to enter Hong Kong. Second, it reinterpreted wording in the Basic Law to the effect that the right of abode should be given to 'Chinese nationals who are children of permanent Hong Kong residents but were born outside Hong Kong' (item 3, section 2, article 24) as meaning that 'the precondition for the children of permanent Hong Kong residents in the interior areas to automatically obtain the right of abode in Hong Kong is that at least one parent was already a permanent Hong Kong resident at the time of birth'. The new ruling was expected to reduce the number of potential immigrants into Hong Kong to 200,000.

Although the NPC decision was greeted by further demonstrations against the alleged erosion of Hong Kong's legal autonomy by human rights groups and (unprecedentedly) lawyers, local majority opinion seemed to find reassurance in the NPC's reinterpretation of the Basic Law. Nevertheless, further demonstrations took place in December, after the CFA had rejected an appeal by 17 mainland Chinese immigrants against the NPC's new ruling, acknowledging the ultimate right of the NPC to interpret the Basic Law and thereby effectively overturning its own original ruling.

On 6 October Tung Chee-hwa delivered his third policy address as Chief Executive, entitled 'Quality People, Quality Home', to a meeting of the HKSAR Legislative Council. He reviewed Hong Kong's achievements in the two years since the 1997 handover, but also spoke of the serious challenges that had faced the SAR during this period. Looking ahead, he unveiled his vision of Hong Kong in the 21st century as a 'knowledge-based and economy-led society', to be attained, first, by nurturing local talent and attracting new skills into the region, and second, by providing a first-class living environment (the 'two essentials'). At the same time, fulfilment of Tung's aspiration that Hong Kong should become a great international metropolis—the 'New York...or London of Asia'—would, he suggested, be facilitated by the SAR's 'four advantages'. These were: its propinquity to the mainland, its unique mix of Chinese and Western cultures, its tradition as a liberal and open society, and the high degree of development of its institutions. In pursuit of the same underlying goal, Tung also referred to the facilitating role of Hong Kong's 'five pillars'—namely, its embodiment of the rule of law, adherence to key principles of 'one country, two systems' and a high degree of autonomy, twin commitments to political development and reform, and the determination to maintain a competitive market-orientated economy.

According to Tung, Hong Kong had passed two recent watersheds. The first was the retrocession of British sovereignty over Hong Kong, effected in July 1997. The second was the successful economic readjustment, which had been made in response to the regional financial crisis. Tung admitted that in summer 1998 speculative attacks had placed foreign exchange and the local stock market under immense pressure. But he insisted that in the face of falling confidence in Hong Kong's financial system, government intervention through the medium of the Hong Kong Monetary Authority had played a critical role in stabilizing the immediate situation. Further measures had strengthened the linked exchange rate regime. Tung was confident that Hong Kong's economic recovery would continue.

Such optimism notwithstanding, economic indicators underlined the seriousness of the ongoing economic recession. Data for the final quarter of 1998 revealed, for example, that unemployment in Hong Kong had risen to a record 5.8 per cent. Deflationary pressures were also in evidence, consumer prices having fallen by 1.6 and 0.7 per cent in November and December 1998-the first such decline in 23 years. However, after 15 months of recession, the attainment of 0.5 per cent growth in the second quarter of 1999 suggested that earlier predictions of a 1.7 per cent GDP contraction for the entire year may were likely to be excessively pessimistic. Evidence of some export recovery also underlined cautious optimism that Hong Kong's economy was beginning to emerge from the worst point of the recession.

Meanwhile, the 1999 budget, presented on 3 March by HKSAR Financial Secretary Donald Tsang, reflected the need for stimulatory measures to revive economic growth. To this end Tsang announced several large-scale investment projects, including the planned establishment of a Disney theme park on Lantau island, which was expected to attract three million more tourists to Hong Kong annually and yield a net return of HK$148,000 million (against projected government investment of HK$22,450 million) over 40 years, following the park's opening in 2005. Tsang also announced the intended creation of a 'cyber-port', designed to enhance Hong Kong's role as an information services centre. Subsequently, a government land auction in October raised HK$706 million, while government sales to the public of shares purchased in August 1998 in support of the local stock market were expected to yield some HK$10,000 million.

Local government elections took place in Hong Kong on 28 November-the first to be held since the establishment of HKSAR. Despite losing ground, the Democratic Party (the main opposition party) remained numerically the single most important political grouping in the region, winning 86 of the contested seats on 18 new district councils. But the most impressive achievement was that of the pro-China Democratic Alliance for the Betterment of Hong Kong, which more than doubled its representation by securing 83 seats.

The final (47th) meeting of the Sino-British Joint Liaison Group (JLG) took place on 8 December, prior to its disbandment at the end of 1999. A celebratory reception marked the successful fulfilment of the JLG's mission.

iii. TAIWAN

CAPITAL: Taipei AREA: 35,981 sq km POPULATION: 21,871,000 ('98)
OFFICIAL LANGUAGE: Chinese POLITICAL SYSTEM: presidential
HEAD OF STATE & GOVERNMENT: President Lee Teng-hui (since Jan '88, popularly elected March '96)
RULING PARTY: Kuomintang (KMT)
PRIME MINISTER: Vincent Siew (since Sept '97)
MAIN IGO MEMBERSHIPS: APEC
CURRENCY: new Taiwan dollar (end-'99 £1=NT$50.53, US$1=NT$31.35)
GDP PER CAPITA: US$12,040 ('98)

Two events dominated events in Taiwan during 1999. The first was the revelation by President Lee Teng-hui that, in the wake of Taiwan's constitutional reforms of 1991, cross-Strait relations had been designated as 'special state-to-state ties'. The statement earned widespread condemnation from the mainland and interrupted the process of non-governmental contacts between the PRC and

Taiwan. The second event was a severe earthquake, which hit central Taiwan on 21 September, causing serious loss of life and widespread damage.

President Lee's statement was wholly unexpected, being made against the background of renewed cross-Strait contacts. In January, for example, it was confirmed that Wang Daohan, chairman of the PRC Association for Relations Across the Taiwan Strait (ARATS), would visit Taiwan in 1999, reciprocating the previous (October 1998) visit to mainland China made by Koo Chen-fu, chairman of the Straits Exchange Foundation (SEF) (see AR 1998, pp. 374-5). In March one of the ARATS deputy secretary-generals travelled to Taipei to discuss arrangements for Wang Daohan's forthcoming visit. In late June the SEF's own vice-secretary-general, Jan Jyh-horng, went to the mainland and reached agreement on two possible dates in September or October for Wang's visit. It was also revealed that the two sides had agreed on a reciprocal exchange of legal experts and agricultural experts in advance of the visit.

Such favourable developments were, however, abruptly halted when, in the course of a video interview with Deutsche Welle on 9 July, President Lee Teng-hui reviewed post-1949 history in order to demonstrate that Beijing's view of Taiwan as a 'renegade province' was at odds with historical and legal realities. Not only did he insist on the continued existence, since 1912, of the Republic of China (ROC) as an independent sovereign state, but also, much more controversially, he argued that since the implementation of Taiwan's constitutional reforms in 1991 'we [Taiwan] have designated cross-Strait ties as special state-to-state ties'. This being the case, he added, the question of Taiwan independence had no meaning, the 1991 amendments having formally acknowledged the geographical limitations of the ROC's legitimate rule, while recognizing the legitimacy of PRC rule over mainland China.

Official mainland sources condemned Lee's statement as a 'flagrant redefinition' of the cross-Strait relationship and reaffirmed Beijing's position that there existed only one China, of which Taiwan was an inalienable part. Official sources in Taipei variously insisted that Lee's 'pragmatic...high-visioned and constructive' remarks presaged no change in Taiwan's policy *vis-à-vis* the mainland, arguing that Lee had merely sought to 'stress Taiwan's status as a sovereign nation without giving up the pursuit of eventual reunification with China'. Premier Vincent Siew reiterated his government's determination to pursue constructive dialogue and reciprocal exchanges with the PRC.

President Lee himself continued to defend the characterization of cross-Strait ties as 'special state-to-state' relations, although he also hoped that 'democratic reunification' might eventually be the basis on which 'one China' could emerge. The director of the government information office in Taipei meanwhile let it be known that the Taiwan government would henceforth refer to the 'special state-to-state relationship' instead of the former 'two states in one nation'. Koo Chen-fu also sent a written statement to ARATS, seeking to give a positive interpretation of Lee's remarks which, he argued, were intended to establish a 'foundation of parity' between China and Taiwan in the interests of more effective cross-Strait dialogue. The letter was, however, rejected by ARATS. Indeed, Tang Shubei (vice-chairman of ARATS) suggested that Lee's new definition of Taiwan's status would 'rudely destroy the one-China principle of the ARATS-SEF relationship'.

As early as 26 July Taiwanese and Japanese sources were reporting that Chinese President Jiang Zemin had decided to cancel Wang Daohan's visit to Taiwan and to suspend all ARATS-SEF exchanges until after Taiwan's presidential election in March 2000-a decision that was subsequently officially confirmed. There was also speculation about the likely military response to Lee's remarks: an unconfirmed report in July noted that armed forces in the Nanjing and Guangzhou military theatres had been placed on second-degree combat readiness. A Taipei source meanwhile referred to two incidents, in which PRC fighter aircraft crossed the centre line (i.e. border) in the Taiwan Strait-albeit 'with no apparent hostile intent'. In the event, as of the end of 1999, there had been no recurrence of the kind of military activity conducted by China on the eve of Taiwan's presidential election in 1996.

In the early hours of 21 September a severe earthquake hit Taiwan, measuring 7.6 on the Richter scale and with its epicentre in Nantou province. The disaster killed 2,256 people and left a further 100,000 homeless. Economic damage was considerable—in September alone lost output cost manufacturing industry over US$2,000 million—and the cost of reconstruction was estimated at over US$33,000 million. Expressions of sympathy and material help were forthcoming from many countries, although Taipei refused an offer of assistance from the PRC.

It was officially announced on 15 November that Taiwan's presidential elections would take place on 18 March 2000. The three front-runners were Vice-President Lien Chan (nominee of the ruling Kuomintang, KMT), Chen Shuibian (for the Democratic Progressive Party) and James Soong (former governor of Taiwan province, standing as an independent). Autumn opinion polls showed Soong to be some 15-20 per cent ahead of Lien Chan, and on 19 November Jason Hu resigned as Foreign Minister in order to direct the KMT's campaign. The following month, however, suggestions that Soong, who had by now been expelled from the KMT, had been implicated in large-scale money-laundering reduced this lead.

Although less affected by the Asian financial crisis than many countries in the region, Taiwan's economic performance in 1998 was the worst for many years. Official GDP growth was just 4.83 per cent, with nominal per capita GDP falling by 5.2 per cent and unemployment reaching 2.69 per cent at the end of the year. A decline of almost 22 per cent in the stock market index, together with sharp falls in export proceeds, retail and financial sales, provided further evidence of Taiwan's economic downturn. Exports provided 40 per cent of Taiwan's GDP and the sharp deterioration in its trade performance, especially *vis-à-vis* its major Asian partners, contributed most to slowing growth. The result of the 9.4 per cent fall in exports, side by side with an 8.5 per cent decline in imports, was to reduce Taiwan's trade surplus by almost 23 per cent to US$5,900 million (the lowest level since 1983). There were, however, signs that early predictions of a further fall in export proceeds in 1999 would be confounded by the faster-than-expected recovery taking place elsewhere in East and South-East Asia.

The government responded to such difficulties with a policy package of financial and other reforms, supplemented by the injection of additional public expenditure designed to stimulate the economy. But even the most optimistic scenarios suggested that GDP growth would remain sluggish through 1999 before showing much stronger recovery in 2000. Such cautious optimism reflected a belief that although the negative economic impact of the regional financial crisis was likely to abate, domestic constraints would continue to impede a more rapid economic recovery.

There were conflicting estimates of cross-Strait trade in 1998. A source in the Ministry of Foreign Trade and Economic Cooperation in Beijing reported that such trade had risen by 3.3 per cent to reach US$20,500 million, with exports to the mainland having risen to US$16,630 million. However, an authoritative source indicated a 7.9 per cent decline in cross-Strait trade, including a remarkable 10.3 per cent fall in exports. It was also reported that during January-May 1999 Taiwanese investment in mainland China had fallen by 69 per cent, the number of approved projects having declined by 46 per cent.

iv. JAPAN

CAPITAL: Tokyo   AREA: 378,000 sq km   POPULATION: 126,000,000 ('98)
OFFICIAL LANGUAGE: Japanese   POLITICAL SYSTEM: parliamentary democracy
HEAD OF STATE: Emperor Tsugu no Miya Akihito (since Jan '89)
RULING PARTIES: Liberal-Democratic Party (LDP) heads coalition with Liberal Party (LP) & New Komeito
HEAD OF GOVERNMENT: Keizo Obuchi, Prime Minister (since July '98)
MAIN IGO MEMBERSHIPS (NON-UN): APEC, CP, OECD, G-8
CURRENCY: yen (end-'99 £1=Y164.97, US$1=Y102.36)
GNP PER CAPITA: US$32,380 by exchange-rate calculation, US$23,180 at PPP ('98)

IN January, after weeks of intense bargaining, the Liberal Party (LP) led by Ichiro Ozawa was brought into coalition with the governing Liberal-Democratic Party (LDP) of Keizo Obuchi, who had become Prime Minister in July 1998 (see AR 1998, p. 378). This alliance, the first realignment of conservative forces since Mr Ozawa left the LDP in 1993, was expected to give the government greater flexibility in pushing its programmes through the upper house, hitherto dominated by the opposition parties. But it was still unfinished business, because the two parties combined still lacked an overall majority there.

By far the most important issues for the Diet sessions early in 1999 were economic. Mr Obuchi promised to give the highest priority to rescuing the economy from its long recession. In March he finally succeeded in getting his budget passed by the legislature. For the long term the economic strategy council stated in its March report that there were three key steps on the path to Japan's recovery: stabilization of the financial system, a return to sustained economic growth and structural reconstruction over the next decade. A plan for the massive infusion of public capital into 15 banks, to help them clean up the bad loans accumulated in the days of the bubble economy, was approved by the financial reconstruction commission. More broadly, the competition commission, consisting of ministers and top business leaders, addressed the question of how to cut excessive production capacity while reducing unemployment from its present unprecedented levels. There was a strong emphasis on encouraging small and middle-sized companies and venture businesses, especially in the high-technology field. But there was a general feeling that it was going to be difficult to translate the varied recommendations for removing the weaknesses of the Japanese economy into effective policies.

In the field of foreign affairs, Mr Obuchi held important talks with President Kim Dae Jung of South Korea in March about how to handle North Korea. After the missile incident in 1998 (see AR 1998, pp. 378-9), Japan had applied financial sanctions of various kinds. Shortly after the meeting, two North Korean fishing boats described as 'spy ships' were found by the Japanese Maritime Self-Defence Force to be sailing without authorization in Japan's territorial waters. This incident exacerbated the relationship further: the two countries embarked on normalization talks, but these broke down at the end of the year.

The long-delayed Japan-US defence cooperation guidelines finally passed the Diet in April in the form of three bills offering cooperation in unspecified areas surrounding Japan and full rearguard support to US forces operating in the East Asian region. The controversial legislation secured approval in advance of Mr Obuchi's six-day official visit to the United States beginning on 3 May. At his meeting with President Clinton, Mr Obuchi was praised for the enhanced regional role which Japan had undertaken, though much of the discussion concerned economic recovery and the trade disputes between the two countries. It was necessary for Japan and the USA to give assurances to the Chinese that these new security guidelines were not aimed against them. Mr Obuchi met with some scepticism on this score when he held important talks with the Chinese President and Prime Minister in July (see IX.2.i).

The changes provided for in the new Japan-US pact gave the Self-Defence Forces (SDF) more responsibility for Japan's own defence and increased its responsibilities for security in the region. This left open, however, the question of increasing SDF participation in UN-led peace-keeping operations. In August Japan and the United States signed an agreement governing 'theatre missile defence' (TMD), whereby Japan would be warned of, and defended against, missiles targeted on its islands.

Regular elections for governors of cities and prefectures took place in the spring. Shintaro Ishihara, the nationalist writer and former Transport Minister (1988-89), was elected governor of Tokyo in April. His success was seen as a particular setback to the LDP for putting forward as its candidate the former prominent UN official, Yasushi Akashi, who suffered a comprehensive defeat.

Mr Ishihara was immediately in trouble with China over his utterances, especially over his right-wing interpretations of the war of 1937-45. Within Japan he pursued one of his election pledges: to secure the return to Japanese control of the US military's airbase at Yokota to the west of Tokyo and to convert it to joint use by Japanese military and civilian authorities. It could thus, he argued, serve as an auxiliary airport to Haneda and Narita and overcome the difficulties which the latter airport was experiencing in finding land for a second runway to cope with traffic expected for the football World Cup in 2002. Meanwhile, Knock Yokoyama, a former comedian, was re-elected as governor of Osaka as an independent candidate—although he resigned unexpectedly in December because of a lawsuit against him.

A significant development was the opening of the Setonaikai bridge between Onomichi and Imabari on 1 May. This completed a three-decade project to link up Japan's southern island of Shikoku by road with the main island of Honshu by building a series of three bridges joining up minor islands (see AR 1998, p. 377). It was hoped that by substituting road communication for sea ferries the opportunities for trade, tourism and investment in Shikoku would be increased. The bridge was a remarkable engineering feat.

A controversial move to the right took place in June when the cabinet adopted a bill to recognize the Hinomaru flag and the Kimigayo anthem as national symbols. Though the flag and anthem from the pre-war period had been in practical use in many circles for some time, their use had not hitherto been officially sanctioned, especially in educational establishments. After its acceptance in the lower house of the Diet, the controversial bill was approved by the upper house on 9 August by the sizeable majority of 166 to 71.

Punishment of members of the Aum Shinrikyo sect had been progressing slowly through the courts since the sarin nerve gas attack in the Tokyo subways in 1995 (see AR 1995, pp. 348-9, 434-5). Several sect leaders were sent to prison in 1999, and one of them, Masato Yokoyama, was sentenced to death on 30 September. In November the Diet initiated steps to impose controls on groups attempting indiscriminate murders, which was allegedly aimed at Aum Shinrikyo.

The Long-Term Credit Bank (LTCB) and Nippon Credit Bank, which had gone into bankruptcy in 1998, were subsequently nationalized until buyers could be found. After a long search, LTCB was bought by a consortium led by US financial group Ripplewood Holdings (see AR 1998, p. 380). Meanwhile, top officials of both banks were put on trial for concealment of bad loans and manipulations. During August the Dai-Ichi Kangyo Bank, Fuji Bank and the Industrial Bank of Japan, in order to safeguard themselves against increased competition from foreign banks, announced their intention to merge as Mizuho Holdings. The plan was that the three would be amalgamated by 2002 into a single structure, likely to become the largest commercial banking group in the world. This was followed by similar announcements of amalgamations between the Sumitomo and Sakura banks and later between the Asahi and Tokai banks.

Corporate restructuring in the manufacturing sector took a major step in March when Nissan Motors concluded a deal that gave practical control of the company to the Renault Motor Company of France. It was stated that the company's survival depended on the management and reorganization to be carried out by the new foreign owners, who decided to close five plants in Japan with the loss of 21,000 jobs over three years. Other car producers also entered into arrangements with foreign manufacturers: Fuji Heavy Industries, Suzuki and Isuzu with General Motors and Mazda with Ford.

On 30 September Japan suffered its worst-ever nuclear accident, at a uranium processing plant at Tokai village, 110 kilometres north-east of Tokyo. Involving nuclear chain reactions, the leakage affected 48 plant employees, who received heavy doses of radiation, and contaminated residential areas where over 300,000 people lived. The major disaster was caused by human error on the part of inadequately trained staff, but revealed lax procedures both in operating the plant and in accident follow-up. It also revealed ineffective inspection systems-extraordinary in a country which had suffered from nuclear attack in 1945. Nor had the lessons of the earlier disaster in 1997 at the same location been learnt (see AR 1997, p. 356). In December one of the operatives died from multiple organ failure as a result of the incident. Many Japanese who had doubted whether nuclear accidents could be severe enough to kill people came to distrust the wider use of nuclear energy which at present supplied more than 30 per cent of Japan's electric power needs.

Thought of earlier as a caretaker Prime Minister, Mr Obuchi on 21 September succeeded in being re-elected to the presidency of the LDP governing party and hence to the premiership. To strengthen his position, he embarked on talks to increase the range of his coalition by bringing in the New Komeito party. Despite some disagreements over the degree to which Japan's Self-Defence Forces should take part in UN-led peacekeeping operations, he succeeded in launching a tripartite coalition of the LDP, the LP and New Komeito in a cabinet reshuffle in October. With the support of the two smaller parties the Prime Minister acquired a majority in the upper house and thus consolidated his grasp on power.

On 22 November the Okinawa prefectural governor agreed to the relocation of Futenma air station, whose use by the US Marine Corps as a heliport had been resented by Okinawan residents for many years (see AR 1998, p. 379), to a coastal district in Nago city within 15 years. This ended the long-standing controversy between local and central government which had held up the ultimate transfer of Futenma to Japanese control.

At the end of November Japan's commitment to Asian development was made clear at an informal summit meeting between Japan and the Association of South-East Asian Nations (ASEAN) (see also XI.6.iii). Leaders from 13 East Asian countries gathered in Manila resolved to expand regional cooperation, while Japan announced its willingness to play a full part in the recovery of the Asian economies.

The government announced in November another in its series of supplementary budget packages. This consisted of public works spending to stimulate the economy amounting to 18,000,000 million yen, although it remained to be seen whether it would succeed when its impact was felt in the new year. The economy had so far proved to be too weak to achieve self-sustaining growth, in spite of previous massive injections of capital, though it saw some recovery in 1999.

At the end of an extraordinary Diet session in December the coalition failed to push through important parts of its programme in the face of unexpected unity between the opposition parties. This left Mr Obuchi's position unstable and unpredictable at the end of the year. Confronted by inconvenient demands from his junior coalition partners and criticisms from anti-mainstream factions in his own party, he had added confirmation that his position was weak from opinion polls showing that his public rating was dropping. There was speculation, therefore, that he might call an election for the lower house before the end of the present Diet in October 2000.

Japan lost two important architects of its post-war industrial progress. On 3 October Akio Morita, one of the founders and later chairman of the Sony Corporation, died at the age of 78. He had seen the company grow from a narrowly Japanese company making transistors to an international company investing widely in overseas factories at the forefront of technological innovation. Another loss was the death of Keizo Saji, latterly chairman of Suntory, the international beer, wine and spirits company. He had promoted the industry and commerce of the Kansai region throughout the post-war period and had been an important ambassador for Japan abroad as well as a great philanthropist for educational and cultural causes.

There was considerable press conjecture over several months that Crown Princess Masako (36), an Oxford- and Harvard-educated former diplomat, who had been married to Crown Prince Naruhito for six-and-a-half years without producing an heir, was pregnant. At the end of the year, however, the Imperial Household Agency announced that she had had a miscarriage, to the great disappointment of the general populace.

v. SOUTH KOREA

CAPITAL: Seoul   AREA: 99,392 sq km   POPULATION: 46,000,000 ('98)
OFFICIAL LANGUAGE: Korean   POLITICAL SYSTEM: presidential democracy
HEAD OF STATE & GOVERNMENT: President Kim Dae Jung (since Feb '98)
RULING PARTIES: National Congress for New Politics (NCNP) & United Liberal Democrats (ULD)
PRIME MINISTER: Kim Jong Pil (ULD), since March '98
MAIN IGO MEMBERSHIPS (NON-UN): APEC, CP, OECD
CURRENCY: won (end-'99 £1=SKW1,825.73, US$1=SKW1,132.80)
GNP PER CAPITA: US$7,970 by exchange-rate calculation, US$12,270 at PPP ('98)

PRESIDENT Kim Dae Jung promised on his election in December 1997 that 'political surveillance' in South Korea would end. However, when opposition Grand National Party president Lee Hoi Chang and supporters broke into room 529 of the National Assembly building in January they found documents suggesting that the Agency for National Security Planning was still collecting information about ruling and opposition party members. The opposition occupied the Assembly, but the ruling coalition managed to form a quorum and, on the nod of the deputy speaker, in three days 'passed' 130 bills and motions, including economic reforms requested by the IMF. Lee won himself a seat in the national assembly in a Seoul by-election in June, but charges of ineffective leadership and scandal in his party weakened early unofficial campaigning for the April 2000 general election.

President Kim held a dinner at the Blue House in April for the heads of five top *chaebols* (conglomerates)—Hyundai, Daewoo, Samsung, LG and SK—to check on their promises to restructure and threaten them with receivership if they had not done so. However, non-performing loans were still rising at mid-year, and the Korea Stock Exchange's index fell 7 per cent in July as a result of investor panic over debt-servicing. Daewoo, the country's second biggest *chaebol*, with debts of $50,000 million and a debt-to-equity rating of 588 per cent, was forced in August to dispose of 16 of its 22 affiliates, including ship-building and construction. Hyundai disposed of 11 subsidiaries in 1999, but new acquisitions in the semi-conductor field required fresh capital. The *chaebols* were splitting up and divesting themselves of non-core activities, supposedly to repay debt, but taking over financial services to channel money illegally into loss-making subsidiaries. President Kim announced plans to curb the *chaebols,* including a ban on cross-shareholdings between subsidiaries.

The economy made a comeback in 1999, GDP growing 10 per cent, having contracted by 5.8 per cent in 1998. The trade surplus in January-November was $22,000 million, foreign reserves reached $73,000 million (compared with $3,800 million in late 1997) and the won reached a two-year high. President Kim declared that South Korea had 'completely overcome' the financial crisis. It had only partly taken up bail-out packages from the IMF, and had begun repaying its debts. However, government borrowing rose from SKW73.3 trillion ($62,900 million) at the end of 1998 to SKW112 trillion ($97,000 million), 22 per cent of GDP, at the end of 1999.

Talks continued in Geneva between North and South Korea, the USA and China on reducing tension in the Korean peninsula and replacing the 1953 armistice with a peace treaty, but made no progress. In February North Korea proposed new talks with the South, subject to the South ending military exercises and other links with the USA. At the end of the month President Kim responded by asking the North to drop its conditions. Prompted by an offer of 100,000 tonnes of South Korean fertilizer, the North met the South in Beijing in June for a new round of talks on the reunification of families, but they proceeded inconclusively and in early July broke down completely.

There was a North-South naval confrontation in the Yellow Sea in June over the disputed 'northern limit line' drawn by the UN Command at the end of the Korean War. Northern crab-fishing boats had been escorted into southern waters; when South Korean naval vessels forced them back North Korean gunboats opened fire. The South Koreans returned fire, sinking one gunboat and damaging others, and killing some 30 North Korean crewmen. North Korea protested at an armistice meeting with the UN Command at Panmunjom. North Korean-US talks on reducing tension in disputed waters were held in mid-

August, a further session in Panmunjom in September dealing with maritime boundary issues; but the North said that it no longer recognized the UN boundary and would enforce a demarcation line of its own, 56 kilometres to the south.

After test-firing its Hyonmu surface-to-surface missile, South Korea in May rejected US plans for theatre missile defence (TMD), on the grounds that it was probably ineffective against North Korean missiles. During his visit to the USA in July President Kim said that, while the framework of his 'sunshine policy' of engagement with the North would continue, he would deal 'resolutely' with military threats. The South wanted to develop a 500-kilometre-range missile to target North Korean military bases. At talks in Seoul in November the USA tried to discourage South Korea from improving its missile capability.

Towards the end of the year investigations were opened into an alleged US 'massacre' of civilians at Nogunri in 1950, at the beginning of the Korean War, and reports that the US military had used Agent Orange defoliant in the demilitarized zone (DMZ) in the 1960s. South Korean Defence Minister Cho Seong Tae met Chinese counterpart Chi Haotian in Beijing in August. Russian Defence Minister Igor Sergeyev visited Seoul in September, following a visit to Moscow by President Kim in May. A state visit to Seoul in April by Queen Elizabeth II 'upgraded our credibility', the South Korean ambassador to Britain, Choi Sung Hong, was reported as saying (see also II.1).

vi. NORTH KOREA

CAPITAL: Pyongyang   AREA: 123,370 sq km   POPULATION: 23,500,000 ('98)
OFFICIAL LANGUAGE: Korean   POLITICAL SYSTEM: people's republic
RULING PARTY: Korean Workers' Party (KWP)
PARTY LEADER: Kim Jong Il, KWP general secretary (since Oct '97)
PRIME MINISTER: Hong Song Nam (since Sept '98)
MAIN IGO MEMBERSHIPS (NON-UN): NAM
CURRENCY: won (end-'99 £1=NKW3.55, US$1=NKW2.20)
GNP PER CAPITA: US$741 ('97 South Korean est.)

US demands for inspection of the supposed secret nuclear facility at Kumchangri and North Korean demands for compensation (see AR 1998, p. 383) were the subject of new US-North Korean talks held in January in Geneva. At a subsequent session in New York in March the North agreed to inspection, setting aside its original admission fee of $300 million in favour of 500,000 tonnes of US grain (mostly wheat) shipped through the World Food Programme. The USA also agreed to ship directly 100,000 tonnes of grain for famine relief on humanitarian grounds and to give help to improve North Korean potato production. When the US inspection team visited Kumchangri in May, the site was virtually empty.

The Kumchangri affair had threatened to undermine the Korean Peninsula Energy Development Organization (KEDO) created under the Geneva framework agreement of 1994. The US Congress wanted to cut off funds for diesel oil shipments to North Korea, and Tokyo threatened to cut Japanese funding for the nuclear power plant. The Japanese self-defence forces fired warning shots when two 'spy ships' from the North intruded into Japanese waters in March.

The day after the Kumchangri inspection, the USA's Korea envoy, former Defence Secretary William Perry, arrived in Pyongyang and met Kim Yong Nam (president of the presidium of the Supreme People's Assembly) and Defence Minister Kim Il Chol. Provided it discontinued the development, deployment and export of missiles, North Korea was told, it would benefit from economic aid, including the lifting of US trade sanctions. Provided it adhered to the Geneva framework agreement, work would proceed on the $5,000 million nuclear power plant.

When North Korean-US missile talks were held in Pyongyang at the end of March, the North reportedly asked for $1,000 million annual compensation in exchange for a pledge to stop making and exporting missiles. When it was rumoured that the new 3,750-mile-range Taepodong 2 was on the launch-pad, US, South Korean and Japanese officials attending an ASEAN meeting in Singapore in July warned of 'serious consequences' if it were launched. US Secretary of State Madeleine Albright called on Pyongyang to 'seize the opportunity' to improve relations. Japan signed up with the USA to begin developing a TMD (theatre missile defence) system and warned that it might freeze foreign currency remittances to North Korea. Following a visit to Pyongyang by US Senator Tony Hall, North Korean-US talks in Berlin in September yielded agreement on postponement, the North signalling that it would 'endeavour to preserve a positive atmosphere conducive to improved bilateral relations and to peace and security'. The KEDO funding was restored, South Korea approving a loan of $3,220 million to finance the two light-water reactors. The November session of the Berlin talks moved on to upgrading representation (for North-South talks and the Yellow Sea clash, see IX.2.v). Following a visit to Pyongyang in December by an all-party group of Diet members, the Japanese government announced the lifting of its ban on food aid and direct charter flights to North Korea and the resumption of talks with the North Korean government. The sanctions had been imposed after North Korea test-fired a rocket over Japan in August 1998 (see AR 1998, p. 383).

When Kim Yong Nam visited Beijing and Shanghai in June, President Jiang Zemin told him that economic might was the leading symbol of a nation's power. China pledged 150,000 tonnes of grain and 400,000 tonnes of coal for North Korea. Thousands of hungry North Koreans were reported to be crossing the Tumen river into China's Jilin province in search of food. Estimates of the numbers of illegal border-crossers in 1998 ranged from 100,000 to 400,000. Most stayed only a few days before returning to their families with food. China's unwillingness to legalize Koreans' status as refugees hindered the work of foreign aid agencies. In China's Yanbian Korean district, border trade with North Korea fell sharply, while across the border in the nearby Rajin-Songbong economic development zone construction work stagnated.

Japanese trade with North Korea was worth $390 million in 1998, 17 per cent less than in 1997. South Korea estimated a 30 per cent drop in trade with the

North in 1998. North Korean trade turnover in 1998 was estimated at $1,400 million. In the first half of 1999 exports were worth $160 million (down 29 per cent) and imports $420 million (down 14 per cent) on the first half of 1998.

It was estimated that in the first half of 1999 North Korea received altogether some $600 million in food, oil, fertilizer and other aid. In May the North allowed the UN World Food Programme access to previously-closed areas of the country. Charity organizations had poured over $1,000 million into the North since the 1995 floods. There were growing demands for the reform of collective agriculture. Cereal production in 1998 (mostly rice) amounted to 3.89 million tonnes, but this was thought to be one million tonnes short of the minimum needed to feed the country's 23,500,000 people.

A North Korean government official said 220,000 people had died from famine-related causes 1995-98, while the American Mercy Corps International estimated the deaths at 1,500,000. South Korean sources reported in April that in three months up to two million people had been moved out of Pyongyang and other towns into the countryside, either to provide additional agricultural labour or to quell dissent. Reports of 'extravagant celebrations' in Pyongyang of Kim Jong Il's 57th birthday in February were dismissed by South Korea as 'a waste of money' in the light of the need to feed the hungry. Kim was said to be grooming his son Kim Jong Nam (28) to succeed him.

vii. MONGOLIA

CAPITAL: Ulan Bator AREA: 1,564,116 sq km POPULATION: 2,458,900 ('98 est.)
PRINCIPAL LANGUAGE: Halh (Khalkha) Mongolian POLITICAL SYSTEM: republic
HEAD OF STATE: President Natsagiyn Bagabandi (since June '97)
RULING PARTIES: Democratic Alliance (of Mongolian National Democratic & Social Democratic parties) has majority in parliament
PRIME MINISTER: Rinchinnyamyn Amarjargal (since July '99)
MAIN IGO MEMBERSHIPS (NON-UN): NAM
CURRENCY: tögrög (end-'99 £1=T1,728.34, US$1=T1,072.37)
GNP PER CAPITA: US$400 by exchange-rate calculation, US$1,520 at PPP ('98)

THE new Democratic Alliance (DA) Prime Minister, Janlavyn Narantsatsralt, who had been appointed in December 1998 (see AR 1998, p. 386) and who completed the formation of his cabinet in the second week of January, lasted only seven months. After a row over his correspondence with the Russian government about privatization of shares of the joint copper-mining enterprise at Erdenet, Mr Narantsatsralt lost a vote of confidence and resigned on 22 July. The rather obscure affair had much to do with rivalries between the two DA coalition parties, the majority Mongolian National Democratic Party (MNDP) and the Mongolian Social Democratic Party (MSDP), which voted against him.

The DA nominated Rinchinnyamyn Amarjargal, who had been Minister of External Relations in 1998, to be the new Prime Minister. However, on the basis of the Constitutional Court's decision the previous October (see AR 1998, p. 386), President Natsagiyn Bagabandi required Mr Amarjargal to give up his seat in the Mongolian Great Hural (National Assembly) before he would even discuss his nomination. After several days of negotiation to work out a procedure whereby the Prime Minister could be appointed and relieved of his Great Hural seat simultaneously, Mr Amarjargal was sworn in on 30 July. He reappointed all the members of Mr Narantsatsralt's cabinet except the Minister of Law, Logiyn Tsog, who did not wish to joint the MNDP and was replaced by Dashpuntsagiyn Ganbold.

In December the DA and the MPRP jointly tabled several amendments to the Mongolian constitution which were approved by the 76-seat Great Hural by 60 votes to one. The first changes to be made to the constitution since it was adopted in 1992 permitted members of the Great Hural to retain their seats in future if appointed to serve in the government, while the President's control over the appointment of the Prime Minister was loosened. The minimum duration of the Great Hural's sessions was reduced to 50 working days, and the simple majority introduced as the basis for a quorum and for voting. The Great Hural threw out President Bagabandi's veto on the amendments, which complained that the President, the constitutional court and non-parliamentary political parties had not been consulted.

The immunity of three DA members of the Great Hural was suspended in April and they were charged with accepting bribes from backers of the Mon-Macau casino, whose legalization had first been approved and then withdrawn. When the case was finally heard in October, sentences of three to five years' imprisonment were imposed.

Banzragchiyn Delgermaa replaced Sharavdorjiyn Tüvdendorj (Defence Minister) as MNDP secretary-general in January, and Dogsomyn Ganbold (deputy speaker of the Great Hural) succeeded Davaadorjiyn Ganbold as MNDP vice-president in April. Mr Amarjargal displaced Mr Narantsatsralt as MNDP president in November. Dissidents in the MNDP gravitated towards the revitalized Mongolian Democratic Union, parent body of the Mongolian Democratic Party, which had merged with the MNDP in 1992. In March the MSDP appointed Adyaagiyn Ganbaatar as vice-chairman in place of Sangajavyn Bayartsogt and Norovyn Altanhuyag as secretary-general in place of Losolyn Byambajargal.

The Mongolian People's Party (MPP) merged with the opposition Mongolian People's Revolutionary Party (MPRP) in March. The MPP had been set up in 1991 by a member of the Mongolian Democratic Union, Lama Baasan, to prevent the MPRP from reverting, as a 1992 general election ploy, to the name Mongolian People's Party that it had itself used from 1919-24. In October poet, nationalist and Great Hural member Ochirbatyn Dashbalbar abandoned the United Heritage (conservative) Party, of which he was chairman, to form the Tradition and Justice Party with Gantömöriyn Galina, chairman of the National Socialist Party. Mr Dashbalbar died of liver disease in October.

The Living Buddha of Mongolia, the Ninth Javzandamba, arrived unexpectedly from Dharamsala in July. Recognized by the Dalai Lama as the successor to the Eighth Javzandamba, the Holy Khan of Mongolia who died in 1924, he was enthroned at Erdene Zuu monastery. The Dalai Lama had not given him permission to visit Mongolia, and he travelled on a tourist visa. Concerned about Chinese views of links with the Dalai Lama, officials kept him out of the way during President Jiang Zemin's state visit. President Kim Dae Jung of South Korea and Prime Minister Keizo Obuchi of Japan also visited Mongolia during the summer. Prime Minister Amarjargal visited North Korea, China and South Korea in November, but denied acting as a go-between for North-South Korean contacts (see IX.2.v; IX.2.vi).

The seventh meeting of the Mongolia Assistance Group was held in June in Ulan Bator for the first time. It approved grants and loans worth $320 million for macro-economic stabilization, financial reform and infrastructure development. Redesignated the Consultative Group, it planned to meet again in December 2000 in Paris.

Foreign trade turnover in 1999 was down some 10 per cent on the previous year at $761.4 million, of which $255.7 million was trade with China. Total imports at $425.8 million were down 15 per cent on 1998 and exports at $335.6 million down 3 per cent. However, gold extraction amounted to 10,902 kg, 34 per cent more than in 1998, and net foreign currency reserves rose 29 per cent to $117 million. There was a more than threefold increase in new foreign investment in Mongolia in 1999 worth $144.8 million, an indicator of foreign confidence in Mongolian reform and stability. Livestock holdings at the year-end census rose to 33.3 million head, a new record.

X AUSTRALASIA AND THE PACIFIC

i. AUSTRALIA

CAPITAL: Canberra   AREA: 7,687,000 sq km   POPULATION: 19,000,000 ('98)
OFFICIAL LANGUAGE: English   POLITICAL SYSTEM: federal parliamentary democracy
HEAD OF STATE: Queen Elizabeth II   GOVERNOR-GENERAL: Sir William Deane
RULING PARTIES: Liberal-National coalition
HEAD OF GOVERNMENT: John Howard, Prime Minister (since March '96)
MAIN IGO MEMBERSHIPS (NON-UN): APEC, PC, PIF, CP, ANZUS, OECD, CWTH
CURRENCY: Australian dollar (end-'99 £1=A$2.46, US$1=A$1.53)
GNP PER CAPITA: US$20,300 by exchange-rate calculation, US$20,130 at PPP ('98)

AUSTRALIA decided not to become a republic by a constitutional referendum, the only method by which such an issue could be resolved. The Australian economy generally improved, with unemployment reduced below 7 per cent by the end of the year. The Liberal-National government of John Howard succeeded in getting much of its proposed goods and services tax (GST) through parliament, although it was forced to withdraw its imposition on food as part of a deal with the Democrats in the Senate. The Australian steel industry faced major restructuring with the closing of the oldest steel works, the BHP plant at Newcastle, on 1 October.

Australian foreign and defence policy was severely tested by the crises in Indonesia and East Timor (see IX.1.vi), while refugee issues were raised in relation to the latter and earlier to Kosovo (see III.2.vi). Timorese and Kosovo refugees were given temporary residence in Australia, but arrivals by boat, mainly from the Middle East, were detained in an atmosphere of some public and official alarm. A new detention facility was opened in the South Australian desert at Woomera for undocumented arrivals, whose numbers had increased sharply. The legal status of undocumented asylum seekers was amended so that they became eligible only for temporary visas rather than permanent residence.

Following the onset of NATO air strikes on Serbia on 24 March, two Australian aid workers were arrested by Serbian police in April while in Yugoslavia and tried for spying, They were released on 1 September after considerable Australian and international pressure.

The collapse of the Suharto government in Indonesia in 1998 had undermined the consistent Australian policy of seeking stability in defence, foreign, trade and investment through good relations with his regime. Australia had been almost alone in recognizing the 1975 Indonesian annexation of East Timor, despite considerable local opposition to this step and the location in Australia of several leading Timorese nationalists. President Bacharuddin Habibie promised a delegation of Australian journalists in April that he would consider East Timorese independence, to which Prime Minister Howard responded by promising substantial aid to supervise the autonomy vote, police and civil personnel for the United Nations supervision and a medical team. This began a process which eventually led to Australian troops taking over command of the United Nations peace-keeping mission and the cancellation of the mutual defence treaty of 1995 (see AR 1995, p. 360).

By September the government was being pressed to intervene but would not do so without an Indonesian invitation, which was eventually forthcoming on 9 September. With UN approval, Australia agreed to send its first detachment of 2,000 men to Timor on 16 September, while Timorese independence leader Xanana Gusmão arrived in Darwin two days later to organize a provisional government. The first troops of what was designated the International Force for East Timor (INTERFET) landed on 20 September under the command of Major-General Peter Cosgrove. Despite threats from the Indonesian forces and demonstrations against Australia in Jakarta, the operation was successful and mainly peaceful. It did, however, commit Australia heavily in military and financial terms to an involvement which it had been seeking to avoid for over 20 years. While very popular at home and supported by the opposition, the new role of Australia in South-East Asia was criticized by Malaysia and was certainly unwelcome in Indonesia. To meet the added costs involved in the operation a specific tax was levied on higher incomes. The future implications suggested greater military expenditure than previous policies had envisaged and this was already being canvassed as the year ended.

A more positive aspect of foreign relations was the visit on 6 September of the Chinese President Jiang Zemin, the first such in Australian history. A Chinese-Australian businessman was released from prison in China as a gesture of goodwill. Among economic benefits discussed at a trade and investment summit meeting in Melbourne were technology transfer in environmental and water conservation projects, the sale of liquefied natural gas and an Australian contract to reform the Chinese welfare system. In return, Mr Howard expressed support for China's entry into the World Trade Organization.

The adoption of the new taxation system, centred around a goods and services tax, required negotiations with the states and with the independents and Democrats holding the balance in the Senate. At the April premiers' conference all the states, regardless of party control, accepted the Commonwealth offer of a massive compensation package for those of their taxes which would be replaced. The Labor Party nationally continued to oppose the tax altogether but the Democrats were prepared to compromise provided that it was not imposed on basic food and some other items. The legislation was eventually passed on 28 June as amended to conform to the Democrats' wishes. This compromise caused some tensions within the Democrats. Party leader Meg Lees survived, though two Democrat senators voted with Labor and the independents against the tax.

The other contentious issue resolved in the Senate was the sale of more of telecommunications giant Telstra, bringing the private holding up to 49.9 per cent (see AR 1997, p. 367; 1998, p. 387). Much of the consequent income would be spent on improving regional and rural services, mainly in response to National Party pressure. The government was forced to withdraw its proposed industrial relations bill when the Democrats decided to oppose it on 29 November. The bill would have imposed secret strike ballots, restricted union access to workplaces and otherwise greatly reduced union influence.

Enthusiasm for the 2000 Olympic Games in Sydney abated in the face of local and international crises within the Olympic movement and the realization of the likely costs involved. Disagreements with sponsors and over ticket sales were among the major problems. Transport arrangements were completed in Sydney and tested satisfactorily by several large events at the Homebush Bay site, where work was completed ahead of schedule. Problems partly reflected tensions between the Commonwealth and New South Wales governments. Prime Minister Howard initially decided to open the Games himself, but was eventually persuaded to cede that role to the Governor-General once the republican issue was resolved. Australia had a good year in sport, winning both the Davis Cup in tennis and the World Cup in rugby union (see Pt XVI).

Labor was easily returned at the New South Wales state election of 27 March. The result for the legislative assembly was: Labor 55 seats (42 per cent of the vote), Liberals 20 (25 per cent), Nationals 13 (9 per cent), others 5 (24 per cent). The high minor party vote reflected dissatisfaction with the major parties and included 7.5 per cent for the populist One Nation. The new legislative council, elected on state-wide proportional representation, included a wide range of minority members, including one from One Nation and one from the new Unity party, which was specifically hostile to One Nation and reliant on Chinese community support.

The apparently secure Victorian Liberal government of Jeff Kennett was defeated at the state election of 18 September, the resultant new Labor premier, Steve Bracks, having the support of three independents for his majority. The final result for the legislative assembly was: Labor 42 seats (45 per cent of the vote), Liberals 36 (42 per cent), National 7 (5 per cent), others 3 (8 per cent). In a by-election arising from the resignation of Jeff Kennett from parliament, his suburban seat fell to Labor for the first time since it was created. The new cabinet included 44 per cent women, an Australian record. Labor thus ruled four of the six states. But it failed to gain support for its republicanism, either from the voters as a whole or from many Labor supporters. Nor was its national support as strong as the state results might have suggested.

Privatization of public services continued, with employment agency work being devolved, partly to religious agencies, at the end of the year. Work for the dole and restricted rights to unemployment benefit were introduced, but the Commonwealth failed to gain support for a reduced youth wage. At the end of the year the Aboriginal and Torres Strait Islander Commission elected Geoff Clarke of Victoria as its first chairman not directly nominated by the Commonwealth. The Northern Territory government signed an agreement on 11 February with two Aboriginal land councils, clearing the way for the long-proposed Alice Springs-to-Darwin railway.

On 6 November a 54.9 per cent majority of Australians in all states and territories except the Capital Territory (Canberra) decided in a constitutional referendum, with compulsory voting, to retain the existing arrangement under which Queen Elizabeth II was the head of state represented locally by a governor-general. There was much confusion and misrepresentation in the preceding campaign. Amid public uncertainty as to what the existing constitution provided, monarchists claimed that the Queen was not head of state, while 'direct election' republicans aligned with the monarchists against the proposal on offer. The results showed that support for a republican model, with a president elected by a parliamentary majority, ranged from 63 per cent in Canberra and almost 50 per cent in Victoria, down to 37 per cent in Queensland. The national vote for the republican model was 45.1 per cent.

Counting by constituencies showed that Labor and Liberal seats were not very different but that National Party seats, predominantly rural and provincial, were overwhemingly against change. Opinion polling suggested that British immigrants were strongly monarchist, while European and Asian immigrants favoured the republic. However, it also perversely suggested that many 'direct election' republicans opposed the new model and consequently voted with the monarchists. Prime Minister Howard was clearly delighted with the result, although his proposed new preamble to the constitution recognizing Aborigines as 'the nation's first people' was even more heavily rejected, by 60.7 to 39.3 per cent. It was clear, therefore, that the referendum exercise was a remarkable defeat for a range of public figures, politicians and media commentators who had predominantly favoured change.

Conflict within the One Nation party escalated in December to the point where the entire Queensland parliamentary group, having numbered 11 as a result of the June 1998 election (see AR 1998, p. 388), disappeared. One member had resigned almost immediately on election in 1998, while five more left the party early in 1999. The party then lost its official registration because it did not conform to membership requirements, thus also losing its electoral funding and status within parliament. In the absence of leader Pauline Hanson overseas, the five remaining Queensland MPs decided to form a new party, which after some debate they called the City-Country Alliance. David Oldfield, elected to the New South Wales legislative council in March, and Senator Len Harris, who had replaced Heather Hill on her disqualification as a dual citizen (see AR 1998, p. 389), were therefore the only remaining One Nation representatives in any parliament. Ms Hill was an active supporter of the breakaway party. Opinion polling support for the party dropped to an average of only 1 per cent.

In another party development, the leader of the National Party, Tim Fischer, resigned and left parliament in July and was replaced by John Anderson. On 9 December the first woman to be president of the Australian Council of Trade Unions, Jennie George, resigned and was expected to be succeeded by another woman, Sharan Burrow.

In December the government announced future plans for television and data broadcasting which were welcomed by media owner Kerry Packer but not by his counterpart Rupert Murdoch. Suitably for one of the first countries to enter the year 2000, there were massive celebrations throughout Australia on the night of 31 December. The 'millennium bug' computer problem did not materialize, possibly because the government spent $A12,000 million on avoiding it.

Among those who died during the year were the former Labor premier of South Australia, Don Dunstan (72); artists Arthur Boyd (78) and John Brack (78); author Morris West (83) (see Pt XVIII: Obituary); transport entrepreneur Sir Peter Abeles (75) of TNT; former judge and Labor minister James McClelland (83); former Solicitor-General Sir Maurice Byers (81); former Speaker of the House of Representatives Jim Cope (91); the first Aboriginal senator, Neville Bonner (76); and the former editor of the *Sydney Morning Herald,* John Pringle (87).

ii. PAPUA NEW GUINEA

CAPITAL: Port Moresby   AREA: 463,000 sq km   POPULATION: 5,000,000 ('98)
OFFICIAL LANGUAGES: Pidgin, Motu, English   POLITICAL SYSTEM: parliamentary democracy
HEAD OF STATE: Queen Elizabeth II
GOVERNOR-GENERAL: Sir Sailas Atopare
RULING PARTIES: People's Democratic Movement (PDM) heads coalition
HEAD OF GOVERNMENT: Sir Mekere Morauta (PDM), Prime Minister (since July '99)
MAIN IGO MEMBERSHIPS (NON-UN): APEC, CP, PC, PIF, ACP, CWTH, NAM
CURRENCY: kina (end-'99 £1=K4.32, US$1=K2.68)
GNP PER CAPITA: US$890 by exchange-rate calculation, US$2,700 at PPP ('98)

THE major social, political and economic problems which had beset Papua New Guinea (PNG) in recent years continued for most of 1999. At the end of the year, though, it was just possible that the first signs of improvement were beginning to emerge.

Certainly there was a sense of a nadir having been reached in the middle of the year. On 7 July Prime Minister Bill Skate resigned. His two-year period in office, latterly at the head of a coalition led by his PNG First Party (see AR 1998, p. 391), had been marked by ubiquitous scandal, the continuing seep of corruption into the fabric of public life and vertiginous economic decline. An intriguing-and saving-characteristic of post-independence politics in PNG was that otherwise ineffective and incompetent coalition governments had been led by a sequence of able Prime Ministers (Michael Somare, Julius Chan, Rabbie Namaliu). This pattern ended with Mr Skate's arrival—and perhaps resumed with his departure.

Mr Skate's resignation followed a bizarre sequence of events which culminated in his announcement on 5 July, after a visit to Taiwan, that PNG would extend full diplomatic recognition to that country. This was done apparently without regard to the implications for the existing relationship with the People's Republic of China. Underpinning this pauline conversion in PNG's Asian diplomacy was a Taiwanese soft loan of some US$2,000 million which was to settle, at a stroke, PNG's desperate financial circumstances. It was also hoped that it would deflate a vote of no confidence in the government due to be debated in parliament a few days later. Threats of 'grave consequences' immediately issued from Beijing, and Australia quickly expressed its unhappiness at the move. Mr Skate's speedy resignation was probably a tactic that he hoped would lead either to his rapid return to office or at least position him as king-maker. In the event, his horse-trading instincts let him down and, after a characteristically shadowy series of inter- and intra-party manœuvres, parliament elected the widely-respected Sir Mekere Morauta, leader of the People's Democratic Movement (PDM), to head a new coalition.

The new Prime Minister moved quickly to reverse the more damaging policies of the previous administration, although, having served for a time as Mr Skate's Deputy Prime Minister, his hands were not entirely clean). As a priority, the plan for diplomatic recognition of Taiwan was abandoned. Speaking on the 24th anniversary of independence on 16 September, the Prime Minister eschewed the self-congratulatory tone by then customary on these occasions. Incompetent and corrupt leadership, he observed, had brought a decline in the social and economic condition of the country since independence rather than the advances which people had reasonably expected.

The country's dire economic predicament began to be addressed in early August with an emergency 'mini-budget' which brought extra taxes and swingeing expenditure cuts. A month later a now less anxious Australian Prime Minister, John Howard, signed an aid package in Port Moresby worth A$1,000 million over the coming three years. Shortly afterwards PNG's fractured relationship with the Bretton Woods system was repaired when, after an evaluation of the new government's proposed budget for 2000, the World Bank and the IMF agreed support measures valued at about US$500 million.

The apparently endless secessionist conflict in Bougainville continued to defy resolution during 1999. Despite a supposed 'final' settlement in 1998 (see AR 1998, pp. 391-2), factionalism within the rebel Bougainville Revolutionary Army (BRA) led again to backtracking on previously agreed positions and the demolition of carefully constructed institutional arrangements. Responsibility for Bougainville was passed by Sir Mekere Morauta to his Foreign Minister, Michael Somare (PNG's independence Prime Minister), in an evident attempt to utilize the latter's national and international prestige.

The backwash from the Bougainville conflict impacted on PNG's other endemic and apparently intractable problems: urban crime and tribal fighting. The easy availability of high-powered weapons, as a result of emergency defence procurements and lax military discipline, had made an already grave series of problems infinitely more deadly than hitherto.

2. NEW ZEALAND–PACIFIC ISLAND STATES

i. NEW ZEALAND

CAPITAL: Wellington   AREA: 270,000 sq km   POPULATION: 4,000,000 ('98)
OFFICIAL LANGUAGE: English   POLITICAL SYSTEM: parliamentary democracy
HEAD OF STATE: Queen Elizabeth II   GOVERNOR-GENERAL: Sir Michael Hardie Boys
RULING PARTIES: New Zealand Labour Party (NZLP) & Alliance
HEAD OF GOVERNMENT: Helen Clark, Prime Minister (since Dec '99)
MAIN IGO MEMBERSHIPS (NON-UN): ANZUS (suspended), APEC, PC, PIF, CP, OECD, CWTH
CURRENCY: New Zealand dollar (end-'99 £1=NZ$3.09, US$1=NZ$1.92)
GNP PER CAPITA: US$14,700 by exchange-rate calculation, US$15,840 at PPP ('98)

NEW Zealand elected a new government in November, ousting the incumbent National Party (NP), which had been in power for nine years. It was replaced by a coalition between the Labour and Alliance parties, with Labour leader Helen Clark as Prime Minister. The election was only the second to be held under the country's proportional electoral system, which was introduced for the first time in 1996. A coalition government between the NP and the New Zealand First (NZF) party had resulted, headed for a year by Jim Bolger and from December 1997 by Jenny Shipley, who had led a minority government since the withdrawal of NZF in mid-1998 (see AR 1998, pp. 393-4).

Accustomed to stable governments, New Zealanders found much of the manœuverings of coalition government distasteful and were critical of the electoral system which produced it. A petition calling for a referendum to reduce the number of members of parliament from 120 to 99—in other words to reverse one of the key aspects of the new electoral system—gathered enough signatures to be put on the November 1999 ballot. The non-binding referendum produced an overwhelming vote in favour of a reduction to 99 MPs, with nearly 82 per cent of those voting supporting such a move. Another referendum, also placed on the ballot by electors (rather than the government), attracted nearly 92 per cent support for changes to aspects of the criminal justice system. Neither referendum was binding and the new government showed little inclination to support either initiative.

Although the rejection of the Shipley government reflected voters' dissatisfaction with the new electoral system, coalition politics and some government policies, there was also a sense that nine years of office had left the NP with little to offer. Its 30.5 per cent share of the vote (giving it 39 seats) was its worst result since its formation in the aftermath of the Labour Party's first election victory in 1935. The performance of its populist erstwhile coalition partner, NZF, was even more miserable, with the party winning less than the 5 per cent of the list vote needed for representation. Its fortunes were salvaged, but only just, when its leader, Winston Peters, held his constituency seat (with a majority down from 8,028 to 63) and thus enabled NZF to qualify for four list seats as well. By contrast, the Labour Party's share of the vote went up significantly from 28 per cent in 1996 to 38.7 per cent and its representation from 37 to 49 seats. As for the left-wing Alliance Party, its support fell to only 7.7 per cent from 10 per cent in 1996 and its representation to 10 seats, while the Association of Taxpayers and Consumers (ACT) advanced to 7 per cent and nine seats and the Greens to 5.2 per cent and seven seats. The remaining seat went to the United New Zealand Party.

Labour's election victory gave the party its fifth chance at governing New Zealand, but with a less convincing mandate than on previous occasions. In the past, Labour had always been able to govern on its own. The 1999 result meant that it had to enter into a coalition with the Alliance (led by Jim Anderton), whose origins lay in a late-1980s rebellion against the economic and social policies of the previous Labour government. The coalition itself was no surprise, because the two parties had entered into a pre-election agreement signalling to voters that they would govern together if given the opportunity to do so. This was a significant change from the acrimony that had existed between them in 1996, when Labour, hoping to govern on its own, had refused to give any pre-election commitment, while the Alliance had declared that it would not take part in any post-election deals unless these were announced to voters in advance.

The new Prime Minister, Helen Clark, had become the first New Zealand woman to lead a political party to victory at a general election. Her government signalled the start of a new era in New Zealand politics with the appointment of seven women to the 20 cabinet positions (compared with only two in the previous government) and the selection of a further four women for an additional six executive positions. Thus the full 26-member ministry included 11 women among its 26 members, giving women near-parity with men.

In other respects, too, the election results were further evidence of the capacity of the new electoral system to produce a more diverse and more representative parliamentary membership. The country's first-ever Asian MP elected in 1996 won a second term, and she was joined by the first Pacific Island woman, a New Zealander of Samoan origin, to win a seat in parliament. The number of women MPs grew slightly, from the record 35 elected in 1996 to 37; and as in 1996 there were 15 Maori MPs, far more than had ever been elected under the previous voting system. Further evidence of cultural change could be seen in the election of a person who had had a sex change operation (apparently the first time that this had happened in any country), as well as the return to parliament of two homosexual male MPs.

Although the Labour and Alliance parties together won only 46.4 per cent of the vote, the election night totals appeared to give them a comfortable majority in parliament, with 63 of the 120 MPs. The final results, however, gave the coalition only 59 seats, since the Greens were able to win a constituency seat in the North Island and therefore qualified for six list seats as well. The party's constituency victory was reportedly the first time that a Green parliamentary candidate anywhere in the world had won a seat in a national legislature in a single-member district. Excluded from the coalition, the Greens were expected to support the government on 'confidence issues'; nevertheless, the late seat adjustments transformed the new coalition into a minority government, dependent for survival on a party which had left the Alliance to compete on its own.

The coalition's declared objectives—to reduce inequality and restore public confidence in parliament and the electoral system—reflected concerns which intensified during the years of NP government. But the Labour-Alliance coalition faced difficulties in reversing of some policies and trends. Plans to cancel the previous government's arrangement with the United States to lease F-16 planes were an immediate source of controversy. Legislation to prevent MPs elected on a party list from changing their party affiliation were also postponed because of opposition from the Greens. The government acted quickly, however, to increase the tax rate on higher incomes and the minimum wage, and to assist students by ending the charging of interest on tertiary student loans.

A highlight of the year in the external policy sphere was the seventh summit of the Asia-Pacific Economic Cooperation (APEC) forum held in Auckland on 12-13 September and attended by US President Bill Clinton and Chinese President Jiang Zemin among other leaders (see XI.6.iii). Shortly after the summit New Zealand troops participated in the Australian-led international force deployed in East Timor to keep the peace as the territory moved to independence from Indonesia (see IX.1.vi).

ii. PACIFIC ISLAND STATES

Fiji

CAPITAL: Suva   AREA: 18,375 sq km   POPULATION: 827,000 ('98)
OFFICIAL LANGUAGES: Fijian, Hindi & English   POLITICAL SYSTEM: republic
HEAD OF STATE: President Ratu Sir Kamisese Mara (since Nov '93)
RULING PARTIES: Fijian Labour Party (FLP) heads coalition
HEAD OF GOVERNMENT: Mahendra Chaudhry (FLP), Prime Minister (since May '99)
MAIN IGO MEMBERSHIPS (NON-UN): CWTH, PC, PIF, CP, ACP
CURRENCY: Fiji dollar (end-'99 £1=F$3.21, US$1=F$1.99)
GNP PER CAPITA: US$2,110 by exchange-rate calculation, US$3,580 at PPP ('98)

Kiribati

CAPITAL: Tarawa   AREA: 1,000 sq km   POPULATION: 85,000 ('98)
OFFICIAL LANGUAGES: English & Kiribati   POLITICAL SYSTEM: republic
HEAD OF STATE & GOVERNMENT: President Teburoro Tito (since Sept '94)
MAIN IGO MEMBERSHIPS (NON-UN): CWTH, PC, PIF, ACP
CURRENCY: Australian dollar (see above)
GNP PER CAPITA: US$1,180 by exchange-rate calculation, US$3,480 at PPP ('98)

Marshall Islands

CAPITAL: Dalap-Uliga-Darrit   AREA: 200 sq km   POPULATION: 62,000 ('98)
OFFICIAL LANGUAGES: English & Marshallese   POLITICAL SYSTEM: republic
HEAD OF STATE & GOVERNMENT: President Imata Kabua (since Jan '98)
MAIN IGO MEMBERSHIPS (NON-UN): PC, PIF
CURRENCY: US dollar
GNP PER CAPITA: US$1,540 by exchange-rate calculation ('98)

Federated States of Micronesia

CAPITAL: Palikir (Pohnpei) AREA: 701 sq km POPULATION: 118,000 ('98)
OFFICIAL LANGUAGE: English
POLITICAL SYSTEM: independent republic in free association with USA
HEAD OF STATE & GOVERNMENT: President Leo Falcam (since May '99)
MAIN IGO MEMBERSHIPS (NON-UN): PC, PIF
CURRENCY: US dollar
GNP PER CAPITA: US$1,800 by exchange-rate calculation ('98)

Nauru

CAPITAL: Domaneab AREA: 21.4 sq km POPULATION: 11,000 ('98)
OFFICIAL LANGUAGES: Nauruan & English POLITICAL SYSTEM: republic
HEAD OF STATE & GOVERNMENT: President René Harris (since May '99)
MAIN IGO MEMBERSHIPS (NON-UN): CWTH, PC, PIF
CURRENCY: Australian dollar (see above)
GNP PER CAPITA: n/a

Palau (Belau)

CAPITAL: Koror AREA: 460 sq km POPULATION: 19,000 ('98)
OFFICIAL LANGUAGE: English
POLITICAL SYSTEM: independent republic in free association with USA
HEAD OF STATE & GOVERNMENT: President Kuniwo Nakamura (since Nov '92)
MAIN IGO MEMBERSHIPS (NON-UN): PC, PIF
CURRENCY: US dollar
GNP PER CAPITA: n/a

Samoa

CAPITAL: Apia AREA: 2,842 sq km POPULATION: 176,000 ('98)
OFFICIAL LANGUAGES: English & Samoan POLITICAL SYSTEM: constitutional monarchy
HEAD OF STATE: Susuga Malietoa Tanumafili II (since Jan '62)
RULING PARTY: Human Rights Protection Party
HEAD OF GOVERNMENT: Tuilaepa Sailele Malielegaoi, Prime Minister (since Nov '98)
MAIN IGO MEMBERSHIPS (NON-UN):: CWTH, PC, PIF, ACP
CURRENCY: tala (end-'99 £1=T4.98, US$1=T3.09)
GNP PER CAPITA: US$1,020 by exchange-rate calculation, US$3,440 at PPP ('98)

Solomon Islands

CAPITAL: Honiara AREA: 28,000 sq km POPULATION: 415,000 ('98)
OFFICIAL LANGUAGE: English POLITICAL SYSTEM: parliamentary democracy
HEAD OF STATE: Queen Elizabeth II GOVERNOR-GENERAL: John Lapli
RULING PARTY: Liberal Party (LP) heads Alliance for Change coalition
HEAD OF GOVERNMENT: Bartholomew Ulufa'alu (LP), Prime Minister (since Aug '97)
MAIN IGO MEMBERSHIPS (NON-UN): CWTH, PC, PIF, ACP
CURRENCY: Solomon Islands dollar (end-'99 £1=SI$8.15, S$1=SI$5.06)
GNP PER CAPITA: US$750 by exchange-rate calculation, US$2,080 at PPP ('98)

Tonga

CAPITAL: Nuku'alofa AREA: 750 sq km POPULATION: 99,000 ('98)
OFFICIAL LANGUAGES: Tongan & English POLITICAL SYSTEM: monarchy
HEAD OF STATE: King Taufa'ahua Tupou IV (since Dec '65)
HEAD OF GOVERNMENT: Baron Vaea, Prime Minister (since Aug '91)
MAIN IGO MEMBERSHIPS (NON-UN): CWTH, PC, PIF, ACP
CURRENCY: pa'anga (end-'99 £1=T$2.46, US$1=T$1.53)
GNP PER CAPITA: US$1,690 by exchange-rate calculation, US$3,860 at PPP ('98)

Tuvalu

CAPITAL: Fongafle AREA: 26 sq km POPULATION: 9,750 ('98)
OFFICIAL LANGUAGE: English POLITICAL SYSTEM: constitutional monarchy
HEAD OF STATE: Queen Elizabeth II GOVERNOR-GENERAL: Tomasi Puapua
HEAD OF GOVERNMENT: Ionatana Ionatana, Prime Minister (since April '99)
MAIN IGO MEMBERSHIPS: PC, PIF, ACP
CURRENCY: Australian dollar (end-'99 £1=A$2.46, US$1=A$1.53)
GNP PER CAPITA: n/a

Vanuatu

CAPITAL: Port Vila AREA: 12,000 sq km POPULATION: 182,000 ('98)
OFFICIAL LANGUAGES: English, French & Bislama POLITICAL SYSTEM: republic
HEAD OF STATE: President John Bani (since March '99)
RULING PARTIES: Melanesian Progressive Party (MPP) heads coalition
HEAD OF GOVERNMENT: Barak Sope (MPP), Prime Minister (since Nov '99)
MAIN IGO MEMBERSHIPS (NON-UN): CWTH, PC, PIF, ACP, Francophonie
CURRENCY: vatu (end-'99 £1=VT208.02, US$1=VT129.07)
GNP PER CAPITA: US$1,270 by exchange-rate calculation, US$3,160 at PPP ('98)

THREE Pacific Island states—Kiribati, Nauru and Tonga—were admitted to UN membership in September, following approval of their applications by the UN Security Council in June and July. Major developments in the region in 1999 included changes of government in several independent states and dependent territories.

In FIJI, parliamentary elections on 8-15 May were the first to take place under the country's reformed constitution as introduced in 1998 (see AR 1998, p. 398), which made substantial changes to the electoral system. The result was a heavy defeat for the ruling Fijian Political Party (SVT) and a decisive victory for the predominantly Indian Fiji Labour Party (FLP), which won 37 of the 71 seats in the House of Representatives. Although commanding an overall majority, FLP leader Mahendra Chaudhry formed a broad-based coalition government which included the Fijian Association Party (FAP) and the Fijian Party of National Unity (PANU), becoming the first Fijian Prime Minister of Indian ancestry. In July former Prime Minister Sitiveni Rabuka stated that the Fijian army had been urged to support a coup by ethnic Fijian nationalists but had declined to do so, adding that 'circumstances are changed' from 1987, when he had led a coup to prevent an Indo-Fijian from becoming Prime Minister. Major-General Rabuka had resigned from parliament on 17 June to become chairman of the Great Council of Chiefs, the highest traditional authority of the indigenous Melanesians. In September the Chaudhry government committed 190 Fijian soldiers to the Australian-led international force deployed in East Timor (see IX.1.vi).

At the beginning of the year Ratu Sir Kamisese Mara had been sworn in for a second five-year term as President, in accordance with the recommendation of the Great Council of Chiefs.

In KIRIBATI, President Teburoro Tito declared a countrywide state of emergency on 3 March because of a prolonged drought caused by an eight-month absence of rain, appealing at the same time for international aid to build desalination plants. In September the President rejected suggestions that the presence of a Chinese tracking station on Tarawa (Kiribati's most populous island) might make the island a target for China's enemies.

In elections in the MARSHALL ISLANDS on 15 November, five of the six cabinet ministers seeking re-election lost their seats and the opposition United Democratic Party (UDP) won at least 18 of the 33 seats in the *Nitijela* (parliament). The government of President Imata Kabua had held a slim 18-15 majority in the outgoing parliament. Its defeat marked the first time that the Marshall Islands electorate had voted to oust a sitting government and paved the way for the prospective election of UDP candidate Kessai Note as President early in 2000.

Following non-party congressional elections in the FEDERATED STATES OF MICRONESIA (FSM) on 2 March, the new Congress on 12 May elected Leo Falcam of Pohnpei state as the country's fifth President (in succession to Jacob Nena), with Redley Killion of Chuuk state winning the vice-presidency. Talks subsequently opened in Hawaii on the renewal of the FSM-US 'compact of free association', which was due to expire in 2001.

President Bernard Dowiyogo of NAURU was defeated in a parliamentary vote of confidence on 28 April and replaced by René Harris, former chairman of the state-owned Nauru Phosphate Corporation. In December Nauru came under criticism from the G-7 countries for allowing its banking system to be used for money-laundering by criminal organizations.

Despite achieving legal independence and UN membership in 1994 in 'free association' with the USA (see AR 1994, p. 406), the Republic of PALAU remained under Washington's direction not only in the areas of foreign policy and defence but also in aspects of domestic policy. Re-elected in November 1996, President Kuniwo Nakamura came into conflict with the legislature over its adoption of legislation seeking to make the republic an offshore financial centre. The issue remained unresolved in 1999, with the US government making clear its disapproval of the plan. Palau raised its regional profile in October when its hosted the 30th summit of the South Pacific Forum, which was renamed the Pacific Islands Forum (PIF).

In SAMOA, Minister of Public Works Luagalau Levaula Kamu was assassinated in Apia on 16 July, dying from a single shot to the heart outside a function celebrating the 20th anniversary of the ruling Human Rights Protection Party. A man arrested by the police on 27 July pleaded guilty to the murder on 7 August and was sentenced to death. Although the death penalty was mandatory, it had never been carried out since independence in 1962, all death sentences having been commuted to life imprisonment by Samoa's head of state. The police subsequently arrested two politicians in connection with the murder, one of them the assassin's father, Leafa Vitale, who was dismissed as Minister of Women's Affairs on 3 August; the other, Toi Aukuso, was a member of the Samoan parliament and former minister opposed to the incumbent government. The trial of the two former ministers was set for January 2000, amid speculation that the real target of the assassination had been Prime Minister Tuilaepa Sailele Malielegaoi.

Ethnic violence on Guadalcanal posed a major challenge to the future of the SOLOMON ISLANDS, as a group known as the Isatambu Freedom Fighters fought to oust immigrants from other parts of the Solomons, notably those from Malaita. The former Prime Minister of Fiji, Sitiveni Rabuka, assisted in securing the signature on 28 June of the 'Honiara peace accord', specifying that the rights of original landowners on Guadalcanal should be respected. A second accord concluded in August, known as the 'Panatina agreement', recommitted the Solomon Islands' government, the police and the Guadalcanal provincial administration to the Honiara accord. In accordance with the Honiara agreement, some members of the Freedom Fighters began to surrender their weapons in September, supervised by peace monitors from Fiji and Vanuatu under the direction of New Zealand police officers.

In TONGA, Legislative Assembly elections were held in two rounds on 10-11 March, with voting for the nine commoners' seats taking place after the elections for the nine nobles' seats. In the polling among Tonga's nobles, held at the King's palace, two of the incumbent representatives were defeated, including the speaker, who lost his seat to one of the King's sons. In the commoners' races, the pro-democracy movement led by Akilisi Pohiva suffered a setback, winning five of the nine seats, one less than previously. Despite having tendered his resignation in December 1998, Baron Vaea continued as Prime Minister through 1999 but was expected to be replaced by one of the King's sons early in 2000.

In TUVALU, a motion of no-confidence did succeed in toppling Bikenibeu Paeniu from his position as Prime Minister. The April vote, which was held on the very last day of the parliamentary session, was followed two weeks later by the election of Ionatana Ionatana, former Minister of Education, as the new Prime Minister.

In VANUATU, Father John Bani was elected as the country's fifth President in March, his election being noteworthy because his predecessor, Jean-Marie Leye, who had sought a further term, did not receive a single vote from the country's 55-member electoral college. In November Father Bani's former colleague, Donald Kalpokas, resigned as Prime Minister rather than lose a no-confidence vote. He was replaced by veteran politician Barak Sope, leader of the Melanesian Progressive Party, who was elected by parliament on a 28-24 vote. In February the Vanuatu Financial Services Commission had rejected a claim by the OECD that local banks were being used by Russian criminals for money-laundering.

Elections in the New Zealand dependency of the COOK ISLANDS in June were the forerunner of a complicated sequence of events, as the Cook Islands Party (CIP) of Prime Minister Sir Geoffrey Henry lost its majority. By the end of the month, however, he was again sworn in as Prime Minister, having succeeded in forming a coalition government with Norman George, leader of the New Alliance Party (NAP). A month later three CIP members unhappy with the coalition formed an alliance with the opposition Democratic Alliance Party (DAP), whereupon Sir Geoffrey unexpectedly resigned (after ten years as

Prime Minister) and one of the three dissident CIP members, Dr Joe Williams, was elected to replace him on a 13-12 vote. The new government preserved the CIP-NAP coalition but lasted only until 17 November, when Dr Williams resigned to avoid a no-confidence vote. Subsequently, DAP leader Dr Terepai Maoate was sworn in as Prime Minister heading a DAP-NAP coalition, with Mr George as his deputy.

In the New Zealand dependency of NIUE, elections in March saw the defeat of the government of Premier Frank Lui, who failed to hold his own seat in the Niue Assembly and retired from politics. The victory of the opposition Niue People's Party was the first time since self-government that a political party had succeeded in winning an election. The government of the new Premier, Sani Elia Lakatani, took power following a 14-6 vote in the Assembly, but in late December it only narrowly avoided losing a motion of no confidence—the vote was 10-10—over controversial plans to establish a Niuean airline company.

French Pacific territories took some small steps towards greater autonomy in 1999. The French National Assembly and Senate each ratified a constitutional amendment changing the status of FRENCH POLYNESIA to that of an 'overseas country', it being envisaged that a new law would further define and guarantee its status within the French Republic. French Polynesia would have the power to negotiate and sign international treaties, and a separate French Polynesian citizenship was also to be established. These moves, however, were unlikely to satisfy those in French Polynesia who were seeking independence. Ironically, the trial on corruption charges of French Polynesia's President, Gaston Flosse, began in October, only a day after the passage of the constitutional amendment by the French Senate. By the end of November M. Flosse had been found guilty, given a two-year suspended gaol term and a fine. He announced his intention to appeal and refused, in the interim, to resign from the presidency.

In the French overseas territory of NEW CALEDONIA, elections in May led to the mayor of Nouméa, Jean Lequès, becoming its first President. These were the first elections to be held under a new statute giving the territory greater self-government. The anti-independence Rally for Caledonia in the Republic took seven of 11 seats in the new cabinet. In October a French constitutional amendment restricted participants in any future referendum on independence to persons who had, at that time, been residents of New Caledonia for at least ten years and were on the electoral roll as of November 1998.

XI INTERNATIONAL ORGANIZATIONS

1. UNITED NATIONS AND ITS AGENCIES

DATE OF FOUNDATION: 1945   HEADQUARTERS: New York, USA
OBJECTIVES: To promote international peace, security and cooperation on the basis of the equality of member-states, the right of self-determination of peoples and respect for human rights
MEMBERSHIP (END-'99): 188 sovereign states; those not in membership of the UN itself at end-1999 were the Holy See (Vatican), Switzerland, Taiwan (Republic of China) and Tuvalu, although all except Taiwan were members of one or more UN specialized agency
SECRETARY-GENERAL: Kofi Annan (Ghana)

ALTHOUGH the year seemed to be dominated by Kosovo and East Timor, other important developments were taking place at the United Nations. The General Assembly held two special sessions and in its 54th ordinary session grappled with the issue of humanitarian intervention. The Security Council terminated two peace-keeping forces and created three others; it established two new sanctions regimes, suspended a third, set out the conditions for suspending a fourth and sought expert advice to enhance the effectiveness of a fifth; and it approved the creation of two new multinational forces and extended the mandate of a third. The Council also continued its attempts to improve its transparency. The organization once again mourned staff lost on active UN service, in Angola, Burundi, Haiti, Kosovo and Sudan.

54TH GENERAL ASSEMBLY. The General Assembly on 14 September elected Foreign Minister Theo-Ben Gurirab of Namibia as president of the 54th session; it also, on the recommendation of the Security Council, admitted to full membership the Pacific Island states of Kiribati, Nauru and Tonga. This increased UN membership to 188 states. In October the General Assembly elected Bangladesh, Jamaica, Mali, Tunisia and Ukraine as new non-permanent members of the Security Council to replace Bahrain, Brazil, Gabon, Gambia and Slovenia, whose two-year terms expired on 31 December 1999. The other five non-permanent members in 2000, elected in October 1998 (see AR 1998, p. 400), were Argentina, Canada, Malaysia, Namibia and the Netherlands.

Speaking in the general debate, UK Foreign Secretary Robin Cook proposed five major priorities for the UN. The root causes of conflicts had to be tackled. The soundest base for peace was prosperity and the best way to prevent conflict was to support sustainable development. Human rights and good governance had to be promoted. The supply of weapons fuelling conflict, particularly small arms, had to be curbed. The illegal trade in diamonds and other precious commodities, which paid for the small arms, and all too often the mercenaries, had to be stopped. And the culture of impunity had to be countered. Those who broke international humanitarian law must know that they would be held to account.

Mr Cook also argued that if the UN was to respond satisfactorily when conflict broke out, it would need to develop three strengths: authority, consensus and capacity. He believed that a small increase in the size of the Security Council would be a modest price to pay for the big increase in its credibility that would come from a more representative permanent membership; that agreement had to be reached on when the UN should act when confronted with genocide, mass displacement of people or major breaches of international law; and that more states should enter into peace-keeping standby agreements to increase the UN's ability to act. To help avoid future difficulties in assembling UN police forces to keep civil order, he announced that the UK would enter into a further standby agreement increasing the number of British police officers available for UN operations, including a commitment to a 'rapid response squad' ready for deployment at short notice. The UK would also establish with the UN a flagship-training course in Britain to train police from around the world for UN missions.

In the first three months of its work the 54th Assembly considered 148 out of 175 agenda items; adopted 250 resolutions, of which about 180 were by consensus, and 77 decisions. Of special note was that the Assembly reached agreement on the development account concept contained in the Secretary-General's suggested reforms tabled by Secretary-General Kofi Annan in 1997 (see AR 1997, pp. 381; 1998, p. 402), whereas agreement remained elusive on the other proposals: results-based budgeting, specific time-limits for new mandates and the 'revolving credit fund.' Nor did the Assembly president believe that any concrete conclusions could yet be drawn on reform of the Security Council structure. Among its other decisions, the Assembly accepted a recommendation from the Secretary-General that it should establish a working group to review the implementation of the proposals in his report on the causes of conflict in Africa. It also adopted resolutions on emergency assistance, assistance in mine-clearing, a nuclear-free-zone in Central Asia, and an International Convention for the Suppression of the Financing of Terrorism.

SPECIAL ASSEMBLY SESSIONS. The 21st special session met from 30 June to 2 July to review the implementation of the plan of action adopted at the International Conference on Population and Development in Cairo in 1994 (see AR 1994, p. 417). The final document adopted by consensus—although some states entered reservations—covered the range of population and development concerns and focused on gender equality, the empowerment of women, and reproductive health and rights. It called for a greater effort by all states to address the shortfall in resources needed to implement the commitments made at Cairo.

The 22nd special session held on 27-28 September reviewed the 1994 programme of action adopted in Barbados at the Global Conference on the Sustainable Development of Small Island Developing States. The Assembly approved a declaration and a statement on progress towards implementation of the programme of action.

BUDGET AND FINANCE. Just before Christmas the General Assembly approved a budget for the 2000-01 biennium of $2,535 million, which was only $2 million more than the budget for 1998-1999 biennium (and $97 million less that the budget for the 1994-95 biennium). Under-secretary-general for management Joseph Connor stated that the virtual 'zero growth' new budget would allow the organization to deliver more value to member-states at about the same cost. The new budget had three unusual features: for the first time a contingency provision of $35 million was included for new political missions; administrative costs were cut and the freed resources were reallocated to the prime functions of the UN (including the maintenance of international peace and security, the promotion of sustained economic growth and sustainable development, and the development of Africa); and a $120 million provision for inflation was offset by further budgetary reductions and favourable exchange rates. The net outcome, however, was that, while the prime UN functions had received a greater percentage of the budget, in real terms many had received no increases, while a few showed decreases.

Since 1992 aggregate assessment levels for the regular budget, peace-keeping and the two international criminal tribunals had reached a peak of over $4,000 million in 1995 and had been reduced to about $2,000 million in 1998. The total rose to $2,400 million in 1999 and was projected to increase to $2,800 million in 2000-01. Regular budget assessments had been fairly level since 1995. The high-point for peace-keeping was in 1995, a low of $907 million being reached in 1998. However, since the assessment levels projected in 1999 included only the start-up phase of the missions in Kosovo, East Timor and Sierre Leone, higher amounts would be required for those missions in 2000-01; in addition, there had been a sustained increase in UN tribunal assessments. Now there would be a sharp change in assessments: the reductions that had characterized the period 1995-1998 would be replaced by increased assessments for 1999, 2000 and beyond.

At the end of 1999 126 member-states had paid their regular assessments, compared with 117 at the end of 1998. Although still hugely in arrears, the United States again avoided losing its vote in the General Assembly under article 19 by paying $350 million between 1 October and 31 December, bringing its contribution for the year to $452 million. This helped to ensure that the organization's regular budget cash balance at the end of the year was $111 million-the first time in six years that there had been a positive balance. There was therefore no need to cross-borrow from the peace-keeping account to finance the regular budget. At year's end there was a cash balance of $957 million in the peace-keeping account, the highest figure for four years, while the UN tribunals had a cash balance of $25 million. The aggregate cash balance was therefore $1,093 million compared with $736 in 1998. This was the highest amount for five years.

At the end of 1999 unpaid assessments for the regular budget, peace-keeping and the tribunals was $1,758 million compared with $2,031 million in 1998. The level of unpaid regular budget assessments was $244 million, which was a reduction of $173 million from 1998. An aggregate of 88 per cent of this debt was owed by the United States, Brazil, Yugoslavia and Argentina. The remaining 12 per cent was owed by 59 other states. Unpaid peace-keeping assessments amounted to $1,482 million, the United States, Ukraine, Belarus and the Russian Federation accounting for 90 per cent of this figure. Unpaid assessments for the UN tribunals were over $32 million at the end of 1999 and had increased since they were established. The growth in unpaid amounts was roughly in proportion to the growth in the level of assessment.

At the end of 1999 the UN owed 72 member-states $800 million for peace-keeping, $72 million less than a year previously. All peace-keeping assessments paid into the account in 1999 had been used to pay bills in Kosovo and East Timor. Arrears payments were immediately dispensed to member-states to keep the debt steady. But the sum could only be repaid if the four major debtors—the United States, Russia, Belarus and Ukraine—continued their arrears payments. If the UN benefited from the second and third stages of the Helms-Biden Bill, which offered staged partial payments of US debt provided the organization met certain conditions, including the reduction of the United States' regular and peace-keeping assessments to 22 and 25 per cent respectively, the money would be used principally to reduce the peace-keeping debt to member-states.

EAST TIMOR. The issue of the right of the people of East Timor to self-determination had been discussed at the UN since 1960, under both Portuguese and Indonesian rule. Since 1982 successive Secretaries-General had had informal discussions with Portugal and Indonesia and consultations with Timorese representatives in an attempt to seek a comprehensive settlement. On 5 May the two states signed agreements that authorized the Secretary-General to organize and conduct a popular consultation to determine whether the East Timorese accepted or rejected special autonomy for the territory within the Republic of Indonesia. Indonesia would remain responsible for security before, during and after the popular consultation. If autonomy was rejected the UN would administer the territory during the transition to independence.

In successive resolutions and presidential statements between 7 May and the end of August the Security Council welcomed the agreement; established the UN Mission in East Timor (UNAMET); approved the form of consultation—a direct, secret and universal ballot; condemned local violence against UN property and staff; reminded Indonesia of its security responsibilities; endorsed Mr Annan's decisions that the consultation process would not begin until the mission was fully deployed and that the referendum should be postponed from 8 to 30 August for technical and security reasons; extended the UNAMET mandate twice; and expanded the number of UN civil police and military.

On 30 August the UN announced that about 98 per cent of the 451, 792 East Timorese registered with UNAMET had voted in the referendum. On 3 September Mr Annan stated that 344,580 East Timorese, or about 78.5 per cent of those registered, had voted against the proposed special autonomy within Indonesia and in favour of independence for the territory. The Security Council then declared that the consultation was an accurate reflection of the views of the people of East Timor; condemned the violence that immediately followed the announcement of the result; urged Indonesia to take the necessary constitutional steps to implement the result; held an open meeting which reflected the broad view that, if Indonesia was unable or unwilling to maintain law and order in East Timor, it should request an international force; and sent a delegation to Jakarta and East Timor. At the end of the delegation's visit, and after receiving telephone calls from Mr Annan, the Indonesian President announced on 9 September that he would accept the deployment of an international force.

Acting under chapter 7 of the UN Charter, the Security Coucnil on 15 September adopted resolution 1264 authorizing deployment of a multinational force—the International Force for East Timor (INTERFET)—to restore peace and security in East Timor, to protect and support UNAMET staff and to facilitate humanitarian assistance operations. The Council then, by resolution 1272 of 25 October, created the UN Transitional Administration in East Timor (UNTAET), with an initial mandate until 31 January 2001. This was a multifunctional peace-keeping mission, with components covering government and public administration, humanitarian assistance and emergency rehabilitation, as well as military requirements. The Council wanted the military component to take over from the Australian-led INTERFET troops as soon as possible. It was expected that the transition from the multinational to the UN force would take place in February 2000.

The UN Human Rights Commission, at a special session in September, requested the Secretary-General to establish an international commission of inquiry to gather and compile systematic information on possible violations of human rights in East Timor. The commission visited the territory in November and would report in January 2000.

KOSOVO. The UN political role in the Kosovo crisis between January and June was very limited, partly because the Security Council permanent members could not reach agreement on preventive action and partly because regional institutions were playing a prominent role. The UN therefore tended to react to events.

In a presidential statement on 19 January, the Security Council strongly condemned the massacre of 45 Kosovar Albanians by Serb forces at Racak in Kosovo (see III.2.vi), calling on the parties immediately to cease all forms of violence and to engage in talks on a lasting settlement; it also warned the separatist Kosovo Liberation Army (KLA) against actions that contributed to tensions. Following the failure of the Rambouillet talks and the launching of NATO air attacks against targets in Serbia on 24 March, the Council held an urgent meeting at which two main views were apparent: the US-UK-French line that the NATO action was legal and necessary to prevent a humanitarian catastrophe, opposed by the Russian and Chinese view that the action was a blatant violation of the UN Charter. On 26 March the Council failed to adopt a draft resolution demanding an immediate cessation of the use of force against the Federal Republic of Yugoslavia; only three states voted in favour (China, Namibia and Russia), the other 12 voting against. Thus the NATO action had neither been condemned nor endorsed by the Security Council.

The Council met on 8 May when the Chinese Government protested strongly against the NATO bombing of its embassy in Belgrade the previous night. A presidential statement was issued that appeared to satisfy the Chinese government. On 14 May the Council, with Russia and China abstaining, called for access for humanitarian personnel working in Kosovo and other parts of Yugoslavia and invited the UNHCR and other international humanitarian organizations to offer relief to the displaced in all parts of the Federal Republic.

Following the signature on 9 June of a 'military technical agreement' by Yugoslavia and NATO bringing the conflict to an end, on 10 June the Council, acting under chapter 7 of the Charter, adopted resolution 1244 by 14 votes with China abstaining (see XVII.1). This authorized the establishment of security and civil presences in Kosovo under UN auspices, with a mandate to deter renewed violence, to demilitarize the KLA and to establish a secure environment for the return of refugees and the operation of the civil presence. The civil presence, designated the UN Interim Administration in Kosovo (UNMIK), was to be established by the Secretary-General, who was requested to appoint a special representative as its head. Its mandate was to promote substantial autonomy and self-government in Kosovo; to facilitate a political process to determine the future status of the province; to support the reconstruction of key infrastructure; to provide humanitarian and disaster relief; to maintain civil law and order; to promote human rights; and to assure the safe and unimpeded return of all refugees and displaced persons to their homes in Kosovo. The presences were established for an initial period of 12 months and would continue unless the Council decided otherwise.

There are some unusual and some controversial features of this new peacekeeping administration. First, the UN was administering part of the territory of a sovereign state, so that some contended that it was colluding in a form of *de facto* partition. Second, the civil and military presences were separated, with no one single person in charge. Third, the UN was cooperating with the European Union in reconstruction and rehabilitation programmes (see XI.4), with the Organization for Security and Cooperation in Europe in institution building (see XI.5.ii) and with the UNHCR in the return of the refugees and the displaced (all of these institutions being under the authority of the UN special representative). Fourth, the political aim of the operation was ambiguous: the Kosovo Albanians wanted independence but the UN representative had to act on the basis that Kosovo remained part of the Federal Republic of Yugoslavia.

IRAQ AND 'OIL FOR FOOD'. On 17 December the Security Council, acting under chapter 7, adopted resolution 1284 by 11-0 (with China, France, Malaysia and the Russian Federation abstaining) as the culmination of a year's quest for agreement among the permanent members on how the UN and Iraq should cooperate to ensure that all relevant resolutions were fulfilled. Council president Sir Jeremy Greenstock (UK) stated that it was little short of miraculous that a result had been obtained on this very difficult subject (see also V.2,vi). The resolution established a new monitoring mission— the UN Monitoring, Verification and Inspection Commission (UNMOVIC)— whose staff would be international civil servants (rather then seconded) and would be drawn from the broadest geographical base. It removed the ceiling on oil exports and asked the Secretary-General to establish a group of experts to report within 100 days on how Iraq's oil production and export capacity could be increased. It also addressed the issue of the repatriation of all Kuwaiti and third-country nationals or their remains and the return of Kuwaiti property, including archives, and set out the conditions for the suspension of sanctions.

Whilst agreement was being sought on the monitoring issue, the Security Council renewed the 'oil for food' programme (see AR 1998, p. 407) for further six-month periods on 21 May and 10 December. In November the Iraqi government had rejected an offer by the Council for a short-term extension while revised terms were considered. In the event, the terms were not revised in the December extension, which was the seventh six-month phase of the arrangement.

PEACE-KEEPING AND PEACE ENFORCEMENT. The Security Council in February did not renew the mandate of the UN Observation Mission in Angola (MONUA) because the conditions for a meaningful UN peace-keeping role in Angola had ceased to exist (see VII.1.vi). In the same month the Council was prevented from renewing the mandate of the UN Preventive Deployment Force (UNPREDEP) in Macedonia by a Chinese veto seen as related to the Skopje government's recent diplomatic recognition of Taiwan (see III.2.iv). In October the Council adopted resolution 1279 which established the UN Mission in Sierra Leone (UNAMSIL), which was mandated to help the government implement the Lomé peace plan (see VI.2.iii), to monitor the ceasefire and to act to ensure security and freedom of movement for its personnel and protection of civilians under imminent threat of physical violence. And in November the Council by resolution 1279 created the UN Observer Mission in the Democratic Republic of the Congo (MONUC), composed of personnel authorized under earlier resolutions and given a liaison, technical assistance, investigative and analytical planning role (see also VII.1.i).

Acting under chapter 7 of the Charter, the Council adopted resolution 1247 in June, authorizing member-states to participate for a further period of 12 months in the multinational Stabilization Force (S-For) in Bosnia & Hercegovina (see III.2.vi).

UNITED NATIONS PEACE-KEEPING MISSIONS

	Established	Present Strength	Renewal Date
UNTSO: United Nations Truce Supervision Organization	June 1948	142 military: 97 international civilian; 115 local civilian.	
UNMOGIP: United Nations Military Observer Group in India & Pakistan	January 1949	46 military; 23 international civilian; 51 local civilian.	
UNFICYP: United Nations Peace-keeping force in Cyprus	March 1964	1,207 military; 35 civilian police; 39 international staff; 188 local civilian.	Resolution 1283 (1999) extended mandate until 15 June 2000
UNDOF: United Nations Disengagement Observer Force	June 1974	1,040 military; 27 international civilian; 99 local civilian.	Resolution 1276 (1999) extended mandate until 20 May 2000
UNIFIL: United Nations Interim force in Lebanon	March 1978	4,494 military; 113 international civilian; 343 local civilian	Resolution 1254 (1999) extended mandate until 31 January 2000.
UNIKOM: United Nations Iraq-Kuwait Observation Mission	April 1991	1,094 military; 52 international civilian; 149 local civilian.	Mandate is reviewed by Security Council every six months
MINURSO: United Nations Mission for the Referendum in Western Sahara	April 1991	208 military; 79 civilian police; 272 international civilian; 109 local civilian.	Resolution 1282 (1999) extended mandate until 29 February 2000.
UNOMIG: United Nations Observer Mission in Georgia	August 1993	102 military; 71 international civilian; 171 local civilian.	Resolution 1255 (1999) extended mandate until 31 January 2000
UNMOT: United Nations Mission of Observers in Tajikistan	December 1994	36 military; 3 civilian police; 52 international civilian; 121 local civilian.	Resolution 1274 (1999) extended mandate until 15 May 2000.
UNMIBH: United Nations Mission in Bosnia & Hercegovina	December 1995	4 military, 1,764 civilian police; 358 international civilian; 1,514 local civilian.	Resolution 1247 (1999) extended mandate until 21 June 2000.
UNMOP: United Nations Mission of Observers in Prevlaka	January 1996	27 military; 3 international civilian; 5 local civilian.	Resolution 1252 (1999) extended mandate until 15 January 2000
MIPONUH: United Nations Civilian Police Mission in Haiti	December 1997	242 civilian police, 63 international civilian; 141 local civilian.	Resolution 1277 (1999) extended mandate until 15 March 2000 to ensure a phased transition to an International Civilian Support Mission in Haiti.
MINURCA: United Nations Mission in Central African Republic	April 1998	801 military; 85 international civilian; 119 local civilian.	Resolution 1271 (1999) extended mandate until 15 February 2000 to ensure a short and gradual transition to a post conflict peace-building presence.

UNITED NATIONS PEACE-KEEPING MISSIONS continued

	Established	Present Strength	Renewal Date
UNMIK: United Nations Interim Administration in Kosovo	June 1999	Authorized strength 38 military; 4,718 civilian police; actual strength 34 military; 1,970 civilian police; 696 international civilian; 2,484 local civilian.	Resolution 1244 (1999) established civilian presence for 12 months, which would continue unless the Council decided otherwise.
UNAMSIL: United Nations Mission in Sierra Leone	October 1999	Authorized strength; 6,000 military; 6 civilian police; actual strength 4841 military; 4 civilian police; 80 international civilian; 56 local civilian.	Resolution 1270 (1999) established mission for six months.
Previous Mission: **UNOMSIL:** United Nations Observer Mission in Sierra Leone	July 1998 until October 1999	210 military observers; 15-personnel medical unit, 5 civilian police and political, civil affairs, information, human rights and child protection units.	
UNTAET: United Nations Transitional Administration in East Timor	October 1999	Authorized strength: 9,150 military;1,640 civilian police. Full military deployment expected by end of February 2,000. Actual strength 480 civilian police; 232 international civilian; 468 local civilian.	Resolution 1272 (1999) extended mandate until 31 January 2001.
Previous Missions: **UNAMET:** United Nations Mission in East Timor	11 June - 30 November 1999	460 civilian police, 300 military liaison; 4,000 international and local staff; 400 UN volunteers; 1600 independent observers accredited.	
INTERFET: International Force for East Timor	15 September 1999 - February 2000	Maximum strength 7,500 military.	
MONUC: United Nations Observer Mission in the Democratic Republic of the Congo	December 1999	Authorized strength 90 military liaison officers. Actual strength 79 military; 24 international civilian; 10 local civilian.	Resolution 1279 (1999) extended mandate until 1 March 2000.
Previous Mission: Military Liaison Group	August-December 1999	Maximum authorized strength 90 military and civilian, political, humanitarian and administrative staff. Located in the capital of states signatories to the ceasefire agreement and the provisional headquarters of Joint Military Headquarters.	

SANCTIONS. In February the Security Council approved in resolution 1227 a voluntary embargo on arms to Ethiopia and Eritrea in light of the border hostilities between the two (see VI.1.i). On 8 April the Council announced that the conditions for suspending the aerial, arms, diplomatic, oil-refining and transport equipment sanctions against Libya had been fulfilled on 5 April. Mr Annan had reported to the Council that the two Libyan nationals suspected of carrying out the 1988 Lockerbie airliner bombing had been transferred from Tripoli into the custody of Dutch law enforcement officials and would be tried in a Scottish court convened in the Netherlands (see V.4.ii).

At the prompting of the Mr Annan and the chairman of the Angolan sanctions committee (Robert Fowler of Canada), the Security Council in May established an independent panel of experts to investigate violations of UN sanctions against the Unita movement in Angola led by Jonas Savimbi. The purpose of the wide-ranging sanctions was to induce Unita to comply with the obligations of the 1991 peace accords and the 1994 Lusaka Protocol and to restrict Unita's ability to pursue its objectives by military means (see VII.1.vi). However, Unita was still able to purchase arms, sell diamonds, evade travel restrictions and maintain unofficial representation abroad. The panel was requested to inform the Council about how the sanctions against Unita were being violated and what could be done to make them more effective.

In February the Council had endorsed the recommendation of the Angolan sanctions committee that states should make sanctions violation a criminal offence; that information should be obtained from companies and private individuals on the transfer of military equipment and on Unita's illicit diamond trade; and that banks should be requested to identify and track the financial flows of Unita, its officials and adult family members. In June-July Mr Fowler visited Africa and Europe, meeting government officials and representatives of the diamond industry and receiving a commitment from De Beers Consolidated, the world's biggest diamond company, that it would support the Council's sanctions. He then provided the Council with a further 19 recommendations on enhancing the effectiveness of the sanctions.

Following the refusal of the Taleban regime in Aghanistan to hand over the indicted suspected terrorist Osama bin Laden as demanded in resolution 1276 of 15 October, the Council on 15 November imposed targeted sanctions-an assets freeze and air travel restrictions-against the Taleban leadership. This provoked a violent reaction in Afghanistan, in which one UN office was burned to the ground and five others attacked (see VIII.1.ii).

OTHER SECURITY COUNCIL PROCEEDINGS. The Security Council held two open briefings and a separate meeting in February to discuss the plight of civilians in armed conflict and requested the Secretary-General to recommend ways in which the Council could improve the physical and legal protection of civilians in armed conflicts. On 17 September, at the end of a two-day debate on Mr Annan's report, the Council decided that it would review further his recommendations and would consider appropriate steps by April 2000.

During the debate the UN High Commissioner for Human Rights, Mary Robinson (Ireland), addressed the Council for the first time.

In August the Council held a two-day debate on children in armed conflict that attracted 48 speakers. In September, in another two-day debate with 54 speakers, the Council reviewed the implementation of the recommendations in the Secretary-General's 1998 report on the causes of conflict and promotion of durable peace and sustainable development in Africa. In November the Council held three meetings on the prevention of armed conflict in which there were 38 speakers. And in December in another open debate the Council explored the UN partnership with Africa.

Other important issues considered by the Security Council included the problem of small arms and violations of arms embargoes, on which the Secretary-General was called upon to develop a reference manual on ecologically-safe methods of weapons destruction and to study the humanitarian and socio-economic implications of the excessive and destabilizing accumulation and transfer of small arms and light weapons. In a debate on threats to peace and security, the Council unequivocally condemned all acts, methods and practices of terrorism as criminal and unjustifiable, regardless of their motivation.

TRANSPARENCY. In December the Security Council, in yet a further effort to improve the transparency of its working methods (see AR 1998, pp. 412-3), decided that it would make all drafts of resolutions and presidential statements available to non-members as soon as they were introduced in informal consultations within the Council; that all non-members should receive weekly situation reports on peace-keeping operations; that there should be increased recourse to public meetings of a type to be decided by the Council from a range of options.

2. DEFENCE AND ECONOMIC ORGANIZATIONS

i. DEFENCE ORGANIZATIONS

North Atlantic Treaty Organization (NATO)
DATE OF FOUNDATION: 1949   HEADQUARTERS: Brussels, Belgium
OBJECTIVES: To ensure the collective security of member states
MEMBERSHIP (END-'99): Belgium, Canada, Czech Republic, Denmark, France, Germany, Greece, Hungary, Iceland, Italy, Luxembourg, Netherlands, Norway, Poland, Portugal, Spain, Turkey, United Kingdom, United States *(total* 19)
SECRETARY-GENERAL: Lord (George) Robertson of Port Ellen (UK)

Partnership for Peace (PFP)
DATE OF FOUNDATION: 1994   HEADQUARTERS: Brussels, Belgium
OBJECTIVES: To provide a framework for cooperation between NATO and the former communist and neutral states of Europe and ex-Soviet Central Asia
MEMBERSHIP (END-'99): Albania, Armenia, Austria, Azerbaijan, Belarus, Bulgaria, Estonia, Finland, Georgia, Irish Republic, Kazakhstan, Kyrgyzstan, Latvia, Lithuania, Macedonia, Malta, Moldova, Romania, Russia, Slovakia, Slovenia, Sweden, Switzerland, Turkmenistan, Ukraine, Uzbekistan *(total* 25)

Western European Union (WEU)

DATE OF FOUNDATION: 1955   HEADQUARTERS: Brussels, Belgium
OBJECTIVES: To provide a framework for defence and security cooperation between European states
MEMBERSHIP (END-'99): Belgium, France, Germany, Greece, Italy, Luxembourg, Netherlands, Portugal, Spain, United Kingdom (*total* 10)
OBSERVER MEMBERS: Austria, Denmark, Finland, Ireland, Sweden
ASSOCIATE MEMBERS: Iceland, Norway, Turkey
SECRETARY-GENERAL: Javier Solana Madariaga (Spain)

FOR some of the world's security alliances and organizations, 1999 was a source of yet more uncertainty and scepticism, rather than a positive affirmation of their role and value in the post-Cold War world. The Commonwealth of Independent States (CIS), for example, was the focus of a concerted attempt by Russia to show that it, too, led a revitalized alliance which, furthermore, was united in its objection to NATO's military action against Serbia. Joint command structures were tightened, and Russian forces on allies' territory were reinforced. Yet, even as the Kosovo air campaign was under way, when it came to negotiating the extension of the CIS 1992 Collective Security Treaty, four allies chose not to renew their membership (Azerbaijan, Georgia, Moldova and Uzbekistan).

Further afield, the Association of South-East Asian Nations (ASEAN) Regional Forum, intended to provide for discussion of regional security matters, was beset by internal disagreement and tension. China's interest in the Spratly Islands—long a source of friction—persuaded the Philippines to agree a new visiting forces agreement with the United States, reversing decisions to expel the US military made seven years earlier (see IX.1.vii; XI.6.iii). Indonesia was wracked by protest movements and by secessionist violence (see IX.1.vi), and its wider intentions were of concern to Singapore. Singapore also continued to feel vulnerable to Malaysia, and tension between them undermined yet another security institution, the Five-Power Defence Arrangements between Malaysia, Singapore, Australia, Britain and New Zealand.

For their part, Australia and New Zealand maintained their defence cooperation with the United States under the 1951 ANZUS Pact, although in the case of New Zealand it had been a lukewarm arrangement ever since the mid-1980s spat over the presence of US nuclear-powered and nuclear-equipped warships in New Zealand ports. ANZUS was put to some use by the USA and Australia in 1999, a joint military exercise being held in Queensland in October. ANZUS meetings also provided a platform for the USA to congratulate and encourage Australia on its involvement in the UN Assessment Mission in East Timor (UNAMET) and for its command of the International Force for East Timor (INTERFET) deployed in September. The United States' other major security partnership in the Asia-Pacific region—the US-Japan Security Alliance—had also suffered in recent years as differences over trade and economic policies threatened to undermine the security arrangement. In 1999 both countries struggled to keep their relationship on a firm footing.

NORTH ATLANTIC TREATY ORGANIZATION. If security pacts around the world continued to experience something of a credibility crisis during 1999, there was at least one alliance—the North Atlantic Treaty Organization—for which the year represented a marked improvement in its fortunes. Having spent much of the 1990s anxious to prove its worth, politically and operationally, NATO experienced something of an *annus mirabilis* in 1999. The summit of NATO leaders in Washington on 23-24 April had long been scheduled as the moment when an enlarged and regenerated Alliance would announce itself ready to meet the challenges of the 21st century. In the event, the summit took place one month after the beginning of the air campaign against Serbia, and it was felt that too much celebration might seem undignified and inappropriate. Inappropriate, or unnecessary? The Kosovo operation was certainly a distraction from the summit, but distractions sometimes have their merits.

'Operation Allied Force', amounting to 79 days of air attacks against Serb military and other targets, began on 24 March and within weeks involved more than 1,000 NATO combat aircraft. Following the signature of a 'military technical agreement' with Yugoslavia on 9 June (see XVII.1), NATO ground forces moved unopposed into Kosovo on 12 June as the lead contingent of K-For (Kosovo Force). Notwithstanding this success, however, both the bombing campaign and the deployment of K-For came under continuing close scrutiny from several perspectives. What was the status of the intervention in international law? Was the intervention morally acceptable? Was it wise, militarily, to forego the use of ground forces initially? Was air power decisive? Did NATO take on a commitment from which it would find it difficult to withdraw?

From NATO's perspective, the Kosovo crisis represented a timely opportunity for the Alliance to reveal its reinvented self. With the end of the Cold War, and the collapse of the Soviet Union and the Warsaw Pact, it had become clear that NATO would have to reorganize itself if it was to have much of a future. During the 1990s the Alliance became preoccupied with its own reorganization. As the reinvention project became more introspective, obsessive and distant, the risk increased that the result would be a *rococo* alliance: expertly designed and pleasing to the eye, but expensive to maintain and useless in the field. The Kosovo operation, therefore, was the chance to prove that NATO had substance. Now the Alliance could show that it had retained the crucial capability to project military power, without which no amount of clever reorganization could ever be worth much. The crisis was also an opportunity to present NATO as a values-based (rather than exclusively territorial) defensive alliance, an idea which was to receive a great deal of attention at the Washington summit.

The summit saw the culmination of several longstanding projects and was, in at least one important respect, a turning-point in the history of the Alliance. In 1998 NATO had agreed to the admission of three new members—the Czech Republic, Hungary and Poland, all former Warsaw Pact adversaries (see AR 1998, p. 414). At the summit the three new members were formally admitted into the Alliance. For the Czechs, Hungarians and Poles, their dogged campaign for membership had finally borne fruit, although their enthusiasm for NATO was perhaps slightly dented by the controversy surrounding the Kosovo operation. But for the Alliance itself, the admission of three new members only brought the thorny issue of enlargement into sharper relief. The issues yet to be resolved included deciding which applicants would be considered for the next tranche of enlargement and when it would take place, coupled with the conundrum of what could be done to placate those applicants frustrated at the pace of enlargement and, in particular, those who would not be included in the next wave.

The Alliance's response to these concerns was to restate the 'open door' policy agreed in Madrid two years earlier, whereby the Alliance reserved the right to consider any candidature for membership, in accordance with Article 10 of the founding Washington Treaty. To underscore this commitment, a new Membership Action Plan was announced in Washington, and the Alliance confirmed its commitment to various other 'outreach' initiatives: an improved Partnership for Peace programme, the Euro-Atlantic Partnership Council, the relationship with Ukraine, a 'Southern Dialogue' with states on the southern Mediterranean coast, and a South-East Europe initiative involving states in and around the Balkans (see XVII.2). However, arguably NATO's most important outreach initiative, the Permanent Joint Council with Russia, was suspended in 1999 following Russian objections to NATO involvement in Kosovo.

The Washington summit also saw the publication of a series of initiatives and documents which, taken together, would constitute the Alliance's *modus operandi* for the near future. The summit communiqué offered a *tour d'horizon* of NATO activities and a summary of other initiatives launched at the summit. The 'Washington Declaration' amounted to a new 'vision statement' for the Alliance. The 'Defence Capabilities Initiative' prepared the way for a high level study of military planning, preparedness and interoperability across the Alliance. The 'Weapons of Mass Destruction (WMD) Initiative' addressed the Alliance's political and military preparedness to respond to the proliferation and possible use of WMD and created a new 'WMD Centre' at NATO headquarters. Finally, and in some respects most importantly, the summit also saw the release of a new 'strategic concept'.

The revised strategic concept had been long awaited. Expectations ran high of a document which was to be the central component of the reinvented NATO and the culmination of NATO's lengthy internal adaptation process, involving a new force posture and a redesigned command system. It was in the preparation of the concept that the double-edged nature of the Alliance's involvement in Kosovo became most apparent. Many of NATO's civilian and military staff, who had been closely involved in preparing the concept, now found themselves over-extended in managing NATO's operation in the Balkans. On the other hand, the Kosovo crisis provided something of a test-bed for the new thinking. In the weeks before the summit, commentators and analysts eager to learn more about the new concept were often told that the document was, in effect, being worked out 'in the air' over Serbia. In the last days of the NATO air campaign against Serbia, Alexander Vershbow, the US permanent representative to NATO, made the connection between Kosovo and concept explicit: 'The two are fundamentally linked. The NATO for the 21st century that we had been planning to launch at the summit turned out to be exactly the NATO we needed to deal with the crisis in Kosovo.'

The new strategic concept set out the Alliance's five 'fundamental security tasks'. The first task—'Security'—amounted to the maintenance of Euro-Atlantic stability and the fostering of democracy and peaceful diplomacy. The second, 'Consultation', referred to the need for discussion among Alliance members of issues affecting their 'vital interests'. 'Deterrence and Defence', the third task, reasserted something of the traditional character of the Alliance as a territorially-defined, collective defence organization. The fourth, 'Crisis Management', entailed a commitment to 'contribute to effective conflict prevention and to engage actively in crisis management, including crisis response operations.' And finally, 'Partnership' reiterated NATO's longstanding commitment to political and military 'outreach' to other states in the 'Euro-Atlantic area'.

Elsewhere, the new strategic concept outlined the Alliance's developing relations with other institutions (UN, OSCE, EU and WEU) and set out the 'security challenges and risks' which the Alliance should be prepared to confront. The scenarios mentioned included everything from the possibility, albeit 'highly unlikely', of a Cold War-style, large-scale conventional aggression directly against the Alliance, to a 'wide variety of military and non-military risks which are multi-directional and often difficult to predict.' The latter included 'uncertainty and instability', 'ethnic and religious rivalries', 'the abuse of human rights' and 'the dissolution of states', all of which could lead to conflict and could thereby indirectly impinge upon the security of the Alliance. The spread of weapons of mass destruction and the technology required to produce advanced conventional weaponry also needed to be taken into account, as did NATO's vulnerability to information warfare and terrorism.

With these new scenarios in mind, the Alliance would have to be prepared to go beyond its traditional function and 'defend' against attacks on its values and interests as much as its territory. The 'transformed NATO' concluded its ambitious mission statement with a pledge 'to contribute to the evolving security environment, supporting security and stability with the strength of its shared commitment to democracy and the peaceful resolution of disputes', to review the strategic concept when necessary, and to exploit every opportunity 'to help build an undivided continent by promoting and fostering the vision of a Europe whole and free'.

EUROPEAN DEFENCE AND SECURITY. With the Kosovo campaign behind it, with much of its programme for reorganization complete at the political level, and with its enlargement and outreach initiatives still full of impetus, 1999 was clearly a good year for NATO. But what remained on the agenda was a diplomatically awkward and intractable issue, one which had dogged the Alliance throughout the 1990s: what should be the nature of the relationship between NATO and the Western European Union (WEU) and, in particular, the European Union (EU) as it sought to develop an 'identity' in the field of security and defence? (see also XI.3). In the December 1991 Maastricht Treaty, the EU had established the framework for a Common Foreign and Security Policy and had set its sights upon a Common Defence Policy and, in time, a Common Defence. This saw the beginning of the long-running dispute between the 'Atlanticists' and the 'Europeanists' over the locus and nature of European defence and security collaboration.

This dispute placed additional strain on NATO: not only did the Alliance have to define a role for itself in the threat-ambiguous post-Cold War world, it also had to prove that it-and not some EU-based initiative-remained the organization best fitted to provide for European defence and security. In formal terms at least, the dispute had been resolved in June 1996, when NATO governments had agreed that, while a more discreetly European effort at security and defence should be welcomed, not least because the cohesiveness of NATO clearly now required the European allies to show willing to take on more of the burden of their own security, any European effort would best be located within the NATO framework, as captured by the slogan 'European security and defence identity (ESDI) within NATO'.

NATO's new strategic concept adopted in April reaffirmed the Berlin compromise, arguing that the object of ESDI, as it continued to develop, should be to strengthen the transatlantic partnership, rather than provide a substitute for it. As ESDI developed, so the strategic concept argued, NATO would have to be willing to cooperate with the WEU and, 'if and when appropriate', the EU. But the most decisive step forward in clarifying the relationship between the various institutions was made later in 1999, by the EU. The Atlanticist/Europeanist debate had been reopened in late 1998 by the Austrian government, concerned to see whether more impetus could be given to the development of EU foreign, security and defence policies. Then, at their summit meeting in St Mâlo in early December British Prime Minister Blair and French President Chirac spoke of the need to make a 'reality' of the Amsterdam Treaty, which had not yet entered into force. The Amsterdam Treaty called for the 'full and rapid implementation of the provisions on CFSP'. With that in mind, Mr Blair and M. Chirac envisaged the 'progressive framing of a common defence policy', albeit in a decidedly inter-governmental framework, making use of the European Council, the General Affairs Council and meetings of Defence Ministers. The EU, they said, should set itself the goal of a 'capacity for autonomous action, backed up by credible military forces,' and in so doing contribute to the 'vitality of a modernized Atlantic Alliance'. The two leaders also acknowledged that, as the EU developed its capacity for action, using military means drawn either from NATO or from 'national or multinational means outside the NATO framework,' account would have to be taken of the 'existing assets of the WEU and the evolution of its relations with the EU'. The use of the word 'autonomous' would later cause some concern in Washington, but in broad terms the St Mâlo initiative appeared to be another endorsement of the formula agreed in June 1996.

The summer of 1999 saw a surge of activity and decision. The Treaty of Amsterdam entered into force on 1 May, but that document was probably not the best explanation for the air of dynamism and determination which hung around the Cologne European Council meeting the following month. Europe's less than decisive performance during the crisis in Kosovo demonstrated to many the urgent need for the EU to have the ability to manage tension and crises at its borders. As a token of its new-found virility, the European Council appointed Javier Solana—outgoing secretary-general of NATO—to the post of secretary-general of the EU Council and high representative for the CFSP, as well as secretary-general of the soon-to-be-subsumed WEU.

It was in the German presidency's 'Declaration on Strengthening the Common European Policy on Security and Defence' that the clearest sense of movement in matters of defence and security could be found. In the declaration, the European Council limited itself to 'the full range of conflict prevention and crisis management tasks' set out in the Amsterdam Treaty; in other words, the EU would not question or challenge NATO's ultimate responsibility for European defence and security. The declaration welcomed the outcome of NATO's Washington summit, particularly 'as regards NATO support for the process launched by the EU and its confirmation that a more effective role for the [EU] in conflict prevention and crisis management will contribute to the vitality of a renewed Alliance.' In order to 'fully assume its tasks in the field of conflict prevention and crisis management', EU members agreed to co-ordinate more closely the various military capabilities available to the EU, and to 'more efficient defence industry collaboration'. Furthermore, EU leaders agreed that the absorption of certain functions of the WEU into the EU's apparatus could now be contemplated. Preparations for the EU/WEU merger would last no more than 18 months, by which point 'the WEU as an organization would have completed its purpose'.

At the Helsinki summit of EU leaders in December agreement was finally reached on the goal of an EU rapid response capability of up to 60,000 troops, deployable at 60 days' notice and sustainable for up to one year, and available from 2003. In addition, various political committees and staff organizations (military and civil) would be set up in Brussels. EU leaders were, however, careful to explain that the initiative should not be construed as undermining NATO. Thus, while the EU's military capability would be expected to carry out the full range of peacekeeping, humanitarian, and crisis response operations, it would not be suitable for anything more demanding militarily, least of all full-scale collective defence. Furthermore, the new permanent bodies—a political and security committee, a military committee and a military staff—would be put in place after March 2000, but would be very firmly within the orbit of the inter-governmental European Council, making little or no concessions to closer styles of EU integration.

In broad terms, the Helsinki summit declaration adopted the 'ESDI-within-NATO' position agreed in NATO in June 1996 and latterly endorsed by Mr Blair and M. Chirac: 'The European Council underlines its determination to develop an autonomous capacity to take decisions and, where NATO as a whole is not engaged, to launch and conduct EU-led military operations in response to international crises. This process will avoid unnecessary duplication and does not imply the creation of a European army.'

The conclusion of the Helsinki summit marked the culmination both of the year-long Anglo-French initiative and of longer-running attempts to effect a durable accommodation between NATO and the EU, dating back at least to the NATO Berlin ministerial meeting in June 1996. Henceforth, this was to be a face-to-face accommodation; with its liaison function no longer thought necessary, the Helsinki summit signalled the end of the WEU as an active defence and security institution. It was nevertheless important to note that much more would have to be achieved before the European defence and security initiative could be considered a success. For all its achievements, the Helsinki declaration remained no more than a statement of intent. Having spent much of the 1990s arguing over the idea of an EU 'identity' in defence and security, only at the end of the decade did EU leaders find themselves in a position to begin considering how to turn that idea into reality. The idea would most certainly come to nothing without a firm financial commitment by EU members and the political will to make European defence spending more coordinated and cost-efficient.

The precise nature of the NATO/EU relationship was expected to become clearer when the practical details of the Helsinki initiative were worked out during 2000. The project would then confront the many organizational hurdles it had to pass before it could be said to have any real meaning. The creation of a 'virtual' (as opposed to a standing) army corps, based upon 'ear-marked' contributions from EU members rather than its own, in-place units, would present difficulties. Some form of headquarters and command structure would need to be established and the force would also need a training programme to achieve the necessary levels of interoperability. A certain amount of equipment standardization would also be necessary, and the EU would need to ensure that its new force had sufficient strategic mobility in the form of heavy-lift aircraft and shipping. In practical terms, therefore, the process leading to the establishment of an effective EU defence and security capability was only just beginning in 1999.

ii. ECONOMIC ORGANIZATIONS

International Monetary Fund (IMF)
DATE OF FOUNDATION: 1945   HEADQUARTERS: Washington DC, USA
OBJECTIVES: To promote international monetary cooperation and to assist member states in establishing sound budgetary and trading policies
MEMBERSHIP (END-'99): 181 UN members plus Switzerland (*total* 182)
MANAGING DIRECTOR: Michel Camdessus (France)

International Bank for Reconstruction and Development (IBRD/World Bank)
DATE OF FOUNDATION: 1946   HEADQUARTERS: Washington DC, USA
OBJECTIVES: To make loans on reasonable terms to developing countries with the aim of increasing their productive capacity
MEMBERSHIP (END-'99): 180 UN members plus Switzerland (*total* 181)
PRESIDENT: James D. Wolfensohn (United States)

World Trade Organization (WTO)
DATE OF FOUNDATION: 1995 (successor to General Agreement on Tariffs and Trade, GATT)
HEADQUARTERS: Geneva, Switzerland
OBJECTIVES: To eliminate tariff and other barriers to international trade and to facilitate international financial settlements
MEMBERSHIP (END-'99): 135 acceding parties
DIRECTOR-GENERAL: Mike Moore (New Zealand)

Organization for Economic Cooperation and Development (OECD)
DATE OF FOUNDATION: 1960 HEADQUARTERS: Paris, France
OBJECTIVES: To promote economic growth in member states and the sound development of the world economy
MEMBERSHIP (END-'99): Australia, Austria, Belgium, Canada, Czech Republic, Denmark, Finland, France, Germany, Greece, Hungary, Iceland, Ireland, Italy, Japan, South Korea, Luxembourg, Mexico, Netherlands, New Zealand, Norway, Poland, Portugal, Spain, Sweden, Switzerland, Turkey, United Kingdom, United States (*total* 29)
SECRETARY-GENERAL: Donald Johnston (Canada)

Organization of the Petroleum Exporting Countries (OPEC)
DATE OF FOUNDATION: 1960 HEADQUARTERS: Vienna, Austria
OBJECTIVES: To unify and coordinate member states' oil policies and to safeguard their interests
MEMBERSHIP (END-'99): Algeria, Indonesia, Iran, Iraq, Kuwait, Libya, Nigeria, Qatar, Saudi Arabia, United Arab Emirates, Venezuela (*total* 11)
SECRETARY-GENERAL: Rilwanu Lukman (Nigeria)

INTERNATIONAL MONETARY FUND. Michel Camdessus, the managing director of the IMF, announced on 9 November his intention to resign in February 2000, rather over half-way through his third five-year term. His successor was again expected to be European: since the Fund's inception its managing director had been drawn from Europe, whereas the president of the World Bank had been a US citizen. However, lack of agreement among key members of the IMF meant that no decision on a replacement had been reached by the end of 1999. On 9 September Gordon Brown, the UK Chancellor of the Exchequer, was elected chairman of the Interim Committee of the Board of Governors of the Fund in succession to Carlo Azeglio Ciampi (who had been elected President of Italy in May); the name of the committee, which had been formed in 1974, was subsequently changed to the International Monetary and Financial Committee of the Board of Governors, reflecting its more permanent standing.

Quotas in the IMF were increased in late January by an average of 45 per cent, after the necessary consent had been obtained from fund members with at least 85 per cent of the total of fund quotas. Total fund quotas thus rose from 145,600 million special drawing rights (SDR) to 212,000 million SDRs (i.e. from about $204,000 million to about $297,000 million). The last increase (of about 50 per cent had taken place following a review of quotas in 1990. The Fund estimated that the latest increase would increase its usable resources by about $63,000 million.

In December 1999 the IMF began selling gold in a complex off-market process which was designed to free funds for debt relief under the World Bank's 'heavily-indebted poor countries' (HIPC) initiative while not at the same time releasing gold onto the free market. Meanwhile, the enhanced structural adjustment facility (ESAF) was in November renamed as the poverty reduction and growth facility (PRGF) and its objectives were changed to support programmes to strengthen balance-of-payments positions substantially and in a sustainable manner, and to foster durable growth, leading to higher living standards and a reduction in poverty.

WORLD BANK. The World Bank (International Bank for Reconstruction and Development) published its annual development report on 15 September in which it drew special attention to the increasing importance of local government in the development process, while at the same time warning that in some instances profligacy on the level of such local government could threaten macro-economic stability. In its annual global development finance report published in April, the Bank had lowered its forecast of growth in the developing countries in 1999 from 2.7 to 1.5 per cent and had noted that development flows from the industrialized countries were at present in effect declining in relative terms.

James Wolfensohn was on 27 September appointed for a second five-year term as president of the World Bank (a post traditionally held by a US citizen).

ORGANIZATION OF THE PETROLEUM EXPORTING COUNTRIES. In the light of continued downward pressure on international oil prices, the 11-member OPEC agreed at a meeting in Vienna on 23 March to cut its members' production levels (excluding Iraq) by a further 1,700,000 barrels per day for the next 12-month period, while four non-OPEC countries (Mexico, Norway, Oman and Russia) also agreed reductions. The OPEC reduction was confirmed in September. After sharp falls in the internationally-recognized forward price for benchmark Brent crude from nearly $17 a barrel in early 1998 to about $10.50 at the end of that year, this price dipped below $10 in February 1999 but then rose to some $15 by late March, to $20 during July and to over $26.50 in November-December.

WORLD TRADE ORGANIZATION. The WTO between 30 November and 3 December held a ministerial meeting in Seattle (United States) designed to launch the ninth round of international trade negotiations in succession to the eight held under the General Agreement on Tariffs and Trade (GATT), most recently in 1986-94. However, because largely of what was widely seen as insufficient preparation of the agenda and sharp differences between important countries or groups of countries—in particular over treatment of agricultural goods, over labour and environmental standards and over anti-dumping policies—the meeting ended in deadlock and without any concluding written statement. Moreover, prior to and during the meeting Seattle had seen massive demonstrations by protesters attacking what they saw as the dominance of the process by rich nations at the expense of the environment and of Third World interests.

Preparation for the Seattle meeting had been slow in getting off the ground as the result of protracted negotiations over the choice of a new director-general in succession to Renato Ruggiero whose term formally ended on 30 April 1999. Eventually it was decided that for the first three years of a six-year period of office the post of director-general should from September be held by Mike

Moore (who had briefly served as Prime Minister of New Zealand in 1990) but that he should himself be followed in 2002 by Supachai Panitchpakdi, currently Deputy Prime Minister and Commerce Minister of Thailand.

Among trade issues concerning the WTO in 1999 were the continued European Union (EU) ban on the import of hormone-treated beef from the USA and Canada and approval for the imposition by those two countries of retaliatory punitive import tariffs on a range of goods, and the imposition by the USA of punitive sanctions over the disputed banana import policy of the EU (see AR 1998, p. 419). The WTO's financial services agreement concluded in December 1997 entered into force on 1 March 1999. The vexed question of China's membership of the WTO remained unsolved at the end of 1999, although provisional agreement had been reached between China and the USA on such accession (see IX.2.i).

ORGANIZATION FOR ECONOMIC COOPERATION AND DEVELOPMENT. The OECD on 28 April launched a set of international principles for corporate governance, designed to protect the rights of shareholders and other stakeholders. The OECD's annual ministerial meeting held in Paris on 26-27 May formally approved these principles but failed to reach agreement on key aspects of the line to be adopted at the forthcoming WTO session in Seattle (see above).

3. OTHER WORLD ORGANIZATIONS

i. THE COMMONWEALTH

DATE OF FOUNDATION: 1931 HEADQUARTERS: London, UK
OBJECTIVES: To maintain political, cultural and social links between (mainly English-speaking) countries of the former British Empire and others subscribing to Commonwealth democratic principles and aims
MEMBERSHIP (END-'99): Antigua & Barbuda, Australia, The Bahamas, Bangladesh, Barbados, Belize, Botswana, Brunei Darussalam, Cameroon, Canada, Cyprus, Dominica, Fiji Islands, The Gambia, Ghana, Grenada, Guyana, India, Jamaica, Kenya, Kiribati, Lesotho, Malawi, Malaysia, Maldives, Malta, Mauritius, Mozambique, Namibia, Nauru, New Zealand, Nigeria, Pakistan (*suspended*), Papua New Guinea, St Kitts & Nevis, St Lucia, St Vincent & the Grenadines, Samoa, Seychelles, Sierra Leone, Singapore, Solomon Islands, South Africa, Sri Lanka, Swaziland, Tanzania, Tonga, Trinidad & Tobago, Tuvalu, Uganda, United Kingdom, Vanuatu, Zambia, Zimbabwe (*total* 54)
SECRETARY-GENERAL: Don McKinnon (New Zealand)

ONE seat was reoccupied and one remained unoccupied when the Commonwealth Heads of Government Meeting (CHOGM) assembled in Durban, South Africa (12-15 November). Suspension had been lifted from Nigeria but imposed on Pakistan. Addressing this last CHOGM of the century and his last as secretary-general, Chief Emeka Anyaoku pointed to a fundamental change that had occurred over recent years: 'We are today in the happy situation where the Commonwealth meets at the summit without any representative of a military regime. In a very real sense the Commonwealth is now a club of democracies.'

Nigeria had returned to full membership on the restoration of civilian rule there on 29 May (see VI.2.ii). For a few months the Commonwealth contained no military government, until General Pervez Musharraf seized power in Pakistan on 12 October (see VIII.2.ii). Commonwealth action was swift. The next day Chief Anyaoku said that overthrow of a democratically-elected government was unacceptable to the Commonwealth and that there was no question of the regime's attending CHOGM. On 18 October the Commonwealth Ministerial Action Group (CMAG), meeting in London, suspended Pakistan 'from the councils of the Commonwealth' and sent a mission of four, led by Lloyd Axworthy, Canadian Minister of Foreign Affairs, to Islamabad. General Musharraf failed to promise an early return to civilian rule or the release of ousted Prime Minister Nawaz Sharif and other political prisoners. CHOGM endorsed the suspension.

The year marked the 50th anniversary of the London Declaration, which historically marked the birth of the modern Commonwealth by enabling India to remain a member and paving the way for other countries to stay in as republics. Its anniversary seemed to mark the close of a chapter of history, as the Durban CHOGM decided to review the role of the Commonwealth. It set up a high-level group of heads of government, chaired by President Thabo Mbeki of South Africa, to advise on how the Commonwealth could best respond to the challenges of the new century. Other members would include Australia, Fiji Islands, India, Malta, Singapore, Tanzania, Trinidad & Tobago, the United Kingdom and Zimbabwe.

The century would start with an innovation. President Mbeki would become the first chairperson-in-office of the Commonwealth for the two years until the CHOGM in Australia in 2001. He would play a representational role, especially in other inter-governmental organizations such as the UN. The chairperson of succeeding CHOGMs would do likewise. This would give the Commonwealth a political focus internationally that the Queen, in her symbolic role, and the secretary-general, in his diplomatic role, could not provide.

Two candidates stood for the succession to Chief Anyaoku as secretary-general: former New Zealand Foreign Minister Don McKinnon and Bangladeshi diplomat Farooq Sobhan. Heads of government voted in Durban for Mr McKinnon.

A record number of heads of state or Prime Ministers (47) attended CHOGM. Notable absentees were the President of Sri Lanka and the Prime Ministers of Malaysia and New Zealand, all of whom were engaged in election campaigns. The leaders, who held their weekend retreat at Fancourt Estate, near George, discussed the future of the CMAG, the committee of eight Foreign Ministers formed in 1995 to monitor serious violations of the 1991 Harare Declaration. A CMAG report recommended widening its operations—for example, that it should act if a government banned, or persistently impeded, the political activities of opposition parties. The proposals were unexpectedly deferred and sent to the high-level group. The CMAG format was revised. No country would now serve for more than two two-year terms. For 2000-01 its members would be: Australia, Bangladesh, Barbados, Botswana, Canada, Malaysia, Nigeria and the United Kingdom. This brought in a South Asian country for the first time, and Australia, the next CHOGM host.

The main topic for discussion in Durban was globalization and concern that its effects would increasingly marginalize small and economically weak states. The Fancourt Declaration on Globalization and People-Centred Development, issued at the retreat, urged the World Trade Organization to ensure that the new global trade round provided better market access for developing countries (see XI.2.ii).

In parallel with CHOGM, the new Commonwealth Business Council became firmly established with a forum in Johannesburg which attracted 600 business leaders. In Durban a huge range of NGO activities were showcased in a Commonwealth People's Centre and a third NGO forum reflected the marked growth in Commonwealth civil society.

The good offices role of the secretariat, sometimes involving personal intervention by the secretary-general, came into play several times during 1999. It produced an agreement between rival political parties in Zanzibar (see VI.1.iii), defused ethnic tensions in the Solomon Islands (see X.2.ii) and mediated a political deal in Guyana providing for early elections (see IV.4.ii). In Sierra Leone the Commonwealth was a moral guarantor to the Lomé peace agreement (see VI.2.iii) and its police task force resumed retraining work in Freetown. The Commonwealth sent observer missions to the four-stage elections in Nigeria and to others in South Africa, Malawi and Antigua & Barbuda. It stepped up technical help in election management, as well as assistance for judicial bodies, parliaments, human rights commissions and government departments.

A meeting of Law Ministers in Port of Spain, Trinidad & Tobago, on 3-7 May adopted a set of Commonwealth 'freedom of information principles' aimed at open and accountable government. It also examined the report of an expert group on concerted strategies based on zero-tolerance for all types of corruption at national and global levels. The report was endorsed by Finance Ministers, meeting in the Cayman Islands in September, who also pushed for a speed-up of the 'heavily-indebted poor countries' (HIPC) initiative. Of the 41 countries classified as HIPCs, ten were Commonwealth members—all but one in Africa.

Under an £8 million settlement at the end of 1999, the Commonwealth Institute in London became, for the first time, an independent pan-Commonwealth agency. After nearly 40 years of dependence on funding from the Foreign and Commonwealth Office, it would now take direct responsibility for its own affairs. Dr Humayun Khan of Pakistan retired as director of the Commonwealth Foundation and was succeeded by Colin Ball of the United Kingdom.

ii. FRANCOPHONE AND PORTUGUESE-SPEAKING COMMUNITIES

International Organization of Francophonie (OIF)
DATE OF FOUNDATION: 1997   HEADQUARTERS: Paris, France
OBJECTIVES: To promote cooperation and exchange between countries wholly or party French-speaking and to defend usage of the French language
MEMBERSHIP (END-'99): Albania, Belgium (French-speaking community), Benin, Bulgaria, Burkina Faso, Burundi, Cambodia, Cameroon, Canada, Cape Verde, Central African Republic, Chad, Comoros, Democratic Republic of Congo, Republic of Congo, Côte d'Ivoire, Czech Republic, Djibouti, Dominica, Egypt, Equatorial Guinea, France, Gabon, Guinea, Guinea-Bissau, Haiti, Laos, Lebanon, Lithuania, Luxembourg, Macedonia, Madagascar, Mali, Mauritania, Mauritius, Moldova, Monaco, Morocco, New Brunswick (Canada), Niger, Poland, Quebec (Canada), Romania, Rwanda, St Lucia, São Tomé & Príncipe, Senegal, Seychelles, Slovenia, Switzerland, Togo, Tunisia, Vanuatu, Vietnam (*total* 54)
SECRETARY-GENERAL: Boutros Boutros-Ghali (Egypt)

Community of Portuguese-Speaking Countries (CPLP)
DATE OF FOUNDATION: 1996   HEADQUARTERS: Lisbon, Portugal
OBJECTIVES: To promote political, diplomatic, economic, social and cultural cooperation between member-states and to enhance the status of the Portuguese language
MEMBERSHIP (END-'99): Angola, Brazil, Cape Verde, Guinea-Bissau, Mozambique, Portugal, São Tomé & Príncipe (*total* 7)
EXECUTIVE SECRETARY: Marcolino Moco (Angola)

FRANCOPHONIE. An important consolidation of the still young International Organization of Francophonie (OIF) came with the summit at Moncton, New Brunswick, Canada, on 3-5 September. This was attended by representatives from 52 countries and territories (of which four were technically observers) compared with the 49 who had attended the previous summit in 1997 in Hanoi (see AR 1997, pp. 393-5). Over 30 heads of state or government attended, as well as, for the first time, delegations from Albania and Macedonia, where French was very marginally spoken, a further indication of the flexible terms of entry for the grouping.

The opening session heard speeches from President Chirac of France; the secretary-general of the OIF, Dr Boutros Boutros-Ghali and his successor as UN Secretary-General, Kofi Annan. France had let it be known before the meeting that it would seek to raise once again the issue of 'cultural exception' in trade, which it would be attempting to bring up at the forthcoming meeting of the World Trade Organization (WTO) in Seattle (see XI.2.ii). As it was, the issues relating to language became submerged in another debate.

The major issue at this summit, raised in particular by the Canadian hosts (both the federal government and the New Brunswick state government), was that of human rights and the allied issue of democracy. The scene had been set by an eve-of-conference report from Amnesty International which suggested that 32 of the 52 countries attending the summit were deficient in matters of human rights and democratic practice. The Canadian media, both English and French-language, took up the issue, suggesting that the OIF might take a leaf from the book of the Commonwealth (to which Canada also belonged), which had more developed mechanisms on issues related to democracy, as invoked against Nigeria between 1995 and 1999 (see XI.3.i).

Prior to the summit Dr Boutros Ghali had resisted the idea that any country should be excluded for deficient practices. President Chirac also repeated his theme from Hanoi: 'Sanctions are not in the tradition of *la francophonie*. They come into the area of the UN. What we want is to convince not constrain.' The amount of time devoted to the subject in his opening speech was an indication of the importance the issue had now attained. The Canadian Prime Minister, Jean Chrétien, said that he was clearly of the view that the grouping should adopt rules to penalize countries which flouted democratic and human rights norms.

After some heated debate, the most the summit could agree on was, on the one hand, to organize a symposium in the year 2000 to prepare 'an inventory of democratic practices, rights and liberties in the francophone area'; and, on the other, to reaffirm a decision taken two years before in Hanoi to establish a human rights 'observatory' in direct cooperation with the UN and the relevant international non-governmental organizations. (The Canadian authorities, again in the manner of other international meetings, had authorized the holding of an 'alternative summit' in the vicinity of the official meeting.) The mandate of the observatory had still to be worked out, however, as Dr Boutros-Ghali clearly indicated at the closing press conference. In view of the continuing interest in the democracy debate, however, it was promised that the next summit, in Lebanon in 2001, would return to the subject.

The Moncton summit broadly approved the attempts of the new secretariat to bring more rigour into the administration of francophone institutions, including the reform of the Francophone Agency (formerly the Agency for Cultural and Technical Cooperation, ACCT). That rigour, it was reported, had created one victim-the director-general of the Francophone University, Dr Michel Guillou, who had been removed for allegedly falsifying expense accounts.

The meeting also heard a report from a meeting of Francophonie Finance and Economy Ministers, who had met in Monaco in April prior to the spring meeting of the IMF/World Bank. This was part of Dr Boutros-Ghali's conscious attempt to widen the remit of the OIF and make it more like the Commonwealth, with which he had been endeavouring to develop good relations. A visit by Dr Boutros-Ghali to the Commonwealth secretariat in London in July saw the signing of a memorandum of understanding between the two organizations and the development of plans to stage a first-ever jointly-organized colloquium on pluralism and democracy in Cameroon in 2000. This would form part of a series of discussions planned by the OIF on democratic themes.

COMMUNITY OF PORTUGUESE-SPEAKING COUNTRIES. At an average rate of five conferences and promotions a month, the CPLP covered an increasingly wide range of cooperative activities in 1999, ranging through defence, international relations, education, medicine, literature, language, agriculture, history, parliamentary and municipal affairs, administration and social policy. One of the highlights of the year was the granting of UN observer status to the CPLP, on a par with the Commonwealth and Francophonie.

Considerable effort was made by the six other CPLP member countries to bring about reconciliation in Guinea-Bissau following the coup which forced President Vieira to seek refuge in the Portuguese embassy before going into exile in Portugal (see VII.1.iii). Within a comparatively short period of time the new government resumed Guinea-Bissau's place in CPLP counsels.

During the year the CPLP permanent coordinating committee also gave close attention to the prolonged conflict in Angola (see VII.1.vi). Both directly and by supporting UN and European Union (EU) resolutions, the CPLP condemned the Unita movement and its leader, Jonas Savimbi, for persistent armed activities and illegal diamond smuggling, inflicting devastation and deprivation in a large part of Angola. In addition to multilateral cooperation with the Angolan government, further bilateral agreements included defence cooperation between Lisbon and Angola.

The most historic events of 1999 for the CPLP concerned two associated Asian territories, namely East Timor and Macao. At the diplomatic level, the first half of the year was dedicated to pressing Indonesia to agree to a UN-supervised referendum in East Timor. The consultation was eventually held on 30 August and resulted in a stunning 78.5 per cent vote in favour of independence (see IX.1.vi), provoking a violent reaction by pro-Indonesian militias aided by the occupying military garrison. The massive destruction and personal suffering were vividly communicated to the world by television and other media, generating an emotional upsurge of support in Portugal and other CPLP countries, especially Brazil and Mozambique (where the Fretilin Timorese liberation movement was based). Following the withdrawal of Indonesian troops and the deployment of an Australian-led and UN-backed peace-keeping force, East Timor became a candidate for full membership of the CPLP, under its newly-adopted name of Timor Soro Lae.

The other major event, the restoration of Macao to Chinese sovereignty on 20 December, ended 450 years of Portuguese rule over the first and last Western colonial outpost in Asia (see also IX.2.i). The political evolution of Macao since the radical decolonization pursued by Portugal in 1974-75 could not have contrasted more sharply with that of East Timor. While East Timor had been invaded and summarily annexed by Indonesia, Beijing preferred a negotiated transfer of Macao to follow the handover of neighbouring Hong Kong by the British in 1997, thus giving ample time for a peaceful and practical transition. While the Chinese enjoyed a further assertion of national independence, the Portuguese left with the thought that the success or otherwise of decolonization depended as much, if not more, on the decolonized as on the decolonizers.

The year ended with preparations being made by the CPLP for the commemoration in May 2000 of the 500th anniversary of the arrival of Portuguese navigator Pedro Alvares Cabral in what became Brazil (see also II.4.iii) and also for the 25th anniversaries of the independence of Mozambique, Angola and São Tomé & Príncipe.

iii. NON-ALIGNED MOVEMENT AND DEVELOPING COUNTRIES

Non-Aligned Movement (NAM)
DATE OF FIRST SUMMIT: 1961   HEADQUARTERS: rotating with chair
OBJECTIVES: Originally to promote decolonization and to avoid domination by either the Western industrialized world or the Communist bloc; since the early 1970s to provide an authoritative forum to set the political and economic priorities of developing countries; in addition, since the end of the Cold War to resist domination of the UN system by the USA
MEMBERSHIP (END-'99): 114 countries (*those listed in AR 1995, p. 386, plus Belarus*)
CHAIRMAN: President Thabo Mbeki, South Africa (since June '99; succeeded Nelson Mandela, who had held post since Sept '98)

Group of 77 (G-77)
DATE OF FOUNDATION: 1964   HEADQUARTERS: UN centres
OBJECTIVES: To act as an international lobbying group for the concerns of developing countries
MEMBERSHIP (END-'99): 133 developing countries (*those listed in AR 1996, p. 385, minus South Korea, plus China, Eritrea & Turkmenistan*)

THE most important gathering of developing countries in 1999 was the ninth ministerial meeting of the Group of 77 (G-77) in Marrakech, Morocco, on 13-16 September. This was held to prepare for the forthcoming session of the United Nations Conference on Trade and Development (UNCTAD) and was preceded in August by regional meetings of Latin American and Caribbean ministers in Santo Domingo and of Asian ministers in Beirut. The African ministers held their regional meeting during the main conference at Marrakech. For the first time, the People's Republic of China was a participant in the G-77's preparatory process for UNCTAD.

After years of despair about the world economy, there was now a sense of optimism at Marrakech that UNCTAD could assist in producing consensus on a 'new development paradigm' based on 'growth, stability and equity with full participation and integration of developing countries in the globalizing world economy'. It was hoped that this would lead to resumption of real dialogue between the industrialized and the developing countries. The decision of the Group of Seven (G-7) summit in Cologne in June to reduce the debt burden of the poorer countries was warmly welcomed, although measures, such as debt swaps and refinancing, were also seen as needed for middle-income countries. There was concern that debt reduction still required submission to performance conditions under the IMF's enhanced structural adjustment facility (ESAF), inhibiting measures to promote development. These concerns were recognized by the IMF when at the end of September the ESAF was reformulated as a 'poverty reduction and growth facility' (PRGF).

The Marrakech conference also focused on the forthcoming World Trade Organization (WTO) meeting in Seattle (see XI.2.ii). The priority was to obtain implementation by the industrialized countries of their obligations, particularly in agriculture, textiles and clothing. At the same time, the G-77 wanted two derogations from the normal WTO rules. Firstly, the least-developed countries should be granted free access to developed-country markets, without any reciprocal concessions. Secondly, WTO must have a mechanism to protect biological resources and traditional knowledge in developing countries from registration by transnational corporations as intellectual property. There was strong opposition to either labour standards or environmental standards being discussed within the WTO.

The 23rd annual meeting of G-77 Foreign Ministers was held in New York on 24 September. It supplemented the Marrakech arguments, by more detailed consideration of the impact of globalization and the need for effective governance. They called for greater involvement of developing-country governments in international policy-making, better integration of trade, finance and development issues, reform of the 'international financial architecture' and the creation of the necessary technological and institutional capacities to prevent weaker countries being marginalized by globalization. This required the United Nations to be the central forum for policy-making. Consequentially, there was great concern with administrative and budgetary questions at the UN (see XI.1). Neither time-limits on UN programmes nor results-based budgeting should be introduced without prior approval by the General Assembly. There should be no budget ceiling and administrative savings should provide continuing annual resources for the UN development account rather than a one-off benefit. The UN Secretary-General was rebuked for proposing a decrease in the budget, below the level previously set by the Assembly.

Two days after the G-77 Foreign Ministers' meeting, six G-77 countries (Argentina, Brazil, India, Saudi Arabia and South Africa plus China) were among 11 major emerging economies included in a new Group of 20 (G-20) set up on the initiative of the G-7 Finance Ministers, meeting in Washington. It was stated that the new grouping—which also included, in addition to the G-7 countries, Australia, South Korea, Mexico, Russia and Turkey, together with the European Union and the IMF/World Bank—would study and review policy issues affecting relations between industrialized countries and emerging-market states with a view to promoting international financial stability. Canadian Finance Minister Paul Martin was selected to chair the G-20 for a two-year term.

The Foreign Ministers of the Non-Aligned Movement (NAM) held their annual meeting on 23 September in New York. The full range of positions adopted at the 1998 Durban summit of the NAM (see AR 1998, pp. 426-8) were reaffirmed, with some updating. The peace agreement for Sierra Leone signed in July (see VI.2.iii) was warmly welcomed and there was a dramatic strengthening of hostility towards the Unita movement's failure to cease fighting in Angola, with Unita leader Jonas Savimbi being labelled a war criminal.

The Kosovo crisis in Yugoslavia (see III.2.vi) caused divisions within the NAM, so the Coordinating Bureau was unable to make a statement until 9 April. There were implicit criticisms of the NATO attacks on Serbia in the reaffirmation of the principle of sovereignty, assertion of the responsibilities of the UN Security Council and a call for the immediate cessation of hostilities. On the other hand, NATO was not directly criticized and deep concern was expressed about the displacement of Kosovo civilians and human rights abuses. At the meeting in September, this precarious balance moved more towards endorsing NATO's actions by calling for full adherence to Security Council resolution 1244 of 10 June, which had authorized a UN civilian administration in Kosovo to cooperate with the K-For security forces (see XVII.1). There was no equivocation in rejecting the addition of crisis response operations to NATO's new strategic concept (see XI.2.i; XVII.2) and in calling on the United States not to develop an anti-ballistic-missile system.

In the Conference on Disarmament and the General Assembly, the NAM countries exerted strong pressure for progress on nuclear disarmament and for the UN to hold a fourth special session on disarmament. The NAM initiative to convene an international conference on the illicit trade in small arms was endorsed by the UN, the NAM being successful in electing Mozambique to chair the preparatory committee.

NAM efforts to help the Libyans break out of their diplomatic isolation bore fruit in 1999 (see V.4.ii). In April the two suspects in the Lockerbie bombing case were delivered for trial at The Hague, whereupon UN sanctions against Libya were immediately suspended. The Security Council statement on lifting sanctions paid particular tribute to the South African and Saudi Arabian governments for their role as mediators. In response to a progress report by Secretary-General Kofi Annan in July, the South Africans demanded on behalf of the NAM that sanctions should be formally terminated, but US pressure prevented the Security Council taking a final decision until the completion of the trial. The NAM Foreign Ministers in September insisted that all parties must comply with whatever verdict was reached by the Scottish court at The Hague.

Detailed preparation started in 1999 for the first summit conference of the G-77, five planning meetings being held in New York. It was agreed that what was designated 'the South Summit' would take place in Havana in April 2000 and would produce both a review of strategy and an action-oriented programme.

When Thabo Mbeki took over the South African presidency from Nelson Mandela in June (see VII.3), he thereby became the chairman of the Non-Aligned Movement. At the end of the year Guyana handed over the chairmanship of the G-77 for 2000 to Nigeria. Neither group of developing countries changed its membership in 1999, the NAM having 114 members and the G-77 132 plus China.

iv. ORGANIZATION OF THE ISLAMIC CONFERENCE (OIC)

DATE OF FOUNDATION: 1970   HEADQUARTERS: Jeddah, Saudi Arabia
OBJECTIVES: To further cooperation among Islamic countries in the political, economic, social, cultural and scientific spheres
MEMBERSHIP (END-'99): Afghanistan, Albania, Algeria, Azerbaijan, Bahrain, Bangladesh, Benin, Brunei, Burkina Faso, Cameroon, Chad, Comoros, Djibouti, Egypt, Gabon, The Gambia, Guinea, Guinea-Bissau, Indonesia, Iran, Iraq, Jordan, Kazakhstan, Kuwait, Kyrgyzstan, Lebanon, Libya, Malaysia, Maldives, Mali, Mauritania, Morocco, Mozambique, Niger, Nigeria, Oman, Pakistan, Palestine, Qatar, Saudi Arabia, Senegal, Sierra Leone, Somalia, Sudan, Suriname, Syria, Tajikistan, Togo, Tunisia, Turkey, Turkmenistan, Uganda, Uzbekistan, United Arab Emirates, Yemen, Zanzibar (total 56)
SECRETARY-GENERAL: Azeddine Laraki (Morocco)

THE OIC Foreign Ministers held their 26th meeting in Ouagadougou, the capital of Burkina Faso, on 28 June-1 July, returning to some of the themes of the 25th meeting in Qatar in 1998 (see AR 1998, pp. 429-30) and also dealing with new developments. In his opening address, President Blaise Campaoré of Burkina Faso recalled the major goals set by the OIC since its establishment in Rabat in 1969, the most important of which was the motto of the 26th meeting, 'Peace and Partnership for Development'.

In a final communiqué, the Ouagadougou session stressed that the question of Palestine and Al-Quds al-Sharif (Jerusalem) was 'the paramount Islamic cause'. The Foreign Ministers called on member states to make efforts within the international community to force Israel to withdraw its troops from all Arab and Palestinian territories to the borders of 4 June 1967, and first and foremost from Jerusalem in order to enable the Palestinian people to achieve their inalienable national rights. They also called on the international community to take immediate action to put an end to 'Israeli colonization and all the inhuman and illegal measures and practices of the Israeli occupation authorities in the city of Al-Quds al-Sharif aimed at judaizing it, namely confiscating land and property, demolishing houses and emptying the city of its Palestinian inhabitants, altering its demographic and geographical set up, obliterating cultural, civilizational, and historical monuments and desecrating Holy Islamic and Christian sites'.

The meeting affirmed its full support of the peace process in the Middle East and its commitment to the principles and parameters of the process. Ministers called on Israel to respect and implement its commitments, pledges and agreements concluded through the peace process and charged that Israeli procrastination and evasion at implementation level had seriously undermined the whole process. Ministers lauded the resistance of the Syrian Arab citizens of the Golan Heights against occupation and strongly condemned Israel for not complying with UN Security Council Resolution 497 (1981). They also strongly condemned Israel for its continuing occupation of parts of southern Lebanon and the western Beqa'a valley, and urged the international community to ensure the implementation of UN Security Council resolution 425 (1978) requiring Israel's immediate and unconditional withdrawal from all occupied Lebanese territory to the internationally-recognized borders.

Ministers reaffirmed their full solidarity with the people of Kosovo to help them overcome the tragedy they had faced as a result of 'the policies of oppression and ethnic cleansing carried out by the Serbian forces' (see III.2.vi). They called for the return of all refugees and deportees to Kosovo, and commended in that regard the invaluable humanitarian aid provided by the member states to the victims.

Meeting as fighting flared in Kashmir (see VIII.2.i; VIII.2.iii), the Foreign Ministers expressed 'deep concern' over the dangerous escalation of the heavy bombing by Indian artillery and Indian air raids across the line of control, which had led to the death of innocent people. They welcomed the diplomatic initiative of the government of Pakistan designed to defuse the 'explosive situation' in Kashmir and called on the two parties to exercise restraint and engage in dialogue to defuse the tension in the spirit of the Lahore Declaration. Declaring full solidarity with Pakistan in its efforts to safeguard its sovereignty, political independence and territorial integrity and security, the session called for the appointment of a special representative of the OIC secretary-general for Jammu and Kashmir.

The Foreign Ministers reaffirmed their support for UN and OIC initiatives for the peaceful settlement of the Afghan crisis (see VIII.1.ii) and called on all Afghan factions to observe an immediate and unconditional ceasefire and to work together to establish a broad-based multi-ethnic national coalition government. They requested all countries to abstain from interfering in internal Afghan affairs and reaffirmed the need for full respect of the sovereignty, unity, territorial integrity, independence and Islamic identity of Afghanistan. The meeting called for the establishment of a fund, under OIC auspices, to assist the Afghan people and invited all Afghan nationals to cooperate in ending to the production and export of illicit drugs. Ministers also reaffirmed their readiness to contribute effectively to the restoration of stability in Somalia and their full commitment to respect for that country's sovereignty and territorial integrity. They called for convening an international conference on peace and national reconciliation in Somalia.

The Foreign Ministers expressed deep concern over the impasse faced by the UN mission regarding the elimination of weapons of mass destruction in Iraq (see V.2.vi; XI.1), and called on Iraq to resume cooperation with the UN Security Council with a view to safeguarding peace and stability in the region. They also reaffirmed support for the sovereignty, territorial integrity and political independence of Iraq and recorded their sympathy for the suffering of the Iraqi people. Great concern was expressed about 'the dangerous and continuing deterioration in the food, health and humanitarian situation of the Muslim Iraqi people, in particular the children, women and the elderly, as acknowledged in the reports of the UN Secretary-General, the specialized agencies and numerous governmental and non-governmental humanitarian organizations'.

On other current international issues, the Ouagadougou meeting reaffirmed the OIC's 'strong support' for the government of Azerbaijan, which had been 'subjected to aggression by the Republic of Armenia, spreading to the extent of threatening the cultural and historical heritage of the Azeri people' (see III.3.iii), and called on Armenia to withdraw its forces from all Azeri territories. On the Cyprus question, the ministers reaffirmed past resolutions expressing solidarity with the Turkish Cypriot people 'in their rightful cause' (see II.4.vi).

The Foreign Ministers expressed deep concern over the growing refugee phenomenon among the Islamic societies and the negative impact created in countries hosting Muslim refugees. They called upon the OIC member-states to mobilize cooperation mechanisms among themselves and within the international specialized bodies to face this phenomenon and to offer the most appropriate solution to it.

Some 40 delegations from Islamic states attended the inaugural session of the OIC Parliamentary Union held in Tehran, Iran, on 15-17 June. The meeting adopted a draft statute and elected a six-member council consisting of representatives from Bangladesh, Chad, Indonesia, Mali, Morocco and Saudi Arabia (the absence of an elected legislature in the last being no apparent disqualification). Earlier in the year OIC secretary-general Azeddine Laraki had urged member-states to pay their affiliation fees to the organization to avert a financial crisis in advance of the ninth OIC summit due to be held in Qatar in 2000.

4. EUROPEAN UNION

DATE OF FOUNDATION: 1952 HEADQUARTERS: Brussels, Belgium
OBJECTIVES: To seek ever-closer union of member states
MEMBERSHIP (END-'99): Austria, Belgium, Denmark, Finland, France, Germany, Greece, Ireland, Italy, Luxembourg, Netherlands, Portugal, Spain, Sweden, United Kingdom (*total* 15)
PRESIDENT OF EUROPEAN COMMISSION: Romano Prodi (Italy)
CURRENCY: euro, introduced on 1 Jan '99 by 11 members, with Denmark, Greece, Sweden & UK not participating (end-'99 £1=Eur1.61, US$1=Eur1.00)

THE launch of the third phase of economic and monetary union (EMU) on 1 January 1999, when the national currencies of 11 European Union (EU) members were subsumed into a single European currency, marked the beginning of a new era in European integration. Over its first 12 months the new currency, the euro, could be declared a qualified success. For the European institutions, though, this was a tense and difficult year, as the European Parliament used its powers to force the resignation of the European Commission before the end of its term, resulting in the appointment of former Italian Prime Minister Romano Prodi to construct a new Commission team.

THE EURO. The 11 countries of the euro zone subsumed their currencies into the euro at the turn of the year on 1 January at rates which had been set by ministers the previous evening. Trading in the new currency began on 4 January. National currencies thus became sub-units of the euro, locked together by fixed exchange rates. The participating countries were Austria, Belgium, Finland, France, Germany, Ireland, Italy, Luxembourg, the Netherlands, Portugal and

Spain. Euro notes and coins would not be introduced until the beginning of 2002, so in its first three years the new currency would primarily be used in capital markets and for transactions between businesses.

The launch of the euro took place with remarkably little dissension. Apart from custard pies thrown at the Dutch Finance Minister by an irate demonstrator, there were no public or political manifestations against this profound development in European politics and economics. Virtually all mainstream parties in the euro zone accepted a step which would remove key instruments of economic policy from national political control. It seemed a relief to many people that so much economic and monetary decision-making had been taken out of national politics and replaced by a set of European rules. Italian Prime Minister Massimo D'Alema, himself a former Communist, said that the new currency signalled the end of an economic model based on budget handouts by the state. One of the two Italian members of the European Commission, Mario Monti, went further, saying that his country had 'won the war of liberation from the lira'.

The president of the European Central Bank (ECB), Wim Duisenberg, said at the launch of the euro that a currency was more than just a medium of exchange: 'A currency is also part of the identity of a people. It reflects what they have in common, now and in the future. The euro has to become a currency which will keep its value over time and contribute to a stable, prosperous and peaceful Europe.'

Four EU countries were missing from the euro zone. Although Britain's Labour government was committed to membership when certain economic conditions were fulfilled, its enthusiasm for a referendum waned during the year as public scepticism grew (see II.1). Denmark and Sweden also stayed outside, although there was increasing internal pressure in both countries for them to join. Greece did not achieve the economic benchmarks required for a euro country, although it was determined to do so by 2001 or sooner.

The constituent currencies of the euro having appreciated against dollar and yen over the previous year, there was steady demand for the new currency on international money markets during the early days of 1999. One euro was worth $1.17 in the first few days of the year. After that, the new currency began to slip, reaching parity with the dollar by the end of the year. Its value against the pound sterling also dropped, from 70p at the start of the year to 62p by the end. For British commentators and public this demonstrated the weakness of the new money; for those inside the euro zone it was a welcome fillip to export-led growth. There was in fact a raft of reasons for the relative weakness of the new currency. Some decline in value was not surprising, given the surge in value of its constituent parts before the euro was launched; furthermore, interest rates were substantially higher in the USA and the UK than in the euro zone. Above all, the strength of the American economy contrasted with the weak condition of several European economies, especially those of Germany and Italy.

Management of the euro was the responsibility of the ECB under the chairmanship of Mr Duisenberg, primarily through control of interest rates. He and his colleagues on the ECB board did not see their task as being to maintain the value of the currency *vis à vis* the outside world: their role was to control inflation—and there were no signs of inflationary pressures. An increase in interest rates might have pushed up the value of the new currency, but it could also have stymied economic growth, which seemed difficult enough to achieve as it was.

Some euro zone economies were growing fast, others not. Output in Ireland, the Netherlands and Spain was expanding rapidly, and the French economy showed signs of recovery from a stagnant period; but Germany and Italy were stubbornly reluctant to join in. The slowness of the German economy to respond was widely attributed to its lack of flexibility, particularly in relation to working practices and company structure. Industrial restructuring was needed, but was politically too difficult to achieve for Chancellor Schröder's government (see II.2.i). The resignation of Oskar Lafontaine as German Finance Minister in March was expected at the time to herald a major change in German policies, but in the event did not.

Herr Lafontaine criticized the ECB for its failure to reduce euro interest rates even further, but Mr Duisenberg resisted his demands, so a 3 per cent basic rate prevailed throughout the year. His intervention was typical of the conflicting comments from various quarters, including some EU Finance Ministers, President Jacques Chirac of France and new Commission president Romano Prodi, all of whom had their own view of what action the ECB should take. Such comments left the currency markets confused as to what the long term policy for the currency was to be.

It was in the bond markets that the euro most quickly found favour, the new currency becoming an increasingly important instrument in industrial restructuring. Whereas governments, constrained by the Maastricht budget disciplines, were reducing borrowings, companies were filling the gap. Over the year as a whole the value of bonds issued by corporations in euros was four times the aggregate level of issue in the predecessor currencies in the previous year, up from Eur30,000 million in 1998 to Eur130,000 million in 1999. Investments and returns in European assets were no longer threatened by currency risk, so a company like Olivetti could raise euro funds on international markets to finance its bid for Telecom Italia, while Vodafone AirTouch of the UK could rely on the market in euro bonds to cover its bid for Mannesmann of Germany.

The launch of the euro also made it possible for pan-European share offerings. Deutsche Telecom aimed at least half of a planned Eur10,000 million share offering to small investors in the euro zone—the first time that any company had deliberately sought to sell shares beyond its own frontiers. There were signs of a new enthusiasm for equity investment, as individual investors put their money into euro-denominated new issues on European stock markets.

INSTITUTIONAL CRISIS. By the beginning of 1999 the tensions between the European Commission and the European Parliament, which had been apparent by the end of the previous year (see AR 1998, p. 438), were beginning to take on new intensity, fed by the prospect of European elections in June. The

Parliament was refusing to give formal clearance to the 1996 budget because of widespread allegations of fraud, nepotism and mismanagement by the Commission. Their particular targets were French commissioner Edith Cresson and Spanish member Manuel Marín. The Commission's president, Jacques Santer of Luxembourg, insisted on the principle of collegiate solidarity and threatened that the whole college of 20 commissioners would resign unless the Parliament gave way. The European Parliament had no constitutional power to sack individual commissioners anyway, and required a two-thirds majority vote to dismiss the Commission as a body.

The political groups in the Parliament were in confusion. The Socialists, who were the largest group, tabled a no-confidence resolution against the Commission, but then announced that they would vote against it. The Christian Democrats accused the Socialists of letting the Commission off the hook, but were still opposed to dismissing the college. The Greens, neo-Fascists and Liberals favoured a motion of censure. At the Strasbourg plenary session in January the vote was taken and the censure motion was defeated by 293 votes to 232, but with major splits in the main groups-about one-third of the Christian Democrats voted for the motion. An alternative resolution severely criticizing the Commission and demanding wide-scale reform of its internal workings was also approved.

It was agreed between Commission and Parliament that a special committee of independent experts be appointed to investigate specific allegations, with full access to all information and including a fundamental review of Commission practices in the awarding of financial contracts. The group was given until 15 March to conclude its report. M. Santer announced an eight-point plan of reform to include codes of conduct covering all Commission officials and individual commissioners.

Although the Commission had escaped the motion of censure, it was severely weakened by the episode. Worse was to come. On 15 March the committee issued its 144-page report on 'Allegations regarding fraud, mismanagement and nepotism in the European Commission'. The report cleared most individual commissioners of direct responsibility for individual instances of fraud and corruption, but was scathing about the culture of the institution, talking of 'an admission of loss of control by the political authorities over the administration that they are supposedly running' and concluding: 'It is becoming difficult to find anyone who has even the slightest sense of responsibility.'

A common theme running through the report was that the Commission had consistently agreed to take on costly programmes for which it simply did not have the available human resources. It was in 'out-sourcing' the work to external consultants or organizations that most of the problems arose. Late in the evening of 15 March the Commission announced its collective resignation, stating that it would continue to transact routine business until its successor was appointed. Its five-year term of office would normally have run until the beginning of 2000.

The German presidency hosted a European Council meeting in Berlin at the end of the month, where Signor Prodi was nominated as successor to M. Santer to preside over a new Commission. The former Italian Prime Minister then began an intensive series of meetings with national governments and with the Parliament to choose the members of the new college. He told Parliament in April that he would 'push Europe towards a great season of reform and change'. All reform should respect three principles: greater effectiveness, absolute transparency and full accountability. 'We will not tolerate corruption under any circumstances', he declared. In May the MEPs formally endorsed his appointment by 392 votes to 72 with 41 abstentions.

EUROPEAN PARLIAMENT ELECTIONS. The Commission was not the only casualty of the crisis, which had served to reinforce general scepticism about the European institutions. Any hopes which MEPs might have had that their aggressive approach would enhance their own standing were not reflected in the turnout for the European elections held on 10, 11 and 13 June. In the EU as a whole, fewer than one in every two voters turned out to vote compared with 57 per cent in the previous elections in 1994. The figure included countries where voting was compulsory. Turnout was particularly low in the United Kingdom, with 24 per cent registering their vote, and in the Netherlands, with 29.9 per cent.

The balance of political strength in the 626-seat Parliament shifted towards the right. The Socialists lost their position as the largest group to the European People's Party (EPP), which consisted primarily of Christian Democrats and British Conservatives. This group had 233 seats in the new Parliament to the Socialists' 180, while the Liberals, Democrats and Reformists had 51, the mainstream Greens and allies 48 and the 'European United Left/Nordic Green Left' 42. Of the remaining seats, 30 went to various Eurosceptic parties in the 'Union for a Europe of Nations' and 16 to outright opponents of the EU grouped as 'Europe of Democracies and Diversities', while 26 of the new MEPs could not be accommodated in any of the official groups.

The UK elections were held under proportional representation for the first time (see AR 1998, p. 18). The success of the British Conservatives, who secured 36 seats to the Socialists' 30 in the UK balloting (see II.1), affected the balance of the Parliament as a whole. When the new body assembled in July, the Socialists were obliged to cede the presidency of the Parliament to an EPP nominee, namely Nicole Fontaine of the New Union for French Democracy, who became the first woman to hold the post since Simone Veil 20 years previously.

NEW COMMISSION. President-designate Romano Prodi worked to put together his team during July and August, taking advantage of the increased powers awarded to the Commission president by the 1997 Amsterdam Treaty (see AR 1997, pp. 402-3), which came into effect on 1 May 1999. Not all the appointees were his first choice, but it was generally regarded as a strong team. Each individual was subject to hearings in the European Parliament before the college as a whole was endorsed by the MEPs in mid-September.

Signor Prodi had undertakings from each of the nominees that they would resign if he requested them to do so.

Four of the old college were reappointed, namely Neil Kinnock (UK), who became a Commission vice-president, Franz Fischler (Austria), who retained agriculture, Erkki Liikanen (Finland), responsible for enterprise and information society, and Mario Monti (Italy), in for the key competition dossier. The other 15 members were new to the post. They included Pascal Lamy (France), once head of Jacques Delors's private presidential office in the Commission, former UK cabinet minister Chris Patten, the last governor of Hong Kong (see AR 1997, p. 350), and Margot Wallström from Sweden.

Signor Prodi matched candidates to portfolios in surprising ways, appointing some to positions where their home country was known to be most critical of EU policy. Allocation of the trade negotiation dossier to France's M. Lamy was the most obvious example. Mr Patten's responsibility for developing the EU's common foreign and security policy in tandem with the newly-appointed high representative of the Council, Javier Solana, could be seen in the same light. The new Commission took office in September, appointed for the remainder of 1999 followed by a full five-year term.

AGENDA 2000. A range of contentious decisions was required of the EU in preparation for the next stage of enlargement (see below), presenting the German presidency with a difficult task in the first half of the year. A compromise agreement was reached at the Berlin summit in March on expenditure for the EU budget for the seven years 2000-06. Prime Minister Tony Blair secured the continuation of the UK's budget rebate; French President Chirac persuaded his colleagues to drop plans for far-reaching cuts in support for cereals and beef and to delay reform of the milk market; and Spanish Prime Minister José María Aznar won concessions over structural fund payments to Spain. Germany and other high net contributors even achieved some reduction in their budget contributions. It was agreed that the ceiling for EU spending should be limited to the current level of 1.27 per cent of GNP, with a progressive reduction in the amount coming from value-added tax (VAT) and an increase in the figure directly related to the size of the economy. In consequence, Austria, Germany, the Netherlands and Sweden were expected to see a reduction of 25 per cent in their contributions.

Average annual spending for agriculture was set at Eur40,500 million over the seven years, plus Eur14,000 million over the full period for rural development and veterinary measures. Reform measures for the milk and cereals sector, which had been agreed two weeks earlier, were watered down by heads of government at M. Chirac's insistence, so guarantee prices for cereals were to be reduced by 15 per cent in two equal steps in 2000 and 2001 (as against the originally agreed 20 per cent) and some 10 per cent of land was to be taken out of production as set-aside. The basic price of beef was to fall by 20 per cent over three years. Reforms to the milk regime were postponed, again at French insistence, so a 15 per cent price cut would not begin to take effect until 2005. The Commission made clear its concern that over-production of dairy products would place such additional burdens on the EU budget that further reforms would be essential. An overall budget of Eur213,000 million was agreed for regional development and training through the structural funds, including Eur3,120 million to help applicant countries in Central and Eastern Europe before their accession to the EU and Eur4,140 million for new members in 2002 rising to Eur14,210 million in 2006.

The Franco-German alliance, which had been the bedrock of European affairs since the 1950s, all but collapsed during the period of the German presidency in the first half of 1999. There was no common ground or mutual understanding between President Chirac and Chancellor Schröder. Apart from the French veto of speedy agricultural finance reform at the Berlin summit, nothing was done to pressurize Spain to lift its objections to energy taxation, In June, moreover, a proposal for recycling scrapped motor vehicles was blocked by the Germans themselves following pressure from the German motor industry just before it was due to be adopted in the Environment Ministers. In the past, consultations between France and Germany would have anticipated such issues.

ENLARGEMENT. Accession negotiations continued with the six priority candidates for EU membership—Poland, Hungary, the Czech Republic, Estonia, Slovenia and Cyprus—but it was clear that there would be substantial problems of adjustment for these countries before the negotiations could be concluded. It was also apparent that second-phase countries such as Bulgaria and Romania needed more sympathetic treatment, especially given the dislocation to some of their economies from the Kosovo conflict (see III.2.vi).

It was left to the Helsinki European Council in December to set the future agenda, softening the distinction between the first and second phase countries. New members, it was agreed, could be admitted from the end of 2002, provided that the EU had modified its own internal procedures appropriately, that the countries concerned had demonstrated that they could accept the obligations of membership, and that the negotiations had been completed. Formal talks were to begin in February 2000 with the other candidate countries—Romania, Slovakia, Latvia, Lithuania, Bulgaria and Malta. In each negotiation, said the Council, 'each candidate state will be judged on its own merits'. Most significant in Helsinki was the EU's acceptance of Turkey as a candidate state 'destined to join the Union on the basis of the same criteria applied to the other candidate states' (see II.4.vii). This decision marked a major evolution in EU policy over a 12-month period, although no date was set for the start of formal accession negotiations with Turkey.

The issue of Cyprus loomed large in the run-up to the Helsinki meeting, with the Council's high representative Javier Solana flying to Ankara for last-minute discussions with the Turkish Prime Minister. The final communique welcomed the renewed UN-sponsored talks for resolving the Cyprus problem (see II.4.vi) but insisted that even if the division of the island had not been resolved by the relevant time, this should not stand in the way of Cyprus becoming an EU member. Turkey, meanwhile, would be able to participate in EU programmes and agencies. None of this new approach would have been possible without changes in Greek policy towards Turkey (see II.4.v).

INTER-GOVERNMENTAL CONFERENCE. Business left unfinished following negotiation of the Amsterdam Treaty in 1997 had to be dealt with before the EU could accept new member states. There was pressure from the Parliament and the Commission for far-reaching reforms on issues such as taxation, revision of the Treaty texts to provide a written constitution and provisions for formal EU agreements between small groups of member countries. The heads of government gathered in Helsinki rejected such a broad agenda and decided to work on minimal changes. They agreed that a new inter-governmental council (IGC) should be convened in February 2000 and concluded by the end of the year.

The range of subjects would be limited to the size and composition of the European Commission; a new weighting of votes in the Council to allow for the fact that countries with large populations could otherwise be outvoted by large numbers of small countries; possible extension of qualified majority voting in the Council; and possible other issues proposed by the incoming presidency.

KOSOVO CONFLICT. Although tensions between member states sometimes threatened EU solidarity during the Kosovo conflict (see III.2.vi), the Union managed to maintain a common position, partly thanks to firm leadership from the German presidency. As the NATO air strikes began in late March, EU leaders urged Yugoslav President Slobodan Milošević to change course by halting Serb aggression in Kosovo and signing the Rambouillet accords. At their meeting in Berlin on 24-25 March they said that Europe could not tolerate a humanitarian catastrophe in its midst, nor could it be permitted that the predominant population of Kosovo should be collectively deprived of its rights and subjected to grave human rights abuses.

As the refugees streamed out of Kosovo, extensive aid was provided from EU funds, especially in Albania, Montenegro and Macedonia, to provide emergency food supplies and equipment. Eur250 million was allocated in April to fund camps, food and medicines.

Sanctions on Yugoslavia were strengthened as the conflict dragged on. A ban on delivery of oil products to Serbia came into force by the end of April and financial sanctions to freeze funds held abroad and prohibit investment were also tightened. In May the EU Foreign Ministers discussed the situation with President Djukanovic of Montenegro and Kosovar leader Ibrahim Rugova. They also supported the role of Finland's President, Martti Ahtisaari, as a peace envoy—appropriate as coming from the country which would have the EU presidency for the second half of 1999 but was not a NATO member. The Council also proposed to convene a conference by the end of July to take forward EU plans for a Stability Pact for South-Eastern Europe.

When the European Council met in Cologne on 3-4 June the NATO bombing had ended. Mr Ahtisaari reported on his mission to Belgrade undertaken with Russian envoy Viktor Chernomyrdin and attention shifted to reconstruction in the Balkans. A European Agency for Reconstruction in Kosovo was to be established by October and a European task-force working on the ground from July. At the end of July leaders from Europe, the USA, Russia and other countries and organizations met in a donor conference to pledge support for emergency assistance for Kosovo. The Stability Pact was also agreed at an international meeting in Sarajevo with the longer-term aim of bringing peace and prosperity to the region.

COMMON FOREIGN AND SECURITY POLICY. The Kosovo crisis was a practical test for the EU common foreign and security policy (CFSP), pointing the way ahead for further initiatives. It gave life to some of the provisions of the Amsterdam Treaty, particularly the appointment of a high representative for the CSFP, the integration of the Western European Union (WEU) into the EU and the strengthening of the EU's own defence identity. Dr Javier Solana (Spain) provided the link between these policy goals. Having coordinated the bombing campaign in Kosovo in his capacity as secretary-general of NATO, he was now appointed secretary-general of the EU Council of Ministers and the EU high representative for the CSFP. He was also named as secretary-general of the WEU (see also XI.2.i).

Addressing the European Parliament in November, Sr Solana was already able to report on his involvement in the Balkans reconstruction process, Chechnya, the Middle East and Algeria. He said that the Bosnia and Kosovo crises had made it clear that more was needed under the CFSP than declarations of intent: 'We need to be able to act. And that means having military capabilities.' Over time, he said, discussion of European defence had become less abstract and more specific.

The Helsinki summit in December duly committed itself to developing the EU's military and non-military crisis management capability, underlining 'its determination to develop an autonomous capacity to take decisions'. It would be able to launch and conduct EU-led military operations in response to international crises. The Council said that this did not imply the creation of a European army, but by 2003 member states as a whole must be able to deploy military forces of up to 50,000 or 60,000 troops within 60 days and sustain them for at least one year in undertaking such tasks as peace-keeping. Political and military bodies would be established to provide political guidance and strategic direction and there would be full consultation, cooperation and transparency between the EU and NATO.

5. EUROPEAN ORGANIZATIONS

i. COUNCIL OF EUROPE

DATE OF FOUNDATION: 1949 HEADQUARTERS: Strasbourg, France
OBJECTIVES: To strengthen pluralist democracy, the rule of law and the maintenance of human rights in Europe and to further political, social and cultural cooperation between member-states
MEMBERSHIP (END-'99): Albania, Andorra, Austria, Belgium, Bulgaria, Croatia, Cyprus, Czech Republic, Denmark, Estonia, Finland, France, Georgia, Germany, Greece, Hungary, Iceland, Ireland, Italy, Latvia, Liechtenstein, Lithuania, Luxembourg, Macedonia, Malta, Moldova, Netherlands, Norway, Poland, Portugal, Romania, Russia, San Marino, Slovakia, Slovenia, Spain, Sweden, Switzerland, Turkey, Ukraine, United Kingdom (*total* 41)
SECRETARY-GENERAL: Walter Schwimmer (Austria)

THE Council of Europe celebrated its 50th anniversary on 5 May. The occasion was commemorated by an official ceremony in the Houses of Parliament in London followed by a reception attended by Queen Elizabeth II in St James's Palace, where the original treaty establishing the organization was signed on 5 May 1949. Throughout the year, member states staged a variety of events and exhibitions designed to publicize the Council of Europe and to look ahead to its future work in promoting democracy, the rule of law and human rights. The Parliamentary Assembly devoted one day of its April part-session to a 'youth parliament' of over 200 young people aged between 16 and 20 from the member states.

The Committee of Ministers continued to implement the action plan agreed at the 1997 second summit in 1997 (see AR 1997, pp. 411-3). In April it responded to the recommendations of the 'committee of wise of persons' on the structure and decision-making processes in the Council of Europe. It was agreed that the organization should give a high priority to the provision of assistance to new members. This emphasis was reflected in the Assembly's continued monitoring of ten member states. The effective abolition of the death penalty in Ukraine, following strong pressure, was viewed as a notable success. Attempts to persuade Russian authorities to cease military action in Chechnya (see III.3.i) met with less success.

A strong commitment to social cohesion was demonstrated by the establishment of a specialized unit on social cohesion which would cooperate with the Social Development Fund and outside partners. The enhancement of cooperation with other international organizations such as the OSCE and EU was supported, although not by the signing of formal agreements. Similarly, the statutory definition of links with the Assembly was resisted, as was the concept of co-decision-making on conventions and budgetary matters, although consultation would continue in these areas. The reform of the structure of the secretariat was completed during the year and proposals for the prioritization of detailed activities in both the Council of Europe and the Assembly were prepared for consideration in early 2000.

In April the Council of Europe welcomed Georgia as its 41st member state at a ceremony attended by the Georgian President, Eduard Shevardnadze. In gaining admission, Georgia was required to implement a series of reforms by specified dates in order to meet Council of Europe standards in certain areas. Mexico was granted observer status on 1 December. Requests for accession by Bosnia & Hercegovina, Monaco, Armenia and Azerbaijan continued to be considered by the Assembly during the year. Consideration of the request for membership by Belarus remained suspended.

The Council of Europe participated in election monitoring in a number of countries throughout the year, in conjunction with the Organization for Security and Cooperation in Europe (OSCE) and the Office for Democratic Institutions and Human Rights (ODIHR) (see also XI.5.ii). Its observers described the campaign during the presidential elections in Ukraine (see III.3.ii) as 'highly questionable', although the result was viewed as a fair reflection of opinion. The Russian parliamentary elections in December (see III.3.i) were thought to represent a 'noticeable improvement' on previous elections and the parliamentary elections in Georgia were also given a relatively clean bill of health (see III.3.iii).

In its response to the Kosovo conflict (see III.2.vi), the Council of Europe provided assistance on the ground and also joined with other international organizations to participate in the Stability Pact for South-Eastern Europe agreed in Sarajevo at the end of July. Areas in which the Council of Europe offered assistance included the establishment of non-judicial machinery for the protection of human rights, expert training in local democracy and police work, the combating of corruption and the support of independent media.

A new secretary-general of the Council of Europe, Walter Schwimmer (Austria), was elected by the Assembly in June. This followed the election in January of Lord Russell-Johnston (UK) as president of the Parliamentary Assembly. There was also a new post created in the organization, that of a commissioner for human rights. The remit of the commissioner was not to deal with individual cases but to promote human rights awareness in member states and to ensure compliance with Council of Europe texts. In September the Assembly elected Alvaro Gil-Robles (Spain) as the first commissioner, to serve for a six-year term.

A proposal for a European Union (EU) 'charter of fundamental rights' emerged late in the year and posed a potential threat to the primacy of the European Convention on Human Rights in the protection of human rights. The exact nature of the proposed EU charter and its relationship with existing treaties were to be determined by the working group drafting the document, on which the Council of Europe was to be represented. In welcoming the increased profile being given to human rights, many were quick to point to the undesirability of two parallel jurisdictions developing in an area which has long been the unquestioned domain of the Council of Europe.

ii. ORGANIZATION FOR SECURITY AND COOPERATION IN EUROPE (OSCE)

DATE OF FOUNDATION: 1975   HEADQUARTERS: Vienna, Austria
OBJECTIVES: To promote security and cooperation among member states, particularly in respect of the resolution of internal and external conflicts
MEMBERSHIP (END-'99): Albania, Andorra, Armenia, Austria, Azerbaijan, Belarus, Belgium, Bosnia & Hercegovina, Bulgaria, Canada, Croatia, Cyprus, Czech Republic, Denmark, Estonia, Finland, France, Georgia, Germany, Greece, Holy See (Vatican), Hungary, Iceland, Ireland, Italy, Kazakhstan, Kyrgyzstan, Latvia, Liechtenstein, Lithuania, Luxembourg, Macedonia, Malta, Moldova, Monaco, Netherlands, Norway, Poland, Portugal, Romania, Russian Federation, San Marino, Slovakia, Slovenia, Spain, Sweden, Switzerland, Tajikistan, Turkey, Turkmenistan, Ukraine, United Kingdom, United States, Uzbekistan, Yugoslavia (*suspended*) (*total* 55)
SECRETARY-GENERAL: Giancarlo Aragona (Italy)

THE main event in the OSCE's calendar for 1999 was the review conference held in Istanbul on 18-19 November, bringing together the heads of state and government and the Foreign Ministers of all 54 participating countries in a huge diplomatic jamboree. The summit's formal purpose was to review the implementation in participating states of OSCE principles, on such matters as human rights and respect for democracy, and also to evaluate the effectiveness of the OSCE's many activities, institutions, structures and instruments. Review conferences took place every three years (the last having been held in Lisbon in 1996—see AR 1996, pp. 401-2), providing the occasion for an intensive round of more informal high-level meetings between OSCE leaders.

The Russian newspaper *Izvestia* commented (20 November) that the Istanbul conference would 'go down in history as "the Chechnya summit"'. Proceedings in Istanbul, and at the preparatory meeting held in Vienna on 20 September-1 October, did indeed take place in the shadow of Vladimir Putin's war in the breakaway Russian republic (see III.3.1). The summit's concluding document thus contained a carefully-worded reference to Chechnya, condemning terrorism, acknowledging the territorial integrity of Russia and voicing concern for the civilian population. Russia agreed to the OSCE chairman-in-office, Knut Vollebaek (Norway's Foreign Minister), leading a fact-finding mission to the region.

The Istanbul summit reached two important decisions. First, the 'adapted CFE' (Conventional Forces in Europe) Treaty was signed by the 30 participating countries involved. This 'adapted treaty' was necessary in order to register the profound changes which had occurred in Europe's strategic landscape since the original CFE treaty was agreed in 1990 (see AR 1990, pp. 433-7)—in particular, the break-up of the Warsaw Pact. Once ratified, the treaty would lead to the destruction of 11,000 weapon systems (a 10 per cent cut in existing arsenals). The second important decision reached at Istanbul was the adoption of a European Security Charter, which included a 'platform for cooperative security'. The Charter defined the OSCE's role in European security and its relationship with other components of Europe's security architecture. It emphasized the OSCE's contribution to preventive diplomacy, crisis management and post-conflict rehabilitation, and created a number of new instruments with which to fulfil these roles. These included 'rapid expert assistance and cooperation teams' (REACT) and an operations centre within the OSCE's Conflict Prevention Centre.

Given the OSCE's primary responsibility for preventive diplomacy and crisis management, it was not surprising that the bulk of the organization's energy was focused throughout the year on the Balkans—in particular Kosovo (see also III.2.vi). The advent of 1999 found the OSCE struggling with its most ambitious and complex responsibility so far-deploying the Kosovo Verification Mission (KVM) set up in October 1998 (see AR 1998, p. 442). The KVM was supposed to verify the ceasefire, assist the return of refugees and displaced persons, and help promote human rights and democracy. Unfortunately, the ceasefire had virtually collapsed by March, while cooperation with officials of the Federal Republic of Yugoslavia broke down totally because the KVM was refused access to many areas. As the situation became increasingly ominous, the 1,400 OSCE verifiers were withdrawn on 19 March. Within a week, NATO began its aerial offensive on Serb positions in Yugoslavia.

During the Kosovo war itself (see III.2.vi), the OSCE took a back-seat to NATO, the European Union (EU) and the UN. Only when a diplomatic solution ended the military campaign in June (see XVII.1) did the OSCE resume a significant role. The mandate for a new OSCE mission in Kosovo was agreed on 1 July, the purpose of the 1,400-strong mission being to 'build a multi-ethnic society on the basis of substantial autonomy respecting the sovereignty and territorial integrity of the Federal Republic of Yugoslavia, pending final settlement in accordance with UN Security Council resolution 1244'. This involved establishing an OSCE police school, as well as training judicial and administrative personnel, developing the infrastructure of civil society, including a free media and a pluralist political party landscape; and working towards free elections. In addition to these responsibilities, the Stability Pact for South-Eastern Europe drawn up by in Sarajevo at the end of July was placed under the auspices of the OSCE by the EU. As the OSCE chairman-in-office noted, the OSCE faced 'its greatest challenge so far' in Kosovo. In taking up the challenge, he said, the OSCE had become 'the most important democracy-building organization in Europe'.

The OSCE was only one of many international organizations involved in efforts to bring peace and stability to the Balkans. This placed a premium on the ability of OSCE personnel to work with their counterparts in NATO, the EU, the Council of Europe and the UN. To this 'alphabet soup' of international organizations, however, the OSCE brought a unique perspective-an emphasis on 'human security'. As the Security Charter agreed at the Istanbul summit made clear, the OSCE sought to foster international security on the basis of 'human rights and fundamental freedoms', democracy and the peaceful settlement of disputes.

The principle of 'human security' provided the rationale for all of the OSCE's many and varied activities. It guided the work of the Office of Democratic

Institutions and Human Rights (ODIHR) in monitoring elections and advising on constitutional arrangements. It also provided the rational for the OSCE representative on freedom of the media (Freimut Duve) and for the OSCE high commissioner for national minorities (Max van der Stoel). During the year the OSCE organized a series of meetings and conferences around themes central to 'human security' in Europe. A 'freedom of religion' symposium was followed by one on 'gender issues' in Vienna in June which drew up a 'gender action plan' for approval and implementation by the OSCE. The rights of children, especially children caught up in armed conflict, and prejudice and discrimination against the Roma (Gypsy) and Sinti communities in Europe were also on the agenda. The OSCE had become increasingly concerned with the Roma and Sinti problem. At the Istanbul summit, participating countries committed themselves to addressing the problems of social exclusion and discrimination suffered by Roma and Sinti.

Whilst events in the Balkans dominated the OSCE's agenda in 1999, the organization was also involved in crisis-management and human security issues elsewhere, particularly in the former Soviet Union. In the Caucasus, the OSCE mission to Georgia was active in trying to negotiate peace in South Ossetia. Unfortunately, the Nagorno-Karabakh problem between Armenia and Azerbaijan remained in deadlock with no prospect for a peaceful political solution, although the five-year-old ceasefire was still holding (see III.3.iii). One positive development in the Caucasus was the opening of an OSCE office in Yerevan (Armenia) along with an agreement to open another in Baku (Azerbaijan). It was hoped that greater OSCE diplomatic influence in the troubled region would result.

One significant development in 1999 was the strengthened influence of the OSCE in the five ex-Soviet Central Asia republics, all OSCE member states. OSCE offices had been opened offices in the five republics, and all five states had signed a memorandum of understanding with the ODIHR. A planned visit to the region by the OSCE chairman-in-office had to be postponed because of the Kosovo crisis, but his personal representative went in his stead. The Central Asian states all stressed their growing concern about terrorism, drugs and arms-trafficking, violent extremism, trans-national criminal organizations, and shortages of water and energy. These problems had been exacerbated by the parlous condition of neighbouring Afghanistan (VIII.1.ii).

As the year drew to a close, the OSCE was able to point to three successes. The first was the closing-down of the Soviet-era Skrunda radar station in Latvia. Second, there was a successful completion of the OSCE mission to Ukraine, which had been tasked with promoting dialogue and understanding between the Russian community in Crimea and the Ukrainian authorities. Third, the process began of OSCE engagement in Belarus designed to facilitate democracy-building and respect for fundamental freedoms.

The approach of the new millennium provided an opportune moment for participating states to reflect on the strengths, weaknesses and potentialities of the OSCE. As the Istanbul document declared, in the three years since the

Lisbon summit the organization had greatly increased the number and size of its field operations. Its common institutions had also grown in number and in the level of their activities. The OSCE was now an established pillar of Europe's security architecture, and made a unique contribution to conflict prevention, crisis-management and post-conflict rehabilitation. Nonetheless, one practical problem had begun to undermine the effectiveness of the OSCE: its employment conditions were abysmal, with result that it was losing experienced and qualified staff to other international organizations. This problem was recognized by the Istanbul summit. Unless a speedy resolution was achieved, the effectiveness of the OSCE as a promoter of 'human security' would be sorely compromised.

iii. EUROPEAN BANK FOR RECONSTRUCTION AND DEVELOPMENT (EBRD)

DATE OF FOUNDATION: 1991   HEADQUARTERS: London, UK
OBJECTIVES: To promote the economic reconstruction of former Communist-ruled countries on the basis of the free-market system and pluralism
MEMBERSHIP (END-'99): Albania, Armenia, Australia, Austria, Azerbaijan, Belarus, Belgium, Bosnia & Hercegovina, Bulgaria, Canada, Croatia, Cyprus, Czech Republic, Denmark, Egypt, Estonia, European Investment Bank, European Union, Finland, France, Georgia, Germany, Greece, Hungary, Iceland, Ireland, Israel, Italy, Japan, Kazakhstan, Kyrgyzstan, South Korea, Latvia, Liechtenstein, Lithuania, Luxembourg, Macedonia, Malta, Mexico, Moldova, Morocco, Netherlands, New Zealand, Norway, Poland, Portugal, Romania, Russia, Slovakia, Slovenia, Spain, Sweden, Switzerland, Tajikistan, Turkey, Turkmenistan, Ukraine, United Kingdom, United States, Uzbekistan (*total* 60)
PRESIDENT: Horst Köhler (Germany)

MARKING the tenth anniversary of the fall of the Berlin Wall on 9 November, the EBRD first vice-president, Charles Frank, recorded that in its first eight years the bank had put 12,500 million euros into 586 projects in its 26 transition states, declaring that the EBRD's 'involvement in projects gives it enormous credibility in the policy dialogue with governments in our countries of operations' and that the bank's focus on private sector investment 'gives us a perspective on government policy issues unique among international financial institutions'.

By that contrast, Mr Frank seemed to be distancing the EBRD from the other institutions, and notably from the 'Washington consensus' of the IMF and the World Bank, which had evoked public criticism for their responses to the Asian and Russian financial crises and for the priority given by them to inflation reduction as condition for credits. The chief economist of the World Bank, Joseph Stiglitz, considered that such policies 'lead to institutional arrangements that reduce economic flexibility without gaining important growth benefits'. His counterpart in the EBRD, Nicholas Stern, wrote in the bank's 'Transition Report 1999' of 'strong and sobering lessons', continuing: 'It is now even more clear that institutional and behavioural underpinnings in much of the region are weak and that this weakness creates difficult and long-term challenges.'

The bank's annual meeting (London, 19-21 April) was indeed sober, for it had for the first time been confronted with a substantial loss, mainly because of the Russian default (see AR 1998, p. 444), and took place during the NATO air-strikes on Serbia, in which region the bank had committed Eur256 million to 24 projects in Albania, Bosnia & Hercegovina and Montenegro. Losses persisted in the first quarter of the year, but the account thereafter turned into a slim profit. Results for the full year showed an operating profit of Eur203.6 million, reduced by provisions of Eur160.9 million to a net profit of Eur42.7 million. In 1999 88 new projects, worth Eur2,200 million, were signed in 25 countries of EBRD operations.

The year's projects were most numerous in the finance of small and medium-sized enterprises and of micro-credits, that is of institutions lending small sums to individual entrepreneurs. But infrastructure—notably for water-supply and railways—was also a substantial part of the additional portfolio. In May a co-financing agreement was made with the Council of Europe's Social Development Fund covering all these objectives. The first beneficiary was the city of Kaunas, the inter-war capital of Lithuania, for improving energy efficiency. But large projects were still acceptable. It was reported in October that the bank was considering a Eur53.7 million investment in a Kosovo steel complex, the capacity of which would generate annually Eur200 million of exports. In the Azerbaijan section of the Caspian Sea the bank and the International Finance Corporation would each invest up to Eur180 million in offshore oil extraction and pipeline facilities. A contract for the first of the decommissioning facilities at the Chernobyl nuclear plant under the Nuclear Safety Account administered by the bank (see AR 1998, p. 445) was awarded in June.

iv. NORDIC, BALTIC AND ARCTIC ORGANIZATIONS

Nordic Council
DATE OF FOUNDATION: 1952   HEADQUARTERS: Stockholm, Sweden
OBJECTIVES: To facilitate legislative and governmental cooperation between member states, with particular reference to proposals of the Nordic Council of Ministers
MEMBERSHIP (END-'99): Denmark, Finland, Iceland, Norway, Sweden (*total* 5)
SECRETARY-GENERAL: Søren Christensen (Sweden)

Baltic Council
DATE OF FOUNDATION: 1992   HEADQUARTERS: rotating
OBJECTIVES: To promote political, economic and social cooperation between the three Baltic republics
MEMBERSHIP (END-'99): Estonia, Latvia, Lithuania (*total* 3)

Council of the Baltic Sea States (CBSS)
DATE OF FOUNDATION: 1992   HEADQUARTERS: Stockholm, Sweden
OBJECTIVES: To promote political, economic and other cooperation between Baltic littoral and adjacent states
MEMBERSHIP (END-'99): Denmark, Estonia, Finland, Germany, Latvia, Lithuania, Norway, Poland, Russia, Sweden (*total* 10)

Arctic Council (AC)
DATE OF FOUNDATION: 1996   HEADQUARTERS: Ottawa, Canada
OBJECTIVES: To promote cooperation between Arctic states (involving indigenous communities) on environmental issues and on the social and economic development of the region
MEMBERSHIP (END-'99): Canada, Denmark, Finland, Iceland, Norway, Russia, Sweden, United States (*total* 8)

THE year was notable for continued attempts to coordinate the work of existing Nordic, Baltic and Arctic regional organizations within the overarching framework of Finland's 1997 initiative on the 'Northern Dimension' (see AR 1997, p. 77). The Nordic Council in particular emerged as a key proponent of such enhanced interaction, sponsoring a number of new departures in regional cooperation.

A good example was the joint session of the Nordic Council and the Baltic Assembly in February, which emphasized the importance of a Nordic-Baltic component to the Northern Dimension. This was followed by the first joint meeting of Nordic and Baltic Ministers of Justice during November, when joint measures to combat juvenile delinquency and improve the functioning of the Baltic states' judicial systems figured high on the agenda. The Nordic grouping also continued to press for Latvia and Lithuania to be admitted to join Estonia as formal negotiators for European Union (EU) membership—a demand satisfied at the EU Helsinki summit in December (see XI.4).

Addressing the 14th session of the Baltic Assembly in Vilnius in May, Estonian Foreign Minister Toomas Hendrik Ilves underlined the 'complementarity' between Baltic cooperation and the respective EU integration strategies of the three countries. Estonia had fought hard to defend the Baltic Free Trade Agreement during its own EU membership negotiations, he added, whilst hinting at Latvia's threat to erect trade barriers as part of the ongoing 'pork war' between the two states. Estonia subsequently assumed the rotating presidency of the Baltic Council of Ministers at Palanga, Lithuania, in July. The latter meeting highlighted the need for further measures to free up movement of labour and services as part of moves to create a common Baltic states' economic area. In the same vein, the Baltic Assembly called for a common energy strategy in order to facilitate EU accession and participation in the proposed Baltic 'energy ring' (see AR 1998, p. 446).

At its eighth ministerial session, held at Palanga in June, the Council of the Baltic Sea States (CBSS) also reaffirmed the importance of the energy cooperation in terms of generating economic growth and long-term regional stability. Building on the establishment of a Baltic energy task force, Energy Ministers from the participating states met in Helsinki in October to discuss further initiatives in this field. At Palanga, the CBSS chairmanship passed to Norway, which began to pipe natural gas via Germany to Poland during the year. However, plans to extend this supply to the Baltic states remained politically sensitive given Russia's current dominance of the eastern Baltic gas market.

Greater economic integration was amongst the priorities identified by the Nordic Council at its 51st session in November. Commenting on a report entitled 'A Borderless Nordic Region', Swedish junior foreign minister Leif Pagrotsky spoke of the need to 'remove all unnecessary irrational and outdated barriers' between the Nordic states. In this regard, Nordic business circles seemed more pro-active than national governments, which continued to appear divided in terms of their attitudes towards EU integration. In keeping with its new-found freedom to discuss security policy, the Nordic Council nevertheless expressed support for the EU crisis management strategy unveiled during the year. It also pledged to maintain a closer dialogue with the European Parliament in matters pertaining to the Northern Dimension.

Another notable Nordic Council initiative was the organization's sponsorship of the first Barents Sea inter-parliamentary conference held at Alta, Norway, during July. As expected, the meeting focused on cooperation with Russia within the overall framework of Barents regional development. Meeting for their sixth session at Bodoe, Norway, during March, representatives of the Barents Euro-Arctic Region (BEAR) approved new initiatives in the spheres of health cooperation and educational exchange. Like their counterparts in the CBSS, however, BEAR participants noted that there was still much work to be done in terms of removing barriers to trade and investment in the region.

Amongst the many observers at the Bodoe meeting was US Deputy Secretary of State Strobe Talbott. Having assumed the two-year presidency of the Arctic Council in 1998, the US government expressed a desire for expanded cooperation and improved coordination with BEAR. The latter did indeed share many common objectives with the Arctic Council, whose senior officials discussed initiatives on public health, education and an action plan for the environment at their meeting in Anchorage, Alaska, in May.

v. OTHER EUROPEAN ORGANIZATIONS

European Free Trade Association (EFTA)
DATE OF FOUNDATION: 1960   HEADQUARTERS: Geneva, Switzerland
OBJECTIVES: To eliminate barriers to non-agricultural trade between members
MEMBERSHIP (END-'99): Iceland, Liechtenstein, Norway, Switzerland (*total* 4)
SECRETARY-GENERAL: Kjartan Jóhannsson (Iceland)

Central European Free Trade Association (CEFTA)
DATE OF FOUNDATION: 1992   HEADQUARTERS: rotating
OBJECTIVES: Reducing trade barriers between members with a view to their eventual membership of the European Union
MEMBERSHIP (END-'99): Bulgaria, Czech Republic, Hungary, Poland, Romania, Slovakia, Slovenia (*total* 7)

Visegrad Group
DATE OF FOUNDATION: 1991   HEADQUARTERS: rotating
OBJECTIVES: Reducing trade barriers between members with a view to their eventual membership of the European Union
MEMBERSHIP (END-'99): Czech Republic, Hungary, Poland, Slovakia (*total* 4)

Central European Initiative (CEI)
DATE OF FOUNDATION: 1992   HEADQUARTERS: rotating
OBJECTIVES: To promote the harmonization of economic and other policies of member states
MEMBERSHIP (END-'99): Albania, Austria, Belarus, Bosnia & Hercegovina, Bulgaria, Croatia, Czech Republic, Hungary, Italy, Macedonia, Moldova, Poland, Romania, Slovakia, Slovenia, Ukraine (*total* 16)

Black Sea Economic Cooperation Organization (BSECO)
DATE OF FOUNDATION: 1992   HEADQUARTERS: Istanbul, Turkey
OBJECTIVES: To promote economic cooperation between member states
MEMBERSHIP (END-'99): Albania, Armenia, Azerbaijan, Bulgaria, Georgia, Greece, Moldova, Romania, Russia, Turkey, Ukraine (*total* 11)
DIRECTOR: Vassil Baytchev

AFTER an eventful 1998 (see AR 1998, pp. 447-8), 1999 was a year in which there were fewer developments relating to the European Free Trade Association (EFTA). Negotiations to establish an EFTA-Canada free trade agreement continued, as did talks on the proposed EFTA-Cyprus free trade agreement. A declaration on cooperation with Lithuania was signed in Geneva on 11 February. In October the Swiss Federal Assembly ratified the free trade agreement negotiated with the European Union (EU) in December 1998 (see AR 1998, pp. 84-5). However, under the terms of the Swiss constitution, opponents of closer integration with the EU were able to force the holding of a referendum on the agreement, to be conducted in May 2000 (see II.3.vii).

The annual summit of the Central European Free Trade Association (CEFTA), held in Budapest on 20 October, was overshadowed by disputes among member states over varying levels of public subsidy for intra-CEFTA agricultural trade.

The forerunner to CEFTA, the Visegrad Group (formed in 1991), had been revived in 1998 partly because of CEFTA antagonisms over agricultural trade and the controversial question of whether there should be a political dimension to the association. Prime Ministers of the three Visegrad nations (Hungary, Poland and the Czech Republic) were joined by Mikulas Dzurinda, Prime Minister of the Slovak Republic, for a summit in Bratislava on 14 May. At a further meeting of the Visegrad four in the Slovak resort town of Tatranska Javorina on 16 October, it was agreed that a commission would be established to prevent cross-border crime. At the October meeting, the four Premiers also agreed to set up a secretariat in Bratislava to deal with issues related to the Roma (Gypsy) people, the treatment of whom had become a source of tension with EU members. At a meeting in the Slovakian town of Gerlachov on 3 December, the four nations announced their intention to create a Visegrad development fund. At a human rights conference in Bratislava on 10 December representatives from the Visegrad four formally requested that the EU provide financial assistance to resolve the social problems of the region's Roma population.

The Central European Initiative (CEI), with 16 member states, continued to be the biggest grouping of nations in Central and Eastern Europe. In 1999 the rotating presidency of the CEI was held by the Czech Republic and its activities were dominated by the Kosovo crisis and its aftermath (see III.2.vi). At a meeting in Lviv (Ukraine) on 15 May, the Presidents of nine CEI nations (Austria, Bulgaria, the Czech Republic, Germany, Hungary, Poland, Romania, Slovenia, and Ukraine) urged the Yugoslav government to accept the G-8 plan for ending the war in Kosovo. The Lviv meeting also proposed a high-level conference on South-Eastern Europe to establish a strategy for the economic reconstruction of the region and condemned ethnic cleansing in Kosovo. Although the leaders issued a statement deploring civilian deaths caused by NATO bombing of Yugoslavia, Ukrainian President Leonid Kuchma was the only head of state at the summit to call on NATO to stop its air strikes.

At a further CEI meeting in Karlovy Vary (Czech Republic) on 24 June, officials agreed that full democratization in Yugoslavia was essential for securing peace and stability in the Balkans. Jan Kavan, the Czech Foreign Minister, said that, whilst the CEI could establish working groups to deal with the region's economic revival, the main financing of regional recovery would have to be provided by the EU.

The CEI held its annual summit meeting in Prague on 3-6 November, together with an economic forum. Attended by 700 government and business leaders, the summit was dominated by the aftermath of the Kosovo crisis. The meeting endorsed UN Security Council resolution 1244 of 10 June and recognized the role of NATO in securing the withdrawal of Serb armed forces from Kosovo (see XVII.1). It also emphasized the importance of international coordination of the reconstruction of Kosovo and of assistance to other countries in the region affected by the crisis. Accordingly, a statement was issued saying that the CEI would 'actively participate' in the Stability Pact for South-Eastern Europe agreed in Sarajevo at the end of July. The summit leaders also noted their 'concern' over the need to remove debris caused by the NATO bombings from the Yugoslav section of the River Danube, as well as calling for the 'prompt start' of EU accession talks with Bulgaria, Romania and Slovakia.

Relations with the EU—specifically the possibility of future membership of the EU for member states—dominated the agenda in 1999 of the 11-nation Black Sea Economic Cooperation Organization (BSECO). Heads of state and government of the grouping met for a summit in the Ukranian town of Yalta on 10-11 September, when a forum entitled 'Baltic-Black Sea cooperation: towards an integrated Europe of the 21st century without dividing lines' was held. Attended by representatives from 22 countries from the Baltic and Black Sea regions, the forum included a scientific conference attended by 150 representatives from international organizations, including NATO, the EU, the Organization for Security and Cooperation in Europe (OSCE) and the Council of Europe. Reflecting on the symbolism of Yalta as a venue for the conference, President Kuchma of Ukraine commented that 'Europe was divided in Yalta once. Our main dream is that this should never happen again.'

In a further development, President Kuchma used the occasion of an informal BSECO summit on 17 November, prior to the OSCE summit in Istanbul on 18-19 November (see XI.5.ii), to propose the establishment of a free-trade zone in the Black Sea region. The Ukrainian President suggested that the creation of such a regional zone could give a 'powerful impetus' to regional cooperation. Observing that eventual membership of the EU was an 'objective necessity' for most members of the BSECO, Mr Kuchma stressed the importance of coordinating political and economic relations with the EU in order to 'prevent the appearance of new dividing lines on the continent'.

A declaration issued by the Istanbul summit 'applauded' the recent decision of the UN General Assembly to grant the BSECO official observer status, thus enabling it 'to join the family of international organizations as an equal partner'. A meeting of BSECO Foreign Ministers in Thessalonika (Greece) on 27 October had considered membership applications from Iran, Macedonia, Uzbekistan and Yugoslavia, but had deferred decisions on whether to accept them.

6. ARAB, AFRICAN, ASIA-PACIFIC AND AMERICAN ORGANIZATIONS

i. ARAB ORGANIZATIONS

League of Arab States
DATE OF FOUNDATION: 1945   HEADQUARTERS: Cairo, Egypt
OBJECTIVES: To coordinate political, economic, social and cultural cooperation between member states and to mediate in disputes between them
MEMBERSHIP (END-'99): Algeria, Bahrain, Comoros, Djibouti, Egypt, Iraq, Jordan, Kuwait, Lebanon, Libya, Mauritania, Morocco, Oman, Palestine, Qatar, Saudi Arabia, Somalia, Sudan, Syria, Tunisia, United Arab Emirates, Yemen (*total* 22)
SECRETARY-GENERAL: Ahmad Esmat Abdel Meguid (Egypt)

Gulf Cooperation Council (GCC)
DATE OF FOUNDATION: 1981   HEADQUARTERS: Riyadh, Saudi Arabia
OBJECTIVES: To promote cooperation between member states in all fields with a view to achieving unity
MEMBERSHIP (END-'98): Bahrain, Kuwait, Oman, Qatar, Saudi Arabia, United Arab Emirates (*total* 6)
SECRETARY-GENERAL: Jameel al-Hujilan (Saudi Arabia)

Arab Maghreb Union (AMU)
DATE OF FOUNDATION: 1989   HEADQUARTERS: Casablanca, Morocco
OBJECTIVES: To strengthen 'the bonds of brotherhood' between member states, particularly in the area of economic development
MEMBERSHIP (END-'99): Algeria, Libya, Mauritania, Morocco, Tunisia (*total* 5)
SECRETARY-GENERAL: Mohammed Amamou (Tunisia)

THE agenda for the ARAB LEAGUE during 1999 was dominated by the issue of Iraq, not least because, for the first time since the invasion of Kuwait in 1990, Iraq took the rotating chair of the organization. The year began with a furious argument in Cairo over the stand to be taken towards the Anglo-American bombing of Iraq in December 1998 (see AR 1998, p. 234). The Iraqi delegation, led by Foreign

Minister Said al-Sahhaf, stormed out of the meeting on 24 January when it refused to ignore the UN sanctions regime, insisting instead that Iraq should recognize Kuwaiti sovereignty and respect the sanctions regime as a first step. Nonetheless, although League secretary-general Esmat Abdel Meguid condemned Iraq in February for threatening to bomb Kuwaiti and Saudi air-bases used by British and American forces, he also led calls within the movement the following month for the bombing of Iraq to stop, after Saudi Arabia had blocked moves within the League for a debate to condemn Western policy.

At the end of April the League welcomed the UN decision to suspend sanctions against Libya in the wake of the Libyan decision to hand over the two accused in the Lockerbie affair for trial in The Netherlands (see V.4.ii). Despite pressure from League members and Libya itself for the organization to ignore the sanctions regime—as members of the Organization of African Unity had done in 1998, in a move which had hastened the final resolution of the Lockerbie crisis—the League had always refused to do this. In response, Libya's Colonel Qadafi directed his interests away from the Arab world and towards Africa during 1999 (see XI.6.ii).

The League also welcomed the decision of the European Union (EU) in March to support an independent Palestinian state, while also calling for greater assistance to the Palestinians and for European support for Syria and Lebanon in recovering control of their occupied territories. In September the organization repeated its condemnation of the US attack on a pharmaceutical plant in Sudan in August 1998 (see AR 1998, p. 245) and reiterated its support for Sudan's territorial integrity. The following month the League secretary-general raised concerns over Mauritania's decision to establish formal diplomatic relations with Israel, arguing that the move was inappropriate in the current diplomatic climate in the Middle East. Iraq responded by severing diplomatic relations with Mauritania, which was the third Arab League state to enter in relations with Israel (after Egypt and Jordan).

At the biannual meeting of League Foreign Ministers in September, the organization resisted calls from the Iraqi chairman of the meeting for a heads-of-state summit to condemn external threats to the region, particularly from the United States, but it did accept calls for a boycott of the Disney and Burger King US corporations. Disney was accused of supporting claims that Jerusalem was the capital of Israel in a new exhibition in its Epcot centre in Florida, whilst Burger King was attacked because its Israeli franchisee intended to open a branch in an Israeli settlement in the occupied West Bank. In the event, Burger King threatened to withdraw its franchise, so that the branch would not be opened, and the League accepted Disney's assurances that Israeli claims to Jerusalem would not be supported. Several League members voiced their disappointment with the outcome, fearing that Disney would do little to correct the error.

Arab League Finance Ministers and central bank governors met in Qatar in April to discuss the proposed Arab free trade area, which the League had put forward in 1996 and approved in principle the following year. They agreed that member states should establish a free trade area by 2007, after national external tariffs had been reduced by 10 per cent each year up to then. The project was given added urgency because of the EU's 'Barcelona process' and the separate economic agreement being negotiated between the EU and the Gulf Cooperation Council. The participants at the meeting also discussed a common economic strategy for the region, to be presented at the World Bank and IMF meetings in December.

Despite disagreements during 1999, the GULF COOPERATION COUNCIL (GCC) was able at the end of the year to launch its most ambitious project to date, the creation of a regional common market, thus marking its definitive transition into an instrument of economic integration 20 years after it was founded. An informal meeting of heads of state in Jiddah, attended by all except Oman and the United Arab Emirates (UAE), had set the tone in May, although no communiqué was issued. In June progress was interrupted by a row between Saudi Arabia and the UAE over the kingdom's apparent willingness to abandon the common GCC position of rejection of Iran's claims to the Tunbs Islands and Abu Musa in favour of a negotiated settlement (see also V.3.iii; VIII.1.i). The shock for the UAE was all the greater since earlier in the year the Arab states of the Gulf, together with the Arab League, had shown solidarity in condemning Iranian moves to integrate the administration of Abu Musa and Iranian naval exercises around the islands in dispute. A compromise was eventually patched together through Qatari mediation so that the UAE grudgingly agreed to consider negotiated solutions.

Even as the row continued, the GCC agreed to link national power grids, with Oman joining in the second phase of the initiative. The agreement seemed largely to have been motivated by a desire to prepare for the effects of economic globalization in the Gulf region. The most important moves in this direction, however, came on 27-29 November at the annual heads-of-state meeting in Riyadh. GCC members agreed to create a customs union by March 2005, with a common external tariff of 5.5 per cent for basic commodities and 7.5 per cent for luxuries. The level set for the union-to be implemented four years after the original schedule-reflected a compromise between the UAE preference for a 4-to-6 per cent band and the Saudi demand for an 8-to-12 per cent range. The summit came just after a Defence Ministers' meeting in the middle of the month at which a common defence strategy was discussed, although no decisions were taken. The customs union decision was to be seen in the context of the 1997 Arab League decision to create a common 10 per cent external tariff (within World Trade Organization rules), which had so far been accepted by 18 of the League's 22 member states. A GCC common market was also to be created by 2015 and member states had five years in which to apply the common external tariff.

The GCC heads-of-state decision was taken as negotiations on a GCC-EU free trade area continued interminably (see AR 1996, p. 410). The EU had made it clear to its prospective GCC partners that negotiations could not meaningfully progress until the GCC had a common external tariff agreement. Nor was the EU side prepared to consider dropping its 6 per cent tariff barrier against Gulf aluminium exports, even though the barrier was discriminatory and did not apply to exports from other parts of Europe. Despite enjoying a $19,000 million trade surplus with the GCC, the EU insisted that aluminium fell outside the scope of the free trade area discussions, although it did offer bilateral negotiations on the issue to the UAE-which were refused. The issue underlined the way in which the GCC was now preoccupied with economic issues as it faced the challenges of globalization, the WTO and the EU. By mutual, if grudging, agreement, the issue of the UAE-Iran dispute over the Tunbs islands and Abu Musa was put into suspension for the six months at the end of the year.

The DAMASCUS DECLARATION organization, which had brought Syria and Egypt together with the six Gulf states in a mutual defence arrangement after the war against Iraq in 1991, did not meet during the year. The ARAB MAGHREB UUNION, which had been in a moribund state since sanctions were imposed on Libya in 1992, appeared to be about to be revived in the wake of the suspension of the UN sanctions regime against Libya. However, despite a preparatory meeting in Algiers in May and Tunisian efforts to reactivate the grouping (see V.4.iii), little progress was made, largely because of the continuing tensions between Algeria and Morocco.

ii. AFRICAN ORGANIZATIONS AND CONFERENCES

Organization of African Unity (OAU)
DATE OF FOUNDATION: 1963   HEADQUARTERS: Addis Ababa, Ethiopia
OBJECTIVES: To promote the unity, solidarity and cooperation of African states, to defend their sovereignty and to eradicate remaining traces of colonialism
MEMBERSHIP (END-'99): Algeria, Angola, Benin, Botswana, Burkina Faso, Burundi, Cameroon, Cape Verde, Central African Republic, Chad, Comoros, Democratic Republic of the Congo, Republic of Congo, Côte d'Ivoire, Djibouti, Egypt, Equatorial Guinea, Eritrea, Ethiopia, Gabon, Gambia, Ghana, Guinea, Guinea-Bissau, Kenya, Lesotho, Liberia, Libya, Madagascar, Malawi, Mali, Mauritania, Mauritius, Morocco, Mozambique, Namibia, Niger, Nigeria, Rwanda, Sahrawi Arab Democratic Republic, São Tomé & Príncipe, Senegal, Seychelles, Sierra Leone, Somalia, South Africa, Sudan, Swaziland, Tanzania, Togo, Tunisia, Uganda, Zambia, Zimbabwe (*total* 54)
SECRETARY-GENERAL: Salim Ahmed Salim (Tanzania)

Economic Community of West African States (ECOWAS)
DATE OF FOUNDATION: 1975   HEADQUARTERS: Abuja, Nigeria
OBJECTIVES: To seek the creation of an economic union of member states
MEMBERSHIP (END-'99): Benin, Burkina Faso, Cape Verde, Côte d'Ivoire, Gambia, Ghana, Guinea, Guinea-Bissau, Liberia, Mali, Niger, Nigeria, Senegal, Sierra Leone, Togo (*total* 15)
EXECUTIVE SECRETARY: Lamine Kouyaté (Guinea)

West African Economic and Monetary Union (UEMOA)
DATE OF FOUNDATION: 1994   HEADQUARTERS: Ouagadougou, Burkina Faso
OBJECTIVES: To promote the economic and monetary union of member states
MEMBERSHIP (END-'99): Benin, Burkina Faso, Côte d'Ivoire, Guinea-Bissau, Mali, Mauritania, Niger, Senegal (*total* 8)

Southern African Development Community (SADC)
DATE OF FOUNDATION: 1992   HEADQUARTERS: Gaborone, Botswana
OBJECTIVES: To work towards the creation of a regional common market
MEMBERSHIP (END-'99): Angola, Botswana, Democratic Republic of the Congo, Lesotho, Malawi, Mauritius, Mozambique, Namibia, Seychelles, South Africa, Swaziland, Tanzania, Zambia, Zimbabwe (*total* 14)
EXECUTIVE SECRETARY: Pakereesamy (Prega) Ramsamy (Mauritius), acting

Common Market for Eastern and Southern Africa (COMESA)
DATE OF FOUNDATION: 1993 (succeeding Preferential Trade Area)   HEADQUARTERS: Lusaka, Zambia
OBJECTIVES: To establish a full free-trade area
MEMBERSHIP (END-'99): Angola, Burundi, Comoros, Democratic Republic of the Congo, Egypt, Eritrea, Ethiopia, Kenya, Lesotho, Madagascar, Malawi, Mauritius, Mozambique, Namibia, Rwanda, Sudan, Swaziland, Uganda, Zambia, Zimbabwe (*total* 20)
SECRETARY-GENERAL: Erastus Mwencha (Kenya)

Economic Community of Central African States (CEEAC)
DATE OF FOUNDATION: 1983   HEADQUARTERS: Libreville, Gabon
OBJECTIVES: To establish a full free-trade area
MEMBERSHIP (END-'99): Angola, Burundi, Cameroon, Central African Republic, Chad, Democratic Republic of the Congo, Republic of the Congo, Equatorial Guinea, Gabon, Rwanda, São Tomé & Príncipe (*total* 11)
SECRETARY-GENERAL: Louis-Sylvain Goma (Republic of the Congo)

East African Commission (EAC)
DATE OF FOUNDATION: 1996 (reviving former East African Community)   HEADQUARTERS: Nairobi, Kenya
OBJECTIVES: To promote economic integration between member states
MEMBERSHIP (END-'99): Kenya, Tanzania, Uganda (*total* 3)

ORGANIZATION OF AFRICAN UNITY. The annual summit of the Organization of African Unity (OAU) was held in Algiers on 12-16 July. There was a very high attendance of heads of state and government, in part because the summit marked the re-entry of Algeria under its new President Abdulaziz Bouteflika to a more active role in African diplomacy after years of being absorbed with its own internal conflicts (see V.4.iv). The summit also saw two other major new faces-President Thabo Mbeki of South Africa, newly-elected successor to Nelson Mandela (see VII.3), and President Olusegun Obasanjo of Nigeria, also newly elected in Nigeria's first properly-conducted (and completed) democratic election since 1979 (see VI.2.ii). The three were said to have formed an operational coalition at the summit which presaged an African revival, in the spirit of South Africa's much trumpeted African renaissance. It was certainly a more conducive atmosphere than the previous year's summit in Ouagadougou (see AR 1998, 453-5), which was ushered in by two coups and a war. However, in spite of a certain euphoria, there was much awareness that all was not well on the African continent. President Bouteflika, the new chairman, stated it bluntly: 'Africa is sick!', he said, while President Mbeki urged Africans not to 'avoid the truth because we want to be polite to one another'.

On the year-old conflict between Ethiopia and Eritrea, in which the OAU's mediation had produced a semi-permanent ceasefire (see VI.1.i), there was a slight move forward at the summit after several false starts. Colonel Qadafi of Libya, attending his first OAU summit since 1977, had been disappointed when Eritrea's President Issaias Afewerki failed to arrive in Tripoli for pre-OAU talks with the Ethiopian Prime Minister, Meles Zenawi. In Algiers it was reported that both sides were persuaded to accept the OAU's negotiating framework, which included a return to pre-May 1998 borders. Mediation would now be conducted by a smaller group headed by President Bouteflika. However, the framework was still felt to be a fragile basis for further discussions, since the full acceptance by both parties was in fact not clear.

Shortly before the summit two peace accords appeared to presage the ending of two of the most serious conflicts afflicting the continent—in Sierra Leone and the Democratic Republic of the Congo (DRC). The ECOWAS-brokered Lomé agreement on Sierra Leone, for which the OAU was a moral guarantor, appeared to be the more improbable of the two in view of the bitterness the conflict had generated, but by the end of the year it was the one which had miraculously held (see VI.2.iii). The Lusaka accord on the DRC barely survived the summit, since the rebels had not signed it; in spite of numerous attempts to apply it, the conflict rumbled on past the end of the year (see VII.1.i).

This perhaps was the measure of 'Africa's first world war', as the DRC conflict was called because so many parties were involved in it, making resolution impossibly difficult. Even so, it was taken as a failure on the part of Africa that the fighting dragged on. Here too President Qadafi appeared to seek an unaccustomed role as peace-maker: it was certainly his intervention at a summit in Sirte in May, attended by the main heads of state involved (though not all the rebel faction leaders), which permitted the disengagement of Chadian troops. Colonel Qadafi later organized an OAU summit of his own in Tripoli to mark his 30th anniversary in power (see V.4.ii). It was attended by 44 African leaders, who approved a vague plan for African unity separate from the OAU's plan for an African Economic Community, which was still due, in principle, to be realized within the next ten years.

One particular issue at the OAU summit was that of coups in Africa—there had been three in April and May (in Niger, Comoros and Guinea-Bissau). Many of the leaders assembled in Algiers were keen to take a strong line condemning those coming to power by force, even if it meant ostracizing some of those present, such as President Sassou-Nguesso of Congo-Brazzaville. One or two recent putschists, such as Major Wanké of Niger (see VI.3.i) were even dissuaded from attending the summit. The anti-coup line was pushed in particular by President Obasanjo, who said: 'We must not have any excuses, diplomatic or expedient, for sitting down with those whose actions have clearly shown that they do not deserve respectability.' The hardliners had sought unlimited retrospective action against any putschist government, but the rule was watered down to apply to governments coming to power through force since the OAU summit in Harare in 1997. The Algiers summit left it to OAU secretary-general Salim Ahmed Salim to assess what regimes that were breaking the rule would have to do to restore constitutional legitimacy.

A gloomier view of Africa came from the executive secretary of the UN Economic Commission for Africa, K.Y. Amoako, who said that there had been growth in only two of Africa's five sub-regions in 1998 and that the economies had contracted in the three sub-regions where 75 per cent of Africans lived. War and political instability had added to the decline, he said, warning that unless OAU member governmentts moved to end the political chaos, the continent would keep going backwards.

The summit approved a broad and general Algiers Declaration on conflict resolution and human rights. Nigeria's proposal that the year 2000 be declared the year of peace, security and solidarity in Africa was also approved.

REGIONAL ORGANIZATIONS. The annual summit of the Southern African Development Community (SADC) held in Maputo, Mozambique, in August (see also VII.2.iv), was inevitably dominated by the SADC-led mediation of President Chiluba of Zambia on the DRC conflict, although any prospect for taking it further was blocked by the non-appearance of President Kabila. The SADC also had tentative discussions on trade liberalization and decided not to renew the contract of Kaire Mbuende (Namibia) as its executive secretary, his deputy, Prega Pakereesamy Ramsamy of Mauritius, succeeding to the post in an acting capacity. Trade questions were strictly speaking the preserve of the wider Common Market for Eastern and Southern Africa (COMESA), which held a summit in Nairobi, Kenya, in May. The summiteers agreed to work towards the elimination of trade barriers by October 2000 and the creation of a common external tariff by 2004. But COMESA's credibility was damaged by Tanzania's withdrawal in September, announced by President Mkapa on the grounds that his government could not cope with membership of so many organizations and that the SADC should have priority.

In East Africa, the East African Commission established in 1997 by Kenya, Tanzania and Uganda had been due to be transformed into a full East African Community by July, but because of a number of hitches the official establishment was postponed. In December, however, the three Presidents signed a framework agreement in Arusha providing for the re-establishment of the Community (which had collapsed in 1977) and envisaging the creation of a customs union and common market leading eventually to monetary union and political federation.

The 1999 summit of Economic Community of West African States (ECOWAS) was held in Lomé, Togo, on 7-8 December. It did little more than endorse the Sierra Leone peace pact and pass its chair from President Eyadéma of Togo to President Konaré of Mali. The departure of Mauritania from the organization, reducing the number of member states to 15, if anything clarified the membership issue. There was always the competition afforded by the West African Economic and Monetary Union (UEMOA), which was much further advanced in economic integration. However, the Côte d'Ivoire coup (see VI.3.i) was not exactly encouraging to investors in the year which saw the opening of the UEMOA stock exchange in Abidjan.

In Central Africa there was a similar symbiosis of groupings between the Economic Community of Central African States (CEEAC) and the francophone Economic and Monetary Community of Central Africa (CEMAC), which held a joint summit in Malabo, Equatorial Guinea, in June. In the same region a 'tropical rainforest summit' of five Central African states (Cameroon, Congo, Gabon, Equatorial Guinea and the Central African Republic), between them covering six million hectares of forest, was held in Yaoundé, Cameroon, in March, with the encouragement of the World Wildlife Fund and attended by the Duke of Edinburgh.

The airline Air Afrique, in which ten francophone African countries had the largest part of the shareholding, began the year sinking into ever-deeper trouble in 1999. The Mauritian Sir Harry Tirvengadum, who had been brought in two years earlier to try and mastermind the airline's putative privatization, announced his departure for 'health reasons'. Although he had been able to bring the airline back to profit, he lacked support from the shareholders for his recapitalization scheme. He was replaced by the Senegalese Pape Sow Thiam, who still faced intact the airline's unacceptable debt burden of 200,000 million CFA francs, for which privatization had been deemed the only solution.

iii. ASIA-PACIFIC ORGANIZATIONS

Association of South-East Asian Nations (ASEAN)

DATE OF FOUNDATION: 1967   HEADQUARTERS: Jakarta, Indonesia
OBJECTIVES: To accelerate economic growth, social progress and cultural development in the region
MEMBERSHIP (END-'99): Brunei, Cambodia, Indonesia, Laos, Malaysia, Myanmar, Philippines, Singapore, Thailand, Vietnam (*total* 10)
SECRETARY-GENERAL: Rodolfo C.Severino (Philippines)

Asia-Pacific Economic Cooperation (APEC)

DATE OF FOUNDATION: 1989   HEADQUARTERS: Singapore
OBJECTIVES: To promote market-oriented economic development and cooperation in the Pacific Rim countries
MEMBERSHIP (END-'99): Australia, Brunei, Canada, Chile, China, Hong Kong, Indonesia, Japan, South Korea, Malaysia, Mexico, New Zealand, Papua New Guinea, Peru, Philippines, Russia, Singapore, Taiwan, Thailand, United States, Vietnam (*total* 21)
EXECUTIVE: Timothy Hannah (New Zealand)

South Asian Association for Regional Cooperation (SAARC)

DATE OF FOUNDATION: 1985   HEADQUARTERS: Kathmandu, Nepal
OBJECTIVES: To promote collaboration and mutual assistance in the economic, social, cultural and technical fields
MEMBERSHIP (END-'99): Bangladesh, Bhutan, India, Maldives, Nepal, Pakistan, Sri Lanka (*total* 7)
SECRETARY-GENERAL: Nacem ul-Hasan (Pakistan)

Indian Ocean Rim Association for Regional Cooperation (IORARC)

DATE OF FOUNDATION: 1997
OBJECTIVES: To promote cooperation in trade, investment, infrastructure, tourism, science, technology and human-resource development in the Indian Ocean region
MEMBERSHIP (END-'99): Australia, India, Indonesia, Kenya, Madagascar, Malaysia, Mauritius, Mozambique, Oman, Singapore, South Africa, Sri Lanka, Tanzania, Yemen (*total* 14)

Pacific Community (PC)

DATE OF FOUNDATION: 1947 (as South Pacific Commission)   HEADQUARTERS: Nouméa, New Caledonia
OBJECTIVES: To facilitate political and other cooperation between member states and territories
MEMBERSHIP (END-'99): American Samoa, Australia, Cook Islands, Fiji, France, French Polynesia, Guam, Kiribati, Marshall Islands, Federated States of Micronesia, Nauru, New Caledonia, New Zealand, Niue, Northern Mariana Islands, Palau, Papua New Guinea, Pitcairn Islands, Samoa, Solomon Islands, Tokelau, Tonga, Tuvalu, United Kingdom, United States, Vanuatu, Wallis & Futuna Islands (*total* 27)
DIRECTOR-GENERAL: Lourdes Pangelinan (Guam)

Pacific Islands Forum (PIF)
DATE OF FOUNDATION: 1971 (as South Pacific Forum)   HEADQUARTERS: Suva, Fiji
OBJECTIVES: To enhance the economic and social well-being of the people of the Pacific, in support of the efforts of the members' governments
MEMBERSHIP (END-'99): Australia, Palau, Cook Islands, Fiji, Kiribati, Marshall Islands, Federated States of Micronesia, Nauru, New Zealand, Niue, Papua New Guinea, Samoa, Solomon Islands, Tonga, Tuvalu, Vanuatu (*total* 16)
SECRETARY-GENERAL: Noel Levi (Papua New Guinea)

ASSOCIATION OF SOUTH-EAST ASIAN NATIONS. Cambodia was formally admitted as the 10th member of the Association of South-East Asian Nations (ASEAN) at a ceremony attended by ASEAN Foreign Ministers in Hanoi, the Vietnamese capital, in April. It had originally been intended that Cambodia would join ASEAN alongside Laos and Burma in July 1997 (see AR 1998, p. 459). However, Cambodian membership was delayed pending a settlement of the internal conflict which had erupted in the country following the seizure of power by Hun Sen. Cambodia's much-delayed entry into ASEAN was hailed by some as marking the formal end to decades of Cold War turmoil in South-East Asia. However, Cambodia's admission came as the region was in the throes of an economic crisis and as differences were growing within ASEAN over issues of democracy and human rights, so that some commentators feared that Cambodia might destabilize ASEAN by bringing its seemingly intractable domestic problems to the forum. Concern was also expressed that the regional grouping's future might be troubled if Cambodia and Laos, along with their mentor Vietnam, formed a lobby group within ASEAN to protect their interests. It was argued that such a faction inside ASEAN could reduce the regional grouping's bargaining power and neutralize any gains expected from increased membership.

Since the Asian financial crisis had erupted in mid-1997, relations between some ASEAN members had been strained, while largest member Indonesia had been shaken by political instability amid fears of a possible break-up (see IX.1.vi). Several disputes had occurred between Singapore and Malaysia over sharing of resources, while the Philippines and Malaysia had exchanged angry words over President Joseph Estrada's open support for imprisoned Malaysian politician Anwar Ibrahim (see IX.1.iii; IX.1.vii).

Against this background, routine ASEAN meetings were held throughout the year. Foreign Ministers held their annual session in July in Singapore. It was followed by a meeting, also held in Singapore, of the ASEAN Regional Forum (ARF), the multilateral group established in 1993 to discuss regional and security issues. Speaking at the latter gathering, US Secretary of State Madeleine Albright expressed concern over rising tensions in the South China Sea caused by sovereignty disputes over the Spratly Islands, which had been the cause of a number of recent incidents. The Spratlys were claimed wholly or in part by ASEAN members Brunei, Malaysia, the Philippines and Vietnam, and also by China and Taiwan.

ASEAN leaders held an informal summit in Manila, the Philippines, in late November. The ten leaders were joined by the heads of government of China, Japan and South Korea in reaching agreement on a framework for East Asian economic cooperation. Although the plan lacked concrete detail, it was regarded as a foundation for a long-term project of integration. The ASEAN leaders committed themselves to accelerating trade liberalization within the region by advancing the final elimination of import duties by the association's 1967 founding members (Indonesia, Malaysia, the Philippines, Singapore and Thailand) and Brunei (1984) from the year 2015 to 2010. For the more recent members (Vietnam, Burma, Laos and Cambodia), the schedule was advanced from 2018 to 2015. The summit also approved a code of conduct to prevent conflicts between members over the disputed Spratly Islands. Although China opposed the code of conduct, Prime Minister Zhu Rongji gave the summit the reassurance that China would 'never seek hegemony' in the region.

The presence of the Myanmar (Burmese) military junta within ASEAN's ranks did little to improve the organization's relations with the European Union (EU) during 1999. It was announced in February that a meeting of ASEAN and EU Foreign Ministers, scheduled to be held in Germany in late March, had been postponed indefinitely because of the UK's objection to the inclusion of Myanmar on the grounds of its poor human rights record. This followed the cancellation of a meeting between EU commissioners and ASEAN officials in January because of the EU's suggestion that the Myanmar delegate should be seated behind a plaque marked 'ASEAN-New Member'.

ASIA-PACIFIC ECONOMIC COOPERATION. The seventh summit of the 21-member Asia-Pacific Economic Cooperation (APEC) forum was held in mid-September in Auckland, New Zealand. The sixth summit, in November 1998, had been a stormy affair which had descended into open bickering between the USA and the host country, Malaysia (see AR 1998, pp. 460-2). By contrast, the Auckland summit was a quiet affair. The closing declaration, summarized by its chairwoman, New Zealand Prime Minister Jenny Shipley, was wholly economic in character, affirming APEC's commitment to promoting economic growth in the region, opening and strengthening markets, enhancing competitiveness and improving financial regulation. APEC leaders also agreed to give strong support to the launch of a new round of multilateral trade negotiations in November under the auspices of the World Trade Organization (WTO) (see XI.2.ii).

Meetings were held on the sidelines of the APEC summit in a bid to secure support for the sending of a UN peace-keeping force to East Timor (see IX.1.vi). In these exchanges South Korea and Japan bridged the gap between countries such as the USA, Australia, New Zealand and Canada, which were pressing for UN intervention, and ASEAN members which feared that interfering in Indonesia's internal affairs might destabilize the country. President Bill Clinton of the USA and President Jiang Zemin of China took the opportunity of their presence in Auckland to hold talks on China's bid for WTO membership and tensions between China and Taiwan (see also IX.2.i). Their meeting marked a relaxation of relations between the two countries which had been strained since NATO's accidental bombing of the Chinese embassy in Yugoslavia in May (see III.2.vi).

At a meeting of APEC Finance Ministers in Malaysia in May, Japanese Finance Minister Kiichi Miyazawa had announced that Japan would guarantee US$17,000 million worth of government bonds to help finance the efforts of emerging economies recovering from financial crisis. The tone of the meeting's closing communiqué was cautiously optimistic, but agreed on the need for further structural reforms in Asian economies. China did not attend the meeting because of a dispute over the composition of the delegation from Taiwan (see IX.2.iii).

SOUTH ASIAN ASSOCIATION FOR REGIONAL COOPERATION. The Foreign Ministers of the seven-member South Asian Association for Regional Cooperation (SAARC) met in Nuwara Eliya, Sri Lanka, in mid-March. The closing statement announced increased cooperation with the EU in several fields, and the decision to set up a committee to plan for a South Asian Free Trade Area (SAFTA), due to be established in 2001. At a meeting on the sidelines the Foreign Ministers of India and Pakistan announced a six-point action programme to accelerate the normalization of bilateral relations-which nevertheless descended into open conflict in Kashmir two months later (see VIII.2.i). The 11th SAARC summit scheduled to be held in late November in Kathmandu, the Nepalese capital, was postponed indefinitely at the request of India because of the October military coup in Pakistan (see VIII.2.ii).

ASIAN DEVELOPMENT BANK. In early 1999 Tadeo Chino replaced Mitsuo Sato as president of the Asian Development Bank (ADB), the region's leading multilateral lending institution. In November the ADB announced that it would henceforth focus on small-scale lending in a change of strategy that would direct its $6,000 million annual lending programme towards alleviating poverty. Micro-finance, alongside rural electrification and farm-to-market roads, would be one of several new areas of focus.

PACIFIC GROUPINGS. Representatives of the 16-member South Pacific Forum (SPF) attended the 30th annual heads of government summit in early October in the Micronesian state of Palau. The Prime Ministers of Australia, Fiji and Papua New Guinea failed to attend the meeting, at which the crisis in East Timor, over-fishing and free trade were amongst the items discussed. President Teburoro Tito of Kiribati told journalists at the close of the meeting that the leaders had agreed unanimously to change the organization's name to the Pacific Islands Forum (PIF).

At the 29th annual conference of the Pacific Community (formerly the South Pacific Commission), held in November in Papeete, French Polynesia, Guam's Lourdes Pangelinan was elected as director-general, thus becoming the first woman to head a Pacific regional organization. The theme of the 1999 conference was 'New Technologies: Knowledge and Information in the Pacific Islands'.

The 13th summit of the Melanesian Spearhead Group (MSG) was held in Port Vila, the capital of Vanuatu, in early July. It was agreed to set up standing committees and a permanent MSG secretariat. Also in Port Vila, representatives from Tonga, Samoa, Vanuatu, Fiji, Marshall Islands and Hawaii held the first meeting in mid-July of the Pacific Islands Kava Council. Shortly afterwards the Marshall Islands hosted a workshop on climate change and sea-level rise for the 32-member Alliance of Small Island States (AOSIS).

iv. AMERICAN AND CARIBBEAN ORGANIZATIONS

Organization of American States (OAS)
DATE OF FOUNDATION: 1951   HEADQUARTERS: Washington DC, USA
OBJECTIVES: To facilitate political, economic and other cooperation between member states and to defend their territorial integrity and independence
MEMBERSHIP (END-'99): Antigua & Barbuda, Argentina, Bahamas, Barbados, Belize, Bolivia, Brazil, Canada, Chile, Colombia, Costa Rica, Cuba (*currently excluded*), Dominica, Dominican Republic, Ecuador, El Salvador, Grenada, Guatemala, Guyana, Haiti, Honduras, Jamaica, Mexico, Nicaragua, Panama, Paraguay, Peru, St Kitts & Nevis, St Lucia, St Vincent & the Grenadines, Suriname, Trinidad & Tobago, United States, Uruguay, Venezuela (*total* 35)
SECRETARY-GENERAL: César Gaviria Trujillo (Colombia)

Rio Group
DATE OF FOUNDATION: 1987   HEADQUARTERS: rotating
OBJECTIVES: To provide a regional mechanism for joint political action
MEMBERSHIP (END-'99): Argentina, Bolivia, Brazil, Chile, Colombia, Ecuador, Guatemala, Mexico, Panama, Paraguay, Peru, Trinidad & Tobago, Uruguay, Venezuela (*total* 14)

Southern Common Market (Mercosur)
DATE OF FOUNDATION: 1991   HEADQUARTERS: Montevideo, Uruguay
OBJECTIVES: To build a genuine common market between member states
MEMBERSHIP (END-'99): Argentina, Brazil, Paraguay, Uruguay (*total* 4)
ADMINISTRATIVE SECRETARY: Ramón Díaz Pereira (Brazil)

Andean Community of Nations (Ancom/CA)
DATE OF FOUNDATION: 1969   HEADQUARTERS: Lima, Peru
OBJECTIVES: To promote the economic development and integration of member states
MEMBERSHIP (END-'99): Bolivia, Colombia, Ecuador, Venezuela (*total* 4)
SECRETARY-GENERAL: Sebastián Alegrett (Venezuela)

Latin American Integration Association (ALADI)
DATE OF FOUNDATION: 1980 (as successor to Latin American Free Trade Association founded in 1960)
HEADQUARTERS: Montevideo, Uruguay
OBJECTIVES: To promote Latin American trade and development by economic preference
MEMBERSHIP (END-'99): Argentina, Bolivia, Brazil, Chile, Colombia, Cuba, Ecuador, Mexico, Paraguay, Peru, Uruguay, Venezuela (*total* 12)
SECRETARY-GENERAL: Juan Francisco Rojas Penso (Venezuela)

Latin American Economic System (SELA)
DATE OF FOUNDATION: 1975   HEADQUARTERS: Caracas, Venezuela
OBJECTIVES: To accelerate economic and social development in member states
MEMBERSHIP (END-'99): Argentina, Barbados, Bolivia, Brazil, Chile, Costa Rica, Cuba, Dominican Republic, Ecuador, El Salvador, Grenada, Guatemala, Guyana, Haiti, Honduras, Jamaica, Mexico, Nicaragua, Panama, Paraguay, Peru, Spain, Suriname, Trinidad & Tobago, Uruguay, Venezuela (*total* 27)
PERMANENT SECRETARY: Carlos Moneta (Argentina)

Caribbean Community and Common Market (Caricom)
DATE OF FOUNDATION: 1973   HEADQUARTERS: Georgetown, Guyana
OBJECTIVES: To facilitate economic, political and other cooperation between member states and to operate certain regional services
MEMBERSHIP (END-'99): Antigua & Barbuda, Bahamas, Barbados, Belize, Dominica, Grenada, Guyana, Haiti, Jamaica, Montserrat, St Kitts & Nevis, St Lucia, St Vincent & the Grenadines, Suriname, Trinidad & Tobago (*total* 15)
SECRETARY-GENERAL: Edwin Carrington (Trinidad & Tobago)

Association of Caribbean States (ACS)
DATE OF FOUNDATION: 1994   HEADQUARTERS: Port of Spain, Trinidad
OBJECTIVES: To foster economic, social and political cooperation with a view to building a distinctive bloc of Caribbean littoral states
MEMBERSHIP (END-'99): Caricom members (*see above*) plus Colombia, Costa Rica, Cuba, Dominican Republic, El Salvador, Guatemala, Haiti, Honduras, Mexico, Nicaragua, Venezuela (*total* 25)
SECRETARY-GENERAL: Simón Molina Duarte (Venezuela)

Organization of Eastern Caribbean States (OECS)
DATE OF FOUNDATION: 1981   HEADQUARTERS: Castries, St Lucia
OBJECTIVES: To coordinate the external, defence, trade and monetary policies of member states
MEMBERSHIP (END-'99): Antigua & Barbuda, Dominica, Grenada, Montserrat, St Lucia, St Kitts & Nevis, St Vincent & the Grenadines (*total* 7)
DIRECTOR-GENERAL: Swinburne Lestrade (Dominica)

AT the 29th regular meeting of the general assembly of the Organization of American States (OAS) in Guatemala City in June César Gaviria Trujillo of Colombia was re-elected for a further five-year term as secretary-general. All 34 active member states in the 35-member organization attended. Among the issues addressed in the 59-item agenda were the modernization of the OAS and renewal of the inter-American system; support for and follow-up on the 'Summit of the Americas' initiatives; and evaluation of the workings of mechanisms for the promotion and protection of human rights with a view to its strengthening and improvement. Earlier, in April, the Prime Minister of Grenada, Dr Keith Mitchell, had called on the OAS to take a role in resolving the trade dispute between the United States and the European Union (EU), stressing the grave social consequences for the island states if they lost their European market (see also XI.4).

Peru withdrew from the jurisdiction if the Inter-American Court of Human Rights (IAHCR) on 7 July, following a ruling by the court that four Chileans given life sentences in military courts, in which they could not contest or even examine the evidence against them, should receive new trials. The IACHR ruled on 27 September that the Peruvian decision to withdraw from the convention, without giving the required year's notice, was 'inadmissible', giving rise to the possibility that sanctions might be imposed by the OAS general assembly in June 2000.

Mexico's partners in the North American Free Trade Agreement (NAFTA) agreed on 15 June to support the Banco de México with US$6,000 million of credit from the US Federal Reserve and US$800 million from the Bank of Canada (see also IV.3.xiv).

A joint declaration on 6 June by their two Presidents that Argentina and Brazil would adopt roughly comparable mechanisms of financial restraint was presented as a step towards enhanced unity within the South Common Market (Mercosur). On 26 July, however, Argentina tried unilaterally to impose measures against excessive imports from any country, including its Mercosur partners. Brazil immediately broke off all negotiations with Argentina, which was forced to withdraw the decree three days later, though restrictions on the import of Brazilian textiles, imposed earlier, remained in place. At the 17th Mercosur summit held in Montevideo, Uruguay, on 8 December, the member states endorsed common standards for financial restraint and agreed to harmonize their national statistics, but failed to agree a new regime for motor vehicles, which made up 30 per cent of intra-regional trade.

Bloc-to-bloc negotiations between Mercosur and the Andean Community (Ancom) had collapsed at the end of March, when existing bilateral trade preferences between invidivual countries, negotiated under the auspices of the Latin American Integration Association (ALADI), were due to expire. Three Mercosur countries (Argentina, Paraguay and Uruguay) agreed to extend them until the end of 1999. Brazil, however, opted to extend bilateral preferences for only six months and in early April opened negotiations for a unilateral free trade agreement with Ancom, though under ALADI terms.

The unilateral decision on 12 May of the new Venezuelan government to close its frontier to Colombian long-haul trucks for a year was denounced by Colombia as a breach of Ancom agreements. On 11 July the Venezuelan ambassador to Bogotá was recalled for consultations following 'disrespectful' criticism of the law by the Colombian Foreign Minister, Marta Lucia Ramírez, while visiting Caracas. However on 13 July the ANCOM secretariat set Venezuela a 30-day deadline for the lifting of the restrictions.

An EU/Latin American/Caribbean summit held in Rio de Janeiro, Brazil, on 28-29 June was attended by 48 heads of state or government. The first of its kind, it was marked by an agreement between the EU and Mercosur to initiate discussions in November with a view to forming an integrated trading bloc some time after 2001. At the same time, Brazil announced the successful conclusion of its negotiations with Ancom.

The ninth Ibero-American summit took place in Havana, Cuba, on the weekend of 13-14 November, to coincide with the first-ever visit of a reigning Spanish monarch to the former colony. Five Presidents refused to attend: those of Chile and Argentina in protest at Spain's proposed extradition of General Pinochet (see II.1; II.4.i; IV.3.iv)); and those of Costa Rica, El Salvador and Nicaragua in protest at Cuba's one-party state. Protests by dissidents were speedily crowded out by Cubans expressing vocal support for President Fidel Castro Ruz and his regime, although delegates were allowed to meet dissident groups. The final conference communique, the Declaration of Havana, as well as expressing a common commitment to democracy, condemned the extraterritorial application of national legislation which breached international law. It was agreed to establish a permanent Ibero-American secretariat in Madrid.

Negotiations on a future Free Trade Area of the Americas (FTAA) made slow progress (see AR 1998, p. 464), the original 12 discussion groups having been reduced to nine negotiating groups, supported by a tripartite committee including representatives of the Inter-American Development Bank (IDB), the OAS and the UN Economic Commission for Latin America and the Caribbean (ECLAC). Following a plan of action originally proposed by the Summit of the Americas in December 1994, the IDB agreed a grant of US$750,000 to set up a corps of volunteers to assist at natural disasters in the region.

A fire at the Caracas headquarters of the Latin American Economic System (SELA) destroyed all installations and caused the suspension of the SELANet communications network.

At the 20th Caribbean Community (Caricom) summit meeting in Port of Spain, Trinidad, on 4-7 July, Haiti formally became Caricom's 15th full member, while Anguilla became the third associate member, along with the British Virgin Islands and the Turks & Caicos Islands. Caribbean leaders resolved to establish a Caribbean Court of Justice during 2000, which would replace the judicial committee of the UK Privy Council as the final court of appeal for, in the first instance, Guyana, Trinidad & Tobago and Barbados. It was expected in due course also to supersede the common High Court of Justice for the Eastern Caribbean states, but the move was criticized by human rights groups as a clear attempt to facilitate the use of capital punishment in several member states. A meeting of Caricom Finance Ministers in Kingston, Jamaica, on 17-18 September was hailed by the secretary-general Edwin Carrington as the occasion for a 'decisive thrust' towards a regional single market.

Agriculture Ministers of the Organization of Eastern Caribbean States (OECS) meeting in St George's, Grenada, in April established a task force to hasten the pace of agricutural diversification in the island group. In June the OECS chairman, Prime Minister Edison James of Dominica, warned government and industry officials in St Lucia and other OECS states against pulling out of the Windward Islands Banana Development and Exporting Company (WIBDECO).

XII RELIGION

RECONCILIATION. On 31 October, the eve of All Saints Day, in the Lutheran church of St Anna in Augsburg, Germany, an historic agreement was signed on the doctrine of justification, after 30 years of study between the Lutheran and Catholic churches. Justification was one of the principal points of dispute during the Reformation in the sixteenth century, centred on whether we are justified by faith alone, as Luther and other reformers held, or by faith and good works. A new 8,000-word declaration stated that justification came 'by grace alone, in faith in Christ's saving work and not because of any merit on our part'. Cardinal Edward Cassidy signed the document for the Vatican, as did Bishop Christian Krause for the Lutheran World Federation, in the city where an 'Augsburg Confession' in 1530 had first tried to heal the breach.

Some supporters of the declaration thought that it meant 'the end of the Reformation' and that inter-communion should be allowed without delay, this being especially urged by the We Are Church movement (see AR 1996, p. 432). But 250 Lutheran theologians signed a protest against it, and some Danish leaders saw the declaration as 'pure politics', with Lutherans capitulating to Rome. Some Austrian Calvinists had also been 'very much disturbed' by the prospect of 'indulgences' (remission of the penalties of sin), another issue at the Reformation, which the Pope had promised to visitors to Rome for the jubilee year in 2000. Nevertheless, supporters of the declaration on justification maintained that Lutheran and Catholic teachings were not fundamentally in conflict.

In May an agreed statement by an Anglican-Roman Catholic International Commission (ARCIC), entitled *The Gift of Authority* and the result of five years of study, received mixed responses. To some, this was a green shoot of spring, after 'a winter of ecumenism', showing a convergence of views by Anglican and Roman Catholic representatives. The statement appeared to accept the primacy of the Pope, not simply in a future reformed and reunited church but 'even before our churches are in full communion'. Moreover, the infallibility of the Pope was accepted, his judgments being described as 'preserved from error', which meant teaching 'infallibly'. But to evangelical Anglicans the statement was a 'betrayal' of Protestantism which did ecumenism 'a disservice', because it bowed to a Roman authority which did not even recognize the validity of Anglican orders.

Fr Jacques Dupuis was further questioned by the Congregation for the Doctrine of the Faith in August on his views of divine and human natures in Christ (see AR 1998, p. 466), on which he sent a 190-page defence. Fr Dupuis received strong support from Cardinal Franz König, former Archbishop of Vienna, who regretted that suspicion was being spread about an author who had done great services to the Church.

CHURCH ACTIVITIES. Pope John Paul II, despite his age (79) and clearly increasing frailty, continued visits to many lands. In Mexico in January he was welcomed by over eight million people at the shrine of the Black Virgin at Guadalupe. On Easter Day he appealed to the authorities in Yugoslavia on behalf of refugees from Kosovo, pleading for an end to war (see III.2.vi). In May he visited Romania, the first visit by a Pope to an Orthodox country for over 900 years, and was hailed by cries of *'unitate'* (unity). The following month he paid a 13-day visit (the longest of his papacy) to his homeland of Poland, for the first time addressing the Polish parliament, where he strongly endorsed Poland's bid to join the European Union. Having called for a 'great harvest of faith' in Asia in the third millennium, the Pope was faced by demonstrations in India in November from Hindu fundamentalists with black flags; he told representatives of seven faiths that people should follow their consciences in choosing a religion and should not be forcibly converted. He gave a large donation for relief work in Orissa, a state where a Catholic priest, Fr Arun Doss, and a Protestant missionary had been killed earlier in the year. The Pope stopped in another Orthodox land, Georgia, on his way back from India, being given a cool reception during which he stressed the importance of Catholic-Orthodox dialogue.

In Rome in May the Pope beatified a 'humble Capuchin friar', Francesco Forgione, known as Padre Pio, who was said to have received the stigmata (the wounds of Christ's crucifixion). He had died in 1968 and his shrine in San Giovanni Rotondo in southern Italy had become a place of pilgrimage at which miracles of healing were claimed. Pope John Paul II had beatified more candidates than any other Pope in history, and more were planned for the jubilee year 2000, so that there were calls for restraint and critical consideration of proposed saints.

A special report on 'Where have all the Catholics gone?' contained statistics showing a sharp decline in church attendance in England and Wales. Other churches showed similar losses (as did public institutions such as trade unions, political parties and other voluntary associations). The number of Roman Catholics was down by more than a quarter compared with 1964, partly as a result of insistence on celibacy and refusal to accept women priests such as had strengthened the ministry in other churches. New Catholic recruits from Ireland, which had helped in the past, were less available after reports of clerical sex scandals in that country. The Roman Catholic population of England and Wales was between 8 and 9 per cent of the total, but showed a continuing decline in baptisms, confirmations, marriages and ordinations. In contrast, denominational schools were a success story, with parents, from the Prime Minister down, seeking a Christian ethic for their children. There were 2,463 Catholic schools, a fairly steady figure over recent years.

British statistics were paralleled across Europe. Although there was less overt membership of religious organizations, Catholics went to church more often than Protestants, and Latin countries were more observant than the northern. The only European country where the priesthood was increasing in numbers was Poland, and its largest decline was in France. The papal ban on contraception, reaffirmed in the encyclical *Humanae Vitae* in 1968, did not appear to have affected church allegiance, since many practising Catholics already used contraceptives, as low birth rates showed, even in Italy. In the USA the number of nuns had fallen steeply, from 180,000 in 1965 to 75,129 in 1999. Most of them were engaged in education but half were over the age of 70.

In the world's population Catholics claimed to number one billion (1,000 million) for the first time in 1999, 17.9 per cent of the total. They had 62.9 per cent of the population in the Americas, 41.4 per cent in Europe, and 14.9 per cent in Africa.

There was special concern at the state of Christianity in the Holy Land, with numbers of Christians dropping from 30,000 in Jerusalem in 1944 to less than 10,000. Historically Christian towns such as Bethlehem and Nazareth now had Muslim majorities. Migration of Christians from Israel was so rapid that holy places were in danger of becoming museums, with a few foreign clergy as caretakers. The decision of the Israeli authorities to allow the building of a mosque near the traditional site of the Annunciation of the birth of Jesus in Nazareth aroused Christian protests, since many pilgrims were expected for the millennium and a planned visit of the Pope in March 2000.

Bishop Carlos Ximenes Belo, the first indigenous bishop of East Timor and Nobel Peace Prize winner in 1996 (see AR 1996, p. 437), defended his people from the Indonesian military after they had voted for independence in August (see IX.1.vi). Called to the Vatican for consultations, he returned to East Timor a month later to find ruin everywhere, with homes and churches destroyed. However, he was able to celebrate Mass in Dili cathedral on 17 October after the arrival of an international peace-keeping force.

ANGLICAN AND ORTHODOX. The Anglican diocese of Sydney in Australia was a stronghold of conservative evangelicalism and rejected the ministry of women as being against the teaching of St Paul. In October, however, the diocesan synod took the untraditional step of voting for laymen to preside at the Eucharist when supported by a local congregation. In November this decision was blocked by Archbishop Harry Goodhew on the grounds that it was against church doctrine and practice, and liable to breach communion with other dioceses in Australia and round the world. There was no shortage of Anglican clergy in Sydney, with 650 active priests and 120 retired, but the demand for lay presidency arose from belief in the dominance of local gatherings of believers rather than the tradition of a wider community with priests and bishops.

An Anglican consultative council, meeting at Dundee in Scotland in September, proposed to transform the ten-yearly Lambeth Conference by uniting it with a larger and more lay-based Anglican Congress. The Lambeth Conference was traditionally for bishops only (see AR 1998, p. 469), but the recommendation was that in future bishops should be accompanied by three lay people, one under the age of 28 and at least one a woman (ordained or lay). Such a Congress could be five times as large and as expensive as the traditional Lambeth Conference with its 850 bishops.

In September the Church of England launched a review of marriage. Despite the number of cohabiting couples, and a UK divorce rate which was the sixth highest in the world, 41 per cent of all first marriages were held in Anglican churches, two million people being married there in the last decade. The remarriage of divorcees in church, forbidden in the Church of England, was allowed in most of the Free Churches. In Eastern Orthodoxy divorced persons were allowed to remarry in church up to three times, though only the first marriage was regarded as sacramental. Despite the rules, few ministers of any church refused Communion to divorcees who presented themselves at the rite.

In August the celebrated composer James MacMillan opened the Edinburgh Festival with a lecture on 'Scotland's Shame', denouncing the anti-Catholic bigotry of Scotland as 'Northern Ireland without the guns and bullets.' Anti-Catholicism was endemic, he maintained, 'in the workplace, in the professions, in academia, in the media, in politics and in sport'. There were Protestant Orange processions in some parts of Scotland, and on the west coast especially Catholics said that careers were closed to those of their religion. Members of the Church of Scotland attacked plans for prayers from other faiths in the new Scottish parliament, demanding only the use of Presbyterian prayers.

In November an ecumenical summit in Moscow considered the effect of Russia's new law on religion (see AR 1997, pp. 449-450), which had not been so severe as feared for non-Orthodox Christians. Orthodox, Catholic and Protestant undertook to halt the feuding that divided them, with Patriarch Alexis of Moscow and Cardinal Cassidy from the Vatican encouraging cooperation.

Investigators into Russian religion spoke of its 'astonishing vitality', from the Baltic states across to the Far East. Many churches now possessed splendid facilities for worship and education, and religious revival followed the collapse of state atheism. The BBC chose to broadcast from the newly-restored Cathedral of the Assumption in the provincial Russian city of Smolensk. Under Stalin all the churches had been closed, and even by 1984 only 35 were open in the diocese of Smolensk; now there were 157, of which 15 were completely new. There were 47 Sunday schools, two high-schools and two kindergartens, while higher Christian education brought together 100 students of both sexes.

JEWISH CONCERNS. The 'war of the crosses' at Auschwitz (see AR 1998, p. 471) was partially resolved when Polish police and army troops removed more than 300 crosses from around the former Nazi concentration camp and took them to a nearby Franciscan monastery. But the 27-foot-high cross which had been brought there from a Mass celebrated in 1979 by the Pope at nearby Birkenau death camp remained in place. The head of Poland's Union of Jewish Councils said that it should also be removed, from the gravel pit where Polish Jews had been massacred, since Jewish tradition did not allow prayers to be offered in the presence of such symbols.

In January Israeli police expelled an American apocalyptic group, Concerned Christians, charged with planning violence in Jerusalem to bring about the second coming of Christ. Founded in Denver, Colorado, in 1980 by Monte Kim Miller, the group claimed him as one of the final witnesses named in the book of Revelation (chapter 11) and said that he would die in Jerusalem and be raised up again.

In February some 200,000 ultra-orthodox Jews blocked streets in Jerusalem, with a 'pray-in' to protest against alleged persecution in the courts. Their total numbers were estimated at about half a million, compared with over three million secular Jews, but they received disproportionate state grants for religious schools and discount on taxes. Many ultra-orthodox did not recognize the state laws and insisted that only the Torah was valid and all Israeli citizens should be governed by it (see also V.1)

In Britain, Chief Rabbi Jonathan Sacks was involved in further controversy over 'chained wives'—orthodox women whose husbands refused them religious divorce after years of separation (see AR 1995, p. 441). In June a visiting rabbi from New York, Moshe Morgenstern, set up his own religious court and presided at the remarriage of a British Jewish woman in London. She had been granted a civil divorce in 1992, but Chief Rabbi Sacks condemned this American-led religious divorce as breaking Jewish law. He claimed to want to help 'chained' orthodox wives, but was accused of inconsistency by both liberals and the rigidly orthodox.

PERSECUTION. In January 17 people were killed by gunfire in a Shia mosque at a village near Multan in Pakistan, amid continuing sectarian violence from the Sunni Muslim community, which formed almost 80 percent of the population. A small bomb in the Roman Catholic cathedral in Karachi was taken as a warning against support for Anglo-American air raids on Iraq. Religious minorities, Muslim and Christian, complained of pressure from the majority fundamentalist Islam, involving social handicaps, denial of jobs of importance and use of the blasphemy laws in disputes over property and party politics.

In October a *fatwa* (judicial sentence) was issued by a *sharia* (Islamic) court in the UK against playwright Terence McNally, whose play *Corpus Christi*, portraying Christ as a homosexual, was showing at the Pleasance Theatre in London. The court said that this was an insult to Jesus, who was acknowledged as a prophet in the Koran, and that the Christian churches were guilty of blasphemy for not taking action against the play.

In India, the secularist aim of religious tolerance was seen as increasingly at risk from Hindu militants. In January extremists forced aboriginal people in Gujerat to renounce Christianity and accept Hinduism as India's one true faith. In February it was stated in the Indian parliament that there were 116 reports of hostilities against Christians in the preceding year, including five murders and the gang rape of four nuns in Madhya Pradesh. Most widely-reported was the murder of an Australian Protestant missionary, Graham Staines, and his two sons aged nine and seven, in the burning of the van in which they were sleeping in Orissa state. Missionaries were also attacked for championing the Dalits (outcasts), while the Vishwa Hindu Parishad (World Hindu Council) described the Nobel Peace Prize award to Mother Teresa (in 1979) as a 'religious plot' to wipe out Hinduism. The Indian Christian churches responded by showing more respect for and interest in Hindu teaching and traditions than at any time in the past.

In January the Vatican accused the authorities in China of sending prostitutes to tempt Catholic priests to break their vows of chastity and loyalty to Rome.

The Chinese government objected to any exercise of papal authority in China, but did not prevent public prayers being said for the Pope. The senior Chinese bishop, Mathias Duan, was not allowed to attend an Asian Bishops' Synod, but he was very active in his diocese of Wanxian, where he faced particular problems. Six of his churches and other buildings would be submerged in the huge reservoir of the Three Gorges Project on the Upper Yangtse, but Bishop Duan planned new churches, kindergartens and ancillary buildings, and launched an international appeal for funds.

From July there was severe crackdown on the largest dissident religious group in China, Falun Gong, which had an estimated 70 million followers, practising a mixture of Buddhist meditation, Daoist philosophy and physical exercise (see also IX.2.i). There were mass arrests, with rumours of torture and deaths in police custody, and charges of treason and subversion. Falun Gong was said to be 'an evil cult, threatening the Chinese people and society', and the press unfairly compared it with the notorious Japanese Aum Shinrikyo (see AR 1995, p. 348). The leader of Falun Gong, Li Hongzhi, was in exile and claimed that the sole aim of the movement was to practise its beliefs in peace.

BOOKS OF THE YEAR. In *Hitler's Pope: The Secret History of Pius XII*, John Cornwell condemned his subject for failing to turn the Catholic Church against Nazism and the Holocaust, despite some of Pius's wartime work for Jews (see also II.3.viii). *The Vatican and the Red Flag: The Struggle for the Soul of Eastern Europe*, by Jonathan Luxmore and Jolanta Babiuch, described as inadequate the Church's response to communism, largely due to its conservative ethics. *Proselytism and Orthodoxy in Russia: The New War for Souls*, edited by John Witte and Michael Bourdeaux, examined new laws on freedom of conscience and religious associations. *Witness to Hope*, by George Weigel, was a new biography of the private and public life of the present Pope John Paul II. *From the Place of the Dead: The Epic Struggles of Bishop Belo of East Timor*, by Arnold S. Kohen, described courageous work for the people. *Patriotism Perverted: Captain Ramsay, the Right Club and British Anti-Semitism 1939-40*, by Richard Griffiths, revealed from primary sources how widespread and almost respectable anti-semitism had been.

No Future Without Forgiveness, by Archbishop Desmond Tutu, gave an account of the South African Truth and Reconciliation Commission. In *The God Experiment* Russell Stannard, a professor emeritus of physics, tested the hypothesis for the existence of God and found in its favour. *One Like Us: A Psychological Interpretation of Jesus*, by Jack Dominian, was an orthodox unquestioning study. *Godless Morality: Keeping Religion out of Ethics*, by Richard Holloway, objected to claims for divine authority or use of infallible texts to resolve questions of conduct. *Khomeini: Life of the Ayatollah*, by Baqer Moin, described the Iranian leader and his religious world. *The Search for the Panchen Lama*, by Isabel Hilton, sketched Tibetan religion up to 1995, when the six-year old Panchen Lama was taken off to China and another proclaimed in his place, amid doubts about both their futures.

XIII THE SCIENCES

1. SCIENTIFIC, MEDICAL AND INDUSTRIAL RESEARCH

SPACE, ASTRONOMY AND PHYSICAL SCIENCES. For the International Space Station (ISS), 1999 was not the spectacular year that some had hoped for. The first two modules, launched the year before (see AR 1998, p. 473), continued in orbit and were visited at the end of May by the space shuttle *Discovery*, receiving supplies and a boost to their orbit. But the planned launch of the Russian habitation module was repeatedly postponed. US space officials expressed their impatience, though some observers suggested that the Americans were not ready either. Russia's reputation was not helped when a *Proton* rocket launch in July ended in disaster with its payload, a military satellite, crashing in Siberia and bits of rocket casing falling on populated areas in Kazakhstan. This led to the Kazakhs banning further *Proton* launches from the Russian-controlled Baikonur cosmodrome, pending an inquiry. Operations continued on the Russian *Mir* space station until the end of August when the last three crew members returned to Earth, the power systems on *Mir* being switched off and the craft put into hibernation. It was thought that the abandoned space station might be lowered for a controlled re-entry into the Earth's atmosphere early in the year 2000.

The new Indian Polar Launch Satellite Vehicle successfully launched the country's first commercial satellites from an island in the Bay of Bengal on 26 May. India was hoping to use the rocket to enter the international satellite launch market and was even considering an unmanned Moon mission. A modified Russian SS-18 nuclear missile was used to launch a civilian satellite for the first time. One of the year's most significant results from the Hubble space telescope came in May with the announcement of the best estimate yet of the 'Hubble constant', a measure of the rate of expansion of the universe. The implied age of the universe was 13,500 million years, a result which seemed to satisfy everyone. If the universe were any younger, it would have been younger than some of the stars within it. If it were much older, it would not fit the acceleration and the density observed in the universe. The new estimate implied that invisible 'dark matter' amounted to about 66 per cent of all matter and not 90 per cent as previously suggested. There were new telescopes for ground-based astronomy, notably the 8-metre Gemini North instrument in Hawaii and three of the four 8-metre reflectors of the European Southern Observatory's Very Large Telescope (VLT) array in Chile.

X-ray astronomy received a big boost in 1999. First came the launch from the space shuttle *Columbia* of the US Chandra X-ray observatory, which became the world's largest X-ray telescope in space. By the end of the year it was already returning high-quality images of X-ray sources such as the regions around black holes and exploding stars. Then, on 3 December, the European

Ariane 5 rocket blasted off successfully from French Guiana carrying XMM, an X-ray telescope with a novel system of concentric and nested X-ray mirrors for producing images and spectra of X-ray sources.

One of the most exciting astronomical events of the year was recorded on the night of 23 January. For nearly 30 years, astronomers had been puzzled by sudden bursts of gamma rays from unidentified sources in the sky. To track down their true origin, an international network had been established, involving the Compton Gamma Ray Observatory, which could detect the flashes quickly, the Dutch-Italian Beppo-SAX satellite, which could narrow down their position in the sky, and a series of telescopes on the ground. On 23 January everything worked perfectly for a particularly powerful gamma ray burst. Within 19 seconds a robotic telescope had recorded images of an optical counterpart to the burst, and within hours giant telescopes had been able to lock on to it showing it to be in a galaxy billions of light years from Earth. That meant that it had to be incredibly energetic, for a few seconds putting out more power than the rest of the universe put together. There was speculation as to its cause: either it was the result of two neutron stars colliding to form a black hole or it was an incredibly powerful exploding star called a hyponova, again forming a black hole and beaming gamma rays in a jet towards us.

The US *Mars Global Surveyor* continued to orbit the red planet, sending back detailed information which included the first global 3-D map of Mars and evidence that there may once have been an ocean in the northern hemisphere of the planet. Otherwise, it was not a good year for research on Mars. Two American space probes had been due to arrive there, but both appeared to end in disaster. First, *Mars Climate Orbiter* lost contact as it arrived and burnt up in the Martian atmosphere. The cause was subsequently found to have been a confusion between the use of metric and imperial units. Then the *Mars Polar Lander* was due to arrive, releasing penetrators and landing near a polar ice cap. Contact was lost as it came in to land and it was feared that it too had crashed.

Space missions to observe our own planet met with greater success. In December the flagship of NASA's Earth Observing System, a satellite called *Terra*, was sent into orbit. NASA emphasized the seriousness of its intention to investigate the possibility of life on other worlds by drawing together allied research at its many centres into a so-called 'Exo-biology programme' under the leadership of Nobel laureate Professor Barruch Blumberg. Research was to include studies of life in hostile environments on Earth as well as missions to other planets and their moons, studies of meteorites and the search for planets around distant stars.

In more distant research, the privately-funded search for radio signals from extra-terrestrial civilizations tapped the resources of millions of home computers with the launch of SETI@home, a screen-saver programme to analyse data from radio telescopes in the search for alien messages. In February a NASA spacecraft called *Stardust* was launched on a mission to collect dust from a comet's tail and return it to Earth in 2006.

Radar evidence from the *Lunar Prospector* mission showed that there might be water buried in a frosty layer on the Moon. When the space probe reached the end of its life in July, it was deliberately crashed towards a shadowy crater near the Moon's South Pole in the hope of throwing out a cloud of water vapour that might be detectable by telescopes on Earth. No sign of water was seen. The crash came two weeks after celebration of the 30th anniversary of the first *Apollo* Moon landing and took the ashes of veteran planetary geologist Eugene Shoemaker to their final resting place.

Further out in the solar system, the Hubble space telescope reported 300-kilometre-per-hour storms on Uranus, as dawn broke in the planet's northern hemisphere for the first time in 20 years, lifting cloud-top temperatures above minus 220°C. Pluto once again became the most distant planet in the solar system, as its 248-year elliptical orbit crossed that of Neptune. The NASA space probe *Deep Space One*, testing a new ion drive propulsion system, passed within 25 kilometres of the surface of an asteroid called Braille. Appropriately, the probe turned a blind eye, pointing its camera in the wrong direction. Scottish astronomers reported the first possible evidence of light reflected from a planet orbiting a star other than the Sun. The first good evidence of a complete solar system came from the perceived wobbling of a star's position in the sky, seemingly due to three orbiting planets.

The most popular astronomical event of the year on Earth was undoubtedly the total eclipse of the Sun on 11 August—the first total eclipse visible from Britain since 1927. The path of 'totality'—from south-west England, across Europe to the Black Sea and eventually India—made it one of the most observed eclipses in history, despite cloud along part of the route. Millions more viewed the partial phase of the eclipse, which was visible to the whole of Europe and parts of North Africa and Western Asia.

In the terrestrial sphere, the US company Moller International made the first brief test flight of a four-seater, petrol-driven 'Skycar' with powerful thrusters which enabled it to take off and land vertically and to travel at nearly 600 kilometres per hour. In Europe, the continent's first hydrogen gas filling station opened in a Hamburg, serving a fleet of commercial vans. Research continued into 'Fullerines', molecules of many carbon atoms related to the football-shaped C60 molecule. There was particular interest in so-called 'nanotubes', consisting of carbon atoms arranged into a microscopic tube which could conduct electricity. Several teams worked independently on control systems which paralysed people might operate by using their brain waves. A team in Germany developed a way in which a patient could learn to move a cursor on a computer screen by conscious control.

MEDICAL AND BIOLOGICAL SCIENCES. Work accelerated on the human genome project, the plan to map the 3,000 million DNA building blocks in the human genetic makeup. US scientists said that 90 per cent of the blueprint of life would be known within a year, while officials of the Wellcome Trust, coordinating British work on the project, announced that they expected to have the entire genome mapped, at least in outline, by the end of February 2000. A commercial US company, Celera, sought to patent more than 6,000 human DNA sequences; other researchers, together with the British and US governments, sought an agreement to make the information freely available. In December genome researchers in Cambridge announced that they had established the full sequence of DNA in chromosome 22, the first human chromosome to be fully sequenced.

The world's population passed 6,000 million during 1999, but there were signs that population growth was slowing. A special session of the UN General Assembly marking the fifth anniversary of the International Conference on World Population in Cairo produced a variety of estimates for future growth. Some suggested that the world population would stabilize at 10,000 or 11,000 million between 2050 and 2100. Others thought that family planning, disaster and famine, disease and conflict would limit the population to about 7,000 million by 2050. The proportion of elderly in the populations of developed countries continued to grow.

Human stem cells were a focus of intense research following the discovery that they could be cloned and grown indefinitely and could, in principle, be used to treat a range of degenerative diseases, even to grow replacement tissues and organs for transplant. Stem cells had been found to exist in most adult human tissues, including the central nervous system and brain, previously thought to have no capacity for regeneration. The most abundant source were foetuses, but suggestions that a foetus might be formed and sacrificed for spare parts evoked strong protests.

The US company Advanced Cell Technology claimed to have created the first cloned human embryo by injecting human DNA into a cow's egg. They said that they let it grow to about 400 cells but destroyed it at the age of 14 days in line with US research rules. They said they had no intention of producing an entire cloned human but wanted to produce tissues for transplant into patients with diabetes and Parkinson's disease.

Cloning was proposed as a way to save endangered species. Scientists at Monash University in Australia said that they planned to clone the endangered northern hairy-nosed wombat, while Chinese scientists claimed to have produced a cloned embryo of a giant panda. Attempts were being made in the USA to clone monkeys to produce genetically identical animals for research purposes. The US company Genzyme cloned goats which gave milk containing a human anti-clotting protein suitable for use in heart patients. Studies of the original cloned sheep Dolly (see AR 1997, p. 457) revealed that her chromosomes showed ageing which matched those of the animal from which she was cloned rather than an animal of Dolly's actual age.

The Council of Europe voted for a moratorium on clinical tests of animal organ transplants into humans. Pigs were being genetically engineered to produce human antigens to reduce rejection, but human transplant trials did not proceed, largely because of fears that pig viruses might cause disease in humans. However, later in the year, at least one common pig virus was found not to transfer into humans. Various genes in humans were linked with diseases but applications were largely limited to diagnosis rather than treatment. Progress with gene therapy continued despite many technical difficulties.

By World AIDS Day on 1 December more than 50 million people worldwide had become infected with the AIDS virus HIV and over 16 million people had died from the disease. The numbers of AIDS patients and victims both rose by more than in any previous year. The most cases were still in Africa and new evidence showed that women infected with HIV outnumbered men by 2 million. It was realized that the number of infected people in India had been grossly underestimated. The fastest rise in numbers of cases was in the former Soviet Union. Several vaccines against HIV were ready to begin human trials. Research showed that the most common form of HIV almost certainly spread to humans from chimpanzees and not from polio vaccine contaminated by monkey cells as had been suggested.

The World Health Organization (WHO) announced that almost a third of the world's population was infected by the bacterium that caused tuberculosis (TB) and that 10 per cent of those would go on to develop the disease. Nine of the 10 worst-affected countries were in Africa, where TB was causing more deaths than AIDS and malaria combined. Doctors at the WHO believed that poor basic health care was more to blame than the spread of drug resistance. British researchers discovered a new chemical signalling system used by TB bacteria to activate them out of latency. Differences in the genetic make-up of TB bacteria in different parts of the world were discovered, possibly explaining why the BCG vaccine was more effective in some regions than others. Although leprosy had almost vanished from the developed world, the WHO had not succeeded in its aim to eliminate the disease as a public health threat by the end of the year. Half-a-million people per year were still contracting the disease in countries including India, Indonesia, Myanmar and parts of Africa. Lack of research, funding and publicity were blamed.

During the year an estimated 2,000 million people were at risk of malaria, 500 million became infected and more than two million, mostly young children, died. Even the city of New York had to be sprayed against disease-carrying mosquitoes. The WHO announced that 60 million African families would be given insecticide-treated bed nets over the next five years. A study in Ethiopia showed that teaching mothers to recognize malaria and giving them cheap anti-malaria drugs could cut infant mortality by 40 per cent. The use of anti-malaria drugs was found to cut the incidence of anaemia in pregnant mothers by 40 per cent. The drug fosmidomycin, already developed and tested against bacteria, was found to be potentially effective against malaria. British scientists discovered the chemical keys used by the parasite to unlock red blood cells. Meanwhile, US scientists produced the first complete map of the parasite's DNA.

An outbreak of encephalitis in Malaysia, which killed more than 100 people and made many more seriously ill, was linked to a virus called the Nipahr virus found in pigs. More than a million pigs were slaughtered in response. The WHO continued its plans to eradicate polio by the end of the year 2000 and appealed for funding for 700 million doses of polio vaccine. The setback of a polio outbreak in Angola prompted the diamond company De Beers to join the coalition for polio eradication. Analysis of body samples from men who died in the 1918 Spanish flu pandemic gave clues which doctors hoped they could use to recognize the most deadly strains of flu in future outbreaks. In preliminary trials, a new vaccine against Rotavirus, a common cause of diarrhoea, was found to offer 90 per cent protection.

Cancer researchers identified four mutations that were common to all types of human cancers and which could provide targets for new anti-cancer drugs. Scientists in the US produced genetically-engineered mice in which leukaemia could be switched on and off. One of the commonest forms of childhood leukaemia was shown to start in the womb, caused by a non-inherited gene defect during the formation of blood cells.

X-ray analysis of hair samples provided a new test to identify women carrying a gene which predisposed them to breast cancer. Trials began in the US of a vaccine against the Human Papilloma Virus, responsible for 95 per cent of cervical cancers. In February, doctors transplanted ovarian tissue into a woman who had had her ovaries removed and some of the tissue frozen. But in November they revealed that whilst the transplanted tissue was producing follicles, no ripe eggs were being released. However, the technique offered hope to young women who had had their ovaries removed or were undergoing radiotherapy that they might still have children.

In the area of brain research, there was strong new evidence that 'mad cow disease', or BSE, could pass from cows to humans. The controversial therapy for Parkinson's disease involving the transplantation of brain cells from an aborted human foetus was shown still to be working ten years after the implant. Researchers showed that Alzheimer's disease in mice could be prevented and even reversed by vaccination with beta-Amyloid protein, the substance believed to cause the damage to the brains of Alzheimer's sufferers. A new brain-scanning technique showed that children with dyslexia used five times the area of their brains to perform simple language tasks than non-dyslexic children.

Genetically-modified (GM) food was frequently in the news (see also XIII.3), with protests, especially in Europe, about its growth and importation. The biotechnology company Monsanto announced that it would cease development of its widely-criticized 'terminator seed' technology whereby genetically-modified crops would yield sterile seeds, forcing farmers to buy fresh seed from Monsanto each year. Meanwhile, Monsanto scientists developed plastic-growing plants by the introduction of genes from plastic-producing bacteria into oilseed rape and cress. The resulting plastic was biodegradable and suitable for commercial use. New Zealand scientists were given permission to raise two herds of cattle genetically modified to produce medicinal compounds in their milk, but the use of human genes was not allowed.

US scientists deduced that the simplest bacterium imaginable would only need about 300 genes to survive. Japanese scientists showed that hydrothermal vents on the sea floor provided suitable conditions for the conversion of glycine molecules into the oligopeptides necessary for protein formation in life.

Fossilized bones were found in central Myanmar of a previously-unknown species of primate that lived 40 million years ago, long before the earliest known African primates. This supported the view that the ancestor of all monkeys and apes lived in Asia, not Africa. Anthropologists unearthed new and convincing evidence that Neanderthals practised cannibalism. Fragments of bone with cuts and fractures found in a cave in south-eastern France suggested that these early distant cousins of modern humans used stone tools to butcher their own species for food. A 13,000-year-old skeleton of a woman, discovered on an island off the coast of California, provided the most ancient example of human remains yet found on the continent. The oldest playable musical instrument, a 9,000-year-old flute fashioned from a bird-bone, was discovered in China. It produced notes similar to those used in modern Western music. Possibly the earliest surviving examples of alphabetic writing were discovered in Egypt. The letters, carved in stone cliffs west of the Nile, were nearly 2,000 years old.

NOBEL PRIZES. The 1999 Nobel Prize for Medicine or Physiology was awarded to the German biologist Günther Blobel for his work on the signal mechanisms used by cells and which break down in some genetic diseases such as cystic fibrosis. The Physics Prize was shared by Dutch physicists Gerardus T'Hooft and Martinus Veltman for their discovery of a way of simplifying quantum calculations of electro-weak interactions; and the Chemistry Prize went to an Egyptian working in the USA, Ahmed Zewail, for his studies on transition states of chemical reactions, lasting less than a billionth of a second.

2. INFORMATION TECHNOLOGY

SOARING Internet stocks on both sides of the Atlantic, alarm about the possible problems which might be occasioned by the 'millennium bug' and the US Justice Department's continuing anti-trust onslaught against Microsoft Corporation, the world's largest software company, were recurrent strands which wove through 1999.

INTERNET STOCKS. So-called 'dot com' stocks, named after the familiar .com address suffix for such companies on the Internet, became an important focus of attention in investment circles. Potential as well as actual performance had always been a factor in valuing a business; but placing a high value upon companies with no track record and even upon start-up enterprises, although not a completely new phenomenon, became more common and inevitably attracted controversy.

Dramatic examples of the effect on investors of the perceived potential of the Net included the UK online auction company QXL.com, which had been valued at £28 million in February 1999, when a venture capital house had acquired 25 per cent of the equity. At the year end, following an initial public offering

(IPO) in October on the London stock exchange and on the New York NASDAQ exchange, QXL.com had a market capitalization of £1,720 million. In another example, in Germany, Freenet.de, the Internet offshoot of the telecommunications company MobilCom, achieved a valuation of Eur478 million at its IPO on the Frankfurt Neuer Markt in December.

Many relatively young Internet companies were not trading profitably, a noteworthy example being the US online bookstore Amazon.com, which nevertheless at the end of the year had a market capitalization of US$12,800 million. Controversy, therefore, attended the initial valuations which Internet companies were achieving; more than once during the course of the year speculation also arose as to whether, and when, a market 'correction' would occur. Major fluctuations in the share prices of Internet stocks did occur, with significant downturns in midyear. At the end of the year, however, no crash had taken place, despite worries about the possible impact of the millennium bug (see below) on trading systems. Indeed, Yahoo!, one of the few profitable Internet service companies, ended the year with a market capitalization of $110,300 million, whilst one of the longest established companies in the sector, America Online (AOL), was valued at $168,600 million. By way of context, these valuations placed the newer companies in the same league as household brands like Coca Cola ($143,900 million) and Ford ($60,800 million).

Concern did manifest itself, however, amongst regulatory authorities during the year. Webvan, a new San Francisco-based company offering online grocery shopping services, was forced to delay its intended IPO in October as a result of intervention by the US Securities and Exchange Commission (SEC). In the course of running road shows to promote itself, Webvan was said to have released price-sensitive information which was not in its formal prospectus. Although the action of the SEC was generally welcomed, it could scarcely be classed as draconian and appeared unlikely to place a long-term damper on the effervescent nature of the sector.

'MILLENNIUM BUG'. Fever over the damage that might be done by the 'millennium bug' problem in computers increased in intensity as the year advanced, although doubts were expressed by some commentators that the magnitude of issue had been overstated. Substantial amounts were spent by governments and international organizations, such as the International Telecommunication Union (ITU), to ensure that computer systems based on two-digit year dates had been identified and adjusted so that the transition from '99' to '00' (see AR 1998, p. 483) would not lead to confusion or break-down. In the developed world, Japan was considered one of the less well-prepared countries, whilst the United States, Canada and the United Kingdom led in this respect. Indeed, the UK government took the step of distributing a booklet to all 25 million households during the year.

Particular concerns existed about less-developed countries and other countries known to be operating older computer systems for critical services, such as former Soviet-bloc republics. One stringent measure intended to reduce the incidence of problems was reported to have been taken by the Chinese government, which was said to have ordered the heads of airlines to be in the air on 1 January 2000. A key problem for China was understood to be the large amount of pirated software in use in the country, which meant that users could not turn to the original suppliers for technical support.

Whilst the millennium bug remained an unknown quantity, an incident in August served to show that other bugs could inflict nasty wounds upon even the mightiest. A flaw in the security software protecting Microsoft's e-mail service, Hotmail, was discovered by a group of hackers, who succeeded in accessing Hotmail accounts without using a password. After having been alerted to the problem by a Swedish journalist, Microsoft switched off the service in order to remedy the problem. The corporation said that it took two hours to do so, but it was widely reported that Hotmail was down for ten hours.

ANTI-TRUST AND OTHER LEGAL ACTION. The proceedings launched against Microsoft in the United States in May 1998 (see AR 1998, p. 483) continued throughout the year. In November Judge Thomas Penfield Jackson issued a 207-page opinion, finding that Microsoft enjoyed monopoly power. Whether, in the view of the court, that power had been abused—and, if so, what penalties and/or remedies should be applied—remained open questions at the end of the year. It seemed unlikely, however, that Microsoft would emerge unscathed. Speculation was therefore rife as to what the outcomes might be, even though expectations were that the issue would go through every available process of appeal. Comparisons were inevitably drawn with the previously most-important US anti-trust suit, which had resulted in the break-up of AT&T in 1984. Notwithstanding this situation, Microsoft ended the year as the largest company in the world in terms of market capitalization, which stood at $604,100 million.

An interesting aspect of the case was the use in evidence of e-mails which had circulated within Microsoft concerning actions taken or contemplated relative to competitors. In general, e-mail had developed as a very informal medium which, through its immediacy, tended to encourage instant reactions and forceful and vivid language. These inherent characteristics of e-mail militated against Microsoft in this case, though this was by no means the only example of internal e-mails being adduced in legal proceedings.

By contrast, Intel, the world's largest manufacturer of semi-conductors, reached a negotiated accommodation over the anti-trust action filed by the US Federal Trade Commission (FTC) more or less contemporaneously with the Justice Department case against Microsoft (see AR 1998, p. 483). Intel agreed not to suspend the supply of chips and necessary technical information to companies with which Intel was in dispute over intellectual property issues. Nevertheless, the FTC intimated that it was still following up other investigations of possible anti-trust infringement by Intel.

'ENEMIES OF THE INTERNET'. Governments deserving of this description were denounced in an August press release issued by Reporters Sans Frontières (RSF), an organization dedicated to campaigning against the oppression of journalists. Of 45 countries identified as restricting their citizens' access to the Internet, usually by means of a state-owned Internet service provider (ISP), 20 were singled out for this particular designation. RSF called on 14 of the countries, which had already signed the International Covenant on Civil and Political Rights, to respect their commitments, including article 19 of the covenant enjoining that 'everyone shall have the right...to receive and impart information and ideas of all kinds, regardless of frontiers'. The remaining six countries—Burma, China, Cuba, Kazakhstan, Saudi Arabia and Tajikistan—were exhorted to sign up to the covenant.

Earlier in the year a Chinese computer engineer, Lin Hai, had been convicted in Shanghai and sentenced to two years in prison for having supplied e-mail addresses to a 'hostile foreign' organization. Washington-based VIP Reference, the organization so described, engaged in the transmission of pro-democracy material to China. It was estimated that there were 6.7 million Internet users in China by the end of 1999.

Some months later Wu Jichuan, the Chinese Minister for the Information Industry, stated that foreign investment in Internet services and in the provision of content through the medium was forbidden in the People's Republic. Shortly afterwards he qualified his remarks, indicating that, while foreign investment in these areas was against current law, the government was reviewing the position with a view to stimulating growth. Nevertheless, existing foreign investors, such as AOL and Dow Jones, remained uncomfortable.

TECHNOLOGY. Developments on the commercial front included the launch in March of Intel's Pentium III micro-processor chip in succession to the Pentium II, which had appeared in 1997 (see AR 1997, p. 463). Intel stated that the Pentium III would facilitate full-screen, full-motion video on the screens of personal computers. In the research arena, the Korean company Samsung announced the development of a one-gigabyte 'synchronous dynamic random access memory' (D-RAM) chip, scheduled for commercial availability early in 2000. The development had been achieved using the same lithographic process as for 256-megabyte D-RAM production, but with a reduced etched-line width of 130 nanometres. Meanwhile, investigations into the possibilities of sub-atomic and quantum particle computing continued in several places, including the Hitachi-funded research laboratory in Cambridge, UK, the Hsinchu Science Park in Taiwan and the Zürich research facility of International Business Machines (IBM).

In the field of telecommunications, concrete progress was made towards the implementation of third generation mobile technology. The first generation of mobile telephones had used analogue technology and the second digital, offering basic fax and e-mail capabilities as well as voice communication. European technology had gained pre-eminence in the second generation since the adoption of a pan-European standard had provided a stimulus for development which did not exist in the United States, where there was no single standard. With the US government clinging to the line that a single standard would be anti-competitive, for the third generation a family of three standard 'modes' had been adopted under the umbrella designation 'International Mobile Communications 2000' (IMT-2000), the expectation being that devices would be able to switch to any of the three modes.

With a much higher transmission rate of up to 2 megabits per second (compared with the existing rate of 9.6 kilobits per second), third-generation technology offered the prospect of major service enhancements, such as mobile access to the Internet, with the ability to download pictures and music, and even mobile video-conferencing. In 1999, therefore, European governments, of which the first was the UK, took practical steps towards the licensing of Universal Mobile Telecommunications Systems (UMTS) operators, UMTS being the European component of IMT-2000.

THE LAZARUS SYNDROME. This syndrome visited the realm of information technology in 1999, as reports of the death of the 'network computer' (see AR 1998, p. 482) proved to be premature when it jumped back up again in a slightly different guise. In the ongoing contest to dislodge Microsoft from its position of primacy in the field of office applications software, Sun Microsystems announced that it would offer word-processing, spreadsheet and other office software as a free Internet service. Initially, users would be expected to download such software to their own personal computers, but it was suggested that at a later date—with higher speed communications—a wider range of software could be rented without the need for downloading. Thus would return the concept of the network computer. Almost immediately, Microsoft reacted by stating that it would similarly make its software available for rental over the Internet.

These manoeuvres served to underline the way in which business models were changing in the networked economy. Another example was the UK company Freeserve, launched in September 1998, which had enjoyed such success as the first ISP to offer free access to the Internet that it was able proceed in 1999 with a billion-pound IPO. An even more striking example, however, was *Encyclopaedia Britannica*, which in October announced that it would make the whole work available via the Internet free of charge. A generation or so previously, the multi-volume printed version had sold for over £1,000, whilst the price of the CD-ROM version, first published in 1994, had initially been fixed at £400 (but had been progressively reduced). By attracting users free of charge, these businesses now aimed to obtain revenues not directly from the users themselves, but by deriving advertising and sponsorship income and commissions on transactions from other businesses which wished to offer products and services to the users.

3. THE ENVIRONMENT

DESPITE the widespread hope that 1999 would set the tone for a bright new millennium, in the event it signally failed to produce any substantive changes in the sphere of environmental policy. Nevertheless, Green campaigners could take some comfort, not from new treaties signed or old ones confirmed, but from the way in which two major institutions with flawed ideologies were humbled by Green activists and public pressure. Monsanto, representing the genetic modification (GM) industry as a whole, was one; the World Trade Organization (WTO), which had until then been pursuing an agenda arguably defined by established business interests and not by human or environmental need, was the other.

In 1998 the questions surrounding genetic modifications to our food had become an issue principally outside the USA (see AR 1998, pp. 484-5). In 1999 that trend became a hot issue, the label 'Frankenstein foods' becoming common on people's lips whilst they fought to keep such products out of their diet. More to the point, by the end of the year what was seen by the public as a cause for serious doubt, and by the GM industry as hysteria, had brought the biggest GM exponent, Monsanto, often seen as the *bête noire* by the anti-GM lobby, virtually to its knees, its GM division viewed by the stock markets as near worthless. Reports suggested that the Wall Street listing of Monsanto shares reflected the value of the non-GM businesses accurately, thus precipitating a reorganization of the company. The WTO was halted in its tracks by ugly scenes outside its Seattle conference headquarters in late November and early December (see XI.2.ii). Just as the GM industry would never be the same, so deliberations at the WTO would never again be able to ride roughshod over all and sundry in the name of unfettered free trade. No doubt it would try. But the battle lines had been drawn.

The year started quietly enough. In retrospect, however, a UK court case in which moves to halt trials of GM crops failed, gave notice that the UK would become the major battleground in the fight against GM. A combination of legal controls and powerful business interests meant that opposition in the USA was stifled. In continental Europe it had not yet reached fever pitch and the gradual introduction of GM foods into stores, accompanied by assurances that it was both beneficial and safe, had been much as the GM industry had planned. In the UK, in contrast, the combination of a pro-GM stance from the government and a vociferous Green lobby headed by Greenpeace, meant that a showdown was inevitable once the legal moves had failed. Analysis of UK newspaper reports showed that GM was very probably the single biggest environmental issue of 1999.

It was not the only one, though. Almost unnoticed was another attempt to fire up the world's imagination and commitment to save what remained of the wild tiger populations, launched from Switzerland in January under the auspices of the UN Convention on International Trade in Endangered Species (CITES). The world's tiger population, once estimated to be over 100,000, was now reduced to well under 10 per cent of that number, with some species having become extinct and a few, such as the Chinese, Sumatran and Siberian tigers, perilously close to joining them. As ever the threats were principally two: the trade in tiger parts for traditional eastern medicines and loss of habitat. Some success could be claimed for moves to limit trade in parts of the dead animals, but raids by police around the world through the year consistently showed it was far from dead.

In February Ethiopia delivered an early-warning shot across the bows of both the GM giants and the WTO as talks over a treaty to regulate trade in GM foods collapsed amid US accusations that developing countries were endangering free trade. The Ethiopians led the counter-attack, arguing that the USA should not be able to decide what the developing world grew and ate. This move came as a surprise, indeed a mystery, to many, since GM foods had been promoted as a technology capable of solving food shortages and hunger. That starvation-prone Ethiopia should lead the revolt illustrated clearly how much the developing world distrusted the pro-GM claims. The move, however, was not restricted to Ethiopia or even Africa: GM soya was banned in Brazil and India's Supreme Court ruled against trials of GM cotton.

Africa was all too often portrayed as a pariah by northern environmental groups, the claim being that it had done far too little to protect its natural resources. February saw what was hailed as the beginning of 'a new green dawn' on the continent when activists in Kenya, led by Wangari Maathai, demonstrated against government plans to allow building on the last remnant of virgin forest: 2,400 acres close to the capital and less than a kilometre from the headquarters of the UN Environment Programme (UNEP).

Meanwhile, in Europe, which had long since destroyed the vast majority of its own forest cover, evidence emerged confirming the apparently inexorable progress of global warming. After surveying weather data from Finland to the Balkans, Munich University reported its finding that spring was officially starting earlier and autumn starting later than ever before recorded. In Europe this might be seen as a benefit, extending the growing season by some ten days.

Elsewhere, the effects of global warming were not likely to be so welcome. Analysis of 1998 data confirmed that it had been one of the stormiest on record, with major weather disturbances that caused more damage than had occurred in the entire 1980s. Analysts cited not just an increased frequency and severity of storms but also a marked increase in the damage they did to life and property. The former had long been predicted as a likely effect of global warming, the inevitable result of the increase in heat energy in the global weather system. The latter was a result of poor planning and housing of some of the world's poorest communities. This was amply and grotesquely proven later in 1999 when storms in Central America left thousands dead and many more homeless when extraordinary rains washed whole communities from destabilized hillsides in rivers of mud. The frequency and severity of storms throughout 1999 suggested the previous year's figures were all too real.

Further fuel for the smouldering GM fire was reported in March. A UK government report highlighted a risk from GM technology: that organisms altered to be virus-resistant would enhance the chances that super-viruses would evolve naturally. What incensed anti-GM activists was that the report was already two years old and had not been published. March also saw the emergence of a new virulent strain of encephalitis in Malaysia. It was initially diagnosed as Japanese encephalitis, which was transmitted by mosquitoes but which had the pig as its host, but DNA analysis placed the blame for some of the deaths elsewhere. A second virus was found, one related to the Australian Hendra virus carried by fruit bats. Fears that the viruses might spread rapidly through both pigs and humans led the Malaysian authorities to act fast: thousands of pigs were slaughtered in early April. The treatment worked and the fear of an epidemic receded.

Rather than support GM technology, the UN Food and Agriculture Organization (FAO) announced that it would be promoting another plan to solve Third World hunger—rabbits. Rabbits bred quickly, produced low-fat high-protein meat and were cheap to farm, eating a wide range of otherwise useless vegetation. Back-yard rabbitries, said the FAO, could be the perfect answer to today's demand for sustainable development. The announcement was greeted with some amusement, but the FAO was serious, the only acknowledged drawback being that rabbits were susceptible to disease.

HIV/AIDS was highlighted in May when the UN announced that the virus had become responsible for more deaths worldwide than any other infectious disease. First identified just 20 years ago, AIDS had now displaced tuberculosis as the world's most potent infectious killer, was fourth in the league table of all diseases and had yet to reach its peak. The World Health Organization (WHO) report projected that deaths from HIV/AIDS would soar in some countries where as many as one in four were infected, including many professional people. The social and political effects of this plague were only just being felt as children were orphaned and the death toll increasingly included people in mid-life—the very people who were most needed to sustain a viable society. Indeed, death rates were rising so fast in Zimbabwe that the country's once-rapid population growth was expected to cease entirely. Malawi was projected to lose half its skilled workers by 2010 and in Tanzania half the nation's teaching staff would succumb in the same decade. In parts of Africa it was now clear that the disease would have an effect as devastating as the Black Death in Europe 700 years earlier.

Whilst treatment (though not a cure) for AIDS was available, the cost remained too high for African states to bear. The picture was not total gloom, however. It became increasingly evident during the year that Uganda, which suffered the epidemic early and acknowledged it sooner than most, had made substantial strides in changing patterns of behaviour and reducing transmission. The biggest single change had been effected by persuading the population to reduce liaisons between older men and young women. Keeping to same-age relationships would in theory vastly diminish HIV spread. Uganda had shown that it worked in practice. On the medical front, research also showed that a short course of anti-AIDS drugs given to an HIV-positive pregnant woman just prior to the birth of her child greatly reduced the chances that the child would be infected, and at relatively affordable cost.

GM hit the headlines yet again in June when the Prince of Wales and UK Prime Minister Tony Blair were reported as having had a heated exchange of views on the issue. The GM debate was not only firmly on the agenda but the signs were now clear that, in the UK at least, something had to happen, because government policy looked increasingly out of step with public opinion. It was also beginning to become clear that UK food retailers would be taking the lead and removing GM foods from shelves in response to public concern, whether valid or not. Faced with threats of a boycott, a farmer carrying out GM trials destroyed his crop before it reached maturity and before anything of scientific value could be learned.

In Bonn, a meeting of officials from 147 countries, ahead of a major conference planned for October, ran into severe difficulties in seeking to iron out details necessary to implement the 1997 Kyoto Climate Change Protocol (see AR 1998, pp. 464-5, 568-72). Instead, it demonstrated all too clearly that major differences remained between developing nations and the USA in particular. The meeting markedly lowered expectations for progress later in the year. As if to underline the problem, a study from the UN International Panel on Climate Change warned that the rapid growth in air travel would contribute as much as 3 per cent to global warming gases by 2050.

In Australia, the Olympics 2000 project was coming under fire. The bid that won the contract for the Games had promised to make the 2000 Olympics the 'greenest' ever. To be built on an old industrial site in Sydney, the Games buildings would not only rehabilitate polluted land but also maximize the use of renewable power sources and dramatically limit environmental impact. But the reality began to look markedly less than the promise. With only a year to go, the plans were redrawn to avoid building on the most polluted areas and thus to avoid the need to clean them up. Ironically, the best technology to cleanse the site had been developed a few miles away at the world-class research centre CSIRO. But the developers failed to use the technology. In addition, opportunities to use state-of-the-art power generators were eschewed in favour of older, less environmentally-friendly, technology. Sydney 2000 might be the 'greenest' Games ever, but the green was looking significantly less brilliant than it might have done.

Representatives of the world's governments met at the UN in New York in June for the 'Cairo plus 5' meeting. Intended to be a review and reaffirmation of the decisions made at the Cairo conference on population control five years earlier (see AR 1994, pp. 485-6), the meeting initially threatened to turn a review into a retreat. The original Cairo document committed signatories to work towards a reduction in population growth by implementing a variety of measures including the empowerment of women and sex education for children. The rationale behind the document followed what had for some time been orthodoxy in non-governmental organization (NGO) circles—that improving the status of women and children resulted in better living conditions for all, lower morbidity and mortality and lower birth rates. However, the implicit focus on sex education and the inclusion of measures to develop family planning services, together with, optionally, facilities for legal and safe abortion, had always been a difficulty for some religious groups.

At 'Cairo plus 5' the Vatican used its special status at the UN in an attempt to reduce the commitment to issues which it felt to be in conflict with Roman Catholic religious beliefs and requirements. Whilst the Muslim states concurred, the rest of the world felt that such concerns were retrogressive, while much of the NGO community was dismayed to discover that a core commitment in the original Cairo document might be lost. The meeting became a desperate struggle to retain the original purpose of the Cairo document, a wording being eventually agreed that was acceptable to all. Later in the year the UN announced officially that the global population exceeded 6,000 million. However, the indications were that the rate of increase was at last slowing and that the outlook was less pessimistic. Despite under-funding and a host of minor concerns, the general view remained that the Cairo agreement was not only an inspired and effective document, but also one that the vast majority of its signatories were implementing with both commitment and success.

The GM tide was ebbing ever faster. In July the European Union (EU) decided to impose tough new GM controls: whilst GM was not entirely banned, the likelihood of any new licences being granted for GM imports in the foreseeable future was effectively nil. By now much of the debate on GM at the political level was as much about politics as food safety. Europe and the USA were at loggerheads over trade issues including bananas, meat and GM foods. Increasingly Europe, along with much of the rest of the world, felt that the WTO rules were in effect forcing countries to accept products that their consumers did not want. For example, soya imported from the Americas could not be traced to GM or non-GM sources and most imports would be a mix of both types. That suited US laws, under which marking products as GM was deemed to be anti-free-trade, but contravened European demands that consumers be given the choice. Likewise with beef: growth hormones, used routinely in the USA, were banned in Europe.

The argument over bananas included all the ingredients of a full-blooded trade conflict with environmental dimensions. Europe, with its historic interests in the Caribbean, wanted to retain the right to buy bananas from its old colonies in the West Indies at above-market prices, contrary to the interests of the massive US-based producers whose products came from plantations in Central America. According to Green activists, those plantations were some of the world's worst examples of exploitation, both of people and of the environment. However, their bananas were cheap, whereas the West Indies' products were grown by small-scale farmers—on land unsuited to anything else (except perhaps drugs)—and were therefore less cheap, though producers claimed that Europe was not only getting a better product but also supporting an ecologically-sustainable banana-growing industry. For the USA and the WTO, EU preference for West Indies' bananas was an illegal practice that denied efficient producers access to lucrative markets. Perhaps as much as any other, therefore, this dispute exposed the ideological weaknesses of the WTO and set the scene for what was to follow in November.

In late July Greenpeace made a characteristic direct strike against GM crops in the UK, invading a trial site at Lyng in Norfolk and destroying the crop. Lord Melchett, the head of Greenpeace UK, was arrested. Later revelations that independent tests had proved that genetically-modified pollen could be tracked miles from its source, carried by wind and bees, blew a hole in the GM companies' assurances that small-scale trials could not have an impact on the environment. If this assertion was false, how much else was questionable?

Further evidence of global warming was announced in August after studies showed that the fish populations of the Mediterranean were changing. Traditional species were disappearing, partially as a result of over-fishing but also because warmer waters attracted new species. Many had taken advantage of a man-made doorway, the Suez Canal. But many others had entered via the Straits of Gibraltar, an entrance open for millennia but hitherto of no interest to fish requiring warmer waters than the Mediterranean once was. In all, over a hundred new species had moved in. On the plus side, Italy, France and Monaco announced that their part of the Mediterranean would be designated a whale sanctuary (see also II.3.viii). Whilst not the home of any of the largest whales, the region had 2,000 of the second largest, the fin whale, along with a dozen smaller species.

Sadly, the wider oceanic outlook was depressing, if an article by marine biologists in *Science* was right. Ocean life was apparently suffering from an unprecedented outbreak of disease caused by a combination of warmer waters and pollution. The potential effects not only on the oceans and the life within, but also on their capability to supply food for an ever increasing world population, could be dire. Whilst loss of ice shelves in Antarctica might be blamed on short-term variations in global temperatures, it was hard to dismiss evidence of change within bodies of water of such volume.

As an announcement from UNEP director Klaus Töpfer made clear in September, the evidence that global warming was upon us was now far too strong to dismiss. He told the world bluntly that the Kyoto protocol, even if fully implemented, would not be enough. And yet the indications remained that even those inadequate proposals were unlikely to be implemented. At a further meeting on climate change in Bonn in October, governments lived up to fears created by earlier bickerings and the event could only be recorded as a failure- if anything a further retreat from the already inadequate provisions of the Kyoto protocol. Far from promising hope for the next millennium, the Bonn meeting signalled that the intransigence of self-interest would maintain its sway even against compelling evidence that action was already long overdue.

The failure came despite new findings not only that climate change was happening but also that the world was heating up faster than ever before. Worse still, the rate of warming was expected to accelerate. This alarming conclusion was reached after a five-year study of forest loss in the Amazon which had discovered that higher temperatures would increase forest 'die-back' and accelerate microbe activity in soils, resulting in further forest loss and massively-enhanced rates of carbon dioxide release. Computer models by the world-renowned Hadley Centre, employing the amended figures, predicted an increase of an extra 1.5°C in global temperatures over the next century.

Throughout October much of the media's attention was focused on the fallout from a small explosion in Japan on 30 September (see also IX.2.iv). At the Tokaimura nuclear plant 110 kilometres north-east of Tokyo, workers operating to inadequate guidelines made a fundamental error—they put too much uranium in too small a space and triggered a nuclear reaction. This could never have created a nuclear explosion, but it might just as well have for the furore it caused as Japan's worst-ever nuclear accident. Already up against the anti-nuclear lobby for its transport of reprocessed fuel from the suspect UK plant at Sellafield (which arrived in Japan just a few weeks after the accident), the Japanese nuclear industry, through arrogance and incompetence, had created a public relations disaster. In the event, the physical damage was minor compared with, for example, the death and destruction caused by the operations of the oil industry. But if the nuclear industry wished to make its case for contributing to a long-term stabilization of global warming, avoidable accidents such as the blast at Tokaimura needed to be eliminated.

If the Bonn climate change meeting was depressing, the WTO gathering in Seattle on 30 November-3 December was a disaster, at least for the WTO and its supporters. The main event began without any of the hoped-for agreements from the preparatory sessions, where detailed texts were supposed to have been thrashed out in private. Despite confident claims from WTO officials that this failure was an inconvenience rather than a real problem, the reality turned out to be far worse. Not only were there no agreements in the conference, but also the streets outside became a riot zone. The 'battle of Seattle', as it was dubbed, involved an unlikely alliance of many forces deeply opposed to the WTO and the way it controlled world trade. Developing nations and their supporters complained of it being damaging to both their prosperity and their food security; Green groups protested that the goal of free trade took precedence over environmental issues; and anti-GM protesters complained that WTO rules would force consumers to swallow a technology they did not want.

WTO staff retreated to their offices in Geneva to plan their next step. As a powerful inter-governmental organization, the WTO was unlikely to back down after just one skirmish. But such was the confidence of the protesters that it was equally unlikely that they would back down either. This conflict was not over. Nor was the dispute over GM foods at an end. By the end of the year Monsanto, described by Greenpeace as 'the devil incarnate' of the GM world, was licking some serious wounds: it had publicly abandoned its so-called 'terminator gene' technology, its share price was dropping and its GM division effectively worthless. Moreover, the fracas in Europe over GM crops was at last having an impact on the US consciousness: farmers were beginning to ask awkward questions, concerned not just by the revelation that GM maize was threatening the Monarch butterfly but that the markets for their products appeared to be shrinking by the day. Consumers were wanting to know why they could not choose between GM and non-GM food. Wall Street saw that US markets overseas would diminish and Monsanto took the fall.

XIV THE LAW

1. INTERNATIONAL LAW—EC LAW

i. INTERNATIONAL LAW

MANY of the most important developments in international law in 1999 concerned the use of force. The NATO air campaign against Yugoslavia gave rise to a fundamental dispute over the legality of humanitarian intervention and the application of the laws of war (see also III.2.vi). Yugoslavia brought an action against ten NATO states to the International Court of Justice. This was part of a recent trend by states to take to the Court cases involving the most controversial subject matter, the use of force. Four judges were re-elected during the year, and one new judge, Awn Shawkat Al-Khasawneh (Jordan), was elected for nine years with effect from 6 February 2000.

Three other new cases also concerned the use of force. The Democratic Republic of the Congo (DRC) brought an action against Burundi, Uganda and Rwanda for acts of armed aggression perpetrated in flagrant violation of the UN Charter (see VII.1.i); it claimed that the invasion by respondent states' troops on 2 August 1998 (see AR 1998, p. 289) was an attempt to overthrow the government and to establish a Tutsi regime and constituted a violation of the DRC's sovereignty and territorial integrity and a threat to peace and security in the Great Lakes region. Pakistan sued India for shooting down a Pakistani aircraft over Pakistani air-space in August 1999 (see VIII.2.i & ii). And Croatia sued Yugoslavia for violations of the Genocide Convention during the 1991-95 conflict through its ethnic cleansing within Serb areas of Croatia. Other new cases were brought by Germany against the USA for violation of the Consular Convention and by Nicaragua against Honduras on legal issues concerning maritime delimitation in the Caribbean. States from all continents having resorted to its jurisdiction, the Court struggled to cope and had inadequate resources to meet its needs.

The Court gave judgment on the merits of one case, between Botswana and Namibia on sovereignty over Kasikili/Sedudu island (see also VII.2.iv). The judgment was based on an Anglo-German Treaty of 1890 which located the dividing line between the spheres of influence of those colonial powers in south-west Africa in the 'main channel' of the Chobe river, but failed to identify the main channel. The Court considered depth, width, flow and navigability and concluded that the north channel was the main channel; it accordingly found by 11 votes to four that the island formed part of the territory of Botswana. It noted, however, that the parties had undertaken that there should be unimpeded navigation for craft of their nationals in the river.

The Court gave an advisory opinion on the Convention on Privileges and Immunities of the UN at the request of the UN Economic and Social Council

(Ecosoc). This was the first request made under Article VIII of the Convention, which provided that in the event of disputes between the UN and one of its members an advisory opinion might be sought and should be accepted as decisive by the parties. The Court held that Cumuraswamy, a Malaysian jurist appointed as special rapporteur by the UN Commission on Human Rights, was protected by the Convention on Privileges and Immunities and was thus entitled to immunity from legal process in the Malaysian courts. The UN Secretary-General had the primary responsibility and authority to assess whether UN agents acted within the scope of their functions and to protect those agents by asserting their immunity.

The Court indicated provisional measures in the case brought by Germany against the USA for violation of the Vienna Convention on Consular Relations; it called on the USA to take all measures at its disposal to ensure that Walter LaGrand, a German national convicted of murder during a bank robbery in 1982, should not be executed pending a final decision by the Court. This was the first time that the Court had indicated provisional measures on its own initiative without giving the parties the opportunity to be heard; it did so because of the urgency of the case, as LaGrand was due to be executed the next day. Despite the Court's order the execution went ahead (see IV.1).

In contrast, the Court rejected provisional measures in the ten cases brought by Yugoslavia against NATO member states. Yugoslavia had sought declaratory judgments: that by taking part in the bombing each respondent state was in breach of the obligation not to use force; that by taking part in training the Kosovo Liberation Army each respondent was in breach of its obligation not to intervene in the affairs of another state; that each respondent state had violated international humanitarian law on the protection of civilian population and objects, the protection of the environment and the use of prohibited weapons; and that each respondent state had violated the obligation in the Genocide Convention not to impose deliberately on a national group conditions of life calculated to bring about the physical destruction of the group. It also requested provisional measures, asking the Court to indicate that each respondent 'shall cease immediately its acts of use of force and shall refrain from any act of threat or use of force against Yugoslavia'; if they did not, claimed Yugoslavia, there would be new losses of human life, physical and mental harm, destruction of civilian targets, heavy environmental pollution and further physical destruction of the people of Yugoslavia.

The Court found that it did not have *prima facie* jurisdiction on the merits of the case under the Genocide Convention, since the allegations by Yugoslavia did not amount to genocide. Moreover, in those cases based on the Optional Clause Yugoslavia's consent was limited to disputes arising after its acceptance of the Optional Clause on 26 April 1999 with regard to situations subsequent to this acceptance. The Court found that the dispute arose when NATO began its air attacks on 24 March 1999 and that therefore the cases were *prima facie* excluded from the Court's jurisdiction.

There were three decisions on procedural matters in the *Cameroon/Nigeria* case. First, the Court authorized Equatorial Guinea to intervene in order to protect its legal rights in the Gulf of Guinea. This was unusual in the jurisprudence of the Court, but neither Cameroon nor Nigeria objected to the intervention. Second, the Court refused Nigeria's request for interpretation of its 1998 judgment on jurisdiction and admissibility (see AR 1998, p. 493), because it attempted to reopen questions already decided by the Court. Third, the Court decided that Nigeria's counter-claims seeking compensation for incursions from Cameroon's side of the border were admissible. This counter-claim was directly connected with the subject matter of Cameroon's claim and rested on facts of the same nature as the corresponding claims of Cameroon.

The International Criminal Tribunal for the former Yugoslavia (ICTY) continued to face lack of cooperation by states. Many of those indicted remained at liberty. In March the president of the tribunal reported to the UN Security Council the continuing refusal of Yugoslavia to cooperate with the tribunal and to allow the prosecutor to enter Kosovo. In August she reported Croatia's failure to cooperate through its refusal to recognize the tribunal's jurisdiction over crimes occurring during 'Operation Flash' and 'Operation Storm' in 1995. On 27 May the ICTY announced indictments of Slobodan Milošević and four other senior Federal Republic of Yugoslavia officials for the actions of forces under their control against the Kosovo Albanian civilian population between 1 January and late May.

Three important judgments were given by the ICTY; in two the characterization of the conflict as internal or international was crucial. In *Aleksovski*, the commander of a prison facility for Bosnian Muslim civilians was found guilty of violations of the laws and customs of war because of physical and psychological maltreatment of prisoners. However, he was found not guilty of grave breaches of the Geneva Conventions because at the relevant time the conflict was between Bosnian Muslims and Bosnian Croats, not an international conflict between Bosnia and Croatia. In contrast, in the *Tadic* case the appeal chamber reversed the judgment of the trial chamber in 1997 (see AR 1997, pp. 473-4) and found that Tadic was guilty of grave breaches under the Geneva Conventions because there was an international conflict between Yugoslavia and Bosnia. In the *Jelisic* case, there was a significant decision on genocide: Bosnian Serb Goran Jelisic was found guilty of 31 of the 32 counts against him for his part in the illegal confinement, mistreatment and killing of Bosnian Muslims and Croats in 1992. He pleaded guilty to the charges of crimes against humanity and violations of the laws or customs of war and was sentenced to 40 years' imprisonment, the harshest sentence yet given by a Trial Chamber of the ICTY. However, he was acquitted on the charge of genocide because the prosecutor had failed to prove beyond a reasonable doubt that he had the required intent 'to destroy in whole or in part a national, ethnical, racial or religious group'. This decision made it unlikely that charges of genocide would be upheld against low-level officials.

Judge Gabrielle Kirk McDonald resigned as president of the ICTY and was replaced by Judge Claude Jorda (France); Louise Arbour was replaced as chief prosecutor by Carla del Ponte (Switzerland). Judge Navanthem Pillay was elected president of the Rwanda Tribunal.

The Rwanda Tribunal (ICTR) decided four genocide cases (see also VII.1.ii). *Omar Serushago* was sentenced to 15 years' imprisonment after pleading guilty to genocide and crimes against humanity. *Clement Kayishema* and *Obed Ruzindana* were found guilty of genocide. Kayishema, former prefect of Kibuye, had been present at massacre sites in April 1994 and had initiated and participated in the killing. Also, with Ruzindana, a wealthy businessman, he had brought soldiers, police and *interahamwe* militia to the Bisesero area and directed them to attack Tutsis throughout April, May and June 1994. Kayishema had criminal responsibility as a superior and had played a pivotal role in the organization and direction of the attacks. He orchestrated the massacres of thousands of civilians. He was sentenced to imprisonment for the remainder of his life. Ruzindana was sentenced to 25 years' imprisonment. The fourth case concerned *Georges Rutaganda*, a former leader of the *interahamwe* who had ordered, incited and carried out murders. He was sentenced to life imprisonment for one count of genocide and two counts of crimes against humanity.

The International Tribunal for the Law of the Sea gave a final decision on the merits of a case first brought before it in 1997, when St Vincent & the Grenadines had sued Guinea for the detention of the *Saiga*, a ship registered in St Vincent which had been bunkering (selling oil and water to fishing vessels) off the coast of West Africa (see AR 1997, p. 476). The tribunal addressed fundamental issues of the law of the sea, including the nationality of ships and the 'genuine link' requirement, but it avoided the controversial issue of the legality of bunkering in exclusive economic zones. It held that the purpose of the requirement that there be a genuine link between a ship and the state whose flag it flew was to seek a more effective implementation of the duties of the flag states, not to establish criteria by reference to which the validity of registration in a flag state might be challenged by other states. It upheld the St Vincent nationality of the *Saiga*. On the merits of the case, the tribunal held that Guinea's arrest and detention of the ship, prosecution of the captain, confiscation of the cargo and seizure of the ship were violations of the Law of the Sea Convention.

The Law of the Sea Tribunal also ordered provisional measures in the *Southern Blue-fin Tuna* cases brought by Australia and New Zealand against Japan in response to Japan's decision vastly to increase its catch of blue-fin tuna as an 'experimental programme'. In this crucial case for the protection of rare marine species, the tribunal said that the parties should act with prudence and caution to ensure that effective conservation measures were taken to prevent serious harm to the stock. It ordered parties to resume negotiations to reach agreement on measures for conservation and management and the restriction of catches.

The caseload of the European Court of Human Rights (ECHR) continued to increase. As in previous years, the largest group of cases concerned the right to a fair trial. Excessive delays in civil and criminal proceedings continued to be a major problem in Italy, France and Portugal. In the UK the public trial in 1993 of two 11-year-old children for the abduction and murder of a two-year-old boy, James Bulger, was held to deny the right of an accused to participate effectively in the trial. The Court considered it essential that a child should be dealt with in a manner that took full account of his age, level of maturity and intellectual and emotional capacities; in respect of a child charged with a grave offence attracting high levels of media and public interest, this could mean that it would be necessary to conduct the hearing in private.

In the first of two important cases concerning the UK military, the ECHR ruled that the UK system of courts martial violated the right to a fair trial. In the second, *Lustig-Prean* v. *UK*, the Court held that the British ban on homosexuals in the armed forces was a violation of the right to privacy (see also II.1). In another case, *Selmouni* v. *France*, the Court made its first decision that a European state was guilty of torture. The victim was a suspected drug-dealer who was subjected to brutal physical assault and rape while in police detention.

Several important treaties were concluded in 1999. The *Convention on the Suppression of the Financing of Terrorism*, adopted by the UN General Assembly on 9 December, was the latest in a long series of treaties on terrorism. It required states to make the provision of funding for terrorist activities a criminal offence under their domestic laws and to confiscate assets allocated for terrorist purposes. On the tenth anniversary of the *Basel Convention on Hazardous Wastes*, the UN Environment Programme (UNEP) adopted a *Protocol on Liability and Compensation for Damage Resulting from the Transboundary Movement of Hazardous Wastes and their Disposal* on 10 December. This established for the first time a mechanism for assigning responsibility for damage caused by accidental spills of hazardous waste during export or import.

An Optional Protocol to the *UN Convention on the Elimination of All Forms of Discrimination against Women* was opened for signature on 7 December; this brought the convention into line with other human rights treaties by creating an individual complaints procedure. On the laws of war, the *UN Convention on the Prohibition of the Use, Stockpiling, Production and Transfer of Anti-Personnel Mines and on their Destruction* (see AR 1997, pp. 475, 566-8) entered into force on 1 March and the Second Protocol to the 1954 *Hague Convention for the Protection of Cultural Property in the Event of Armed Conflict* was opened for signature on 26 March. This applied to internal as well as to international armed conflict. One of its most important provisions was the limitation of the doctrine that military necessity could justify attacks on cultural property.

ii. EUROPEAN COMMUNITY LAW

BY 1999 the European Union (EU) and its legal system had quite clearly entered into a new phase. The travails of the Maastricht and Amsterdam Treaties constituted a watershed on the hither side of which a sort of tense maturity could now be detected. No longer was the emphasis, political and legal, placed on building the Union. That had been done. The *acquis communautaire*, a term used so much in successive enlargement negotiations and intergovernmental conferences (IGCs), was truly acquired and could now be taken for granted. Instead, the mentalities had switched from construction to change of what had been constructed. For the first time, there seemed to emerge an awareness of the antiquity of the European Community (EC), created in another and remote historical era nearly two generations ago: not only were current law students not alive when the Community was created, often neither were their parents. Increasingly, administrators, politicians and lawyers could be heard saying that, while EC rules and, more particularly, procedures might have been appropriate for the original Community of six or nine, they would not suit a Union of 20 or even 25. In any case, the world had moved on and the Union now had different priorities.

The catalyst for this new mood—EU expansion to the east (see also XI.4)—was not new, but acquired added force from the failure of the Amsterdam Treaty to agree on the necessary structural reforms and the consequent need for a new IGC to complete that task. Accordingly, the establishment of this ICG was formally agreed at the Helsinki Council in December. At that same meeting it was also agreed to include in the accession negotiations not only the six Central and East European countries (CEECs) which had already been collaborating with the Commission throughout the year, but also the 'second tranche' of the remaining six applicants together, *mirabile dictu*, with Turkey (see also II.4.vii). At the same time the potential geographical border of the EU was clearly placed beyond the Black Sea with the entry into force of partnership agreements with the three Caucasian states of Georgia, Armenia and Azerbaijan. In fact, the 'boundary' of Europe was pushed well into Central Asia, since similar agreements had been signed not only with Uzbekistan and Turkmenistan but also with Kazakhstan. In addition to this geographical dimension, the EU also pursued a far-reaching alteration of the Lomé Convention governing relations with the African, Caribbean and Pacific (ACP) developing countries, due to expire in 2000, and also of the parallel convention on Overseas Countries and Territories (OCT)—neither of which, however, reached final stage in 1999.

The second political catalyst was the entry into force on 1 May of the Amsterdam Treaty. By the end of the year lawyers had for the most part accustomed themselves to use of the new numbering of the EC and EU Treaties and such old favourites as Articles 177 and 85 were sounding distinctly old-fashioned as 234 and 81 replaced them in books and conferences. A more serious consequence was the alacrity with which the Commission used the partial transfer of 3rd Pillar matters, particularly judicial cooperation, out of the EU Treaty and into the EC Treaty (the new Title IV on a so-called 'area of freedom, security and justice'), in order to convert to a regulation and thus bring under its control the Brussels Convention on jurisdiction and enforcement of civil and commercial judgments.

Another Amsterdam innovation, the incorporation of the Schengen Agreement *acquis* into the two Treaties (partly into the 3rd Pillar and partly into Title IV of the EC Treaty), began with the publication of a more or less definitive list of instruments forming the *acquis*. At the same time, the 3rd Pillar Europol (European Police Office) was set up organizationally by a long series of published texts and a 1st Pillar Community anti-fraud office (OLAF) was set up within the Commission. On the other hand, the Corpus Juris proposal for an EU public prosecutor system, although strongly urged by new Commission president Romano Prodi among others, was not adopted at the Helsinki Council, but neither was it killed.

The usual activity of the courts and legislature in applying and developing Community law continued, and included what was probably the last of very many judgments in the Factortame series: the UK House of Lords on 28 October applying the ruling of the European Court of Justice in *Brasserie du Pêcheur* and holding that the Spanish fishermen in that case were indeed entitled to damages (see also II.1). But the outstanding hard law event of the year was undoubtedly the enactment by the Council on 13 December of the Electronic Signatures Directive 1999/93, a trail-blazing text of great legal difficulty which would have much influence over the development of commercial law generally.

The high drama of the year was, however, none of these. It was the open recognition at last that the EC legal system had become overloaded and could no longer cope with the demands placed upon it. This had two manifestations, both of which reflected a need for radical reassessment of the scope and manner of enforcement of Community law. Both surfaced in the spring of 1999 at about the time that the Treaty of Amsterdam came into force and were linked to the watershed changes in the EU referred to above.

The first related to EC anti-trust law. It had long been recognized that this was not solely concerned with competition but also had an important inter-state trade element. The virtual completion of the internal market reduced the importance of that concern and hence of the overriding need for supranational enforcement against the will or inertia of the member states. At the same time, the Commission, and particularly its Competition Directorate General (formerly DG IV), found the pressure on its resources had become intolerable. It therefore produced a white paper in May which proposed a fundamental reorganization both of the anti-trust rules in Article 81 of the EC Treaty and of the procedures for enforcing them. This would involve a redrafting of Article 81 itself (i.e. Treaty amendment) and the repeal and replacement of the indispensable procedural Regulation 17, which had been the keystone of the EC anti-trust system since its beginning in 1962.

The reform had two main components, both revolutionary. First, the existing presumption that restrictive agreements were anti-competitive and prohibited unless authorized ('exempted') by the Commission, either individually or through 'block exemption' regulations, would be replaced by a presumption that they were not prohibited. This would be accomplished by replacing the various regulations with one virtually universal block exemption for all vertical agreements, thus leaving the Commission free to concentrate on horizontal cartels. A draft regulation to that effect was debated throughout the year. The second component, assisted by the first, was to transfer most of the competition policing from the Commission to the anti-trust agencies of the member states. An essential feature of that was abolition of the burdensome—for the Commission as well as for companies—procedures of prior notification of dubious agreements, on which EC anti-trust law had relied from the beginning.

As if these proposals were not cataclysmic enough (anti-trust law and its procedures had formed the central core of EC legal practice throughout its history), the very epicentre of Community law, the Court of Justice (ECJ) itself, embarked upon a root-and-branch re-examination of its own role and structure. It shared with the Commission the sense of losing grip of its growing workload, but unlike the Commission it could not escape the prospect of an exponential increase in that load as five or ten new member states joined the Union during the next decade, all full of courts and lawyers seeking the help of the ECJ, and as huge quantities of new law worked their way through the court system and new specialist tribunals such as the Community Trade Mark Office (OHIM) began to send large numbers of appeals to Luxembourg. The Court had been concerned for many years at its delays in throughput and the failure of successive attempts to solve them. It was also frustrated by its inability to alter its own rules of procedure without the unanimous approval of all the member states in the Council as well as by the refusal of the Council and the European Parliament to provide the financial resources to do so. Its budget remained the lowest of all the EU institutions and only just above that of the Economic and Social Committee.

In April the Commission set up a committee chaired by Ole Due, a former president of the ECJ, to examine the problems and propose solutions. In May the Court itself presented to the Council a major memorandum analysing the issues and proposing some minimal reforms. These included transferring more cases to the Court of First Instance (CFI) and encouraging national courts not to make Article 234 references to it. For its part, the CFI introduced the possibility for cases to be heard by a single judge, a very counter-intuitive step in the eyes of most continental lawyers. Much would depend on the IGC in 2000.

2. LAW IN THE UNITED KINGDOM

CONTINUING the radical constitutional changes of recent years, by a short section of a short statute parliament removed the rights of hereditary peers to sit in the House of Lords (see II.1);[1] an argument that it was in breach of the *Act of Union 1707* was rejected by the Privileges Committee of the House of Lords, as was an argument that it could not affect hereditary peers summoned to the present parliament.[2] On the boundary between English and European law, the House of Lords ruled that where the UK government had failed to implement legislation required by European Community law, knowing that it was the view of the European Commission that such legislation was obligatory, substantial damages would be awarded against the government to those who had suffered loss.[3] Individual rights were boosted by the decision of the House of Lords, in what was described as a case 'of fundamental constitutional importance', that the public's right of access to the highway were not restricted to a right of passage along it; a group of demonstrators peacefully protesting on the highway in the vicinity of Stonehenge were held not to have committed any offence.[4]

The *Greater London Authority Act* set up the framework for the Greater London Authority, and provided for the election of a Mayor of London. The *Local Government Act* introduced regulations affecting local authorities, with a view to improving their economy, efficiency and effectiveness. It was held that a Local Government Commissioner had been justified in finding that there had been maladministration when planning consent had been given for the erection of a new stand at a football stadium when several councillors were season ticket holders of the relevant club;[5] but the Court of Appeal, reversing an earlier decision, held that the existence of a party political motive did not in itself make unlawful a decision by the ruling group of a local authority.[6]

Both parliament and the courts dealt with the law relating to refugees. The *Immigration and Asylum Act* aimed to improve the operation of rules relating to entry into the United Kingdom, both by streamlining the system for those with a right of entry and by introducing further controls on those without. Important questions about the granting of refugee status were considered by the House of Lords in *R* v. *Immigration Appeal Tribunal, ex parte Shah*;[7] regulations allowing the grant of asylum to individuals fearing persecution because of their 'membership of a social group' were held to be sufficiently wide to extend to Pakistani women, on proof that women in Pakistan suffered discrimination. The Divisional Court interpreted the UN Convention relating to the Status of Refugees 1951, holding that individuals seeking asylum were not precluded from doing so merely because they had not claimed it at the earliest possible moment;[8] and the Court of Appeal held that it was wrong to insist on the return of applicants for asylum to other European countries when those countries did not apply the convention properly.[9] The *Protection of Children Act* plugged gaps in the system of child protection, introducing further regulations to ensure that those unsuited to work with children would not find child-related employment.

The far-reaching changes embodied in the *Civil Procedure Rules 1998* were brought into force: their effect was to bring the trial process more firmly under judicial control, with a view both to improving the efficiency of legal process and so far as possible reducing its cost. Within weeks the rules were applied to debar an expert witness from giving evidence, despite his being acceptable to both parties, on the grounds that he was failing to comply with his responsibilities to the court.[10] The House of Lords, vacating a previous decision of its own, laid down guidelines for the circumstances in which a judge should not sit in judgment in a case in which he might be thought to be biased;[11] a subsequent decision of the Court of Appeal clarified the circumstances in which such apparent bias should be a disqualification.[12] On the rehearing of the case, the substantial effect of the previous decision was upheld;[13] in doing so their lordships further clarified the law relating to extradition and to the immunity from prosecution of heads of state.[14] Alongside this, the procedures of the Court of Appeal were streamlined,[15] and rules were laid down for the conduct of Welsh legal proceedings in the light of the *Government of Wales Act 1998*.[16]

The *Access to Justice Act* brought about substantial changes in the provision of legal services and legal aid. Amongst other things it provided for the setting up of a Community Legal Service and a Criminal Defence Service, charged with overseeing the availability and operation of legal aid services, and amended the rules relating to rights of audience and conditional fee agreements. Speedier procedures in magistrates' courts were introduced.[17] The Court of Appeal laid down guidelines for the imposition of custodial sentences,[18] and for the imposition of sentences by courts-martial.[19] Further reforms in the youth justice system were introduced by the *Youth Justice and Criminal Evidence Act*; the act also brought in measures to make it easier for young or vulnerable witnesses to give evidence in legal proceedings. A bill was introduced into the House of Lords designed to remove the right to trial by jury for various offences of middle-ranging seriousness and to class them with minor offences suitable for trial in magistrates' courts;[20] research published by the Home Office revealed that the vast majority of individuals summoned for jury service were in fact excused from serving.[21] The Law Commission issued important consultation papers on fraud and on the compatibility of the law of bail with the *Human Rights Act 1998*,[22] and the Lord Chancellor announced a sweeping review of criminal procedures.[23]

The House of Lords held that the *Computer Misuse Act 1990* was directed at any form of gaining unauthorized access to computer data, not merely unauthorized access from outside; it was therefore appropriate to extradite to the United States an employee charged with the fraudulent manipulation of data.[24] The defence of duress was held not to be open to a person who had brought the duress on himself;[25] and it was held that positive acquiescence in another's inaccurate belief might constitute criminal deception.[26]

Several decisions stressed the paramountcy of the interests of children in litigation touching them. Balancing the interests of a child and the need to maintain an effective and consistent immigration policy, the House of Lords held that a judge had been right to allow a Jamaican child to be adopted by her grandparents who were resident in England.[27] A mother was held to have the right to refuse consent to the circumcision of her son,[28] and a natural father was not entitled to insist that the child be known by a name different from that in which he had been registered by his mother.[29]

New procedures relating to the working of trades unions were incorporated in the *Employment Relations Act*; the Act also provided for enhanced rights for maternity and parental leave, and for leave to care for dependants. The employment rights of disabled people were dealt with by the courts in *Clark v. TDG Ltd*,[30] the first case to interpret the *Disability Discrimination Act 1995*. The *Disability Rights Commission Act* replaced the National Disability Council with a more powerful Disability Rights Commission, designed to reduce discrimination in employment suffered by the disabled. The House of Lords held that an employment decision might be discriminatory, and hence unlawful, when the complainant had been treated unfavourably for one of the reasons listed in the Race Relations Act 1976, whether or not the employer had been consciously motivated by discriminatory reasons.[31] Significant changes were made to the rules relating to pension schemes and other social security benefits by the *Welfare Reform and Pensions Act*.

The *Contracts (Rights of Third Parties) Act*, giving effect to recommendations made by the Law Commission, made inroads into the long-standing rules of privity of contract by providing that in certain circumstances individuals might gain enforceable rights under contracts to which they were not parties. The circumstances in which money paid under a mistake of law should be recoverable were given sharper delineation.[32] The House of Lords held that a professional body carrying out regulatory functions was not doing so in the course of business, so that it was not able to recover value added tax paid by it;[33] but a stockbroker's legal costs in defending himself before a regulatory body were held to have arisen in the course of his business and were hence legitimately deductible expenses in calculating his tax liability.[34] In determining whether a minority shareholder in a company was being unfairly prejudiced by the majority shareholders, the House of Lords laid down that regard should be had to equitable principles and not simply strict legal rights.[35] The Court of Appeal refused to allow enforcement of a foreign arbitration award consequent upon an admittedly illegal contract, holding that such a course of action was contrary to public policy;[36] where the contract was to be performed abroad, though, it was held that different considerations should apply.[37]

The House of Lords gave further consideration to the circumstances in which tortious liability might arise when a public authority had negligently exercised its statutory powers; it was held that an action in negligence might lie where the complaint was concerned with the way in which the authority had acted after having taken a child into care rather than with the decision to take the child into care in the first place.[38] In reaching its decision the court drew attention to the very real problems caused in English law by the decision of the European Court of Human Rights in *Osman v. UK*,[39] which hugely restricted the circumstances in which it would be proper to strike out a claim in advance of a hearing. The British Boxing Board of Control was held to owe a duty of care to boxers fighting under its auspices;[40] and in *Gower* v. *Bromley London Borough Council* the Court of Appeal held that a school might owe a duty of care to a pupil with special educational needs.[41] The police were held to owe a duty of care to a prisoner known to have suicidal tendencies, but in an action brought by the family of the deceased prisoner damages were reduced by 50 per cent to take account of contributory negligence;[42] and a police officer was held to have been under a duty to come to the aid of a colleague who was being attacked.[43]

The Court of Appeal held that where the victim of another person's negligence had received a benefit from a third party to offset the cost of the injury, the value of this benefit could not be recovered in damages from the negligent party.[44] Receivers managing mortgaged property were held by the Court of Appeal to owe a duty of care to the mortgagor, not simply a duty to act in good faith.[45] This was distinguished in *Starling* v. *Lloyds TSB Bank plc*,[46] where the Court of Appeal said there was no more than a duty of good faith owed by a mortgagee to a mortgagor in determining whether to give permission for the property to be leased to a third party. Where a vasectomy operation had been unsuccessful as a result of doctors' negligence, it was held that damages were recoverable for the pain and suffering of the unwanted pregnancy but not for the expenses associated with the bringing up of the child.[47]

In the first defamation action in the English courts arising out of a publication on the Internet, it was held that an Internet service provider could be liable for the innocent publication of defamatory material; and if the material was not deleted on receipt of a complaint from the plaintiff the defendant would not be permitted to rely on the defence of innocent dissemination provided by the *Defamation Act 1996*.[48] The Court of Appeal allowed an action for defamation by a former member of parliament (Neil Hamilton) to proceed notwithstanding the results of a previous parliamentary investigation; it was held that there was no breach of the Bill of Rights of 1688 so long as there was no direct challenge to parliament.[49] The action, which attracted huge publicity (see II.1), was unsuccessful.[50] In another high-profile action involving a politician, the House of Lords declined to apply the defence of qualified privilege to every publication of 'political information', preferring the traditional approach of the Common Law to that adopted in the United States.[51]

The *Trustee Delegation Act* further allowed trustees of land to delegate some of their management powers. A trivial boundary dispute between neighbouring householders, though with far-reaching implications for farmers, reached the House of Lords.[52] It was held that the normal presumption that a boundary ran down the middle of a hedge was displaced when the hedge was adjacent to a ditch; in such a case the boundary was presumed to lie along the edge of the ditch most distant from the hedge. In a similar type of case the Court of Appeal held that where an old fence had been replaced by a wall by the agreement of both neighbours, the boundary between their properties was presumed to be determined by reference to the position of the present wall.[53]

The House of Lords held that the inhabitants of a village were entitled to register land as a village green under the *Commons Registration Act 1965*, and so to prevent building development, when the land had been used for recreational purposes for more than 20 years, even though none of the villagers was shown to have given thought to the question whether the recreational use was a matter of right; it was further held that the words 'sports and pastimes' in the Act were not limited to communal activities such as shooting at butts or dancing round a maypole, but included any informal recreational use.[54] The House of Lords reiterated that a grant of the exclusive possession of property for a fixed period would constitute a lease rather than a licence, whatever language the parties had used to describe the arrangement;[55] and the provisions of the Rent Act 1977 allowing a member of a tenant's family to succeed to the tenancy on the death of the tenant were extended to include a homosexual partner.[56]

The Court of Appeal applied 'commercial good sense' in holding that a person who received property knowing that it had been obtained in breach of fiduciary duty would not automatically be treated as holding it on constructive trust,[57] and stated that the proof of the requisite dishonesty had to be established to a high degree of probability.[58] The Court of Appeal held that a local authority would not be liable in nuisance simply because it had not prevented its tenants harassing other nearby property owners; for liability to arise it would have to be shown that the authority had expressly or impliedly authorized the acts complained of;[59] and the House of Lords held that landlords would not be liable for noise created by their tenants when the tenants themselves would not have been liable in nuisance.[60] On the other hand, where the complaint was of the conduct of the authority's licensees rather than their tenants it was held that an action for nuisance would lie.[61]

Parliament having provided over 60 years earlier that hospitals providing treatment for the victims of road accidents might recover some of their costs from those responsible for the accidents, the *Road Traffic (NHS Charges) Act* provided an administrative framework for the achievement of this. The House of Lords held that the Home Secretary had acted unlawfully in laying down a blanket policy that interviews of prisoners by journalists would be permitted only if an undertaking was given not to publish any part of the interview.[62] The Tribunal set up to investigate the events of 'Bloody Sunday' in Northern Ireland was held by the Court of Appeal to have acted improperly in providing that military witnesses should not give evidence anonymously[63].

Lord Denning, the most influential English lawyer of the twentieth century, died on 5 March at the age of 100 (see XVIII: Obituary).[64]

1. *House of Lords Act*, s.1
2. *Lord Gray's Motion, Lord Mayhew of Twysden's Motion, The Times*, 12 November
3. *R* v. *Secretary of State for Transport, ex parte Factortame Ltd* [1999] 4 All ER 906
4. *Director of Public Prosecutions* v. *Jones* [1999] 2 All ER 257
5. *R* v. *Local Commissioner for Administration in North and North East England, ex parte Liverpool City Council* [1999] 3 All ER 85 (Hooper J.)

XIV.2. LAW IN THE UNITED KINGDOM 497

6. *Porter* v. *Magill, The Times,* 6 May
7. [1999] 2 All ER 545
8. *R* v. *Uxbridge Magistrates' Court, ex parte Adimi* [1999] 4 All ER 520
9. *R* v. *Secretary of State for the Home Department, ex parte Adan* [1999] 4 All ER 774
10. *Stevens* v. *Gullis (Pile, third party), The Times,* 6 October
11. *R* v. *Bow Street Metropolitan Stipendiary Magistrate and others, ex parte Pinochet Ugarte (No 2)* [1999] 1 All ER 577
12. *Locabail (UK) Ltd* v. *Bayfield Properties Ltd, The Times,* 19 November
13. *R* v. *Bow Street Metropolitan Stipendiary Magistrate and others, ex parte Pinochet Ugarte (No 3)* [1999] 2 All ER 97
14. For subsequent proceedings, see *The Times,* 9 October
15. *Practice Direction* [1999] 2 All ER 490
16. *Practice Note* [1999] 3 All ER 466
17. *The Times,* 2 November
18. *R* v. *Howells* [1999] 1 All ER 50
19. *R* v. *Cooney* [1999] 3 All ER 173
20. *Criminal Justice (Mode of Trial) Bill*
21. *The Times,* 11 November
22. Law Commission Consultation Paper 155, *Legislating the Criminal Code: Fraud and Deception*; Consultation Paper 157, *Bail and The Human Rights Act 1998*
23. *The Times,* 15 December
24. *R* v. *Bow Street Metropolitan Stipendiary Magistrate, ex parte Government of the United States of America* [1999] 4 All ER 1
25. *R* v. *Heath, The Times,* 15 October; cf *R* v. *Baker, The Times,* 28 April
26. *R* v. *Rai, The Times,* 10 November
27. *Re B (a minor) (adoption order: nationality)* [1999] 2 All ER 576
28. *The Times,* 26 November
29. *Dawson* v. *Wearmouth* [1999] 2 All ER 353
30. [1999] 2 All ER 977
31. *Nagarajan* v. *London Regional Transport* [1999] 4 All ER 65
32. *Nurdin & Peacock plc* v. *D B Ramsden & Co Ltd* [1999] 1 All ER 941
33. *Institute of Chartered Accountants in England and Wales* v. *Customs and Excise Commissioners* [1999] 2 All ER 449
34. *McKnight* v. *Sheppard* [1999] 3 All ER 491
35. *Re a company (No 00709 of 1992)* [1999] 2 All ER 961
36. *Soleimany* v. *Soleimany* [1999] 3 All ER 847
37. *Westacre Investments Inc* v. *Jugoimport-SDPR Holding Co Ltd* [1999] 3 All ER 864
38. *Barrett* v. *Enfield London Borough Council* [1999] 3 All ER 193
39. (1998) 5 BHRC 293
40. *Watson* v. *British Boxing Board of Control, The Times,* 12 October
41. *The Times,* 28 October
42. *Reeves* v. *Commissioner of Police for the Metropolis* [1999] 3 All ER 897
43. *Costello* v. *Chief Constable of the Northumbria Police* [1999] 1 All ER 550
44. *Dimond* v. *Lovell* [1999] 3 AE 1; *Hardwick* v. *Hudson* [1999] 3 All ER 426
45. *Medforth* v. *Blake* [1999] 3 All ER 97
46. *The Times,* 12 November
47. *McFarlane* v. *Tayside Health Board* [1999] 4 All ER 961 (House of Lords)
48. *Godfrey* v. *Demon Internet Ltd* [1999] 4 All ER 342
49. *Hamilton* v. *Al Fayed* [1999] 3 All ER 317
50. *The Times,* 22 December
51. *Reynolds* v. *Times Newspapers* [1999] 4 All ER 609
52. *Alan Wibberley Building Ltd* v. *Insley* [1999] 2 All ER 897
53. *Burns* v. *Morton* [1999] 3 All ER 646
54. *R* v. *Oxfordshire County Council, ex parte Sunningwell Parish Council* [1999] 3 All ER 385
55. *Bruton* v. *London and Quadrant Housing Trust* [1999] 3 All ER 481

56. *Fitzpatrick* v. *Sterling Housing Association Ltd* [1999] 4 All ER 705
57. *Satnam Investments Ltd* v. *Dunlop Heywood & Co Ltd* [1999] 3 All ER 652
58. *Heinl* v. *Jyske Bank (Gibraltar) Ltd* , *The Times*, 28 September
59. *Hussain* v. *Lancaster City Council* [1999] 4 All ER 125
60. *Southwark London Borough Council* v. *Mills* [1999] 4 All ER 449
61. *Lippiatt* v. *South Gloucestershire Council* [1999] 4 All ER 149
62. *R* v. *Secretary of State for the Home Department, ex parte Simms* [1999] 3 All ER 400
63. *R* v. *Lord Saville of Newdigate, ex parte A* [1999] 4 All ER 860
64. *The Times*, 6 March

3. UNITED STATES LAW

COURTS' decisions about respective spheres of the federal and state governments' sovereignty continued, in 1999, the contraction of the powers of the federal government that began with the Supreme Court's decision in 1995. In *Alden* v. *Maine* the Supreme Court held that Alden, a state probation officer in Maine, could not sue his state government employer in a state court for a violation of the federal Fair Labor Standards Act without the consent of that state. In *Florida Prepaid Postsecondary Education Expense Board* v. *College Savings Bank* the Court held that a Florida state agency could not, without its consent, be sued by College Savings Bank in a federal court for a violation of patents held by that bank or for a violation of federal laws prohibiting false advertising because states were immune, under the Eleventh Amendment, from such suits in federal courts.

A federal circuit court of appeals held unconstitutional a provision in the federal Violence Against Women Act which entitled a rape victim to sue her attackers for a violation of her civil rights; the court held that because the law lacked a link to economic conduct or interstate commerce, Congress did not have power to enact it under the commerce clause. A federal district court, however, held unconstitutional a statute enacted by the Massachusetts legislature that prohibited the state and its agents from purchasing goods or services from anyone doing business with the Union of Myanmar (Burma) because the law infringed on the federal government's exclusive authority to regulate foreign affairs. The case was expected to be appealed, because of similar boycott laws adopted by other state and local governments.

The Supreme Court, in *Saenz* v. *Roe*, held unconstitutional a California law that entitled the welfare recipients who had recently moved to that state to benefits lower than it entitled the welfare recipients who already lived in there; that law violated the newcomers' 'privileges and immunities' protected by the Fourteenth Amendment privileges and immunities clause. Because the Court, in 1873, had held that there were no nationally recognized privileges and immunities protected by that clause, the Court's decision in 1999 was viewed as a major precedent for enlarging the protection of human rights.

A federal district court in Texas held unconstitutional another provision in the federal Violence Against Women Act which prohibited from owning a gun a man who was under an order that restrained him from going within a specified distance of a woman; the court held that the law violated the Second Amendment right to bear arms. The decision was the first ever to hold that the Second Amendment prohibited the power of Congress to limit ownership of guns.

In contrast to its decision in 1998, in *Bragdon v. Abbott*, where the Supreme Court liberally interpreted the Americans With Disabilities Act to cover a dental patient with HIV but no symptoms of AIDs, the Court, in three cases in 1999, restricted the scope of that law to disabilities that substantially limited major life activities. In *Murphy v. United Parcel Service*, the Court held that United Parcel Service had not illegally discriminated against Murphy when it denied him a job as a truck driver because he had high blood pressure that he controlled with medication. In *Sutton v. United Airlines*, the Court held that United Airlines had not illegally discriminated against Sutton when it denied him a job as an airline pilot because he had poor vision, which he corrected with eye glasses. In *Albertson's v. Kirkingburg*, the Court held that Albertson's had not illegally discriminated against Kirkingburg when it denied him a job as a truck driver because he had poor vision in one eye, for which he had learned to adjust. No disability existed in these cases because the plaintiff had ameliorated its effects such that no 'major life activity' was 'substantially limited'.

Law suits against tobacco and gun manufacturers created major precedents in products liability law (see also IV.1). Juries in California and Oregon, in separate cases, awarded verdicts against Philip Morris of $1.5 million and $1.6 million, respectively, in compensatory damages for smoking-related illnesses and $50 million and $79.5 million, respectively, in punitive damages. The judges reduced these punitive damages to $26.5 million and $32.8 million, respectively. The verdicts were the largest to date against a tobacco company for such diseases. In Florida, a district court of appeal held that a class action on behalf of 500,000 smokers could be prosecuted against tobacco companies for making a defective product and conspiring to conceal the dangers of smoking. The Florida supreme court undertook to review the decision. A jury in a federal court in Ohio delivered a verdict in favour of the tobacco companies in a suit by 114 union trust funds for the costs of health-care benefits provided to union members. The federal government initiated a suit against to tobacco companies for additional costs of federal health care plans that result from covering smoking-related illness.

Following the precedent in the state and local government suits against tobacco companies, 27 municipalities initiated suits against gun manufacturers for the additional costs of policing and health care that resulted from the negligent manufacture and distribution of hand guns. Courts in New York and Georgia ruled that the cases could proceed, while courts in Florida, Ohio and Connecticut dismissed such cases. A jury in a New York court awarded a victim of a shooting $560,00 in damages against the manufacturer of the handgun used in the shooting. It was the first case in which a verdict was awarded against a gun manufacturer for its negligent marketing of its guns.

The Supreme Court held unconstitutional as too vague a Chicago anti-gang ordinance that required the police to order any group of people standing around with no apparent reason to move if the police officer believed one of the group belonged to a gang. Similar ordinances had been enacted over the last six years in other cities to reduce crimes by gangs.

XV THE ARTS

1. OPERA—MUSIC—BALLET & DANCE—THEATRE— CINEMA—TELEVISION & RADIO

i. OPERA

THE fortunes of the Royal Opera improved steadily throughout the year when its new executive director, the American Michael Kaiser, took up his post and began to oversee the rebuilding and to supervise a reorganization of the company's financial resources. The glamorously rebuilt theatre in Covent Garden opened on schedule at the beginning of December, though a projected staging of Ligeti's *Le Grand Macabre* had to be abandoned in order to achieve this. After a royal gala evening of opera and ballet excerpts, a few days later the first new opera production was staged. This was Verdi's *Falstaff* with the opera world's current favourite baritone, the Welshman Bryn Terfel, in the title-role. At the wildly enthusiastic curtain-calls after the first performance, Terfel was presented with the BBC's 'Artist of the Year' award.

English National Opera (ENO) presented a full season of opera in London. Their first new production was Wagner's *Parsifal*, which the composer envisaged as an opera about an elite group of Aryan knights opposed to an evil magician who represented Judaism. The work could possibly be viewed as a homo-erotic fantasy about the knights, who allowed no woman to invade their realm; but, whatever else it might be, *Parsifal* was a complex work of art whose music was, at least intermittently, as powerful as anything Wagner ever composed. Nikolaus Lehnhoff's production turned the knights into 20th century German soldiers, with Parsifal and Kundry made up, confusingly, to resemble members of an African tribe. However, musically all was superb, with Mark Elder conducting beautifully, Kim Begley a fine Parsifal, and Kathryn Harries a sensuous Kundry.

ENO's new production of Arrigo Boito's *Mephistopheles* was less enjoyable. Boito's score was uneven, with a bombastic orchestral prelude, and no more than one or two attractive arias and a fine quartet. Despite sympathy with the director Ian Judge's attempts to enliven the proceedings, a staging that restored something of the atmosphere of Goethe's *Faust*, on which the composer's libretto was based, would have been preferable. Alastair Miles's voice was not really weighty enough for Mephistopheles, but David Rendall's Faust, though uncharismatic, was sung in clear, ringing tones. A third new production, *The Carmelites* (taken up later in the year by Welsh National Opera) was exemplary, doing full justice to Poulenc's moving opera about the sufferings of a group of nuns at the time of the French Revolution. Elizabeth Vaughan gave a performance of Bette Davis-like intensity as the dying Prioress, Joan Rodgers was superb as the novice Blanche, and Paul Daniel conducted with evident love of the music.

The regional opera companies all contributed interesting and enjoyable new productions, as well as some decidedly disappointing ones. Opera North's *Arabella*, in one of those misconceived stagings perpetrated by directors who think themselves superior to the composers they are meant to be interpreting, was at least sung and played superbly. The decor for *La Traviata* was economical, but its cast of singing-actors was first-rate. Janis Kelly's Violetta was dramatically convincing, and vocally exquisite, and Thomas Randle's Alfredo was a most compelling interpretation of the role.

Benjamin Britten's *Peter Grimes* is not the easiest of his operas to stage, mainly because of the composer's ambivalent attitude to Grimes, whom he turned into an unsatisfactory combination of visionary and thug. Welsh National Opera's new staging by Peter Stein was grim, Germanic, and dramatically unconvincing. As Grimes, John Daszak lacked variety of timbre and seemed not to have decided on any particular characterization. The company's 15-year-old staging of *La Bohème* still looked miraculously fresh, as did its even older production of *The Magic Flute* (first seen in 1979) with an ideal Pamina in Franzita Whelan, Andrew Shore's sympathetic Papageno, and Toby Spence's eager Tamino. Another successful revival was Yannis Kokkos's 1993 staging of *Tristan und Isolde*, with Jeffrey Lawton a stalwart Tristan and Mary Lloyd-Davies a fearless Isolde.

The summer season at Glyndebourne opened with Nicholas Hytner's impressive production of Mozart's final opera, *La Clemenza di Tito*, in David Fielding's elegant, though meaninglessly tilted decor and gender-confusing costumes. All the cast were performing their roles at Glyndebourne for the first time, with Monica Groop and Lisa Larsson magnificent as Sesto and Servillia, and Hans-Peter Blochwitz making the most of what opportunities he was given in the dramatically passive title-role. Glyndebourne also offered a new staging of *Pelléas et Mélisande*. Debussy's only opera was a problematical and rather precious work, easier to admire than to warm to. Its characters were shadowy, and its music sought not so much to define them as to create atmosphere. Graham Vick's staging was set in luxurious but highly inappropriate decor by Paul Brown, against which a strong cast, led by Richard Croft, Christiane Oetzre and John Tomlinson fought a losing battle. Also at Glyndebourne, Smetana's folksy Biedermeier comedy *The Bartered Bride* was updated by its director, Nikolaus Lehnhoff, and staged as a grim social drama set in a drab village hall in 1950 Czechoslovakia. Solveig Kringelborn brought an attractive presence and a pleasing lyric soprano to Marenka, and Kim Begley was convincing as her unpleasant lover, Jenik.

Alfredo Kraus, one of the greatest tenors of his generation, died in September at the age of 71. Other singers who died during the year included Victoria Sladen who was one of the most popular sopranos in Great Britain in the decade following World War II; Donald Smith, the Australian tenor who was a great favourite with Sadler's Wells' audiences in the 1960s; Maria Stader, the famous Swiss soprano, whose only British appearance was as the Queen of Night in *The Magic Flute* (in English) at Covent Garden in the 1949-50 season;

Constance Shacklock, a leading mezzo-soprano who was popular in a wide variety of roles at Covent Garden in the 1950s; and Nell Moody, soprano, translator and teacher, who was a notable figure in British operatic life over a period of more than 50 years.

ii. MUSIC

THE year 1999 was for classical music globally one of much varied, occasionally brilliant, activity. It took place, however, against a background of a contracting market, with attendant financial and artistic implications, an ever-encroaching trend towards the mindless vacuity of pop music, and a lack of aesthetic certainty about what constituted excellence in the musical art.

The established repertoire made up the greater part of performances. One of the leading magazines of the record industry, *Gramophone*, nailed its colours firmly to the traditional mast in a succinct summary of 20th century popular taste, by listing the ten 'best recordings ever', that is to say those so voted by its readers. Some dated back to the 1950s: Wagner, *The Ring* (VPO/Solti); Elgar, *Cello Concerto* (Jacqueline du Pré); Beethoven, *Symphony No. 5* (VPO/Kleiber); Puccini, *Tosca* (Maria Callas); Bach, *Goldberg Variations* (Glen Gould); Mahler, *Das Lied von der Erde* (Ferrier, Patzak, VPO/Walter); Beethoven, *Choral Symphony* (Bayreuth Festival Orchestra/Fürtwängler); Wagner, *Tristan und Isolde* (Philharmonia/Fürtwängler); Schubert, *Lieder* (Fischer-Dieskau/Moore); R. Strauss, *Four Last Songs* (Schwarzkopf, Berlin RSO/Szell).

A musical tradition begins nationally, even locally. It lives, grows, and is judged according to the place it affords to its living composers. On such a basis of established and familiar classics, performances of new music provided the leaven; and there were some notable recordings in 1999, including two of major works by Elliott Carter: *Symphonia: Sum Fluxae Pretium Spei* (BBC SO/Oliver Knussen) (see AR 1998, p. 513), and the earlier (1946) *Piano Sonata*, brilliantly played by Charles Rosen. Examples of performance of music from the previous generation were Roberto Gerhard's neo-classic *Harpsichord Concerto* and *Piano Concerto* (Barcelona SO/Lawrence Foster), and, from today's *avant-garde*, Simon Bainbridge's four orchestral songs *Ad ora incerta* (BBC SO/ Martyn Brabbins), and Louis Andriessen's *Trilogy of the Last Day* (Schoenberg Ensemble/ Reinherdt de Leeuw) .

The year also saw an event of the greatest potential importance for British music: the release of the first ten discs in the 'British Musical Heritage' series, focusing on chamber music groups and solo performers, and including composers from 1800 to the present day. The reissue of long-held recordings proved an inexhaustible asset to record companies, who catered for the discriminating collector in series: great pianists, great conductors, great orchestras. Twentieth-century opera fared particularly well under this system: Berg, *Wozzeck*

(Hamburg State Opera/Metzmacher); Busoni, *Doktor Faust* (Opéra National de Lyon/Nagano); Messiaen, *St François d'Assise* (Arnold Schoenberg Choir, Halle Orchestra/Nagano); R. Strauss, *Ariadne auf Naxos* (Schwarzkopf, Seefried, Streich, Philharmonia/Karajan); Emmerich Kalman, *Die Herzogin von Chicago* (Berlin Radio Choir, SO/Bonynge) .

Concert performances too were preponderantly weighted in favour of the established repertoire. Orchestras performed globally, and the same music was heard internationally. The Kirov Ballet, and the Kirov Opera, on their annual visit to London, in 1999 performed Shostakovich's *Lady Macbeth of Mtsensk* at the Barbican. Also at the same venue, in June, one of the most exciting performances of the year was given, by the St Petersburg Philharmonic, under Yuri Temirkanov, of Shostakovich's searing *Leningrad Symphony*. As an encore, and as a gesture to their hosts, they played *Nimrod* from Elgar's *Enigma Variations*. This was no chance. Elgar was getting better known internationally, and his music had a surge in popularity throughout Europe in 1999. The *Cello Concerto* was played in eight cities on various occasions, with a different soloist each time.

Other performances were promoted because of the composer's date of birth. It helped if the anniversary was divisible by five. The fiftieth anniversary of Richard Strauss's death fell in 1999, and was accordingly celebrated with operatic highlights, chiefly in Germany (Munich, Berlin, Dresden, Salzburg, Vienna), but also in New York and Garsington. A new edition of his works was brought out, and three books in English, which dealt largely with Strauss's relations with the Nazis before 1945. Charles Ives was another such composer with a doubly fortunate anniversary—the 125th of his birth, the 45th of his death. This was duly marked with concerts in Tuscson, Arizona (*Symphony No. 3*) , London (*Emerson Concerto*, in a reconstruction by David G. Porter), and Edinburgh (*Symphony No. 4*).

There were two centenaries in 1999. The first, at the lighter end of the stylistic spectrum, was that of the birth of the French composer Francis Poulenc. His *L'Histoire du Babar* was toured in Europe-Stavanger Festival, Geneva, Bonn, Wüppertal—while his opera *Dialogue of the Carmelites* was performed by both the Welsh National Opera, and the English National Opera at the Coliseum. The second, and most colourful anniversary, was that of the legendary jazz musician Duke Ellington—the 100th of his birth, the 25th of his death. He would have been mightily surprised at such attention from so many classical Big Bands. Concerts of his music were mainly in the USA, in Chicago (*Grand Slam Jam*), in Denver (*Harlem*), in Philadelphia (*Three Black Kings*), in Erie (*Black, Brown and Beige*), and in Los Angeles (*Night Creatures*); but it was also featured in London, at a South Bank jazz festival in November; and in April at, a concert in Amsterdam, Louis Andriessen contributed his own jazz interpretation to the festivities, *Passagiata in tram in America e ritorno*. In short, the Duke was accorded cult status.

Apart from Ellington, 1999 was a positive year for many other American composers. Charles Ives and Leonard Bernstein had by now become familiar beyond the point when their work called for explanation. Among the other most frequently performed composers were John Adams, Samuel Barber, John Corigliano, Philip Glass, John Harbison, Joan Tower. Each had many important performances in 1999. The most successful and prestigious was the world premiere in December, at the Metropolitan Opera in New York, of John Harbison's opera *The Great Gatsby*, for which the composer wrote his own libretto to F. Scott Fitzgerald's classic. The music was a fusion of the 'jazz age' of the 1920s, the age of 'flappers' and champagne, and the style of contemporary classicism. Thus America celebrated both the American 20th century opera tradition, and the 25th year at the Met of the distinguished conductor and artistic director James Levine.

Viewing the 20th century as a whole, and the musical trends working through it, the opening years witnessed a mood of radical idealism in the musical art, whose common language was not yet divided. The close of the century was therefore a time for reflection on some of the developments, fresh endeavours, artistic dead ends, that had marked the intervening years. In the early years of the 20th century there were two prime creative forces in music: jazz, which originated in America, and serialism, which originated in Vienna. As a cultural force jazz quickly spread, until it permeated the classical art-forms worldwide, through the work of leading composers such as Stravinsky, Copland, Weill, Tippett. By the end of the century it could be seen as part of the American tradition. Serialism on the other hand was a philosophical/intellectual movement, originating in Vienna in the 1920s, which gradually spread through Europe and America in the mid-century years, until by the 1950s the tide was running at the flood in the work and electronic research of Boulez and Stockhausen. Its features gradually became apparent. It led to a self-perpetuating complexity of the musical language, and a denial of creativity; and these factors made its decline inevitable. By the 1980s the tide had ebbed; by the 1990s total serialism was outplayed as a creative force.

To offset the gloom and complexities of serialism, several compensating trends developed: in America, minimalism; in Europe, particularly Britain, the early music movement, with the use of 'authentic or 'period' instruments; beyond Europe, folk music. The later years of the 20th century were characterized by pluralism in music; and just as the musical language itself became fragmented and diversified, so did its aesthetic standards. In Britain the divisions within the musical culture became more evident than elsewhere. The proportion of performance-time allotted to the living British composer reduced from about 8-9 per cent in the 1970s to about 3-4 per cent in the 1990s. As the century neared its close there was markedly less curiosity and interest among audiences about new British music than there had been 30 years earlier. The long-term effect of this lack of interest, as each generation added its quota to the list of unheard composers, was that the British musical tradition became like an immense iceberg, with only a tiny part visible, or audible.

Paradoxically, this trend seemed to affect in no way at all the surge of musical activity in Britain, particularly in London, and in the number of composers of every stylistic allegiance actively working and resident. In 1999 they totalled some 500. It would be possible to mount ten festivals of British music, not one of which would overlap with the other nine. Yet there seemed to be some inbuilt reluctance in the British musical culture to exploit the talent of its composers. Whereas the Americans greeted the new millennium with a new American opera at the Met, the British greeted it with pop music at the Greenwich Millennium Dome. An opportunity was spectacularly missed, particularly since the potential was so rich.

Among those who died in 1999 were the composers Einar Englund, Howard Ferguson and Gérard Grisey; the conductors Harry Blech, Paul Sacher, Robert Shaw and Georg Tintner; the violinists Viktor Liberman, Yehudi Menuhin and Eli Goren, founder of the Allegri String Quartet; the opera intendant Rolf Liebermann; the pianist and teacher György Sebök; the singer Ilse Wolf; and the percussionist James Blades. (For Blades and Menuhin, see XVIII: Obituary).

BOOKS OF THE YEAR. *Richard Strauss*, by Tim Ashley; *The Life of Webern*, by Kathryn Bailey; *Richard Strauss*, by Matthew Boyden; *Berlioz 1803-1832: The Making of an Artist*, by David Cairns; *The Life of Mussorgsky*, by Caryl Emerson; *The Life of Charles Ives*, by Stewart Fedar; *The Atonal Music of Anton Webern*, by Allen Forte; *Richard Strauss: Man, Music, Enigma*, by Michael Kennedy; *Alan Rawsthorne: Portrait of a Composer*, by John McCabe; *The Life of Debussy*, by Roger Nichols; *Beethoven's Concertos: history, style, performance*, by Leon Plantinga.

iii. BALLET & DANCE

IN 1999 London could, at last, claim to be attracting major international dance companies. The rebuilt Sadler's Wells, with its large stage, provided the opportunity for classical ballet and larger contemporary companies to be seen, complementing the work seen on smaller stages such as the Place. It was not the very largest companies that were attracted to Sadler's Wells-those like the Bolshoi needed and were indeed seen at the Coliseum—but the range of important companies including Pina Bausch in *Viktor*, Mark Morris's Company, and Cloud Gate from Taiwan could be enjoyed. The productions they brought were well established but for London audiences the backlog of works that remained unseen was substantial. At the same time Edinburgh Festival, which had served as Britain's major showcase for dance, was less interesting than in recent years. The festival's programme included the Cullberg Ballet performing choreography by Mats Ek, Dutch National Ballet, and American choreographer Susan Marshall.

Londoners had opportunities to gauge the strength of the dance scene in the USA with visits from Pacific Northwest and San Francisco Ballets at Sadler's Wells, and Stars of New York Ballet and Atlanta Ballet at the Royal Festival Hall. Pacific Northwest presented their superb staging of *A Midsummer Night's Dream*, and George Balanchine's *The Four Temperaments* (mounted by Francia Russell in an earlier staging than was generally seen) which riveted the audience although, it must be said, their other productions were less inspiring. San

Francisco's mixed programmes showed off the company from principals to *corps de ballet* in works by Morris, Balanchine and Helgi Tommasson and in a well-chosen gala programme. Most interesting was their performance of Jerome Robbins' *The Cage*. This work about predatory females had been tiresome by some people, but in 1999 two strong performances led to reconsideration of the work and recognition of its power. The first was by New York City Ballet with Alexandra Ansanelli and Monique Meunier in the leads; the second by San Francisco with Lucia Laccara as the novice who kills the intruders.

Dancers from New York City Ballet formed the major part of the group performing on the South Bank. They were excellent but the quality of presentation a little slap-dash. The only American ballet company which was not first class was Atlanta Ballet. Specializing in family entertainment their *Peter Pan* provided Christmas fare. This very Disneyish production seemed to be enjoyed by the young but was uninspiring choreographically. One other American visitor was worthy of note. Twyla Tharp's *Diabelli* at the Barbican Concert Hall showed she was back on form. With a new team of dancers in which long-serving members, including Jamie Bishton, were joined by new ones such as the excellent Dane, Thomas Lund, her production echoed the music with its rich tapestry of quotations. The music was played by the pianist Nikolai Demidenko who shared the stage with the dancers. Tharp attracted quite a lot of attention in Britain when both Birmingham Royal Ballet and Rambert Dance Company acquired works from her. Birmingham did better with *In the Upper Room,* as *The Golden Section,* which entered the Rambert Repertoire, now looked dated; but the dancers in both companies were happy to be challenged by Tharp's choreography and it was interesting to note which dancers got to grips with her fast quirky movements. Rambert revived a second work created, like *The Golden Section*, in 1981, but *Ghost Dances* by Christopher Bruce, illustrating the plight of persecuted people in South America, was as powerful and relevant as ever particularly when the former Chilean dictator Augusto Pinochet's extradition from Britain was under consideration.

In 1999 New York City Ballet celebrated their 50th anniversary with a year-long celebratory programme of 100 ballets presented in thematic groups. The ballets by Robbins were well performed whilst less attention was given to those by Balanchine. Included in the season were works by a number of other choreographers and a major event was the staging of the company's first complete *Swan Lake*. This was the Peter Martin's production originally choreographed for the Royal Danish Ballet. A surprising fact was that the average age of the dancers was only 20 and whilst it was delightful to see the young dancers bring a freshness to certain works there was definitely a lack of maturity in their approach to many ballets.

One curious feature of 1999 was the interest in 'aerial dances', as three significant artists showed works in London using equipment to defy gravity. In *Furioso*, created in 1993, Meryl Tankard, in Australia Dance Theatre's final performances before disbanding, showed her women swooping across the stage on ropes, their hair streaming behind them, although the men remained largely earthbound. Elizabeth Streb, from New York, brought her physical theatre for which the stage was filled with equipment, a flying-machine and piles of acrobatic mats. As the climax of the first half a 'dancer' catapulted through a pane of glass! More artistry was seen in *Rota* by Deborah Colker, from Rio de Janiero, in which eight performers hooked onto a revolving wheel. Apparently this was intended as a metaphor for life rather than heralding the fun-fair rides planned for the millennium.

The opening of London's rebuilt Royal Opera House dominated the end of the year. Although the Royal Ballet made a strong impact at the opening gala with a divertissement that documented its history at Covent Garden, it was not otherwise a notable year of activities for that company. William Tucket created a version of *The Turn of the Screw* for Irek Mukhamedov as Quint and Bruce Samson as Miss Jessel; Adam Cooper was invited to return to the company as guest to dance with Sarah Wildor (now promoted to principal dancer) in *Ondine*. Most exciting was the strengthening of the male part of the company. Cuban dancer Carlos Acosta proved to be a real asset being particularly impressive as the Brother in Kenneth MacMillan's *My Brother, My Sisters*. Johann Kobborg, a Dane, created a role in Michael Corder's *commedia dell'arte* evocation, *Masquerade*, the highlight of the company's last Dance Bites tour. As the House reopened Angel Corella, from Spain, and Ethan Steifel, from America, arrived as guest artists. The Royal Ballet's team of men was suddenly more exciting than it had been in years, the dancers being vastly more interesting than those who defected to Tetsuya Kumakawa's K Company in Japan. It should be noted, nevertheless, that the K Company sold out all its performances, a feat unrivalled in Japan by even the Kirov and Bolshoi.

The Bolshoi returned to London, revitalized now that Alexei Fadeyechev had taken over as artistic director. The highlight of the season was Fadeyechev's fresh staging of *Don Quixote* (scintillatingly danced by Nina Aniashvalli and Andrei Uvarov). Such a captivating and lively production was most encouraging after the dreary presentations of their previous visit and it was also intriguing to see *Paganini*, a neo-romantic Soviet drama.

Dancers of the calibre of Mikhail Baryshnikov, Irek Mukhamedov and Altynai Asylmuratova created excitement when they appeared but none were seen to great advantage in London. Baryshnikov returned with his White Oak, appearing in the Japanese-inspired *Dance with Three Drums and Flute* by Tamasaburo Band and Mark Morris's *The Argument* (which looked very different danced by Baryshnikov and three women instead of the Morris Company version with three men and three women). More significant was Baryshnikov's partnership with Merce Cunningham as part of Cunningham's 80th birthday programme in New York in July. Mukhamedov starred in Arc's cinematic-inspired *Return of Don Juan* and added Asylmuratova to his own showcase divertissement company. They smouldered together in *When Angels Fly* but acclaim depended on their personalities not the productions.

The Norwegian Ballet showed Corder's *Romeo and Juliet* which, with lively choreography, told Shakespeare's story clearly but was let down by dull dancers and toytown settings. Northern Ballet Theatre created an updated *Carmen* with choreography by Didy Veldman. Set in South America, this used an arrangement of Bizet's score and was an excellent example of clarity of narrative through dance. Using elements of Chaucer's *The Canterbury Tales* proved more of a challenge for Christopher Bruce in *God's Plenty* for Rambert. This was an ambitious production and while the choreography was interesting many had reservations about the introduction of spoken word. Siobhan Davies created her first full-evening work, *Wild Air*, for her company, luminous, languid and beautifully danced.

English National Ballet devoted several months to performing their huge arena *Swan Lake* tour in Hong Kong and Australia as well as Britain. The company, however, really showed its strength on their autumn tour with Ronald Hynd's enduring *Coppélia* and an excellently-programmed triple bill of *La Bayadère, Sphinx* and MacMillan's *Rite of Spring*. Nevertheless, it was Paris Opéra which once again provided the best dancing. Its tribute to Jerome Robbins was all that perfectionist choreographer could ever have demanded.

iv. THEATRE

THE most striking feature of the theatre year in London, and to a lesser degree in New York, proved to be the paucity of new plays possessing the stature to win awards or in other ways make the year memorable for new writing. The judges of the *Evening Standard* awards, for which only plays produced in the London area were eligible, decided to make no award at all for best play. In part this reflected their anger that *The Late Middle Classes*, written by one of Britain's leading dramatists, Simon Gray, and directed by Harold Pinter, was denied the West End theatre it had been led to expect. In its place the management preferred to install a fatuous musical about an imaginary boy band, inevitably titled *Boyband*. Greeted with excited squeals of delight from adolescent girls in the audience, this show's run was brief.

Gray's play had already toured the provinces, thus qualifying for the Barclays Theatre Awards, the judges of which had no hesitation in naming it best play. The author acknowledged this recognition with a careful smile but few words, and there was no disputing that the prize could only be a second-best. Set in a complacent corner of 1950s England, in fact the Isle of Wight, the play showed the baleful effects of emotional reticence and sexual duplicity in a troubled middle-class family where xenophobia and anti-semitism were never far away. The pathologist father vehemently attacked his son's piano-teacher, an Austrian refugee, for not being 'straight'—in the usage of that time meaning 'English', although there was platonic paedophilia in the music room—yet was himself deceiving his wife with another woman. Gray's sensitivity to the pressure parents exerted over their children and their manipulative power created a funny, sad, deeply compassionate play, and Pinter's atmospheric production elicited superb acting from a cast led by Harriet Walter and Nicholas Woodeson. London's West End became the poorer for this play's absence from it.

A play with over a dozen names listed as authors opened too late for the *Evening Standard* awards, which ended its theatrical year in September, but was the runaway winner in the best play category of the Critics' Circle awards. This was *Mnemonic* (Riverside) by the much-travelled Théâtre de Complicité, whose past achievements had included *The Street of Crocodiles*, *The Three Lives of Lucie Cabrol* and a revival of *The Chairs*, all multi-award-winning productions. Though listed as being 'devised by the company', *Mnemonic* was conceived and directed by Complicité's artistic director, Simon McBurney, and roamed freely and imaginatively around the twinned themes of memory and the search to recover the past. Its most striking component was the pattern of fact and speculation it wove around the Ice Man, the Neolithic mountaineer whose mummified body emerged in 1991 from the Alpine glacier that had entombed it for 5,000 years. At various times all seven performers took on the role of the Ice Man, with McBurney also playing a contemporary man whose sometime lover scoured Eastern Europe for her missing father. In leading us over this complex, whirling terrain the company shifted between character and setting like figures in an animated cartoon, tumbling between scenes, folding past into present and clouding the accepted boundaries between fact, memory and imagination. Text, performance, sound and lighting combined to create an evening that was both beautiful and awesome.

The worldwide tour of *Mnemonic* was destined to include a season in New York and, mirroring this journey, all but one of the original cast of *Sideman* were due to cross the Atlantic in the other direction. Warren Leight, author of this Tony award-winner for best play, was himself once a sideman, as struggling jazz musicians were called in the years from 1950. He based his play on the difficulties these players encountered and the sacrifices their families were forced to make. It was always gratifying when a play that had begun Off-Broadway made the successful climb to Broadway (John Golden Theatre) and won the top prize.

Curiously, its three rivals for the Tony all originated in Britain-Patrick Marber's *Closer* (Music Box), set in an up-to-the-minute London, yet another of Martin McDonagh's improbably murky views of rural Ireland, *The Lonesome West*, and a play written by Tennessee Williams at the very start of his career, *Not About Nightingales* (Circle in the Square). The manuscript of this grim play, based on a true incident that took place in a hellish prison in Philadelphia, lay unnoticed in a university archive for 60 years until brought to the attention of Vanessa Redgrave and subsequently produced in London at the National Theatre.

As a further example of the mutually-enriching two-way traffic between London and New York, the *Evening Standard* award for most promising playwright was given to American-born Rebecca Gilman for her unnerving drama of moral nullity set in the Deep South and ironically named *The Glory of Living* (Royal Court). The play followed a young psychopath and his besotted teenage moll across a landscape of cheap motels picking up under-age vagrant girls for him to rape and for her to kill afterwards. What Gilman hauntingly revealed was the girl's pitiful contradictions in which the vague sense that her behaviour was somehow wrong tussled with a desperate longing to be liked, first by her psychotic partner and then by her bemused lawyer. Monica Dolan and Tony Curran formed a vivid partnership as the morally-vacant pair, products and victims of a sleazy world, in a precisely-choreographed production by Kathryn Hunter, an actress now fast establishing herself as a first-class director.

The shortage of good new plays was strikingly illustrated at the National Theatre (NT), where a procession of feeble or downright wretched plays coincided with sensationally-good productions of classics. So poor were audiences for *Remember This*, Stephen Poliakoff's rambling play about the difficulty of preserving the past, that the play was hastily withdrawn—a measure seldom resorted to at this theatre—and a touring production of *Closer* brought in to fill the yawning gap.

There appeared to be some blind spot or cloth ear in the department responsible for presenting new writing, though Nick Darke's *The Riot*, presented at the National's Cottesloe auditorium was a refreshing exception. This exhilarating adventure pitting fishermen against Sunday observance in 19th century Cornwall became a popular success, but was a co-production with Cornwall's small touring company, the attractively-named Kneehigh Theatre.

The great achievements of the National's year emerged from the work of the NT Ensemble, established by Trevor Nunn, the artistic director, and John Caird. A core of about three dozen actors worked together throughout the year on a series of large-scale productions, developing singing and dancing skills, finetuning the art of verse-speaking and creating the sense of delight that comes from seeing an actor playing the lead in one play and a tiny, sharp-etched cameo in the next. Gilz Terera, scarcely out of drama school at the start of the year, when he played a servant in *Troilus and Cressida* and a monkey in *Candide*, finished as the lead in the Christmas show *Honk!* (a musical version of the *The Ugly Duckling*).

The chosen plays spanned the centuries, posed ever-urgent questions and reflected different dramatic styles. Within the compass of a few days audiences were able to take in Edward Bulwer-Lytton's *Money* from 1840, an hilarious yet touching drama from a notoriously thin period of playwriting; the superb sweep of Gorky's *Summerfolk* (1904), almost a pendant to Chekhovian drama, where the newly-prosperous middle-classes fritter their lives away in houses built where there might once have been a cherry orchard; and the greatest production in living memory of *The Merchant of Venice*. Trevor Nunn chose Mussolini's Italy of the 1920s as the period in which to relocate a play so steeped in antisemitism and distaste for men of 'complexion', i.e., black, that not a scene of it could be staged if it had been written today. Rich in telling details that brought new life to the multiple narrative strands, subtly hinting at the horrors only twenty years ahead, this compelling revival enabled Henry Goodman to give the performance of his career as a weary, wary Shylock, an irascible but doting father, isolated, implacable yet sensitive and troubled to the heart of his being.

At the Royal Shakespeare Company (RSC), producing and then transferring productions between the Barbican Centre in London and the three theatres at Stratford-upon-Avon, revivals ranged from the triumphant to the faintly disappointing. Nigel Hawthorne's doughty portrayal of the doomed monarch in *King Lear* did not find the tragic reach that marks out this mad sovereign as very different from his celebrated King George III. Director Yukio Ninagawa's difficulties with the English language cannot have helped his cast. Other Shakespeare productions fared much better: Michael Boyd's *A Midsummer Night's Dream*, ecstatic and boldly erotic; an *Othello* thrillingly directed by Michael Attenborough with the first black actor (Ray Fearon) to play the role on the main Stratford stage since Paul Robeson in 1959, and a smarmily devilish Iago from Richard McCabe. Alan Bates and Frances de la Tour played an *Antony and Cleopatra* (directed by Steven Pimlott) that emphasized how age had withered these once great lovers; and in a season dominated by the tragedies—there was also a *Macbeth* with Antony Sher—Gregory Doran revived the rarely-performed *Timon of Athens* with Michael Pennington, an accomplished verse-speaker, as the madly generous host who becomes an even madder misogynist when fortune and friends desert him. An intriguing feature here was the music, a jazz score by Duke Ellington written in 1963 for a production of this play at Stratford, Ontario.

In the centenary year of Noël Coward (born 16 December 1899), almost every British management felt duty bound to mount a Coward work be it play, musical or cavalcade. *Cavalcade* itself, his elegy for the first 30 years of the century, was successfully produced at Glasgow's Citizens' Theatre but his major plays fared badly in London, a disappointingly flat *Private Lives* at the National and a *Hay Fever* (Savoy) misjudged and coarsened by the normally reliable Declan Donnellan. A more interesting revival brought a magnetic Vanessa Redgrave and her brother Corin Redgrave together in *Song at Twilight* (Gielgud), Coward's last play, in which a famous writer is forced out of the closet. Directed by Sheridan Morley, one of Coward's godsons and better known as a theatre critic, his production was first seen at a pub theatre (King's Head, Islington) before its transfer to the West End.

However, it was Broadway that saw the most succesful Coward revival: *Waiting in the Wings* (Walter Kerr), his affectionate tribute to elderly actresses living in a retirement home. Written in 1960, Michael Langham's production was the American premiere and, while Lauren Bacall's performance was only politely noticed, uniform praise came to her co-star, the redoubtable Rosemary Harris who turned 70 even as rehearsals began.

Two of Arthur Miller's major plays were seen on Broadway in the course of the year: *Death of a Salesman* (Eugene O'Neill), directed by Robert Falls, for which Brian Dennehy and Elizabeth Franz each won Tony awards; and *The Price* (Royale), still an underrated drama, in which Harris Yulin's performance won greater praise than James Naughton's production.

In a Broadway season that saw Bernadette Peters triumph in a joyful revival of *Annie Get Your Gun* (Marquis), the musical that might be thought to have had the unlikeliest chance of success was *The Dead* (Belasco), based on the profound, and final, story in James Joyce's collection of short stories, *Dubliners*. With a book by Richard Nelson (who at last achieved a deserved American success) and music from Shaun Davey, directed by James Hofsiss, and presented first at Playwrights' Horizons before its Broadway run, this touching show was welcomed by one critic as 'a quiet revolutionary; a musical that dares to be diffident'.

Diffidence was a word that could be applied to few musicals, on Broadway or in the West End, and 'difference' was another with little significance when the same musicals were to be seen on both sides of the Altantic (and in many other countries too): *Beauty and the Beast, Cats, Chicago, Les Misérables, The Lion King, The Phantom of the Opera, Saturday Night Fever, Miss Saigon, Smokey Joe's Café* and *Rent* were all running in New York and in London at some time during the year, and several had been running already for a decade or more. A revival of Cole Porter's 1948 musical *Kiss Me, Kate* arrived on Broadway during the year (Martin Beck), to great acclaim, joining *Fosse*, a tribute to the celebrated director and choreographer, which had yet to cross the Atlantic.

In London *The Lion King* (Lyceum) left some critics underwhelmed but all agreed, along with the audiences, that the costumes, masks and staging by master-puppeteer Julie Taymor, along with spectacular scenery by Richard Hudson, made this Disney production a far more imaginative and theatrical recreation of a cartoon film than was achieved by the earlier *Beauty and the Beast*. The untranslated Zulu songs from the South African composer Lebo M added a welcome authenticity to the show, in striking contrast to Elton John's conventional pop music and Tim Rice's insipid lyrics. Whenever the show relied upon words the spell was broken: when spectacle took over, as in the sensational opening scene, the effect was breathtaking.

Where *The Lion King* brought an idea of the hot, dry, African veldt onto the stage, the West End's other new musical successes gave a glimpse of old Yorkshire and an ironic travel-brochure Greece. *Spend Spend Spend* (Piccadilly) by the colourfully-named Steve Brown and Justin Greene, tracked the story of Viv Nicholson who famously won a football pool prize in 1961 and gave that answer when asked what she would do with the money. Essentially, the musical was a tale of the rise, fall and resurrection of a cheeky working-class girl, filled with tunes as bouncy as its heroine (a vivacious Barbara Dickson), where folksy miners' chants were given equal place with pastiches of the pop songs of 40 years ago.

In total contrast came *Mamma Mia!* (Prince Edward) where 22 songs by the Swedish group Abba were fitted into a cherishably-absurd plot supplied by Catherine Johnson. Unlike so many compilation shows, doing little more than punch songs into what purports to be a biography of the singer, Ms Johnson created an original tale, with a little help from the ancient Greek dramatists, about an Irish owner of a Greek taverna, an illegitimate daughter who wanted to meet her father before she got married, and the three suspects who unwittingly accepted invitations to the wedding. Wittily knowing and ironic, yet with moments of genuine feeling, allowing audiences to groan with delight whenever the cast, led by a feisty Siobhan McCarthy, uttered another shameless cue for the next Abba number, the show may have been supremely silly but was nonetheless tremendous fun. A genre that could embrace three such different musicals as well as *The Dead* had life in it yet.

v. CINEMA

ON the crest of the new millennium, dozens of experts all over the world were requested to write about the future of cinema and film—how celluloid would soon be dumped, how films could be made infinitely cheaper on tiny cameras by the merest amateur, how we would all see our movies downloaded from the Internet. Maybe, but not yet. Not in the year in which James Cameron's *Titanic*, which cost $200 million, succeeded in grossing well over $1,000 million. And a little British film, financed by the Americans, carried off Oscars and caused its main writer, Tom Stoppard, to be knighted by the Queen. *Shakespeare in Love* gave smaller fry than James Cameron hope that the kind of independent work Hollywood would not contemplate making itself could reach for the skies—and not through the Internet.

The cinema, it seemed, was still very much alive and kicking, capable of making fortunes for the lucky even if frequently failing to do so for the less fortunate. The new technology—best expressed on the screen so far with handheld video cameras boosted up to 35mm and labelled 'Dogma' by the Danish film-makers who reinvented the idea, and computer animation which resulted in the successful *Toy Story II* and the rather less-highly-praised *Fantasia 2000*-seemed well short of revolutionary.

As mentioned in *The Annual Register* in previous years, the ever-increasing cultural dominance of Hollywood, not just in America but over at least three-quarters of the globe, inevitably meant that the success or failure of a year for the film world was determined by the triumph or disaster of American film. In this respect 1999 was certainly not a failure, even though the studios were consistently complaining about the inordinate cost of their films and the acquisitiveness of their stars. They also complained that only a few of the 500 films produced survived more than a week or so as top-flight attractions, which meant more and more product had to be pumped hopefully into the cinemas before being dumped unceremoniously into the video bin. But a studio could exist on two or three hits in a year, and most of them had that number. Abroad, their product, good or bad, dominated cinemas almost everywhere, except in China and India. But even there *Titanic* did titanic business.

The year's major attraction was the new *Star Wars* film which, despite a feeble script and characters of straw or possibly wood, proved a huge draw.

George Lucas, who vowed never to make another film as director after the troubles he had experienced convincing Hollywood that the first edition was worth its salt, scarcely proved himself a better film-maker. But it did not seem to matter. Nor did it seem to matter that Mike Meyers's *Austin Powers: The Spy Who Shagged Me* was considerably poorer than the first Powers movie. The sequel also triumphed at the box-office.

There were not too many prestige productions to write home about, though Terrence Malick's *The Thin Red Line*, an audacious war story that outdid Steven Spielberg's *Saving Private Ryan* in thoughtfulness if not in technique, was well worth arguing about in quality terms. So was Martin Scorsese's *Bringing Out The Dead*, hardly his best work but at least back on the mean streets of New York after the *longueurs* of his slow-motion Tibetan epic *Kundun*. There was also Stanley Kubrick's *Eyes Wide Shut* too, years in the making, and even more hyped after his sudden death (see XVIII: Obituary). None of these films made much money but each of them gave hope that Hollywood was not entirely concerned with satisfying avid teenagers with spectacular special effects.

Europe's major coup, after Roberto Benigni's triumphant *Life Is Beautiful* had proved the most successful foreign film ever shown in America, was Pedro Almodovar's splendid *All About My Mother*. Made by a gay man, this beautifully-acted tribute to women proved—as Benigni's film had-that it was still possible to produce a seriously intelligent film that was also popular around the world. There was much argument at Cannes in 1999 when Almodovar only got the best director prize and the Dequenne brothers from Belgium won the Palme d'Or for *Rosetta*. But that little film, unlikely to appeal widely, was another that proved that Europe could still do what Hollywood could not with highly personal material.

Other European art-house hits included the Dogma-oriented *Mifune*, from Denmark, the controversial *L'Humanité*, from France, and two British films— Lynne Ramsay's *Ratcatcher*, about a Glaswegian childhood, and Damian O'Donnell's *East Is East*, taken from a play by Ayub Khan about a mixed-race English-Pakistani family and its inter-generational conflicts. This last took £10 million at the British box-office, an unheard of feat considering the subject matter and absence of recognizable stars. Tim Roth's first effort as director, *The War Zone*, about the tricky subject of child abuse, did not do well at the box-office but was another British film recognized abroad and gaining the Fassbinder Award.

On the popular front in Europe, there was the British-American *Notting Hill*, which united Hugh Grant and Julia Roberts in a comedy from the shrewd pen of Richard Curtis, the writer of *Four Weddings and a Funeral*, and the French *Asterix and Obelix*, a hugely-expensive, rather clumsy, but very successful, screen version by Claude Zidi of the famous comic-strip. But Almodovar predictably won the European Film Academy's accolade for Best European Film, and deserved almost every compliment bestowed upon it.

One country to benefit greatly from the increasingly international nature of film was India, whose Hindi film industry, nicknamed 'Bollywood', began to realize that it could make movies for the world rather than just for the admittedly huge and film-obsessed population of the sub-continent. There had, of course, always been a market for Bollywood outside India, specifically in the Middle East, Africa and the former Soviet Union. The late Raj Kapoor, star, producer and director, was as well-known in the USSR as he was in India. But now Britain began to show Bollywood films in multiplexes around the country, daring to take on and beat the video versions, often pirated, that the immigrant population seemed previously to favour. America also became a big market, with Canada following. Several Bollywood films, in fact, were more successful abroad than they were at home, notably *Straight from the Heart*, a three-hour music and dance spectacular of some originality. This was partly made in the Czech Republic, which stood in for Vienna, and many other Bollywood films used foreign locations as well. The Scottish glens, Sydney Bridge and New York were now as likely to feature as song and dance settings in Bollywood films as hillside locations in India.

Additonally, the Indian diaspora managed to produce a number of films by NRIs (non-resident Indians), many of which detailed Indian experiences as immigrants but some of which were popular successes with no reference to their origins. The two most astonishing productions were M. Night Shyamalan's highly-successful *The Sixth Sense*, made in Hollywood with Bruce Willis starring in a psychological ghost story of particularly Indian sensibility, and Shakur Kapur's *Elizabeth*, made in Britain and giving a decidedly new take on the early years of Queen Elizabeth I. Indians, it seemed, now did not mind where they made movies or who financed them.

No other Asian country could match the Indian achievement, although some had successes on the festival circuit. China, for instance, won the Golden Lion at Venice with Zhang Yimou's *Not One Less*, about a young supply teacher losing a pupil from her country school in the big city. But the other blue-riband Chinese director, Chen Kaige, saw his expensive historical epic *The Emperor and the Assassin*, made with money raised from China, Japan and France, get a mixed reception at Cannes.

Iran's top director, Abbas Kiarostami, whose *The Taste of Cherries* won at Cannes in 1997, continued to prosper with *The Wind Will Carry Us Away*, which took the Special Jury Prize at Venice—before the director announced that he had had enough of competition and would henceforward show his films without vying with others. Iran produced several more good films, proving that the Iranian cinema was no one-man band.

Africa contributed little of note, largely because of serious money problems, but Latin America, suffering from much the same fate in recent years, began to wake up. There were no palpable hits, but several outstanding first features were shown at festivals around the world. Alas, there was little to write about from either Russia or Japan, except perhaps two films from Russia—Alexander Sokurov's *Moloch*, an impressive, if eccentric, study of the banality of evil, exploring the relationship between Hitler and Eva Braun; and Alexander Rogozhkin's *Checkpoint*, which viewed Russia's military attempts to control its former provinces with a very beady eye. Russia also produced what many thought the worst large-scale film of the year. This was Nikita Mikhalkov's *The Barber of Siberia*, made in English and equipped with every Hollywood cliché in the book. It opened Cannes, but closed pretty soon everywhere else.

Among others who died in 1999 were the British actors Sir Dirk Bogarde and Chili Bouchier, and the American actor George C. Scott (see XVIII: Obituary).

vi. TELEVISION & RADIO

THE world of broadcasting might be changing dramatically in technological terms but some things remained constant. An altercation at Sharon's wedding helped *Coronation Street* once again to take the top programming slot on British television for the year, with an audience of 19.82 million on 7 March.

The Street just managed to edge out the programming phenomenon of the year, *Who Wants to be a Millionaire?* with Chris Tarrant, from the top spot on the same evening. Many people probably wanted to be a millionaire, but no contestants actually made it to the big prize on ITV's new quiz show programme, with a format that was quickly exported around the world. The lack of a million-pound winner did not rob the show of excitement, the top-rated edition in March attracting an audience of 19.21 million. It also, with the help of no less than three editions on Christmas Day, helped ITV to get within a whisker of reaching its demanding self-imposed target for the year of 39 per cent of total viewing in prime time.

Managing to produce a real increase in the ratings for one single channel in the face of the spread of digital multi-channel television was judged to be a considerable achievement by Richard Eyre, chief executive of the ITV Network. Criticism continued, however, over the decision to axe *News at Ten* and ITV's failure to put much of substance into the vacated prime-time slot. Although there was controversy over its broadcasting of soft-porn late at night, Channel 5 also increased its share of the audience, to 6 per cent, and was estimated to be worth £1,000 million. Channel Four's subscription film service, FilmFour, was established as a business success.

In the 100 most-viewed programmes of 1999, the best the BBC could manage was 11th place with an episode of its soap opera *Eastenders*. The Corporation did, however, produce a number of memorable programmes, the most notable being *Walking with Dinosaurs*, which was the highest-rated documentary of the year with an audience of 15 million. There were other BBC successes in drama, ranging from *David Copperfield* to *Wives and Daughters*. The BBC also attracted audiences of more than 10 million to its ambitious, but occasionally technically-flawed, continuous millennium coverage from around the globe. On Monday 26 April, moreover, there was a 10.3 million audience for the BBC's *Nine O'Clock News* on the day that television presenter Jill Dando was shot dead outside her London home—a murder that remained unsolved at year-end.

The BBC dominated the headlines in other ways, as the controversial reign of Sir John Birt as director-general came to an end and the search began for a successor. Greg Dyke, the multi-millionaire former managing director of London Weekend Television and current chief executive of Pearson Television, was widely believed to be the first choice of BBC chairman Sir Christopher Bland. The £400,000-a-year job was advertised and a tense battle ensued between internal and external candidates. One of the few to break coverbecause he was an outside chance at best—was Andrew Neil, former editor of the *Sunday Times*. Mr Neil warned that those who worked for the BBC 'need to have their fading loyalty and morale restored by clear and consistent statements of what the BBC is about and the distinctive direction in which it should be going'. Licence-fee payers, he added, needed to 'recaptured' through the sorts of programmes that should be the hallmark of BBC broadcasting.

The three top names on the final shortlist were Greg Dyke, Tony Hall chief executive of BBC News, and Richard Eyre of ITV. In June the job finally went to Mr Dyke but only after a vehement campaign against his appointment by *The Times* on the grounds that his political payments to the Labour Party, and the office of Tony Blair in opposition, rendered him unsuitable (see also II.1). *The Times* emphasized that the donations, totalling £55,000, were important because the director-general was also head of BBC journalism as editor-inchief. Overcoming these objections, Mr Dyke quickly made it clear that he wanted to reduce the layers of management in the BBC and end its reliance on external management consultants. He had not been due to become director-general until April 2000, but the date was brought forward after Sir John Birt was made a life peer in the New Year's Honours list.

By chance, the long-winded process of choosing a new BBC director-general was in full swing when Mark Booth, chief executive of satellite broadcaster BSkyB, unleashed a digital price war by announcing on 5 May that digital boxes were going to be offered free until further notice. Until then, since the launch of digital television in the autumn of 1998 (see AR 1998, p. 529), Sky had signed up more than 550,000 digital subscribers. Said Mr Booth: 'We have had the most successful digital launch anywhere. But it's not good enough when there is so much more to play for. We want to be the leading integrated consumer product into the home.' ONdigital, the digital terrestrial television service owned by Granada and Carlton Communications, were immediately forced to follow suit with a free box offer. The offers greatly stimulated the market for digital television: by the end of the year BSkyB had more than two million digital subscribers and ONdigital had 552,000. The leading cable companies had also begun to sign up digital subscribers, with the additional carrot of being able to offer high-speed Internet access.

In October a consortium of companies led by BSkyB launched an interactive digital television service called 'Open....', offering everything from home banking and shopping and even pizza delivery to viewers. Users could also get Internet access and send and receive emails via the television screen. In the run-up to Christmas sales were running at the rate of £1 million a week and the first mortgages initiated on a television had been approved. In a more traditional area of viewer interest, football, a big worry for BSkyB was the threat to its all-important exclusive deal with the English Premier League, after its £623 million bid for premier club Manchester United (see AR 1998, p. 529) had been vetoed by Trade and Industry Secretary Stephen Byers on the advice of the Competition Commission in April. Negotiations for the next contract to run from the 2001-02 season were due to get under way in the spring of 2000.

The fastest-possible spread of digital television was a central plank of the government's media policy. The aim was to encourage the digital revolution so that every home had access to digital information. When achievement of that goal was close, the government would be able to auction off the existing analogue frequencies for mobile communications, for perhaps £10,000 million. In September Culture, Media and Sport Secretary Chris Smith told delegates to the Royal Television Society conference in Cambridge that he wanted the process of switching off analogue television to begin in 2006 and end in 2010—an ambitious target. A final date would be set for switch-off only when 95 per cent of the population had digital television. Even that proportion would leave more than one million homes to be, in effect, coerced into buying new television equipment. At the same time, Mr Smith made it clear that the government wanted to see the BBC properly financed to play its full part in the digital world.

A panel on the future financing of the BBC chaired by Goldman Sachs economist Gavyn Davies reported in July. The committee produced a majority report arguing that the BBC should get an additional digital licence fee of £24 a year—around one-third of the extra funding asked for by the BBC. Most of the Davies panel argued that it would be wrong to make general licence-fee payers contribute more to provide new digital services for the minority who had digital television, most of them better off than the average. Lord Gordon of Strathblane, founder of Radio Clyde and the only broadcaster on the panel, argued that it would be better to boost BBC revenues with two 'one-off' £5 increases to the general licence fee.

Commercial broadcasters were quick to point out that not only had digital viewers been promised that they would not have to pay extra, but that a digital licence fee would inevitably slow down the spread of digital television. By year's end the government seemed torn between introducing a digital licence fee, raising the general licence or combining a mixture of the two. Before the decision was taken, however, Chancellor Gordon Brown produced a licence-fee shock of his own. He decided that everyone over the age of 75 should be given a free television licence, at the taxpayers' expense.

Commercial radio saw the arrival of its first digital channels, to compete with the BBC services which had been broadcasting for a number of years. Only a few thousand listeners could hear the broadcasts, because the cost of a digital receiver, though likely to fall rapidly, was still more than £600. Revisions to the methods of measuring the radio audience produced an unexpected bonus for the BBC: by the end of 1999 BBC Radio was back in the lead, with a total audience share of more than 51 per cent.

While the government wrestled with problems such as how best to finance the BBC, huge newly-rich forces were gathering in the form of expanding telecommunications companies and Internet organizations (see also XIII.3). Freeserve, the Internet access company controlled by the Dixons store chain, was almost overnight more wealthy than television groups such as Carlton Communications. The first big media merger came in the USA in September when Viacom, owners of everything from Paramount studios and MTV to Blockbuster video, bought the US network company CBS in a $37,000 million deal. Most observers thought that it would be only a matter of time before there were even-larger mergers, following the industrial pattern of everything from banking to pharmaceuticals.

In the UK, a further round in the consolidation of the cable industry got under way when NTL beat Telewest to merge with Cable & Wireless Communications. NTL was able to mount its bid because of the financial help of France Telecom, which provided finance in return for a 25 per cent stake. Uncertainty over the deal continued because the merger was referred to the Competition Commission for a full investigation. Another French investment in the UK suffered the same fate. Vivendi, the French company which controlled the subscription television group Canal Plus, acquired a 24 per cent stake in BSkyB. Although Rupert Murdoch—chairman of News Corporation, which had a 40 per cent stake in BSkyB—ruled out any chance of a merger, the deal was referred by Industry Secretary Stephen Byers. The minister expressed concern that BSkyB and Canal Plus could together dominate television sports rights in Europe.

The clearest example of the pressures driving the media to consolidation came in November when two ITV rivals, Carlton Communications and United News & Media (UN&M), announced a friendly £8,000 million merger. The deal was surprising for two reasons. Together the companies would control around 34 per cent of television advertising, whereas five years earlier UN&M had agreed that it would not increase its control of advertising beyond 25 per cent without the approval of the Office of Fair Trading. Both sides noted that the 25 per cent limit was already under review. Even more surprising was the idea of two notoriously spikey characters, Carlton chairman Michael Green and UN&M chief executive Lord Hollick, cooperating in a single company.

The proposed Carlton-UN&M merger shocked Granada, which liked to see itself as the leading ITV company but would be pushed into second place if the deal went through. After pondering for a while, Granada chairman Gerry Robinson asked the OFT for permission to make takeover bids for either Carlton or United, with United the more likely target of the two. The entire

Granada-Carlton United issue was also likely to end up before the Competition Commission, which would mean that the Commission rather than the government would set out the changing framework for commercial television in the UK. The government, if re-elected, was not planning to introduce substantive broadcasting legislation before 2002.

There was little doubt in 1999 that technology was moving faster than government regulation. The first commercial video-on-demand services down the telephone line had already been launched and Internet television was coming closer in terms of quality. Digital television receivers were becoming sophisticated computers. The latest models would be able to record automatically up to ten hours of the receiver's favourite programmes straight into the equivalent of a computer hard disk. Even in such a world, however, *Coronation Street* and *Who Wants to be a Millionaire?* were expected to dominate the ratings for some time to come.

2. VISUAL ARTS—ARCHITECTURE

i. VISUAL ARTS

'SENSATION', the exhibition of young British artists from the Saatchi Collection which had been the subject of considerable controversy when first shown in London at the Royal Academy in 1997 (see AR 1997, p. 510-11), had even greater repercussions when restaged at the Brooklyn Museum in New York City in 1999. Whereas in London a portrait of the serial child-killer Myra Hindley (by Marcus Harvey) had been the subject of public outrage, in New York the focus of contention was a representation of the Virgin Mary by Chris Ofili, an artist of African descent who depicted the Mother of God as a caricatural black woman, adorned his canvas with cut-out details of pornography and encrusted the surface with dried elephant dung (a trademark motif of this artist). Ofili's work excited the indignation of New York City's mayor, Rudolph Giuliani, who objected to a publicly-funded institution exhibiting objects likely to offend religious sensibilities. He made strenuous attempts to block the exhibition—disrupting public transport in the area on the evening of the opening—and threatened to cancel the museum's funding, which was heavily dependent on the city. This threat was successfully resisted through the courts on First Amendment grounds, but the issue of future capital funding remained. The controversy provoked extensive press coverage, turning the exhibition into a *cause célèbre* and ensuring massive attendance.

Back in the UK, Charles Saatchi donated 100 pieces from his collection to the Arts Council of England. The young artists he collected, meanwhile, began achieving prices at auction to match their critical notoriety. The year was generally marked by sharp increases in the values of contemporary artists at auction, which experts attributed to stock market escalations. When the Dow Jones index reached a new all-time high at mid-year, for instance, a typical work by the contemporary American artist Robert Gober—a cast of the artist's leg protruding from a wall—fetched a record $720,000 shortly afterwards. In other areas the art market also saw marked increases, with new records established for masters old and new, including Velazquez and Lucian Freud.

Issues of restitution continued to proliferate in the museum world—often, though not exclusively, to do with claims relating to World War II and the Cold War. Committees were established in various countries to investigate claims, while the National Gallery in London launched an inquiry into 120 works in its own collection whose provenances raised queries. Heirs of the dealer Paul Rosenberg (brother of the famous promoter of Cubism, Leonce Rosenberg), whose collection had been appropriated by the Nazis but not returned to the family upon its repatriation to France at the end of the war, were able finally to retrieve works from the Seattle Museum in the USA and from the National Museum of Modern Art in Paris (at the Pompidou Centre). The Museum of Modern Art in New York also agreed the return of a work, as well as settling a long dispute with heirs of the Russian painter Kasimir Malevich, a large group of whose works had been lodged with the museum since the 1930s. The Austrian government decided to return to the Austrian branch of the Rothschild family some 250 works which had been confiscated by the Nazis and retained by the government of the day in exchange for export permission on other items. The returned works included three paintings by Frans Hals held by the Kunsthistoriches Museum. However, the Austrian government did not agree that paintings in state collections by Gustav Klimt should be returned to the Bloch-Bauer heirs; these works had been sold by court order in 1938 to settle punitive taxes imposed, at the time, on Jews.

The Getty Museum in Los Angeles took the initiative in returning three works to the Italian government when the museum's own researches revealed them to be stolen property. All three were important classical artefacts. The British Museum, meanwhile, paid $3 million for a classical artefact—its most expensive single acquisition since 1982—that was controversial for its subject-matter rather than its provenance. Depicting acts of homosexual love-making, the *Warren Cup*, was named after the expatriate American collector who once owned it; in the 1950s, when the work was under offer to the Metropolitan Museum in New York, it had been refused entry by US Customs on grounds of immorality.

Twenty years of controversial restoration work was completed in 1999 on Leonardo da Vinci's *Last Supper* frescoes in Milan and received mixed reviews. Critics pointed out that less than a quarter of Leonardo's original painting remained and believed that the restorers had been over-inventive. Plans began to be made for another the world's most celebrated threatened cultural treasures, the Parthenon in Athens, after it was decided that the temple would have to be moved from the Acropolis, to be replaced there by a replica. Comparably radical plans to save the city of Venice from the ravages of the sea by constructing sea barriers were vetoed by Green-aligned politicians in the Italian government.

The millenium year was to be the focus for a number of new museums and extensions in the UK, but in 1999 several establishments were unveiled. The Guildhall Museum in the City of London, which had been destroyed during the blitz in 1941, reopened in new premises, while in Scotland two important developments took place: a centre for contemporary art opened in Dundee which included art galleries, art school premises and facilities for the city's famed print-making workshop, while the Dean Gallery, an outhouse of Edinburgh's Scottish National Gallery of Modern Art stationed in a fine neo-classical building, presented the Surrealist collection of Gabrielle Keiller, together with other surrealist material from the collection of Sir Roland Penrose and the donated studio archive of Scottish-born Pop artist Sir Eduardo Paolozzi. Plans were unveiled for two important museum projects in London: a new Queen's Gallery, at Buckingham Palace, which was to be built in the classical style of the earlier part of the palace and to be opened in the Golden Jubilee year, 2002; and a new store for the British Museum offering unprecedented ease of access to scholars and members of the public to the museum's collections of textiles, ethnography and Romano-British materials. The store was to be converted from an old post office sorting house nearby in Bloomsbury in a commercial development which would include a hotel and shops.

The Tate Gallery and the Victoria & Albert Museum undertook an important exchange of materials which made sense of the changing identities of each institution. The V&A's extensive holdings of John Constable transferred to Millbank, where they could be displayed alongside Constable's historic rival Turner in the Clore Galleries (the Turner wing), while the Tate in turn surrendered various eighteenth-century works. The V&A, meanwhile, secured planning permission for its controversial new wing by American architect Daniel Libeskind, to be built in a radical 'deconstructivist' style in marked contrast to the Renaissance style of the rest of the museum (see AR 1997, p. 515). The year saw the opening of another museum by Liebeskind, this time at Osnabrück in Germany for the magic realist painter Felix Nussbaum, a victim of the Nazis who had made highly significant works depicting the Holocaust.

The Boston Museum of Fine Arts joined a growing trend in the globalization of prominent institutions. Following the lead of the Guggenheim Museum, which had various American and European satellites, the BMFA opened a partnership museum at Nagoya, Japan. This move, together with plans for an extensive redevelopment of the mother museum in Boston, followed on the heels—critics felt ominously—of the director's decision to sack a considerable number of longstanding curators, many of them eminent scholars in their field. In Australia, a museum appointment also proved controversial, and gained international attention. When John McDonald, the lively critic of the *Sydney Morning Herald*, was named head of Australian art at the National Gallery of Australia, 400 artists, academics and professionals signed petitions of protest. Many of these people had been victims of McDonald's critical pen.

The Venice Biennale, organized by the German curator Harald Szeemann, excited little critical enthusiasm with its heavy bias in favour of new media, in particular video installation. More noteworthy were two exhibitions which ran concurrently in the city: an ensemble of sculptures by Sir Anthony Caro, displayed in a disused church on the Guidecca, dealing with the theme of the Last Judgment; and a monumental survey of the influences running between Venice and northern Europe during the Renaissance.

There were, in fact, many major exhibitions organized around the world in 1999, some of them ground-breaking. A survey of the seventeenth-century Dutch master Pieter de Hooch was the first for this artist in the UK and the USA, shown at the Dulwich Picture Gallery in London and the Wadsworth Athenium in Hartford, Connecticut (the oldest art museums in each country). But the year might be remembered by museum visitors for a coincidental focus on portraiture, as several major exhibitions dwelt on this genre. Besides fullscale retrospectives of Anthony Van Dyck and John Singer Sargent, both of whom excelled at portraiture, there were exhibitions which looked specifically at Ingres's portraits, and Rembrandt's self-portraits. These shows were at important venues in London and the USA. London and New York also shared an in-depth reconsideration of the Abstract Expressionist painter Jackson Pollock. A show devoted to Monet's paintings in the twentieth century—the artist's late works, including his monumental lily pond series—drew record attendances at London's Royal Academy, which introduced the innovation of round-the-clock opening hours to cope with visitor demand. A major display of Chardin began its international tour in Paris.

Some institutions launched revisionist surveys of the modern period to mark the change of century. The Whitney Museum of American Art in New York, for instance, organized a mammoth two-part survey of its collections entitled 'The American Century', bringing many *recherché* items out of store for the first time in ages. The Museum of Modern Art launched an even more ambitious three-part re-examination of its holdings of turn of the (last) century art in a troika of shows, 'People', 'Places' and 'Things', grouped under the collective title 'Modern Starts'. It was a significant departure for this institution, the premier modern art museum in the world, to organize its displays around genres, mixing different schools and mediums (paintings, prints, design objects etc.). It was even perceived as a radical break with its own traditions that the museum walls, usually white, were appointed in rich and diverse colours, as if to mark a transition from a purist curatorial vision to an eclectic one.

Among those in the British art world who died in 1999 were Ronald Alley, curator at the Tate Gallery; Harry Blacker, cartoonist; Sir Hugh Casson, former president of the Royal Academy; Alex Gregory Hood, art dealer; David Smith, marine painter; and Patrick Heron, abstract painter and art critic. Internationally, the year marked the loss of Leo Castelli, New York art dealer; Horst Horst, photographer; Norman Bluhm, American abstract painter; Bernard Buffet, French realist painter; Albert Tucker; Rudy Burckhardt, Swiss-born New York artist and experimental film-maker; Werner Haftmann, German art historian; Olivier Debré, French painter; César, French sculptor; Saul

Steinberg, American cartoonist; Paul Mellon, collector and benefactor of the Yale Center for British Art; and Oswaldo Guayasamin, Ecuadorian painter. (For obituaries of Buffet, Casson, Castelli, Heron and Mellon, see Pt XVIII.)

ii. ARCHITECTURE

As the twentieth century drew to a close, Berlin became a focus for architectural symbols denoting on the one hand the emergence of a new democracy in Germany (and by implication anywhere, given political will), and on the other a reminder of the evil of genocide. The building representing the brightest future was the rehabilitated and extended *Reichstag* parliament building, designed by Foster & Partners. Opened with appropriate celebrations (marred only by a subsequent spat over fees), the building, with its glazed dome providing new views across the city, was an immediate hit with the public, who queued in their thousands to visit the visible representation of the uniting of East and West Germany.

By and large, the critics approved of the Berlin building. Controversial decisions, such as to leave the graffiti of the Russian army when it took control of the building in 1945, were generally applauded, although a section of German politicians objected. There was some criticism that the transparency of the building was more apparent than real, and that the public could not in fact see into the parliamentary chamber from the dome. Nevertheless, the public approved, and the sight of the dome, especially at night when lights beamed out from it, became a natural part of the city's skyline. Lord (Norman) Foster of Thames Bank was given high honours by the German government, reinforcing his reputation as, probably, the world's leading architect.

The other key building to open in Berlin during 1999 was the Jewish Museum, designed by Daniel Libeskind. The extraordinary concrete structure, twisting and turning on itself, attempted to convey the idea of absence: of the Jews of Berlin who were taken from the city by the Nazis, never to return. This *tour de force* ran the gamut of architectural experience: dramatic stairways; a room in which you heard the sounds of street life while feeling utterly remote from it; slit windows arranged as reminders of particular people who lived at particular addresses in the city; a garden of skewed concrete columns representing the Jewish diaspora. Taken together, the museum and the *Reichstag* building could be read as the story of a city and a country coming to terms with its past, without flinching and without attempting to disguise the worst aspects of that past.

In Britain, the architecture of democracy was also a prominent feature of the year. After a closely-fought competition, Foster & Partners' glass sphere was chosen as a home for the new Greater London Authority on the south bank of the Thames close to Tower Bridge. Construction was due to finish in 2001, so the new mayor, who was to take up office in June 2000, would have to make do with temporary accommodation. The Foster partnership also designed an extraordinary spiral glass office tower for the City of London.

The Scottish Parliament continued in its temporary home while designs for its new building, by the Spanish architect Enric Miralles, neared completion amidst complaints about rising costs. The year's most significant building in Edinburgh was the Museum of Scotland, which opened to widespread approval, representing the entire history of the country without ever resorting to narrow nationalism. The neo-Corbusian design by Benson & Forsyth, too full of ideas for some tastes, gave the city what might be its finest building of the 20th century, providing an enriching architectural experience which justified repeated visits.

In Wales, complaints about cost were heard in relation to the planned new Welsh National Assembly building in Cardiff designed by the Richard Rogers Partnership, but the city's new millennium stadium by the Lobb Partnership won broad approval. The replacement design for the ill-fated Zaha Hadid opera house (see AR 1996, p. 492), a millennium centre designed by the Jonathan Adams/Percy Thomas Partnership, was unveiled to an approving audience. Hadid, meanwhile, had a resounding architectural success, winning the competition to design a new museum of modern art in Rome.

While Londoners pondered on the idea of the mayor's glass bubble, they came to grips with three extraordinary structures: the Millennium Dome, designed by the Richard Rogers Partnership (who also completed a spectacular new City of London office building for Daiwa); the Millennium Wheel, or more accurately the 'London Eye', designed by David Marks and Julia Barfield; and the media centre at Lord's, home of cricket, designed by Future Systems. Neither of the entertainment buildings formally opened until the new year, but each helped redefine the mental map of London, particularly the tourist map. The Lord's media centre won a string of awards, concluding with the Stirling Prize for architecture. Future Systems (Jan Kaplicky and Amanda Levete) had long promised a truly extraordinary public building, and this was it: descriptions ranged from a flying saucer on stilts to an espresso machine without the levers. This was one of a series of highly innovative buildings commissioned by a very establishment client; on completion it became an instant icon for cricket and for London. The head of Selfridges department store, on seeing it, promptly commissioned Future Systems to design a new store in Birmingham.

However, the most significant architectural event in the UK capital was the completion of the extension to the Jubilee Line of the London Underground. This project was overspent and late, but its importance to the redevelopment of London was undeniable and its station architecture, won widespread congratulation. The 11 stations, each designed by a different architect under the guidance of Roland Paoletti, were showcases for the best of British design. They ranged from little gems (such as Ian Ritchie's Bermondsey) to major set-pieces at Canary Wharf (Foster & Partners), North Greenwich (Alsop Lyall & Störmer), which served the Millennium Dome, and Stratford (Wilkinson Eyre). It was difficult to overestimate Paoletti's achievement in bringing an architectural aesthetic to an organization heavily dominated by engineers. The scheme set new standards for future infrastructure developments, and more than paid for itself by the added value it is brought to swathes of property across east London.

Elsewhere in London, arts buildings began to emerge after several years of National Lottery funding, and in some cases controversy. The most prominent building to be inaugurated was the new Royal Opera House, produced by an architectural team comprising BDP, Jeremy Dixon and Edward Jones. After many years of planning disputes, changes of programme and design, and a fraught building contract, the completed scheme won instant approval from audiences and, more important, performers. For the first time the Royal Ballet could rehearse and train on site. Less successful was the reopening of Sadler's Wells in Islington, to designs by RHWL and Nicholas Hare, mainly because of contractual problems.

Two of the capital's most significant schemes continued apace: on the south bank of the Thames the Tate Gallery's new Tate Modern offshoot was largely completed to spectacular design by Herzog & de Meuron. Work began on the pedestrian bridge linking the City of London with the gallery, to designs by Foster & Partners. At the British Museum a huge glass roof by the same architect was installed over the court housing the round reading room. On a smaller scale, but spectacular in its context, was the Peckham Library, designed by Will Alsop, full of colour and supported on his trademark huge pilotis (columns). Another colourful contribution to the London scene was an IMAX cinema on the south side of Waterloo Bridge, designed by Bryan Avery, with a blow-up Howard Hodgkin painting enclosing the 360° structure.

Meanwhile, the entire adjacent South Bank Centre arts complex was the subject of an international competition to find a master-planner, following the demise of the Richard Rogers' designs for the site. The competition was won by the London-based American, Rick Mather, who began the job of improving circulation without destroying the character of the complex, with its 1960s concrete landmark buildings continuing to cause controversy.

On the world stage, sustainability continued to be a key driver for concerned architects, while gurus such as the Dutch architect and theorist Rem Koolhaas grappled with the dilemmas implied by rapid urban change in China and other Far East economies. In Britain, the big new concern was the regeneration of existing cities, brought into focus by Lord (Richard) Rogers' report *Towards an Urban Renaissance*, proposing design-led solutions to the need for new housing and city renewal. The Royal Gold Medal for Architecture was won by the city of Barcelona (the first time a city rather than an individual or individuals had received it). The Pritzker Prize was won by Lord Foster.

Among those who died were Sir Hugh Casson (see XVIII: Obituary), director of the 1951 Festival of Britain, and Aldo van Eyck, one of the greatest humanist architects of the century.

3. LITERATURE

A century which had seen the defeat of Germany in two world wars ended with its last Nobel Prize for Literature bringing overdue recognition to the great German novelist Günter Grass. Though no longer the fashionable writer he became when his *The Tin Drum* (*Die Blechtrommel*) was published in 1959, the award of the Nobel Prize was greeted everywhere as just acknowledgement not only of Grass's influential work but of the place of German writing in the European mainstream and of the centrality of fiction in post-war literary forms. Evidence of this continuing tradition was amply provided by W.G. Sebald's admired new work, *Vertigo*, well translated by Michael Hulse.

In Britain the Booker Prize was for the first time given to an author who had won it before. For the second time J.M. Coetzee was unable to attend the ceremony in London at which his victory was announced, but no-one seriously challenged the appropriateness of Coetzee's post-apartheid novel *Disgrace* winning the pre-eminent book award in the country. This South African success, alongside the achievements of the Australian novelist Murray Bail in winning the Commonwealth Writers' Prize and the American Suzanne Berne receiving the Orange Prize for Women's Fiction, gave some force to the arguments of the chairperson of the latter award, Lola Young, who was quoted as saying British fiction today is 'piddling'.

The controversy surrounding Professor Young's remarks were rooted in serious critical debate, but the media connived to give them a frivolous spin. Increasingly in the American and British literary press comments on books were being couched in personal terms, with much emphasis on celebrity interviews and on semi-manufactured rivalries. In the United States the publication of a previously-unpublished novel by Ernest Hemingway, *True at First Light*, was said to have offended members of the author's family, and the issuing, as though a completed work, of Ralph Ellison's posthumous novel, *Juneteenth*, resulted in considerable criticism of its academic editor, John F. Callahan, with accusations that he had virtually constructed the novel himself.

Cutting down tall poppies had long been a feature of literary journalism, which in Britain often manifested itself by attempts to create tensions among writers. Many commentators on the Booker Prize, for example, set up a non-existent rivalry between two novelists of Indian origin, Salman Rushdie and Vikram Seth, intrigued by the fact that both had taken music as the subject of their latest books. Mercifully, Coetzee's win meant that no *coup de grace* was delivered to the reputation of either writer. Some more dispassionate observers felt, however, that the failure of Rushdie to land a major award for *The Ground Beneath Her Feet* would astonish future generations, who might well regard this book as one of the masterpieces of the century.

The appointment of a new Poet Laureate in Britain resulted in the press indulging in some of the most pointed personality-slanging ever to have surrounded a literary issue, with essentially very private poets being labelled simplistically as 'lesbian', 'metropolitan', 'provincial' or 'republican'. Andrew Motion emerged as the late Ted Hughes's successor as Poet Laureate, a post which had been in existence in some form or other since Ben Jonson held it in the early seventeenth century and which had become the prototype of all such laureateships around the world. Perhaps in recognition of the doubts which many had expressed about his suitability for the role, it was announced that Motion, currently professor of creative writing at East Anglia University, would hold the post for a ten-year period rather than for life. Another change was that the post's emolument became £5,000 per annum, instead of the long-prevailing £170.

Though Ted Hughes had died the previous year (see AR 1998, pp. 538, 591), his last works continued to dazzle. *Birthday Letters* remained in the best sellers throughout the year, posthumously winning for him the T.S. Eliot Prize for Poetry. The Royal National Theatre staged his superb new version of the *Oresteia* of Aeschylus; and what may have been his final work, a translation of the *Alcestis* of Euripides, was published to acclaim. Yet even as Hughes was being celebrated in the months after his death, which was marked by a state memorial service in Westminster Abbey, so there appeared accounts by second-rate writers claiming to have had affairs with him.

Translated poetry rarely sold in large quantities, but an exception was Seamus Heaney's highly-original reworking of *Beowulf*. Alexander Solzhenitsyn's massive *November 1916*, first published in Russia in 1984 and written in 1973, was very well translated by H.T. Willetts. Patrick Chamoiseau, a French-language novelist from Martinique, began to make a truly international impact. In many parts of the world one could cautiously point to an increasing interest among book buyers in translated works of literature.

In fiction, apart from novels already mentioned, it was not regarded as a major year, though several new names emerged which were thought to be worth watching closely. They included the New Zealand novelist Catherine Chidgey, the daring British writer David Mitchell, and yet another crop of outstanding young writers in English from the Indian sub-continent, among them Kamila Shamsie of Pakistan. More established authors, including Anita Desai, Doris Lessing, Alice Munro and José Saramago, published good new novels. The Egyptian novelist Ahdaf Soueif won plaudits for her lengthy novel *The Map of Love*, and her compatriot Nawal El Saadawi wrote her autobiography, *A Daughter of Iris*. Michael Holroyd's family memoir *Basil Street Blues* was thought by many to be a minor classic. There was no doubt that V.S. Naipaul's *Letters Between a Father and a Son* would enjoy such a status, being the tender exposition of a relationship founded as much in the love of words as in its natural bond.

In poetry, the publication, in time for his 70th birthday, of the Australian Peter Porter's *Collected Poems* was a major event. New volumes by Wislawa Szymborska, Adrienne Rich and, among younger poets, Jo Shapcott and Michael Hofmann, made a firm mark. Ted Hughes's daughter Frieda Hughes was read with interest, critics agreeing that *Wooroloo* was a work of individual talent.

Whereas a decade ago new plays were often published only if they enjoyed commercial success, it had become common practice by the end of the century for them to be printed either alongside their first production, in which case they would be sold as a programme, or immediately afterwards. Apart from making them more easily available for revival, this guaranteed that they would be read as literature as well as seen as stagecraft. However, no indubitably front-ranking play emerged in the year, though Arthur Miller had interesting, if minor, new work staged in America, David Williamson in Australia and Alan Bennett in Britain. Simon Gray's *The Late Middle Classes*, an enigmatic look at the England of the 1950s, was probably the best dramatic text of the year, though it failed to get a staging in the West End of London (see XV.1.iv). For the first time in its history the prestigious *Evening Standard* Award for Best Play was not given because the judges had seen nothing they sufficiently valued. There began to be an anxiety that the writing of new plays was facing a crisis.

Coinciding with constitutional devolution in Scotland and Wales, and the progress towards a new governance in Northern Ireland, the year saw a spate of books on the nature of Britishness. Of these, Norman Davies's *The Isles: A History* was the most challenging, with its notion that the United Kingdom was a fabrication with no true national coherence.

Undoubtedly the literary phenomenon of the year was the extraordinary rapidity with which the Scottish children's writer J.K. Rowling became the fastest-selling author, her *Harry Potter* sequence of stories for young people topping all best-seller lists. Indeed, no sooner had Thomas Harris's *Hannibal* broken all records in America and Britain for sales on the day of publication than Rowling's latest Potter book capped it. By the end of the year she was at the head of Internet bookselling lists for her fourth Potter tale, a truly remarkable situation, since she had not yet written the book: it was at the head of the list on the basis of advance orders. The Harry Potter books were rapidly being translated all over the world and their author seemed to be in universal demand for personal appearances.

There were rapid developments in bookselling techniques. In large cities across the world the remorseless advance of the large bookshops continued, with mega-stores opening in many capitals. They were rivalled, however, by the growth in usage of Internet bookselling. In particular Amazon.com became the world's most successful site (see also XIII.3), with a reputation for fast delivery and fair pricing which threatened the long-term survival of more traditional methods of buying books.

As momentum gathered for millennium celebrations throughout the world, there was much discussion about the place of books and reading in the development of civilizations in the past 1,000 years. In opinion polls about the most significant single event of the period, the majority choice was usually Johann Gutenberg's invention of printing in the fifteenth century. Similarly, the most-cited 'person of the millennium' was William Shakespeare. World Book Day on Shakespeare's birthday, 23 April, was deemed an international success. On the other hand, there was adverse comment in Britain that the vastly expensive Millennium Dome, opened on the last night of the century, had paid little regard to literary inheritance. Around the world, in contrast, there was evidence that the millennium was being recorded and celebrated in the story-telling and poetry of ordinary people. In this, more than any government-led project, lay testimony to the continuing power of the word.

Sadly, the last year of the century was also the last year of many long-lived writers of consequence. Two had been born in 1897 and only just missed living in three centuries, Nirad C. Chaudhuri and Naomi Mitchison. Chaudhuri, originally from Bengal but resident in Britain for nearly 30 years, was one of the greatest essayists of modern times and a consummate artist of English prose. Mitchison was a versatile Scottish writer who had lived in the thick of intellectual and political *milieux* throughout her long life. In France Nathalie Sarraute, in her experimentations with form one of the most innovative and influential of twentieth-century novelists, died in her late 90s. Dame Iris Murdoch also died, perhaps the most celebrated of British novelists at the end of the century. Her philosophical comedies had surprised and entertained readers of all kinds for nearly 50 years. Other deaths in 1999 included those of the great Arabic poet Abdel Wahab al-Bayyati, the Australian novelist and playwright Morris West, the Jamaican poet John Figueroa, the Spanish poet Rafael Alberti and the American creator of *Catch 22*, Joseph Heller. Another American author of note, Paul Bowles, died in Tangier where he had lived for many years as one of the century's most famous literary exiles. Brian Moore, who hailed originally from Northern Ireland but who had become Canadian, was one of the most admired novelists of recent years, his books filled with Catholic resonance. (For Alberti, Chaudhuri, Heller, Mitchison, Murdoch, West and Sarraute, see XVIII: Obituary).

British authors who died included the playwright Jim Allen, whose *Perdition* had been, in 1987, the only play ever withdrawn before its opening night from the repertoire of the radical Royal Court Theatre in London on account of the political offence it might give. By coincidence it was receiving its belated première at the time of Allen's death. Another playwright committed suicide early in the year, Sarah Kane, by general consent the outstanding new talent in the generation of British writers for theatre still in their 20s. Her death compounded the sense of malaise in contemporary playwriting. Sir Dirk Bogarde, an internationally-celebrated film actor who in later years had become a much admired novelist and autobiographical writer, also died (see XVIII: Obituary), as did the poet Patricia Beer, the novelist Penelope Mortimer and the Welsh-language author Robert Gerallt Jones.

Though she was not an author, the premature death of Clarissa Luard, senior literature officer at the Arts Council of England, shocked the literary community in Britain. She had been married to Salman Rushdie, who himself continued to live under tight protection despite some alleviation brought about by the Iranian government's reiteration of its assurance that it would not seek implementation of the 1989 *fatwa* on him.

Among the leading titles published in 1999 were the following:

FICTION. Ackroyd, Peter, *The Plato Papers* (Chatto & Windus); Axtaga, Bernard (trans. Jull Costa, Margaret), *The Lone Woman* (Harvill); Barker, A.L., *The Haunt* (Virago); Barrett, Andrea, *The Voyage of the Narwhal* (HarperCollins); Baylis, Matthew, *Stranger than Fulham* (Chatto & Windus); Blackburn, Julia, *The Leper's Companions* (Cape); Brady, Joan, *The Emigré* (Secker & Warburg); Brookner, Anita, *Undue Influence* (Viking); Burnside, John, *The Mercy Boys* (Cape); Chamoiseau, Patrick (trans. Rejouis, Rose-Myriam and Vinokurov, Val), *Solibo Magnificent* (Granta); Chidgey, Catherine, *In a Fishbone Church* (Picador); Coetzee, J.M., *Disgrace* (Secker & Warburg); Crace, Jim, *Being Dead* (Viking); Dabydeen, David, *A Harlot's Progress* (Cape); Desai, Anita, *Fasting, Feasting* (Chatto); Doyle, Roddy, *A Star Called Henry* (Cape); Dunant, Sarah, *Mapping the Edge* (Virago); Duncker, Patricia, *James Miranda Barry* (Serpent's Tail); Dunmore, Helen, *With Your Crooked Heart* (Viking); Dunn, Suzannah, *Commencing Our Descent* (HarperCollins); Ellison, Ralph, *Juneteenth* (Hamish Hamilton); Fell, Alison, *The Mistress of Lilliput* (Doubleday); Foden, Giles, *Ladysmith* (Faber); Forster, Margaret, *The Memory Box* (Chatto); Francis, Richard, *The Fat Hen* (Fourth Estate); Frayn, Michael, *Headlong* (Faber); Gowdy, Barbara, *The White Bone* (Flamingo); Greig, Andrew, *When They Lay Bare* (Faber); Gunn, Kirsty, *This Place You Return to is Home* (Granta); Guterson, David, *East of the Mountains* (Bloomsbury); Hill, Tobias, *Underground* (Faber); Harris, Thomas, *Hannibal* (Heinemann); Kennedy, A. L., *Everything You Need* (Cape); Klima, Ivan (trans. Turner, Gerald), *Lovers for a Day* (Granta); Le Carré, John, *Single and Single* (Hodder & Stoughton); Lessing, Doris, *Mara and Dann* (Flamingo); McCabe, Patrick, *Mondo Desperado* (Picador); McKay, Shena, *The World's Smallest Unicorn and Other Stories* (Cape); Middleton, Stanley, *Necessary Ends* (Hutchinson); Mitchell, David, *Ghostwritten* (Sceptre); Minot, Susan, *Evening* (Chatto & Windus); Mo, Timothy, *Renegade, or Halo 2* (Padleless); Munro, Alice, *The Love of a Good Woman* (Chatto); O'Hagan, Andrew, *Our Fathers* (Faber); Parks, Tim, *Destiny* (Secker); Proulx, Annie, *Close Range—Wyoming Stories* (Fourth Estate); Pullinger, Kate, *Weird Sister* (Bloomsbury); Roberts, Michèle, *Fair Exchange* (Little, Brown); Rogers, Jane, *Island* (Little, Brown); Rubens, Bernice I., *Dreyfus* (Little, Brown); Rushdie, Salman, *The Ground Beneath Her Feet* (Cape); Saramago, José (trans. Jull Costa, Margaret), *All the Names* (Harvill); Sebald, W.G. (trans. Hulse, Michael), *Vertigo* (Harvill); Selvaduri, Shyam, *Cinnamon Gardens* (Anchor); Seth, Vikram, *An Equal Music* (Phoenix); Shamsie, Kamila, *In the City by the Sea* (Granta); Sher, Antony, *The Feast* (Little, Brown); Solzhenitsyn, Alexander (trans. Willetts, H.T.), *November 1916* (Cape); Soueif, Ahdaf, *The Map of Love* (Bloomsbury); Srivastava, Atima *Looking for Maya* (Quartet); Toibin, Colm, *The Blackwater Lightship* (Picador); Tremain, Rose, *Music and Silence* (Chatto & Windus); Unsworth, Barry, *Losing Nelson* (Hamish Hamilton); Waters, Sarah, *Affinity* (Virago).

POETRY. Abse, Dannie, *Arcadia, One Mile* (Hutchinson); Carson, Anne, *Autobiography of Red* (Cape); Clanchy, Kate, *Samarkand (Picador);* Conn, Stewart, *Stolen Light: Selected Poems* (Bloodaxe); Crawford, Robert, *Spirit Machines* (Cape); D'Aguiar, Fred, *Bill of Rights* (Chatto); Dove, Rita, *On the Bus with Rosa Parks* (Norton); Duffy, Carol Ann, *The Pamphlet* (Anvil); Durcan, Paul, *Greetings to Our Friends in Brazil* (Harvill); Forbes, Peter (ed.), *Scanning the Century: the Penguin Book of the Twentieth Century in Poetry* (Viking/Poetry Society); Hamilton, Ian, *Sixty Poems* (Faber); Harrison, Tony, *Prometheus* (Faber); Heaney, Seamus, *Beowulf: A New Translation* (Faber); Hill, Geoffrey, *The Triumph of Love* (Penguin); Hofmann, Michael, *Approximately Nowhere* (Faber); Hughes, Frieda, *Wooroloo* (Bloodaxe); Hughes, Ted, *A translation of The Oresteia by Aeschylus* (Faber); Kay, Jackie, *The Frog Who Dreamed She Was an Opera Singer* (Bloomsbury); Kay, Jackie, *Off Colour* (Bloodaxe); Kramer, Lottie, *Selected and New Poems 1980-1997* (Rockingham/ European Jewish Publication Society); Longley, Michael, *Selected Poems* (Cape); McGough, Roger, *The Way Things Are* (Viking); Michaels, Anne, *Skin Divers* (Bloomsbury); Motion, Andrew, *Selected Poems 1976-1997* (Faber); O'Donaghue, Bernard, *Here Nor There* (Chatto & Windus); Ondaatje, Michael, *Handwriting* (Bloomsbury); Padel, Ruth, *Rembrandt Would Have Loved You* (Chatto); Paterson, Don, *The Eyes: Versions of Antonio Machado* (Faber); Paulin, Tom, *The Wind Dog* (Faber); Porter, Peter, *Collected Poems, Vol.1: 1961-81; Vol.2: 1984-99* (OUP); Reynolds, Oliver, *Almost* (Faber); Rich, Adrienne, *Midnight Salvage: Poems 1995-1998* (Norton); Romer, Stephen, *Tribute* (OUP); Rumens, Carol, *Holding Pattern* (Blackstaff); Shapcott, Jo *My Life Asleep* (OUP); Shuttle, Penelope, *Selected Poems: 1980-1996* (OUP); Sisson, C.H., *Collected Poems* (Carcanet); Szymborska, Wislawa (trans. Baranczak, Stanislaw and Cavanagh, Clare), *Poems New and Collected 1957-1997* (Faber); Thorpe, Adam, *From the Neanderthal* (Cape); Tomlinson, Charles, *Selected Poems 1955-1997*

(OUP); Tranter, John, *Late Night Radio* (Polygon); Wallace-Crabbe, Chris, *Whirling* (OUP); Woodward, Gerard, *Island to Island* (Chatto & Windus).

AUTOBIOGRAPHY AND BIOGRAPHY. Adams, R.J.Q., *Bonar Law* (John Murray); Arnold, Bruce Jack, *Yeats* (Yale); Beatty, Laura, *Lillie Langtry: Manners, Masks and Morals* (Chatto & Windus); Callow, Simon, *Love is Where It Falls: an Account of a Passionate Friendship* (Nick Hern); Cameron, Jamie, *James V: The Personal Rule 1528-1542* (Tuckwell); Dallas, Roland, *King Hussein: A Life on the Edge* (Profile); de Klerk, F.W., *The Autobiography: The Last Trek, A New Beginning* (Macmillan); Denniston, Robin, *Trevor Huddleston: a Life* (Macmillan); Enright, D.J., *Play Resumed: A Journal* (OUP); Grundy, Isabel, *Mary Wortley Montagu: Comet of the Enlightenment* (OUP); Guinness, Alec, *A Positively Final Appearance: A Journal 1996-98* (Hamish Hamilton); Guralnick, Peter, *Careless Love: The Unmaking of Elvis Presley* (Little, Brown); Holden, Anthony, *Shakespeare* (Little, Brown); Holroyd, Michael, *Basil Street Blues: A Family Story* (Little, Brown); Jack, Belinda, *George Sand: A Woman's Life Writ Large* (Chatto & Windus); Jones, Kathleen, *Catherine Cookson: the Biography* (Constable); Lock, F.P., *Edmund Burke, Vol. One: 1730-1784* (OUP); Logue, Christopher, *Prince Charming: A Memoir* (Faber); MacDonogh, Giles, *Frederick the Great: a Life in Deed and Letters* (Weidenfeld); McLeod, Kirsty, *Battle Royal: Edward VIII and George VI: Brother Against Brother* (Constable); Mango, Andrew, *Ataturk* (John Murray); Morton, Andrew, *Monica's Story* (Michael O'Mara); Murray, Alexander (ed.), *Sir William Jones 1746-1794, A Commemoration* (OUP); Naipaul, V.S., *Letters Between a Father and a Son* (Little, Brown); Omissi, David (ed.), *Indian Voices of the Great War: Soldiers' Letters 1914-18* (Macmillan); Prince, Alison, *Hans Christian Andersen: The Fan Dancer* (Allison & Busby); Roberts, John Stuart, *Siegfried Sassoon 1886-1967* (Richard Cohen); Rogers, Ben, *A.J.Ayer: a life* (Chatto & Windus); Saadawi, Nawal El, *A Daughter of Iris: The Autobiography of Nawal El Saadawi* (Zed); Sampson, Anthony, *Mandela* (HarperCollins); Schiff, Stacy, *Vera (Mr. Vladimir Nabokov)* (Picador); Shakespeare, Nicholas, *Bruce Chatwin* (Harvill/Cape); Schama, Simon, *Rembrandt's Eyes* (Penguin); (Shannon, Richard), *Gladstone: Heroic Minister 1865-1898* (Allen Lane/Penguin); Short, Philip, *Mao: A Life* (Hodder & Stoughton); Sheridan, Alan, *André Gide: A Life in the Present* (Hamish Hamilton); Stallworthy, Jon, *Singing School: the Making of a Poet* (Murray); Thorpe, Jeremy, *In My Own Time: Reminiscences of a Liberal Leader* (Politico's); Thurman, Judith, *Sins of the Flesh: A Life of Colette* (Bloomsbury); Walter, Harriet, *Other People's Shoes* (Viking); Walvin, James, *An African's Life: The life and times of Olaudah Equiano, 1745-1797* (Cassell); Wheen, Francis, *Karl Marx* (Fourth Estate); White, Edmund, *Proust* (Weidenfeld & Nicolson); Wilton, Iain, *C.B. Fry: An English Hero* (Richard Cohen); Wroe, Anne, *Pilate:The Biography of an Invented Man* (Cape).

OTHER BOOKS. Barber, Elizabeth Wayland, *The Mummies of Urumchi* (Macmillan); Booth, Martin, *The Dragon Syndicates* (Doubleday); Brittain, Victoria, *Death of Dignity: Angola's Civil War* (Pluto); Campbell, James, *This is the Beat Generation* (Secker); Davies, Norman, *The Isles: A History* (Macmillan); Devine, T.M., *The Scottish Nation 1700-2000* (Allen Lane The Penguin Press); Edwards, Ruth Dudley, *The Faithful Tribe* (HarperCollins); Fenton, James, *Leonardo's Nephew* (essays) (Viking); Ferguson, Niall, *The World's Banker: The History of the House of Rothschild* (Weidenfeld & Nicolson); Foot, Michael, *Dr. Strangelove, I Presume* (Gollancz); Greer, Germaine, *The Whole Woman* (Doubleday); Hochschild, Adam, *King Leopold's Ghost* (Macmillan); Keneally, Thomas, *The Great Shame: a Story of the Irish in the Old World and the New* (Chatto); Pavord, Anna, *The Tulip* (Bloomsbury); Rae, Jonathan, *I See a Voice: a Philosophical History of Langauge, Deafness and the Senses* (HarperCollins); Soyinka, Wole, *The Burden of Memory, the Muse of Forgiveness* (OUP); Thubron, Colin, *In Siberia* (Chatto & Windus); Wood, James, *The Broken Estate: essays on literature and belief* (Cape).

XVI SPORT

THE 114-member International Olympics Committee (IOC) and its president, Juan António Samaranch (Brazil), survived a turbulent year, but with damaged reputation in both cases. The crisis centred on the disclosure of the bribery of some IOC members in the bidding for the 2002 Winter Games in Salt Lake City (USA) and reports of similar chicanery in earlier Games awards. It was perhaps ironic that the scandal broke shortly before the death in April of Lord Killanin, Sr Samaranch's predecessor as IOC president (see XVIII: Obituary).

Holding only the second extraordinary session in its 104-year history, in Lausanne (Switzerland) in March, the IOC expelled six of its members (from Chile, Congo, Ecuador, Mali, Samoa and Sudan) and issued warnings to ten others, including the South Korean representative, who had been seen by some as a potential successor to Sr Samaranch. Nevertheless, the 78-year-old IOC president, who had held the post since 1980, easily survived a vote of confidence and commented afterwards: 'What happened you can call corruption, but I accept only 50 per cent responsibility for IOC members. The other 50 per cent is from the people who are offering [bribes].' The Lausanne meeting set up both an ethics committee and an 'IOC 2000' reform committee, including former US Secretary of State Henry Kissinger among its members. In its final meeting on 30 October, the reform committee submitted 49 recommendations, including new rules for the bidding approval process.

Meanwhile, IOC representatives had been called to testify before the US Senate commerce committee, although Sr Samaranch himself declined to attend. The committee later issued a report damning the IOC for its 'culture of bribery and gift-taking'. More directly damaging to the Olympics movement was the decision of the US healthcare products corporation Johnson & Johnson to withdraw its planned $30 million sponsorship of the 2002 Winter Games.

Disarray of a different sort beset the International Amateur Athletics Federation (IAAF) and UK Athletics, the new body set up to oversee the sport in Britain following the bankruptcy of the previous one. In their case, the problem was about doping policies, in particular whether or not certain athletes had taken the banned substance nandrolone. In clearing Dougie Walker, Gary Cadogan and semi-retired Olympic champion Linford Christie, who had all tested positive to nandrolone, UK Athletics accepted the contention that the drug could be taken accidentally. However, the IAAF refused to endorse the UK decision and continued to take a hard line against the use of nandrolone by athletes.

Drugs likewise cast a shadow over rugby union in 1999, as the result of a sting by undercover journalists who persuaded England captain Lawrence Dallaglio to boast in a taped conversation that he had taken cocaine and supplied drugs to team-mates. Dallaglio resigned as team captain, admitting that he had 'experimented' with drugs as a teenager but contending that he had made up his claims to the journalists. A Rugby Football Union (RFU) tribunal later fined him £15,000 (plus £10,000 in costs) for bringing the game into disrepute, but decided that there was no evidence against him of drug-taking or supply 'as a professional rugby player'. Dallaglio was quickly reinstated in the England team, though not as captain.

The English Football Association (FA) was also in trouble. Chairman Keith Wiseman resigned, as had FA chief executive Graham Kelly in December 1998 (see AR 1998, p. 547), over an unapproved loan of £3 million to the Welsh FA. There was also unprecedented political intervention over the England team manager, Glenn Hoddle, who had been appointed in 1998 (see AR 1998, p. 503). Prime Minister Tony Blair and other ministers called for Hoddle's sacking over a media interview in which he had declared his belief in reincarnation and suggested that people born disabled were paying the price for sins committed in a former life. The FA complied by dismissing Hoddle and later appointing former England captain Kevin Keegan as his successor (see below).

ASSOCIATION FOOTBALL. The most dramatic finish ever to a European Champions League or its predecessor European Cup, saw Manchester United complete a unique treble. They had already beaten Arsenal by a single point in the English Premier League and had crushed Newcastle in the FA Cup Final. On the way to completing the double at Wembley, United had come from a goal down to beat Liverpool by scoring twice in the last three minutes. In the semi-final against main rivals Arsenal, Ryan Giggs had scored a remarkable winner in added time with United down to ten men. However, none of these matched their epic come-back in the Champions League final against Bayern Munich of Germany in Barcelona. Manchester United went behind in the fifth minute and were outplayed by the German side for the rest of the 90 minutes. Only fine goal-keeping by United's captain, Denmark's Peter Schmeichel, in his last game for the club, kept them from going further behind. As the end approached, manager Alex Ferguson sent on two substitutes, Teddy Sherringham of England and Ole Gunner Sølksjær of Norway. In the second minute of injury time Sherringham put them level; seconds later, with almost the last kick of the game, Sølksjær stabbed in the winning goal from Sherringham's flick. No wonder the Bayern side collapsed in tears, while United's supporters exulted.

To complete a remarkable season, Manchester United then won the World Club Championship in Japan, defeating South American champions Palmeiras of Brazil. In the last ever European Cup Winners' Cup, holders Chelsea went out to Spain's Real Mallorca, who were beaten in the final by Italy's Lazio.

Trebles were the order of the day in British football in 1999. In Scotland, Rangers also completed one. They won the Scottish Premiership for the tenth time in 11 years, clinching their victory in a bad-tempered match against holders and Glasgow rivals Celtic. The referee was injured by a missile from the crowd, as a flurry of red cards helped Rangers to an emphatic win. Rangers then won both Scottish cups, defeating Celtic again in the Scottish FA Cup Final.

In the qualifying rounds for the European Nations championship finals in 2000, England started so badly that Sweden became uncatchable in their group. Following the dismissal of Glenn Hoddle as team manager in February, the charismatic Kevin Keegan was appointed in his place, at first on a part-time basis as he managed London club Fulham to the second division championship and later in a full-time capacity. England made an inspiring start under Keegan, with a 3-1 victory over Poland at Wembley; but a 0-0 draw in Poland still left England depending on Sweden beating Poland in the final match. This they did, so that England, like Scotland, made it to the play-offs for best-placed group runners-up. Huge interest was aroused when the two home countries were drawn together for the two-match play-off. England won the first leg at Glasgow's Hampden Park 2-0, but then struggled to survive at home at Wembley. They were lucky to lose only 0-1 and so go through to the finals.

The 16 countries which would contest the 'Euro-2000' finals were the joint hosts Belgium and the Netherlands and the holders Germany, together with the Czech Republic, Denmark, England, France, Italy, Norway, Portugal, Romania, Slovenia, Spain, Sweden, Turkey and Yugoslavia. Both in these finals and in the qualifying rounds for the 2002 World Cup, England were drawn in the same groups as old rival Germany.

ATHLETICS. The world athletics championships in Seville were, as usual, dominated by America. The outstanding athlete of the games was Maurice Greene, who won gold medals in the 100 and 200 metres and in the sprint relay. Another American, Marion Jones, was expected to go one better. But having stormed away in the 100 metres, she then injured herself too badly to continue. In the men's 400 metres, Michael Johnson again proved himself invincible, a real world-beater.

The outstanding Briton of the championships was Wales's Colin Jackson, who won the short hurdles; but this was Britain's only gold medal in a meeting which highlighted the decline of British athletics since the 'glory days' of the Coe-Ovett-Cram era. The most unexpected British success was that of the unheralded Dean Macey, who outstripped all his previous performances to take silver in the decathlon. In the heptathlon, Denise Lewis won a silver medal for Britain, as did the British team in the 4 x 100-metres relay. Dwain Chamberlain took a bronze medal in the 100 metres, as did European champion Jonathan Edwards, still short of his best, in the triple jump.

BOXING. The heavyweights had always been the main attraction of boxing—the chief crowd-pullers and money-spinners. They were certainly the focus of attention in 1999, at first in a damaging way for the sport. The centre-piece was the 'unification' fight in the USA in the spring between American Evander Holyfield and Britain's Lennox Lewis. Between them these two held all three of the separate world heavyweight boxing 'titles' sponsored by competing 'authorities', so the contest was rightly billed as a fight for the undisputed championship of the world. It lasted the full 12 rounds, with Lewis the very clear winner in everyone's view except the judges, who scored it a tie. There was outrage and inquiry over this absurd decision. Further damage was done when former world champion Mike Tyson was allowed to box again, despite his two prison sentences and his disgraceful conduct in the ring (see AR 1997, p. 525). Happily, the re-match between Lewis and Holyfield evoked no further controversy. Again the fight went the distance, but this time was much closer. No doubt with the earlier injustice in mind, the judges gave Lewis the unanimous decision, which was generally agreed to be fair, although there was very little between the two. So Lewis became the first Briton in the twentieth century to be undisputed world heavyweight champion, and was later voted BBC 'sports personality of the year'. In a double for boxing, former heavyweight champion Muhammad Ali was voted 'sports personality of the century'.

CRICKET. The World Cup held in England in the summer confirmed Australia as the top team in one-day cricket as well as in Tests. But it was a close-run affair, after Australia lost to both New Zealand and Pakistan in the group matches. To become champions, the Australians had then to win their next seven matches. They did so, but only after two desperately close encounters with South Africa in which the luck went with them. Their semi-final meeting ended as a tie, but turned into a 'win' because Australia's overall run-rate was just 0.19 better that South Africa's. The other major contender was the eventual runner-up, Pakistan, who were either totally dominant or strangely submissive. Having beaten the West Indies and Australia in their group matches, the Pakistanis were outplayed by Bangladesh; but that surprising defeat made no difference to their qualifying for the last 'super six' with a four-point credit.

The real shock of the competition was that Zimbabwe became the other team to qualify for the last six with the maximum four-point bonus. Their narrow defeat of India was followed by the turn-up of the championship when they beat South Africa. That remarkable result let Zimbabwe through to the last six at the expense of a disappointing England side, who had defeated Zimbabwe as well as holders Sri Lanka and Kenya but lost to South Africa and India. Apart from the early exit of the West Indies, the other surprise in the group matches was New Zealand's defeat of Australia, which sent them through to the 'super six' stage, where they reached their fourth World Cup semi-final after a five-wicket defeat of India. As in their previous three, however, the New Zealanders were again the losers, overwhelmed by Pakistan in a one-sided match in which Saeed Anwar's unbeaten century was the basis of a nine-wicket victory.

Before their titanic semi-final struggle, the 'super six' match between Australia and South Africa provided the competition's most dramatic encounter to that stage. South Africa seemed poised for victory after totalling 271, with opener Herschelle Gibbs scoring 101, and reducing Australia to 48 for 3. However, a marvellous 120 off 110 balls by captain Steve Waugh had given Australia victory with two balls to spare, the turning-point being an extraordinary slice of luck for Waugh, then on 56, when Gibbs took a simple catch at mid-wicket, but then let the ball slip from his hands as he prepared for a celebratory throw into the air.

Unbelievably, the semi-final between Australia and South Africa proved to be even more thrilling, providing the game of the tournament for entertainment, skill and excitement. Thanks to Michael Bevan and Steve Waugh (again), Australia reached a modest 213, to which South Africa replied by cruising to 48 without loss. On came master leg-spinner Shane Warne, who in just eight balls dismissed Gary Kirsten, Gibbs and captain Hansie Cronje (the last suffering from a wrong decision by the umpire). Warne continued to restrict the South African scoring, taking 4 for 29 (and later being named 'man of the match'). With three wickets left, South Africa still needed 39 runs from five overs. Enter Lance Klusener, their leading all-rounder, who had so far scored 250 runs from 214 balls in the championship. With his heavy bat he duly clubbed South Africa towards victory. Nine runs were needed off the last over from Damien Fleming, with nine wickets down. Klusener smote the first two balls to the boundary, but he suddenly lost confidence and tried to scramble the winning single from the next two. His suicidal calls nearly ran out Allan Donald from the first, and did so from the second. It was a sad end for Klusener, who had done so much for his team throughout, although he had the partial consolation of being named 'player of the tournament'.

The final between Australia and Pakistan was a dreary contrast, as the Pakistanis were overrun. Once again Warne was 'man of the match' with 4 for 33, while Glen McGrath, Australia's other outstanding bowler, took 2 for 13 in nine niggardly overs. Pakistan slumped to 132 all out, enabling Australia to win by eight wickets with almost 35 overs to spare. It was a disappointing end to what was generally rated a successful World Cup, which had provided a series of riveting matches and had been watched by more spectators than any previous cricket tournament.

The Test matches which followed in 1999 were an anti-climax, except for two surprising results. England won the first of their four Tests against New Zealand, thanks to an unbeaten 99 from Alex Tudor, but then contrived to lose the series 1-2. Later in the year, moreover, World Cup champions Australia lost a Test series in Sri Lanka for the first time.

GOLF. Playing at home on the Brookline course, America finally regained the Ryder Cup in another very tense finish following Europe's narrow victory to retain the cup in 1997 (see AR 1997, pp. 526-7). Going into the singles Europe had a four-point lead, but this was steadily eroded as the American golfers fought back. Despite wins by the outstanding Colin Montgomerie (Scotland), Ireland's Padraig Harrington and British Open champion Paul Lawrie (Scotland), all depended on Spain's José Maria Olazabal's contest with Justin Leonard. Olazabal was four up with only seven holes to play, but in a stirring fight-back Leonard squared the match to give the Americans a one-point victory. On the way, another kind of tension soured their win. On the 17th green, Leonard putted first and holed from near the edge of the green. At once the watching American players and their wives rushed out for a victory dance all over the green. In fact, Leonard's putt had not settled the match, since Olazabal could still have won had he holed his putt. Upset by the lengthy celebrations, he missed, before collecting himself bravely to win the last hole with a birdie and to tie his match. The American captain had to apologize for the unruly and unsporting behaviour of his players, and also for the crowd's relentless and vicious heckling of Montgomerie. In his long-running radio series, *Letter from America*, the veteran broadcaster Alistair Cooke deeply regretted the demise of the last bastion of real sportsmanship which golf and the Ryder Cup had previously represented for him.

There was, however, much good sportsmanship in the amateur Walker Cup, as the golfers of Great Britain and Ireland also recovered from a bad start to beat America by a record margin. Nor was the quality absent from the 1999 majors, despite a British Open at Carnoustie which challenged the metal and temperaments of the world's leading players. Stiff breezes compounded the difficulty of Carnoustie's narrow fairways, thick rough and small greens, so that good scores were at a premium. Spain's Sergio Garcia, an outstanding player for the rest of the season, was so put off his game that he finished last. Instead of the leaders being many strokes better than par, none of them beat it. Whilst some stars complained about the conditions, a couple of moderate players went steadily on to reach a three-man play-off. In fact, France's little-known Jean Van de Velde had been poised to win comfortably as he stood on the final tee with two strokes in hand. However, a wayward drive and a hack into the Carnoustie burn left him in real trouble. He will always be remembered for the agonizing minutes he spent paddling in the water trying to decide whether to play his ball from there. Common sense prevailed; after dropping out, he finished bravely to tie with Paul Lawrie (another with a very low previous ranking) and the highly-regarded American Justin Leonard. In the four-hole play-off all three were in trouble over the first two, until Lawry took charge with two birdies to become an unexpected Open champion.

Colin Montgomerie had an outstanding season, winning six times in Europe as well as giving a fine performance in the Ryder Cup, unphased by the disgraceful barracking. He became the first player who had never won a major to win the World Matchplay championship at Wentworth. In the semi-finals he destroyed Padraig Harrington, while holder Mark O'Mara (USA) beat Nick Price (Zimbabwe) by chipping in from off the green at the final hole. Montgomerie was always ahead in the final, winning by 3 and 2. Olazabal had fluctuating form and fortune during the season, his second US Masters victory being the highlight. The winners of the other two majors were the Americans Tiger Woods and Payne Stewart, the latter being tragically killed soon afterwards (see IV.1).

In the Dunhill Nations championship at St Andrews Spain defeated South Africa in the semi-final then took the cup by beating Australia in the final. Garcia was in that winning Spanish team and had such an impressive season that he was spoken of as a potential young rival to Woods. For the present, however, it was Woods who remained golf's indisputable number one both for performance and star status.

GRAND PRIX MOTOR RACING. All's well that ends well was an appropriate summary for Finland's Mika Hakkinen's up-and-down season, which finished with his second successive world championship. The fact that he started the final race four points behind Ferrari's Eddie Irvine was the result of some unusual errors of his own, some mechanical problems in his McLaren Mercedes car and some forced errors as his partner David Coulthard still fought to be champion. Early on it was clear that McLaren Mercedes cars were comfortably fastest, but not as reliable as Ferrari. They still built a lead, with 11 pole positions for Hakkinen proving their speed. Germany's Michael Schumacher, however, took advantage of every slip and was pressing hard for his own and Ferrari's world championship.

Then disaster stuck as a mechanical fault sent Schumacher's car careering across a gravel trap, which slowed him just enough so that, in an horrendous crash, a broken leg was all the injury he sustained. That kept him out until the penultimate Grand Prix on the new circuit in Malaysia. So it all seemed plain motoring for McLaren and Hakkinen. Instead, Eddie Irvine, and Schumacher's replacement Mika Salo, kept Ferrari in the title race as the McLaren drivers squandered their opportunities in a tragedy of errors. When Schumacher returned, the impact was enough to indicate that he might well have been world champion again, but for his long lay-off. In wet and difficult conditions he dominated the Malaysian race, letting Irvine through for victory then holding up Hakkinen to ensure a Ferrari first and second.

That left Ferrari four points ahead in both the constructors' and the drivers' championships. Drama then mounted when both Ferrari drivers were disqualified from their Malaysian placings when a barge-board on their cars was found to be a centimetre longer than the rules allowed. This decision seemed to have virtually decided the championship. However, they were quickly exonerated on appeal, which was no surprise given Formula One's reputation for preferring exciting finishes to strict judgments.

So once again Hakkinen had to win at Suzuka, Japan, to be champion. Once again he proved himself one of the greats by doing so, despite being second on the grid behind Schumacher. A racing start enabled Hakkinen to take the lead at the first corner and go on to win comfortably, with good McLaren tactics to aid him. David Coulthard played his part by holding up Irvine and later Schumacher, until he spun off, enabling Ferraris to take second and third places and giving them the constructors' championship. Jordan also had a fine season, coming third in both the constructors' championship and, through the German Heinz-Harald Frenzen, in the individual title race. Damon Hill played a minor part in Jordan's success and retired after a sad end to a great career at Suzuka.

RUGBY UNION. The rugby union World Cup, officially hosted by Wales, was a success in financial terms, because it netted a £48 million profit, with a further

£30 million in ticket sales being divided between the five nations which actually staged matches. Otherwise the tournament suffered from justified criticism of the ticketing, scheduling and marketing arrangements, and even of the state of the pitch in Cardiff's new Millennium Stadium, which was not completely ready in time. The main weakness, however, was on the field: the lack of exciting open play, the endless free kicks, the predictability of results, the humiliation of the 'minnows' and the continuing domination of the southern hemisphere sides, with only France making a dent in their effortless superiority. In the early stages not only were there long gaps between matches, but also, for many of those played, there were small crowds and no excitement. Many countries were not of a standard to compete at this level, both England and New Zealand scoring 100 points in otherwise pointless matches against modest opposition.

The few honourable exceptions included Samoa's victory against Wales and Argentina's narrow defeat by the hosts in the opening match. Fiji were also unlucky not to defeat France in a hard-fought match. In a key group game, England kept level with favourites New Zealand until Jonah Lomu , the highest try scorer of the tournament, finally broke English resistance. England therefore finished runners-up in their group and so had to play Cup holders South Africa in the quarter-finals, where they succumbed to the superior Springboks without much resistance.

Only in the semi-finals did the 1999 World Cup come to life, starting with a battle between old rivals Australia and South Africa. In a grim struggle, decided by penalty-kicking and a record number of dropped goals, South Africa levelled the scores with the last kick of full time-a long-range acutely-angled penalty. Despite having victory snatched away like this, Australia remained the stronger side in extra time, a dropped goal sealing their victory. New Zealand entered the other semi-final against France with total confidence. They were tri-nations champions and had beaten France 54-7 in an earlier friendly, while France had taken the 'wooden spoon' in the recent Five Nations' championship. That confidence seemed justified as the All Blacks built a 24-10 lead, helped by a couple of Lomu tries, in one of which he forced his way over the line through six abortive French tackles. But in a remarkable second-half reversal, France scored 26 points without reply, playing with a dash and flair which disconcerted their opponents and produced the one major upset of the tournament. They could not repeat the feat in the final, when the Australians' superior strength and discipline ground them down. Two late tries did nothing to arouse excitement in a final as uninspiring as the championship itself.

In contrast, the Five Nations' tournament was highly entertaining, despite the northern hemisphere's lower levels of skill. England and France were expected to continue their dominance, only to find Wales and Scotland staging a welcome revival. A lacklustre French team had the humiliation of ending bottom of the table. England appeared certain to win another 'grand slam' after beating Scotland, France and Ireland. But at Twickenham England went down to a last-minute try by Wales, which left Scotland as overall winners-level with England on points but with a better scoring record. It was the last Five Nations' tournament, because in 2000 Italy were to be admitted to what would become the Six Nations' championship.

TENNIS. In both men's and women's tennis it was an old star who shone brightest. Andre Agassi (USA), who at one stage had sunk to 150th in the world ratings, came back to form by winning in Paris, the only major he had not won previously. Agassi seemed on course for another win at Wimbledon; but fellow-American Pete Sampras, having disposed of Britain's Tim Henman in the semifinals, proved too strong for him. Even so, Agassi took over from Sampras as world number one. Another win in the US Open ensured that Agassi kept that rating at the season's end.

Neither Henman nor fellow-Briton Greg Rusedski had a great season. Rusedski, however, did make a huge improvement in his bank balance by winning the ATP tour championship. Both then helped Britain to keep its place in the top Davis Cup division. The Davis Cup final was between France (the holders and hosts) and Australia. With Patrick Rafter injured, Australia brought in 18-year-old Lleyton Hewitt, who promptly lost his two singles matches. But Mark Philipoussis won his two, and the experienced Mark Woodforde and Todd Woodbridge took the doubles to give Australia the cup.

In ladies' tennis, Germany's Steffi Graf was back to her best in winning the French Open in a gruelling match with Martina Hingis of Switzerland. At Wimbledon, however, she was swept aside in the final by America's Lindsay Davenport and announced her retirement from top-class tennis. Hingis had been so upset by her narrow defeat in France that she had thrown a tantrum. Coming to Wimbledon as holder, she was still so out-of-sorts that she lost her first match to 16-year-old Australian qualifier Jelena Dokic 6-2, 6-0. Dokic went on to reach the quarter-finals, where she lost to another young qualifier, Alexandra Stevenson (USA), who became the first qualifier to reach a Wimbledon semi-final. Hingis had started the season well by winning the Australian Open and soon regained her composure after the Wimbledon upset. By the season's end she was again the player everyone else had to beat.

THE TURF. On the flat, here was no doubt about the horse of the year, as Daylami climaxed a season of success by winning the Breeders' Cup at Gulfstream, Florida. That was his seventh win in group one competition from a mile to 12 furlongs, including victories in the Coronation Cup, the King George and Irish Champion Stakes. The only disappointment for Daylami was a poor run on heavy ground in the Prix de l'Arc de Triomphe in France. For jockey Frankie Dettori Daylami's Breeders' Cup win was a special delight: the previous year he had been mercilessly criticized for allowing Swain to drift right-handed to lose this race. As he commented: 'I made a mistake then, but you can't write off a 10-year career on one ride.'

To underline his continuing excellence, Dettori flew straight to Italy and 20 hours later was a winner on Godolphin's Oriental Fashion in the Premio Ribot.

For Sheikh Mohammed's Godolphin stable this was a year of triumph, starting with Almutawakel's win in the Dubai World Cup. Altogether they had 18 group one wins worldwide, becoming the year's champion owners, while Godolphin's Saeed Bin Suroor was champion trainer.

In England, Oath won the Derby, Highland Sands the 2000 Guineas, Wince the 1000 Guineas and Ramruma the Oaks. Once again Kieran Fallon was the champion jockey by a distance, but it was Pat Eddery who set a new record, riding over 100 winners for the 26th time.

In National Hunt racing, Bobbyjo jumped impeccably to win the Grand National, as did See More Business to take the Gold Cup at Cheltenham. Tony McCoy retained the jockeys' championship, once again riding over 200 winners.

AMERICAN ASPECTS. In American football, Super Bowl XXXIII in Miami belonged to the Denver Broncos and their quarter-back John Elway. For Elway the 34-19 thrashing of the Atlanta Falcons was particularly sweet. The taunt that he was incapable of winning the big one, after three Super Bowl defeats, was exorcized, finally and unquestionably. As retirement loomed, Elway finished in style. He made one of Denver's touch-downs and so master-minded the play that he was unanimously voted the game's 'most valuable player' on performance rather than sentiment. Another outstanding player for Denver was Terrell Davis, who rushed over 100 yards to add to a season's total already exceeding a remarkable 2,000. Howard Griffith also shone with two touchdowns and forceful blocking which created space for Davis. For the Falcons it was a sad day. Coach Dan Reeves had been sacked by Denver after three losing Super Bowls, and now suffered another defeat at his former team's hands. Quarter-back Chris Chandler was also out of form, as interceptions and fumbles due to his throwing helped to swing the game to the Broncos. The only bright moments for the Falcons were a field goal in the first drive of the game and a 94-yard touch-down. The big surprise of the game was that the season's two best kickers missed three simple field goals between them.

Lance Armstrong became the second American ever to win the prestigious Tour de France cycle race, finishing more than seven minutes ahead of his nearest rival in one of the world's toughest races. Most remarkable was the fact that he had been diagnosed as suffering from testicular cancer only three years before.

Both in America and Britain, Muhammad Ali was voted 'sports personality of the century'. In athletics Carl Lewis was voted the century's top athlete ahead of Jesse Owens, whom many felt had had the greater impact back in the 1930s.

XVII DOCUMENTS AND REFERENCE

1. KOSOVO AGREEMENT AND UN RESOLUTION 1244

Published below are (i) the 'Military Technical Agreement' ending the Kosovo conflict, signed on 9 June 1999 between the NATO-led International Security Force ('K-For') and the governments of the Federal Republic of Yugoslavia and the Republic of Serbia; and (ii) UN Security Council resolution 1244, adopted on 10 June 1999 by 14-0 (the People's Republic of China abstaining). A map illustrating the Agreement appears on p. 142. (Sources: NATO and UN)

MILITARY TECHNICAL AGREEMENT
Article I: General Obligations

1. The Parties to this Agreement reaffirm the document presented by President Ahtisaari [of Finland] to President Milošević [of Yugoslavia] and approved by the Serb parliament and the federal government on 3 June 1999, to include deployment in Kosovo under UN auspices of effective international civil and security presences. The Parties further note that the UN Security Council [UNSC] is prepared to adopt a resolution, which has been introduced, regarding these presences.

2. The state governmental authorities of the Federal Republic of Yugoslavia [FRY] and the Republic of Serbia understand and agree that the International Security Force ('K-For') will deploy following the adoption of the UN Security Council resolution referred to in paragraph 1 and operate without hindrance within Kosovo and with the authority to take all necessary action to establish and maintain a secure environment for all citizens of Kosovo and otherwise carry out its mission. They further agree to comply with all of the obligations of this Agreement and to facilitate the deployment and operation of this force.

3. For purposes of the agreement, the following expressions shall have the meanings as described below:

a. 'The Parties' are those signatories to the Agreement.

b. 'Authorities' means the appropriate responsible individual, agency or organization of the Parties.

c. 'FRY Forces' includes all of the FRY and Republic of Serbia personnel and organizations with a military capability. This includes regular army and naval forces, armed civilian groups, associated paramilitary groups, air forces, national guards, border police, army reserves, military police, intelligence services, federal and Serbian Ministry of Internal Affairs local, special, riot and anti-terrorist police, and any other groups or individuals so designated by the International Security Force ('K-For') commander.

d. The Air Safety Zone (ASZ) is defined as a 25-kilometre zone that extends beyond the Kosovo province border into the rest of FRY territory. It includes the airspace above that 25-kilometre zone.

e. The Ground Safety Zone (GSZ) is defined as a 5-kilometre zone that extends beyond the Kosovo province border into the rest of FRY territory. It includes the terrain within that 5-kilometre zone.

f. Entry Into Force Day (EIF Day) is defined as the day this Agreement is signed.

4. The purposes of these obligations are as follows:

a. To establish a durable cessation of hostilities, under no circumstances shall any Forces of the FRY and the Republic of Serbia enter into, re-enter, or remain within the territory of Kosovo or the Ground Safety Zone (GSZ) and the Air Safety Zone (ASZ) described in paragraph 3 of Article I without the prior express consent of the International Security Force ('K-For') commander. Local police will be allowed to remain in the GSZ.

The above paragraph is without prejudice to the agreed return of FRY and Serbian personnel which will be the subject of a subsequent separate agreement as provided for in paragraph 6 of the document mentioned in paragraph 1 of this Article.

b. To provide for the support and authorization of the International Security Force ('K-For') and in particular to authorise the International Security Force ('K-For') to take such actions as are required, including the use of necessary force, to ensure compliance with this Agreement and protection of the International Security Force ('K-For'), and to contribute to a secure environment for the international civil implementation presence, and other international organizations, agencies and non-governmental organizations (details in Appendix B).

XVII.1. KOSOVO AGREEMENT AND UN RESOLUTION 1244

Article II: Cessation of Hostilities

1. The FRY Forces shall immediately, upon entry into force (EIF) of this Agreement, refrain from committing any hostile or provocative acts of any type against any person in Kosovo and will order armed forces to cease all such activities. They shall not encourage, organise or support hostile or provocative demonstrations.

2. Phased Withdrawal of FRY Forces (ground): The FRY agrees to a phased withdrawal of all FRY Forces from Kosovo to locations in Serbia outside Kosovo. FRY Forces will mark and clear minefields, booby traps and obstacles. As they withdraw, FRY Forces will clear all lines of communication by removing all mines, demolitions, booby traps, obstacles and charges. They will also mark all sides of all minefields. International Security Forces' ('K-For') entry and deployment into Kosovo will be synchronized. The phased withdrawal of FRY Forces from Kosovo will be in accordance with the sequence outlined below:

   a. By EIF+1 day, FRY Forces located in Zone 3 will have vacated, via designated routes, that Zone to demonstrate compliance (depicted on the map at Appendix A to the Agreement). Once it is verified that FRY forces have complied with this subparagraph and with paragraph 1 of this Article, NATO air strikes will be suspended. The suspension will continue provided that the obligations of this agreement are fully complied with, and provided that the UNSC adopts a resolution concerning the deployment of the International Security Force ('K-For') so rapidly that a security gap can be avoided.

   b. By EIF+6 days, all FRY Forces in Kosovo will have vacated Zone 1 (depicted on the map at Appendix A to the Agreement). Establish liaison teams with the K-For commander in Pri_tina.

   c. By EIF+9 days, all FRY Forces in Kosovo will have vacated Zone 2 (depicted on the map at Appendix A to the Agreement).

   d. By EIF+11 days, all FRY Forces in Kosovo will have vacated Zone 3 (depicted on the map at Appendix A to the Agreement).

   e. By EIF+11 days, all FRY Forces in Kosovo will have completed their withdrawal from Kosovo (depicted on map at Appendix A to the Agreement) to locations in Serbia outside Kosovo, and not within the 5-kilometre GSZ. At the end of the sequence (EIF+11), the senior FRY Forces commanders responsible for the withdrawing forces shall confirm in writing to the International Security Force ('K-For') commander that the FRY Forces have complied and completed the phased withdrawal. The International Security Force ('K-For') commander may approve specific requests for exceptions to the phased withdrawal. The bombing campaign will terminate on complete withdrawal of FRY Forces as provided under Article II. The International Security Force ('K-For') shall retain, as necessary, authority to enforce compliance with this Agreement.

   f. The authorities of the FRY and the Republic of Serbia will cooperate fully with International Security Force ('K-For') in its verification of the withdrawal of forces from Kosovo and beyond the ASZ/GSZ.

   g. FRY armed forces withdrawing in accordance with Appendix A, i.e. in designated assembly areas or withdrawing on designated routes, will not be subject to air attack.

   h. The International Security Force ('K-For') will provide appropriate control of the borders of FRY in Kosovo with Albania and FYROM [Former Yugoslav Republic of Macedonia] until the arrival of the civilian mission of the UN.

3. Phased Withdrawal of Yugoslavia Air and Air Defence Forces (YAADF)

   a. At EIF+1 day, no FRY aircraft, fixed wing and rotary, will fly in Kosovo airspace or over the ASZ without prior approval by the International Security Force ('K-For') commander. All air defence systems, radar, surface-to-air missile and aircraft of the Parties will refrain from acquisition, target tracking or otherwise illuminating International Security Force ('K-For') air platforms operating in the Kosovo airspace or over the ASZ.

   b. By EIF+3 days, all aircraft, radars, surface-to-air missiles (including man-portable air defence systems, MANPADS) and anti-aircraft artillery in Kosovo will withdraw to other locations in Serbia outside the 25-kilometre ASZ.

   c. The International Security Force ('K-For') commander will control and coordinate use of airspace over Kosovo and the ASZ commencing at EIF. Violation of any of the provisions above, including the International Security Force ('K-For') commander's rules and procedures governing the airspace over Kosovo, as well as unauthorised flight or activation of FRY Integrated Air Defence (IADS) within the ASZ, are subject to military action by the International Security Force ('K-For'), including the use of necessary force. The International Security Force ('K-For') commander may delegate control of normal civilian air activities to appropriate FRY institutions to monitor operations, deconflict International Security Force ('K-For') air traffic movements, and ensure smooth and safe operations of the air traffic system. It is envisioned that control of civil air traffic will be returned to civilian authorities as soon as practicable.

Article III: Notifications

1. This Agreement and written orders requiring compliance will be immediately communicated to all FRY forces.
2. By EIF+2 days, the state governmental authorities of the FRY and the Republic of Serbia shall furnish the following specific information regarding the status of all FRY Forces:

   a. Detailed records, positions and descriptions of all mines, unexploded ordnance, explosive devices, demolitions, obstacles, booby traps, wire entanglement, physical or military hazards to the safe movement of any personnel in Kosovo laid by FRY Forces.

   b. Any further information of a military or security nature about FRY Forces in the territory of Kosovo and the GSZ and ASZ requested by the International Security Force ('K-For') commander.

Article IV: Establishment of a Joint Implementation Commission (JIC)

A JIC shall be established with the deployment of the International Security Force ('K-For') to Kosovo as directed by the International Security Force ('K-For') commander.

Article V: Final Authority to Interpret

The International Security Force ('K-For') commander is the final authority regarding interpretation of this Agreement and the security aspects of the peace settlement it supports. His determinations are binding on all Parties and persons.

Article VI: Entry Into Force

This agreement shall enter into force upon signature.

Appendices

A. Phased withdrawal of FRY Forces from Kosovo

MAP

B. International Security Force ('K-For') Operations

1. Consistent with the general obligations of the Military Technical Agreement, the state governmental authorities of the FRY and the Republic of Serbia understand and agree that the International Security Force ('K-For') will deploy and operate without hindrance within Kosovo and with the authority to take all necessary action to establish and maintain a secure environment for all citizens of Kosovo.

2. The International Security Force ('K-For') commander shall have the authority, without interference or permission, to do all that he judges necessary and proper, including the use of military force, to protect the International Security Force ('K-For'), the international civil implementation presence, and to carry out the responsibilities inherent in this Military Technical Agreement and the Peace Settlement which it supports.

3. The International Security Force ('K-For') nor any of its personnel or staff shall be liable for any damages to public or private property that they may cause in the course of duties related to the implementation of this Agreement. The Parties will agree a Status of Forces Agreement (SOFA) as soon as possible.

4. The International Security Force ('K-For') shall have the right:

   a. To monitor and ensure compliance with this Agreement and to respond promptly to any violations and restore compliance, using military force if required. This includes necessary actions to: (i) enforce withdrawals of FRY forces; (ii) enforce compliance following the return of selected FRY personnel to Kosovo; (iii) provide assistance to other international entities involved in the implementation or otherwise authorized by the UNSC.

   b. To establish liaison arrangements with local Kosovo authorities, and with FRY/Serbian civil and military authorities.

   c. To observe, monitor and inspect any and all facilities or activities in Kosovo that the International Security Force ('K-For') commander believes has or may have military or police capability, or may be associated with the employment of military or police capabilities, or are otherwise relevant to compliance with this Agreement.

5. Notwithstanding any other provision of this Agreement, the Parties understand and agree that the International Security Force ('K-For') commander has the right and is authorised to compel the removal, withdrawal, or relocation of specific Forces and weapons, and to order the cessation of any

activities whenever the International Security Force ('K-For') commander determines a potential threat to either the International Security Force ('K-For') or its mission, or to another Party. Forces failing to redeploy, withdraw, relocate, or to cease threatening or potentially threatening activities following such a demand by the International Security Force ('K-For') shall be subject to military action by the International Security Force ('K-For'), including the use of necessary force, to ensure compliance.

UN SECURITY COUNCIL RESOLUTION 1244 (1999)

The Security Council,
Bearing in mind the purposes and principles of the Charter of the United Nations, and the primary responsibility of the Security Council for the maintenance of international peace and security,
Recalling its resolutions 1160 (1998) of 31 March 1998, 1199 (1998) of 23 September 1998, 1203 (1998) of 24 October 1998 and 1239 (1999) of 14 May 1999,
Regretting that there has not been full compliance with the requirements of these resolutions,
Determined to resolve the grave humanitarian situation in Kosovo, Federal Republic of Yugoslavia, and to provide for the safe and free return of all refugees and displaced persons to their homes,
Condemning all acts of violence against the Kosovo population as well as all terrorist acts by any party,
Recalling the statement made by the Secretary-General on 9 April 1999, expressing concern at the humanitarian tragedy taking place in Kosovo,
Reaffirming the right of all refugees and displaced persons to return to their homes in safety,
Recalling the jurisdiction and the mandate of the International Tribunal for the Former Yugoslavia,
Welcoming the general principles on a political solution to the Kosovo crisis adopted on 6 May 1999 (S/1999/516, annex 1 to this resolution) and welcoming also the acceptance by the Federal Republic of Yugoslavia of the principles set forth in points 1 to 9 of the paper presented in Belgrade on 2 June 1999 (S/1999/649, annex 2 to this resolution), and the Federal Republic of Yugoslavia's agreement to that paper,
Reaffirming the commitment of all member states to the sovereignty and territorial integrity of the Federal Republic of Yugoslavia and the other States of the region, as set out in the Helsinki Final Act and annex 2,
Reaffirming the call in previous resolutions for substantial autonomy and meaningful self-administration for Kosovo,
Determining that the situation in the region continues to constitute a threat to international peace and security,
Determined to ensure the safety and security of international personnel and the implementation by all concerned of their responsibilities under the present resolution, and acting for these purposes under Chapter VII of the Charter of the United Nations,
1. Decides that a political solution to the Kosovo crisis shall be based on the general principles in annex 1 and as further elaborated in the principles and other required elements in annex 2;
2. Welcomes the acceptance by the Federal Republic of Yugoslavia of the principles and other required elements referred to in paragraph 1 above, and demands the full cooperation of the Federal Republic of Yugoslavia in their rapid implementation;
3. Demands in particular that the Federal Republic of Yugoslavia put an immediate and verifiable end to violence and repression in Kosovo, and begin and complete verifiable phased withdrawal from Kosovo of all military, police and paramilitary forces according to a rapid timetable, with which the deployment of the international security presence in Kosovo will be synchronized;
4. Confirms that after the withdrawal an agreed number of Yugoslav and Serb military and police personnel will be permitted to return to Kosovo to perform the functions in accordance with annex 2;
5. Decides on the deployment in Kosovo, under United Nations auspices, of international civil and security presences, with appropriate equipment and personnel as required, and welcomes the agreement of the Federal Republic of Yugoslavia to such presences;
6. Requests the Secretary-General to appoint, in consultation with the Security Council, a Special Representative to control the implementation of the international civil presence, and further requests the Secretary-General to instruct his Special Representative to co-ordinate closely with the international security presence to ensure that both presences operate towards the same goals and in a mutually supportive manner;
7. Authorizes member states and relevant international organizations to establish the international security presence in Kosovo as set out in point 4 of annex 2 with all necessary means to fulfil its responsibilities under paragraph 9 below;
8. Affirms the need for the rapid early deployment of effective international civil and security

presences to Kosovo, and demands that the parties cooperate fully in their deployment;

9. Decides that the responsibilities of the international security presence to be deployed and acting in Kosovo will include:

a. Deterring renewed hostilities, maintaining and where necessary enforcing a ceasefire, and ensuring the withdrawal and preventing the return into Kosovo of Federal and Republic military, police and paramilitary forces, except as provided in point 6 of annex 2;

b. Demilitarizing the Kosovo Liberation Army (KLA) and other armed Kosovo Albanian groups as required in paragraph 15 below;

c. Establishing a secure environment in which refugees and displaced persons can return home in safety, the international civil presence can operate, a transitional administration can be established, and humanitarian aid can be delivered;

d. Ensuring public safety and order until the international civil presence can take responsibility for this task;

e. Supervising de-mining until the international civil presence can, as appropriate, take over responsibility for this task;

f. Supporting, as appropriate, and coordinating closely with the work of the international civil presence;

g. Conducting border monitoring duties as required;

h. Ensuring the protection and freedom of movement of itself, the international civil presence, and other international organizations;

10. Authorizes the Secretary-General, with the assistance of relevant international organizations, to establish an international civil presence in Kosovo in order to provide an interim administration for Kosovo under which the people of Kosovo can enjoy substantial autonomy within the Federal Republic of Yugoslavia, and which will provide transitional administration while establishing and overseeing the development of provisional democratic self-governing institutions to ensure conditions for a peaceful and normal life for all inhabitants of Kosovo;

11. Decides that the main responsibilities of the international civil presence will include:

a. Promoting the establishment, pending a final settlement, of substantial autonomy and self-government in Kosovo, taking full account of annex 2 and of the Rambouillet accords (S/1999/648);

b. Performing basic civilian administrative functions where and as long as required;

c. Organizing and overseeing the development of provisional institutions for democratic and autonomous self-government pending a political settlement, including the holding of elections;

d. Transferring, as these institutions are established, its administrative responsibilities while overseeing and supporting the consolidation of Kosovo's local provisional institutions and other peace-building activities;

e. Facilitating a political process designed to determine Kosovo's future status, taking into account the Rambouillet accords (S/1999/648);

f. In a final stage, overseeing the transfer of authority from Kosovo's provisional institutions to institutions established under a political settlement;

g. Supporting the reconstruction of key infrastructure and other economic reconstruction;

h. Supporting, in co-ordination with international humanitarian organizations, humanitarian and disaster relief aid;

i. Maintaining civil law and order, including establishing local police forces and meanwhile through the deployment of international police personnel to serve in Kosovo;

j. Protecting and promoting human rights;

k. Assuring the safe and unimpeded return of all refugees and displaced persons to their homes in Kosovo;

12. Emphasizes the need for coordinated humanitarian relief operations, and for the Federal Republic of Yugoslavia to allow unimpeded access to Kosovo by humanitarian aid organizations and to cooperate with such organizations so as to ensure the fast and effective delivery of international aid;

13. Encourages all member states and international organizations to contribute to economic and social reconstruction as well as to the safe return of refugees and displaced persons, and emphasises in this context the importance of convening an international donors' conference, particularly for the purposes set out in paragraph 11(*g*) above, at the earliest possible date;

14. Demands full cooperation by all concerned, including the international security presence, with the International Tribunal for the Former Yugoslavia;

15. Demands that the KLA and other armed Kosovo Albanian groups end immediately all offensive actions and comply with the requirements for demilitarization as laid down by the head of the international security presence in consultation with the Special Representative of the Secretary-General;

16. Decides that the prohibitions imposed by paragraph 8 of resolution 1160 (1998) shall not apply to arms and related matériel for the use of the international civil and security presences;

17. Welcomes the work in hand in the European Union and other international organizations to

XVII.1. KOSOVO AGREEMENT AND UN RESOLUTION 1244

develop a comprehensive approach to the economic development and stabilization of the region affected by the Kosovo crisis, including the implementation of a Stability Pact for South-Eastern Europe with broad international participation in order to further the promotion of democracy, economic prosperity, stability and regional cooperation;

18. Demands that all states in the region cooperate fully in the implementation of all aspects of this resolution;

19. Decides that the international civil and security presences are established for an initial period of 12 months, to continue thereafter unless the Security Council decides otherwise;

20. Requests the Secretary-General to report to the Council at regular intervals on the implementation of this resolution, including reports from the leaderships of the international civil and security presences, the first reports to be submitted within 30 days of the adoption of this resolution;

21. Decides to remain actively seized of the matter.

Annex 1

Statement by the Chairman on the conclusion of the meeting of the G-8 Foreign Ministers held at the Petersberg Centre on 6 May 1999

The G-8 Foreign Ministers adopted the following general principles on the political solution to the Kosovo crisis:
- Immediate and verifiable end of violence and repression in Kosovo;
- Withdrawal from Kosovo of military, police and paramilitary forces;
- Deployment in Kosovo of effective international civil and security presences, endorsed and adopted by the United Nations, capable of guaranteeing the achievement of the common objectives;
- Establishment of an interim administration for Kosovo to be decided by the Security Council of the United Nations to ensure conditions for a peaceful and normal life for all inhabitants in Kosovo;
- The safe and free return of all refugees and displaced persons and unimpeded access to Kosovo by humanitarian aid organizations;
- A political process towards the establishment of an interim political framework agreement providing for a substantial self-government for Kosovo, taking full account of the Rambouillet accords and the principles of sovereignty and territorial integrity of the Federal Republic of Yugoslavia and the other countries of the region, and the demilitarization of the KLA;
- Comprehensive approach to the economic development and stabilization of the crisis region.

Annex 2

Agreement should be reached on the following principles to move towards a resolution of the Kosovo crisis:

1. An immediate and verifiable end of violence and repression in Kosovo.

2. Verifiable withdrawal from Kosovo of all military, police and paramilitary forces according to a rapid timetable.

3. Deployment in Kosovo under United Nations auspices of effective international civil and security presences, acting as may be decided under Chapter VII of the Charter, capable of guaranteeing the achievement of common objectives.

4. The international security presence with substantial North Atlantic Treaty Organization participation must be deployed under unified command and control and authorised to establish a safe environment for all people in Kosovo and to facilitate the safe return to their homes of all displaced persons and refugees.

5. Establishment of an interim administration for Kosovo as a part of the international civil presence under which the people of Kosovo can enjoy substantial autonomy within the Federal Republic of Yugoslavia, to be decided by the Security Council of the United Nations. The interim administration to provide transitional administration while establishing and overseeing the development of provisional democratic self-governing institutions to ensure conditions for a peaceful and normal life for all inhabitants in Kosovo.

6. After withdrawal, an agreed number of Yugoslav and Serbian personnel will be permitted to return to perform the following functions:
- Liaison with the international civil mission and the international security presence;
- Marking/clearing minefields;
- Maintaining a presence at Serb patrimonial sites;
- Maintaining a presence at key border crossings.

7. Safe and free return of all refugees and displaced persons under the supervision of the Office of the United Nations High Commissioner for Refugees and unimpeded access to Kosovo by humanitarian aid organizations.

8. A political process towards the establishment of an interim political framework agreement pro-

viding for substantial self-government for Kosovo, taking full account of the Rambouillet accords and the principles of sovereignty and territorial integrity of the Federal Republic of Yugoslavia and the other countries of the region, and the demilitarization of UCK. Negotiations between the parties for a settlement should not delay or disrupt the establishment of democratic self-governing institutions.

9. A comprehensive approach to the economic development and stabilization of the crisis region. This will include the implementation of a Stability Pact for South-Eastern Europe with broad international participation in order to further promotion of democracy, economic prosperity, stability and regional cooperation.

10. Suspension of military activity will require acceptance of the principles set forth above in addition to agreement to other, previously identified, required elements, which are specified in the footnote below (1). A military-technical agreement will then be rapidly concluded that would, among other things, specify additional modalities, including the roles and functions of Yugoslav/Serb personnel in Kosovo:

Withdrawal

Procedures for withdrawals, including the phased, detailed schedule and delineation of a buffer area in Serbia beyond which forces will be withdrawn;

Returning personnel
- Equipment associated with returning personnel;
- Terms of reference for their functional responsibilities;
- Timetable for their return;
- Delineation of their geographical areas of operation;
- Rules governing their relationship to the international security presence and the international civil mission.

Notes

1. Other required elements:
- A rapid and precise timetable for withdrawals, meaning, e.g., seven days to complete withdrawal and air defence weapons withdrawn outside a 25-kilometre mutual safety zone within 48 hours;
- Return of personnel for the four functions specified above will be under the supervision of the international security presence and will be limited to a small agreed number (hundreds, not thousands);
- Suspension of military activity will occur after the beginning of verifiable withdrawals;
- The discussion and achievement of a military-technical agreement shall not extend the previously determined time for completion of withdrawals.

2. NATO'S NEW STRATEGIC CONCEPT

Published below is the 'Strategic Concept' document approved by the heads of state and government of the 19-nation North Atlantic Treaty Organization (NATO) meeting in Washington DC, USA, on 23-25 April 1999, to mark the 50th anniversary of the creation of the Alliance. (Source: NATO)

INTRODUCTION

NATO has successfully ensured the freedom of its members and prevented war in Europe during the 40 years of the Cold War. By combining defence with dialogue, it played an indispensable role in bringing East-West confrontation to a peaceful end. The dramatic changes in the Euro-Atlantic strategic landscape brought by the end of the Cold War were reflected in the Alliance's 1991 Strategic Concept. There have, however, been further profound political and security developments since then.

The dangers of the Cold War have given way to more promising, but also challenging prospects, to new opportunities and risks. A new Europe of greater integration is emerging, and a Euro-Atlantic security structure is evolving in which NATO plays a central part. The Alliance has been at the heart of efforts to establish new patterns of cooperation and mutual understanding across the Euro-Atlantic region and has committed itself to essential new activities in the interest of a wider stability. It has shown the depth of that commitment in its efforts to put an end to the immense human suffering created by conflict in the Balkans. The years since the end of the Cold War have also witnessed important developments in arms control, a process to which the Alliance is fully committed. The Alliance's role in these positive developments has been underpinned by the comprehensive adaptation of its approach to security and of its procedures and structures. The last ten years have also seen, however, the appearance of complex new risks to Euro-Atlantic peace and stability, including oppression, ethnic conflict,

economic distress, the collapse of political order and the proliferation of weapons of mass destruction.
  The Alliance has an indispensable role to play in consolidating and preserving the positive changes of the recent past, and in meeting current and future security challenges. It has, therefore, a demanding agenda. It must safeguard common security interests in an environment of further, often unpredictable change. It must maintain collective defence and reinforce the trans-Atlantic link and ensure a balance that allows the European Allies to assume greater responsibility. It must deepen its relations with its partners and prepare for the accession of new members. It must, above all, maintain the political will and the military means required by the entire range of its missions. This new Strategic Concept will guide the Alliance as it pursues this agenda. It expresses NATO's enduring purpose and nature and its fundamental security tasks, identifies the central features of the new security environment, specifies the elements of the Alliance's broad approach to security, and provides guidelines for the further adaptation of its military forces.

PART I: THE PURPOSE AND TASKS OF THE ALLIANCE

  NATO's essential and enduring purpose, set out in the Washington Treaty, is to safeguard the freedom and security of all its members by political and military means. Based on common values of democracy, human rights and the rule of law, the Alliance has striven since its inception to secure a just and lasting peaceful order in Europe. It will continue to do so. The achievement of this aim can be put at risk by crisis and conflict affecting the security of the Euro-Atlantic area. The Alliance therefore not only ensures the defence of its members but contributes to peace and stability in this region. The Alliance embodies the trans-Atlantic link by which the security of North America is permanently tied to the security of Europe. It is the practical expression of effective collective effort among its members in support of their common interests. The fundamental guiding principle by which the Alliance works is that of common commitment and mutual cooperation among sovereign states in support of the indivisibility of security for all of its members. Solidarity and cohesion within the Alliance, through daily cooperation in both the political and military spheres, ensure that no single Ally is forced to rely upon its own national efforts alone in dealing with basic security challenges. Without depriving member states of their right and duty to assume their sovereign responsibilities in the field of defence, the Alliance enables them through collective effort to realise their essential national security objectives. The resulting sense of equal security among the members of the Alliance, regardless of differences in their circumstances or in their national military capabilities, contributes to stability in the Euro-Atlantic area. The Alliance does not seek these benefits for its members alone, but is committed to the creation of conditions conducive to increased partnership, cooperation, and dialogue with others who share its broad political objectives.
  To achieve its essential purpose, as an Alliance of nations committed to the Washington Treaty and the United Nations Charter, the Alliance performs the following fundamental security tasks:
  Security: To provide one of the indispensable foundations for a stable Euro-Atlantic security environment, based on the growth of democratic institutions and commitment to the peaceful resolution of disputes, in which no country would be able to intimidate or coerce any other through the threat or use of force.
  Consultation: To serve, as provided for in Article 4 of the Washington Treaty, as an essential trans-Atlantic forum for Allied consultations on any issues that affect their vital interests, including possible developments posing risks for members' security, and for appropriate coordination of their efforts in fields of common concern.
  Deterrence and Defence: To deter and defend against any threat of aggression against any NATO member state as provided for in Articles 5 and 6 of the Washington Treaty.
  And in order to enhance the security and stability of the Euro-Atlantic area:
  Crisis Management: To stand ready, case-by-case and by consensus, in conformity with Article 7 of the Washington Treaty, to contribute to effective conflict prevention and to engage actively in crisis management, including crisis response operations.
  Partnership: To promote wide-ranging partnership, cooperation, and dialogue with other countries in the Euro-Atlantic area, with the aim of increasing transparency, mutual confidence and the capacity for joint action with the Alliance.
  In fulfilling its purpose and fundamental security tasks, the Alliance will continue to respect the legitimate security interests of others, and seek the peaceful resolution of disputes as set out in the Charter of the United Nations. The Alliance will promote peaceful and friendly international relations and support democratic institutions. The Alliance does not consider itself to be any country's adversary.

PART II: STRATEGIC PERSPECTIVES
The Evolving Strategic Environment

The Alliance operates in an environment of continuing change. Developments in recent years have been generally positive, but uncertainties and risks remain which can develop into acute crises. Within this evolving context, NATO has played an essential part in strengthening Euro-Atlantic security since the end of the Cold War. Its growing political role; its increased political and military partnership, cooperation and dialogue with other states, including with Russia, Ukraine and Mediterranean Dialogue countries; its continuing openness to the accession of new members; its collaboration with other international organizations; its commitment, exemplified in the Balkans, to conflict prevention and crisis management, including through peace support operations: all reflect its determination to shape its security environment and enhance the peace and stability of the Euro-Atlantic area.

In parallel, NATO has successfully adapted to enhance its ability to contribute to Euro-Atlantic peace and stability. Internal reform has included a new command structure, including the Combined Joint Task Force (CJTF) concept, the creation of arrangements to permit the rapid deployment of forces for the full range of the Alliance's missions, and the building of the European Security and Defence Identity (ESDI) within the Alliance.

The United Nations, the Organization for Security and Cooperation in Europe (OSCE), the European Union (EU) and the Western European Union (WEU) have made distinctive contributions to Euro-Atlantic security and stability. Mutually reinforcing organizations have become a central feature of the security environment.

The *United Nations Security Council* has the primary responsibility for the maintenance of international peace and security and, as such, plays a crucial role in contributing to security and stability in the Euro-Atlantic area.

The *OSCE*, as a regional arrangement, is the most inclusive security organization in Europe, which also includes Canada and the United States, and plays an essential role in promoting peace and stability, enhancing cooperative security, and advancing democracy and human rights in Europe. The OSCE is particularly active in the fields of preventive diplomacy, conflict prevention, crisis management and post-conflict rehabilitation. NATO and the OSCE have developed close practical cooperation, especially with regard to the international effort to bring peace to the former Yugoslavia.

The *European Union* has taken important decisions and given a further impetus to its efforts to strengthen its security and defence dimension. This process will have implications for the entire Alliance, and all European Allies should be involved in it, building on arrangements developed by NATO and the WEU. The development of a common foreign and security policy (CFSP) includes the progressive framing of a common defence policy. Such a policy, as called for in the Amsterdam Treaty, would be compatible with the common security and defence policy established within the framework of the Washington Treaty. Important steps taken in this context include the incorporation of the WEU's Petersberg tasks into the Treaty on European Union and the development of closer institutional relations with the WEU.

As stated in the 1994 summit declaration and reaffirmed in Berlin in 1996, the Alliance fully supports the development of the European Security and Defence Identity within the Alliance by making available its assets and capabilities for WEU-led operations. To this end, the Alliance and the WEU have developed a close relationship and put into place key elements of the ESDI as agreed in Berlin. In order to enhance peace and stability in Europe and more widely, the European Allies are strengthening their capacity for action, including by increasing their military capabilities. The increase of the responsibilities and capacities of the European Allies with respect to security and defence enhances the security environment of the Alliance. The stability, transparency, predictability, lower levels of armaments and verification which can be provided by arms control and non-proliferation agreements support NATO's political and military efforts to achieve its strategic objectives. The Allies have played a major part in the significant achievements in this field. These include the enhanced stability produced by the CFE Treaty, the deep reductions in nuclear weapons provided for in the START treaties; the signature of the Comprehensive Test Ban Treaty, the indefinite and unconditional extension of the Nuclear Non-Proliferation Treaty, the accession to it of Belarus, Kazakhstan and Ukraine as non-nuclear-weapons states, and the entry into force of the Chemical Weapons Convention. The Ottawa Convention to ban anti-personnel landmines and similar agreements make an important contribution to alleviating human suffering. There are welcome prospects for further advances in arms control in conventional weapons and with respect to nuclear, chemical and biological (NBC) weapons.

XVII.2. NATO'S NEW STRATEGIC CONCEPT

Security Challenges and Risks

Notwithstanding positive developments in the strategic environment and the fact that large-scale conventional aggression against the Alliance is highly unlikely, the possibility of such a threat emerging over the longer term exists. The security of the Alliance remains subject to a wide variety of military and non-military risks which are multi-directional and often difficult to predict. These risks include uncertainty and instability in and around the Euro-Atlantic area and the possibility of regional crises at the periphery of the Alliance, which could evolve rapidly. Some countries in and around the Euro-Atlantic area face serious economic, social and political difficulties. Ethnic and religious rivalries, territorial disputes, inadequate or failed efforts at reform, the abuse of human rights, and the dissolution of states can lead to local and even regional instability. The resulting tensions could lead to crises affecting Euro-Atlantic stability, to human suffering, and to armed conflicts. Such conflicts could affect the security of the Alliance by spilling over into neighbouring countries, including NATO countries, or in other ways, and could also affect the security of other states.

The existence of powerful nuclear forces outside the Alliance also constitutes a significant factor which the Alliance has to take into account if security and stability in the Euro-Atlantic area are to be maintained.

The proliferation of NBC weapons and their means of delivery remains a matter of serious concern. In spite of welcome progress in strengthening international non-proliferation regimes, major challenges with respect to proliferation remain. The Alliance recognizes that proliferation can occur despite efforts to prevent it and can pose a direct military threat to the Allies' populations, territory, and forces. Some states, including on NATO's periphery and in other regions, sell or acquire or try to acquire NBC weapons and delivery means. Commodities and technology that could be used to build these weapons of mass destruction and their delivery means are becoming more common, while detection and prevention of illicit trade in these materials and know-how continues to be difficult. Non-state actors have shown the potential to create and use some of these weapons.

The global spread of technology that can be of use in the production of weapons may result in the greater availability of sophisticated military capabilities, permitting adversaries to acquire highly capable offensive and defensive air, land, and sea-borne systems, cruise missiles, and other advanced weaponry. In addition, state and non-state adversaries may try to exploit the Alliance's growing reliance on information systems through information operations designed to disrupt such systems. They may attempt to use strategies of this kind to counter NATO's superiority in traditional weaponry.

Any armed attack on the territory of the Allies, from whatever direction, would be covered by Articles 5 and 6 of the Washington Treaty. However, Alliance security must also take account of the global context. Alliance security interests can be affected by other risks of a wider nature, including acts of terrorism, sabotage and organised crime, and by the disruption of the flow of vital resources. The uncontrolled movement of large numbers of people, particularly as a consequence of armed conflicts, can also pose problems for security and stability affecting the Alliance. Arrangements exist within the Alliance for consultation among the Allies under Article 4 of the Washington Treaty and, where appropriate, coordination of their efforts including their responses to risks of this kind.

PART III: THE APPROACH TO SECURITY IN THE 21ST CENTURY

The Alliance is committed to a broad approach to security, which recognizes the importance of political, economic, social and environmental factors in addition to the indispensable defence dimension. This broad approach forms the basis for the Alliance to accomplish its fundamental security tasks effectively, and its increasing effort to develop effective cooperation with other European and Euro-Atlantic organizations as well as the United Nations. Our collective aim is to build a European security architecture in which the Alliance's contribution to the security and stability of the Euro-Atlantic area and the contribution of these other international organizations are complementary and mutually reinforcing, both in deepening relations among Euro-Atlantic countries and in managing crises. NATO remains the essential forum for consultation among the Allies and the forum for agreement on policies bearing on the security and defence commitments of its members under the Washington Treaty.

The Alliance seeks to preserve peace and to reinforce Euro-Atlantic security and stability by: the preservation of the trans-Atlantic link; the maintenance of effective military capabilities sufficient for deterrence and defence and to fulfil the full range of its missions; the development of the European Security and Defence Identity within the Alliance; an overall capability to manage crises successfully; its continued openness to new members; and the continued pursuit of partnership, cooperation, and dialogue with other nations as part of its co-operative approach to Euro-Atlantic security, including in the field of arms control and disarmament.

The Trans-Atlantic Link

NATO is committed to a strong and dynamic partnership between Europe and North America in support of the values and interests they share. The security of Europe and that of North America are indivisible. Thus the Alliance's commitment to the indispensable trans-Atlantic link and the collective defence of its members is fundamental to its credibility and to the security and stability of the Euro-Atlantic area.

The Maintenance of Alliance Military Capabilities

The maintenance of an adequate military capability and clear preparedness to act collectively in the common defence remain central to the Alliance's security objectives. Such a capability, together with political solidarity, remains at the core of the Alliance's ability to prevent any attempt at coercion or intimidation, and to guarantee that military aggression directed against the Alliance can never be perceived as an option with any prospect of success.

Military capabilities effective under the full range of foreseeable circumstances are also the basis of the Alliance's ability to contribute to conflict prevention and crisis management through non-Article 5 crisis response operations. These missions can be highly demanding and can place a premium on the same political and military qualities, such as cohesion, multinational training, and extensive prior planning, that would be essential in an Article 5 situation. Accordingly, while they may pose special requirements, they will be handled through a common set of Alliance structures and procedures.

The European Security and Defence Identity

The Alliance, which is the foundation of the collective defence of its members and through which common security objectives will be pursued wherever possible, remains committed to a balanced and dynamic trans-Atlantic partnership. The European Allies have taken decisions to enable them to assume greater responsibilities in the security and defence field in order to enhance the peace and stability of the Euro-Atlantic area and thus the security of all Allies. On the basis of decisions taken by the Alliance, in Berlin in 1996 and subsequently, the European Security and Defence Identity will continue to be developed within NATO. This process will require close cooperation between NATO, the WEU and, if and when appropriate, the European Union. It will enable all European Allies to make a more coherent and effective contribution to the missions and activities of the Alliance as an expression of our shared responsibilities; it will reinforce the trans-Atlantic partnership; and it will assist the European Allies to act by themselves as required through the readiness of the Alliance, on a case-by-case basis and by consensus, to make its assets and capabilities available for operations in which the Alliance is not engaged militarily under the political control and strategic direction either of the WEU or as otherwise agreed, taking into account the full participation of all European Allies if they were so to choose.

Conflict Prevention and Crisis Management

In pursuit of its policy of preserving peace, preventing war, and enhancing security and stability and as set out in the fundamental security tasks, NATO will seek, in cooperation with other organizations, to prevent conflict, or, should a crisis arise, to contribute to its effective management, consistent with international law, including through the possibility of conducting non-Article 5 crisis response operations. The Alliance's preparedness to carry out such operations supports the broader objective of reinforcing and extending stability and often involves the participation of NATO's Partners. NATO recalls its offer, made in Brussels in 1994, to support on a case-by-case basis in accordance with its own procedures, peacekeeping and other operations under the authority of the UN Security Council or the responsibility of the OSCE, including by making available Alliance resources and expertise. In this context NATO recalls its subsequent decisions with respect to crisis response operations in the Balkans. Taking into account the necessity for Alliance solidarity and cohesion, participation in any such operation or mission will remain subject to decisions of member states in accordance with national constitutions.

NATO will make full use of partnership, cooperation and dialogue and its links to other organizations to contribute to preventing crises and, should they arise, defusing them at an early stage. A coherent approach to crisis management, as in any use of force by the Alliance, will require the Alliance's political authorities to choose and coordinate appropriate responses from a range of both political and military measures and to exercise close political control at all stages.

Partnership, Cooperation and Dialogue

Through its active pursuit of partnership, cooperation and dialogue, the Alliance is a positive force in promoting security and stability throughout the Euro-Atlantic area. Through outreach and

XVII.2. NATO'S NEW STRATEGIC CONCEPT 555

openness, the Alliance seeks to preserve peace, support and promote democracy, contribute to prosperity and progress, and foster genuine partnership with and among all democratic Euro-Atlantic countries. This aims at enhancing the security of all, excludes nobody, and helps to overcome divisions and disagreements that could lead to instability and conflict.

The *Euro-Atlantic Partnership Council* (EAPC) will remain the overarching framework for all aspects of NATO's cooperation with its Partners. It offers an expanded political dimension for both consultation and cooperation. EAPC consultations build increased transparency and confidence among its members on security issues, contribute to conflict prevention and crisis management, and develop practical cooperation activities, including in civil emergency planning, and scientific and environmental affairs.

The *Partnership for Peace* [PFP] is the principal mechanism for forging practical security links between the Alliance and its Partners and for enhancing interoperability between Partners and NATO. Through detailed programmes that reflect individual Partners' capacities and interests, Allies and Partners work towards transparency in national defence planning and budgeting; democratic control of defence forces; preparedness for civil disasters and other emergencies; and the development of the ability to work together, including in NATO-led PFP operations. The Alliance is committed to increasing the role the Partners play in PFP decision-making and planning, and making PFP more operational. NATO has undertaken to consult with any active participant in the Partnership if that Partner perceives a direct threat to its territorial integrity, political independence, or security.

Russia plays a unique role in Euro-Atlantic security. Within the framework of the [1997] NATO-Russia Founding Act on Mutual Relations, Cooperation and Security, NATO and Russia have committed themselves to developing their relations on the basis of common interest, reciprocity and transparency to achieve a lasting and inclusive peace in the Euro-Atlantic area based on the principles of democracy and co-operative security. NATO and Russia have agreed to give concrete substance to their shared commitment to build a stable, peaceful and undivided Europe. A strong, stable and enduring partnership between NATO and Russia is essential to achieve lasting stability in the Euro-Atlantic area.

Ukraine occupies a special place in the Euro-Atlantic security environment and is an important and valuable partner in promoting stability and common democratic values. NATO is committed to further strengthening its distinctive partnership with Ukraine on the basis of the NATO-Ukraine Charter, including political consultations on issues of common concern and a broad range of practical cooperation activities. The Alliance continues to support Ukrainian sovereignty and independence, territorial integrity, democratic development, economic prosperity and its status as a non-nuclear weapons state as key factors of stability and security in central and eastern Europe and in Europe as a whole.

The *Mediterranean* is an area of special interest to the Alliance. Security in Europe is closely linked to security and stability in the Mediterranean. NATO's Mediterranean Dialogue process is an integral part of NATO's cooperative approach to security. It provides a framework for confidence building, promotes transparency and cooperation in the region, and reinforces and is reinforced by other international efforts. The Alliance is committed to developing progressively the political, civil and military aspects of the Dialogue with the aim of achieving closer cooperation with, and more active involvement by, countries that are partners in this Dialogue.

Enlargement

The Alliance remains open to new members under Article 10 of the Washington Treaty. It expects to extend further invitations in coming years to nations willing and able to assume the responsibilities and obligations of membership, and as NATO determines that the inclusion of these nations would serve the overall political and strategic interests of the Alliance, strengthen its effectiveness and cohesion, and enhance overall European security and stability. To this end, NATO has established a programme of activities to assist aspiring countries in their preparations for possible future membership in the context of its wider relationship with them. No European democratic country whose admission would fulfil the objectives of the Treaty will be excluded from consideration.

Arms Control, Disarmament and Non-Proliferation

The Alliance's policy of support for arms control, disarmament and non-proliferation will continue to play a major role in the achievement of the Alliance's security objectives. The Allies seek to enhance security and stability at the lowest possible level of forces consistent with the Alliance's ability to provide for collective defence and to fulfil the full range of its missions. The Alliance will continue to ensure that-as an important part of its broad approach to security-defence and arms control, disarmament and non-proliferation objectives remain in harmony. The Alliance will continue to actively contribute to the development of arms control, disarmament and non-proliferation agreements as well as to confidence and security building measures. The Allies take seriously their distinctive role in promoting a broader, more comprehensive and more verifiable international arms control and disarmament process. The Alliance will enhance its political efforts to reduce dangers arising from the proliferation of weapons of mass destruction and their means of delivery. The principal non-proliferation goal of the Alliance and its members is to prevent proliferation from occurring or, should it occur, to reverse it through diplomatic means. The Alliance attaches great importance to the continuing validity and the full implementation by all parties of the CFE Treaty as an essential element in ensuring the stability of the Euro-Atlantic area.

PART IV: GUIDELINES FOR THE ALLIANCE'S FORCES

Principles of Alliance Strategy

The Alliance will maintain the necessary military capabilities to accomplish the full range of NATO's missions. The principles of Allied solidarity and strategic unity remain paramount for all Alliance missions. Alliance forces must safeguard NATO's military effectiveness and freedom of action. The security of all Allies is indivisible: an attack on one is an attack on all. With respect to collective defence under Article 5 of the Washington Treaty, the combined military forces of the Alliance must be capable of deterring any potential aggression against it, of stopping an aggressor's advance as far forward as possible should an attack nevertheless occur, and of ensuring the political independence and territorial integrity of its member states. They must also be prepared to contribute to conflict prevention and to conduct non-Article 5 crisis response operations. The Alliance's forces have essential roles in fostering cooperation and understanding with NATO's Partners and other states, particularly in helping Partners to prepare for potential participation in NATO-led PFP operations. Thus they contribute to the preservation of peace, to the safeguarding of common security interests of Alliance members, and to the maintenance of the security and stability of the Euro-Atlantic area. By deterring the use of NBC weapons, they contribute to Alliance efforts aimed at preventing the proliferation of these weapons and their delivery means.

The achievement of the Alliance's aims depends critically on the equitable sharing of the roles, risks and responsibilities, as well as the benefits, of common defence. The presence of United States conventional and nuclear forces in Europe remains vital to the security of Europe, which is inseparably linked to that of North America. The North American Allies contribute to the Alliance through military forces available for Alliance missions, through their broader contribution to international peace and security, and through the provision of unique training facilities on the North American continent. The European Allies also make wide-ranging and substantial contributions. As the process of developing the ESDI within the Alliance progresses, the European Allies will further enhance their contribution to the common defence and to international peace and stability including through multinational formations.

The principle of collective effort in Alliance defence is embodied in practical arrangements that enable the Allies to enjoy the crucial political, military and resource advantages of collective defence, and prevent the renationalization of defence policies, without depriving the Allies of their sovereignty. These arrangements also enable NATO's forces to carry out non-Article 5 crisis response operations and constitute a prerequisite for a coherent Alliance response to all possible contingencies. They are based on procedures for consultation, an integrated military structure, and on cooperation agreements. Key features include collective force planning; common funding; common operational planning; multinational formations, headquarters and command arrangements; an integrated air defence system; a balance of roles and responsibilities among the Allies; the stationing and deployment of forces outside home territory when required; arrangements, including planning, for crisis management and reinforcement; common standards and procedures for equipment, training and logistics; joint and combined doctrines and exercises when appropriate; and infrastructure, armaments and logistics cooperation. The inclusion of NATO's Partners in such arrangements or the development of similar arrangements for them, in appropriate areas, is also instrumental in enhancing cooperation and common efforts in Euro-Atlantic security matters.

Multinational funding, including through the Military Budget and the NATO Security Investment Programme, will continue to play an important role in acquiring and maintaining necessary assets and capabilities. The management of resources should be guided by the military requirements of the Alliance as they evolve. The Alliance supports the further development of the ESDI within the Alliance, including by being prepared to make available assets and capabilities for operations under the political control and strategic direction either of the WEU or as otherwise agreed.

To protect peace and to prevent war or any kind of coercion, the Alliance will maintain for the foreseeable future an appropriate mix of nuclear and conventional forces based in Europe and kept up to date where necessary, although at a minimum sufficient level. Taking into account the diversity of risks with which the Alliance could be faced, it must maintain the forces necessary to ensure credible deterrence and to provide a wide range of conventional response options. But the Alliance's conventional forces alone cannot ensure credible deterrence. Nuclear weapons make a unique contribution in rendering the risks of aggression against the Alliance incalculable and unacceptable. Thus, they remain essential to preserve peace.

The Alliance's Force Posture: The Missions of Alliance Military Forces.

The primary role of Alliance military forces is to protect peace and to guarantee the territorial integrity, political independence and security of member states. The Alliance's forces must therefore be able to deter and defend effectively, to maintain or restore the territorial integrity of Allied nations and-in case of conflict-to terminate war rapidly by making an aggressor reconsider his decision, cease his attack and withdraw. NATO forces must maintain the ability to provide for collective defence while conducting effective non-Article 5 crisis response operations.

The maintenance of the security and stability of the Euro-Atlantic area is of key importance. An important aim of the Alliance and its forces is to keep risks at a distance by dealing with potential crises at an early stage. In the event of crises which jeopardize Euro-Atlantic stability and could affect the security of Alliance members, the Alliance's military forces may be called upon to conduct crisis response operations. They may also be called upon to contribute to the preservation of international peace and security by conducting operations in support of other international organizations, complementing and reinforcing political actions within a broad approach to security.

In contributing to the management of crises through military operations, the Alliance's forces will have to deal with a complex and diverse range of actors, risks, situations and demands, including humanitarian emergencies. Some non-Article 5 crisis response operations may be as demanding as some collective defence missions. Well-trained and well-equipped forces at adequate levels of readiness and in sufficient strength to meet the full range of contingencies as well as the appropriate support structures, planning tools and command and control capabilities are essential in providing efficient military contributions. The Alliance should also be prepared to support, on the basis of separable but not separate capabilities, operations under the political control and strategic direction either of the WEU or as otherwise agreed. The potential participation of Partners and other non-NATO nations in NATO-led operations as well as possible operations with Russia would be further valuable elements of NATO's contribution to managing crises that affect Euro-Atlantic security.

Alliance military forces also contribute to promoting stability throughout the Euro-Atlantic area by their participation in military-to-military contacts and in other cooperation activities and exercises under the Partnership for Peace as well as those organised to deepen NATO's relationships with Russia, Ukraine and the Mediterranean Dialogue countries. They contribute to stability and understanding by participating in confidence-building activities, including those which enhance transparency and improve communication; as well as in verification of arms control agreements and in humanitarian de-mining. Key areas of consultation and cooperation could include inter alia: training and exercises, interoperability, civil-military relations, concept and doctrine development, defence planning, crisis management, proliferation issues, armaments cooperation as well as participation in operational planning and operations.

Guidelines for the Alliance's Force Posture

To implement the Alliance's fundamental security tasks and the principles of its strategy, the forces of the Alliance must continue to be adapted to meet the requirements of the full range of Alliance missions effectively and to respond to future challenges. The posture of Allies' forces, building on the strengths of different national defence structures, will conform to the guidelines developed in the following paragraphs. The size, readiness, availability and deployment of the Alliance's military forces will reflect its commitment to collective defence and to conduct crisis response operations, sometimes at short notice, distant from their home stations, including beyond the Allies' territory. The characteristics of the Alliance's forces will also reflect the provisions of relevant arms control agreements. Alliance forces must be adequate in strength and capabilities to deter and counter aggression against any Ally. They must be interoperable and have appropriate doctrines and technologies. They must be held at the required readiness and deployability, and be capable of military success in a wide range of complex joint and combined operations, which may also include Partners and other non-NATO nations.

This means in particular:
• that the overall size of the Allies' forces will be kept at the lowest levels consistent with the requirements of collective defence and other Alliance missions;
• that they will be held at appropriate and graduated readiness; that the peacetime geographical

distribution of forces will ensure a sufficient military presence throughout the territory of the Alliance, including the stationing and deployment of forces outside home territory and waters and forward deployment of forces when and where necessary. Regional and, in particular, geo-strategic considerations within the Alliance will have to be taken into account, as instabilities on NATO's periphery could lead to crises or conflicts requiring an Alliance military response, potentially with short warning times;

• that NATO's command structure will be able to undertake command and control of the full range of the Alliance's military missions including through the use of deployable combined and joint headquarters, in particular CJTF headquarters, to command and control multinational and multiservice forces. It will also be able to support operations under the political control and strategic direction either of the WEU or as otherwise agreed, thereby contributing to the development of the ESDI within the Alliance, and to conduct NATO-led non-Article 5 crisis response operations in which Partners and other countries may participate;

• that overall, the Alliance will, in both the near and long term and for the full range of its missions, require essential operational capabilities such as an effective engagement capability; deployability and mobility; survivability of forces and infrastructure; and sustainability, incorporating logistics and force rotation. To develop these capabilities to their full potential for multinational operations, interoperability, including human factors, the use of appropriate advanced technology, the maintenance of information superiority in military operations, and highly qualified personnel with a broad spectrum of skills will be important. Sufficient capabilities in the areas of command, control and communications as well as intelligence and surveillance will serve as necessary force multipliers;

• that at any time a limited but militarily significant proportion of ground, air and sea forces will be able to react as rapidly as necessary to a wide range of eventualities, including a short-notice attack on any Ally. Greater numbers of force elements will be available at appropriate levels of readiness to sustain prolonged operations, whether within or beyond Alliance territory, including through rotation of deployed forces. Taken together, these forces must also be of sufficient quality, quantity and readiness to contribute to deterrence and to defend against limited attacks on the Alliance;

• that the Alliance must be able to build up larger forces, both in response to any fundamental changes in the security environment and for limited requirements, by reinforcement, by mobilising reserves, or by reconstituting forces when necessary. This ability must be in proportion to potential threats to Alliance security, including potential long-term developments. It must take into account the possibility of substantial improvements in the readiness and capabilities of military forces on the periphery of the Alliance. Capabilities for timely reinforcement and resupply both within and from Europe and North America will remain of critical importance, with a resulting need for a high degree of deployability, mobility and flexibility;

• that appropriate force structures and procedures, including those that would provide an ability to build up, deploy and draw down forces quickly and selectively, are necessary to permit measured, flexible and timely responses in order to reduce and defuse tensions. These arrangements must be exercised regularly in peacetime;

• that the Alliance's defence posture must have the capability to address appropriately and effectively the risks associated with the proliferation of NBC weapons and their means of delivery, which also pose a potential threat to the Allies' populations, territory, and forces. A balanced mix of forces, response capabilities and strengthened defences is needed;

• that the Alliance's forces and infrastructure must be protected against terrorist attacks.

Characteristics of Conventional Forces

It is essential that the Allies' military forces have a credible ability to fulfil the full range of Alliance missions. This requirement has implications for force structures, force and equipment levels; readiness, availability, and sustainability; training and exercises; deployment and employment options; and force build-up and mobilization capabilities. The aim should be to achieve an optimum balance between high readiness forces capable of beginning rapidly, and immediately as necessary, collective defence or non-Article 5 crisis response operations; forces at different levels of lower readiness to provide the bulk of those required for collective defence, for rotation of forces to sustain crisis response operations, or for further reinforcement of a particular region; and a longer-term build-up and augmentation capability for the worst case-but very remote-scenario of large scale operations for collective defence. A substantial proportion of Alliance forces will be capable of performing more than one of these roles.

Alliance forces will be structured to reflect the multinational and joint nature of Alliance missions. Essential tasks will include controlling, protecting, and defending territory; ensuring the unimpeded use of sea, air, and land lines of communication; sea control and protecting the deployment of the Alliance's sea-based deterrent; conducting independent and combined air operations; ensuring a secure air environment and effective extended air defence; surveillance, intelligence, reconnaissance and electronic warfare; strategic lift; and providing effective and flexible command and control facilities, including deployable combined and joint headquarters.

The Alliance's defence posture against the risks and potential threats of the proliferation of NBC weapons and their means of delivery must continue to be improved, including through work on missile defences. As NATO forces may be called upon to operate beyond NATO's borders, capabilities for dealing with proliferation risks must be flexible, mobile, rapidly deployable and sustainable. Doctrines, planning, and training and exercise policies must also prepare the Alliance to deter and defend against the use of NBC weapons. The aim in doing so will be to further reduce operational vulnerabilities of NATO military forces while maintaining their flexibility and effectiveness despite the presence, threat or use of NBC weapons.

Alliance strategy does not include a chemical or biological warfare capability. The Allies support universal adherence to the relevant disarmament regimes. But, even if further progress with respect to banning chemical and biological weapons can be achieved, defensive precautions will remain essential.

Given reduced overall force levels and constrained resources, the ability to work closely together will remain vital for achieving the Alliance's missions. The Alliance's collective defence arrangements in which, for those concerned, the integrated military structure plays the key role, are essential in this regard. The various strands of NATO's defence planning need to be effectively coordinated at all levels in order to ensure the preparedness of the forces and supporting structures to carry out the full spectrum of their roles. Exchanges of information among the Allies about their force plans contribute to securing the availability of the capabilities needed for the execution of these roles. Consultations in case of important changes in national defence plans also remain of key importance. Cooperation in the development of new operational concepts will be essential for responding to evolving security challenges. The detailed practical arrangements that have been developed as part of the ESDI within the Alliance contribute to close allied cooperation without unnecessary duplication of assets and capabilities.

To be able to respond flexibly to possible contingencies and to permit the effective conduct of Alliance missions, the Alliance requires sufficient logistics capabilities, including transport capacities, medical support and stocks to deploy and sustain all types of forces effectively. Standardization will foster cooperation and cost-effectiveness in providing logistic support to allied forces. Mounting and sustaining operations outside the Allies' territory, where there may be little or no host-nation support, will pose special logistical challenges. The ability to build-up larger, adequately equipped and trained forces, in a timely manner and to a level able to fulfil the full range of Alliance missions, will also make an essential contribution to crisis management and defence. This will include the ability to reinforce any area at risk and to establish a multinational presence when and where this is needed. Forces of various kinds and at various levels of readiness will be capable of flexible employment in both intra-European and trans-Atlantic reinforcement. This will require control of lines of communication, and appropriate support and exercise arrangements.

The interaction between Alliance forces and the civil environment (both governmental and non-governmental) in which they operate is crucial to the success of operations. Civil-military cooperation is interdependent: military means are increasingly requested to assist civil authorities; at the same time civil support to military operations is important for logistics, communications, medical support, and public affairs. Cooperation between the Alliance's military and civil bodies will accordingly remain essential.

The Alliance's ability to accomplish the full range of its missions will rely increasingly on multinational forces, complementing national commitments to NATO for the Allies concerned. Such forces, which are applicable to the full range of Alliance missions, demonstrate the Alliance's resolve to maintain a credible collective defence; enhance Alliance cohesion; and reinforce the trans-Atlantic partnership and strengthen the ESDI within the Alliance. Multinational forces, particularly those capable of deploying rapidly for collective defence or for non-Article 5 crisis response operations, reinforce solidarity. They can also provide a way of deploying more capable formations than might be available purely nationally, thus helping to make more efficient use of scarce defence resources. This may include a highly integrated, multinational approach to specific tasks and functions, an approach which underlies the implementation of the CJTF concept. For peace support operations, effective multinational formations and other arrangements involving Partners will be valuable. In order to exploit fully the potential offered by multinational formations, improving interoperability, inter alia through sufficient training and exercises, is of the highest importance.

Characteristics of Nuclear Forces

The fundamental purpose of the nuclear forces of the Allies is political: to preserve peace and prevent coercion and any kind of war. They will continue to fulfil an essential role by ensuring uncertainty in the mind of any aggressor about the nature of the Allies' response to military aggression. They demonstrate that aggression of any kind is not a rational option. The supreme guarantee of the security of the Allies is provided by the strategic nuclear forces of the Alliance, particularly those of the United States; the independent nuclear forces of the United Kingdom and France, which have a deterrent role of their own, contribute to the overall deterrence and security of the Allies.

A credible Alliance nuclear posture and the demonstration of Alliance solidarity and common commitment to war prevention continue to require widespread participation by European Allies involved in collective defence planning in nuclear roles, in peacetime basing of nuclear forces on their territory and in command, control and consultation arrangements. Nuclear forces based in Europe and committed to NATO provide an essential political and military link between the European and the North American members of the Alliance. The Alliance will therefore maintain adequate nuclear forces in Europe. These forces need to have the necessary characteristics and appropriate flexibility and survivability, to be perceived as a credible and effective element of the Allies' strategy in preventing war. They will be maintained at the minimum level sufficient to preserve peace and stability.

The Allies concerned consider that, with the radical changes in the security situation, including reduced conventional force levels in Europe and increased reaction times, NATO's ability to defuse a crisis through diplomatic and other means or, should it be necessary, to mount a successful conventional defence has significantly improved. The circumstances in which any use of nuclear weapons might have to be contemplated by them are therefore extremely remote. Since 1991, therefore, the Allies have taken a series of steps which reflect the post-Cold War security environment. These include a dramatic reduction of the types and numbers of NATO's sub-strategic forces including the elimination of all nuclear artillery and ground-launched short-range nuclear missiles; a significant relaxation of the readiness criteria for nuclear-roled forces; and the termination of standing peacetime nuclear contingency plans. NATO's nuclear forces no longer target any country. Nonetheless, NATO will maintain, at the minimum level consistent with the prevailing security environment, adequate sub-strategic forces based in Europe which will provide an essential link with strategic nuclear forces, reinforcing the trans-Atlantic link. These will consist of dual capable aircraft and a small number of United Kingdom Trident warheads. Sub-strategic nuclear weapons will, however, not be deployed in normal circumstances on surface vessels and attack submarines.

PART V: CONCLUSION

As the North Atlantic Alliance enters its sixth decade, it must be ready to meet the challenges and opportunities of a new century. The Strategic Concept reaffirms the enduring purpose of the Alliance and sets out its fundamental security tasks. It enables a transformed NATO to contribute to the evolving security environment, supporting security and stability with the strength of its shared commitment to democracy and the peaceful resolution of disputes. The Strategic Concept will govern the Alliance's security and defence policy, its operational concepts, its conventional and nuclear force posture and its collective defence arrangements, and will be kept under review in the light of the evolving security environment. In an uncertain world the need for effective defence remains, but in reaffirming this commitment the Alliance will also continue making full use of every opportunity to help build an undivided continent by promoting and fostering the vision of a Europe whole and free.

3. THE SHARM EL SHAIKH MEMORANDUM

Published below is the 'Memorandum on Implementation Timeline of Outstanding Commitments of Agreements Signed and the Resumption of the Permanent Status Negotiations', signed by Israel and the Palestine Liberation Organization (PLO) at Sharm el Shaikh, Egypt, on 4 September 1999. (*Source:* Keesing's Record of World Events).

The government of the State of Israel and the Palestine Liberation Organization commit themselves to full and mutual implementation of the Interim Agreement and all other agreements concluded between them since September 1993 (hereinafter 'the prior agreements'), and all outstanding commitments emanating from the prior agreements.

Without derogating from the other requirements of the prior agreements, the two sides have agreed as follows:

1. Permanent Status Negotiations

a. In the context of the implementation of the prior agreements, the two Sides will resume the Permanent Status negotiations in an accelerated manner and will make a determined effort to achieve their mutual goal of reaching a Permanent Status Agreement based on the agreed agenda, i.e. the specific issues reserved for Permanent Status negotiators and other issues of common interest.

b. The two sides reaffirm their understanding that the negotiations on the Permanent Status will lead to the implementation of Security Council resolutions 242 and 338 [of 1967 and 1973 respectively];

c. The two sides will make a determined effort to conclude a Framework Agreement on all Permanent Status issues in five months from the resumption of the Permanent Status negotiations.

d. The two sides will conclude a comprehensive agreement on all Permanent Status issues within one year from the resumption of the Permanent Status negotiations;

e. Permanent Status negotiations will resume after the implementation of the first stage of release of prisoners and the second stage of the first and second further redeployments and not later than 13 September 1999. In the [1998] Wye River Memorandum [WRM], the United States has expressed its willingness to facilitate these negotiations.

2. Phase One and Phase Two of the Further Redeployments

The Israeli side undertakes the following with regard to phase one and phase two of the further redeployments:

a. On 5 September 1999, to transfer 7 per cent from Area C to Area B.[*]

b. On 15 November 1999, to transfer 2 per cent from Area B to Area A and 3 per cent from Area C to Area B.

c. On 20 January 2000, to transfer 1 per cent from Area C to Area A, and 5.1 per cent from Area B to Area A.

3. Release of Prisoners

a. The two sides shall establish a Joint Committee that shall follow-up on matters related to release of Palestinian prisoners.

b. The government of Israel shall release Palestinian and other prisoners who committed their offences prior to 13 September 1993 and were arrested prior to 4 May 1994. The Joint Committee shall agree on the names of those who will be released in the first two stages. Those lists shall be recommended in the relevant authorities through the Monitoring and Steering Committee.

c. The first stage of release of prisoners shall be carried out on 5 September 1999* and shall consist of 200 prisoners. The second stage of release of prisoners shall be carried out on 8 October 1999 and shall consist of 150 prisoners.

d. The Joint Committee shall recommend further lists of names to be released to the relevant authorities through the Monitoring and Steering Committee;

e. The Israeli side will aim to release Palestinian prisoners before next Ramadan.

4. Committees

a. The Third Further Redeployment Committee shall commence its activities not later than 13 September 1999.

b. The Monitoring and Steering Committee, all Interim Committees (i.e., CAC, JFC, JSC, legal committee, people to people), as well as Wye River Memorandum committees shall resume and/or continue their activity, as the case may be, not later than 13 September 1999. The Monitoring and Steering Committee will have on its agenda, *inter alia*, the Year 2000, Donor/PA projects in Area C, and the issue of industrial estates.

c. The Continuing Committee on displaced persons shall resume its activity on 1 October 1999 (Article XXVII, Interim Agreement).

d. Not later than 30 October 1999, the two sides will implement the recommendations of the Ad-Hoc Economic Committee (Articles 111-6, WRM).

5. Safe Passage

a. The operation of the southern route of the safe passage for the movement of persons, vehicles, and goods will start on 1 October 1999 (Annex I, Article X, Interim Agreement) in accordance with the details of operation, which will be provided for in the Safe Passage Protocol that will be concluded by the two sides not later than 30 September 1999.

b. The two sides will agree on the specific location of the crossing-point of the northern route of the safe passage as specified in Annex 1, Article X, provision e-4, in the Interim Agreement not later than 5 October 1999.

c. The Safe Passage Protocol applied to the southern route of the safe passage shall apply to the northern route of the safe passage with relevant agreed modifications.

d. Upon the agreement on the location of the crossing-point of the northern route of the safe passage, construction of the needed facilities and related procedures shall commence and shall be ongoing. At the same time, temporary facilities will be established for the operation of the northern route not later than four months from the agreement on the specific location of the crossing-point.

e. In between the operation of the southern crossing-point of the safe passage and the northern crossing-point of the safe passage, Israel will facilitate arrangements for the movement between the West Bank and the Gaza Strip, using non-safe passage routes other than the southern route of the safe passage.

f. The location of the crossing-points shall be without prejudice to the Permanent Status negotiations (Annex 1, Article X, provision *e*, Interim Agreement).

6. Gaza Sea Port

The two sides have agreed on the following principles to facilitate and enable the construction works of the Gaza Sea Port. The principles shall not prejudice or pre-empt the outcome of negotiations on the Permanent Status:

a. The Israeli side agrees that the Palestinian side shall commence construction works in and related to the Gaza Sea Port on 1 October 1999.

b. The two sides agree that the Gaza Sea Port will not be operated in any way before reaching a joint Sea Port Protocol on all aspects of operating the port, including security.

c. The Gaza Sea Port is a special case, like the Gaza Airport, being situated in an area under the responsibility of the Palestinian side and serving as an international passage. Therefore, with the conclusion of a joint Sea Port Protocol, all activities and arrangements relating to the construction of the port shall be in accordance with the provisions of the Interim Agreement, especially those relating to international passages, as adapted in the Gaza Airport Protocol.

d. The construction shall ensure adequate provision for effective security and customs inspection of people and goods, as well as the establishment of a designated checking area in the port.

e. In this context, the Israeli side will facilitate on an ongoing basis the works related to the construction of the Gaza Sea Port, including the movement in and out of the port of vessels, equipment, resources and material required for the construction of the port.

f. The two sides will coordinate such works, including the designs and movement, through a joint mechanism.

7. Hebron Issues

a. The Shuhada Road in Hebron shall be opened for the movement of Palestinian vehicles in two phases. The first phase has been carried out, and the second shall be carried out not later than 30 October 1999.

b. The wholesale market Habashe will be opened not later than 1 November 1999, in accordance with arrangements which will be agreed upon by the two sides;

c. A high-level Joint Liaison Committee will convene not later than 13 September 1999 to review the situation in the Tomb of the Patriarchs/Al-Haram al-Ibrahimi (Annex I, Article VII, Interim Agreement and as per the 15 January 1998 US Minute of Discussion).

8. Security

a. The two sides will, in accordance with the prior agreements, act to ensure the immediate, efficient and effective handling of any incident involving a threat of act of terrorism, violence or incitement, whether committed by Palestinians or Israelis. To this end, they will cooperate in the exchange of information and coordinate policies and activities. Each side shall immediately and effectively respond to the occurrence or anticipated occurrence of an act of terrorism, violence or incitement and shall take all necessary measures to prevent such an occurrence.

b. Pursuant to the prior agreements, the Palestinian side undertakes to implement its responsibilities for security, security cooperation, ongoing obligations and other issues emanating from the prior agreements, including, in particular, the following obligations emanating from the Wye River Memorandum: i. continuation of the programme for the collection of illegal weapons, including reports; ii. apprehension of suspects, including reports; iii. forwarding of the list of Palestinian policemen to the Israeli side not later than 13 September 1999; iv. beginning of the review of the list by the Monitoring and Steering Committee not later than October 15, 1999.

9-11. Other Clauses

The two sides call upon the international donor community to enhance its commitment and financial support to the Palestinian economic development and the Israeli-Palestinian peace process.

Recognizing the necessity to create a positive environment for the negotiations, neither side shall initiate or take any step that will change the status of the West Bank and the Gaza Strip in accordance with the interim agreement.

Obligations pertaining to dates which occur on holidays or Saturdays shall be carried out on the first subsequent working day.

This memorandum will enter into force one week from the date of its signature.*

*It is understood that, for technical reasons, implementation of Article 2*a* and the first stage mentioned in Article 3*c* will be carried out within a week from the signing of this memorandum.

4. UNITED KINGDOM LABOUR GOVERNMENT

(as at 31 December 1999)

Members of the Cabinet

Prime Minister, First Lord of the Treasury and Minister for the Civil Service	Rt. Hon. Tony Blair, MP
Deputy Prime Minister and Secretary of State for the Environment, Transport and the Regions	Rt. Hon. John Prescott, MP
Lord Chancellor	Rt. Hon. The Lord Irvine of Lairg
Chancellor of the Exchequer	Rt. Hon. Gordon Brown, MP
Secretary of State for the Home Department	Rt. Hon. Jack Straw, MP
Secretary of State for Foreign and Commonwealth Affairs	Rt. Hon. Robin Cook, MP
Secretary of State for Trade and Industry	Rt. Hon. Stephen Byers, MP
President of the Council and Leader of the House of Commons	Rt. Hon. Margaret Beckett, MP
Lord Privy Seal, Leader of the House of Lords and Minister for Women	Rt. Hon. Baroness Jay of Paddington
Secretary of State for Education and Employment	Rt. Hon. David Blunkett, MP
Secretary of State for Social Security	Rt. Hon. Alistair Darling, MP
Secretary of State for Health	Rt. Hon. Alan Milburn, MP
Secretary of State for Defence	Rt. Hon. Geoff Hoon, MP
Secretary of State for Northern Ireland	Rt. Hon. Peter Mandelson, MP
Secretary of State for Scotland	Rt. Hon. John Reid, MP
Secretary of State for Wales	Rt. Hon. Paul Murphy, MP
Secretary of State for Culture, Media and Sport	Rt. Hon. Chris Smith, MP
Chief Secretary to the Treasury	Rt. Hon. Andrew Smith, MP
Minister of Agriculture, Fisheries and Food	Rt. Hon. Nick Brown, MP
Chancellor of the Duchy of Lancaster and Minister for the Cabinet Office	Rt. Hon. Marjorie (Mo) Mowlam, MP
Secretary of State for International Development	Rt. Hon. Clare Short, MP
Chief Whip	Rt. Hon. Ann Taylor, MP

Other Senior Ministers

Minister of State for Transport and the Regions	Lord MacDonald of Tradeston
Financial Secretary to the Treasury	Stephen Timms, MP
Economic Secretary to the Treasury	Melanie Johnson, MP
Paymaster-General	Dawn Primarolo, MP
Minister of State for the Environment	Michael Meacher, MP
Minister of State for Local Government and the Regions	Hilary Armstrong, MP
Minister of State for Housing, Planning and Construction	Nick Raynsford, MP
Minister of State for Foreign and Commonwealth Affairs	Peter Hain, MP
Minister of State for Foreign and Commonwealth Affairs	John Battle, MP
Minister of State for Foreign and Commonwealth Affairs	Keith Vaz, MP
Minister of State for Home Affairs	Paul Boateng, MP
Minister of State for Home Affairs	Charles Clarke, MP
Minister of State for Home Affairs	Barbara Roche, MP
Minister of State for Education and Employment	Tessa Jowell, MP
Minister of State for Education and Employment	Estelle Morris, MP
Minister of State for Education and Employment	Baroness Blackstone
Minister of State for Energy and Competitiveness in Europe	Helen Liddell, MP
Minister of State for Trade	Richard Caborn, MP

Minister of State for Small Businesses and E-Commerce	Patricia Hewitt, MP
Minister of State for Agriculture, Fisheries and Food	Joyce Quin, MP
Minister of State for Agriculture, Fisheries and Food	Baroness Hayman
Minister of State for Defence Procurement	Baroness Symons of Vernham Dean
Minister of State for the Armed Forces	John Spellar, MP
Minister of State for Health	John Denham, MP
Minister of State for Health	John Hutton, MP
Minister of State for Social Security	Jeff Rooker, MP
Minister of State for Scotland	Brian Wilson, MP
Minister of State for Northern Ireland	Adam Ingram, MP
Minister of State in the Cabinet Office	Lord Falconer of Thoroton
Minister of State in the Cabinet Office	Ian McCartney, MP

Law Officers

Attorney-General	Lord Williams of Mostyn
Solicitor-General	Ross Cranston, MP

5. UNITED STATES DEMOCRATIC ADMINISTRATION
(as at 31 December 1999)

Members of the Cabinet

President	Bill Clinton
Vice-President	Al Gore
Secretary of State	Madeleine K. Albright
Secretary of the Treasury	Lawrence Summers
Secretary of Defence	William S. Cohen
Secretary of the Interior	Bruce Babbitt
Secretary of Agriculture	Dan Glickman
Secretary of Commerce	William M. Daley
Secretary of Housing & Urban Development	Andrew M. Cuomo
Secretary of Transportation	Rodney E. Slater
Secretary of Health & Human Services	Donna E. Shalala
Attorney-General	Janet Reno
Secretary of Labour	Alexis M. Herman
Secretary of Energy	Bill Richardson
Secretary of Education	Richard W. Riley
Secretary of Veterans' Affairs	Togo D. West

Other Leading Executive Branch Officials

White House Chief of Staff	John Podesta
Director of Office of Management & Budget	Jacob J. Lew
Chairman of Council of Economic Advisers	Martin N. Baily
National Security Adviser	Samuel D. Berger
Head of Environmental Protection Agency	Carol Browner
Director of Central Intelligence Agency	George Tenet
Representative for Trade Negotiations	Charlene Barshefsky
Ambassador to United Nations	Richard C. Holbrooke
Director of National Economic Council	Gene Sperling
Director of Small Business Administration	Aida Alvarez

6. INTERNATIONAL COMPARISONS: POPULATION, GDP AND GROWTH

The following table gives population, gross domestic product (GDP) and growth data for the member states of the Organization for Economic Cooperation and Development plus selected other countries. (Source: World Bank, Washington)

	Population		GDP ($000mn)		GDP growth %	
	1998mn	%growth	1997	1998	1998	1999-03*
Argentina	36.1	1.3	292.9	298.1	3.9	4.2
Australia	18.8	1.2	399.5	364.2	3.6	6.1
Austria	8.1	0.4	206.2	212.1	3.3	n/a
Belgium	10.2	0.3	242.5	247.1	2.9	n/a
Brazil	165.9	1.4	820.4	750.8	0.2	3.0
Canada	30.6	1.2	607.7	598.8	3.0	n/a
Chile	14.8	1.5	74.1	78.7	3.4	4.9
China	1,248.1	1.0	902.0	960.9	7.8	7.0
Czech Republic	10.5	-0.1	53.0	56.4	-2.3	n/a
Denmark	5.3	0.4	171.1	174.3	2.9	n/a
Egypt	61.5	1.9	75.5	84.3	5.7	6.1
Finland	5.2	0.4	119.8	125.7	5.3	n/a
France	59.0	0.4	1,392.1	1,432.9	3.2	n/a
Germany	82.2	0.3	2,100.5	2,142.0	2.5	n/a
Greece	11.0	0.4	119.5	120.3	3.0	n/a
Hungary	10.2	-0.3	45.7	47.8	5.1	n/a
Iceland	0.3	0.8	7.4	8.2	5.1	n/a
India	979.1	1.7	407.9	419.7	6.3	6.2
Indonesia	203.7	1.6	215.7	94.2	-13.2	5.1
Irish Republic	3.7	0.6	75.8	80.9	9.0	n/a
Israel	6.0	2.6	98.1	101.0	2.0	n/a
Italy	57.5	0.2	1,145.4	1,171.0	1.5	n/a
Japan	126.3	0.3	4,197.8	3,783.1	-2.8	n/a
South Korea	46.4	1.0	476.5	320.7	-5.8	5.4
Luxembourg	0.4	1.4	15.8	16.5	4.2	n/a
Malaysia	22.2	2.5	100.2	72.5	-7.5	5.1
Mexico	95.9	1.8	401.7	410.3	4.8	4.8
Netherlands	16.0	0.6	363.3	382.5	3.7	n/a
New Zealand	3.8	1.6	64.6	54.1	0.2	1.7
Nigeria	121.3	2.9	39.9	41.4	1.8	2.1
Norway	4.5	0.5	153.4	145.9	2.0	n/a
Pakistan	130.6	2.5	63.0	63.4	3.3	n/a
Philippines	75.1	2.3	82.2	65.1	-0.5	4.8
Poland	38.6	0.1	147.9	157.5	4.8	5.2
Portugal	10.0	0.1	101.3	106.6	3.9	n/a
Russia	146.0	-0.2	436.0	276.6	-4.6	0.5
Saudi Arabia	20.7	3.5	140.4	125.8	1.2	n/a
Singapore	3.2	1.9	95.1	84.4	1.5	n/a
South Africa	41.3	2.0	147.6	133.4	0.5	2.9
Spain	40.2	0.1	530.8	551.9	3.8	n/a
Sweden	9.0	0.4	227.8	225.0	2.9	n/a
Switzerland	7.1	0.6	255.3	264.4	2.2	n/a
Thailand	61.1	1.1	149.1	111.3	-9.4	,2.7
Turkey	63.5	1.5	190.7	198.8	2.8	5.0
United Kingdom	59.1	0.3	1,283.3	1,357.4	2.5	n/a
United States	270.0	1.0	7,823.3	8,210.6	3.9	3.8
Venezuela	23.2	2.1	84.4	95.0	-0.7	3.1

*Forecast

XVIII OBITUARY

Alberti, Rafael (b. 1902), leading Spanish poet and playwright who was forced to spend many years in exile during the Franco period because of his communist beliefs. He began his career as a painter in impressionist style, but turned to poetry when he became ill. His first book, *Marinero de Terra*, recalled the attractions of the Andalusian seascapes of his childhood, and his second, *Sobre los Angeles*, which was published in 1929 and which was to establish his reputation, examined the conflict between nature and industrialized society. It was after the publication of this book that he turned to communism. After championing the Republican cause during the Spanish civil war he was forced to flee when Franco came to power, and remained in exile for nearly 40 years. His memoirs, *La Arboleda Perdida*, were translated as *The Last Grove* and were widely praised. On his return to Spain in 1977 he was elected to the Cortes as a member of the Communist Party, but resigned after a few months in order to devote the rest of his life to painting. Died 28 October

Barnes, Dame Josephine, DBE (b. 1912), British obstetrician and gynaecologist, became first woman president of the British Medical Association. Born in Sheringham, Norfolk, she read medicine at Lady Margaret Hall, Oxford, where she had to have anatomy classes on her own as it was regarded as unsuitable for men and women to carry out dissections together. After completing her training at University College Hospital in London she decided to specialise in gynaecology, joining the Samaritan Hospital in 1939 as well as having a private practice in Wimpole Street. In 1945 she was given her first consultancy post at the Elizabeth Garrett Anderson Hospital, and stayed there (helping to save it from closure) until officially retiring in 1977, while also acting as consultant gynaecologist at Charing Cross Hospital. She was elected vice-president of the Royal College of Obstetricians and Gynaecologists in 1974 and president of the BMA in 1979. She continued in private practice but also acquired a formidable workload of committee memberships and other activities on many aspects of medicine and on improving the position of women. Died 28 December

Beloff, Lord (Max) (b. 1913), Gladstone professor of government and public administration at Oxford University from 1957-74 and founding principal of the University College at Buckingham from 1974-79, controversial author, historian and journalist whose political opinion and affiliation changed from left to right during the 1970s. Educated at St Paul's School and Corpus Christi College, Oxford, he was awarded a research fellowship which resulted in the publication of *Public Order and Disturbances 1660-1717* and to his appointment as assistant history lecturer at Manchester University. In 1947 he became a fellow of Nuffield College, Oxford, and began studying foreign affairs, with particular interest in the policies of the Soviet Union and in American history (publishing *Thomas Jefferson and American Democracy* in 1948). He expanded these interests when he became Gladstone professor, publishing *New Dimensions in Foreign Policy* in 1961 and *The United States and the Unity of Europe* in 1963, before turning to a study of Britain's withdrawal from its imperial role. He was also deeply interested in education, and it was his concern that educational standards were falling that led to his decision to retire from Oxford and nurture the development of a new independent university at Buckingham. After many years as a member of the Liberal Party, he resigned over its education policy and allied himself with the Conservatives, largely because of its recognition of the need to curb the dominance of the trade unions. He subsequently became an outspoken critic of European federalism. Died 22 March

Benda, Václav (b. 1946), Czech mathematician, philosopher and dissident, was one of the most determined opponents of the communist regime in his country. He was one of the first signatories of Charter 77, the movement set up in 1977 to monitor the Czechoslovak government's compliance with the Helsinki accords on human rights, and was subsequently subjected to frequent police interrogations, searches and other harassment, including a restriction to manual labour. In 1979 he was arrested, together with Václav Havel and others, and sentenced, after a dramatic show trial, to four years' imprisonment. On his release he resumed his Charter activities and was again subjected to intimidation, but refused to keep silent. After the communists were overthrown in 1989 Benda joined the Christian Democratic Party, becoming its chairman in the Federal Assembly. He was elected to the Senate in 1996, but his persistent attempts to pursue those believed to be guilty of communist crimes separated him from many former political colleagues who wished to look to the future rather than the past. Died 1 June

Blackmun, Harry (b. 1908), associate judge of the US Supreme Court who wrote the majority opinion establishing the constitutional right of a woman to have an abortion. Appointed to the Court by President Nixon in 1970, Blackmun was seen as a Republican and a conservative but he regarded such labels as misleading, believing that justices should grow constitutionally during their term of office. The case of *Roe v. Wade* in 1973 established Blackmun's liberal reputation as well as securing him a huge pile of hate-mail. The case involved a 21-year-old waitress from Texas who became pregnant after being raped by three men, and Blackmun delivered the 7-2 ruling which overturned anti-abortion laws in 46 states. Before being appointed to the Supreme Court, Blackmun was a judge in a circuit court of appeals. He gained his degree in the Harvard Law School and initially specialized in tax and civil litigation before becoming resident counsel for the Mayor Clinic. When the Supreme Court vacancy occurred, Blackmun was Nixon's third choice to fill it, the other two being voted down by the Senate. He retired in 1994. Died 4 March

Blades, James (b. 1901), British percussion player who recorded the morse code V-for-Victory signal for the BBC's wartime radio broadcasts to occupied Europe. He used subsequently to describe it as the greatest noise he ever made, but his musical reputation had already been established by his remarkable ability to produce any of the frequently challenging sounds demanded by modern composers, including Stravinsky, under whom Blades played on occasion. Subsequently he worked with Benjamin Britten and the English Opera Group, where his inventive genius was challenged to the full, notably in the effects for Britten's church parables. Later Blades became professor of timpani and percussion at the Royal Academy of Music and a leading authority on the history of percussion instruments, publishing what has become the standard work on the subject in 1970. He also became an entertaining lecturer. Died 19 May

Bogarde, Sir Dirk (b. Derek Van Den Bogaerde, 1921), British actor and author who justly earned a high reputation in both arts. He began his career on the stage but never made much impact there, suffering from stage fright and eventually abandoning the theatre in favour of films, where he quickly achieved success, beginning with *The Blue Lamp* in 1949 and going on to make a popular series of films based on Richard Gordon's Doctor novels, in one of which, *Doctor at Sea*, he starred with Brigitte Bardot. These were followed by a short and fairly disastrous experience in Hollywood, after which Bogarde returned to Britain to make a number of highly-rated films, including *The Servant, King and Country, Darling* and *Accident*. In 1968 he and his partner and manager, Tony Forwood, moved to France, where Bogarde began to work with continental film-makers, giving one of his most memorable performances in

Visconti's film of Thomas Mann's *Death in Venice*. He subsequently made a number of other films but most of his energies, particularly following the death of Forwood, were now devoted to writing. He wrote seven novels and eight volumes of autobiography, of which the first, *A Postillion Struck by Lightning*, was published in 1977 and the last, *Cleared for Take-Off*, in 1994. All were greeted with considerable popular and critical approval, the later ones revealing much of his private melancholy and despair at the nature of modern society. Died 8 May

Bouchier, Chili (b. Dorothy Irene Boucher, 1909), British film star who made her debut at the age of 17 in the 1927 silent film *Shooting Stars* and became internationally known for her performance in *You Know What Sailors Are*, when American journalists named her 'the Brunette Bombshell'. In 1930 she starred in *Carnival*, directed by Herbert Wilcox, and was much sought after by Hollywood, where she signed a contract with Warner Brothers. She hated it so much that she never made a film there, but returned to Britain where she continued to act in films and on the West End stage, including two years in *The Mousetrap* and playing opposite James Stewart in a revival of *Harvey*. In 1985, at the age of 76, she was delighting audiences with her singing of *Broadway Baby* in Stephen Sondheim's *Follies*, and in 1989 appeared in the West End in his musical *A Little Night Music*. She was married three times, had no children, and turned down a proposal from (among many others) Howard Hughes. Died 9 September

Boyd, Arthur, AC, OBE (b. 1920), Australian artist whose powerful visionary work often centred on the themes of love and redemption. Born near Melbourne, Boyd left school aged 14 to work in a paint factory, attending art classes in the evening and beginning to paint landscapes which were good enough to be exhibited in 1937. For the next ten years Boyd became one of those associated with what became known as the 'angry decade', producing work that combined scenes of love and suffering, but he also painted landscapes which were much admired. In the 1950s a visit to central Australia produced a series of paintings called *Love, Marriage and Death of a Half-Caste*, and in 1960 Boyd moved to London, where he held his first exhibition at the Zwemmer Gallery, with a retrospective at the Whitechapel Gallery two years later. Commissions followed for theatre set designs in London and New York, and he began work on a series of 35 large pictures about Nebuchadnezzar for the Adelaide arts festival. He was now dividing his time between Europe and Australia, and in 1993 joined with his friend Sir Sidney Nolan in donating property for the establishment of an arts and environment centre in his home country. He was voted Australian of the Year in 1995. Died 24 April

Broakes, Sir Nigel (b. 1934), former chairman of Trafalgar House and of the London Docklands Development Corporation, was for a time one of Britain's most successful businessmen, reflected in his ownership of a number of high-profile properties. Educated at Stowe, Broakes worked first with a company of Lloyd's underwriters but left them to go into the property business on his own account. By the age of 28 he was managing director of Trafalgar House, diversifying from property into a conglomerate with the help of Victor (later Lord) Matthews, whose building firm became part of the company. The Cunard shipping line was acquired in 1971, the Ritz hotel in London in 1976 and the former Beaverbrook newspapers *Daily Express* and London *Evening Standard* in the following year. In 1980 he was appointed chairman of Docklands, and for the next few years this took most of his time and energy, though he was also involved with the early moves for the Channel Tunnel and became a trustee for the Royal Opera House and a number of museums. Trafalgar House meanwhile was running into difficulties. A bid for the P&O shipping group failed and the company began reporting losses. Broakes was eased from the chairmanship in 1992 with the title of honorary president. Died 28 September

Buffet, Bernard (b. 1928), French post-war artist whose work was highly praised at the start of his career but was more recently dismissed by critics as superficial. His thick lines and cold colours, ascetic figures and landscapes were judged perfectly to reflect the grim times that followed the ending of World War II, and his paintings quickly found their way into public and private collections all over the world (there is a Buffet Museum in Japan). He held his first exhibition in Paris in 1946, won the Prix de la Critique at the age of 20 and was invited to the Venice Biennale in 1956, having already held a most successful show in New York. He worked at a prodigious rate, completing most of his paintings in a couple of days, and soon began to be criticized as being repetitive and mannered. The Pompidou Centre did not include any of his paintings in its exhibition of 1950s art. Nonetheless his work continued to hold its value and he remained defiant of his critics, continuing to paint in his own style until he developed Parkinson's disease, when he took his own life. Died 4 October

Burg, Josef (b. Dresden 1909), Israeli statesman, was deputy speaker of the Knesset and a cabinet minister for 35 years. He qualified as an ordained rabbi after studying at Leipzig University and worked in the Palestine Office in Berlin for some years after the Nazis came to power but, after escaping arrest in 1938 left for Palestine. When the state of Israel was created he became deputy speaker of the Knesset as well as holding a number of ministerial posts, and in 1956 founded the National Religious Party, which was to play a moderating role in Israeli politics and form a significant part of most of the coalition governments, most notably in 1977, when the party broke away from the Labour Party to join with the Herut, led by Menachem Begin. But in the following years Burg found himself increasingly opposed by his party on proposals to give Palestinians living in the occupied territories a degree of autonomy, which he favoured, and in 1986 he gave up the party leadership and resigned from the Cabinet. Died 31 January

Casson, Sir Hugh, CH, KCVO (b. 1910), British architect, designer, watercolourist, journalist, teacher and president of the Royal Academy, first made his mark with the Festival of Britain in 1951, for which he was director of architecture. It was his imagination and ability to get people of varying talents to work together that ensured the success of the South Bank exhibition, which was the most memorable feature of the festival. He was knighted for this work. As an architect one of his most striking buildings was the elephant house at the London Zoo and as an interior designer his work included many offices, restaurants, passenger liners and the royal yacht *Britannia*. He taught architecture and design at the Royal College of Art for more than 20 years and in 1976 was elected president of the Royal Academy, where he was able to transform its rather dusty image and rocky finances with his innovative ideas, energy and ability to communicate. He also served on many other public bodies, and spent much of what little spare time he had painting in watercolour, holding several exhibitions and illustrating many books and other publications. Died 15 August

Castelli, Leo (b. Leo Krauss, 1907), New York art dealer widely regarded as the century's most influential modern art dealer. He was involved with all the American new art movements since the 1950s, showing the work of post-abstract expressionists which paved the way for pop art, and representing artists such as Jasper Johns, Andy Warhol and Roy Lichtenstein. Born in Trieste, Castelli opened his first gallery in Paris in 1939 and made a great impact with an exhibition of surrealists. He moved to New York when war broke out, studying art history until drafted into the US army. After World War II he worked in the garment industry but began dealing in works of art by Jackson Pollock and others, turning the living room of his apartment into a gallery. Subsequently he opened a gallery in New York's SoHo. He continued to foster new art and artists, moving from pop art to minimalist and conceptual artists and to the neo-expressionists of the 1980s, often giving artists a monthly stipend to keep them going and encourage them to remain within the Castelli orbit. Died 21 August

Chamberlain, Wilt (b. 1936), American basketball player whose size and skill dominated the game during a professional career of 14 years. Standing an inch or two over 7ft and weighing more than 17 stone, he complemented his size with surprising agility. His brilliance was such that the administrators of the game changed the rules and redesigned the court in an attempt to reduce his dominance, but to no effect. In 1962, playing for the Philadelphia Warriors, he scored 100 points in a single game, a record that still stands. But for all his individual brilliance Chamberlain's team seldom won the basketball championship, and off the court his extravagant lifestyle deprived him of the popularity he felt he deserved. Died 12 October

Charteris of Amisfield, Lord, GCB, GCVO, OBE, QSO, PC (b. 1913), was private secretary to the Queen from 1972-77. Educated at Eton and Sandhurst, Charteris was commissioned into the King's Royal Rifle Corps in 1933, serving with the regiment in Burma and in Egypt. He was invalided home with glandular fever when war broke out, but on recovery was returned to the Middle East, where he joined the intelligence staff of the GOC, General Macmillan, and where he met and married Gay, daughter of Viscount Margesson, Secretary of State for War from 1940-42. In 1950 Charteris was appointed private secretary to Princess Elizabeth and was travelling with her *en route* to Australia when her father died and she became Queen. Charteris then joined the team serving the royal household. On the retirement of Sir Michael Adeane he became private secretary and keeper of the archives, devoting himself whole-heartedly and enthusiastically to the post and to the task of showing the Queen to her people as she really was, and being credited with successfully revealing her natural sense of humour. In 1978 he was appointed provost of Eton, was a trustee of the British Museum from 1979-89, and in 1980 set up the National Heri-tage Memorial Fund. Died 23 December

Chaudhuri, Nirad C. (b. 1897), controversial Indian author and broadcaster whose first work, *The Autobiogra-phy of an Unknown Indian,* was published in England in 1951. Dedicated to the memory of the British Empire in India which, he wrote, shaped 'all that was good and living within us', the book was well received outside India and led to an invitation to Britain, from which emerged a book of observations on British life, *A Passage to England.* In 1965 he wrote *The Continent of Circe,* a controversial study of India and its peoples which again did not go down well in his own country but was awarded the Duff Cooper Memorial Prize in Britain. While studying the papers of the German scholar Max Müller, Chaudhuri settled near Oxford, where he lived for the rest of his long life. His last book, published in 1997, *The Three Horsemen of the New Apocalypse,* was strongly critical of Britain's 'descent into decadence'. Died 1 August

Chebrikov, Viktor (b. 1923), hardline Soviet communist who spent most of his career in the KGB, which he headed between 1982 and 1988. After serving in the army during World War II, Chebrikov joined the KGB. He was sent to Budapest before the crushing of the Hungarian revolt in 1956, where he was put in charge of the day-to-day running of the Soviet embassy under Yuri Andropov, who was then the ambassador. When Andropov became head of the KGB, Chebrikov became his deputy, working with him on the successful operation to seize the American communications ship *Pueblo,* which yielded much information about American surveillance and code systems. When Andropov succeeded Leonid Brezhnev as Soviet leader in 1982, Chebrikov became head of the KGB, and it was he who, in 1983, ordered the shooting-down of a Korean airliner which strayed off course into Soviet airspace. All 269 people on board were killed. Following the deaths of Andropov and of his successor, Konstantin Chernenko, Chebrikov gave his support to new leader Mikhail Gorbachev and was rewarded in 1985 by being appointed to the politburo. But he became critical of the policy of *glasnost,* was sacked from his KGB post and, in 1989, from the politburo, along with four other opponents of Gorbachev's reforms. Died 2 July

Clark, Alan (b. 1928), maverick and outspoken British Conservative MP who became a junior minister but whose frankness, unpredictable opinions and irrepressible sense of humour deprived him of the high political office he had hoped for. The son of Kenneth (later Lord) Clark, he grew up at Saltwood Castle, which he eventually inherited, was educated at Eton and Christ Church, Oxford, where he read history, but it was not until he was in his thirties that he began to make a mark. He did so first as a historian, in 1961 publishing *The Donkeys*, a history of the British Expeditionary Force in World War I (which later inspired the musical satire *Oh! What a Lovely War*). This was followed by *The Fall of Crete* (1963), *Barbarossa* (1965), an account of the Russo-German conflict 1941-45, and *Aces High: the War in the Air over the Western Front* (1973). His parliamentary career began in 1974, when he was elected MP for Plymouth Sutton, but it was not until 1983 that he was rewarded with office, when Mrs Thatcher appointed him junior minister for employment. His ministerial career nearly ended there, when after attending a wine-tasting he read a statement to the House of Commons in a manner which suggested that he was drunk. The Prime Minister forgave him, and subsequently appointed him to the Ministry of Trade and finally to the Ministry of Defence as minister of state; but his career foundered when he was forced to admit that he had been 'economical with the *actualité*' during a trial of Matrix-Churchill executives on evading arms embargoes. He decided not to stand for re-election in 1992, but hit the headlines in the following year with the publication of his *Diaries*, in which he was rude about many of his parliamentary colleagues and devastatingly frank about his own sexual experiences. In 1995 he sought and won the nomination for the safe Conservative seat of Kensington and Chelsea, for which he was duly returned to parliament in the general election of 1997. Died 5 September

Cockerell, Sir Christopher, CBE, FRS (b. 1910), British engineer who invented and developed the hovercraft in the 1950s. Before turning his mind to the problem of friction between boats and water, Cockerell was engaged in research into radio, working with the Marconi company for 15 years. During World War II he led a design team that produced the direction finder loop for RAF bombers and equipment which was able to identify the location of German radar stations along the Channel coast. During his period with Marconi, Cockerell devised 36 inventions for the company. He started work on the hovercraft in 1950, taking out a patent on what he said was neither an aeroplane, nor boat, nor wheeled land vehicle, but which was supported over land or water by a cushion of air. The government classified the vehicle as secret and set up a company to develop it, with Cockerell as its director, and in 1959 the first practical hovercraft was launched. Cockerell regretted that subsequent development in the UK was slow, and disagreed strongly with the policy of licensing overseas companies. He resigned from Hovercraft Development in 1966, though staying on as a consultant until this was terminated in 1970. He was knighted in 1969 and continued to work as an inventor, though he was bitter about his career's frustrations and lack of reward. Died 1 June

Couve de Murville, Maurice (b. 1907), Prime Minister of France 1968-69, during de Gaulle's last year as President, and Foreign Minister 1958-68, he also led the French delegation in Brussels during Britain's attempt to enter the Common Market in 1962, and was equally opposed to the second attempt in 1967. During his term as Foreign Minister he also put into effect the French withdrawal from NATO and the threatened boycott of the EEC in the dispute over the common agricultural policy in the mid-1960s. Born in Reims, Couve de Murville studied law before becoming an inspector of finance in 1930. For a short time after the outbreak of World War II he was director of external finances under the Vichy government but was dismissed because of his alleged republican symathies. Subsequently he made his way to Algiers, where he became secretary to General Giraud before transferring his allegiance to General de Gaulle. After the war he was appointed director-general of political affairs at the French Foreign Ministry and for a number of years was French representative at the UN General Assembly in New York. From 1950 to 1954 he was ambassador to Egypt, and in the following years served as French permanent representative to NATO, ambassador in the US and then in West Germany before returning to France as Foreign Minister. His political career was distinguished by his determination, which he shared with de Gaulle, to fashion an independent policy that served the interests of France. Died 24 December

Denning, Lord, OM, PC (b. 1899), Master of the Rolls 1962-82 and holder of many other judicial offices in Britain, was always ready to challenge orthodoxy and many of his judgments had a profound influence on the shape of English law. Born in Hampshire (he never lost the local burr), he was educated at Andover Grammar School and Magdalen College, Oxford (his education being interrupted by World War I service in the Royal Engineers), where he eventually obtained a double first in mathematics. After teaching for a year at Winchester he went back to Oxford, where he gained a first in law. He was called to the bar at Lincoln's Inn in 1923 and quickly established a reputation for mastering all the details of his briefs as well as the finer points of law. He took silk in 1932 and in 1944 was appointed Recorder of Plymouth, but in less than a year was raised to the High Court. In 1948 he was on the Court of Appeal and, for five years from 1957, went to the House of Lords. But most unusually he decided to return to the Court of Appeal as Master of the Rolls, largely because his radical views and enthusiasm for reform did not go down too well with some of the other law lords.

Lord Denning became more widely known outside legal circles in 1963, when he was appointed by the Prime Minister, Harold Macmillan, to examine the Profumo affair. The Denning Report, as it was popularly known, became an immediate bestseller, memorably described in *The Times* as reading 'like a Mills and Boon novel'. Many of the judgments in his Court of Appeal also brought Denning into the public eye, notably his attempts to safeguard the rights of separated women (which eventually became law), the decision that the Education Secretary had misdirected himself in trying to force comprehensive education on a reluctant local authority, and the declaration that the Home Office was acting unlawfully in trying to make people pay more for television licences before new rates had come into force. Such decisions earned him a popular reputation as a judge who would defend the rights of the individual against bureaucracy and the misuse of power. At the age of 80 Denning wrote a series of books on the law, but the last of these, setting out his thoughts on law reform (published in 1982), led directly to his retirement because comments made in the book had offended members of the black community. Even after retiring Denning continued to deliver opinions on current legal and other issues, many of them controversial and, like his legal judgments, some radical and some deeply conservative. Died 5 March

Devlin, Paddy, CBE (b. 1925), Northern Ireland politician who was one of the founders of the Social Democratic and Labour Party (SDLP) and Minister for Health and Social Services in the short-lived power-sharing executive of 1973. Born in the Falls Road district of Belfast, he left school at 14 and joined the youth wing of the IRA. He was interned from 1942-45 and resigned from the IRA in 1949, haunted, as he later said, by the knowledge that intelligence gathered by the organization during World War II had been passed directly to the Germans. He joined the Northern Ireland Labour Party and was elected to the Belfast city council in 1956. In 1969 he became a member of the Stormont parliament for the Falls Road constituency and in the following year joined with Gerry Fitt and John Hume in setting up the cross-community (though mainly Catholic) SDLP in response to the violence propagated by the new Provisional IRA. After the suspension of the Stormont parliament in 1972, Devlin worked to secure an IRA ceasefire, and then for the creation of the power-sharing executive. When that collapsed and direct rule from Westminster was resumed in 1974, Devlin continued to try to secure cooperation between the SDLP and the Unionists, but his criticisms of the SDLP's policy of involving the Irish government in Northern Ireland's affairs led to his expulsion from the party. He remained active on the Belfast council until losing his seat in 1981, when he turned to writing until forced to give up by failing eyesight. Died 15 August

DiMaggio, Joe (b. 1914), American baseball player who became a star within his own country for his feats on behalf of the New York Yankees, both as centre field and at bat, and later achieved international recognition by marrying Marilyn Monroe. He was taken on by the Yankees at the age of 21, and stayed with them until his retirement soon after his 37th birthday, missing only the years from 1943-45 when he served in the US air force. During his playing years the Yankees won nine World Series and ten league championships, his part in their success being vital. In 1938 he hit 46 home runs and in the following year won the first of three Most Valuable Player awards. In 1941 he recorded a hit in every game for 56 consecutive games, a sequence that remains a record in American baseball history. He ended his career with a batting average of .325 and a total of 365 home runs. An introspective and reserved man, he surprised many when he became the second husband of Marilyn Monroe. The marriage, which inevitably became the focus of much media attention, was not a success, though the couple maintained a strong association after their divorce. He did not marry a third time, retiring quietly to Florida. Died 8 March

Eccles, Viscount, PC, CH, KCVO (b. 1904), British cabinet minister who served in administrations run by Churchill, Eden, Macmillan and Heath. Born in London and educated at Winchester and New College, Oxford, Eccles went into the City until World War II, when he was sent to Madrid and Lisbon as economic adviser, or what he described as 'an apostle of bribery', to ensure that Spain and Portugal retained their neutrality. He returned to London in 1942 and at Churchill's suggestion stood for parliament in a by-election at Chippenham. In 1951, when the Conservatives were returned to power, Eccles was appointed Minister of Works, a fairly mundane assignment which was transformed when King George VI died and Eccles had to take charge of arrangements for the 1953 coronation, for which he was knighted by the new Queen. In 1954 he was appointed Minister of Education and in 1957 became President of the Board of Trade. In both positions he proved energetic in fighting his corner in the Cabinet. He was returned to Education in 1959 but was then sacked by Harold Macmillan, along with six other ministers, in the notorious 'night of the long knives' reshuffle of 1962. Resuming his business interests, he became a director of Courtaulds, but was unexpectedly recalled to government by Edward Heath in 1970 as Paymaster-General with responsibility for the arts, a post he held until 1973. He then became first chairman of the British Library. Died 24 February

Ehrlichman, John (b. 1925), American domestic policy adviser in President Nixon's White House, imprisoned for his role in the Watergate scandal. Trained as a lawyer and practising for some years in Seattle, he was appointed presidential adviser by Nixon in 1968 and quickly began to share the new President's paranoia about the political enemies aiming to bring him down. It was this which led to the break-in at the Washington headquarters of the Democratic national committee in 1972, during the re-election campaign which Nixon won convincingly. Ehrlichman, with his colleague John Haldeman, was involved with the break-in from the beginning and with the attempted cover-up once the affair began to become public. In 1973 both Ehrlichman and Haldeman were sacked by the President, and in the following year Ehrlichman was found guilty on charges of obstructing justice, conspiracy and perjury. He served 18 months in prison before being released on parole, after which he accepted his guilt and became a radio commentator and writer. Died 15 February

Evans, Godfrey, CBE (b. 1920), English cricketer who kept wicket for England with great style and panache from 1946-59. He began playing cricket for Kent in 1937, appearing in his first first-class match in 1939. He played some cricket during his wartime service in the army, and was spotted by a former England captain while playing in a match at Aldershot. He was quickly recruited to the national side when first-class cricket resumed after World War II, played in a Test match against India in 1946 and travelled to Australia to play for England in the winter tour. His early success as a wicket keeper can be gauged from the fact that, during the first two Tests in Australia, the home team scored more than 1,000 runs before Evans conceded a bye, a record which stood for many years. He stood up to Alec Bedser and all but the very fastest bowlers, and his agility behind the stumps was the stuff of cricketing legend. He was also a competent batsman, scoring two Test centuries and once batting for 95 minutes against Australia without scoring a run, a feat which helped to save the match. Had he been prepared always to exercise such patience he would no doubt have scored many more runs during his career. He retired in 1959 at the conclusion of his 91st Test match. Died 3 May

Fanfani, Amintore (b. 1908), Prime Minister of Italy six times between 1954 and 1987, some of the terms of office lasting no more than a week or two. Born near Arezzo in Tuscany, Fanfani attended the Catholic University of the Sacred Heart in Milan where, after gaining a degree in economic and social sciences, he was appointed to the chair of economic history. He was not a supporter of fascism and during World War II moved to Switzerland. In 1946 he returned to Italy and helped devise the country's new constitution before becoming a deputy of the constituent assembly and joining the government with a variety of ministerial responsibilities. He was appointed Prime Minister for the first time in 1954, but this administration lasted no more than 12 days. Subsequently he took on the role of party secretary for the Christian Democrats and became Prime Minister again in 1958, but again his government was defeated within a short time. He gave up the leadership of the party but was summoned to form another administration in 1960, when some of his major social reforms, including compulsory education, came into effect. He was elected president of the UN General Assembly in 1965, but his government was defeated and he had to resign. He returned to the political limelight in 1969, as president of the Italian Senate. He was once again called upon to form a government in 1987, but this final attempt at a coalition lasted only 10 days. Died 20 November

Farmer, James (b. 1920), American civil rights' campaigner who founded the Congress of Racial Equality (CORE) and pioneered many of the methods followed by others struggling for civil rights in the 1950s and '60s. Born in Texas, the son of a Methodist minister, Farmer moved to Mississippi with his family while he was still a child. There he experienced the full effects of racial prejudice, discrimination and segregation. He was much influenced by the non-violent civil disobedience methods practised by Mahatma Gandhi against the British in India, and when he founded CORE in 1942 its early campaigns included the organization of sit-ins where segregation was practised and the ignoring of segregated seating in public places. In 1961 CORE arranged the first Freedom Ride following the Supreme Court ruling that segregation of passengers on inter-state buses was illegal, a decision that was largely ignored in the South. The bus was attacked by white mobs and the Attorney-General, Robert Kennedy, was forced to order the authorities in Alabama and Mississippi to provide protection for the members of CORE, Farmer having refused to agree to Kennedy's suggestion of a cooling-off period. During one of these demonstrations Farmer was arrested and imprisoned. As the campaigning became more militant Farmer began to lose his influence and he resigned as director of CORE in 1965, concentrating instead on the problems of illiteracy among blacks in America. He served for a time under President Nixon as assistant secretary for administration in the Department of Health., Education and Welfare, and also lectured and wrote on labour and race relations problems. He was awarded the Presidential Medal of Freedom in 1998. Died 9 July

Fuchs, Sir Vivian, FRS (b.1908), British explorer, leader of the first surface crossing of the Antarctic in 1957-58 and director of the British Antarctic Survey from 1958-73. His first contact with the polar regions came while he was an undergraduate at St John's College, Cambridge, as geologist on an expedition to Greenland led by J.M. (later Sir James) Wordie, Master of the College, who had been chief scientist on Shackleton's Imperial Trans-Antarctic Expedition of 1914-17. Fuchs spent much of the next decade in Africa, leading the Lake Rudolf Rift Valley Expedition in 1933-34 and the Lake Rukwa Expedition in 1937-38. On the outbreak of war he was posted to the Gold Coast and later took part in the north-west Europe campaign. In 1947 he was appointed to command the Falkland Islands Dependencies Survey, spending two years there before returning to Cambridge. He now began planning an expedition to accomplish Shackleton's ambition for a trans-Antarctic crossing, designing it as a scientific expedition during which, among other things, the thickness of the Antarctic ice would be measured. He organized the expedition in two parts, with Sir Edmund Hillary leading a New Zealand team halfway across Antarctica from the Ross Sea to establish depots for the trans-polar party during the second half of their journey. Fuchs and his team took 99 days (one short of their estimate) to travel the 2,200 miles to the shore of the Ross Sea, which they reached on March 2, 1958. Fuchs was knighted three days after his return to Britain, and became director of the FIDS, which was subsequently renamed the British Antarctic Survey (BAS). One of his achievements in the post was to ensure that the Halley station was maintained as a centre for upper atmospheric research, and it was from this station that the hole in the ozone layer was detected in 1985. Fuchs was president of the British Association for the Advancement of Science in 1971, elected a fellow of the Royal Society in 1974 and was president of the Royal Geographical Society from 1982-84. He published a history of the BAS in 1982 and an autobiography in 1990. Died 11 November

Gorbachev, Raisa (b. Raisa Maximovna Titorenko, 1932), wife of Mikhail Gorbachev, the former Soviet President, proved a potent ally in his attempts to reform the Soviet Union and to win the goodwill of other countries, particularly those of the West. Trained as a sociologist and carrying out postgraduate work when she married in 1955, Mrs Gorbachev had to give up this work when her husband moved to Stavropol to further his political career. She gained a part-time job as a teacher and continued her sociological studies, finally achieving a doctorate from the Moscow State Pedagogical Institute. When Mr Gorbachev was promoted to the central committee the family moved to Moscow, where Raisa was appointed lecturer in marxist-leninist philosophy at Moscow State University, a post she was obliged to resign when her husband became Soviet leader. As first lady, Raisa shared her husband's reforming vision and was happy to play her part in public appearances and trips abroad, displaying an elegance and assurance that was unusual in the wives of Soviet leaders. At home she campaigned energetically for *perestroika* but was not wholly surprised by the 1991 coup attempt which preceded the demise of the Soviet Union at the end of the year and her husband's departure from office. She suffered a small stroke when they were imprisoned in their dacha during their 1991 holiday in the Crimea, and a heart attack two years later. Died 20 September

Hassan II, King, of Morocco (b. 1929), succeeded to the throne in 1961 and ruled his country with a firmness that successfully overcame a number of attempted coups and a good deal of domestic unrest. Claiming descent from the prophet Mohammed, and bearing the titles of Commander of the Faithful and Allah's Deputy on Earth, he maintained an Islamic state without religious extremism and an effective dictatorship with some democratic trimmings. Born when his country was divided into a French and Spanish protectorate, Hassan was given a Koranic education before taking a law degree at Bordeaux University and serving in the French navy. He and his father were deported from Morocco in 1953 but were returned three years later when Morocco received its independence. When he came to the throne his country was deeply in debt, largely illiterate and had a high rate of unemployment. During his reign the population rose from about 10 million to some 30 million, an increase which virtually negated such economic progress as was achieved during these 38 years. A moderate and neutral foreign policy secured some economic and cultural support from abroad, while at home Hassan combined toughness with a degree of political reform, organizing in 1963 a general election for a two-chamber legislature (though reserving to himself the right to appoint and dismiss ministers and to preside at cabinet meetings). When rioting broke out in Casablanca and other parts of the country two years later, he declared a state of emergency and assumed direct rule.

During this time there were several attempts on his life, the most serious of which came from the armed forces. In 1971 some 1,500 armed soldiers and cadets stormed his palace, killing many of the guests who were celebrating his birthday. Hassan reportedly approached the rebel leader, quoted the Koran to him and brought the rebellion to an abrupt end. A year later the King's aircraft was attacked by planes of the Moroccan air force, on the orders of the Defence Minister, but the attack ended when Hassan announced over the radio that the King was dead. Both incidents were followed by executions, and added to Hassan's popular reputation as a man of good luck. In 1975 he added to his prestige by leading a 'green march' of some 350,000 unarmed Moroccans into Western Sahara, a Spanish colony claimed by Morocco. Spain gave up the colony in the following year, but the Moroccan army became involved in a costly conflict against the Polisario Front, a liberation movement supported by Algeria and Libya. During these years Hassan also became active in promoting peace in the Middle East. His father had protected Morocco's Jews during World War II, and although the Jewish population had greatly reduced by exodus to Israel Hassan continued to regard them as a demonstration that the two races could live and work together. At a meeting of Arab leaders he supported a peace plan that recognized Israel's right to exist, and in 1986 met Israeli Prime Minister Shimon Peres, a gesture which prompted Syria to break off diplomatic relations. In the final years of his reign, faced with increasing international criticism of Morocco's human rights record, Hassan released hundreds of political prisoners and embarked on a new programme of constitutional reform. Elections to a two-chamber parliament were held in 1997 and a socialist Prime Minister appointed in the following year, though the King retained the right of dismissal and the right to dissolve both chambers. Died 23 July

Heller, Joseph (b. 1923), American novelist, author of *Catch-22*, which became a classic of its kind, reflecting the lunacies of war, its title taken up everywhere to reflect circumstances which present human beings with an impossible set of choices. Heller was born in Brooklyn and served during World War II with the US army air force in Italy. On demobilization he took a BA at New York University, an MA at Columbia, and went to Oxford on a Fulbright scholarship. After this education he began to write and had a number of short stories published in American magazines, then worked in advertising. At the same time he began writing *Catch-22*, which he worked on for more than eight years before it was finally published in 1961. Set on a small island in the Mediterranean where a bomber squadron of the US army air force is based, the title refers to the dilemma faced by pilots not wanting to fly. The sane were obliged to fly, whereas the insane were excused. But not wanting to fly was a clear indication of sanity, which meant that there was no escape from further flying. At first the novel attracted only a cult following, but when its paperback edition appeared its sales soared. In the next 10 years more than seven million copies were sold, and it remains in print. Though he continued to write, with difficulty, his next novel, *Something Happened*, was not published until 1974. *Good as Gold* followed in 1979, *God Knows* in 1984 and *Picture This* in 1988. In 1994 Heller brought back some of the characters from *Catch-22* in *Closing Time*, but neither in this nor his other novels was he able to match his original masterpiece. Died 12 December

Heron, Patrick, CBE (b. 1920), English painter, was one of the St Ives group of imaginative artists who gathered in this small Cornish town in the 1940s and '50s. Born in Leeds, Heron's father was a textile manufacturer for whom Paul Nash and other artists designed fabrics, as did Patrick in the 1930s. He became a part-time student at the Slade School of Fine Art in 1937, but failed to complete the course. Being a conscientious objector he was sent to work on the land during World War II until 1943, when he was released to join Bernard Leach at his pottery in St Ives. There he met other St Ives artists such as Ben Nicholson, Barbara Hepworth and Naum Gabo, but he left the pottery in 1945, when he married and returned to London. Two years later he rented a studio at St Ives, which he kept until 1955. At the same time he ventured successfully into art criticism, writing for the *New Statesman* and later for the New York magazine *Arts*. He took up abstraction and in 1957 painted the first of his horizontal stripe paintings, which were followed by his development into large rectangles of colour. He believed that colour was then the only direction in which paintings could travel, and he continued to develop his paintings along these lines. He had retrospective exhibitions at the Whitechapel Gallery in 1972, the Barbican in 1985 and at the Tate Gallery in 1998. Died 20 March

Hetherington, Alastair (b. 1919), editor of the *Manchester Guardian*, subsequently The Guardian, from 1956 to 1975. The son of a university professor, he too seemed destined for an academic career until World War II intervened and he joined the army. When the war ended in 1945 he was asked to set up a newspaper for the Germans and created the paper that became *Die Welt*. On being demobilized in the following year he continued in journalism, working for four years on the *Glasgow Herald* before joining the *Manchester Guardian* as defence correspondent and leader writer. He was appointed foreign editor in 1953 and took over the editorship at the height of the Suez crisis three years later. It was a tough initiation for a man of only 36, but Hetherington stuck firmly to his editorial policy against military intervention. Subsequently he pushed ahead with the move of the paper to London, first dropping Manchester from the title and then, in 1961, setting up the office in the capital. It was initially a disastrous move, plunging the paper into serious financial crisis which almost led, in the mid-1960s, to a merger with *The Times*. The paper survived, its circulation for a while overtaking that of *The Times*, and when, in 1975, Hetherington was approached about becoming controller of BBC Scotland he accepted, feeling that he had had enough of Fleet Street and being keen to return to his Scottish roots. The job did not work out and after three years he left, running Radio Highland in Inverness for a short time before taking on a research professorship in media studies at Stirling University. He wrote a number of books, including his memoirs which he called *Guardian Years*. Died 3 October

Hodson, Henry Vincent (Harry) (b. 1906), former editor of *The Sunday Times* and more recently of *The Annual Register*, turned to mainstream journalism after embarking initially on an academic career. The son of a professor of anthropology, he was educated at Gresham's and Balliol College, Oxford, and was subsequently elected a prize fellow of All Souls. His early interest was in the British Empire, and in 1931 he joined *Round Table*, the journal established by 'Lord Milner's kindergarten', which he edited from 1934 until the outbreak of World War II in 1939, when he was appointed director of the Empire division of the Ministry of Information. In 1941 he was sent to India as reforms commissioner, but returned a year later to head a division of the Ministry of Production. After the war he applied for a job on *The Sunday Times*, was appointed assistant editor and became editor in 1950. His style may have been more All Souls than Fleet Street but he ran an increasingly successful paper, first under the proprietorship of Lord Kemsley and later under Roy (later Lord) Thomson. The new, brasher, less conservative style of journalism that came in with the Thomson regime was not to Hodson's taste, and in 1961 he gave up as editor to become the first director (or provost, as he liked to call it) of the new Anglo-American conference centre at Ditchley Park, an ideal forum for one of his knowledge and experience of international affairs, as indeed was the editorship of *The Annual Register*, which he took on in 1973, soon after leaving Ditchley. He edited *The Annual Register* with great assurance for 15 years, introducing changes gradually and without flourish, and adding his own elegantly-written contributions, including an editorial (his first innovation, together with a chapter on sport) and, for a time, also taking on the record of events in the United Kingdom, always one of the longest and most difficult chapters in the book. Following his retirement he continued to act as a contributor, editorial consultant and chairman of the advisory board until his death at the age of 92. Died 27 March

Hume, Cardinal Basil, OM (b. George Hume, 1923), Roman Catholic Archbishop of Westminster from 1976-99, was able by personal example and spirituality to win the respect of many outside his church as well as within it, and to re-establish Catholicism as a generally accepted part of English life. Born in Newcastle-upon-Tyne, George Hume (he adopted the name Basil when joined the Benedictines) was educated at Ampleforth, where he spent most of his early life. He became a monk at Ampleforth Abbey at the age of 18 and was sent to the Benedictines' house, St Benet's Hall, at Oxford, where he read history, and then to Fribourg in Switzerland before returning to teach at Ampleforth. He was elected Abbot in 1963, and during his leadership there experienced the pressures put upon the unity of the Catholic Church following the Second Vatican Council. He later wrote that what unites people had to be very deep, and that this was the life of prayer. His way of achieving unity, both at Ampleforth and later in the English Catholic Church as a whole, was by listening and by understanding the views of others. It was a painstaking process that sometimes aggravated but more often impressed those who came into contact with him, and who often left his company convinced that they had indeed been communing with a man of God.

When Cardinal Heenan died in 1975 Basil Hume was a surprise choice as his successor. The front-runner was Bishop Derek Worlock of Portsmouth, who had formerly been secretary to three Cardinal Archbishops of Westminster, but the intervention of the Apostolic Delegate in London, Archbishop Bruno Heim, was decisive in persuading Rome to choose Hume, who was only 53 when he was consecrated bishop and cardinal. His diffident style but powerful personality soon made its impression on both Catholics and non-Catholics. The latter were attracted by his apparent simplicity and lack of dogma, while Catholics were appreciative of the sensitive way in which he steered a course between the conservative and liberal elements in his Church, maintaining good relations with Rome while contriving to suggest that he might have handled some delicate issues rather differently. He never contradicted the Vatican's orthodox teachings, such as that homosexual acts were objectively wrong, but softened their impact by advising homosexuals not to develop a sense of guilt and by reminding people that homosexuals were precious in the eyes of God. He was undoubtedly shocked by the decision of the Church of England to ordain women priests, publicly wondering whether the Church of England, representing 4 per cent of Christianity, could decide an issue like this on its own. It was a crisis for the Church of England that could have become one also for the Catholic Church; but when several hundred Anglican clergy, many of them married, became Catholic priests Hume managed to negotiate special arrangements for them with the Vatican without alienating either the rigid doctrinalists of his own Church or the authorities of the Church of England. It was a typical example of the exercise of those qualities of patience, tact, humility and quiet determination that made Hume so much respected. Died 17 June

Husain, King, of Jordan (b. 1935), survived many assassination attempts, transformed his small country into an effective and well-ordered state, and was a great influence towards peace in the Middle East. Born when his newly-created country depended for its existence on grants from the UK, Husain was 15 when his grandfather Abdullah was shot dead by a Palestinian gunman, an event he witnessed and which brought home to him the dangers that he and his family faced. He was completing his education at Harrow in 1952 when his father, who was suffering from schizophrenia, was forced to hand over the throne. The prospects were not good, either for Jordan or its new young king. Arab nationalism was rampant and there was widespread hostility towards any connection with outside powers. Husain negotiated subsidies from other Arab nations to replace the British grant, dismissed General Sir John Glubb from the command of his army and, after the Israeli invasion of Sinai during the Suez crisis of 1956, declared his readiness to prepare an armed response, though he did not do so. Cairo radio continued to denounce him for refusing to join with Egypt and Syria in the new United Arab Republic. Husain countered by allying with Iraq, but his position became more precarious when his cousin, King Faisal of Iraq, was murdered during the military coup of 1958. The arrival of British troops helped to stabilize the situation, though Husain's own position remained vulnerable. The Six-Day War of 1967 aggravated his difficulties. He could not avoid Jordan's involvement, though he knew his army could not compete in battle with Israel, and as a result his country lost the West Bank and East Jerusalem.

The rise of the Palestine Liberation Movement and the *fedayeen* under Yassir Arafat, culminating in the hijacking of Western airliners in the Jordanian desert, brought a new crisis for Husain which he resolved by driving out the PLO by force, and by chasing Syrian tanks from his borders when they sought to intervene. He again became the target of Arab anger and his Prime Minister, Wasfi al-Tal, was murdered. Preoccupied with security at home, he refused to allow the country to become involved in further struggles with Israel, though he also refrained from signing a bilateral peace treaty as Egypt had done and as US President Carter was urging him to do (and which he finally did in 1994). He supported Iraq in its war against Iran, allowing Jordan to become Iraq's main supply route, refused to condemn Saddam Husain for his action against Kuwait in 1990 and opposed the dispatch of Western forces to Saudi Arabia. It was a typically bold and independent stance which infuriated some and endeared him to others, including many of his old critics, but added to his growing popularity at home, which was at its highest during his final years, when he was battling with the cancer that finally killed him. Died 7 February

Iotti, Nilde (b. 1920), Italian Communist who was president of the Italian Chamber of Deputies for 13 years. Daughter of a laundress and a railwayman, Nilde Iotti won a scholarship to the Catholic University of Milan, where she gained a degree in literature and philosophy. Elected to the new constituent assembly in 1946 as an independent on the Communist Party list, she met the leader of the party, Palmiro Togliatti, and began a relationship that lasted 20 years. But since he was a married man the affair had, in theory, to be clandestine, though they lived together and adopted a child. Nilde Iotti joined the party's central committee in 1956 and was put in charge of the women's section in 1961. After Togliatti's death in 1964 she supported the compromise that was designed to take the Communists into the Italian government, a deal which failed to materialize following the murder of Aldo Moro in 1978. Nilde Iotti became the lower house's first woman president in 1979, refusing to accept nomination as a senator 12 years later because she wished to continue with her work in the Chamber, where she served for more than 50 years. She retired in 1999. Died 3 December

Isa bin Sulman al-Khalifa, Shaikh, Emir of Bahrain (b. 1933), came to the throne in 1961 when the fervour of Arab nationalism was running strongly throughout the region and when his small state was facing considerable economic problems. The first Gulf state to strike oil, its reserves were now running out and the Emir had to fashion a new basis for his country's future prosperity. Shaikh Isa set about diversifying the economy, opening the state's doors to international banking and encouraging the development of shipbuilding, iron and steel production, mining and the production of aluminium. Politically the Emir had to steer a course between the state's powerful neighbours and its position as a British protectorate, and he demonstrated his personal hold on his people when he persuaded an angry mob to abandon attempts to attack British property. Britain's decision to end the protectorate treaties in 1971 gave Bahrain its independence (though not until the Iranian claim to the territory had been settled), but also left it more exposed to the volatility and vagaries of its neighbours. Shaikh Isa followed the Arab consensus where he could, and developed particularly close relations with Saudi Arabia, but continued to have difficulties with Iran. At home he allowed a brief experiment with democracy but after a few years reverted to personal rule. Died 6 March

Jakobovits, Lord (Immanuel) (b. 1921), Chief Rabbi of the United Hebrew Congregations of the British Commonwealth from 1967-91, was a supporter of conservative values who believed that the commandments of God should be applied to the ethics of the nation. Born in Germany, the son of a rabbi who fled to England from Nazi persecution, Jakobovits was a graduate of London University and became minister of the Brondesbury Synagogue at the age of 20. In 1949 he became Chief Rabbi of Ireland and 1958 Rabbi of the Fifth Avenue Synagogue in New York. He returned to Britain in 1967 when invited to become the Chief Rabbi. At his induction sermon he made clear his adherence to the belief in the divine origin of the whole corpus of Jewish law and tradition, but would also do all within his power to close the gaps within the Jewish people. The gaps he referred to were those caused by Rabbi Louis Jacobs, the orthodox scholar whose progressive views deeply divided Anglo-Jewry in the 1960s, and Jakobovits largely succeeded in healing the rift by holding firm to old traditions and by introducing some changes in the way things were done. He set up an advisory group of rabbinical colleagues, founded a trust for expanding Jewish education and spoke in favour of increasing the participation of women (without actually removing any of the limitations imposed on them). Once established within his own community he began to express himself in terms that brought him a wider audience, advocating self-help rather than relying on state welfare, calling for the adherence to moral values, condemning homosexuality, divorce and abortion. He was knighted in 1981 and made a life peer in 1988. Died 31 October

Johnson, Frank M., Jr (b. 1918), US federal judge who was described by the Ku Klux Klan as 'the most hated man in Alabama'. The reason for the Klan's dislike was a series of judgments Johnson made from the bench in Montgomery, Alabama, which helped to remove the last vestiges of state-supported racism in the American South. Born and brought up in Alabama, he became, after serving in the army during the war, a state manager in General Eisenhower's presidential campaign, being rewarded in 1953 with an appointment as US attorney for Northern Alabama. In 1955 he was appointed federal district judge for Middle Alabama, and the first of his memorable cases came before him within a few weeks of his joining the bench, when a black seamstress called Rosa Parks defied the city law by refusing to give up her seat to a white passenger on a local bus. Johnson ruled that the city's bus segregation law was unconstitutional. Many similar judgments followed, involving the removal of segregation in schools, colleges, airports, restaurants, libraries and other public buildings and organizations, including the Alabama state police. In 1965 he ruled that a civil rights march led by Martin Luther King could not be banned, as state governor George Wallace had proposed, as the right to assemble and demonstrate was inviolable. King described him as a judge who had given true meaning to the word justice. In 1979 Johnson was appointed to the US court of appeals for the fifth circuit. In 1995 he was awarded the Presidential Medal of Freedom. Died 23 July

Kendall, Professor Henry W. (b. 1926), American physicist who shared a Nobel Prize for the discovery of quarks, the basic building-blocks of matter. Born in Boston, Massachusetts, he trained at the American Merchant Marine Academy, and it was while there in 1945 that the first atom bombs were exploded over Japan, an event which made him decide to leave the navy and take up science. He enrolled in Amherst College, graduating in mathematics, later studying physics and working at the Massachusetts Institute of Technology and then Stanford University. At that time Stanford had an electron accelerator of 60 metres, and was planning a new one two miles long. Kendall returned to MIT in 1961, but when the new accelerator came into being he went back to Stanford to start work with Jerome Friedman and Richard Taylor, with whom he subsequently shared the Nobel Prize. Their work involved the firing of electron beams into the heart of atoms, at protons, the nuclei of hydrogen atoms, and at neutrons. They discovered that the electron beams were sometimes violently deflected, indicating that there was within protons and neutrons a deeper more fundamental layer of matter, confirming the earlier theory of Murray Gell-Mann, who had adopted the term quark for what was then a hypothetical idea. The experiments of Kendall and his colleagues confirmed its truth. While carrying out his scientific work Kendall became increasingly concerned at the proliferation of nuclear weapons. During the Vietnam War he was co-founder of the Union of Concerned Scientists and in 1992 led an appeal, headed 'Warning to Humanity', by 1,500 scientists against the continuing destruction of the earth's natural resources. He was keen on outdoor pursuits, and died while scuba-diving to take photographs. Died 2 February

Kennedy, John Fitzgerald, Jr (b. 1960), American lawyer, was the only son of President John F. Kennedy. Born shortly after his father had beaten Richard Nixon in the 1960 presidential election campaign, Kennedy's earliest years were spent in the White House until, three days before his third birthday, his father was assassinated, following which Jacqueline Kennedy moved the family to New York. After attending schools in the city he went to Brown University, Rhode Island, where he graduated in history. He then studied for a short time at the University of Delhi before enrolling in the New York University law school, finally passing his exams at the third attempt. He was called to the bar in 1990 and worked for five years in the Manhattan district attorney's office. Though he proved a capable prosecutor he did not enjoy the work, and his name was more often associated with pretty women than with the law or, as many had expected, with politics. In 1995 he changed direction and launched a glossy political magazine called *George*, which proved to have some serious political intent in spite of its glitzy illustrations and layout, and which he later sold to the French company Hachette Filipacchi. His death occurred when the aircraft he was piloting, with his wife and sister-in-law as passengers, plunged into the sea. Died 16 July

Killanin, Lord (b. 1914), was president of the International Olympic Committee during some of the Games' most critical years. Born Michael Morris in Ireland and succeeding to the title as third Baron in 1927, he was educated at Eton and Magdalene, Cambridge. He then became a journalist, working as a war correspondent in the Sino-Japanese war and subsequently political correspondent for the *Daily Mail*. He joined the army in World War II and took part in the D-Day landings, and after the war became president of the Irish Olympic Council and a member of the IOC from 1952. He was elected president in 1972 shortly before Israeli athletes were killed by Arab terrorists during the Munich Olympic Games. The next Games, held in Montreal in 1976, were marred both by delays in preparations and by disputes between China and Taiwan and a boycott by African nations. Killanin's last Games, held in Moscow in 1980, proved even more troublesome following the Soviet Union's invasion of Afghanistan in the previous year. As a result, many nations, including the USA and West Germany, refused to attend, but the Games went ahead, with 80 of 150 nations taking part, and a grateful IOC created the post of honorary life president for Killanin on his retirement. Died 25 April

Kubrick, Stanley (b. 1928), American film director who moved to Britain in 1961 in search of greater independence for his work. Born in New York, Kubrick's first job was as a staff photographer on *Look* magazine. In 1950 he made a short documentary film about a boxer and three years later made his first feature film with money borrowed from friends, and for which he acted as director and producer as well as scriptwriter and cameraman. This was followed by a thriller and, in 1957, by *Paths of Glory*, a powerful film about three French soldiers on the Western Front in World War I. The film established Kubrick as a leading film-maker, and he was given a Hollywood epic, *Spartacus*, to direct. Though the film was a success Kubrick did not like the controls exerted on him and decided to settle in Britain, where his first film was *Lolita*, a striking adaptation of the Nabokov novel. His next was an even greater critical and popular success, *Dr Strangelove, or How I Learned to Stop Worrying and Love the Bomb*, a black comedy about the destruction of the world in which Peter Sellers gave a memorable performance as the mad doctor running the American nuclear deterrent. This was followed by the equally successful *2001: A Space Odyssey*, for which Kubrick devised some original and dramatic special effects to illustrate a voyage to Jupiter. He then made what was to become his most controversial film, *A Clockwork Orange*, based on the novel by Anthony Burgess, which Kubrick himself eventually withdrew because the mindless thuggery it depicted was seen by many as likely to inspire similar real-life violence. Kubrick's later films, which included *Barry Lyndon* and *The Shining*, had less impact and were generally seen as disappointing. His last, *Eyes Wide Shut*, was released shortly after his death. Died 7 March

Lini, Father Walter (b. 1942), first Prime Minister of Vanuatu, was an Anglican priest credited as founding father of the new Pacific state (formerly the Anglo-French condominium of the New Hebrides) which acquired its independence in 1980. Born on Pentecost Island, Lini was educated in the Solomon Islands and in New Zealand, where he was ordained priest in 1970, serving in the diocese of New Hebrides from 1975. At a time of political moves towards independence he joined the New Hebrides National Party, which was sponsored by Anglican Church missions and was soon to be renamed the Vanuaaku Party. Lini became its president, and negotiated an agreement with Britain and France for the introduction of an elected representative Assembly. In the elections for the first independent state his party won a majority and he was voted Prime Minister. An archipelago of some 80 coral and volcanic Pacific islands occupied by varying races speaking a number of different languages, much of it owned before independence by foreigners, Vanuatu was not an easy state to run. On one of its largest islands, Espiritu Santo, the opposition leader declared in 1980 that it would secede. A party of British marines was initially sent in as a peace-keeping force, but this was replaced by troops from Papua New Guinea under a defence pact concluded by Lini. These quickly overcame the rebellion and restored Espiritu Santo to Vanuatu. Subsequent crises within his own party damaged Lini's leadership, he suffered a stroke and, in 1991, was replaced as Prime Minister and party leader following a vote of no confidence. Died 21 February

Lowry, Lord, PC (b. 1919), Lord of Appeal in Ordinary from 1988-94 and Lord Chief Justice of Northern Ireland from 1971-88, presided over the constitutional convention in 1975 which attempted to establish a structure of democratic local government for Northern Ireland. It failed, but there was general admiration for his objective running of the convention, just as there was for the independent justice and fair treatment he administered between the two communities during his term in Northern Ireland. The son of an Ulster Unionist politician, Robert Lowry was educated at the Royal Belfast Academical Institution amd Jesus College, Cambridge, taking a degree in classics before serving in the army during World War II. After reading for the bar he practised in Northern Ireland before joining the Northern Ireland bench in 1964. His appointment as Lord Chief Justice coincided with the escalation of strife in the province and he was himself not immune to its dangers, twice surviving assassination attempts. His judgment in 1984, acquitting all 35 defendants in an IRA terrorist trial on the grounds that the evidence of an informer was unworthy of belief, marked a turning-point in the use of informers to try to obtain mass convictions. As a law lord he earned a reputation for his patience, courtesy and carefully-worded judgments. Died 15 January

Lynch, Jack (b. 1917), was twice Taoiseach of the Republic of Ireland, from 1966-73 and 1977-79, and inevitably spent much of his time in office preoccupied with the conflict in Northern Ireland and its impact on his own country. It had not been his ambition to become a politician.

His first job was in the civil service, as an assistant to the registrar in the probate office in Cork, but at the same time he read law and was called to the Irish bar in 1945. Within a few years of beginning to practice he was invited to join Fianna Fáil and won the Cork constituency for the party in 1948. When Éamon de Valera was returned to power in 1951 Lynch was appointed parliamentary secretary to the government. He became Minister for Education in 1957, Minister for Industry and Commerce in 1959, Minister for Finance in 1965 and was elected party leader and Taoiseach in 1966. When violence erupted in Northern Ireland Lynch pursued a moderate line, though initially calling for a UN peace-keeping force to be sent to the province and urging the British government to persuade the Protestant majority to accept unification. But he condemned IRA violence, dismissed two of his ministers charged with illegal gun-running and agreed with Britain that the border could not be changed by force. He welcomed the introduction of direct rule from Westminster in 1972, strengthened the Republic's laws against terrorism and agreed that the status of Northern Ireland could only be changed with the agreement of the majority of its inhabitants, a position which provided the basis for discussions between the governments long after Lynch had retired. Within the Republic his most significant achievements as Taoiseach were to lead the Republic into the European Community in 1973 and into the European monetary arrangements in 1978. When economic problems arose and Fianna Fáil lost two by-elections in Cork in 1979, Lynch decided to retire. Died 20 October

Marshall, Malcolm (b. 1958), Barbadian cricketer, played for the West Indies in 81 Tests and was never in a losing series. He was a great fast bowler, taking 376 Test wickets at an average of 20 runs, the highest wicket-taker in West Indies history until that record was surpassed by Courtney Walsh (who played in more Tests). He was not a tall man, obtaining his speed through rhythm and the flexibility of his wrist. Over a career which lasted from the late 1970s until the 1990s, and included playing for Hampshire and, for a season after apartheid, for Natal in South, he took 1,524 first-class wickets at an average of 18 runs. Died 5 November

Mellon, Paul (b. 1907), American philanthropist and collector, gave more than $600 million during his lifetime for the benefit of education, the arts, conservation, science and many other causes. Born in Pittsburgh, the son of a wealthy banker, Andrew Mellon, and a British woman, Nora McMullen, who were later divorced, Paul spent his childhood half in America and half in England. He was educated at a school in Connecticut, at Yale University and then at Clare College, Cambridge, before joining the Mellon Bank in Pittsburgh. After three years he gave up banking, to his father's chagrin, turning instead to collecting books and pictures and to breeding and training racehorses. He was made an honorary member of the Jockey Club in 1968 and established his reputation as an owner with the colt Mill Reef, which he bred in America and brought to England in 1969. Mill Reef won the Derby in 1971 and his other victories included the Eclipse, the King George VI and Queen Elizabeth Stakes and the Prix de l'Arc de Triomphe. As a collector of British paintings, Mellon bought nearly 2,000 during his lifetime, as well as twice as many prints and some 20,000 rare British books. He gave large amounts to many British institutions, including Oxford and Cambridge universities, the Tate Gallery and the Royal Veterinary College, but his greatest single gift, $165 million, was for the founding of the Yale Centre for British Art. He also paid for the building of the east wing of the National Gallery of Art in Washington, with which he was connected, as president and chairman, for more than 40 years until he retired in 1985. Died 2 February

Menuhin, Lord (Yehudi), OM (b. 1916), British (b. American) violinist who had his first professional engagement at the age of eight. From then on he had to live with the descriptions child prodigy and genius, having played in New York, London, Berlin and Paris by the time he was 13. He was educated at home by his Russian Jewish parents, who were so determined that he should succeed that many normal childhood activities were forbidden in case his fingers were damaged. He was given his first lessons, aged four, by Louis Persinger and subsequently studied under the Romanian violinist George Enescu. In 1927 he performed the Beethoven Violin Concerto under Fritz Busch in Berlin and under Bruno Walter in London the following year, returning to London in 1932 to record Elgar's Violin Concerto with the composer. During World War II he gave more than 500 concerts to Allied troops and made many broadcasts, including the difficult Bartok Concerto No 2, a performance which so impressed the composer that Bartok wrote his final major work, the Sonata for Solo Violin, for him. In 1945 Menuhin played with Benjamin Britten at the concentration camp in Belsen, which had been liberated a few weeks before, an occasion he remembered vividly for the rest of his life. He set up home with his second wife in London in 1959, and began broadening his interests and activities. He founded the Yehudi Menuhin School in Surrey, which had Nigel Kennedy among its pupils, the Menuhin Music Academy in Gstaad, where he had a second home, and Live Music Now, an organization enabling young people to attend concerts cheaply. He also began to conduct, as well as continuing to give solo recitals. For a time he had his own chamber orchestra, and he also conducted many of the world's major symphony orchestras, becoming associate conductor of the Royal Philharmonic in 1982 and principal guest conductor of the English String Orchestra from 1988. He became interested in Indian music and in jazz, memorably performing duets with the jazz violinist Stephane Grappelli, and remained in the public eye in his later years because of his interest in and espousal of many causes, including those issues which were subsequently labelled 'green'. He was knighted in 1956, appointed OM in 1987 and created a life peer in 1993. Died 12 March

Meynell, Dame Alix, DBE (b. 1903), was, as Alix Kilroy, one of the first women to reach the highest ranks of the British civil service, serving as under-secretary at the Board of Trade from 1946-55. Educated at Malvern Girls' College and Somerville College, Oxford, where she gained what she called a 'modest second' instead of the first-class degree her tutor had expected, she joined Lincoln's Inn but instead of sitting the bar exams decided to go for the administrative class of the home civil service exams, which were being opened to women between the ages of 22 and 24. She was one of two women out of 200 successful candidates, coming 12th in the order of merit, and joined the Board of Trade, where she quickly began to make her mark. She was appointed first woman principal in 1932 and principal assistant secretary, in charge of a new industries' and manufacturers' department, in 1942. Between 1949, when she was appointed DBE, and 1952 she was seconded to the Monopolies and Restrictive Practices Committee. After returning to the Board of Trade for another three years, she resigned from the civil service, later serving on the South-Eastern Gas Board and a number of other bodies before becoming managing director of the Nonesuch Press after the death of her husband, the typographer, publisher and poet Sir Francis Meynell, whom she had married in 1946 and who had set up the press in 1923. Died 31 August

Mitchison, Naomi, CBE (b. Haldane, 1897), British author who was a political and religious radical, an early supporter of birth control and nuclear disarmament, and writer of historical novels. She was born into the Scottish Haldane family and brought up in Oxford, where her father was a fellow of New College and her brother the geneticist J.B.S. Haldane. During the World War I she worked as a nurse, marrying, in 1916, Gilbert Richard Michison, a lawyer who was wounded while serving with the army in France. After the war they lived in London, where he practised as a barrister and she began producing a family of seven children, and started writing. Her first novel, *The Conquered*, about the Roman conquest of Gaul, was published in 1923, and during the rest of her life she produced more than 80 books, an average of more than one a year. These included *The Corn King and the Spring Queen*, another historical novel set in ancient Greece and Scythia, *The Blood of the Martyrs*, *The Big House* and *Memoirs of a Spacewoman*, three volumes of autobiography, books about Scotland (where she settled in the late 1930s), about philosophy (including Socrates, on whom she wrote with R.H.S. Crossman), and many books on subjects that reflected the political and social concerns of the times. After meeting James Watson, the American joint co-unraveller of DNA, she also helped to edit *The Double Helix* (1968), which was dedicated to her. She was apponted CBE in 1985. Died, aged 101, 11 January

Murdoch, Dame Iris, DBE (b. 1919), novelist and philosopher, was born in Dublin of Anglo-Irish parents, educated at Badminton School and Somerville College, Oxford, where she gained a first in greats. She worked during World War II in the civil service, joining the Treasury under Evelyn Sharp, and was posted first to Belgium and then to Austria on secondment to the UN Relief and Rehabilitation Administration. She returned to academic life after the war, studying philosophy for a year at Newnham, Cambridge, before returning to Oxford as a tutor and lecturer in philosophy, becoming a fellow of St Anne's College in 1948. Her first book, *Sartre: Romantic Rationalist*, was inspired by her early enthusiasm for existentialism, but she became critical of his views, and of analytic philosophy, as was reflected in her later volume of essays, *The Sovereignty of Good*. She began writing novels at the age of 35, developing existential themes in her first, *Under the Net* (narrated by a male), which was published in 1954. There followed many other successful novels, including *The Sandcastle* (1957), *The Bell* (1958), *A Severed Head* (1961, later dramatized by J.B. Priestley as a play which ran for three years in London's West End), *The Red and the Green* (1965), *The Black Prince* (1973) and *The Sea, The Sea* (1978, a novel which finally won for her the Booker Prize, for which she was six times shortlisted). Her last book, *The Green*

Knight, was published in 1993, shortly before the onset of Alzheimer's disease brought her career to an end. In 1956 Iris Murdoch had married John Bayley, a literary critic and later professor of English literature at St Catherine's College, Oxford, who cared for her during her final illness and subsequently wrote movingly about it. Died 8 February

Nkomo, Joshua (b. 1917), Vice-President of Zimbabwe, was for many years the leading figure in the liberation movement in his country, then the British colony of Southern Rhodesia, but failed to become its leader once independence was achieved and political parties divided along tribal lines. Nkomo, recognized champion of the Ndebele people (though himself a Kalanga) and leader of the Zimbabwe African People's Union (ZAPU), lost out to Robert Mugabe's Zimbabwe African National Union (ZANU), which was supported by the Shona majority. Nkomo's apprenticeship in African politics began in Johannesburg, where he was training in social work and came to know Nelson Mandela and other prospective young black leaders; but it was not until 1957, when he was elected president of the African National Congress (ANC) in Southern Rhodesia, that he began to be recognized as leader of the country's nationalist movement. When a state of emergency was declared and the ANC banned, Nkomo created a new party, followed by others, including ZAPU. However, when he accepted an offer of a minority of black parliamentary seats Mugabe and others broke away to form ZANU. Violence followed and most of the leaders of both movements were detained by the Ian Smith government, Nkomo himself being confined to the south-east of the country for ten years. Attempts to reunite the parties failed, and when elections were held shortly before independence (in 1980) ZANU won 57 of the 100 seats and ZAPU only 20. Mugabe became Prime Minister and Nkomo was given a few minor jobs until, a year later, he was sacked and accused of plotting to overthrow the government. He escaped to London, as many of his supporters in Matabeleland were killed; but it soon became evident that his influence was needed to run that part of the country and a deal was struck giving him a vice-presidency of the country. His physical and mental health declined in his last years, which were mainly preoccupied with business interests. Died 1 July

Nyerere, Julius (b. Kambarage, 1922), was Prime Minister of Tanganyika from 1961 and President of the United Republic of Tanzania, formed after the union with Zanzibar, from 1964-85. One of 26 children of a chief of the Zanaki tribe, Nyerere was educated at Tabora and Makerere University College in Uganda, and at Edinburgh University. He adopted the Christian name Julius after his baptism as a Roman Catholic at the age of 20, but he became widely known in his own country as Mwalima, the teacher, a title earned from his early career, which he gave up after a few years in order to devote his time to politics. Appointed to the legislative council, which he used largely to campaign for education for the black population, he founded the Tanganyika African National Union (TANU) in 1954, with a policy committed to the achievement of independence for the British colony. He was banned from public speaking after touring the country to drum up support for the party, and resigned from the legislative council. Brought back in 1958, he helped to prepare the way for independence, which was achieved in 1961 after TANU had won all but one of the seats in the new Legislative Assembly. Becoming Prime Minister, Nyerere introduced a new constitution making the country a one-party state with a Preventive Detention Act enabling the government to arrest its critics. In 1967 he made his Arusha Declaration, establishing an agricultural collective system which involved the resettlement of millions of Africans into cooperative villages, with state marketing boards through which farmers had to sell their produce. It was a disastrous move, as he was later to acknowledge, reducing his naturally fertile country into over-dependence on overseas aid (Tanzania becoming the highest per capita recipient of foreign aid in Africa). Burdened by expensive social services, the country's economy began to collapse, as Nyerere's rule became more impatient and dictatorial at home, though his reputation abroad remained high. He was one of the founders of the Organization of African Unity and a man of international influence, particularly in the developing world. He sent in troops to assist with the removal of President Amin in Uganda, and in 1985 persuaded Colonel Qadafi to release British hostages held in Libya. Nyerere handed over power to his Vice-President in 1986, but continued to retain a dominant position in Tanzania as chairman of the only legal political party until finally retiring to his farm on the shores of Lake Victoria in 1990. Died 14 October

Papadopoulos, George (b. 1919), was dictator of Greece from 1967-73, having organized the military coup which overthrew the country's democratic government. He graduated from the Greek Officers' Cadet Academy shortly before the country was invaded by Italy in 1940. After the German occupation he carried out a number of military assignments before being recruited into the Greek intelligence service, where he concentrated on combating communism. He was appointed the army's deputy chief of operations in Athens in 1966, and it was here that he planned, with other officers, a coup timed to forestall the elections planned for the spring of 1967. The coup succeeded, and the military government confirmed its hold on the country in December, when King Constantine fled to Italy after failing to organize a counter-coup. Some initial popular support for Papadopoulos, or relief that a weak and vacillating civilian government had been replaced, gradually evaporated as he refused to set a timetable for elections and, in 1973, proclaimed himself President (after formally abolishing monarchy). He was himself deposed in a swift coup later in 1973. Following the restoration of democratic rule in 1974, he was eventually put on trial and found guilty of treason, his death sentence being commuted to life imprisonment by the newly-elected Karamanlis government. His last years were spent under guard in hospital. Died 27 June

Peyrefitte, Alain (b. 1925), French author and statesman, was a Gaullist who held eight ministerial portfolios from the 1960s until the early '80s. Educated at the École Normale Supérieure and the École Nationale d'Administration, Peyrefitte began his career as a diplomat, serving in West Germany, Belgium and Poland, but he switched to politics in 1958, joining the Gaullist party. He was appointed Minister of Information by Georges Pompidou in 1962, a job which entailed weekly meetings with President de Gaulle. In 1967 he became Minister for Education, embarking on a number of reforms, but he resigned after the student revolt in the following year, having failed to anticipate its seriousness. He later became secretary-general of his party, but the publication of two books in the mid-1970s, *Quand le Chine s'éveillera* (a study of maoism based on a visit to China in 1971) and *Le Mal français* (a critical account of the country's bureaucracy), brought him new fame and popular respect. In 1977 he served as Minister of Justice in Valéry Giscard d'Estaing's government, putting through a series of authoritarian reforms which somewhat marred his liberal reputation, lost him his seat in the 1981 elections and made him the target of a terrorist assassination attempt, which he survived. In 1983 he became editor-in-chief of *Le Figaro*, which he made use of to criticize President Mitterrand. Died 27 November

Ramsey, Sir Alf (b.1920), was manager of the England football team that won the World Cup in 1966. His first opportunity in the game came during service with the army during World War II, when he occasionally turned out for the local Southampton team. He began his professional career with Southampton when the war ended, winning his first England cap in 1948, and was recruited by Tottenham Hotspur, where his tactical skill earned him the nickname 'the General'. In 1955 he was appointed manager of Ipswich, then in the third division of the English League. He took the team into the second division, then won the divisional and the

League championships in consecutive seasons. Approached to become the England's first full-time manager in 1962, after the team had failed in the World Cup of that year, he accepted the job on condition that there would be no interference with the way he did it. His first decisive move was to appoint the 22-year-old Bobby Moore as captain, and he continued to make his own decisions, and stand by them, during the 1966 World Cup. His failure to recall Jimmy Greaves for the final was bitterly criticized, until a hat-trick by replacement Geoff Hurst vindicated his judgment-just as the 4-2 defeat of West Germany finally silenced all other opposition to his tactics. Ramsey was knighted in the following year, but he was not able to repeat England's triumph in his two subsequent World Cup campaigns, the first in Mexico in 1970 and again in 1974, when England failed to qualify and he was sacked. Though he temporarily managed Birmingham City in 1977, his exit from the England post was in effect the end of his career. Died 28 April

Reilly, Sir Patrick, GCMG, OBE (b. 1909), was British ambassador in Moscow from 1957-60 and in Paris from 1965-68. Born in India (his father was chief justice of Mysore), Reilly was educated at Winchester and New College, Oxford, and was elected a fellow of All Souls in 1932. He came top in the Foreign Office exam the following year and was posted to Tehran in 1935. In London at the start of World War II he became assistant to the head of MI6 before moving to Algiers in 1943 to serve with Harold Macmillan, the minister-resident in North Africa. When Paris was liberated in 1944 he became head of chancery there for a short spell before being posted to Athens. He returned to London in 1948 and then went back to the embassy in Paris as minister. In 1956 he was back at the Foreign Office as under-secretary during the Suez crisis, then went to Moscow during the Khrushchev era, when tension was high because the position of West Berlin, surrounded by communist territory, was being threatened. Reilly returned to London in 1960, where he worked on Britain's first attempt to enter the Common Market. When he became ambassador in Paris four years later, Harold Wilson's Labour government, with George Brown as Foreign Secretary, sought to persuade President de Gaulle to drop his veto on Britain's entry, though Reilly's advice was that there was no chance of Britain being admitted while de Gaulle remained in power. Brown was reluctant to accept this view and in his aggressive way made life difficult for Reilly, eventually replacing him and hastening his retirement from the diplomatic service. Reilly nonetheless maintained his links with France, becoming chairman of the British and French Bank, later renamed the Banque Nationale de Paris. Died 6 October

Richardson, Elliot (b. 1920), was US Attorney-General for a time during President Nixon's administration, and later ambassador to the UK. Born in Boston and educated at Harvard, Richardson served in the US army during World War II, winning a Bronze Star and Purple Heart as an infantry lieutenant in the Normandy landings. He was admitted to the Massachusetts bar in 1947, joining the Republican Party during Eisenhower's presidency and becoming assistant secretary of health, education and welfare in 1957 and US attorney for Massachusetts in 1959. He was elected lieutenant-governor of the state in 1965 and state attorney-general in 1967. He joined the Nixon administration in 1969, becoming successively under-secretary of state, Secretary of Health, Education and Welfare, Secretary of Defence and finally, in 1973, US Attorney-General. This post led him into direct conflict with Nixon when he refused the President's instruction to order Archibald Cox, who had been appointed by Richardson as special prosecutor in the Watergate affair, to abandon his inquiries, and then to remove him from office. Richardson resigned, and after Nixon's own resignation was appointed ambassador in London by the new President, Gerald Ford. He was recalled to Washington in 1976 to become Secretary of Commerce. When Jimmy Carter took office in 1977 Richardson was appointed head of the American delegation to the third UN Conference on the Law of the Sea, an assignment that was near completion when President Reagan ordered a complete re-examination and dismissed the entire American delegation. Richardson resumed private practice and was awarded the Presidential Medal of Freedom in 1998. Died 31 December

Rodrigues, Amália (b. 1920), *fado* singer who was popularly known as the 'Voice of Portugal' and largely responsible for this traditional, melancholy Portuguese music becoming more widely appreciated. Born in Lisbon, Amália Rodrigues in later life declared that her background and upbringing provided the essential elements of *fado*: poverty and a feeling of hopelessness. *Fado*, the Portuguese for 'fate', emerged from the poor areas of the country in the nineteenth century, seemingly deriving from a mixture of African, Arab and Portuguese music. Amália, as she was universally called in her own country, began singing in Lisbon's taverns and in local festivals; as her fame spread in the 1940s she made many records and a number of films. In the following decade she took her *fado* songs to other countries, including the USA, France, Russia and Japan. Her last stage appearance was in Lisbon in 1998, and on her death the Portuguese government declared three days of official mourning (see II.4.iii). Died 6 October

Sarraute, Nathalie (b. Natasha Tcherniak, 1900), was a French author born in Russia whose parents split up when she was two, forcing her to divide her childhood between them, one living in St Petersburg and the other in Paris. Eventually she settled in Paris (where her father and his second wife lived), studying English literature at the Sorbonne. She read history for a year at Oxford, then spent a year in Berlin before returning to Paris to read law. She married a fellow law student, who encouraged and supported her desire to write, though she did not begin until after the birth of her three children. Her first book, *Tropismes*, was published in 1938, its title a metaphorical term which she used to refer to the semi-conscious impulses that determine human actions. During the German occupation she went into hiding after being denounced as Jewish, but she continued to write and her first novel, *Portrait d'un inconnu*, was published in 1948, part of it being featured by Jean-Paul Sartre in *Les Temps modernes*. Since the novel failed to attract much critical attention, Sarraute turned to writing essays, a volume of which was published in 1965 with the title *L'Ère du soupçon*. The essays brought her into the heart of the literary debates then taking place in Paris about the future form of the novel. In 1959 she wrote *Le Planetarium*, a novel which established her reputation in this genre, and after the publication of her next, *Les Fruits d'or*, she was awarded the 1964 Prix Internationale de Littérature. During this time she also wrote a number of plays for radio, two of which were produced in a stage version by Jean-Louis Barrault. More novels and other works continued to be published, including *Entre la vie et la mort*, which closely reflected her own preoccupation with death, the fear of which she believed lay behind much human behaviour. Died, aged 99, 19 October

Schawlow, Arthur (b. 1921), American scientist who, with Charles Townes, invented the laser. Born in Mount Vernon, New York state, Schawlow read radio engineering at Toronto University before going to Columbia University where he worked with Townes on microwave spectroscopy. In 1955 the two men published a book on the subject and in 1957 worked together on a device that could operate at shorter wavelengths than the maser (the microwave precursor of the laser). They published their findings in *Physical Review*, the journal of the American Physical Society, in 1958, and received a patent for the laser, though they did not profit financially since they were working for Bell Laboratories, and at first no uses could be identified for their invention. In 1961 Schawlow left Bell to join the physics department at Stanford, where he continued working on laser and microwave spectroscopy, being made chairman of the department in 1966. He was jointly awarded the Nobel Prize for Physics in 1981 for his contribution to the development of laser spectroscopy. Died 28 April

Scott, George C. (b. 1927), American actor who won an Oscar, which he refused to accept, for his portrayal of General Patton in the 1970 film *Patton*. After leaving school in Detroit, Scott joined the marine corps, but World War II ended before he had finished his training. After his discharge, he enrolled in a journalism course at the University of Missouri, but decided to take up acting instead, appearing in many university stage productions. He had little success as a professional actor until he moved to New York in 1956, when he was given the title role in *Richard III* in the New York Shakespeare Festival. He went to Hollywood in 1959 to make his first film, *The Hanging Tree*, starring Gary Cooper, and in the same year also appeared in *Anatomy of a Murder* with James Stewart, both actors receiving Oscar nominations for their performances. Scott won another Oscar nomination for his role in the 1961 film *The Hustler*, but he refused to accept it, denouncing the awards ceremony as a 'self-serving meat parade'. His next film was *Dr Strangelove, or How I learned to Stop Worrying and Love the Bomb* directed by Stanley Kubrick (q.v.), in which he gave a memorable performance as a US air force general dealing with a rogue nuclear attack on Russia. After being sacked from a film for failing to turn up on time, he did some stage work, then in 1970 was cast as Patton. In spite of his previous refusal, he was awarded an Oscar, and became the first actor to turn down this coveted award. He continued to make films but also began working in television, winning an Emmy award for his performance in Arthur Miller's play *The Price*. Again he refused to accept the award. Died 22 September

Seaborg, Glenn (b. 1912), American nuclear scientist who won the Nobel Prize for Chemistry in 1951 and later became the first living scientist to have an element named after him. Born in Michigan, Seaborg moved with his family to California where he studied chemistry at Berkeley, staying on to work with the team synthesizing elements. In 1940 they synthesized plutonium 238 by bombarding uranium with deuterons in the cyclotron at Berkeley, and in the following year, when the USA entered World War II, created plutonium 239, the element used in the second of the nuclear bombs dropped on Japan in 1945. At the outbreak of war, Seaborg was seconded to the Manhattan Project, as a section chief in Chicago, working with J. Robert Oppenheimer to develop the atomic bomb. When the bomb was made, Seaborg was one of those who signed an abortive appeal to President Truman that it be demonstrated to Japanese scientists before being used as a weapon of war. Seaborg returned to Berkeley after the war, identifying, after plutonium (element 94 in the periodic table), americium (95), berkelium (97), einsteinium (99), fermium (100) and nobelium (102). Element 106 was given the name seaborgium in 1997. Seaborg shared the 1951 Nobel Prize with Edwin McMillan, who synthesized the element neptunium (93) in 1940. Died 25 February

Silva Henríquez, Cardinal Raúl (b. 1907), was Archbishop of Santiago and a determined defender of human rights during the dictatorship of General Pinochet in Chile, once declaring that he would hide opponents of the regime under his bed rather than hand them over to the security forces. Born in the southern city of Talca, he was educated at the Catholic University in Santiago, where he gained a degree in law before travelling to Italy and, in 1938, becoming ordained in Turin. He returned to Chile in 1939 and was appointed Bishop of Valparaiso in 1959 and Archbishop of Santiago in 1962, becoming a cardinal in the following year. When President Allende was overthrown by the military coup in 1973 the Cardinal drafted a strongly-worded condemnation, on behalf of his bishops, of the violence used and rejected Pinochet's request for a *Te Deum* in Santiago cathedral to give thanks for the country's salvation. As the nature of the military persecution became evident he founded an ecumenical peace committee, but was forced to close it down in 1975. Though receiving death threats he responded within two months by setting up the Vicaria de Solidaridad which documented cases of disappearance, helped men and women released from months of torture, and provided refuge for other victims of the regime. Many widows of the 'disappeared' stayed in the mansion and brought up their children there. Evidence compiled in the vicariate, which included the names of more than 3,000 people killed or who had disappeared during the dictatorship, was used in the report of the commission of inquiry appointed by the democratic government that eventually succeeded General Pinochet. Cardinal Silva Henriquez's persistent efforts to mediate between the General and his opponents played a significant part in bringing about the change of government, though ill-health had forced his retirement in 1983, while Pinochet was still in power. Died 9 April

Stoph, Willi (b. 1914), was Chairman of the Council of Ministers in the German Democratic Republic for two terms, from 1964-73 and from 1976-89, working under two general secretaries of the East German Communist Party, first Walter Ulbricht and then Erich Honecker. Born in Berlin, Stoph joined the communist youth party when he was an apprentice bricklayer, and the Communist Party in 1931. He served in the artillery during World War II, after which he worked in various economic posts in the Soviet zone until he was appointed Minister of the Interior, setting up what was to become the GDR's army. In 1956 he was appointed Minister of Defence, which enabled him to develop the army into one of the most efficient in the Warsaw Pact. Stoph's career did not progress as he had hoped when Ulbricht decided in favour of Honecker as his successor in 1971, though he was brought back in 1976 to help cope with the country's increasing economic difficulties. When the GDR finally collapsed in 1989, Stoph was among those put on trial on charges of manslaughter, but was eventually excused on medical grounds. Died 13 April

Tudjman, Franjo (b. 1922), President of Croatia, was a ruthless leader whose ambition to create an independent state contributed to the break-up of Yugoslavia and precipitated 'ethnic cleansing' and slaughter on a scale equivalent to that of fellow Balkan leader Slobodan Milošević. During World War II Tudjman had joined Tito's communist partisans and was appointed a general in the Yugoslav national army after the war, but he left the army in 1961 to devote himself to promoting Croatian nationalism, maintaining that Tito had favoured the Serbs in the development of the country. When the Croatian establishment demanded greater political autonomy, Tito arrested the leaders, sending Tudjman to prison. After Tito's death in 1980 Tudjman founded the Croatian Democratic Union, a party dedicated to complete independence, and when his party won the election of 1990 the collapse of the federation became inevitable. As President of an independent Croatia from 1991, Tudjman launched a campaign of discrimination against the Serbs, removing them from positions of influence on the pretext that they were communists. His policies provoked a rebellion of the Serbs in Krajina, and war broke out in earnest in 1991. The Croatian army could not contain the Croatian Serbs, and about a third of Croatian territory, including Krajina and east and west Slavonia was lost and some 20,000 Croatians killed before a ceasefire, mediated by the UN, was agreed. Returned to power in the presidential election of 1992, Tudjman set about training a new army which he decided was ready for action by 1995. In that year both western Slavonia and Krajina were recaptured and some 250,000 Serbs fled the country. Under US auspices an agreement was reached in November 1995 at Dayton, Ohio, which divided Bosnia, 51 per cent going to the Muslim-Croat federation and 49 per cent to the Serbs. Tudjman and Milošević also agreed that eastern Slavonia should be placed under UN administration for three years before being restored to Croatia. Tudjman thereafter tightened his control of the country, refusing to allow a free press and making virtually all important decisions himself. Cancer, which was first diagnosed in 1996, seemed the only threat he could not control, and this was a battle he ultimately lost. Died 10 December

Valiani, Leo (b. Weiczen, 1909), Italian senator and lifelong opponent of fascism, was born in Fiume (Rijeka) when it was part of the Austrian Empire. The family italianized the name in the 1920s, when Fiume was annexed by Italy. Valiani at first hoped to be a professional footballer, but turned to sports journalism when it became evident that he was not good enough on the field. At the same time he became a member of a clandestine communist organization, and in 1928 was sent to prison for distributing anti-fascist propaganda. He soon got into trouble again on his return to Fiume, and was sentenced to 12 years' imprisonment but was released after five years. He acted as correspondent for some Italian newspapers covering the Spanish Civil War and was subsequently imprisoned in a French concentration camp in the Pyrenees. These experiences persuaded him to give up communism. He escaped from France and made his way to Mexico in 1941, returning to Sicily and walking to Rome in 1943. He moved on to Milan to take charge of the northern Italian national liberation committee on behalf of the Liberal-Socialist Action Party, and in April 1945 he signed Mussolini's death warrant after the dictator had refused to surrender to the partisans. Following the end of World War II Valiani helped to frame the new Italian constitution and was elected to the constituent assembly in 1946, but lost interest in active politics after failing to establish an independent Socialist Party. He worked in a bank in Milan while writing a series of books on the history of twentieth-century Italian politics and was nominated a life senator of the Italian Republic in 1980. Died 18 September

West, Morris, AO (b. 1916), Australian author who studied for the Roman Catholic priesthood but turned instead to writing novels, many of them best-sellers and several successfully filmed. After early education at a local school in Melbourne West moved to a Christian Brothers' seminary in Sydney, but growing doubts prevented him from taking his vows. It was 1939 and he was 23. He worked in military intelligence in Melbourne for a time during World War II, but after the bombing of Darwin by the Japanese was posted to the Northern Territory, where he also began to write his first novel, based on his experience of monastic life. It was published in 1943. That same year he worked for a short period as secretary to former Prime Minister William Hughes, after which he worked in commercial radio. More novels came in the 1950s, most with exciting if sometimes far-fetched plots which nonetheless raised real issues in the Catholic Church, in politics or in international affairs. Particular successes were *Children of the Sun* (1957), a study of a Catholic priest's efforts to help street urchins in Naples, *The Devil's Advocate* (1959), about an inquiry by a dying priest into the claims to sainthood of a British army deserter, and *The Shoes of the Fisherman* (1963), about the election of a Russian Pope. Two later novels were also set in the Vatican- *Clowns of God* (1981) and *Lazarus* (1990). During his lifetime West wrote 27 novels which sold some 60 million copies. Died 9 October

Whitelaw, Viscount (William), KT, CH, MC, PC, (b. 1918) served in the cabinets of two markedly different Conservative administrations, those of Edward Heath and Margaret Thatcher (against whom he had stood for the party leadership in 1975). Born a Scot, he was educated at Winchester and Trinity College, Cambridge, where he had an undistinguished academic career but achieved a golfing Blue. When war came he joined the army and served as a regular officer in the Scots Guards until 1947, earning the Military Cross during the Normandy campaign and being twice mentioned in dispatches. A compassionate man, he began a political career on release from the army, finally getting elected in 1955 for the Penrith and the Border constituency, which he continued to represent until 1983. In 1956 he was appointed parliamentary private secretary to the President of the Board of Trade, Peter Thorneycroft, moved to the Treasury in the same capacity and then became parliamentary under-secretary at the Ministry of Labour. He was made chief whip when the Conservatives were in opposition from 1964-70, then became Lord President of the Council and Leader of the House of Commons in the Heath government formed in 1970. In 1972 he was appointed to his most testing political assignment, the new post of Secretary of State for Northern Ireland, which he took on when Stormont was suspended and direct rule from Westminster imposed. By the time he left, at the end of 1973, he had succeeded in bringing together politicians from both communities in a power-sharing administration responsible to an elected Assembly. It did not last, but Whitelaw was given much credit for achieving what at the time seemed a minor miracle. There was also regret in Ulster at the suddenness of his departure, but the government was in severe trouble at home and Heath wanted Whitelaw's conciliatory gifts to help resolve the dispute with the miners. He was appointed Secretary of State for Employment, but was not able to make much progress before the Prime Minister called an election in February 1994, which Whitelaw strongly opposed, and which the Conservatives lost. When Mrs Thatcher won the election of 1979 Whitelaw combined the role of her deputy with the post of Home Secretary until 1983, when he was persuaded, rather against his wishes, to accept an hereditary viscountcy and become Leader of the House of Lords. He left this post in 1988 but retained the unofficial title of Deputy Prime Minister until 1991. Though sometimes critical of Mrs Thatcher's policies, and of Thatcherism, he was always loyal to her, and worked, both at the Home Office and in the Lords, to find a middle way acceptable to the party as a whole. On his retirement Mrs Thatcher acknowledged his value with the memorable words 'Every Prime Minister needs a Willie'. Died 1 July

CHRONICLE OF PRINCIPAL EVENTS IN 1999

JANUARY

1 Eleven EU countries (excluding Denmark, Greece, Sweden and the UK), with a combined population of 290 million people, merged their national currencies, replacing them with the euro; circulation of notes would begin from January 2002.
3 Pakistan's PM Nawaz Sharif narrowly escaped assassination when bomb exploded on his route home to Lahore.
  In Sierra Leone, ECOMOG warplanes attacked rebel hideout near Freetown, killing 200 insurgents supporting deposed junta.
4 In India, 16 died when gunmen fired on Shia Muslims at prayer in mosque in eastern Punjab.
  In Angola, some UN flights suspended following shooting-down of two of its planes; future of 1994 peace agreement was in jeopardy.
5 In Democratic Republic of Congo, 500 civilians reported massacred in eastern area.
6 In Sierra Leone, rebel forces supporting ousted junta entered Freetown, seizing public buildings, killing civilians and freeing scores of prisoners from gaol.
  UK PM Tony Blair on three-day visit to S. Africa.
7 In USA, impeachment trial of President Clinton formally opened in US Senate; it was the first Senate trial of a President since Andrew Johnson in 1868; prosecution opened on 14 Jan., Mr Clinton being accused of 'egregious and criminal conduct' (see 12 Feb.).
10 In Kazakhstan, Nursultan Nazarbayev re-elected President amid allegations of unfair practice.
11 In Turkey, Bülent Ecevit formed pro-secular minority government, ending six-week crisis.
   In Mali, former President Moussa Traoré and his wife sentenced to death for embezzlement; his 23-year rule had ended in 1991.
13 Brazil, world's eighth-largest economy, devalued its currency by 9 per cent amid mounting fears of economic collapse.
   In Sierra Leone, Nigerian-led ECOMOG troops regained control of Freetown, driving out rebel forces who had destroyed most public buildings (see 7 July).
15 In Kosovo, 45 ethnic Albanians found massacred in village of Racak; the West claimed that Serbian forces were responsible.
18 In Grenada, the ruling New National Party led by PM Keith Mitchell won all 15 seats in elections to House of Representatives.
19 In USA, President Clinton delivered State of Union address, focusing on domestic policy, social security in particular.
20 In Barbados, PM Owen Arthur and his Barbados Labour Party retained power in general election.
22 Pope John Paul II on visit to Mexico and USA; on 26 Jan. he met President Clinton at St Louis, Missouri.
26 In south-west Colombia, over 900 people died in earthquake measuring 6.1 on Richter scale; 250,000 left homeless.
28 Kosovo warring parties given ultimatum by six-nation Contact Group, meeting in London, to attend peace talks and agree deal within 21 days, or face NATO bombing.

FEBRUARY

4 Out of N. Korea's population of 20 million, some 3 million reported to have died in years of starvation.
6 On Kosovo crisis, talks opened in Rambouillet, France, between Contact Group and Yugoslav and ethnic Albanian leaders in effort to agree peace plan; talks suspended on 19 March because of failure of Serbs to negotiate in good faith.
  King Husain of Jordan died (see XVIII: Obituary); 50 world leaders attended his funeral in Amman on 8 Feb.; he was succeeded by his eldest son, King Abdullah II.

12 In USA, Senate impeachment trial ended with acquital of President Clinton on two charges of perjury and obstruction of justice; Mr Clinton declared his sorrow at his role in these events and called for reconciliation.
16 Kurdish rebel leader Abdullah Öcalan captured by Turkish agents in Kenya and flown back to Turkey to face terrorism charges, arousing worldwide Kurdish protests (see 29 June); on 17 Jan. security guards shot dead three Kurdish protesters attempting to storm Israeli consulate in Berlin.
23 In Austria, over 30 people died in avalanche in Tyrolean resort of Galtur, the country's worst since 1954.
    In UK, PM Blair launched 30-month campaign to increase awareness of potential benefits of joining single European currency.
24 In UK, report of Sir William Macpherson's inquiry into controversial case of black teenager Stephen Lawrence, murdered in 1993, accused Metropolitan Police of 'pernicious and institutional racism' in its investigation of the murder.
26 EU leaders held special summit in Petersberg, Germany, to discuss reform of EU finances, changes to common agricultural policy and admission of new members from Central and Eastern Europe.
27 In Nigerian presidential election, former military leader Gen. Olusegun Obasanjo defeated Olu Falae to be returned as elected civilian President; he was sworn in on 29 May.

MARCH

1 In Uganda, Rwandan Hutu rebels kidnapped 14 Western tourists on a safari holiday near Congolese border and subsequently murdered eight of them.
4 A dispute over banana imports into Europe led to USA imposing 100 per cent tariffs on a wide range of European goods.
7 In Bahrain, Shaikh Hamad sworn in as Emir following death of his father, Shaikh Isa bin Sulman al-Khalifa.
    Estonia held a general election; a coalition government, headed by Pro Patria Union leader Mart Laar, was formed on 25 March.
    In El Salvador, Francisco Flores Pérez of the National Republican Alliance gained outright victory in presidential election; he was sworn in on 1 June.
    In Equatorial Guinea, ruling Democratic Party retained large majority in National Assembly elections.
8 President Clinton began four-day visit to Central America.
9 In UK, budget day; Chancellor announced measures to help families with children and reduction of standard rate of tax by 1p to 22p in 2000, its lowest rate for 70 years.
    Prince of Wales on official visit to Argentina, Uruguay and Falkland Islands.
    Iran's President Khatami on official visit to Rome and Vatican, first Iranian leader to visit Europe since overthrow of Shah in 1979.
    In Antigua & Barbuda, the Antiguan Labour Party led by PM Lester Bird retained power in general election.
12 In Tonga, parliamentary elections resulted in pro-democracy candidates winning five of nine popularly-elected seats.
14 In Kosovo, seven died in worst weekend of violence since start of Rambouillet peace talks.
    Afghanistan's ruling Taleban and opposition representatives reached agreement in Turkmenistan talks on power-sharing in hope of finding permanent end to 20-year civil war.
15 In N. Ireland, death of leading nationalist lawyer Rosemary Nelson in car-bomb explosion caused new threat to ongoing peace process.
16 Entire EU Commission headed by Jacques Santer (Luxembourg) resigned over damning report by outside auditors on its failure to deal with fraud and corruption.
18 International Olympics Committee (IOC) concluded two-day emergency session in Lausanne by expelling six members and cautioning ten, following disclosures of extensive bribery influencing decisions on Games' locations; but veteran IOC president Juan António Samaranch easily survived no-confidence vote.

20 In Kosovo, OSCE monitors abandoned mission as Serbs began renewed offensive against ethnic Albanians.

Bertrand Picard (Switzerland) and Brian Jones (UK) completed first-ever circumnavigation of Earth in balloon *Breitling Orbiter 3*; their voyage lasted 20 days.

21 In Kosovo, thousands of ethnic Albanians fled their homes in face of renewed Serb offensive.

In Finnish general election, ruling Social Democratic Party remained largest parliamentary party; its leader, Paavo Lipponen, formed new coalition on 13 April.

23 NATO secretary-general ordered air-strikes against Yugoslavia after failure of last-ditch talks between US special negotiator Richard Holbrooke and President Milošević to find peace deal for Kosovo.

OPEC Oil Ministers in Vienna agreed aggregate 1.7 million barrels per day cut in production in move to boost world oil prices (see 23 Sept.).

24 In 'Operation Allied Force', NATO launched massive bombing of strategic targets in Yugoslavia, the biggest military operation in Europe since World War II.

EU leaders opened summit in Berlin; they named former Italian PM Romano Prodi as new President of EU Commission.

In Indonesia, more than 200 reported dead in ethnic violence on Borneo island.

In Vanuatu, Fr John Bani elected President for five-year term.

Over 40 people died when lorry caught fire in Mont Blanc tunnel through Alps linking France and Italy; ten died in second Alpine tunnel fire on 30 May.

In Kenya, 32 died when Nairobi-Mombasa train was derailed in Tsavo National Park.

25 In Kosovo, Serbian forces began a new murderous campaign of 'ethnic cleansing' against Albanian population; by 6 April more than one million refugees were reported to have fled their homes in province, seeking sanctuary in Albania, Macedonia and Montenegro.

28 In Yugoslavia, as NATO bombing continued, American combat forces mounted daring operation to rescue pilot of US 'Stealth' bomber shot down in Serbia.

29 In Paraguay, President Raúl Cubas resigned and was granted political asylum in Brazil: he was facing possible impeachment for abuse of power; Congress appointed Senate president Luís González Macchi as President.

30 Russian PM Yevgenii Primakov held talks in Belgrade with President Milošević but no agreement was reached on withdrawal of Serb forces from Kosovo.

In Benin elections, opposition alliance led by former President Nicéphore Soglo won narrow parliamentary majority.

APRIL

1 In N. Ireland, following three days of talks in Belfast UK PM Blair and Irish PM Bertie Ahern issued so-called Hillsborough Declaration including measures to break deadlock over arms decommissioning and to bring Sinn Féin into new power-sharing executive; Sinn Féin rejected plan on 2 April.

In northern Canada, 'Nunavut' came into being as country's largest territory, its population being 85 per cent native Inuits.

In UK, Anthony Sawoniuk (78) received two life sentences at Old Bailey for murder of Jews in Belarus in World War II.

5 Libya surrendered two men suspected of bombing of Pan Am plane over Lockerbie in 1988 for trial by a Scottish court sitting in the Netherlands; UN acted immediately to suspend sanctions imposed against Libya because of its refusal to hand over suspects.

7 Macedonian authorities forcibly evicted 30,000 Kosovo refugees from camp on border; Serbia closed all border crossings to Albania, forcing refugees to turn back.

9 In Niger, President Mainassara assassinated by members of presidential guard; on 11 April Maj. Daouda Malam Wanké (commander of presidential guard) appointed head of National Reconciliation Commission to rule pending democratic elections (see 24 Nov.).

10 In UK, Grand National won by Bobbyjo at 10-1.

11 India carried out test-firing of its *Agni II* ballistic missile, arousing concern in UK and USA.

12 NATO admitted that a missile attack on railway bridge in Serbia had hit a passenger train, killing nine people.
14 NATO bombs accidentally hit a convoy of Albanian refugees near Davovica, Kosovo, killing 75 people; EU leaders held special summit on Kosovo in Brussels: they rejected a German ceasefire plan.
15 In Algeria, Abdelaziz Bouteflika of National Liberation Front (FLN) elected President with 73.8 per cent of vote, against six minor candidates; main opposition parties had withdrawn over allegations of ballot fraud.
Malaysia's former Deputy PM Anwar Ibrahim gaoled for six years for corruption; Amnesty International condemned trial as politically motivated.
Pakistan's former PM Benazir Bhutto and her husband sentenced to five years in gaol and fined £5 million for corruption; Ms Bhutto, who was abroad, claimed political victimization.
UK Home Secretary ruled that former Chilean dictator Gen. Augusto Pinochet must face formal proceedings on Spanish application for his extradition to stand trial in Spain.
16 UNHCR said that thousands more ethnic Albanians were fleeing Kosovo as Serbs stepped up 'ethnic cleansing'.
18 Turkey held general election; Democratic Left Party led by Bülent Ecevit gained largest share of vote with far-right Nationalist Action Party in second place (see 29 May).
In India, government of Atal Bihari Vajpayee defeated in parliament; on 26 April President Narayanan dissolved parliament pending general election, India's third in three years (see 4 Sept.).
In East Timor, 30 died in weekend of violence as Indonesian-backed armed militiamen conducted purges against pro-independence activists.
In UK, London Marathon won by Abdelkader El Mouaziz of Morocco in 2hr 7 min 57 sec.
19 In Germany, newly-renovated *Reichstag* in Berlin formally inaugurated as seat of German parliament, which met there for first time since World War II.
Queen Elizabeth II began four-day state visit to S. Korea.
20 In USA, 15 students and staff died in shooting incident at a school in Denver, Colorado; two fellow students, who shot themselves, were responsible.
21 UK PM Blair in Washington for talks on Kosovo with President Clinton.
Kyrgyzstan's legislature approved appointment of Amangeldy Muraliyev as PM following death of Jumabek Ibrahimov.
23 NATO leaders began three-day summit in Washington, marking 50th anniversary of Alliance by adopting a new 'Strategic Concept' (see XVII.2); Czech Republic, Hungary and Poland formally accepted as new NATO members.
25 First Kosovo refugees arrived in UK at start of emergency airlift.
26 In Serbia, NATO planes destroyed last bridge over Danube at Novi Sad.
In Malaysia, Salahuddin Abdul Aziz Shah, Sultan of Selangor, invested for five-year term as Supreme Head of State.
28 In Yugoslavia, Vuk Draskovic sacked as Deputy PM after criticizing government for lying to Serbian people about NATO bombing.
30 Russian negotiator Viktor Chernomyrdin held unsuccessful talks on Kosovo with President Milošević.
In UK, three died, 65 injured in nail bomb explosion at public house in London's Soho frequented by homosexuals; a man was later charged with this and two other bombings in London earlier in the month targeted against ethnic minorities.
In Comoros, President Massounde overthrown in bloodless military coup led by Col. Azili Assoumani, who was later sworn in as President.

MAY

1 In Kosovo, more than 40 died when NATO bombs accidentally hit a bus; a second bus was hit on 3 May, killing 17.
2 Yugoslav authorities released three US servicemen held in Serbia since 1 April, after mediation by US civil rights leader Rev. Jesse Jackson.

3 UK PM Blair visited Kosovo refugee camps in Macedonia.
In USA, at least 47 died, thousands homeless, when tornado struck Oklahoma and Kansas.
A US expedition on Mount Everest claimed to have found remains of British mountaineer George Leigh Mallory who attempted Everest in 1924: it was not known whether he and his companion Andrew Irvine had reached summit.
6 In UK, Scotland and Wales held elections for new devolved legislatures: Labour gained largest number of seats in both elections but failed to achieve majority in either, because of large nationalist vote; in countrywide local elections Conservatives made net gain of 1,336 seats and took control in 48 more councils, overtaking Liberal Democrats as second-strongest party locally.
7 Four died when NATO mistakenly bombed Chinese embassy in Belgrade; action strongly condemned by Chinese leaders.
In Guinea-Bissau, 70 died in military coup which overthrew President Vieira; Malam Bacai Sanha appointed acting President on 14 May (see 28 Nov.).
Pope John Paul II on first papal visit to Romania, with 90 per cent Orthodox population.
8 In Iceland, a general election resulted in continuation of two-party coalition led by PM Davíd Oddsson.
10 King Abdullah II of Jordan on first official visit to UK.
In Russia, President Yeltsin dismissed government of Yevgenii Primakov, naming Sergei Stepashin as PM (see 9 Aug).
In Wales, Alun Michael (Labour) elected First Secretary by new National Assembly, heading minority Labour administration.
13 In Kosovo, 100 ethnic Albanian refugees reported killed in NATO attack on village of Korisa, near Albanian border.
In Italy, Carlo Azeglio Ciampi elected President in succession to President Scalfaro.
15 In Fiji, two-round parliamentary elections concluded with ruling Fijian Political Party being heavily defeated by ethnic Indian Fijian Labour Party led by Mahendra Chaudhry, who formed broad-based coalition government on 21 May.
17 In Israel, Ehud Barak (Labour Party) won landslide personal victory in general election and Labour-led alliance gained ground; Mr Barak formed broad coalition government on 30 June.
In Scotland, Donald Dewar (Labour Party) took office as First Minister, forming coalition with Liberal Democrats.
In Nepal, parliamentary elections concluded, resulting in victory for Nepali Congress Party (NCP); on 31 May NCP leader Krishna Prasad Bhattarai sworn in as PM.
18 In Lithuania, Rolandas Paksas appointed PM following resignation of Gediminas Vagnorius (see 3 Nov.).
23 In Germany, Johannes Rau (Social Democrat) elected President in succession to Roman Herzog (Christian Democrat); he was sworn in on 1 July.
24 NATO announced doubling of land force deployed in Macedonia (to 48,000), intended to enter Kosovo to secure province for return of ethnic Albanians.
26 In Wales, Queen Elizabeth II opened new National Assembly in Cardiff.
Indian jets launched air attacks on Muslim guerrilla positions in Indian-held region of Kashmir; on 27 May Pakistan shot down two Indian fighter planes, killing one pilot; fighting between Indian and Pakistani ground forces intensified over several days.
27 UN War Crimes Tribunal indicted President Milošević of Yugoslavia and four others for crimes against humanity.
29 In Slovakia, Rudolf Schuster defeated former PM Vladimir Meciar in presidential election; he was sworn in on 15 June.
30 In Armenia, parliamentary election brought Unity (Miasnutiun) group to dominance; on 11 June Unity leader Vazgen Sarkisian named as PM (see 27 Oct., 2 Nov.).

JUNE

2 In S. Africa's second democratic post-apartheid elections, the ANC gained almost two-thirds majority in parliament (see 16 June).
3 In Kosovo negotiations, Russian envoy Chernomyrdin and Finnish President Ahtisaari obtained President Milošević's agreement to G-8 plan for withdrawal of all Serb forces from Kosovo.
  Supermarkets across Europe cleared thousands of products after a scandal in Belgium where animal feed had been contaminated with dioxin.
5 Pope John Paul on two-week visit to his native Poland; on 11 June he addressed the *Sejm*, first Pope ever to addresss a national parliament.
  In UK, Derby won by Oath at 13-2.
7 Indonesia held its first free elections for 45 years; results, declared on 16 July, gave victory to Indonesian Democratic Party (PDI) led by Megawati Sukarnoputri (see 20 Oct.).
8 NATO ended its air campaign against Serbia.
9 In Kosovo, talks between NATO commander Sir Michael Jackson and Serb generals concluded with signature of a military technical agreement (see XVII.1) paving way for withdrawal of Serb forces from Kosovo and entry into province of international security force ('K-For').
  In UK, former Conservative cabinet minister Jonathan Aitken gaoled for perjury and conspiracy to pervert the course of justice in his abortive 1997 libel action against *The Guardian*.
10 UN Security Council adopted resolution 1244 providing for establishment of international security force in Kosovo.
  Throughout EU, voting began in fifth direct elections for European Parliament (some countries voting on 11 or 13 June); turnout across Europe was lowest ever recorded; balance of power shifted from Socialists to centre-right in 626-member parliament.
12 NATO forces, led by British paratroops, advanced into Kosovo from Macedonia at start of 'Operation Joint Guardian' to secure province for return of ethnic Albanian refugees.
  In USA, Governor George W. Bush of Texas announced that he would seek Republican Party nomination for 2000 presidential election; on 16 June Vice-President Al Gore announced his candidacy for Democratic nomination.
13 In Belgium, general election resulted in defeat of centre-left coalition of Jean-Luc Dehaene; Flemish Liberals and Democrats (VLD) emerged as largest single party (see 12 July).
  In Luxembourg, general election resulted in Christian Social-Socialist coalition losing ground; on 7 Aug. Christian Socials formed centre-right coalition with Democratic Party, with Jean-Claude Juncker continuing as PM.
15 Malawi held presidential and legislative elections: incumbent President Bakili Muzuli and his United Democratic Front returned for further term, although results were disputed.
16 In South Africa, ANC leader Thabo Mbeki sworn in as President in succession to Nelson Mandela, who had retired.
18 G-7 summit opened in Cologne: debt relief package for poorest countries was agreed and genetically-modified (GM) foods were among other matters discussed; on 20 June G-7 leaders joined by President Yeltsin of Russia, to become G-8.
19 In UK, the marriage took place at Windsor Castle of the Queen's youngest son Prince Edward and Miss Sophie Rhys-Jones, who became the Earl and Countess of Wessex.
20 Serb forces completed their withdrawal from Kosovo; President Clinton visited Kosovo refugee camps in Macedonia.
21 In Kosovo, two UK soldiers on bomb-disposal duty were killed, the first British casualties in the operation.
22 President Arpad Göncz of Hungary began four-day state visit to UK.
29 In Turkey, Kurdish rebel leader Abdullah Öcalan sentenced to death for treason, sparking international protest.
  In Serbia, thousands took part in demonstrations demanding resignation and indictment of President Milošević.
30 Duty-free shopping ended for travellers within European Union.

JULY

1 Queen Elizabeth II opened new Scottish Assembly, Scotland's first parliament for 292 years.
   In French Alps, 20 died in cable-car accident.
3 In Kuwait, early elections to 50-member National Assembly strengthened liberal and Islamist opposition groups; new government sworn in on 14 July.
4 In UK, Pete Sampras (USA) beat Andre Agassi (US) in final of Wimbledon tennis championships: it was his sixth win, a twentieth-century record.
6 Price of gold fell to a 20-year low following sale by Bank of England of 25 tonnes of its reserves.
7 Sierra Leone's eight-year civil war was supposedly ended by a power-sharing deal between President Kabbah and rebel leader Foday Sankoh signed in Lomé, Togo.
   UK embassy in Tripoli, Libya, reopened, having been closed since 1984 following the murder of a young policewoman outside Libyan embassy in London.
8 Japanese PM Keizo Obuchi in China for summit talks with President Jiang Zemin.
   In Latvia, Vaira Vike-Freiberga sworn in as President, having been elected on 17 June.
9 New 20-member EU Commission unveiled by new president Romano Prodi, containing four of the team which had resigned in March.
11 A peace accord between Democratic Republic of Congo government of President Kabila and supporters of rebel forces was signed in Lusaka, Zambia, but ceasefire was ignored by two other rebel groups seeking overthrow of regime.
12 In Iran, many injured as thousands of pro-democracy protesters took to streets of Tehran in most violent clashes since overthrow of Shah in 1979.
   In Belgium, a new coalition government of Liberals, Socialists and Greens, led by Guy Verhofstadt, took office.
14 Northern Ireland peace process effectively collapsed over Ulster Unionists' refusal to form a power-sharing executive with Sinn Féin without prior decommissioning of IRA weapons; plans for establishment of a devolved Northern Ireland government were put on hold (see 27 Nov., 2 Dec.).
   In Papua New Guinea, Sir Mekere Morauta elected as PM to replace Bill Skate.
15 New Israeli PM Ehud Barak on five-day visit to Washington for talks on Middle East peace process; he held talks in London with PM Blair on 21 July.
16 In Latvia, a new government was formed under Andris Skele, following resignation of PM Vilis Kristopans on 4 July.
   In USA, John F. Kennedy Jr, son of late President, his wife and sister-in-law, died when plane he was piloting crashed off Massachusetts (see XVIII: Obituary).
19 Syria ordered members of radical Palestinian organizations based in Damascus and Hizbullah guerrillas in southern Lebanon to end armed struggle against Israel.
22 In Belarus, thousands demonstrated against President Lukashenka, who had extended his term of office until 2001.
   Former New Zealand PM Mike Moore appointed director-general of World Trade Organization, in compromise arrangement whereby rival candidate Supachai Panitchpakdi (Thailand) would take over after three years.
23 King Hassan II of Morocco died after 32-year reign (see XVIII: Obituary); he was succeeded by his son, King Mohammed VI.
   In Kosovo, 14 Serbian farmers massacred while harvesting in village of Kracko; ethnic Albanians were believed responsible.
25 In Morocco, following funeral of King Hassan in Rabat, President Clinton, Israeli PM Barak and PLO leader Yassir Arafat held talks on Middle East peace process.
   In Venezuela, left-wing ruling coalition of President Chávez gained landslide victory in elections for constituent assembly.
26 In Switzerland, 20 died in 'canyoning' accident in flooded ravine in Interlaken.
28 In UK, PM Blair announced extensive changes to lower ranks of his government.
29 In USA, 12 died when Mark Barton went on shooting rampage in Atlanta, Georgia, before turning gun on himself.

30 Leaders of 40 nations attended summit conference in Sarajevo to discuss regeneration of Balkans, signing an ambitious Stability Pact for South-Eastern Europe.
31 UK PM Blair visited Kosovo to meet local people and British troops.

AUGUST

1 EU lifted three-year-old ban on export of British beef, imposed because of fears over BSE ('mad cow disease') (see 8 Dec.).
2 In India, some 300 died in head-on collision between two express trains in West Bengal.
4 UK Defence Secretary George Robertson named as next secretary-general of NATO, in succession to Javier Solana.
5 In China, 60 million people reported to be affected by severe flooding along Yangtse river basin; some 5.5 million feared homeless.
9 In Russia, President Yeltsin dismissed government of Sergei Stepashin and named Vladimir Putin as PM: it was fourth government he had dismissed in 17 months
  In UK, Charles Kennedy elected leader of Liberal Democrats in succession to Paddy Ashdown.
10 Indian combat planes shot down Pakistani naval jet over Arabian Sea, killing 16; India claimed Pakistan plane had violated its airspace; on 11 Aug. Pakistan opened fire on Indian fighter jets in retaliation.
  In Russian Caucasian republic of Dagestan, Islamic rebels led by Chechen warlord Shamil Basayev declared an independent Islamic state; on 25 Aug., after two weeks of fighting, Russian forces claimed to have subdued uprising.
11 An estimated two billion people witnessed a total eclipse of the sun visible over a three-hour period from Cape Cod to Bay of Bengal.
13 UN demographers said that India's population, growing at a rate of 15 million a year, had reached 1,000 million and would overtake China's within 20-30 years.
17 In north-western Turkey, some 15,000 died amid massive damage in earthquake measuring 7.4 on Richter scale.
  Preliminary US-Russian negotiations opened in Moscow on a third strategic arms reduction treaty (START-III).
25 Presidents Yeltsin and Jiang Zemin held summit talks in Bishkek, Kyrgyzstan during meeting of 'Shanghai Five' alliance (China, Russia, Kyrgyzstan, Kazakhstan and Tajikistan).
30 In East Timor referendum, voters overwhelmingly approved proposal to become independent after 24 years of Indonesian rule, and 400 years of colonial (Portuguese) domination; on 31 Aug. three UN staff killed by anti-independence militiamen as violence erupted in capital Dili.

SEPTEMBER

1 In Singapore, S.R. Nathan sworn in as President following his election in April as sole eligible candidate.
  In Panama, Mireya Moscoso (Arnulfist Party) sworn in as country's first female President following her election victory on 2 May.
4 In India, four weeks of polling began in general election; results declared on 6 October gave clear majority to alliance led by Bharatiya Janata Party headed by PM Atal Bihari Vajpayee.
  PLO leader Arafat and Israeli PM Barak signed new peace agreement, the Sharm el Shaikh Memorandum (see XVII.3), setting out 12-month timetable for ending Israel-Palestinian conflict.
5 In East Timor, anti-independence militiamen went on rampage forcing 150,000 to flee their homes.
7 In Greece, more than 60 died in earthquake in Athens area.
9 In Russia, 84 died in terrorist bomb explosion in Moscow apartment block; a further 70 died in a similar explosion on 13 Sept.

XIX CHRONICLE OF PRINCIPAL EVENTS IN 1999 603

In N. Ireland peace process, a report by commission chaired by Chris Patten proposed controversial reforms of Protestant-dominated Royal Ulster Constabulary, including a new name.
11 In UK, *The Times* named 87-year-old Melita Norwood as most important female British agent recruited by KGB, citing the 'Mitrokhin Archive' of KGB files copied by a defector and also revealing names of other alleged KGB agents; on 20 Dec. Solicitor-General ruled that Mrs Norwood should not face prosecution.
12 Indonesian government agreed to allow UN peace-keeping force into East Timor to restore order following reign of terror by anti-independence militiamen which had forced thousands from their homes in wake of 30 Aug. referendum.
15 UN Security Council adopted resolution 1264 authorizing dispatch of Australian-led peace-keeping force to East Timor; first contingent of troops arrived in Dili on 20 Sept.
16 In USA, seven died when lone gunman went on rampage in church in Fort Worth, Texas.
19 In Central African Republic, presidential polling resulted in re-election of Ange-Félix Patassé of People's Liberation Party.
21 In central Taiwan, 2,000 people died and 100,000 made homeless in earthquake measuring 7.6 on Richter scale.
23 Russia launched air-strikes against separatist rebels in Chechnya; a ground campaign by Russian troops commenced on 30 Sept.
   In Yemen, first-ever direct presidential election returned incumbent Ali Abdullah Saleh.
   OPEC Oil Ministers in Vienna agreed to maintain production cut decided in March 'until at least the end of March 2000'; world oil price had risen to $23 per barrel, from under $10 in February.
   In USA, NASA scientists lost contact with *Climate Orbiter* spacecraft about to orbit Mars; on 1 Oct. they admitted that confusion between imperial and metric measurements had caused the failure (see 7 Dec.).
26 In Egypt, referendum endorsed Husni Mubarak for fourth six-year term as President; the following month Atif al Ubayd appointed as new PM.
27 In South Africa, 27 British tourists died in coach crash near Lyndenburg.
30 In Japan, 14 workers exposed to high levels of radiation in Japan's worst nuclear accident at a uranium processing plant in Tokaimura.

OCTOBER

3 At general election in Austria, the ruling Socialists and People's Party lost ground, as far-right Freedom Party led by Jörg Haider became second-strongest party; a new coalition had not been formed by year-end.
   In UK, 31 died when two trains collided outside London's Paddington station.
7 In Mexico, 600 died and over half-a-million made homeless in mud-slides in central Puebla state.
10 In Portuguese general election, Socialist Party led by PM António Guterres re-elected for second term, but without absolute majority.
   In Kazakhstan, first round on parliamentary elections; second round on 24 Oct. confirmed dominance of presidential Fatherland Party (Otan); on 12 Oct. Kasymzhomart Tokayev approved as new PM.
11 In UK cabinet reshuffle, Peter Mandelson returned to office, replacing Mo Mowlam as Northern Ireland Secretary; Geoff Hoon became Defence Secretary, Alan Milburn Health Secretary and Andrew Smith Chief Secretary to the Treasury.
12 In Pakistan, government of Nawaz Sharif overthrown in military coup; army chief Gen. Pervez Musharraf subsequently declared himself Chief Executive Officer of Pakistan.
14 US Senate voted 51 to 48 against ratification of Comprehensive Nuclear-Test-Ban Treaty signed by President Clinton in 1996.
15 EU leaders opened two-day summit in Tampere, Finland: they discussed action to curb cross-border crime and measures on asylum-seekers.
   Nobel Peace Prize awarded to Médécins sans Frontières for its humanitarian work in wars and disasters.

16 In Botswana, presidential and parliamentary elections returned President Festus Mogae his Botswana Democratic Party for further term.
19 President Jiang Zemin began four-day state visit to UK, first-ever by a Chinese leader; visit marked by demonstrations by pro-democracy and pro-Tibet groups and by vigorous police action to contain them.
20 Indonesia's parliament elected Abdurrahman Wahid (Gus Dur), leader of National Awakening Party, as President; Megawati Sukarnoputri, winner of June elections, elected Vice-President.
22 In Chechnya, where Russian offensive had been continuing for a month, 160 died in Russian missile attack on central Grozny.

East Timorese independence leader José Xanana Gusmão received hero's welcome on return to Dili.
24 In Switzerland, parliamentary election strengthened right-wing Swiss People's Party, a member of four-party coalition in power since 1959.

In Argentina, presidential election won by Fernando de la Rúa of Radical Civic Union-National Solidarity Front (see 10 Dec.).

In Tunisia, President Ben Ali re-elected with 99 per cent of vote; his Constitutional Democratic Party again won large parliamentary majority; on 17 Nov. Mohammed Ghannouchi sworn in as new PM.
26 In UK, House of Lords voted overwhelmingly in favour of government bill to end voting rights of hereditary peers after 800 years.
27 In Armenia, PM Vazgen Sarkisian and seven others died when gunmen opened fire inside parliament building (see 1 Nov.).
29 In India, thousands died in a cyclone in Orissa on east coast, the country's worst natural disaster this century.

In Chechnya, President Aslan Maskhadov said that over 3,000 had died since start of Russian offensive in September.

In Albania, Ilir Meta appointed PM to replace Pandeli Majko, who had resigned after failing to be elected leader of ruling Socialist Party.
31 In USA, 217 died when Egypt Air Boeing 767 crashed into Atlantic off Nantucket.

Indonesia withdrew its last troops from East Timor, ending 24 years of military occupation.

NOVEMBER

2 Aram Sarkisian appointed PM of Armenia in succession to his elder brother assassinated on 27 Oct.

Pope John Paul II arrived in Delhi at start of his second visit to India.
3 In Lithuania, Andrius Kubilius (Conservative) replaced Rolandas Paksas as PM.
6 Australians voted in a referendum to reject a proposal that the country should end its links with the British monarchy and become a republic.

In Tajikistan, Imamali Rakhmanov re-elected President almost unopposed.
8 Queen Elizabeth II on two-day state visit to Ghana, later visiting South Africa and Mozambique.
9 In UK, Chancellor of Exchequer delivered autumn economic statement: he promised a crackdown on the £50,000 million black economy and free TV licences for over-75s.

In Indonesia, one million people took part in rally demanding a referendum on independence for northern province of Aceh.

In Germany, celebrations were held in Berlin to mark tenth anniversary of dismantling of the Wall.
11 In UK, hereditary peers sat in House of Lords for last time before prorogation of parliament and granting of royal assent to House of Lords Reform Bill.
12 Four-day Commonwealth Heads of Government Meeting (CHOGM) opened in Durban, South Africa; Don McKinnon, former Foreign Minister of New Zealand, elected new Commonwealth secretary-general; CHOGM confirmed suspension of Pakistan in wake of military coup; Nigeria readmitted to membership.

In north-western Turkey, some 700 died in another earthquake, measuring 7.2 on Richter scale, centred on Düzce.
In northern Kosovo, a UN aid plane crashed, killing 24.
14 In Ukraine, President Leonid Kuchma re-elected for second term.
In Georgia, completion of parliamentary election gave further majority to Citizens' Union of Georgia led by President Shevardnadze.
UN Security Council imposed limited sanctions on Afghanistan for its refusal to deliver Afghanistan-based Islamic militant Osama bin Laden to US authorities for trial on terrorism charges.
President Clinton arrived in Ankara at start of 10-day tour of eastern Mediterranean countries.
15 China and USA concluded a deal paving way for China's admission to World Trade Organization.
16 In N. Ireland peace process, after 11 weeks of talks chaired by former US Senator George Mitchell, Sinn Féin leader Gerry Adams pledged total opposition to use of violence for political purposes (see 27 Nov., 2 Dec.).
17 In UK, state opening of parliament: Queen's Speech foreshadowed over 30 bills including new measures on crime, racial discrimination, welfare, transport and freedom of information.
18 Representatives of 54 countries, attending a two-day summit conference of OSCE in Istanbul, denounced Russian bombing of Chechnya.
Pakistan's former PM Nawaz Sharif charged with treason, conspiracy to murder and hijacking
19 In Greece, Athens police fired tear gas to disperse left-wing demonstrators opposed to visit by President Clinton.
20 A weekend 'Third Way' conference of centre-left leaders was held in Florence, Italy, attended by President Clinton, UK PM Blair, German Chancellor Gerhard Schröder and French PM Lionel Jospin.
21 In UK, Lord (Jeffrey) Archer withdrew from forthcoming election for mayor of London after new revelations of deception relating to a 1987 libel trial (see AR 1987, pp. 449, 587).
22 Royal Ulster Constabulary awarded George Cross (Britain's highest award for gallantry) for 30 years of fighting terrorism in N. Ireland.
24 In Niger, presidential election won by Mamadou Tandja of National Movement for a Development Society.
25 UK-French summit held in London: a joint declaration included proposals for setting up European-only rapid deployment force.
In UK by-election, former Conservative cabinet minister Michael Portillo elected MP for Kensington & Chelsea.
27 Ulster Unionist Party agreed to admit Sinn Féin to new N. Ireland devolved government without prior decommissioning of IRA weapons; talks on disarmament would continue (see 2 Dec.).
28 At New Zealand general election, Labour Party defeated ruling National Party and later formed minority coalition with Alliance with Helen Clark as PM.
In Uruguay, presidential election won by Jorge Batlle of ruling Colorado Party; his father had been President in 1948.
In Guinea-Bissau, opposition Social Renewal Party (PRS) won parliamentary election and PRS leader Kumba Yalla headed first round of presidential poll (to be decided in Jan. 2000).
In Chechnya, 500 deaths reported in three days of intensive bombardment of Grozny by Russian troops.
In Spain, Basque separatist ETA announced that its 14-month ceasefire would end on 3 Dec.
In UK, man wielding sword ran amok in south London church, wounding 11 worshippers.
29 In Malaysian general election, ruling National Front gained convincing victory; its leader, Mahathir Mohamad, in office for 18 years, returned for further five-year term as PM.
30 Delegates from 130 countries attended four-day summit of World Trade Organization in Seattle, USA; severely disrupted by demonstrators, the conference ended in failure, with delegates unable to reach agreement on agenda for further talks.

DECEMBER

1   In Namibia, ruling SWAPO led by Sam Nujoma gained landslide victory in Namibia's second post-independence election.
     In UK, Royal Opera House, Covent Garden, reopened after three-year renovation, costing £214 million.
2   In N. Ireland, new power-sharing devolved government, led by David Trimble as First Minister, took office at Stormont; Republic of Ireland amended its constitution to end its territorial claim to province, maintained since 1937.
3   Cypriot President Glafkos Clerides and Turkish Cypriot leader Rauf Denktash met in New York for UN-sponsored 'proximity' talks.
5   In Macedonia, re-run second round of presidential election (after disputed poll on 14 Nov. and first round on 31 Oct.) gave victory to Boris Trajkovski of nationalist VMRO-DPMNE, who was inaugurated on 15 Dec.
     In Uzbekistan, ruling People's Democratic Party remained largest single party in parliamentary election.
6   Russia gave inhabitants of Chechen capital Grozny ultimatum to leave via safe corridor within five days pending final assault on city.
7   In USA, NASA scientists abandoned hope of re-establishing contact with *Polar Lander* probe to Mars, lost on 3 Dec. as spacecraft approached planet.
8   France announced that it would not lift its ban on British beef without further guarantees over safety.
10   In Croatia, President Franjo Tudjman died at age of 77 (see XVIII: Obituary).
     Chechen President Maskhadov left Grozny for his own safety: the city was surrounded by 100,000 Russian troops.
     Two-day EU summit opened in Helsiniki: it decided to begin membership negotiations with a further six countries; Turkey assigned status of candidate.
     In Argentina, Fernando de la Rua inaugurated as President in succession to Carlos Menem.
12   Maltese tanker *Erika* split in two in Bay of Biscay spilling 12,000 tonnes of oil off Brittany coast, causing extensive environmental damage.
     In Turkmenistan, ruling Democratic Party of President Niyazov won all seats in parliamentary election.
13   In N. Ireland, inaugural session of North-South Ministerial Council, attended by delegates from Ulster and Irish Republic, was held in Armagh.
14   In Panama, ceremonies were held to mark handover of Panama Canal, which had been controlled by USA since its opening in 1914 (see AR 1977, p. 65).
15   In Chechnya, more than 100 Russian troops reported dead in fighting as Russian tanks advanced on capital Grozny.
     In Romania, President Constantinescu dismissed PM Radu Vasile, who was replaced by Mugur Isarescu.
     Israeli PM Barak and Syrian Foreign Minister Faruq al-Shara attended talks in Washington, hosted by President Clinton, on Middle East peace process.
16   In Venezuela, some 50,000 died in flash floods and mud-slides along the Caribbean coast.
19   In Russia, 100 million were eligible to vote in third parliamentary elections since collapse of communism; Communist Party narrowly remained largest formation but lost control of Duma to centre-right groupings led by Kremlin-backed Unity movement.
     Macao returned to Chinese rule after 442 years as Portuguese colony.
21   In Sri Lanka, Chandrika Kumaratunga re-elected President for second term: she had survived assassination attempt on 18 Dec.
     In UK, former Conservative MP Neil Hamilton lost a libel action against Mohamed al-Fayed arising from 1997 'cash for questions' parliamentary scandal.
     Mozambique held presidential and parliamentary elections: Joaquim Chissano was re-elected President and Frelimo retained Assembly majority.
22   In UK, four died when South Korean Boeing 747 cargo jet crashed near Stansted airport.

23 In Côte d'Ivoire, President Konan Bédié overthrown in military coup; Gen. Robert Guei suspended constitution and assumed power on 25 Dec.
24 Grand Duke Jean of Luxembourg announced that he would abdicate in 2000 in favour of his son Prince Henri.
  Indian Airlines Airbus 300, with 187 people aboard, hijacked on flight from Kathmandu to New Delhi by Kashmiri Muslim militants who murdered one passenger; week-long siege at Kandahar airport in Afghanistan ended on 31 Dec. following release of three Kashmiri militants from Indian gaol.
26 In Guatemala, right-wing Guatemalan Republican Front candidate Alfonso Portillo gained decisive victory in presidential election.
  France was hit by two days of violent storms in which 87 died; 3.5 million homes were without power and an estimated 270 million trees were lost.
29 In Germany, Bonn public prosecutor opened criminal investigation of former Chancellor Helmut Kohl following disclosure of illegal financial donations to Christian Democratic Union under his leadership.
31 In Russia, Boris Yeltsin unexpectedly resigned as President, naming PM Vladimir Putin acting President pending elections in March 2000.
  In Indonesia's northern Molucca Islands, more than 300 reported dead in week of Christian-Muslim ethnic violence.
  Millions gathered in towns and cities around the world to view spectacular fireworks displays celebrating the advent of the new millennium; in UK, Queen Elizabeth opened the £758 million Millennium Dome at Greenwich, south-east London.

INDEX

Page references in bold indicate location of main coverage.

Abacha, Gen. Sani, 257, 261
Abdelaziz, Mohammed, 244
Abdelaziz bin Abdullah al-Sheikh, Shaikh, 227
Abdildin, Serikbolsyn, 309
Abdic, Fikret, 133
Abdul Aziz Shah, Salahuddin, Sultan of Selangor, 342, 598
Abdulaziz bin Baz, Shaikh, 227
Abdullah II, King of Jordan, 210, 211, 216, 217, 220, 580, 595, 599
Abdullah ibn Abdul Aziz, Crown Prince, of Saudi Arabia, 225, 226, 227
Abeid, Lt.-Col. Said, 336, 337
Abeles, Sir Peter, 383
Aberchan, Mustafa, 92
Abse, Dannie, 532
Abu Dhabi, 229
Abu Musa & Tunbs Islands, 233, 303, 446, 447
Abubakar, Harune, 257
Acharya, Mahesh, 328
Ackroyd, Peter, 532
Acosta, Carlos, 508
Acosta, Jorge, 175
Adamkus, Valdas, 113, 115
Adams, Gerry, 51, 52, 605
Adams, John, 505
Adams, Jonathan, 526
Adams, R.J.Q., 533
Adeane, Sir Michael, 571
Adoboli, Eugène Koffi, 263
Afewerki, Issaias, 235, 245, 448
Afghanistan, 2, 3, 33, **304-7**, 311, 313, 319, 324, 402, 423, 437, 595
African Economic Community (EAC), 449
African Organizations & Conferences, 447-51
Agassi, Andre, 542, 601
Agathe, Berger, 334
Ahern, Bertie, 71, 72, 597
Ahmed, Shahabuddin, 324, 326
Aho, Esko, 82
Ahtisaari, Martti, 80, 81, 140, 431, 432, 544, 600
AIDS/HIV, 62, 285, 286, 289, 291, 292, 293, 294-5, 296, 298, 469, 478-9
Air Afrique, 451
Aishworya, Queen, 329
Aitken, Jonathan, 23, 600
Akashi, Yasushi, 369
Akayev, Askar, 308, 313

Akihito, Emperor Tsugu no Miya, 368
Akilov, Akil, 308, 310
Alanis of Urgel, Bishop Joan Martí, 88
Alatas, Ali, 347, 348
Albania, 5, 64, **128-31**, 140, 416, 431, 439, 603
Albar, Hamid, 343
Albert II, King of Belgium, 67, 68
Alberti, Rafael, 531, 567 (obit.)
Albright, Madeleine K., 115, 193, 210, 212, 219, 223, 351, 375, 452, 565
Alden, 498
Alegrett, Sebastián, 455
Alemán Lacayo, Arnaldo, 190, 192
Alexander, Lamar, 160
Alexis, Jacques Édouard, 189
Alexis of Moscow, Patriarch, 462
Algeria, 2, 35, 62, **240-2**, 243-4, 277, 298, 432, 447, 597
Ali, Amina Salum, 252
Ali, Muhammad, 537, 543
Alier, Abel, 234
Aliyev, Geidar, 152, 153
Allen, David, 203
Allen, Jim, 531
Allende, Salvador, 180, 591
Alley, Ronald, 524
Alliance of Small Island States (AOSIS), 455
Alliot-Marie, Michèle, 60
Almodovar, Pedro, 515
Almunia, Joaquín, 91
Alsop, Will, 527
Altanhuyag, Norovyn, 377
Alvares, Elcio, 178
Alvarez, Aida, 565
Alvarez Cascos, Francisco, 91
Amadou, Hama, 263, 270
Amamou, Mohammed, 444
Amarjargal, Rinchinnyamyn, 376, 377, 378
Amato, Giuliano, 65
Amazon rain forest, 482
American & Carribbean Organizations, 455-8
Amin, Idi, 588
Amnesty International, 268, 416
Amoako, K.Y., 449
Amor, Mohammed Belhaj, 239
Amour, Salmin, 250, 251
Andean Community of Nations (CA/Ancom), 455, 457
ANZUS Pact, 404

Anderson, John, 382
Anderton, Jim, 386
Andorra, 88-9
Andrade, Alberto, 185
Andreotti, Giulio, 66
Andrew, Christopher, 28
Andrew, Prince, 17
Andrews, David, 52, 74
Andrianarivo, Tantely, 338
Andriessen, Louis, 503, 504
Andropov, Yuri, 571
Angola, 2, 273, 275, **283-5**, 286, 290, 295, 298, 299, 393, 399, 402, 418, 470, 594
Anguilla, 202, 203, 458
Aniashvalli, Nina, 508
Annan, Kofi, 104, 313, 347, 352, 393, 394, 396, 397, 402, 416, 421
Ansanelli, Alexandra, 507
Antarctica, 481
Anthony, Kenny, 200, 201
Antigua & Barbuda, 200-1, 415, 595
Antrobus, Charles James, 200
Anwar, Saeed, 537
Anwar Ibrahim, 343, 350, 452, 598
Anyaoku, Chief Emeka, 413, 414
Apotheker, Haijo, 70
Aquino, Corazon, 349
Arab League, 224, 247, 336, **444-6**
Arab Maghreb Union (AMU), 240, **444, 447**
Arab States of the Gulf, 217, 224, **229-34**, 446
Arab World, 211-4
Arafat, Suha, 161
Arafat, Yassir, 3, 78, 170, 208, 210, 211, 212, 213, 214, 217, 222, 224, 242, 580, 601, 602
Aragona, Giancarlo, 435
Arbour, Louise, 487
Archer of Weston-super-Mare, Lord (Jeffrey), 19, 20, 21, 27, 605
Archer, Mary, 21
Architecture, 525-8
Arctic Council, 440, 441
Arenas, Javier, 91
Argaña, Nelson, 184
Argaña Ferraro, Luís María, 183
Argentina, 14, **175-7**, 184, 393, 396, 420, 456, 457, 603, 605
Arias, Arnulfo, 193
Arias Mendoza, Rubén, 183
Aris, Michael, 339
Arizaga, Alfredo, 183
Armenia, 152, 153, 423-4, 434, 437, 489, 598, 603
Armijos, Ana Lucia, 183
Arms Control, see Defence, Disarmament & Security
Armstrong, Hilary, 564
Armstrong, Lance, 543
Arnold, Bruce Jack, 533
Art, see Visual Arts

Arthur, Owen, 197, 595
Aruba, 205, 206
Arzilli, Giuseppe, 88
Arzú Irigoyen, Alvaro, 190
Asad, Bashar al-, 219
Asad, Hafiz al-, 210, 216, 219, 220
Asad, Rifa'at al-, 219
Åsbrink, Erik, 79
Ashbook, Larry Gener, 165
Ashcroft, Michael, 23
Ashdown, Paddy, 24, 602
Ashi Dorji Wangmo Wangchuk, Queen, 330
Ashley, Tim, 506
Asia-Pacific Economic Cooperation (APEC), 170, 361-2, 387, 451, **453-4**
Asia-Pacific Organizations, 451-5
Asian Development Bank (ADB), 454
Asian Economic Recovery, 14, 452
Asmal, Kader, 300
Asrat Woldeyes, Prof., 247
Association of Caribbean States (ACS), 456
Association of South-East Asian Nations (ASEAN), 325, 339, 340, 345, 351, 353, 375, 404, **451, 452-5**
Assoumani, Col. Azili, 335, 336, 337, 598
Asylmuratova, Altynai, 508
Atatürk, Kemal, 107
Atopare, Sir Sailas, 383
AttaMills, John, 255
Attenborough, Michael, 512
Aubry, Martine, 59
Aukuso, Toi, 390
Aura, Matti, 81
Australia, 39, 312, **379-83**, 384, 389, 397, 404, 414, 415, 418, 420, 453, 454, 461, 463, 468, 479, 487, 537, 538, 541, 542, 568, 592-4, 603
Austria, 82-4, 120, 424, 429, 434, 443, 459, 522, 595, 602
Avery, Bryan, 527
Axtaga, Bernard, 532
Axworthy, Lloyd, 174, 175, 414
Ayala Lasso, José, 183
Aydid, Hussein, 246, 248
Ayu, Chief Iyorchia, 257
Azerbaijan, 152, 153, 304, 423-4, 434, 437, 439, 489
Aznar López, José María, 91, 93, 94, 429

Baasan, Lama, 377
Babbitt, Bruce, 565
Babiuch, Jolanta, 464
Baburin, Sergei, 115
Bacall, Lauren, 512
Baccar, Tawfik, 239
Bach, J.S., 503
Badawi, Abdullah Ahmad, 343
Bagabandi, Natsagiyn, 376, 377
Bahamas, The, 199
Bahçeli, Devlet, 107

Bahrain, 230, 232, 233, 393, 579, 595
Bail, Murray, 528
Bailey, Kathryn, 506
Baily, Martin N., 565
Bainbridge, Simon, 503
Bakhius-Trinidad, Josephine, 205
Balaguer Ricardo, Joaquín, 190
Balanchine, George, 506, 507
Balcerowicz, Leszek, 111
Balgimbayev, Nurlan, 310
Ball, Colin, 415
Ballet & Dance, 506-9
Baltic Council/Assembly, 439, 440
Bananas, 1, 201-2, 413, 458, 480-1
Band, Tamasaburo, 508
Banda, Dr Hastings, 286
Bandaranaike, Sirimavo, 331
Bandelj, Mirko, 137
Bangladesh, 232, 320, **324-7**, 393, 414, 415, 424
Bani, Fr John, 389, 391, 597
Banzer Suárez, Hugo, 177
Bao Tong, 356
Barak, Ehud, 3, 78, 170, 171, 207, 208, 209, 210, 211, 212, 213, 214, 217, 219, 242, 599, 601, 602, 606
Baranczak, Stanislaw, 532
Barbados, 198, 415, 458, 584, 594
Barbaso, Fabrizio, 129
Barber, Elizabeth Wayland, 533
Barber, Samuel, 505
Bardot, Brigitte, 568
Barents Euro-Arctic Region (BEAR), 441
Barfield, Julia, 526
Barker, A.L., 532
Barnes, Dame Josephine, 567 (obit.)
Barrault, Jean-Louis, 590
Barrett, Andrea, 532
Basque question, 92-3
Barshefsky, Charlene, 359, 565
Bartok, Béla, 585
Barton, Mark, 601
Baryshnikov, Mikhail, 508
Basayev, Shamil, 146, 602
Bashir, Omar Hasan Ahmed al-, 234
Basri, Driss, 243, 244
Basuta, Manjit, 164
Bates, Alan, 512
Batlle Ibáñez, Jorge, 186, 605
Battle, John, 564
Bausch, Pina, 506
Bayartsogt, Sangajavyn, 377
Baykal, Deniz, 107
Bayley, John, 587
Baylis, Matthew, 532
Baytchev, Vassil, 442
Bayyati, Abdel Wahab al-, 531
Baz, Usama al, 215
Beache, Vincent, 202
Beatrix, Queen of the Netherlands, 69

Beatty, Laura, 533
Beckett, Margaret, 17, 564
Bédié, Henri Konan, 266, 267, 607
Bedser, Alec, 575
Beer, Patricia, 531
Beethoven, Ludwig van, 503, 506
Begin, Benny, 207, 209
Begin, Menachem, 570
Begley, Kim, 501, 502
Beilin, Yossi, 210
Belarus, 13, 130, 147, **149-50**, 396, 434, 437, 596, 600
Belgium, 67-8, 201, 424, 536, 599, 600
Belize, 23, 198
Beloff, Lord (Max), 567 (obit.)
Bemba, Jean-Pierre, 275
Ben Ali, Zayn al-Abdin, 238, 239, 240, 604
Ben Ami, Shlomo, 210
Ben Yahya, Habib, 239
Benaissa, Mohammed, 243
Benbitour, Ahmed, 240, 241
Benda, Václav, 568 (obit.)
Bendtsen, Bendt, 75
Benigni, Roberto, 515
Benin, 263, 269, 596
Benn, Hilary, 22
Benn, Tony, 22
Bennett, Alan, 530
Benton, Mark, 165
Berg, Alban, 503
Berger, Samuel D., 565
Berger Perdomo, Oscar, 191
Berisha, Sali, 131
Berlioz, Hector, 506
Berlusconi, Silvio, 65, 66
Bermuda, 202, 203
Berne, Suzanne, 528
Bernstein, Leonard, 504
Berry, Shawn Allen, 163
Berzins, Indulis, 115
Bessette, Lauren, 155
Bevan, Michael, 538
Bhagwat, Adm. Vishnu, 315
Bhattarai, Krishna Prasad, 327, 328, 329, 599
Bhumibol Adulyadej (Rama IX), King of Thailand, 340, 341
Bhutan, 330-1
Bhutto, Benazir, 321, 322, 323, 598
Bicakcic, Edhem, 131
Biernacki, Marek, 112
Bignone, Gen. Reynaldo, 175
Bildt, Carl, 80
bin Laden, Osama, 162, 215, 306, 402, 605
Bird, Lester, 199, 200, 596
Bird, Sir Vere, 201
Bird, Vere, Jr, 200
Birendra Bir Bikram Shah Deva, King of Nepal, 327, 329
Birt, Sir John, 518
Bishara, Azmi, 207, 208, 209

INDEX

Bishton, Jamie, 507
Biwott, Nicholas, 249
Biya, Paul, 270, 272
Bizet, Georges, 509
Bizimungu, Pasteur, 278
Black Sea Economic Cooperation Organization (BSECO), 442, 443-4
Blackburn, Julia, 532
Blacker, Harry, 524
Blackmun, Harry, 568 (obit.)
Blackstone, Baroness, 564
Blades, James, 506, 568 (obit.)
Blair, Cherie, 20
Blair, Tony, domestic affairs, 16, 20, 22, 24, 25, 26, 29, 36, 51, 479, 518, 535, 564, 596, 597, 601; external relations, 41, 72, 168, 208, 329, 361, 408, 409, 429, 564, 598, 599, 601, 605
Blakely, Rev. Keith, 166
Bland, Sir Christopher, 518
Blech, Harry, 506
Blobel, Günther, 471
Blocher, Christoph, 85, 86, 87
Blochwitz, Hans-Peter, 502
Bluhm, Norman, 524
Blumberg, Barruch, 466
Blumenthal, Sidney, 158
Blunkett, David, 564
Boateng, Paul, 564
Boatswain, Anthony, 199
Bogarde, Sir Dirk, 517, 531, 568 (obit.)
Boito, Arrigo, 501
Bojars, Juris, 114
Bol, Kerubino Kuanyin, 234
Bolger, Jim, 385
Bolivia, 177, 182
Bolkiah, Sir Hassanal, Sultan of Brunei, 344
Bollini, Marino, 88
Bondevik, Kjell Magne, 77, 78
Bongo, Omar, 271, 272, 273
Bonino, Emma, 65
Bonner, Neville, 383
Bonnet, Bernard, 62
Booker Prize, 528
Booth, Mark, 518
Booth, Martin, 533
Borneo, 349
Borrell, Josep, 91
Bosnia & Hercegovina, 70, 80, 84, **131-4**, 134, 174, 399, 400, 434, 439, 486
Botswana, 9, 277, **290, 291-2**, 293, 415, 484, 603
Botticelli, Sandro, 89
Bouchard, Lucien, 173
Bouchier, Chili, 517, 569 (obit.)
Bougainville, 384
Boulez, Pierre, 505
Boungnang Volachit, 353
Bourdeaux, Michael, 464
Bourne, Nick, 48

Bouteflika, Abdulaziz, 240, 241, 242, 448, 598
Boutros-Ghali, Boutros, 416, 417
Bower Montalto, Walter, 184
Bowles, Paul, 531
Boyd, Arthur, 383, 569 (obit.)
Boyd, Michael, 512
Boyden, Matthew, 506
Boyea, Ken, 202
Brabbins, Martyn, 503
Brack, John, 383
Bracks, Steve, 381
Bradley, Bill, 160, 162
Brady, Joan, 532
Braghis, Dumitru, 149, 151
Bramble, Percival Austin, 204
Brandt, David, 202, 204
Brazil, 13, 14, 98, 177, **178-9**, 181, 184, 393, 396, 418, 420, 456, 457, 477, 534, 535, 594
Brdjanin, Radislav, 133
Brewer, Lawrence, 163
Brezhnev, Leonid, 571
Brezzo, Luis, 186
Brinkhorst, Laurens Jan, 70
British Virgin Islands, 202, 203, 458
Brittain, Victoria, 533
Britten, Benjamin, 502, 568, 585
Brizuela de Avila, María Eugenia, 192
Broadcasting, see Television & Radio
Broaddrick, Juanita, 158
Broakes, Sir Nigel, 569 (obit.)
Brookner, Anita, 532
Brown, Charlie, 156
Brown, George, 589
Brown, Gordon, 12, 25, 36, 37 411, 519, 564
Brown, Nick, 41, 564
Brown, Paul, 502
Brown, Steve, 513
Browner, Carol, 565
Bruce, Christopher, 507, 509
Brunei, 344, 452, 453
BSE (bovine spongiform encephalopathy), 40, 470
Buchanan, Pat, 160
Buffet, Bernard, 524, 570 (obit.)
Buhari, Alhaji, 257
Bulatovic, Momir, 138
Bulgaria, 98, 105, **126-8**, 136, 430, 443
Bulger, James, 488
Bulwer-Lytton, Edward, 511
Bunwaree, Vasant, 334
Burckhardt, Rudy, 524
Burford, Earl of, 18
Burg, Josef, 570 (obit.)
Burgess, Anthony, 583
Burkina Faso, 263, 268, 422
Burma, see Myanmar
Burnside, John, 532
Burrow, Sharan, 382
Burundi, 275, **278-9**, 393, 484
Busch, Fritz, 585

Busch, Gary, 163
Bush, George, 159, 179
Bush, George W., 159, 160, 162, 600
Busoni, Ferrucio, 504
Bustamante Belaúnde, Alberto, 184, 185
Buthelezi, Chief Mangosuthu, 297
Butler, Richard, 223
Buyoya, Pierre, 278
Buzek, Jerzy, 110, 111
Byambajargal, Losolyn, 377
Byers, Sir Maurice, 383
Byers, Stephen, 519, 520, 564
Byrd, James, 163
Byrne, David, 74

Cabral, Pedro Alvares, 98, 418
Cadogan, Gary, 534
Caird, John, 511
Cairns, David, 506
Callahan, John F., 528
Callas, Maria, 503
Callow, Simon, 533
Câmara, Dom Hélder, 178
Cambodia, 352-3, 452, 453
Camdessus, Michel, 178, 410, 411
Camelia-Römer, Susanne, 205
Cameron, James, 514
Cameron, Jamie, 533
Cameroon, 270, 272, 417, 450, 486
Campaoré, Blaise, 422
Campbell, James, 533
Canada, 15, 50, 114, **171-5**, 196, 236, 393, 402, 413, 414, 415, 416, 417, 420, 442, 453, 456, 472, 516, 596
Canavan, Denis, 43
Canterbury, Archbishop of, 223, 234
Cape Verde, 280, 281
Caprivi Strip, 294, 295
Cárdenas Solórzano, Cuauhtémoc, 194
Cardoso, Fernando Henrique, 177, 178
Caribbean Community (Caricom), 456, 458
Carl XVI Gustav, King of Sweden, 79
Carlisle, Sir James B., 199
Carlos Rios, Juan, 185
Caro, Sir Anthony, 524
Caroline of Monaco, Princess, 90
Carrington, Edwin, 456, 458
Carson, Anne, 532
Carter, Elliott, 503
Carter, Jimmy, 193, 320, 589
Carter, Jonathan Erik, 166
Caruana, Peter, 94, 95
Carvalhas, Carlos, 96
Cassidy, Cardinal Edward, 459, 462
Casson, Sir Hugh, 524, 527, 570 (obit.)
Castañeda Lossio, Luis, 185
Castelli, Leo, 524, 570 (obit.)
Castillo, Oscar, 176
Castro Ruz, Fidel, 94, 188, 457

Cauchi, Bishop Nikol, 98
Caushi, Myrteza, 130
Cavallo, Domingo Felipe, 176
Cavanagh, Clare, 532
Cayman Islands, 203-4, 415
Cegielska, Franciszka, 111
Cem, Ismail, 101, 105
Central African Republic, 266, **271, 273**, 400, 450, 602
Central Asian Economic Union (CAEU), 314
Central Asian Republics, 308-14, 437
Central European Free Trade Association (CEFTA), 442
Central European Initiative (CEI), 442, 443
Cernak, Ludovit, 120
César, 524
Çetin, Himet, 303
Ceuta and Melilla, 92-3
Chad, 2, 236, **270, 271-2**, 424
Chakwanda, Gwanda, 287
Chamberlain, Dwain, 536
Chamberlain, Wilt, 571 (obit.)
Chamoiseau, Patrick, 529, 532
Chan, Anson, 363
Chan, Julius, 383
Chand, Lokendra Bahadur, 327
Chandler, Chris, 543
Chaouch, Ali, 239
Chaovalit Yongchaiyudh, 341
Chardin, Jean-Baptiste-Siméon, 524
Charles, Prince, see Wales, Prince of
Charles II, King, 18
Charnock, Job, 321
Charteris of Amisfield, 571 (obit.)
Chaucer, Geoffrey, 509
Chaudhry, Mahendra, 387, 389, 599
Chaudhuri, Nirad C., 321, 531, 571 (obit.)
Chávez Frias, Hugo, 186, 187, 196, 601
Chavunduka, Mark, 288
Chebrikov, Viktor, 571 (obit.)
Chechnya, 1, 4, 13, 58, 116, 144, 145, 146 (*map*), 147, 171, 432, 433, 435
Chee Soon Juan, 345
Chen Kaige, 516
Chen Shui-bian, 367
Chernenko, Konstantin, 571
Chernomyrdin, Viktor, 140, 145, 432, 598, 600
Cheuang Sombounekhanh, 353
Chi Haotian, 356, 374
Chidgey, Catherine, 529, 532
Chidyausiku, Judge Godfrey, 288
Chile, 14, 25, 40, 93-4, 177, **179-80**, 456, 457, 465, 534, 590-2
Chiluba, Frederick, 275, 285, 450
China, 354-62; cinema, 516; economy & society, 8, 10, 14-5, 356-9; external relations, 39-40, 84, 147, 169-70, 223, 277, 305, 311-2, 313, 315, 319, 320, 325, 329, 345, 350, 351, 353, 359-62, 366-7, 370, 373,

374, 375, 378, 380, 383, 387, 390, 399, 404, 419, 420, 421, 452, 453, 454; Falun Gong, 354, 355, 464; Hong Kong, 363-5; human rights, 7, 39; information technology, 472-3, 474; Kosovo conflict, 5, 6, 140, 169, 360, 361, 398, 453; Macao, 7, 97, 362, 418; population, 321, 358; science, 468, 471; WTO, 1, 170, 355, 361, 413
Chino, Tadeo, 454
Chirac, Jacques, 59, 60, 61, 63, 88, 93, 242, 267, 268, 361, 408, 409, 416, 417, 426, 429, 430
Chissano, Joaquim Alberto, 282, 283, 606
Cho Seong Tae, 374
Choi Sung Hong, 374
Choinquitel, Virginia, 180
Chrétien, Jean, 171, 172, 173, 417
Christensen, Søren, 439
Christie, Linford, 534
Chronicle of 1999, 594-606
Chuan Leekpai, 340, 341, 342
Chygir, Mikhas, 149, 150
Ciampi, Carlo Azeglio, 63, 65, 66, 411, 599
Çiller, Tansu, 107
Cinema, 514-7
Ciroma, Adamu, 257
Ciubuc, Ion, 151
Claes, Willy, 67
Clanchy, Kate, 532
Clark, Alan, 26, 572 (obit.)
Clark, Helen, 385, 386, 605
Clark, Joe, 172
Clark, Lord (Kenneth), 572
Clark, Gen. Wesley, 138
Clarke, Charles, 564
Clarke, Geoff, 381
Clarke, Kenneth, 24
Clarkson, Adrienne, 171, 172
Clerides, Glafkos, 103, 104, 105, 106, 606
Clerides, Takis, 106
Clinton, Bill, domestic affairs, 154, 156-7, 159, 161, 162, 163, 165, 166, 167, 168, 565; external relations, 1, 4, 51, 64, 78, 102, 105, 109, 126, 137, 147, 168-71, 186, 188, 191, 193, 194, 206, 208, 211, 216, 219, 242, 307, 320, 323, 360, 369, 387, 453, 361, 453, 598, 600, 601, 603, 605, 606; impeachment, 4, 154, 156, 157-8, 595, 596
Clinton, Hilary Rodham, 161
Cockerell, Sir Christopher, 572 (obit.)
Codett, Anthony, 205
Coetzee, J.M., 528, 532
Cohen, William S., 141, 169, 233, 565
Colker, Deborah, 508
Colom Caballeros, Alvaro, 191
Colombia, 14, **181-2**, 186, 193, 457, 594
Colt, Sam, 166
Combs, Sean ('Puff Daddy'), 166
Common Market for Eastern & Southern Africa (COMESA), 251, **448, 450**
Commonwealth of Independent States (CIS), 147, 153, 310, 311, 404
Commonwealth, The, 39, 204, 251, 293, 301, 322, **413-5**, 416, 417, 604
Community of Portuguese-Speaking Countries (CPLP), 98, **417-8**
Comoros, 335, 336-7, 449
Compaoré, Blaise, 263, 268
Compaoré, François, 268
Condé, Alpha, 265, 266
Condon, Sir Paul, 31, 33
Conference on Cooperation and Confidence-Building Measures (CCCBMA), 314
Congo, Democratic Republic of the, 2, 235, 238, 253, **275-7**, 279, 285, 289, 290, 299, 300, 399, 401, 449, 484, 594, 600
Congo, Republic of, 2, **271**, **272-3**, 449, 450, 534
Conn, Stewart, 532
Connor, Joseph, 395
Constable, John, 523
Constantine, ex-King, 588
Constantinescu, Emil, 123, 124, 606
Conté, Lansana, 261, 262, 266
Contreras Sepúlveda, Gen. (retd) Manuel, 180
Cook Islands, **390-1**
Cook, Robin, 27, 40, 94, 393, 394, 564
Cooke, Alistair, 539
Cooke, Sir Howard, 195
Cooper, Adam, 508
Cooper, Gary, 591
Cope, Jim, 383
Copland, Aaron, 505
Corder, Michael, 508
Corella, Angel, 508
Corigliano, John, 505
Cornwell, John, 89, 464
Corsica, 62, 90
Cort, Errol, 200
Cosgrove, Maj.-Gen. Peter, 380
Cossiga, Francesco, 64, 67
Cossutta, Armando, 64
Costa Rica, 191, 193, 457
Côte d'Ivoire, **262**, 264, **266-8**, 450, 606
Cotti, Flavio, 86
Coulibaly, Gen. Abdoulaye, 267
Coulthard, David, 540
Council of Europe, 84, **433-4**, 439, 443, 468
Council of the Baltic Sea States (CBSS), **440, 441**
Couve de Murville, Maurice, 572 (obit.)
Cova, Errol, 205
Coward, Noël, 512
Cox, Archibald, 589
Cox, Morrel, 201
Cox, Pat, 74
Cozma, Miron, 123

Craborn, Richard, 564
Crace, Jim, 532
Cranston, Ross, 565
Crawford, Robert, 532
Craxi, Bettino, 66
Cresson, Edith, 427
Crimea, 437
Croatia, 134-5, 137-8, 484, 486, 591-3, 605
Croft, Richard, 502
Cronje, Hansie, 538
Crossman, R.H.S., 586
Cuba, 93, 94, 184, **189-90**, 421, 457, 474
Cubas Grau, Carlos, 183
Cubas Grau, Raúl, 183, 184, 597
Cubie, Andrew, 43
Cumuraswamy, 485
Cunningham, Jack, 26
Cunningham, Merce, 508
Cuomo, Andrew M., 565
Curran, Tony, 511
Curtis, Richard, 515
Curuvija, Slavko, 140
Cyprus, 102, **103-6**, 108, 109, 171, 400, 430-1, 442, 605
Czech Republic, 5, 13, 33, 105, **117-8**, 120, 405, 430, 442, 443, 516, 536, 567

da Costa, Guilherme Posser, 280, 282
da Silva, Afonso da Graça Varela, 282
da Vinci, Leonardo, 522
D'Aguiar, Fred, 532
D'Alema, Massimo, 63, 64, 65, 67, 89, 238, 425
d'Auvergne, Judge Suzie, 201
Dabydeen, David, 532
Dacko, David, 273
Dafis, Cynog, 47
Dagestan, 146
Daim Zainuddin, 343
Dalai Lama, 377, 378
Daley, William M., 565
Dallaglio, Lawrence, 534, 535
Dallas, Roland, 533
Dalli, John, 99
Damascus Declaration Group, 447
Dando, Jill, 518
Daniel, Paul, 501
Danjuma, Gen. Theophilus, 257
Darbinian, Armen, 152
Darke, Nick, 511
Darling, Alistair, 564
Daschle, Tom, 156
Dashbalbar, Ochirbatyn, 377
Daszak, John, 502
Davenport, Lindsay, 542
Davey, Shaun, 513
David, Adelino Castelo, 282
David, Ivan, 117
Davies, Gavyn, 519
Davies, Norman, 530, 533

Davies, Omar, 195
Davies, Ron, 46, 47
Davies, Siobhan, 509
Dávila, Roberto, 180
Davis, Terrell, 543
Dåvøy, Laila, 77
de Chastelain, Gen. John, 50, 51, 52
de Gaulle, Gen. Charles, 60, 573, 588, 589
de Hooch, Pieter, 524
de Klerk, F.W., 533
de la Rúa Bruno, Fernando, 175, 176, 604, 606
de la Tour, Frances, 512
de Leeuw, Reinherdt, 503
de Marco, Prof. Guido, 98, 99
de Piña Moura, Joaquim Augusto, 97
de Sousa, Rebelo, 96
de Sousa Franco, António, 97
de Valera, Éamon, 584
Deane, Sir William, 379
Debré, Olivier, 524
Debussy, Claude, 502, 506
Déby, Col. Idriss, 270, 271
Decibe, Susana, 176
Defence, Disarmament & Security, defence organizations, **403-10**; comprehensive test-ban treaty, 170, 319-20; India/Pakistan, 315, 320, 322; landmines treaty, 488; NATO strategic concept, 406-7, 408, **549-60**
Degn, Helle, 135
Dehaene, Jean-Luc, 68, 600
Deiss, Joseph, 87
Dejeu, Gavril, 123
del Ponte, Carla, 487
Delgermaa, Banzragchiyn, 377
Delors, Jacques, 429
Demaqi, Adem, 139
Demidenko, Nikolai, 507
Demirchian, Karen, 152
Demirel, Süleyman, 107, 108, 313
Denham, John, 565
Denktash, Rauf, 103, 104, 105, 106, 606
Denmark, 74-5, 313, 425, 459, 536, 594
Dennehy, Brian, 512
Denning, Lord, 573 (obit.)
Denniston, Robin, 533
Depasquale, Bishop Annetto, 98
Dequenne brothers, 515
Deri, Aryeh, 209
Desai, Anita, 529, 532
Dettori, Frankie, 542
Developing Eight (D-8), 326
Devine, T.M., 533
Devlin, Paddy, 573 (obit.)
Dewar, Donald, 16, 43, 44, 599
Dhlakama, Afonso, 282, 283
Di Pietro, Antonio, 65, 66
di Tella, Guido, 176
Diabaté, Henriette, 267

INDEX 615

Diack, Abdoulaye, 263
Diallo, Ali, 265
Diallo, Amadou, 163
Diana, Princess of Wales, 28, 30
Díaz Pereira, Ramón, 455
Dickson, Barbara, 513
Didier, Garnet, 201
DiMaggio, Joe, 574 (obit.)
Dimitrov, Georgi, 128
Ding Guangen, 354
Dingake, Michael, 292
Dini, Lamberto, 64
Diouf, Abdou, 262, 263, 264
Disasters & Accidents (see also Environmental Questions), Austria, 82; Bahamas, 199; Central America, 477; France, 62-3; India, 321; Mexico, 195; Norway, 78; Taiwan, 367; Turkey/Greece earthquakes, 101, 108; UK, 25; USA, 154-6, 469; Venezuela, 188
Disney, Walt, 7, 445
Dixon, Jeremy, 527
Djermakoye, Moumouni, 270
Djibouti, 245, 248-9
Djukanovic, Milo, 138, 139, 431
Dlamini, Sibusiso Barnabas, 290
Dlamini-Zuma, Nkosazana, 300
do Espirito Santo, Paolo Jorge Rodrígues, 282
Dobson, Frank, 19, 20, 26
Documents & Reference, 544-66
Dodds, Nigel, 53
Dodik, Milorad, 131, 132
Dokic, Jelena, 542
Dolan, Monica, 511
Dole, Bob, 160
Dole, Elizabeth, 160
Doleguele, Anicet Georges, 271, 273
Dominian, Jack, 464
Dominica, 200, 201, 458
Dominican Republic, 189, 190
Donald, Allan, 538
Donnellan, Declan, 512
Doran, Gregory, 512
Dørum, Odd Einar, 77
dos Santos, José Eduardo, 283, 284
Doss, Fr Arun, 460
Doué, Lt.-Col. Mathieu, 267
Douglas, Denzil, 200
Douglas, Rosie, 201
Dove, Rita, 532
Dowiyogo, Bernard, 390
Doyle, Roddy, 532
Draskovic, Vuk, 139, 140, 598
Dreifuss, Ruth, 85
Driberg, Tom, 29
Drnovsek, Janez, 137
du Pré, Jacqueline, 503
Duan, Bishop Mathias, 464
Dubai, 232, 319
Dubs, Lord, 53

'Duch', 352
Due, Ole, 491
Duffy, Carol Ann, 532
Dugan, Angel Serafin Seriche, 271, 274
Duhalde Maldonado, Eduardo, 176
Duisenberg, Wim, 425, 426
Dujakovic, Rade, 132
Dumas, Roland, 61
Dunant, Sarah, 532
Dunbar, Charles, 244
Duncker, Patricia, 532
Dunmore, Helen, 532
Dunn, Suzannah, 532
Dunstan, Don, 383
Dupuch, Michel, 267
Dupuis, Fr Jacques, 459
Dur, Gus, 346, 604
Durão Barroso, José Manuel, 96
Durcan, Paul, 532
Duval, Xavier, 334
Duve, Freimut, 437
Dyke, Greg, 22, 518
Dzurinda, Mikulas, 119, 120, 442

Eagleton, William, 244
East African Commission (EAC), 448, 450
East Timor, 2, 74, 97, 174, 347, 348 (map), 379-80, 389, 401, 404, 418, 453, 454, 461, 597, 601, 602, 603
Eccles, Viscount, 574 (obit.)
Ecevit, Bülent, 104, 105, 106, 107, 109, 595, 598
Echeverría, Rodolfo, 194
Eclipse of the Sun, 467
Economic and Monetary Community of Central Africa (CEMAC), 274
Economic Community of Central African States (CEEAC), 274
Economic Community of West African States (ECOWAS), 259, 264, 269, 280, **447**, 449, **450**
Economic Organizations, 410-13
Ecuador, 14, 181, **182-3**, 186, 534
Eddery, Pat, 543
Edinburgh, Duke of, 17, 30, 254, 450
Edlinger, Hans, 84
Edward, Prince, 600
Edwards, Jonathan, 536
Edwards, Ruth Dudley, 533
Egypt, 210, 211, 212, **214-6**, 222, 223, 232, 234, 235, 236, 298, 326, 445, 602
Ehrlichman, John, 574 (obit.)
Eichel, Hans, 56
Eisenhower, Dwight D., 589
Ek, Mats, 506
El Salvador, 190, 191, **192**, 457, 595
Elchibey, Abulfaz Ali, 153
Elder, Mark, 501
Elgar, Edward, 503, 504, 585
Elgin Marbles, 102, 103

Elizabeth II, Queen of England etc., 16, 27, 39, 171, 195, 197, 198, 199, 200, 216, 254, 374, 379, 382, 383, 385, 388, 389, 433, 571, 598, 599, 601, 604, 607
Ellington, Duke, 504, 512
Ellington, Ralph, 504
Ellison, Ralph, 528, 532
Elway, John, 543
Eman, Jan Hendrick (Henny), 205
Emerson, Caryl, 506
Enescu, George, 585
Englund, Einar, 506
Enoksen, Odd Roger, 77
Enright, D.J., 533
Environmental matters (see also AIDS/HIV, BSE, Disasters & Accidents), **476-83**; Caribbean, 198, climate change, 479, 481; El Niño, 182; food scares, 68; GM crops, 62-3, 470, 476, 477, 478, 479, 480-1, 482-3; Hurricane Floyd, 154; Indian Ocean, 336, 337; pollution, 62, 70; population, 479-80; whales, 90, 481; nuclear issues, 80, 84, 115, 118, 120, 137-8, 371, 482
Equatorial Guinea, 271, 273-4, 450, 486, 595
Eritrea, 2, 235, **245**, 246, **247**, 402, 448
Ermán González, Antonio, 176
Ernst August, Prince of Hanover, 90
Eroglu, Dervis, 106
Ershad, Hussein Mohammed, 325
Erwin, Alec, 297, 301
Escobar Fariña, Gen. Guillermo Rolando, 184
Estonia, 105, **113-4**, 115, 116, 430, 440, 595
Estrada, Joseph Ejercito, 349, 350, 452
Ethiopia, 2, 235, **245-7**, 248, 249, 402, 448, 477
European Bank for Reconstruction & Development (EBRD), 438-9
European Community Law, 489-91, 492
European Court of Human Rights (ECHR), 42, 60, 89, 95, 108, 488
European Court of Justice (ECJ), 40, 42, 491
European Free Trade Association (EFTA), 441, 442
European Space Agency (ESA), 465-6
European Union (see also European Community Law), **424-32**; ACP states, 202, 269, 489; Africa, 98; Agenda 2000, 429-30; Angola, 418; Arabs-Israel, 212, 214, 445, 446, 447; ASEAN, 453; Baltic states, 441; bananas, 1, 480-1; Belarus, 150; Black Sea, 444; British beef, 3, 16, 40-2, 62; budget, 429-30; CEI, 443; China, 359; Commission, 63, 64-5, 74, 75, 424, 426-9; Côte d'Ivoire, 267; Council of Europe, 433, 434; defence/security policy, 8, 39, 63, 407-9, 432; ECB, 11, 425-6; economies, 1, 11, 59, 71, 80, 96; enlargement, 58, 84, 93, 98, 102, 103, 104, 105, 109, 110, 111, 113, 115, 117, 119, 120, 121, 122, 125, 126, 129, 137, 430-1, 440, 441, 460; euro launch, 8, 15, 16, 25, 35-6, 71, 90, 95, 424-6; Euro-elections,22, 44, 48, 49, 57, 60-1, 65, 68, 69, 70-1, 74, 75, 79, 82, 91-2, 96, 102-3, 428; Europol, 490; fisheries policy, 40; G-20, 420; Gibraltar, 95; GM crops, 480; immigration/asylum, 35, 92; institutional crisis, 426-8; intergovernmental conference, 431; Iran, 303; Kazakhstan, 309; Kosovo crisis, 8, 74, 81, 82, 140, 398, 430, 431-2, 436; Latin America/Caribbean, 457; Libya, 237; Malta, 98; NATO, 407-9; Northern Dimension, 81, 440; SAARC, 454; SADC, 290; South Africa, 291, 301; Switzerland, 85, 87, 442; Togo, 268; Turkey, 102, 103, 104, 105, 108-9, 430-1; UK attitude, 16, 22, 24-5; USA, 63, 413, 456; withholding tax, 71
Evans, Godfrey, 575 (obit.)
Ewerem, Evan, 257
Ewing, Dr Winnie, 43
Extracts from Past Volumes, xvi-xx
Eyadéma, Gen. Gnassingbé, 263, 268, 450
Eyre, Richard, 517, 518

Fabius, Laurent, 62
Fadeyechev, Alexei, 508
Fadul, Francisco, 264, 280
Fahd ibn Abdul Aziz, King of Saudi Arabia, 225, 227
Fahima, Al-Amin Khalifa, 237
Faisal, King, 580
Faisal, Prince, 227
Faisal Husaini, 213
Falae, Olu, 256, 257, 596
Falcam, Leo, 388, 390
Falconer of Thoroton, Lord, 565
Falkland Islands/Malvinas, 177, 179
Fallon, Kieran, 543
Falls, Robert, 512
Fanfani, Amintore, 575 (obit.)
Farmer, James, 575 (obit.)
Faroe Islands, 75
Faulder, Joseph, 164
Fayed, Dodi, 28
Fayed, Mohamed al-, 28, 29, 30, 606
Fearon, Ray, 512
Fedar, Stewart, 506
Fell, Alison, 532
Fenech Adami, Edward, 98
Ferchiou, Ridha, 239
Ferguson, Sir Alex, 535
Ferguson, Howard, 506
Ferguson, Niall, 533
Fernandes, George, 315, 320
Fernández, Leonel, 189
Fernández Estigarribia, José Félix, 184
Ferrier, Kathleen, 503
Fico, Robert, 119
Fielding, David, 502
Figueroa, John, 531

Fiji Islands, **387**, **398**, 391, 414, 454, 455, 541, 598
Filali, Abd al-Latif, 243
Finland, 41, 68, **80-2**, 93, 126, 127, 140, 201, 424, 429, 440, 477, 596
Fischer, Joschka, 54, 56, 58, 115
Fischer, Tim, 382
Fischer, Vaclav, 117
Fischer-Dieskau, Dietrich, 503
Fischler, Franz, 429
Fisher, Rich, 351
Fitt, Gerry, 573
Fitzgerald, F. Scott, 505
Five-Power Defence Arrangements, 404
Fleming, Damien, 538
Fletcher, Raphael, 198
Fletcher, Raymond, 29
Flores Bermúdez, Roberto, 192
Flores Facussé, Carlos Roberto, 190, 192
Flores Pérez, Francisco, 190, 192, 596
Flosse, Gaston, 392
Foden, Giles, 532
Folador, Maria Dorcelina, 178
Fontaine, Nicole, 428
Food & Agriculture Organization (FAO), 478
Foot, Michael, 533
Forbes, Peter, 532
Forbes, Steve, 160
Ford, Gerald, 589
Forgione, Francesco, 460
Forné Molné, Marc, 88
Forster, Margaret, 532
Forte, Allen, 506
Forwood, Tony, 568
Foster, Lawrence, 503
Foster of Thames Bank, Lord (Norman), 525, 527
Fowler, Robert, 402
Fraga Neto, Arminio, 178
France, 59-63; accidents & disasters, 62-3; British beef, 3, 40-2; Corsica, 62; economy, 9, 11, 12, 59, 424, 426; elections, 60-1; EU, 424, 426, 429, 430; external relations, 34, 35, 39, 63, 74, 89, 90, 93, 104, 138, 141, 219, 223, 237, 242, 248, 258, 267, 268, 272, 337, 361, 397, 399, 408, 409; Francophonie, 416-7; obituaries, 569, 571, 587, 589; Pacific dependencies, 392; religion, 460; scandals, 61-2; sport, 536, 539, 541, 542; torture, 488; whales, 90, 481
Francis, Richard, 532
Franco, Itamar, 178
Franco, Vice-Adm. (retd) Rubén Oscar, 175
Francophone Agency, 417
Francophone Community, see International Organization of Francophonie
Frank, Charles, 438
Franz, Elizabeth, 512

Frayn, Michael, 532
Free Trade Area of the Americas (FTAA), 458
Frei Rúis-Tagle, Eduardo, 179
French Guiana, 466
French Polynesia, 392, 454
Frenkel, Prof. Jacob, 211
Frenzen, Heinz-Harald, 540
Freud, Lucian, 522
Frick, Mario, 88, 90
Friedman, Jerome, 582
Fuchs, Sir Vivian, 576 (obit)
Fujimori, Alberto Keinya, 184, 185
Furrow, Buford Oneal, 165
Fürtwängler, Wilhelm, 503

Gabo, Naum, 578
Gabon, 271, 272, 273, 393, 450
Galina, Gantömöriyn, 377
Galindo, Celvin, 191
Galtieri, Leopoldo, 175
Gama, Jaime, 347
Gambia, The, 260-1, 264, 393
Ganbold, Dashpuntsagiyn, 377
Ganbold, Davaadorjiyn, 377
Ganbold, Dogsomyn, 377
Gandhi, Indira, 319
Gandhi, Mahatma, 575
Gandhi, Priyanka Vadhra, 319
Gandhi, Rajiv, 331
Gandhi, Sonia, 315, 316, 318
Ganic, Ejup, 131
Ganzuri, Kamal, 215
Gaolathe, Baledzi, 292
Garang, Col. John, 234, 235
Garbah, Sam, 255
Garcia, Sergio, 539
Garcia Medina, Amalia, 194
García Pérez, Alan, 185
García Sola, Manuel, 176
Garrigoza, Gen. Expedito, 184
Garzón, Baltasar, 175
Gates, Bill, 168
Gatkouth, Gatwich, 235
Gaviria Trujillo, César, 455, 456
Gayoom, Maumoun Abdul, 327, 335
Geingob, Hage, 290
Gell-Mann, Murray, 582
Genscher, Hans-Dietrich, 57
George, Jennie, 382
George, Norman, 391, 392
George VI, King, 574
Georgia, 152, 153, 313, 400, 433-4, 437, 460, 489, 604
Georgievski, Ljubco, 136, 137
Gerardi Conedera, Mgr Juan José, 191
Gerhard, Roberto, 503
Germany, 54-8; Berlin, 54, 525-6; CDU scandal, 54, 56-7; economy, 9, 11-12, 38, 55-6, 226, 424, 426; elections, 55-6; EU, 424,

425, 426, 429, 430, 431; external relations, 35, 41, 42, 54, 56-7, 58, 93, 104, 118, 129, 138, 141, 169, 175, 212, 214, 309, 313, 441, 443, 453, 484, 485; Internet, 472; religion, 459; sport, 535, 536
Ghana, 39, **254-5**
Ghannouchi, Mohammed, 238, 239, 604
Ghirlandaio, Domenico, 89
Gibbs, Herschelle, 537, 538
Gibraltar, 40, 93, **94-5**, 481
Gidada, Negaso, 245
Giggs, Ryan, 535
Gil, Jesús, 95
Gil-Robles, Alvaro, 434
Gilman, Rebecca, 510, 511
Gimblett, Sheriff Margaret, 45
Giraud, Gen. Henri, 573
Giscard d'Estaing, Valéry, 588
Giuliani, Rudolph, 161, 163
Gizikis, Gen. Phaidon, 103
Glass, Philip, 505
Glickman, Dan, 565
Gligorov, Kiro, 136, 137
Glistrup, Mogens, 75
Gloucester, Duke of, 17
Glubb, Gen. Sir John, 580
Gober, Robert, 522
Goethe, Johann Wolfgang von, 501
Goh Chok Tong, 344
Goldenberg Schreiber, Efraín, 185
Goldwyn, Rachel, 340
Goma, Louis-Sylvain, 448
Göncz, Arpád, 39, 120, 600
Gonsalves, Dr Ralph, 202
González, Elian, 189
González Fernández, José Antonio, 194
González Macchi, Luís, 183, 184, 597
Goodhew, Archbishop Harry, 461
Goodman, Henry, 511
Gorbachev, Mikhail, 571, 576
Gorbachev, Raisa, 576 (obit)
Gordon, Richard, 568
Gordon of Strathblane, Lord, 519
Gore, Al, 159, 160, 162, 165, 313, 565, 600
Goren, Eli, 506
Gorky, Maxim, 511
Gould, Glen, 503
Gouled Aptidon, Hassan, 248
Gourad Hamadou, Barkat, 245, 248
Gowdy, Barbara, 532
Graf, Steffi, 542
Graham, Billy, 23
Gramm, Phil, 160
Grant, Hugh, 515
Grappelli, Stephane, 585
Grass, Günter, 528
Gray, Simon, 509, 530
Greaves, Jimmy, 589
Greece, 60, 95, **100-3**, 105, 118, 130, 136, 140, 171, 313, 425, 431, 444, 587, 594, 601, 604

Green, Michael, 520
Greene, Justin, 513
Greene, Maurice, 536
Greenspan, Alan, 10, 11, 167
Greenstock, Sir Jeremy, 399
Greer, Germaine, 533
Greig, Andrew, 532
Grenada, 198, **199**, 456, 458, 594
Griffith, Howard, 543
Griffiths, Richard, 464
Grímsson, Ólafur Ragnar, 76
Grisey, Gérard, 506
Groop, Monica, 502
Group of Seven/Eight (G-7/G-8), 104, 140, 169, 285, 301, 390, 419, 443
Group of 20 (G-20), 109, 301, **420**
Group of 77, 419-20
Grundy, Isabel, 533
Guadalcanal, 391
Guam, 454
Guardado, Facundo, 192
Guatemala, 190-1, 456, 606
Guayasamin, Oswaldo, 525
Guazzaloca, Giorgio, 66
Gueï, Gen. Robert, 262, 266, 267, 607
Guelendouksia, Ouaido, 272
Guillou, Michel, 417
Guinea, 261, **262**, **265-6**, 280, 487
Guinea-Bissau, 2, 260, 264, **280-1**, 418, 449, 598, 604
Guinness, Sir Alec, 533
Gulf Cooperation Council (GCC), 226, 233-4, 303, **444**, **446-7**
Gunn, Kirsty, 532
Guralnick, Peter, 533
Gurirab, Theo-Ben, 393
Guseinov, Surat, 153
Gusmão, José Xanana, 347, 380, 604
Gutenberg, Johann, 530
Guterres, António, 95, 96, 603
Guterson, David, 532
Guy, Verhofstadt, 601
Guyana, 188, **196-7**, 415, 421, 458
Gwynn, Nell, 18
Gwyther, Christine, 47
Gypsies (Roma), 33, 118, 120, 437, 442

Habibie, B.J., 345, 346, 347, 348, 379
Hachani, Abdelkader, 241
Hadid, Zaha, 526
Haftmann, Werner, 524
Hague, William, 16, 21, 23, 24, 25, 26, 27
Haider, Jörg, 82, 83, 603
Hain, Peter, 564
Haiti, 174, **189-90**, 393, 400, 458
Hajdari, Azem, 129, 130
Hakkinen, Mika, 540
Haldane, J.B.S., 586
Haldeman, John, 574
Hall, Tony, 375, 518

Halonen, Tarja, 82
Hals, Frans, 522
Hamad bin Isa al-Khalifa, Shaikh of Bahrain, 230, 233, 596
Hamad bin Khalifa al-Thani, Shaikh of Qatar, 229
Hameed, A.C.S., 333
Hamilton, Ian, 532
Hamilton, Neil, 29, 495, 606
Hammarberg, Thomas, 352
Hamzik, Pavol, 120
Hanchar, Viktar, 149, 150
Hanish Islands, 247
Hannah, Timothy, 451
Hans Adam II, Prince of Liechtenstein, 88, 89, 90
Hanson, Pauline, 382
Harach, Lubomir, 120
Harald V, King of Norway, 77
Harbison, John, 505
Hardie Boys, Sir Michael, 385
Hare, Nicholas, 527
Hariri, Rafiq, 222
Harper, Robin, 43
Harries, Kathryn, 501
Harrington, Padraig, 538, 539
Harris, Eric, 164
Harris, Len, 382
Harris, René, 388, 390
Harris, Rosemary, 512
Harris, Thomas, 530, 532
Harrison, Tony, 532
Harvey, Marcus, 521
Hasan, Nacem ul-, 451
Hasan, Prince of Jordan, 216, 217
Hasikos, Socrates, 106
Hasina Wajed, Sheikh, 324, 325, 326
Hassan II, of Morocco, 219, 242, 244, 577 (obit.), 601
Haughey, Charles, 72
Havel, Václav, 111, 117, 568
Hawthorne, Nigel, 512
Hayman, Baroness, 565
Heaney, Seamus, 529, 532
Heath, Sir Edward, 574, 593
Heenan, Cardinal, 579
Heim, Archbishop Bruno, 579
Heller, Joseph, 531, 577 (obit.)
Hemingway, Ernest, 528
Henderson, Russell, 166
Henman, Tim, 542
Henri, Prince of Luxembourg, 71, 607
Henry, Graham, 48
Henry, Sir Geoffrey, 391
Hepworth, Barbara, 578
Hercus, Dame Ann, 104
Herman, Alexis M., 565
Heron, Patrick, 524, 578 (obit.)
Herzog, Roman, 54, 599
Heseltine, Michael, 24

Heston, Charlton, 165
Hetherington, Alastair, 578 (obit.)
Hewitt, Lleyton, 542
Hewitt, Patricia, 564
Hiebert, Murray, 344
Hierro López, Luis, 186
Hill, Christopher, 138
Hill, Damon, 540
Hill, Geoffrey, 532
Hill, Heather, 382
Hill, Tobias, 532
Hillary, Sir Edmund, 576
Hilton, Isabel, 464
Hindley, Myra, 521
Hinds, Sam, 196
Hingis, Martina, 542
Ho Chi Minh, 351
Ho Hao Wah, Edmund, 362
Hoddle, Glenn, 535, 536
Hodgkin, Howard, 527
Hodson, Henry Vincent (Harry), 578 (obit.)
Hofmann, Michael, 529, 532
Hofsiss, James, 513
Holbrooke, Richard C., 139, 565, 597
Holden, Anthony, 533
Hollick, Lord, 520
Holloway, Richard, 464
Holocaust issues, 62, 84, 89, 116, 122, 522
Holroyd, Michael, 529, 533
Holy See, see Vatican
Holyfield, Evander, 536, 537
Honduras, 190, 191, 192, **193**, 484
Honecker, Erich, 592
Hong Kong, 14, 39, 358, 360, **363-5**, 418, 429
Hong Song Nam, 374
Hood, Alex Gregory, 524
Hoon, Geoff, 26, 564, 603
Horn of Africa, 246-50
Horst, Horst, 524
Hoss, Salim al-, 221, 222
Hossain, Anwar, 325
Houngbedji, Adrien, 269
Houphouët-Boigny, Félix, 267
Howard, John, 379, 380, 381, 382, 384
Hu, Jason, 367
Hu Jintao, 354, 360
Hubbell, Webster, 159
Hudson, Richard, 513
Hughes, Frieda, 529, 532
Hughes, Howard, 569
Hughes, Hubert, 202, 203
Hughes, Simon, 24
Hughes, Ted, 529, 532
Hughes, William, 593
Hujilan, Jameel al-, 444
Hull, Jane, 164
Hulse, Michael, 528, 532
Hume, Cardinal Basil, 579 (obit.)
Hume, John, 49, 573
Hun Sen, 352, 353, 452

Hung Pacheco, Gen. Mario Raúl, 192
Hungary, 5, 13, 39, 105, **120-2**, 405, 430, 442, 443, 599
Hunter, Kathryn, 511
Hurst, Geoff, 589
Hurtado González, Jaime, 182
Husain ibn Tal, King of Jordan, 211, 216, 217, 580 (obit.), 595
Husain Qusay, 224
Husain Uday, 224
Husbands, Sir Clifford, 197
Hutton, John, 565
Hyde, Henry, 156
Hyland, Tom, 74
Hynd, Ronald, 509
Hytner, Nicholas, 502

Ialá, Kumba, 281
Ibero-American Summit, 94, 184, 457
Ibrahim, Foundi Abdallah, 337
Ibrahimov, Jumabek, 310, 313, 598
Iceland, 76, 598
Idris, Moussa Ahmad, 248
Idris, Salih, 235
Ilunga, Emile, 276, 277
Ilves, Toomas Hendrik, 113, 440
India, 2, 84, 175, 231, 307, **314-21**, 323, 324, 325, 329, 331, 400, 414, 420, 423, 454, 460, 463, 465, 469, 484, 516, 537, 570, 594, 596, 597, 598, 601, 603, 606
Indian Ocean Rim Association for Regional Cooperation (IORARC), 451
Indonesia, 2, 3, 14, 97, 174, 326, **346-9**, 379, 380, 396, 397, 418, 424, 452, 453, 461, 469, 596, 599, 602, 603, 606
Information Technology, 9-10, **471-5**
Ingraham, Hubert, 199
Ingram, Adam, 565
Ingres, Jean Auguste Dominique, 524
Insulza, José Miguel, 179
Inter-American Court of Human Rights (IACHR), 456
Inter-American Development Bank (IADB), 182, 187, 458
Inter-Governmental Authority on Development (IGAD), 234, 248
International Comparisons, 565
International Court of Justice (ICJ), 179, 233, 292, 484-6
International Finance Corporation (IFC), 439
International Monetary Fund (IMF), 13, 109, 125, 129, 135, 150, 178, 182, 183, 185, 186, 236, 250, 251, 252, 255, 258, 267, 272, 281, 282, 287, 298, 323, 338, 340, 341, 353, 384, **410-2**, 417, 419, 420, 446
International Organization of Francophonie (OIF), 416-7
International Telecommunication Union (ITU), 472

Ionatana, Ionatana, 389, 391
Ionescu, Constantin Dudu, 123
Iotti, Nilde, 580 (obit.)
Iran, 84, 215, 224, 225, 227, 230, 235, **302-4**, 305, 326, 424, 444, 446, 447, 517, 595, 600
Iraq, 23, 217, 218, 220, **222-5**, 233, 240, 399, 400, 444, 445
Ireland, Northern, see Northern Ireland
Ireland, Republic of, 51, 52, 53, **71-4**, 403, 424, 539, 542, 583
Irian Jaya, 349
Irvine, Andrew, 599
Irvine, Eddie, 540
Irvine of Lairg, Lord, 564
Iryani, Abdulkarim al-, 227
Isa bin Sulman al-Khalifa, Shaikh of Bahrain, 581 (obit.), 596
Isaac, Mark, 199
Isarescu, Mugur, 123, 124, 125, 606
Ishihara, Shintaro, 369, 370
Islamic Conference Organization, see Organization of the Islamic Conference
Islamic Development Bank (IDB), 236
Islamic militancy, 3, 146, 215, 222, 236, 241, 243, 253, 257-8, 307, 311, 424
Ismail, Azizah, 343
Ismail Omar Guellah, 245, 248
Israel, 3, 78, 170, 171, **207-11**, 212, 213, 214, 216, 217, 219, 221, 222, 242, 303, 422, 445, 461, 462, 559, 569, 598, 600, 605
Italy, 9, 11, 12, **63-7**, 90, 104, 107, 130, 138, 140, 174, 216, 237-8, 258, 313, 411, 424, 425, 426, 428, 429, 460, 461, 481, 488, 535, 536, 574, 579-1, 592, 598
Ives, Charles, 504
Izaguirre Porras, Martiza, 187

Jabir al-Ahmad al-Jabir al-Sabah, Shaikh, 229
Jack, Belinda, 533
Jackson, Colin, 536
Jackson, Glenda, 20
Jackson, Judge Thomas Penfield, 473
Jackson, Lt.-Gen. Sir Michael, 141, 600
Jackson, Rev. Jesse, 169, 598
Jacobs, Rabbi Louis, 581
Jagan, Janet, 196
Jagdeo, Bharrat, 196
Jagland, Thorbjørn, 78
Jakobovits, Lord (Immanuel), 581 (obit.)
Jamaica, 195-6, 393, 458
James, Edison, 200, 201, 458
Jammeh, Col. Yahya, 260, 261
Jamri, Shaikh Abdulamir al-, 233
Jan Jyh-horng, 366
Japan, 368-72; art, 524; Aum Shinrikyo, 370, 464; cinema, 517; economy, 8, 9, 10, 14, 226, 255, 313, 368-9, 370-2; external relations, 320, 354, 356, 358, 362, 375, 378, 404, 452, 453, 454, 600; law of the sea,

487; nuclear accident, 371, 482; politics, 368, 369-70, 372; science, 470; sport, 535, 540
Jarquín, Agustín, 192
Jaruzelski, Gen. Wojciech, 112
Jay of Paddington, Baroness, 564
Jayalalitha Jayaram, 315, 316
Jazi, Daly, 239
Jean, Grand Duke of Luxembourg, 70, 71, 607
Jefferson, Thomas, 203
Jefri, Prince, 344
Jegham, Muhammad, 239
Jelavic, Ante, 131
Jelisic, Goran, 133, 486
Jeri, Mohammed, 239
Jiang Zemin, 39, 170, 313, 354, 355, 356, 360, 361, 362, 367, 375, 378, 380, 387, 453, 601, 602, 604
Jigme Singye Wangchuk, Dragon King of Bhutan, 330
Jóhannsson, Kjartan, 441
John, Elton, 513
John Paul II, Pope, 64, 88, 89, 113, 194, 234, 460, 464, 595, 599, 600, 604
Johns, Jasper, 570
Johnson, Andrew, 154, 595
Johnson, Catherine, 513
Johnson, Frank M., Jr, 581 (obit.)
Johnson, Melanie, 564
Johnson, Michael, 536
Johnston, Donald, 411
Jonah, Sam, 254
Jones, Brian, 597
Jones, Edward, 527
Jones, Ieuan Wyn, 47, 48
Jones, Kathleen, 533
Jones, Marion, 536
Jones, Paula, 156, 158, 159
Jones, Robert Gerallt, 531
Jonson, Ben, 529
Jorda, Claude, 487
Jordan, 210, 211, 212, **216-8**, 219, 220, 224, 445, 484, 579, 594, 598
Jordan, Vernon, 158
Joseph, Fred, 189
Joseph, Patrick, 201
Jospin, Lionel, 41, 60, 62, 63, 242, 605
Jowell, Tessa, 564
Joyce, James, 513
Juan Carlos, King of Spain, 91, 94
Juárez, Juan Carlos, 95
Judge, Ian, 501
Jull Costa, Margaret, 532
Juncker, Jean-Claude, 70, 600
Juppé, Alain, 61
Jusko, Marian, 119

Kâ, Djibo, 263
Kabbah, Alhaji Ahmed Tejan, 259, 260, 601
Kabila, Laurent, 238, 253, 275, 276, 277, 279, 289, 294, 450, 601
Kabua, Imata, 387, 390
Kaiser, Michael, 501
Kalejs, Konrad, 116
Kallas, Siim, 114
Kallel, Abdallah, 239
Kalman, Emmerich, 504
Kalpokas, Donald, 391
Kalua, Kamulepo, 287
Kamal ud Din Husain, 216
Kamilov, Abdulaziz, 313
Kamotho, Joseph, 249
Kamu, Luagalau Levaula, 390
Kane, Sarah, 531
Kaplicky, Jan, 526
Kapoor, Raj, 516
Kapur, Shakur, 516
Karadzic, Radovan, 133
Karajan, Herbert von, 504
Karimov, Islam, 308, 313
Karlsson, Peter, 80
Karran, Ralph Ram, 196
Kasal, Jan, 118
Kashmir, 307, 314, 316-7, 319, 320, 322, 323-4, 423, 454, 598
Kaura, Katuutire, 294
Kavan, Jan, 117, 443
Kay, Jackie, 532
Kayishema, Clement, 487
Kazakhstan, 13, **308-10**, 311, 312, 313, 314, 465, 474, 489, 594, 602
Kazhegeldin, Akezhan, 309
Ke Kimyan, Gen., 352
Keegan, Kevin, 535, 536
Keiller, Gabrielle, 523
Keita, Ibrahim Boubakar, 262
Kelly, Graham, 535
Kelly, Janis, 502
Kelly, John, 203
Kemsley, Lord, 579
Kendall, Prof. Henry W., 582 (obit.)
Keneally, Thomas, 533
Kennedy, A.L, 532
Kennedy, Charles, 24, 25, 602
Kennedy, Edward, 155
Kennedy, Jacqueline, 582
Kennedy, John F., 582
Kennedy, John F., Jr., 155, 582 (obit.), 601
Kennedy, Michael, 506
Kennedy, Nigel, 585
Kennedy, Robert, 575
Kennedy, Judge William, 164
Kennett, Jeff, 381
Kent, Duke of, 17
Kenya, 100, 107, 246, **249-50**, 450, 477, 537, 596
Kérékou, Mathieu, 263, 269
Kervorkian, Dr Jack, 164
Keyes, Alan, 160
Khadka, Puma Bahadur, 328

Khakamada, Irina, 147
Khalifa bin Sulman al-Khalifa, Shaikh, 230
Khamenei, Ali, 302, 303
Khamphoui Keoboualapha, 353
Khamtay Siphandon, Gen., 353
Khan, Ayub, 515
Khan, Dr Humayun, 415
Kharrazi, Kamal, 225
Khasawneh, Awn Shawkat Al-, 484
Khatami, Mohammed, 3, 225, 233, 302, 303, 596
Khatim, Gen. Abd al-Rahman Sirr al-, 236
Khieu Samphan, 352
Khin Nyunt, Gen., 339
Khrysokhoidis, Mikhalis, 101
Kiarostami, Abbas, 516
Killanin, Lord, 534, 583 (obit.)
Killion, Redley, 390
Kim Dae Jung, 369, 372, 373, 374, 378
Kim Il Chol, 375
Kim Il Sung, 276
Kim Jong Il, 374, 376
Kim Jong Nam, 376
Kim Jong Pil, 372
Kim Yong Nam, 375
King, John William, 163
King, Martin Luther, 582
Kinnock, Neil, 429
Kiribati, 387, 389-90, 393, 454
Kirienko, Sergei, 147
Kirkingburg, 499
Kirsten, Gary, 538
Kissinger, Henry, 179, 534
Klebold, Dylan, 164
Klestil, Thomas, 82, 84
Klima, Ivan, 532
Klima, Viktor, 82, 83
Klimt, Gustav, 522
Klusener, Lance, 538
Knussen, Oliver, 503
Kobborg, Johann, 508
Koch, Ursula, 85
Kocharyan, Robert, 152
Kohen, Arnold S., 464
Kohl, Helmut, 57, 607
Köhler, Horst, 438
Koirala, Girija Prasad, 327
Kok, Wim, 69
Kokkos, Yannis, 502
Kolélas, Bernard, 273
Kolingba, André, 273
Koller, Arnold, 86
Koma, Kenneth, 292
Konaré, Alpha Oumar, 262, 450
König, Cardinal Franz, 459
Kony, Joseph, 253
Koo Chen-fu, 362, 366
Koolhaas, Rem, 527
Koolman, Olindo, 205
Kordic, Dario, 133

Korea, Democratic People's Republic of (North Korea), 276, 369, 373, **374-6**, 378, 594
Korea, Republic of (South Korea), 10, 14, 39, 226, 231, 358, **372-4**, 378, 420, 452, 453, 534
Koroma, Johnny, 260
Kosovo crisis, 5-6, 7, 16, 33, 57, 58, 63, 64, 65, 74, 81, 82, 83, 84, 89, 101, 102, 118, 121, 125, 127, 128, 129, 130, 131, 136, 138-41, 142 (*map*), 143, 168, 169, 174, 206, 354-5, 356, 360, 361, 379, 393, 397-8, 401, 405, 406, 420-1, 423, 430, 431-2, 434, 436, 443, 460, 485, **544-50**
Kostov, Ivan, 126, 127
Kouchner, Bernard, 141
Kouyaté, Lamine, 447
Kouyaté, Seydou Badian, 265
Kovác, Michal, 119
Kowlessar, Sasenarine, 196
Kramer, Lottie, 532
Kramer, Susan, 21
Kranidiotis, Yiannos, 102
Kraus, Alfredo, 502
Krause, Bishop Christian, 459
Kringelborn, Solveig, 502
Kristopans, Vilis, 114, 601
Kubilius, Andrius, 113, 115, 604
Kubrick, Stanley, 515, 583 (obit.), 591
Kucan, Milan, 137
Kuchma, Leonid, 149, 150, 151, 443, 444, 605
Kuffour, John, 255
Kumakawa, Tetsuya, 508
Kumaratunga, Chandrika Bandaranaike, 329, 331, 332, 333, 606
Kurdish question, 33, 100-1, 107, 108, 220, 224, 303, 595, 599
Kuwait, 217, 223, 224, 225, 226, **229**, 230, 231, 399, 400, 444, 445, 600
Kwasniewski, Aleksander, 110, 111
Kyaw Wunna, 340
Kyprianou, Spyros, 106
Kyrgyzstan, 308, 310, 311, 312, 313, 314, 597

La Kha Phieu, 351
Laar, Mart, 113, 114, 596
Labastida Ochoa, Francisco, 194
Lacalle Ibáñez, Luis Alberto, 186
Laccara, Lucia, 507
Lader, Philip, 51
Lafontaine, Oskar, 55, 56, 426
Lagos Escobar, Ricardo, 180
LaGrand, Walter, 164, 485
Lahoud, Émile, 221, 222
Lakatani, Sani Elia, 392
Lakhova, Yekaterina, 148
Lamy, Jean, 190
Lamy, Pascal, 429
Langham, Michael, 512

INDEX

Lansky, Egon, 117
Laos, 353-4, 452, 453
Lapid, Yosef (Tommy), 208
Lapli, John, 388
Laraki, Azeddine, 422, 424
Larsson, Lisa, 502
Latin American Economic System (SELA), 455, 458
Latin American Integration Association (ALADI), 455, 457
Latvia, 98, 105, **113, 114**, 115, 116, 430, 440, 600
Laurier, Sir Wilfrid, 172
Lavín Infante, Joaquín, 180
Law & Legal Affairs (see also European Court of Human Rights, International Court of Justice, War Crimes Tribunals), **484-500**; European Community Law, **489-91**; international law, **484-8**; UK law, **492-8**; US law, 163-6, **498-500**
Lawrence, Doreen & Neville, 30
Lawrence, Stephen, 30, 31, 33, 596
Lawrie, Paul, 45, 538, 539
Lawton, Jeffrey, 502
Layva, Silvio, 166
Le Carré, John, 532
Le Kha Phieu, Gen., 350, 351
Le Pen, Jean-Marie, 60
Leach, Bernard, 578
Leakey, Richard, 250
Lebanon, 218, 219, 220, **221-2**, 400, 417, 445
Leblanc, Camille, 189
Lee Hoi Chang, 372, 373
Lee Hsien Loong, 344, 345
Lee Kuan Yew, 345
Lee Teng-hui, 354, 362, 365, 366, 367
Lees, Meg, 380
Lehnhoff, Nikolaus, 501, 502
Leight, Warren, 510
Leon, Rose, 196
Leonard, Justin, 538, 539
Leonowens, Anna, 341
Lepper, Andrzej, 110
Lequès, Jean, 392
Lesotho, 290, 291, **293**
Lessing, Doris, 529, 532
Lestrade, Swinburne, 456
Letelier, Orlando, 180
Letsie III, King of Lesotho, 290
Lévêque, Michel, 88
Levete, Amanda, 526
Levi, Noel, 452
Levine, James, 505
Levy, David, 207, 208, 210
Lew, Jacob J., 565
Lewinsky, Monica, 5, 156, 157, 158, 159, 162
Lewis, Carl, 543
Lewis, Denise, 536
Lewis, Lennox, 536, 537
Leye, Jean-Marie, 391

Li Hongzhi, 464
Li Lanqing, 354
Li Peng, 354, 356
Li Ruihuan, 354
Li Zhaoxing, 361
Liberia, 259, **261**, 266
Liberman, Viktor, 506
Libeskind, Daniel, 523, 525
Libya, 100, 215, 234, **237-8**, 240, 247, 275, 402, 421, 447, 448, 449, 596, 600
Lichtenstein, Roy, 570
Liddell, Helen, 564
Lieberman, Avigdor (Yvette), 208, 209
Liebermann, Rolf, 506
Liechtenstein, 88, 89-90
Lien Chan, 367
Ligeti, György, 501
Liikanen, Erkki, 429
Lim Kit Siang, 343
Lin Hai, 474
Ling, Syargey, 149
Lini, Father Walter, 583-5 (obit.)
Lipponen, Paavo, 80, 597
Lissouba, Pascal, 273
Literature, 528-34
Lithuania, 98, 105, **113, 114-5**, 116, 430, 439, 440, 442, 598, 603
Living Buddha of Mongolia, 377
Livingstone, Ken, 19, 20
Lloreda Caicedo, Rodrigo, 181
Lloyd-Davies, Mary, 502
Lock, F.P., 533
Lockerbie affair, 237, 402, 421, 445
Logue, Christopher, 533
Lomu, Jonah, 541
Longchamp, Emmanuel Fritz, 189
Longley, Michael, 532
Lopes, Francisco, 178
Lopez, Jennifer, 166
López, Leopoldo, 177
Lott, Jonathon, 166
Lott, Trent, 156
Louima, Abner, 163
Louisy, Perlette, 200
Loum, Mamadou Lamine, 262
Løwer, Eldbjørg, 77
Lowry, Lord, 584 (obit.)
Luard, Clarissa, 531
Lucas, George, 515
Luce, Sir Richard, 94
Lucinschi, Petru, 149, 151
Lui, Frank, 392
Lukashenka, Alyaksandr, 149, 150, 601
Lukman, Rilwanu, 411
Lund, Thomas, 507
Lundgren, Bo, 80
Luo Gan, 354
Luxembourg, 42, **70-1**, 109, 174, 424, 427, 599, 606
Luxmore, Jonathan, 464

Luzhkov, Yuri, 147
Lynch, Jack, 584 (obit.)
M, Lebo, 513
Maathai, Wangari, 477
McAleese, Mary, 52, 71
Macao, 7, 97, 362, 605
Macapagal-Arroyo, Gloria, 350
McBurney, Simon, 510
McCabe, John, 506
McCabe, Patrick, 532
McCabe, Richard, 512
McCain, John, 160, 162
McCarthy, Siobhan, 514
McCartney, Ian, 565
McCartney, Robert, 49
McClelland, James, 383
McCoy, Tony, 543
McCreevey, Charlie, 73
McDonagh, Martin, 510
McDonald, Gabrielle Kirk, 487
MacDonald of Tradeston, Lord (Gus), 564
McDonald, John, 523
MacDonogh, Giles, 533
McDougal, Susan, 159
Macedonia, 5, 126, **136-7**, 138, 169, 399, 416, 431, 444, 596, 605
Macejko, Jozef, 120
Macey, Dean, 536
McFall, John, 53
McGough, Roger, 532
McGrath, Glen, 538
McGuinness, Martin, 50
Machar, Riak, 235
Machinea, José Luis, 176
McKay, Shena, 532
MacKilligin, David, 202
McKinney, Aaron, 166
McKinnon, Don, 413, 414, 604
McLeod, Kirsty, 533
McMillan, Edwin, 591
Macmillan, Gen., 571
Macmillan, Harold, 573, 574, 589
MacMillan, James, 462
MacMillan, Kenneth, 508, 509
McMullen, Nora, 585
McNally, Terence, 463
Macpherson, Sir William, 30, 596
'Mad cow disease', see BSE
Madagascar, 336, **338**
Madani, Abassi, 241
Madrazo Pintado, Roberto, 195
Mahajan, Pramod, 315
Maharaj, Ramesh Lawrence, 197
Mahat, Ram Sharan, 328
Mahathir Mohamad, Dr, 342, 343, 350, 605
Mahdi, Sayyid Sadiq al-, 234
Maher, Ted, 90
Mahler, Gustav, 503
Mahuad Witt, Jamil, 182

Mainassara, Gen. Ibrahim Baré, 269, 270, 597
Maiyaki, Ibrahim Assane, 269
Majid, Ali Husain al-, 224
Majko, Pandeli, 128, 129, 131, 604
Makhuba, Bheki, 296
Maktoum bin Rashid al-Maktoum, Shaikh, 229
Malawi, **286-7**, 478, 599
Malaysia, 14, 326, **342-4**, 345, 350, 380, 393, 399, 404, 414, 415, 452, 453, 454, 469, 478, 485, 540, 597, 605
Maldives, **327**
Malevich, Kasimir, 522
Mali, **262**, 264, **265**, 393, 424, 450, 534, 594
Malick, Terrence, 515
Malielegaoi, Tuilaepa Sailele, 388, 390
Malikova, Anna, 120
Mallon, Seamus, 49, 50, 51, 52
Mallory, George Leigh, 599
Malta, **98-100**, 105, 414, 430
Mandela, Nelson, 297, 300, 419, 421, 448, 587, 600
Mandelson, Peter, 25, 51, 52, 53, 564, 603
Mane, Gen. Ansumane, 264, 280, 281
Mango, Andrew, 533
Mankahlana, Parks, 300
Mann, Thomas, 569
Manning, Preston, 172
Manos, Stephanos, 103
Manqoush, Mohammed Ahmed al-, 237
Manuel, Robert, 189
Manuel, Tevor, 297, 298
Mao Zedong, 276
Maoate, Dr Terepai, 392
Maples, John, 24
Mara, Ratu Sir Kamisese, 387, 389
Maragall, Pasqual, 91
Marber, Patrick, 510
Marchuk, Yevhen, 151
Marcos, Ferdinand, 349
Marek, John, 47
Margesson, Viscount, 571
Margrethe II, Queen of Denmark, 74
Marín, Manuel, 427
Marín Millie, Gladys, 180
Marjanovic, Mirko, 138
Marks, David, 526
Marshall Islands, **387, 390**, 455
Marshall, Malcolm, 584 (obit.)
Marshall, Romell, 197
Marshall, Susan, 506
Martin, Paul, 172, 174, 420
Martin, Peter, 507
Martina, Don, 205
Martinovic, Vinko, 135
Marulanda Vélez ('Tirofijo'), Manuel, 180, 181
Masakhalia, Francis, 249, 250
Masako, Crown Princess of Japan, 372
Masari, Abu Hamza al-, 227

Masefield, Thorold, 202
Masire, Sir Quett Ketumile, 277
Maskhadov, Aslan, 604, 606
Massounde, Tajiddine Ben Said, 336, 598
Masud, Gen. Ahmed Shah, 304, 305
Matesa, Zlatko, 134
Mather, Rick, 527
Mathilde d'Udekem et d'Acoz, 68
Matos, Gen., 284
Matthews, Lord (Victor), 569
Matutes, Abel, 94
Mauritania, 262, **264-5**, 445, 450
Mauritius, 333-4, 336, 450, 451
Mawdsley, James, 340
Mazak, Jan, 119
Mbeki, Thabo, 293, 297, 298, 299, 300, 414, 419, 421, 448, 600
Mbuende, Kaire, 450
Meacher, Michael, 564
Meciar, Vladimir, 119, 120, 599
Medical Research, see Scientific, Medical & Industrial Research
Megawati Sukarnoputri, 346, 600, 604
Megrahi, Abd al-Basset al-, 237
Mégret, Bruno, 60
Meguid, Ahmad Esmat Abdel, 444, 445
Mejdani, Rexhep, 128, 129
Melanesian Spearhead Group, 454-5
Melchett, Lord, 481
Meles Zenawi, 245, 448
Mellon, Andrew, 585
Mellon, Paul, 525, 585 (obit)
Menem, Carlos, 606
Menuhin, Lord (Yehudi), 506, 585 (obit.)
Mercieca, Archbishop Joseph, 98
Mercosur, see Southern Common Market
Merdassi, Fethi, 239
Meri, Lennart, 113, 114
Meridor, Dan, 209
Mertlik, Pavel, 117
Messiaen, Olivier, 504
Meta, Ilir, 128, 131, 604
Metzler, Ruth, 87
Meunier, Monique, 507
Meyers, Mike, 515
Meynell, Dame Alix, 585 (obit.)
Meynell, Sir Francis, 586
Mexico, 182, **194-5**, 225, 230, 412, 420, 434, 456, 460, 602
Michael, Alun, 16, 20, 46, 47, 599
Michaelides, Dinos, 106
Michaels, Anne, 532
Michel, Louis, 68
Michelini, Rafael, 186
Michison, Gilbert Richard, 586
Micronesia, Federated States of, 388, 390
Midaoui, Ahmed, 243
Middleton, Stanley, 532
Mihajlovic, Svetozar, 131
Mihdar, Zine el-Abidine al-, 227

Mikhalkov, Nikita, 517
Milburn, Alan, 26, 564, 603
Miles, Alastair, 501
Millennium bug, 472-3, 606
Miller, Alan Eugene, 165
Miller, Arthur, 512, 530, 591
Miller, Billie, 197
Miller, Monte Kim, 462
Milner, Lord, 579
Milo, Paskal, 128
Milo, Roni, 209
Milošević, Slobodan, 6, 64, 138, 140, 141, 169, 431, 486, 592, 597, 598, 599, 600
Milutinovic, Milan, 138
Minot, Susan, 532
Mintoff, Dom, 99
Miquelena, Luis, 187
Miralles, Enric, 526
Mish'al, Khalid, 217
Mitchell, David, 529, 532
Mitchell, George, 50, 51, 52, 72, 605
Mitchell, Sir James, 200, 201
Mitchell, Keith, 198, 198, 456, 595
Mitchison, Naomi, 531, 586 (obit.)
Mitrokhin, Vasili, 28, 29
Mitterrand, François, 61, 588
Miyazawa, Kiichi, 454
Mjartan, Ivan, 119
Mkapa, Benjamin, 250, 251, 450
Mo, Timothy, 532
Mobutu Sese Seko, 276
Moco, Marcolino, 416
Mocumbi, Pascoal, 282
Mogae, Festus, 290, 292, 604
Mohajerani, Ataollah, 302
Mohammed, Sheikh, 543
Mohammed VI, King of Morocco, 242, 243, 244, 601
Mohohlo, Lena, 292
Moi, Daniel arap, 249
Moin, Baqer, 464
Moldova, 13, 130, **149, 151**
Molina Duarte, Simón, 456
Monaco, **88, 90,** 417, 434, 481
Monet, Claude, 524
Moneta, Carlos, 455
Mongkut, King of Thailand, 341
Mongolia, 313, **376-8**
Monroe, Marilyn, 574
Monteiro, Antonio Mascarenhas, 280
Monteiro Filho, Agildo, 178
Montenegro, Yugoslav Republic of, 134, 138, 140, 143, 431, 439
Montesinos, Vladimiro, 185
Montgomerie, Colin, 538, 539
Monti, Mario, 425, 429
Montserrat, 203, 204
Moody, Nell, 503
Moore, Bobby, 589
Moore, Brian, 531

626 INDEX

Moore, Mike, 411, 412, 601
Morauta, Sir Mekere, 383, 384, 601
Mordechai, Yitzak, 207, 209
Morgan, Rhodri, 46, 47
Morgenstern, Moshe, 463
Morita, Akio, 372
Morley, Sheridan, 512
Moro, Aldo, 581
Morocco, 92, 219, 240, **242-4**, 419, 424, 447, 576, 600
Morris, Estelle, 564
Morris, Mark, 506, 507, 508
Mortimer, Penelope, 531
Morton, Andrew, 159, 532, 533
Morton, Sir Alastair, 37
Moscoso de Gruber, Mireya Elisa, 191, 193, 602
Moshin, Mohammed, 328
Mosisili, Bethuel Pakalitha, 290
Motion, Andrew, 529
Mouaziz, Abdelkader El, 598
Mowlam, Marjorie (Mo), 25, 26, 49, 50, 51, 564, 603
Moynihan, Daniel Patrick, 161
Moyongo, Mishake, 295
Mozambique, 9, 39, **282-3**, 291, 418, 450, 606
Mozart, Wolfgang Amadeus, 502
Mswati III, King of Swaziland, 290, 296
Mubarak, Mohammed Husni, 210, 212, 214, 215, 603
Mufarech, Jorge Jamil, 185
Mugabe, Robert, 276, 287, 288, 289, 587
Mukhamedov, Irek, 508
Müller, Max, 571
Mulroney, Brian, 172
Muluzi, Bakili, 286, 287
Mundell, Robert A., 15
Munro, Alice, 529, 532
Muraliyev, Amangeldy, 308, 310, 598
Murdoch, Dame Iris, 531, 586 (obit.)
Murdoch, Rupert, 382, 520
Murerwa, Herbert, 289
Murphy, Paul, 17, 564
Murray, Alexander, 533
Musa, Said, 198
Museveni, Yoweri, 252, 253, 275, 278
Musharraf, Gen. Pervez, 315, 319, 321, 322, 323, 414, 603
Music, 503-6
Musoke, Kintu, 252
Musonge, Peter Mafany, 270
Mussolini, Benito, 593
Mussorgsky, Modest, 506
Mutangelwa, Imasiku, 295
Muzenda, Simon, 289
Muzuli, Bakili, 600
Mwencha, Erastus, 448
Mwila, Benjamin, 286
Myanmar (Burma), 325, **339-40**, 342, 452, 453, 469, 471, 474
Mzema, Augustine, 251
Nagano, Kent, 504
Nagorno-Karabakh, 152, 153, 437
Naidu, Chandrababu, 319
Naimi, Ali al-, 225
Naipaul, V.S., 529, 533
Najafabadi, Qorbanali Dorri, 302
Nakamura, Kuniwo, 388, 390
Namaliu, Rabbie, 383
Namibia, 275, 284, **290**, 291, 292, **294-5**, 393, 398, 450, 605
Nana Opuku Ware II, 254
Nano, Fatos, 130, 131
Narantsatsralt, Janlavyn, 376, 377
Narayanan, Kocheril Raman, 314, 316, 598
Naruhito, Crown Prince of Japan, 372
Narváez, Ivar, 177
Nash, Paul, 578
Nasim, Mohammed, 324
Nasser, Gamal Abdel, 215
Nathan, S.R., 344, 602
Naughton, James, 512
Nauru, 388, 389, **390,** 393
Nazarbayev, Nursultan, 308, 309, 313, 314, 595
Ndadaye, Melchior, 278
Ndi, John Fru, 272
Neil, Andrew, 518
Nelson, Francis, 201
Nelson, Richard, 513
Nelson, Rosemary, 596
Nemtsov, Boris, 147
Nena, Jacob, 390
Nepal, 307, 319, **327-30,** 331, 454, 598
Netanyahu, Binyamin, 207, 208, 210, 211, 212, 213, 214, 217
Netherlands, The, 38, **69-70**, 104, 237, 393, 424, 425, 426, 429, 445, 536
Netherlands Antilles, 205-6
New Caledonia, 392
New Zealand, 170, 361, **385-7**, 391, 392, 404, 413, 414, 453, 470, 487, 537, 538, 541, 600, 604
Ngo Xuan Loc, 351
Niasse, Moustapha, 263
Nicaragua, 191, 192-3, 457, 484
Nichols, Roger, 506
Nicholson, Ben, 578
Nicholson, Jim, 49
Nicholson, Viv, 513
Nielson, Poul, 75, 301
Niger, 2, 237, **263, 269-70,** 449, 596, 604
Nigeria, 2, **256-9,** 261, 298, 326, 413, 414, 415, 416, 421, 448, 450, 486, 595
Nimairy, Jafar, 236
Ninagawa, Yukio, 512
Niue, 392
Nixon, Richard, 568, 574, 576, 582, 589
Niyazov, Gen. Saparmurad, 308, 606

Nkomo, Joshua, 289, 587 (obit.)
Nobel Prizes, chemistry, 471; economics, 15, 423; literature, 528; medicine, 471; peace, 603; physics, 471
Nolan, Sir Sidney, 569
Non-Aligned Movement (NAM), 325-6, **419, 420-1**
Noor, Abdul Rahman, 343
Noor, Fadzil, 343
Nordic Council, 439, 440-41
Noriega Moreno, Gen. Manuel Antonio, 193
Norris, Steven, 21
North American Free Trade Agreement (NAFTA), 456
North Atlantic Treaty Organization (NATO) (see also Partnership for Peace), **403-7;** Canada, 175; Chechnya, 4; enlargement, 115, 118, 120, 405; Europe, 8, 79, 82, 83, 84, 100, 407-10, 432; Kosovo crisis, 5, 6, 16, 38-9, 58, 64, 65, 84, 93, 106, 118, 121, 125, 126, 127, 129, 136, 138, 139, 140, 147, 168-9, 174, 354, 360, 361, 397-8, 420-1, 431-2, 436, 439, 443, 453, 484, 485, 544-50; secretary-general, 26, 27, 93, 432; strategic concept, 406-7, 408, **549-60**
Northern Ireland, 2, 16, 22, 25, **48-54,** 72, 572-4, 595, 596, 600, 602, 604, 605
Norway, 77-8, 136, 225, 230, 412, 435, 440, 441, 536
Norwood, Melita, 29, 603
Note, Kessai, 390
Nouri, Abdollah, 303
Nsibambi, Apolo, 252
Ntoutoume-Emane, Jean-François, 271, 272
Nujoma, Sam, 290, 294, 295, 606
Nunn, Trevor, 511
Nuon Chea, 352
Nuon Paet, 352
Nussbaum, Felix, 523
Nyachae, Simeon, 249
Nyerere, Julius, 251, 279, 587 (obit.)

O'Donnell, Damian, 515
O'Donaghue, Bernard, 532
O'Hagan, Andrew, 532
O'Mara, Mark, 539
O'Neal, Ralph, 202
O'Rourke, Mary, 74
Obasanjo, Gen. Olusegun, 256, 448, 449, 596
Obiang Nguema Mbasogo, Brig.-Gen. Teodoro, 271
Obituaries, 566-94
Obote, Milton, 253
Obuchi, Keizo, 601
Obuchi, Keizo, 313, 339, 362, 368, 369, 371, 372, 378, 601
Öcalan, Abdullah, 100, 105, 107, 108, 596, 600
Ocampo Alfaro, Rear-Adm. José, 184
Oddsson, Davíd, 76, 599

Oetzre, Christiane, 502
Ofili, Chris, 521
Ogi, Adolf, 86
OheneKena, Fred, 254
Olazabal, José Maria, 538, 539
Oldfield, David, 382
Olympic Games, 103, 381, 479, 534, 582, 595
Oman, 229, 230, 231, 232, 412, 446
Omar, Mola Mohammad, 304, 305, 306, 307
Omar Abdulrahman, Shaikh, 215
Omar Guellah, Ismail, 248
Omissi, David, 533
Ondaatje, Michael, 532
Ong Teng Cheong, 344
Opera, 501-3
Oppenheimer, Robert, 591,
Orban, Viktor, 120, 121, 122, 313
Organization for Economic Cooperation & Development (OECD), 8, 9, 10, 11, 13, 14, 143, 201, 391, **411, 413**
Organization for Security & Cooperation in Europe (OSCE), 109, 116, 131, 134, 135, 138, 147, 171, 309, 314, 398, 407, 433, 434, **435-8,** 443, 444
Organization of African Unity (OAU), 98, 238, 240, 242, 246, 267, 269, 275, 277, 336, 445, **447-50**
Organization of American States (OAS), 455, 456
Organization of Eastern Caribbean States (OECS), 456, 458
Organization of the Islamic Conference (OIC), 422-4
Organization of the Petroleum Exporting Countries (OPEC), 224, 225-6, 230, **411, 412,** 596, 602
Ortiz, Benjamín, 183,
Oscar awards, 514
Otkir, Sultonov, 308
Otumfuor Osei Tutu II, 254
Ouattara, Alassane, 267
Ouedraogo, Kadre Desiré, 263
Ould Daddah, Ahmed, 264
Ousmane, Mahamane, 270
Overviews of the year, 1-15
Oviedo Silva, Gen. (retd) Lino César, 183, 184
Owen, Robert, 132
Owens, Jesse, 543
Öymen, Altan, 107
Ozawa, Ichiro, 368

Pacific Community (PC), 451, 454
Pacific Islands Forum (PIF), 390, **452, 454**
Pacific states, 387-92
Packer, Kerry, 382
Padel, Ruth, 532
Paeniu, Bikenibeu, 391
Pagrotsky, Leif, 441
Paisley, Rev. Ian, 49

Paiva, Paulo, 178
Pakistan, 2, 33, 175, 232, 305, 306, 307, 314, 315, 316-7, 319, **321-4**, 326, 329, 400, 413, 414, 415, 423, 454, 463, 484, 537, 538, 594, 597, 598, 601, 602, 604
Paksas, Rolandas, 115, 599, 604
Palacka, Gabriel, 120
Palau, 388, 390, 454
Palenfo, Gen. Lansana, 267
Palestinian entity and people, 3, 78, 170, 207, 208, 209, 210, **211-4**, 217, 219, 222, 224, 242, 303, 422, 445, 559, 601
Panama, 181, 182, **191, 193,** 206, 601, 605
Panchen Lama, 464
Panday, Basdeo, 197
Pandey, Ramesh Nath, 328
Pangalos, Theodoros, 101
Pangelinan, Lourdes, 451, 454
Pant, Kamala, 328
Paoletti, Roland, 526
Paolozzi, Sir Eduardo, 523
Papadopoulos, Alexandros, 101
Papadopoulos, Col. George, 103, 588 (obit.)
Papandreou, Andreas, 101
Papandreou, George, 101, 105
Papandreou, Vasso, 101
Papazoi, Elisavet, 101
Papon, Maurice, 62
Papua New Guinea, 2, **383-4**, 454, 600
Paraguay, 183-4, 457, 596
Paris Club, 218, 282
Parks, Rosa, 582
Parks, Tim, 532
Partnership for Peace, 74, **403**
Pasqua, Charles, 60, 61
Pastrana Arango, Andrés, 180, 182
Patassé, Ange-Félix, 271, 273
Paterson, Don, 532
Patten, Chris, 429, 603
Patterson, Percival J., 195
Paulin, Tom, 532
Paulino, Alberto, 282
Pavarotti, Luciano, 51
Pavle, Patriarch, 135
Pavletic, Vlatko, 134, 135
Pavord, Anna, 533
Pawar, Sharad, 316, 319
Pecorelli, Mino, 66
Pennington, Michael, 512
Penrose, Sir Roland, 523
Peprah, Richard Kwame, 254
Peres, Shimon, 208, 577
Peretz, Amir, 208
Perez, Rafael, 163
Pérez Roque, Felipe, 188
Pérez Yoma, Edmundo, 179
Perry, William, 375
Persinger, Louis, 585
Persson, Göran, 79
Peru, 182, 183, **185-6**, 456

Peters, Bernadette, 512
Peters, Higman, 202
Peters, Winston, 385
Petritsch, Wolfgang, 84, 132
Petsalnikos, Phillipos, 101
Peyrefitte, Alain, 588 (obit.)
Phan Van Khai, 350, 351
Phatswe, Chris, 292
Philipoussis, Mark, 542
Philippe, Crown Prince of Belgium, 68
Philippines, 349-50, 351, 404, 452, 453
Picard, Bertrand, 597
Pillay, Navanthem, 487
Pimlott, Steven, 512
Pinochet Ugarte, Gen. (retd) Augusto, 25, 40, 179, 180, 507, 591, 592, 598
Pinter, Harold, 509
Pio, Padre, 460
Pique, Josep, 91
Pius XII, Pope, 89, 464
Plantinga, Leon, 506
Poci, Spartak, 130
Podesta, John, 565
Pohiva, Akilisi, 391
Poland, 5, 13, 105, **110-3**, 405, 430, 441, 442, 443, 460, 452, 536, 599
Poliakoff, Stephen, 511
Pollo, Genc, 131
Pollock, Jackson, 524, 570
Pompidou, Georges, 588
Poole, Alan, 202
Poplašen, Nikola, 131, 132
Portas, Paulo, 96
Porter, Cole, 513
Porter, David G., 504
Porter, Peter, 529, 532
Portillo Cabrera, Alfonso Antonio, 190, 191, 607
Portillo, Michael, 26, 27, 605
Portugal, 95-8, 201, 258, 281, 347, 362, 396, 418, 424, 488, 536, 589, 602
Poulenc, Francis, 501, 504
Pourier, Miguel, 205
Poznyak, Zyanon, 149
Prabhakaran, Velupillai, 332
Prescott, John, 25, 564
Préval, René, 189
Previti, Cesare, 66
Price, Nick, 539
Priestley, J.B., 586
Primakov, Yevgenii, 144, 147, 148, 597, 599
Primarolo, Dawn, 564
Prince, Alison, 533
Pringle, John, 383
Prodi, Romano, 63, 64, 65, 66, 67, 237, 424, 426, 428, 429, 490, 597, 601
Proulx, Annie, 532
Puapua, Tomasi, 389
Puccini, Giacomo, 503
Puerto Rico, 206

Puey Ungpakorn, 342
Pujol, Jordi, 92
Pullinger, Kate, 532
Putin, Vladimir, 4, 144, 145, 435, 602, 607

Qaboos bin Said, Shaikh, 229
Qadafi, Col. Muammar, 237, 238, 240, 275, 445, 448, 449, 588
Qarwi, Hamid, 239
Qatar, 229, 230, 231, 232, 233, 247, 422, 424, 445, 446
Qian Qichen, 313
Quayle, Dan, 159, 160
Quebec, 171, 172, 173, 174
Quin, Joyce, 565
Quintero Payán, Juan José, 194

Rabbani, Mohammed, 304
Rabin, Yitzhak, 170
Rabuka, Maj.-Gen. Sitiveni, 389, 391
Rachid, Gen. Lallali, 277
Radhakishum, Pretaapnarain, 204
Rae, Jonathan, 533
Rafter, Patrick, 542
Rainier III, Prince of Monaco, 88
Rais, Amien, 346
Rakhmanov, Imamali, 308, 310, 313, 604
Ramadan, Taha Yazid, 224
Rameau, Jean Coles, 190
Ramgoolam, Navin, 333, 334
Ramírez, Marta Lucia, 457
Ramírez Durand ('Feliciano'), Oscar, 185
Ramos, Fidel, 349
Ramsamy, Pakereesamy (Prega), 447, 450
Ramsay, JonBenet, 166
Ramsay, Lynne, 515
Ramsey, Sir Alf, 588-90 (obit.)
Ranabhatt, Tara Nath, 328
Randle, Thomas, 502
Rangel, José Vicente, 187, 196
Rasizade, Artur, 152
Rasmussen, Poul Nyrup, 74, 75
Ratsiraka, Didier, 338
Rau, Johannes, 599
Rawabidah, Abdul Rauf, 216, 217
Rawlings, Jerry, 254, 255
Rawsthorne, Alan, 506
Ray, Robert, 161
Raynsford, Nick, 564
Razak, Najib, 343
Razaleigh, Tengku, 343
Reagan, Ronald, 156, 590
Red Cross, International Committee of the, 340
Redgrave, Corin, 512
Redgrave, Vanessa, 510, 512
Reed, Oliver, 100
Rees-Jones, Trevor, 28
Reeves, Dan, 543
Rehn, Elizabeth, 82

Rehnquist, William, 156
Reid, John, 17, 44, 564
Reid, Kevin, 44
Reilly, Sir Patrick, 589 (obit.)
Rejouis, Rose-Myriam, 532
Religion, 213-4, 355, **459-64**
Rembrandt, 524
Rendall, David, 501
René, France-Albert, 335
Reno, Janet, 565
Ressam, Ahmed, 162
Reynolds, Oliver, 532
Rhys-Jones, Sophie, 600
Rice, Tim, 513
Rich, Adrienne, 529, 532
Richards, Rod, 48
Richardson, Bill, 225, 565
Richardson, Elliot, 589 (obit.)
Riley, Richard W., 565
Ringholm, Bosse, 79
Rio Group, 455
Risal, Basudev, 328
Ritchie, Ian, 526
Robbins, Jerome, 507, 509
Roberts, John Stuart, 533
Roberts, Julia, 515
Roberts, Michèle, 532
Robertson of Port Ellen, Lord (George), 26, 44, 403, 602
Robeson, Paul, 512
Robiana González, Roberto, 188
Robinson, Arthur N.R., 197
Robinson, Gerry, 520
Robinson, Mary, 403
Robinson, Peter, 53
Roche, Barbara, 564
Rød-Larsen, Terje, 78
Rodgers, Joan, 501
Rodrigues, Amália, 96, 590 (obit.)
Rodríguez, Edgardo Dumas, 192
Rodríguez Echeverría, Miguel Angel, 190
Rodríguez Saá, Adolfo, 176
Rogers, Ben, 533
Rogers, Jane, 532
Rogers, Lord (Richard), 526, 527
Rogozhkin, Alexander, 517
Rohee, Clement, 196
Rojas, José, 187
Rojas Penso, Juan Francisco, 455
Rokophyllos, Christos, 102
Roma, see Gypsies (Roma)
Roman, Petre, 123
Román, Rafael, 95
Romania, 98, 105, 122, **123-5,** 130, 430, 443, 460, 536, 598, 605
Romer, Stephen, 532
Rooker, Jeff, 565
Rosen, Charles, 503
Rosenberg, Leonce, 522
Rosenberg, Paul, 522

Rosselló, Pedro J., 206
Roth, Tim, 515
Rowling, J.K., 530
Rubens, Bernice I., 532
Rubin, Robert, 167
Rubio, Humberto Gordon, 179
Ruckauf, Carlos, 176
Ruggiero, Renato, 412
Rugova, Ibrahim, 140, 431
Ruiz Massieu, José Francisco, 194
Ruiz Massieu, Mario, 194
Rumens, Carol, 532
Ruml, Jan, 118
Rusedski, Greg, 542
Rushdie, Salman, 303, 528, 531, 532
Russell, Francia, 506
Russell-Johnston, Lord, 434
Russian Federation, 144-8; Chechnya, 1, 3, 4, 58, 116, 144, 146 (*map*), 147, 171, 303, 433, 435; cinema, 517; corruption, 144-5; economy, 4, 10, 13, 110, 144, 145, 412, 439; elections, 145, 147-8, 434; external relations, 147, 150, 151, 153, 171, 211, 219, 220, 229, 305, 310-11, 312, 313; 361, 396, 398, 399, 406, 420, 441; Kosovo crisis, 5-6, 64, 81, 138, 141, 398, 432; obituaries, 570-2, 575; politics, 144-5; religion, 462; social affairs, 130; space, 465
Rutaganda, Georges, 487
Ruzindana, Obed, 487
Rwanda, 238, 275, 276, **278, 279-80,** 290, 300, 484, 487
Rwigyema, Pierre-Célestin, 278
Ryan, George, 189

Saad al-Abdullah as-Salim as-Sabah, Crown Prince, 229
Saadawi, Nawal El, 529, 533
Saadi, Ramón, 176
Saatchi, Charles, 521
Sacher, Paul, 506
Sacks, Chief Rabbi Jonathan, 463
Saddam Husain, 222, 223, 224, 580
Sadio, Leopold, 264
Safir, Howard, 163
Safra, Edmond, 90
Saguier, Miguel Abdón Tito, 184
Sahbani, Ismail, 239
Sahhaf, Said al-, 445
St Albans, Duke of, 18
St Kitts & Nevis, 200, 201
St Lucia, 200, 201-2, 458
St Vincent & the Grenadines, 198, **200, 202,** 487
Saitoti, George, 249
Saji, Keizo, 372
Salas Wenzel, Gen. (retd) Hugo, 179
Saleh, Ali Abdullah, 227, 228, 603
Saleh, Jaime M., 205
Salim, Salim Ahmed, 447, 449

Salinas de Gortari, Carlos, 194
Salinas de Gortari, Raúl, 193
Salmond, Alex, 43
Salo, Mika, 540
Samaranch, Juan António, 534, 596
Samoa, 388, 390, 455, 534, 541
Sampaio, Jorge, 95, 362
Sampras, Pete, 542, 601
Sampson, Anthony, 533
Samson, Bruce, 508
San Marino, 88, 90
Sanders, Ronald, 200
Sandoval, Mauricio, 192
Sanguinetti Cairolo, Julio María, 186
Sanha, Malam Bacai, 280, 281, 599
Sankoh, Foday, 259, 260, 601
Sant, Dr Alfred, 98, 99
Santer, Jacques, 70, 427, 428, 596
Santiago, Manuela, 206
São Tomé & Príncipe, 280, **281-2,** 418
Saramago, José, 529, 532
Sardinia, 90
Sargent, John Singer, 524
Sarkisian, Aram, 152, 604
Sarkisian, Vazgen, 152, 599, 604
Sarraute, Nathalie, 531, 590 (obit.)
Sartre, Jean-Paul, 590
Sarwar, Mohammad, 44
Sassou-Nguesso, Denis, 271, 272, 273, 449
Sato, Mitsuo, 454
Saucedo Sánchez, Gen. César, 185
Saudi Arabia, 215, 217, 219, 223, 224, **225-7,** 230, 233, 237, 254, 303, 420, 421, 424, 445, 446, 474
Sauri Riancho, Dulce María, 194
Sauter, Christian, 61
Savage, Frank J., 202
Savimbi, Jonas, 284, 295, 402, 418, 420
Savisaar, Edgar, 113
Sawoniuk, Anthony, 597
Sayegh, Hani Abderrahman Hussein al-, 227
Scalfaro, Oscar Luigi, 65, 599
Schama, Simon, 533
Schäuble, Wolfgang, 57
Schawlow, Arthur, 590 (obit.)
Schiff, Stacy, 533
Schmeichel, Peter, 535
Schmied, Roberto, 179
Schröder, Gerhard, 54, 55, 56, 58, 111, 129, 430, 605
Schubert, Franz, 503
Schultz, Charles, 156
Schumacher, Michael, 540
Schüssel, Wolfgang, 83
Schuster, Rudolf, 119, 599
Schwartz, Charles, 163
Schwarzkopf, Elizbeth, 503, 504
Schwimmer, Walter, 84, 433, 434
Scientific, Medical & Industrial Research, 465-71

INDEX 631

Scognamiglio, Carlo, 64
Scorsese, Martin, 515
Scotland, 2, 16, 17, 22, 38, **43-5**, 237, 402, 421, 461, 462, 530, 535, 538, 542, 598, 600
Scotland of Asthal, Baroness, 204
Scott, George C., 517, 591 (obit.)
Seaborg, Glenn, 591 (obit.)
Sebald, W.G., 528, 532
Sebastian, Sir Cuthbert, 200
Sebök, György, 506
Segovia Voltes, Gen. José, 184
Séguin, Philippe, 60
Sellers, Peter, 583
Selvaduri, Shyam, 532
Senegal, **262, 263-4**, 280, 451
Senghor, Abbé Diamacoune, 264
Serbia, see Yugoslavia, Federal Republic of
Serfaty, Abraham, 243
Sergeyev, Igor, 374
Serushago, Omar, 487
Šešelj, Vojislav, 143
Seth, Vikram, 528, 532
Severino, Rodolfo C., 451
Seychelles, **335-6**
Shabi, Najib Qahtan al-, 228
Shacklock, Constance, 503
Shahak, Amnon Lipkin, 209
Shakespeare, Nicholas, 533
Shakespeare, William, 530
Shalala, Donna E., 565
Shamkhani, Ali, 303
Shamsie, Kamila, 529, 532
Shanghai Five, 311-2
Shannon, Richard, 533
Shapcott, Jo, 529, 532
Shara, Faruq al-, 171, 211, 220, 606
Sharansky, Natan, 209
Sharif, Nawaz, 315, 317, 321, 322, 323, 414, 595, 603, 605
Sharjah, 229
Sharon, Ariel, 212
Sharp, Dame Evelyn, 586
Shaw, Robert, 506
Shaw, Vernon, 200
Shephard, Matthew, 166
Sher, Antony, 512, 532
Sheridan, Alan, 533
Sheridan, Tommy, 43
Sherringham, Teddy, 535
Shevardnadze, Eduard, 152, 153, 313, 433, 605
Shi Guangsheng, 359
Shipley, Jenny, 385, 453
Shochat, Avraham (Beiga), 210
Shoemaker, Eugene, 467
Shoigu, Sergei, 147
Shore, Andrew, 502
Short, Clare, 204, 564
Short, Philip, 533

Shostakovich, Dmitry, 504
Shuttle, Penelope, 532
Shyamalan, M. Night, 516
Sibanda, Gibson, 288
Sierra Leone, 2, 74, **259-60**, 261, 266, 269, 300, 401, 449, 450, 594, 600
Siew, Vincent, 365, 366
Signorelli, Luca, 89
Sihanouk, Norodom, King of Cambodia, 352, 353
Silajdzic, Haris, 131
Silva Henríquez, Cardinal Raúl, 180, 591 (obit.)
Silva Nogales ('Comandante Antonio'), Jacobo, 194
Simeonov, Teodosii, 127
Simitis, Kostas, 100
Simpson, O.J., 166
Sin, Cardinal Jaime, 349
Singapore, 236, **344-5**, 375, 404, 414, 452, 453, 601
Singh, Jaswant, 315, 319, 320, 329
Singh, Karpal, 343
Sinha, Yashwant, 315
Sirin Nimmanahaeminda, 341
Sisavath Keobounphanh, Gen., 353
Sisson, C.H., 532
Skate, Bill, 383, 384, 601
Skele, Andris, 113, 114, 601
Skinner, Dennis, 24
Sladen, Victoria, 502
Slater, Rodney E., 565
Slovakia, 33, 98, 105, 115, 118, **119-20**, 121, 430, 442, 443, 598
Slovenia, 105, 115, **137-8**, 393, 430, 443, 536
Smetana, Berich, 502
Smith, Alan, 26
Smith, Andrew, 564, 603
Smith, Benjamin, 165
Smith, Chris, 519, 564
Smith, David, 524
Smith, Donald, 502
Smith, Ian, 587
Smith, Jennifer, 202, 203
Smith, Peter John, 202, 203
Soares, Mário, 96
Soares da Silva, Agripino, 178
Sobchak, Anatolii, 145
Sobhan, Farooq, 414
Sobhuza II, King of Swaziland, 296
Sock, Mademba, 264
Sodano, Cardinal Angelo, 88
Soglo, Nicéphore, 269, 597
Soglo, Rosine, 269
Sokurov, Alexander, 516
Solana Madariaga, Javier, 58, 93, 404, 409, 429, 430, 432, 602
Sølksjær, Ole Gunner, 535
Solomon Islands, **388, 391**, 415
Soloman, Thomas J., 165

Solti, George, 503
Solzhenitsyn, Alexander, 529, 532
Somalia, 2, 33, 35, **245, 247-8,** 423
Somaliland, 248
Somare, Michael, 383, 384
Sondheim, Stephen, 569
Soong, James, 367
Sope, Barak, 389, 391
Soueif, Ahdaf, 529, 532
Soukhan Maharaj, 353
South Africa, 2, 39, 237, 276, 290, 291, 292, 293, 295, **297-301,** 414, 420, 421, 448, 537, 538, 541, 594, 599, 602
South Asian Association for Regional Cooperation (SAARC), 320, 323, 325, 329, **451, 454**
South Ossetia, 437
South Pacific Forum, see Pacific Islands Forum (PIF)
Southern African Customs Union (SACU), 291
Southern African Development Community (SADC), 251, 290, 293, 300, **447, 450**
Southern Common Market (Mercosur), 455, 456-7
Soyinka, Wole, 533
Space Research, see Scientific, Medical & Industrial Research
Spain, 40, **91-4,** 95, 179, 201, 227, 258, 425, 426, 427, 434, 457, 490, 535, 536, 538, 539, 566, 604
Spellar, John, 565
Spence, Toby, 502
Sperling, Gene, 565
Spidla, Vladimir, 117
Spielberg, Steven, 515
Sport, 45, 48, 155, 381, **534-44**
Spratly Islands, 350, 351, 404, 452, 453
Sri Lanka, 2, 33, 35, 320, 325, 329, **331-3,** 414, 454, 537, 538, 606
Srivastava, Atima, 532
Ssendawula, Gerald, 252
Stability Pact for South-Eastern Europe, 432, 434, 436, 443
Stader, Maria, 502
Staines, Graham, 463
Stallworthy, Jon, 533
Stamper, Norm, 162
Stanley, Francisco 'Paco', 194
Stannard, Russell, 464
Starr, Kenneth, 159, 161
Steel of Aikwood, Lord (David), 43
Steifel, Ethan, 508
Stein, Peter, 502
Steinberg, Saul, 524
Stepashin, Sergei, 144, 145, 599, 602
Stephanopoulos, Kostas, 100, 313
Stern, Howard, 160
Stern, Nicholas, 438
Stevenson, Alexandra, 542

Stewart, James, 569, 591
Stewart, Payne, 155, 539
Stiglitz, Joseph, 438
Stockhausen, Karlheinz, 505
Stojkovski, Radovan, 136
Stoph, Willi, 592 (obit.)
Stoppard, Tom, 514
Stoyanov, Petar, 126, 128
Strauss, Richard, 503, 504, 506
Strauss-Kahn, Dominique, 59, 61
Stravinsky, Igor, 505, 568
Straw, Jack, 26, 28, 29, 30, 31, 33, 34, 40, 564
Streb, Elizabeth, 508
Sturza, Ion, 151
Suárez Mason, Gen. (retd) Guillermo, 175
Sudan, 234-6, 246, 247, 253, 300, 393, 445, 534
Suharto, Gen. 346, 347
Sultan bin Abdul Aziz, Prince, 303
Sultonov, Otkir, 308
Sumairsingh, Hansraj, 197
Sumaye, Frederick, 250
Summers, Lawrence, 167, 565
Summit of the Americas, 456, 458
Supachai Panitchpakdi, 413, 601
Surayud Chulanont, Gen., 342
Suriname, 204-5
Suroor, Saeed Bin, 543
Sutton, 499
Suu Kyi, Aung San, 339, 340
Svoboda, Ivo, 117
Swaziland, 290, 291, **296**
Sweden, 79-80, 82, 425, 429, 536, 594
Switon, Kazimierz, 112
Switzerland, 85-8, 313, 442, 476, 487, 534, 596, 600, 603
Symonds, John, 29
Symonenko, Petro, 150, 151
Symons of Vernham Dean, Baroness, 565
Syria, 3, 100, 171, 210-1, 217, 218, **219-20,** 221, 222, 223, 303, 422, 445, 600, 605
Szeemann, Harald, 523
Szymborska, Wislawa, 529, 532

T'Hooft, Gerardus, 471
Ta Mok, 352
Tadic, 486
Taiwan, 7, 15, 100, 169, 170, 353, 354, 356, 361, 362, **365-8,** 383, 399, 452, 453, 454, 474, 602
Tajikistan, 305, **308, 310,** 311, 312, 313, 314, 400, 474, 603
Tal, Wasfi al-, 580
Talat, Mehmet Ali, 106
Talbott, Strobe, 171, 319, 441
Talic, Col.-Gen. Momir, 133
Tamils, 33, 331-3
Tandja, Col. Mamadou, 263, 270, 605
Tang Jiaxuan, 360
Tang Shubei, 367

Tankard, Meryl, 507
Tanoh, Augustus 'Goosie', 255
Tanumafili II, Susuga Malietoa, 388
Tanzania, 235, **250-2,** 276, 278, 279, 414, 450, 478, 586-8
Tarar, Mohammed Rafiq, 321, 322
Tariq Aziz, 224
Tarmidi, Bianfrifi, 335, 337
Tarrant, Chris, 517
Tarrin Nimmanahaeminda, 341
Taufa'ahua Tupou IV, King of Tonga, 388
Taya, Col. Moaouia Ould Sidi Mohammed, 262
Taylor, Ann, 564
Taylor, Charles, 261
Taylor, Derek H., 203
Taylor, John, 52
Taylor, Richard, 582
Taymor, Julie, 513
Television & Radio, 517-21
Temirkanov, Yuri, 504
Tenet, George, 169, 565
Terera, Gilz, 511
Terfel, Bryn, 501
Terragno, Rodolfo, 176
Thaci, Hacim, 143
Thackeray, Bal, 317
Thailand, 14, 325, 339, **340-2,** 354, 413
Thaksin Shinawatra, 341
Than Shwe, Gen., 339
Thani, Hassan bin Jassem bin Hamad al-, 233
Thapa, Surya Bahadur, 327
Tharp, Twyla, 507
Thatcher, Baroness (Margaret), 24, 25, 572, 593, 594
Theatre, 509-14
Thiam, Pape Sow, 451
Thomas, Percy, 526
Thompson, Elizabeth, 197
Thomson, Lord (Roy), 579
Thorneycroft, Peter, 593
Thorpe, Adam, 532
Thorpe, Jeremy, 533
Thubron, Colin, 533
Thurman, Judith, 533
Tiberi, Jacques, 61
Tibet, 7, 39
Timms, Stephen, 564
Timor Sorolae, see East Timor
Tintner, Georg, 506
Tippett, Sir Michael, 505
Tiruchelvam, Neelan, 333
Tirvengadum, Sir Harry, 451
Tito, Josip Broz, 592
Tito, Teburoro, 387, 389, 454
Tlili, Abderrahmane, 239
Togliatti, Palmiro, 580
Togo, 259, **263,** 265, 267, **268-9,** 280, 450
Togoimi, Youssouf, 271
Toibin, Colm, 532

Tokayev, Kasymzhomart, 308, 309, 603
Tomlinson, Charles, 532
Tomlinson, John, 502
Tomlinson, Richard, 28
Tommasson, Helgi, 507
Tonga, 388, 389, **391,** 393, 455, **595**
Töpfer, Klaus, 481
Topize, Joseph, 334
Tornay, Cedric, 89
Torres, Juan José, 177
Torres Heyn, Gen. Eligio, 184
Torrijos Espinoso, Martín, 193
Torrijos Herrera, Gen. Omar, 193
Touré, Bamou, 265
Toussaint, Yvon, 189
Tower, Joan, 505
Townes, Charles, 590
Trajkovski, Boris, 136, 137, 606
Tran Duc Luong, 313, 350
Tranter, John, 533
Traoré, Moussa, 595
Tremain, Rose, 532
Trigueros, José Luis, 192
Trimble, David, 48, 49, 50, 51, 52, 72, 606
Trinidad & Tobago, 196, **197,** 198, 414, 415, 458
Tripp, Linda, 162
Trøjberg, Jan, 75
Trovoada, Miguel, 280, 282
Trulock, Notra, 169
Truman, Harry S., 591
Trump, Donald, 160, 161
Truong Dinh Tuyen, 351
Tsang, Donald, 365
Tsog, Logiyn, 377
Tsvangirai, Morgan, 288
Tucker, Albert, 524
Tucket, William, 508
Tudjman, Ankica, 134
Tudjman, Franjo, 134, 135, 138, 592 (obit.), 606
Tudjman, Miroslav, 134
Tudor, Alex, 538
Tulio Espinosa, Gen. Marco, 191
Tung, Brian Kuei, 197
Tung Chee-hwa, 363, 364
Tunisia, 238-40, 298, 393, 603
Turabi, Hasan al-, 234
Turajonzade, Haji Akbar, 310
Turkey, 3, 33, 100, 101, 103, 104, 105, 106, **107-9,** 153, 171, 220, 223, 224, 258, 303, 313, 326, 420, 430, 431, 536, 594, 595, 597, 599, 601, 604
Turkish Republic of Northern Cyprus (TRNC), 105, 106
Turkmenistan, 305, **308,** 310, 312, 489, 595, 605
Turks & Caicos Islands, 203, 204, 458
Turnbull, Charles, 206
Turner, Gerald, 532

Turnquest, Sir Orville, 199
Tutu, Archbishop Desmond, 464
Tuvalu, 389, 391
Tüvdendorj, Sharavdorjiyn, 377
Tynan, Bill, 44
Tyson, Mike, 537

Ubayd, Atif al, 214, 215, 603
Uddin, Baroness, 35
Uganda, 2, 235, 238, 250, **252-3**, 275, 276, 277, 278, 290, 450, 478, 484, 595
Ukraine, 13, 130, **149, 150-1**, 393, 396, 406, 433, 437, 443, 444, 604
Ulbricht, Walter, 592
Ulenga, Ben, 294
Ulufa'alu, Bartholomew, 388
United Arab Emirates (UAE), 229, 230, 231, 232, 233, 236, 303, 307, 446, 447
United Kingdom (see also Northern Ireland, Scotland, Wales)**, 16-54;** Afghanistan, 306; Archer affair, 19, 20-1; Argentina/Falklands, 177; arts, 501-34; Ashcroft affair, 23; Australia, 381-2; BBC director-general, 22; beef exports, 3, 16, 40-2, 62, 74; Commonwealth, 414, 415; Council of Europe, 433, 434; defence, 39, 42, 63, 404, 408, 409, 488; devolution, 2, 16-7, 43-4, 46-7, 52; East Timor, 39; economy, 9, 12-3, **35-8**, 254; elections, 22, 26-7, 44, 428; EU/euro, 16, 24-5, 35-6, 425, 426, 428, 429; external relations, 16, **38-42**, 63, 75, 93, 100, 102, 103, 177, 196, 197, 204, 214-5, 312, 339, 359, 360-1; fox-hunting, 26; Gibraltar, 94-5; GM crops, 470, 476, 477, 478, 479, 480-1, 482-3; government changes, 17, 19, 25-6, 47, 51, 563-5; Gurkhas, 329; Hamilton affair, 29-30; homosexualism, 26, 27, 488; Hong Kong, 365; House of Lords, 17-9, 492; IMF, 411; immigration, 35; information technology, 471-2, 474, 475; Iran, 303; Iraq, 445; Kosovo crisis, 6, 16, 38-9, 168, 397-8; law, 45, **492-8**; Libya, 237, 238; London bombings, 32; London mayor, 19-21, 492; Macpherson report, 30-2; Millennium Dome, 27, 526; nuclear issues, 482; obituaries, 566-94; Paddington crash, 25; political asylum, 33-5; politics, 22-5, 26-7; Pinochet affair, 25, 179; Portillo's return, 26-7; race relations, 30-3; religion, 460, 461-2, 463; science, 469; security/espionage, 27-30, 116, 117; sport, 45, 48, **534-44**; transport, 25, 37-8; UN, 393-4, 399; welfare reform, 18; Yemen terrorists, 227-8
United Nations, 393-403; Afghanistan, 305, 306, 307, 423; Angola, 283, 284-5, 418; Arabs-Israel, 78, 422; Bangladesh, 325; Bosnia, 133; BSECO, 444; budget/finance, 395-6; Cambodia, 352; Central African Republic, 266, 273; Charter, 484, 485; China, 359-60; Congo-Kinshasa, 276, 277; Cuba, 183; cultural property, 488; Cyprus, 103-5; East Timor, 39, 97, 347-8, 380, 393, 396-7, 453; endangered species, 476-7; environment, 477, 481; Eritrea/Ethiopia, 246; G-77, 420; General Assembly, 393-4; hazardous wastes, 488; human rights, 215, 402-3; Iraq, 223-5, 399, 423, 445; Japan, 371; Kazakhstan, 313; Koreas, 373-4; Kosovo crisis, 5, 6, 38, 139, 140, 360, 393, 397-8, 420-1, 436, 486; landmines treaty, 488; Laos, 354; law of the sea, 487; Libya, 237, 238; Macedonia, 136; membership, 389, 393; Myanmar, 340; NATO, 407; peace-keeping missions (*table*), 399-401; population, 394, 468, 479-80; Puerto Rico, 206; Rwanda/Burundi, 278-9; sanctions, 402, 417; Sierra Leone, 260; small island states, 394; South Africa, 301; Sudan, 235, 236; Switzerland, 85; terrorism, 488; transparency, 403; UNCTAD, 9, 298, 421; UNDP, 292; Vatican, 89; Western Sahara, 244; women, 488
United States of America, 154-71; arts, 506-7, 509, 513, 514-5, 521-2; bananas, 480-1; climate change, 479; Clinton impeachment, 4-5, 154, 156-7, 158-9; Clinton, Mrs, 161; death penalty, 164, 485; defence/security, 7, 39, 162, 404; disasters & accidents, 155-6, 216; economy, 1, 8, 9, 10, 11, 12, 38, 157, 163, 166-8; EU, 413, 456; external relations, 1, 3-4, 7, 51, 63, 64, 78, 102, 105, 108, 115, 126, 129, 134, 137, 147, 150, **168-71**, 175, 180, 188, 189, 191, 192, 193, 194, 196, 201, 206, 210-1, 212, 213, 214, 215, 216-7, 218, 219, 223, 225, 227, 233, 235, 237, 242, 267, 303-4, 305, 306, 307, 313, 315, 319-20, 322, 323, 331, 351, 355, 359, 360, 361, 362, 369, 371, 373, 374-5, 404, 387, 390, 404, 441, 445, 452, 453, 484, 485; GM crops, 477, 482-3; government list, 564; gun control, 165-6, 499-500; IMF, 411; information technology, 471, 472, 473, 474-5; Kosovo crisis, 5, 7, 16, 64, 121, 138, 139, 141, 168-9, 360, 397-8; law, 163-6, 498-500; Lewinsky affair, 156, 158, 159, 162; medical research, 467-8, 469-70; obituaries, 567, 569, 570, 573, 574-6, 576-8, 580-3, 584, 588-91; presidential candidates, 159-61, 162; racial tensions, 163-4, 165; religion, 461; shooting incidents, 165-6; space, 465-7; sport, 534, 536-8, 538-40, 542, 543; State of the Union address, 156-7; tobacco issues, 164, 499; UN, 396; weather problems, 154; Whitewater affair, 159, 161; World Bank, 412; WTO, 1-2, 7, 162, 413
Unsworth, Barry, 532

INDEX 635

Uriburu, José Alberto, 176
Uruguay, 184, **186,** 457, 604
US Virgin Islands, 206
Usmon, Davlat, 310
Uteem, Cassam, 333
Uvarov, Andrei, 508
Uyesugi, Bryan, 165
Uzbekistan, 305, **308,** 310, 313, 314, 444, 489, 605

Vaea, Baron, 388, 391
Vagnorius, Gediminas, 114, 599
Vajpayee, Atal Bihari, 314, 315, 316, 317, 318, 323, 598, 602
Valdés, Juan Gabriel, 179
Valiani, Leo, 593 (obit.)
Van de Velde, Jean, 539
van der Stoel, Max, 437
Van Dyck, Anthony, 524
van Eyck, Aldo, 527
Vanuatu, 389, 391, 454, 455, 582, 596
Vasile, Radu, 124, 606
Vatican, 3, **88, 89,** 90, 113, 179, 183, 194, 224, 234, 459, 460, 461, 463
Vaughan, Elizabeth, 501
Vaz, Keith, 564
Vázquez, Tabaré, 186
Veiga, Carlos, 280, 281
Veil, Simone, 428
Velazquez, 522
Veldman, Didy, 509
Veltman, Martinus, 471
Venezuela, 1, 14, 181, **187-8,** 197, 230, 457, 600, 605
Venizelos, Evangelos, 101
Vennamo, Pekka, 81
Vera Esteche, Pablo, 184
Verdi, Giuseppe, 501
Verhofstadt, Guy, 67, 68
Vershbow, Alexander, 406
Vetere, Eduardo, 244
Vick, Graham, 502
Videla, Jorge Rafael, 175
Vieira, João Bernardo, 280, 281, 418, 599
Vietnam, 169, 313, **350-1,** 452, 453
Vike-Freiberga, Vaira, 113, 114, 116, 601
Villanueva Madrid, Mario, 194
Villanueva Ruesta, José, 185
Villar Benítez, José, 184
Vinokurov, Val, 532
Visconti, Luchino, 569
Visegrad Group, 442
Visual Arts, 521-5
Vitale, Leafa, 390
Vojvodina, 121
Vollebaek, Knut, 138, 435
Volpe, Justin, 163
von Sydow, Björn, 79
Vujanovic, Filip, 138
Vulterin, Karel, 117

Wade, Abdoulaye, 263
Wagner, Richard, 501, 503
Wahid, Abdurrahman, 345, 346, 604
Wakeham, Lord, 17
Waleed bin Talal bin Abdulaziz al-Saud al-, Prince, 254
Wales, 2, 16, 17, 20, 22, 45, **46-8,** 530, 541, 542, 598
Wales, Charles, Prince of, 17, 40, 176, 216, 479, 596
Walker, Dougie, 534
Walker, William, 138
Wallace, George, 582
Wallace, Jim, 43
Wallace-Crabbe, Chris, 533
Wallström, Margot, 429
Walsh, Courtney, 584
Walter, Bruno, 503, 585
Walter, Harriet, 510, 533
Walvin, James, 533
Wamba dia Wamba, 276, 277
Wang Daohan, 362, 366, 367
Wanké, Maj. Daouda Malam, 269, 449, 597
War Crimes Tribunals, 133, 135, 141, 279, 486-7, 598
Warhol, Andy, 570
Warne, Shane, 538
Waters, Sarah, 532
Watson, James, 586
Waugh, Steve, 537, 538
Way Rojas, Víctor Joy, 185
Wazzan, Shafiq al-, 222
Webern, Anton, 506
Wei Jianxing, 354
Weigel, George, 464
Weill, Kurt, 505
Weiss, Birte, 75
Weizman, Ezer, 207
Wen Ho Lee, 169
Wen Jiabao, 354
Wessex, Earl and Countess of, 600
West African Economic & Monetary Union (UEMOA), 268, **447, 450**
West, Morris, 383, 531, 593 (obit.)
West, Togo D., 565
Westendorp, Carlos, 84, 132
Western European Union (WEU), 93, **404,** 407-9, 432
Western Sahara, 242, **244,** 400
Wheen, Francis, 533
Whelan, Franzita, 502
White, Edmund, 533
Whitelaw, Viscount (William), 593 (obit.)
Wickremasinghe, Ranil, 331, 332
Widdecombe, Anne, 23
Wiegel, Hans, 69
Wigley, Dafydd, 47, 48
Wijdenbosch, Jules, 204
Wiktorin, Gen. Owe, 79
Wilcox, Herbert, 569

Wildor, Sarah, 508
Wille, Herbert, 89
Willetts, H.T., 529, 532
Williams, Sir Daniel, 198
Williams, Jesse, 164
Williams, Joe, 392
Williams, Tennessee, 510
Williams of Mostyn, Lord, 565
Williamson, David, 530
Willis, Bruce, 516
Wilson, Brian, 565
Wilson, Harold, 589
Wilton, Iain, 533
Windward & Leeward Islands, 200-2, 458
Winsor, Tom, 37
Wiranto, Gen., 347, 348
Wiseman, Keith, 535
Witte, John, 464
Wolde Semayat, Dr Taye, 247
Wolf, Ilse, 506
Wolfensohn, James D., 410, 412
Wood, James, 533
Woodbridge, Todd, 542
Woodeson, Nicholas, 510
Woodforde, Mark, 542
Woods, Tiger, 539, 540
Woodward, Gerard, 533
Woodward, Louise, 164
Woodward, Shaun, 27
Wordie, Sir James (J.M.), 576
World Bank, 129, 192, 214, 247, 250, 251, 255, 281, 282, 320, 326, 327, 338, 384, **410,** 411, **412,** 417, 420, 438, 446
World Food Programme (WFP), 284, 374, 376
World Health Organization (WHO), 469, 478
World Trade Organization (WTO), 1-2, 7, 129, 170, 198, 226, 301, 355, 359, 361, 362, 380, **411, 412-3,** 416, 419-20, 446, 447, 453, 476, 477, 481, 482
Worlock, Bishop Derek, 579
Wroe, Anne, 533
Wu Jichuan, 474
Wutzow, Jacek, 111
Wye River Accords, 210, 212, 214

Ximenes Belo, Bishop Carlos, 461

Yadav, Mulayam Singh, 316
Yakovlev, Vladimir, 148
Yalla, Kumba, 605
Yamassoum, Nagoum, 270, 272
Yankah, Kojo, 255
Yeltsin, Boris, 4, 144, 145, 147, 150, 171, 361, 599, 600, 602, 607
Yemen, 216, **227-9,** 247, 602
Yerima, Ahmad Sani, 257
Yılmaz, Mesut, 107

Yokoyama, Knock, 370
Yokoyama, Masato, 370
Yona, Daniel, 251
Yordanov, Emanuil, 127
Young, Lola, 528
Young, Sir Colville, 198
Youssoufi, Abderrahmane, 242, 243
Yugoslavia, Federal Republic of, 5-6, 7, 8, 16, 33, 38-9, 81, 93, 106, 121, 125, 126, 127, 133, 135, **138-43,** 147, 168, 169, 174, 379, 396, 398, 405, 406, 420, 431, 436, 439, 443, 444, 453, 460, 484, 485, 536, 544, 596, 597
Yulin, Harris, 512
Yushchenko, Viktor, 149, 151

Zaïre, see Congo, Democratic Republic of the
Zaldívar, Andrés, 180
Zambia, 276, 277, 284, **285-6,** 290, 295, 336, 450
Zanzibar & Pemba, 251-2, 415
Zayad bin Sultan al-Nahayyan, Shaikh, 229
Zayas Chirife, Federico, 184
Zedillo Ponce de León, Ernesto, 193, 194
Zeman, Milos, 117
Zeng Qinghong, 354
Zéroual, Liamine, 240
Zewail, Ahmed, 471
Zhang Wannian, 354
Zhang Yimou, 516
Zhao Ziyang, 356
Zhirinovsky, Vladimir, 148
Zhotev, Petur, 127
Zhu Rongji, 345, 354, 355, 359, 361, 453
Zia, Begum Khaleda, 324, 325
Zia, Gen., 321
Ziauddin, Lt.-Gen., 322
Zidi, Claude, 515
Zimbabwe, 275, 277, 285, **287-9,** 290, 292, 298, 414, 478, 537, 586
Zongo, Norbert, 268
Zorrilla, Ignacio, 186
Zouari, Abderrahim, 239
Zuabi, Mahmud, 219
Zuma, Jacob, 297

REF D 2.A7 1999